A LEVEL

ACTIVE SOCIOLOGY

SHAUN BEST

JANIS GRIFFITHS

TANYA HOPE

ADVISER: JONATHAN BLUNDELL

Pearson Education Limited
Edinburgh Gate
Harlow
Essex CM20 2JE
England
and Associated Companies throughout the world

ISBN 0 582 40541 6

First published 2000
Second impression 2000

Printed in Singapore (KKP)

The Publisher's policy is to use paper manufactured from sustainable forests.

Contents

Introduction

These are testing times for Sociology as a discipline and for teachers of Sociology in schools and colleges. Major changes are taking place in society. These changes are reflected in many of the new concerns that challenge sociologists and social order. Traditional ways of thinking about issues such as social class and gender no longer apply as we are all challenged by the advent of a new media and technologically dominated culture.

Even if the old ways of perceiving society have changed, sociology has a massive contribution to make towards an understanding of what is happening within it. Sociology has a body of knowledge and a tradition of research methodology, which still challenges commonplace assumptions about the nature of the socially constructed worlds in which we live. This book has attempted to answer these challenges by placing theory and research methodology where they belong, as the starting point for all of the debates that are studied within the new AS/A Level Sociology specifications. The key sociological writers have also been placed in context with the 'Sociologists in Profile' sections, enabling students to really understand where the concepts they are using have come from.

For teachers and students the challenge of taking AS/A Level Sociology is further compounded by changes imposed by Curriculum 2000. We believe that these developments are a practical improvement on what has gone before. Sociology is a discipline that is concerned with the real problems of our culture. Theory without practical application remains a form of meditation or an intellectual exercise, empty and meaningless, hence the stress on realistic and tried teaching activities and practical ways of applying theory to the world to which students belong. For this reason we have also included 'Sociology in Practice' sections that enable students to apply their sociological knowledge and understanding to 'real life' sociological case studies.

Of all subjects, we believe Sociology to be one of the most relevant and useful to an understanding of the way in which we negotiate our world. Very few academic or practical disciplines have been untouched by the influence of sociological thought. However, the terminology, concepts and theory can often be confusing and off-putting for new students of Sociology. We have attempted to demystify Sociology and create a book that is accessible and easy to understand for all 'wannabe' 'A' grade Sociologists, regardless of their academic background. To this end we have done as much as we can to support and help learning; with 'Hints and Tips' sections, 'Discussion Points' and identification of the key skills and assessment objectives within all of the 'Activities'. It is useful to remember that the key skills identified can also be applied to students' personal portfolios, as wells as to signal the personal development of transferable study skills that are generic to all subjects.

It is worth noting that the assessment objectives for both the AQA and OCR AS/A Level Sociology course specifications have been split into sections:

AO1 – knowledge and understanding of theories, methods, concepts and studies communicated in a clear and effective manner.

AO2 – identification, analysis, interpretation and evaluation of area/module content applied in an appropriate manner.

In all the activities we have identified the specific skill that the student has to demonstrate in relation to the assessment objectives:

- Knowledge and understanding (AO1) – knowing what is meant by the sociological theories, methods, concepts and studies being used.
- Identification and interpretation (AO2) – realising which sociological evidence is appropriate, what it is suggesting and its relevance to the question in hand.
- Analysis and evaluation (AO2) – a balanced judgement based on an examination of the evidence's strengths and weaknesses in relation to the question.

Finally we recognise that the ultimate aim of a Sociology course for many students is instrumental: they want to pass the examination. We live in a qualification-bound society and this need to acquire certification should be acknowledged. We have therefore aimed to cover all the main specification points of both the AQA and OCR examination boards so that the student has a thorough understanding of the knowledge and skills necessary for examination success.

This book has been a challenging task, but one which we have enjoyed and gained much pleasure from. We would like to take the opportunity to thank all of those involved in the project from its conception, families, friends, each other and staff at Pearson Education. Most particularly we would like to thank our advisor, Jonathan Blundell for his wide knowledge and excellent good sense and our publisher, Andrew Thraves for all of his generous support and time.

Shaun Best
Janis Griffiths
Tanya Hope

Acknowledgements

We are grateful to the following for permission to reproduce copyright material:

Figures 3.17 and 3.18, Marisa Rueda.

We are grateful to the following for permission to use photographs:

Figure 2.1, Popperfoto; Figure 3.1, John Stillwell; Figure 3.13 [top], Gamma; Figure 3.13 [second top], Rex Features; Figure 3.13 [second bottom], Tony Stone; Figure 3.13 [bottom], Tony Stone; Figure 3.19, Bubbles; Figure 3.20, Popperfoto; Figure 5.2, Popperfoto; Figure 5.4, Digital Vision; page 302, Friedrich Engels, Popperfoto; page 303, Simone de Beauvoir, Reuters; Figure 6.2, Reuters.

We are grateful to the AEB, AQA and OCR examination groups for permission to reproduce questions that have appeared in their examination papers. The guidance given for answering these questions is solely the responsibility of the authors.

Area 1

Sociological Theory

This area covers:

- The application of theory within sociology
- An historical and contemporary overview of sociological theory
- A critical examination of structural-consensus theories, structural-conflict theories, structuration theory, interpretive theories and relativist theories
- The future of sociological theory.

By the end of this area you should be able to:

- understand, apply and evaluate a variety of sociological theories
- interpret the theoretical perspective/s used by different sociologists

Key terms

structural	Marxism
conflict	postmodernism
consensus	phenomenology
interpretivism	functionalism
structuration	Weberianism

Area 1   Contents

Introduction

What is sociological theory and why do we use it?

6 *Theory: a systematic and general attempt to explain phenomena, and in the case of sociology, the social world around us. Theories are advanced to cover general areas of social life, yet they are often partial in that they are put forward by sociologists from a particular sociological perspective.*

Lawson, T. and Garrod, J. (1996:279)

Human beings are constantly trying to make sense of the world around them, by exploring and attempting to understand their lives in comparison to others'. Therefore, the majority of people engage in theoretical thought or thinking that tries to explain something. The difference between common sense and sociological theory is that sociologists use social concepts, such as socialisation or ideology, to establish detailed theories (or explanations) about the society in which we live. Unlike common-sense theories, which are based on the individuals' experiences, sociological theories tend to be more objectively informed and systematic. For example, sociologists can establish a theory about the 'underclass' through clear, coherent and detailed research (see Area 2): they do not have to be members of that alleged class. A common-sense theory could not provide this information.

Theory is therefore essential to sociology. It enables the sociologist to explain social phenomena in a way that can be critically examined and challenged by other sociologists. Consequently, sociology has developed as a discipline with a diverse set of theoretical approaches, all contributing to the richness of sociological explanations of the social world. It is important to understand fully the main theoretical perspectives, because this will provide an understanding of the concepts that can be applied to, and interpreted in, sociological debates.

By now it should be fairly clear that sociological theory, offering explanations of society, individuals and the relationship between them, is fundamental to the study of the social world. It enables social concepts to be classified, which in turn gives them a common meaning and people a general understanding of the world around them.

> **HINTS AND TIPS**   *It is useful to know the difference between a* **theory** *and a* **perspective**. *A theory is a specific explanation of a social phenomenon, while a perspective represents a particular viewpoint, such as Marxism, functionalism, feminism, structural or interpretive sociology. Perspectives tend to focus on a particular principle and are therefore partial representations of the social world. They also change as society changes, making it difficult for sociologists to pledge allegiance to one perspective.*

Therefore sociological theories are both:

a   **An attempt at generalisations** about society, such as; class conflict causes inequality (Marxist theory). These generalisations can never fully represent society, because each theory will focus on a different social feature and therefore focus on specific concepts. However, a combination of theories may present a more representative picture of the social world. For example, a poor market situation (Weberian theory) based on class (Marx), gender (feminist theory) and ethnicity (anti-racist theory) may provide a more complete explanation of social inequality.

b   **Contradictory of each other** and therefore need rationalising. Each theory will claim to be the most important explanation of a social phenomenon, but this is impossible; one must be more valid than the other. For example, structural theorists claim that inequalities in the social structures cause crime, while phenomenologists claim that the forces of social control cause crime (see Area 12): it is the responsibility of the sociologist to decide which one is closest to the 'truth'. This is perhaps the most difficult task for an experienced sociologist, let alone an AS/A level student, because it involves an evaluation of the logic within the argument, i.e. does it make sense?, and the evidence provided by the research, i.e. is the empirical data reliable and/or valid?

Consequently, it should be remembered that theories prioritise particular concepts or ideas and are consequently selective in their portrayal of social reality. At AS and A Level it is important to understand a variety of sociological theories and perspectives, in order to attain a balanced conclusion when explaining a social phenomenon. Therefore, despite the limitations of sociological theory, without it society would exist as a mass of unrelated social facts. Kirby et al. (1997) clearly summarise these points:

> ❛ ... *we need theory to get facts and then we also need theory to try and make sense of these facts ... So think of theories as ways of understanding and you will see they are there to help you make sense of the world you live in. Of course, you yourself have to decide whether the theories are any good, but this is a matter of choosing between the theories rather than choosing between theory and no theory.*

Kirby, M. et al. (1997:11)

Macro/micro – structural/interpretive perspectives

Sociological theories can be differentiated from one another according to the perspective they fall into, such as **macro**/structural or **micro**/interpretive. Dividing social theory by reference to these terms or **dualisms** (two related but opposing concepts) enables sociologists to think about their explanations of the social world from a specific viewpoint.

Macro/structural and micro/interpretive perspectives differ in their explanations of how society works. The macro/structural perspective explains social phenomena with reference to the structure of society, a structure which exists outside the people who inhabit it and which determines their behaviour. On the other hand, the micro/interpretive perspective is concerned with explaining the meaning people attach to their lives and the way in which this meaning is interpreted and used as the basis of action. Turner (1998) identified the theoretical distinction between the two approaches:

> ❛ *In commonsense terms the micro level is the level of everyday interaction typically involving face-to-face negotiation between individuals. By contrast the macro level refers to the global structures of societies, and the analysis of major institutions such as the interface between the economy and politics; it also deals with large-scale collective action such as global social movements. The majority of social theorists recognise implicitly some form of this distinction.*

Turner, B. S. (1998:222)

> **MACRO/STRUCTURAL THEORY**
> **Society (through socialisation and control)**
> ⟶ **Influences the individual to act**
>
> > **MICRO/INTERPRETIVE THEORY**
> > **Shared understanding of the world**
> > ⟶ **Action** ⟶
> > **Interpretation** ⟶ **Action**

It should be noted that the divide between macro/structural and micro/interpretive perspectives is not a clear one; for example, Weber applied both structure and individual action to his theory. There have also been attempts to bridge the gap between macro/structural and micro/interpretive perspectives, with sociologists asking such questions as 'In what ways could the interpretations of individuals come from, yet at the same time create, the social structure?' Therefore theoretical pluralism, or drawing information from diverse perspectives to explain social phenomena, could become more popular in contemporary sociology.

> ## REASONS FOR USING SOCIOLOGICAL THEORY
>
> 1 Theory enables an explanation or description of social phenomena, by putting social facts into categories and by determining their relative importance.
>
> 2 Theoretical assumptions can result in questions being raised about specific aspects of the social world.
>
> 3 It is a two-way relationship between theory and methods; you cannot have one without the other.
>
> 4 Sociological theory can result in social, economic and/or political change.
>
> 5 Many sociologists do not stick to one theory rigidly; the dynamic nature of theorising means that an appropriate selection of theories may be used to explain social phenomena.

It should be noted that it does not matter which approach sociological theory takes, it will still seek to explain the same fundamental questions about society. These questions revolve around the way in which

A C T I V I T Y **KS** WORKING WITH OTHERS

KNOWLEDGE AND UNDERSTANDING	IDENTIFICATION AND INTERPRETATION

Sociological theory is necessary if you want to have a clear view of society, because it allows you to focus on and explain a particular concept.

1 In pairs discuss what is meant by the term 'theory' and how theory is useful and relevant to sociology.

2 Make a list of the most important functions sociological theory has for the study of society and share this list with the rest of the class.

society is structured and the way it works. In fact, if any sociologist could answer these questions categorically, then social life would at last be clear. However, different approaches come to different conclusions about the structure and workings of society … and that is where the difficulty of understanding sociological theory lies.

HINTS AND TIPS   *If you are having trouble remembering what a particular theory argues about a specific area, such as stratification, use the following questions to guide your response:*

1 How does x theory describe the structure of society?

2 How does x theory say that society works?

3 How does x theory explain the inequalities between social groups?

4 How does x theory explain changes in society?

5 How does x theory explain the relationship between society and the individual?

Historical overview

Sociology is a relatively new academic discipline, in fact even the first sociologists did not think of themselves as such, but as political and economic philosophers. This said, the theories that they used to investigate society were clearly sociological. Consequently, **Karl Marx** (1818–83), **Émile Durkheim** (1858–1917) and **Max Weber** (1864–1920) have become known as the 'founding fathers' of sociology. Their work has had a huge impact on the development of sociology and remains influential today.

Marx, Durkheim and Weber lived during periods of massive social change. The effects of the Industrial

Revolution in Europe, the Democratic Revolutions of the USA and France and the intellectual/philosophical revolution in Europe, known as 'The Enlightenment', were still being felt. The Enlightenment involved intellectuals demonstrating that human reason could be used to understand the world and create knowledge, and that this knowledge could be used to make a better world. The reason why these ideas were considered so radical was that they were based on reason and logic, rather than faith in God, the leading ideology at the time.

The 'revolutions' occurring in Europe involved the overthrow of agriculture and the aristocracy by industry and democracy. This presented the population of Europe with unimaginable changes. Peasants went to work in squalid conditions in the cities and the landed gentry were forced to invest in the growing manufacturing industries. The emerging middle class had to struggle for power against the aristocracy, for example the right to vote. Social theorists wanted to investigate and understand these changes in Europe, therefore issues of stratification, such as class inequalities, became prevalent in the writings of the founding fathers.

Marx, Durkheim and Weber were developing their social theories in a dynamic social world, a world in which the economy, politics and culture were subject to massive transformations. The tradition of the past was being swept away by what is now known as **modernity**. Modernity refers to the 'revolutions' mentioned above and how they affected the world from the seventeenth century to the middle of the twentieth century. It enabled theorists to present rational explanations about the world, based on scientific principles and the belief that knowledge was fixed and solid. However, it should be noted that social thinkers were also influenced by moral and political issues, such as social reform to free people from oppression, as well as by social change (Holton, 1998).

HINTS AND TIPS   *The easiest way to remember the changes involved with the world becoming 'modern' is as follows:*

MODERNITY = ECONOMIC, POLITICAL AND CULTURAL CHANGE.

MODERNITY = INDUSTRIAL, DEMOCRATIC AND SCIENTIFIC REVOLUTION.

During The Enlightenment the natural sciences appeared successful in their explanations about the natural world, which encouraged social thinkers to apply scientific method to social enquiry. Also, religion no longer presented the barrier it once had presented to alternative explanations of social conditions. Sociological thought at this time was focused on using rational explanations of the social world as the basis for social change. The scientific approach to social research (see Area 2 on Sociological Research Methodology) was believed, in the spirit of The Enlightenment, to be the most appropriate basis for an attempt to explain the way in which society functioned. Using this, the founding fathers (Marx, Durkheim and Weber) developed clear models explaining the social system, models that consequently shaped modern sociology.

A C T I V I T Y   **KS** COMMUNICATION

KNOWLEDGE AND UNDERSTANDING	IDENTIFICATION AND INTERPRETATION

The hymn 'All things bright and beautiful' contains the verse:

> The rich man at his castle,
> The poor man at his gate,
> God made them high and lowly
> And ordered their estate.

Explain how the words of this hymn may have acted as a barrier to social scientific investigation into the stratification of society at the beginning of The Enlightenment.

❛ *The achievement of classical social theory, as it evolved in the nineteenth and early twentieth centuries, was to identify and elaborate most of the major generic issues that arise in the construction of a theory of society. This exercise is founded on a sense of the distinctiveness of society from nature.*

Holton, R. J. (1998:27)

HINTS AND TIPS   *The terms used in sociological theory are often complicated and confusing. If you are having difficulty understanding the terminology used in this area, the key terms are explained in the revision section at the end of the area.*

Contemporary situation

There have been major developments in sociological theory over the past 50 years. The founding fathers' focus on structure, or the way in which social systems act upon the individual, has been accepted, developed and rejected to varying degrees to provide an ever widening spectrum of social theories. These new or contemporary explanations of social phenomena range from interpreting the interactions of individuals (**interpretivism**), to examining the effect of socially constructed stratification systems, other than class position, on social groups (**feminism**).

It has been argued that contemporary social theory has highlighted culture, or the way of life of a society, in attempting to explain the social world (Jameson, 1984). Classical social theory neglected the cultural aspect of social existence, something contemporary theorists could not do considering the massive effect of consumerism, i.e. the production and consumption of culturally acceptable goods.

However, the consideration of culture is not the most radical turn sociological theory has taken recently. Postmodernists have argued that 'the social' can no longer exist in a world of mass communication systems (Baudrillard, 1983), that everything is a story or representation of a simulation. Therefore society cannot be studied, because any theory that attempts to explain it is creating yet more stories, or **narratives**, because social life is not real.

The pessimistic postmodern approach has not discouraged social theorists from their pursuit of explaining social phenomena, although it has been argued that contemporary sociological theory has not made much progress:

❛ *One of the basic criticisms of social theory is that it has failed in any significant or genuine fashion to resolve some of the fundamental problems, dichotomies, and puzzles which have been the perennial issues within the twentieth-century theoretical activity ... new topics have been discovered, while old problems are abandoned.*

Turner (1998:11)

Also, sociologists appear confused about what actually constitutes social theory, finding it difficult to decide whether it is a framework for research or a collection of concepts. Postmodernism has helped only to increase this uncertainty. However, this said, sociologists have continued to use theory well for the purposes of empirical research and/or examining public issues. For example, poverty was believed to be a thing of the past in 1950s Britain, but in the 1960s it was 'rediscovered' by Abel-Smith and Townsend and resulted in social policy to alleviate the harsher edges of inequality. Therefore, contemporary sociological theory remains necessary for the pursuit of knowledge about our society.

Structural theories

Sociologists who decide to use a **structural** approach when explaining social phenomena have decided that it is society that affects individual and group behaviour (instead of individuals and groups affecting society, as interpretive approaches argue). For example, if a theory attempts to explain people's position in the stratification system by their class origin or importance in maintaining a functioning society, then the theory would be considered structural.

It is interesting to note that both Marxism and functionalism are based on structural theories, despite appearing so different at first. Both approaches view society and the economy as the most important factors in determining our lives. However, Marxism, by arguing that conflict or struggle drives society, has become known as a structural-**conflict** theory; while functionalism, by arguing that consensus or agreement maintains a balanced society, has become known as structural-**consensus** theory. Structural-consensus theory in the form of functionalism dominated theoretical debate in the 1930s to 1950s, but its limitations were highlighted by structural-conflict theories. Marxism, for example, provided questions and answers about social life that functionalism could not and this led to the demise of structural-consensus theory in the 1960s. In fact, the growth in popularity of structural-conflict theory and alternative theories, such as interpretivism (discussed later), was a consequence of the criticisms they put forward about functionalism.

Structural-consensus perspective

Individual and group behaviour is determined by an equal society, a society in which social divisions are a response to consensus between all members of society.

Structural-consensus theory explains social life through the learning and acceptance of shared cultural norms and values. **Socialisation**, or the way that human beings learn how to behave appropriately, is central to structural-consensus theory. Socialisation explains why societies are different, but also why a particular society remains stable. For example, in the UK our socialisation involves learning about and accepting capitalism, while in China people are socialised into communist principles, but accept that private enterprise is necessary to exist in the world economy. Both countries are stable, even though they have different rules that govern behaviour, these rules being part of the way of life, or culture, of that society (see Area 4 on Society and Cultural Identities). Therefore, socialisation results in an agreement, or consensus, between members of society about what constitutes appropriate behaviour.

Structural-consensus theory argues that a society's culture determines, or structures, individual behaviour, which is driven in a particular direction. For example, as an AS/A Level student your choice to continue in education has been directed by the culture of your society, with great worth being attributed to further education and the future reward it can bring you. You know what is expected of you as a student and, on the whole, you tend to behave appropriately while at school or college. Structural-consensus theorists claim that social structures also constrain individuals through the cultural rules that determine the position they occupy. Therefore, socialisation into society's cultural rules structures behaviour and guarantees consensus on appropriate behaviour, ensuring social stability.

HINTS AND TIPS   Positions in the social structure are known as roles. Rules that structure behaviour are called norms. Cultural rules not attached to any role are referred to as values. Structural-consensus theorists, such as functionalists, always refer to these elements in their theories.

Sometimes differences in behaviour and values will arise that do not agree with prevailing norms. Structural-consensus theorists explain this with reference to the existence of alternative cultural influences, such as class, 'race' or gender, which affect behaviour. For example, the different socialisation experienced by girls and boys has been used to explain the different roles they later inhabit in the occupational structure. However, this does not mean that overall consensus is threatened. Even though cultural differences may exist within society, socialisation into the **core values**, indisputable values on which all societies are based, ensures that the status quo is never challenged.

Individualistic theory

Herbert Spencer (1820–1903) established an individualistic theory of society that can be linked to structural-consensus theory, by arguing that society was regulated by the mutual self-interest of individuals. This can be seen as a type of unconscious consensus or agreement between social actors. Spencer stated that individual initiative was the basis for economic development and that minimum state intervention was the key to sustaining this (ideas later adopted by the New Right).

Auguste Comte (1798–1857) disagreed with Spencer on how individual freedom could be maintained in the social world. Comte advocated a strong state presence, while Spencer argued that civilised trade between people would sustain social stability. This debate emphasises a fundamental issue of sociological theory – the relationship between individuals and the social structure, an issue examined at length by functionalist theorists.

Functionalism

Functionalism is a structural-consensus theory linked very closely to the advances of nineteenth-century science. Social life was explained using the language of biology, with references being made to 'structure' and 'function'. The first major exponent of the functionalist approach was Émile Durkheim (1858–1917), who argued that individuals are directed by the social system and have little control over their own actions. Durkheim's work influenced the research of anthropologists Malinowski and Radcliffe-Brown in the 1920s, who used functionalism to explain social organisation in primitive societies. It also had a huge effect on Talcott Parsons (1902–79) who, along with Robert Merton (b. 1910), developed functionalism as the guiding theoretical perspective of the period from the 1930s to 1950s.

Émile Durkheim

The concept applied by structural theorists that social forces are independent of the individual became established through the theory of French sociologist Durkheim in the late nineteenth century. Durkheim took a consensus approach, arguing that social structures are created from norms and values established during socialisation (see earlier information on structural-consensus theory). Social life is therefore a consequence of learning societal culture, a process that is structured by society and peoples' positions within it. For example, as Durkheim (1964:7) wrote, children are not born knowing the norms and values of the society into which they are thrown, they have to learn them from others in order to survive:

> ... all education is a continuous effort to impose on the child ways of seeing, feeling and acting which he would not have arrived at spontaneously. From the very first hours of his life, we compel him to eat, drink, and sleep at regular hours; we constrain him to cleanliness, calmness, and obedience; later we exert pressure upon him in order that he may learn proper consideration of others, respect for customs and conventions, the need for work, etc. If, in time, this constraint ceases to be felt, it is because it gradually gives rise to habits and to internal tendencies that render constraint unnecessary; but nevertheless it is not abolished, for it is still the source from which these habits were derived.

Durkheim referred to the agreed rules or culture of a society, that constrain behaviour in order to maintain society, as **social facts**, for example moral codes. These social facts, or cultural rules, determine individual behaviour and were seen to exist *prior* to the individual. However, if this is the case, then a different explanation is needed to show how these rules were established in the first place.

Organic analogy

As suggested earlier, functionalism has its origins in the scientific tradition. Durkheim attempted to explain social structures by comparing them to (making an analogy with) biological organisms. He argued that a living organism is dependent on the functioning of all the organs within it to survive. All organs are interdependent and indispensable because each has a specific, but integrated function, which makes the system work properly. For example, your body requires all its organs to be functioning correctly and working together in order for you to feel completely healthy. If one organ fails, this can jeopardise your life or make your body function less effectively. Durkheim argued that the character of society could be explained in exactly the same way.

Social systems, or working social structures, were seen by Durkheim to consist of structured cultural rules (norms, values and belief systems) to which society's members conform (become **institutionalised**). The institutions of society, such as education and the family, perform necessary functions that help to maintain the social system. Therefore, a social system is made up of interdependent parts that are indispensable, just as in an organism, and society would falter if part of the system collapsed (see Figure 1.1).

It should be noted that Durkheim used the organic analogy:

a To show the way in which the whole of the social system can be understood only by examining the parts that make it up.

b To highlight the difference between the cause and effect of social facts, in that the functions performed by social facts are separate from the consequences of them. In other words, effects are what happen after an event and cause is what initiates the event.

Human nature

Durkheim argued that social order, or as he called it social solidarity, exists because of 'human nature', or the inherent tendency and unquenchable desire to be constrained by attainable goals. Moral codes were seen to be the social fact that regulated individual desires. For example, in pre-industrial societies individuals performed similar tasks, had shared interests

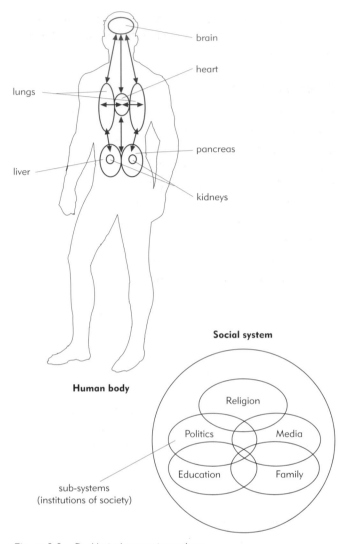

Figure 1.1 Durkheim's organic analogy

(**mechanical solidarity**) and therefore only required simple moral codes to guide them. Durkheim argued that religion offered the moral codes of '**collective conscience**' that secured social order by making people accept and be satisfied with their fate.

In complex industrial societies shared interests have been replaced by different, but interdependent economic needs (**organic solidarity**). Durkheim argued moral codes, have weakened (**anomie**) as a consequence of specialised and individual roles in the social system. However, Durkheim maintained that anomie would not threaten social solidarity by allowing 'human nature' to run wild with its desires, but would be controlled by the moral codes of associations at work.

For further information on the work of Durkheim see Area 2 on Sociological Research Methodology and Area 9 on Religion.

Talcott Parsons

Parsons' structural functionalist theory dominated American sociology until the 1960s and was both revered and criticised. Parsons took his theoretical framework from Durkheim, but surprisingly was also influenced by Weber's social action theory. Parsons' work has consequently been grouped into four phases, which identify specific themes within his theorising:

1   **Simple social-action phase** – the actor was seen to have choice in social action, but is also guided by social facts, social forces, situations and goals. Parsons called this the 'action-situation frame of reference' (1951).

2   **Developed social-action phase** – Parsons elaborated on the role of 'actors', 'orientations' and 'situations', allowing the individual to be seen as a thinking and feeling being prior to action. However, he also pointed out that all actions are directed by the structural context that surrounds them.

3   **Social-systems phase** – Parsons examined the connections and interrelations between social subsystems and the rest of society, for example the economy. He argued that four **functional imperatives/prerequisites**, or problems that need to be solved in order for society to function, exist in all social systems:

- Adaptation – the system must accommodate the demands of the environment.
- Goal attainment – objectives and priorities must be defined, agreed and realised.
- Latency – individuals must generally agree with and be committed to social and group values and resolve any tension that arises as a consequence of this.
- Integration – relationships in society must be organised and regulated to appear legitimate.

4   **Action meets function phase** – Parsons developed his theory on four main 'systems of action' (1966) that made society function:

- Cultural system – beliefs, ideas and values.

- Social system – patterns of expectations institutionalised in social structures, such as norms, values, collectivities and roles.
- Personality system – motives, predisposition and temperaments.
- Organic system – biological and psychological needs.

It was also at this stage that he examined the role of **structural differentiation**, the specialisation of particular institutions on social problems, in society. He argued that structural differentiation had 'adaptively upgraded' society (socially evolved) or changed to support more complex and specialised functions. For example, as industrialisation developed social evolution supported by structural differentiation changed the role of family from a unit of production to a unit of social support. Social equilibrium or balance is maintained by improved prosperity and sustained value consensus (agreement on what is good and worthwhile).

ACTIVITY KS **COMMUNICATION, WORKING WITH OTHERS**

KNOWLEDGE AND UNDERSTANDING	IDENTIFICATION AND INTERPRETATION	ANALYSIS AND EVALUATION

In pairs write a list of all the social structures (cultural rules and values) that you think are good and worthwhile. Justify your choices. Then consider whether there are any social structures that you do not agree with in society and write them down too. Based on the evidence in front of you, evaluate whether you agree with the functionalist concept of 'value consensus'. Present your findings to the rest of the group.

Robert K Merton

Merton attempted to develop functionalism as a theory so that it could incorporate the issues of complex, highly differentiated industrial societies (1949). In fact, his functionalist theory has become known as Mertonian functionalism, because of its differences from traditional functionalism.

Merton began his overhaul of functionalism by examining the social consequences of specific institutions. To do this he redefined the term 'function' as:

1   Social function – the objective and observable consequences of a person's action.

2   Manifest function – when something has intended and recognised social consequences.
3   Latent function – when something has unintended or unrecognised social consequences.

His precise definitions of 'function' displayed his belief that functionalism and sociology should be interested only in 'outcomes', not subjective motives.

Merton also challenged the assumption that all aspects of the social system have a positive function. He identified '**dysfunctions**' within society, which meant that social practice could have harmful as well as positive effects, depending on the structural context in which they occurred. For example, religion has been argued by some theorists to be an institution that integrates social groups and societies, however this is not always the case, as wars in the Balkans have shown recently.

The idea that societies can have dysfunctional practices led Merton to argue that the concepts of '**functional unity**' and '**functional universality**' were incorrect. Early functionalists had assumed that society is always integrated and harmonious (functional unity) and that every persistent social practice and cultural item is necessary to the maintenance of society. Merton suggested that the degree of societal integration is variable and that the functions of some institutions may be carried out by other institutions (functional alternatives) just as well. For example, the role of 'the family' was taken over by the whole community in Israeli Kibbutzim. As a structural-consensus theorist Merton maintained that these varying degrees of societal integration and the appearance of functional alternatives were still dependent on the structural context in which they occur.

Merton managed to address some of the major criticisms that functionalism was facing from the 1940s to the 1960s. His concept of functional alternatives removed the tautology of his predecessors by showing that items do not always have to fulfil the needs of the social system. He also identified the possibility of dysfunctional practices, to counter the obvious negative effects of some institutions on society. Likewise Durkheim provided valuable insights into the working of contemporary society as a system. However, despite these achievements functionalist theory remains heavily challenged by a diverse range of sociologists.

Evaluation of functionalism

1   It provides insight into the working of the social system.
2   It is **teleological**, which means that it explains cause by effect. For example, functionalism argues that institutions exist because they benefit the social system, which is rather like saying 'You overeat because you are fat'. Getting fat is the effect of overeating not the cause!
3   It is difficult to assess the benefits an institution has for society. Therefore, a theory based upon the assumption that social institutions continue to exist because of the beneficial effects they have for society is unfounded.
4   The idea of value consensus maintaining social order is a hypothesis only and has yet to be shown to exist.
5   The concept of human behaviour being dictated by the social system has been said to ignore free will and interaction (social-action/interpretivist theories).
6   It has ignored a fundamental part of the social system – coercion and conflict (structural-conflict theories).

Strengths	Weaknesses
1 The role of socialisation in determining behaviour is recognised.	1 Violent and radical social change cannot be explained adequately by a theory that emphasises consensus.
2 The importance of culture in structuring society is identified.	2 Society does not have a life of its own (organic analogy), it is dependent on the people that make it up.
3 The importance of understanding how society is an integrated whole with independent parts is identified.	3 It supports conservatism and thereby justifies social equilibrium.
	4 Too deterministic, ignores possibility that individuals have free choice to resist social forces.
	5. Teleological.

Figure 1.2   Structural-consensus theory

Neo-functionalism

'Neo' means new, and in relation to functionalism it refers to theorists who have adapted that theory to the contemporary world or updated it. Neo-functionalists have in common the inclusion of social norms and value consensus when explaining society and a less deterministic approach to the role of the individual. Kingsley Davis is one of the most noted neo-functionalists, despite the fact that he started theorising while Parsons was still going strong. Davis argues that all sociological theory is reliant upon functionalism's understanding of the social system, in that it seeks to account for persistent forms of social action and behaviour in the maintenance of society:

> ❛ ... consensus on the definition of structural-functional analysis does not exist, but the examination of the features most commonly mentioned and of the work actually done under this label shows it to be, in effect, synonymous with sociological analysis.

Davis, K. (1959:757)

In the mid-1980s there was a neo-functionalism revival led by Alexander (1985), which called for the reworking of macro sociology and the theories of Parsons. In fact, Luhmann (1982) attempted to rebuild Parsons' systems theory to remove the actor from any account of structure. This shows that functionalism retains some relevance to sociological theory; however, based on the many original criticisms of the approach, it is unlikely that it will resume dominance in the foreseeable future:

> ❛ ... it seems almost inconceivable now that any grand theory of the scale and scope of the functionalism-systems theory paradigm could reemerge to dominate the discipline in the near future.

Hamilton in Turner (Ed.) (1998:169)

New Right

As mentioned previously in this section, the New Right perspective adopted the principles of individualistic theory. It is a particular type of individualism, focusing on minimal state intervention and control and maximum individual freedom, which has shaped New Right theory and politics.

The most famous manifestation of New Right theory is within the politics of Margaret Thatcher's and John Major's Conservative governments. New Right Conservative politics emphasised not only the benefits

of a capitalist 'free market' in sustaining personal freedom, but also moral and cultural consensus. National campaigns were initiated under grand titles, such as 'Back To Basics', which were aimed at bringing the community together over commonly held moral beliefs, for example the value of the family unit. New Right theory within sociology has been relatively slow to develop, but since the late 1980s sociologists, such as Peter Saunders (1990), have provided explanations of social issues using New Right theory.

Peter Saunders

The basis for Saunders' theory of society lies in the economic thinking of Hayek (1960) and Friedman (1980) in that equality of opportunity in a free market economy provides the most efficient form of society. Saunders argues that competition is open and based on ability, but that this ability is naturally unevenly distributed. Rewards provide motivation to compete and are recognition of effort and ability. Social stratification is therefore considered to be fair, as it reflects biological inequality in society (see Area 3 on Social Stratification and Differentiation). It also means that outcomes will never be equal, i.e. people will never have the same access to material and cultural resources; but Saunders argues that this is functional and acceptable.

Saunders does support **selectivist provision** (see Area 10 on Wealth, Poverty, Welfare and Social Policy) for the very needy, such as the homeless, but rejects state intervention in the balance of equality. He states that capitalism will raise living standards generally and that any remaining inequality will act as a motivating force for people. Saunders also realises that for capitalism to work at optimum efficiency society must provide a structure that supports and reinforces a 'set of core values which bind people together through ties of mutual obligation and social responsibility' (1995:119). In this way it can be argued that New Right theory has a structural-consensus approach, expecting social actors to agree on how society functions based on legitimating social norms and values, in the interests of society.

New Right theory has been challenged for assuming that individuals all aspire to a higher morality that will make them behave in the 'right' way. However, most people's needs and relationships are highly structured and institutionalised. For example, the basic human need of shelter is institutionalised in the form of renting or buying accommodation; while family life revolves around parent/s and offspring. Therefore, if people were suddenly given total individual freedom, it would potentially cause chaos, because people would be able to do whatever they wanted. For example, bivouacs might suddenly be erected on the motorway or children might be left to be raised by packs of dogs.

Perhaps the most challenged assumption of New Right theory is that there are biological inequalities between individuals and that these are fairly reflected in the social structure. The majority of sociologists would argue that most inequalities are socially constructed, such as class and gender divisions (see Area 3 on Social Stratification and Differentiation). Charles Murray and Richard Herrnstein (1994) displayed how dangerous this argument could be if developed by claiming in *The Bell Curve* that ethnic minorities in the USA were at the bottom of the stratification system because of their 'race'. Not only did their argument lack objective evidence, but it also fuelled racist beliefs and nationalistic tendencies. However, despite these criticisms the New Right theoretical approach has sustained political support in both the UK and the USA.

Structural-conflict perspective

Individual and group behaviour is determined by an unequal society, a society in which social divisions are created by the conflict of interests between those who 'have' and those who 'have not'. In other words, all groups in society have different interests, with the social structure benefiting some at the expense of others.

The structural-conflict perspective argues that people are constrained by their position in an unequal society. It emphasises the effects of an 'unequal distribution of advantage' (Jones, 1990) on the behaviour of an individual, such as unequal amounts of power, wealth and prestige. Theories that fall under the structural-conflict umbrella believe that the advantaged groups have power and control over the disadvantaged groups to maintain social inequality, i.e. it sustains a conflict of interests.

Structural-conflict theories also argue that it is the reward system of a society and the advantages it gives people that determine behaviour (not socialisation as other perspectives may argue). In an unjust system you would expect people to complain; however inequality is accepted, which enables society to work or function. This acceptance of disadvantage is intentionally or unintentionally forced upon the individual, through methods such as the threat of death or by creating norms and values (culture), which through socialisation, makes them think that their situation is acceptable and even just.

HINTS AND TIPS   *Consider Area 10 dealing with poverty and the concept of relative deprivation. It explains clearly how people put up with inequality until they realise that other people are actually much better off than they are for no apparent reason.*
If you apply this concept to structural-conflict theories it is easier to understand how inequality is perpetuated, but sometimes challenged. In the words of 1980s/90s pop group James in the song **Sit Down***, 'If I hadn't seen such riches I could live with*

Marxism

Marxism, or, as it has come to be referred to, traditional Marxism, is based on the work of Karl Marx (see profile on page 19). It is a structural-conflict theory that argues that society is controlled by the way in which people organise it to survive. This organisation can lead to conflict, because some people may benefit (the ruling class) at the expense of others (the subject class), resulting in massive inequality. In turn, this inequality has to appear fair and acceptable for society to function, therefore Marx investigated the history and importance of class conflict in structuring the social system. He also examined the potential for change within a society based on class inequality.

HINTS AND TIPS   *The easiest way to remember the essence of Marxist theory is to think of it as having three main beliefs:*
1 *The economy is the most important thing in society.*
2 *To analyse society you have to take into account class conflict.*
3 *Class conflict will eventually lead to communism.*

However, it should be acknowledged that there is a general disagreement among sociologists about what

Marx actually meant. His theory is full of inconsistencies: for example, he started off as a phenomenological sympathiser, concentrating on the individual's interpretation of the situation, but came to rely more and more on a material/structural emphasis as his writing developed. As a consequence different sociologists have adopted different elements of his work to explain social phenomena, giving rise to many interpretations of Marxism.

Infrastructure and superstructure

Central to Marxism is the idea of subsistence, or economic activity that produces material goods necessary for survival, which refers to food, clothing and shelter. Marx argued that the way in which a society organises its production of material goods affects the whole social structure, from politics to religion. For example, if a society shares out its resources equally, ensuring a basic subsistence for all its members, then the other institutions in that social structure will reflect that. In this way the economic base or **infrastructure** dictates the activities of all the other institutions, value and belief systems in society, known as the **superstructure**. The superstructure in turn maintains and reflects the infrastructure, thereby sustaining the status quo.

Marx therefore theorised that the ideas, values and beliefs in the superstructure would perform an important role in society. Class-based societies are founded on exploitation and oppression. These social inequalities have to be tolerated, accepted or go unnoticed by the most disadvantaged for that society to survive. This is where the superstructure comes in: it perpetuates ruling-class control (**hegemony**), promoting the infrastructure as legitimate and/or desirable. For example, religion reflected and supported the infrastructure of the feudal mode of production by encouraging serfs to accept their terrible lives on earth by promising rewards in heaven. In other words, we learn to see inequality as legitimate, because the superstructure hides from us the real factors of a class society.

History

Marx argued that different societies in different historical periods organised the production of material goods in very different ways. However, it was the labour of human beings in producing material goods

SUPERSTRUCTURE

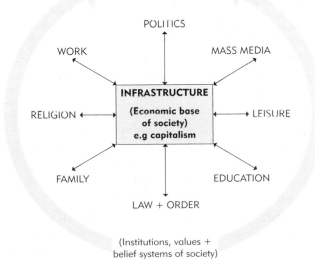

(Institutions, values + belief systems of society)

Figure 1.3   A representation of Marx's concept of superstructure infrastructure

that Marx saw as essential in understanding history and social life. This concept has been referred to as **historical** or **dialectical materialism**. Dialectic simply means a process of change that occurs through a conflict of opposing forces. Marx argued that these forces were material conditions (unlike Hegel who said that they were ideas), such as capitalism, and that they determined social change, hence dialectical materialism. Therefore Marx believed that social change lies in the conflict inherent in the economic system. However, Marx himself only ever referred to these ideas as 'the materialist concept of history'.

Marx's picture of history was not based on any empirical evidence, but outlined a theory of what might have been. He argued that there have been five different ways of societies organising production (producing material goods). Sometimes these modes of production are referred to as **epochs**, or a period of historical change with a specific way of organising its production, which are:

- primitive communism – based on subsistence and equality
- ancient – class-based on masters and servants
- feudal – class-based on nobility and serfs/peasants
- capitalism – class-based on bourgeoisie and proletariat
- communism – based on equality.

Class

Primitive communism was classless, in that everybody was equal in fulfilling his or her basic human needs for subsistence. Marx defined **class** as a group's or individual's relationship to the **means of production** (the things necessary to produce the goods and services needed by an individual). Therefore, in primitive communism everyone shared the same relationship to the means of production, resulting in only one class. However, ancient, feudal and capitalist systems of organisation are based on two basic class divisions, between those who own the means of production (**the ruling class**) and those who do not (**the subject class**). For example, in capitalism the bourgeoisie own the factories and companies necessary to produce the materials needed by people to survive. Whether you own the means of production or not is known as your **class relation**.

Owning the means of production gives the ruling class more power, wealth and prestige than those who do not. In fact, those who do not own the means of production have only their labour to sell or bargain with in order to survive. However, class-based societies need the labour power of the subject class to run effectively, which makes the ruling class dependent upon them, but it is an unequal dependency. The subject class makes up the mass of the population and is therefore expendable. For example, if a member of the subject class complains about conditions of employment in capitalism, he or she can be sacked and replaced by someone who needs the work to feed, clothe and house his or her family. Therefore the relationship between the classes is one of exploitation and oppression, or conflict.

Changes <u>in</u> systems of production

Marx argued that all societies would eventually pass through the first four epochs and enter a communist mode of production. It may not happen at the same time, but he was certain that as the final epoch was reached, conflict would no longer exist and as class conflict was the driving force of social change, history would end with communism.

> *The history of all hitherto existing society is the history of class struggle.*

> Karl Marx and Friedrich Engels (1998:34)

Class-based epochs have been based on the domination and exploitation of the subject class by the ruling class. The conflicting basis of the classes remains the same in each epoch, although the classes themselves are different. For example, in the feudal mode of production the ruling class was the nobility or lords, because they owned the land which was the means of production, while the subject class was the peasants or serfs who worked the land. However, in capitalism the ruling class is the bourgeoisie because they own the factories that produce material goods, while the subject class is the proletariat who work for them.

Marx argues that historical and social change occurs when one mode of production withers as another one begins to flourish. Primitive communism's lack of technology and a hostile environment meant that existence was based on subsistence, or producing the basics necessary for survival. It is suggested that it was the arrival of new technologies that led to the development of surplus and private property. Previously, this mode of production had been unable to produce a surplus and therefore there were no 'haves' and 'have nots', no classes. The occurrence of private surplus property meant that some people had more than others and that a class division was evident. This new property-owning class became the ancient masters.

Ancient society depended on the power of the state, but as this crumbled it became more difficult to force people to do as the state decreed. Therefore, slavery disintegrated and a new mode of production emerged based on the power of local nobility and lords. It was a smaller and more sustainable system than ancient society, with regional warlords controlling pieces of land and coercing an agricultural labour force to work on it to secure a tenancy. The tenancies cost the peasants dearly, but were their only means of survival.

Gradually, however, state control of the feudal territories grew and national trading developed. Also, agricultural production became more efficient, forcing the serfs to seek alternative methods of subsistence, as they became landless. The only thing they had at their disposal was their labour power, which they had to sell to survive. The consequence of this was a labour market, in which property owners paid a wage to this new **proletariat**.

Capitalism therefore developed before industrialisation, but when things other than agricultural goods began to be produced, the factories of industrial capitalism took over. These factories were owned and controlled by the bourgeoisie, a ruling class like all the others, who exploited and oppressed the proletariat in order to sustain their advantaged position in society. The dominance of the bourgeoisie became based upon the surplus value or profit they attained from the difference between the cost of producing goods and the price they were sold at. The proletariat will always receive less in wages than the product costs to produce, reinforcing their exploitation by the bourgeoisie.

However, despite the superstructure legitimating the exploitation of the proletariat by the bourgeoisie, massive inequality can be justified only for as long as the masses accept it. The realisation of their own oppression by the proletariat is known as class

consciousness. Marx predicted that this would emerge as capitalism developed, because the bourgeoisie would exploit the proletariat more and more:

> *The development of modern industry, therefore, cuts from under its feet the very foundation on which the bourgeoisie produces and appropriates products. What the bourgeoisie therefore produces above all, are its own grave-diggers. Its fall and the victory of the proletariat are equally inevitable.*

Karl Marx and Friedrich Engels (1998:50)

The increased automation of factories means that labour is not needed at the same level and unemployment rates rise. The consumers include the unemployed and therefore the demand for goods may go down. The capitalists still have to produce the goods at a profit, which means further cuts to employment levels or wages. Also, small businesses will not be able to compete with large organisations, leading to all intermediate groups entering the ranks of the proletariat. As the gap between rich and poor grows ever wider, the proletariat will start to awake from their false class consciousness (lack of realisation about their oppression and exploitation). Polarisation, or the division of the two classes into even more distinct groups, will result in the proletariat becoming a class 'in itself' (class conscious) and 'for itself' (class solidarity). At this point it will have reached the stage where a revolution to overthrow capitalism is possible. Marx and Engels (1998:77) argued in *The Communist Manifesto* that 'the proletarians have nothing to lose but their chains', enticing the masses into a violent revolution, the final goal being a society in which the means of production would be communally owned.

Alienation

Capitalism, according to Marx, is a bad thing not only because it oppresses and exploits the mass of society, but also because it separates them from the product of their labour. **Alienation** is therefore the separation of workers from the tools of their trade and the final product, as a result of increased mechanisation, automation and specialisation in capitalist industry. It reaches it height in capitalism, because the workers have to labour to survive, which means that work becomes a means to an end, rather than an end in itself.

Marx argued that alienation is soul destroying for the workers, who never have the satisfaction of seeing what has been produced by their toil. Human labour is the most vital part of human activity, its essence. To be deprived of a connection with the creations of one's work results in the workers feeling that they have no control over their life.

The concept of alienation is crucial to an understanding of Marxism. It shows how the workers are separated from their purpose in life under capitalism and how this division perpetuates the inequality in the system, by making people underestimate their potential and abilities. For example, Marx argued that by giving supernatural powers, such as God, the credit for creating the world people were duped into accepting their alienation. Instead, people should have realised that it was they, not the economy or God, that controlled their own destiny. Therefore for people to rediscover their 'human essence', their ability to labour and shape the world according to human needs, capitalism must be overthrown and replaced with a system in which all own and control the means of production.

Strengths	Weaknesses
Taken-for-granted institutions, such as employment and the legal system, are examined critically.	Ownership or non-ownership of the means of production (class relation) is seen as the most important factor when examining society: all other factors are secondary. The superstructure can play a directing role in social change.
Major inequalities are challenged through examining conflict in society, such as lack of power and wealth.	The ruling class is seen to be in a 'conspiracy' to maintain the oppression of the subject class.
It provides an explanation for the maintenance of existing social systems, by showing that various parts of society are interrelated.	History has not supported Marx's claims about the route of social change – class has become more complex rather than polarised, communism in eastern Europe has been replaced by democracy.
It is not a deterministic theory, because 'Man makes his own history'. The economy was created by people and can therefore be changed only by people.	Has been accused of economic determinism and some forms of Marxism appear to do this.

Figure 1.4 Marxism

Neo-Marxism

The term neo-Marxism refers to sociological theories that apply Marxism to societal conditions in the second half of the twentieth century. In other words, the social change that Marx predicted – class conflict causing a proletarian revolution in which the means of production in advanced industrial societies would be seized and given to the masses resulting in communism – did not happen. Russia experienced a communist revolution, but its industry was underdeveloped and did not meet the conditions Marx said would be necessary for a revolution. Therefore, contemporary Marxists have attempted to explain why a revolution in the West has not happened. They are called neo-Marxists because of their new or 'neo' approach.

Louis Althusser

Louis Althusser, a neo-Marxist, argued that Marxism is scientific and **reductionist**. By this he meant that Marxism is not concerned with a quest for a humane society or in explaining social change as resulting from anything other than the economy (unlike the Frankfurt School who argued that Marxism is humanistic, as we will see later). Althusser took a structuralist approach, in that people are controlled by the structure of society and its relations of production, but not by history. Therefore class conflict is inherent in society, but the potential for class consciousness is not: this has to be released by freeing the masses from their conditioning into the dominant **ideology** (norms, values and beliefs of those in power) (see Area 4 on Society and Cultural Identities). However, according to Althusser the dominant ideology is sustained by ideological state apparatus, or agencies of the state, such as the education system, which have the primary function of making sure that the masses accept capitalism. Therefore the liberation of the subordinate group into class consciousness appears difficult under the conditioning of ideological state apparatus.

Western Marxism and later humanist Marxists, such as Thompson (1978), have criticised the concepts of Althusser for ignoring the active role that people play in social change. Throughout history people have fought their oppressors. However, because of the huge range of interpretations of Marx's writings, humanist Marxists have in turn been challenged for underplaying the economic conditions of these people's existence.

Karl Marx

(1818–83)

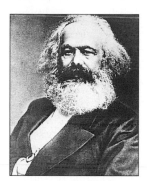

Marx, a German political philosopher, was born in Trier, Germany and educated in Bonn, Berlin and Jena. He started writing by contributing to a newspaper (*Rheinische Zeitung*) in Cologne in 1842. He soon became the editor and used the newspaper to criticise social conditions in Germany. His views led to the paper being closed down and Marx went to Paris, where he developed his communist perspective. Engels joined Marx in Paris in 1844 and they collaborated in producing a theory of principles of communism (scientific socialism) and in organising a working-class movement based on those principles.

Marx's revolutionary activities led to him being forced to leave Paris in 1845. He went to Belgium and continued to mobilise the European working class through Communist Correspondence Committees, which became the Communist League in 1847. Marx and Engels formulated a statement of principles for the League called *The Communist Manifesto*, which became the first systematic modern socialist doctrine. *The Communist Manifesto* contained a materialist conception of history, or historical materialism, that was developed in Marx's *Critique of Political Economy* (1859).

The Belgian government, afraid of a revolution occurring as it had in France and Germany, turned Marx out in 1848. Marx went first to Paris and then back to Germany, where he established a communist paper (*Neue Rheinische Zeitung*). In 1849 Marx was arrested for provoking revolutionary tendencies; he was acquitted but was expelled from Germany. He went to France, but was also expelled from there and so went to England. He led the remainder of his life in London and is buried there.

While in England, Marx devoted himself to writing, philosophising and to establishing an international communist movement. His work at this time included: *Das Kapital* (volume 1, 1867; volumes 2 and 3, edited by Engels and published after his death in 1885 and 1894, respectively; translated 1907–09), *The Civil War in France* (1871) and *The Gotha Program* (1875; translated 1922). He also contributed articles on contemporary political and social events to newspapers in Europe and the USA, such as the *New York Tribune*.

The last few years of Marx's life were filled with a struggle against ill health. After his death, documents were found and these were later published by the German socialist Karl Johann Kautsky as *Theories of Surplus Value* (4 volumes, 1905–10; translated 1952). Marx may not have influenced society a great deal during his life, but after his death the labour movement grew rapidly. His theories have made him one of the most influential thinkers in the world, supplying the basis for modern socialist doctrine.

Althusser has also been criticised for applying the term 'ideological state apparatus', because of the assumed conspiracy among those who operate under state control.

Western Marxism

Western Marxism is also neo-Marxism, but the term refers more specifically to the work originating from 1920s sociologists who based their theories on the **humanistic** writing of Marx. Humanism refers to the way in which society's members are seen to construct social order. As mentioned earlier, Marx thought that 'Man makes his own history' and this led to a humanist interpretation of Marx's theory. Western Marxism rejected what it saw as the 'base' or 'vulgar' type of Marxism which reduced everything in social life to economic interests or the relationship between the infrastructure and the superstructure.

Western Marxism also attempted to explain the lack of a proletarian revolution, which Marx had predicted, by showing that the working-class consciousness had been shaped in such a way as to prevent the true nature of capitalism being realised.

George Lukacs

George Lukacs was the first western Marxist and he argued that the main element in Marxism is **social totality**. Social totality is when:

> ❛ *... the true identity of things is provided by their relationship to a whole. For example, the individual characteristics of a person do not make a person a slave, and nothing in the constitution of a particular machine makes it an item of capital. These items acquire those identities only as part of a system.*

> Cuff. E. C., Sharrock. W. W., and Francis. D. W., (1990:185)

In other words, society as a whole dictates what the pieces are that make it up. Lukacs therefore rejected the traditional Marxist view that economic conditions alone could cause class consciousness, it must instead be caused by society as a whole. He also argued that only the working class could understand totality, because after the communist revolution they will be humanity.

Lukacs also addressed the traditional Marxist notion that people, on the whole, believe that the world operates independently of them, rather than being a consequence of their actions. He called this **reification**, or a mystification of reality, and linked it to the idea of totality by suggesting that it stopped people understanding the whole of the capitalist economic system.

Antonio Gramsci

Antonio Gramsci (1891–1937) was another western Marxist who argued that ideas and economic interests are of equal value for social life, because ideas play an important role in social change. Gramsci argued that cultural and intellectual (ideological) domination by the ruling class, or hegemony, of the subject class is a necessary part of class conflict.

Gramsci argued that hegemony referred to an accepted form of leadership that can operate alongside coercive rule or instead of it. In fact, hegemonic rule could be argued to be more effective than force, especially if the subordinate group accepts as legitimate the dominant group. For example, the ideology of the bourgeoisie may be seen as part of popular culture in advertising. Advertising legitimates the desire of people to consume the products of capitalism, while at the same time sustaining a committed workforce who must work to be able to afford to consume. Therefore Gramsci's work suggests that cultural and ideological struggle should be included within a general concept of Marxist struggle. Only by seizing this hegemony from the bourgeoisie is it possible for the proletariat to escape it oppression.

Gramsci argued that this hegemony varies over time and therefore strategies for further socialist revolution would have to take into account that it had not been as embedded in Russia as it was in western Europe. Therefore, the revolution witnessed in Russia would not necessarily be the route of transformation taken in western Europe. Gramsci suggested that the bourgeoisie is often divided and that the proletariat experiences a **dual consciousness**, which reflects the ideas of the bourgeoisie and its own lives. Therefore the bourgeois ideology may never become coherent, allowing the proletariat to see through it, change its ideas and challenge the dominant ideas imposed upon it.

The concept of hegemony has directly influenced the work of the Centre for Contemporary Cultural Studies (CCCS) in Birmingham, which has developed cultural theory since the 1970s under the directorship of Stuart Hall (see Area 4 on Society and Cultural Identities). Consequently, Gramsci's use of Marxism has become known as cultural Marxism. However, the CCCS has adopted the approach that cultural and ideological struggle is the most important type of struggle, rather than seeing it as part of the political struggle against capitalist domination, as Gramsci intended.

The Frankfurt School/Critical Theory

The Frankfurt School was constituted of a collection of western Marxists, including Herbert Marcuse, who were associated with the Institute for Social Research at the University of Frankfurt. The main ideas of the School were put forward between the 1920s and the 1960s, but were most influential between the 1960s and 1980s. Although there were variations in the theorists' application of Marxism, there was a general agreement that capitalism destroys the critical thought necessary for challenging the whole system (hence the identification of their work as 'critical theory'). For example, in a mass society people become the same and are controlled, directly and indirectly, by the state and through the 'culture industry', which provide (superficial) meaning in their lives (see Area 4 on Society and Cultural Identities). Also, in common with Lukacs, the Frankfurt School emphasised the role of ideas, focusing on The Enlightenment, in social change.

The Frankfurt School argues that economic affluence and The Enlightenment had stripped the working class of its identity, included it in capitalism and made it unable to undertake a communist revolution. According to Marcuse the working class has the appearance of freedom, but really it experiences a repressive tolerance, a system that allows it to express ideas as a way of stopping any potential revolutionary tendencies.

The Enlightenment resulted in the domination of nature and some humans by science. The Frankfurt School/Critical Theory has argued that the scientific method, with its systematic and organised approach, has been adopted for the administration of society. Therefore the social system has ended up being controlled by science, with the illusion of freedom, but with the actuality of tight government control over what questions are asked. Consequently, Critical Theory challenged the idea of science, suggesting that it manipulates people into passively accepting capitalism, rather than supporting their welfare.

Jurgen Habermas

Habermas (1972, 1981, 1989) has developed critical theory from a contemporary perspective by including the influence of Durkheim, Mead and Parsons. He argues that it is possible to understand the world and use knowledge to construct a better one. This support of The Enlightenment ideas (see introduction) and refusal to accept postmodernist claims that it is impossible rationally to understand society, shows Habermas's aim to restructure the meaning of rationality. He believes that humans can change their environment and use signs to communicate (language), creating a stage for rational communication.

Habermas may accept ideas from The Enlightenment, but he is critical of the distortions introduced to the meaning of rationality by **positivism**. Like the Frankfurt

Structural	Humanistic
Althusser, Gramsci (both)	**Frankfurt School, Thompson, Marcuse, Lukacs, Gramsci (both)**
Scientific approach.	Humane approach.
Reductionism (everything in society is driven by the economy/relations of production) or economic determinism.	Non-reductionism (the economy is important in driving society, but so are ideas).
Economic struggles will cause social change.	Ideological and cultural struggles, as well as economic struggles, are necessary to cause social change.
A proletarian revolution is possible within capitalism, because the system is based on inherent conflict.	A proletarian revolution is unlikely within capitalism, because the system manipulates people's needs.

Figure 1.5   Differences between two types of neo-Marxism

> ### Rationalisation
> Habermas's notion of rationalisation involves the growth of rational standards of interpersonal behaviour and the way in which we reflect on our actions and communicate through arguments judged by their logic and truth.

School, Habermas argues that science can never be objective, as claimed by positivism, because understanding involves both an object *and* a subject. Therefore rationalisation is both a process concerned with the achievement of organised goals (objective) and the development of knowledge in humans through active pursuit (subjective). In this way Habermas challenges Weber's notion of rationalisation, which ignores the cultural process involved, i.e. how people can develop mutual self-understanding.

Communication is seen as a tool in the struggle for political freedom by Habermas. Language is necessary for understanding and social actors are seen to enter into agreements during communicative rationality and action. Therefore, communication/reason is argued to be a liberating force, because it can be used to arrive at agreements and maintain social relationships. Logical argument allows consensus to be achieved by presenting all relevant evidence without subjectivity or constraint (Habermas called this the 'ideal speech situation'). This communicative rationality removes the pessimistic ending of Weber's rational world (see section on Weberianism, page 32), allowing rationality to play a role in making society better.

New Left

The ideas of the Frankfurt School, such as the proletariat accepting capitalism, were used in the development of the New Left. The New Left refers to a range of movements that emerged in the 1960s to challenge elements of inequality or unacceptable actions in society, such as sexual and racial discrimination or the Vietnam War. The New Left was seen as an alternative to the working-class struggle.

Traditional Marxists, however, challenge this approach by arguing that the working class, because of its position in the economic structure, is the only group or movement with the power to transform society. The New Left is simply forwarding radical ideas that lack the power to instigate social change.

It should be noted that Area 12 on Crime and Deviance examines New Left Realism: this takes a Marxist approach but emphasises subculture, relative deprivation and marginalisation as explanations of crime in the UK. It is therefore a radical alternative to traditional Marxism, but utilises the concept of working-class disadvantage to explain crime.

Post-Marxism

Post-Marxism refers to the collapse of Marxist theory since the USSR and eastern bloc countries in Europe abandoned their communist principles. The expansion of liberal free-market economies based on democracy has led many sociologists and political commentators to claim that Marxism is dead. In western Europe there has been a notable absence of organised class action. Changes in employment have reduced the numbers of manual workers, which has fragmented the workforce. A consequence of this has been seen as a weakening of political orientation in society, with class no longer determining political behaviour to the same extent (see Area 14 on Power, Politics and Protest). Without class solidarity the predictions of Marx seem unlikely to occur.

The position of socialism in the West has also been weakened by the crisis of confidence in and within left-wing politics over the last 20 years. Post-Marxism, or literally 'after Marxism', offers an attempt to modernise Marxism in the face of social and political changes, taking into account the contemporary relationship between class and individuals (as Great Britain's Communist Party – CPGB – acknowledged in its *Manifesto for New Times* in 1990). Some Marxists, such as Baudrillard (see section on Postmodernism), may have abandoned Marxism. The social changes noted above and the difficulties of applying traditional Marxist notions to contemporary society do present a challenge in applying Marxism today, but modern Marxists are attempting to make their theories more relevant to contemporary problems. Also, issues of power and social inequality will always be central to a social world based upon capitalism. Therefore, the insights provided by Marxism (see section on Marxism, page 14) will continue to be of relevance and use in our society and will inform sociology for years to come (see Jameson in Area 4 on Society and Cultural Identities).

Conflict and gender – feminist theories

Sociology was, until relatively recently, 'malestream' (Abbott and Wallace, 1997) or dominated by male thought and concerns. As a consequence of female subordination in society, women did not have much influence on the topics or content of sociological debate. Therefore the theories that emerged, such as traditional Marxism, ignored the lives and experiences of females. However, as society changed, giving women more freedom and equality of opportunity, so did sociology as an academic discipline.

That is not to say that women had always been unequal in social history. Some writers have claimed to have evidence that for 20,000 years women controlled social existence under the influence of Mata Devi, or the mother goddess, who gave power to women through the gift of creating life (*Sociology Review*, 1990). Recent history, such as the feudal era or twentieth-century socialist countries, shows that women and men were working together, doing the same physically demanding jobs.

Female inequality is therefore a relatively modern social construction. It was the creation of the mother-housewife role (Oakley, 1974) during industrialisation, that separated women's work from men's work through legislation created by male politicians, such as the Mines Act (1842) and the Factories Act (1819). The social (Queen Victoria supported the idea that 'a woman's place was in the home'), political (legislation) and economic (industry moved work into factories and the family ceased to be a unit of production) climate all supported a subordinate role for women in society. Housework and childcare became the primary role of women and was seen as less important than paid employment, now the province of men.

In the late 1960s the feminist movement raised questions about the situation of women in society. These questions, such as 'Why do women have fewer opportunities for success in the labour market than men?' entered the arena of sociological debate and have remained there ever since. Feminist sociology was born. Therefore feminism is a theoretical approach that explains the unequal position of women in society from the viewpoint of women (see Area 3 on Social Stratification and Differentiation). It is also a conflict perspective, because it focuses on the oppression of women by men, i.e. the conflict in society between the sexes.

The language of sociology also changed to support this development, removing its masculine assumptions and replacing them with gender-neutral terms. Feminism has changed a great deal since the 1960s, with early feminist assumptions being challenged for appearing:

- **racist** – Black feminists argue that the focus on white women's experiences in early feminism ignores the very different situation of black women in industrial societies;

- **toothless** – Radical feminists argue that a peaceful assault on patriarchy using legislation will not remove female subordination, only a radical reversal in the distribution of power from men to women will do this;

- **classless** – Marxist/socialist feminists argue that female equality lies in the hands of a working-class revolution that releases women from the exploitation of capitalism and their oppression by men.

Therefore, contemporary feminism should be referred to as feminisms, because of the variety of theoretical approaches contained within the perspective.

MISINTERPRETATIONS OF FEMINISM

Do you know what feminism is?
Yes. Well, you can have a woman who is very feminine and one who's not. (Agnes, 78)
Feminism? Well, the only thing I can think of is like a man acting like a woman. Is that what you mean? (Yvonne, 75)
Well, you say, very feminine. I suppose it is someone who doesn't like to get their hands dirty, you know … And always doing their hair and doing their eyelashes. (Carol, 38)

Feminism or women's liberation as 'equal rights'
Oh well, that's a thing that (laughs) … you can be a bus driver. Women's lib, is that. (Doreen, 70)
People who want women's lib., who want all the freedom of everything. (Dorothy, 79)
Fight for the rights of women, for equality, to make decisions to do what they want to do with their lives... (Cynthia, 53)
Well, to achieve equal opportunities for women and to change attitudes towards women. (Pauline, 39)
They want to be equal in life … they don't think that men should be superior to them … They don't think they should dress up. They don't think women should have to make themselves attractive for men. (Kristy, 19)
I think it is like an awareness of yourself as a woman and how you can live your life … to be aware of the limitations and lack of opportunities … that stop you living your life how you want to because you are a woman. (Hayley, 23)

Negative images of feminism and feminists
Of course, there's quite a few women's libbers on the telly, which sometimes can be taken to the extreme. (Sarah, 64)
Well, I think they go over the top with it. (Vera, 56)
I don't think they're that feminine, you know. (Joan, 51)
Well, they are usually all sort of for themselves. I think … (Carol, 38)
I still don't think you got to be as extreme as feminists. (Karen, 29)
… I thought of somebody, I don't know why, somebody on Greenham Common, like a lesbian. (Wendy, 22)

Source: 'Misinterpretations of Feminism' Jane Pilcher, *Sociology Review*, Novermber 1993, p.5

Liberal feminism

Liberal feminism was the earliest form of feminism and focused on the legal restrictions women faced. It advocated the introduction of new legislation as a way of achieving female equality. Therefore liberal feminists realised that women's disadvantage in society was socially constructed. This perspective has been criticised for ignoring patriarchy and therefore not challenging malestream ideas. It also fails to tackle class and 'race' differentiations that women experience and which may change their social life.

Ann Oakley was one the first feminists in the UK to examine female oppression from a sociological position and her work influenced the development of liberal feminism. Her theoretical approach was based on a critique of functionalist assumptions that gender divisions (see Area 3 on stratification) were natural and desirable in society (1972). Oakley argued that social divisions based on gender were social constructions designed to subordinate women in a patriarchal society.

Oakley's work encouraged liberal feminists to investigate the effect of legislation on the social construction of gender disadvantage. The liberal feminists raised the public profile of female inequality in the workplace, resulting in the government passing legislation in the form of the Equal Pay Act, 1970 and the Sex Discrimination Act, 1975, which gave women equal rights to men.

ACTIVITY   KS **COMMUNICATION**

> KNOWLEDGE AND
> UNDERSTANDING

Outline three characteristics of liberal feminism and three criticisms that could be made of this viewpoint.

Gender inequality, however, did not disappear from society. This is not surprising considering:

a The difficulties of imposing the laws. For example, equal pay for equal work is difficult to judge when women are doing different jobs from men (horizontal segregation).

b The small sanctions imposed for breaking these laws, such as a £50 fine for not allowing women to wear trousers at work.

c The fact that sex discrimination had become part of our culture (see Area 4 on Society and Cultural Identities) and is therefore taken for granted and perpetuated.

Radical feminism – Millet

Radical feminism concentrates on the universal nature of **patriarchy** (the control of society by men) and the role of men in oppressing women. All men are in an opposing group to women and benefit from patriarchy. Women should actively challenge patriarchy and live in a way that frees them from male exploitation. Radical feminism has been criticised for overlooking the different forms that patriarchy takes over time and place and the different experiences that women have.

Radical feminism developed in the early 1970s through the work of Shulamith Firestone (1970) and Kate Millet (1971), who saw the 'personal as political'. The personal referred to the domestic sphere, where women were seen to be just as oppressed as in the public sphere (e.g. employment). The political referred to the power people have in influencing others, but particularly in the way **sexual politics** operates allowing men to dominate women in the family and relationships.

Millet (1971) observed that institutions, such as the family, reproduced patriarchy through socialisation, ideologies and culture. Men are guaranteed a superior status to women, gender roles ensure masculinity is enshrined with aggression and force, disallowing women the temperament to challenge male dominance.

> *Sexual politics obtains consent through the 'socialization' of both sexes to the basic patriarchal politics with regard to temperament, role and status ... Patriarchy's chief institution is the family. It is both mirror of and a connection with larger society; a patriarchal unit in a patriarchal whole. Mediating between the individual and the social structure, the family effects control and conformity where political and other authorities are insufficient.*

Millet, K. (1971:43–44)

Millet made some reference to violence and sexuality in her work, but not to the same extent as recent radical

A group of young people wanted to go swimming together but there were only single-sex pools in the area.

MEN ONLY ←

WOMEN ONLY →

No
Neither sex was being treated less favourably

A man applied for a job as a paper sorter and was turned down. He was told that the job was more suited to a woman 'because it was boring, repetitive work which a woman wouldn't mind doing'. He took the firm to a tribunal

Yes
The firm paid him £100 compensation

Source: *Rights, Responsibilities and the Law* (Edmunds, 1987)

Figure 1.6   Is sexual discrimination against the law?

feminists (Rich, 1981; Dworkin, 1981). Sexuality, violence and social control have developed as the central theme of radical feminism. Sexuality (feelings that arouse and give pleasure) is argued to be socially constructed by men to satiate their own desires. Men, in making women their 'play things', have constructed, for example, the notion of women being sexual 'objects', as on page 3 of *The Sun*. Rich (1981) refers to this as 'compulsory heterosexuality', by which she meant that heterosexuality is seen as the norm and women have to comply. However, some radical feminists argue that only through lesbianism can women achieve a non-oppressive, enjoyable sexual relationship.

Masculine behaviour is seen by radical feminists to be aggressive, with rape and domestic violence being an extension of the male role. The threat of violence and actual violent behaviour by men controls women. For example, women may not wear the short/tight clothes that they like to in a nightclub, because the cultural belief is that they would be 'asking for trouble'. Therefore, sexuality, violence and social control are tightly linked to patriarchy. The fear of rape controls female behaviour (Brownmiller, 1976).

Kate Millet – 'What Kate Did Next'

Kate Millett is broke: other feminist pioneers have killed themselves or gone mad, rejected by their disciples. What happened to the sisterhood?

Most household names have short shelf lives. Not so Kate Millett. Even though it's almost 30 years since she wrote *Sexual Politics*, she is still the world's most famous radical feminist. In the eyes of her enemies, especially, her influence knows no bounds. Whenever Paul Johnson and his ilk blame the women's movement for eroding the fabric of society, she always gets a personal mention. She doesn't get quite that much credit in academia, but many of her most controversial ideas have become the common currency of gender studies, and those that are not still provoke angry debate.

Millett did not, and never intended to become, a career feminist. She was far too interested in her art and her other causes. She made her bohemian outlook clear in the often brilliant, always shocking autobiographical books that followed on from *Sexual Politics*. None of them were blockbusters, partly because most touched on issues that were a lot less fashionable than feminism – things like torture, political imprisonment and the mistreatment of the mentally ill. They alluded to her periodic financial difficulties, but we all thought these were of the cash-flow variety, because when someone has this kind of name-value, you naturally assume that they're also worth something at the bank.

But recently, Millett disabused us of this notion in a furious article she wrote for an American magazine called 'On the Issues'. It later appeared in a shortened version in the *Guardian*, with the headline, 'Read this and weep'. The news was that at 63 she was broke, out of print in her own country and unable to find a job.

She claimed to be mystified by her hard luck. When she first rang her contacts at various women's studies departments, she said: 'The academic voices were kind and welcoming, imagining I am rich and am doing this for amusement … a real faculty appointment seems an impossibility, in my case as in so many others now … surely I'm qualified? I ask, not as a "celebrity" but as a credentialled scholar with years of teaching and a doctorate with distinction from Columbia, an Oxford First, eight published books. They'll get back to me. But they never do. I begin to wonder what's wrong with me. Am I "too far out" or too old? … Or is it something worse? Have I been denounced or bad-mouthed? By whom? What is the matter with me, for God's sake?'

When the article went to press, her future was still uncertain, but when I rang her to ask for an update, she was somewhat affronted by my concern. She never meant to present herself as a charity case or to suggest that the world of women's studies owed her a living. Her main intention was to show how bad things are these days for so many of the women who were in the movement at the beginning and what little respect they get for devoting their lives to the cause. 'If it's this hard for me,' she says, 'think what it's like for the others.'

After all, she's not the only original founder to be out of print. Other big names of the time like Ti-Grace Atkinson and Jill Johnston have suffered the same fate. Some, like Shulamith Firestone, have spent the last quarter of a century locked up in asylums. She's out now and has just published a 'tough little book' called Airless Space, about lives ruined by incarceration. Firestone counts as a success story next to the suicides – Maria del Drago went this way, as did Ellen Frankfurt and Elizabeth Fischer, founder of *Aphra*, the first feminist literary journal.

What makes Millett most angry, though, is that no one wants to give these women credit for what they did when they were alive – or even remember that they existed. 'Why do women seem particularly unable to observe and revere their own history?' she asks.

For too many of her contemporaries, the question is not academic. Take her friend and associate Cindy Cisler, who was the only woman in a class of 100 when she trained as an architect at Yale. She became one of the first abortion activists, and went on to devote her life to that cause.

When I caught up with her, she was sitting in a friend's apartment, trying to locate a mini-storage and a van. Three months ago, she was evicted from her apartment. The landlord disposed of almost all of her belongings, including the 'best abortion archive there is'. For years, she's been trying to get a grant so that she can put it into order. 'But instead, they give the money to people who are going to start goddess circles or teach women horse-riding.'

And women's studies institutes? I should forget I even asked. The people who run these places are busy writing themselves into their 'cartoon history' of the early movement, and writing her out. So now the archive is gone forever. She could sue the landlord if she could find a lawyer. But first she has to find a place to live or she is going to be 'literally pushing a shopping cart by the weekend'. 'Had I understood 30 years ago that things would come to this,' she says, 'I would have settled for architecture and clapped from the sidelines.'

But how did it come to this? Why have these early activists become so desperately unfashionable, so tainted, that even women's studies programmes don't want to preserve them, if only as museum pieces? When I asked this question of a number of other people who were 'there at the beginning' or arrived only a few seconds afterwards, they insisted that many of the reasons had very little to do with feminism and an awful lot to do with what they darkly alluded to as the 'larger context'.

The women's movement did not rise fully formed out of Betty Friedan's head. I am reminded of this by Anita Bennett, who was one of the founders of Female Liberation at Berkeley and went on to help set up the first Women's Strike for Equality in 1970. Many of the earliest feminists were also activists in civil rights and the anti-war movement. As such, they were open to the sort of harassment that the FBI vented on all 'un-American' groups. When abortion became the key issue in the early Seventies, that harassment stepped up. And even in New York, it was hard to keep an apartment if your landlord got the idea you were a 'red'. Unless you were independently wealthy or had the good fortune, very rare in those days, of having parents who sympathised with your political views, you really had to struggle to make ends meet. Hence the horrible tales from the breadline.

But the full story is not perhaps as dire as Kate Millett implied, according to Cora Kaplan, now Professor of English at Southampton. The ones who had managed to claw their way into academia had done well enough for themselves and it wasn't true, she said, that all women's studies institutes were in the hands of Johnny-come-latelies without real activist credentials. She cited as an example Charlotte Bunch, who now runs the institute at Rutgers in New Jersey where Kaplan taught in the early Nineties.

Bunch was certainly a very active activist during those early days, and if the radical label now no longer applies, it is not, says Kaplan, because Bunch and her fellow survivors have sold out but because they have changed with the times. There is no point using the old rhetoric to reach young women, Kaplan explains, because they aren't going to listen to you if you do.

In any event, it is not the feminism these young women object to, but the Sixties wrapping. 'It's the Sixties that haven't done well in our imagination,' she says. Kate Millett and Co are out of style not because of their views on women, lesbianism and patriarchy, but because their names are inextricably linked with the S-word.

But if Kate Millett had studies the history of the women's movement in the way she claims that rest of us haven't, she will have known all along that she was going to have to face at least temporary oblivion. The wild Mary Wollstonecraft was not honoured by the more respectable campaigners who took up where she left off. The dashing, fearless Amelia Earharts of the Thirties had little patience with the dowdy, librarian suffragettes who won them the vote. They in turn got written out of the story by Betty Friedan, who was so convincing in her claim that nothing feminist had happened in the 40 years before her book was written, that most women of my generation still aren't aware that the truth was very different.

It's a strange little pattern, which itself probably tells you more about human nature or the way history gets written than it tells you about feminism. You could argue that it's a pattern Millett and her contemporaries are doomed to repeat, because they still haven't acknowledged that it's been a problem all along. I can afford to keep a distance on this subject, because I was never a radical feminist in the first place. My life will be much the same, whether they're on that record or off it. All the more reason, then, to take this opportunity to say it just isn't right.

Source: *The Observer*, 3 January 1999

1   Define radical feminism.   **(2)**

2   Make a list of reasons that might explain why Millet was not offered an academic position, despite excellent qualifications.   **(4)**

3   Explain how the different feminisms would answer the following question posed in the article: 'Why do women seem particularly unable to observe and revere their own history?   **(8)**

4   What is 'the larger context' mentioned in the article that has resulted in early feminists being treated poorly?   **(3)**

5   Examine the idea of different feminisms having historical waves of popularity and impact, which may explain the current demise of radical feminism.   **(9)**

Marxist/socialist feminism

Marxist feminists view female inequality as rooted in capitalism, explaining women's oppression in terms of its function to the economic system. Marxist feminists, such as Beechy (1987), have interpreted the economic and domestic position of women in Marxist terms, seeing it as the same as male waged labourers in the way that it serves the interests of those who own and control the means of production. However,

Marxist/socialist feminists have overlooked female oppression in pre-capitalist and non-capitalist societies.

Women are oppressed and exploited in both the domestic and public sphere. For example, women receive the lowest pay and lowest status jobs, because their primary role is as unpaid mother-housewife, which in turn ensures a cheap supply of healthy, educated workers. Therefore, women are seen as expendable in the workforce (a **reserve army of**

labour), their wages being an extra bonus for the family, rather than essential like the husband's wages. Consequently, Marxist feminists argue that female subordination supports capitalism by ensuring a cheap supply of waged and domestic labour with which to sustain the economic system.

Feminist Marxists (rather than Marxist feminists) or socialist feminists, as they preferred to be called, employ a **dual-systems approach**. They believe that capitalism maintains female subordination in its own interests, but argue that patriarchy and ideology reinforce this oppression, resulting in both concepts being as important as each other. Michele Barrett (1980) argued that by examining ideology feminist Marxists could explain why women accept as inevitable the family as their only route to fulfilment. Therefore, to achieve social equality women will have to be freed not only from the constraints of capitalism, but also from the ingrained assumptions about the relationship between men and women. The ideology of gender must be transformed so that the sexes are free to be as they choose.

> *Ideology – as the work of constructing meaning – cannot be divorced from its material conditions in a given historical period. Hence we cannot look to culture alone to liberate us... Nonetheless the struggle over the meaning of gender is crucial. It is vital for our purposes to establish its meaning in contemporary capitalism as not simply 'difference', but as division, oppression, inequality, internalized inferiority for women. Cultural practice is an essential site of this struggle. It can play an incalculable role in the raising of consciousness and the transformation of our subjectivity.*

Barrett, M. (1980:112–113)

Black feminism

Black feminism concentrates specifically on the oppression and disadvantage suffered by black women of all cultural backgrounds, such as African-Caribbean or Asian. It is written by black women for black women and developed to redress the white, middle-class bias of previous feminist theory (Anthias and Yuval-Davis, 1983). In fact, all the feminist theory so far examined in this book has been in reference to white

women, which can therefore provide only a partial view (like all theory) of the situation.

Black feminism has accused feminist theory of being racist, because it ignores the fact that the situation of black women (and men) is different from that of white. For example, patriarchy is assumed to be inherent in society and therefore affects all women; however, black men have different experiences from white men in society, with racism creating a different relationship between black men and women (see Area 3 on Social Stratification and Differentiation). Black women appear to be invisible in the majority of feminist theory. Black feminism aims to make the disadvantage suffered by black women visible in its own right, as a different type of oppression from that experienced by white women, because black women experience racism alongside sexism (Hooks, 1984).

> *Black women have no other institutionalized 'other' that we may discriminate against, exploit, or oppress... It is essential for continued feminist struggle that black women recognize the special vantage point our marginality gives us and make use of this perspective to criticize the dominant racist, classist, sexist hegemony... I am suggesting that we have a central role to play in the making of feminist theory and a contribution to offer that is unique and valuable.*

Hooks, b. (1984:14–15)

ACTIVITY   KS **COMMUNICATION**

KNOWLEDGE AND UNDERSTANDING	IDENTIFICATION AND INTERPRETATION

Create a table that summarises the main viewpoints and main criticisms of the different feminist approaches. You will find that this will help you to compare and contrast feminist theories.

Post-feminism

Post-feminism (a term first used by Stacey, 1986) refers to a school of thought that emerged in the 1980s, developed by women who refused to define themselves as feminists. It was interpreted as a reaction to feminism, which was seen by some to have gone 'over the top' in its criticism of men and femininity. At the same time the women's movement was becoming more differentiated, resulting in internal divisions and difficulties (Oakley, 1984).

Any backlash against feminism could be seen as a response to:

- the economic, social and political climate of the 1980s – Conservative right-wing politics and policies emphasised the benefits of 'family values' and continued to allow women to be paid less than men on average and to remain in lower status jobs;

- disagreements in the women's movement – the public received an image of the movement as disorganised and therefore ineffective (especially considering that the majority of people thought equality for women had been achieved);

- the growth of alternative feminisms, such as black feminism and radical feminism – new feminisms could be seen to be too extreme and therefore to challenge the status quo.

Some attempts have been made by governments and individuals to reassert traditional sex roles by undermining women's claims for equality through research and via popular culture (Faludi, 1992), for example media reports on the psychological damage inflicted on children of working mothers. However, this assumes that women have reached a position of equality in employment and the domestic sphere. Inequalities clearly continue to exist between men and women (see Area 3 on Stratification, Inequality and Differentiation) and therefore the notion that feminism has 'gone too far' is hard to sustain.

Postmodern feminism, a contemporary feminist approach reacting to post-feminist concerns, believes that the oppression women experience differs radically from woman to woman and therefore there cannot be an accurate theory about female disadvantage in society. Postmodernism can help to deconstruct the assumptions surrounding terms such as 'woman' (Jardine, 1985), showing the myths about femininity that are created by patriarchy, but it can never offer a universal truth. Identities, including gender role, have become uncertain in this postmodern world.

Post-feminism is a vaguely defined approach and is hard to support if it assumes that women have attained political, legal, social and economic equality. However,

it has made sociologists more reflective about feminist theories. Feminists, such as Friedan (1983), have considered their first ideas on gender inequality and revised them in developments in feminist theory. For example, in the 1970s feminists were expected to challenge traditional gender roles, but 30 years later it is acceptable to value the differences between men and women, realising it is the interpretation of gender roles that makes men and women unequal, not the roles themselves.

Outside postmodern feminism, contemporary feminisms appear to be entering a 'power' phase, where women are no longer seen as the victims, but are instead seen as powerful and capable. Women are encouraged to take all opportunities to empower themselves (Wolf, 1993). This 'power feminism' has been helped in the UK by the media coverage of the better educational attainment of girls compared to boys in secondary school examinations. Women may not have achieved social equality yet, but the social and political climate of the UK in the twenty-first century has encouraged most feminists to enter an optimistic phase.

Conflict and 'race'/ethnicity – theories on race relations

Many sociologists from a variety of theoretical backgrounds, such as Cox (1970), Miles (1993), Rex (1967) and Hall (1980), have contributed either structural and/or cultural explanations of racial inequality in industrial society (see Area 3 on Social Stratification and Differentiation). These theories can be seen as conflict theories, because of the struggle involved for ethnic minorities in a society that still possesses racialist legislation, such as the 1981 Nationality Act.

Marxist/neo-Marxist theory on 'race'

The variety of interpretations of Marxism can be applied to theories on 'race' and ethnicity. Traditional Marxists who emphasise structure argue that capitalist countries dominate others in the quest for profit. The dominated countries suffer from underdevelopment, so their citizens migrate for work but become disadvantaged in the host country. Conflict is seen to be inevitable between the ruling and subject classes. Ethnic minorities join the lowest ranks of the working class after migration and therefore suffer the same disadvantages as the rest of the working class.

Marxists who highlight 'action', or a humanistic approach, also believe that the state creates and perpetuates racist and racialist ideology. This ideology is argued to sustain racial divisions, which are exploited by capitalists to further divide the working class and thereby suppress class consciousness (Cox, 1970; Miles, 1982). For example, ethnic groups are targeted as 'different', which creates a discriminatory ideology that separates them from the rest of the working class.

Traditional Marxism saw 'race relations' as a part of general class oppression. Neo-Marxists, such as Hall and Gilroy (1982) at the Centre for Contemporary Cultural Studies (CCCS), moved on from this position to see 'race' and ethnicity as **relatively autonomous** from class, which just means that it is not determined by the economy, but that it does affect it. Neo-Marxists attempted to explain the causes of racial discrimination and how it can be analysed in association with class. However, some neo-Marxists claimed that this could only be done in autonomy, or as a product of contemporary social and historical relations, rather than as a by-product of general economic and social relations (Ben-Tovim and Gabriel, 1979). Solomos (1988) has attempted to bring some unity to neo-Marxist theory by arguing that:

■ racism and racialism are connected to and structured by wider economic and social conditions;

■ race relations also has autonomy, because it is a consequence of a specific historical and social context.

Overall, Marxist theories on 'race' and ethnicity are diverse in their approach, but they all agree that there is a material basis for racial oppression and that it is linked to social and economic conditions. However, the Marxist approach has been criticised for:

a marginalising 'race' and ethnicity through the focus on class

b assuming that all ethnic minorities are part of the working class, disadvantaged and similar in their life experiences (**homogeneous**)

c not examining widely enough racial prejudice and discrimination

Weberian theory on 'race'

The Weberian approach to 'race' and ethnicity is examined here, because there appear to be many similarities between this and Marxism. Both theories argue that race relations have to be seen first of all in relation to the economy and class, and then in a specific historical context and the ideologies that have developed around race relations (Rex, 1967).

However, it should be noted that the Weberian approach does allow the concept of power to be employed in relation to racial disadvantage. For example, the **status** of ethnic groups, or the amount of esteem they hold in society, was low compared to white people, resulting in real disadvantage and a lack of power. This inequality suffered by ethnic minorities, in areas such as employment or education, led Weberian theorists to suggest that black people formed an '**underclass**' in the UK (Rex and Tomlinson, 1979) (see Area 3 on Social Stratification and Differentiation).

Weberian theorists have been criticised by Marxists, even though they agree on the basics of race relations, for focusing on status rather than class and for ignoring the position of ethnic minorities in the working class. However, the major criticism is that this approach separates racial discrimination from wider inequality, when it can be understood only as a whole.

'New racism' and the New Right

It is strange to think that the work of the concepts on culture established by neo-Marxist Gramsci have been used as the basis for theory constructed by the New Right. The New Right as a sociological perspective argues that the most important features of society are:

■ freedom of the individual

■ free trade and capitalist enterprise.

To support these beliefs, an ideology has to be constructed by the state (Gramsci's notion of hegemony). This ideology has encouraged the idea of differences between cultures (hence it is a conflict theory), in order to strengthen the concept of **nationalism** (a unified nation based on a single cultural background) and weaken the position of ethnic minorities (see Area 4 on Society and Cultural Identities).

This 'new racism' (seeing 'race' in terms of culture, rather than biology) has been witnessed in politics (Margaret Thatcher's speech in 1979 when she claimed that the UK might be 'swamped' by ethnic minorities) and general society through racial discrimination (the British National Party or Combat 18). Therefore the New Right has linked national identity with culture, with ethnic minority groups being identified as having a different culture and consequently being some kind of threat to national stability. However, it does serve the purpose of dividing the masses and sustaining the primary goal of a functioning, exploitative free market economy. (See Area 3 for more information on 'new racism'.)

Postmodern theory and 'race'

Postmodernism considers race relations to be a part of general inequality and conflict in society, rather than being tied to capitalist class relations, as the Marxists argue. The reason for examining 'race' and ethnicity in this way is based on the fundamental assumption of diversity. Postmodernists, such as Modood (1992), argue that ethnic groups are distinctive and different and therefore respond to racial disadvantage in different ways. Ethnic groups cannot, therefore, be referred to as if they were homogeneous (similar), although that is precisely what other theories and the state do. Negative ideologies about ethnic groups are constructed through discourse (language) and inequality is perpetuated.

Postmodern theories on 'race' and ethnicity have been challenged for playing down the material disadvantages and the consequences of these for ethnic groups. However, interpreted as a conflict theory, it does provide an alternative examination of racial disadvantage in contemporary industrial society.

Social-action theory

Individual and societal action is determined by interaction with others. Behaviour expresses meaning and intention and is interpreted in this way by others. In other words, individuals understand what happens when relating with others and respond to this with social actions.

Weberianism

Weber shared Marx's concern with the nature of capitalism and the importance of the economy in influencing social action. He also acknowledged the inequality present in society and how this struggle for power was influenced in part by material factors. However, he differed from Marx by arguing that capitalism could not be explained by a general theory, because it comes in many forms. Weber claimed that the economy was only one factor in the struggle for power in society, with power being exerted through other categories of people, such as status groups. Therefore, society is shaped not only by material forces, such as the economy, but by the ideas of people, too.

Historical development and social change

‘ *The impulse to acquisition, pursuit of gain, of money, of the greatest possible amount of money, has itself nothing to do with capitalism. This impulse exists and has existed among waiters, physicians, coachmen, artists, prostitutes, dishonest officials, soldiers, nobles, crusaders, gamblers, and beggars. One may say that it has been common to all sorts and conditions of men at all times and in all countries of the earth, wherever the objective possibility of it is or has been given.*

Weber, M. (1974:17)

Weber differed from Marx in his explanation of the origins of capitalism. Marx interpreted the history of capitalism as a consequence of primarily structural processes, such as the development of industry. Weber emphasised the effect meaningful activity by human actors had on the cause of capitalism, such as the belief in the Protestant ethic of hard work and self-discipline. Therefore Weber argued that society is constructed through social interaction, but that action is constrained by the structure of society in which people live. It was this combination of structure and agency that led to Weberian theory being referred to as social-action theory. Weber has also been called the father of interpretive theory (see later).

> *Sociology … is a science which attempts the interpretive understanding of social action in order thereby to arrive at a causal explanation of its course and effects.*
>
> Weber, M. (1974:12)

The principle of Weberian theory is based on the concept that history and society consists of only human individuals. These individuals make decisions and take actions, which means that history cannot have a purpose, as Marx suggested. It also meant that Weber did not make generalisations about society, realising that any sociological 'law' was only a statement about the activities of individuals, or as he put it an '**ideal type**'. An ideal type is a social construction that represents a typical phenomenon against which to measure and compare real examples.

However, Weber realised that ideal types did enable theorists to categorise and organise their findings. In considering social action, an area which later became adopted as a specialist field and is referred to as 'rational choice theory' or 'action theory' (Abell, 1998), Weber identified four ideal types of action that he presented from the social actors' point of view:

- **Zweckrational** or instrumentally rational – this is action that enables a social actor to reach a goal, it is a means to an end. However, if the action is too difficult it may be abandoned. For example, taking AS or A Levels is zweckrational action.

- **Wertrational** or value-rational – this is action that has to be completed, however difficult, to achieve the final goal. For example, joining the army to serve one's country, despite the risk of death, is wertrational action.

- **Traditional** – this is action that is taken because it has always been that way, it is part of tradition. For example, drinking alcohol to excess on your 18th birthday could be considered traditional action.

- **Affective** – this is action that is caused by emotion based on unusual circumstances. For example, getting into a fight at school because you have found out that someone has been spreading malicious rumours about you.

Capitalism and Protestantism

Weber identified that capitalism (the organised pursuit of profit) has come in different shapes and sizes over the years, ranging from bartering to pirating, and that the type of capitalism experienced in the West was just one type. Weber's theory was based on the **rational capitalism** of Europe and the USA. The term 'rational' was used by Weber to refer to a way of understanding the means to an end, in this case a specific form of capitalism that consisted of:

- a commitment to the continuous accumulation of profit as an end in itself

- the identification of this profit as morally justified, rewarding hard work.

The second point separated western capitalism from other forms, because work was seen as positive and the way to fulfilment, rather than as a means to an end. Weber identified this work ethic or 'spirit' in Calvinist Protestantism.

Protestants in Europe in the 1800s took part in daily life with rigorous dedication as a way of celebrating God's glory. Weber found that their energy for their secular (non-religious) role was similar to that of the capitalists. Consequently, Weber attempted to understand this connection, in order to show how rational capitalism could have developed out of the Protestant ethic (see Area 9 on Religion).

Weber argued that social action is a result of interpretations that lead to a situation having meaning, or a rational and chosen outcome. He did not claim to demonstrate cause and effect, just the possibility of connections based on empathetic understanding, which he called **verstehen** (see Area 2 on Sociological Research Methodology). Weber argued that by looking at the world as if you were in the position of the individual/s you want to understand, you could imagine what their world was like.

Idealism versus materialism?

Weber believed that ideas could cause changes in social history. If Marx is interpreted in a humanistic way, then his ideas can be seen to be similar to Weber's; however, some interpretations of Marx argue that only material (structural) forces, i.e. the economy can cause social change. Weber argued that the ideas of a religion, such as Calvinist Protestantism, could affect historical activity. But this belief did not make Weber an idealist, because he acknowledged that history consisted of material human beings, not ideas. He supported the concept of economic relations being important to an understanding of society, but unlike Marx he did not consider it to be the most important factor. Weber considered social life to be too complex and variable to have a single explanation.

Social inequality and power

Weber argued that society was organised on the basis of struggles for power (the ability to influence others, with or without their consent). Therefore, like Marx, he believed that social existence revolved around inequality. However, unlike Marx, he saw this inequality as not only economic (although economic inequality was important). The main focus of Weber's social theory is social stratification (which is discussed at length in Area 3), with all forms of inequality being viewed as inequalities of power.

According to Weber power forms the basis of struggle between and among three categories:

1 **Class** – It can be defined as a collection of people with a similar market situation (position in the economic system from which to command rewards). It is similar to Marx's concept of class and can also be divided into those who own only their labour and those who own what produces wealth. However, differentiating between the skills possessed by those who own only their labour can increase the number of classes. For example, the manual working class has a very different market situation to the skilled white-collar workers. Therefore classes are based on economic inequalities.

2 **Status** – It can be defined as a group of people who share the same amount of social honour,

which is recognised and accepted by both themselves and others. Marx did not acknowledge status as a form of division in society, but belonging to a privileged status group does assume an economic position that can support an associated lifestyle. For example, Queen Elizabeth II and her family belong to a high-status group in UK society (royalty) and have the wealth to support the accompanying lifestyle. Quite often status groups have a high degree of **social closure** (they are difficult to get into), such as the Royal Family, resulting in solidarity and common interest. Therefore status groups are based on inequalities of prestige (the amount of social esteem given and held by others).

3 **Party** – It can be defined as an organisation developed with the sole purpose of attaining power. A party does not have to be political; it includes any organisation that seeks to maximise its chances of winning power, such as religious or business organisations. Membership of **parties** can represent the interests of class and/or status groups, but it does not have to.

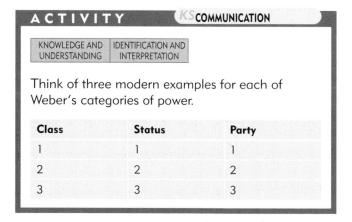

ACTIVITY **KS** COMMUNICATION

KNOWLEDGE AND UNDERSTANDING	IDENTIFICATION AND INTERPRETATION

Think of three modern examples for each of Weber's categories of power.

Class	Status	Party
1	1	1
2	2	2
3	3	3

It appears that Weber is presenting a conflict theory, with struggle existing in all areas of society. However, this is not the case; in fact, Weber emphasised how non-confrontational the mass of the population was. He explained this lack of conflict by the fact that power has two elements – coercion and authority. Coercion involves power without consent by force, while authority relies on consent and acceptance of that power as legitimate. Weber argued that rational capitalism was based on three kinds of authority:

1 **Charismatic** – with leaders offering strong personality traits and the ability to exert their will over others. For example, the Reverend Jim Jones (leader of the cult 'the People's Temple') asked his followers to commit suicide by taking cyanide, which they did.

2 **Traditional** – the person who assumes power does so by right of established entitlement, such as inheritance. For example, a king or queen may hold power through rights of birth.

3 **Rational-legal** – people holding this type of power do so through formal processes, such as election or interview. It is based on the statutes of law and is impersonal compared to the other two forms of authority, in that leaders are not selected from followers, family or friends. For example, the adult population via a large-scale administrative system (bureaucracy) elects the Prime Minister.

Therefore society is bureaucratic and the majority of the population accepts the authority of those who control society.

It should be noted that Weber feared the development of bureaucracy and the way in which this would limit the freedom of the individual or, as he put it, create an 'iron cage'. He argued that the best way to stop bureaucracy taking over society was through balancing it with a strong leader, whether charismatic or traditional.

KNOWLEDGE AND UNDERSTANDING	IDENTIFICATION AND INTERPRETATION	ANALYSIS AND EVALUATION

Construct a table consisting of two columns, one headed 'Marxism – main features' and the other 'Weberianism – main features'. Fill in all the main features you can think of for each. Using this table construct a second table with two columns labelled 'Similarities between Marxism and Weberianism' and 'Differences between Marxism and Weberianism'. Fill in the table and you will find that it improves your evaluation skills enormously!

Evaluation

1 Weber provided insight into the nature of social inequality in relation to power.

2 The role of social actors was explained by the way in which they take into account the behaviour of others when planning their own action. Therefore people were identified as having conscious intentions, something ignored by theories that stressed only the causes and consequences of the social structure on behaviour.

3 He provided insight into the way the social world could be seen to be constructed by people's social interactions.

4 The nineteenth-century liberal view of the individual used by Weber limits his theory on action and meaning. The individual is seen to be totally subjective, rather than having inter-subjective relations with others, i.e. concentrating on conscience rather than morality, which stops his theory developing as an interpretive approach.

5 Structural theorists claim that Weber fails to acknowledge the controlling influence of material forces, outside personal control, on the lives of individuals.

6 Capitalism is believed to have existed before Protestantism and therefore Protestantism could not have a causal effect on capitalism.

Conflict theory

Conflict theory rose in opposition to the functionalist concept of consensus structuring society. It is a combination of Weberian and Marxist theory and claims that society is organised through conflict. Conflict theory was mainly influenced by Weber and his notion of conflict existing at more than just an economic level, such as between status groups. For example, Rex and Tomlinson (1979) demonstrated how conflict and 'race'/ethnicity showed divisions in society that existed outside the Marxist definition of conflict. This has been explained in more depth in the section headed 'Conflict and 'race'/ethnicity' on page 30.

Conflict theory has been criticised for not developing a way of showing whether conflict is inherent in a social system. Functionalists have claimed that conflict theory shows only that conflict is possible (Craib, 1992) and does not distinguish between real consensus and coercion.

Max Weber

(1864–1920)

Max Weber was a German economist and social historian born in Erfurt, Germany, and educated in Heidelberg, Berlin and Gottingen. He was a professor in economics at Freiburg, Heidelberg and Munich.

Weber combined economics with sociology in an attempt to establish that historical causation was not influenced merely by economic factors. His work established a link between structure and agency, now known as social-action theory. *The Protestant Ethic and the Spirit of Capitalism* (1904–5) became one of his most famous pieces of work and in it he attempted to show a link between religious ideas and capitalism. Therefore Weber was influential in challenging the dualism of structure and action, by showing that they both affect social behaviour.

Structuration theory

Giddens

Structuration theory was developed by Anthony Giddens to get rid of the stark division between structural and social-action/interpretive theories. Structuration emphasises the interconnections between the role of social structures and interpretive creation of social action. For example, social structures are argued to exist as a consequence of organised interactions between individuals, who need social structures to enact those interactions.

Giddens, Director of the London School of Economics and adviser to the Prime Minister, is a prominent contemporary British sociologist. His theory of structuration developed from his readings of Marx, Weber, Mead, etc. and an attempt to utilise their most relevant and important points in one sociological theory. Giddens wanted to establish a theory that showed that society could both make and be made by individuals. In other words, Giddens attempted to create a theory that brought to an end the 'structure' versus 'agency' debate.

The dualism of agency and structure

Giddens identified that many sociologists had highlighted the role of human action and beliefs in explaining social phenomena, but had not incorporated the structural features of society into these theories. Likewise, sociologists who emphasised social structures dismissed the influence of individuals on society. Giddens argued that structures shape individual action, but that it is these actions that make structures effective or modify them. He referred to this concept as the 'duality of structure'. Giddens wanted to remove this 'dualism of agency and structure' to create a synthesis between the two approaches, because he argued that they were really the same thing.

The basis of Giddens' structuration theory is that societal structures, such as factories or schools, are created by the actions (or agency) of humans. These actions are controlled by the society in which they take place, because of predefined patterns of organisation. However, social structures would not be maintained if it were not for social action. In other words, schools, for example, would not exist if humans using social rules and resources did not reproduce them. To Giddens, structures are the rules and resources of society; by this he means that structure is the cultural and material means that enable people to act. Therefore social structure and social action work hand in hand to create and maintain society.

Social structures and social systems

Giddens distinguishes between social structures and social systems in the shaping of society.

- **Social structures**: these are the result of the unintended outcomes of human behaviour, which in turn control individual action. Structures can be both enabling and constraining for individual action. For example, cultural expectations or material position can limit behaviour or encourage new outlooks. Structure has three dimensions:

  1 **Signification** – social actions are made to conform to social rules through communication and interaction.
  2 **Domination** – inequality exists in the distribution of resources.
  3 **Legitimation** – shared norms and values result in the sanctioning of different forms of conduct.

- **Social systems**: these are collections of social beings that exist for a long time, because of the structures entrenched in them.

Evaluation

Structuration theory has highlighted the ability of structural and social-action theory to coexist in an explanation of society. However, it has been challenged for not realising how structures can influence how much they can be changed by social action. In other words, social rules and regulations will not enable social change to take place as and when social actors desire it (Archer, 1982).

Interpretive perspective

Individual behaviour is a reaction to, and an understanding of, interactions with others. Daily behaviour expresses meaning and intention and is interpreted in this way by others. Society is based on the interactions of individuals. In other words, individuals understand what happens when relating with others and this is what constitutes society.

Interpretivist theories attempt, like Weber's social-action theory (see earlier in this section), to show the importance of the individual social actor in understanding society. Weber has, in fact, been referred to as the 'founding father of interpretive sociology', because he was the first sociologist to thoroughly examine the relationship of the individual to society. Before Weberian theory, sociological debate had focused on the importance of structure in understanding society (Marxism).

Despite Weber's commitment to interpreting individual experience and meaning, he was part of The Enlightenment movement, which emphasised the use of scientific method in research. Therefore social-action theory can be distinguished from interpretivist theories by the generalisations made about social action and consequently society. Interpretivist theories focus on the micro level (see earlier) and validity rather than the macro and reliability (see Area 2 on Sociological

Research Methodology). Interpretivists argue that society is the outcome of interpretations and therefore 'reality' is not as structural theorists see it (determined by the social structure), it is the outcome of interpretations that are different for all people and therefore not generalisable.

> **HINTS AND TIPS**   To help you understand the interpretivist concept of 'reality' being relative to the interpretation of the situation, consider the following recent television advertisement. The advert portrayed a young skin-headed man running after and tackling an older suited man – was he attacking him or saving him? From one angle the 'reality' appears to be an attack, because all we see is the older man being wrestled to the floor. From another angle we see scaffolding collapsing and the young man pushing the older one out of the way, therefore the 'reality' changes to a save. It all boils down to how the situation is interpreted by **each** onlooker and how they **choose** to see things.

The main theories that have attempted to interpret the variety of individual meaning and intention include **symbolic interactionism**, which was inspired by George Mead (1863–1931), **ethnomethodology**, which was founded by Harold Garfinkel in the 1950s and **phenomenology**, which is a philosophical theory developed by Edmund Husserl. These theories may emphasise different elements of individual behaviour, but they all agree that the individual creates society (rather than the structural theorists' belief that society determines the individual). In other words, society is the end result of human interaction.

Interpretivists recognise that some human interaction lacks intention, for example belching or shaking. Sometimes we behave in **involuntary** ways because our body makes us. However, human action is largely **voluntary**, in that it is a consequence of a conscious decision. We choose to behave in certain ways to achieve a specific goal and therefore our action and interactions are **meaningful**. For example, when you embarked on this course you were performing a meaningful action, realising that a good education in a capitalist society is one of the best ways to achieve your goals.

Meaningful actions are carried out by individuals who have interpreted the world around them, made sense of it and responded appropriately. For example, if you were involved in a bank robbery it is likely that you would make the conscious decision (meaningful act) to do as you were told by the robbers (appropriate act) in order to protect your life (make sense of situations). It should, however, be remembered that interpretations of situations occur as part of interactions with others and that these interpretations can be changed by others to create the definition of the situation that *they* want. For example, people's mannerisms, dress and language (symbols) can all change the way in which others interpret a situation. Also, because society is based upon arbitrary interpretations it should be recognised as a fragile structure open to change.

ACTIVITY   KS**COMMUNICATION**

KNOWLEDGE AND UNDERSTANDING	IDENTIFICATION AND INTERPRETATION

1   Write down three different groups of people who wear a uniform.
2   Consider how each of these uniforms communicates information about that group, for example does it put them in a position of authority? Record your responses.
3   How would an interpretivist theorist explain the use of uniforms in society?

Symbolic interactionism

6   *If men define situations as real, they are real in their consequences.*

Thomas, W. I. (1863–1947)

Symbolic interactionism is a theoretical approach that examines the use of 'symbols', such as language or mannerisms, in the interactions of humans. It is the most popular interpretive theory and has offered an alternative approach to functionalism and Marxism (structural theories) since the interwar years, when the Chicago School in the USA developed it. However, as with all theoretical approaches, different sociologists have emphasised different parts of the theory. Therefore symbolic interactionism focuses on different aspects of human interaction, such as Mead's identification of 'self' to the **dramaturgical** approach of Erving Goffman (see later).

Symbolic interactionism is primarily concerned with how people make their world meaningful. For example, how do you know how to behave when in

school? Herbert Blumer (1969) identified the three main features of symbolic interactionism:

1   Humans act towards objects on the basis of the meanings that the object has for them.
2   These meanings are constructed through social interaction.
3   These meanings are experienced and changed by an interpretive process that all individuals encounter in dealing with their environment.

Put another way, symbolic interactionists believe that humans act towards others on the basis of meanings given, but that these meanings are constantly being altered (negotiated) through interaction. Therefore all social situations need to be defined by the people involved in the interaction (definition of the situation).

Symbolic interactionism also emphasises the idea that individuals can be understood only through interaction with others. In other words, a person's identity is constructed by how others see them and how that person thinks others see them. For example, you may consider yourself to be generous, but this understanding of yourself will be negotiated through interactions with others, which confirm or deny this part of your 'self'. This area of symbolic interactionism has been called 'labelling theory' and has been particularly associated with the sociology of deviance and mental illness (see Area 12 on Crime and Deviance).

George Herbert Mead

As mentioned earlier, the Chicago School had an important influence on the development of symbolic interactionism. **George Herbert Mead** (1863–1931) taught at the University of Chicago and has been credited as the most important figure in the development of symbolic interactionism. Mead, a social psychologist, wanted to understand how the ability to communicate through symbols developed in human beings.

Mead (1934) began his investigation into social interaction by stating that the mind, or as he called it 'the self', could be studied scientifically. He argued that the way the mind works is displayed in human conduct. Mead compared the working of the human mind to that of animals and realised that the human mind was capable of reflection and anticipation (**symbolic capacity**), something animals could not do. This showed Mead that human beings could control their behaviour.

George Herbert Mead

(1863–1931)

George Herbert Mead was born in South Hadley, Massachusetts, USA. He taught, as a social psychologist, at the University of Chicago from 1894 until his death.

Mead was influential in the development of symbolic interactionism. His psychology background led him to emphasise 'the self'. He argued that the self emerges out of a social process in which the organism interacts with its environment and becomes self-conscious. The mind, or intelligence, is a social product developed by the individual to solve problems. Mead published only articles while he was alive; his books were published after his death. His publications included: *The Philosophy of the Present* (1932) and *Mind, Self, and Society from the Standpoint of a Social Behaviorist* (1934).

A person's psychological character, or self, is developed through symbolic interaction. This 'social self' is constructed by the way other people act, it is learnt through socialisation and watching others. For example, you may have learnt from imitating your brothers or sisters (**significant others**) how to behave like a student. Therefore the social self also enables individuals to see things from a vast collection of other people's points of view, a view which Mead termed '**the generalised other**'.

The concept of the 'generalised other' displays the importance of social interaction to Mead's theory. Even the self, an individual mind, can be seen as social in character. Mead divided the concept of 'self' into the 'I' and 'me'. 'I' refers to the part of you that looks at yourself, while 'me' refers to how other people see you. 'The self', according to Mead, is developed through the continual interplay between 'I' and 'me'. In other words, we come to be who we are based both on how we see ourselves (we shape our own social experience) and how others see us (our social experience is shaped by society). Therefore, the 'I' can be seen as active, being able to control 'the self', while the 'me' is passive, making the individual 'act' according to others' perceptions him/her.

❛ *I have been undertaking to distinguish between the 'I' and the 'me' as different phases of the self, the 'me' answering to the organised attitudes of the others which we definitely assume and which determine consequently our own conduct so far as it is of a self-conscious character. Now the 'me' may be regarded as giving the form of 'I'. The novelty comes in the action of the 'I', but the structure, the form of self is one which is conventional.*

Mead, G.H. (1934:209)

Mead also examined the use of language as a form of communication and expression of meaning. Mead rejected the idea that language is purely an imitation and instead claimed that it provides meaningful symbolism. Language enables people to negotiate social roles, roles that may enable one person in a similar situation to another to behave differently. Language also provides the common structure of meaning that links different groups together.

Herbert Blumer

Blumer (1969) supported Mead's argument about the nature of symbols being different in particular groups, with a common structure, language, enabling these groups to integrate into society. He argued that people use accepted meanings during interactions, which form part of that societal culture and a framework within which meaning can be constructed for any other interaction. However, Blumer did note that meanings and situations are constantly changing and therefore the framework is fluid, enabling meanings to be modified if inappropriate.

Blumer argued that action involves interpretation, with behaviour being dependent on how people perceive situations (reality). As Thomas' statement at the beginning of this section shows, people respond to what they believe is real (even though it may not be considered real by others, such as psychic power). The actor, therefore, determines the meaning of the situation through the way in which that situation is interpreted. This interpretation is not based entirely on culture, but also on improvisation, because each situation is different and cannot be anticipated. Consequently, social interaction involves the reworking of social structures, i.e. norms, rules and values in its creation of group life:

> *It is the social process of group life that creates and upholds the rules, not the rules that create and uphold group life.*
>
> Blumer, H. (1969:18)

Case studies and symbolic interactionism

Everett Hughes developed an approach to sociology that involved using symbolic interactionism and case studies to understand the social world. Later Howard Becker, Erving Goffman and Anselm Strauss developed an approach termed 'urban anthropology'. The research was seen as an open-ended pursuit, with the structure of the case study being dictated by interactions with those being studied. The case studies tended to be about people in disadvantaged situations and were accused of being sentimental in their identification with the underprivileged.

Many of the case studies focused on occupations and the 'sense of self' associated with low-status work. The 'sense of self' refers to a person's feeling of self-worth in his or her own eyes and in the eyes of others. Glaser and Strauss (1968) conducted a case study of the medical profession and concluded that a high 'sense of self' could improve a person's life chances in hospital. For example, a doctor has to decide whether to resuscitate a person whose heart has stopped; if that person is considered important by the doctor, he or she may try harder to revive the person. Therefore Glaser and Strauss showed that some individuals in society are considered to have less worth than others, which does, in part, justify the interest of some symbolic interactionists in the position of the underdog in society.

Erving Goffman – a dramaturgical approach

Goffman is the most successful interactionist, in that he has developed a distinct concept of the roles individuals have in social life. He argues that social life is like a play or drama (hence the term dramaturgical) in which we take on different roles. These roles are tied to the expectations that others have of us. We create and manage our roles in every social interaction, our social roles being defined by our performances. These performances may incorporate elements of our other 'roles', such as a student exhibiting signs of a 'son/daughter role' when pleading for more time to complete an assignment. Life, according to Goffman, is therefore one big act in which we are all social actors.

In his research Goffman displayed how the social actor constructs and communicates a sense of self during interaction and how this interaction is managed and organised by the actor. For example, Goffman carried out fieldwork in the Shetland Islands to see how people 'presented themselves in everyday life'. He witnessed the local people using particular **regions** to construct reality, a region being 'any place that is bounded to some degree by barriers to perception' (1987:109). Goffman argued that 'front' and 'back' regions elicited different behaviour:

- Front region – where collective 'front'-of-house action is displayed in teamwork. It is the area where a **performance** is given.

- Back region – the 'back' stage area where the action occurs related to the performance, but is inconsistent with the performance.

The Shetland Islanders allowed the outside of their cottages to look shabby so that the landlord would keep their rent the same, thereby displaying a 'front' region unity in their performance, with the action to organise this taking place in the 'back' region. The actual behaviour of the Islanders was termed **'impression management'**, which Goffman refers to as social actors controlling the image of their performance:

> *... when an individual appears before another he will have many motives for trying to control the impression they receive of the situation.*
>
> Goffman, E. (1987:26)

ACTIVITY KS COMMUNICATION, WORKING WITH OTHERS

| KNOWLEDGE AND UNDERSTANDING | ANALYSIS AND EVALUATION |

In pairs identify in the table below the main features of Goffman's theory in relation to the 'self'. As a group discuss which feature you consider to be the most important to his theory and why you hold this belief.

Feature of Goffman's theory	Explanation of feature
1	
2	
3	

'Institutions'

Goffman investigated the treatment of deviant behaviour in official institutions, such as in mental hospitals, and discovered that it did not conform to his theory of front and back regions. Inmates were not given privacy or therapy, but were instead re-socialised by having their self-image totally remodelled by the institution. For example, labelled deviants in prison have all their personal possessions removed, are told what to do and when to do it and are treated the same as all the other deviants/criminals. Therefore, Goffman argues, individuals who are labelled deviant and enter institutions to 'rectify' that deviance, often become institutionalised (they have their self-image taken away by the institution and replaced with one that is acceptable to the institution).

Institutionalisation, according to Goffman, makes deviants accept that there is something psychologically wrong with them, rather than their actions being seen as a rational response to their environment (as Goffman would argue). For example, a patient in a mental hospital may decide to keep a pea from dinner in his or her pocket. This hoarding behaviour appears strange at first, until you consider that the patient has no private possessions and that the pea is the only thing that makes the patient different from everyone else in the institution. The pea represents individuality and is therefore quite a rational reaction to the situation. The inmate's sense of self is totally mortified or destroyed (mortification of self) by the rituals imposed by the institution, such as strip searches, enforced showers, obedience and public degradation. Once the inmates have lost their old self-image and accepted the institution's version, they can 'recover'.

As a symbolic interactionist theorist (social identities are socially created) Goffman argues that institutionalisation is an interactive process between inmate and institution and therefore the inmate can resist or accept the process of re-socialisation. Consequently, individuals labelled deviant by institutions can be converted, rebel or 'play along' by assuming the role that is seen as desirable by the institution. Goffman (1963) also identified inequalities of power in his examination of institutions and the mortification of self, something early symbolic interactionists ignored. He asserted that external social constraints, such as a mental hospital, could have an effect on shaping our individuality. His later work, however, moved away from this view towards a more structural approach.

> **HINTS AND TIPS**   A good way to remember Goffman's symbolic interactionist theory of institutionalisation is to watch the film **One Flew Over The Cuckoo's Nest**. In this film a man is convicted of raping an underage girl, but to avoid prison he claims to be mentally ill. He is institutionalised in a mental hospital for psychological evaluation. His behaviour, to the viewer, can be seen to be normal (especially when compared to the other inmates), but the hospital interprets it as a symptom of his illness. Eventually his 'normal' behaviour is classed as too disruptive to the other patients/institution and the hospital takes drastic action to remove his sense of self. Remember that you can apply the information in this film to support an argument in the examination.

Labelling theory

Labelling theory is part of symbolic interactionist theory, but concentrates specifically on how organisations, such as the police, have publicly identified someone as a deviant or criminal. This identification becomes the 'label' by which that person is recognised by others. For example, a person identified by the police as a 'child molester' will be seen by that label by others. Therefore, labelling theorists argue that the difference between 'normal' people and deviants is not their individual characteristics, but the way in which they have been treated by public organisations enforcing social rules. Consequently, labelling theorists investigate how some people become labelled as deviant and others do not.

Labelling theorists identify power as the main reason for some people being assigned negative labels. The weak and the powerless are seen to be the victims of damaging labels (Becker, 1963), with deviant and criminal behaviour being a product of labelling. The creation of labels is seen as part of a power struggle between 'us' and 'them' or 'rich' and 'poor', with the powerful forcing the weak into deviant activities. Laws are created in the interests of the powerful. The weak, such as the working class, are much more likely than those in high-status positions to have their behaviour interpreted as criminal or deviant. The label once given encourages a self-fulfilling prophecy or behaviour, which supports the label given. Therefore, labelling theory focuses on the social construction of crime by social actors. (This approach is examined in detail in Area 12 on Crime and Deviance.)

Evaluation of symbolic interactionism

1 It is ahistorical.
2 It ignores the wider features of the social structure and their influence on behaviour.
3 Individuals are presented as totally rational and unemotional in their actions, which may not be the case.
4 People are seen in a very optimistic light, with individuals being expected to respond humanely and rationally to 'freedom'. History has shown this is not always the case.
5 It overemphasises the degree to which social actors consciously interpret their environments.
6 It provides information on power and control at group or small organisation level, such as between teacher and pupil, or the labels given by others to the mentally ill.
7 A clear framework of analysis is provided to show how individuals could be perceived as 'social actors'.
8 It is not deterministic. Social actors are consciously involved in social life.
9 Human behaviour is seen as meaningful, which makes the social actors' interpretation of their actions essential in understanding behaviour.

Phenomenology

Phenomenology is a theory of social life that focuses on the concept that 'things' have no meaning in themselves and therefore only mean what they are taken to mean by social actors. Phenomenologists argue that members of a socially created world must have shared meanings for things if there is to be any kind of order. In other words, people in every society, however different, teach its offspring, as part of socialisation, how to see things in that society. Berger and Luckmann (1985) support the belief that we learn how to 'know' our world:

> *The man in the street inhabits a world that is 'real' to him, albeit in different degrees, and he 'knows', with different degrees of confidence, that this world possesses such and such characteristics.*
>
> Berger, P. and Luckmann, T. (1985:13)

Consequently, what we have learnt becomes taken for granted and appears to be 'natural'. For example, gender roles are assumed to be a natural extension of the sex differences between men and women, when they are really a relatively modern social construction (see Area 6 on Families and Households).

Phenomenologists argue that shared meanings are the common-sense understanding people have of the world. These common-sense meanings are supported through language. Language provides us with the knowledge we need to make sense of social life. For example, few of us can experience everything we know about, therefore knowledge about the world around us is passed on by language.

Alfred Schutz (1899–1959) developed phenomenology (from the work of his teacher Edmund Husserl) to show that the 'reality' we experience is based on taken-for-granted knowledge that has come to represent the social world. In other words, we do not experience the world ourselves, but interpret it in ways that are meaningful to us. For example, a plate has meaning because we know about plates; if we did not understand the concept of plate it would simply be a flattish round object. Therefore, all social actors possess common-sense knowledge that is attained through living and experiencing life, and this makes people feel as though they know and understand the world they live in.

Phenomenology has been charged with many problems, the most common of which comes from the structural perspective and criticises the focus on the meaning of everyday life at the expense of understanding social structures, such as inequality and power. Also sociologists using the phenomenological approach have been argued to offer only their own interpretation of the actors' meaning, rather than an objective account. However, these criticisms aside, phenomenology can be seen to have significantly affected sociology by challenging many common-sense assumptions that needed to be investigated. Phenomenology has provided explanations of areas of social life, such as crime and deviance, by deconstructing taken-for-granted meaning, such as official statistics (see Area 12 on Crime and Deviance). Also, the type of interpretivist stance taken by phenomenology has enabled a theory to develop, which emphasises the dynamic nature of common-sense knowledge. This theory is ethnomethodology.

Ethnomethodology

Ethnomethodology grew out of the work of Alfred Schutz (see section on 'Phenomenology'). It appears to be similar to other interpretivist theories, in that all attempt to show how people define situations, constructing social organisation from the interactions of individuals. However, ethnomethodology does not treat interactive situations as part of common-sense knowledge (as Schutz did): it argues that members of society have constantly to make sense of situations. Therefore, unlike other interpretivist theories which are concerned with the outcome of interpretations such as 'the self' or 'labels', ethnomethodology studies how interpretations occur. Ethnomethodologists investigate how interaction is accomplished, with ethnomethodology being literally defined as the study of the methods used by ordinary people to make sense of everyday life.

Lawson and Garrod (1996) argue that ethnomethodology was developed to:

> *... stress the infinite ambiguity of language and action. Rather than assume that we understand what another person means when they say or do something, 'ethnos' argue that we have to struggle for their meaning, and that every situation is characterised by the search for common understandings. The social world is therefore built up of arbitrary rules, made up of dense and often contradictory sets of tacit understandings about what is going on.*

Lawson, T. and Garrod, J. (1996:91)

Therefore, ethnomethodology can be seen to based on three assumptions (Jones, 1990):

1 Social interaction is variable and anything could happen within it.
2 Social actors never realise that interactions are precarious.

3 Social actors can unconsciously make the social life appear ordered.

Ethnomethodology began as a criticism by Harold Garfinkel of all other sociological theories and methods, because they did not question the use of the common-sense meanings employed. It is these common-sense, taken-for-granted meanings of social life that ethnomethodologists examine. Garfinkel identified three elements that aid the investigation of common-sense understanding of society:

1 Indexicality of meaning – language can change in meaning depending on the situation in which it is used. Interaction involves a context that is constantly being redefined and re-evaluated. Therefore, the production of conversation is a skill at which we are well practised and this is the only reason why it appears natural.
2 Reflexivity – there is an inherent relationship between talk and action. By describing a situation people can construct it and then make it occur.
3 Rules – reality is created by the assumption that rules exist, rather than by the rules themselves. These rules are not absolute, but are instead fragile, always being modified during interactions. The modification or elaboration of the rule depends on the context of the interaction (Garfinkel termed this the **etcetera clause**).

Ethnomethodology has been criticised for its lack of methodology and evaluation, for being trivial and lacking sociological relevance (Gouldner, 1975). However, it is not surprising that it was treated with some contempt when you consider that *it* condemned all other forms of sociology. This said, ethnomethodology has failed to evaluate objectively different members' accounts of situations. Also the lack of theoretical perspective has created a near relativist position (see section on relativist theories on page 47), with ethnomethodologists postulating that there is no 'real' social world, but instead a body of interaction individuals creating meaning. Some ethnomethodologists have sought to address this criticism by developing a more focused approach, such as **conversation analysis** (see Area 2 on Sociological Research Methodology). Conversation analysis aims to construct a theory on the way conversation is organised by those taking part in the conversation and how action is produced by everyday chit chat.

Symbolic interactionism	Ethnomethodology
Assumes prior existence of symbolic order and language structure.	Symbolic order and language structure is an accomplishment and should not be assumed.
Meaning is negotiated during interaction.	Concentrates on the invisible, taken-for-granted processes that make meaning possible.
Assumes 'social actor' is aware during interaction and examines his or her point of view	Assumes that the individual is unaware of how meaning is constructed.

Figure 1.7   Differences between symbolic interactionism and ethnomethodology

TASK

KS COMMUNICATION, APPLICATION OF NUMBER

KNOWLEDGE AND UNDERSTANDING	IDENTIFICATION AND INTERPRETATION	ANALYSIS AND EVALUATION

Hypothesis – 'Social action is a consequence of the social structure'.

Context – The great dualism in sociological theory is between structure and action – does the social structure determine social action or does human action determine the social structure? The hypothesis above presents a structural perspective, which is supported by both functionalism and Marxism. However, interpretivists present a radical alternative to this view, arguing that social action actually determines the social structure. To make matters even more complicated, this dualism has been challenged and social-action theorists have argued that structure and action are linked and therefore interact to affect each other.

Conduct a literature search to establish which theories are relevant to the dualism debate and which theorist's work can be applied to the hypothesis. A literature search may be conducted using a computer in your local library, school or college to find out what books are available on the subject/topic you are interested in. The usual format is that you enter an introductory page and you can enter either the name of the subject, book or author on whom you are looking for information. The computer will then provide a list of relevant books held in the library. Remember to include the alternative theories in your review, such as structuralism and postmodernism.

Method – The data collected from your literature search for your context may also provide some information for your methodology. For example, evidence from Weber's examination of Protestantism and capitalism can be used as secondary data to support the argument that both structure and action

influence behaviour. Consider also the research of Durkheim on suicide and Goffman on mental illness as secondary data evidence for the other sides of the argument.

Conducting primary research is difficult for this hypothesis, but possible with careful organisation and planning. You will have to use triangulation to ensure that both the structural and interpretivist perspectives are investigated fairly. Establish a random sample of the adult population in your area and conduct a closed questionnaire to establish how they respond to the social structure and how they affect the social structure. Include questions such as 'Do you think that your job (or lack of one) has been determined by the class you were born into?' (structure) or 'Do you think that society has changed as a consequence of social protests?' (action). Add detail to your quantitative data by conducting interviews with a selection of those from your sample.

Remember to record all the positive and negative outcomes of your research as you go along, such as access to secondary sources or poor response rates. Also, concentrate on the way in which the research is working, rather than the data being collected, to assess whether your chosen methods are suited to your purposes.

Evaluation – Assess the advantages and disadvantages of using your chosen research methods for examining whether social action is a consequence of the social structure. Compare and contrast the findings of the secondary data to your results. Examine the successes and problems with using the quantitative and qualitative techniques you applied to your research, linking these evaluations to the structure (positivist methods) versus action (interpretivist methods) debate.

Alternative theories

Sociobiology

Sociobiology is probably the most alternative of the alternative sociological theories, because it rejects the fundamental basis of most sociological theorising – that human behaviour is influenced by cultural factors. Sociobiology, which also goes under other names such as **evolutionary psychology**, argues that human behaviour is affected by biology (hence 'socio-biology') and was developed in the 1970s. It offers an interesting and much debated theory that challenges most sociological thinking, with theorists, such as E. O. Wilson, explaining social behaviour through biological evolutionary theory.

Sociobiology has interpreted and developed the evolutionary theories and Charles Darwin. It believes that all species, including humans, evolve over time through a process of natural selection. Therefore human beings are governed by a genetic make-up that encourages them to pass on their genes through reproduction. Men and women, however, behave differently in their attempts to maximise their reproductive prospects. Men will take every opportunity to have sex, in order to impregnate as many women as possible and thereby pass on their genes. Women, on the other hand, want to save their limited supply of eggs for the best possible mate and therefore limit the number of males with which they have intercourse.

Unfortunately, this approach has been used to justify socially unacceptable behaviour. For example, the rape of women by men could be argued to be part of their biological need to reproduce, while the primary role of women as mother-housewife could be seen as an extension of their need to protect and nurture their limited number of offspring.

The debate between nature (biology) and/or nurture (culture – see Area 4 on Society and Cultural Identities) determining human behaviour has been around for a long time. Sociologists and biologists have examined the degree to which our behaviour is learnt and/or inherited, but have failed to agree on the influence of each. It is, however, an important debate, because the outcome affects our understanding of issues such as 'race', educational attainment, gender roles and deviant behaviour. For example, the subordinate position of women in the modern industrial world can be explained differently depending on whether the nature-or-nurture debate is supported. Theorists who advocate a biological explanation (nature) suggest that men and women have different genetic make-up that predisposes them for different social roles. Theorists who explain gender differences socially (nurture) argue that we learn to see biological differences as inequalities and that gender roles are socially constructed on that basis. Therefore, sociobiology has the potential to change our understanding of social stratification and differentiation (see Area 3 on Social Stratification and Differentiation), or why certain people experience varying degrees of social inequality. If the sociobiologists are correct, you could be born a criminal or destined for a lifetime of subordination because of the colour of your skin!

Sociobiologists are aware of the controversial nature of their theorising. For example, Van den Berghe (1988) noted that he was 'touching on practically every raw nerve in the Social Sciences' when he put forward a sociobiological explanation of 'race' and ethnicity. Sociobiologists remain committed to explaining social behaviour as an interaction between biology and culture, examined through scientific methods. However, sociobiology has been widely criticised by feminists, who argue that it is just an excuse to justify patriarchy. Also, other sociological theorists have, while acknowledging the importance of nature, challenged a sociobiological explanation that fails to take into account the huge diversity in behaviour between different cultures. For example, we may have evolved to ensure the reproduction of our species, but different societies have different norms and values that control sexual behaviour and assign it significance beyond reproductive purposes, such as as a sign of love.

Structuralism

Structuralism is an approach that has been adapted from the study of structural linguistics, anthropology and psychoanalysis and is based upon the idea that human consciousness does not determine meaning in language. Ferdinand de Saussure (1857–1913), Claude

Levi-Strauss and Sigmund Freud (1856–1939) have all been influential in developing this theory that analyses cultural phenomena. Saussure, a structuralist linguist, argued that linguistics, or language, can be seen as a system of words (or **signifiers**) that have meaning only because they contrast with other signs (a contrast that Levi-Stauss later termed **oppositions**). For example, a 'tree' has meaning because it is not a 'flower' or a 'bush'. Therefore signifiers are not connected to objects in the real world, only the concepts (signified) of those objects. Freud, along with Jacques Lacan (1901–81), argued that 'the unconscious' is constructed like a language and therefore the structures that govern human thought can be explained. Consequently, structuralists have attempted to discover the unconscious structures that make the mind work and how these structures shape conscious thought.

Levi-Strauss, an anthropologist, developed the structuralist movement in Paris after 1945. He linked the ideas of language and the mind together to explain the system of unconscious rules of thought within the mind. Levi-Strauss (1969) considered whether 'primitive' minds think differently from 'advanced' minds. He discovered that in primitive societies, which practise totemism, people's minds work in the same way as the minds of people in advanced societies, they just have different conditions (systems) under which to think and alternative means of expressing themselves. Therefore, Levi-Strauss concludes that there are universal processes of the mind, which is not surprising considering we all have to rely on our brains to think.

Levi-Strauss's (1970, 1981) later work was on primitive societies' myths, such as stories involving trips to heaven and help from animals. For people from advanced societies these myths are hard to understand, appearing illogical and contradictory, because they address the complex nature of human beings' relationship with nature and culture. Levi-Strauss argued that myths are not arbitrary, but are instead concerned with deep intellectual problems and have underlying structures that are very logical. In fact, the myths serve to **mediate**, or resolve, the oppositions, or contradictions, of people's lives. For example, the contradiction of good and evil can be resolved in a myth that shows supernatural beings that are neither.

In some ways Levi-Strauss's work is very similar to Marx's concept of ideology, in that myths are used for collective self-delusion. However, Levi-Strauss was anti-humanist, with myths being seen as a product of the operation of the unconscious mind, rather than the ingenuity of the storyteller. The structuralist approach of Levi-Strauss has encouraged the use of semiology in sociology (the study of systems of signs, such as food) and the development of cultural studies.

Semiology

Roland Barthes (1915–86) developed the sociology of signs from both a structuralist and poststructuralist framework. His early structuralist work analysed French culture through an emphasis on the centrality of language in a bourgeois society, which displays some Marxist assumptions. This Marxist tendency is also present in Barthes' explanation of **myth** (or a system of communication), which like Levi-Strauss he views as a construct, but in addition sees it as an ideological construction designed to obscure reality:

> ❛ … *mythology: it is part both of semiology inasmuch as it is a formal science, and of ideology inasmuch as it is an historical science: it studies ideas in form.*

> Barthes, R. (1989:121)

For example, wearing clothes appears natural, but it is also cultural and therefore has meaning. Certain types of clothes communicate specific meanings, for example wearing a short skirt and tight, low-cut top is considered sexually provocative in most western cultures. Consequently, myths naturalise things, making them seem inherent to social life, obscuring the fact that they may stem from an exploitative history.

ACTIVITY   KS **COMMUNICATION**

KNOWLEDGE AND UNDERSTANDING	IDENTIFICATION AND INTERPRETATION

List five things in your social world that appear natural or taken for granted, but which on closer examination could be cultural constructs that have a meaning of their own, such as a red rose or a box of chocolates. Justify your choice for each item, explaining clearly the cultural meaning that each item holds.

Barthes also examined **realism**, which is a literary style that presents itself as a natural way of writing. Barthes argues that realism is ideological, because it attempts to present a version of the world as reality by claiming that writing is only a way of presenting facts. Barthes maintains that realism cannot act as a window to the real world, because it, too, is a literary style just like any other form of writing and therefore affects the reader's perceptions of reality. In fact, we are all prisoners of language according to Barthes, because our only access to reality is through culture schemes, such as language, which makes an independent representation of reality impossible.

Evaluation of structuralism and semiology

Structuralism has been criticised for interpreting signs using underlying rules, which could generalise the meaning in signs when really subtle differences exist. Also, if underlying structures determine action, then any change within that structure is difficult to explain. This said, structuralism has provided valuable insights for the development of sociological theory. Both structuralism and semiology provide a way of examining human culture. They display how human consciousness does not determine the meaning in language and how phenomena that appear natural can be seen as being the outcome of underlying structures.

Relativist theories

Truth is not universal, it is relative to the individual or social group and therefore varies according to their beliefs. One truth cannot therefore be superior to another truth.

Relativist theory is based on the idea that there is no such thing as valid or invalid knowledge. Contrary to the claims of modernism (science and positivism), relativism argues that it is impossible to produce *a truth*, because even the most apparently scientific methods are based upon a theoretical judgement. Therefore, all knowledge is relative to the way, time and place in which it is acquired. For example, witchcraft offers an alternative form of understanding the world to scientific explanations; relativism argues that both are based on uncertain assumptions that make them equally plausible explanations for the parties involved.

Postmodernism and poststructuralism are theoretical approaches that adopt a relativist position. They attempt to deconstruct (break down) sociological theory to confirm the impossibility of producing any valid knowledge. Any theory based on an alleged ability to demonstrate 'the truth' is disregarded, because, as postmodernists would say, 'all truth is meaningless except for this truth'. Social existence is constructed from multiple versions of reality (narratives or stories), which determine our identity in a fragmented and constantly changing world.

Poststructuralism

The terms postmodernism and poststructuralism are often used interchangeably, because they are based on the same relativist assumptions. However, unlike postmodernism, poststructuralism grew out of an established theory, **structuralism** (see section on 'Structuralism', page 43), and reacted against it. Poststructuralism, like many traditional sociological theories, is based on a variety of themes, which are used differently by those labelled as poststructuralists. For example, both Michel Foucault and Jacques Derrida are labelled poststructuralists, but they do not agree with some of each other's ideas. Therefore, poststructuralism can be interpreted in different ways, which has led to it being seen as a complex and elusive theoretical approach.

Poststructuralism is based on the abandonment of the idea that there is a universal and rational order to social thought and progress in social development. Friedrich Nietzsche (1844–1900) was the first to doubt the ability of reason and rational thought to be objective and reflective. Western Marxism had developed a way of thinking that assumed sociology could reveal the truth about society or expose ideological 'untruths'. However, the poststructuralists claimed that this assumption, that knowledge brings freedom through rational and science-based organisation of society, was itself an ideology.

Poststructuralists saw The Enlightenment as an ideological conception that promised human freedom, but which really acted as a form of social control. Poststructuralists see even sociology as ideological, which questions the whole basis of theoretical knowledge and its use in making the human condition better.

Foucault (1979, 1980) supports the idea that sociology can never provide a scientific understanding of the social world, because the concepts applied no longer have any connection with the real world. He argued the link between language and reality has disappeared, making society a confusing mass of discourses or statements. In a world where language has a variety of meanings, where ideas and words are not connected, the 'truth' is hard to find. He continues that knowledge is connected to power and therefore those who have power can also dictate which concepts are seen as true. Scientific enquiry is just one discourse taking part in the power struggle. Consequently, any researcher searching for 'truths' is maintaining the power struggle to make his or her discourse the dominant one and sustaining the problem of non-reality.

Evaluation

1   It challenges traditional thinking about sociological theory.
2   The rejection of scientific knowledge could speed the downfall of civilisation.
3   It is a pessimistic theory with nihilist outcomes (there is nothing to believe in) and therefore makes social enquiry pointless.

Structuralism	Poststructuralism
Scientific aspirations i.e. to be rational and objective.	Abandoned scientific aspiration i.e. realised objectivity is not possible.
Ideology is virtually inescapable.	There is a paradox in explaining the inescapable nature of ideology through that ideology.
Language is power that dominates people's understanding of 'reality'.	Language is power that dominates people's understanding of 'reality' and acts as a form of social control.
Marxist politics.	Anarchistic politics.

Figure 1.9   Structuralism versus poststructuralism

Modernity and postmodernism

> *Postmodern thought is characterized by a loss of belief in an objective world and an incredulity towards meta-narratives of Legitimation. With a delegitimation of global systems of thought, there is no foundation to secure a universal and objective reality. There is today a growing public acknowledgement that 'Reality isn't what it used to be.'*
>
> Kvale, S. in Anderson (Ed.) (1996:19)

Modernity

Modernity (see Area 2 on Sociological Research Methodology) refers to the period of enlightenment in the eighteenth and nineteenth centuries that saw science/human reason being used to make sense of the world. It involved the development of a social, intellectual, cultural, economic and political system in the West. Sociologists, such as Comte, Durkheim and Marx, attempted to use scientific methods to explain society, considering themselves to be objective in their observations and assumptions.

Positivism (see Area 2 on Sociological Research Methodology) was accepted as the dominant perspective from which to develop 'laws' about society and the basis on which to solve social problems. Modernity saw a massive break from tradition, which was based on ritual and symbolic practices that socialise people into the norms and values that link them to a real or imagined past. The importance of the church/religion, feudalism and a unified community was replaced by state and political authority, capitalism, new classes, scientific thinking and new communities (Hall, 1980). However, tradition did survive in some forms into modernity; for example the House of Lords is a reflection of Britain's feudal past.

Giddens (1994) has clearly separated tradition from modernity. He argues that modernity has the four characteristics that distinguish it from tradition; industrialisation, capitalism, surveillance and total war capacity. In other words, the modern society has the physical and social relations that can support industrialisation, such as machinery and social class, capitalism and war.

Sociology can be seen as a product of modernity, with theorists attempting to explain their social world through reason and the application of scientific method. As a consequence of this, many sociological theories have been based on the approach of the natural sciences (positivism), for example structural theories, such as traditional functionalism tend to use 'scientific' models (see section on 'Structural theories' page 8). The main assumptions that support modernity and which apply to sociology may be summarised as follows:

1   The production of objective knowledge as both possible and desirable.
2   Impartial professionals base valid knowledge on systematic and vigorous methods.
3   Valid knowledge can be applied to societies and the structures within them.

HINTS AND TIPS   *Modernity is characterised by the dominance of traditional, scientific thought. Issues raised by theory (and methods) questions in the examination, for example the scientific status of sociology, are closely related to the three assumptions of the modern period.*

Around the middle of the twentieth century, as sociologists developed greater understanding of the social world, interpretivism emerged to challenge the dominant position of positivism. This was seen as the great 'dualism' (or battle of opposites), highlighting the division in theory between society versus individual, macro versus micro perspectives and science versus personal.

Contemporary sociological theory has offered an alternative to the 'dualisms' of traditional sociology. The gap between structural and interpretive theories has been bridged by the idea of 'duality' (see Giddens on structuration theory), which links the concepts of structure and action (agency or individual behaviour) together. It is possible that this change in sociological thinking has developed in line with the recent transition of modern society. The last few decades have witnessed a massive transformation in how with live, with **globalisation** (see Area 13 on World Sociology) playing a crucial role in this process.

Globalisation involves increasing political, cultural and economic interdependence between societies across the globe. For example, the recent European War in Yugoslavia involved NATO and its affiliated countries (political), the war was played out to a worldwide audience on television (cultural) and it has supported both economic production (arms) and consumption

(aid) for many countries. Globalisation has therefore been identified as part of the social change into a postmodern era.

Postmodernism

Sociologists have come to some agreement that the last three decades of the twentieth century witnessed massive and swift social change. This social transformation from modernity to postmodernity, supported by the development of globalisation, is potentially quite radical. Postmodernism has emerged as a theoretical approach that seeks to explain these changes. Postmodernism challenges the assumptions of modernity, in that it questions the supposed 'certainties' and 'realities' of a global society with no definite rules. Therefore, postmodernists argue that the accepted rationality of The Enlightenment is misplaced is a constantly changing world, a world that is actually irrational and that cannot be explained by macro theories.

HINTS AND TIPS   *Some sociologists, such as Giddens, do not believe that society has become postmodern. Instead they argue that the social world has entered a phase of **late modernity**. Late modernity can be defined as a period in which sociologists and other researchers have become much more critical of modernist assumptions, but accept that the potential for progress still exists. A growth in critical awareness is also known as **reflexivity**.*

Postmodernism can be seen to oppose each of the three assumptions of modernity (see section on 'Modernity', page 48) through three countering arguments:

1   Relativism – **there is no such thing as valid or invalid knowledge**. Modernism argued that belief/knowledge may be based on things such as common sense, tradition, authority, etc., but that valid knowledge is desirable. Therefore 'the truth' should be capable of proof through appropriate methods. However, postmodernists claim that 'appropriate' methods can be based on theoretical judgements, but may also be based on convenience or other considerations. Consequently, any form of knowledge is seen as being value laden and relative, because the evidence collected is shaped by external, non-factual influences that cannot be scientifically validated.

Postmodern ideas of relativism also incorporate the notion of **deconstruction**, or breaking down into parts. Through deconstructing sociological theories, postmodernists have implied that they are based on assumptions that are no more certain than those that inform witchcraft or fortune telling. However, the intention of deconstruction is not to substitute new and more acceptable criteria for old theories, but rather to affirm the impossibility of producing any demonstrably valid knowledge at all. All knowledge is seen as equally uncertain and any theory that claims to show 'the truth' should be disregarded.

2   Death of the subject – **knowledge is seen as a form of control rather than of liberation**. In modernism the researcher is the originator of knowledge, knowledge that can be used to intervene in the world to improve social situations, such as reducing poverty. Therefore in modernist theory tradition is subject centred, with humans being at the centre of the production of knowledge. Postmodernists, however, believe there is no one truth, only multiple versions of reality (narratives or stories) that determine our social world and our identity within it. Therefore, the lack of an objective reality means that intervention is not rational. Knowledge cannot consequently liberate the human condition, subject centredness is undermined and the death of the subject (importance of the researcher) occurs.

3   Grand theories are inadmissible – **macro theories, such as Marxism, make truth claims that they cannot substantiate**. Postmodernism uses the critical term 'metanarratives' to refer to the grand theories of sociology, such as Marxism, functionalism, interactionism, etc. Metanarratives mean 'big stories' and are seen as one version of reality that make truth claims about themselves, such as that they are universal. Metanarratives also utilise the notion of social planning and intervention, which postmodernists consider as subject centred and invalid. Postmodernists therefore conclude that grand theories are thoroughly modernist and as such are inappropriate and misleading.

Postmodernist theory in sociology critically examines (is reflexive in) the following areas:

■   'Metanarratives' (big stories) or totalistic theories that claim to explain social life, e.g. Marxism and

the claim of an inevitable communist revolution (Lyotard, 1984).

■   Science, e.g. the damage caused to humans by increasing scientific technology (Bauman, 1992), such as the effects of genetically modified food.

■   Globalisation, e.g. the effects of the increasing ease of communication between nations (Hall, 1992).

■   Culture, identity and social pluralism, e.g. the establishing of pick-and-mix identities, based on global media and multicultural societies (Strinati, 1995; Willis, 1990).

■   Social movements, e.g. the growth of 'life politics', such as Greenpeace, as an alternative to traditional politics.

■   Connections between society and the individual (duality), e.g. structure and action are interconnected and therefore work together.

■   The environment, e.g. the effects of human action on the nature, such as global warming (Beck, 1992).

Postmodernism, however, does not claim to explain social life completely (it is not totalistic or universalistic). Instead, postmodernism argues that all individuals, groups and cultures are different and therefore not predictable, consequently any attempt to construct a theory that attempts to explain a universal behaviour is impossible. Hence, postmodernism is relativist in its theoretical assumptions, suggesting society be examined in an open and provisional way.

Whether it has been loved or loathed by sociologists, it cannot be doubted that postmodernism has had an effect on sociology. It may be rather remote from many of the difficulties faced by people in their day-to-day lives, but it does present another way of seeing society. The central theme of reflexivity (or being critically evaluative of something) has been integrated into sociology generally and has made researchers aware of the potential negative effects of the pursuit of progress. For example, sociologists tend to consider the negative effects/values, ethics of research on humanity. The sociology of globalisation and culture has developed through postmodernism's awareness of the importance of culture (communication, consumption and lifestyle). Also, postmodernism has suggested connections in sociology, rather than dualisms, allowing the relationship of the individual and society to be seen as a process.

A C T I V I T Y   KS COMMUNICATION, WORKING WITH OTHERS

KNOWLEDGE AND UNDERSTANDING	IDENTIFICATION AND INTERPRETATION

Visit a museum that has an anthropological display, i.e. it includes artefacts from a variety of societies' social histories, such as clothes, jewellery, etc. (The Pitt Rivers Museum in Oxford has an excellent collection of different peoples' past possessions … including shrunken heads!) Make a note of all the exhibits that bear some resemblance to objects found in modern western society. Also note down the date and place that the exhibit comes from. At the end of your visit you should be able to identify the pick-and-mix culture we experience. Discuss the items you discovered that were borrowed from the past and used as the trends we have today, such as patterns on clothing or body jewellery, with other sociology students.

Jean Baudrillard

Postmodernists, such as Baudrillard (1983), argue that culture has become the main part of social life, because of improved global communications/development of the mass media. For example, Avon make-up is a known cosmetic brand around the world; it has even been marketed effectively in remote areas of the Amazon. We see ourselves, and define reality, through the cultural and media images that surround us. For example, Baudrillard argues that signs (words and images) used to reflect reality; however, these signs (signifiers) have become distorted to the point that they have lost all connection with reality.

Baudrillard continues that the objects produced and consumed in social life have become signifiers, or products of the mass media that are produced and consumed instead of the 'real' object. The ultimate signifier is a **simulacrum**, or an image that does not exist and never has done. A prime example of a simulacrum is the recent 'radio marriage' that invited two people who had never met to get married. The marriage and their life together were both fiction and reality, and all events were documented on radio and television. After a few months of marriage (and documentary intrusion) the couple split up, the signifier (image of a marriage) destroyed the reality (actual marriage). This is also an example of '**hyperreality**',

which refers to a reality that is created by the media and its production of signs, a state of being that, according to Buadrillard, is common to the postmodern world where reality and image can no longer be told apart.

Jean-François Lyotard

Baudrillard's work has been criticised for its abstract and unsubstantiated approach, however this is a feature of postmodernist theorising. Lyotard (1984) also refused to be constrained by a systematic research methodology when postulating his theories. He argued that postmodernism could be summed up as follows:

> I define 'post-modernism' as incredulity towards metanarratives. This incredulity is undoubtedly a product of progress in the sciences.

Lyotard, J-F. (1992:356)

Lyotard argues that science itself has shown that it is impossible to devise universal laws by challenging the 'truths' established by scientific enquiry in previous years, such as Newton's laws of physics.

Postmodernism rejects the usefulness of metanarratives and instead Lyotard concentrates on '**language games**'. Language games are discussions in which things are claimed to be correct and are used to legitimise behaviour. In The Enlightenment language games were replaced by scientific reason, but the theories established by science still relied upon narratives or stories to provide them with meaning. In the postmodern world knowledge is based on the language games and these games allow diverse groups to be heard. Metanarratives are, according to Lyotard, being replaced by a plurality of discussions that put forward different versions of reality, allowing previously marginalised people, such as women, to argue their cause.

Postmodernism is a confusing theoretical approach, because it has been used and interpreted in a variety of ways. Everyday language has incorporated the term 'postmodern', such as the band The Sneaker Pimps' song 'Postmodern Sleaze', without really understanding what it means. On top of this, postmodernism challenges the fundamental assumptions of traditional theories (metanarratives), such as the inadmissible nature of grand theories. It also presents a view diametrically opposed to that of the traditional structural theorists, who argue that culture does not dominate the economy, the economy dominates culture. However, despite all the controversy surrounding postmodernism, it cannot be denied that the massive amount of social change witnessed in western society and the scepticism towards scientific research tends to support a move away from modernism.

Evaluation

1 Postmodernism challenges the way in which traditional theories have been accepted as 'the truth' and therefore provides an alternative way of thinking about society.

2 Postmodernism has been argued to be a metanarrative itself for postulating a theoretical perspective as Bruce (1999:110) argues:

> ❛ Postmodernists write books and lecture; they try to communicate their claims to others. They do so because they believe that they are right and others are wrong. If they took a full-strength dose of their own medicine, they would shut up shop. If no reading is superior to any other, then why destroy trees to announce that to the world? If it is not possible to distinguish truth from error, why do postmodernists argue with those who do not share their views?

3 It is relativistic and therefore does not provide any explanations of social life (Gellner, 1991).

4 Individuality is seen as directed by ideologies (Baudrillard) and therefore postmodernism has been accused of being deterministic.

5 Postmodernism emphasises the cultural at the cost of the socio-economic (traditional Marxism).

6 Postmodernists largely ignore the fact that capitalism continues to cause massive social inequality across the globe (structural conflict theorists).

7 Postmodernism does not analyse contemporary society adequately (provide a 'total' theory).

8 Postmodernism has not provided any convincing evidence for ignoring traditional sociological concepts, such as inequality, power, structure and action (in fact, Giddens has expanded the postmodernist approach to include the above).

ACTIVITY KS**COMMUNICATION**

KNOWLEDGE AND UNDERSTANDING	IDENTIFICATION AND INTERPRETATION	ANALYSIS AND EVALUATION

The social construction of reality is a concept put forward by both postmodernist and interpretivist theory. Despite this similarity, the two approaches are based on fundamentally different assumptions. Explain how the two theories are in opposition.

The future of sociological theory

Sociology emerged as a discipline that saw society as an independent world open for scientific examination. Sociological theory developed alongside this positivist (see Area 2 on Sociological Research Methodology) outlook and was based upon logical deductions that could be grouped together as propositions leading to coherent concepts. Structural sociological theory was, therefore, as Turner (1998) argued, a means of explaining social research:

> ❛ Social theory is developed as a tool of social research which seeks to provide coherent and relatively simple explanations of events in the real world by, for example, the development of models and causal accounts.
>
> Turner, B. S. (1998:7)

Sociological theory has, however, never been a unified body of thought. Structural theorists may have applied scientific methods, but the explanations they developed fell clearly into opposed fields of conflict and consensus theory. Twentieth-century sociological theory can be seen to provide a variety of explanations, not only of human behaviour, but also of the nature of theory itself. For example, interpretivist theorists view theory as an interpretation of social reality that results in understanding through detailed description. This understanding is based on revealing the social actor's meaning of a social action.

The diversity of social theory did not end with the great dualism of structure versus action (or positivism versus interpretivism). Some theorists attempted to construct a theory that explained causal links and the understanding of meaning (social action theory), thereby showing the duality or link between structure and action. Others have abandoned theory completely, arguing that it is merely one 'narrative' or story showing a version of events that can never be real (postmodernism), which has led to some sociologists questioning the value of theory at all.

Sociology and social policy

Sociological theory is, as stated at the beginning of this area, essential in explaining social phenomena. Postmodernism may claim that theories are useless, but surely it, too, is a theory claiming that its version of reality is correct. Social policy refers to the legislation implemented by the government to deal with 'social problems'. Social problems are social phenomena that have been labelled as undesirable in society, in accordance with the social and legal rules of that society. For example, in the UK poverty and crime are considered to be social problems that require further investigation in order to reduce their occurrence in society.

To draw up social policies the government often relies on the research of sociologists, who approach the social problem being investigated using a variety of theoretical structures and perspectives. Sociologists have the expertise to apply the most appropriate theoretical approach and research methodology, thereby producing data that should help the

government understand how and why people behave as they do. Therefore sociological theory and research contribute towards government decision-making on social policy. Consequently, the relationship between sociology and social policy is essential for understanding social issues and acting upon this understanding. In this way, sociological theory cannot be seen as useless.

The contribution of sociology to social policy

The government has commissioned sociological research in many areas, such as:

- household income
- race relations
- gender inequality.

The data produced by this research has resulted in social policy, such as Family Credit (which provides extra income for families on a low income); the Race Relations Act, 1976 (based on the work of Rose and Deakin, 1969 for the Institute of Race Relations) and the Sex Discrimination Act, 1975.

Therefore, what is a good student of sociology to believe? The most straightforward approach is to understand that sociology has developed as a discipline with a diverse set of theoretical approaches, all contributing to the richness of sociological explanations of the social world. Sociological theory provides people with a general understanding of the world around them, dependent on the type of theory they choose to accept. Consequently, the future of sociological theory appears to be as diverse and pluralistic as the subject matter it attempts to explain.

Area summary

Sociology is fundamentally linked with theory, relying on its 'more-than-common-sense' explanations of social phenomena. Sociological theory is wide-ranging and diverse and sometimes even theorists within the same tradition fail to agree on the best way to explain the social world. This said, structural, interpretivist, social-action and the alternative theories to these traditional ones, such as postmodernism, all add, in varying degrees, to our understanding of the complex world that we both live in and create.

1800s	1900s	2000s ?
The Enlightenment (modern)		Postmodernism
(S)	Marxism	Critical theory
	Functionalism	New Right
		Feminism
		Race relations
(I)	Social Action	Symbolic Interactionism
		Phenomenology/Ethnomethodology
(R)		Poststructuralism/Postmodernism
(A)		Sociobiology

Key: S = Structural, I = Interpretivist, R = Relativist, A = Alternative.

Figure 1.10   Time line of sociological theory

Links between theory and method

Macro		Micro
Structural	Social action	Interpretivist
Marxism	Weberianism	Symbolic interactionism
Functionalism		Phenomenology
Feminisms		Ethnomethodology
Positivist	Realist	Anti-positivist
Quantitative		Qualitative
Reliable		Valid
Generalisable		Specific
Comparative method		Participant observation
Closed questionnaires		Informal interviews
1		
2		

ACTIVITY   KS **COMMUNICATION**

KNOWLEDGE AND UNDERSTANDING	IDENTIFICATION AND INTERPRETATION

1 Explain the diagram opposite. Remember to show how the ideas link together in each column.
2 When you have done this add two further points to each column.
3 Name a sociologist who has conducted a study using the research methods identified.

Definitions

Alienation	A Marxist concept that argues that the worker becomes detached from the product of their labour during industrialisation
Anomie	A condition identified by Durkheim and refers to the normlessness experienced by people in times of social transition
Capitalism	A society based on the accumulation of profit/surplus value
Class	A group or individuals with a similar position in the social stratification system
Class relation	Refers to whether an individual owns the means of production or not
Collective conscience	A term used by Durkheim to refer to the existence of a social/moral order of shared commitments that operates outside of the individual, but directly acts upon them
Conflict	This means disagreement and is used in theory to reflect social struggle through divided interests and hostility
Consensus	This means agreement and is used in theory to reflect social cohesion through accepted norms and values
Conversation analysis	A theory of the way in which conversation is organised by those taking part and how it can result in action
Core values	The indisputable beliefs on which a society is based
Deconstruction	A postmodernist concept that refers to the way in which paradoxes in text are highlighted, despite conventional attempts to identify a coherent and fluent text
Discourse	A term used in poststructuralism to refer to a way of speaking/writing that operates according to social and historical rules. It is not fixed or universal, but emerges at certain times in history
Dramaturgical	A sociological approach developed by Goffman, which assumes that social life is like a play or drama in which humans take on different roles
Dual consciousness	A term developed by Mann to refer to the way in which the working class accept middle-class values, but at the same time develop their own opposing values

Dualism	Refers to opposites, specifically the split between structural explanations of the social world and explanation based on individual actions
Duality of structure	A term used by Giddens to explain the way in which structures shape individual action and how individual actions modify structures
Dual-systems approach	A term used by socialist feminists to refer to the way in which they explain female subordination in relation to both capitalism and patriarchy
Dysfunctions	These refer to when the social structure experiences things that do not support its well-being and maintenance
Epoch	A period of historical change with a specific way of organising production
Etcetera clause	A term used by Garfinkel to refer to the way in which any modification to a rule is dependent on the context of the interaction
Ethnomethodology	A theory that emphasises the taken-for-granted nature of language and action and the way in which we understand what other people mean
Evolutionary psychology	This is a theoretical perspective that examines the constantly progressing nature of human behaviour
Feminism	A sociological perspective that develops sociological theory from the viewpoint of women
Functional alternatives	These are structures in society that could carry out the same job as another structure and achieve similar results
Functional imperatives/ prerequisites	These refer to the basic needs that society has to have met if it is to continue
Functional unity	Refers to the functionalist belief that society works as a balanced system, with all parts working together to maintain the whole
Functional universality	This refers to the functionalist belief that functional prerequisites (see above) are necessary for society to exist and therefore must be a part of every social system
Functionalism	A theory that explains that social structures exist through their role in sustaining the social system; it is a structural-consensus theory that examines the social structure as a set of interrelated parts ensuring the smooth running of the whole
Globalisation	Refers to the way in which societies have become increasingly interdependent politically, culturally and economically
Hegemony	Cultural and intellectual activities are subject to ruling-class ideology and are therefore a place for social conflict
Historial/dialectical materialism	This is a Marxist concept and refers to a process in which the conflict that exists between the social classes causes social change (or history)
Homogeneous	This means similar or alike
Humanistic	A theory that advocates the freedom of the individual
Hyperreality	A term used to refer to a reality that is created by the media
Ideal type	A Weberian concept that identifies that 'sociological laws' are simply generalisations about society or the activities of individuals

Ideology	A system of ideas that systematically misrepresents reality to serve the interests of particular social groups, such as the ruling class
Impression management	A term used by Goffman referring to the way in which social actors control the image of their performance
Infrastructure	A term used to refer to the economic base of society, such as capitalism
Institutionalised	Refers to the way in which an individual within an institution loses self-image and has it replaced with one that is acceptable to the institution
Interpretivism	Theories that analyse society from the level of the individual, because society would not exist without the individuals that make it up
Involuntary	Refers to action or behaviour beyond our control
Language games	A concept put forward by Lyotard that refers to the way in which the claims made during discussions are used to legitimate behaviour
Late modernity	A period in which researchers accepted that progress could still exist, but had become more critical of the ability of scientific principles to provide all knowledge
Macro	Large-scale; used in sociology to refer to structural theories
Marxism	A structural-conflict theory based on the works of Marx, which explains the role of class struggle in maintaining and overthrowing capitalism
Meaningful	An interpretivist term used to refer to voluntary behaviour
Means of production	Refers to the elements necessary to produce the goods and services needed by an individual
Mechanical solidarity	A term used by Durkheim to refer to the way in which the people of rural communities identify with each other based on shared experiences
Mediate	To resolve
Metanarratives (Grand narratives)	Narratives, or stories, that have attempted to provide a comprehensive explanation, which is seen as worthy, of the social world
Micro	Small-scale; used in sociology to refer to interpretivist theories
Modernity	A condition in social history from The Enlightenment of the seventeenth century to the middle of the twentieth century; it was based on the understanding that rational, scientific principles could and should be used to determine knowledge
Myth	A term used in semiology to refer to a system of communication
Narrative	The common, predominant form within which knowledge is conveyed, such as story or conversation
Nationalism	The belief in a unified nation based on a single cultural background
Norms	The rules that structure social behaviour
Oppositions	The way in which some signs differ other signs
Organic solidarity	This is a term used by Durkheim to refer to the way in which the people of industrial communities integrate through needing different things from different people
Parties	Self-conscious organisations pursuing power

Patriarchy	A term used to explain the control of society by men, in the interests of men
Performance	A term used by Goffman representing the acting out of a social role
Perspective	A particular concept or idea that affects the interpretation of a theory
Phenomenology	A theoretical approach based on understanding everyday interactions and the common-sense understandings that surround them
Positivism	A perspective that believes all phenomena should be studied scientifically
Postmodernism	A perspective that focuses on the global and fragmented nature of the postmodern world around us; the credibility of scientific explanations is challenged, based on a social world that is constantly changing and in which there are no absolute rules
Proletariat	Marx's term for the subject class in capitalist society
Rational capitalism	A concept that identifies capitalism as being bound by logic and order
Realism	An ideological concept that seems to portray how things really are in the world
Reductionist	This means bringing things back to a basic level
Reflexivity	Can be defined as a growth of critical awareness
Regions	A term used by Goffman to describe a 'place' in the social world that is constructed by people's perceptions
Reification	This refers to the treatment of something as real or concrete, when it may only be a theory or model
Relatively autonomous	A neo-Marxist concept used to explain race relations; 'race' is seen to exist in a way that is not determined by class, but class is seen to affect it
Relativism	This approach argues that all knowledge is partial and directly linked to the social position of the individual; there is no such thing as 'truth'
Reserve army of labour	Refers to a section of the workforce, particularly women and ethnic minority groups, who are seen as expendable in times of recession or accessible in times of an expanding labour market
Roles	The positions that people have in the social structure
Ruling class	A Marxist term; refers to those who own the means of production in a class-based social stratification system
Selectivist provision	This is the belief that welfare services and resources should only be provided to the most needy in society, such as means-tested benefits
Sexual politics	A term used by radical feminists to refer to the way in which men have been enabled by society to dominate women in the family and relationship
Significant others	The people in our lives who have a direct influence on our behaviour
Signifiers	Systems, such as words or language, that have meaning only through the way in which they differ from other signs
Simulacrum	A term used by Baudrillard to refer to an image that does not exist, but may be seen as real
Social closure	This refers to when a society has no social mobility, or movement between stratum

Social facts	The agreed rules or culture of a society that constrain behaviour in order to maintain that society
Social totality	Everything in society
Socialisation	Learning to be social by understanding social values
Status groups	A collection of people who see themselves as equals with a shared understanding of their position in society
Structural differentiation	A concept identified by Parson that argues all social structures become progressively more specialised as time goes by, e.g. the family
Structural theories	Explanations that give the social structure priority over the individual are seen as structural; individuals carry out actions dictated by their position in the social structure
Structuralism	Language is seen as the basic structure in society and everything that is produced by humans is a form of language
Structuration	Continuing from the work of Weber, Giddens emphasised the interdependence of structure and action
Subject class	A Marxist term; refers to those who do not own the means of production in a class-based social stratification system
Superstructure	A term used by Marxists to refer to the institutions, values and beliefs systems that reflect the infrastructure (see above), while at the same time maintaining that infrastrucrture
Symbolic capacity	A term used by Mead to describe the way in which the human mind is capable of reflection and anticipation (unlike animals)
Symbolic interactionism	An interpretive theory that assumes that the social world is based on symbols with shared meanings; society is therefore understood by the meanings that individuals attach to events or phenomena and transmitted by language
Teleological	An approach that explains something by the purpose it serves, e.g. norms and values exist because they serve the maintenance of social order
The generalised other	The vast collection of people in our life whose views we know and take into account, but that may not affect us directly
Theory	A systematic explanation of phenomena that is open to challenge by others
Underclass	A term used to refer to a class or group with similar characteristics that has a status below that of the working class
Values	A set of cultural beliefs about how society should be that are installed in the main parts of society and regulate its activities
Verstehen	A Weberian concept; refers to the way in which social action results from the meaning of interactions; it literally means 'to understand' and results from empathy with others
Voluntary	Refers to action or behaviour derived from a conscious decision
Weberianism	A social-action theory based on the work of Weber, which explains social structures as a consequence of both structural and human influences

Data response questions

The history of all hitherto existing society is the history of class struggles. Freeman and slave, patrician and plebeian, lord and serf, guild-master and journeyman, in a word, oppressor and oppressed, stood in constant opposition to one another, carried on uninterrupted, now hidden, now open fight, a fight that each time ended, either in revolutionary reconstitution of society at large, or in the common ruin of the contending classes.

In the earliest epochs of history, we find almost everywhere a complicated arrangement of society into various orders, a manifold gradation of social rank … The modern bourgeois society that has sprouted from the ruins of feudal society has not done away with class antagonism. It has but established new classes, new conditions of oppression, new forms of struggle in place of the old ones.

Marx, K. and Engels, F. (1998:34–5; first published 1888)
The Communist Manifesto. New York, Verso.

When an individual enters the presence of others, they commonly seek to acquire information about him or to bring into play information about him already possessed. They will be interested in his general socio-economic status, his conception of self, his attitude towards them, his competence, his trustworthiness, etc. Although some of this information seems to be sought almost as an end in itself, there are usually quite practical reasons for acquiring it. Information about the individual helps to define the situation, enabling others to know in advance what he will expect of them and what they may expect of him. Informed in these ways, the others will know how best to act in order to call forth a desired response from him.

Goffman, E. (1987:13; first published 1959)
The Presentation of Self in Everyday Life. Harmondsworth, Penguin.

The Modern Age, which sounds as if it would last forever, is fast becoming a thing of the past … The Post-Modern Age is a time of incessant choosing. It's an era when no orthodoxy can be adopted without self-consciousness and irony, because all traditions seem to have some validity. This is partly a consequence of what is called the information explosion, the advent of organised knowledge, world communications and cybernetics. It is not only the rich who become collectors, eclectic travellers in time with superabundance of choice, but almost every urban dweller. Pluralism, the "ism" of our time, is both the great problem and the great opportunity: where Everyman becomes a Cosmopolite and Everywoman a Liberated Individual, confusion and anxiety become ruling states of mind … This is the price we pay for the Post-Modern Age, as heavy in its way as the monotony, dogmatism and poverty of the Modern epoch. But, in spite of many attempts in Iran and elsewhere, it is impossible to return to a previous culture and industrial form, impose fundamentalist religion or even Modernist orthodoxy. Once a world

communication system and form of cybernetic production has emerged to
create their own necessities and they are, barring a nuclear war, irreversible.

Jencks, C. (1996:26–7) 'What is Post-Modern?' in Anderson, W. T. (Ed.)
The Fontana Post-Modernism Reader. London, Harper Collins.

a   What theoretical position is the author of Item B taking?   **(2)**

> **GUIDANCE**   *This is a question that requires you to understand what the item is*
> *saying and relate it to a sociological theory. The source and the terms used in the*
> *text always provide extra help in associating an idea to a theoretical context.*
>
> KNOWLEDGE AND
> UNDERSTANDING

b   Explain what is meant by 'The history of all hitherto existing society is the
history of class struggles.' (Item A)   **(5)**

> **GUIDANCE**   *Refer to the source for a clue about the theoretical*
> *context of the question. You should refer to Marxism as a structural*
> *conflict theory and how the quote reflects the concept about social change in class-based systems.*
>
> KNOWLEDGE AND | IDENTIFICATION AND
> UNDERSTANDING | INTERPRETATION

c   Structural and interpretivist theorists examine the modern world, a world
that Item C claims disappearing. Assess the strengths and weaknesses
of a postmodern analysis of society.   **(9)**

> **GUIDANCE**   *Outline the social and historical*
> *context into which postmodernism falls, i.e.*
> *challenging the authority of rational explanation that exploded in The Enlightenment (modern) era.*
> *Link the social/historical context to the traditional theories (structural, social-action and interpretive) and*
> *explain how postmodernism interprets these theories.*
>
> KNOWLEDGE AND | IDENTIFICATION AND | ANALYSIS AND
> UNDERSTANDING | INTERPRETATION | EVALUATION
>
> *Any question that calls for evaluation **must** present a balanced argument ... even if a particular theory*
> *appears useless. Remember to include an examination of the strengths of postmodernism, for example*
> *how it explains the global nature of the social world, **and** its weaknesses, for example that it, too, is a*
> *metanarrative and cannot therefore provide the 'truth'.*

Structured questions

a   Briefly explain the meaning of conflict and consensus.   **(4)**

b   Identify and describe two features of interpretivism.   **(4)**

c   Outline the contribution of social-action theory to sociology.   **(7)**

d   Assess the strengths and weaknesses of postmodern theory as an
explanation of social life.   **(10)**

(25)

Essay titles

1 Assess the claims made by interactionists that the social world has to be
  explained in terms of the meanings actors give to their actions. **(25)**

  (AEB, June 1994)

*GUIDANCE Begin by interpreting the question, which in this case suggests that there is a debate
surrounding the interactionist belief (particularly Goffman) that society is determined by people.
Introduce the essay by showing that you fully understand the question and the terminology used in it,
such as interactionism and actors. This displays your interpretation skills. Also, attempt to make brief
reference to a study conducted by an interactionist that supports the essay title, such as **Asylums**
(Goffman, 1963) to show your knowledge, understanding and application. You should also decide at
the beginning of the essay whether:*

*a The social world does have to be explained by the meaning given by social actors to their actions i.e.
   what alternative theories are there that explain society?*

b The strengths of the interactionist argument outweigh its weaknesses.

*c The alternative arguments that explain the social world are as strong as the interactionist
   explanation.*

*By making these decisions at the beginning of the essay your evidence in the main body will have
reflected your arguments fluently. It also means that your conclusion is much easier to write, because
you know that it is based on your first decisions about the title.*

*The main body of the essay should demonstrate your knowledge and understanding of the content of
the essay by evaluating the strengths and weaknesses of interactionist theory. In other words, show the
advantages of using the meaning given by social actors to their behaviour as a way of explaining the
social world, providing examples from studies. Also, examine alternative explanations of the social
world, such as structural and social-action theories. Show the differences between the structural
explanations and interactionist ones and why they would always challenge each other (see section on
macro versus micro approaches, page 5). Show the differences and similarities between social-action
and interactionist theory, remembering to link an evaluation back to the title. It is always useful to
include relevant studies or theorists to emphasise your knowledge of the area, but do not be tempted
to write a list of names and ideas at the expense of making your essay relevant and evaluative. Always
remain focused on the question.*

*Evaluation should have been used throughout the essay, however the conclusion is the place to weigh
up your argument in relation to the title, considering the evidence you have presented in the main
body of the essay. Make reference to the decisions you made about the title at the beginning of the
essay, such as whether the interactionist claim is a valid one, but provide a little more detail related to a
study or argument applied in the main body of the essay. It may not be possible to support the essay
title totally or reject it completely; as long as your argument is well balanced then it is acceptable to 'sit
on the fence'. In other words, you may decide that interactionism has contributed to our
understanding of the social world, but it is not the only way of explaining it. Lastly, if you can apply a
relevant piece of information that is up to date, such as a quotation or data from research, this will
leave the examiner in no doubt of your sociological skills.*

2 Evaluate the main strengths and weaknesses of functionalist approaches
  to the sociological study of society. **(25)**

  (AEB, November 1994)

3   Compare and contrast the contributions of structural theories and interactionist theories to the understanding of social life.   **(25)**

(AEB, June 1995)

> **HINTS AND TIPS**   *The OCR examination does not have specific essay questions on sociological theory, however theoretical knowledge, understanding and application are expected in all of the other areas. For example, the following Deviance and Control question requires knowledge of symbolic interactionism and theories critical of it:*
>
> *'Discuss the strengths and weaknesses of labelling theory as an explanation of deviant behaviour.'*
>
> **(25)**
> (IBS (now OCR), 1997)

Further reading and references

Cuff, E. C., Sharrock, W. W. and Francis, D. W. (1998) *Perspectives in Sociology*. London, Routledge.
This text appears complicated when approached initially, but it provides some excellent and detailed information on sociological theories and theoretical debates. Students looking for further information on particular theorists and theory will find this book very useful.

Jones, P. (1990) *Theory and Method in Sociology: A Guide for the Beginner*. London, Unwin Hyman.
This is a straightforward and accessible book, which students attempting to understand basic sociological theory will find helpful.

Maynard, M. (1989) *Sociological Theory*. Harlow, Longman.
This book is small, well organised and easy to understand. A good read for students struggling with the terminology and complex ideas of sociological theory.

Turner, B. S. (1998) *The Blackwell Companion to Social Theory*. Oxford, Blackwell.
This is a book that would challenge the thoughts of students who have conquered the basics of sociological theory. It is by no means straightforward, but it is worth reading for the detailed and informed account it provides of all the theoretical perspectives.

Internet sites

http://www.pscw.uva.nl/sociosite/TOPICS/sociologists.html (Sociologists: Dead and Very Much Alive) An excellent site that concentrates on sociological theory and provides assorted links.

http://www.ctheory.com/ (CTheory) A useful online journal of social theory.

http://www.stg.brown.edu/projects/hypertext/landow/cpace/theory/Mobius/links.html (Baudrillard Resources) This is a website that provides information on the postmodernist Baudrillard.

http://sosig.ac.uk/ (Sosig) A good starting point from which to find other links to sociological theory and theorists.

http://www.anu.edu.au/polsci/marx/marx.html (Marxism Page) A website dedicated to the works of Marx. It seems a bit complicated at first, but those radicals among you will find it worth the effort.

http://www.freespace.virgin.net/chris.livesey/home.htm (Sociology Central) An impressive site specially written for AS/A level students. You will find the revision cards on theory particularly useful.

Bibliography

Abbott, P. and Wallace, C. (1997) *An Introduction to Sociology: Feminist Perspectives*. London, Routledge.

Abel-Smith, B. and Townsend, P. (1965) *The Poor and the Poorest*, London, bells and Sons.

Abell, P. (1998) 'Sociological Theory and Rational Choice Theory', in Turner, B. S. (Ed.) *The Blackwell Companion to Social Theory*. Oxford, Blackwell.

Alexander, J. C. (1985) *Neofunctionalism*. London, Sage.

Althusser, L. (1969) *For Marx*. London, Allen Lane.

Anderson, W. T. (1996) *The Fontana Post-Modernism Reader*. London, Fontana.

Anthias, F. and Yuval-Davis, N. (1983) 'Contextualising Feminism: Gender, Ethnic and Class Divisions'. *Feminist Review*, No. 15.

Archer, M. S. (1982) 'Morphogenesis versus structuration: on combining structure and action'. *British Journal of Sociology*, Volume 33.

Barrett, M. (1980) *Women's Oppression Today: Problems in Marxist Feminist Analysis*. London, Verso.

Barthes, R. (1989) *Mythologies*. London, Puladin.

Baudrillard, J. (1983) *In the Shadow of the Silent Majorities*. New York, Semiotext.

Bauman, Z. (1992) *Intimations of Postmodernity*. London, Routledge.

Beck, U. (1992) *Risk Society*. London, Sage.

Becker, H. (1963) *Outsiders*. New York, Free Press.

Beechy, V. (1987) *Unequal Work*. London, Verso.

Ben-Tovim, G. and Gabriel, J. (1979) 'The politics of race in Britain: a review of major trends and of recent literature', Sage, *Race Relations Abstracts*, 4, 4:1 56.

Berger, P. and Luckmann, T. (1985) *The Social Construction of Reality*. Harmondsworth, Penguin.

Blumer, H (1969) *Symbolic Interactionism: Perspective and Method*. New Jersey, Prentice-Hall.

Brownmiller, S. (1976) *Against Our Will*. London, Penguin.

Bruce, S. (1999) *Sociology: A Very Short Introduction*. Oxford, Oxford University Press.

Cox, O. (1970) *Caste, Class and Race*. New York, Monthly Preview Books.

Craib, I. (1992) *Modern Social Theory*. Hemel Hempstead, Harvester Wheatsheaf.

Cuff, E. C., Sharrock, W. W. and Francis, D. W. (1990) *Perspectives in Sociology*. London, Routledge.

Davis, K. (1959) 'The Myth of Functional Analysis as a Special Method in Sociology and Anthropology'. *American Sociological Review*, 25:757–72.

Derrida, J. (1981) *Writing and Difference*. London, Routledge.

Durkheim, E. (1964, first published 1895) *The Rules of Sociological Method*. New York, Free Press

Dworkin, A. (1981) *Pornography*. London, Women's Press.

Edmunds, J. (1987) *Rights, Responsibilities and the Law*. Surrey, Thomas Nelson.

Faludi, S. (1992) *Backlash: The Undeclared War Against Women*. London, Chatto and Windus.

Firestone, S. (1970) *The Dialectic of Sex*, London, Women's Press.

Foucault, M. (1979) *The History of Sexuality*. London, Allen Lane.

Foucault, M. (1980) *Power/Knowledge: Selected Interviews and Other Writing 1972–77*. Brighton, Harvester.

Freely, M. (1999) 'What Kate Millet Did Next'. *The Observer*, 3 January 1999.

Friedan, B. (1983) *The Second Stage*, London, Abacus.

Friedman, M. (1980) *Free to Choose*. Harmondsworth, Penguin.

Gellner, E. (1991) *Nations and Nationalism*, Oxford, Blackwell.

Giddens, A. (1984) *The Constitution of Society: An Outline of the Theory of Structuration*. Cambridge, Polity Press.

Glaser, B. G. and Strauss, A. L. (1965) *Awareness of Dying*, Chicago, Aldine.

Goffman, E. (1963) *Asylums: Essays on the Social Situation of Mental Patients and Other Inmates*. Harmondsworth, Penguin.

Goffman, E. (1987) *The Presentation of Self in Everyday Life*. Harmondsworth, Penguin.

Gouldner, A. (1975) *For Sociology*. Harmondsworth, Penguin.

Gramsci, A. (1971) *Selections from the Prison Notebooks of Antonio Gramsci*, New York International Publishers.

Habermas, J. (1972) *Knowledge and Human Interests*. London, Heinemann.

Habermas, J. (1976) *Legitimation Crisis*. Oxford, Heinemann.

Habermas, J. (1981) *The Theory of Communicative Action*. London, Heinemann.

Habermas, J. (1989) *The New Conservatism*. Cambridge, Polity Press.

Hall, S. (1980) *Race, Articulation and Societies Structured in Dominance in Sociological Theories: Race and Capitalism*. Paris, UNESCO.

Hall, S. (1992) 'New Ethnicities' in Donald, J. and Rattansi, A. (Eds.) *Race, Culture and Difference*. London, Sage.

Hall, S. and Gilroy, P. (1982) *The Empire Strikes Back: Racism in 1970's Britain*. London, CCCS/Hutchinson.

Hamilton, P. (1983) *Talcott Parsons*. London, Tavistock.

Hayek, F. (1960) *The Constitution of Liberty*. London, Routledge.

Herrnstein, R. and Murray, C. (1994) *The Bell Curve: Intelligence and Class Structure in American Life*. New York, Free Press.

Holton, R. J. (1998) 'Classical Social Theory' in Turner, B. S. (Ed.) *The Blackwell Companion to Social Theory*. Oxford, Blackwell.

Hooks, b. (1984) *Feminist Theory: From Margin to Centre*. Boston, South End Press.

Hughes, E. (1958) *Men and Their Work*, New York, Free Press.

Jardine, A. (1985) *Gynesis: Configurations of Women and Modernity*. London, Cornell University Press.

Jameson, F. (1984) 'Postmodernism or the Cultural Logic of Late Capitalism'. *New Left Review*, 146:53–92.

Jones, P. (1990) *Theory and Method in Sociology*. London, Unwin Hyman.

Kautsky, K. (1953) *Foundations of Christianity*, New York, Russell.

Kvale, S. (1996) 'Themes of postmodernity' in Anderson, W. T. (ed.) *The Fontana Post-Modern Reader*, London, Harper Collins.

Kirby, M., Kidd, W., Koubel, F., Barter, J., Hope, T., Kirton, A., Madry, N., Manning, P. and Triggs, K. (1997) *Sociology in Perspective*. Oxford, Heinemann.

Lawson, T. and Garrod, J. (1996) *The Complete A–Z Sociology Handbook*. London, Hodder & Stoughton.

Levi-Strauss, C. (1969) *Structural Anthropology*. New York, Basic Books.

Levi-Strauss, C. (1970) *The Savage Mind*. London, Weidenfeld and Nicolson.

Levi-Strauss, C. (1981) *The Naked Man*. London, Cape.

Luhmann, N. (1982) *The Differentiation of Society*. New York, Columbia University Press.

Lukacs, G. (1971) *History and Class Consciousness*, London, Merlin.

Lyotard, J. (1984) *The Postmodern Condition: A Report on Knowledge*. Manchester, Manchester University Press.

Malinowski, B. (1954) *Magic, Science and Religion and Other Essays*, New York, Anchor Books.

Marcuse, H. (1955) *Reason and Revolution*. London, Routledge.

Marx, K. and Engels, F. (1998, first published 1888) *The Communist Manifesto*. New York, Verso.

Maynard, M. (1989) *Sociological Theory*. Essex, Longman.

Mead, G. H. (1934) *Mind, Self and Society*. Chicago, University of Chicago Press.

Merton, R. K. (1949) *Social Theory and Social Structure*. New York, Free Press.

Miles, R. (1982) *Racism and Migrant Labour*. London, Routledge.

Miles, R. (1993) *Racism and After 'Race Relations'*. London, Routledge.

Millet, K. (1971) *Sexual Politics*. London, Verso.

Modood, T. (1992) *Not Easy Being British*. Stoke on Trent, Trentham Books.

Oakley, A. (1972) *Sex, Gender and Society*. London, Temple Smith.

Oakley, A. (1974) *Housewife*. London, Allen Lane.

Oakley, A. (1984) *The Captive Womb*. Oxford, Blackwell.

Parsons, T. (1966, first published in 1951) *The Social System*. London, Routledge.

Pilcher, J. (1992) 'I'm Not a Feminist But … Understanding Feminism'. *Sociology Review*, November 1993.

Radcliffe-Brown, A. R. (1950) *African Systems of Kinship and Marriage*, New York, Free Press.

Rex, J. and Moore, R. (1967) *Race, Community and Conflict: A Study of Sparbrook*. Oxford, Oxford University Press.

Rex, J. and Tomlinson, S. (1979) *Colonial Immigrants in a British City: A Class Analysis*. London, Routledge and Kegan Paul.

Rich, A. (1981) *Blood, Bread and Poetry*. New York, W. W. Norton.

Rose, E. and Deakin, N. (1969) *Colour and Citizenship*. Oxford, Oxford University Press.

Saunders, P. (1990) *Social Class and Stratification*. London, Routledge.

Saunders, P. (1995) *Capitalism: A Social Audit*. Buckingham, Open University Press.

Solomos, J. (1988) 'Varieties of Marxist Conceptions of 'Race', Class and The State: A Critical Analysis', in Rex, J. and Mason, D. (Eds.) *Theories of Race and Ethnic Relations*. Cambridge, Cambridge University Press.

Stacey, J. (1986) 'Untangling Feminist Theory' in D. Richardson and V. Robinson (Eds.) *Introducing Women's Studies*. London, Macmillan.

Strauss, A. (1963) 'The hospital and its negotiated order' in Freidson, E. (ed.) *The Hospital in Modern Society*, New York, Macmillan.

Strinati, D. (1995) *An Introduction to Theories of Popular Culture*. London, Routledge.

Thompson, E. P. (1978) *The Poverty of Theory and Other Essays*. London, Merlin Press.

Turner, B. S. (1998) *The Blackwell Companion to Social Theory*. Oxford, Blackwell.

Van den Berghe, P. (1988) 'Ethnicity and the Sociobiology Debate', in Rex, J. and Mason, D. (Eds.), *Theories of Race and Ethnic Relations*. Cambridge, Cambridge University Press.

Weber, M. (1944) *The Theory of Social and Economic Organisation*. New York, Oxford University Press.

Weber, M. (1974, first published 1905) *The Protestant Ethic and the Spirit of Capitalism*. London, Unwin.

Willis, P. (1990) *Common Culture*. Buckingham, Open University Press.

Wilson, E. O. (1975) *Sociobiology: The New Synthesis*, Cambridge, Harvard University Press.

Wolf, N. (1993) *The Beauty Myth*. London, Vintage.

Sociological Research Methodology

This area covers:

- The historical and contemporary basis of sociological research
- The theoretical context of research methodology
- The types of methodology used to collect social data
- The advantages and disadvantages of using different types of methodology
- The problems encountered by sociologists when embarking on research.

By the end of this area you should be able to:

- understand, apply and evaluate all the different types of research methods applicable to sociology
- make a connection between the theoretical outlook of the researcher and the methodology used.

Key terms

quantitative	qualitative
valid	reliable
positivism	representativeness
interpretivism	secondary data
primary data	sampling

Area 2 Contents

Introduction

Why conduct sociological research?

The truth is out there!

Figure 2.1   Everyone is looking for sociological understanding

You will have witnessed, or may have been involved with, discussions about social issues, such as drug usage or teenage drinking. These discussions tend to be based on common-sense arguments or personal experience and therefore carry the bias and prejudice of a subjective opinion. Sociological research is an attempt to investigate social phenomena in a systematic and unbiased way, in order to attain more accurate (**reliable** and/or **valid**) data.

When practised appropriately, sociological research can lead to the government or institutions taking action about a social issue; this is known as social policy. Therefore, sociological research is useful to society, fuelling objective debate and decision-making on social changes, such as educational initiatives and health services.

Links between theory and method

Sociologists want to gain a better understanding of social life, and **empirical research** (empirical meaning 'based on objective observations') coupled with a theoretical base usually allows this aim to be met. A theoretical base is useful for interpreting the 'facts' obtained by the research. A theory is a general explanation of how social 'facts' are related to one another. Therefore, a theoretical base allows the data collected from sociological research to be interpreted and given meaning in a social context.

There are various sociological theories (see Area 1 on Sociological Theory) that can be used as the basis for a research methodology and/or applied to the data collected from sociological research. The theoretical perspective of a sociologist will usually have a direct effect on the type of methodology used. A structural sociologist, for example, will approach social issues from a macro perspective and therefore will use a research methodology, such as social surveys, to investigate effectively large-scale issues which have their cause in the social structure. The theoretical perspective also affects the way in which sociologists apply data that has already been collected. Interpretivist sociologists, for example, would interpret the meaning of expressive documents, such as diaries, for a social issue, but would find no meaning in statistics. (The issue of structural versus interpretivist research methodology will be explored further in the next section).

Sometimes, however, sociologists will use a variety of research methods that fit loosely with their theoretical base, usually because that base reflects a combination of theoretical approaches. A Marxist feminist, for example, may use structured questionnaires to support the structuralist nature of her theoretical base, i.e. she can make universal claims about their research, but conduct unstructured interviews to discover in-depth information about female inequality which can be used only in that context. Applying a variety of research methods to one piece of social research is known as **triangulation**.

Whatever the theoretical perspective held by sociologists, the data that they collect through their research has the potential to influence social issues. However, the information gathered on social phenomena is only as good as the research methodology used to investigate it. Therefore the whole credibility of sociology rests on excellent research methodology, making its study central to sociology:

> *The status of sociological knowledge – the value of the claims made by sociology – rests ultimately on the methods used being seen as valid.*
>
> Kirby et al. (1997:60)

ACTIVITY		KS COMMUNICATION
KNOWLEDGE AND UNDERSTANDING	IDENTIFICATION AND INTERPRETATION	ANALYSIS AND EVALUATION

Imagine that you are a Weberian sociologist conducting research into crime rates. What type of research methodology would you use? Justify the use of this method from your theoretical perspective.

HINTS AND TIPS *Remember that Weberian sociologists are social-action theorists (see Area 1 on Sociological Theory) and would therefore prefer a research technique that employs both a macro or large-scale standpoint and a micro or individual approach.*

Sociological research methodology

What is research?

Sociological research is knowledge based on evidence from the social world. This knowledge may be

descriptive, describing a social issue such as family violence in detail; or explanatory, explaining the existence of a social issue such as gender inequality. The evidence collected depends on the theoretical approach used. Structural theorists (positivists) generally argue that sociology can be scientific and that research should be conducted in this way. This is a traditional approach to research and has its basis in The Enlightenment of the seventeenth and eighteenth centuries, i.e. historically valid knowledge is scientific, because it is systematic, reliable and establishes laws.

> *Basic research is the pursuit of scientific knowledge that may or may not have commercial uses ...*
>
> Bullock et al. (1988: 741)

However, the infinite variety of social attitudes and behaviours was seen to challenge the application of rigid scientific procedures and interpretive (**phenomenological**) sociologists argued that research should not and could not be based on scientific methods. Consequently, sociological research is based on the quest for social knowledge, but the methods employed to obtain this knowledge are wide ranging (see section on 'Doing Sociological Research Methodology'):

> *... sociologists adopt various research techniques, often using different ones simultaneously, in order to explore or explain some particular area of social life.*
>
> Bilton et al. (1996: 100)

What is methodology?

The term 'methodology' is often used instead of 'methods' and refers to the analysis of the ways in which data was collected and the justification of these processes. Lawson and Garrod clearly summarise methodology as:

> *The study of the types of method used by sociologists, the reasons for their choice of method, and how they collect, select, interpret and analyse their data.*
>
> Lawson, T. and Garrod, J. (1996:166)

As suggested earlier, the theoretical base of the sociologist will affect the type of research methodology employed, but he or she will always be expected to evaluate the processes involved in the collection of social data. It is always worth remembering that excellent methodology results in accurate, more reliable and/or more valid information about society.

ACTIVITY KS **COMMUNICATION, INFORMATION TECHNOLOGY**

KNOWLEDGE AND UNDERSTANDING	IDENTIFICATION AND INTERPRETATION	ANALYSIS AND EVALUATION

Look up and record different definitions of 'research' and 'methodology' from alternative sources, such as:

- The Internet
- Encarta on CD-ROM
- The *Oxford English Dictionary*
- *Macmillan's Encyclopaedia of Sociology.*

Compare the definitions you have found and assess their relative merits and problems in relation to the sociological meaning of 'research' and 'methodology'. Share your findings with the rest of the class.

HINTS AND TIPS   *Remember that the general meaning of these words will be different from the social scientific meaning and that even this can vary. For example, positivists favour a scientific interpretation, while phenomenologists prefer a more open definition.*

Historical overview

The changing face of Europe in the nineteenth century became the subject of social enquiry for classical sociologists, such as Comte (1798–1857), Marx (1818–83) and Durkheim (1858–1917). The modern world influenced these early social thinkers, who were largely theorists rather than actual researchers. They utilised secondary data collected by historians and governments instead of collecting their own data. Therefore, they relied heavily on the comparative method, a scientific approach which involves comparing data about social issues or societies in order to explain the causes of variations. For example, Durkheim's study of suicide sought to explain the social cause of different suicide rates by comparing different social contexts, such as religion and integration into society. Therefore, modernity and the desire for objective and scientific 'truths' about social

issues and society itself influenced early sociological research methods.

Evidence of primary sociological research could be seen at the turn of the twentieth century. Between 1891 and 1903 Charles Booth (1840–1916) published *Life and Labour of the People in London*, which was one of the first social surveys. The aim of this survey was to discover the true extent of poverty among the working classes. His methodology was based on quantitative and qualitative techniques, such as recording the number of rooms in a house, the number of residents, income, etc. (quantitative), but also observing and recording the lives of families in these houses while boarding with them (qualitative).

The twentieth century saw anthropological research becoming established, which involved living with primitive tribes and recording information about their lives. Evans-Pritchard (1902–73) and Malinowski (1884–1942) initiated methods of research which argued that the only valid way to collect information about a society or group was to live as part of it. Robert E. Park (1864–1944), of the Chicago School of symbolic interactionists (see Area 1 on Sociological Theory), applied anthropological methods to sociology to investigate Chicago lifestyles. Consequently, the quantitative approaches using scientific method conducted by classical sociologists were joined by more qualitative methods, which relied on participant observation and more expressive documents, such as unstructured interviews (see 'Doing sociological research methodology' on page 85).

The 1950s saw the resurgence of scientific method in sociology. It was believed that sociological research could and should be value-free and that the only way to achieve this was through systematic data collection based on natural scientific technique, such as the hypothetico-deductive method (see 'Doing sociological research methodology' on page 85). As a result of this belief, statistical data, which was assumed to be free of bias in its information about society, became the most valued of social knowledge. The emphasis at this time was therefore on social surveys, but other research methods remained.

In the 1960s and 1970s a debate developed between sociologists about the value of data collected by different research methods. Supporters of more scientific methods argued that their work was more objective and reliable than interpretive techniques, while advocates of phenomenological research methods claimed that the validity of their work made it more useful than the constructed categories of the positivists. Therefore, sociologists spent a lot of time during this period arguing about the methodology, rather than actually doing the research!

Contemporary situation

Contemporary sociology appears to have accepted both quantitative and qualitative approaches to research, which can only be beneficial in that it encourages a deeper exploration of social phenomena. A variety of sociological research is going on in the world and a variety of methods is employed to investigate different social issues, as the chart (Figure 2.2) demonstrates.

The trend for sociological methodology appears to support variety, as McNeill aptly states:

❛ ... *it has become perfectly acceptable to use a wide variety of research techniques in one study, and to use different techniques for the study of different topics.*

McNeill, P. (1985:6)

This trend could also explain the current development of realism (see later section, page 81), which rejects the idea that sociology should be based on a natural scientific approach, studying only things that can be directly observed (positivism), or the view that subjective experience is the only basis for research (interpretivism). Realism argues that there are real structures in society, but that these structures may not be observable; however, they still require investigation. Therefore, sociologists who employ a realist approach would link their methodology tightly to their theory in order to explain the unobservable. For example, fundamental structures of society, such as stratification, have an underlying cause that may not be observable by applying traditional research methods.

Realism, in relation to methodology, can therefore be summarised as a belief that there are deeper structures in society than the surface phenomena, phenomena that most researchers see as the main 'truth'. Therefore, there is an independent reality and our theories should support that, even though this reality cannot be objectively researched. Realists seek to avoid postmodernist conclusions (see Area 1 on Sociological Theory), which challenge any certainty about the social world and research from this perspective offers an unlimited amount of interpretations about society and our everyday lives.

Feminist research

The rise of a feminist research methodology is argued to be based upon a need for a non-sexist, non-hierarchical and subjective approach that values the experience of

Sociologist	Sociological issue	Research method/s	Publication
Chris Barker	The use of soap operas in developing female Asian identities in the UK	In-depth recorded discussion between British-Asian girls on soap operas.	*Sociology* (1998) Vol. 32. No. 1
Beverly Skeggs, Carole Truman and Les Moran	The relationship between sexuality and safety in public spaces	Triangulation – large-scale survey, in-depth interviews, and citizen's enquiry.	(1999) ESRC project 'Violence in Society'.
Janet Holland, Caroline Ramazanoglu, Sue Sharpe and Rachel Thomson	Young peoples' sexual attitudes and practices.	Detailed interviews with 194 young men and women on their sexuality and sexual experiences.	(1998) *The Male in the Head: young people, heterosexuality and power.* Tufnell Press, London.
John Balding	Illegal drug usage among teenagers.	Questionnaires.	(1997) *Young People and Illegal Drugs in 1997*. Schools Health Education Unit, University of Exeter.
Daniel Miller	The connection between shopping and social relationships.	Participant observation.	(1998) *The Theory of Shopping*. Polity, Cambridge.

Figure 2.2   Recent sociological research

HINTS AND TIPS   Use all information available, including details above, notes from your teacher and other texts. Compare your findings to those of other members of the class and share information.

women. Feminists have identified the patriarchy (or androcentrism) inherent in academic institutions and the traditional research methods employed. For example, universities are predominantly the domain of males, with the subject areas researched being of more interest to men, and the methods used tend to reflect male values such as objectivity and distance.

Feminists who attempted to reconstruct women's history found that the research methods available to them were quite inadequate. Evidence of female contributions to history was sparse, thereby disallowing a positivist approach. Consequently, feminist research adopted a more qualitative/interpretivist approach (see later section on 'Quantitative versus qualitative research methods') to reveal the social experiences of women, experiences which had been hidden from sociological view by previous patriarchal research. Feminist research can therefore be seen as **'standpoint' research** (see section on 'Quantitative versus qualitative research methods'), because it entails taking a particular 'stand' on, or view of, society, which challenges the assumptions inherent in traditional sociology.

Maria Mies (1997) argued that feminist research is not compatible with quantitative methods, because positivism is inextricably linked to male ideas and interests and cannot therefore support female liberation:

> *... there is a contradiction between the prevalent theories of social science and methodology and the political aims of the women's movement.*

Mies, M. (1997:66)

The quest for a value-free, objective and uninvolved approach to research is seen to undermine women's experience of oppression. Feminist researchers argue that there should be a reciprocal relationship between the research object and subject, because female researchers also have experience of sexism in male dominated academic institutions. Therefore women must, according to Mies, 'integrate their repressed, unconscious female subjectivity, that is, their own experience of oppression and discrimination into the research process'.

Feminist researchers should not control the research situation (as many male methods are held to do), but instead allow the respondents to set their own agendas and 'tell their own stories'. This method, it is argued, can reveal more about the respondent's common-sense world, enabling the researcher to document it and provide information that may empower all women.

Mies (1997) has argued that there are seven methodological guidelines for feminist research:

1 **Conscious partiality** – the researcher should partially identify with the research objects, realising that they are part of a social whole, but enabling the correction of distortion on both sides.

2 **View from below** – research is seen to serve the interests of those who are dominated, exploited and oppressed, particularly women.

3 **Active participation in actions, movements and struggles** – feminist research grew out of the women's movement and should therefore support female emancipation.

4 **Change of the status quo** – to understand patriarchy, feminist research must fight against female oppression, rather than examining the surface consequences of it, such as housework. A breakdown of 'normal' life for women will reveal their consciousness.

5 **Conscientisation** – the research process must by carried out by the objects of oppression, thereby the objects of research (women) become the subject (female social scientists) of their own research and action.

6   **Study of women's individual and social history** – women have not made history their own, therefore their struggles and dreams have not been heard. This history must be seen in order for women to have a collective conscience and challenge patriarchy.

7   **Women must collectivise their own experiences** – research must be for the good of all women, based on shared methodology with other feminists and group discussions. Realising a collective experience can provide diversified information and remove structural isolation for women.

Feminist researchers claim that social scientific research has a masculine bias and therefore produces a male view of social life that ignores the experiences of women. For example, the examination of 'work' is a reference in sociology to paid employment and ignores the work that women do in the home. However, feminist research methodology has been criticised for being biased itself (Hill Collins, 1991). For example, a great deal of feminist research can be seen to have a white and eurocentric bias that ignores the situation of 'black' women in non-western societies. It may also ignore class oppression by focusing only on the situation of women or by drawing samples for qualitative research from predominantly white middle-class women (Cannon et al. 1991).

Primary versus secondary data

There are many different ways in which you can find out things about society. The research method chosen will depend on the problem or the social issue being investigated, and the practicalities of what is possible in the time given and with the resources available. Consideration should be given to the advantages and disadvantages of using primary or secondary data.

Primary data

Information collected by the researchers themselves, whatever the research method used, is known as **primary data**. The main ways in which original research can be operationalised (put into action) and primary data can be collected are as follows:

■   **Social surveys** – Townsend, for example, administered a 120-page questionnaire to 150 households to investigate the amount and causes of poverty in and around London in the 1960s.

■   **Case studies** – Laing, for example, studied the day-to-day experiences of particular patients to discover the social causes of schizophrenia.

■   **Unstructured interviews** – Dobash and Dobash, for example, interviewed 109 women for between two and 12 hours each in an informal setting in an attempt to describe and explain wife-battering in modern society.

■   **Observation** – Pryce, for example, became a participant observer among Bristol's West Indian community in the 1970s in order to describe their way of life.

Different research methods have different strengths and weaknesses in relation to the data they produce (as shown in the section on 'Difficulties of research methodology'). The main advantage of primary data, however, is that the researcher knows the exact methodology used to investigate that social issue and therefore the value of the data. The main disadvantage of using primary data is that it has to be conducted from scratch and therefore the researcher has to ensure that the methodology is appropriate and effective, despite any potential practical constraints, such as time or money. Unreliable research methodology produces unreliable and/or invalid data.

Secondary data

Useful information that is gathered by another researcher is known as **secondary data**. Any existing piece of data may be re-analysed and used as a secondary source if it applies to your topic of research:

❛   *Almost any data can be used in a study providing they are used relevantly and accurately.*

O'Donnell, M. (1997:35)

Secondary data can be collected from a variety of sources, which include:

■   **Official statistics** – The census, for example, is the main source of quantitative secondary data and is collected by the government.

■   **Historical** – Laslett, for example, used parish records to investigate the composition of households before industrialisation.

- **Expressive documents** – These documents can be personal or public. An example of personal documents being used as a secondary source of data could be the diaries used by Thomas and Znaniecki in 1919 to study the migration of Polish peasants to the USA and Europe. An example of a public document being used for sociological information could be the Black Report conducted by Townsend and Davidson (1982), but commissioned by the government to investigate health inequalities in the UK.

- **Mass media** – Content analysis of media documents and programmes, such as the Glasgow Media Group's analysis of the press coverage of AIDS between 1988 and 1991, provides useful information to social researchers.

The strengths and weaknesses of different sources of secondary data are specific to the research method used to collect them (see section on 'Difficulties of research methodology'). However, the general advantages of using secondary data are that:

- it provides useful ideas about the subject you intend to research

- existing data can be compared to primary data

- it may be more easily accessible, cheaper to collect and less time-consuming than embarking on primary research.

The main disadvantages of using secondary data are that:

- someone else has collected it and therefore the methodology may not be accurate

- the information may not be relevant to your research.

It is worth remembering that although primary and secondary data are often discussed separately, they are frequently used to complement each other within one piece of research. For example, official statistics may be used to support primary data collected on the amount of poverty experienced by unemployed people in the UK.

Sociology and science

Sociology is the study of human social life, which may be researched using any effective method, as long as it

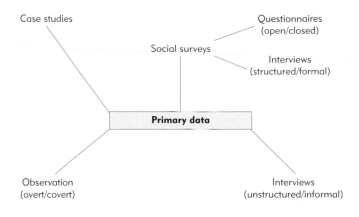

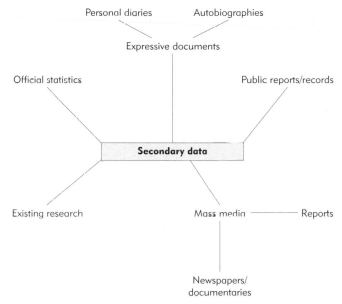

Figure 2.3   Research methods that produce primary and secondary data

adds to our knowledge and understanding of society. Natural science is the systematic testing of hypotheses in order to accumulate verifiable data about the world around us. These definitions are important, because they inform the debate about whether sociology is a science, or whether it should even strive to be scientific.

Through science and technology we have been able to explain and control our environment, sending people to the moon and creating test-tube babies. The research methods used by scientists are systematic and reliable and therefore attractive when attempting to create understanding and knowledge, whether it is about the natural or social world. The methods followed by natural scientists are explained in the section on 'Difficulties of research methodology' on page 109.

The Founding Fathers

The attitude of sociologists towards the notion of sociology as a science has changed since the 1950s. Until the 1960s it was generally agreed that the natural scientific method was desirable in the social sciences. Natural scientists had made great discoveries about the living world, which, not surprisingly, influenced all the great thinkers of the nineteenth and early twentieth centuries. Classical sociologists, such as Auguste Comte (1798–1857) and Émile Durkheim (1858–1917), approached their research using scientific/positivist methods, because it was seen to enable systematic objective enquiry. Comte actually referred to sociology as 'social physics' and believed that the 'laws' of science (see the hypothetico-deductive method on page 84) could and should be applied to society. 'Social facts' were assumed to interact with other 'social facts' in an ordered and observable way, thereby making predictions about future actions possible. This **positivist** approach argued that 'social facts' were external to individuals and caused their responses. Durkheim agreed with Comte on this point, but did not apply the natural scientific method fully to his research. Realising that human beings could not be legitimately 'experimented upon', he applied the comparative method (see the section on 'Difficulties of research methodology') to systematically observe and measure social relationships.

Max Weber (1864–1920) identified the differences between the subject matter of sociology and the natural sciences at the turn of the twentieth century. He highlighted the importance of the meaning of social action for those involved, using **interpretivist** research methods, which did not attempt to explain social action by external causes, but instead investigated the individual actors' part in the social world. This, however, did not attain credibility until the 1960s.

The 1960s saw the scientific establishment being challenged as 'the fount of all knowledge'. Phenomenologists argued that the subject matter of sociology has always made the collection of reliable data problematic, despite being as rigorous and systematic in its methodology as the natural sciences. 'Social facts' are different from inanimate natural facts. 'Facts' such as suicide (see Area 12) are social constructs, which have no meaning outside the meaning given to them by people, but trees and mountains exist whether people are there to see and label them or not. Consequently, when writers such as Thomas Kuhn challenged the sacred process of natural scientific enquiry, the legitimacy of using 'not so scientific' research methods, such as participant

Émile Durkheim
(1858–1917)

Émile Durkheim was born in Épinal, France, to an academic family. He taught law and philosophy to start with, moved to the University of Bordeaux to teach Sociology in 1887 and then to the University of Paris. He investigated social change and the factors that kept societies together. Durkheim adopted a scientific approach to social research, being influenced by modern thinking and the industrial revolution.

Durkheim's use of the comparative method, considerations on value consensus and the functioning of the modern world, could be seen to make him influential in the development of functionalism. Functional consensus theory has led to him being accredited with developing modern sociology. Durkheim proposed that groups or structures had characteristics that were different from individuals' characteristics or behaviours. He argued that social stability was based upon the common values (collective conscience) shared by a society, such as morality and religion.

Durkheim's most famous methodological and theoretical study was of suicide, which he explained as a result of an individual's lack of integration in society (*Suicide: A Study in Sociology* (1897; translated 1951)). He displayed how social scientific research could be used to explain seemingly individual acts as socially determined. Suicide was seen as a 'social fact', rather than an individual act. He also conducted research into how society governed religion and divisions in labour, and developed the concept of 'anomie', in works that included: *The Division of Labour in Society* (1893; translated 1933), *The Rules of Sociological Method* (1895; translated 1938) and *The Elementary Forms of Religious Life* (1912; translated 1915).

observation, was confirmed. Social investigation that involved the researcher in the process, but that still allowed the collection of valid knowledge-enhancing data about the social world, became accepted and expected within sociological research.

Karl Popper

Karl Popper (1959) described the process of scientific research as conjecture and refutation. He argued that science developed through researchers putting forward conjectures, or ideas, about their subject matter, which they then try to refute, or disprove. If they cannot do so, these unrefuted conjectures provide the basis for scientific theories. This process is also referred to as **falsification theory**. Such tests aim to ensure that theories are well-founded and objective, but they do not prove that scientific theories are completely true, only that so far no one has disproved them. It can therefore be assumed that scientific knowledge always remains provisional. Consequently, the main difference between natural scientific and social scientific research methods may be the claim to provide a path towards 'true knowledge' about the world. Science has been assumed to be correct in its theories (until a better one comes along), while sociological research is assumed to be relative in its assumptions. The rise of postmodernist doubts about the value of any 'truth' claims for scientific or social knowledge has added further interest to the debate about sociology as a science.

Thomas Kuhn

Thomas Kuhn (1970) identified that the sciences tend to jump from one major theory to another, rather than follow a gradual path to a 'universal truth'. He described this process as similar to a political revolution, where the old order no longer works and a new and more interesting approach replaces it. According to Kuhn, a scientific revolution occurs when one scientific paradigm (a model of how things should be done) breaks down and another one comes along to take its place. It is not a cumulative process, but rather an erratic affair made up of discontinuous phases and periods of intense struggle between competing paradigms. It was in this way that Darwin's theory of evolution overturned religious views of human development.

Kuhn's view that science is not some kind of sacred cow makes it easier to compare to sociology. Both physics and sociology, for example, are equally haunted by the spectre of subjectivity.

Modern sociologists, armed with quantitative techniques based on computers, are able to conduct large surveys into social behaviour (see section on 'Difficulties of research methodology'). They can isolate and interrelate key variables to explain cause and effect. However, humans do not respond like chemical compounds! Humans think for themselves and therefore their behaviour is variable and not easily reducible to mathematical formulae. It is difficult for sociologists to remain totally objective, but scientists are people too and are subject to the same type of subjective influences.

Whether sociology is a science or not depends ultimately on the definition employed. If science is the collection of verifiable data, then sociology is a science. If science is hypotheses testing, then sociology is not a science. However, what sociology does share with science is its desire to attain knowledge and understanding through systematic and rigorous research methodology. Both disciplines should ideally be aiming to produce empirical evidence through methods that are critically executed, thoroughly recorded and totally accountable to any other interested party. If the precise and systematic nature of scientific research is a myth, then the debate on whether sociology is a science becomes redundant. Perhaps the question that academics should now ask is just whether sociological research is rigorous and open (see section on value freedom, page 105).

Quantitative versus qualitative research methods

> *... social scientists are deeply divided over what constitutes a proper approach to social research.*
>
> Andrew Sayer (1997:1)

There are two broad types of sociological research methods: quantitative and qualitative. **Quantitative research** methods are used to produce numerical data, such as statistics. This 'facts-and-figures' data usually represents a relationship between social issues, for example the degree of negative attitudes towards minority ethnic groups in the UK in relation to social class. The main research methods used to provide quantitative data are questionnaires and structured interviews. Both of these methodologies allow the research to be structured in a way that elicits clear and quantifiable answers. Researchers who favour quantitative methods argue that these methods secure objective data, data that reflects external 'facts' about 'social reality'. Therefore, quantitative methods are argued to produce impartial, reliable data that operates 'outside' of the individual.

Qualitative research methods are generally used to achieve a more in-depth understanding of a social issue or situation, by producing information about experiences or meanings. For example, asking respondents open-ended questions could be used to gain a more detailed understanding of why men rape women (Scully, 1990). The main research methods used to collect qualitative data are unstructured interviews and observation, although other types of methodology, such as diaries, can be applied. Advocates of qualitative research methods argue that the subjective data collected about feelings and experiences is as 'true to life' and 'honest' as it is possible to achieve through research. Therefore, qualitative methods are said to produce valid data which reflects the role of the individual in society.

Some qualitative research is seen as 'standpoint' research, in that it takes a fixed view dependent on the particular beliefs of the researcher, which usually stands against the traditional sociological practice, i.e. white, male and middle class (see section on 'Feminist research'). For example, many of the contemporary perspectives developing in sociology, such as Race Relations theory, could be seen to employ standpoint research, because they have taken a stand against traditional sociological research. In other words, ethnic minorities were ignored in traditional sociological research and therefore Race Relations theory has made a stand against this to establish the importance and significance of ethnic groups' status in society. Consequently, standpoint research has been accused of bias (see section on 'Value freedom'), in that it favours a particular social group for analysis. However, this argument has been countered by arguing that in the past these groups received little, if any, sociological attention.

Positivism versus interpretivism

As mentioned earlier, the theoretical perspective of the researcher can directly affect the choice of method employed by the researcher. The different theoretical perspectives, however, can be broadly divided into two main schools of thought: positivism and interpretivism.

Positivism

Positivists are usually **structural** theorists (see Area 1 on Sociological Theory) who believe that the social world is made up of 'facts', which can be studied like the natural world. They prefer to use research methods that are considered objective, quantitative, replicable, systematic, standardised, verifiable and therefore able to produce generalisable findings.

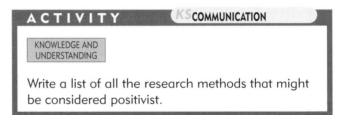

ACTIVITY KS **COMMUNICATION**

KNOWLEDGE AND UNDERSTANDING

Write a list of all the research methods that might be considered positivist.

Structural theory, such as Marxism and functionalism, is usually described as employing positivism, because it has followed the principles of scientific research. For example, Durkheim in his study of suicide (1897) identified a problem, set a hypothesis, collected data, analysed the results, interpreted the results and concluded whether his hypothesis was true or false.

Positivism is about getting at the 'facts' of social behaviour. It believes that with careful methodology precise generalisations can be made about the causes of social behaviour and future trends can be predicted for society.

It is assumed that the generalisations made by positivists are based on objective research; however:

■ No technique can be completely unbiased (consider the social construction of official statistics).

■ The researcher has to impose a frame of reference on the respondent, asking questions which he or she considers to be important.

■ All interactions are subjective and this may affect data, however carefully the research tool is constructed (consider the health of the respondent when being questioned).

- Controlled experiments may elicit responses different from whatever might take place in the 'real' world (consider the 'Hawthorne effect').

Interpretivism

Interpretivist researchers (also known as anti-positivists or phenomenologists) are diametrically opposed to positivists, in that they argue that the social world is very different from the natural world. Sociological subject matter has free will, which makes social life unpredictable and therefore impossible to study in any rigid or structured way. Social 'facts' are seen as social constructs, which require in-depth analysis in order to understand the meaning we attach to behaviour. Therefore interpretivist theorists apply research methods that reveal the subjective experience of those being studied, while accepting that the researcher is part of that experience and can therefore never be truly objective.

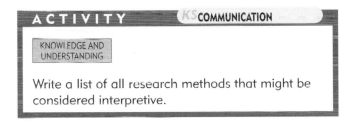

In assuming that a subjective account of society produces more 'true to life' data, interpretivists encounter several problems:

- The data may be little different from fictional accounts of the social world found in novels or tabloid newspapers.

- The presence of the research may affect the behaviour of those being studied (consider again the 'Hawthorne effect'), producing a social situation different from that originally being studied.

- It does not provide a systematic or unbiased look at social life.

While dividing the approaches provides a clear framework for understanding the concepts, it should be realised that real research is a mass of contradictions. Not all structuralists use positivist approaches and phenomenologists do not always employ interpretivist stances. In fact, there are now computer programmes,

such as NUDIST, which are used by interpretivists to analyse qualitative data! However, positivism and interpretivism as research methodologies do agree that sociology is an empirical discipline (in that studies produce data), even though they approach their research in different ways.

Realism

Realism has been seen as an answer in the debate about sociology and science (see earlier section). It is an approach that centres on the nature of society as a whole and how individual activity and institutions, on both a surface level and through underlying causes, create this. Realism therefore applies elements of both positivism (scientific approaches) and interpretivism (anti-scientific approaches).

Realism rejects positivism in two ways:

1 Theory can be established from non-observable data, as well as empirical data.
2 Sociology cannot discover universal laws, because society is based on dynamic and complex social relations.

Realism also rejects interpretivism for the following two reasons:

1 Sociological research should attempt to use a realistic scientific approach (but not the positivist interpretation of scientific research).
2 There are surface structures in society, as well as underlying causes.

Consequently, realism as a methodology offers an alternative to the main two approaches. An example of realism in action can be found in the work of Durkheim (1897) on suicide. He analysed surface structures (suicide rates compared with religiosity, etc.) in order to understand the underlying causal factors (the amount

Positivism	Realism	Interpretivism
Structural	Scientific	Phenomenological
Macro	Macro/micro	Micro
Universal	Dynamic	Individual
Generalisable	Dynamic	Specific
Laws	Underlying structures	Relative
Quantitative	Quantitative/ qualitative	Qualitative

Figure 2.4   The relationship between positivism, realism and interpretivism

social integration or moral regulation directly affects suicide rates). This approach appears to be growing in support (Pawson and Tilly, 1996), but has yet to become as popular as positivism or interpretivism.

Ethnomethodology

Ethnomethodology is the study of the ways in which people create and construct their way of life. It is an approach that examines everyday life according to a set of accepted assumptions, such as understanding what is meant when something is said. Life is considered to be very orderly and is a consequence of daily interactions. Garfinkel (1967) argued that people make sense of the world and that this enables them to behave appropriately in a variety of social situations.

Therefore ethnomethodologists study how people achieve the unwritten rules of society. For example, Garfinkel devised an experiment that would upset normal social life to see what would happen. He asked his students to behave as if they were lodgers, while still living in their own homes. The students' formality and politeness caused problems and showed Garfinkel the socially constructed nature of 'ordinary' life.

ACTIVITY KS **COMMUNICATION, WORKING WITH OTHERS**

KNOWLEDGE AND UNDERSTANDING	IDENTIFICATION AND INTERPRETATION

Practise some ethnomethodology by challenging a taken-for-granted assumption. For example, when people ask, 'How are you?' or say 'All right?' they are not really enquiring about your health. Challenge this by telling them in detail about how you are feeling. Note down their reactions. Decide whether Garfinkel was correct about ordinariness being socially constructed.

Reliability, validity and representativeness

Reliability, validity and representativeness are terms associated with the data collected by different research methods. They are important concepts, because they represent, in their fullest form, the ideals that all research strives for.

Reliability refers to the extent to which a method of data collection gives a consistent and replicable result, when used in similar circumstances by different researchers or applied at different times. In other words, if researchers were to investigate the same social issue using the same method, they would get the same results. Some research methods, such as closed questionnaires, are considered to be more reliable than others, such as participant observation, because they are more systematic and structured (and therefore replicable) in their approach. Positivists tend to adopt methods that produce reliable data, because reliability is associated with the ability to make generalisations about the phenomenon being studied.

Validity refers to the extent to which a research method represents or measures the social phenomenon it claims to represent or measure. In other words, valid data is believed to be a true-to-life representation of what is being studied. Qualitative research methods, such as unstructured interviews, are believed to be more valid than quantitative research methods, such as structured interviews, because the techniques involve understanding the social issue from the view of the respondent, rather than imposing the researcher's frame of reference upon it. Interpretivists, in their quest for meaning behind social behaviour, opt for more validity in their research.

It should be noted that reliability and validity are rarely witnessed within the same piece of research, unless the researcher adopts a variety of methods (triangulation). For example, a study might accurately measure the amount of people who smoke, meaning that the data was reliable (showing the same results if repeated), but it would not be valid if its original aim was to discover the cause of smoking.

Representativeness refers to the group under study being the same as the larger population from which it is taken. In other words, if the researcher is investigating the types of music listened to by teenagers in the UK, the group being studied should be typical of all teenagers in the UK to assume that their tastes in music can be generalised. If a piece of research is not representative (see the section on 'Sampling'), then the data produced has no relevance to anything else, except the issue it was designed to investigate.

ACTIVITY KS COMMUNICATION, APPLICATION OF NUMBER

| KNOWLEDGE AND UNDERSTANDING | IDENTIFICATION AND INTERPRETATION |

Create a piece of sociological research to investigate the amount of people who read novels regularly, the 'typical' regular novel reader and the reasons behind why people may or may not read novels regularly. Show you could achieve reliability, validity and representativeness.

HINTS AND TIPS Revise the definitions of reliability, validity and representativeness and apply these. For example, you will have to consider both quantitative and qualitative research methods. The sample you choose will have to be taken from the whole population, because if you sampled a specific group, say people coming out of the library, they would not be typical of the British public (they would be more likely to read novels regularly).

SOCIOLOGY IN PRACTICE

Helen Benedict (1992) Virgin or Vamp: How the Press Covers Sex Crimes.

This is first and foremost a critique of the way the print press covers sex crimes. In it, I will demonstrate that the pervasiveness of rape myths and the habits of the newsroom have led the press to consistently cover these crimes with bias and, sometimes, even cruelty.

I have chosen this subject not only as an exercise in press criticism, however, but as a way of examining public attitudes toward women, sex, and violence, and the role the press plays in establishing or reinforcing those attitudes. Sex crimes have a unique ability to touch upon the public's deep-seated beliefs about gender roles. Whereas people may put on a tolerant front when discussing those roles in marriage or the job market, their true opinions are often shocked out of them by the news of a rape or sex-related murder. For example, the very person who declares that a woman has a right to be paid as much as a man for the same work might well blurt out, "Well, what did she expect?" upon hearing of a gang rape in a seedy bar. Sex crimes have the ability to evoke such beliefs because they involve aggressive, sexual interaction between men and women, and call into play age-old myths and assumptions about rape and sex.

As has been well documented (Ericson, Graber, Gitlin, and others), the press both reflects and shapes public opinion. Sometimes, by reporting events and echoing what is said out in the field, it merely reinforces established opinions by mirroring them. At other times it takes a more active role, suggesting new views and challenging old ones. It usually does both, in a constant give and take with the public. When the press reports a sex crime, therefore, it is also reflecting the public opinion elicited by that crime. In this book, I will show how sex-crime reporting exposes the press and the public's view of both the crime and of sex roles and women in general.

Method

The book is based on an examination of four specific sex-crime cases, all of which were among the most prominent of the past decade. Each case became a major event for print and television, and they were all either analyzed in books or magazines after they were over, or turned into motion pictures. The fact that these crimes were so widely reported and therefore so frequently discussed makes them particularly useful as vehicles for public opinion about sex roles.

The cases are the 1979 Greta and John Rideout marital rape case in Oregon, which provoked national debate about the rights of husbands over wives; the 1983 pool table gang-rape of a woman in a New Bedford, Massachusetts bar, which resulted in clashes between feminists and local residents; the 1986 sex-related killing of Jennifer Levin by Robert Chambers in New York, which outraged feminists and press critics; and, finally, the 1989 gang rape and beating of the Central Park jogger in New York, which divided men against women, blacks against whites in the furor that accompanied it.

Each case symbolizes a critical factor in public opinion about gender roles. Marriage (the Rideouts), ethnicity (New Bedford), class (Levin), and race (the jogger) are revealing windows through which to look at press and public attitudes toward sex crimes and women. (The rape case against William Kennedy Smith, very much on the public's mind during 1991 and 1992, will be referred to in the conclusion. I did not include it as one of my major four cases because it was primarily a story about celebrities – its notoriety was entirely due to the Kennedy name – and thus it does not play the symbolic role of the other cases.)

I analyzed the language of the original newspaper and magazine stories about each case, and interviewed the reporters and editors responsible for those stories. For background, I conducted research in the fields of media analysis, history, press ethics, the sociology of crime, rape and sexual assault, and linguistics.

I concentrated on the local and national papers that devoted the most coverage to each case, and managed to interview a fair sample of reporters from each one of those papers. My findings, of course, were greatly affected by the types of newspapers that covered the crime, the location of those papers, and the time that had elapsed between the case and my interviews. The Rideout case, for example, was covered primarily by traditional, family-oriented newspapers, which are staid and careful and not subject to much competitive pressure. The New Bedford and New York cases, on the other hand, were covered by splashy tabloids as well as by big city broadsheet newspapers in a much more competitive atmosphere.

Likewise, the Rideout and New Bedford cases both occurred many years ago, ten and five, respectively, at the time I interviewed the reporters who had worked on the original stories. This lapse of years, I found, had a twofold effect upon the interviewees: their memories of details were more inexact but, at the same time, their distance from the cases enabled them to analyze their own performances with less emotion and defensiveness than the reporters interviewed about more recent stories.

As I went through the clips about each case, reading the day-to-day coverage, I looked for certain specifics: The attitudes toward women brought to bear on the case by the reporters, how they were expressed and how they interplayed with public reaction to the story; the public and local attitudes toward sex and violence, race, and class reflected by the coverage; the sort of vocabulary used; which issues raised by the case were picked up by the papers and which were ignored; how the accused were treated; and, above all, how the victims were portrayed.

Because I approached my research as a social critic rather than as a social scientist, I did not use formal methods of contest analysis, although I sometimes referred to others' work that did. However, I did count the number of male versus female reporters on each case, and found that all the cases except the Rideouts were covered predominantly by men. This points to an irony intrinsic to the newspaper coverage of rape and sex crimes: Because rape is a crime, and because crime reporters are traditionally male, rape is covered mostly by men. In addition, as most editors are still men, rape stories tend to be edited by men. (The Rideout case was an exception because it was not covered until it reached trial, and trials, unlike crime stories, are not primarily the domain of male reporters. The editors on the story, however, were almost all men.) The paradoxical fact that rape, a crime that happens overwhelmingly to women, is usually covered by men may partly explain why the press has been so slow to change its approach to sex crimes.

My examination of the way men and women report sex crimes, however, did not show that women automatically do a better job. More important than the reporter's gender, I found, was that reporter's understanding of sex crimes and rape myths. A myth-saturated woman will be just as insensitive to the subject of rape as a myth-saturated man, especially given the conditions and habits of newsroom behavior. Women, however, are more likely to have read about rape than are men, who do not usually consider themselves at risk of an attack and so are simply not as interested in the subject as women. (Beneke and others have shown that men are often reluctant to understand rape and unable to empathize with victims.) Also, women, especially newspaper women, are more likely to have a relatively modern attitude toward women's role in society than are their male counterparts, perhaps because of the battles they have had to fight to get their jobs. Nevertheless, opinion pieces and columns were the only forums in which I found women consistently more enlightened than men in their treatment of rape cases.

Source: Oxford, Oxford University Press

1   Does this case study use primary data, secondary data or both?   **(1)**

2   List the types of data used by Benedict.   **(2)**

3   Describe the research methods Benedict has used in this study.   **(4)**

4   What alternative research method could be used to investigate social attitudes towards 'sex crimes'? Justify and explain your answer.   **(6)**

5   How would you operationalise the method you have chosen above?   **(8)**

6   Outline the strengths and weaknesses of Benedict's research methodology.   **(9)**

Doing sociological research methodology

Before undertaking research there are four questions that every researcher must ask, regardless of the sampling and research method preferred. Only when these questions have been answered satisfactorily should the research proceed. The questions are as follows:

1   What am I trying to discover? (What am I looking for? Does the phenomenon exist?)
2   What is the context of my study? (What studies have already been conducted in this area?)
3   Which research method is most appropriate for my study? (Should the data collected be quantitative or qualitative?)
4   How should I evaluate my findings? (What is the best way to present my data?)

Other questions will arise when conducting research, such as 'Is the method morally correct?', 'Should the researcher report illegal activities discovered?', but the four questions above are essential.

Sampling

All primary research that seeks to generalise about society, except for the census, has to employ a **sampling** method. The practical constraints of investigating the whole population of a society, or even a group within a society make it necessary to use a sample. The researcher will firstly identify the population or group to be studied, for example Sixth Formers. A list, or sample frame, will then be constructed to represent the population, for example a selection of post-16 educational establishments and the class lists within them. A sample will then be chosen from the sample frame, using an appropriate sampling method, to represent the population, for example 1,000 Sixth Formers chosen by a random sampling method from the sample frame. A sample is therefore a small representative group selected from the population. If a sample is not representative of the population, when it is intended to be (see section below on 'representativeness') then the study will be inaccurate, unreliable and invalid.

ACTIVITY **KS** COMMUNICATION

KNOWLEDGE AND UNDERSTANDING

A list of names for the complete population is known as the **sample frame**. Suggest four sources from which a sample frame could be obtained for a study of the people in your area.

Representativeness

If a sample contains the typical characteristics in the same proportion as the population, then it is considered to be representative. Representativeness can also be affected by the sample size, which should vary according to the population and issue being surveyed. It should be noted that non-representativeness can be employed in sampling to subject the study to the ultimate testing of the hypothesis, in other words, if a theory can be established from an atypical proportion of the population, then it must be correct for the majority.

HINTS AND TIPS   If you are embarking on research for your coursework, or for a class project, remember to ensure that your sample is representative. No matter which research method you use, it is worth taking time to consider the relevance of your sample frame (list of people from whom the sample is selected) to your study and to ensure that the sample from it represents that group.

ACTIVITY **KS** COMMUNICATION

KNOWLEDGE AND UNDERSTANDING	IDENTIFICATION AND INTERPRETATION	ANALYSIS AND EVALUATION

In her book **The Captive Wife** (1966) Hannah Gavron investigated the position of women, and women with young children, in the family and society. Her work derived from that of earlier studies of family life, such as Young and Wilmott's **Family and Kinship in East London** (1957). Gavron attempted to assess the changes that had taken place in family and social life for women in the intervening years. Her research involved ordinary working- and middle-class people (she claimed that many previous studies had used atypical or extreme examples of working-class/middle-class families). Gavron's sample involved 48 middle- and working-class families, the former drawn from a GP's patient list in Kentish Town and the latter a doctor's list in West Hampstead and from a 'housebound wives' register.

1   To what extent would it be reasonable for Gavron to generalise from her findings about all women with young children?   **(9)**

HINTS AND TIPS   Remember that Gavron studied only particular samples, which inevitably would have influenced her findings.

2   How important is it to choose typical groups for a study of this kind?   **(8)**

The census

The census is a national survey carried out on behalf of the government to find out about the whole of the British population. However, the purpose of the census is not to produce data about individuals, but to provide statistical facts about the community, and groups within the community, as a whole. It is against the law to disclose individual or single household data collected through the census. Citizens are legally obliged to take part in this massive piece of research and will be fined if they do not. It is such an extensive survey that, due to cost and time, it can be conducted only every 10 years. It does not, therefore, have to rely on any sampling methods, because the whole population is surveyed. As such it should be an incredibly representative piece of research.

The census has provided information about the UK since the nineteenth century. It involves every household completing a compulsory questionnaire (a requirement since the Census Act 1920) on topics such as sex, age, country of birth, illness, etc. However, 2 million people were missed from the 1991 census through non-response. To check that the estimate of how many people have been missed is accurate, a follow-up survey, called a census validation survey, is always carried out. The non-response rate was explained in terms of:

a   A high level of homelessness (census data is based on collecting information from a residential address).

b   A deliberate attempt not to be included (the 'poll tax' was in operation and people hid their presence from official records in order not to pay).

c   A technical problem in estimating numbers in institutions, such as universities.

The Office of Population Censuses and Surveys (OPCS) has stated that young adults aged between 20 and 34 years old, particularly young men, featured prominently among those missing from statistics.

The 1991 census should have been reliable and representative, but the degree of non-response makes its accuracy dubious. Quite apart from the fact that official statistics are socially constructed (see below), there are technical problems, such as the questionnaires being too difficult to fill in, with the research method. These problems mean that even the census, the most widespread, costly and formal of social surveys, suffers from the same problems as all quantitative research methods.

Official statistics

Any numerical data produced by the state, about society and the communities/groups within it, constitutes official statistics. The census provides the government with data from which to construct official statistics; however, official statistics are available through many pieces of research and on many different topics. Governments use official statistics to build their policies and make projections about future social needs.

There are both advantages and disadvantages to be considered when employing official statistics in your research. Positivists argue that an accurate and objective picture of society can be drawn with official statistics. Interpretivists state that official statistics are socially constructed, government officials having

HINTS AND TIPS   A prime source of official statistics is the Central Statistical Office (CSO). When conducting your own research it is worth contacting the CSO for its 'In Figures' year summary, which provides insightful secondary data. The summary covers issues such as education, income and wealth, birth rates, death rates, divorce rates, employment, crime, etc. Another source to consider from the CSO is the annually published **Social Trends***, which also provides quantitative data on areas such as the family, health, religion, politics, etc.* **Sociology Update** *also provides summaries of official statistics in a small and easily accessible annual pamphlet.*

decided what issues should be defined as important and what the data collected means, and can therefore never hope to measure social reality objectively. However, without the generalisations obtained from numerical data, government policy makers would never be able to do their jobs.

The table below offers some advantages and disadvantages of using official statistics in sociological research.

Official statistics	
Advantages	**Disadvantages**
Inexpensive to use.	The way in which concepts have been defined and measured has to be accepted, which may provide false results. Definitions and measurements can change between studies and over time.
Readily available on a wide range of issues.	Misleading to accept them as objective social reality.
Analysis can be relatively quick since time is saved by not doing primary research. Findings can therefore be more up to date.	People's feelings are not considered.
Patterns and trends can be examined over time.	Difficult to accept the data without considering the way it was collected, i.e. what was the purpose of the research? Who funded the research? Did any external forces influence the results?
Hypotheses can be tested.	
The statistics themselves can be studied in order to show their construction.	

Figure 2.5   Advantages and disadvantages of official statistics

" *Official statistics are a secondary source of data compiled by officials for practical reasons like the formation of policy, government administration, and financial accountability. Social scientists need to be constantly reminded of this because, however objective the figures may appear to be, the collection of the information they contain is a social process. One consequence of this is that official statistics vary in their reliability.*

Lane, J. K. (1985:28)

Sampling methods

Various sampling methods or procedures can be employed by a researcher once the sample frame has been established. The choice of sampling method depends on the type of data the researcher wants to collect, such as totally random or proportional to the gender split in the population, and on practical considerations, such as access to the population and time constraints (see Figure 2.6).

Scientific research methods

The natural sciences follow systematic enquiry based on the collection of data that can be proven true or false. Most scientific investigations begin with observations, such as 'Sample A reacts differently from sample B when exposed to substance C', and then progress to experiments to test and verify those observations. Scientists use the following research methods to construct theories about the natural world:

- **Observation** – All scientific activity depends on the systematic observation, recording and describing of its subject matter.
- **Conjecture** – This involves providing a plausible reason for the occurrence of an observable fact.
- **Hypothesis formation** – The conjecture is put into a form that allows the scientist to determine how well it explains the occurrence of the observation. It essentially predicts the result of the test.
- **Testing** – The hypothesis is subjected to rigorous tests, such as experiments, to show whether it can be proved wrong.
- **Control** – All scientific tests must take place under conditions that the scientist can control, such as conducting experiments in a laboratory.

- **Generalisations** – If the test has not proven the hypothesis incorrect, it shows that the conjecture explains the occurrence of the observation. The hypothesis may then be generalised into either:
  1. A law-like statement, such as 'Light rays bend at an angle dependent on the density of the medium they enter', which shows that factors will interact in the same way given the same conditions, or:
  2. A probabilistic statement, such as 'There is a 95% probability that c will occur when d is also present under the condition b.'

  Generalisations also provide the basis for predictions about how the natural world will behave in the future.

- **Theory formation** – This is the ordering of a number of generalisations into a coherent model or theory that explains a given range of phenomena.
- **Objectivity** – The elimination of bias or value judgement on the part of the researcher is crucial in scientific methodology. Researchers are expected to be totally neutral and impartial, otherwise their work will be seen as a piece of propaganda. Laboratory experiments are argued to be the best method for testing a hypothesis, because they allow all variables to be controlled, which makes the test very accurate and reliable.

This approach has also been termed the hypothetico-deductive method, and was outlined succinctly by McNeill and Townley (1981) (see Figure 2.7).

Experiments

Natural scientists assume that the world has an independent existence and must therefore be governed by observable laws, which the researcher can discover using the correct research tool, such as the experiment. Experiments are seen as being objective and factual and therefore a sound basis for testing a hypothesis. The laboratory experiment is used to measure causal effect (something that is almost impossible to do in the social sciences, which explains the relative absence of the experiment as a research method in this field), such as 'adding heat to water *causes* it to boil'. However, in order to make sure that heat is the independent variable (causal factor), the experiment must be controlled, i.e. take place in an environment, such as a laboratory, where all the variables (factors) are held

Sampling methods

Type	Explanation	Advantages	Disadvantages
Random	Everybody in the population has an equal chance of selection. Sometimes known as probability sampling. Names may be selected at random from the sample frame by a computer or by drawing names from a hat.	1 Statistically reliable. 2 The sample can be checked for representativeness.	1 Can be expensive if population is large. 2 Can be time-consuming if sample is large. 3 Sometimes complex if population is large.
There are three subtypes of random sampling:			
Stratified	Population divided by relevant factors, such as age or gender, and a random sample is taken from each stratum.	Particularly useful when the population is small.	Division of population means that the data may not be representative.
Multistage/cluster	For a dispersed population the sample is subdivided into clusters. For example, to sample people over 18 a random set of political constituencies is chosen, then a sample of wards within them, then a sample of polling districts within them, and finally a random sample of people in that district from the electoral roll.	Useful when a sample frame is not readily available.	
Multiphase	After a survey is complete, a sample of the original sample is selected for further questioning.	Provides more detailed information.	
Quota	Not based on the principles of randomness. If the population is known, then it can be subdivided proportionately according to social factors, such as age and gender. For example, 20 men and 10 women. Researcher questions a specified number (quota) from each group.	1 Simple. 2 Relatively inexpensive. 3 Relatively quick. 4 Low non-response rate.	1 Researcher selection of sample can lead to bias. 2 Representativeness of sample cannot be checked.
A type of quota sampling is:			
Opportunity	Used by market researchers. Respondents are stopped and questioned when other sampling methods are impossible, such as finding out users' attitudes to a new shopping centre.	100% response rate (ask all that are needed).	Researcher bias in selection of respondents. Certain sections of the population may be missed out.
Snowball	A sample is established through recommendations and 'contacts'. For example, a contact in the crime world may recommend other criminals to interview.	1 Provides a sample when a sample frame is not available. 2 Enables more data to be gathered on sensitive social issues.	Data unlikely to be representative.
A related type of sampling is:			
Volunteer	Individuals volunteer to be studied.	Responsive respondents.	Potentially biased respondents, interested in research.

Figure 2.6   Advantages and disadvantages of sampling methods

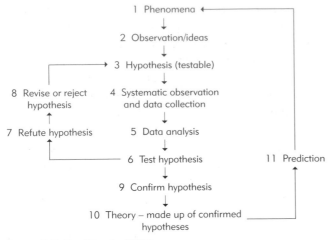

Source: McNeill and Townley (1981)

Figure 2.7   The hypothetico-deductive method

constant, in order to determine the dependent variable (affected factor). Once the experiment has been conducted, the scientist can refute or generalise the results and establish a law or redefine the experiment/hypothesis.

Experiments have been used as a basis for theory in sociology, but confining humans to laboratory conditions has ethical problems, therefore the experiments have been relatively short. Milgram (1965) conducted a famous experiment into the effects of authority upon human behaviour. He invited participants in the experiment to act as 'teacher' or 'learner'; the teacher saw the learner bound to a chair and was then taken to another room. The teacher was asked to give electric shocks to the learner if he or she made an error while learning a series of linked words. The learner responded to the shocks with protests, screams and eventually silence. The learner, however, was part of the experiment and was faking receipt of the shocks. The teacher was not aware of this and 65 per cent of teachers were found to be prepared to administer shocks to the maximum level when instructed to do so.

Milgram's experiment demonstrated that social behaviour could be conditioned. People were found to obey the orders of others who were seen to hold more authority. However, the ethics of making those involved in the experiment believe that they were inflicting pain on others is questionable. It is possible that the 'teachers' may have long-term negative experiences as a consequence of being involved with

the experiment, which is a reason why experiments are rarely used in sociological research.

A more sociologically-based experiment was carried out by Atkinson, Kessel and Dalgaard (1975) to examine the socially constructed nature of suicide rates. Case details of 40 'suicides' were sent to Danish and English coroners to establish verdicts. Atkinson et al. wanted to see if the coroners constructed the meaning of each death as suicide. The Danish coroners declared 29 of the 40 cases to be suicides, while the English coroners found 19 of the cases to be suicides. The coroners came to these vastly different conclusions based on the definitions of suicide applicable in each country.

In Denmark a suicide is recorded when it appears likely on the balance of probability. In England definite suicidal intention has to be apparent to the cause of death. The experiment showed that coroners' verdicts on suicide are socially constructed. This research therefore demonstrates how experiments can be of use in establishing a sociological theory. The experiment also shows that ethics and morality do not have to be sacrificed with this research method, because the subject being researched does not directly have to affect the people involved. In other words, the coroners were not affected personally by the experiment, because their interpretations of the suicides were not linked to their professional expertise. However, in general, experiments result in the application of generalisations, which have been strongly contested as a reflection of human social life (see section on 'Positivism versus interpretivism').

The Hawthorne Effect

The feasibility of carrying out experiments rests upon two conditions:

1   The control and experimental groups must match.
2   These groups must be isolated from the effects of other variables.

In practice, both these conditions are virtually impossible to meet in sociology. First, although you can match members of society by characteristics, such as sex or age, you can never find two people with exactly the same histories. Second, it is impossible to control the large number of variables acting on human beings in the social world. Conducting the experiment in a laboratory is one solution, but a major problem is that those in the experiment change their behaviour when being observed. The Experimental Effect or the Hawthorne Effect are terms used to refer to the way in which the researcher affects the subject and thereby influences the outcome of the experiment.

Comparative method

The comparative method is considered by positivists to be a valuable alternative to the practically problematic experiment. Using this method the research assembles data about the 'real' world and then compares one society/group with another, in an attempt to identify the independent variable/s that explain the presence of a particular phenomenon in a particular context. In a sense, this method could be seen as a 'natural experiment'. Classical sociologists, such as Durkheim (1897) and Weber (1905), used the comparative method to investigate society. Durkheim compared different societies' legal systems, religious systems and social integration. His most famous study, however, was into the causes of suicide. He collected the official statistics on suicide for a number of different European countries and showed that the rates were stable over time. He also showed that suicide rates were higher in areas where there were more Protestants, in cities and among the unmarried and childless, but lower where there were more Catholics, in rural areas, among the married and among those with children. Based on these observations Durkheim tested and confirmed a whole series of hypotheses until he had proven his case enough for it to be considered a theory. Durkheim's work is often considered to be the clearest example of positivist methodology in sociology.

Weber applied the comparative method when examining reasons for the emergence of capitalism in western Europe. Weber compared the socio-economic systems of China, India, some Islamic countries and ancient Palestine with Europe. He found that the independent variable present in western Europe was Protestantism/Calvinism and that this led to the emergence of capitalism. There was no evidence of Protestantism in the other countries he studied. Weber also showed that there was a connection between Calvinists' beliefs and their actions, such as God had chosen each person's destiny, but success and reinvestment in work and trade suggested a greater likelihood of heaven than hell as the final resting place.

The presence of a connection or correlation, such as those found by Weber and Durkheim, has been referred to as **concomitant variation**, which simply means a relationship exists between two factors and that one factor may be a causal one. Contemporary sociologists, such as Fletcher (1981), have continued to support the comparative method in sociological research, stating that as a procedure for testing theories in sociology, it is the only alternative to carrying out experiments. In fact, many recent sociological studies have used the comparative method to examine potential correlation in social phenomena, such as gender and educational achievement (Arnot et al., 1996) and class and racial discrimination (The Rowntree Foundation, 1995).

> **HINTS AND TIPS**   It should be noted that a systematic and large-scale comparative analysis requires a complex methodology, such as a social survey (see section on 'Social Surveys' below).

Social surveys

 The aim of a survey is to obtain information which can be analysed and patterns extracted and comparisons made.

Bell, J. (1987:8)

Surveys come in many different forms, for example the census is a social survey and so is an opinion poll. Most surveys will employ a sample of the population (see above), which will represent the attitudes, beliefs and actions of the population. Social surveys find out 'factual' information about social issues, communities and groups. This research method is generally used when a large amount of, typically statistical, data is needed quickly. Consequently, questions are standardised and refined, i.e. everyone is asked the same questions in the same order in an understandable unambiguous way, to gather reliable data.

Social surveys can collect two types of data:

1 **Explanatory/analytical** – the information collected explains something about the phenomenon being researched. (Usually conducted by sociologists.)
2 **Descriptive** – the information describes features/attitudes of the phenomenon. (Usually commissioned by the government.)

The General Household Survey, which has been conducted since 1971 in the UK and is based on a sample of 12,000 private household residents, is a good example of a large-scale survey. Ann Oakley's small-scale social survey, *The Sociology of Housework* (1974), provides information on women's attitudes to housework based on a sample size of 40. Both surveys provide informative data, but in very different ways. The first focuses on reliability, the other takes a more qualitative approach. The researcher must decide which type of survey meets his or her methodological needs best.

ACTIVITY   KS **COMMUNICATION**

KNOWLEDGE AND UNDERSTANDING	IDENTIFICATION AND INTERPRETATION

Find a newspaper article that cites an explanatory and/or a descriptive social survey. Remember that lots of media reports mention opinion polls, or surveys, or research findings to give weight to their arguments. Write a report on the use of the survey in the article.

Surveys involve careful planning in order to elicit reliable (and possibly valid) data. Most commonly, questionnaires will be used to gather data for a social survey, but sometimes structured interviews may be used. The main reason for using these methods is because they produce generalisable data, which is the aim of a survey. Bilton et al. (1996:113) suggest a series of steps that should be adopted when planning a survey:

- *identification of the 'problem' which the survey addresses (the research question, its relation to prior work and the principal proposition or hypotheses to be tested)*
- *identification of the population of respondents to be surveyed*
- *selection of the sample of respondents that represent the total population*
- *pilot interview schedule to refine questions and topic*
- *preparation and dispatch of final questionnaire*
- *follow-up interviews*
- analysis of data *collected*
- *results and dissemination of findings*

It is important to understand the procedures involved with planning and operationalising (carrying out) a social survey, because at some stage every researcher is likely to undertake this common form of primary data collection.

Types of social survey

Cross-sectional social survey: This is a study of a representative cross-section of the population at a particular time. Opinion polls are an example of a survey used within this type of study. Cross-sectional social surveys provide only a 'snapshot' of what is happening at any one time and therefore do not provide data on social change.

Longitudinal social survey: This is a study conducted over a long period of time. A cohort is surveyed and any changes over time are recorded. An interesting example of a longitudinal survey is the '7UP' television documentary that has followed the lives of several children since they were 7 years old. A more conventional sociological survey is the National Child Development Study (NCDS). The disadvantages of this method are loss of respondents and time consumption.

Questionnaires – closed and open-ended

The main type of research method used for social surveys is the questionnaire. The researcher will have considered alternative research methods, such as interviews or observation, and decided that a questionnaire will provide the most appropriate data to answer the research question. However, as simple as a questionnaire may seem, it is one of the most difficult research tools to construct and operationalise effectively.

In order to construct, deliver and evaluate well the data of a questionnaire, several important points must be considered:

1. **What does the researcher want to find out?**
   The hypothesis should have been considered when deciding which questions to ask.

2. **What types of questions elicit the most appropriate information?**
   There are two basic forms of questions – open-ended and closed. **Open-ended questions** allow

the respondent to answer the question freely, providing more detail and depth to the data. It is hard to quantify this type of response, because each respondent can answer differently, but the data may be more valid. An example of an open-ended question is 'What are the characteristics of a good teacher?'. **Closed questions** restrict answers to categorised responses, such as 'Yes' or 'No', thereby providing easily quantifiable data. Data may be more reliable, but it also reflects the researcher's ideas of what needs to be found out about that social issue. An example of a closed question is 'Is your Sociology teacher a good teacher?' Closed questions usually have 'tick box' responses, which make it easier to quantify the responses.

Closed questions can be subdivided into categories, in order to attain specific types of information and also to facilitate coding. **Codification** means that the researcher gives a value to each answer (e.g. 'Yes' = 1, 'No' = 2), which allow responses to be quantified more easily when the data has been gathered. The following types of closed questions are often used:

- **Lists** – a choice of responses is given in list form (e.g. qualifications).
- **Categories** – a response is given to one category (e.g. age range).
- **Ranking** – responses are placed in order, usually from highest to lowest priority (e.g. most important qualities of a student).
- **Scales** – a response is given about the importance of an issue on a predefined scale (e.g. how much a student likes school).

Coding and quantifying open-ended questions is much more difficult, such as putting responses into categories and then coding those categories, and is not always desirable.

3   How should the questions be worded?

Good questions should be clear, unambiguous (mean the same thing to all respondents), simple to respond to and relevant to the respondent. The researcher should think of the respondent when phrasing questions and consider:

- **Understanding** – Will the respondent understand what is being asked? Every effort

should be made to use familiar words, and to avoid imprecise or complicated words, two questions in one or vague concepts.

- **Willingness** – Will the respondent be willing to answer the questions? The researcher should recognise the difficulty of asking questions on taboo or embarrassing subjects or the possibility of implying morality.
- **Ableness** – Will the respondent be able to answer the question? The respondent may not know the answers, because the questions are too technical or intricate, or the respondent cannot remember, or just does not know!

Consequently, all questions should be worded to optimise respondent participation. When constructing a questionnaire, questions which have a double meaning, lead the respondent towards a 'correct' answer, assume knowledge, make presumptions, are hypothetical, are offensive or require feats of memory, should be avoided.

4   What should the questionnaire look like?

Appearance and layout are very important, because the respondents should want to read and complete the questionnaire. A scruffy or ill-prepared document will not elicit many responses. Remember the following when drafting a questionnaire:

a   Type it.
b   Give clear instructions.
c   Put spaces between questions.
d   Keep response boxes tabulated to the right-hand side.
e   Be critical of the final format.
f   Start with the easy questions.

A good-looking, well-structured questionnaire will help the researcher attain a much higher response rate.

5   How should the questionnaire be administered and collected?

Before administering a questionnaire a **pilot** questionnaire, which tests the sample itself, how long it takes to complete the questionnaire, the questions etc., should be conducted. The pilot should be considered a trial run, a chance to rectify any problems with the questionnaire before distribution. The researcher should use it as an opportunity to ask the respondents about the

Please have this **NATIONAL RESEARCH SURVEY** No. *093*
questionnaire filled out by the main shopper in your household. Thank you.

Instructions:
1) Please let us know the answers that apply to you and/or your partner by putting a "✓" in the appropriate boxes.
2) In order to incorporate your opinions into our report, we need your reply within 14 days.
3) When you return your completed survey, don't worry about postage - it's already been taken care of.

If you would prefer not to complete some of the questions, please just ignore them and pass on to the next one.

EXAMPLE: **Do you drink tea** 1 ✓ Yes   9 ☐ No

1. HOBBIES AND ACTIVITIES

1 Please tick ALL the leisure interests and activities you and your partner enjoy regularly:

01 ☐ Avid Book Reading
02 ☐ Charities/Voluntary Work
03 ☐ Coin/Stamp Collecting
04 ☐ Collectables
05 ☐ Cooking
06 ☐ Crosswords/Puzzles
07 ☐ Current Affairs
08 ☐ Do-It-Yourself/DIY
09 ☐ Eating Out
10 ☐ Fashion Clothing
11 ☐ Fine Art/Antiques
12 ☐ Fishing
13 ☐ Foreign Travel
14 ☐ Gardening
15 ☐ Playing Golf
16 ☐ Gourmet Foods/Wines
17 ☐ Grandchildren
18 ☐ Hiking/Walking
19 ☐ Home Computing
20 ☐ Active Sport/Exercise
21 ☐ Knitting
22 ☐ National Trust
23 ☐ Photography
24 ☐ Going to the Pub
25 ☐ Records/Tapes/CDs
26 ☐ Religious Activities
27 ☐ Self Improvement
28 ☐ Sewing/Needlework
29 ☐ Snow Skiing
30 ☐ Theatre/Cultural/Art Events
31 ☐ Wildlife/Environment
32 ☐ Wines by Mail Order
33 ☐ Football
34 ☐ Rugby
35 ☐ Cricket
36 ☐ Sailing

2 Please write the numbers of your four favourite activities from the list above:
You: 1 ☐ 2 ☐ 3 ☐ 4 ☐
Partner: 1 ☐ 2 ☐ 3 ☐ 4 ☐

3 On average how many hours TV do you watch in a day?
1 ☐ 0-1   2 ☐ 1-2   3 ☐ 2-3   4 ☐ 3-4   5 ☐ 4-5   6 ☐ 5 +

4 How often do you eat a meal in a Pub-Restaurant?

	Weekly	Monthly	Quarterly	Yearly	Never
Any Pub-Restaurant	01 ☐	05 ☐	09 ☐	13 ☐	17 ☐
Beefeater	02 ☐	06 ☐	10 ☐	14 ☐	18 ☐
Brewers Fayre	03 ☐	07 ☐	11 ☐	15 ☐	19 ☐
Other	04 ☐	08 ☐	12 ☐	16 ☐	20 ☐

5 Do either of you bet on: (Please tick all that apply)
1 ☐ Pools   2 ☐ Bingo   3 ☐ Horseracing   4 ☐ Other

6 How many prize draws, competitions or lotteries did you enter in the last year excluding the National Lottery? 9 ☐ None
1 ☐ 1-3   2 ☐ 4-6   3 ☐ 7-10   4 ☐ 11 plus

7 Where have you been on holiday in the last 3 years?
(Please tick all that apply)
1 ☐ UK   2 ☐ Europe   3 ☐ USA   4 ☐ Rest of World

8 What type of holiday(s) do you take?
1 ☐ Camping/Caravanning
2 ☐ Hotel/Hotel Package
3 ☐ Self Catering
4 ☐ Winter Sun
5 ☐ Weekend or City Breaks
6 ☐ Winter Snow

9 Please tick all the newspapers that are REGULARLY read by your family: 99 ☐ None

	Daily	Sunday		Daily	Sunday
Express	01 ☐	21 ☐	Financial Times	10 ☐	
Independent	02 ☐	22 ☐	Guardian	11 ☐	
Mail	03 ☐	23 ☐	Star	12 ☐	
Mirror	04 ☐	24 ☐	Sun	13 ☐	
Sport	05 ☐	25 ☐	News of the World		29 ☐
Telegraph	06 ☐	26 ☐	Observer		30 ☐
Times	07 ☐	27 ☐	People		31 ☐
Other/Local	08 ☐	28 ☐	Post		32 ☐
Daily Record	09 ☐		Sunday Mail (Scotland)		33 ☐

10 From the list above, please write the number of your main newspaper: Daily: ☐☐   Sunday: ☐☐

11 Is your main daily newspaper delivered? 1 ☐ Yes   9 ☐ No

12 On what day(s) do you buy your main daily newspaper?
(If not everyday, please tick all that apply)   9 ☐ Do not buy
1 ☐ Every day   3 ☐ Tuesday   5 ☐ Thursday   7 ☐ Saturday
2 ☐ Monday   4 ☐ Wednesday   6 ☐ Friday

13 How often do you buy your main Sunday newspaper?
1 ☐ 3-4 times a month   2 ☐ 1-2 times a month   3 ☐ Less often

14 How often do you use the following to plan your TV viewing?
(Please tick all that apply)

	Every week	Most weeks	Occasionally	Xmas	Never
Radio Times	01 ☐	05 ☐	09 ☐	13 ☐	17 ☐
Other paid for listing	02 ☐	06 ☐	10 ☐	14 ☐	18 ☐
Daily Paper	03 ☐	07 ☐	11 ☐	15 ☐	19 ☐
Weekend Newspaper/ TV Supplements	04 ☐	08 ☐	12 ☐	16 ☐	20 ☐

15 What causes have you contributed to in the past year?
01 ☐ Environmental
02 ☐ Health Research
03 ☐ Third World Causes
04 ☐ Children's Welfare
05 ☐ Helping the Elderly
06 ☐ Disaster Relief
07 ☐ Wildlife
08 ☐ Animal Welfare
09 ☐ Disabled/Handicapped
10 ☐ Other

16 Would you consider sponsoring a child in a third world country?
1 ☐ Yes   2 ☐ Possibly   9 ☐ No

17 How do you contribute? (Please tick all that apply)
1 ☐ By covenant   2 ☐ In street/at door   3 ☐ By post

18 Would you donate to any of the following charities?
01 ☐ RNIB
02 ☐ Salvation Army
03 ☐ RSPB
04 ☐ OXFAM
05 ☐ SCOPE
06 ☐ Amnesty International
07 ☐ RSPCA
08 ☐ PDSA
09 ☐ Save The Children
10 ☐ NSPCC
11 ☐ NCH Action For Children
12 ☐ Christian Naval Charity

2. SHOPPING

1 Which of the following stores do you use for food and grocery shopping? (Please tick all that apply)
01 ☐ Aldi
02 ☐ Alldays/Circle K
03 ☐ Asda
04 ☐ Budgen
05 ☐ Co-op
06 ☐ Food Giant
07 ☐ Gateway/Solo
08 ☐ Garage Shop
09 ☐ Iceland
10 ☐ Kwik Save
11 ☐ Mace/Spar/VG
12 ☐ Marks & Spencer
13 ☐ Morrisons
14 ☐ Netto
15 ☐ Presto
16 ☐ Safeway
17 ☐ Sainsbury
18 ☐ Savacentre
19 ☐ Somerfield
20 ☐ Tesco
21 ☐ Tesco Metro
22 ☐ Waitrose
23 ☐ Corner Shop/Other

2 Please write the number of the store where you do your main shopping: ☐☐

3 Where do you buy most of your tobacco products?
1 ☐ Corner Shop   3 ☐ Newsagent
2 ☐ Supermarket   4 ☐ Other
If Supermarket, please indicate from the list of stores above, the number of your store: ☐☐

4 Do you or your partner use any of the following supermarket club cards on a regular basis?

	You	Partner		You	Partner
Safeway - ABC	01 ☐	07 ☐	Tesco - Club Card Plus	04 ☐	10 ☐
Sainsbury - Reward	02 ☐	08 ☐	Asda - Club	05 ☐	11 ☐
Tesco - Club Card	03 ☐	09 ☐	Other	06 ☐	12 ☐

WHEN DOING YOUR MAIN SHOPPING:

5 Why do you buy where you do? (Please tick a maximum of 2)
1 ☐ Distance
2 ☐ Convenience
3 ☐ Quality of Products
4 ☐ Parking Facilities
5 ☐ Range of Products
6 ☐ Prices
7 ☐ Store Loyalty Card
8 ☐ Customer Service

6 How far is the store from your home?
1 ☐ Less than 1 mile   3 ☐ 3-4 miles   5 ☐ 8-10 miles
2 ☐ 1-2 miles   4 ☐ 5-7 miles   6 ☐ more than 10 miles

7 What do you spend on groceries a week?
Main shopping   1 ☐ Under £15   3 ☐ £30-44   5 ☐ £60-74
2 ☐ £15-29   4 ☐ £45-59   6 ☐ £75+
Other Grocery shopping   7 ☐ Under £10   8 ☐ £10-19   9 ☐ £20+

8 How often have you bought the following products in the past 3 months?

	1	2-3	4+	None
Environmentally Friendly Products	1 ☐	3 ☐	5 ☐	7 ☐
Recycled Products	2 ☐	4 ☐	6 ☐	8 ☐

9 How many times in the last year have you bought goods/services via the mail? 9 ☐ None
1 ☐ 1   2 ☐ 2-3   3 ☐ 4-5   4 ☐ 6 plus

Please turn to the next page →

1

Figure 2.8 National Research Survey – an example of closed questionnaire construction utilising lists, categories, ranks and scales.

questionnaire design itself (e.g. clarity of questions, layout and time to complete etc.).

There are three main ways of administering/collecting a questionnaire:

a   **By post** – The questionnaire is posted to the sample and a prepaid reply envelope is included. The questionnaire is **self-administered**, i.e. completed by the respondent. Postal surveys are expensive and tend to have a low response rate; however, they are a good way of reaching a large, difficult-to-survey sample.

b   **'Drop and collect'** – The questionnaire is delivered (usually by hand) to the sample and collected from the respondent's house. This method is time-consuming, but the response rate is generally higher than for postal questionnaires.

c   **Interview** – The questionnaire is read to the respondent (**researcher-administered**) and the questions filled in by the interviewer. The interview may be formal, in that the interviewer does not deviate from the questions at all, or informal, where the interviewer may explain what a question means to elicit a response. Interviews may also take place over the telephone, a method often used by businesses seeking information from clients. Interviews ensure a higher response rate than other questionnaire administering techniques and can result in more reliable/valid data, but are extremely time-consuming. Telephone interviews, however, can experience low response rate, because the respondent perceives it as an invasion of privacy or the call comes at an inconvenient time. However, telephone interviews can enable access to respondents who may have otherwise been unavailable for questioning.

6   **How should non-response be dealt with?**
Respondents should be given a date by which to complete and return questionnaires. The researcher should decide whether to follow up non-respondents with a further questionnaire; however, if anonymity was assured to the respondent, then this may not be possible. It is worth considering that the response rate is affected by all the factors discussed above, hence the importance of constructing and administering a questionnaire as well as possible. A low response rate will distort findings, because the sample will no longer be representative of the population, which in turn will make evaluation of data difficult, unreliable and invalid.

7   **How should the data be analysed?**
Ideally, the researcher should wait for all questionnaires to be returned before embarking on an analysis; however, limited time may make it necessary to record responses as soon as they appear. The researcher should prepare a summary sheet on which to record responses for all respondents. Coding will have made this process easier, because the codes of each response can replace the actual response. For example, if 'Yes' = 1, 'No' = 2, and Respondent A answers 'Yes' to question 1 and 'No' to question 2, the summary sheet reads:

Respondent	Question 1		Question 2	
	1	2	1	2
A	×			×
B				
C				

However, if the questionnaire contains open-ended questions these may be coded by similar responses, or added as prose to the summary sheet.

Coded data may be analysed by quantifying it, or turning it into a statistic, such as a percentage. Variations in response can be seen according to such factors as age or sex, which may be interesting to the study. The quantitative data can be presented in graph or chart form, which enables the reader to understand it more easily. Qualitative data will have to be examined for similarities of theme and frequency of occurrence of these themes, if a generalisation is to be made. Whether the researcher uses quantitative and/or qualitative data on which to base the evaluations, he or she will still be expected to produce a written evaluation of the findings, in relation to the context of the study, the original research question and the successfulness of the methodology.

Advantages and disadvantages of using questionnaires

There are many reasons for choosing to use questionnaires, rather than other research methods, and as many reasons against choosing them. Ultimately, whether a researcher uses a questionnaire or not will depend on what it is the researcher is trying to find out about society. For example, Shere Hite's *The Hite Report: Growing Up Under Patriarchy* (1994), was based on research to examine parent–children relationships in the family. Hite employed the use of 3,000 questionnaires in a large-scale survey of parents and children in different countries. She used open-ended anonymous questionnaires (here referred to as essay questionnaires), in order to attain detailed, unconstructed primary data:

> *I have always preferred to use the probing, in-depth format of essay questions, rather than the more usual and simplified multiple-choice, as I wanted to get a picture of childhood unblemished be preconceptions, a fresh picture built on primary data. A multiple-choice questionnaire would have presented people with pre-set categories from which to choose, limiting their responses. Additionally, I have always preferred the arduous task of distributing a questionnaire to anonymous participants because of the rewards: the freedom and beauty of the voices.*

Hite, S. (1994:xv)

Hite could have used unstructured interviews to obtain her detailed, qualitative data, but she would not then have reached such a large sample. Therefore, she decided to use a method that could be operationalised on a large scale, but that could also elicit qualitative data – the open-ended questionnaire.

Numerical data – tables, charts and graphs

The data produced by quantitative research methods, such as social surveys and questionnaires, is numerical and can therefore by assimilated into tables, charts and graphs. Tables, charts and graphs are useful for showing information in a clear and simple way. For example, a table may sum up in a few lines what it takes two pages of text to explain. It is therefore important to understand the meaning of tables and graphs.

Tables, charts and graphs tend to represent:

■ Similarities or differences between or within groups, for example by sex or income, or between times, for example 1990 and 2000.

■ Patterns in the data, such as a trend in the population growth (see Figure 2.9).

■ Generalisations in society through statistics or figures, such as the percentage of female MPs or the number of people who passed Sociology A Level in 2000.

HINTS AND TIPS   The following diagrams represent the most common and likely form of tables, charts and graphs you will encounter in Sociology. Study them carefully and look for the meaning within them, for example what does each of them tell you?

You will be expected to understand the meaning of tables, charts and graphs throughout the course.

Births outside marriage and levels of cohabitation
(England and Wales)

	% of births outside marriage	% of illegimate births where parents live apart
Manchester	54.0	55.9
Liverpool	53.1	65.1
Nottingham	50.9	47.5
Middlesbrough	50.1	58.0
Rhondda	49.6	50.7
Lewisham (S.E. London)	46.2	52.9
Brighton	44.9	31.2

Source: *Population Trends 91*, March 1998

Figure 2.9   Example of a table

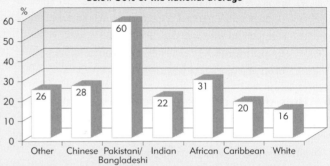

Note: the report warns against placing too much confidence in the estimates for the African and Chinese households because the samples were small.

Source: R. Berthoud *The Incomes of Ethnic Minorities*, Joseph Rowntree Foundation, 1998

Figure 2.10   Example of a chart

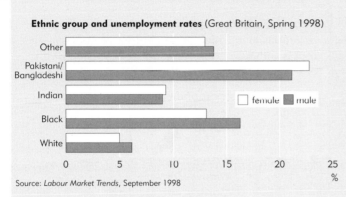

Ethnic group and unemployment rates (Great Britain, Spring 1998)

Source: *Labour Market Trends*, September 1998

Figure 2.11   Example of a chart

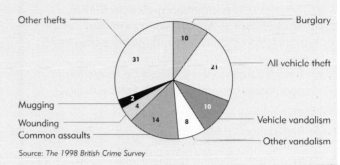

Source: *The 1998 British Crime Survey*

Figure 2.12   Example of a pie chart

Number of violent incidents against men and women in 1997

*The % of incidents against men and women within violence types do not sum up to 100 because they are based on the number of incidents.

Source: *The 1998 British Crime Survey*

	Number of incidents (thousands)			% of all incidents	% against men and women, within violence type*		
	All	**Men**	**Women**	**All**	**Men**		**Women**
All violence	**3381**	**2043**	**1382**	**100**	**60**		**41**
Domestic	835	234	582	25	28		70
Mugging	390	232	164	12	68		42
Stranger	681	568	139	20	83		20
Acquaintance	1462	992	499	43	68		34

Figure 2.13   Example of a table

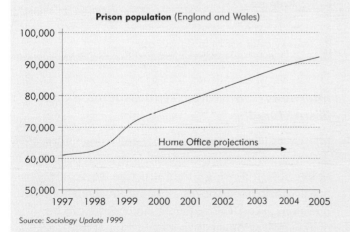

Prison population (England and Wales)

Home Office projections

Source: *Sociology Update 1999*

Figure 2.14   Example of a graph

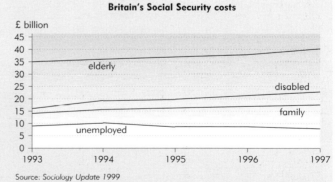

Britain's Social Security costs

£ billion

elderly

disabled

family

unemployed

Source: *Sociology Update 1999*

Figure 2.15   Example of a graph

KNOWLEDGE AND UNDERSTANDING	IDENTIFICATION AND INTERPRETATION

Using the table below identify the following:
a The trend in population growth in the UK.
b The similarities and differences in the population growth rates of the countries that make up the UK.
c Any generalisations that can be made about population growth in the UK for the future.

	1961	1971	1981	1991	1996	2011*
England	43,561	46,412	46,821	48,208	49,089	51,161
Wales	2,635	2,740	2,813	2,891	2,921	2,989
Scotland	5,184	5,236	5,180	5,107	5,128	5,059
N. Ireland	1,427	1,540	1,538	1,601	1,663	1,720
UK	52,807	55,928	56,352	57,807	58,801	60,929

* projected

Sources: Office for National Statistics, General Register Office for Scotland, Northern Ireland's Statistics and Research Agency

Figure 2.16   Population of the UK

Advantages	Disadvantages
Information can be collected from a large sample of the population, making data more representative and generalisations easier.	Potentially low response rate.
It is fairly cheap to produce and distribute large numbers of questionnaires.	Those who respond to questionnaires may be different from the rest of the sample who do not respond – this makes their representativeness doubtful.
The interviewer is unlikely to affect results.	Respondents may respond in an appropriate, rather than honest, way.
Postal respondents have time to consider answers, rather than guessing or answering hastily.	Questions are imposed on the respondent, who could reflect the researcher's values, rather than the respondent's.
Post may be the only way to reach the sample.	
Responses to quantitative questions can be compared and analysed statistically.	

Figure 2.17   Advantages and disadvantages of questionnaires

KNOWLEDGE AND UNDERSTANDING	IDENTIFICATION AND INTERPRETATION	ANALYSIS AND EVALUATION

Read the questionnaire below. Identify and explain any faults in it. Think of an alternative question that is without a fault. Type out your version of the questionnaire.

Please tick the appropriate answer.

1 Age   under 18   ☐
                18–30   ☐
                30–50   ☐
2 Family   Bachelor/spinster   ☐
                Widow/widower   ☐
                Married with children ☐
                Married without children ☐
3 Class   Upper   ☐
                Middle   ☐
                Working   ☐
4 'The majority of people think school is useless and rubbish.'
                Strongly agree   ☐
                Agree   ☐
                Disagree   ☐
                Strongly disagree   ☐
5 'Ms Hope is an excellent Sociology Teacher'.
                Agree   ☐
                Disagree   ☐
6 Would you like to live in Oxford?
                Yes   ☐
                No   ☐
7 How frequently do you skive off from school?
                Too often   ☐
                Average   ☐
                Not enough   ☐

Thanks a lot for helping me out.

Interviews – structured, semi-structured and unstructured

Interviews involve the researcher collecting information directly from the respondent. Meetings can be formal or informal, following a rigid structure, such as a questionnaire (see above), or being flexible about the questions asked. Consequently, interviews can be quantitative or qualitative or even a bit of both. Whichever approach the researcher decides to take, the same careful research procedures outlined above for conducting questionnaires must be applied to conducting interviews. A research question must be asked, questions devised, a schedule (list of questions) prepared and piloted and tools for analysis considered.

Interview techniques

There are three types of interview available to the researcher; structured interviews, semi-structured interviews and unstructured interviews. The researcher should choose the type most appropriate to the research question being posed, bearing in mind the strengths and weaknesses of each method.

Structured interviews

This is a formal interview, usually based on a questionnaire, where the interviewer reads the questions and fills in the respondent's answers. It is a quantitative technique designed to produce statistical data. Structured interviews tend to be the least time-consuming of all the interview techniques, with the researcher having a good idea of how long the interview will last.

Arber (1993) conducted a large-scale survey of the range of services provided to local authority housing tenants using structured interviews. One of her reasons for choosing this research tool was to gain information quickly to inform the local authority that was funding the research. The sample frame was a list of local authority tenancies, from which 1,225 were selected through a 'disproportionate' stratified sample (reflecting representation from housing estates of different sizes). Arber chose to use structured interviews based on a questionnaire to obtain reliable, generalisable data:

> *Large scale surveys generally require identical question wording for each respondent so that the results are reliable and so that comparable information is obtained from each respondent, facilitating data entry and statistical analysis.*

Arber, S. (1993:40)

The questionnaires contained open-ended and closed questions and were operationalised by a team of 40 interviewers. Each interviewer was expected to interview 25 respondents in a six-week period, with interviews lasting about an hour and a quarter. All of the interviewers underwent a two-day training programme, the intention being to standardise the interview technique and process, thereby obtaining more reliable results.

Semi-structured interviews

This is a semi-formal interview, usually based on predefined questions, but allowing the interviewer to deviate from the schedule to ask further relevant questions as appropriate. It is both a quantitative and qualitative technique designed to produce both statistical and in-depth data. Semi-structured interviews can vary in length, but are not usually as long as unstructured interviews.

Dobash and Dobash (1980) investigated wife-battering in modern society using a semi-structured interviewing technique. Their sample consisted of 109 women from Scotland, 93 of whom lived in refuges for battered women and 16 of whom had recently left a refuge. The women were both middle- and working-class, aged between 16 and 30 years old and had two or three children. The women were usually interviewed soon after arrival at a refuge and no one refused to take part.

Trust needed to be established between the interviewers (two female research assistants) and the respondents, because of the sensitive nature of the investigative area. This was done by placing the researchers in continual contact with the refuges and over a period of months. An informal approach was adopted during the interviews, the interview schedule being based on standardised questions that could be changed or clarified if appropriate. Dobash and Dobash stated that this open-ended type of semi-structured interview increased their understanding of the respondents' answers, perceptions and motivations. Also, by establishing a rapport between interviewer and interviewee richer and more valid data could be collected.

The use of semi-structured interviews allowed Dobash and Dobash to provide both detailed accounts of battered women's experiences and statistics on common occurrences, such as frequency of beatings and injuries. Therefore, they were able to describe what being battered meant to the women interviewed, but also back it up with quantifiable data to identify patterns between women who were beaten.

Unstructured interviews

This is an informal interview, usually based on a few pertinent questions relating to what the researcher wants to find out. The interviewer may deviate totally from the interview schedule should any interesting data emerge. It is a qualitative technique designed to produce in-depth information. Unstructured interviews are a useful tool when embarking on research in an unknown area, because the respondent can provide detailed information, which the researcher can apply to more structured/quantitative data-collection techniques, thereby producing more valid data. This is generally the most time-consuming interview technique.

Kelly (1988) used unstructured interviews and a strong feminist rationale to investigate sexual violence. As an active campaigner for the equality of women, Kelly was able to find access to a constant stream of information about sexual abuse towards women. Her research was based on four pilot interviews (with friends), which enabled her to redraft the interview 'guide', making her questions more relevant and valid. Kelly interviewed 60 respondents and gave the interviewees the interview tapes to think about, the result being that they could consider the information they gave her and add to it if necessary. This informal approach was used for the interviews because of the sensitive nature of the subject. Kelly also wanted the interviewees to get something back from the process, such as the ability to reflect:

> *The women who did the pilot interviews felt that hearing their own tape gave them time to reflect on and add to what they had said and this resulted in the decision to return a transcript of the interview to each woman and to do follow-up interviews with them.*

Kelly, L. (1988:8)

Kelly's interview schedule followed a chronological pattern, beginning with reflections on childhood and gradually moving to adulthood. Difficult questions about sexual violence were left until near the end of the interview, although the last area to be covered was about the future (ending on a positive note). Structuring the question areas in this way helped the respondents to relax and feel comfortable talking about such sensitive and personal issues. Unstructured interviews take a lot of preparation, in order to avoid rambling and irrelevance, and skill on the part of the interviewer:

> *Interviewing is a skill. My skill developed over time as I sensed where to ask a further question, when just to listen, and where to leave space for women to think. It is not just talking, although a good interview may feel*

> *like a stimulating conversation. It involves the interviewer being aware of a number of things at the same time and juggling priorities.*

(1988:9)

It is interesting to note that almost 75 per cent of the women remembered further relevant information between the first interview and follow-up interview, and several women added detailed comments to their original transcripts. By giving control to the interviewees, Kelly was able to gain valuable insight into the experiences of women who had been subjected to sexual violence.

unstructured	semi-structured	structured
INFORMAL **Qualitative**		**FORMAL** **Quantitative**

Figure 2.18   Interview methodology choices

Interviewees

Interviewees should be selected using the same principles applied to questionnaires, i.e. a representative sample. Sometimes this is not possible because of the nature of interviews, that is that people may not want to talk to a researcher, or give up their time. Therefore, the researcher should always have a reserve list of interviewees selected from the population.

The sample selected for interviewing can be interviewed as a group, as well as, or instead of, individually. This may provide the researcher with information about interviewee responses within that group (it can provide more authentic information or more deliberated answers – see 'Hawthorne Effect', page 86) and provide more data more quickly.

Recording information

Unless an interview is structured, it is difficult for the researcher to write down responses during the interview. Handling an interview takes skill, particularly if the interviewer is expected to 'pick up' on areas of interest and develop more probing questions in that direction. Writing notes may also distract the interviewee, making him or her less relaxed and therefore less able to reveal the 'truth'. Consequently, many researchers tape-record interviews, which are later transcribed.

The following instructions are given to interviewers by a market research company:

1. When you approach someone to ask for an interview, do it with confidence. You will find that most people enjoy the chance to give you their opinion. Before you start the questions show the respondent your Identity Card. You should be familiar with the questionnaire and have everything that you need ready. You can then lead the respondent straight into their first question.

2. If you are asked how long the interview will take give a fair assessment. Do not let the respondents wander off the subject, but politely repeat questions and be business-like in recording their replies.

3. Always face your respondent so that they can see and hear you clearly. DO NOT let them read the questionnaire.

4. Do not show surprise or distrust about anyone's replies either by comments or by the expression on your face. You are there simply to record their opinions and attitudes.

5. Likewise you should NEVER give your own opinion on the subject or the questions during an interview. This could influence the way the respondent answers subsequent questions.

6. Always aim to leave a respondent feeling that s/he would like to be interviewed again. Even if a respondent does not fit your quota and you are not completing a questionnaire with him/her, s/he should feel that he has contributed to the research.

7. A respondent may refuse to continue or to give you personal information. Do not allow this to alter your pleasant manner and your usual thanks.

8. NEVER interview someone you know, or anyone involved in market research. Do not interview people whom you have interviewed in the previous six months. Their responses are likely to be quite different from a stranger's and might bias the results.

9. ALL information you collect is confidential. Your professional manner should reassure respondents that you are involved in RESEARCH, not selling something.

10. At the end give the respondent a THANK YOU leaflet (with your name and interviewer number).

Figure 2.19   A guide to conducting market research – the interview.

Transcribed tapes can, however, also have their disadvantages. A researcher has to make sure that what was said in an interview has the same meaning on paper. This is sometimes hard to do, because the tone of voice or pauses may alter the meaning of the written word. Video-tape recordings may offer an alternative and display not only gestures and tone, but also body language, thereby providing more information for the interview. However, it should be remembered that the presence of a video camera could cause the interviewee to change his or her behaviour.

Advantages and disadvantages

All three types of interview have different advantages and disadvantages. The researcher who uses a

structured interview should consider the same benefits and drawbacks as described for questionnaires. Any research tool that produces quantitative data will enable generalisations to be made, but lack validity. However, the response rate should be better than for a self-administered questionnaire and the problem of ambiguity should be removed by interviewer intervention. The data from structured interviews, unlike unstructured interviews, can be compared, because the conditions of the research should have been the same.

A researcher who opts for an unstructured interview approach should be able to collect qualitative data on the interviewee's real feelings, attitudes and experiences, which can lead to new discoveries. Collecting this data takes skill but can produce incredibly valid information. However, because of the informal nature of unstructured interviews, it should be considered whether the interviewer has influenced the respondent, consciously or unconsciously. If the interviewer has influenced responses, or not considered certain points relevant, this is known as interviewer **bias**. Interviewer bias jeopardises the validity of the data.

Generalisations cannot be made from the information collected by unstructured interviews, which is why some researchers opt for semi-structured interviews. Semi-structured interviews combine the quantitative and the qualitative approaches to data collection, allowing some generalisation and some detailed information to enrich it.

ACTIVITY   KS **COMMUNICATION**

KNOWLEDGE AND UNDERSTANDING	INTERPRETATION AND APPLICATION	EVALUATION

Using the information above on the advantages and disadvantages of interviews, fill in the table below.

Interviews	
Advantages	**Disadvantages**

Content analysis

Figure 2.20 Is what we see or read really what it seems? Only content analysis has the answers!

> *Content analysis is a technique for systematically analysing the content and meaning of media messages. It has been applied to newspapers, magazines, comics, television programmes and films by various sociologists. Content analysis leads the researcher to encode the content of the medium studied: to, in other words, break the content down into recorded sections or types.*

Howe, N. (1994:70)

Content analysis is an approach to research that uses secondary data or sources. It is important actually to examine secondary sources, because the information they portray may reflect bias and therefore distort understanding and behaviour. In content analysis the researcher examines the content of documents produced by social institutions, typically the mass media, as evidence of a specific social phenomenon, such as the way in which black people are portrayed.

Conducting content analysis

Content analysis can be approached in two ways:

1 Quantitative data can be analysed statistically, for example gender stereotypical advertisements in men's magazines could be categorised and counted for frequency. This was popular in the 1970s and early 1980s and was applied by sociologists such as the Glasgow University Media Group (GUMG).

2 Qualitative data can be analysed to understand the meanings of the presentations, for example the message inherent in soap operas that depict happy nuclear families. It attempts to uncover 'messages' and suggest the type of behaviour these may support. This type of content analysis has become more popular since the late 1980s and has been applied by sociologists such as A. McRobbie (1983).

However, both approaches require the researcher to identify specific themes and examine how these have been developed. The Women in Journalism (WIJ) Research Committee (1996) utilised content analysis to investigate a specific theme: the way women were portrayed in the national press in the UK. They analysed the newspaper stories of two similar political events that happened shortly after one another, but one involved a man and the other a woman. Alan Howarth MP and Emma Nicholson MP swapped political allegiance (or 'crossed the floor') in 1995. The WIJ committee examined 10 newspapers covering five days of the story and including daily tabloids, daily broadsheets, Sunday tabloids and Sunday broadsheets. They counted the number of articles, number of paragraphs and average length of story and found that there was no gender bias in the frequency and length of reporting.

ACTIVITY KS COMMUNICATION

| KNOWLEDGE AND UNDERSTANDING | IDENTIFICATION AND INTERPRETATION |

Record three television advertisements about a similar theme, such as breakfast cereals. Analyse them using content analysis, for example count the number of times any sociological issues arise, such as use of a nuclear family. Investigate whether there are any hidden meanings present in the advertisements. Present your findings in both quantitative and qualitative form.

The WIJ also analysed the 'attitude' of the coverage by classifying the tone of the reports as 'favourable',

Content analysis	
Advantages	**Disadvantages**
Relatively cheap.	Assumes the media has an effect on audience behaviour.
Data is easily available and accessible.	The audience is not considered in the analysis.
Relatively quick compared to primary research data-collection methods.	Researcher can exert influence/bias when interpreting data (subjectivity).
Very reliable/repeatable.	
No researcher influence/bias on original data.	

Figure 2.21   Advantages and disadvantages of content analysis

'unfavourable' or *'neutral'*. They discovered that differences did exist in the attitudes of the press to each MP. Lastly, the text and headlines were examined for differences in the use of language, such as sexism. This last area uncovered gender bias, with Nicholson being referred to as menopausal, while Howarth was said to be 'an honourable man', both supporting gender stereotyped ideologies. The WIJ concluded, based on their content analysis based research, that Howarth was portrayed as having made a hard, but balanced decision, while Nicholson had made an emotional and irrational choice.

Conversation analysis

Conversation analysis can be seen as a more detailed form of content analysis, which concentrates on specific interaction situations, such as a conversation between a pupil and a teacher. The aim of this method is to interpret how the meaning of the conversation is constructed. It is a strand of ethnomethodology developed by Sacks, which shows that meaning is based on taken-for-granted rules of conversation that enable us to see the world in similar ways. It is argued that by **deconstructing**, or breaking down, the **discourse**, or conversation, the 'reality' that is established by the interaction will become clear.

Dramaturgical sociology (where everyday interactions are seen to be based on generally understood 'scripts', which develop freely during interaction) has utilised conversation analysis to find out more about the meaning within everyday conversations.

HINTS AND TIPS   *The term '**verstehen**', which literally translated from the German means 'to understand', is a good word to use in relation to conversation analysis. In fact, the concept of verstehen can be applied to all data collected from a phenomenological or interpretivist perspective, because it is about the researchers putting themselves in the position of the subjects, in order to understand their experiences. From the interpretivist perspective it is essential to apply verstehen, because only then will the researcher understand the subjective meanings, or social consciousness, that the individual assigns to the things that they do.*

Ethnography

Ethnography is an interpretivist approach to research, which has its roots in early anthropological studies of non-industrialised societies and the workings of their cultures. Ethnography focuses on qualitative data collection:

> *it involves the ethnographer participating, overtly or covertly, in people's daily lives for an extended period of time, watching what happens, listening to what is said, asking questions – in fact, collecting whatever data are available to throw light on the issues that are the focus of the research.*

> Hammersley, M. and Atkinson, P. (1995:1)

In its simplest form ethnography refers to 'recording a way of life', in that the researcher describes the culture and lifestyles of individuals and/or groups. It is hoped that these descriptions will be as accurate a reflection of the subjects' life experiences as is possible. As McNeill (1985:54–5) stated:

> *The idea is not so much to seek causes and explanations, as is often the case with survey-style research, but rather to 'tell it like it is'.*

The sociological researcher who chooses to employ an ethnographic approach will want to gain insight into the lives of the people that he or she is studying. One of the main methods for doing this is through observation.

Observation

To understand the lives of a social group, a researcher may decide to observe that group in its natural setting, either by becoming a member of that group or purely by observing what goes on.

Non-participant observation

Where the researcher chooses to observe the group without becoming involved, for example the relations between employers and employees in a factory, this is known as **non-participant observation**. The data collected may be analysed quantitatively, even though the subject matter is phenomenological, because the researcher can observe and record precise interactions. It is hard for the researcher to record the views and attitudes of the group, unless they occur during observations, but the data recorded should be relatively uninfluenced by relations with the group. An example of research utilising non-participant observation is that of Hargreaves (1967), who investigated the labelling of deviant pupils by teachers by observing classroom interactions. A researcher using non-participant observation as the method will be overt, or known to the group being studied, in order to gain access.

Participant observation

Active involvement in the lives of those under study, such as being accepted as a member of a gang, is known as **participant observation**. It is the most qualitative of all research methods, producing information that is descriptive rather than quantifiable. It enables the researcher to find out detailed data about the thoughts, feelings and behaviour of the group he or she is studying. It allows the researcher to get a feel for the 'reality' of the group's lives. An example of research conducted using the principles of participant observation is that of Pryce (1979), who studied the way of life of members of a West Indian community in Bristol. Participant observation enables the researcher to make sense of the group's 'world', their social reality, without imposing preconceived ideas or expectations upon it. It allows the researcher to have an 'insider's view'.

Participant observation can be carried out using one of two approaches, **covert** (disguised) observation or **overt** (open) observation. The researcher must decide which is the best way to obtain a rich and valid body of data, without influencing the group. Both approaches have their advantages and disadvantages and should be considered carefully before they are used.

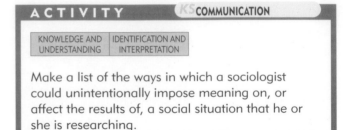

ACTIVITY   KS COMMUNICATION

KNOWLEDGE AND UNDERSTANDING	IDENTIFICATION AND INTERPRETATION

Make a list of the ways in which a sociologist could unintentionally impose meaning on, or affect the results of, a social situation that he or she is researching.

HINTS AND TIPS   *It is interesting to note that while researching the effect of changes on productivity in Hawthorne Electricity Plant, Chicago, Mayo realised that his team of researchers was having the largest effect on production levels. He had employed an open or overt method of non-participant observation, in that the employees knew of the researchers' presence, and this knowledge had encouraged the employees to work harder. The principle of the 'Hawthorne Effect' had become established.*

Covert observation

The researchers' true identity and purpose is concealed from the group under study. An example of research using covert participant observation was Humphries' study of homosexual activity in Tearoom Trade (1970). Humphries investigated illicit meetings between homosexual men in public toilets in America by pretending to be a 'watchqueen' or lookout for the liaisons. Taking this role meant that Humphries could avoid participating in homosexual activity, but still be accepted as part of the group without raising any suspicion about his presence.

The advantages and disadvantages of covert observation are as follows:

■ It does not disturb the natural setting as much as overt observation, because the researcher appears to be another member of the group. Therefore, the information collected is true to the group's way of life. However, if the researcher's cover is blown, then this will affect the social reality of the group and the continuation of the sociologist's research.

■ Activities that the group may not wish to reveal, such as deviant behaviour, can be observed, because the group continues to act normally. Social investigations, such as Humphries', could not be conducted using any other type of research method, because access to the group would have been denied. However, this may also present ethical and potentially legal difficulties for the researcher. Social phenomena that necessitate qualitative inquiry tend to be sensitive or taboo, for example drug-taking or child abuse, and therefore raise issues about the nature of observing people without their consent and obligations to the law.

■ Researchers may become too involved in the group that they are studying and become, at the worst, non-observing participants or subjective in their accounts. The risk of being accepted into a group is that you become like them and therefore research loses its objectivity and becomes bias.

Overt observation

The researcher's identity is revealed to the group under study, but sometimes the true nature of the research is withheld. An example of research conducted using overt participant observation is that of Williams (*Cocaine Kids* (1990)), who investigated the lives of teenage crack-cocaine sellers in New York. Williams was in his thirties when he embarked on his research and therefore had to apply overt participant observation as his method. Also, by revealing his work to those he was studying, he was able to avoid any ethical difficulties, such as being offered illegal drugs.

The advantages and disadvantages of using overt observation are as follows:

■ Any ethical problems about recording information without the group's knowledge are removed. However, the group may behave differently as a response to being observed (the Hawthorne Effect).

■ The researcher is less involved with the group he or she is studying and can therefore be more objective about what is observed. It should be realised, however, that by distancing him or herself from the group, the researcher might fail to get a 'real life' understanding of the group's behaviour and beliefs.

■ Access to, and acceptance by, a group can be difficult for the researcher attempting covert observation, i.e. the researcher will have to look and behave like a member of that group. Overt observation allows the researcher to access the group on their own terms. However, by acknowledging that he or she is a researcher, the researcher risks being excluded by the group from witnessing specific behaviour or from collecting certain information.

Participant observation	
Advantages	**Disadvantages**
The group under observation is unaffected in its behaviour.	The researcher may affect the working of the group.
Provides insights into the 'real lives' of social groups.	Difficult to make generalisations based on observations.
Detailed qualitative information.	Time-consuming.
Valid information based on actions, norms and values of the actors within the group.	The researcher chooses which information to record, resulting in a potentially subjective account.
	The researcher may become a participant rather than an observer, resulting in a biased account.
	It is difficult to record information accurately.
	It can be dangerous.

Figure 2.22   *Advantages and disadvantages of participant observation*

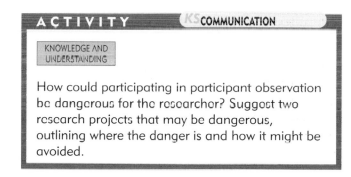

ACTIVITY   **COMMUNICATION**

KNOWLEDGE AND UNDERSTANDING

How could participating in participant observation be dangerous for the researcher? Suggest two research projects that may be dangerous, outlining where the danger is and how it might be avoided.

Conducting observational research

The process involved with carrying out observational research may be more dynamic than with quantitative methods, but it requires as much preparation and rigour in its application. The following stages should be followed to achieve maximum validity:

1   **Topic choice** – Decide who and what is to be studied, for example teenagers into the rave scene.

2   **Assess methodology** – Evaluate whether your choice of topic is best served by investigation through participant observation, i.e. will participant observation reveal more information about that topic than an interview or questionnaire?

3 **Access** – Find a group that you can successfully join. Use contacts to introduce you or start to 'hang around' with potential groups.

4 **Define your role** – Decide on overt or covert observation. If you reveal your identity, decide how much information you will give to the study group about your research. If you decide to disguise your identity, construct a convincing cover story about who you are and where you came from.

5 **Recording information** – Once within the group you must remain objective and receptive to all that is going on around you. You will have the doubly difficult role of being a member of the group, but also having to document its way of life. For covert observations make inconspicuous notes about the group's actions and attitudes as often as possible during your time with them (e.g. by writing up in the toilet), but at the latest by the end of the day. Overt observation allows more obvious note-taking or even the use of video and/or tape recorders. Once a rapport has been established, overt observation may allow for key group members to be interviewed.

6 **Analysing information** – Patterns of behaviour may be observed within the group and put into a theoretical framework. The way of life of the group should be portrayed accurately and any possible sociological ideas/concepts relating to this way of life inferred.

7 **Anonymity** – All groups should have their identities hidden, unless you have asked for their permission to reveal who they are.

> **HINTS AND TIPS** *Conducting sociological research using participant observation may be difficult if time is limited, for example for an A Level coursework project. It may be easier to use non-participant observation, which allows an investigation into a qualitative area, but does not have the problems of access, time and ethics.*

Expressive documents

Any pieces of information that are created by individuals about their personal experiences are important for sociological research, because they provide insight into social relations. As Plummer (1983) argues, these useful pieces of information (also known as **life documents**) could be anything from a letter written to a friend or graffiti scrawled on a wall to a journal kept about daily events. **Expressive documents**, qualitative pieces of information that tell us something about someone's life and feelings from their own perspective, provide an interpretivist approach to research.

The use of expressive documents was first noted in the work of Thomas and Znaniecki (1918), who studied the life story of a Polish peasant, Wladek Wisniewski, who migrated to Germany and then to America. Their study provided valuable insight into the life of a poor immigrant to the USA at the beginning of the twentieth century. The methodology, however, was challenged by positivist sociology for its lack of scientific application and consequently became less popular until recently. This said, some interesting studies were conducted using expressive documents in the 1970s and 1980s, such as Lewis' research on a poor rural family in Mexico (1970), Oakley's study of housework (1974) and Harding's investigations into the criminal underworld (1981). The changes to research methodology in the 1990s, such as the triangulation of methods and theoretical perspective determining the method, has enabled expressive documents to find new credibility. In fact, the government's annual Family Expenditure Survey (1998) was based on the diaries of 6,400 households. Each household was asked to record spending for two weeks and then to take part in a follow-up interview about income. Using this method the government was able to compare household expenditure between social groups, over time and what was purchased.

Two methods for collecting data that utilise the expressive document approach are:

1 **Diaries** – These are a personal record of events in that person's life. They are kept regularly and are often kept a secret. As a sociological method it provides detailed accounts about the life, thoughts and experiences of an individual. However, it does have the problem of being a **selective** account, in that the respondent decides what information to include, rather than the researcher. Also, the researcher should try to ensure that the diary (usually recorded for between one and two weeks) is **typical** or reflects life as it usually happens. If the diary is untypical, then it will not present a valid or representative picture of that individual's life.

2   **Biographies** – These are the life stories of respondents, recorded through an interview or conversation, to elicit detailed information about the individual's life and interpretations of experiences. A biography can add depth and 'reality' to research, making the sociologist focus on the person rather than the 'theory'. However, biographies are not representative and may therefore be challenged by all the quantitative arguments. Also, the accuracy of the respondents' memory when recounting events is always open to doubt.

The advantages of using expressive documents as a research method are as follows:

1   The data collected can provide validity and depth to a piece of contemporary sociological research. For example, when Valerie Hay (1997) investigated the friendship groups of girls in two London schools, she examined the 'secret' notes that they wrote to each other and the diaries that they kept (as well as observing their behaviour), which provided insight into the girls' relationships with each other.

2   It may be the only way to collect information about events or attitudes that occurred in the past. For example, historical documents, such as letters or diaries written by the suffragettes at the turn of the twentieth century, may be the only source of data to reveal how people actually felt and the social relationships that they experienced.

3   The researcher does not have to be present to find out information, therefore this method is less time-consuming in its collection stage than observation or interviewing. However, it should be noted that the recording of an individual's life through such methods as a diary can take many years.

The disadvantages of using expressive documents are as follows:

1   The information recorded by the individual may not be an accurate reflection of events. For example, a student with a crush on his or her teacher may not record an accurate account of social interactions with that teacher in a diary; the account may be biased. Therefore, the validity of this method may be challenged, as it may not reflect the 'reality' if the situation. However, it should be noted that interactionists would argue

that these interpretations of events have interest for sociologists.

2   The information collected will not be reliable, because it focuses on the individual and is unlikely to be a representative sample. Therefore, expressive documents cannot be used to make generalisations or universal statements about society or the individuals within it.

Conducting research involving expressive documents

When embarking on research employing expressive documents, the researcher must approach it with as much preparation and rigour as other methods. The following stages should be followed to achieve maximum validity:

1   **Topic choice** – Decide who and what is to be studied, for example the elderly and the daily routines that they follow.

2   **Assess methodology** – Evaluate whether your choice of topic is best served by investigation through expressive documents, i.e. will a diary kept by an elderly person reveal more information about that topic than an interview or non-participant observation?

3   **Access** – Find a group from whom you can successfully request information. It may be difficult to find people who are willing to commit so much time. Keeping a diary or recording a life history (biography) is incredibly time-consuming for the people involved.

4   **Recording/collecting information** – Decide whether to provide a clear framework for the respondents in your research. For example, if you require them to keep a diary, you may decide to provide them with detailed information about how to keep it. However, some interpretivist researchers argue that a structured framework imposes meaning on the data and thereby reduces validity. If the research involves documents that were written/collected in the past, make sure that the respondent is as thorough as possible in his or her declaration of them.

5   **Analysing information** – The data collected should provide rich and detailed information about human elements of experience in individual lives. Therefore, generalisations will not be a desired outcome, but insight into people's lives will be.

6 **Anonymity** – All groups should have their identities hidden, unless you have asked for their permission to reveal who they are.

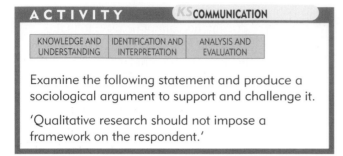

ACTIVITY KS COMMUNICATION

| KNOWLEDGE AND UNDERSTANDING | IDENTIFICATION AND INTERPRETATION | ANALYSIS AND EVALUATION |

Examine the following statement and produce a sociological argument to support and challenge it.

'Qualitative research should not impose a framework on the respondent.'

Case studies

Case studies employ interpretivist principles to examine an individual, a group or a social institution in detail to elicit valid information. A variety of qualitative and quantitative methods may be chosen from as the basis of the research, as Howe (1994:68) elucidates:

> *A case study is an in-depth examination, often through direct primary data-gathering methods such as participant observation, of a particular institution or (in the guise of the life document) of an individual.*

Case studies have been challenged for not being representative of a population; however, this approach has never claimed to be representative or reliable. Therefore, this method could be seen as having the disadvantages of not being able to make generalisations about social life, not being replicable and not being objective. However, case studies do provide valuable insight into specific social phenomena, such as a single parent's way of life. Therefore, the advantages of using this approach are that it could act as the basis for a larger study by giving the researcher ideas about areas to investigate further, or it could highlight a broad typicality to similar social areas.

Researchers who decide to use case studies must adhere to the following steps, according to Brewer (1994):

1 State the relevance of the case study to other cases.
2 State the area of focus, areas ignored and provide a justification for this.

3 State the theoretical framework.
4 State problems encountered when conducting the research.
5 Justify interpretations of the data collected.
6 Show how the context may have affected the respondents.

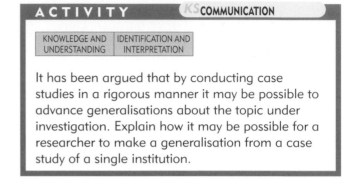

ACTIVITY KS COMMUNICATION

| KNOWLEDGE AND UNDERSTANDING | IDENTIFICATION AND INTERPRETATION |

It has been argued that by conducting case studies in a rigorous manner it may be possible to advance generalisations about the topic under investigation. Explain how it may be possible for a researcher to make a generalisation from a case study of a single institution.

Sociological research has utilised case studies to examine a variety of social areas. For example, Goffman (1968) investigated the definitions of mental illness that an asylum in the USA gave to its patients, by entering that institution as a covert participant observer (employee). Lane and Roberts (1971) examined a strike in a UK factory by employing a variety of methods, such as surveys of the strikers, interviews with the management and content analysis of newspaper reports on the event. Other areas in which case studies have been employed are education (Ball, 1981), marriage (Rapoports, 1971) and even closed-circuit television (Pawson and Tilly, 1996).

Triangulation

Triangulation is when a researcher decides to use a variety of research methods. For example, a study may be conducted based on observation and structured interviews, or closed questionnaires and diaries. The reason for employing triangulation is that different types of data can be collected, which enables the researcher to do one or more of the following:

■ Support quantitative data with qualitative examples, thereby providing reliability and validity in a study.

■ Examine the reliability of the research using different sources.

- Cross-reference the researcher's interpretations to other data collected to check for accuracy.

- Provide balance between methods; one may be weaker than another in that particular area of research.

Triangulation, however, is time-consuming and expensive, as Barker (*The Making of a Moonie – Choice or Brainwashing?* (1984)) discovered when she embarked on research into the Unification Church (Moonies). Barker decided to use in-depth interviews, participant observation and questionnaires to investigate the Moonies' beliefs and the media hype about them 'brainwashing' members. She was actually invited to study the Moonies by the Church itself, which was concerned about the representation it were getting in the press. This allowed Barker access and co-operation, which was unusual but necessary, considering the research took six years.

Barker's choice of research methods was based on her desire really to understand the Moonies. She interviewed a random sample of 30 members for six to eight hours about themselves, their joining and life in the Church. She then lived with members of the Church at different centres in the UK and abroad and attended workshops and seminars. Barker believed that employing these ethnographic methods would enable her to attain a 'true to life' knowledge of the Unification Church. This knowledge was used to justify a quantitative approach. It provided her with the appropriate questions to ask in a 41-page questionnaire that was issued two years after the start of her study. The data from the questionnaire enabled Barker to compare the Moonies with the UK population, on characteristics such as class, age and sex.

ACTIVITY   KS COMMUNICATION

KNOWLEDGE AND UNDERSTANDING	IDENTIFICATION AND INTERPRETATION

Triangulation was the only research approach Barker could use to obtain the information she wanted to find out; however, there were many problems she could have encountered with each of the methods. Write a list of the methodological difficulties Barker may have encountered with each research method.

Difficulties of research methodology

Value freedom

Max Weber based his methodological approach on the idea of **value freedom**. He argued that all sociological research should be free of political or moral beliefs. Positivist sociologists, in their belief that social facts can be studied scientifically, support Weber's idealism. They suggest that social facts can and should be investigated without reference to the researcher's own values. However, the idea of 'value-free' research has been widely debated in sociology.

Interpretivists argue that the values of the researcher affect many elements of methodology, from the choice of topic to the type of research method employed, therefore value freedom is not possible. Sociologists are social beings and are therefore subject to socialisation into the norms and values of their society, which will inevitable affect their choices as a researcher. Becker (1967) stated that sociologists would always present a biased account of their research, because as social beings they can never be neutral in their outlook.

The debate of value freedom in sociology has moved on. Many sociologists have accepted that research cannot be value-free and are claiming that it should not pretend to be so (Gouldner, 1973). Sociologists have been encouraged to declare their personal and political beliefs, in an attempt to show the values and possible bias within the research. The acceptance that the researcher shapes and is reflected in the research (and affects the research) is known as **reflexivity**. Sociologists who practise reflexivity examine their own values in relation to their research to establish the extent to which the findings reflect their beliefs. It is argued that the critical awareness of reflexivity brings more validity to social research, by creating a more honest picture of social reality.

In conclusion, the debate over value freedom continues between positivists and interpretivists. However, McNeill (1985:123–4) offered an alternative view by stating that values will have some effect on research methodology, but should not bias the way in which the method is employed:

6 *Choice of topic to study will be value-laden, but methods must avoid all personal bias and in this sense be value-free.*

Ethics

6 *Ethical constraints: factors which prevent a particular method or research study being used because of a belief that it would be morally wrong.*

Lawson, T. and Garrod, J. (1996:89)

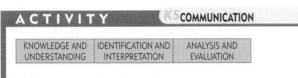

KNOWLEDGE AND UNDERSTANDING	IDENTIFICATION AND INTERPRETATION	ANALYSIS AND EVALUATION

Choose one piece of feminist sociological research, one piece of positivist sociological research and one piece of interpretivist research. Assess how much the researcher's values may have influenced each piece of methodology. Compare the pieces of research on levels of value freedom. Which piece of research appears to have the most value freedom and why?

Sociologists should consider the effects of their research on the people being studied before they start. The aim of sociological research may be to get a better understanding of the world, but not at the cost of affecting those being studied: this would be seen as immoral. Consequently, laboratory experiments are not used in sociology, because they directly affect the subject. For example, if a researcher favoured a positivist approach and wanted to conduct an experiment on the effects of material deprivation in childhood on role allocation in later life, it would be considered unethical to construct a situation of deprivation for the children. The researcher would be expected to wait for incidences of material deprivation to occur and use these as part of the study, rather than impose a situation on the respondent that affects his or her life.

Controlling human behaviour as part of a research project is not the only ethical consideration; the following questions should be posed before embarking on the study:

1   Have all the participants consented to take part in the research? Is it all right to study people without their knowledge to further understanding?

2   Will the researcher witness any illegal activities? Is it the duty of the researcher to report illegal activities to the police?

3   Has the anonymity of the participants been maintained in the final report? Will the report affect the participants?

The researcher, having deliberated these questions, will have to decide whether the **ethical constraints**, such as participant consent, are worth accepting for the final outcome of the study. Participant observation, for example, would not work if the people being studied were aware of that fact. Consequently, some researchers believe that this method is an invasion of privacy and unethical, while others believe that the negligible influence of the researcher and the rich and valid data collected override the morality issue.

Practical constraints

Apart from the practicality of choosing an accessible research topic, the other main practical constraints that affect what research is possible are:

■ time

■ labour power

■ cost.

The researcher should consider the time available to conduct the study and choose the research method appropriately. For example, if the government directs the researcher to produce an account of British attitudes towards teachers' pay in two months, they would be wise to use a closed questionnaire, rather than an unstructured interview, because it is quicker and gets the desired results.

Labour power is also a crucial factor in determining the type of research carried out. If the sociologist has a large team of researchers working on the study, then time-consuming methods, such as unstructured interviews, can be considered. If the researcher is working alone, then this may result in a smaller study, using less time-consuming methods, such as questionnaires, or concentrating on a specific group of people through participant observation or case studies.

Of all the practical constraints, money is the biggest dictator of the type and scale of research that can be conducted. Without money, then time and labour power are limited. For example, a research team will expect to be paid for its work and a lone ethnographer will need financial support while getting to know his or her subject.

HINTS AND TIPS   *When conducting your own research, think about how much it costs to get photocopies of your questionnaires or secondary data. Your project will be small by comparison to some sociological studies and therefore cheaper, but funding it may still be a problem.*

Alternative sources of knowledge for sociological research

Source	Examples
Broadsheet and tabloid newspapers/magazines	*The Independent, The Guardian, The Times* and even *The Mirror* are all useful sources of data. Look out for relevant articles and examples of research.
Television/films	Documentaries, such as *Heart of the Matter* and *Panorama*, soap operas, such as *EastEnders* and feature films, such as *ID*, all provide useful secondary data and sometimes material on research methods.
Central Statistics Office (CSO)	Provides up-to-date statistics on the UK. CSO Library, Cardiff Road, Newport, Gwent NP9 1XG
The Internet	Conduct a word search of your research topic using a web browser and apply relevant material. Alternatively, construct a website and use the Internet to conduct your own research.

Figure 2.23   Alternative sources of information

TASK

COMMUNICATION, INFORMATION TECHNOLOGY, APPLICATION OF NUMBER

KNOWLEDGE AND UNDERSTANDING	IDENTIFICATION AND INTERPRETATION	ANALYSIS AND EVALUATION

Hypothesis – 'The World Wide Web (WWW) has made all other forms of social research redundant.'

Context – The world is a constantly changing place. Contemporary western society has made great technological breakthroughs in accessing information. The WWW has enabled a great deal of people to have super-fast access to what is effectively the world's library. Consequently, it could be argued that all primary and secondary research could be conducted on the WWW, such as interviews and questionnaires, or literature searches.

However, qualitative approaches are harder or impossible to conduct on the WWW, such as participant observation. Also, the researcher may reach only a bias sample, i.e. those who have a computer and those who are interested in the research area. All of these issues should be addressed within a context of the social construction of knowledge. Is knowledge a reflection of hegemony (Marxism), or value consensus (functionalism), or patriarchy (feminism)? Conduct a literature search to discover which sociological theories and studies have addressed the issue of the social construction of knowledge. Apply what the WWW is, what it can do and what it offers within this context.

Method – Conduct both a quantitative and qualitative piece of research on the WWW about using the Internet as a research tool. It may be easier to create your own website with chat page, in order to place a questionnaire on it and conduct interviews on-line. Record all the research pros and cons as you go along, such as poor response rate or false respondents. Remember to concentrate on the way in which the research is working (representativeness, reliability and validity), rather than the data itself.

Evaluation – Assess the advantages and disadvantages of using all the sociological research methods on the WWW. Compare and contrast traditional sampling methods to those applicable when conducting research on the WWW. Examine the successes and problems with using the quantitative and qualitative techniques you applied to your research. Link these evaluations to the idea of the social construction of knowledge and research bias.

KNOWLEDGE AND
UNDERSTANDING

Use what you have learned from Area 2 to write a one-sentence definition of the following research methods:

Experiment	Open questionnaires
Comparative study	Unstructured interviews
Official statistics	Expressive documents
Closed questionnaires	Case studies
Structured interviews	Conversation analysis
Content analysis	Observation – covert/overt

Area summary

Sociology is fundamentally linked with research. Sociological research enables society to be informed about its citizens, institutions, values and belief systems, in a general or specific way. Research can be primary or secondary, quantitative or qualitative, positivist or interpretivist, valid or reliable, but whichever approach is employed, it must be accurate, representative and appropriate.

Positivism		Interpretivism	
Method	**Qualities**	**Qualities**	**Method**
Experiment	Quantitative	Qualitative	Participant observation (covert)
Hypothetico-deductive	Scientific	Phenomenological (anti-scientific)	Observation (overt)
Comparative	Macro	Micro	Case studies
Closed questionnaires	Universal/generalisable	Specific/relative	Diaries
Structured interviews	Reliable	Valid	Unstructured interviews
Official statistics	Structuralist (Marxism/ functionalism)	Behaviouralist (Interactionism/ ethnomethodology)	Open questionnaires
		Social action (Weberian) Scientific realism Feminisms Content analysis (postmodernism)	
		Triangulation	

Figure 2.24 Sociological research methodology

Definitions

Bias	Not presenting representative or accurate (reliable/valid) data in research
Closed questions	Questions that have categorised responses, such as 'yes' or 'no'
Codification	When the researcher gives a value to each answer on a questionnaire, which allows responses to be quantified more easily
Concomitant variation	Refers to a relationship existing between two factors, with one factor potentially being the causal one
Covert observation	A term used to describe how a researcher watches those being studied without them being aware of the researcher's presence
Deconstruction (1)	A term used in conversation analysis to refer to the breaking down of conversation to reveal the 'reality' of interaction
Deconstruction (2)	This is a concept applied by Derrida to text, in that there is no meaning in text other than in its relationship to other texts. Therefore all texts are ultimately ambiguous
Discourse	Conversation
Dramaturgical	A sociological approach developed by Goffman, which assumes that social life is like a play or drama in which humans take on different roles
Empirical research	Information or data collected from primary research, such as questionnaires or interviews
Ethical constraints	Moral beliefs that stop research, such as it being wrong to experiment on humans
Expressive documents	Qualitative pieces of information that tell us something about someone's life from the individual's own perspective
Falsification theory	Refers to the way in which science develops through researchers putting forward conjectures, or ideas, about their subject matter, which they then try to refute, or disprove. If they cannot do so, these unrefuted conjectures provide the basis for scientific theories
Interpretivism	Sociological theories that emphasise the analysis of the individual rather than the social structure, such as interactionism
Life documents	Any pieces of information created by individuals about their personal experiences, such as letters
Non-participant observation	A research method that involves the researcher observing a group, but without becoming involved
Open-ended questions	Questions that allow the respondent to answer the question freely with a detailed response
Overt observation	A term referring to a researcher who reveals his/her identity to those being studied
Participant observation	A type of research based on the researcher becoming actively involved in the lives of those being studied

Phenomenology	Approach that argues that each individual has unique experiences, but that all interaction is based on common-sense understandings that everybody knows
Pilot	A term used when a research tool is 'tried out' on a small scale to test whether it will work
Positivism	The application of scientific method to the investigation of phenomena
Primary data	Information collected by the researcher
Qualitative research	Investigations that collect information shown in written form, such as interview transcripts
Quantitative research	Investigations that collect information shown in numerical form, such as statistics
Reflexivity	This can be defined as a growth of critical awareness
Reliability	Research can be repeated and the same results collected
Representativeness	How far the sample reflects accurately the population it was taken from
Researcher-administered	Refers to when the researcher conducts the research and completes the data with a respondent, such as in a structured interview
Sample frame	The list of the population that has been chosen for the sample
Sampling	To select a representative section of the population being researched
Secondary data	Information used by sociologists, but collected by other researchers
Selective	A term used to refer to data that has been chosen by someone for their own reasons
Self-administered	Refers to when a questionnaire is completed by the respondent
Standpoint research	A type of research, such as a feminist approach, that entails taking a particular 'stand' on, or view of, society, which challenges the assumptions inherent in traditional sociology
Structural	Sociological theories that emphasise the analysis of the social structure rather than the individual, such as Marxism
Triangulation	The application of more than one research method when conducting research
Typical	A reflection of life as it normally happens
Validity	Research measures what it set out to measure
Value freedom	The degree to which research has not been affected by the researcher's values and beliefs
Verstehen	A Weberian concept, refering to the way in which social action results from the meaning of interactions; it literally means 'to understand' and results from empathy with others

Data response questions

As long as the process of selecting and interviewing a sample is carried out with proper care, the information collected from it will provide a reliable guide to the larger group from which it is drawn. Bowley, a pioneer of sampling in social research, carried out a series of surveys on poverty in English towns from 1912 on; in the report of his first survey he discussed the errors due to sampling, and was able to show that they were relatively small... The value of sampling is no longer in question. The method is widely used by research workers in all sorts of subjects, from agriculture to medicine, as well as by sociologists.

Young, M. and Willmott, P. (1983:201–2)
Family and Kinship in East London.
London, Routledge and Kegan Paul.

The interview data was augmented with extended participant observation. This included attending council meetings, election campaigns, demonstrations and related forums. This dimension of the research aimed to provide an insight into how issues of race featured in the daily workings of the local state and the forms of dialogue and consultation that were taking place between the local political sphere and minority organisations and representatives.

Solomos, J. and Back, L. (1995:216) *Race, Politics and Social Change.*
London, Routledge.

Given these different ways of understanding intelligence, you will naturally ask where our sympathies lie and how they shape this book. We will be drawing most heavily from the classical tradition. That body of scholarship represents an immense and rigorously analyzed body of knowledge. By accepted standards of what constitutes scientific evidence and scientific proof, the classical tradition has in our view given the world a treasure of information that has been largely ignored in trying to understand contemporary policy issues. Moreover, because our topic is the relationship of human abilities to public policy, we will be dealing with relationships that are based on aggregated data, which is where the classical tradition has the most to offer.

Herrnstein, R. and Murray, C. (1994:19)
The Bell Curve. New York, Free Press.

a   Explain briefly what is meant by triangulation. (Item B)   **(2)**

b   Outline the main considerations for a researcher using a sample. (Item A)   **(5)**

> **GUIDANCE**   *It is worth 'brainstorming' this question when you first read it. Write a list of all the terms associated with sampling, such as population, representativeness and the types of samples. This information will help you explain how a researcher achieves an accurate and appropriate sample.*
>
> | KNOWLEDGE AND UNDERSTANDING | IDENTIFICATION AND INTERPRETATION |
> |---|---|

c   Assess the strengths and weaknesses of using scientific research methods in sociological investigations. (Item C)   **(9)**

> **GUIDANCE**   *It is important to remember that you **must** present both sides of the argument relating to scientific/quantitative research methods, however much you may disagree with one argument. Evaluation requires a balanced conclusion based on all the evidence.*
>
> | KNOWLEDGE AND UNDERSTANDING | IDENTIFICATION AND INTERPRETATION | ANALYSIS AND EVALUATION |
> |---|---|---|
>
> *Do not be tempted to provide detailed information on the strengths of qualitative methods; the question is not asking you to do this and you will lose Interpretation marks if you do (not to mention valuable time). However, you may refer to alternative methods when explaining the weaknesses of scientific methods in the social sciences.*
>
> *Consider applying information on social/historical events, such as the use of human experimentation in Nazi Germany, linking it carefully to the question for Application marks.*
>
> *Lastly, it is worth citing examples of research which have employed scientific research methods, such as Durkheim's **La Suicide**, in order to attain full Knowledge and Understanding marks.*

Structured questions

a   Identify and explain two advantages for a researcher witnessing social behaviour.   **(4)**

b   Briefly explain two methods which are usually associated with positivist sociologists.   **(4)**

c   Outline the reasons given by interpretivist sociologists for using unobtrusive research methods.   **(7)**

d   Assess the advantages and disadvantages of quantitative research methods in sociology.   **(10)**
                                                                                                                   (25)

Essay titles

1   Evaluate the advantages and disadvantages of using interviews in different types of sociological research.   **(25)**
                                                                                                                   (AEB, November 1993)

2   Outline and assess the advantages and disadvantages of primary and secondary data as sources of information in sociological research.   **(25)**

(AEB, June 1994)

3   'No matter how well designed research may be, if the sample is unrepresentative, the results, and any generalisations made from them, may be flawed.'

Assess the extent to which sample selection influences the quality of data collected. Illustrate your answer with examples from research with which you are familiar.   **(25)**

(IBS, June 1997)

4   'Some sociological studies are not restricted to one research method but employ a range of methods in the pursuit of validity.'

Examine the strengths and weaknesses of a multiple methods approach to sociological research. Illustrate your answer with examples from studies employing more than one method.   **(25)**

GUIDANCE *Begin by interpreting the question, which in this case is making reference to the advantages and disadvantages of* **triangulation**. *Introduce the essay by showing that you fully understand the question and the terminology used in it, such as validity and multiple methods. This displays your Interpretation skills. Also, attempt to make brief reference to a piece of research that uses triangulation, such as Eileen Barker's* **The Making of a Moonie**, *to show your Knowledge, Understanding and Application. You should also decide at the beginning of the essay whether:*

a   one method **is** *actually restrictive to sociological research*

b   validity is the actual outcome of triangulation

c   the strengths of triangulation outweigh the weaknesses.

By making these decisions at the beginning of the essay your evidence in the main body will have reflected your arguments fluently. It also means that your conclusion is much easier to write, because you know that it is based on your first decisions about the title.

The main body of the essay should demonstrate your Knowledge and Understanding of the content of the essay by evaluating the strengths and weaknesses of using triangulation as a research method. In other words, show the strengths and weaknesses of using different research methods in the same piece of research, using examples from research that has employed that method. Also, because the title suggests that validity is the main reason for using triangulation, demonstrate how using multiple methods does not always result in either valid or reliable data. Lastly, if you have employed triangulation in any research/projects during your course, you can, and should, make reference to it in a relevant way to obtain Application marks.

Evaluation should have been used throughout the essay; however, the conclusion is the place to weigh up your argument in relation to the title, considering the evidence you have presented in the main body of the essay. Make reference to the decisions you made about the title at the beginning of the essay, such as 'Is one method inferior to triangulation?' but provide a little more detail related to a study or argument applied in the main body of the essay. Lastly, if you can apply a relevant piece of information that is up to date, such as a quotation or data from research, this will leave the examiner in no doubt of your sociological skills.

(IBS, June 1997)

Further reading and references

Hammersley, M. (Ed.) (1997) *Social Research: Philosophy, Politics and Practice*. London, Sage.
A detailed book on the less traditional approaches to sociological research. A useful text for the more confident, inquisitive and 'aspiring researcher' student.

Kidd et al. (1998) *Readings in Sociology*. Oxford, Heinemann.
This is an unusual, but incredibly valuable, text for AS/A level students, because it presents extracts from original sociological research in an easy-to-understand format. It provides students with the opportunity to see exactly what the researchers themselves aimed to discover and how.

Kirby et al. (1997) *Sociology in Perspective*. Oxford, Heinemann.
This book provides a clear, well-structured and accurate account of research methods. It is particularly useful in providing references of further researches that could be used in contexts for coursework.

McNeill, P. (1985) *Research Methods*. London, Tavistock Publications.
A straightforward account of different sociological research methods, although the more contemporary approaches have yet to be included. This text is especially useful to those students who need a bit more insight into the basic research methodology.

Internet sites

http://www.socioweb.com/-markbl/socioweb/ (Socioweb) is a useful website, providing access to information on research methods.

http://www.sociresearch.com/ (Research resources for the Social Sciences) provides useful resources when embarking on sociological research for your coursework.

http://www.socsurvey.ac.uk/sru/sru/html (Social research update) is a full-text quarterly journal about social research.

http://www.scpr.ac.uk/cass (CASS: Centre for Applied Social Surveys) will provide information on methods and formats of data collection.

Alternatively, go to a search engine, such as 'Yahoo', and type 'sociology' or http://www.cla.ufl.edu/users/gthursby/socsci/index.htm and you will be provided with various Internet sites to choose from.

Bibliography

Arber, S. (1993) 'The Research Process', in N. Gilbert (Ed.) *Researching Social Life*. London, Sage.
Arnot, M., David, M. and Weiner, G. (1996) *Educational Reforms and Gender Equality in Schools*. Manchester, Equal Opportunities Commission.
Atkinson, W.M., Kessel, N. and Dalgaard, J. (1975) 'The Comparability of Suicide Rates', *British Journal of Psychiatry*, Vol. 127.

Ball, S. (1981) *Beachside Comprehensive: A Case Study of Secondary Schooling*. Cambridge, Cambridge University Press.

Barker, E. (1984) *The Making of a Moonie: Choice or Brainwashing*. Oxford, Blackwell.

Becker, H. (1967) 'Whose Side Are We On?', *Social Problems*, Vol. 14.

Bell, J. (1987) *Doing Your Research Project*. Buckingham, Open University Press.

Benedict, H. (1992) *Virgin or Vamp: How the Press Covers Sex Crimes*. Oxford, Oxford University Press.

Bilton, T., Bonnett, K., Jones, P., Skinner, D., Stanworth, M. and Webster, A. (1996) *Introductory Sociology*. Basingstoke, Macmillan.

Booth, C. (1902) *Life and Labour of the People in London*, London, Williams and Northgate.

Brewer, J. (1994) 'The Ethnographic Critique of Ethnography: Sectarianism in the RUC', *Sociology*, Vol. 28, No. 1, pp. 231–44.

Bullock, A., Stallybrass, O. and Trombley, S. (1988) *The Fontana Dictionary of Modern Thought*. London, Harper Collins.

Canon, L., Higginbotham, E. and Leung, M. (1991) 'Race and class bias in qualitative research on women' in M. Fonow and J. Cook (Eds.) *Beyond Methodology: Feminist Scholarship as Lived Research*. Bloomington, Indiana University Press.

Dobash, R. E. and Dobash, R. P. (1980) *Violence Against Wives: A Case Against Patriarchy*. Shepton Mallett, Open Books.

Dunsmuir, A. and Williams, L. (1994) *How To Do Social Research*. London, Collins Educational.

Durkheim, E. (1897) *Suicide: A Study in Sociology*. London, Routledge and Kegan Paul.

Fletcher, R. (1981) *Sociology: The Study of Social Systems*. London, Batsford.

Garfinkel, H. (1967) *Studies in Ethnomethodology*. Englewood Cliffs, Prentice-Hall.

Gavron, H. (1966) *The Captive Wife*, London, Routledge.

Glasgow University Media Group (1976) *Bad News*. London, Routledge and Kegan Paul.

Goffman, E. (1968) *Asylums*. Harmondsworth, Penguin.

Gouldner, A. W. (1973) *For Sociology: Renewal and Critique in Sociology Today*. Harmondsworth, Penguin.

Hammersley, M. and Atkinson, P. (1995) *Ethnography: Principles in Practice*. London, Routledge.

Harding, S (1981) *Feminism and Methodology*, Milton Keynes, Open University Press.

Hargreaves, D. H. (1967) *Social Relations in Secondary School*. London, Routledge and Kegan Paul.

Hay, V. (1997) *The Company She Keeps: An Ethnography of Girls' Friendships*. Buckingham, Open University Press.

Herrnstein, R. J. and Murray, C. (1994) *The Bell Curve: Intelligence and Class Structure in American Life*. New York, Free Press Paperbacks.

Hill Collins, P. (1991) 'Learning from the outsider within: the sociological significance of black feminist thought' in M. Fonow and J. Cook (Eds.) *Beyond Methodology: Feminist Scholarship as Lived Research*. Bloomington, Indiana University Press.

Hite, S. (1994) *The Hite Report on the Family: Growing Up under Patriarchy*. London, Bloomsbury Press.

Howe, N. (1994) *Advanced Practical Sociology*. Surrey, Thomas Nelson.

Humphries, L. (1970) *Tearoom Trade*. London, Duckworth.

Kelly, L. (1988) *Surviving Sexual Violence*. Cambridge, Polity.

Kirby, M., Kidd, W., Koubel, F., Barter, J., Hope, T., Kirton, A., Madry, N., Manning, P. and Triggs, K. (1997) *Sociology in Perspective*. Oxford, Heinemann.

Kuhn, T. (1970) *The Structure of Scientific Revolutions*. Chicago, University of Chicago Press.

Laing, R. D. (1976) *The Politics of the Family*, Harmondsworth, Penguin.

Lane, J. K. (1985) *A Practical Guide to A-Level Sociology*. Surrey, Thomas Nelson.

Lane, T. and Roberts, K. (1971) *Strike at Pilkingtons*. London, Collins.

Laslett, P. (1972) *Household and Family in Past Time*, Cambridge, Cambridge University Press.

Lawson, T. and Garrod, J. (1996) *The Complete A–Z Sociology Handbook*. London, Hodder & Stoughton.

Lewis, O. (1970) *The Children of Sanchez*, New York, Random House.

Mayo, E. (1933) *The Human Problems of an Industrial Civilisation*, Basingstoke, Macmillan.

McNeill, P. (1985) *Research Methods (Society Now)*. London, Tavistock Publications.

McNeill, P. and Townley, C. (1981) *Fundamentals of Sociology*. London, Hutchinson.

McRobbie, A. (1983) 'Teenage Girls, Jackie and the Ideology of Adolescent Feminity,' in B. Waites, T. Bennet and G. Martin (Eds.) *Popular Culture: Past and Present*. London, Croom Helm.

Mies, M. (1997) 'Towards a Methodology for Feminist Research' in Hammersley, M. (Ed.) *Social Research: Philosophy, Politics and Practice*. London, Sage.

Milgram, S. (1965) 'Some Conditions of Obedience and Disobedience to Authority', *Human Relations* 18:57–74.

O'Donnell, M. (1997) *Introduction to Sociology*. Surrey, Nelson.

Pawson, R. and Tilly, N. (1996) 'How (and how not) to design research to inform policy making', in Samson, C. and South, N. (Eds.) *The Social Construction of Social Policy*. Basingstoke, Macmillan.

Popper, K. (1959) *The Logic of Scientific Discovery*. London, Hutchinson.

Plummer, K. (1983) *Documents of Life: An Introduction to the Problems and Literature of the Humanistic Method*. London, George Allen and Unwin.

Pryce, K. (1979) *Endless Pressure*. Harmondsworth, Penguin.

Rapoport, R. and Rapoport, R. N. (1971) *Dual-Career Families*. Harmondsworth, Penguin.

Rowntree Foundation (1995) *Inquiry into Income and Wealth*. Joseph Rowntree Foundation.

Sayer, A. (1997) *Method in Social Science: A Realist Approach*. London, Routledge.

Scully, D. (1988) *Understanding Sexual Violence*. London, Harper Collins.

Solomos, J. and Back, L. (1995) *Race, Politics and Social Change*. London, Routledge.

Thomas, W. L. and Znaniecki, F. (1918) *The Polish Peasant in Europe and America*. New York, Dover Publications.

Weber, M. (1905) *The Protestant Ethic and the Spirit of Capitalism*. London, Unwin (1985).

Williams, T. (1990) *Cocaine Kids*. London, Bloomsbury.

Women In Journalism Research Committee (1996) *Women in the News: Does Sex Change the Way a Newspaper Thinks?* London, Women in Journalism.

Young, M. and Willmott, P. (1957) *Family and Kinship in East London*. London, Routledge and Kegan Paul.

Area 3

Social Stratification and Differentiation

This area covers:

■ The nature of social stratification and differentiation

■ The relevance of social stratification and differentiation in western industrial societies

■ The theoretical context of social stratification and differentiation

■ Contemporary social inequalities based on class, gender, 'race', ethnicity, age and disability.

By the end of this area you should be able to:

■ know, understand and evaluate all areas of social stratification and differentiation in modern industrial societies

■ interpret and apply your understanding of social inequality to other sociological issues, concepts or debates.

Key terms

social stratification	age
social class	differentiation
gender	sex
sexual discrimination	'race'
ethnicity	disability

Area 3   Contents

Introduction

What is social stratification and differentiation?

So what's this I hear about us being a classless society now?!

Figure 3.1

The terms **stratification** and **differentiation** may seem confusing and imply sociological jargon, but their meaning covers an area of great sociological and public importance – social inequality and difference. Inequality is a taken-for-granted aspect of our everyday lives. For example, you may be studying for your A/AS Levels in either a local authority-run Sixth Form as part of a secondary school, an independently run and privately funded Sixth Form boarding school, or a Further Education College. In whichever institution you have 'decided' to complete your further education, your choice was based upon unequal provision and unequal

factors shaping your decision, such as do you agree with private education, have you the status to access it and do you have the wealth to fund it? Therefore, even something that appears relatively equal, such as deciding on your education, accepts as normal the inequality already evident in our social system.

Social equality, or **egalitarianism**, is a social state in which no one person is ranked above another and all people have equal amounts of power, wealth and status. This utopian or ideal social system has not been much in evidence throughout human history. Communist societies have been identified as aspiring towards egalitarian principle, by ensuring that the means of production (what produces wealth in that society) is owned by everybody. However, there has been evidence of stratification existing alongside communism, such as in East Germany before the capitalist revolution, based upon criteria such as gender or military status. Therefore, the possibility of ever achieving a fully egalitarian society has been widely debated (see section on 'Is stratification inevitable?').

Factors affecting a group or individual's position in a social stratification system, based on the theories of Max Weber

Power: The ability of individuals and/or groups to exert their will over others, with (authority) or without (coercion) their consent.

Wealth: What is deemed valuable by a particular society, usually material possessions of some sort, such as land or money.

Status: The degree of prestige or social esteem given to social positions, individuals and lifestyles.

The terminology for stratification has been borrowed from geology, which identified stratification or layers in rock formations. Social stratification means the social ordering of different groups one above the other into different layers or strata. For example, class, gender, 'race' or age could be the basis for ordering people into different and unequal social strata. This hierarchical social system is dependent on unequal social factors between the groups, such as power, wealth and status. Each layer or stratum will have a similar identity, similar life chances and similar amounts of power, wealth and status. Therefore social stratification is a

Figure 3.2   Social stratification is a hierarchical ranking system made up of unequal amounts of power, wealth and status

system of socially created inequalities and sociologists who study social stratification have attempted to identify and explain these social inequalities.

Social differentiation means the distinctions and differing access to resources that exist between groups and individuals, such as varying amounts of income or the different types of education available dependent on wealth and status. Therefore social stratification is the actual social inequality and differentiation is the criteria for categorising and comparing strata. Consequently, it could be argued that social differentiation causes social stratification, in that it is the differences between the strata that ultimately makes them unequal.

HINTS AND TIPS   *It may be helpful to use the following chart to remember the distinctions between social stratification, types of social stratification and social differentiation:*

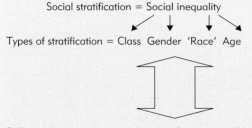

Different systems of social stratification have been identified, one of the oldest and most widespread being slavery. Slavery means the ownership of one human being by another, resulting in two main strata –

free citizens and 'unfree' slaves. Those who are free possess the highest amount of power, wealth and status, while those who are slaves have none. Many societies' historical development was based upon slave labour, such as Ancient Greece, Rome and the southern states of the USA. Figure 3.3 identifies a selection of social stratification systems that exist, or have existed, as ways of dividing people up in different countries around the world.

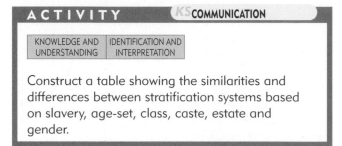

ACTIVITY   **COMMUNICATION**

KNOWLEDGE AND UNDERSTANDING	IDENTIFICATION AND INTERPRETATION

Construct a table showing the similarities and differences between stratification systems based on slavery, age-set, class, caste, estate and gender.

HINTS AND TIPS   *There are some excellent books and films dealing with the experience of slavery and the low status of ex-slaves in the USA. You might gain something from watching* **The Colour Purple** *or* **Amistad** *on video. Do not expect the films to be a comfortable experience, however. Ask English or History teachers to see if they can recommend texts. Do not be ashamed to read books that are intended to explain slavery to people younger than you.*

It should be noted that there are many differences between individuals within groups: for example, not all women or ethnic minorities are subject to a disadvantaged position in a stratification system. Social inequality is a social construction and is therefore constantly changing according to the demands of the social system and social actors within it. Consequently, studies on social stratification may make generalisations about social strata, for example by talking about the 'working class', but contemporary sociologists never forget that it is the diversity that exists within social groups which makes society dynamic.

Closed stratification systems: Very little social mobility (movement between strata). Status is usually ascribed (given at birth).

Open stratification systems: High degree of social mobility (movement between strata). Status is largely achieved (gained by merit).

Type	Characteristics	Example
Slavery	■ Clear division between strata – powerful freemen and oppressed slaves. ■ Social rights to human ownership. ■ Status is ascribed (given at birth) or achieved (gained by actions), but generally no social mobility exists.	■ Old colonies on the West Indies ■ Southern states plantations in the USA ■ Ancient Greece ■ Ancient Rome
Age-set	■ Strata are based on age – the older a person is, the more important he or she is. ■ The first stratum or age-set is based on a group of children roughly the same age, who stay together, resulting in a *closed* stratification system (no social mobility). ■ Status is ascribed, with age allowing certain rights, such as marriage, to the individual.	■ Same parts of Africa ■ Aboriginal communities in Australia
Caste	■ Very rigid divisions between strata that are decreed by religion. ■ Five main strata with Brahmins having the most power, wealth and status, and untouchables or outcastes having little or none of the above. ■ Status is ascribed and can be changed only through reincarnation, resulting in a *closed* stratification system (no social mobility). ■ It has been illegal since 1949 in India, but still affects the occupations and life chances of the Hindu population.	■ India ■ Parts of Asia
Estate	■ Divisions between strata are based on land ownership. ■ The nobles, who owned the land, held most power, wealth and status. Merchants and craftsmen had less importance and serfs or peasants were relatively powerless. ■ Status was ascribed and individuals accepted their estate in life (educational inequality restricted opportunities for achieved status). ■ A relatively *closed* stratification system (no social mobility), but occasional social movement occurred.	■ Feudal societies in England and Europe ■ China and Russia before their communist revolutions ■ Japan, before the Second World War
Class	■ Least rigid division between strata based on unequal amounts of power, wealth and status. ■ Status achieved by merit, although birth can affect social position. ■ Individuals can change class position (social mobility), resulting in an *open* stratification system, through a change of occupation.	■ Modern industrial societies, such as United Kingdom, USA, Germany, etc.
Gender	■ Varying degrees of division exist between men and women. ■ Status is ascribed and used to justify unequal amounts of power, wealth and status. ■ The system is *closed*, although mobility between sexes is possible, but not common.	■ Modern industrial societies, such as United Kingdom, USA, Germany, etc. ■ Africa ■ Asia ■ Australasia ■ India

Figure 3.3 Forms of stratification

Historical overview

Traditional sociologists, such as Marx and Weber, examined social stratification through class inequalities, which is not surprising considering that their writing had been affected by a period of social, political and economic revolutions (see Area 1 on Sociological Theory). Massive differences in wealth between rich and poor had been revealed and required an explanation. Marx investigated the historical development of class-based stratification systems leading to capitalism and the potential for communism.

He defined class in terms of economic production by the relationship each group had to the means of production. In other words, if you owned the means of production in any system you were ruling class and if you did not own the means of production you were a member of the subject class.

Weber, like Marx, examined the economic basis of stratification in the formation of classes and found that class was linked to a person's ability to command scarce resources in the labour market (**market situation**). Hence a class could be defined as a group of people with a similar market situation. However, he also argued that social stratification is based on factors outside the economy or wealth, such as status and party membership (power) in varying combinations. Therefore, Weber suggested that there were differences between the 'propertyless' classes, i.e. those who did not own the means of production, in terms of power, wealth and status that resulted in four classes:

1 The propertied upper class (landowners, factory owners)
2 The propertyless white collar workers (clerical workers)
3 The petty bourgeoisie (small business managers)
4 The manual working class (labourers).

Both Marx and Weber identified stratification in terms of social-class position (see later sections for further details), which is interesting considering that slavery had existed before industrialisation and was an obvious form of social inequality based on economic power. Issues of 'race' and ethnicity did not emerge as a subject for stratification theorists in sociology until relatively recently. The reason for this can be seen in the assumption of 'race' being a biological rather than social construction. Sociologists had accepted the scientific categorisations of ethnic groups and the justification of social inequalities as being a consequence of biological inferiority, i.e. white people were superior to black people. Therefore, classical sociologists did not consider 'race' an area for social investigation.

A similar attitude existed to stratification by gender. The history of academic research is the province of male scholars. Women have not had access to the same educational opportunities as men and have not, therefore, until recently, had the ability to research their position. Men conducted sociological research without much consideration for the position of women, an unequal position accepted as 'normal' and therefore not requiring investigation. Feminism from the 1960s onwards exposed the malestream bias of sociology and examined the stratified position of women in society. Therefore, contemporary sociologists have changed the way in which social stratification has been examined and the way in which we think about social inequality, i.e. what it consists of and who is affected by it.

Contemporary situation

Any form of structured social inequality is an example of stratification. The biggest difference between contemporary studies of social stratification and differentiation and classical ones is that we now realise that many assumed 'natural' divisions between people, such as **gender** or 'race' or even **age**, are actually socially constructed divisions that have justified the unequal treatment of members of specific strata.

A good example of how different stratified groups have become the focus of recent sociological investigation can be seen through 'age'. It has been generally accepted that physical deterioration makes people economically redundant to society at 65. Contemporary sociologists have challenged the assumption that this is a natural decline necessitating a social division. Older workers are more expensive than younger ones and society cannot sustain full employment, therefore retirement provides an excuse to remove a costly part of the workforce. Older people are physically and mentally capable of continuing in employment past 65 years of age; think of the hectic role played by the Queen, after what is normally considered the retirement age. Social myths of fragility and dementia ensure that retirement appears 'natural'.

Traditional forms of stratification remain important to the investigation of social stratification, such as **social class**, and many sociologists continue to refine theories and research in those areas. Contemporarily identified forms of stratification, such as 'race' and gender have also been linked to the concept of class, merging old and new perceptions of stratification in the work of Marxist feminists, for example. However, some feminist and 'race relations' sociologists have argued that gender and racial inequality respectively should be examined, at last, in their own right (Oakley, 1972; Modood, et al. 1997). This said, we live in a class-based stratification system, the social inequalities of which affect us every day of our lives. For example, class, as the dominant division in society, determines who our friends are, where we live, our life chances and even the food we eat. Class is a dimension of society that affects our morals and our values, so that many sociologists even think in terms of separate class cultures. Therefore 'class' appears to be an appropriate place to begin a detailed analysis of social stratification and differentiation.

Class

The relevance of class

❛ *The Diana mystique was nothing without her class and title; in any other context, her remarkable capacity to relate to the 'downtrodden' would have generated precious little 'magic' ... But the role was age old. So was the public adulation of the stunning, outspoken, fragile, 'excluded' Royal, standing up for 'us' against 'them' in a society where 'they' are still widely seen, particularly by the less well-off, as a class apart.*

Adonis, A. and Pollard, S. (1998:x–xi)
A Class Act: The Myth of Britain's Classless Society

Contemporary politicians, journalists and celebrities have made popular the idea that Britain is now a 'classless society'. Specific social events, such as the mourning for the death of Diana, Princess of Wales, have been interpreted as a sign of national and class unification. However, sociologists would argue that such national displays of unity do not dispel the notion of class, but instead act to emphasise the divisions between the wealthy and the not so wealthy (Adonis and Pollard, 1998), as the quotation above displays.

Based on the inequalities apparent in education, health provision, housing and lifestyle, Britain appears to be far from 'classless'. The class to which we are assigned at birth, i.e. that of our parents, tends to dictate our life chances from then on. For example, if you are born to working-class parents you are much less likely to enter further education and therefore achieve a professional-status job and all the associated consumer durables (big house, flashy car, etc.). As Gerth and Mills (1961:240) stated:

❛ *No matter what people believe, class structure as an economic arrangement influences their life chances according to their positions in it.*

The term 'class' originally referred to property divisions in Roman times and implied an inherited social position. The modern use of 'class' is linked to the Industrial Revolution and modern capitalism (late

HINTS AND TIPS   *You are advised to collect and pool with the rest of your group as much data as you can from **Social Trends** that offers class as a variable. It could even form the basis of a wall display. Look for death rates, incidence of criminality, life expectancy and unemployment and family breakdown. You will see from this data that class is a very significant factor in people's life experience.*

eighteenth century). Industrialisation brought with it new classes based on achievement, and transformed the class structure from its ascribed roots based on privilege of birth. Social class, therefore, became a central issue in sociology, with theorists providing a range of definitions dependent on their school of thought (see later section on 'Classical theories' page 128), but agreeing that social class was dependent on an individual's position in the labour market. In other words, the better someone's occupation is, the more power, wealth and status that person has and the higher his or her class is. Social classes are therefore groups of people who share a similar position in the market economy (or have a similar job) and develop similar norms, values and attitudes.

> **Capitalism**: An economic system based on the private ownership of money used to finance (capital) the production of commodities with the aim of maximising profit (surplus value).

Social class has been a prominent type of social stratification, in one form or another, since Roman times. In modern industrial societies based on capitalist economies, such as the UK, the USA and western Europe, people are ranked according to their position in the labour market. This ranking affects their lifestyles, such as accent and dress, and life chances, such as education and health, because of differentiation in income, power and status. Even in the eastern bloc, the collapse of socialism has signalled the emergence of capitalist/free-market economies and the associated class divisions that accompany this mode of production (see later sections on Marx p. 128 and Weber p. 130). Consequently, it is important to examine the class structure, because it enables us to explain one form of social inequality that affects all our lives.

Theoretical perspectives on class

Classical

Marx

Karl Marx (1818–83) never actually used the term social stratification, but he was the first academic to attempt a systematic analysis of the social inequalities in industrial society. Marx argued that in all stratification systems there exist two major social groupings (with minor groups, such as the **relative surplus population** – the 'scum' of society, standing outside the main divisions in society):

1 **The ruling class** – Those who control and own the means of production (what produces wealth in that society).
2 **The subject class** – Those who own only their labour.

Class position is determined by an individual's relationship to the means of production. In other words, if people own and control what produces wealth, then they are members of the ruling class and if they do not then they are members of the subject class. The ruling class has the best position in a class-based stratification system, possessing the most power, wealth and status. This position enables the ruling class to oppress and exploit the subject class, which has to work to survive.

The relationship between the ruling class and the subject class is based on an unequal, but mutual dependency. The members of the ruling class need the members of the subject class to work for them to sustain their privileged position and the subject class needs the ruling class to survive. However, the subject class forms the mass of the population, yet has no power, which makes it expendable and easy to exploit, i.e. if one labourer will not work for a certain wage, there will always be another who will. This

relationship between the ruling class and the subject class also creates a conflict of interests – a conflict that Marx argued was inherent in any class-based social system.

Marx stated that society has not always had class-based divisions, a statement that provided the basis for his belief that a classless society would eventually be achieved through communist revolution (Marx, K. and Engels, F.: 1998, 1888). Marx argued that western society had developed through four main epochs (or transitional stages):

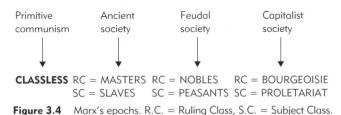

Figure 3.4 Marx's epochs. R.C. = Ruling Class, S.C. = Subject Class.

Marx believed that in primitive societies based on subsistence (where only the basic needs, such as food, clothing and shelter, have to be met) no classes existed. Social classes developed only as a consequence of surplus wealth, or when people started producing more than they needed to survive. This surplus wealth was used in exchange and developed into the trading of private property. Now some groups could be argued to own the means of production and others own only their labour.

It should be noted that Marx argued that the final stage of historical development would be communism; however, this cannot be called an epoch, because it was not considered to be transitional. As Marx and Engels (1998:34) wrote:

❦ *The history of all hitherto existing society is the history of class struggle …*

As class struggle is based on conflict between the classes, history would end with communism (in other words there would be no more social change), because society would be classless.

Marx argued that every historical stage has:

- **infrastructure** – economic base of society, such as capitalism

- **superstructure** – major institutions, values and belief systems of society, which reflect the economic system and the ideology of the ruling class that dominates it.

The infrastructure shapes the superstructure through the relations of production, which support ruling-class ideology. Therefore, the superstructure reflects, supports and maintains the interests of the infrastructure. In other words, if our infrastructure is capitalism, then the way in which capitalism operates affects our institutions, such as schools and the mass media, values, such as individual competition, and belief systems, such as trying to have the best living conditions possible. If the infrastructure changed, say we had a communist revolution, then our superstructure would change to reflect and maintain this, because it is governed by the interests of the infrastructure. Schools and the mass media would emphasise the benefits of community support, which would change our values, making us less competitive and less consumer orientated (see Figure 1.3 in Area 1 on Sociological Theory).

HINTS AND TIPS There is a lot of information on the Internet on Karl Marx. Political groups who wish to convert people to Marxist political ideas have put some of it there, but you will find sociological accounts too. Marx is also well covered by most of the CD-ROM encyclopaedias, and you can add work to your folder. Do not worry if some of it appears difficult at first. You will soon grow to understand the complexities of the debate as you progress through the course. Many of the main ideas of Marx are in **The Communist Manifesto** *by Marx and Engels. It is a relatively short book because it is a piece of journalism, and it is not particularly difficult to read compared with some of the later writing. You may find it interesting, if challenging.*

Marx believed that conflict was the driving force of social change, propelling epochs inevitably into their next form. For example, he believed that the potential ruling class of capitalist society emerged in feudal society. The two minority classes entered into conflict over who had most power and control – the rising industrialists or the landed nobles. The industrialists, or bourgeoisie, with their new technology and ability to produce surplus value (profit), had more power than the nobility, whose estates were becoming too expensive to manage

and maintain. Consequently, the bourgeoisie became the ruling class in the new epoch of capitalism.

Marx, however, saw the capitalist epoch running a course different from the minority battles of the previous epochs. Marx's experience of capitalism was of extremes. For the proletariat of Germany there existed nothing more than a life of poverty, squalor and endless hardship, while the ruling class lived comfortable and enjoyable lives. The massive social inequality of Marx's day directed his theorising, for he argued that in capitalism the majority proletariat would overthrow the minority bourgeoisie in a communist revolution.

Marx envisaged a growing chasm between the lives of those who owned the means of production and those who did not. This polarisation (growing further apart) of the two main classes would be based on:

- the de-skilling of jobs uniting the proletariat

- the proletariat becoming poorer and poorer in comparison to the bourgeoisie

- the growth of successful companies and the destruction of small ones (the petty bourgeoisie), who enter the proletariat.

Marx argued that when the proletariat became larger and poorer it would become:

- a '**class for itself**' – attaining class consciousness (awareness of the true situation of exploitation and oppression) and solidarity (working together in collective action)

- a '**class in itself**' – attaining the same relationship to the means of production (equality through communism).

The conflict inherent in communism (Marx referred to the bourgeoisie as 'its own grave-diggers' (1998:50)) would eventually anger the masses so much that they would revolt and challenge their oppressors, after all as Marx and Engels (1998:77) wrote, 'the proletarians have nothing to lose but their chains'. The proletariat would overthrow the ruling class and seize power and control of the means of production and a communist society:

> *In place of the old bourgeois society, with its classes and class antagonism, we shall have an association, in which the free development of each is the condition for the free development of all.*

Marx, K. and Engels, F. (1998:62)

HINTS AND TIPS Remember that Marx was writing about a society that was different from our own. The gap between rich and poor was extreme. To appreciate the differences fully you should attempt to look at some of the great stately homes, particularly those built in Victorian times and then remember that much of this wealth was built on the exploitation of an extremely poor urban working class. Victorian society was reminiscent of the conditions that we expect in developing countries today.

Criticisms of Marxist theory on class

Although Marx provided a clear account of what he saw to be the cause of social inequalities in society, an account that is still used today, his theory of class-based social divisions has been challenged in the following ways:

- His concept of polarisation, where the bourgeoisie and the proletariat become further apart, is seen to be too simplistic. In the late 1800s, when Marx was writing, the structure of capitalism appeared to be becoming more complex. Also, there is little evidence of polarisation in modern industrial societies.

- The proletariat does not appear to be a homogeneous (similar) group, with similar norms, values and attitudes, and is therefore unlikely to become class-conscious or solidaristic.

- Marx emphasised the importance of class conflict in securing historical social change, but he has been criticised for exaggerating the role of class struggle. The proletariat (working class) has not developed into a revolutionary mass on the basis of class conflict.

- Increased cultural homogeneity (similarity), based on shared access to the media, across modern western industrial societies has blurred class divisions.

- Marx has been accused of allowing his ideological and political beliefs to affect his analysis of class, resulting in a biased account.

- Marx argued that social class was directly related to economic position (economic determinism) and therefore ignored the influence of status and subjective differences. This view also underestimates the influence people can have on determining unpredictable social change.

- Marx made reference only to paid employment, which ignores the inequality experienced by women engaged in unpaid domestic labour.

ACTIVITY KS **COMMUNICATION**

KNOWLEDGE AND UNDERSTANDING

Define the following terms (without referring to the text above) to test your knowledge of Marx and social stratification:

- capital
- epoch
- surplus value
- superstructure
- infrastructure
- polarisation
- class in itself
- 'class for itself'
- proletariat
- bourgeoisie

Weber

> ... capitalism is identical with the pursuit of profit, and forever **renewed** profit, by means of continuous, rational, capitalistic enterprise. For it must be so: in a wholly capitalistic order of society, an individual capitalistic enterprise which did not take advantage of its opportunities for profit-making would be doomed to extinction.

Weber, M. in Andreski, S. (Ed.) (1983:24)
***Max Weber on Capitalism, Bureaucracy and Religion: A Selection of Texts**. London, Allen and Unwin.*

Looking at the extract above written by Max Weber (1864–1920), it is easy to see the comparisons with Marx's theory of class. Weber agreed with Marx that capitalism is intrinsically linked with the making of profit (surplus value) at any cost, including exploitation and oppression of the waged labourer. He also agreed that it was a period in social history unlike any other, because of the conflicting class relationship between those who had power in capitalism and those who had to work for them:

> Class struggles between creditor and debtor classes, landowners and the landless, serfs and tenants, and conflicts between trading interests and consumer landlords, have been occurring everywhere in various combinations ... The modern conflict of the large-scale industrial entrepreneur and the free wage labourers has no equivalents anywhere.

Weber, M. in Andreski, S. (Ed.) (1983:27)
***Max Weber on Capitalism, Bureaucracy and Religion: A Selection of Texts**. London, Allen and Unwin.*

Therefore, both Marx and Weber supported the idea that social stratification has an economic basis, in that people in market economies compete for scarce resources for economic or financial gain. They also acknowledged that the major class division was between those who owned the means of production and those who did not. However, this is where the similarities in their theories of class end.

Class

Weber, as a social-action theorist (see Area 1 on Sociological Theory), examined the wider causes and cases of social inequality, such as status and ethnic stratification, not just the economic explanation. Weber was not a socialist like Marx, instead he supported the rationality of capitalism (Edgell, 1993) and the chances it allowed people in the labour market. Therefore Weber defined class as a group of people with a similar situation in a market economy (market situation). By this he meant a group who had similar amounts of power to command similar resources, such as money, housing, lifestyle etc., and thereby had similar life chances.

For Weber, class divisions were not based solely on the ownership of the means of production. Weber argued that there were a number of classes in modern capitalist societies, positively privileged property and commercial classes at the top of the stratification system, negatively privileged property and commercial classes at the bottom and in between these were a variety of middle classes:

■ *Positively privileged classes*

1   **property/ownership classes** which own different kinds of property, such as land or people
2   **commercial/acquisition classes** which consist of people who possess goods, services and skills that can be offered in the labour market. It includes professionals, merchants and bankers.

■ *Middle classes* – These classes included workers with exceptional credentials and/or skills, such as craftsmen or peasants.

■ *Negatively privileged classes* (**property**)

1   the unfree
2   the declassed
3   the paupers

These classes do not own any property.

■ *Negatively privileged classes* (**commercial**)

1   skilled workers
2   semi-skilled workers
3   unskilled workers

These classes do not possess sought-after services in the labour market.

To make matters even more complicated (or just more representative of the actual class structure), Weber also identified four social classes or class situations:

1   The working class
2   The petty bourgeoisie
3   The propertyless intelligentsia
4   The propertied upper class.

He argued that class situation, i.e. membership of one of the social classes above, was determined by market situation allowing the possession of property or not (the main category of all class situations). Therefore, the market value of skills of the propertyless is seen as important in the formation of social classes.

By identifying middle classes, and arguing that they expand with capitalism to support the growing bureaucracy needed to run it, Weber dismissed the Marxist concept of polarisation. He also challenged any idea of a proletarian revolution through the acknowledgement of plural classes, which would not allow for class solidarity or consciousness – the foundation of Marx's communist revolution.

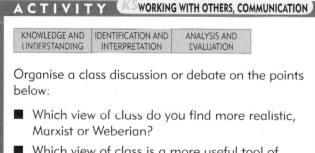

ACTIVITY   KS **WORKING WITH OTHERS, COMMUNICATION**

KNOWLEDGE AND UNDERSTANDING	IDENTIFICATION AND INTERPRETATION	ANALYSIS AND EVALUATION

Organise a class discussion or debate on the points below:

■ Which view of class do you find more realistic, Marxist or Weberian?

■ Which view of class is a more useful tool of sociological analysis?

■ Remember to justify (identify strengths and weaknesses) your answers to improve your evaluation skills.

Status and party

Weber strongly disagreed with Marx's concept of power. Power enables a group or individual to have control of or influence others and is therefore central to issues of social stratification. Marx argued that political power derives from economic power, or the ownership of the means of production. Weber argued that economic power is only one type of power and that **status** (social power) and **party** (political power) have a direct effect on social inequality too.

Weber argued that there is a complex relationship between class, status and party in the formation of power. One may act independently of the other, but it is more common that they operate together. The **status situation** of an individual or group refers to the degree of social honour or prestige they are given. For example, a **status group** will share the same amount of social honour. In the caste-based stratification system mentioned earlier, a Brahmin is a member of a high-status group and therefore has power. However, an untouchable is a member of a low-status group and has no power. Therefore status situation can provide access to economic power (class) and political power (party).

Status groups were considered by Weber to represent a collective identity or 'community', where members know each other. He argued that social closure resulted from this shared identity, where non-members would not be allowed within that status group. For example, the ascribed status of the caste system does not allow movement from one status group (stratum) to another. Therefore, status groups are different from classes, because classes are not 'communities' who know each other. This could explain why the proletariat has not achieved class consciousness as Marx predicted. This said, status groups can traverse classes, for example 'travellers' have become a status group in the UK, sharing the same amount of social honour and community, yet come from a variety of class backgrounds.

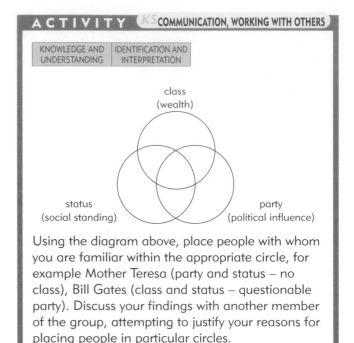

ACTIVITY COMMUNICATION, WORKING WITH OTHERS

| KNOWLEDGE AND UNDERSTANDING | IDENTIFICATION AND INTERPRETATION |

Using the diagram above, place people with whom you are familiar within the appropriate circle, for example Mother Teresa (party and status – no class), Bill Gates (class and status – questionable party). Discuss your findings with another member of the group, attempting to justify your reasons for placing people in particular circles.

Party refers to Weber's concept of groups that are concerned with influencing policy in the interests of members. The whole purpose of party membership is to attain political power in a planned and organised way, i.e. through a political party, organised interest group or pressure group. Parties may represent the interests of classes, such as the Conservative Party following the interests of the middle class; or status groups, such as the British Nationalist Party (BNP) supporting white supremacy; or neither, such as Greenpeace which wants power to protect the environment. Weber argued that party membership was a useful and necessary tool in advancing social change, especially considering that social conflict as a route to change had been dulled by the blurring of class/status/party boundaries.

Criticisms of Weber's theory of social stratification

Weber provided a complex and pluralistic examination of social inequality, introducing alongside class the ideas of status and party as determinants of power. As a social-action theorist he provided a model of society that was both ordered around the economic structure, yet allowed for the actions of class/status/party group members to affect that structure. However, his approach is also a conflict theory, like Marx's, based on the emphasis on the constant struggle for power and wealth among competing groups.

HINTS AND TIPS The following sentences may be useful in remembering Weber's concept of class, status and party:

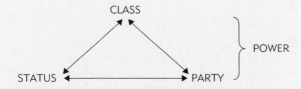

STATUS NOT CLASS = COMMON IDENTITY
A CLASS MAY CONTAIN DIFFERENT STATUS GROUPS
PARTIES REPRESENT CLASSES +/- STATUS GROUPS OR NEITHER

Weber's theory of social stratification has been challenged for reducing the significance of social class as a way of analysing social inequality. By identifying many different classes he made it difficult to differentiate between the groups. Marxists have criticised Weber for allowing status and party a value equal to class in determining power, a criticism that has been hard to sustain in a social order where nobility may have high social status, but a low class through lack of wealth and party representation. They have also argued that linking social division, such as 'race'/ethnicity and gender, to status groups, rather than class differences, ignores the root cause of that conflict.

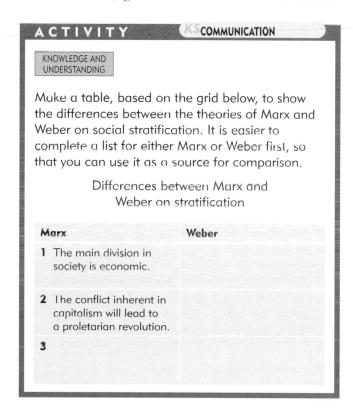

ACTIVITY KS COMMUNICATION

KNOWLEDGE AND UNDERSTANDING

Make a table, based on the grid below, to show the differences between the theories of Marx and Weber on social stratification. It is easier to complete a list for either Marx or Weber first, so that you can use it as a source for comparison.

Differences between Marx and Weber on stratification

Marx	Weber
1 The main division in society is economic.	
2 The conflict inherent in capitalism will lead to a proletarian revolution.	
3	

Functionalism

Functionalists, such as Durkheim and Spencer (see Area 1 on Sociological Theory), believed that as society develops it becomes more complex and requires a large variety of social roles or positions to make it function effectively. They identified role differentiation in the evolution of most societies based on 'tribe' and 'tribe chief', the latter role carrying more status than the other. The ability of some to gain a more important position in society than others was justified by arguing that people are born with different capabilities and that

this is functional for society, i.e. it keeps society balanced and working effectively.

As a structural-consensus theory (see Area 1 on Sociological Theory) functionalism argues that people agree that society has to be organised to make the best use of the different capabilities people have. Social inequality is, therefore, seen as a device through which those with the scarcest talents and skills are justifiably more highly rewarded (wealth and status act as motivation to perform successfully) and given most power (to represent the interests of the society). Consequently, functionalists argue that social stratification is inevitable, because it functions to maintain a stable and efficient society.

Functionalists argue that social stratification can work to everyone's benefit only if everyone has been socialised into accepting that inequality is just. Talcott Parsons (1951) supported this view by arguing that social order is based on value consensus, or general agreement on what is good and worthwhile. Value consensus is established through primary socialisation (see Area 4 Society and Cultural Identities and also see Area 6 on Families and Households), where children learn about the norms and values of society. It is at this stage that they become aware of the importance of social achievement, or successfully achieving societal values.

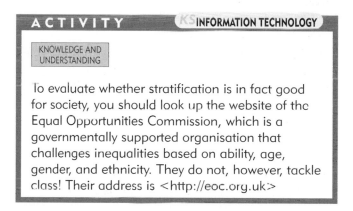

ACTIVITY KS INFORMATION TECHNOLOGY

KNOWLEDGE AND UNDERSTANDING

To evaluate whether stratification is in fact good for society, you should look up the website of the Equal Opportunities Commission, which is a governmentally supported organisation that challenges inequalities based on ability, age, gender, and ethnicity. They do not, however, tackle class! Their address is <http://eoc.org.uk>

Parsons argued that all societies have social stratification systems, because without social inequality it would be difficult to motivate people and make them work together for a common goal. Power, wealth and status are a reflection of hard work and importance to society.

Kingsley Davis and Wilbert Moore (1945), like Parsons, argue that stratification is universal. They believe that all societies have **functional prerequisites**, or things needed to make society work, such as providing people with roles to perform. However, these roles have unequal rewards, depending on their importance to the maintenance and survival of society. Therefore, a role that achieves the highest rewards is considered to be functionally unique (no other role like it) and/or other positions are totally dependent on that role. The people who engage in these roles do so based on their superior talent and skills.

ACTIVITY · COMMUNICATION, WORKING WITH OTHERS

KNOWLEDGE AND UNDERSTANDING	IDENTIFICATION AND INTERPRETATION	ANALYSIS AND EVALUATION

It could be argued that the Prime Minister's role in the UK is functionally unique and that all other positions are dependent upon it and therefore it should justifiably receive the highest reward. In reality, the wife of Labour Prime Minister Tony Blair earned considerably more as a lawyer than did her husband. This raises serious questions about why one would want the job of a politician! In pairs, using your own knowledge and research, find out the salary of the Prime Minister and the duties of the role. Do you think your findings support Davis and Moore's theory of social stratification? Justify your answer in order to develop your evaluation skills.

Criticisms of functionalist theory on social stratification

Parsons and Davis and Moore have been criticised for their functionalist approach to social inequality. Melvin Tumin (1967) offered a critique of Davis and Moore's theory, challenging their measure and use of the importance of positions/roles to society. For example, how can talent be measured? Examination results? Do unequal rewards really attract talented workers? Is talent really necessary for highly rewarded roles? Tumin argued that Davis and Moore failed to take into account the influence of power in attaining highly rewarded social roles. For example, directors of large, powerful companies have salaries far in excess of headteachers', yet both could be considered equally talented and as functionally important to society as the other.

Tumin concluded that social stratification is not functional to the balance and smooth running of society: it does, in fact, stop skilled and qualified

people from achieving high-ranking positions. Those at the bottom of the stratification system may hold that position because of discrimination, such as élite self-recruitment (where members of the middle class employ people from a background similar to their own), or forms of social inequality other than 'talent', such as gender, 'race' or age. Consequently, both Parsons and Davis and Moore could be accused of ignoring the dysfunctions of social stratification. Lastly, from a Marxist perspective, it could be argued that stratification is not inevitable or even necessary for a functioning society, such as in communism.

HINTS AND TIPS   An easy way to remember the classical theories of social stratification is to divide them into consensus and conflict approaches.
Consensus approach (Functionalism) – Inequality is to everyone's benefit, rich or poor, powerful or powerless, because it allows society to be efficient and stable.
Conflict approach (Marxism, Weberianism) – Inequality is to the benefit of whoever is winning the social struggle.

Contemporary

Neo-Marxist

Neo or modern Marxists maintain Marx's original theory of stratification, in that the basic class division is between those who own the means of production and those who do not. However, neo-Marxists have had to adapt their theories to include the complex range of occupations that have arisen in modern industrial societies, occupations that blur the boundaries between the bourgeoisie and the proletariat. Neo-Marxists, such as Harry Braverman (1974) and Erik Olin Wright (1976, 1985), have included occupational diversity in their theories in order to understand class conflict in contemporary society, as Wright (1976:3–4) stated:

> It matters a great deal for our understanding of class struggle and social change exactly how classes are conceptualized and which categories of social positions are placed in which classes.

Through identifying the contradictory nature of intermediate groups, such as managers who have an interest in the success of the business, but remain paid labourers and are still fundamentally selling their labour power and subject to the power of the ruling class. As an intermediate group, managers have similarities to

Ruling class	Bourgeoisie	Small employers	Petty bourgeoisie	
Subject class	Expert managers	Expert supervisors	Expert non-managers	EXPERTS
	Semi-credentialled managers	Semi-credentialled supervisors	Semi-credentialled	SKILLED
	Uncredentialled managers	Uncredentialled supervisors	Proletarians	UNSKILLED
	(lots of employees) MANAGERS	(some employees) SUPERVISORS	(no employees) NON-MANAGEMENT	

Figure 3.5   Adapted from Erik Olin Wright's neo-Marxist class model (1997)

the bourgeoisie, but are not part of it for the reasons stated above. Therefore, groups that appear 'middle class' become accounted for in neo-Marxist explanations of inequality.

Wright also moved beyond Marx's industrially based model of control. Wright argued that capitalist economic control not only involved physical control of the means of production and labour power, but also control over investment capital or financial services and organisational power. By this he meant that intermediate groups could exploit other groups by having better skills or qualifications, which gives them more power than other members of the subject class, creating a **contradictory class location**.

Wright (1997) developed a model of class in modern capitalism, which looks remarkably similar to Weber's class structure (Figure 3.5). It is designed to show the overall exploitative nature of the class system. Groups within the system experience varying degrees of exploitation.

Wright challenges the notion of his model approaching a Weberian theme, by arguing that he places

contradictory classes only within the objective structure of overall material exploitation, not within the subjective position of the individual. In this way, Wright would see that the difference between the classes is based on whether one survives by earning a wage. Bank employees may earn £100,000 a year and shop-owners considerably less, but the bank employees can always be made redundant. In practical terms, this is an interesting analysis of social relationships, but almost impossible to apply to the real world in any useful sense.

Neo-Weberian

Neo or modern Weberians, such as John Goldthorpe (1987), have adapted Weber's explanation of class inequality to provide a unified model of the class structure in contemporary capitalist societies. Goldthorpe, in a study of social mobility (Oxford Mobility Study, 1972), combined Weber's two distinct concepts of work situation and market situation into seven occupational categories defined by income, job security and promotion prospects (market situation) and occupational position (work situation) (Figure 3.6).

Service class	Intermediate class	Working class
1 Higher professionals, high-grade administrators, managers of large industrial companies and large proprietors	3 Routine non-manual (clerical and sales)	6 Skilled manual workers
2 Lower professionals, higher-grade technicians, low-grade administrators, small-business managers and supervisors of non-manual workers	4 Small proprietors and self-employed artisans	7 Semi-skilled and unskilled manual workers
	5 Lower-grade technicians and supervisors of manual workers	

Source: Adapted from Goldthorpe (1980)

Figure 3.6   Goldthorpe's neo-Weberian class model

Following a further large-scale study of social mobility, Goldthorpe redesigned his class groupings to make them more representative of contemporary class structures in other countries (Figure 3.7).

Despite the alterations Goldthorpe made to his explanation of class divisions, he has been challenged on the following issues:

- The model is based on common sense, rather than systematic research, with an arbitrary placing of classes, such as routine non-manual workers being higher than small proprietors in his first model and a complete lack of clearly defined class categories (Ahrne, 1990).

- The ruling class seems to have been ignored (Penn, 1983)

- His work ignored the position of women in the class structure (he examined male heads of households) and therefore failed to include female-dominated occupations, such as personal service workers.

Class I & II	All professionals, administrators, managers, higher-grade technicians and supervisors of non-manual workers
Class III	Routine non-manual employees in administration, sales and clerical workers
Class IV ab	Small proprietors, self-employed artisans and other 'own account' workers
Class IV c	Farmers, small-holders and other self-employed workers in primary production
Class V & VI	Low-grade technicians, supervisors of manual workers and skilled manual workers
Class VII a	Semi- and unskilled manual workers
Class VII b	Agricultural workers

Source: Adapted from Goldthorpe (1987)

Figure 3.7 Goldthorpe's revised neo-Weberian class model

ACTIVITY KS **PROBLEM SOLVING, STUDY SKILLS**

KNOWLEDGE AND UNDERSTANDING	IDENTIFICATION AND INTERPRETATION	ANALYSIS AND EVALUATION

As a classroom exercise, see if you can develop a better way of analysing social class. Begin by taking a positive approach and thinking of different indices of class and different social groupings, and develop as many different categories and solutions to the problem as possible.

Now take a problem-centred approach and criticise your own and each other's work as fully as possible.

The point of the exercise is to examine the methodological difficulty of constructing a model of social class. Your conclusions should centre on the problems that you experienced in the exercise rather than on the success or lack of success you felt that you had in creating a model of class.

Linking Marxism and Weberian theory

Marxist explanations of class refer only to the ownership and non-ownership of the means of production, making little reference to the occupational position. On the other hand, Weberian theory of class concentrates on the market situation of the individual without emphasising the class inequalities that arise from not owning the means of production. Therefore it could be argued that a theory is needed that combines wealth (ownership of the means of production) and income (market situation) in an explanation of class inequality.

Structuration, a theory developed by Anthony Giddens (1984) to link structure and action, could be applied in this context. Giddens used the concept of social structure (social practices that create order in the social system) to explain class inequalities. Marx believed that the structure of society constrained the individual, for example not owning the means of production resulted in the proletariat having to sell labour in order to survive. Giddens argued that individuals have choices within the structure in which they live, for example the choice to work and survive or not work and die. Therefore, like Weber, Giddens has explained class position in relation to human action, as well as the structure of society.

Giddens has been criticised for using a non-traditional definition of structure (usually 'structure' is formed before the individual and therefore affects the individual, not vice versa) that fails really to link Marxist and Weberian concepts. W. G. Runciman (1990), however, has attempted to combine traditional Marxist notions of structure or ownership of the means of production and Weberian ideas of market situation.

Runciman has established the concept of economic role as the basis of class. An economic role refers to a socially structured position in society that has a relative amount of power that places that individual in a position in the class structure. Runciman states that economic power is linked to:

- ownership – of the means of production (in whole or part)
- marketability – a recognised skill/ability that can be sold on the labour market
- control – accepted right to direct production of fixed, financial or labour assets.

Based on the criteria of ownership, marketability and control, Runciman has constructed a seven-class model of contemporary British society:

1 **Upper class** – owners of the means of production, senior managers and individuals with exceptional marketability.
2 **Upper middle class** – higher-grade professionals, senior civil servants and managers.
3 **Middle middle class** – lower professionals, middle managers and small proprietors.
4 **Lower middle class** – routine white-collar workers.
5 **Skilled working class** – carpenter, builder.
6 **Unskilled working class** – shop assistants, assembly line workers.
7 **Underclass** – benefit claimants, long-term unemployed, those unable to work.

Although Runciman does not show a clear division between the class boundaries offered, he has provided a useful examination of both structure and market situation as a way of explaining class inequality. By moving away from the traditional division between ownership and non-ownership of the means of production, he has been able to emphasise the diversity of middle-class positions within a framework of ownership, marketability and control. He also displays the importance of identifying the upper class as a separate group, which is important in a society where a small section of the population still retain more power, wealth and status than the rest of the population.

New Right

The New Right is an individualistic theory that believes the free market economy is the most efficient way to organise society, because individuals make choices

TASK

Hypothesis: 'Equality of opportunity is the backbone of modern Britain'

Context: New Right theorists argue that equal opportunities exist in the UK, resulting in the opportunity for some people to be unequal. Therefore social inequality is a reflection of some people's lack of ability and talent to reach positions of power, wealth and status in the stratification system. Other sociological theorists, such as Marxists, Weberians and feminists, have argued that equal opportunities do not exist in a capitalist and patriarchal system, based on the exploitation of those not in the ruling class, or with the wrong ethnic origin or the wrong sex.

Method: Conduct a social survey to examine whether social inequality is based on lack of talent/ability or structural/ideological constraints, such as class, gender, 'race', age or disability. A straightforward data-collection tool would be a structured questionnaire to discover people's attitudes on this issue. Attempt to identify an accessible population, such as your local community, and perform a stratified sample using the electoral roll. Issue your questionnaire and quantify the resulting data.

Evaluation: Analyse your data in relation to the question and context. Remember to cross-reference your results to the appropriate theory in order to achieve application marks. Assess the strengths and weaknesses of your research method, considering how the sampling process went, the ease or difficulties associated with distributing and collecting questionnaires, and the response rate.

about their own behaviour, such as what to buy, whether to sell their labour, etc. New Right theory supports the notion of equality of opportunity, in that those who have the ability are seen to be able to attain the highest rewards. Therefore, New Right theorists reject state intervention on the basis that it could restrict the development of equality by removing rewards from those who have earned them.

It is the New Right theorists' notion of equality of opportunity that also acts as the basis of their belief in inequality. They argue that social inequality acts as a motivating force for economic growth. For example, in free-market economies the value of commodities is accurately calculated, and individuals knowing these values work to achieve the means of obtaining what they can afford. (See the profile of Hayek in Area 10 on Wealth, Poverty, Welfare and Social Policy.)

Peter Saunders (1990, 1995) presents a theory, similar to that of Davis and Moore, which justifies social inequality based on the rewarding of talent. Unlike functionalists, he does not argue that stratification is inevitable, merely that it is the best way of organising a capitalist society. To maintain a free-market economy, therefore, equality of opportunity (equal chance of becoming unequal) and legal equality (everyone is equal in the eye of the social norms and laws) have to run alongside the inequality that keeps it functioning. It appears to be a bit of a paradox that New Right theorists should value equality in the maintenance of social inequality. However, by emphasising equal access to all rewards, New Right theorists such as Saunders and Marsland (see Area 10 on Wealth, Poverty, Welfare and Social Policy) argue that income and wealth are fairly distributed. If you work hard and have the ability you will achieve an excellent class position; if you do not work hard you have only yourself to blame for your inferior class position.

It could be argued that the New Right approach to inequality promotes individual self-interest, a statement Saunders would support, despite Marxists and New Left (see later) theorists offering a criticism. Saunders argues that self-interest and inequality promote economic expansion, because people want to achieve the best quality of life that they can and this depends upon economic factors. Saunders does acknowledge that not all wealth is acquired by talent; in the UK inherited wealth undermines the notion of equality of opportunity. However, he maintains that even if Britain is not a meritocracy, opportunities for social mobility have increased, which shows a certain degree of equality in the opportunity of becoming unequal.

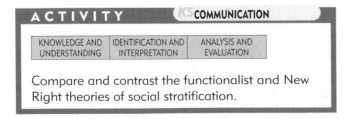

ACTIVITY KS **COMMUNICATION**

KNOWLEDGE AND UNDERSTANDING	IDENTIFICATION AND INTERPRETATION	ANALYSIS AND EVALUATION

Compare and contrast the functionalist and New Right theories of social stratification.

New Left

Will Hutton (1995) is an economist who has provided a damning critique of New Right theory on class inequality. Although Hutton recognises that inequality is a necessary part of free-market economies, he argues that social inequality, in the form of low wages, low skill and high unemployment, has resulted in a clearly divided and economically unstable society. Hutton has put forward the 30-30-40 thesis to show the three-way split in contemporary British class relations, a split that can be overcome only by reforming capitalism through the strengthening of public funds.

Hutton argues that there is a growing divide between rich and poor that has been caused by the reliance of the former Conservative government on the free market. Our society can now be seen to consist of:

- ◼ 30% – unemployed, low paid, insecure work
- ◼ 30% – some job security and quality of life
- ◼ 40% – privileged workers in secure and regular employment

Therefore, the only solution to class-based inequality is to create a 'stakeholder' society, where businesses support the community, not just their shareholders. Basically, like most New Left theorists, Hutton supports the idea of an extended welfare state that removes the emphasis on finance capital, but retains the positive aspects of free-market decision-making.

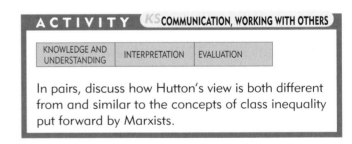

ACTIVITY KS **COMMUNICATION, WORKING WITH OTHERS**

KNOWLEDGE AND UNDERSTANDING	INTERPRETATION	EVALUATION

In pairs, discuss how Hutton's view is both different from and similar to the concepts of class inequality put forward by Marxists.

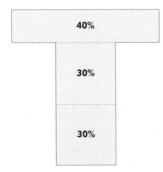

Figure 3.8 Hutton's 30-30-40 thesis

Hutton's thesis has been criticised for providing too rigid a structure of class division. He has not taken into account:

■ the way in which his three sections may overlap

■ how people may move between sections

■ the diversity of life chances and lifestyles within each section

■ the varying status associated with social positions within each section (e.g. gender or ethnicity).

Overall it could be argued that Hutton simplifies the impact of social class on the labour market and therefore on differentiations in social inequality.

Class and gender

Feminists have accused classical theories of class of focusing on the economic position of men in society, while ignoring the role of women. For example, theories such as Marxism rely on a person's relationship to the means of production to identify their class position – either they work or they do not work. Therefore, paid employment becomes the key factor in determining class, which ignores the unpaid domestic labour undertaken by women, which makes them invisible when allocating class positions or allocates them to their husband's class. Sociologists have presented alternative models for allocating class positions to women, which have taken into account feminist arguments. Currently, five broad models have been identified in the debate over class and gender:

1   The conventional model
2   The cross-class model
3   The class accentuation model
4   The individualistic model
5   The patriarchal model

The classical approach to class and gender has been called the conventional model (Goldthorpe et al. 1980), because the male is seen as the breadwinner and the female as dependent on her spouse for her standard of living and life chances. This model was widely accepted until the 1970s when feminism began to challenge the assumption of female dependence on men. The conventional model did not take into account the role of women in the family or in paid employment. For example, a full-time working wife could dramatically alter the life chances of the whole family through increased income.

The realisation that female employment could affect the class position of a couple or family resulted in the cross-class model (Britten and Heath, 1983). The cross-class model recognises that women should be seen as independent people who, in a relationship or family, may improve the social class position of the household through higher earnings. For example, a bricklayer husband (working class) and teacher wife (middle class) would have a higher family income than a bricklayer husband (working class) and a shop-assistant wife (working class), which would affect the life chances of the whole family.

The cross-class model has been accused of blurring class inequality, a criticism taken on board by the class accentuation model (Bonney, 1988). This model argues that homogamy occurs, which means that like marries like, and therefore partners tend to have similar class backgrounds. Having a similar class to one's mate is seen to accentuate the social class inequalities. In other words, working-class men usually marry working-class women, and middle-class women tend to marry middle-class men, which increases the class divisions between middle-class and working-class families. Women who have been successful in paid employment are seen to have come from middle-class backgrounds and have married men who have achieved similar success.

Gender and class is an area that presents a wide range of theoretical approaches to explain the differences in life chances not only between men and women, but between families and households. It has been argued that class should be given only to the individual, not to a family, and therefore women would be assigned a class position independently of men (Marshall et al. 1988). This individualistic model is based upon occupation and does not include unemployed people, retired people or housewives. Thus, the individualistic model has been criticised for not taking into account the consequences of domestic partnership, such as the effect of marriage and children on the employment prospects of women. Domestic arrangements do have an effect on employment, single women tend to be in full-time, well-paid employment more often than single mothers or married mothers with dependent children.

The interrelationship between domestic and labour-market roles has been identified in the first three models. However, feminists have maintained that women should be given a class that shows them acting autonomously or independently of men. The patriarchal model (Walby, 1990) argues that women are made dependent by men and are consequently exploited by them. Women's roles are subsumed within the males' roles and therefore women are subject to gender conflict in the home and in paid employment. The patriarchal model has gender stratification at its core (see later section, page 178) rather than class stratification and assumes a negative relationship between partners.

Class may not be the only basis on which inequality is defined, but gender inequality (see later section, page 178) as an aspect of the modern industrial world is related to the class position that a woman holds. Women experience discrimination in the workplace, in education and in the way in which others interpret their behaviour, which directly affects their life chances and class position, especially considering the association between class and occupation in the UK.

ACTIVITY   KS **WORKING WITH OTHERS**

IDENTIFICATION AND INTERPRETATION	ANALYSIS AND EVALUATION

Which model of women's position in the class structure do you find most realistic? Test this by asking women who are married what occupations they and their spouses have. Are they of a similar class and background? Do women give way to their partners' ambitions and move in relation to their partners' work? Remember that your analyses will be based on small samples but they may offer some insight into the theory discussed above.

Class and 'race'/ethnicity

Like women in relation to men, ethnic groups have been identified to hold a disadvantaged position in the socio-economic structure of the UK (The Rowntree Foundation, 1995) in relation to white people (see later section, page 186). Marxist and Weberian sociologists have argued that ethnic minority groups have experienced occupational segregation in the struggle over scarce resources, being cast into an '**underclass**' (Rex and Tomlinson, 1979) at the bottom of the stratification system. Therefore 'race' is seen by some structural-conflict theorists as a social construct that promotes racial conflict to fragment the working class,

which in turn hides the real problem of class conflict and thereby sustains capitalism (Miles, 1988). The ethnic minority groups become the disadvantaged scapegoats of capitalism with the poorest class positions and subject to **racial discrimination** in all areas of social life.

Ethnic minorities, however, like women and classes, consist of diverse and differentiated groups and cannot be seen to have exactly the same life chances or class positions. In fact, there is a growing section within the middle class that is made up of ethnic minority group professionals (Cross, 1992). Asian businessmen, for example, are more likely to become self-employed than white men (Labour Force Survey, 1994) and 'buppies' (black yuppies) have provided inspiration and support for other aspiring ethnic minorities. Consequently, it should not be assumed that the social class position of all ethnic minorities in the UK is poor; there is evidence to support class diversity in this group as among the white population.

ACTIVITY   KS **COMMUNICATION, WORKING WITH OTHERS**

IDENTIFICATION AND INTERPRETATION

In pairs construct a list of ethnic minority group members who have achieved a high social class position in the UK. Consider television journalists/newsreaders, academics, actors/actresses, sportsmen/women, members of parliament, business people, etc. Do certain ethnicities have a higher profile than others? To what extent are ethnic minority achievers restricted to certain areas of activity such as sport and popular music?

Changing class structure

Class-based stratification systems are constantly changing, because the distribution of resources or material wealth is never fixed. Those who own the source of wealth (what Marxists termed the means of production) are constantly striving to increase the amount of resources they possess, while those who work for the wealthy struggle to increase their share of resources as much as possible.

The twentieth century has witnessed many changes in the class structure, primarily as a consequence of changes in the occupational structure of the UK. These changes have had an effect on social inequality. The distribution of income and wealth (see Area 10 on Wealth, Poverty, Welfare and Social Policy) has become more unequal in the UK than in any other industrialised country, except New Zealand, since the 1980s (Hills, 1995). A report by Johnson and Webb (1997) identified that the top 10 per cent of the population possess the same income as the bottom 50 per cent of the population, while *Social Trends 1995* revealed that the most wealthy 10 per cent of the population own 49 per cent of all wealth in the UK, but that the bottom 50 per cent of the population own only 8 per cent of all wealth.

The changing class system has been accounted for in the following ways:

■ **The changing occupational structure.**

There has been a rise in the number of service industry jobs, i.e. employment that does not produce goods, such as the leisure and tourism industry, and a decline in employment in the manufacturing industry, i.e. jobs that have an end product, such as furniture manufacturers. This shift between manufacturing and servicing has been referred to as a post-industrial or **post-Fordist** economy (see Area 1 on Sociology Theory). Between 1971 and 1993 the numbers employed in the manufacturing industries declined by over $3\frac{1}{2}$ million, while the service industries increased their numbers by over 3 million (*Sociology Update*, 1996).

The consequence of this shift for the class structure of the UK has been to increase the number of middle-class/intermediate occupations and to reduce the amount of working-class jobs. The need for professional workers to run the huge bureaucracy of the service industries has expanded the middle class (see later section on the middle classes, page 148). Some sociologists now consider the middle class, as the mass of the population, to be the most important section to examine in order to understand society. The problem with this approach to class is that it has the potential to ignore the massive inequality experienced by the bottom 10 per cent of the population who are unemployed or in what is left of manual employment since the decline of the manufacturing industries.

More women are entering employment each year, but women are not employed evenly throughout the occupational structure. Many women enter and remain in poorly paid non-manual work, although by 1995 women made up 40 per cent of professionals (Pascall, 1995).

The effect on the class structure of more women being in paid employment is evident through the way in which it has altered family income/status (see section on 'Gender and class') or allowed women to achieve an independent class status. Sociological studies on social class have been forced by this change to examine the way in which female employment is part of the class structure.

■ **The increasing social inequality between the rich and poor in Britain.**

There has been a decrease in the average income of workers in poorly paid occupations. Between 1979 and 1994 the income of the poorest 10 per cent fell by 17 per cent (1994 Family Expenditure Survey). Tax changes have also reduced the income of the poor, which has served only to widen the gap between the middle and the working classes.

Class still exists and is a powerful influence on our life chances; however, it is changing like the society it reflects.

Measuring class

Changes in the class structure have been widely explained by changes in the occupational structure. The reason for this connection is the way in which class has been measured empirically. Several factors could be used to assess social class, such as:

■ occupation

■ income and wealth

■ status

■ lifestyle and life chances

■ family background

However, the major factor found to correlate with most criteria associated with class, such as power, wealth and status, is occupation. Occupation is a good single indicator of a whole range of characteristics, for example:

- occupations are rewarded differently
- employment controls up to 66 per cent of a person's life
- different occupations require different levels of education
- work puts people into social situations where they interact with others of a similar social type
- occupation indicates economic situation (wealth)
- employment is likely to affect the type of home a person lives in
- occupation can influence leisure pursuits
- different styles of accent and clothes may be linked to occupation
- person's job is used to 'make sense' of someone
- our behaviour is affected by the role expected of us by our occupation

However, problems can arise from using occupation as the only measure of class, such as:

- the very wealthy, such as the owners of large companies, are left out of studies
- the unemployed and unwaged workers are not included in studies
- similar occupational titles may mean different things in different companies or circumstances, for example a teacher in a private school receives better pay and conditions of service than a teacher in a state school
- people in similar occupations may have different access to resources, creating different lifestyles

However, taking into account the advantages and disadvantages of using occupation as an indicator of class, sociologists have applied the concept of occupation, as we shall see later, as a way of measuring class objectively in the UK.

Subjective and objective class

Social class is probably the most significant influence on our lives. It affects us in two ways: subjectively, i.e. through our norms, values and attitudes, and objectively, i.e. by the possessions we have and our health. **Subjective class** refers to the class a person thinks that he or she is in. It is incredibly difficult to construct an accurate measure of subjective class, because a person's perception of his or her own class

may be based on many different variables. However, it is important to understand that a person's subjective class measurement can affect the way he or she acts. For example, if you believe that you are working class, despite having a professional occupation, you are likely to live in a working-class neighbourhood, partake in working-class leisure activities and have working-class norms and values.

Objective class refers to the way in which others perceive a person's class. In sociology an objective class measure is one that can be applied to the whole population through a common criterion, such as occupation (for the reasons explained above). It is possible to measure objective class quite accurately. However, it should be noted that objective class measurements could be very different (see section on contemporary theories of class, page 130), which can have real consequences for the findings. Occupation may be considered an objective measure, but by concentrating on occupation only there may be a tendency to ignore wealth and power as crucial aspects of social differentiation. For example, the Queen would be ignored in class measures based on occupation, but she is influential and could be argued to reside at the top of the class system!

Subjective	Objective
Politics – voting is related to social class (e.g. more professionals vote Conservative).	**Infant mortality** – the children of unskilled working-class parents are three times more likely to die in their first year of life than the children of professionals.
Leisure – the greater income, longer holidays and higher levels of education of the middle class tend to result in leisure interests different from those of the working class.	**Health** – working-class people are three times more likely to have a long-term serious illness compared to middle-class people.
Social views – the working class are more likely to be sympathetic towards trade unions based on their social history.	**Death** – an unskilled working-class man is likely to live, on average, seven years less than a professional man.
	Education – 60 per cent of professionals are graduates, while 47 per cent of unskilled manual workers have no educational qualifications.

Figure 3.9   Examples of subjective and objective class

NB: The subjective and objective differences between social classes are termed **life chances**. Evidence suggests that a person's chances of success or failure in the UK are strongly influenced by the social class into which the person was born.

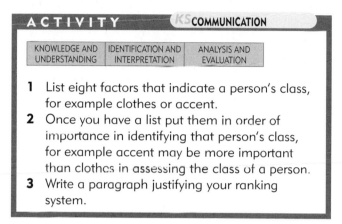

Classifications of social class

Occupation has been the objective measure applied by sociologists and governments examining social class in Britain. Classifications have been established to determine the proportion of the population within specific occupational groupings, based on a hierarchical notion that highest occupations equate with the highest social-class status. In other words, scales have been devised to reflect a person's status in the community based on the skills and educational qualifications of that person's job. The following classification systems all use occupation as an objective measure of social class:

- The Registrar-General's Scale
- The Standard Occupational Classification
- The National Statistics Socio-Economic Classification (NSSEC)
- The Essex University Class Scale
- The Surrey Occupational Class Scale
- Olin Wright's Neo-Marxist Scale (see section on 'Contemporary theoretical perspectives on class – neo-Marxist')
- Goldthorpe's Neo-Weberian Scale (see section on 'Contemporary theoretical perspectives on class – neo-Weberian')
- Runciman's combined Marxian and Weberian Scale (see section on 'Contemporary theoretical

perspectives on class – linking Marxism and Weberian theory')
- Hutton's 30:30:40 Thesis Scale (see section on 'Contemporary theoretical perspectives on class – New Left')

The Registrar-General's Scale

The Registrar-General's Scale classifies the workforce into six classes (with class III being divided between non-manual and manual work, reflecting the assumed division in the lifestyles and norms of similarly paid but different occupations), as shown in the table below.

The government uses the Registrar-General's Scale as its official measure of class in Britain. The census (see Area 2 on Sociological Research Methodology) has been the vehicle for the government to operationalise the Registrar-General's Scale since 1911. The way in which the scale is structured assumes shared values with regard to status based on occupation, such as unskilled workers being less valued than skilled. This assumption means that the Registrar-General's Scale fits into a functionalist perspective of stratification, i.e. value consensus and justifiable social inequality.

Criticisms

- There is not a direct relationship between the earning power of relative occupations in the same class (e.g. university lecturers earn a lot less than architects, in general).
- The scale is based on status, which is a subjective assessment and throws doubt on the objectivity of this measure of class.

Class	Occupation
I	Professional – doctors, architects, solicitors
II	Managerial and technical – farmers, shop owners, teachers
III NM	Skilled non-manual – shop assistants, clerical workers
III M	Skilled manual – builders, electricians
IV	Semi-skilled manual – fishing industry workers, farm labourers
V	Unskilled manual – porters, labourers, cleaners

Figure 3.10 The Registrar-General's Scale

- Using occupation as the defining measure of class ignores the position of the 40 per cent of the population without paid employment. For example, the Registrar-General's Scale cannot examine the unemployed and women who undertake full-time domestic labour.

- According to the 1991 census, groups II and IIINM made up 91 per cent of the middle class, which means that the scale does show the differences in lifestyles and life chances between different middle-class occupations.

The Standard Occupational Classification

The Standard Occupational Classification (SOC) was developed by the Institute for Employment Research to replace the Registrar-General's Scale as the basis for all official information on occupational groupings in the UK. It was argued in *Employment Gazette* (1988:214) that:

' *Occupational Classifications need to be kept up to date if planners are to remain fully informed about the changing job market.*

Therefore, the SOC has updated existing scales to co-exist with the International Standard Classification of Occupations, which meant adding more groups for 'female occupation', such as clerks and teachers, and cover more types of jobs. The SOC classifies occupations based on two criteria:

1 the type of work
2 the level of competence

This means that the status or 'social standing' (a measure used by the Registrar-General's Scale) is not used in classifying people's position in the stratification system.

The SOC classifies occupations as 9 major groups, 76 minor groups and 364 unit groups. The 9 major groups are shown in Figure 3.11.

Criticisms

- The SOC treats occupation as an isolated factor that does not affect, and/or is not affected by social status. It has been argued that this treatment removes the notion of class from occupational classifications.

| Managerial/Administrative |
| Professional |
| Associated professional/technical (do not require a degree) |
| Clerical |
| Skilled manual |
| Personal and protective services |
| Sales |
| Machine |
| Other |

Figure 3.11 Standard Occupational Classification

- By changing the classification system it prevents comparisons between classes or groups over time, which potentially removes the information about class-based social inequality.

The National Statistics Socio-Economic Classification

The NSSEC is the newest social classification system developed for the government by Goldthorpe, Marshall and Rose. It will replace the Registrar-General's Scale, being used for all government official statistics and for the census from 2001. The new system takes into account the massive changes in the occupational structure that have been witnessed over the last 30 years. It acknowledges that a division between manual and non-manual employment, as a reference for class, is no longer appropriate.

The NSSEC is based on occupation, but the categories used are based on employment conditions and relations, rather than skills associated with the occupation (like the RGS). Employment conditions refers to the conditions experienced in that job, such as salary, promotion prospects, sick pay, autonomy, etc. Employment relations refers to the status of being an employee, employer or self-employed. The intention of these categories is to show that social class is not based on hierarchies, but on social difference. For example, earnings are less important than job security, status is less important than long-term prospects in pay and promotion, and skills are less important than power to control your own working environment. These distinctions in employment have resulted in a scale of seven categories, with an optional eighth (see diagram).

National Statistics Socio-Economic Classification

1 **Higher managerial and professional occupations**
   1.1 **employers and managers of large organisations**, e.g. company directors, senior civil servants, corporate managers
   1.2 **higher professional**, e.g. doctors, barristers, teachers, clergy, architects.

2 **Lower managerial and professional occupations**, e.g. nurses, journalists, police officers, musicians

3 **Intermediate occupations**, e.g. secretaries, computer operators, clerks, driving instructors

4 **Small employers and self-employed**, e.g. taxi drivers, window cleaners, publicans, decorators

5 **Lower supervisory, craft and related occupations**, e.g. train drivers, shop assistants, bus drivers, hairdressers

6 **Semi-routine occupations**, e.g. traffic wardens, shop assistants, bus drivers, hairdressers

7 **Routine occupations**, e.g. cleaners, couriers, road sweepers, labourers

8 **Never worked/long-term unemployed**.

Criticisms

- The NSSEC does not show inequalities in earning power or social status and, therefore, may not be of much use in explaining the relationship between social inequality and employment.

- The scale emphasises social difference rather than social inequality and may, therefore, have a political agenda for its implementation in all official publications.

- A hierarchy may be read into the findings of the scale.

The Essex University Class Scale

The 1988 Essex University Class study by Marshall, Newby, Rose and Vogler (*Social Class in Modern Britain*) applied the definitions of class used by Goldthorpe and Wright (see earlier section in this Area on contemporary class theories, page 134) to examine the position of both men and women in the British stratification system. They found that Goldthorpe's 7-class classification scale was more appropriate for

their data than Wright's 12-class scheme, because it allowed them to analyse more accurately the level of skill required by a job and the freedom employees had within work.

Criticisms

Any Marxist classification of class groupings ignores the importance of wealth and power in determining social status and ultimately class. For example, Goldthorpe identifies capitalists in the same group as higher professionals, which underestimates the differential in power between members of that class. Consider the power, wealth and status held by Richard Branson (capitalist) compared to a local government director of services.

The Surrey Occupational Class Scale

The Surrey Occupational Class Scale (SOCS) was developed through feminist research (see Area 2 on Sociological Research Methodology) by Arber, Dale and Gilbert (Surrey University, 1986). It rejected the commonly held assumption that the head of the household (until recently typically seen as the male preserve) should be used as the basis for class analysis. The SOCS employed the individual as the basis for classifying class, which allowed for precise differentiation between female, as well as male, occupations.

The SOCS identified eight classes and examined them in relation to employment status and sex (Figure 3.12).

The scale showed the way in which women are grouped in particular occupations and the continuation of male dominance in higher employment and full-time employment (19.5 per cent men, 6.5 per cent women). Therefore, the consideration of female workers has

1	Higher professionals
2	Employers and managers
3	Lower professionals
4	Secretarial and clerical
5	Supervisors, self-employed manual
6	Sales and skilled manual
7	Semi-skilled
8	Unskilled

Figure 3.12   The Surrey Occupational Class Scale

provided this scale with clear advantages over its predecessors, in that:

- It distinguishes between employers and managers and lower professionals (displays the separation of men and women into different jobs – vertical segregation).

- It differentiates shop work from secretarial/clerical work and sales representatives (displays the number of women in full-time employment in secretarial/clerical work).

- It differentiates personal-service workers from semi-skilled factory workers (displays number of women in part-time employment in these areas).

Criticisms

Employment status was used as a category for analysing socio-economic position, which included male and female full-time employment and female part-time employment and unwaged work. Using part-time employment and unwaged work as categories could be misleading, because these are often transitional states of 'employment' that should not be used as a fixed determinant of class position. For example, the occupational status of a woman after the birth of a child may be different from her typical employment and should not therefore be used as an indicator of class.

Class groupings

Sociologists have tried to show and explain the differences between social classes for many years. However, as has already been suggested, the division between classes is not always clear or applied in a useful manner (see section on Measuring class, page 141). This said, massive social inequality and differentiation continues to exist in modern Britain, and differences/relations in the class structure can be used to illustrate this. Theoretical and research interests dictate how each sociologist perceives the class structure, resulting in a fractured picture of class groupings. Consequently, separating the class structure into four groupings (dominant/upper, intermediate/middle, subordinate/working and lower/underclass) may create a false sense of fluency in class division, but it is useful when attempting to understand the main social divisions in society.

Dominant/Upper class

The power and influence held by the dominant/upper class (also known as the ruling class (Marxist) or super class (Adonis and Pollard, 1998)) in modern western industrial society make it an area of sociological interest. It contains the wealthiest business people and property owners, who have opportunities for control over cultural, political and economic life. As a class they have shared a particular class culture and background, based upon late nineteenth-century notions of nobility and plutocracy (power based on money). However, the growth of New Right Conservatism in the 1980s encouraged businesses to prosper and the 'new wealth' has entered the upper class just like their industrialist forefathers.

The wealth, as a percentage of total wealth, of the dominant/upper class may have been reduced over this century, but it remains huge. For example, in 1923 the top 1 per cent owned 61 per cent of all wealth (Lord Diamond Commission), while in 1993 the top 1 per cent owned 17 per cent of all wealth based on Inland Revenue statistics (Labour Research, February 1997). The dominant/upper class's wealth is based upon inheritance, such as the ownership of shares, property, land, jewellery, art and historical antiquities. It also has the advantage of 'cultural capital' (social skills/contacts that allow someone to achieve in society) as part of its class culture, which enables it to use class position and associated qualities, such as accent, values, confidence, schooling etc. to attain high-grade employment (if necessary).

Britain has 20,000+ millionaires, most of whom have a dominant/upper class background (although the occasional 'newcomer' does infiltrate the ranks, especially with the introduction of the National Lottery). *The Sunday Times* newspaper produces a list of the *Top 100 richest people in the UK* every year, which shows how interested we are in the wealthy. Giddens (1976) has divided 'the rich' into three main groups: jet set/pop aristocracy, landowning aristocracy and the entrepreneurial rich. The first group includes entertainers and sports people, such as Jim Carey, George Michael or Michael Jordan, who have made a great deal of money from their jobs. The second group includes the old landed gentry whose status, wealth and power derive from the land they own. The last group is based upon people who have been active in business and made fortunes through enterprise, such as Richard Branson, Anita Roddick and the Rothschilds'.

Super class

Adonis and Pollard (1998) argue that social class is still a big issue in contemporary Britain, especially considering that the dominant/upper class is being reinforced by an emerging 'super class'. This super class consists of the managerial and professional élite who, through their incredibly high salaries, have become the 'fat cats' of industry and business. For example, Brandon Gough, Chairperson of Yorkshire Water, earns £120,000 per day; Nicola Horlick, fund manager at Morgan Grenfell, had an annual salary of £1.15 million in 1997.

ACTIVITY   KS **COMMUNICATION**

KNOWLEDGE AND UNDERSTANDING	IDENTIFICATION AND INTERPRETATION

Watch the film *The Rogue Trader*, which tells the story of Nick Leeson, a boy from the working class who became a top trader for Barings Bank in Asia. Consider the salary and lifestyle of Leeson before his deception was discovered. Was Leeson a member of the 'super class'?

The super class is submerged into the traditional British financial services of the City of London, with its Oxbridge and gentleman's club heritage. The rapid growth in financial services, supported by the Thatcher years of privatisation and reform in taxation, has enabled the super class to flourish. The super large earnings have been influenced by international trading, especially with the USA, and are seen as a justifiable reflection of ability and achievement. The culture and wealth of the super class could support their inclusion in the dominant/upper class.

> *The thirty years since the mid-1960s have seen the rise of the Super Class – a new elite of top professionals and managers, at once meritocratic yet exclusive, very highly paid yet powerfully convinced of the justice of its rewards, and increasingly divorced from the rest of society by wealth, education, values, residence and lifestyle. It is a seminal development in modern Britain … The aristocracy has been substantially absorbed into the Super Class: old money found its*

> *way into the City a century ago and into business earlier still, and old families no longer care for the tradition of public service.*
>
> (Adonis and Pollard, 1998:67–68)

The dominant/upper class in modern Britain appears to be alive and kicking, despite having changed considerably since its origins as a landed class in early capitalist development (Scott, 1982). Scott (1986) presents a Marxist analysis of the dominant/upper class. He argues that the large estate holders who rented out land (landed magnates) and the small estate holders who farmed the land (landed gentry) can be seen as the original dominant/upper class. However, in the eighteenth century industrialists and financiers challenged the privileged position of the landowners. Development in British industry enabled people to achieve upper-class status through entrepreneurialism. The nineteenth century therefore witnessed three upper classes: landed, commercial and manufacturing.

By the twentieth century a unified upper class emerged based upon social, economic, political and cultural ties linking land, commerce and manufacturing together (Scott, 1986). The three separate classes intermarried and developed similar lifestyles. Wealthy businessmen married the daughters of the landowners to acquire social status and the fathers of the brides, who were experiencing depleted wealth, improved their financial status.

HINTS AND TIPS   To gain a full understanding of the social history surrounding the emergence of the new dominant/upper class, it may be useful to watch the old BBC 1 television series **Buccaneers**, a story about the fate of the daughters of rich American industrialists at the turn of the century. The fathers wanted to improve their social position and business connections and married their daughters into British upper-class families to do this.

The unification of the upper class supported the growth of a concentrated number of larger businesses and the development of joint stock companies (companies in which shares can be bought and sold). However, Scott argues that this has not depleted the power of the dominant/upper/ruling class, because the new larger companies are controlled in the interests of those who own them. He has termed those who control big business as 'the business class' and it is made up of three groups: entrepreneurial capitalists, internal capitalists and finance capitalists. The first group has invested money in the company and is concerned with long-term profits. Internal capitalists are senior executives who work for one company and are concerned with salary and job security, which are linked to company performance. The last group have shares in, manage and finance more than one company, and therefore need to maintain long-term profits to repay loans. Finance capitalists have a 'constellation of interests' and create a network of interlocking directorships, i.e. the business of one company is known and has an effect on other companies. Consequently, the business class has a great deal of political and economic power and is part of the dominant/upper class in modern Britain.

Scott's analysis of the dominant/upper class in Britain is critical of cruder Marxist accounts of the ruling class (bourgeoisie) that fail to acknowledge that not all capitalists are politically active and that not all those with power are members of the bourgeoisie (as argued by Westergaard, 1995). Traditional Marxists argue that the ruling class is capitalists whose economic interests are maintained by the state. The ruling class maintains political power by taking top political jobs, ensuring that its interests are the same as the state's, manipulating the state through threats and bribery and continuing to operate in a capitalist economic system (Miliband, 1973).

Dahrendorf (1959) examines the dominant/upper class from a Weberian perspective in a process he refers to as the 'decomposition of capital'. He argues that it is the highly paid businessmen/managers that hold the power in advanced industrial societies and they therefore receive the highest rewards, putting them at the top of the stratification system. Dahrendorf believes that the growth of joint stock companies (businesses in which the general public can buy shares) has changed the power balance in capitalist societies. The capitalist class, i.e. the very rich who form part of the economic élite and own companies, has less power than the large organisations that operate in the interest of their shareholders. Consequently Dahrendorf argues that modern industrial societies are 'managed' societies, where the rules of large organisations control the managers, stopping them from following their own interests, because they are answerable to outside interests, such as shareholders, the government and the public:

> *Never has the imputation of the profit motive been further from the real motives of men than in the modern bureaucratic managers.*
>
> (Dahrendorf 1959:46)

Dahrendorf's argument about the changing nature of modern industrial society has been criticised by Giddens on two levels. Firstly, Giddens argues that despite the growth of joint stock companies the motive of enterprise is still profit, the basis of capitalism, and therefore capitalism remains (it is not 'decomposing'). Secondly, managers and capitalists do not have conflicting interests, rather both are concerned with the success of the company. This shared interest is based on the fact that top managers usually have shares in the company they manage and therefore control it in their own interest, which is to achieve profit. Consequently Giddens agrees with Scott that modern western societies remain capitalist.

Dahrendorf and Giddens/Scott disagree on who makes up the dominant/upper class. Saunders, arguing from a New Right perspective, adds a further possibility to the debate, by suggesting that the capitalist class is fragmented and instead forms an economic élite whose power is derived from its economic situation. This is an important division, because each theorist sees a different group controlling society for a different reason. Giddens and Scott argue that the ruling class or capitalists dominate society in their own interest; Dahrendorf argues that it is the impersonal control of large organisations that shapes society; and Saunders suggests that position in the stratification system is based on wealth earned through work. It could be argued that we do have large companies managed by specialists in our society, that economic situation does affect class position and that a wealthy and powerful upper class with a distinct culture and access to the best jobs exists. Therefore, it may be concluded that the dominant/upper class is changing in modern Britain, but that its position at the top of the stratification system ensures continued privilege and power.

Middle classes

The middle class in modern capitalist societies has been argued to have expanded and fragmented more in this century than ever before. The middle class is therefore seen as a collection of classes located in the middle of the social stratification system. However, this 'collection of classes' presents a 'boundary problem', in that sociologists have had trouble agreeing where the middle classes start and finish. Sociologists used to apply a boundary of 'non-manual' work to the middle class; in other words, if the employment did not involve manual labour then it secured middle-class status. However, this distinction was considered inadequate, because it did not take into account the diversity of employment that constituted non-manual work and the differences in lifestyles and life chances associated with them (see also section on objective class measurements, page 142).

The middle classes have been referred to as the petit bourgeoisie, white-collar class and non-manual class, which has resulted in an attempt to make a distinction between the 'old' propertied middle class and the 'new' propertyless middle classes (Mills, 1956).

The 'old' propertied middle class

The 'old' middle class is seen as entrepreneurial and both to own and work the means of production, being self-employed, with or without employees. Marx and Weber both argued that this 'lower stratum of the middle class' would disappear with the growth of large capitalists. Marx argued that it would be absorbed into the proletariat (see section on Proletarianisation, page 151), while Weber believed that it should become technically trained and attempt to attain higher status within the middle class (see section on embourgeoisement, page 154). Edgell (1993) outlines three developments that could happen to the petit bourgeoisie/'old' middle class:

1   **The demise thesis** – 10 per cent of the workforce were self-employed in the 1990s; however this is not seen as positive, but negative. Edgell explains that self-employment can be seen as a 'refuge' for the unemployed, particularly those made redundant, acting as a holding place until the petit bourgeoisie disappears for good.

2   **The marginalisation thesis** – the petit bourgeoisie continues to exist, but does not develop and flourish, taking instead a marginal role. It acts as support for capitalist values of self-development and as a reserve employment route if unemployment needs absorbing, based on continual entrepreneurial opportunities.

3   **The demarginalisation thesis** – the petit bourgeoisie can be seen to develop and expand, based on:

   - the need of the service industry for small, labour-intensive businesses
   - the ability of small companies to compete with large ones through the use of information technology
   - small businesses being seen as more ethically sound than large ones
   - the meritocratic nature of small businesses.

The developments of the demarginalisation thesis have been identified in the relative stability of self-employment over the last 10 years, and its improved status through association with finance and technology consultancy. However, there is still a strong argument to support the concept that self-employment acts as a cover for problems in the labour market. Evidence suggests that the 'old' middle class has remained, because although large companies dominate the socio-economic structure, small businesses have remained, albeit in a marginal position.

The 'new' propertyless middle classes

The 'new' propertyless middle classes range from routine white-collar workers to skilled professionals. Marx and Weber differed in their forecasts for this section of the stratification system. Marx argued that white-collar workers would increase in number, based on the availability of public education and the division of labour in the office, causing them to be devalued and enter the ranks of the proletariat (see section on proletarianisation, page 151). Weber predicted an opposite trend; he argued that increased bureaucracy would raise the status of workers with specialist knowledge (see section on embourgeoisement, page 150).

Despite their different interpretations, both Marx and Weber acknowledged a developing growth in the middle class (see section on Changing class structure, page 140). Based on the occupational changes and expansion of higher education, it could be argued that they were both correct. Fragmentation has occurred in the middle class, with different classes emerging in the middle of the stratification system. For example, the situation of clerical workers has declined as capitalism has progressed, but the position of professional workers in the class structure has strengthened.

Roberts et al. (1977) identified, using a Weberian approach, that the term 'middle class' has different interpretations. In a study of 243 white-collar workers, they found that half saw themselves as part of a massive group situated between the powerful dominant/upper class and the weak subordinate/working class, while 14 per cent felt that they had more in common with the working class. What this shows is that the self-images of the middle class vary and that the so-called 'middle class' has been replaced by a fragmented range of 'middle classes' with different lifestyles and life chances. Giddens, however, argues that this conclusion ignores the fact that the middle classes are united as a stratum by educational qualifications that separate them from the other classes.

The professions

The professions are a stratum in the middle of the class structure and have commonly been referred to as upper middle class (the opposite of which is the routine white-collar worker, who is referred to as lower middle class). The professions are one of the fastest growing sectors of the occupational structure, based on the need for specialised and expert knowledge for increasingly complex and bureaucratic organisations. Professional skills are essential for the development and expansion of industrial economies.

The professions are typically divided into two groups:

1 **The higher professions** – judges, solicitors, doctors, dentists, university lecturers, etc.
2 **The lower/semi-professions** – teachers, nurses, social workers, librarians, etc.

The lower professions have an inferior market situation to the higher professions, experiencing less pay, less independence, little self-regulation and poorer working conditions. Millerson (1964) outlined six characteristics that he believed make up a professional occupation:

1 A skill based on theoretical knowledge, e.g. practising medicine.
2 The skill requires training and education, e.g. becoming a solicitor.
3 The profession must demonstrate competency by passing a test, e.g. taking accountancy examinations.

4 Integrity is maintained by sticking to a code of conduct, e.g. the Hippocratic oath.
5 The service is for the public good, e.g. university lecturers passing on knowledge to new professionals.
6 The profession is organised, e.g. the Law Society.

He argued that the higher professions possess all six traits, while the lower professions tend to lack the final characteristic (which may explain their lower market situation). Millerson's criteria for professional status are very similar to that put forward by functionalist Barber. Barber (1963) argued that the professions have four essential attributes that enable them to maintain the functional well-being of society:

■ Systematic and generalised knowledge that can be applied to a variety of problems (Millerson's characteristics 1–3)

■ The professions are concerned with the community and not self-gain (Millerson's characteristic 5)

■ The professions are controlled by a code of ethics (Millerson's characteristic 4)

■ High rewards show achievement and the value of the profession to society (Millerson's characteristic 6).

Although it is difficult to argue with the first four characteristics put forward by Millerson, it is harder to sustain trait number 5 and the idea that the professions make important contributions to all members of society and work in their interests. For example, how can accountants be seen to be working for society and its members when they support members of the ruling class in efforts to evade paying taxes that could help a poorer member of society?

Parry and Parry (1976) offer a Weberian perspective on the professions. They argue that the professions have succeeded in controlling the labour market to maximise rewards, as Millerson identified in characteristic 6. However, unlike Millerson and Barber, Parry and Parry argue that the professions are organised primarily in their own interests through a system of self-government. For example, the medical profession restricts entry by having tough qualifying procedures. Once accepted, the trainee finds it difficult to succeed, which results in a reduced supply of doctors, a continued demand for treatment and therefore high rewards. The medical profession ensures that it is beyond reproach by maintaining a strict code of conduct around the

Hippocratic oath. In case of problems the profession is organised enough to have its own regulating and disciplinary body, the British Medical Association, which deals with issues and problems privately (preventing public scrutiny). The whole medical profession is organised to protect the interests of the profession, to ensure that it appears committed to the public good and to maintain the claim that it alone is qualified to practise medicine.

Goldthorpe (1982) employs a Weberian approach for examining the 'new' propertyless middle class. He argues that a distinct middle class of professional/managerial workers exists and that they provide specialist services and/or knowledge. They are highly rewarded and share a similar experience in the workplace, making their positions interchangeable. This service class or '**salariat**' is seen as largely meritocratic and heterogeneous (different), with 60 per cent coming from alternative class backgrounds. The consequence of the way the service class has developed is that it lacks cohesion and, therefore, is unlikely to take any class action. Goldthorpe concludes that the service class is a conservative force, content with maintaining its relatively privileged position in the stratification system.

Marxists have challenged this image of the middle class, particularly Savage et al. (1992). Savage et al. argue that the 'new' propertyless middle class is a diverse group based on differing cultural or economic factors. They argue that professionals and managers are facing less job security than ever before, for example in the form of fixed-term contracts, rather than permanent employment. Therefore, Goldthorpe's contented service class is difficult to identify among the contest for employment, especially among managers. In fact, it appears that there is a new conflict emerging among the 'new' middle classes, a conflict based on economic survival and prosperity.

Wright (1976, 1985) developed the Marxist theory of contradictory class locations. He argued that professional workers find that they have things in common with the bourgeoisie, such as sharing in profits, but that they are also members of the proletariat. This contradiction in their class location (are they middle class, working class or what?) provides them with a vague class position, somewhere between the dominant class and the subordinate one.

Neo-Marxists have also attempted to explain the position of the 'new' propertyless middle class so evident in modern industrial society. Gouldner (1979) identified a group of 'humanistic intellectuals' (people with a social and political awareness) who possessed the social knowledge (cultural capital) to be able to transcend class boundaries. This 'new class' is argued to be concerned with human freedom and takes part in new social movements that express a political conscience.

The Weberian approach presents the professions as a market strategy, which could explain why the lower professions occupy a lower market situation than the higher professions – they are not as well organised. For example, doctors attained professional status before the state had a chance to intervene, while teachers failed to organise themselves before state intervention and control. However, Marxists, who argue that the professions serve the interests of the ruling class, challenge the idea that the professions work in their own interests. Wright argues that the professions teach large companies how to do what they want within the law, while poorer members of society cannot afford their services. Therefore the position of the professions at the top of the middle class is based on their value to the rich and powerful. The neo-Marxist Ehrenreichs (1979) argue that the professional–managerial class has developed to support capitalist culture and capitalist class relations. In other words, the skills of the professions have been put to use in organising capitalism to maintain and sustain the maximum profit for the bourgeoisie. Therefore, it would appear that the role of the professions is dependent on the theory used to explain it.

Proletarianisation

Mar argued that the expansion of white-collar employment would result in the devaluing of petit bourgeois occupations and increasing polarisation between the proletariat and the bourgeoisie (see Area 1 on Sociological Theory). Routine white-collar workers (clerks, secretaries and shop assistants) were predicted to leave the middle class and become part of the proletariat, hence the term **proletarianisation**.

Marx identified three types of proletarianisation:

1 **Proletarianisation of work** – wage labour enslaves the workers and condemns them to being a commodity. Increased use of machinery and

Can marriage change your social class?

Old aristocracy: extremely wealthy but care about society.

Suburbanites: work hard for financial security.

New money: typically from lower strata.

Figure 3.13 Are we all middle class now?

specialised divisions in labour result in the de-skilling of work and a loss of autonomy (being able to control what you do).

2 **Proletarianisation of society** – the tendency of the working class to increase in size, live in urban areas and experience relative poverty as a consequence of capitalism.

3 **Political proletarianisation** – after experiencing a proletarianisation of society and work, the proletariat will unite to improve its working conditions and wages.

Braverman (1974), an American Marxist, examined proletarianisation of work and society. He argued that the de-skilling of routine non-manual jobs, where the skills associated with white-collar jobs have decreased over the last century, is based on the separation of tasks, computerisation and 'feminisation'. In other words, routine non-manual jobs have become sliced up and taken over by computers and women, all of which has resulted in a decrease in rewards for those still employed. He also argues that professional workers have experienced proletarianisation, to the point that they have become the slaves of capitalism. Consequently, all workers, i.e. anyone who has to work to survive, are the new proletariat.

Braverman does not take into account political proletarianisation and has been criticised for 'removing' the potential class consciousness of the working class. He has also been criticised for not showing whether de-skilled workers were forced into that employment from a higher status job (Erikson et al. (1983)). Lockwood (1989), using a Weberian perspective, denies the claim that routine white-collar workers have been proletarianised (although he acknowledges that they have received a drop in wages). He argues that clerks have distinct advantages over manual workers, such as better job security and working conditions. Therefore, the lower stratum of the middle class has not entered the ranks of the working class. However, Lockwood's study did not include female clerical workers, who do appear to have been proletarianised. Crompton and Jones (1984) found that 91 per cent of clerical workers, including female clerks in typical 'women's work', in their study of 887 had no control over their jobs. Marshall et al. (1988) in their study of 1770 routine white-collar workers found that personal-service workers (typically women), such as receptionists and shop assistants, had a similar lack of autonomy to the working class. Both neo-Marxists and neo-Weberians agree that women in routine white-collar employment have experienced de-skilling:

' *Women in routine clerical jobs are very closely comparable to men in manual wage-earning ones in that they occupy essentially subordinate positions within the organisation of production.*

(Goldthorpe, 1984:495)

Working class

The working class is typically seen as manual workers. For example, occupational scales, such as the Registrar-General's Scale, place the working class in groups IIIM, IV and V, which is manual employment (see section on Measuring class, page 141). The changes that have occurred in the occupational structure have affected the position of the working class in Britain. The decline of the manufacturing industries (traditional area for working-class employment), increased affluence (wealth) among the working class, a growth in white-collar employment and the increasing number of women in the labour force have all acted upon the position of the working class in the stratification system.

The most notable change to the structure of the working class in post-war Britain has been the decreasing

Anthony Giddens	There is a single middle class based on educational and/or technical qualifications. Have to sell mental and physical labour.
John Goldthorpe	The middle class consists of two groups: 1 **The intermediate class** – clerical workers, personal-service workers and low-grade technicians 2 **The service class** – professional, managerial and administrative workers. The service class has a better market situation than the intermediate class.
Roberts, Cook, Clark and Semeonoff	The middle class is made up of a number of strata with a distinctive view of their place in the stratification system. The middle class is becoming increasingly fragmented.
Braverman/ Crompton and Jones	White-collar work has been de-skilled and proletarianised. The middle class has become divided, with the routine non-manual workers entering the ranks of the proletariat and the professional non-manual workers moving closer to the bourgeoisie.

Figure 3.14   Positions on the intermediate/middle class/es

number that participates in manual employment. The expansion of white-collar work within the middle class has provided non-manual employment opportunities for those who would previously have been employed in manual work (see section on Embourgeoisement, page 154). This movement between social groups (know as **social mobility**) has been seen as a positive change by Liberal theorists.

The Liberal perspective argues that high rates of social mobility are a sign of increasing affluence and a more positive working environment in an industrial society. The Liberal perspective assumes that as industrial society moves into a post-industrial phase (from manufacturing to information processing), work becomes more enjoyable and the traditional attitudes of the working class become more middle class (see section on embourgeoisement, page 150).

Traditional working class

Sociologists have tended to see the traditional working class as having norms, values and attitudes distinct from the middle class. The traditional worker is seen to be:

- manually employed
- fatalistic (believes social situation will not improve)
- poor at deferring gratification (lives for the present)
- good at supporting the working class as a whole (group solidarity)
- socialising with workmates
- seeing society as divided between employers and workers (a power model)
- less wealthy and have poorer working conditions than non-manual workers
- inferior in market situation to non-manual workers, i.e. more likely to become ill, die young, have less educational qualifications, be convicted of a crime, etc.

Marxist theorists, however, argue that the working class is not enjoying work more as the service industries expand, in fact it is becoming more alienated, or cut off, from its labour (see Area 1 on Sociological Theory). Braverman (1974) argued that de-skilling had become a major feature of manual employment, which meant that workers' tasks were being simplified and controlled by the owners (see section on proletarianisation, page 151). Therefore, far from developing attitudes and values similar to the middle class, Braverman argued that manual workers, and the proletariat in general, would become more conscious of who they are (the oppressed mass) and resist control.

The working class is central to Marxism as a theoretical perspective (see Area 1 on Sociological Theory). Marx argued that the working class, or proletariat in capitalist society, was an oppressed mass who would eventually become unified as a class in itself, and for itself, to overthrow the bourgeoisie and seize control of the means of production. Marxist theory gave rise to the belief in a traditional working class (see page 153) who worked together in the interest of each other (solidaristic collectivism), rather than for individual interest (instrumentalism). This image of the working class in Britain has been supported by obvious and recognised collective class action, such as the miners' strikes in 1984/5 and the continuation of the Labour Party. However, the action that has taken place has not secured a redistribution of wealth or communal ownership of the means of production. Working-class action has secured reforms for workers within contemporary capitalism. The radical and militant class-conscious proletariat that Marx envisaged has not arisen in the UK to challenge the structure of society.

Marshall et al. (1988) argue that the working class retains an image of itself as being part of the 'us' and 'them' power model. An opinion poll by Gallup (1993) found that class identity was important to the British public, with the working class having an awareness of how its class position affected workers' lives (Abercrombe and Warde, 1994). However, it has been argued (Marshall et al., 1988) that the working class has not translated this identity into class action for the following reasons:

- Instrumentalism – the working class uses capitalism to serve its own interests. Militant class action is a tool to ensure that it receives higher rewards to improve general living standards.
- Indifference – the working class does not have a unified attitude towards capitalism, it is ambivalent or indecisive/indifferent. Therefore, Marxist claims

that there is a dominant ideology (see Area 1 on Sociological Theory) are difficult to support. The ruling class cannot be seen to have indoctrinated the working class into a meek acceptance of capitalism. The working class utilises the areas of capitalism that it benefits from and challenges the parts that it does not. This ambivalent attitude is better explained by the neo-Marxist concept of hegemony (Gramsci, 1971) (see Area 1 on Sociological Theory), which shows the transient nature of working class attitudes that are influenced by the ruling class through cultural and political devices.

Sociologists have, therefore, explored the question of whether the working class will ever become class-conscious, realise its social inequality and challenge the stratification system that has supported it. Contemporary answers to this question have rested on the idea that the working class has become increasingly heterogeneous or divided in relation to the work that it does and the political views that it holds (Dahrendorf, 1992; Crewe 1986) and will not be able to take collective action. However, it should be noted that Marxist sociologists, such as Westergaard and Resler (1976), believe that the potential for class consciousness remains and may be stimulated by the growing affluence identified among the working class (see section on Embourgeoisement below). Westergaard argues that instrumental workers expect higher wages and rising living standards and this is their motivation to work. Consequently, if this criterion fails to be met, it may trigger a radical reaction in the workplace.

Embourgeoisement

Embourgeoisement is a term that refers to an increasing number of manual workers becoming more affluent (wealthy) and thereby entering a more middle-class lifestyle. It is a hypothesis (see Area 2 on Sociological Research Methodology) that emerged in the 1950s, when there was a general increase in the wealth of advanced industrial societies. The UK was experiencing the post-war economic boom and Harold Macmillan, the Prime Minister, summed up the nation's positive outlook by stating that Britain had 'never had it so good'. Sociologists were interested in the social, economic, political and cultural position of the increasingly well-off working class, especially with the 1959 defeat of the Labour Party and an apparent loss of traditional working-class support. In other words, sociologists wanted to know whether the working class was becoming more middle class.

The social stratification system appeared to be changing in structure, with increasing affluence placing the majority of the population within the middle stratum (see diagram below).

It was argued that the changing occupational structure demanded a more highly skilled and educated workforce to operate modern technology, which in turn necessitated higher rewards. These higher wages were also seen as a way of supporting mass consumerism, a feature necessary for the functioning of an industrial economy. Therefore, the relative affluence of the working class was argued to be a sign of it adopting a middle-class lifestyle, with supporters of the embourgeoisement thesis suggesting that the working class was almost impossible to distinguish from the white-collar middle class.

In 1963 Goldthorpe, Lockwood, Bechhofer and Platt embarked on an empirical test of the embourgeoisement hypothesis to see whether the presumed phenomenon was actually occurring. Goldthorpe et al. took a sample of 229 manual workers in the increasingly affluent area of Luton, and a comparative group of 54 white-collar workers. Their study took two years and examined the migrant labour force of Vauxhall Cars, Skefco Engineering and LaPorte Chemicals. Nearly half of their sample had come to the south east in search of well-paid employment and held few political views. All the people in the sample were married men, 57 per cent

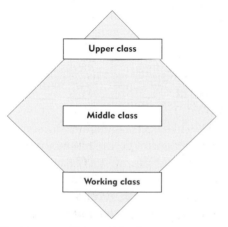

Figure 3.15   More people are middle class

were homeowners and their wages were comparable to white-collar workers.

From the beginning of their research Goldthorpe et al. were clear that wages alone could not determine a person's position in the class structure. It was obvious that the earnings of the working-class men in their sample did place them in reach of a middle-class lifestyle and that they took advantage of 'middle class' consumer durables, such as televisions and automatic washing machines. However, their economic position did not show any other similarities to that of the middle class. For example, the working class experienced a lack of promotion prospects, few fringe benefits, overtime as a means of securing high wages and little satisfaction derived from work. In relation to their political position, this inferior economic situation to the middle class appeared to ensure strong support of trade unions and less support for the Conservative Party (in 1959, 80 per cent of the sample voted Labour). Therefore, the affluent workers were instrumental in voting Labour; in other words they voted as a way of improving their economic position.

On a cultural level, Goldthorpe et al. discovered that the working-class sample did not seek middle-class friends or a middle-class lifestyle. It did not have a traditional working-class community life, which was to be expected considering that half had moved to find work, but the family was still an important part of social life. In fact, the majority of the working class socialised with kin, workmates and close neighbours in informal situations. Therefore, the cultural behaviour of the affluent working class was not moving towards a middle-class lifestyle, but was changing as a response to geographical mobility and increased use of the home for leisure time.

Supporters of the embourgeoisement thesis have argued that the manual working class has become increasingly middle class, but Goldthorpe et al. (1968) found little evidence of this in their study. They argued that the affluent working class was different to the traditional manual class, but was by no means middle class. There were common characteristics emerging between the manual workers and the white-collar workers, but these characteristics were not evidence of class convergence (see Figure 3.16). In this situation, class relationships were not determined by economic forces, the small increase in wages did not make the manual workers middle class. It could be concluded that Goldthorpe et al. identified an affluent working class in Luton that may be termed the 'new working class'.

Despite general agreement existing within the sociological world that embourgeoisement has not occurred, the idea of a 'new' privatised, home-centred, instrumental working class has been disputed (Marshall, Newby, Rose and Vogler, 1988). Marshall et al. claim that the working class has exhibited the traits identified in Goldthorpe et al.'s 'new working class' since the nineteenth century. Penn (1983) also argues that the working class has used trade unions to represent its interests in an instrumental way for hundreds of years, through the sectional representation of specific types of workers. These arguments not only dispute the idea of a 'new working class', but suggest that divisions have existed within the working class since the nineteenth century. The importance of this argument is that if historically occupation, industry, area and skill have stratified the working class, then any solidarity, then or now, is hard to imagine. This said, the Labour Party did develop within these social conditions to represent the interests of the working class, so divisions within the working class may not prevent class action in the future.

Underclass or lower strata

The social stratification system in Britain has traditionally been imagined as having three main strata; the upper class, the middle class and the working class. Giddens

Working class	Middle class
Work is instrumental or a means to an end, with little intrinsic satisfaction from work.	Expects job satisfaction and career progression.
Does not view work in the context of making friends; social life revolves around kin and neighbours.	Makes friends at work.
Practises instrumental collectivism, i.e. works together to improve situation.	Practises instrumental collectivism, i.e. works together to improve situation.
Privatised, home-centred existence.	Privatised, home-centred existence.
Generally votes Labour.	Generally votes Conservative.

Figure 3.16 Differences and similarities between the affluent working class and the white-collar middle class in the 1960s

(1973), however, identified in the 1970s the potential for a fourth strata in advanced industrial societies; a lower strata, or **underclass**, facing social inequalities harsher than those experienced by the working class. Since the identification of this possible new social class division sociologists have been keen to examine and explain the position of the underclass.

Giddens (1973) suggested that the underclass was made up of people who were restricted to employment in the secondary labour market, with poor pay, conditions and chances of promotion. He argued that the underclass was in a very different economic situation compared to the working class, because the underclass lacked any kind of work-related support or rights. Jordan (1973) supported the idea of a new lower stratum, arguing that a new 'claiming class' had emerged that was reliant on welfare benefits for survival. Unlike Giddens, Jordan identified this new subordinate class as jobless, an idea that linked the most underprivileged sections of the population to the underclass thesis: ethnic minorities and women.

Rex and Tomlinson (1979) conducted a study of the social position of ethnic minorities living in Birmingham and declared that ethnic minorities were part of the underclass. They argued that the life chances of ethnic minorities, including employment, housing and education opportunities, were inferior to that of white people living in Birmingham. Therefore, ethnic minority groups had a different and disadvantaged social position compared to white people that made them an underclass in British society.

The work conducted by sociologists in the 1970s on the possible existence of an underclass has been widely adopted by contemporary sociologists. However, it should be noted that it has not been agreed what constitutes the 'underclass' and, therefore, whether it actually exists. In fact, the term itself has become highly emotive, being adopted by the media to represent a section of society that is not only in an undesirable situation, but is itself undesirable.

The underclass has been highlighted by some sociologists as a deviant group at the bottom of the stratification system (Murray, 1990; Saunders, 1990), a group that causes problems rather than a group that is caused by social problems, such as unequal distribution of resources (Field, 1989). The first explanation of the underclass can be seen as a cultural view, the latter a structural view (the debate between cultural and structural views can be seen in Area 1 on Sociological Theory). Throughout Britain's social policy-making history public support has swung between a cultural and a structural view (see Area 10 on Welfare). In times of economic prosperity, the poor were not blamed for their situation and were given relief by the state; during recession poverty was seen as a justified consequence of laziness.

Cultural explanations

In 1989 Charles Murray was sponsored by *The Sunday Times* to visit Britain to uncover the 'underclass' that was claimed to exist. He identified a group of people living in a culture of poverty (See Area 10 on Poverty) where they had become dependent on welfare benefits, had turned to crime and had no respect for family values:

> *Then there was another set of poor people, just a handful of them. These poor people didn't just lack money. They were defined by their behaviour. Their homes were littered and unkempt. The men in the family were unable to hold a job for more than a few weeks at a time. Drunkenness was common. The children grew up ill-schooled and ill-behaved and contributed to a disproportionate share of the local juvenile delinquents.*

(Murray, 1996:23)

Based on the ideas of Lewis (1968), Murray blamed the poor for their own poverty. He argued that the underclass chose not to seek employment, but to live within their culture of dependency:

> *... the definitive proof that an underclass has arrived is that the large numbers of young, healthy, low-income males choose not to take jobs.*

(Murray, 1996:37)

Increasing illegitimacy, crime and unemployment made Murray state that the disease of the underclass was growing in Britain.

His findings in Britain supported what he had found in the USA (Murray, 1984), that dependency on welfare provision had increased poverty rather than reduced it. Murray argued that welfare benefits supported a rise in illegitimacy and destructive behaviour. Therefore he

considers the underclass to be a growing threat to both American and British society.

Unfortunately Murray wrote about Britain's growing underclass at a time of economic recession and found support for his cultural explanation among the public, encouraging further racialism and anger against 'dole bludgers'.

Saunders (1990) supports the cultural view of Murray, identifying the way of life of those in poverty as the cause of their disadvantaged social position. Saunders argues that the British underclass shares four social characteristics:

1   Multiple deprivation (many aspects to its poverty)
2   Marginalisation (cut off from the rest of society)
3   Welfare State dependency (relies on benefits to survive)
4   Fatalistic (resigned to its inferior position).

These characteristics present a very negative picture of a dependent culture of the underclass. Both Murray and Saunders present a New Right perspective that is explained in further detail in Area 1.

Structural explanations

Sociological research in Britain has favoured a structural approach, with Field (1989) identifying government economic and social policies as the cause of an underclass of old age pensioners, the unemployed and single parents. Field argues that full employment, an improved welfare state and a redistribution of wealth would enable the disadvantaged underclass to enjoy full citizenship rights.

Dahrendorf (1987) argues that although the underclass has negative cultural characteristics, such as 'laid-back sloppiness', these characteristics are a consequence of structural changes in society. He believes that developments in information technology have both removed the need for a large workforce and made the service industry too expensive for many consumers. Consequently, with few employment prospects, except in low-paid jobs, the underclass continues to grow.

Dahrendorf also states that the underclass does not have the same position in society as other employed members. By this he means that members of the underclass, such as young people and ethnic minorities, do not have full citizenship rights, because they do not have an economic place in the structure of society. It is for this reason that Dahrendorf sees the underclass developing a less than desirable culture. If members of the underclass are treated as second-class citizens, with very little opportunity for improving their economic position, what is the point of conforming? It seems, therefore, a rational reaction for the underclass to establish an alternative set of norms and values, but the problem is that these norms are seen to threaten members of mainstream society.

According to Dahrendorf the underclass is an issue that is difficult to address. Full employment is unlikely, although a fairer spread in employment, such as job sharing, could offer some relief and potentially give the underclass full citizenship rights. He also suggests that local communities should develop initiatives to help the underclass escape its disadvantaged economic situation. Unfortunately, Dahrendorf does not provide an accurate picture of what 'the underclass' actually is; rather he provides stereotypical images of a group 'who have suffered misfortune'. In fact, he concludes that he is not convinced that 'the underclass' is actually a class at all. If this is the case, then it is difficult to accept his explanation of its development as a group with an alternative set of norms and values.

Ideologically, the structural approach is much more acceptable than cultural theories, because it blames the inequalities evident in the social system for the subordinate position of members of society. However, the structural approach does fail to acknowledge that the term 'underclass' actually includes very diverse groups of people that are affected differently by, and react differently to, social inequality. Therefore, it is very difficult to measure the structural impact of poverty on, for example, ethnic minorities, single parents and old age pensioners when their experiences are all so diverse.

The structural argument for the existence of an underclass has been supported and criticised in relation to the position of ethnic minorities. Racial inequality has been argued by Weberians to be an example of status inequality, placing ethnic minorities in a disadvantaged social position. The notion of a black underclass is seen to elicit support through the restriction of many ethnic minorities to the poorest areas of employment (Parkin, 1979); their status disadvantage has become a class disadvantage.

ACTIVITY KS **COMMUNICATION, WORKING WITH OTHERS**

KNOWLEDGE AND UNDERSTANDING	IDENTIFICATION AND INTERPRETATION	ANALYSIS AND EVALUATION

Make a list identifying the three social factors that you think affect the following 'underclass' groups most. In a group, discuss your findings and examine whether it is possible to talk about 'the underclass' as a homogeneous (similar) group with shared norms, values, attitudes and life chances.

Ethnic minorities	Racialism
Single parents	Low income
Old age pensioners	Unemployment
Unemployed	Welfare dependency

HINTS AND TIPS   *It is useful to remember that 'the underclass' has not been clearly defined and is therefore very difficult to identify and measure. Consequently the size of 'the underclass' in advanced industrial societies is hard to determine, because sociologists cannot agree on what or who comprises it. The following characteristics of 'the underclass' have all been identified, but not agreed upon, by sociologists:*

- *members of the secondary labour market*
- *unemployed*
- *single parents*
- *ethnic minorities*
- *benefit claimants*
- *old age pensioners*
- *criminals*
- *those in poverty*
- *drug users*
- *truants*
- *homeless*
- *chronically sick*
- *those without paid employment for at least 2.5 years*
- *those who exhibit deviant behaviour*

A useful concluding point has been given by Murray (1990:41), which can be used to question the validity of attempting to identify 'an underclass' at all:

> *... it all depends how one defines its membership ... The size of the underclass can be made to look huge or insignificant, depending on what one wants the answer to be.*

Marxists, such as Miles (1982), however, are critical of a separate underclass of ethnic minority workers and instead see them as the lowest stratum of the working class. Ethnic minority workers are seen to have a relatively distinct economic, political and ideological position in the UK, but this position operates within the working class.

Both Weberians and Marxists agree that British capitalism, and the racialism that exists within it, maintains the subordinate position of black people in the stratification system. They also agree that it is important to look at employment when placing ethnic minorities in the class structure and to realise that their interests are different to white workers. However, it is important to realise that the situation of ethnic minorities in Britain is changing and that although as a whole ethnic minorities are disadvantaged, as separate ethnic groups they are no longer restricted to unskilled manual work. In fact, there is much evidence of increasing access to professional employment for specific ethnic groups, such as African Asians (Modood, 1991).

There is no doubt that the existence of an underclass in Britain and USA is a controversial issue. There are obviously sections of these populations that are seriously materially and socially disadvantaged. Such groups have been identified by classical sociologists; Marx's lumpenproletariat consisted of vagabonds and tinkers unfit to be members of the working class. However, whether these sections of society form a poorer stratum of the working class, or constitute a separate group with similar norms and values, is highly debatable, as we have seen.

> 6 *There is no doubt that Britain has become a more polarised society, but whether this has resulted in the growth of a distinct underclass, cut off economically from the working class and characterised by distinct attitudes and behaviour, is debatable.*
>
> (Pilkington, 1992:32)

Social mobility

Social mobility refers to the amount of movement from one stratum to another. In a class-based stratification system social mobility can be seen by changes of members of society in class position. Class-based stratification systems, such as in Britain, are called 'open' societies, because they have a high degree of social mobility meaning that the classes have relatively open access. Status in open societies is usually achieved by merit, which would allow someone to 'work their way up' the class structure. 'Closed' societies are ones that have very little social mobility and therefore do not allow movement between strata, such as in the Indian caste system of stratification. Status is generally ascribed, or given at birth, in closed societies, which means that members have to accept the position into which they are born.

Sociologists continue to examine social mobility because it provides information on all types of stratification issues, such as:

■ how classes are formed

■ the size and shape of classes

■ the way classes respond to high and low social mobility

■ the way individuals respond to social mobility

■ life chances

■ the pattern of people's class-based lives

■ the functioning of meritocratic ideals (fairness) and equal opportunities in society.

Consequently social mobility has been widely researched, traditionally concentrating on the employment of men, but more recently acknowledging the position of women in the occupational class structure. Whether the studies have been on men, women or both, they have applied their measures to either:

1 **INTRAgenerational mobility** – social mobility within a single generation, i.e. comparing the occupational position of a single person at two or more points in time.

2 **INTERgenerational mobility** – social mobility between generations, i.e. comparing the occupational position of father and son, father and daughter and in the future possibly mother and daughter.

HINTS AND TIPS   *An easy way to remember the difference between intragenerational and intergenerational mobility is to think:*

■ *INTRA means within, such as intravenous (within the vein), so it must be within an individual life.*

■ *INTER means between, such as intercity (going between different cities), so it must mean between two people's lives.*

Social mobility can be long-range, for example from one class to another; short-range, such as from the lower middle class to the middle middle class; and upwards or downwards (vertical mobility) or sideways (horizontal mobility into a similar, but different, occupation) within the stratification system. As well as individuals having various opportunities for social mobility, stratum mobility exists too. Stratum mobility refers to the movement of a whole social group, for example the improved status of the working class during post-war affluence. However, it is interesting to note that despite the potential for social mobility in open societies, most people stay in the class into which they were born.

Social mobility can also be classified as absolute or relative. Absolute social mobility is the total amount of social mobility that occurs in a society. For example, absolute mobility can be seen in a study (see explanations of social mobility) that measures the total number of people in each class that has experienced social mobility. Relative social mobility refers to the comparative chances of different social groups achieving social mobility at the same point in time. For example, the expansion of the service industries in the 1990s allowed for more social mobility, because there was a demand for more workers in this area. However, the relative chances of a middle-class person getting a service-industry job would be higher than that of a working-class person. Therefore the relative social mobility of the working class is lower than the intermediate class, which in turn is lower than the service class. Social mobility that is relative to your class position has been summed up as the '1:2:4 rule'. This rule means that the service class is four times more likely than the working class to get a service-class job and the intermediate class is twice as likely as the working class to get a service-class job. It is interesting to identify relative social mobility when attempting to assess how open or meritocratic a society is.

Problems in measuring social mobility

There are many difficulties associated with studying and measuring social mobility, such as:

- Different occupational scales may be used for different studies (see section on Measuring class, page 141), which makes comparing studies very difficult and often misleading.

- Individuals may not have stable career paths, which makes comparisons in mobility difficult to target, i.e. at which point should a person's occupational status be compared?

- The extremely wealthy may be unidentifiable in studies of social mobility, because their private investments are unlikely to be reflected by their occupations.

- Female social mobility has only recently been examined as a separate entity to that of their husbands and therefore does not enable historical comparison.

- The amount of mobility may depend on the measure employed.

Explanations of social mobility

Social mobility in England and Wales, 1949

Glass (1954) conducted the first major investigation into male intergenerational mobility in England and Wales in 1949. He identified a reasonably high level of social mobility, with two-thirds of the men interviewed being in a different status group to their fathers. The vertical mobility of these men had been $\frac{1}{3}$ upward and $\frac{1}{3}$ downward, although the change in status was not great. Short-range mobility, where the sons had moved into a status category adjacent to their fathers, was typical. Long-range mobility was hard to find, which could be explained in part by the considerable amount of élite self-recruitment (employing people for higher level jobs who already had fathers in that type of employment).

Glass found that the class status of the family directly affected the life chances of the individual. In other words, if the father had a high occupational status, then the son was more likely to find a good job. Glass identified high levels of absolute mobility but low relative mobility levels. There was evidence of high levels of total social mobility, but this mobility was relative to class status. This suggests that in 1949 England and Wales were not as open to social mobility as it may have appeared and that there was actually a high level of inequality of opportunity.

The validity of Glass's study has been challenged, because it is argued that he did not take into account the expansion of white-collar work before 1949. This would affect his findings by underestimating the amount of social mobility. However, Glass's findings inspired sociologists to examine future patterns of social mobility.

The Oxford Mobility Study (Nuffield College), 1972

The next major study to be conducted into intergenerational social mobility in England and Wales was by a team at Nuffield College, Oxford, in 1972. Although the findings are not strictly comparable, because of the use of different criteria to establish social mobility, the team did find higher rates of long-range mobility than in 1949. This suggests that relative mobility rates were decreasing, with 7.1 per cent of the sons with semi-skilled fathers entering the higher professionals. The study also discovered high rates of absolute social mobility, with over 50 per cent of the sample originating from a different social class.

The study found higher chances for upward vertical mobility than downward, which seemed to support the idea that Britain was becoming a more open society. However, although the relative mobility levels appeared to be increasing, there was still evidence of massive inequality of opportunity to achieve upward social mobility for the lower class. For example, 45.7 per cent of higher professional workers had fathers in the same occupational status (compared to 7.1 per cent having fathers who were semi-skilled). The relative chances of the sons of those from classes outside the professions taking advantage of increasing room at the top (see section on changes in the occupational structure, page 140) of the stratification system had not improved very much at all. Therefore, in 1972 Britain had not become a more open and meritocratic system; class boundaries were still in evidence despite high levels of absolute mobility.

Female social mobility

Female mobility has been ignored for a long time, yet females make up half the adult population. Both the Oxford Mobility Study and Glass's study can be criticised for ignoring the occupational position of women. However, studying female mobility is technically difficult, because many women are not in paid employment and those who are may be in part-time jobs or have career breaks to raise children. Consequently women's relationship to the occupational structure has often meant that women's class, and the

class of the household, has been set by the occupation of the husband. However, the difficulty of measuring female social mobility is no excuse for neglecting the female occupational and class experience.

Harris and Clausen (1964) had conducted an intragenerational mobility study on both men and women between 1953 and 1963. They discovered a high rate of élite self-recruitment, which resulted in only 4 per cent of women being employed in the professions. There were high rates of absolute mobility, but less chance of relative mobility, based on very little evidence of long-range mobility. Women tended to stay in the occupational status group they had first entered, but there was evidence of more downward than upward social mobility compared to men. For example, 65 per cent of women and 78 per cent of men remained in routine white-collar work, but 26 per cent of women and only 13 per cent of men moved down into manual work over the 10-year study.

Heath (1981) attempted to examine the intergenerational mobility of women using the General Household Surveys of 1972–1975. He compared the occupational status of daughters to that of their fathers. He found that women from a professional background were more likely to experience downward vertical mobility compared to men of the same class background although women from the working class experienced more upwardly vertical mobility to the middle class compared to men of the same class origin.

Heath's findings can be explained in part by the changing occupation structure in Britain, which has progressively provided more employment opportunities for women, but with lower wages than their male counterparts. It could also be argued that women are less likely to achieve high-grade qualifications that would enable them to achieve the professional occupation that their fathers had. Therefore, the inequality of opportunity for women in the occupational structure can be seen to have a direct effect on their class position and life chances.

The Essex Mobility Study, 1988

Marshall, Rose, Newby and Vogler conducted a study of social class (see section on occupational class groupings, page 145), which included collecting data on social mobility. It was the first large-scale study of

British Class to investigate the intergenerational and intragenerational social mobility of both men and women. In order to operationalise their study, intergenerational mobility was based on a comparison of occupational status between respondent and the person he/she considered the main supporter as a child, i.e. mother or father. The occupational status was recorded at the same age for respondent and main childhood supporter.

The Essex Mobility Study discovered similar absolute levels of social mobility to previous studies, because there had been a continued expansion of white-collar work. Male social mobility rates were very similar to the Oxford Mobility Study, while female mobility patterns tended to support the findings of Heath, presenting a very different picture to male mobility rates. Women's social mobility was seen to be both upwardly and downwardly vertically mobile into routine white-collar work.

Relative social mobility was found to be similar for both the men and the women in the study. Class background affects the relative chances of each sex of attaining employment in an alternative class occupation. However, absolute social mobility is different for men and women, because women tend to be concentrated in particular occupational status groups.

In relation to intragenerational mobility, the Essex Mobility Study found that sex influenced the first type of employment gained, but had less of an effect on subsequent jobs. However, the first job had a strong effect on the class people ended up in, as did the class of origin. For example, 84 per cent of men and 77 per cent of women from a service-class background and with a service-class job had started their careers in the service class. However, 64 per cent of men and 43 per cent of women from the working class who started their career with a service-class job had remained employed in the service class. This shows that class background has a direct influence on life chances and position in the stratification system.

From the studies outlined above it becomes clear that class-based stratification systems are based on inequality, despite claims that social mobility can make them more open or equal. Entry to a different social class is a complex matter and necessitates a change in norms, values and behaviour, which is not always possible and/or acceptable to those entering the class

or those already within it. The result of this can be seen in behaviour that restricts entry to 'newcomers', such as élite self-recruitment. Also, **sexual discrimination** appears to have a direct effect on the occupational opportunities and class position of women. Therefore there may be evidence of great economic and educational opportunity in Britain since 1945, but the chances of the whole population enjoying this are relative to their class origin and sex.

Social mobility rates explained

- A decline in the manufacturing industries and a rise in the service industries can be seen to explain the increase in white-collar jobs and the need for members of the working class to fill them. Also, men have taken advantage of women entering the low-status white-collar jobs, by filling the new professional, administrative and managerial positions created by the service industries. This occupational change resulted in the upward social mobility identified by the Oxford Mobility Study.

- The manual working class has higher fertility rates than the sedentary middle class, which means that middle-class workers do not produce enough offspring to replace themselves. The consequence of this is the upward mobility of the children of manual workers to fill vacant jobs in non-manual occupations.

- Educational opportunities are considered to be more available than ever before, which allows more equality in the labour market and higher rates of social mobility (see Area 8 on Education). However, the concept of a meritocratic society based on equality of opportunity has not been that evident in studies of social mobility. Élite self-recruitment and the concentration of women in low-grade white-collar work suggests that class and sex still have an effect on an individual's opportunities in the stratification system.

Is a classless society possible?

❝ Ever since Marx, the word 'class' has been heavily loaded. Yet virtually all modern social analysis – whether by Whitehall, the media, academics or market

ACTIVITY   KS COMMUNICATION

KNOWLEDGE AND UNDERSTANDING	IDENTIFICATION AND INTERPRETATION	ANALYSIS AND EVALUATION

Based on the summary of the theories of social mobility below and your knowledge of stratification, make a list of the criticisms of each perspective on social mobility.

Theories of social mobility

Functionalism

- Society is based on value consensus and equality of opportunity, therefore everyone has an equal chance of social mobility, because occupational status is achieved by merit.

- Improved opportunities in education allow access to occupational success and enable society to operate effectively, because the most talented people are doing the most important jobs.

- High rates of social mobility should be encouraged, because they increase economic and social efficiency.

Weberianism

- Conflict can be reduced by a relatively high rate of social mobility, therefore it is important to sustain an open society.

- Educational and occupational opportunities increase social mobility.

- Status can be improved by access to different classes and parties.

- Competition for scarce resources in an open society makes class solidarity unlikely.

Marxism

- Social mobility is short-range to adjacent classes, rather than long-range across classes.

- The ruling class is a closed group, which does not allow social mobility into this class.

- Proletarianisation means that there is less chance of social mobility, as the working class becomes larger and more homogeneous (similar).

- Unequal distribution of power and opportunity maintains class boundaries and education will never compensate for this, because that would challenge the basis of capitalism.

researchers – divides people by class, sex or age, often by all three. And standing back from the various schemes of class categorisation on offer, it is the degree of agreement, not disagreement, which is remarkable … What, then, are we to make of the idea of the 'classless society'?

(Adonis and Pollard, 1998:6–14)

Politicians (particularly right-wing politicians) have argued that class divisions no longer exist in modern Britain (see section on multi-class classlessness, page 164). Increased affluence among the working class in the 1980s, allowing the purchase of home comforts and consumer durables, was used to support the idea that poverty was over. However, research continued to show that there was a massive divide between rich and poor. In the 1990s it was clear that those who used the term 'classless society' did not mean a society without class, but a society based on meritocracy or equality of opportunity.

John Major envisaged an 'opportunity society', a Britain where the functionalist ideal of the most talented people attaining the highest position was the goal:

❛ *I think we need a classless society, and I think we need to have what I refer to as social mobility. And what I mean by social mobility is the capacity of everybody to have the help necessary to achieve the maximum for their ability.*

(John Major, Prime Minister, **The Guardian** 28 November 1990)

However, Major clearly forgot to acknowledge the constraints to social mobility, such as élite self-recruitment, sex discrimination and racialism. He also, by supporting the principles of meritocracy, allowed the argument of class differences being based on genetic traits to be raised. At the beginning of the 1990s New Right theorists were claiming that intelligence is inherited and therefore the offspring of intelligent people (the middle class) will also be intelligent (middle class) and vice versa (Herrnstein and Murray, 1994; Saunders, 1996). The consequence of these claims was to justify the social inequality that existed in Britain. Therefore the 'classless society' of opportunity appeared to be a smoke screen for the justification of social stratification.

The inheritance of intelligence has not been proved, but even if it had the likelihood of all intelligent people being grouped together at the higher end of the stratification system seems difficult to support. It is even harder to believe that this assumed genetic division happened in the three generations where social mobility was achievable by merit (previously class was more likely to be ascribed). Also, despite the claims that education now provides equality of opportunity to all children, it is clear that schools are still identified by class divisions. Parents who have the means can choose to send their children to schools that offer the potential for a higher chance of success. Where is the equality of opportunity in that? As Adonis and Pollard (1998:19) claim, 'In Britain's class meritocracy, all children are equal but some are more equal than others.'

Away from the political arena sociologists have debated the advent of a classless society and arrived at three main concepts:

- **total classlessness**
- **one-class classlessness**
- **multi-class classlessness.**

Total classlessness is based on a radical transformation of society through the abolition of private property. It is a neo-Marxist approach that advocates the removal of economic inequality and inheritance and the instigation of free welfare services. Total classlessness therefore challenges functionalist claims that stratification is necessary for the organisation of society. However, the possibility of changing the infrastructure and superstructure to reach total classlessness, while retaining a motivated workforce, has been received with some scepticism.

One-class classlessness is a theory based on the idea that society could become either totally working class or totally middle class. The experiences of communist Russia could be seen as one-class classlessness based on a working-class model. In societies based on working-class one-class classlessness differences in social and economic position could exist, but high rates of social mobility and the non-ownership of the means

of production were believed to remove class divisions. However, evidence in Russia displayed that the Communist Party enjoyed economic advantages over the citizens and became a bureaucracy that monopolised state power. Middle-class one-class classlessness has been argued to exist in Britain, based on theories of embourgeoisement (see section on embourgeoisement, page 150). However, the increased affluence experienced by some sections of the working class has not been shown to lead to their entry into the middle class.

Multi-class classlessness is based on the equality of opportunity to be unequal. In other words, multi-class classlessness occurs in societies where classes have become divided, but the potential for social mobility is made clear. It is the type of classlessness that is supported by right-wing politicians (see discussion above) and has been termed non-egalitarian classlessness (Ossowski, 1963). However, despite the attraction of seeing a meritocratic society as classless, i.e. it is good to think that all barriers to social mobility are transcendable, it remains clear that social inequality is justified by this approach and therefore class divisions are accepted and expected within it. Consequently, multi-class classlessness appears extremely contradictory, because it ignores the social and economic inequalities perpetuated by a class-based stratification system, inequalities that cannot always be overcome by talent.

Is a classless society possible? Will egalitarianism always remain a Utopian ideal? Based on the evidence of social history and contemporary social change, it seems fair to conclude that it is unlikely that we will see the end of a class-based stratification system in our lifetime. Class is etched into the infrastructure and superstructure of modern Britain, affecting individuals in areas such as educational opportunities, health, employment prospects, self-perceptions, lifestyles, patterns of consumption and overall life chances. Therefore, as Edgell (1995:122) concluded, 'Class rules and classlessness remains a dream rather than a reality.'

C A S E   S T U D Y

Class and Class Consciousness

G. Marshall, H. Newby, D. Rose and C. Vogler (1988), *Social Class in Modern Britain*. London, Unwin Hyman.

Class is one of the central concepts of sociology. Much of the research carried out by sociologists in Britain between the 1950s and 1970s was centrally concerned with class. A person's class position has been used to explain differences of culture, politics and health. More specifically, one of the main themes of the British sociology of class has been the changing nature of the working class and the class basis of politics.

Social Class in Modern Britain is the definitive study of class and the class basis of politics in contemporary Britain. The aim of the study is to examine the declining significance of class in British social and political life. The authors use data from a national survey to consider a wide range of issues in class analysis including: How should sociologists conceptualise and measure social class? How have class processes, such as social mobility, changed recently in Britain? To what extent is class still an important source of social identity and basis for political action in Britain?

Research Design

The study was based on structured interviews with a national sample of 1770 men and women. This sample was obtained from addresses on the electoral register selected in three stages. Firstly, 100 parliamentary constituencies were selected, after being stratified according to their social characteristics, such as the percentage of people owning their own houses.

Secondly, in each constituency two polling districts were selected in a similar way. Finally, 19 addresses in each polling district were selected at random. It was not a simple random sample, but a *multi-stage stratified random sample*, which goes to show how complex survey research is becoming before any questions are even asked!

The questions covered a range of issues about people's economic position, and their political attitudes. Most importantly they asked questions which enabled the authors to create a variety of models of class structure.

Principal Findings

Marshall et al. consider several important themes: social mobility, proletarianization, class identity and voting.

(i) Social mobility

On social mobility their results broadly support those of the Nuffield studies (see Goldthorpe, 1987). Whilst absolute social mobility had increased – there is more upward mobility – relative social mobility had not changed. By absolute social mobility sociologists mean the overall pattern of movements between class positions, or the total amount of mobility. In contrast, relative social mobility refers to the comparative chances of social mobility for people from different backgrounds (see Haralambos, 1990, p. 104). In these terms Goldthorpe had found that the chances of someone from the middle class staying in the middle class were much greater than someone from the working class entering the middle class. Absolute social mobility has increased only because of the expansion of middle class places in the class structure, but relative social mobility remained much the same.

Marshall *et al.* challenge Goldthorpe's conventional view of class analysis, which suggests that sociologists should only consider men's mobility. They show that, whilst men's and women's relative mobility chances are the same, men's absolute mobility chances are much better than women's. Women are at a disadvantage in terms of inter-generational mobility and in their own careers. Men are more likely to enter *both* the service class *and* the working class than women. However, women are more likely to enter the intermediate class of routine white-collar workers than men. Whatever their class origins, most women enter the intermediate class when they start employment.

(ii) Proletarianization

Marshal *et al.* distinguish four types of proletarianization discussed by sociologists. Firstly, some, such as Wright, have argued that the working class is growing in size, so the class structure as a whole is being proletarianized. Secondly, for Goldthorpe, the crucial issue is whether individuals are being proletarianized due to downward social mobility. Thirdly, for sociologists such as Crompton, the question is whether or not *types of jobs*, such as clerical work, are being proletarianized. Finally, there is the question of socio-political proletarianization, …

They conclude that the size of the working class is declining – refuting Wright. People, furthermore, tend not to be downwardly mobile, refuting that model of proletarianization. Marshall *et al.*'s data also contradict Stanworth's feminist claims that women are downwardly mobile. They found that women's relative mobility is the same as that of men.

They consider the proletarianization of clerical jobs by asking not only whether or not people felt that their jobs had been deskilled, but also questions about what people did in their jobs. Their results, they argue, justify placing clerical workers in an intermediate class category. Clerks are not deskilled like many manual workers, but they do not have the autonomy and control at work that is reported by many professionals and managers. In terms of measures of socio-political proletarianization, such as class identity and union membership, clerical workers are more like the middle class than manual workers. This suggests, according to Marshall *et al.*, that it is legitimate to consider them an intermediate class that has not been proletarianized in any sense.

(iii) Class identity and **class consciousness**

The authors also assess whether or not class is still a source of social identity and political conflict in Britain. At the time of their study, in the mid-1980s, there appeared to be a convincing case for the reduced salience of class in British society. Changes in the economy were transforming the class structure. The growth of service industries and the decline of manufacturing meant that traditional male manual working class factory jobs were disappearing. Simultaneously, professional, managerial and administrative jobs had grown in number. So the traditional working class was shrinking and the new middle class or service class was growing.

It was thought during the 1980s that people no longer had a strong attachment to class identity, with, for example, fewer working class people voting Labour. People were engaging in 'privatized consumption', i.e. people were aspiring to buy homes and fill them with consumer goods. The working class had become divided between affluent home owners voting Conservative, and the poor trapped in council estates and voting Labour. Not only had the working class declined in size, but it had lost its traditional solidarity and patterns of community life. There appeared to be new, and increasingly significant, divisions *within* the working class.

Marshall *et al.* summarise their conclusions here in terms of *instrumental collectivism*. This means that people join and support working class organizations, such as trade unions, for instrumental reasons of self-interest. These instrumental reasons are to do with their own economic well-being. In other words, people join unions to obtain pay rises and to give them security in their jobs.

People perceive the distribution of income and wealth in Britain as both unequal and unfair. Many believe that this situation *could* be changed towards a more equitable order without radically transforming capitalism. However, respondents are cynical and fatalistic about the ability and commitment of politicians to effect such changes. This they describe as *informed fatalism*. Informed fatalism involves a recognition of class inequality. This recognition is what Marshall *et al.* call the *cognitive sphere* of people's attitudes. In addition, this informed fatalism involves a belief in the impossibility of change. This is what Marshall *et al.* refer to as the evaluative sphere of people's attitudes; how people judge what is desirable or possible. Informed fatalists are pragmatic, putting up with the present situation and supporting organizations such as trade unions for their own personal instrumental reasons, such as pay rises. Social order in British society thus does not depend on shared values and beliefs, but upon the fatalism of the lower classes:

> We find that class is still the most common source of social identity and retains its salience as such. It is true that the collectivism of our respondents can most appropriately be characterised as instrumental. To that extent it reflects the pursuit of self-interest rather than collective improvement. However, our data also suggest that such instrumentalism is an entirely pragmatic response to a distributional order and distributional mechanisms that are perceived to be unjust, but are accepted as largely unalterable facts of life. This general perspective may be summarized as one of 'realism', 'resignation', 'cynicism', or – as we would prefer to describe it – 'informed fatalism'. Its origins lie in the evaluative rather than the cognitive sphere. People are often aware of alternatives but they are, on the whole, resigned to the fact that they can do little or nothing to help achieve these. Our findings suggest, then, that contemporary British society lacks a moral order, and that its cohesion is rooted more in resignation and routine than consensus and approval. (Marshal *et al.*, 1988, p. 143)

Class was the most accessible source of identity for most people in their survey, but this made little impact on their individual capacities for class action, as people believed that such action would be ineffectual. Furthermore, Marshall *et al.* found that people held complex and contradictory views about society. With so little ideological consistency, they show that there are no clear class ideologies among the population at large. They argue that only class based organizations such as political parties and trade unions develop coherent class ideologies. However, they believe that this does not mean that class is entirely irrelevant to individual attitudes and behaviour.

The authors maintain that class position remains the most important social structural factor shaping people's attitudes. Class position was better than employment sector, housing tenure, welfare dependency, sex, income or education in explaining people's sympathy for working class views of society. Furthermore, there were no age differences in class consciousness, and this, they argue, shows that class consciousness is not declining over time.

According to Marshall *et al.*, divisions within the working class have been well established since the nineteenth century. Similarly, the instrumental collectivism of the contemporary working class was widespread over a hundred years ago, when people joined trade unions to obtain wage increases. In short, little has changed in their view.

iv Class and voting behaviour

The main point of reference for Marshall *et al.*'s discussion of class and politics – voting behaviour – is the debate around the class dealignment thesis. This was developed most thoroughly by Ivor Crewe, who argued that classes are becoming less and less attached to their 'natural' class parties. Fewer middle class people are voting Conservative and fewer working class people are voting Labour.

They argue that the class dealignment thesis is wrong. It is not the case that the working class is deserting Labour. In relative terms the working class still votes disproportionately for the Labour Party and the middle class still votes disproportionately for the Conservatives. What explains Labour's electoral weakness, according to Marshall *et al.*, is their loss of votes across all social classes, in addition to the decline in the overall size of the working class. Divisions within the working class, such as housing tenure, have only a limited effect. Council house tenants only appear to vote disproportionately for the Labour Party because most of them are working class. Similarly the sector of employment has a limited effect on the relationship between class and voting. Its only real impact is on the service class, where those employed in the public sector, such as teachers, doctors, nurses, etc., are more likely to vote Labour. So the authors conclude that class is still the most important factor shaping people's voting behaviour.

Source: Bagguley, P. (1994) 'Class and Class Consciousness' in Warde, A. and Abercrombie, N. (Eds.) (1994:25–29) *Stratification and Social Inequality*. Lancaster, Framework Press.

1   Why is class 'central' to the study of society?   **(2)**

2   How did Marshall et al. operationalise the concept of class?   **(2)**

3   Explain whether Marshall et al.'s study finds Britain to be an 'open' society?   **(3)**

4   What were the four types of proletarianisation identified by Marshall et al.?   **(4)**

5   Has proletarianisation occurred in modern Britain?   **(1)**

6   Is class, according to Marshall et al., still a source of social identity?   **(1)**

7   Is class consciousness a possibility for the working class in the UK?
    Justify your answer.   **(4)**

8   Examine the political position adopted by the working class in   **(8)**
    Marshall et al.'s study.

Gender

Throughout much of modern western historical development, females have been seen as the property of their menfolk. Until the late twentieth century this was so much part of western culture that this point was rarely questioned, but the inequality and injustice that some women have experienced over the centuries has been terrifying. (See Area 6 on Families and Households for development of this point). Until recently, females in Britain did not have their own surnames but were named after their fathers and then, on marriage, their husbands. A church wedding service asks the nearest male relative of the bride to give her away to her husband and, even today, a woman may vow to obey her husband. Today, these elements of a wedding service are mere convention and form, but they were real promises in the past. Note that even Karl Marx who argued so persuasively for the emancipation of women and was famously adoring of his wife, Jenny, fathered a child on his servant and added her to his household, expecting his wife and daughters to tolerate the situation.

Feminist historians and academics have attempted to reclaim a place in the history of western culture for women and to examine their contribution to the development of western society. While many females may have been content to live domestic and family-centred lives, others have gone to quite extraordinary lengths to play a more active role in the world; even to the extent of masquerading and living successfully as men throughout portions of their adult lives! Usually, however, the chance of an active life was the privilege of the wealthy woman or the widow. Others could be seen as the victims of both their gender and their poverty and this is a theme of much early female literature.

HINTS AND TIPS   *If you have not already done so, have a look at the novels of Jane Austen, in particular* **Persuasion**, *and of the Brontë sisters, especially* **The Tenant of Wildfell Hall**. *Both have been filmed recently as BBC drama productions. Do not look at them merely as romantic stories but as historical documents, and you will gain an understanding of how cruel life could be for intelligent women in the nineteenth century.*

ACTIVITY   KS **COMMUNICATION, WORKING WITH OTHERS**

IDENTIFICATION AND INTERPRETATION

Talk to a woman who is much older than yourself about how attitudes to gender and to women have changed in this century. Ask her to tell you stories about her childhood, her expectations of life, and the conditions in her home. Would she like to live and work in the kind of home that her own mother ran? Remember that there may be class differences in responses, however – wealthy women in the past would have had many servants.

Gender, sex and sexuality

Sociology has specific meanings for the terms **sex** and gender. Sex generally refers to biological processes, in other words the biological sex you are born. Gender refers to social processes that occur because of your sex, such as behaving in a feminine way if you are female. The cultural approach argues that males and females are trained from the instant of birth to behave in certain socially appropriate ways, despite the fact that new babies have few gendered characteristics. The very first thing a new mother is told is the sex of her child. However, biological arguments have been put forward to explain the differences in behaviour between girls and boys/women and men.

Sex roles	= The physical/biological differences between men and women
Gender roles	= The 'masculine' and 'feminine' roles adopted in society based on the attitudes and behaviour imposed by the culture.

NB: Gender does not have to be linked to sex, i.e. you do not have to be feminine to be a woman, or masculine to be a man.

Scientists have argued that hormones influence behaviour, personality and emotions, so because males produce more androgens (sex hormones) than females they are more aggressive and inclined to criminal activity. While it cannot be disputed that men and women have different hormones, it should not be forgotten that we are socialised into a particular culture, i.e. we learn the norms, values and appropriate behaviour of our society. Therefore, any claims that men cannot control their behaviour because of their hormones dismisses their ability to respond to social norms. Sociological studies show that socialisation (culture) supersedes biological factors of sex by highlighting how gender is more influential than sex. For example, there is evidence of children being born with male external genitalia, but actually having female internal organs, yet because they were raised as boys they were masculine in their behaviour.

A C T I V I T Y   KS COMMUNICATION

KNOWLEDGE AND UNDERSTANDING	IDENTIFICATION AND INTERPRETATION

Look in any shop for cards for new babies. What symbols are typical of cards for girls and for boys? What differences in language style do you note? How easy is it to find a non-gendered card that would be suitable for either a boy or a girl?

Sexuality is directly influenced by sex and gender roles and refers to attitudes and behaviour associated with sexual intercourse/intimacy. It is hard to believe that something as intimate as sexuality is conditioned by society, but our sex and gender indicate the type of appropriate sexual experience we should have. In other words, in contemporary Britain men are socialised into seeing sex with women as the norm, as women are with men (heterosexuality). Also, men are assumed to have a different sexual identity to women, in that men have a higher desire and need for sex and that this is a sign of masculinity; the same behaviour in women is deemed unacceptable. Sociobiologists (see later) have even used the high sex drive of men and their quest to pass on their genes as a way of justifying male sex crimes.

The media representation of female sexuality has helped to sustain gender roles and social inequalities based on sex, through emphasis primarily on two areas:

■ **Pornography** – Dworkin (1981) outlines how pornography can be seen to exploit women by supporting the idea that women like to be controlled by men and that they are there for the sole purpose of giving men pleasure. It could be argued that hard-core pornography that involves sadist behaviour could encourage male violence towards women. Whether this is true or not, pornography helps to define female sexuality by establishing women as the pleasure things of men. It is interesting to note that feminists have attempted to establish pornography for women, in order to demonstrate that women have similar sexual desires to men. However, female pornography magazines, such as *For Women* and *Playgirl*, have not been able to show erect penises in their photo shoots, while *Penthouse* and *Playboy* remain free to show all female genitalia.

■ **The 'Body Beautiful'** – Increasing incidence of anorexia among teenaged girls has been blamed on the image of female beauty represented in the media. Waif-like models are seen as the epitome of beauty and splashed all over magazines and television shows. Women are socialised into associating beauty with happiness, i.e. a pretty face and a thin body will make you attractive to men and result in a fulfilling life. Consequently sexuality becomes tied up with looks (Wolf, 1990) and can cause some women to submerge their sexuality in a sea of diets and beauty products.

The media pay a great deal of attention to the sexuality of women, portraying many negative stereotypes of how women should look and act to be the perfect sexual being. As in industry the media are controlled by men, which could explain why images of women are generally as objects of men's lust. It has been argued that men have shaped female sexuality to suit their own needs, creating sex objects or mother-housewives. As Jerry Hall, actress and mother, is famously quoted as saying, men want a 'whore in the bedroom and a cook in the kitchen'. However, recent television programmes have been portraying women in roles that challenge previous stereotypes of female sexuality. For example, *This Life* (BBC 1) portrayed the lives of six 20-somethings living in London and Anna, the female barrister, was seen to be in touch with her sexuality and open to new sexual experiences without guilt or repression.

The problem women have had with enjoying their supposed sexual freedom since the 1960s has been the associated fear of unwanted pregnancy, sexually transmitted diseases, poor reputation and violent crime. Female sexuality remains controlled by society through myths and realities of negative sanctions. Women are still afraid to walk alone at night in clothes considered overtly sexual for fear of attack or abuse and of being seen as 'asking for it'. Girls are still reluctant to experiment with different sexual partners for fear of attaining a reputation for being a 'slag' (Less, 1993). Sexuality is a double-edged sword for women, who are expected to be sexy, but only when it is appropriate, whatever that might mean. However, female sexuality has become a subject of much debate and these discussions have brought new sexual consciousness to the younger generations, with old taboos, such as female masturbation, being brushed slowly aside.

The following is an exact copy from a 1950s Home Economics textbook:

Good Wives Guide

Have dinner ready. Plan ahead, even the night before, to have a delicious meal ready on time for his return. This is a way of letting him know you have been thinking about him and are concerned about his needs.

Most men are hungry when they come home and the prospect of a good meal (especially his favourite dish) is part of the warm welcome needed.

Prepare yourself. Take 15 minutes to rest so you'll be refreshed when he arrives. Touch-up your makeup, put a ribbon in your hair and be fresh-looking. He has just been with a lot of work-weary people.

Be a little gay and a little more interesting for him. His boring day may need a little lift and one of your duties is to provide it.

Clear away the clutter. Make one last trip through the main part of the house just before your husband arrives. Gather up schoolbooks, toys, paper, etc. and then run the dustcloth over the tables.

Over the cooler months of the year you should prepare and light a fire for him to unwind to. Your husband will feel he has reached a haven of rest and order, and it will give you a lift too. After all catering for his comfort will provide you with immense personal satisfaction.

Prepare the children. Take a few minutes to wash their hands and faces (if they are small), comb their hair, and if necessary change their clothes. They are little treasures and he would like to see them playing their part.

Minimise all noise. At the time of his arrival, eliminate all noise of the washer, dryer or vacuum. Try to encourage the children to be quiet. Be happy to see him.

Greet him with a warm smile and show sincerity in your desire to please him.

Listen to him. You may have a dozen or more things to tell him, but the moment of his arrival is not the time. Let him talk first   remember, his topics of conversation are more important than yours.

Make the evening his. Never complain if he comes home late or goes out to dinner or other places of entertainment without you. Instead, try to understand his world of strain and pressure, and his very real need to be at home and relax.

Your goal. Try to make sure your home is a place of peace, order and tranquillity where your husband can renew himself in body and spirit.

Don't greet him with complaints and problems. Don't complain if he's late home for dinner or even if he stays out all night. Count this as minor compared with what he might have gone through that day.

Make him comfortable. Have him lean back in a comfortable chair or have him lie down in the bedroom. Have a cool or warm drink ready for him. Arrange his pillow and offer to take off his shoes. Speak in a low, soothing and pleasant voice.

Don't ask him questions about his actions or question his judgement or integrity. Remember, he is the master of the house and as such will always exercise fairness and truthfulness .You have no right to question him. A good wife always knows her place.

The debate on sexuality has also included an investigation into homosexuality (having a sexual relationship with someone of the same sex), which has been seen as not only deviant, but criminal in recent history. Homosexuality has been argued to be deviant because it goes against the gender norms and sexual values of industrial societies. Engels argued that men developed control over women's sexuality with the ownership of private property to ensure the inheritance of their offspring. Marxist feminists have argued that patriarchy ensures that capitalism has a plentiful and healthy workforce through the control of women in the family unit. Both arguments show the importance of heterosexuality to capitalism, which means that homosexuality has no benefits for capitalism.

Homosexuality is generally assumed not to produce children (a workforce) and therefore is not a motivating institution for workers (no family, no work ethic to support them). Homosexual acts were commonplace 400 years ago when 'manservants' looked after their masters' every need and lords took lovers from women and young men. Consequently, it could be argued that it is not the sexuality of homosexuality that has made it become seen as deviant and differentiating, but the way in which the lifestyle apparently fails to support capitalism.

Theoretical perspectives on gender

The academic world had few women working in it until the 1960s and these were usually considered exceptional and unusual creatures. Their lack of conventional attractiveness was often underlined as though brains and beauty in a woman were mutually exclusive. Thus, in much early sociology, certain assumptions about the role and nature of women were so universally held that there was virtually no debate. Dale Spender underlined this point when she considered *Invisible Women: The Schooling Scandal* (1982) in her study of gender and education. Early studies of deviance barely noticed the existence of females either as victims or as criminals.

This sociological perspective ignores the point that feminism and female emancipation movements have a long and venerable history, but women needed to target basic social injustices before they could turn their full attention to the world of academic debate. It was

not until the 1970s that feminism gained mainstream acceptance as a sociological perspective, despite the impressive contributions of women such as Simone de Beauvoir, who was writing in the 1930s and beyond, to the field of gender studies.

Biological determinism

A mode of thought known as **biological determinism** acts on the assumption that the differences that there are between male and female gendered behaviours depend on their relative biology. Women have babies, therefore they are natural carers and want to nurture. Males, however, are natural hunters and act in a dominant manner reflecting their evolutionary path as hunting animals. This type of thinking in its most overt form is typical of writers such as media zoologist Desmond Morris and functionalist theorists such as Murdock (1949) and Parsons (1959). All human behaviour is reduced to a set of biological imperatives, so females wear lipstick simply to excite males through the imitation of sexual flushes. At a superficial level, this type of theory is amusing and attractive, but it dismisses the possibility of human beings rationalising their motives for action. They are merely responding to sexual instinct.

Biological determinism has been criticised from a number of perspectives and this discussion is even more significant in psychology where it is often described as the Nature–Nurture debate:

- Historical rejections of biological determinism stress that human behaviour changes over time.
- Anthropological rejections stress the role of culture in behaviour.
- Case studies of humans who have been brought up without the benefit of other people show that they do not behave as humans do but imitate animals around them.

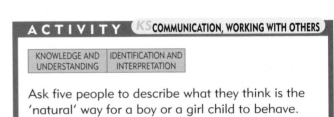

ACTIVITY KS **COMMUNICATION, WORKING WITH OTHERS**

KNOWLEDGE AND UNDERSTANDING	IDENTIFICATION AND INTERPRETATION

Ask five people to describe what they think is the 'natural' way for a boy or a girl child to behave. How many people subscribe to biological beliefs about the way that the genders behave?

Structural functionalism

This biological type of thinking about the nature of gender underpins much functional analysis of the family and gender relations, because functionalism as a theory originated before there had been sincere and widespread criticism of traditional views of family and gender. Functionalist theorist Murdock (1949) assumed that there are different roles within the family for each gender and that these are, in fact, the best possible for society. Women were considered to have inherent advantages associated with their biology, which make them suited to their role as mother-housewives. Likewise men's superior biological strength is believed to enable them to conduct the male gender role effectively. Murdock concludes that **gender roles** are not only practical, efficient and organised, but that they are universal.

It is worth noting at this point that functionalism frequently overlooks the individual in its social analyses and may actually disregard massive human unhappiness if the outcome is judged as positive for society. You will note in the family area that females are considered as emotional supports for males whereas males must be providers. Even at the time when functionalism was most popular as a theoretical perspective, this overlooked the social reality of working-class women who frequently worked to support children or parents.

Even though many thinkers were aware of Marxism and early feminism, the ideas proposed did not enter mainstream academic discussion until the 1960s, when all of the previous racist and sexist assumptions about society came under attack. Probably one of the first and most influential books was Betty Friedan's (1963) *The Feminine Mystique* which suggested that women remained unfulfilled by conventional housewife roles. This book created a huge sensation because it was both accessible to ordinary women in the way that other thinkers such as Simone de Beauvoir were not, and because it fitted the mood of the time.

Later in the decade, Greer had exactly the same effect with her book, *The Female Eunuch* (1971), in which she suggested that women had effectively been sexually neutered and had little concept of what femininity meant because they only saw themselves reflected in the eyes of men. These public debates triggered the rise of what was then called in the late 1960s and early 1970s, 'female liberation'. Women's liberation was initially a political movement but it later became incorporated into a series of philosophical and academic approaches to gender studies which are broadly known as feminism. Homosexual males were also fighting a battle for 'Gay Liberation' which in many ways was a more difficult fight because homosexuality was actually illegal. These two areas of thought were so attractive and vibrant, provoking expression through art, popular music and literature, that towards the end of the 1980s, a serious appraisal of the nature of gender itself became possible in a way that could not have been considered in the 1950s.

> **HINTS AND TIPS**   You are advised to read **The Female Eunuch** *(1971) both for the analysis that it offers, and for a flavour of the language and style of some of the feminism typical of the 1970s and before. It is eminently readable; Greer has an excellent style which is, in places, deliberately provocative and shocking.*

Cultural theories

The cultural approach challenges the biological assumptions of biological determinism and structural functionalism by arguing that gender roles do not flow naturally from sex roles. Children may be born a particular sex (although the media has recently highlighted cases of children being born of indeterminate sex and later having problems with birth certificates if the chosen sex is found to be inappropriate), but they are socialised into a specific gender. Gender socialisation takes place in the home and is continued at school. Feminists have identified that many resources used to teach young children reinforce gender roles of masculinity and femininity. Boys are displayed in scenarios that involve activity and mending things, while girls stand by watching admiringly or are helping their mothers. Gender roles are also learnt by watching adults who act as role models. Children unconsciously internalise the way in which their mothers and fathers act, which can reproduce different perceptions of power and authority between women and men.

McRobbie (1991), a Marxist feminist, used the teenage girls magazine *Jackie* to illustrate the socialisation of female adolescents. She found that the process of learning the female role begins in babyhood within the family and is reinforced through the media, school and work. Magazines, such as *Jackie*, are characterised by a

Here we are at home, says Daddy.

Peter helps Daddy with the car, and Jane helps Mummy get the tea.

Good girl, says Mummy to Jane.

You are a good girl to help me like this.

Good good girl

Figure 3.17 The transmission of gender roles

lightness of tone, small repertoire of concerns, concentration on personal matters, romance, fashion and beauty. Girls are therefore encouraged by the media to see the female role as one that is concerned more about appearance for attracting a mate, than intelligence for developing a career.

Oakley (1974), using data collected by Murdock (1949), demonstrated that a division of labour by sex was not universal. For example, Oakley found that although Murdock claimed that labour was divided by sex in all 224 societies that he examined, he ignored the 14 societies in which lumbering was done either exclusively by women or shared with the men. Oakley concluded from this that there are no exclusively female roles, because physical characteristics do not bar women from doing certain jobs. Consequently it can be assumed that gender roles are a social construction that suit the purposes of society.

Margaret Mead, in her classic and often quoted study, *Sex and Temperament in Three Primitive Societies* (1935) took an anthropological stance and pointed out that there are considerable cultural variations in the notions of what is feminine and masculine behaviour. Indeed, in many cultures, it is the female role to act as the worker at heavy tasks whereas in our society, women are considered unable to lift heavy weights. In the USSR, women were regularly used as fighter pilots and combat troops. Afghani women are expected to fight as well as their men, if required. Tom Wolfe pointed out in his study of the American space race *The Right Stuff* (1983), that women outperformed men in many of the skills required to pilot spacecraft, and

had the added advantage of being lighter and smaller generally in a situation where weight was of considerable significance. They could not, however, go into space because it would have challenged male notions of superiority endemic at the time. The first nation to put a woman into space was the USSR.

Ethnomethodologists Kessler and McKenna (1978) argue that it is impossible to differentiate between women and men until you learn to do so. The culture of western industrial society has created such structured gender roles and stuck to them so rigidly that they are now seen as the norm and taken for granted. However, Kessler and McKenna state that it is clear gender is a social construction based on the following evidence:

- Some individuals are born with male chromosomes but do not react to them, appear female and are treated as such. Therefore genetic make-up does not dictate gender behaviour.

- The biology of some individuals is neither male (XY) or female (XX), but the indeterminate XO, which gives them a female appearance but no definitive sex (Turner's Syndrome).

- Some babies are born with male and female genitalia (hermaphrodites) and it is left to the parents to decide which sex to raise them and arrange appropriate surgery.

- A third gender is recognised in some societies, such as the 'berdache' of North American Indians, who are men who take on the role of women. They are accepted as a separate gender with full status rights. In Thailand the youngest son of some large families is raised as a girl and expected to carry out feminine tasks. These 'boys' are treated as special and considered quite a symbol of status for the family.

Generally gender and genitals go together in modern Britain, but Kessler and McKenna observe that this assumption is part of learnt behaviour. When we meet people we assess a person's speech, physical appearance and any history they offer to reach a conclusion about their sex. Therefore the most basic division in society, between men and women, can be seen as being a social construct, at least in part.

Feminisms

Feminism is not a single perspective as such, but illustrates a significant point within sociological debate, which is that people who work within one perspective do not agree (see Area 1 on Sociological Theory). They will spend as much time arguing within the tradition as with those who do not share their perspectives. In-fighting within feminism has been especially bitter and unpleasant even to the point where noted writers, such as Germaine Greer and Suzanne Moore, had a public and extremely personal battle across newspaper columns in the mid-1990s. Similar squabbles take place regularly in the academic press about a variety of topics but are not so newsworthy because fewer people understand the basis of the argument. Feminists agree that women are not equal in status and power with men, but then divide into a number of debates, which can be roughly classified in the following manner (see Area 1 for further information on feminisms).

- Marxist feminism is similar to Marxism in that society is seen as unequal and that people are exploited. The difference between Marxism and feminism is that feminists see patriarchy or the rule of men as a more significant problem than capitalism. The revolution will be against men and capitalism!

> **HINTS AND TIPS**   Note that not all Marxist or left-wing thinkers subscribe to the view that women are the equals of men. One renowned example might be the traditional Marxism which flourished in the industrial working areas of the South Wales valleys and the English and Scottish coal-mining areas. The Labour Party and trade unions talked of 'brothers' and allowed affiliated drinking clubs to run men-only bars.

- Liberal feminism works towards gradual social change, believing that it cannot be imposed on society. It points to the inequality which is built into our society, so that males may not be aware of the injustices that females experience, or consider that the exploitation of women is insignificant compared to other injustices experienced by other groups in society.
- Radical feminism is extreme and writers in this tradition tend to have a one-sided perspective which, at its most critical of society, suggests that lesbianism is the only solution to the oppression of women by men. This is the type of feminism that is often pilloried by the mass media, and the stereotype is of fat, dungaree-wearing, unattractive

Figure 3.18   Feminist realisation

women who resort to lesbianism because no man would have them. Marxist and liberal feminists tend to argue that both males and females need to be freed from gender restrictions, but radical feminism is more concerned with proving the superiority of females as the caring and effective gender.

- Since the 1980s there has been the emergence of black feminism which unites the insights offered by feminism into the 'malestream' nature of our society with the perspectives offered by non-white, non-Europeans into white **ethnocentric** views of society. Ethnocentrism is the view that one's own culture is the main or only culture. Black feminists point to the dual exploitation and injustice experienced by black women who suffer from both sexism and racism. This is known as an **aggregation of inequalities** and was used first by Rosemary Deem who considered working-class women to suffer from both sexism and social-class bias.

> **HINTS AND TIPS**   Much literature has given voice to the black feminist view and you should look at writing by modern American writers such as Toni Morrison. Many of you will already be familiar with Maya Angelou's **I know why the caged bird sings** (1983) which also puts forward this perspective. In sociology in Britain, this view is associated with Dr Heidi Safia Mirza, among others.

Masculinity

Increasingly, gender is not just an issue for feminists who wish to understand the processes that have made women lower in status than men in western societies. The debate has broadened out. Masculinity has become part of the contemporary discussion about gender roles. Modern industrial society has changed rapidly and the position of men has been altered more than at any

Health

● Boys are four times more likely to be autistic than girls, and nine times as likely to have Asperger syndrome
● Males aged 16 to 24 years are more likely to suffer from high blood pressure than women
● 25 per cent of boys suffer from asthma, compared with 18 per cent of girls
● Prostrate cancer is predicted to be the UK's most common cancer by 2018

Alcohol

● Men are three times more likely than women to be dependent on alcohol. The highest rates are for men aged 20 to 24
● Six million men drink more than the recommended weekly limit of 21 units of alcohol a week compared to 14 per cent of women; six per cent of men drink dangerous quantities
● Among 15-year-olds, 15 per cent of boys drink 15 or more units compared with seven per cent of girls

Drugs

● Men are more likely than women to use illegal drugs
● Between April and September 1996, three times as many men as women attended counselling centres dealing with drug abuse
● More than half of the users who attended drug clinics were in their twenties

This is Harry. He's six months old, he's beautiful, and his parents love him (and his big brother) very much. But statistically, as he grows up he's now more likely to fail at school or to lose his job, more likely to have an accident, more likely to be violent or to be the victim of violence than a girl. He's more likely to commit a crime, and if he gets caught, he's far more likely to end up in prison. But there's a lot we all can do to change this future. And, in the end, few of us would want to change Harry. Vive la difference, and thank heaven ... for little boys

Problems

● Four times as many girls call Childline as boys, but when they call, boys tend to report more severe problems, such as physical abuse, bullying and homelessness
● Childline refers more girls than boys to social services or the police; 45 per cent of the referrals were dealing with runaways or homelessness
● Males over 18 are twice as likely to go missing than females, according to the Missing Person's Helpline

Work

● 17 per cent of all men have lost a job or been made redundant, compared with seven per cent of women
● Redundancy is most common in young, single men
● In the past five years, 21 per cent of men have been working longer hours, compared with 13 per cent of women

Life and death

● Suicide is the biggest killer of young men after road accidents; twice as many young men die from suicide than from cancer
● The most common age for male suicide is 29
● There has been a 71 per cent increase in suicide among young men in the past 10 years; they are now three times as likely to kill themselves as women

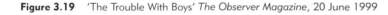

Figure 3.19 'The Trouble With Boys' *The Observer Magazine*, 20 June 1999

other time in recent history. The decline in working-class industrial jobs, increased female participation in employment, the rise in divorce and increased unemployment have all had a significant effect on what it means to be a man and/or masculine. Advances in technology, male contraception and continuing female equality are all creating new challenges for men in the new millennium. Consequently a number of areas of significance need to be looked at:

■ Masculinity varies from society to society and appears to exaggerate biological potential in different ways (Gilmore, 1990). The social construction approach supports this relative concept of masculinity, with male gender roles varying across time and place. For example, for the Semai tribe of Malaysia our idea of masculinity would be out of place, because aggressive and selfish behaviour is taboo. Carrigan et al. (1985) identified 'hegemonic' and 'subordinate' masculinities, the former being white, middle class, heterosexuals and the latter black, working class or gay. Therefore it would seem that not only is masculinity relative historically and between cultures, it is relative to a man's position in the stratification system of his own society.

■ Gender behaviour can be seen as a point on a continuum of behaviours rather than as two opposite ends of a spectrum. Masculinity is subject to change in line with social expectations, changes and demands. Men have been encouraged to look at alternative forms of behaviour and there was much media talk of the New Man who was in touch with his feelings and able to explore his feminine side. This is probably more myth than reality. (Examine later discussions on changes in the family for a deeper explanation of this point.) However, men are now able to express themselves openly in forms that would have been completely unacceptable to the mid-twentieth-century working-class male.

■ There is a cultural dimension to this debate. Masculinity in the early days of the cinema was often characterised by the myth of the cowboy. To be a man, it was necessary to be inarticulate, careful of the feelings and sensibilities of women and to be driven by a sense of duty. Problems could be solved by the application of brute force and the 'good' man would often resort to fist fighting to prove his masculinity and the right of his

case. Gilmore (1990) has summed up this type of masculinity as having three characteristics:

1 Man the impregnator – men are expected to compete for the attention of women.
2 Man the provider – women need looking after, especially once they are pregnant.
3 Man the protector – men should protect their women and children against danger.

■ Beverley Skeggs (1991) and Bea Campbell (1995) argued more recently that working-class masculinity has changed to the point where it is defined in two ways. In the first, a male is a man because he is different from females. This means that working-class males in particular need to express their masculinity by being 'other' or 'not female'. This leads them to reject anything they view as female

Figure 3.20   The ideal of masculine behaviour was often seen as embodied in roles taken by the actor, John Wayne.

behaviour. They also point to the media image of masculinity that is offered as a role model for young males in terms of *Robocop* and the *Terminator* films. In these films, men are defined as masculine by their ability to exert power and control over others, rather than their ability to care for and to protect the weak, which was so much an element of cowboy films.

■ Postmodern writers have pointed out that gender is better described in terms of a point on a scale rather than as two opposites. The traditional social differences have blurred so that it is acceptable for females to wear male clothing. Some males have pioneered the wearing of skirts and sarongs by men. The degree to which men are willing to accept the roles of females is probably overstated in our society. However, it is clear the male role has become more uncertain or ambiguous over time, both in the workforce and in the family unit.

ACTIVITY KS **COMMUNICATION**

KNOWLEDGE AND UNDERSTANDING	IDENTIFICATION AND INTERPRETATION

On scrap paper, which you must throw away at the end of the lesson, collect a series of terms of abuse for the following:

■ a masculine female
■ a feminine female
■ a masculine male
■ a feminine male.

It is probable that you were able to come up with far more terms of abuse, some very unpleasant, for the feminine male. This shows something significant. To adopt the perceived behaviour of a female in our society implies a significant loss of status for a male. It is difficult to think of abusive terms to describe a masculine male which do not also imply some form of admiration – think of the expression 'a right bastard' which can be used to suggest admiration as well as dislike.

Gender-based stratification and differentiation

Whatever the theoretical debate on feminism and the role of women suggests, there is a huge amount of

---

HINTS AND TIPS *An excellent and quick book to read (only 55 pages) is* **The Future of Men** *(1997) by Dave Hill. It provides an overview of the changes that have occurred in modern Britain, such as the decline of industry, breakdown in family life, sexuality etc., that have affected the role of men. To give you a taster, Hill states that:*

> *Even present-day first impressions hint at how much more relaxed and elastic the category of masculinity is becoming: men do not look alike any more. Looks aren't everything, as every sensible girl knows. But the adventurous male wardrobe is astonishing compared with fifty years ago. (pp.47–48)*

quantitative evidence to suggest that females suffer from inequality in all societies. As a general overview of the debate, there are real issues for women at the beginning of the new millennium all over the planet and these should be evident in every area of this book:

■ Women tend to earn less than men do (but it should not be assumed that all men are better paid than women). Professions and employment which are feminised, such as teaching, nursing and cleaning, are low-pay occupations. For example, the average hourly earnings for men in 1995 in non-manual jobs was £11.33, for women it was £7.76 (New Earnings Survey, 1995). This type of work is treated as an extension of female domestic roles within the family (Benet, 1972). For further information on women and employment see Area 7 on Work, Organisations and Leisure.

■ Women are more likely to be the victims of abusive relationships, or be attacked by someone they know. For further information on women and crime, see Area 12 on Crime and Deviance.

■ Women are often the scapegoats for social ills: there is seen to be a direct relationship between crime rates in young men and poor mothering, for instance. Other variables are not really considered fully. This reinforces the ideology that women's primary role should be that of mother-housewife. For further information on socialisation and the mother-housewife role, see Area 6 on Families.

■ Even if women have the same qualifications as men, they are less likely to be promoted. For example, in the Civil Service women are concentrated in the lower grades, with 68.8 per cent of Administrative Officers being women in 1994, but only 5.7 per cent being on Grade 1. For further information on women and employment see Area 7 on Work, Organisations and Leisure.

■ There are fewer women in positions of power and status in our society than there are men. For further information see Area 14 on Power, Politics and Protest.

■ Girls are doing better in education, up to the age of 18 years old, than ever before and are even out-achieving boys. However, the results for females in higher education are not as encouraging, with fewer women getting high-grade degrees than men and women continuing to enter gender-specific subject areas. For further information see Area 8 on Education.

■ Many women are not in charge of their own fertility and do not have access to contraception. For further information on women and fertility see Area 6 on Families and Households.

■ Women in developing countries have additional problems due to social custom. Female circumcision is traditional in parts of Africa but results in death, mutilation and suffering for women and can also damage and kill their children. For further information on women around the world, see Area 13 on World Sociology.

Certainly, women's lives are changing dramatically and young women have expectations today that their mothers would not have believed possible. The pendulum has apparently swung so far in favour of girls that now it is argued that males experience a sense of inferiority in our society (see section above on Masculinity).

Women and paid employment

Women generally face four main disadvantages in the labour force that situate them in the secondary labour market and result in **vertical and horizontal segregation**. Vertical segregation refers to the way men and women in the same occupation are concentrated at different levels; men tend to occupy the high-level jobs and women the lower-level. Horizontal segregation refers to the way in which men and women have different occupations, men are situated in industries such as manufacturing and construction, while women are in catering and personal services. The four disadvantages are:

1   lower pay than men
2   low-status jobs
3   concentration in the lower-level occupations
4   a greater chance of part-time/casual/temporary work than men.

These disadvantages have been explained as being based on women being the secondary earner (men are still considered the breadwinner), because they may leave their job to raise a family. Therefore it is less likely that a woman will receive a high-status job with associated training and promotion prospects. Consequently women become seen as and treated as

a reserve army of labour, providing a flexible, cheap and expendable workforce (Caplow, 1954; Beechy, 1983). However, it is also important to consider the following changes in female employment:

■ Increasing numbers of women have been entering paid employment since the end of World War II.

■ It has become increasingly the norm for women to return to work after having children.

■ Employment for women outside the home is nothing new. British women have been traditionally engaged in farming and in the seventeenth century women formed a significant part of the textiles, retail and provision trade workforce in a variety of skilled occupations. During the eighteenth and nineteenth centuries women's labour formed an important part in the building blocks of the industrial revolution in factories, mills and coal-mines.

■ Women's labour was essential during the world wars, but after the First World War women had to be enticed back to the home through a government campaign on the joys of housework and the duty of mothers.

'Race' and ethnicity

'Race' itself is a profoundly misused and misinterpreted term. There is an assumption made on the 'scientific' grounds of the turn of the twentieth century that human beings divide into races. Implicit within this science is the belief or value judgement that some races are also 'better' than others are. This idea is actually an old one in western culture; the poet Rudyard Kipling who profoundly admired the peoples of modern-day India and Pakistan also wrote of the 'White man's burden' which was to bring civilisation to these areas of the world. A notion of race was actually being used as a justification for war and political annexation of other lands.

While many would find these ideas merely amusing today, there is a distinctly frightening element when one considers the racism and ethnic violence which was endemic in the world at the end of the twentieth century. Notions of race are used to justify the most appalling barbarity. In practical terms, there are few physical differences between the various anthropological human groupings and most of those are associated with distribution and quality of hair type, bone structure and eye shape (phenotypes).

Skin colour, which is seen as significant by some racists, is not a good indicator of race. There are considerable variations of skin colour within each of the distinctive human groups so that anthropologists would argue that the white-skinned peoples of northern Europe belong to the same human type as the black-skinned people of Sri Lanka and Southern India. Indeed, elements of language remain similar over much of this region arguing strongly for a common cultural root deep in prehistory. Much racism, therefore, is actually based on a profound misunderstanding of the anthropological bases of racial types. You should also note that few modern anthropologists are concerned with the typing and categorising of human racial characteristics as they are now operating at the genetic level in order to trace the development and geographical movement of human social groups.

Immigration and legislation

Ethnic minorities within the UK have been treated as second-class citizens based on their 'immigrant' status. An immigrant is commonly seen as any person who has recently arrived from another society in which he/she habitually lived. Therefore it is fair to say that the term has often been misused to refer to non-whites, and has consequently become a derogatory or negative label. This is interesting considering that the majority of UK residents are descended from immigrants, such as the Romans, Vikings, Angles and Saxons. The Irish have been settling in Britain for centuries and many Europeans migrated to Britain after the Second World War, but their presence has gone virtually unnoticed because of their skin colour. Also, the descendants of migrants to Australia, New Zealand and Canada have not met with the harsh immigration laws experienced by some new Commonwealth country members.

After the Second World War Indian, Sri Lankan, West Indian and Bangladeshi citizens with British passports were encouraged to migrate to Britain to fill labour shortages. Most of these migrants were black and they were treated as different from the white population from their arrival. They were filtered into unskilled, poorly-paid jobs, despite many having held skilled occupations in their countries of origin. They had been promised the opportunity of a better life, but experienced difficulties in attaining adequate accommodation and education. Language difficulties and cultural differences differentiated them from the majority of the population, which was used by right-wing politicians, such as Enoch Powell, and the media to scapegoat ethnic minority groups for any social ills.

New Commonwealth migrants had only begun to enter Britain in relatively large numbers around 1948, when the British Nationality Act enabled all Commonwealth citizens to enter the UK to work and settle. By 1962 the Conservative government had produced the Commonwealth Immigration Act which restricted further immigration for black people, without appearing overtly racist. Labour supported immigration control and even the 1969 Immigration Appeals Act, which gave migrants the right to appeal, limited the number of dependants allowed to enter Britain. By 1971 the Immigration Act removed the ability for black Commonwealth members to settle in the UK. Conservative legislation on immigration continued with the 1981 Nationality Act, the Immigration Act of 1988, the Asylum and Immigration Appeals Act of 1993 and the Asylum and Immigration Act, 1996. All the Acts tightened control on the entry of black people into Britain, by restricting entry to those with at least one British parent and who had independent funding to sustain them on entry to the country.

Legislation to improve the position of ethnic minority groups living in the UK has not been very effective in challenging racialism. The Race Relations Act of 1965 was established by the Labour Government to stop discrimination of the basis of colour, race or ethnic origin, when providing goods, services or facilities. In 1968 the Act gave more power to the Race Relations Board and created the Community Relations Committee to foster good race relations. Labour continued to introduce race relations legislation with the 1976 Race Relations Act, which made all acts of discrimination illegal, irrespective of intention. Labour

had realised, based on research (Daniel, 1968; McIntosh and Smith, 1975), that discrimination on the grounds of colour was still widespread, despite anti-discrimination legislation.

The Scarman Report, 1981, requested that there should be more positive race relations legislation, but very little has happened. A Home Office Report in 1983, on Ethnic Minorities in Britain, confirmed high levels of discrimination in employment and in the choice of worker to be made unemployed (see Area 7 on Work, Organisations and Leisure). The Policy Studies Institute, 1984 reported that opportunities had scarcely changed for ethnic minority groups since the 1950s.

In today's Britain it has been suggested that ethnic minorities form part of an underprivileged underclass, based on the disadvantages generally experienced in the labour market, housing and education. None of this continued racialism is surprising considering the mixed messages being sent out by the government in their immigration and race relations legislation. On the one hand, immigration legislation implies that the darker a person's skin colour, the more likely he/she is to be problem, but race relations legislation has made it illegal to act on the basis of someone's colour. In addition to this, in cases where racial discrimination has occurred, very little is done by the state to bring the offenders to justice. For example, with the death of Stephen Lawrence, it was his father who had to campaign for an inquiry, the MacPherson Report, into how his son's tragic race-related murder had been mishandled by the police.

Theoretical perspectives on 'race' and ethnicity

Biological/racial formation approach

'Scientific racism' in the nineteenth century was used to justify political oppression. People who were poor and in low-paid jobs were deemed to be in that position because they were of inferior racial stock. Large numbers of 'scientific' books were produced to show that various ethnic groupings were weaker and poorer physical specimens of humanity. Their poverty was due to their natural inferiority. This position was widely held in the southern states of the USA, in South Africa and also in Britain. Sometimes, attitudes were not cruel so much as paternalistic and kindly, for example: 'These poor Africans cannot look after themselves so they need us white people to do it for them.' Whatever the underlying motive, the effect was the same. People were denied the power and the right to determine their own futures.

Scientists had therefore formed a catalogue of characteristics, determined by biology/physiology, which they argued separated the 'races'. When the idea that a person's skull size and skin colour could determine level of intelligence and/or social development was undermined, scientists turned to a genetic argument. Contemporary geneticists, such as Jones (1991), have argued that the five racial categories identified by Morton in 1839 (Caucasian, Mongolian, Malay, American and Ethiopian) do possess a different genetic make-up that predispose them to different behaviour. Sociobiologists, such as Van den Berghe (1988), support the idea that genes interact with culture to ensure the survival of the fittest genes; in this case the dominant races. Even sociologists, such as Kohn (1995) and Herrnstein and Murray (1994) have utilised the idea that biological race differences can be used to classify people into racial groups with different potentialities.

Numerous empirical studies by scientists and social scientists after the Second World War concluded that all humans have the same origin and, therefore, gene pool. The only difference between humans has been the environment in which they have lived, which has had an effect on their physical features. For example, continued exposure to a hot sun has resulted in a darker skin that protects the owner from the damaging effects UV light can have. Generally sociologists are in agreement that 'race' is socially constructed rather than biologically formed.

Many ethnic minority groups have displayed signs of resistance to biological race formation ideology. For many people in developing countries, the history of the twentieth century has been very much a history of the struggle for liberation from the attitudes of the past. Many students will be familiar with the history of apartheid in South Africa and it remains a fascinating case study into the origins and practical application of the beliefs of scientific racism.

Sociological approaches

Marxism

Marxists, such as Cox (1970) and Miles (1982, 1993), maintain that racial inequality is directly linked to social inequality. Racial discrimination, particularly within employment, is a consequence of a capitalist economic structure. Capitalists exploit the racial divisions that already exist in society to divide the working class, and thereby suppress solidarity and potential class consciousness. Racialism is therefore a means of control for the ruling class, an ideological construction that sustains hostility and conflict within the mass of society.

Consequently, Marxists argue that any hostility displayed towards ethnic minorities by the working class is evidence of false class consciousness. Ethnic minorities become part of a surplus pool of labour, open to exploitation and easily dispensable. As a result Marxists conclude that they are forced to live in the poorest areas, work in specifically migrant occupations and face high levels of unemployment at times of economic recession. Ethnic minorities are faced with constant denigration in the media, where the negative image of the 'immigrant' is deeply embedded in the culture of the host society.

ACTIVITY   KS **INFORMATION TECHNOLOGY, COMMUNICATION**

KNOWLEDGE AND UNDERSTANDING	IDENTIFICATION AND INTERPRETATION	ANALYSIS AND EVALUATION

Choose one developing nation or area such as South Africa or perhaps the Indian subcontinent. Attempt to make a short timeline of its history throughout the twentieth century using CD-ROM information or the Internet to help you. Use children's books to support your study. Adult books are far more interesting but

may offer too much detail for you to process quickly. If you are fortunate to have access to someone whose ethnic origins lie in the region you are attempting to study, then see what perspective he/she can add to the events. This might be a useful whole-group exercise where people each contribute a small piece of information and between you, you could create a wall display.

Neo-Marxists, such as Hall (1980) and Ben-Tovim and Gabriel (1979), cannot agree whether 'race' should be examined relatively autonomously from class, i.e. it operates separately from other social relations, but at the same time affects class; or autonomously, i.e. race is a separate issue to general class conflict. Both approaches have added a cultural dimension to traditional Marxist analysis of race relations, allowing racialism to be examined in its own right. Solomos (1988), however, has brought both the relative autonomy and autonomy models together. He states that racism does have wider social connections, because race relations form part of the structural features of society, but that each historical race relations situation also has autonomy and should be examined in its own right. Economic and social conditions are seen to help in the construction of racist ideology and as a specific set of practices.

Although Marxist and neo-Marxist approaches examine racial discrimination in capitalist society and thereby highlight the disadvantaged position of ethnic minorities in the workforce, they make massive generalisations about their position in the stratification system. It should be remembered that not all members of ethnic minority groups are in the lowest social classes, live in the poorest areas, go to the worst schools or have low-status jobs. Much differentiation exists within different minority groups and there is evidence to show that the position of some groups, such as Indians, in the occupational structure is better than whites. For further information on Marxism and 'race'/ethnicity see Area 1 section on race relations theories.

Weberianism

The Weberian approach acknowledges that it is largely irrelevant whether real racial differences exist or not. The fact that 'race' is perceived to exist, and is used as the basis of discrimination, is enough to explain the hostility that results in society (Rex, 1967, 1988). Therefore Marxists and Weberians agree that 'race' is a form of ideology used to disadvantage the assumed inferior group. It is based on the perceptions of people in everyday life, where there is a constant struggle for scarce resources, such as jobs and homes. Ethnic minorities may be seen as a threat to the acquisition of these resources and targeted for hostility.

Rex and Tomlinson (1979) suggested that ethnic minority groups may be considered an 'underclass'

with life chances and conditions operating below that of the working class. Rex (1988) added that white members of society were now experiencing the social disadvantage experienced by members of ethnic minority groups. The economic recession appeared to have created an opportunity for all deprived members of the working class and unemployed to unite; but the underlying racialist ideology present in the UK may result in some whites challenging with whom they are in competition.

The Weberian approach offers a potentially positive outcome, because it argues that the market situation of ethnic minorities can change. However, this change is dependent on a very fluid, or socially mobile society, which in reality may not actually exist. Evidence suggests that there are limited opportunities for social mobility among ethnic minorities in the UK (see section on Social mobility for further discussion on this area). For further information on Weberianism and 'race'/ethnicity see Area 1 on race relations theories.

Functionalism

Functionalists, such as Patterson (1963), argue that it may be functional to have ethnic minorities in society because:

- they meet a specific demand for certain types of labour
- their presence may be used to explain social disorders and conflicts, making them a convenient scapegoat for the real cause
- over time they will come to accept the dominant values of the host society.

This approach argues that conflict in society is based on cultural differences and that it is 'natural' for the host society to be suspicious of 'dark strangers' who could be a threat to the status quo. Therefore, ethnic minorities would be free from hostility and domination if they assimilated mainstream social values.

The functionalist view assumes that cultural consensus, or the agreement of ethnic minority groups to abandon their own culture for the host society's results in a functional society. It is also assumed that ethnic groups will experience equal opportunities, their talent and ability allowing them access to rewards. This optimistic theory ignores the social inequalities experienced by ethnic minorities on the basis of ethnicity, class and sex. Functionalist theory on race relations has also acted as the foundation for the development of New Right theory and ideas of nationalism and assimilation. For further information on functionalism and 'race'/ethnicity see Area 1 on race relations theories.

John Rex

John Rex was brought up in South Africa and arrived in Britain in the late 1940s. He is currently Professor Emeritus at Warwick University but has also taught at Durham University where he set up the Department of Sociology in 1964.

His work has been associated with the problem of racism and ethnicity, and among his most influential works are the following studies: *Key Problems of Sociological Theory* (1964), *Race Relations in Sociological Theory* (1970), *Race and Ethnicity* (1986). Recent publications include *Ethnic Minorities in the Modern Nation State: Working Paper in the Theory of Multi- Culturalism and Political Integration* (1996).

John Rex is one of the pioneers of the study of ethnicity and race in Britain. He draws widely on a number of perspectives in his sociology and is described as a Weberian who also applies Marxist theorising. He has identified the social creation of a 'black underclass' in British society caused by discrimination and inequality and his work has been influential among politicians working in the field of race relations.

Symbolic interactionism

Symbolic interactionists stemming from the Chicago School, such as Park (1950) and Blumer (1969), argued that racial conflict was generated during times of real or imagined threats to the way in which social life operated. For example, as long as ethnic minorities did not challenge the status quo they were left alone, but should they compete for jobs or housing, then all hell would break loose. Park (1950) argued that racialism was a consequence of poor communication about different self-perceptions. The host society did not understand the history or culture of the ethnic groups.

However, Park could not see how this understanding would be attained and concluded that racial conflict would vanish as ethnic groups became assimilated.

The nature of symbolic interactionism is that it concentrates on individual situations and therefore it has been criticised for not being 'generalisable' about the race relations situation as a whole. It also fails to take into account class and the effect that this has on ethnic minorities. This said, it does provide an alternative approach to understanding how ethnic minorities interact with the indigenous population. For further information on symbolic interactionism and 'race'/ethnicity see Area 1 on race relations theories.

Postmodernism

Postmodernists challenge the grand theories, such as Marxism, about their interpretations of race relations as secondary aspects of a capitalist stratification system. Postmodern theorising, such as in the work of Cohen (1992) and Modood (1992), has created an anti-racist school of thought that stresses differences and diversity among ethnic groups and attacks the idea that they are victims by examining identity. It has been argued that identity is a dynamic feature of social life that has become more fluid through globalisation. Different cultural groups have had closer contact than ever before, which has brought a whole new set of identities for people to 'pick and mix'. Consequently, postmodernists claim that individuals no longer have a fixed identity, such as Asian working class; they can now choose to be black, male, home boy, brother.

These new identities should blur the boundaries between ethnic groups, but it has been argued that they could instil a stronger sense of nationalism as new identities threaten the established ones. Also, the ideas on racial identities put forward by postmodernists remain vague and ambiguous and do not allow for the value placed on traditional culture by Britain's minority ethnic groups (Modood, 1994). Postmodernism is an interesting and challenging new perspective, but it does seem to ignore the material and social disadvantages experienced by many ethnic minorities that might prevent them from taking part in a global society. For further information on postmodernism see Area 1 on Sociological Theory.

Approaches to the race debate

Sociobiological	More recent analyses of race which emphasise racial differences tend to rely on the view that cultures are very different and that these cultural differences have an impact on intelligence and achievement. Arguments based on these principles are a little more difficult to refute than those based on overt and clearly racist principles but they remain essentially racist because they stress differences between cultures but resist social explanations for those differences beyond those of notions of 'superior' cultures. Psychologists such as Eysenck (1970) are associated with such views.
New Right	Writers from this perspective adapt the functionalist view that members of ethnic minorities should adapt their own culture to that of the country in which they have settled. Attempts at multi-culturalism have no value because they exist to 'appease' ethnic minorities. Note that intellectuals such as Roger Scruton and politicians such as Norman Tebbit have made public statements to this effect.
Marxists/neo-Marxists	Marxists see all conflict as being class-related and claim that the divisions, which are engendered by racism, are a way of dividing the working class in order to rule them. This is a simplistic view of the work of Stuart Hall and others. Nationalism is a way of creating a false sense of unity among people who have little in common other than a shared sense of culture. To illustrate the point, the Queen Mother was famously admired during the Second World War for visiting bomb victims in the East End slums wearing 'only' her pearls rather than diamonds and was loved for identifying with them because Buckingham Palace had also been bombed.
The underclass debate	The notion of an underclass is drawn from Marxism and Weberianism (the concept of the lumpenproletariat or reserve army of labour and the dual labour market). These are people of even lower status than the working class who remain essentially outside society until required by employers to undercut the wages of the authentic working class. Women and immigrant workers fit into this category as they can be drawn upon to support factory owners in times of high productivity such as war. Rex and Moore (1967) developed this argument to point out that the position of the black workers is even more precarious in a capitalist society because they are disliked by the working class whose jobs they threaten and because they are subject to exploitation as cheap labour by employers. Black children are not able to be socially mobile in the same way as white children because they are handicapped by the racism of others.
Anti-racism	This view suggests that people who are of Afro-Caribbean, Asian or African origin in Britain share economic exploitation on the basis of notions of race. Just as feminists have taken Marxism and adapted it to their own analyses, so anti-racists have developed a perspective. People in this position do not identify with the separate cultural identities among the ethnic groups but refer to those of non-European origin as 'black' and emphasise a shared and common experience of slavery and oppression. The term 'black', despite its origins as a slogan of pride in non-European status, has become a term that is criticised by members of minority ethnic groups because it fails to take account of the different cultural experiences of people. Not all West Indians have a black skin, but many experience a secondary status in our society. The 'black' debate is one that has given rise to a huge political and sociological controversy. The argument against 'black' consciousness has been led by Modood (1992) who objects to the loss of

individual cultural heritage implied by the notion of 'blackness'. He sees the whole debate as one of more complexity than the anti-racist view offers.

Liberal views of race   Liberal perspectives tend to encourage the view that people should become colour blind and unaware of racial differences. Many writers object to the blurring of ethnic differences because the suggestion is that significant cultural differences and understandings will be lost. Liberal views of race can blur into New Right thinking.

Radical views of race   This is a perspective which is more typical of American research traditions, but which does appear in British writing. In this view of the race debate, all 'white' people are seen as potential racists. It is critical of the liberal perspective and encourages people of colour to take a pride in their differences from European cultures. It is a political movement as well as a sociological movement. Radical writers attempt to 'reclaim' historical figures as black and their rhetoric is similar to that of radical feminism and radical gay activists.

Racial stratification and differentiation

Employment

■ In general, ethnic minorities are found in lower-level employment more often than white workers. However, it should be remembered that different ethnic groups have different levels of success in the occupational structure and that upward social mobility is now becoming more evident for Indians and African Asians. In fact, 22 per cent of African Asians are now in professional and managerial work, a higher figure than for whites.

■ Female ethnic minorities in paid employment have greater similarity with white female workers. Both groups tend to be concentrated in low-level, white-collar or semi-skilled manual employment.

■ Ethnic minorities in employment are more likely to be found doing shift work than whites and to have fewer opportunities for promotion.

■ Members of ethnic minorities are much more likely than whites to experience unemployment, which is particularly acute among the younger members of the population.

■ Differences in language ability and educational qualifications between ethnic minorities and whites cannot explain the massive differences in the levels of jobs and lack of promotion.

NB: For further information on 'race' and employment, please refer to the relevant areas in the rest of the book.

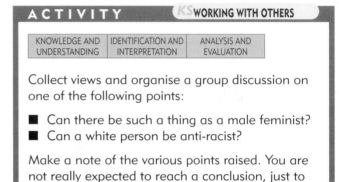

ACTIVITY   KS **WORKING WITH OTHERS**

KNOWLEDGE AND UNDERSTANDING	IDENTIFICATION AND INTERPRETATION	ANALYSIS AND EVALUATION

Collect views and organise a group discussion on one of the following points:

■ Can there be such a thing as a male feminist?
■ Can a white person be anti-racist?

Make a note of the various points raised. You are not really expected to reach a conclusion, just to develop a fuller understanding of the issues.

Age and disability

This is probably one of the least well-studied areas of sociology. **Age** and **disability** are both factors that differentiate us in society and can lead to disadvantaged positions in the stratification system. For example, old age pensioners may experience a drop in income once paid employment has stopped, which results in a lowering of their living standards. Likewise many people will, at some point in their lives, experience a degree of bodily dysfunction as a result of natural ageing processes, which could easily affect their life chances.

Age

Biology is the basis of age. Everyone who lives a full life cycle is born, grows up, ages and dies. At each stage the body reaches a given stage of development, although variations between individuals are common. Sociologists are mainly interested in how different age groups are treated differently in society and how this treatment changes over time. For example, in some societies older people have much more status and power than in others; but the status of the elderly may change as the society develops. Therefore sociologists argue that society constructs the way of life for people of a given age.

A full life cycle is made up of 'age stages' between life and death. The main stages are:

- childhood
- youth
- adulthood
- old age

In the UK, childhood is associated with dependence on parents, and turns into 'youth' when the child has started to establish independence and self-reliance. This period carries on throughout the teenage years and may not change into adulthood until the mid-twenties, when commitments to other people and things ensure responsibility. Adulthood, however, is a very vague stage, because in Britain you are legally an adult at 18 years of age, but may not actually experience an adult lifestyle until much later on. Conversely, a 16-year-old who has a child may have adulthood thrown on him/her prematurely, but still be a youth. Old age has the same relative nature. Biologically bodies mature at different rates and the 65-year marker of old age may be premature for some people still in the prime of adulthood. As Pilcher (1995:8) states:

> *For sociologists ageing, or the process of growing up and growing older, is socially constructed. In other words, sociologists argue that whilst the physiological aspects of growing up and growing older are both universal and natural, the ways of understanding the ageing process are neither of these.*

Childhood

It has been argued that the idea of childhood is a relatively new phenomenon (Airies, 1962). It was not until the eighteenth century that the notion of treating children as 'little people' in need of care and support emerged. Children older than five had always been treated as 'mini adults' capable of working to support the family. For example, in the Middle Ages the children of peasants were expected to work the land and formed an essential part of the economy. There were no separate children's clothes, no organised education, and even the children of the wealthy were trained for their future duties from a very early age.

The early eighteenth century saw the newly rich traders begin to treat their children differently, particularly in the way they gave them a long period of training/ education in order to enable them to run the family businesses. At the same time academics and theologians were introducing a new concept relating to children, suggesting that they were born pure and innocent. The wealthy, acknowledging these ideas, began to supervise the upbringing of their children to protect them from corruption. They also had the money to dress their children in clothes specifically designed for them.

The nineteenth century saw a turn in social and religious attitudes towards children. It was now believed that children were born wicked and had to be firmly controlled, in order to learn the best way to behave (beatings were regularly given for misconduct). In Victorian England the lives of middle-class children were tightly regimented, with the authority of adults being absolute. Children were 'seen and not heard'. Wealthy families sent their boys to public schools to learn to become gentlemen, and girls were taught to become good wives and mothers. The lives of working-class children continued as they had done since the Middle Ages; they worked to sustain the family economy as soon as was possible.

The awareness of childhood as a truly distinctive period in the life cycle of all social classes emerged with the passing of various employment acts in the 1820s controlling the number of hours children could work. The eventual introduction of a national system of schooling in 1870 consolidated the notion of childhood. However, the ideas of child-rearing involving beating them and allowing them no views continued well into this century.

The twentieth century brought another change in attitude towards children, which involved showing them love and attention. From the 1950s onward the idea that children were precious and in need of nurturing and protection became common among all social classes. However, important differences appeared in the way children were socialised:

- Class – working-class parents are more likely to give commands to their children, while middle-class parents tend to explain their wishes. Also, the working class tends to dismiss children's views and punish them more erratically than the middle classes.
- Gender – girls are more closely supervised by their parents.
- Ethnic group – West Indian and Asian parents are stricter with their children and place a high value on obedience.

Children in other cultures have also been treated differently over time, dependent on economic and social factors. An interesting example of this is the behaviour of the Ik, a tribe living in the mountains

between Uganda and Sudan. Turnbull (1961) investigated the lifestyle of the Ik in the 1960s and identified that a forced move from their homeland, in a fertile game reserve to the mountains, had changed the way in which they treated their children. The Ik were originally hunters, but had no choice but to develop agriculture in the harsh conditions of the mountains. Food was in short supply and a culture developed to ensure their survival despite inadequate supplies. Consequently children came to be seen as a curse or 'another mouth to feed' when there was not enough food. Parents treated their offspring harshly in the hope that they would die. At three years old children were thrown out of their homes and expected to look after themselves. The children tended to band together in age groups to survive and girls would prostitute

---

ACTIVITY   KS **COMMUNICATION**

KNOWLEDGE AND
UNDERSTANDING

Fill the gaps using the words provided. Use the completed text for revision of this area.

CHILDREN

Complete the following:

The role of children in the family has changed enormously as their ability to contribute to the household _____ has diminished. This is mainly the result of successive _____ restrictions on the age at which the young may work for payment, and where they may work. Moreover, the family itself has become much more _____-_____ as families have turned in on themselves. The consequences of this are varied. Certainly the lives of young children are different from the past, if only in _____ terms. Generally speaking they are better fed, clothed and sheltered than they were. Some families in _____, however, still cannot provide a decent standard of living for their children. In the family they are more likely to be consulted in decision-making although they may not have any final say.

Some sociologists have, therefore, argued that childhood is _____-_____ and is the product of changing social forces, not a _____ state at all. In the past children were treated as little adults and have only recently come to be seen as children. Others have argued that, when the personal accounts of parents in the past are examined, a

much more child-centred view of parenthood emerges.

However, not all children find the family a safe and attractive place. There is increasing evidence that many children suffer from battering and sexual abuse by _____ members of the family. Many may suffer from psychological disturbance because of the intensity of family life and the _____ phenomena such as rising unemployment can increase the tensions of family life. Arguing and divorcing parents may produce strain on the children as they try to cope with the conflicting demands on their affections. In the USA thousands of children disappear from the family each year. Not all are abducted; many leave voluntarily and this suggests that all is not rosy in the nuclear family.

Sociologists often find it difficult to investigate these problems precisely because they are so _____. Moreover, these sorts of issue arouse emotion, and it is a problem for investigators to divorce themselves from the passions that may be present during the investigations. By their nature, many of the issues are hidden from view and family members may be reluctant, or even frightened, to talk about them. Yet sociologists continue, by a variety of methods, to examine these personal problems.

CLOSE   NATURAL   LEGAL   ECONOMY
PERSONAL   MATERIAL   STRUCTURAL
SOCIALLY-CONSTRUCTED   POVERTY
CHILD-CENTRED

themselves in exchange for food. Childhood in the Ik contained no preconceptions of love and support.

In modern Britain the introduction of free state education, welfare services and smaller family units (see Area 6 on Families and Households) meant that the life of children in the twentieth century became gradually more comfortable both emotionally and physically. However, children do continue to suffer in a variety of ways. The most basic reason for this suffering tends to be the pressure that parents find themselves under in the stress of everyday living. For example, divorce and separation do not necessarily harm the child, but the arguments and the pain that is associated with them can do.

An area that displays the unequal position that children have in the social structure is child abuse. It is very difficult to measure the extent of child abuse, because it often occurs in private and is not realised by the victim until they get older, when it is more difficult to report. Child abuse can be divided into four types:

1 physical violence
2 physical and emotional neglect
3 emotional abuse
4 sexual exploitation.

Much child abuse occurs within the family, although evidence suggests that children are more likely to be sexually abused by a stepfather than a natural father.

*HINTS AND TIPS   Consider the television programmes and news reports that have highlighted child abuse cases in the UK. For example, Mandy on **Hollyoaks** (Channel 4) was sexually exploited and experienced physical violence at the hands of her fathers for years. Fred and Rosemary West exposed their children to all forms of child abuse and even killed some before they were arrested by the police for killing a number of vulnerable young women in their Gloucestershire home. Both examples display the reverse side of childhood in the west, a dark side that should be identified to show the lack of power children have in society.*

Youth

Young people are identified as being in a distinct stage in their life cycle in western industrial societies. It has become a stage of transition between the dependency of childhood (and the associated lack of power) and adulthood with all its associated rights, privileges and responsibilities. Youth involves moving from education to employment and from the parental home to supporting and sustaining oneself. It is a time of self-discovery and exploration, which tends to involve participating in previously adult-only activities, such as drinking alcohol and having sex. This could explain the large number of sociological studies examining youth culture (see Area 12 on Crime and Deviance and Area 5 on Mass Media for further information on youth culture).

Adulthood

Adulthood has been examined throughout this book, for example any study that investigates employment will use an adult population. Therefore sociologists, unless specifically examining a different life course stage, will conduct studies based on an adult population. Adulthood, in physiological terms, should be when puberty has occurred, although in modern western industrial societies it is more closely linked with cultural expectations of emotional maturity, independence and employment. For example, a 12-year-old may have a fully matured 'adult' body, but not have any adult rights until 18 years old and then not be treated as an adult until he/she is seen as fully independent.

Old age

Old age appears to be a prime example of how age can be seen as a social construction, as well as being a biological fact. For example, in societies where life expectancy is low the old people are of an age which would be considered relatively young in societies with a longer life expectancy. In modern Britain the most common stereotypes of the old are that they are 'useless' and that they 'have problems'. These labels have resulted in much negative thinking about old age and have put most old people in a low-status position. However, as it is the society itself that dictates how age should be viewed, the social inequality faced by the aged is not inevitable.

There is a biological basis to old age. The body does 'run down' and eventually die. However, humans have managed to affect the ageing process itself. Medicine has both lengthened old age and made at least the earlier part of it healthier for most. Old age now tends to be separated into two stages:

1 Early old age (65–75) – travelling, seeing friends, leisure time, classes.

We are an ageing society

- Since 1950 the number of people living to over 100 years of age has risen by 7 per cent a year.

- In 1991 there were 4,400 people in the UK aged 100 years or over.

- The Office for National Statistics estimates that there will be 45,000 centenarians (100+ years old) in 2031.

- Women are seven times more likely to become centenarians than men.

- Life expectancy has increased from 43 years for women and 41 years for men in 1841 to 80 years for women and 74 for men in 1991.

- A man in France lived to 121 years of age!

Adapted from *Sociology Update* (1998)

2   Late old age (76+) – increased physical and mental health problems, community care.

It should be noted that these are generalisations and, as such, ignore the important differences between old people based on class, gender and ethnicity, which produce differences in lifestyles. For example, what do a retired train driver and the Queen Mother have in common? Not much, apart from the right to draw a pension!

It is interesting to realise that old age in other societies can bring status, but in modern industrial societies, where status is associated with occupation, the termination of employment (retirement) results in a loss of status. The respect shown to elders in other societies is lost in our ageing population, where increasing numbers of old age pensioners tend to be seen as a drain on resources, rather than a fount of knowledge and experience. In fact, in societies based on rapid

ACTIVITY KS **COMMUNICATION, WORKING WITH OTHERS**

KNOWLEDGE AND UNDERSTANDING	IDENTIFICATION AND INTERPRETATION

Interview an elderly member of your family/local community about his/her experiences of the ageing process. Pay particular attention to the social inequalities he/she may have experienced.

social change, the skills of the old are virtually redundant as technology moves ahead to create a whole new area of expertise. This, too, reduces the value of the old to society and weakens their position in the stratification system. The whole ageing process may gradual disengage or separate the elderly from the rest of society, making this life course stage the most disadvantaged of all.

Disability

A number of points should be raised about disability in order to develop your understanding of this little-studied area of sociology.

- Disability is not necessarily a handicap. In the early days of the settlement of the Canadian island of Newfoundland, nearly one-quarter of the population was profoundly deaf due to a genetic disorder in the community. Everyone used sign language and deafness was merely seen as another dimension of 'normal'.

- In our culture there is a strong residual belief that disability is a punishment for a wrong committed by a family member. This is expressed in biblical terms as 'the sins of the father shall be visited upon the son'. We may be ashamed and embarrassed by disability among family members. Certainly, in the past, learning disability was considered a huge disgrace so those children would be locked away from public sight.

- Disability and handicap are not the same thing. The inability to walk is not a problem if the person has access to a wheelchair or another aid. Public buildings that can only be accessed by stairs are the problem for people who have little use of their legs. People who experience disability are handicapped as much by society as by their own bodies.

- A dual standard of morality has operated in many societies so that the disabled are seen as not fully human and therefore not worthy of life. A less well-publicised aspect of the Holocaust was the Nazi drive towards purification of the race by the deliberate killing of those who experienced physical or learning disability and mental instability. Disabled children were often starved to death and it is estimated by the Holocaust Museum that over 200,000 handicapped people were murdered in the T-4 programme. In America, mentally handicapped and troubled children who attended the Fernald State School in Waltham, Massachusetts, were fed radiation-spiked cereals without the consent of their parents throughout the 1940s and 1950s.

■ The handicapped and disabled can be seen in terms of well-meaning but ultimately humiliating stereotypes. This can be seen in soap opera where disability is often introduced as a plot line which offers two distinct perspectives – the disabled person is bitter and twisted by the disability or the disabled person is more saintly and virtuous than other people. In nearly all cases, the disability itself and responses to it run the plot rather than the character of the person who is disabled.

ACTIVITY   KS **WORKING WITH PEOPLE, COMMUNICATION**

KNOWLEDGE AND UNDERSTANDING	IDENTIFICATION AND INTERPRETATION	ANALYSIS AND EVALUATION

Organise a discussion to the effect that just as it would be completely unacceptable for a white person to play the part of a black person in films, so it is equally unacceptable for the able-bodied to play disabled in feature films and television programmes.

■ The dual element of bitter versus saintly is a key theme in discussions of disability, so that Jacques Lusseyran is described on a website devoted to Practical Philosophy <http://world.std.com/~socrates/lusseyrn.html> as being unusually compassionate *because of his*

HINTS AND TIPS   If you are interested in the experience of disability and how it affects people, there is a surprisingly wide variety of materials on the web. You are advised simply to type in a key search word referring to disability in general or to refer to a more specific problem such as impaired vision. As many of these sites are run by people who themselves experience disability, or for academics and interested professionals who need to develop their own knowledge, they are mercifully free from the stereotypes of dependence and/or charity case. Many sites are political and angry. They offer a great deal of interest to the novice sociologist.

---

blindness. One of the weirder expressions of this popular myth-making is the way that able-bodied actors who portray the disabled in Hollywood films seem likely to receive Oscar nominations.

ACTIVITY   KS **PROBLEM SOLVING**

ANALYSIS AND EVALUATION

Attempt a small research exercise based on the following questions.

How many recent Hollywood films can you think of which have disability as a theme? What view of disability do these films offer?

How many of them resulted in major awards for the actor or actress concerned?

PROFILE

Dr Tom Shakespeare

Tom Shakespeare was brought up in Aylesbury and gained his first degree in Social and Political Science from Cambridge University in 1987. He gained his doctorate from Cambridge University in 1995, where he studied sociological perspectives on disability. He has been a lecturer at the University of Sunderland, and a research fellow at the University of Leeds, and is now developing a research centre with the Universities of Newcastle and Durham, exploring the ethical and social implications of the new genetics.

Tom Shakespeare has worked to develop social theories on disability, and to research the lives of disabled people: his publications include **The Sexual Politics of Disability** (1996) and several sociological introductions to disability studies. He is also interested in the relationship between biological and social factors in human experience, and in the impact of new scientific knowledge. He has always tried to make his work accessible and relevant, and pops up regularly in the media talking about disability and about genetics: he believes he is the only person ever to have appeared on *Newsnight* wearing a Newcastle United strip.

Theoretical perspectives on age and disability

Marxism

The issue of social inequality resulting from old age and/or disability has been explained using a Marxist approach. It has been built into the broad theory of class-based inequality, by recognising that all social inequalities are based on the hegemony (ruling class ideology). It is argued that old people and the disabled are forced into a 'structured dependency' through the way in which capitalism works (Phillipson and Walker, 1986).

Structured dependency refers to the way in which capitalism is structured to ensure maximum profit for the ruling class, while keeping the workers dependent on the system for survival. Age is one basis for structuring society, particularly in the area of employment. For example, there are laws that dictate at what age we can first undertake paid employment and at what age we should stop (retirement). The same principle applies to disability, in that there are areas of employment that are restricted for the disabled. Therefore, the elderly and the disabled experience differentiation in society to ensure that capitalism can maintain maximum profits, i.e. old people and the disabled are considered to be less efficient and/or effective in the workplace than adults or the able-bodied.

It would seem that the labour market, according to Marxists, is structured to support social inequalities based on age and ability. This is supported by social ideology that identifies old age and disability as something negative in a capitalist society, because it reduces the ability to work. Marxists argue that work is directly related to people's identity and therefore retirement or unemployment is coupled with a loss of status. Also, not working is seen as a drain on resources, which reinforces the idea that being old and/or disabled is a bad thing for society. (For further information on dependency on welfare services, see Area 10 on Wealth, Poverty, Welfare and Social Policy).

Weberianism

The Weberian approach to age inequality is similar to status inequality (see Area 1 on Sociological Theory), in

that society is divided up into different age strata (Riley, 1988). These strata are subject to social change based on the way they are affected by what is going on in society. For example, being a child today is very different to what it would have been like being a child in the 1800s (see section on Childhood, page 187). Therefore this approach explains how age stratification works, but does not, unlike the Marxist approach, show how age-based social inequality developed.

> **HINTS AND TIPS** *In relation to both age and disability it is relatively straightforward to apply Weberian theory. Consider the concepts of market situation, class, status and party. The old and the disabled have a very weak market situation compared to the rest of society and, therefore, are at the bottom of the stratification system when competing for scarce resources. Their status in society is also weak, which results in them having very little party representation. Have you heard of a political party or pressure group that has campaigned on behalf of the elderly or the disabled?*
>
> *With knowledge and understanding you should be able to apply any sociological theory to a particular concept that you are examining. Start by identifying the main points of the theory, then use them to explain the concept, as shown above.*

Functionalism

The concept of age is applied by functionalists, such as Eisenstadt (1956), in a typically functional manner. They argue that age-based strata only have significance in societies that have general, rather than specific, norms, values and rules. For example, in societies where position in the stratification system is determined by family membership, a specific rule, age division is not common. However, in societies where status is based on a number of things, age differentiation can develop. This shows how modern societies, where achievement allows social mobility, give age more importance than where status is ascribed.

Eisenstadt suggests that dividing society into age groups supports the stability and well-being of society. Society becomes more integrated through age-based divisions, because they connect families to the outside world by making young adults leave home and function beyond kinship-based relationships. It is useful to see age as a social construction, but suggesting it integrates society does not explain the dysfunctions of age-based social divisions, such as the social inequality faced by the elderly. It could be argued that stratification by age, far from being an integrative force in society, is in fact a differentiating one that allows different rights and privileges to different strata.

Life-course

Structural theories, such as Marxism and Weberianism, emphasise the economy and labour market as the most important part of society. In relation to children, the retired and the profoundly disabled, this disqualifies them from investigation. The life-course approach builds in a moral and cultural aspect that takes into account policies and issues that have a direct effect on their lives. For example, the elderly experience 'structured dependency' (see Marxism, page 192), which means that their living standards are decided by politicians, relatives and care homes (Vincent, 1995). Individual lives are subject to structures of inequality, such as exclusion from the labour market, which are constantly changing throughout their life-course. The individual or group responds to these inequalities, accepting or rejecting them, which results in social change.

Vincent has argued that ruling-class ideology has helped to reproduce the inequalities of old age. The elderly are exploited in the workforce based upon the cultural myths that are perpetuated. For example, there has been recent media coverage about the poor pay and conditions of retired people working in part-time jobs, such as in DIY stores. We tend to classify people by age and associate them with the leading stereotype. For example, old people are useless, disabled people will not be able to cope with employment. This shows that the construction of class-, gender- and 'race'-based differentiations have the same basis as social inequalities dependent on age and disability.

Conclusion

Is stratification inevitable?

Different historical periods and societies have seen various reformers and revolutionaries committed to equality attempt to end systems of social stratification. The French Revolution of 1789 and the Russian Revolution of 1917 both had an egalitarian society as the goal. Marx's theory was developed to encourage a proletarian revolution where each person would have his or her needs met under a communist regime. Even clause 4 of the British Labour Party constitution (adopted in 1918, abandoned 1996) supports the development of an equal society:

> *To secure for the workers by hand or by brain the full fruits of their industry and the most equitable distribution thereof that may be possible upon the basis of the common ownership of the means of production, distribution and exchange, and the best obtainable system of popular administration and control of each industry or service.*

The support for an egalitarian society, however, has not resulted in a society that is equal in all respects. This has led functionalists and New Right theorists to claim that social inequality is inevitable and necessary for a balanced and efficient society. However, it could be argued that these consensus theorists' view of stratification is a way of justifying privilege. Marx's theory of a classless society may be a Utopian dream, but it is a dream that attempts to remove the harsh realities of life for those at the bottom of the stratification system. To end on a positive note, just because social equality has not been achieved in one society in all respects, does not mean that at some time in the future of humankind it will not appear.

Area summary

Stratification

- Difference and power causes social inequality.
- Occupation affects income and this affects lifestyles and life chances.
- Material inequalities are often, but not always, referred to as class inequalities.
- Inequalities of status arise because some kinds of people are more highly regarded than others.
- Inequalities of power are inequalities in the ability to influence and control other people.
- Scales based on occupation ignore status.
- Status may be achieved or ascribed.
- Sociologists do not create systems of stratification, they merely use terms, such as social class, to point out the differences between people that already exist.

Social class

- Social class is usually measured by occupation.
- Social class can be subjective or objective.
- Britain is a relatively affluent society.
- Living standards for the whole population have never been higher.
- Some sections of the population have received a steady increase in their level of income over the past few years.
- The real level of income of the lowest-paid workers has barely increased since the mid-1980s, unlike for the higher earners.
- A large and increasing proportion of the UK population is in poverty, including workers in low-paid jobs.
- Independent Institute for Fiscal Studies (1994):

  6 *The gap between the highest and the lowest paid workers has been getting bigger in recent years. The gulf between top and bottom incomes is now greater that at any time this century.*

Gender

- Women tend to be in low-paid, part-time, low-status employment.
- Women's primary role is usually seen as that of mother/housewife.
- Most new jobs created over the last two decades have gone to women, especially 'working mums'.
- Women contribute an increasing share of the household income.
- Women are becoming better represented among the professions.
- The under-35s tend to share a common set of values in relation to sex equality, which has opened up the way for the blurring of gender differences.
- The gap between women and men in earnings is slowly decreasing.

Ethnicity

■ Racial attacks and harassment are on the increase.

■ Ideas of assimilation and a harmonious multi-racial society are not being supported by empirical evidence. The Anti-Racist Alliance estimated that 14 people died in racially motivated attacks in 1992–1993. Also, the 1991 Census identified that ethnic minorities tend to be concentrated in certain areas of the UK, particularly in inner cities.

■ There are no official figures for 'race-related' offences.

■ Ethnic minorities are much more likely to find themselves in lower-status, lower-paid and lower-skilled jobs than members of the white population. However, recent studies have shown that some ethnic groups are achieving upward social mobility.

Age and disability

■ Different age stages have different experiences of social inequality, childhood has little power, but may bring wealth or poverty; old age may result in loss of power, wealth and status.

■ Disability is used to differentiate part of the population, which tends to result in a lower position in the stratification system, with reduced access to jobs, wealth and power.

Definitions

Achieved status	The amount of social esteem or honour given to an individual based on his or her own achievements or merits
Age	Stage of biological maturity, which is related to cultural rights/expectations
Aggregation of inequalities	The way in which disadvantages can mount up and be grouped together
Ascribed status	The amount of social esteem or honour given to an individual based on their origin of birth
Biological determinism	An approach that believes a person's biology, or genetically inherited traits, determine or affect the rest of their social and physical existence
Class consciousness	The subject class (proletariat) becoming aware of its disadvantaged and exploited position at the hands of the ruling class
Closed society	Society that has no social mobility, or movement between strata
Contradictory class location	Concept used by Wright (Marxist) to describe social positions in contemporary capitalism that exist outside of the bourgeoisie, proletariat and petit bourgeoisie, but that occupy semi-permanent class position in relation to politics, ideology and economics

Differentiation	Separation into different groups
Disability	Physical or mental incapacity
Egalitarianism	Principle that advocates social equality, in that there should be no social stratification within the society
Embourgeoisement	The merging of the working class into the middle class based on a new affluent lifestyle
Ethnicity	Cultural heritage
Ethnocentric	Seeing something from your own cultural viewpoint (or ethnicity) and reflecting your cultures bias in your observations
Functional prerequisite	A basic need of society that must be met if society is to continue
Gender	Socially-constructed role based on societal norms and values associated with that sex
Gender roles	Masculinity or femininity, as defined by the society
Life chances	The specific opportunities or outcomes that an individual or group may have as a consequence of their position in the social stratification system, such as longevity, risk of heart disease, educational attainment etc.
Market situation	A term used by Weberians to describe an individual's position within the labour market based on their qualifications, experience and general employability
Objective class	Social class position of an individual based on external categorisations, such as occupation or income
Open society	A social stratification with a high degree of social mobility, usually based on status being achieved by merit
Party	Term used by Weber to refer to a group that represents the interests of its members and to which association may affect your social position
Post-Fordist	View of society where the reliance on computer technology changes the nature of the workforce, making employees flexible and multi-skilled
Proletarianisation	The merging of the middle class into the working class (or proletariat), based on increasing divisions between the rich and poor
'Race'	Real or perceived biological differences that have been given a social meaning in relation to the colour of someone's skin or place of origin
Racial discrimination	Negative or hostile behaviour towards a person, or group, because of their presumed 'race'
Racial prejudice	Negative or hostile feeling towards a person, or group, because of their presumed 'race'
Relative surplus population	A term used by Marx to describe people who exist outside of the proletariat at the bottom of the stratification system
Salariat	Salaried workers
Sex	Biological definition of difference between men and women
Sexual discrimination	Negative or hostile behaviour towards a person, or group, because of their sex

Social class	Hierarchically arranged groups in a capitalist system, based on similarity in wealth, income, occupation and status
Social mobility	Movement from one stratum to another in a social stratification system
Social stratification	A hierarchical ranking system made up of unequal amounts of power, wealth and status
Status	The type of role held in society
Status group	A collective of people who all hold the same amount of social honour or esteem in that society
Status situation	The consciousness of clerks to their relationship with their employers, providing them with a sense of prestige higher than that of manual workers
Structuration	A term developed by Giddens to link structure and action together in a theory of mutual inter-dependence, i.e. individual actions create structures, but those structures are necessary to perform the actions in the first place
Subjective class	The social class position of an individual based on their own opinions and beliefs, rather than any external categorisations
Underclass	A group of people with life chances below that of the working class in the stratification system

Data response questions

Item A

When trying to estimate what's happening to the underclass, I focus on three symptoms: crime, illegitimacy, and economic activity among working aged men.

Murray, C. (1996) 'Underclass: The Crisis Deepens' in **Charles Murray and the Underclass: the Developing Debate**. London, Institute of Economic Affairs.

Item B

Analysis of the Labour Force Survey (LFS) data for 1987, 1988 and 1989 reveals that 41 per cent of men in employment of Indian origin were found in managerial and professional occupational groupings, compared with 35 per cent for the white population. The relatively high proportion for Indian men in this occupational band is partly explained by the significantly larger proportions of people of Indian origin in self-employment.

Skellington, R. (1996:212) **'Race' in Britain Today**. London, Sage.

Item C

Despite the seemingly feminine, or certainly less macho nature of so much of indie music's lyrical content, almost all of the genre's leading 'scenes' have, over the years, been quite male-dominated, if not laddish ... Bands like Primal Scream were fusing post-Jesus and Mary Chain feedback with fey vocals ... However, no matter how harmlessly wimpy the likes of Lawrence from Felt or Stephen of The Pastels seemed, they still belonged to a movement made up entirely of blokes. The Soup Dragons, The Bodines, and Mighty Lemon Drops – not only does it read like a list of major label signing failures, but there isn't a female band among them.

Davies, L. L. (1995:128) 'Velocity Girls: Indie, New Lads and Old Values' in S. Cooper (Ed.) **Girls, Girls, Girls**. London, Cassell.

a Describe briefly what sociologists mean by the term 'underclass'. (Item A) **(2)**

> **GUIDANCE** *To answer this question you need to have learned about the concept of the 'underclass'. However, Murray hints at the groups he considers are most at risk of entering that 'class'.* | KNOWLEDGE AND UNDERSTANDING |

b Identify and explain three similarities between women and ethnic minorities in British society. (Items B and C) **(6)**

> **GUIDANCE** *Items B and C suggest that ethnic minorities and women have different experiences in society compared to whites and men. In Item B Indian workers are seen to occupy high-status jobs, but as a consequence of self-employment. In Item C women are shown to have had little clout in the indie music industry. Using this information, and what you have learned in class, you should attempt to cite three clear examples of similarities between ethnic minorities and women, such as discrimination in employment, and then explain them with an example.* | KNOWLEDGE AND UNDERSTANDING | IDENTIFICATION AND INTERPRETATION |

c Using evidence from the Items above and elsewhere, assess the view that social stratification is socially constructed. **(9)**

> **GUIDANCE**   *This question requires all the skill domains, which means that you should approach*
>
> | KNOWLEDGE AND UNDERSTANDING | IDENTIFICATION AND INTERPRETATION | ANALYSIS AND EVALUATION |
> |---|---|---|
>
> *it as if it were a mini essay. Outline the argument in your introductory paragraph (try to use a relevant up-to-date quotation or example). In the main body of the answer, examine the argument for social stratification being a social construct and the arguments against (nurture versus nature). Remember to apply examples from sociological studies/theories on all the areas of stratification, including age/disability. Your conclusion should be based on the strengths and weaknesses of the evidence you have presented, which is very likely to support the idea that social inequality has been devised by society for its own purposes.*

Structured questions

1 To what does the term 'institutional racism' refer? **(2)**

> **GUIDANCE**   *This question is worth only two marks and requires you to reflect your knowledge and understanding of the term 'institutional racism'. Provide two sentences explaining what it is in about 3–4 minutes.*
>
> | KNOWLEDGE AND UNDERSTANDING |
> |---|

2 Identify and explain any one sociological explanation of the inequalities faced by ethnic minorities in the UK. **(5)**

> **GUIDANCE**   *For this question you are expected to recall a sociological theory or approach that has been used to explain the*
>
> | KNOWLEDGE AND UNDERSTANDING | IDENTIFICATION AND INTERPRETATION |
> |---|---|
>
> *disadvantage, such as poor employment prospects, experienced by ethnic minority groups in Britain. The question should take you about 10 minutes and should focus on how the theory you have chosen, such as labelling, is applied to the concept of racial inequality. Remember to develop your answer to cover at least four different elements briefly. It would be acceptable to answer in bullet points to save time.*

3 To what extent do sociologists face problems when trying to research institutional racism? **(8)**

> **GUIDANCE**   *To answer this question you should identify a range of research probelms facing sociological research into institutional*
>
> | KNOWLEDGE AND UNDERSTANDING | IDENTIFICATION AND INTERPRETATION |
> |---|---|
>
> *racism, such a ethnocentricity of the researcher, the hidden nature of institutional racism, problems of operationalisation etc. and weigh up their impact on the data collected. This question should take you about 16 minutes to write and should be in prose rather than bullet points.*

4   Outline and assess the view that the disadvantage faced by women, the poor, the unemployed and some ethnic minority groups is caused by economic inequality rather than by cultural attitudes.   **(10)**

> **GUIDANCE**   *The question requires you to display a wide-ranging and detailed knowledge and*
>
> | KNOWLEDGE AND UNDERSTANDING | IDENTIFICATION AND INTERPRETATION | ANALYSIS AND EVALUATION |
> |---|---|---|
>
> *understanding of the economic explanations of stratification, such as Marsixm, neo-Marxism, Weberianism, neo-Weberianism and Feminism, applying evidence from sociological studies to support your arguments. You also need to balance this by establishing cultural approaches, such as sub-cultural theory and labelling, within the argument as a contrast for th evaluation. Consider using and applying different types of data to support your argument, such as theoretical and empirical. Remember that this answer is worth 10 marks and should therefore be planned and structured like a mini essay to provide a coherent and fluent framework for your balanced argument.*

Essay titles

1   Does the evidence about social mobility indicate that Britain is an 'open' or 'closed' society?   **(25)**

OCR, Paper 1 (1991)

2   Critically assess sociological explanations of racism which seek to show why 'black workers seem to be paid less than white ones simply because they are black' (Item B, lines 13–14).   **(16)**

OCR, Paper 1 (1996)

3   Outline and critically assess the view that class remains the most significant aspect of social inequality.   **(25)**

> **GUIDANCE**   *The first thing you should do is identify the theoretical perspective of the argument. This statement supports the Marxist approach, and therefore this perspective will form the centre of your essay. However, you must also know the alternative arguments, which aver that class is just one aspect of social inequality, for example, feminisms and race relations theory.*
>
> *Start the essay by introducing the concept of social stratification and the place that class has within this. Also identify the other features of social stratification; gender, 'race', age and disability. Use an appropriate quotation and contemporary piece of information on the area to achieve application marks. Also, hint at your conclusion to show that you evaluated the question before you began.*
>
> *The main body of the essay should examine the arguments for and against the question. Support your theoretical knowledge with examples from sociological studies wherever possible. You may want to use evidence from other Areas in this book, such as Work and Leisure, to show that employment disadvantages are based on more than just class associations; colour, sex, age and disability all have an effect on employment prospects. You should be aiming to display not only your knowledge and understanding in this section, but also your application and evaluation skills.*

Evaluation should have been used throughout the essay, however the conclusion is the place to weigh up your argument in relation to the title, considering the evidence you have presented in the main body of the essay. Make reference to the decisions you made about the title at the beginning of the essay, such as whether class is the most important factor in creating social inequality, but provide a little more detail related to a study or argument applied in the main body of the essay. Lastly, if you can apply a relevant piece of information that is up-to-date, such as a quotation or data from research, this will leave the examiner in no doubt of your sociological skills.

OCR, Paper 1 (1997)

Further reading and references

Edgell, S. (1993) *Class*. London, Routledge.
A detailed account of class from a variety of sociological perspectives. A useful text for the sociology student who wants to know more about this highly debated area of sociology.

Modood, T., Berthoud, R., Lakey, J., Nazroo, J., Smith, P., Virdee, S. and Beishon, S. (1997) *Ethnic Minorities in Britain: Diversity and Disadvantage*. London, Policy Studies Institute.
An up-to-date book providing empirical evidence on the position of ethnic minorities in the UK. The research conducted for the Policy Studies Institute has been used to inform political debate on the area of 'race relations'. An interesting and informative read.

Jenks, C. (1996) *Childhood*. London, Routledge.
This is a welcome text because it illuminates the little-written-about area of childhood from a sociological perspective. Not only does it examine the issue of inequality that arises in childhood, but the additional historical account provides the context for sociological discussion of stratification issues.

Barker, D. L. and Allen, S. (Eds.) (1976) *Sexual Divisions and Society: Process and Change*. London, Tavistock.
Although this book is relatively old, it provides an interesting starting point for students interested in gender division. The selection of essays covers a variety of issues relating to the differentiated lives of women in Britain and abroad.

Internet sites

http://longman.awl.com/thio/chaptermenu_10.htm
Sociology online is an excellent website for revising any of the areas of sociology covered in this book. Chapter 10 concentrates on social stratification and class and provides a list of things you should know about the topic and a set of questions and answers to test your understanding of the concepts.

http://www.cso.uiuc.edu/admin_manual/Courses/C_D/latest/soc223.html
This website examines inequalities in power, prestige, income, privilege and lifestyles in the USA and other countries.

http://www.uia.org/uiademo/pro/b5577.htm
A sociological perspective of class, race and gender is presented at this site.

http://risya3.hus.osaka-u.ac.jp/shigeto/ssm/ssmE.html
This displays research for a social stratification and social mobility survey (SSM Survey) based on personal histories. It is concerned with social status and inequality for a national representative sample.

NB: It is useful to know that if you use Lycos as your search engine and type in 'social stratification' it will recover many useful sites for you to browse through.

Bibliography

Abercrombie, N. and Warde, A. (1994) *Contemporary British Society*. Cambridge, Polity Press.

Adonis, A. and Pollard, S. (1998) *A Class Act: The Myth of Britain's Classless Society*. London, Penguin.

Ahrne, G. (1990) 'Class and society: a critique of John Goldthorpe's model of social classes' in J. Clark et al. (Eds.) *John H. Goldthorpe: Consensus or Controversy*. Basingstoke, Falmer Press.

Airies, P. (1962) *Centuries of Childhood*. London, Jonathan Cape.

Angelou, M. (1983) *I Know Why the Caged Bird Sings*, New York, Bantam Books.

Arber, S., Dale, A. and Gilbert, N. (1986) 'The limitations of existing social class classifications and women' in Jacoby, A. (ed.) *The Measurement of Social Class*, Guildford, Social Research Association.

Bagguley, P. (1994) 'Class and class consciousness' in A. Warde and N. Abercrombie (Eds.) *Stratification and Social Inequality*. Lancaster, Framework Press.

Barber, B. (1963) 'Some problems in the sociology of professions' *Daedalus* vol. 92, no. 4.

Barker, D. L. and Allen, S. (Eds.) (1976) *Sexual Divisions and Society: Process and Change*. London, Tavistock.

Barker, M. (1981) *The New Racism*. London, Junction Books.

Beechy, V. (1983) 'The sexual division of labour and the labour process: a critical assessment of Braverman' in Wood, S. (ed.) *The Degradation of Work, Skill, Deskilling and the Labour Process*, London, Hutchinson.

Benet, M. K. (1972) *Secretary: An Enquiry in to the Female Ghetto*, London, Sidgwick and Jackson.

Ben-Tovim, G, and Gabriel, J. (1979) 'The politics of race in Britain: a review of the major trends and of recent literature', *Sage Race Relations Abstracts*, 4, 4: 1–56.

Blumer, H. (1969) *Symbolic Interactionism: Perspective and Method*, Englewood Cliffs, Prentice-Hall.

Bonney, N. (1988) 'Gender, household and social class'. *British Journal of Sociology*, Volume 39, No. 1, March.

Bonney, N. (1992) 'Theories of social class and gender'. *Sociology Review*, February.

Braverman, H. (1974) *Labor and Monopoly Capital*. New York, Monthly Review Press.

Britten, N. and Heath, A. (1983) 'Women, men and social class' in E. Gamarnikow et al. (Eds.) *Gender, Class and Work*. Oxford, Heinemann.

Campbell, B. (1995) 'Granddaddy of the Backlash', *The Guardian*, 1 April.

Caplow, T. (1954) *The Sociology of Work*, New York, McGraw-Hill.

Carrigan, T., Connell, R. and Lee, J. (1985) 'Towards a new sociology of masculinity', *Theory and Society*, Vol. 14.

Cohen, P. (1992) 'It's racism what dunnit: hidden narratives in theories of racism', in Donald, J. and Rattansi, A. (eds.) *'Race', Culture and Difference*, London, Sage.

Cox, O. (1970) *Caste, Class and Race*. New York, Monthly Preview Books.

Crewe, I. (1986) 'On the death and resurrection of class voting: some comments on how Britain votes'. *Political Studies* 34: 620–38.

Crompton, R and Jones, G. (1984) *White Collar Proletariat*, Basingstoke, Macmillan.

Cross, M. (1992) 'Introduction', *New Community*, Vol. 19, No. 1.

Dahrendorf, R. (1959) *Class and Class Conflict in an Industrial Society*. London, Routledge.

Dahrendorf, R. (1987) 'The erosion of citizenship and its consequences for us all'. *New Statesman*, 12 June.

Dahrendorf, R. (1992) *Understanding the Underclass*. London, Policy Studies Institute.

Daniel, W. W. (1968) *Racial Discrimination in England*. Harmondsworth, Penguin.

Davis, A. (1979) *Women, Race and Class*. London Women's Press.

Davis, K. and Moore, W. E. (1945) 'Some principles of stratification analysis' in R. Bendix and S. M. Lipset (Eds.) *Class, Status and Power*. London, Routledge and Kegan Paul.

Davies, L. L. (1995) 'Velocity Girls: Indie, New Lads and Old Values' in S. Cooper (Ed.) *Girls, Girls, Girls*. London, Cassell.

Denscombe, M. (1996) *Sociology Update 1996*, Leicester.

Dworkin, A. (1981) *Pornography*. London, Women's Press.

Edgell, S. (1995) *Class*. London, Routledge.

Ehrenreich, B and Ehrenreich, J. (1979) 'The professional-managerial class' in Walker, P. (ed.) *Between Labour and Capital*, Sussex, Harvester Press.

Eisenstadt, S. N. (1956) *From Generation to Generation*. London, Macmillan.

Elliott, J. E. (1991) 'Demographic trends in domestic life, 1945–87' in Clark, D. (ed.) *Marriage, Domestic Life and Social Change*, London, Routledge.

Employment Gazette, April 1988, 214.

Erikson, R., Goldthorpe, J. H. and Portocareoro, L. (1983) 'International social mobility and the convergence thesis', *British Journal of Sociology*, 34: 313–43.

Eysenck, H. J. (1970) *Crime and Personality*, London, Paladin.

Family Expenditure Survey (1994), Central Statistics Office, HMSO, London.

Field, F. (1989) *Losing Out: The Emergence of Britain's Underclass*. Oxford, Blackwell.

Firestone, S. (1979) *The Dialectics of Sex*. The Women's Press Ltd.

Friedan, B. (1963) *The Feminine Mystique*. London Gollancz.

Friedan, B. (1983) *The Second Stage*, London, Abacus.

Gerth, H. H. and Mills, C. W. (Eds.)(1961) From Max Weber, *Essays in Sociology*. London, Routledge and Kegan Paul.

Giddens, A. (1973) *The Class Structure in Advanced Societies*. London, Hutchinson.

Giddens, A. (1984) *The Constitution Society: An Outline of the Theory of Structuration*. Cambridge, Polity Press.

Giddens, A. (1976) *The New Rules of Sociological Method*, London, Hutchinson.

Gilmore, D. D. (1990) *Manhood in the Making: Cultural Concepts of Masculinity*. New Haven, Yale University Press.

Gilroy, P. (1987) *There ain't no black in the Union Jack: The cultural politics of Race and Nation*. London, Hutchinson.

Gilroy, P. (1993) *The Black Atlantic: Modernity and Double Consciousness*. London, Verso.

Glass, D. V. (1954) *Social Mobility in Britain*. London, Routledge and Kegan Paul.

Goldthorpe, J. H. (1982) 'On the service class: its formation and future' in A. Giddens and G. Mackenzie (Eds.) *Social Class and the Division of Labour*. Cambridge, Cambridge University Press.

Goldthorpe, J. H. (1987/8) *Social Mobility and the Class Structure in Modern Britain*. Oxford, Clarendon Press.

Goldthorpe, J. H., Lockwood, D., Bechhofer, F. and Platt, J. (1968) *The Affluent Worker*. Cambridge, Cambridge University Press.

Goldthorpe, J. H. (1984) 'Women and class analysis: a reply to replies', *Sociology*, 17: 465–88.

Goldthorpe, J. H., Llewellyn, C. and Payne, C. (1980) *Social Mobility and Class Structure*, Oxford, Oxford University Press.

Gouldner, A. (1979) *The Future of Intellectuals and the Rise of the New Class*. Basingstoke, Macmillan.

Gramsci, A. (1971) *Selections from Prison Notebooks*, London, Lawrence and Wishart.

Greer, G. (1971) *The Female Eunuch*. St. Albans, Paladin.

Hall, S. (1980) 'Race, articulation and societies structured in dominance', in *Sociological Theories: Race and Colonialism*, Paris, UNESCO.

Haralmabos, M. (ed.) (1990) *Developments in Sociology*, Vol. 6, Ormskirk, Causeway Press.

Harris, A. and Clausen, R. (1966) *Labour Mobility in Great Britain 1953–63*, London, HMSO Report 5333.

Heath, A. (1981) *Social Mobility*. Glasgow, Fontana.

Herrnstein, R. and Murray, C. (1994) *The Bell Curve: Intelligence and Class Structure in American Life*. New York, Free Press.

Hill, D. (1997) *The Future of Men*. London, Phoenix.

Hills, J. (1995) *Inquiry into Income and Wealth*, York, Joseph Rowntree Foundation.

Hutton, W. (1995) *The State We're In*. London, Jonathan Cape.

Jenks, C. (1996) *Childhood*. London, Routledge.

Johnson, P. and Webb, S. (1997) *Counting People with Low Incomes*, London, Institute of Fiscal Studies.

Jones, S. (1991) 'We are all cousins under the skin'. *The Independent*, 12 December.

Jordan, B. (1973) *Pauper*. London, Routledge.

Kessler, S. J. and McKenna, W. (1978) *Gender: An Ethnomethodological Approach*, New York, John Wiley and Sons.

Kirby, M. (1999) *Stratification and Differentiation*. Basingstoke, Macmillan.

Kohn, M. (1995) *The Race Gallery*. London, Jonathan Cape.

Labour Force Survey (1994), Central Office of Statistics, London, HMSO.

Labour Research (February 1997) Inland Revenue.

Lees, S. (1993) *Sugar and Spice*, Harmondsworth, Penguin.

Lewis, O. (1968) *La Vida*. Harmondsworth, Penguin.

Lockwood, D. (1986) 'Class, Status and Gender', in Crompton, R. and Mann, M. (eds.) *Gender and Stratification*, Oxford, Polity.

Marshall, G., Newby, H., Rose, D. and Vogler, C. (1988) *Social Class in Modern Britain*. London, Hutchinson.

Marsland, D. (1989) 'Universal welfare provision creates a dependent population, the case for', *Social Studies Review*, November 1989.

Marx, K. and Engels, F. (1998, first published 1888) *The Communist Manifesto*. London, Verso.

McRobbie, A. (1991) *Feminism and Youth Culture*. Basingstoke, Macmillan.

Mead, M. (1935) *Sex and Temperament in Three Primitive Societies*. New York, Morrow.

Miles, R. (1982) *Racism and Migrant Labour*. London, Routledge.

Miles, R. (1988) 'Racism, Marxism and British Politics', *Economy and Society*, Vol. 17, No. 3.

Miles, R. (1993) *Racism After 'Race Relations'*. London, Routledge.

Miliband, R. (1973) *The State of Capitalist Society*. London, Quartet.

Millerson, G. (1964) *The Qualifying Associations*, New York, Free Press.

Millet, K. (1970) *Sexual Politics*. New York Doubleday.

Mills, C. W. (1956) *White Collar*. Oxford, Oxford University Press.

Mills, C. W. (1956) *The Power Elite*, Oxford, Oxford University Press.

Modood, T. (1992) *Not Easy Being British*, Stoke on Tent, Trentham Books.

Modood, T. (1994) 'Political blackness and British Asians', Sociology, Vol. 28, No. 4.

Modood, T., Berthoud, R., Lakey, J., Nazroo, J., Smith, P., Virdee, S. and Beishon, S. (1997) *Ethnic Minorities in Britain: Diversity and Disadvantage*. London, Policy Studies Institute.

Murdock, G. (1949) *Social Structure*. Basingstoke, Macmillan.

Murray, C. (1984) *Losing Ground*. New York, Basic Books.

Murray, C. (1990) *The Emerging British Underclass*, London, Institute of Economic Affairs

Murray, C. (1994/6) *Underclass: The Crisis Deepens*. London, Institute of Economic Affairs.

New Earnings Survey (1995), London, HMSO.

Oakley, A. (1972) *Sex, Gender and Society*. London, Temple Smith.

Oakley, A. (1974), *Housewife*, London, Allen Lane.

Ossowski, S. (1969) *Class structure in the Social Consciousness*, London, Routledge and Kegan Paul.

Park, R. (1950) *Race and Culture*, New York, Free Press.

Parkin, F. (1979) *Marxism and Class Theory: A Bourgeois Critique*, London, Tavistock.

Parry, N. and Parry, J. (1976) *The Rise of the Medical Profession*, London, Croom Helm.

Parsons, T. (1951) *The Social System*. New York, Free Press.

Parsons, T. (1959) 'The social structure and the family' in Anshen, R. (ed.) *The Family: Its Function and Destiny*, London, Harper and Row.

Pascall, G. (1995) *Social Policy: A Feminist Analysis*, London, Verso.

Patterson, S. (1963) *Dark Strangers*, Harmondsworth, Penguin.

Penn, R. (1983) 'Skilled manual workers in the labour process' in S. Wood (Ed.) *Skilled Workers in the Class Structure*. Cambridge, Cambridge University Press.

Phillipson, C. and A. Walker (1986) *Ageing and Social Policy: A Critical Assessment*. Aldershot, Gower.

Pilcher, J. (1995) 'Growing up and growing older: the sociology of age'. *Sociology Review*.

Pilkington, A. (1992) 'Is there a British underclass?' *Sociology Review*, February.

Rex, J. and Moore, R. (1967) *Race, Community and Conflict: A Study of Sparbrook*. London, Institute of Race Relations.

Rex, J. and Moore, R. (1967) *Race, Community and Conflict*, Oxford, Oxford University Press.

Rex, J. (1970) *Race Relations in Sociological Theory*, London, Weidenfeld and Nicholson.

Rex, J. and Tomlinson, S. (1979) *Colonial Immigrants in a British City: A Class Analysis*. London, Routledge and Kegan Paul.

Rex, J. (1976) *Race and Ethnicity*, Buckingham, Open University Press.

Rex, J. (1988) 'The role of class analysis in the study of race relations: a Weberian Perspective' in Rex, J. and Mason, D. (eds.) *Theories of Race and Ethnic Relations*, Cambridge, Cambridge University Press.

Riley, M. W. (1988) 'On the Significance of Age in Society', in M. W. Riley, B. J. Huber and B. B. Hess (Eds.) *Social Structures and Human Life*. London, Sage.

Roberts, K. et al (1977) *The Fragmentary Class Structure*. Oxford, Heinemann.

Rowntree Foundation (1995) *Inquiry into Income and Wealth*. Joseph Rowntree Foundation.

Runciman, W. G. (1990) 'How many classes are there in contemporary British society?' *Sociology*, Volume 4, No. 3.

Saunders, P. (1990) *Social Class and Stratification*. London, Routledge.

Saunders, P. (1995) *Capitalism: A Social Audit*. Buckingham, Open University Press.

Saunders, P. (1996) 'A British bell curve? Class, intelligence and meritocracy in modern Britain', *Sociology Review*, Vol. 6, No. 2.

Savage, M., Barlow, J., Dickens, P. and Fielding, T. (1992) *Property, Bureaucracy and Culture*. London, Routledge.

Scott, J. (1982) *The Upper Classes*. London, Macmillan.

Scott, J. (1986) 'Does Britain Still Have a Ruling Class?' *Social Studies Review*, Volume 2, No. 1.

Shakespeare, T. (1996) *The Sexual Politics of Disability*, London, Cassell.

Skeggs, B. (1991) 'Postmodernism: what is all the fuss about?' *British Journal of Sociology of Education*, Vol. 12, No. 2.

Skellington, R. (1996) *'Race' in Britain Today*. London, Sage.

Solomos, J. (1988) 'Varieties of Marxist conceptions of 'race', class and the state: a critical analysis', in Rex, J. and Mason, D. (eds.) *Theories of Race and Ethnic Relations*, Cambridge, Cambridge University Press.

Solomos, J. (1993) *Race and Racism in Contemporary Britain*. Basingstoke, Macmillan.

Smith, A. D. (1986) *The Ethnic Origin of Nations*. Oxford, Blackwell.

Spender, D. (1982) *Invisible Women: The Schooling Scandal*. Writers and Readers Co-Operative.

Tumin, M. M. (1967) 'Some principles of stratification: a critical analysis' in R. Bendix and S. M. Lipset (Eds.) *Class, Status and Power*. London, Routledge and Kegan Paul.

Turnbull, C. (1961) *The Forest People*, London, Jonathan Cape.

Van den Berghe, P. (1988) 'Ethnicity and the sociobiology debate' in J. Rex and D. Mason (Eds.) *Theories of Race and Ethnic Relations*. Cambridge, Cambridge University Press.

Vincent, J. (1995) *Inequality and Old Age*. London, UCL Press.

Walby, S. (1990) *Theorising Patriarchy*. Oxford, Blackwell.

Watkins, S. A., Rueda, M. and Rodriguez, M. (1992) *Feminism for Beginners*. Cambridge, Icon Books.

Weber, M. in S. Andreski (Ed.) (1983) *Max Weber on Capitalism, Bureaucracy and Religion: A Selection of Texts*. London, Allen and Unwin.

Westergaard, J. (1995) *Who Gets What? The Hardening of Class Inequality in the Late Twentieth Century*, Cambridge, Polity Press.

Westergaard, J. and Resler, H. (1976) *Class in a Capitalist Society: A Study of Contemporary Britain*. Harmondsworth, Penguin.

Wilson, E. (1975) *Sociobiology: The New Synthesis*. Cambridge, Mass. Harvard University Press.

Wolf, N. (1990) *The Beauty Myth*, London, Vintage.

Wolfe, T. (1983) *The Right Stuff*, New York, Bantam Books.

Wright, E. O. (1976) 'Class boundaries in advanced capitalist societies'. *New Left Review*, No. 98.

Wright, E. O. (1985) *Classes*. London, Verso.

Wright, E. O. (1997) *Class Counts*. Cambridge, Cambridge University Press.

Society and Cultural Identities

This area covers:

- The sociological literature on culture, self, human agency and identity
- The relationship between identity, society and culture
- A consideration of the sociological debates about the nature of culture and social relationships
- Ideas about how culture can define how we behave as individuals and how we see others.

By the end of this area you should be able to:

- have an understanding of culture, self, human agency and identity
- identify what sociologists have said about self and its relationship to the culture that we live in
- identify and evalute theories relating to the differing forms of culture identified by writers working in this field.

Key terms

self identity	mores
socialisation	structuration
norms	human agent
culture – high/low/folk/mass/popular	ideology
values	globalisation

Area 4   Contents

Introduction

Identity is a highly personal thing; it is what we use to define who we are as individuals. However, at the same time identity is cultural in nature because our culture defines us as individuals and affects how we see ourselves. This area will look at culture and its relationship with social identity, and consider how we can be either the products or the creators of our cultures. Culture is a wider term than society, because it describes social relationships and also considers the ideas that we have about our society.

There is a significant debate in this area as many sociologists argue that our ideas about ourselves, our sense of self, are created by the culture that we live in. For example, we know who we are because we are made by factors outside individual control such as economic factors, our beliefs or our language. In contrast, other sociologists argue that the self is an 'agent', it has control over its own destiny and it creates the culture of the society and all the structures within the society.

There are also important debates for sociologists about the nature of culture. It is not easy to define in any practical sense, though we all belong to it and understand it because it forms part of the rules by which we live. Many writers consider that our cultures are created as we go along, the rules are made and changed so that our culture is fluid and to a certain extent personal. The culture in which your parents grew up is similar to the one in which you have grown up, but as your parents' generation will tell you, there are also significant differences in what was expected of them and what is expected of you in the practice of your daily lives. Other writers, particularly those who have been influenced by Marxism, see culture as a conspiracy, created for us in order to control and manipulate our ideas and behaviour. We are the products of mind control exercised by powerful agencies and individuals.

This area is concerned with some of the fundamental philosophical and sociological questions which have occupied generations of writers.

- What is a person?
- How is society possible?

- What are the bonds that link people in terms of shared values, attitudes and beliefs? What is the nature of culture?

HINTS AND TIPS   *This area of the syllabus is ideal for drawing upon your own personal experience, and thereby scoring marks for interpretation and application. Make use of yourself and others, as a resource! After all, you are a* **person**; *you are a human agent. Who are you? How do you define yourself? Ask people that you know the same questions. You may find that you define yourself in terms of the role that you play: I am a student, a daughter or son, etc. Are you anything other than the roles that you play? Draw up a list of what you think are the characteristics of a person and give some justification for the points you make. This will allow you to draw upon your personal experience to evaluate the sociological theories of self and identity in this chapter.*

Alternatively, you may wish to organise a discussion in which you ask people the question 'What does it mean to be a person?' Make notes on the main points raised by individuals. Whatever you decide a person is, that person will exist within a culture.

Creating cultures and social identities

From the moment of birth to the instant of death, other people define us and tell us who we are (social identity) and how to think and behave (culture). A new-born child has a number of social identities before it is ever conscious of individual thought:

- it has a gender
- it is a baby (age)
- it has an ethnicity, a family identity and a social class which it derives from its parents
- if it is sick, then it is a patient

As the child grows, it is constantly being told how to behave, what to believe and who it is. In this sense, there is real strength to the argument that we have little individuality, that we are the creation of other people. However, this sort of belief is deterministic, it denies us the right to make choices or to freedom of action.

Obviously we are more than the products of society because we are not all the same. People are reflective or reflexive, which means that they can think about their lives; this leads to series of questions which revolve around the point that although we are ruled by other people, we also have a sense of who and what we are. We can think and we can influence others in our turn. Together, we create a culture or even a variety of cultures and it is the process of creating and maintaining a culture which is discussed in this area.

IDENTIFICATION AND INTERPRETATION

1 Write down 10 words which you think apply to you.
2 Write down 10 words which describe your neighbour.
3 How many of these words are social definitions which describe relationships or are social labels such as: 'student', 'Asian', 'old', 'mother', 'child'?
4 What does this tell you about the way that your sense of who you are comes from other people and from society?

Socialisation

Culture is transmitted to the individual through a life-long process called **socialisation**. Socialisation is the process of learning to behave in a way that is appropriate for your society. It is an idea that derives from a form of thought known as functionalism, but most sociologists agree that this is a correct description of what takes place in society. We all need to learn a series of rules about our cultures. These are unwritten codes and although we live by them, we are not always aware of their effect upon us until we break one. Through socialisation people learn the appropriate ways of behaving and the various forms of these are described below. These are key terms for sociology and should appear in all your writing and thinking about the subject.

Norms – These are rules which direct our actions. It is easier to understand them as a series of unwritten but completely understood laws about what we consider as normal behaviour for any given situation. It is normal to sit at a desk. Sitting at a desk is a norm for a school or college.

Values – These are general ideas of what is important. These may feel personal such as a set of religious ideas, but they can be social and cultural in that they are shared by others. A person may consider that all life is sacred; this is a value.

Mores – These are a sense of what is right and wrong. They are similar to values but differ in that they refer to actual behaviour. A value tells people that life is sacred, a more is that it is wrong to eat dead animals, and so they become vegetarian.

Norms, values and mores derive from culture and are part of daily life from birth. They may originate in religious belief or in family ideas about how to conduct yourself. Norms, mores and values tend to be at their strongest in the most intimate areas of people's lives such as the eating of certain foods, property rules, sexual behaviours, toilet behaviours and in family relationships. They are so much part of thinking that people probably obey them even if on their own.

HINTS AND TIPS   To understand the significance of norms, mores and values try asking people you know questions of morality such as:

■ Could they have sex with strangers for money even if no one knew it had happened?
■ Could they steal property from a friend even if they would not get caught?
■ Could they kill someone if they thought they would get away with it?

While some people undoubtedly could do these things, or say they could, there are many who would not and who may even be shocked at the suggestion that they could.

An important notion to note here is that cultures vary. This idea is known as cultural relativity and it suggests that everything that our society considers morally correct, valuable and good, another culture would consider bizarre, unpleasant and morally obscene. Inuit society sanctions the killing of girl babies, the expulsion of the old from the tribe to certain death and the offering of females to visiting males for sex as a friendly social gesture. These are Inuit norms, in that no one in the culture would consider these actions exceptional. Whilst our culture would be deeply offended by these actions, from the point of view of the values and the mores of the Inuit, they ensure the control of population, the survival of the culture and the spreading of genetic material in a harsh and difficult landscape.

> **HINTS AND TIPS**   *It is easy to pick out examples of cultural relativity from anthropology texts and you are advised to look up some examples of cultural beliefs which are significantly different from our own.*
>
> *You may find it useful to learn something of the significance of Margaret Mead's famous 1935 study* **Sex and Temperament in Three Primitive Societies**. *Her study was of three societies in New Guinea: the Arapesh, Mundugumor and Tchambuli. She wanted to find out if the view of male and female temperament in western society was 'universal'. This is very readable although available only on library loan currently. It is also well discussed in textbooks.*

ACTIVITY   **KS COMMUNICATION**

IDENTIFICATION AND INTERPRETATION

Within western society, there are examples of cultural variations between nations. Using general knowledge and ideas taken from films and television, list a series of differences between American culture and British culture. Here is a rough guide for ideas: language, law, food, sport, education.

Processes of socialisation

The concept of socialisation assumes that although people may have biological drives, they do not have animal instincts. If people had fixed patterns of biologically determined behaviour this would prevent different processes of socialisation taking place.

Socialisation can be deliberate, or formal, for example we are given instruction by parents or teachers in the skills we need, such as reading or cooking.

Socialisation can also be unintentional, or informal. Events or situations have a significant effect upon us which was never planned.

In our society, a number of agencies of socialisation can be identified, including:

- family
- peer group

Figure 4.1   Elements of culture

- school
- mass media
- work
- religious groups and clubs

Three forms of socialisation into culture are identified by sociologists:

1   **Primary socialisation** is the socialisation of young children in the family. In addition to learning essential skills such as language, children learn rules in relation to how to dress, customs and traditions which are appropriate to their role. Socialisation is informal at this stage, and based on personal relationships.

2   **Secondary socialisation** starts when a child starts school. During this phase children are judged according to universal criteria, such as exam success. Children also have formal socialisation in the teaching of skills that they will need to fulfil their adult roles, for example in the labour market.

3 **Adult socialisation** is concerned with life-long processes of learning and development. In addition, people who enter total institutions, such as prisons, boarding schools or some other closed community, have to go through a process of re-socialisation into the norms and values of the institution.

Although socialisation is thought to produce a degree of conformity, it should be noted that the child is active in the socialisation process, in other words the child has agency – the ability to think of itself as a separate person and to act on that assumption.

Contemporary societies are culturally diverse and may contain a number of subcultures. A subculture is a group in society which has values, norms and mores which are different from those of mainstream culture. There is some considerable debate in sociology as to whether subcultures with values different from mainstream culture actually exist. This takes place within the functionalist tradition. Even if they do not exist, the concept is a useful one. It can be used to describe the way that some social groups are expected to have norms, values and mores which are different from those of other social groups in the same society. This is a topic which will be revisited in this area.

HINTS AND TIPS   Use your 'elements of culture' diagram (Figure 4.1) to consider whether men and women in our society belong to different cultures and do in fact form subcultures. There are certainly considerable differences in the way that they are expected to behave.

Note that although the processes of socialisation are the same for men and women, the intended outcomes of socialisation are quite different so that men and women have grown experiencing quite different norms, morals and values. Gender roles vary considerably in different societies and Ann Oakley in a range of books over many years has demonstrated that gender roles in our society are acquired via the process of socialisation rather than biologically determined. Oakley (1981) argues that gender socialisation has four central elements:

1 **Manipulation** – Parents encourage or discourage ways of behaving in their children on the basis of what they consider to be normal or abnormal behaviour for a male or female child.

2 **Canalisation** – Parents direct their children's interests towards appropriate games and toys for

their gender. Drawing upon his own experience, Stephen Pfohl (1992) talks about how he asked his parents if he could have a baby brother or sister. When they refused, he asked if he could have a doll instead. Reluctantly, his parents agreed. While in his bedroom with the window open, Stephen heard his parents discussing the doll and their concerns about it. On hearing this, Stephen went downstairs and asked his parents to take the doll back to the shop and exchange it for a gun. His parents were pleased.

3 **Verbal appellations** – The use of language to label children in a way that reinforces appropriate gender identification. Think of the pet names applied to children according to gender.

4 **Different activities** – Girls are encouraged to participate in indoor activities which are often 'domestic' in nature. Boys are encouraged to participate in more outdoor activities.

In summary, it is through this gendered socialisation process that we develop our personality, our sense of self and our identity as female or male. Diverse cultures have diverse forms of socialising the people that live with those cultures so that gender roles also vary considerably in different societies.

ACTIVITY   KS **COMMUNICATION, PROBLEM SOLVING**

KNOWLEDGE AND UNDERSTANDING	IDENTIFICATION AND INTERPRETATION

Read the passage and answer the questions below.

❛ *Indian emperor, Akbar (who ruled from 1542 to 1602), ordered a group of children be brought up without any instruction in language, to test the belief that they would eventually speak Hebrew, the language of God. The children were raised by deaf mutes. They developed no spoken language and communicated solely by gestures.*

McLeish (1993: 694)

a What do you understand by the term 'socialisation'?

b Why did the children fail to develop spoken language?

c How is culture transmitted from one generation to the next?

Boy's life as a dog

A BOY of four who had only dogs for company has shocked welfare workers.

Berci Kutrovics moved on all fours and growled rather than talked.

He also sniffed and lapped up his food and slept curled up in corners – but unlike Mowgli, the boy in Rudyard Kipling's *Jungle Book* who was brought up by animals, little Berci was not an orphan.

His mother has shamed the village of Szil in Hungary for her neglect and now the 'dog-boy' has been taken into care.

Villager Csilla Horvath said: 'The whole episode has brought shame on us and no one has said a word to the mother since.'

Berci's father had disappeared and the mother left him alone with the family's mongrel dog and bitch which were kept in an outside shed.

District nurse Maria Kokedi said she had suspicions about the boy when she tried to visit him two years ago.

'The mother refused to let me see him,' she said. 'She was afraid she would lose her child benefit allowance if we took him away, and as we don't have the necessary legislation, we had no powers to enforce a decision to take the boy into care.'

Mihaly Szechenyi, director of Gyor County children's home, said he had never seen a case like it.

'When Berci first came he couldn't stand up,' he said. 'He lapped his food directly from the plate and when we put him in a bed he got out and curled up in the corner of the room.'

Berci's mother told the authorities she believed her son was retarded, but Mr Szechenyi said that after the boy had been taken into custody, he was found to be properly developed mentally, although damaged psychologically.

However, Mr Szechenyi said Berci has made satisfying progress in the three weeks he has been in the home.

He went on: 'He can use a spoon now and he's already walking. He says "One, two – one, two" as he makes his tentative steps. He's captivated by the other children and is learning incredibly fast.

'No one can believe how bright a child brought up by dogs can be. He's almost become a normal child already.'

Since Mr Szechenyi made an appeal for foster parents a week ago the home has been inundated with applications. However he is in no hurry to make a decision.

He said: 'Berci has been so deprived of parental love we want to make sure his new parents make up for it.'

Legends abound of wolfboys such as the twins Romulus and Remus – who were brought up outside Rome by a wolf – but they have had modern counterparts.

Last July, Romania reported that an abandoned boy in an orphanage was suckled by a dog.

The child yelped instead of talked, and shared his food with the bitch which raised him. In the 1940s, an American girl called Isabelle, found at the age of six after being shut away in a darkened room with her deaf mute mother, not only subsequently learnt to speak but caught up to a normal educational level.

Czechoslovakian twin boys who had suffered extreme neglect within their family made excellent progress after being found in 1967, including successful relationships in a new foster family. However, they hated any reminder of their early deprivation.

Duncan Shiels *Daily Mail* 17 December 1994

1   How did the dog boy behave?   **(1)**

2   How did the boy's behaviour differ from that of a normal four-year-old child?   **(1)**

3   Could such a case occur in Britain? Consider arguments both for and against the suggestion that it could.   **(3)**

4   How did the child's community react when it heard of the case?   **(3)**

5   What skills do the authorities think that the boy will need to acquire to be a normal child?   **(5)**

6   What are the chances of the child learning to behave in a normal way for a child of his age? Use information from the article to support your point of view.   **(8)**

7   What does the case of the dog boy have to tell sociologists about the significance of socialisation in the development of a personality?   **(9)**

Forms of culture

Culture is created by people; it is a key element in our social heritage. Culture provides us with our guiding values, norms and ideals, and it provides the context for our 'taken-for-granted' world. Culture provides a foundation for our thoughts and actions, and guides our responses to the actions of others. As Clyde Kluckholm (1951:86) argued, culture is the 'distinctive way of life of a group of people, their complete design for living'.

Kluckholm argued that we human beings share the same biology and have the same psychic nature. However, how we respond to a range of tastes, smells and sights will be culturally determined. The study of culture directs us to look at social aspects of behaviour rather than biological influences.

For many social scientists 'culture' and 'social organisation' are one and the same. Until now, this area has used the notion of culture in its very broadest sense as being a discussion about the ways of living within a

society, shared meanings, shared consciousness and taste. However, there are common-sense meanings used in the term culture in that it often refers to the creative and artistic productions of a society. Be cautious, because within the debates the two notions are often blurred and it can be difficult to know which meaning is being used. Some of the debate that follows uses an artistic sense of culture in addition to a wider sense of culture.

> **HINTS AND TIPS**   *The mass media are an enormously important agency of socialisation and are significant in giving us ideas about our culture. You should be certain that you refer to Area 5 on Mass Media and Popular Culture with relation to most of the debates within this area, even if it does not form one of your specialist areas.*

To illustrate the point, Herbert Gans (1974) gave a useful insight into the sociology of culture when he stated that all humans have aesthetic urges, and a need to spend time away from their work routine. Culture develops to satisfy the needs of the people. From this he develops the notion of 'taste publics', which includes a range of divisions within a culture. For Gans there is a continuum of cultures and tastes in a society, which he terms: high, upper middle, lower middle, low and 'quasi-folk low'. Basically, this means that different people within a society have different tastes and that some forms of cultural production are more valued than others.

ACTIVITY   **KS WORKING WITH PEOPLE**

| IDENTIFICATION AND INTERPRETATION | ANALYSIS AND EVALUATION |

Offer people a variety of artistic and cultural forms such as football, classical music, hip-hop, television, comics, clubs, opera, film, modern art and erotic dancing.

Ask them to list those which they consider to be most important to society. You could vary the question and ask which should receive government subsidy or lottery funding.

1   Are all cultural forms equally valuable?
2   Are there social patterns in what people consider to be valuable?
3   Are the cultural forms associated with rich and educated people seen as more valuable than the cultural forms associated with poorer people and children?

'High' and 'low' culture

Throughout many public debates on culture, the artistic notion of culture is significant and there is a common assumption that the cultural tastes and productions of wealthy and educated people (**high culture**) have more value than the culture which is enjoyed by common people (**low culture**). This belief is reflected in Arts Council funding and lottery funding where opera is subsidised and bingo is not. However, if the common people have created the culture themselves and it represents a historical tradition, then it is no longer low culture but art (**folk culture**). You should however note that the culture of ordinary people is often more commercially profitable and therefore mass-produced for wide audiences (**popular culture**) because the market for the productions is generally larger. Because the products of high culture and folk culture require education to be appreciated and because they are challenging intellectually, they are frequently unpopular. In order to be commercially successful to a wide audience, anything which is too complex must be removed. This process of removing the difficulty and individuality from a cultural product in order to make it commercially popular is known as 'dumbing down'.

High culture	Low culture
ballet, classical music, theatre, jazz broadsheet newspapers	disco, musicals, soap opera, quiz shows, pop and rock music tabloid press, sport, bingo, sporting shows
for the educated and 'cognoscenti' hard to understand not always in English	very accessible to anyone instantly has youth orientation often with an American flavour
often produced in past can be popular culture of past	usually modern and instant ephemeral (short-lived)
often complex characters and emotions romanticises poverty women are often portrayed as victims	shallow analysis stereotypical celebrates sex or is overtly sexual
often expensive to produce or enjoy	often cheap to produce and highly profitable to producer
only affects a few people but these are opinion-makers usually middle/upper class more valued as 'art'	designed for maximum exposure to broad mass of working classes devalued as 'entertainment'
tends to be 'dead white European male' culture has high status is associated with European production companies	draws on cross-culture (esp. American black) tends to be male-orientated in production often reflects culture of greed and materialism may swamp indigenous cultures with mass produced American cultural artefacts

Figure 4.2   A working guide to differences between high and low culture

Dominic Strinati (1995) raises the following questions about popular culture:

- Where does popular culture come from? Is it created for people by sellers of media products or does it actually get popular because it emerges from the people themselves?

- Does popularity inevitably mean that the products are intrinsically less valuable or of lower quality? Is it possible that the money-making possibilities of anything popular mean that the originality and the ideas that made it popular in the first place have to be removed to make it even more popular?

- Is popular culture ideological? Does popular culture mean that people stop thinking about issues of real importance because they are so concerned and mind-controlled by popular culture that they are no longer able to think for themselves?

Popular culture

Popular culture is commercially produced and was seen by sociologists, particularly critical sociologists such as Marxists and feminists, as a site for the transmission of ideology and patriarchy. The value of looking at cultural products such as advertisements, film and television was that they were meant to represent power relationships within social systems.

ACTIVITY KS COMMUNICATION

ANALYSIS AND EVALUATION

Watch some American wrestling on television. Look at it in an analytical way to see what norms, values and mores are represented.
1 What images of masculinity and femininity are on offer?
2 Can you offer reasons why it is so popular with so many people?
3 Can you suggest reasons why some people would find the sport objectionable in terms of the values that it represents?

However, since the 1970s popular culture has become a site for negotiation in that people have criticised the representations of themselves which are available to

them through the media. A politics of diversity, which takes its starting point from Foucault and Deleuze has been taken up by a range of new social movements. Since the urban riots in 1981 there has been a shift towards anti-racism and a deconstruction of negative imagery so that people can explore their minority identities. The examples of the Pet Shop Boys and Elton John show that it is now possible to see positive imagery of homosexuality. It is arguable that the Spice Girls represented a new and aggressive feminine culture where sexual imagery is designed as a challenge to masculinity.

Feminists also realised that popular culture, such as soap opera, was enjoyed by thousands of women and that to dismiss this as just rubbish in favour of class-based ideas that certain forms of high culture are 'more valuable' is to reject the women who actually enjoyed popular culture. Indeed, it became apparent that soap opera provided many examples of strong and dominant female characters partly because the market for this drama is female. The opening up of television and other mediums in the 1990s because of the development of cable and satellite has made popular culture more varied in nature so that people are more aware of different forms of culture.

ACTIVITY KS WORKING WITH PEOPLE, COMMUNICATION

| IDENTIFICATION AND INTERPRETATION | ANALYSIS AND EVALUATION |

Watch *EastEnders* or *Coronation Street*. What images of women and the lives of women are on offer to the audiences? How does this differ from the imagery and the behaviour of women as shown on popular game shows or in tabloid newspapers such as the *The Sun*?

Folk culture

Folk culture is commonly used to refer to the traditional culture of local communities. This form of self-regenerating culture is passed on from one generation to the next by rituals, folk wisdom and folklore. For instance, superstitions, musical forms and singing will be passed on by the old people to children. Some of these cultural forms are limited geographically.

Others, however, are very widely popular with people who do not come from the original cultural tradition; consider the recent commercial adaptations of Irish folk music and dance. Here folk culture has become commercialised pop culture. Black American music has been developed into modern rock and pop in a similar process. Folk culture, however, is seen as a cultural form which responds to local needs in a traditional way. It was extremely popular with the Nazis who usurped the term 'folk' to argue that traditional German forms of culture were superior to other forms and who wished for a return to the traditional values of the past. They rejected forms of culture which were not Germanic in form, especially Black American music such as jazz, which they considered to be degenerate. Folk cultural forms are the subject of considerable interest and debate to sociologists, particularly Anthony Giddens, who argues that older, traditional forms of wisdom and cultural knowledge are under threat from processes of globalisation.

> **HINTS AND TIPS**   *What do people understand by the term 'folk' in folk music, folk literature and folk art? You might even enjoy an evening at a local folk music club. Find out from the local library where the club meets.*

> **HINTS AND TIPS**   *You may wish to look at what Anthony Giddens has had to say about the issue of culture and globalisation by looking at <http://www.lse.ac.uk/Giddens>*

Global culture

Global culture refers to the increasingly popular idea that as communication between countries and population movements increase, local cultures are being overtaken by a single world culture, which is dominated by the values of American commercialism.

Does **globalisation** mean that a local or folk culture is disappearing? Mike Featherstone (1990) argued that there is no one country which is imposing its culture on the rest of the world. However, there are cultural processes, such as those associated with the products of multi-national companies, which cross national boundaries and in many respects people have to fit into a range of cultures as 'cosmopolitans'. This view builds on the notion of a 'global village' or the 'small world' theory.

Globalisation is the idea that the whole world is becoming a single place; as a process globalisation directly affects the lives of all the people in the world. Drugs, sex tourism, the nature of the work we do, eating disorders, plastic surgery and more, all have a global dimension to them.

> **ACTIVITY**   **KS PROBLEM SOLVING**
>
> | IDENTIFICATION AND INTERPRETATION | ANALYSIS AND EVALUATION |
> | --- | --- |
>
> Look at the products which you have used today, the food that you have eaten and the clothes that you are wearing. Where were they made? Did the styles originate in your own country and reflect your own personal culture or are they the kinds of products that young people in all countries wear?
>
> As suggestions, consider lager, hamburger, pizza, and trainers and then develop the list. Now consider if American culture is dominating your own culture or if you are engaged in a form of cultural 'pick and mix'. It is this question that forms the basis of the debate.

These processes of globalisation have a significant effect upon the self and upon our sense of identity in that they generate feelings of uncertainty. We no longer know exactly who we are in terms of our culture and we experience a loss of identity as a result. As Roland Robertson stated:

> *The fact and the perception of ever increasing interdependence at the global level, the rising concern about the fate of the world as a whole and of the human species (particularly because of the threats of ecological degradation, nuclear disaster and AIDS), and the colonisation of the local by global life (not least via the mass media) facilitate massive processes of relativization of cultures, doctrines, ideologies and cognitive frames of reference.*
>
> Robertson (1992:87)

What does Robertson mean by this?

- There is increasing interdependence between people in the world, which is truly global in nature.

- In addition, part of this interdependence is a global concern about the future of the human species itself;

because of ecological degradation, nuclear disaster and AIDS, human beings may become extinct.

■ The 'colonisation of the local by global life (not least via the mass media)' means that local cultures are been destroyed by global cultures which are spread all over the globe by the mass media.

■ In addition to the destruction of local cultures, we accept global doctrines, ideologies and ways of thinking about the world which Robertson terms 'cognitive frames of reference'.

The following activity is an example of the points that Robertson was raising.

ACTIVITY KS **PROBLEM SOLVING**

IDENTIFICATION AND INTERPRETATION

How 'global' is the mass culture that we consume through our television set and video? Read the following passage from Marsh et al. (1999) and explain what you think the significance of the information is.

' What follows is a folk tale, I have no idea as to its validity! After the completion of the film **Star Trek: Generations**, William Shatner and his wife decided to go on holiday. The Shatners wanted to 'get away from it all' and decided to spend a holiday deep in the jungle of Cambodia. When their plane landed they took a taxi to the river and headed for its source; after changing boats several times because of the river becoming narrower, they eventually made their way up river in a rowing boat. Eventually the Shatners made their way deep into the jungle and their long journey came to an end. As they were taking their luggage out of the boat a figure came out of the jungle to help them. The figure from the jungle stared at William Shatner and said in astonishment 'Capt. Kirk'. Is the significance of the passage above, that even people deep in the jungle are fans of **Star Trek**?

The significance of these points for sociological theories of social identity is complex. On the one hand, the process of globalisation can be seen as liberating. It enhances the choice of resources available to people in the construction of an identity that they feel both

happy and comfortable with. People today know much more about how others lead their lives; this helps to break down traditions and local ignorance.

In contrast, the process of globalisation can be seen to destroy local cultures; this is not only unsettling for individuals but gives their lives an uncertain feel. This is what Robertson called the processes of relativisation. Rather than creating tolerance of others who may have different ways of living, people in communities may attempt to reinvent traditions, in an effort to give themselves a sense of identity. In religious terms there may be a growth of fundamentalism and rejection of people from other cultural traditions. The proof of belonging to such new or what some sociologists have termed 'imagined communities' is active involvement in acts of great cruelty against others who are seen to be different.

Arjun Appadurai explains that the processes of globalisation are brought about by a number of flows or patterns of social exchange:

■ **Ethnoscapes** – the flow of people, tourists, immigrants, refugees, exiles and guest workers

■ **Technoscapes** – the movement of technology

■ **Finanscapes** – the rapid movement of money via money markets and stock exchanges

■ **Mediascapes** – information and images generated and distributed by film, television, newspapers and magazines

■ **Ideoscapes** – the movement of political ideas and ideologies

In 1993 Leslie Sklair outlined a number of different models of globalisation. Firstly, there is a world system model which is Marxist in orientation, as put forward by Immanuel Wallerstein. In this model there is an international division of labour within the world economy. A nation's economy is linked in a number of ways to the international economy and can be at it core, semi-periphery or periphery. Those nations which are at the periphery are much more likely to be in poverty. However, this model is said to be too determined by economic factors and ignores cultural factors.

HINTS AND TIPS Marx's model of society is generally applied to individual countries and that was Marx's own perception. Does it have more relevance when applied to the politics of the whole world at once?

The second model is one of 'cultural imperialism', in which local or traditional cultures are destroyed by the cultural products of multi-national corporations in the advanced countries. Ulf Hannerz (1996) outlines a number of possible types of cultural unification; one of which is 'global homogenisation' – this suggests complete domination of the world by 'lowbrow' western lifestyles, western products in the shops, western cars in the streets, western films at the cinema and western soaps on television. This spread involves *Dynasty* and the products of low, popular culture rather than Shakespeare.

The third model is Sklair's own model, which is that the global system is built upon transnational practices. These practices are formed by transnational corporations and they allow economic, political and cultural or ideological practices, like consumerism, to travel across state borders.

> **HINTS AND TIPS**   *Consider this question. Who has more power, the Coca-Cola Company or the British Government?*

According to David Held (1995), governments find it difficult to regulate their own economies as global financial dealings can diminish the worth of a country's money. Environmental issues cross national boundaries. Although transnational governmental organisations, like the European Union, NATO and the IMF have expanded their influence in the world, it is still the case that bringing people together from diverse cultures can increase the chances of conflict between people of different ethnic identities. Globalisation can diminish what were commonly accepted political and economic structures without inevitably leading to the foundation of new systems, which are clearly needed.

Globalisation can then generate nationalist conflict in the world, because political decisions are no longer taken by governments within nation states. In addition, as a process, globalisation can destroy a person's cultural identity; people fight to protect their local ways of living. Although there is no one acceptable definition of nationalism from this perspective it is a counter-politics of the local. This is known as the politics of resistance.

On the other hand, Mark Kirby (1996:208) has suggested that two critical points can be made against the globalisation thesis:

- The extent of the changes is overstated particularly when it is implied that the whole world is involved.

- Longstanding changes that result from larger historical trends are wrongly identified as being products of the 1980s and 1990s.

Subcultures

The notion of 'subculture' was very popular in sociology from the 1950s to the 1970s and has already been discussed in relation to socialisation. It is also significant in terms of crime and in education (see Areas 12 and ? respectively). Functionalism suggests that society is held together by consensus and agreement. The fundamental flaw in this logic is that within any society there are groups of people who do not represent agreement with society but are rejected by that society or who reject society. The solution used by American functionalism to explain this anomaly, or problem, in its logic was the idea that subcultures develop with aims and values which are different from those of mainstream society. The theory of subculture is of less significance to Marxism which accepts that social groups can be in conflict and have differing interests.

ACTIVITY   **PROBLEM SOLVING**

IDENTIFICATION AND INTERPRETATION	ANALYSIS AND EVALUATION

Think of various societies which have groups within them who do not share the values of the majority of the people. Think of groups within British society who may not feel themselves to be fully part of the culture.

In the 1990s the term 'subcultures' is rarely used by researchers. It was never clear within functional debate what the main determinants of a subculture were. Subcultures are discussed in Area 12 on Crime and Deviance and it is possible to see that the definition of a subculture varies with the researcher.

With the spread of postmodern ideas, most researchers are less willing to accept the idea of one dominant culture which the notion of subculture assumes. Culture is now characterised by diversity and choice.

David Muggleton (1995) even goes so far as to argue that there were no authentic subcultures, they were an invention of the sociologists who discussed them. The theory, as it was used in the 1950s and 1960s by American researchers, suggested that delinquent working-class boys had low self-esteem and joined subcultures to fight back against middle-class culture. As Bordua said at the time:

> The delinquent subculture functions simultaneously to combat the enemy without and the enemy within, both the hated agents of the middle class and the gnawing internal sense of inadequacy and low self-esteem. It does so by erecting a counterculture, an alternative set of status criteria.

Bordua (1961:125)

However, even at the time there were objections to this theory. Miller (1958) argued such boys were not hitting out at middle-class culture, but were emphasising 'masculinity', which was always regarded as a positive thing to strive for in lower-class neighbourhoods.

ACTIVITY KS COMMUNICATION

ANALYSIS AND EVALUATION

Research and plan an essay answer or a debate on this question:

Would you accept or reject the view of Paul Willis (1990) that 'The spectacular (youth) sub-cultures of the 1950s and 1960s are now impossible'?

Culture and social definitions

Western society changed dramatically in the late 1960s and early 1970s. The German term *Zeitgeist* is used to describe the spirit of the age, the feelings and the mood of the time. At that time, there was a mood of rejection of traditional ideas and people were optimistic that they could change the world. This led to a whole

series of new questions about society and a rejection of many ideas that had never been criticised before. In America, young people rejected the Vietnam War and, for some, Marxism became a popular theory.

Under the influence of the then new social movements, such as the women's movement and the Black Panthers, 'culture' was seen as significant in the manufacture of significant social inequalities such as racism, sexism and homophobia. Sociologists began to query the nature of social identity and to look at the way that it is created. It is these arguments that will be considered in a general sense, before moving onto a deeper consideration of varying theories of culture and its role in the creation of a social identity. There are two dimensions to the debates:

■ How do people acquire and create social identities?

■ What impact do these identities then have on society?

HINTS AND TIPS *You are advised that you should look at Area 5 on Mass Media and Popular Culture for development of some of the themes presented in this area because it can be through the media that we acquire and consolidate our notions of age, gender, ethnicity and class.*

Two key terms are important for our understanding of much of this area:

■ **Cultural relativism** – This is the argument that all cultures are different, but of equal validity. Cultures simply reflect the shared meaning within a given context.

■ **Ethnocentrism** – This is the idea that one's own culture is superior to any other. Think of the view of culture held by Nazism or the British before the Second World War, for instance.

ACTIVITY KS COMMUNICATION, PROBLEM SOLVING

IDENTIFICATION AND INTERPRETATION

In the text we suggested that all cultures are different, but of equal validity. Cultures simply reflect the shared meaning within a given context. However, are some cultures better than others? Is high culture superior to popular culture?

Gender and sexuality

There are two terms which are in common use to describe the differences between males and females.

Sex refers to biological differences. These are actually fewer between the sexes than might be imagined. There is greater variation between individuals within each sex than there is between the sexes taken as a whole.

Gender refers to the social differences between males and females. These vary considerably from culture to culture and at different times within a culture. Gender behaviour is learned behaviour. It is this area which is being questioned by sociologists and by people within society as a whole.

The debate about the nature of gender and sexuality began with the rejection of traditional female roles which became part of public debate in the 1970s and 1980s. Oakley's work established a sociology of gender, and some excellent studies were to follow. One example is Sue Sharpe's classic study *Just like a Girl* (1976) which demonstrated the role that secondary school plays in girls' socialisation. She argued that the school curriculum was gender-based; girls were discouraged from studying science. In Sharpe's study the girls' ambitions were children, husbands, jobs, and careers – in that order. You should develop these ideas by considering the notion of the hidden curriculum which is discussed in Area 8 on Education. From the perspective of early feminists, women were the victims of the rule of men, which is known by them as patriarchy. More recently males have begun to question traditional gender roles so that there is now a debate as to the nature of gender itself.

HINTS AND TIPS   *Any view which offers the perspective that only women are victims of gender stereotyping is a shallow analysis. Certainly, by many measures of power and influence, women have suffered at the hands of males, but males too have experienced suffering. The nature of that suffering is merely different. One has only to look at the graveyards of the battlefields of the First World War and other more recent wars to recognise that the individual males who knowingly went to almost certain death were also the victims of their class, their time and their gender.*

ACTIVITY   KS WORKING WITH OTHERS

| KNOWLEDGE AND UNDERSTANDING | IDENTIFICATION AND INTERPRETATION |

How does one learn to act as a male or a female? Take a mail order catalogue, or go through a shopping centre with all the big chain stores. Identify the products that are targeted at children of each sex and identify the gender messages they are being given by the goods that are on offer. Look at toys, reading materials, hair-styles, clothing, computer games, bedlinen and other interior furnishings.

What do children learn of the expectations of their social behaviour from what they are presented to play with?

Can it be argued that gender is taught to children through the products which they consume? This is a particularly easy and very interesting area to develop as part of a coursework module.

There has already been discussion on how girls learn to be female. Note that the debate and the research has often centred on three main agencies of socialisation, although it is now taking in other areas of society and culture. Develop your notes by referring to the following areas in this text:

■ Families and Households (Area 6)
■ Education (Area 8)
■ Mass Media and Popular Culture (Area 5)

Oakley, Sharpe and others assumed that the process of socialisation acted to fix a woman's identity. In other words, they assumed that the concept woman had firm foundations, that it was an 'essential subject'. However, in recent years, the category woman has become problematic. What is it that constitutes the category woman? It is not something that we can simply assume. This criticism came initially from 'black' feminists who were unable to develop any form of sisterhood with 'white' feminists. If there is no foundation, then the category woman is of little value to us. This idea has been fully explored by Judith Butler of the University of California, who is also associated with 'queer theory' and a questioning of traditional gender identities (see section on page 225).

HINTS AND TIPS *At this stage consider the question of whether 'woman' or 'man' exist as categories except in biological terms. Are class differences more significant in dividing women from each other than gender differences in dividing women from men? This is a complex area of thought and you may wish to return to the ideas. Do not expect to find easy answers to your debates.*

A C T I V I T Y KS **COMMUNICATION**

IDENTIFICATION AND INTERPRETATION	ANALYSIS AND EVALUATION

Buy or borrow copies of a variety of weekly and monthly magazines aimed at adult women. Categorise them as for middle-class women readers and for working-class readers. You can do this on the price and the amount of reading in the content.

1 What view of femininity do the magazines present to their readers?

2 What differences are there in the assumptions that the magazines are making about the interests and opinions of their readers?

You could develop this type of thinking by adding men's magazines to the analysis and considering their representations of women and men!

Another strand of thought has suggested that there has been a blurring of the traditional differences between males and females in our society. At the turn of the twentieth century these were marked and obvious. Females were concerned with domesticity and care. They wore dresses and skirts and had long hair. Males wore trousers and worked in jobs outside the home. In most families, the father was seen as the dominant decision-maker and he certainly could control expenditure if he wished. Violence against women, if not acceptable, was arguably commonplace in many families. The questioning of the continuance of traditional gender roles began with the work of Young and Willmott in the 1960s and 1970s. They suggested that males and females were breaking traditional patterns of domestic labour, but they did it from the patriarchal stance that it was the female role to work in the home caring for her husband and children. Feminist backlash against their research picked up methodological problems and claimed that the oppression of women continued. However, there were

social changes taking place in society with regard to gender roles; broader cultural differences appeared between generations so that traditional patterns associated with hair-styles and clothing were being challenged by young people. Younger women wore trousers in public and young males grew their hair. These actions were not merely fashion although they were fashionable. They were used at the time to express an opinion and were read by other people as statements of political position. This wider cultural change translated into sociology as the belief that one could 'be' anything one desired by taking the appropriate cultural and social actions.

Agnes the transsexual

In 1967 these arguments were taken to the limit by the ethnomethodologist Harold Garfinkel in his case study 'Passing and the managed achievement of sex status in an intersexed person', which is more commonly known as his study of Agnes the transsexual.

In our society the transfer of sexual status is not possible. The legal change of the birth certificate is not allowed. 'Our society prohibits wilful or random movement from one sex status to another' (Garfinkel 1967:125). Garfinkel's case study is of a 19-year-old who had been born and brought up as a boy, with male genitalia. However, physically, she looked like a woman; she had ample breasts, a thin waist and a complexion free of facial hair.

Most of us are brought up with a very clear sense of our sexual and gender identity. It is the very first thing that our parents know of us as babies. Girls are socialised into the appropriate ways of behaving for a young female adult. This learning process involves observing adult females and attempting to adopt their ways of behaving in an effort to 'pass' as a female. Agnes appeared to be female but she lived her life as a female by a range of techniques which Garfinkel refers to as 'passing'. These involved quite complex strategies to hide the fact that 'she' could also legitimately be described as 'he'.

Passing was not simply a matter of desire for Agnes; it was a necessity. What Agnes feared above all else was 'being noticed' while passing; it was for this reason that the security of her identity was to be fiercely protected.

A C T I V I T Y *KS* WORKING WITH OTHERS, COMMUNICATION

IDENTIFICATION AND INTERPRETATION	ANALYSIS AND EVALUATION

According to Harold Garfinkel, passing is something that we all feel that we have to do in our everyday lives. Identify some occasions in which you have attempted to 'pass', giving the impression that you had an identity which you feel was not really yours. Explain to yourself what you did and how you did it. How, for example, would a person under the age of 18 'pass' for an 18-year-old to gain entry to a public house or cinema?

HINTS AND TIPS As a word of warning, Garfinkel is an ethnomethodologist and he is attempting to make visible the common-sense notions which we take for granted in our every day lives. In other words, he is attempting to move beyond common sense in an effort to explain common sense. This often gives his work an incomprehensible feel; there do not seem to be words in the language to explain common sense. The whole point is that it needs no explanation. Garfinkel always has to use inappropriate tools for the task he has set himself.

One of the techniques Agnes used was 'anticipatory following', learning from attempting to analyse questions and situations in an effort to find clues hidden within them on 'normal' ways of behaving. Agnes was taught how to cook, what clothes to wear, what styles to adopt and skills in home management by an older woman and a boyfriend taught Agnes detail on how to behave in front of other men. Agnes observed other women, how they acted and reacted in various situations, so as to fine-tune her own femininity. After a sex change operation, Agnes went on to lead an active and sexually enjoyable life as a woman.

What conclusions did Garfinkel draw from his study? All aspects of our lives, including our identity or selves as people, are created by our own **human agency** – in other words, by our self. Agnes actively desired status as a female. The success of any of our creations, including our creation of an identity for our self, involves us working to make the setting for our creations 'feel natural' and as such be treated by others as a fact. Agnes had to act a part which other females would have been taught from conception.

A C T I V I T Y *KS* PROBLEM SOLVING

IDENTIFICATION AND INTERPRETATION	ANALYSIS AND EVALUATION

Harold Garfinkel raises important questions about gender; you might find it useful to answer the questions:
1 What does it mean to be a woman?
2 What social skills and knowledge would any person need to have to be able to pass as a person of the opposite gender?
3 Was Agnes, in reality, a woman? Garfinkel claimed she was. Germaine Greer would argue strongly that she was not because one needs to experience socialisation as a woman to be a woman. Offer a variety of points of view.

Queer theory

A recent form of theorising is 'queer theory'. It builds on the suggestion that people are free to 'become' whatever they wish, and it has allowed various groups who share an identity to develop their own analyses of their position in society.

Conventional descriptions of sexuality viewed heterosexual sex as a natural feature of human life. So what does it mean to be homosexual or 'queer'? Over the course of the 1990s there was a notable increase in the level of political activism amongst gays and lesbians who had 'come out' since AIDS was first diagnosed. In Britain, the activist group OutRage found itself in the news headlines because of their tactic of 'outing' closet homosexuals (forcing individuals to state their homosexuality openly).

Taking as their starting point the work of Michel Foucault (1977), who attempted to explain how notions of sexuality were produced, OutRage has been striving to change the identity of homosexual men and lesbian women. Their argument is that they are moving away from the notion of 'gay' and labelling themselves as 'queer'. They suggest that people who define themselves as 'homosexuals' have accepted a marginalised, heterosexual vision of their sexuality. People who accept a 'homosexual' or 'gay' identity are merely attempting to assimilate themselves into heterosexual cultural life because they have accepted a role as a member of a distinct minority. They ask for tolerance; but will always be regarded by other cultures as sexually 'wrong'. Elements of queer cultural theorising include the following points:

- It is highly political, but claims to be above party politics.

- It rejects the rational sexual categories imposed upon us all, both homosexual and straight, male and female, in which we are asked to define ourselves as sexually 'normal'/heterosexual or otherwise.

- It aims to destabilise the power relations that maintain sexual identities and categorisations which force homosexuals into a private world.

- It replaces the civil rights campaigns with a politics of 'carnival' which is about refusing to accept homosexuals as a minority group in the population.

- It draws on highly theoretical modern writing which makes it inaccessible to many people.

Queer theory draws upon a number of poststructuralist theories:

- Jacques Lacan's model of a decentred and unstable identity.
  Lacan believes that no personality is stable, and that we are engaged in a constant redefining of ourselves as individuals.

- Jacques Derrida's notions of deconstruction and 'performativity'.
  Deconstruction is the idea that we should disassemble social ideas to see what makes them work. This notion of deconstruction is used by queer theorists to look at ideas such as masculine/feminine or male/female upon which patriarchy is based. Performativity is one of the most influential concepts within queer theory. Performatives are when we do things with the use of words, such as marrying people. They generate a conventional procedure that participants agree to abide by. There are 'proper' ways of behaving for men and women, which are practices that are conventional and make use of appropriate words. Masculinity and femininity are such practices, they are neither true nor false, and they simply exist and guide our behaviour in appropriate situations.

- Foucault's model of discourse, knowledge and power.
  Discourses are sets of practices which both exist within and support institutions. They take the form

of a social and moral debate about the nature of certain social practices so that the meaning of ideas such as 'male' and 'female' have actively changed over the centuries.

HINTS AND TIPS In many schools, children use the terms 'gay' or 'woman' as terms of abuse to be directed at those who annoy or fail to conform. What does this suggest about modern culture? Is there a movement to accept a shift in gender patterns in broader society or is this merely the concern of a small number of individuals?

New masculinities

Just as women have been questioning what it means to be female, so this has provoked a debate among males as to the nature of masculinity. The question is, 'What does it mean to be a man?' Women have challenged males in their traditional areas of superiority and many have argued that this has caused a crisis of confidence among men. We know a great deal about what it means to be a part of society, which is a male social construction, but there has been very little attention paid to a qualitative analysis of the social construction of masculinity itself.

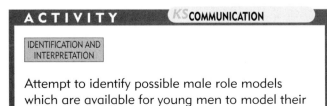

ACTIVITY KS COMMUNICATION

IDENTIFICATION AND INTERPRETATION

Attempt to identify possible male role models which are available for young men to model their male identity on. Use magazines for ideas and create a wall display of male role models.

Segal (1990) points to a historical masculine ideal of the Victorian male which is very different from what would be expected of men today. The masculine man of the middle classes was expected to repress his sexuality with cold baths, to cultivate a lack of emotion and to express great physical bravery in the face of overwhelming odds. The poetry of Sir Henry Newbolt was widely taught in schools and emphasises an ethos of fairness and muscular Christianity which is embodied by the cricket-playing values of the traditional public schoolboy. However, there is a class dimension to this model in that working-class men at the same time were expected by their peers to be hard-drinking, hard-working and hard-playing.

Brittan (1989) suggests that there is a difference between masculinity and masculinism. Masculinity is socially constructed and changes through history. It has been associated with care for the weak and with paternalism, but equally the New Man offered a new masculinity in the 1980s. Masculinism is apparent throughout society and takes the form of a desire to dominate and control a social relationship or situation.

The most recent social identity for males which has been identified and discussed widely in the media is the 'new lad'. This is in essence a form of youth culture because laddism is more typical of the young than of mature men. Comedians such as Frank Skinner and David Baddiel seem to represent the laddism of male culture. It appears in magazines such as *FHM* and *Loaded*. It can be identified on the type of game shows which reject familiar game-show formats, such as *They Think It's All Over* and *Shooting Stars*. Symptoms of laddism include an obsession with sport, drink and sex, an immature attitude to social relationships, a rejection of femininity and a desire to 'have a laugh'. Laddism has many of the features of traditional working-class culture; however, in the media, it is often middle-class educated men who seem to be linked with it. This is certainly true of its literary expression where the writers most closely associated with laddism (perhaps unfairly) are Nick Hornby and Martin Amis. Amis is himself the son of an extremely well-known writer and comes from a privileged background. Nixon and others see the rise of the new lad as a return to many of the masculinities of the past. Note that the desire to care for and protect

the weak is no longer part of laddism although it was certainly part of the masculinities of the 1930s and before.

Class and culture

This area is explored in both Area 5 on Mass Media, which follows, and later in this area at a theoretical level when Marxism is discussed far more fully. It is also significant in Area 8 on Education, because the different achievement of working-class and middle-class children in school is often said to be caused by serious differences in culture between the two classes. Note that it has been part of the discussion of masculinity which precedes this topic.

Throughout the centuries, there has been a difference of culture between the various social classes, so that in Tudor times, there were laws of sumptuary, which required that people wear clothing appropriate to their position in life. Anyone who wore certain good forms of clothing would be fined heavily for attempting to go above their status in life. Even in the 1930s, people could be recognised by specific class identifiers such as the wearing of a flat cap for working men or an apron for working-class women. There were a variety of indicators of class and this may be a good moment to return to the elements of culture diagram (Figure 4.1) and identify cultural differences between upper- and working-class people. The questions which are now under discussion include:

- Are there differences of culture between working- and middle-class people? The evidence suggests that there are and that these have a huge impact on people's life chances.

- If there are differences of culture, what are the features which differentiate the classes? These are probably more significant now than in the past, and reflect morals, norms and values.

Some of the most significant work in this area was done in the 1950s and the 1960s in Britain. Sociologists at the time were aware that massive changes in the nature of industrialisation were having an impact on the culture and behaviour of working people. There was an intense burst of activity which looked at class,

---

ACTIVITY   KS **COMMUNICATION**

IDENTIFICATION AND
INTERPRETATION

1 What are the typical characteristics and attitudes of a 'new lad'? Use male magazines aimed at the younger male such as *Loaded* and *FHM* to identify some of the social attitudes and interests in them.

2 To what extent is the 'grl pwr' or 'girl power' of the late 1990s an extension of 'new lad' cultural expression into female behaviour?

but from the perspective that it did exist, that it was significant in people's lives. The methods used were ethnographic in that people looked at working-class cultures from the point of view of outsiders, which of course, they were. Academics would generally have been drawn from the middle classes so working-class cultures were to a limited extent alien. Middle-class people would not have mixed in the ordinary way with people who were not of their own class and culture, and there is sometimes a slight tone of cultural superiority in the writings of middle-class people about the lives of the working classes.

Among the most significant writers in this area were Goldthorpe and Lockwood. They suggested that the culture of the working classes was bound up with the form of work which they undertook, a classic Marxist position. They identified a culture among workers in the heavy industries of mining and shipbuilding which was based on mutual care, living for the present and

which was very aware of the difference between themselves and the middle classes. Other writers in this tradition include Hoggart, who is discussed later under a consideration of Marxism, and the sociologists who carried out detailed studies of Bethnal Green in London. This was during the 1950s and 1960s when the traditional employment and settlement patterns were being broken up by slum clearance and industrial relocation.

Postmodernists, however, do not recognise that modern culture is class-based and reject notions of class as significant in the creation of culture. Their theorising is supported by the work of Ivor Crewe, who is well-known for his work on class and political party allegiances. He suggests that class is significantly less important as a cultural identifier because people define themselves by their ownership of possessions and their geographical location. Fiona Devine (1992), however, suggested that people do define themselves in terms of their social class.

TASK

Hypothesis – Children are aware of the social class to which they belong and this is an element of their social identity.

Context – There is a strong argument that Britain is a classless society. This opinion is held by many, both on the left and the right of the political spectrum. Certainly the behaviours expected of the various social classes have changed so that some of the more obvious differences of culture as applied to social class have now been lost. However, if children are aware of their social class, this implies that they are also aware at some level of differences of culture between the social classes. This awareness may not be more sophisticated than 'posh' and 'snob' or 'common' but it will impact on their attitudes and their awareness of their own social identity.

Method – You will need a sample of children. You are advised to make sure that they are not too young to understand the questions that you will ask. A top junior school or a lower secondary school group would be ideal.

Qualitative or quantitative methods will work with this question, but you might be better to look at harder quantitative methodologies because you are asking about the meaning of social class and children's

perceptions of their class positions. Devise a questionnaire, or an interview schedule, and ask questions about their own class position. You would be better to make sure that these are objective and use a class index such as the Registrar-General's Scale. Do people in their homes work? If so, what jobs do they do?

From that starting point, ask whether they understand the meaning of class, if they have heard the term before. It is possible that they may not have done. If not, use the terminology 'ordinary people' and then see what they mean by the term ordinary. Are they ordinary? They will say 'yes', so what to them, does ordinary mean? Are there people who are better or richer, or who are poorer than they are?

Evaluation – This is quite a difficult question in terms of questionnaire design and this will give you a great deal to talk about regarding your methodology and your evaluation. If children have difficulty with your questions, you will have proved your point, however, which is that class is not significant in social identity among modern children. However, if children are reasonably accurate about their class position and can identify themselves correctly, then in modern culture, class is a significant component of social identity.

At a more theoretical and analytical level, Marxists are concerned with the reproduction of social classes across generations, for example by parents buying advantages for their children. This notion of class **structuration** involves the transference of 'cultural capital' from parent to children. In Education Area 8 on Pierre Bordieu describes a situation in which cultural knowledge, forms a habitus (or a set of norms, mores and values) which can be used by children to become successful in schools. He calls this cultural capital. In other words some children have greater access to high culture in that they have ways of speaking and notions of good taste which teachers regard as superior and indicators of intelligence.

A more recent theory in this debate originates with Giddens who looks at class structuration. Class structuration theory is concerned with the process by which individual human agents create and recreate class structures. Giddens talks of proximate structuration. This is a cultural concept. It is concerned with the involvement of individuals in the division of labour, authority relations and consumption groups, all of which can help to reproduce class relationships. The class structure is, for Giddens, both the medium and the outcome of the activity by individual agents. Clothes and body shape can be used to judge the relative worth of people. Parents play a key role in developing styles of accent, dress and demeanour in their children, as well as teaching children how to hide away their natural functions, which can have a significant impact upon future life chances.

Race, ethnicity and nationalism in contemporary Britain

There are three elements involved here and it can be difficult to separate the various strands in the debate because they are so interconnected in people's behaviour and attitudes.

'Race' and racism are always used in connection with people's negative social attitudes to those who are seen as different from themselves. Often they target those of differing skin colour, so that people who have African ancestry can be targets. However, this is not always the case. The Irish, too, have been the victims of negative images in popular culture. Think of the Irish joke.

Ethnicity involves a form of self-identification so that a person may identify with a nationality or a cultural tradition. Within Britain there are varying ethnicities which are endemic to this culture; think of the Scottish, the Welsh and Northern Irish Catholics and Protestants. There may even be more localised ethnicities such as Yorkshire people or the Cornish. To complicate the issues, there are also many members of minority cultural groups whose families came to Britain at some time in the historical past through immigration. Some cities may have large populations of such people. There is an unsubstantiated claim that more people speak Asian languages in Cardiff than speak Welsh as a first language. These people are part of British culture, but may still be referred to in a way that implies that they are not fully of it. For example, the terms 'Asian', and more insultingly 'Paki', are in common use to describe people who were born in Britain, some of whose families may actually have come to Britain from Africa, but whose cultural traditions are from the Indian subcontinent. A sense of ethnic identification needs only to exist as a result of emotion, heritage or history, but it can make an individual's identity and will certainly affect his/her behaviour. The history of the twentieth century should act as proof to the point.

> **HINTS AND TIPS**   *We all have ethnicity and the term should not be used in a way that implies that only those from different or minority cultures are in some way 'ethnic'. This is grossly misleading and may even have tones that are racist. Be cautious in your use of this language.*

Nationalism refers to geographical and political movements. Many of us have a sense of nation or nationality and it is a political term to describe a legal status as a citizen of a given country. Hechter suggests that nationality is a relatively recent concept in history; it only came about because of modern communications and the development of nation states in the nineteenth century. Within Britain, there are political parties with nationalist aims who make specific demands with regard to areas that are bounded by a clear border – the Scottish National Party and Plaid Cymru in Wales. Nationalism as a political ideology has two separate strands:

- Patriotism – this is a sense of belief and particular pride in one's country.
- Separatism – this is a belief that one's country should develop apart from another.

Norman Tebbit, a former Conservative government minister, famously suggested that a person could reveal nationality by deciding which side to support in a cricket match. This comment, which was heavily criticised for racism, was aimed at British Asians who support the Pakistan team. At what times do you feel that your nationality is important to you as a person? You may wish to return to your cultural map and consider what makes you feel as though you belong to a nation. Develop the idea by asking other people what nation they feel they belong to and how they know.

Questions of nationality are also deeply connected to regionalism in Britain. There is great inequality of wealth so that the income per head of the population is lower in Scotland and Wales than in England.

There are two ways in which a sense of ethnicity can be reinforced in the individual. Ethnocentricity suggests that one's own culture is superior and racism offers the belief that others are inferior. These are areas that require discussion.

- **Gaining a sense of identity** – Durkheim offers some of the best answers to the question of why many people feel a need to develop a sense of nation. He suggests that people need to feel part of society and gain from a sense of being integrated into society. In contrast, Aitchison and Carter (1990) suggested that, for many, the desire to reject the development of a global culture is enough to prompt a separatist movement among people determined to hold on to their own cultural identifiers. They will then take positive steps to encourage a sense of nation in the population. Both positions agree that a sense of ethnicity and nation can confer a sense of social identity on a person.

- **Rejecting the other** – A number of thinkers offer the view that nationalism grows out of a sense of other. Miles (1989) offers the view that people create a real or mythic stereotype of other people which can then be rejected. Many cultures have words to describe people who are not of their own ethnicity in terms that can also imply inferiority. To develop the point, foreigners and non-English people were often represented in popular literature and media forms before the 1970s in stereotyped and derogatory ways.

HINTS AND TIPS *For your own education only, just think of all the words in the English language which insult the non-English as having undesirable characteristics. These terms may seem harmless, such as 'frog' for French people, but they probably originated as abuse. If you write these words down, be certain that at the end of the lesson, you throw your paper away. If your first language is not English, then what words in your own tongue insult other nationalities?*

Overt racism is increasingly rejected by society, but few people would deny its existence. Barker (1981), for instance, has suggested that the gross racism associated with rejecting people on the basis of skin colour has been replaced in recent years by a marginally more sophisticated form which he terms New Racism where commentators reject those of different ethnicity on cultural grounds. Moslems, for instance, are rejected for their 'failure' to adapt to British cultural traditions.

Use a good dictionary and discover just how many common English words have been absorbed into the language from other cultures. You may wish to begin by looking up the following:
bungalow, jodhpur, pyjama, algebra, juggernaut, veranda, balcony, reggae.

To develop the idea, you might like to consider the extent to which Britain has become or is a multi-cultural society, absorbing ideas into its culture and making them its own. Begin with the popularity of ethnic foods.

Within Britain, there are two forms of nationalism:

- Welsh and Scottish nationalism is associated with the rejection of English political domination over the lives of their populations. They are also associated with the preservation of traditions which are significantly different from those of the dominant English. In particular, the preservation of languages which are very unlike English is a political issue. There are also religious and class elements to the debate.

■ English nationalism has few such direct political objectives as Welsh or Scottish nationalism, except for concerns which are frequently expressed in the media about the loss of English culture to the European Community. There is a British National Party which has leanings to the far right and is racist in intent. This group, however, is not particularly significant in the politics of the nation.

> **HINTS AND TIPS**   *Expressions of English nationalism tend to focus on sporting events and on public celebrations such as royal weddings. You might like to consider why this is so.*

Welsh and Scottish nationalism had such an impact on the politics of these areas that under the Labour government of the late 1990s, there has been devolution. This means that political power has been given to regional organisations. In Scotland, there has been the development of a Parliament and its website is <http://scottish-devolution.org.uk>. The Welsh people have a National Assembly which can be accessed in English at <www.wales.gov.uk>. These groups will have considerable local powers, but it will take time for them to develop fully and for their contribution to the cultural development of the areas they serve to be fully appreciated.

Culture and self identity

In everyday life, we commonly assume culture to be either 'high' culture such as great art, literature and classical music or 'popular' culture such as Oasis, *Coronation Street* and tabloid newspapers. For sociologists however, 'culture' has a much wider meaning and includes all human creations: the clothes we wear, the house we live in, and the food we eat are all products of our common culture. It is at this point that it is necessary to return to the notion of the self as a product of a culture and the idea that our notions of self are inextricably bound up with the cultures into which we were born and which we create.

All sociologists are concerned with the relationship between the individual human being and the culture he/she lives in. People may produce culture but at the same time the culture of a society will help to shape the personality of the individual. People have to learn how to become a member of society, and this learning process is called the process of 'socialisation'. This is an ongoing process of development which starts at birth and continues throughout our lives. This area looks at the very nature of the self which is affected by such cultural factors as race, ethnicity, class and gender. Note, too, that with the advent of postmodernism it has become to talk about sexual identity, culture politics or even sexuality with any common agreement. It is argued that we have become 'decentred'; in other words, there is not one sexuality but many, not one gay identity but many, each with its own set of cultures constructed and politicised. Nothing can be taken for granted.

> **HINTS AND TIPS**   *This area contains a great deal of discussion about social theory. Don't view social theory as simply a chore, as something that you have to learn in order to pass the exam. Social theories are invented and developed by sociologists and others to aid our understanding of the world. If a theory does not sound as if it helps you to make sense of your world, this may be because the theory is flawed in some way. Point out the flaw and explain clearly why the theory does not adequately explain how the real world works. This is the skill of evaluation.*

Individual people have knowledge of their own existence, and a belief that they are the creators of their own behaviour. We can say that the self is an 'agent'. In other words, people feel that they are responsible for their actions. In addition, individual people have an identity, a feeling of being part of a wider group, of being part of a number of wider associations, yet at the same time, a feeling of being unique. People who do not believe that they are themselves are thought to be suffering from some form of mental illness, such as Capgrass Syndrome – a condition where individuals believe that either themselves or those close to them have been taken over by other hostile agents. In summary, a person is an agent, a unique individual with an identity. It is necessary to look at some of the cultural factors which help to create that **self identity**.

Symbolic interactionism

Symbolic interactionism is a perspective within sociology which is concerned with how sustained social interaction is possible. Interestingly, symbolic interactionists take the view that there is no culture as such, merely interactions between individuals and from these we create a view of the world. Nevertheless the impact of their work on sociology and the study of society has been enormous.

In 1934 G. H. Mead defined 'the self' with the short words 'I' and 'Me'. The self was viewed as a 'social construction' arising out of social experience. For Mead, selves can exist only in definite relationships to other selves; moreover, the essence of the self is 'cognitive'. In other words, self is formed through the knowledge we gain from the 'negotiated' nature of the experience we have with others. The 'I' and the 'Me' form a 'cognitive structure' with the concept of the 'generalised other' – which Mead understood to be 'the attitude of the whole community' to which a person belongs. It is the 'essential basis and prerequisite of the fullest development of that individual's self' (Mead, 1967:219).

The 'I' is the impulsive and disorganised part of the individual. The 'Me' is the situated self, it is the self that we find playing roles within a structured environment. The 'Me' is the self that we present to others, while the 'I' is our subjective and reflexive self. When we do reflect upon ourselves we make use of what Mead referred to as the 'generalised other' which is made up of what we understand to be the accepted attitudes and beliefs within our community. This points to the significance of culture in our self concept, even if Mead finds the concept one that he must reject. In the last

analysis, for Mead: 'It is a structure of attitudes which makes a self' (Mead 1967:226).

PROFILE

George Herbert Mead
(1863–1931)

George Herbert Mead was one of sociology's nicest theorists. He seems to have inspired genuine affection and regard in all who knew him. He came from an educated and religious background, though his family was not wealthy. He struggled to gain an education, his father died young and his mother worked as a teacher to support her family.

His training and work were in philosophy and psychology and he studied for a time in Germany and at Harvard University. In 1893 he joined the new University of Chicago and stayed there until his death. He worked with a wide variety of enormously respected American scholars and gained a reputation as someone who could break with traditional modes of thought.

Mead worked on a variety of educational projects and even edited a journal, but he found writing difficult, and he genuinely felt that he could not do justice to his ideas or explain them in print. He actually published very little in his lifetime and much of the work that is associated with him came from the lecture notes of his students. He would probably have been surprised by the impact that his work would eventually make on the development of social sciences in the USA and in Europe.

Erving Goffman on the self

Goffman is regarded as one of the most influential writers of symbolic interactionism. Goffman makes a distinction between the 'official self', the self that we present to others in our everyday encounters with them, and the 'unofficial self', which he has also referred to as the 'unsocialised self'. This is the self which hides behind the mask of the official self. Individuals present a 'front' when they are carrying out any social action. The 'front' forms part of what

Goffman terms our 'expressive equipment'. 'Front' includes two key elements:

- **Setting** – which is concerned with the manipulation of the geographical aspects of where the social action takes place. This can include such things as reorganising furniture or choosing to meet a person in a particular place, in an effort to change the other person's perception of us.
- **Personal front** – which includes aspects such as rank, gender, age and race.

'Fronts' are selected, according to Goffman, not created. The notion of 'front' is used by Goffman to provide the clearest outline of the official and unofficial self:

> *Behind many masks and many characters, each performer tends to wear a single look, a naked unsocialised look, a look of concentration, a look of one who is privately engaged in a difficult, treacherous task.*

Goffman (1959:228)

ACTIVITY **WORKING WITH OTHERS**

IDENTIFICATION AND INTERPRETATION

If you were going to an interview for a job for which you did not feel fully qualified, but which you desperately wanted, what would you do to manage the image of yourself that others would believe?

In 1963, Goffman wrote an influential book called *Stigma: Notes on the Management of a Spoiled Identity*. He offers a different view of socialisation from the one that was discussed earlier in this area and which derives from functionalism. He does not, however, look at 'normal' socialisation but uses the case of those who are or feel themselves to be different in order to examine the processes by which we all learn to develop a sense of who we are and to manage ourselves in our societies. In this book he attempted to explain how individuals who have a problem with their official self, usually their outward appearance, cope. Goffman identified three different types of stigma:

- abominations of the body – different physical deformities

- blemishes of individual character – such as 'unnatural passions', mental disorders, addiction, suicide attempts
- tribal stigma – such as race, nation, and religion

Stigma involves having shameful differences which are used by others to give a person an identity, which is different from the identity of 'normal' people. Note, however, that two of Goffman's types of stigma actually refer to social definitions of a problem with identity: ethnicity and a failure to behave in a way that fulfils norms or values. 'Normal' people regard the stigmatised as not fully human and construct ideologies to explain why the stigmatised are both inferior and pose a threat to the community. Goffman refers to this as 'rationalizing an animosity' (Goffman, 1963:15).

However, the categories of 'normal' and 'stigmatised' are not concrete groups of people, but rather they are 'perspectives'. They are simply ways of labelling people. Almost all individuals carry with them some degree of stigma. Learning how to manage our stigma is part of our process of socialisation, and Goffman refers to this learning process as a 'moral career'. Most of us make use of a variety of techniques to restrict information about ourselves and hence minimise our stigma. For Goffman, we live in constant fear that our stigma will be exposed. Among the many examples discussed by Goffman are the cases of girls who examine themselves in a mirror after losing their virginity to see if their stigma shows. They only slowly accept that they look no different.

Perhaps the most important form of information control is 'covering'. This involves not displaying the things about ourselves which we believe are abnormal. This can include such things as name changing, or in disabled people learning to behave in such a way to minimise the obtrusiveness of their stigma.

HINTS AND TIPS *You may wish to consider the following questions:*
Do the concepts of 'official self' and 'unofficial self' apply to you? Explain to yourself how your 'official self' differs from your 'unofficial self'.

If you have a job, is there a distinction between 'front region' and 'back region'? If you have ever worked in a restaurant, for example, did the waiters ever behave differently when dealing with the public from the way they did in the kitchen?

What is the body?

This is a more recent discussion in sociology and the most influential theorist on matters concerning the body is **Michel Foucault**. He has been influenced by the work of Marxists and this shows in his theories. He wrote about how the state attempted to manipulate, regulate and control all aspects of the **body** in relation to gender, sexuality, madness, criminality and medical issues. This is motivated by a search for the causes of 'abnormality'; the state is searching for answers to the question of what makes some bodies sick or disobedient.

> **HINTS AND TIPS** *Before progressing with this particular section, it might help you to think in an abstract way if you attempt to consider the question 'What is normal?'*

Within Foucault's work it is possible to identify three organising principles used by him to explain how bodies are controlled:

■ **Dividing practices**. This involves the removal of anybody who is believed to be a threat to the community. The most famous example of this is the enforced removal of lepers from the community into leper colonies during the Middle Ages, which did result in the elimination of leprosy from Europe. It was believed that other dangers to the community could be cleared up by similar exclusions. Hence,

  ▪ the poor were forced into workhouses

  ▪ criminals were forced into prison

  ▪ the insane were forced into mental hospitals, or 'ships of fools' (said to be ships pushed out to sea, loaded with insane individuals seeking their sanity)

Although the ship of fools may have been imaginary, it is unquestionably true that the insane once had a recognised position within local communities, for instance as the village idiots, and that this role was taken away from them when they were excluded from everyday society.

■ **Scientific classification**. The Age of Enlightenment (1760s onwards) brought with it a number of new sciences which were concerned

Michel Foucault
(1926–84)

Foucault was an enormously influential figure in academic circles in his own lifetime in France and in later years, the USA. It is only in recent years that his work is reaching a wider audience. Foucault was a philosopher and psychologist by training and although he began as a Marxist, he finally came to criticise Marx and develop his original ideas into a new form of thinking.

He was educated in Paris and rose to high academic status relatively quickly. He was in one of the most prestigious academic jobs in France by the time he reached his late forties! It was at this stage in his life that he began an active lecturing career travelling around the world. It was in America that many of his ideas took hold.

He was particularly interested in key themes related to the nature of the self and studied madness, criminality, sexuality and welfare. He was concerned with the nature of social control and the way that society has power over individuals and the self. He encouraged people to resist the power of the state and traditional forms of authority by developing their own personal systems of ethics.

There are a number of common themes running through his work. For Foucault the state was a political structure which emerged in the sixteenth century and its purpose was to look after the interests of the whole community. Towards this end, the state gathers information about all forms of bodily activities: birth rates, death rates, unemployment, public health, epidemic diseases and crime. All these things could be pointers to a serious threat to the community. Foucault referred to the activity of the state gathering information about potential threats as bio-power, and it formed the basis of new developments in disciplinary technology – new ways of controlling people.

with understanding the 'nature' of both the mind and the body. New sciences, such as psychiatry, defined what is 'normal' in all sorts of areas: sexuality, passions, body shape and belief. In addition, the 'abnormal' body could be treated. The key tool for these new sciences was the examination, which transformed visibility into power, classified people into cases, which clearly stated if they were normal or not. In Foucault's work, power relationships are based upon surveillance, observing people and documenting what they do. Power need not be based upon physical punishment.

■ **Subjectification**. Here Foucault is concerned with the process of self-formation, which is understanding how people construct a 'self' for themselves. This includes both self-understanding and the way in which obedience is placed in people's minds. Individuals define themselves as 'normal' in relation to a number of factors: sex, health, race and many more. This is primarily concerned with what Foucault was to call the 'power of the norm': all individual actions were compared with the behaviour of others which pressurises people to behave 'normally'. Normal people could then justifiably regard themselves as members of the society.

HINTS AND TIPS   You may like to consider how people in any institution treat people whom they consider to be different or who do not behave in a way that reflects the norms of that particular culture. Think, for instance, of those whose personal hygiene is not good! This will help to illustrate the points that Foucault is making about identity and normality.

However, in recent years many people have questioned what is a normal body. Reshaping the body in an effort to reshape self and self identity is now less likely to be viewed as abnormal. This is usually associated with the emergence of a postmodern condition, in which commonly held beliefs and certainties are questioned. There has been an explosion of interest in the body in recent years. Think of the following examples: aerobics and the more aggressive forms of gym culture, piercing, tattooing and cutting. There is even a new tolerance for the sexual reallocation operation, what we used to call 'the sex change'. This has major implications for the sociology of gender.

The body is viewed as the 'visible carrier' of the self, something to be manipulated in an effort to improve self-image. In this sense the body can play a key role in our self-defined identity, but is one still the same person when the body changes?

ACTIVITY   KS **PROBLEM SOLVING**

ANALYSIS AND EVALUATION

Since the day you were born, everything about you has changed. You are taller, you look different, you can do more and virtually every cell of your body has changed! What is it that makes you the same person as the baby that you once were? Brainstorm some ideas around this question.

Food provides us with the link between a notion of 'the body' and 'culture'. As Pasi Falk (1994) argues, edible versus inedible is one of the key distinctions within any culture. However, the distinction is a 'fuzzy' one. Not everything that is edible is eaten; for example, insects are rich in protein but not eaten in our culture. Yet some poisons are consumed, for example, tobacco. Edmund Leach (1964) defines three categories of edible/inedible:

■ edible substances consumed as part of the everyday diet

■ edible substances which are allowed to be eaten under certain conditions

■ edible substances which are not defined as food

These categories clearly have a greater significance; they make a distinction between people who are regarded as 'us' or 'not us'. Hence, food and what we eat play a role in defining our cultural identity.

HINTS AND TIPS   You may wish to talk to a Moslem or a Jew about the importance of food laws in religion and in culture.

Think about the ritual significance of certain foods such as turkey at Christmas or cake at a wedding.

What foods would you find it totally unacceptable to eat even though you know other cultures would regard them as delicacies?

In terms of the effect of body shape upon life chances, research was published in 1994 by David Blanchflower and John Sargent, based upon the 12,536 children born in the first week of March 1958, who were included in the National Child Development Study and have been tracked since. This research found that girls born in Britain who were in the heaviest 10 per cent

Hypothesis – Many young people are interested in and attempt to alter their body image.

Context – There is considerable debate attempting to link the media with conditions such as anorexia. It is very difficult to prove a direct relationship between the media and an illness and establishing that the media cause excessive dieting is impossible. Nevertheless, our culture values extreme thinness. Does a cultural value placed on thinness cause people to feel uncomfortable with their body shape? This case has been argued for a long time by feminists about women, but there is increasing evidence to apply the same generalisation to young men and Susan Faludi, among others, is associated with this view.

Methods – A simple quantitative survey of a number of people asking whether they diet, go to gyms or attempt to control their body shape by the use of tight and baggy clothing should give you the answers that you need. Develop the questionnaire by asking people which parts of their body give them most dissatisfaction and what they would change about themselves if pressed. You might even ask how they feel about people who are too fat, or too thin.

Evaluation – This is a simple study and should work well with little to make it go wrong, as long as your sample is large enough and willing to be fairly truthful with you. You will almost certainly discover that a number of people actively control their body image, or wish that they could. Your efforts should be spent on making sure that the context section is interesting and detailed.

of their age group at 16 earned 7.4 per cent less than the non-obese girls in the sample. The top 1 per cent, the heaviest of the teenaged girls, earned 11.4 per cent less than other girls in the sample. In addition, women who were still fat at age 23 were at a significant disadvantage in terms of income. As Shelly Bovey has explained: '… the stress caused by being stigmatised for being fat can cause high blood pressure and stress' (Bovey, *The Times*, 20 March 1994).

Culture and classical sociology

Many classical sociologists argue that culture should be understood as 'common ways of behaving' within a community. This notion has a considerable role to play in the creation of our identity. Several classical social theorists, notably Durkheim, Weber and Marx, sought to understand the relationship between the political system, the economic system and culture. These analyses are found in:

- Durkheim's conception of the collective conscience
- Marx's conception of ideology

Durkheim and the collective conscience

Durkheim believed in the notion of a social fact. He thought that this was something bigger and more significant than the individuals concerned which influenced people's behaviour. Think of how it feels to be in a crowd where people are sharing an emotion. A rugby or football match offers an example and the emotion which people feel when they are all together offers a good view of how Durkheim viewed the way that society works. He believed that a social fact was something which was external to the individual but which affected the way that the individual behaved. For Durkheim, the clearest example of a 'social fact' was the collective conscience.

The collective conscience is where individual people interact with each other and have expectations of each other's behaviour. These expectations come together to form a normative order, or common ways of behaving in society. These are over and above the individual. These shared expectations which make up the normative order are external to the individual and at the same time exercise constraint upon individual behaviour. This normative order is the collective conscience. The collective conscience is Durkheim's contribution to our understanding of culture.

HINTS AND TIPS   *If you are discussing Durkheim's work in an essay or data response question, one of the issues you might want to look at is the relationship between the individual and the social structure or collective conscience.*

Durkheim assumes that individual people are pushed about by forces outside their control. Ways of behaving are determined by external forces so that people are powerless and have limited choice in their ways of behaving. For Durkheim, the individual human agent is a 'cultural dope'. People do what they are told, and follow the rules, without question. Are people pushed about by forces outside their control or are people in control of their own lives? What is your view? You should give evidence to support your answer, whatever you decide to argue.

Marx on class, culture and ideology

Marxism is a class-based theory. However, what does Marx understand by the term 'class relations'? For Marx, capitalist society is a form of society in which factories, shops and offices are privately owned, rather than communally owned or owned by the government.

Within capitalism there are a number of economic classes, but two are investigated by Marx: the ruling class, which he refers to as the bourgeoisie who own the means of production, and the working class or proletariat, who do not own the means of production. Marx explains the relationship between the bourgeoisie and the proletariat as an exploitative one. The rich people are rich, because the poor people work for them and create wealth. However, the poor people are unable to buy the things that they make. The two groups have a fundamental conflict of interest: to make profits the bourgeoisie must take advantage of the proletariat at an economic level; but to improve its own living standards the proletariat must reduce the profits of the bourgeoisie by transferring more profit to the workers as wages.

Marxism and the dominant ideology

Obviously, this creates the question that if people are rich and exploit poor people, why do the poor people tolerate the situation? The answer for Marxists lies with **ideology**; the bourgeoisie not only rule economically, they also rule intellectually. The bourgeoisie dominate the ideas of the proletariat. This is known as the concept of the 'dominant ideology'. Through the mass media, the education system and organised religion together with other institutions which are concerned with ideas, working-class people have their ideas manipulated by the bourgeoisie and are made to support capitalism. Ideas are shaped by class interests and the bourgeoisie distort the ideas of the proletariat by imposing a 'false consciousness' upon it. Working-class people make use of their false consciousness to excuse their own reliance upon the bourgeoisie within capitalism.

The Marxist concept of 'dominant ideology' could mean at least two different things. Dominant ideology proposes that there is one ideology which all people embrace because it is imposed upon everybody. In contrast, dominant ideology could mean that there is one dominant ideology and any number of non-dominant ideologies.

The Marxist analysis of ideology is very simplistic; people have their ideas manipulated and this legitimises both the position of the bourgeoisie and the exploitation of the working class, against its own interests. In practical terms, the working classes have a culture created for them, which reflects the needs of the bourgeoisie and not their own needs. It is this culture which is used to control, dominate and subdue the proletarians because it stops them from questioning the fundamental inequalities of society.

Marxists treat working-class people as 'cultural dopes'. People are said to believe what capitalists need them to believe. Individuals are simply pushed about by economic factors outside their control. In contrast to this Marxist view we could argue that working-class people are not passive and helpless.

The Marxist analysis of ideology undervalues the role of the human agent. The deterministic assumption, shared by all Marxists, that working-class people are pushed about by economic forces which are outside their control, may not be correct. Recent sociologists have been finding evidence of resistance to many forms of cultural domination in a variety of spheres of society.

Marxists do not explain how ideology works. What goes on inside the mind of a working-class person for him or her to reject his or her own economic interests so fully and totally?

The Mode of Production

Superstructure:

- this is the sphere of culture, ideas and ideology
- the Superstructure is determined by the Economic Base

The Economic Base:

this is made up of two parts

- the Relations of Production – this means Class Relations
- the Forces of Production – is made up of all the things from nature that we need to produce commodities

An individual's identity is built upon his or her class interests.

Economic factors are at the heart of any explanation of human behaviour.

Non-economic factors are of no significance in any explanation.

Our ideas are decided by economic factors.

Figure 4.3   Key assumptions of Marxism

How can the 'agency' – the ability to make decisions in our own interests for our own reasons – of working-class people be so completely destroyed without their revolutionary potential also being destroyed?

Just as Durkheim is very good at explaining the common ways of behaving within a society, so is Marx. However, in a similar fashion to Durkheim, Marx's understanding of the human agent is also limited. Marx assumes that individual people are pushed about by economic forces outside their control. He assumes that ways of behaving are determined by economic forces, most notably ideology, which is outside the individual's ability to control. In the same way as in Durkheim, people are powerless and have limited choice in terms of ways of behaving, what to do and how to do it. Marx also assumes that the individual human agent is a 'cultural dope', doing what it is told, following the ideology, without question.

> **HINTS AND TIPS**   Marx and Durkheim have many views in common. The difference tends to lie in their views of whether society works in favour of or against individuals. You are advised to revise this topic by looking at the similarity between Marx and Durkheim as well as the differences.

All sociological theories make assumptions about the nature of the self and its relationship with the social structure. Interactionists and other theorists, who place a great deal of emphasis on social action, argue that the self has the ability to make a difference in the world. In other words, interactionists argue that the person is a human agent; as such, the person is the author of his own actions. Marxists, feminists and functionalists, by contrast, believe that people are pushed about by forces outside the control of the self. For Marxists, feminists and functionalists, the self has very little 'agency' – unable to control its own thoughts and having little or no ability to make a difference in the world. When evaluating any theory outline the assumptions that the researcher is making about the human agent, state the assumptions and state if you agree or disagree with those assumptions giving your reasons.

The Frankfurt School

One of the most significant twentieth-century approaches to the sociology of culture was that developed by a group of neo-Marxists known as the Frankfurt School. Their stance must be understood in the context that the Frankfurt School developed in Hitler's Germany. Many of them were Jewish and intellectual and so they were frightened by the developments that they saw in the way that the mass media were used as a form of mind control to indoctrinate people into Nazism. They developed what became known as Critical Theory, and in terms of culture adopted an interdisciplinary approach in order to understand the 'industrialisation' of culture. The Frankfurt School claimed that culture was becoming:

- commodified – this means that culture is now a commodity to be sold rather than a creation of the individual
- standardised – this means that all cultural commodities are similar and that individuality is no longer prized
- massified – this means that the relationship we have with culture is that it belongs to the masses and that popularity means that it loses quality

However, it is easier to outline the notions of culture that the School rejected. They did agree that artistic culture should be regarded as something more than simply the reflection of class interests. For the director of the School, Max Horkheimer, culture originated in the way that society is organised. The Marxist approach, which regarded culture as something that simply emerged from the economic base, was rejected as too simplistic.

For the Frankfurt School it was important to develop a sociology of 'mass culture', in order fully to understand the changes that had taken place since the 1930s, such as:

- the emergence of the 'mass media'
- the emergence of an entertainment industry
- the manipulation of culture by the Nazis

All these factors pointed to significant changes in patterns of culture. The school focused on assessing how ideas were transmitted by 'the culture industry', and how this influenced personal and private lives. Horkheimer and Adorno rejected the idea that 'culture' could arise spontaneously from the masses. Culture was not something which emerged from the demands of people – but was brought about by manipulation. Local and folk cultures are destroyed in this process. The culture industry, via commercial entertainment, aims to bring about an attentive but passive welcome from the mass. The culture industry reproduces and reinforces the dominant interpretations of reality. At the same time audience responses are standardised, as each product contains cues to the appropriate response, for example 'canned' laughter to induce laughter from the audience. The culture industry was said to prevent individual people from developing into independent individuals who were capable of critical thought. The media develops a state of dependence and weakness which helps to reinforce the status quo.

David Held (1980) gives the following summary of one of the leading figures in the School, Herbert Marcuse, on the culture industry:

❛ *The development of mass culture:*
establishes a (false) harmony between public and private interests
reinforces privatisation and consumption orientations
spreads an advertising aesthetic
undermines indigenous working class culture

increases the domination of instrumental reason, and manipulates sexuality – leading to a (general) … pursuit of false and limited wants and needs.

Held (1980:108)

The Frankfurt School argued that the culture industry has a significant effect upon the formation of our identity. Again Marcuse suggests that the individual, as understood by Freud, is likely to become extinct, according to Held (1980:138). This is because:

- severe limits are placed on the development of the personality
- there is a decline in the position of the father
- individuals do not develop a personal sense of conscience
- values and prohibitions become less central to the individual's concerns and reflections
- social control is reinforced at an unconscious level

In summary, the School argued that the function of the culture industry was to reinforce capitalist society by ideological means.

Douglas Kellner (1997) has made a number of critical comments about the position of the Frankfurt School:

- the School made a number of assumptions about a rigid distinction between high culture and low culture, but such a distinction is blurred
- the School argued that only high culture can be critical, subversive and emancipatory, but popular mass culture can also have critical moments
- the School assumed that all popular culture is ideological in nature
- the School did not take into account the way that audiences can produce their own meanings for the products of the culture industry; the audience is not totally passive.

British Cultural Studies

From the 1950s to the present day, a group of British writers from Richard Hoggart (1957) to Raymond Williams and the Centre for Contemporary Cultural Studies at Birmingham University have attempted to develop an understanding of culture. British Cultural Studies rejects the elitism of the Frankfurt School and in particular its distinction between 'high' culture and 'popular' culture.

Hoggart, who rejected the Marxist approach, felt that the Frankfurt School was particularly insulting to the working classes because it was not itself working class. He said it offered the following view of culture:

> *A middle class Marxist's view of the working classes ... He pities the betrayed and debased worker, whose faults he sees as almost entirely the result of the grinding system which controls him. He admires the remnants of the noble savage ... Usually, he succeeds in part-pitying and part-patronising working-class people beyond any semblance of reality.*
>
> Hoggart (1957:16)

Hoggart described the Hunslet area of Leeds without over-romanticism, but points out that the territory was mapped and familiar for residents. Hoggart argued that working-class communities grew up around industry. With people living and working so closely together, they formed strong social bonds and a distinct sense of social solidarity. As well as shared leisure pursuits, cultural groups celebrated rituals and festivals, many rooted in their shared experience of work. This culture was passed on by club singing and other rituals. In fact, he describes a local folk culture. The culture of Hunslet was based on the belief in 'us' and 'them', with 'us' being the working-class community and 'them' being the 'hegemonic leadership' or 'the bosses'.

Hoggart's model of working-class culture presents the Hunslet residents as passive and receptive to the culture they found themselves in. Nevertheless, he supported some of the findings of the Frankfurt School because he said that the working-class folk culture rooted in churches, social clubs and family groups he described in the 1950s was disappearing because of the 'interplay'

between material improvement, cultural loss, and the effect of popular culture. Free from the hardship they had experienced during the 1930s, working-class people no longer needed the security that loyal membership to working-class groups once gave:

> *No doubt many of the old barriers of class should be broken down. But at present the older more narrow but also more genuine class culture is being eroded in favour of mass opinion, the mass recreational product and the generalised emotional response ... The old forms of class culture are in danger of being replaced by a poorer kind of classless ... 'faceless', culture, and this is to be regretted.*
>
> Hoggart (1957:280)

The community that Hoggart described no longer exists; it was razed to the ground to make way for the M621 motorway.

ACTIVITY   KS **WORKING WITH OTHERS**

ANALYSIS AND EVALUATION

Have communities lost their cultural traditions or have they merely changed? List some of the social and activity groups which exist in your town or area. You may need to talk to a retired person or a mother with young children to get a view of the full range of activities which people can participate in.

In contrast to Hoggart, Williams suggested that popular culture had an active and critical audience, who could evaluate everything from sporting events to film. However, drawing upon Gramsci's notion of hegemony which is discussed in Area 5 on Mass Media, British cultural theorists still argued that culture was used to reproduce capitalist society and induce consent.

This approach was built upon by Stuart Hall who argued that in the transformation of traditional society into modern society, new communities were constructed which developed their own identity in ideas, religion, symbols, views of the past and through creating their own traditions. For example, the French national identity is developed from the 1789 Revolution which overthrew the old regime and rejected the monarchy. In contrast, the British monarchy is a national symbol. Hall and the others at the CCCS distanced themselves from the traditional Marxian approach to ideology, on the grounds that it was too deterministic.

The development of youth culture

In place of ideology, Hall and his colleagues developed notions of the 'relative autonomy' of the superstructure, which allowed young people in particular to develop their own forms of cultural resistance to authority. One of the many interesting books that came out of the CCCS was Hebdige's *Subculture: The Meaning of Style* (1979). This made use of a range of semiological concepts to read the youth subcultures as a form of resistance, from teddy boys in the 1950s to punks in the late 1970s. You will read more about semiology in Area 5 on Mass Media and Popular Culture. These groups were radically different in the styles that they adopted, but were concerned with the same thing: showing their contempt for authority and capitalist ideology. They did this by developing forms of resistance through loud music with radical lyrics, unconventional forms of dress and aggressive behaviour. Youth culture was, then, deliberate resistance to capitalist ideology.

There were always problems with this position. Youth groups were in conflict with each other. This represented disagreement between groups of working-class people, for example the Mods and the Rockers. This contradicts the idea that young people are rejecting middle-class society.

Youth cultures are also commercialised so that popular musicians, rather than representing a rejection of capitalism, can actually become very rich. Consider the case of Mick Jagger of the *Rolling Stones*, who were once seen as rejecting authority; he is currently conventional enough to appear in *Hello!* magazine.

It is difficult to theorise about middle-class youth cultures. Many of the American hippies of the 1960s were rejecting extremely wealthy and comfortable lives. There is also a failure to take into account the views of people who make use of the culture. Many young people did not see youth culture as a form of resistance to capitalism – it was simply about having a good time.

More recent studies of youth culture include investigations into club culture. Sarah Thornton (1995) identified a view of club culture among young people which suggested that knowledge of the culture was used to exclude those who did not have the knowledge and to gain status or 'cool' for those who did. Questions of good and bad taste dominate the culture and the identifying features among those in the know include certain clothing brands and items and a rejection of commercial mainstream popular music.

There has been an interest in black youth subculture because sociologists have wanted to find in it evidence of resistance to white culture. The most notable writers were Hall, Gilroy and Pryce. It is interesting to study black culture, because often black youth cultural fashions set the trend for white youth to follow. There has been a development of Asian youth cultural forms such as Bhangra which are distinctive from white culture. Again, non-Asian people have taken Asian dress styles and adapted them to form part of white culture. Madonna was photographed in the late 1990s with henna patterns on her hands and arms.

> *HINTS AND TIPS If you are a member of a youth culture, or know people who do belong, then you may find it interesting to discover more about its norms and values as part of a coursework project. You are advised to move beyond mere description however and to analyse the implications of the culture for society. Does it represent a rejection of society or a rebellious phase in an individual life?*

Ethnicity, Stuart Hall and rewriting Marxism

In the 1990s Hall, in particular, moved away from what he saw as increasingly redundant Marxian concepts towards concerns with identity which have a more postmodern feel to them. In *New Ethnicities* (1992), he argues that the notion of 'black' is now uncertain. Black politics in the 1970s and 1980s was based upon the notion of an essential black subject, or fixed black identity. However, there are significant differences within the black community in terms of ethnic background, religion and culture. Writers such as

Modood object to the term 'black' as obscuring the distinct cultural tradition of Asians.

Moreover, there are significant political differences between 'black' people, based upon their sense of their cultural identities. This deconstruction of the category 'black' has generated a significant literature which suggests that racism is based upon skin colour. 'Racial formations' or the 'process of racialisation' should include factors such as religion and nationality.

Returning to Marxism

A number of people have attempted to save the Marxist analysis that Hall moved away from. Williams (1990), for example, attempted to argue within Marxian analysis that individual people were responsible for producing culture, but to remain within a Marxian framework he still had to make comments such as:

> At one level, 'popular culture'… is a very complex combination of residual, self-made and externally produced elements, with important internal conflicts between these. At another level, and increasingly, this 'popular' culture is a major area of bourgeois and ruling-class cultural production, moving towards an offered 'universality' in the modern communications institutions …
>
> Williams (1981:228)

In other words, people have an active role to play in culture, even popular culture, but in the last analysis

---

ACTIVITY KS**COMMUNICATION**

IDENTIFICATION AND INTERPRETATION

How are capitalists in popular culture represented? For example:

- Ian Beale – *EastEnders*
- Mike Baldwin – *Coronation Street*
- Quark – *Deep Space Nine*

In the cases that you can identify, does popular culture present a positive image of capitalism and capitalist values?

---

people are pushed about and have the ideas inside their own heads manipulated by the capitalist media.

Recent contributions to the debate

Many postmodernists consider people to be reflexive. According to Giddens, to be reflexive is to have a life narrative, to choose a character we would love to be. We mould our personal identity and decide upon what moral or rational principles we might want to make use of in order to make sense of our own subjective experience. This narrative is what we use to 'authenticate' ourselves as a self. In other words, the life narrative is what we use to make ourselves different from other selves. Individuals, then, have to create and constantly recreate themselves, choosing from lifestyle resources – cultural artefacts such as books, films, therapy and music to create, develop and monitor their chosen life narrative.

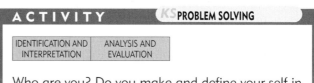

ACTIVITY KS**PROBLEM SOLVING**

| IDENTIFICATION AND INTERPRETATION | ANALYSIS AND EVALUATION |

Who are you? Do you make and define your self in the way that is described above? If your answer is yes, outline which resources you have made use of.

In Giddens' analysis, the late modern world is becoming very uncertain. For Giddens, individuals have become reflexive in order to compensate for the breaking down of the basic security system of customs and cultural traditions within local communities. Individuals find this breakdown of community to be personally troubling, because the local community provided a protective framework of psychological support to individuals. Without such support, individuals may feel 'ontological insecurity': personal meaninglessness and dread. But what is ontological insecurity? An ontology is a theory of what reality consists of and people who have a feeling of ontological insecurity feel that they are losing touch with reality, hence their feelings of meaninglessness and personal dread.

ACTIVITY   **KS WORKING WITH PEOPLE**

IDENTIFICATION AND INTERPRETATION	ANALYSIS AND EVALUATION

According to Giddens one element of the self is the ability to make 'rules' and 'routines' which help to make people feel comfortable and secure. Think of rules and routines that you make; do you make these rules for reasons of security or are these rules made for other reasons? Your answers to this activity will allow you to evaluate Giddens' theory, by saying either that his theory is true in your experience or that it is not.

Baudrillard and the culture of commodity

The work of Baudrillard is an attempt to make intelligible the significance of the proliferation of communication via the mass media. He argues that a new cultural form has emerged which traditional theories such as those of Durkheim, Weber and Marx cannot make sense of. Culture is now dominated by simulations – objects or discourses which have no firm origin and no foundation. Baudrillard is a former Marxist who became a postmodernist; he turned his back on the Marxist theory of culture and ideology because of its inadequacy in dealing with issues of culture and value.

In contrast to Marx, Baudrillard suggests that objects are not given value because of 'use value', but because we want them. Baudrillard argues that classification within our social order is now based upon consumption. Objects have 'meaning' for a consumer, and advertising turns products into a system of signs. This system of signs is a network of floating signifiers which invite desire. We no longer define ourselves by the old markers of class, gender and ethnicity but by new social identifiers created by the mass media. We identify ourselves by what we buy. In order to become an object of consumption, the object must become a sign; that is, in some way it must become external to a relation that it now only signifies. For example, perfume is sold not as a smell, but as a desirable lifestyle. It is in this way that a product becomes 'personalised' in that it has an identity.

HINTS AND TIPS   *To understand this, collect advertisements from glossy magazines. Can you decide what is being sold? Is it products or is it a personal image with which people would like to associate themselves? Which products are most closely associated with desirable lifestyle signs?*

You may like to consider the branding of clothing items. Would people still buy the items if they did not have identifiable logos and brand associations?

Baudrillard suggests that we exist in hyperreality. This is a world of self referential signs. For example, the television newscast which creates the news so that it can narrate it. We live in a world which is so media-created that there can be no objective reality. There is no subject, and no categories such as 'truth' and 'fiction'. Simulations are immune from rational critique. If we take the case of advertising, in the 1950s adverts were straightforward, the message was 'buy this–it is nice'. The situation today is rather different. We conceive the meaning of a product through advertising. However, we do not agree as to the meaning because it is based upon nothing but faith. An arbitrary sign induces people to be receptive, it mobilises our consciousness, and reconstitutes itself as a collective meaning. Advertising creates its own meaning. There can be no culture which we all share, despite the fact that we buy the same goods. We buy goods which are signs for other people, and we become the sum of what we buy.

The postmodern self

The term postmodernism suggests a radical break with the past. For Jean-François Lyotard, the postmodern condition is a situation in which individuals have lost faith in what he calls 'grand narratives', 'big ideas' or belief systems which we once accepted and which gave us a feeling of security. The bonds which once held communities together no longer have the same force they once had. As a social formation postmodernity has no foundations, no shared culture to give us a feeling of security, no grand theory to help us explain or understand the situation we are in. The self is isolated in the postmodern condition without logic, rationality, or morality to guide it. The postmodern condition is a world which is becoming fragmented, a world without certainty. However, everyone is said to have a need for both meaning and predictability in their lives and relationships. As Peter Marris (1996) makes clear:

> ' *Meanings are intentional structures which perceive, create and reiterate relationships for a purpose.*

Marris (1996:33)

Marris argues that meaning has a variety of forms, all of which are associated with the creation of certainty in everyday life:

- **Personal meanings** – these originate from the attachment people have to the world and the people around them; they underlie both our search for relationships and our personality

- **Mutual meanings** – these are influenced by the shared expectations within a relationship

- **Public meanings** – these are based on a conceptual set of interpretations, such as the law, which are independent of specific relationships

- **Meta meanings** – these relate to 'appropriate' ways of understanding a given situation

Meanings generate a basis or foundation for predictability in our social relationships. In other words 'meanings' provide us with an understanding of the world which is safe and predictable. What is the purpose of 'meaning' in modern culture and what is the foundation that meaning provides?

However, in the postmodern condition there is no legitimate order to provide such a foundation. Postmodern meanings take the form of

- Kitsch – which implies 'bad taste' with bragging; people boast about the things they have or the things they have given but are oblivious of the bad taste of the items

- Camp – this suggests the culture of a minority circle usually constructed around a secret language

- Simulacrum – a phrase first used by Baudrillard to explain that media products are continually reconstructed to the point where they take on a meaning mainly by referral to earlier versions of

'meaning' is an indicator	– it stands for something that we understand
'meaning' is a cause	– it gives us an idea of what made something happen
'meaning' is an effect	– it gives us an understanding of the result of something
'meaning' is intention	– it tells us why people behave in the way that they do
'meaning' is explanation	– it tells us why something happened
'meaning' is purpose	– it tells us about the function of things
'meaning' is implication	– it tells us about the consequences of our actions
'meaning' is significance	– it tells us about the importance of things

similar media products. We live in a world of 'hyperreality'. It is not possible to perceive any division between the 'real' and the 'representation'. Media representations give us a feeling for our environment which gives us the experience of being 'realer' than real.

HINTS AND TIPS *Recent films which illustrate this view perfectly are Kevin Smith's cult classics,* **Clerks and Mallrats** *about American youth culture. These are grossly offensive films in terms of dialogue although there is little in terms of action to shock or annoy. They are sometimes shown on television late at night. You will either loathe them or find them the funniest things you have ever watched. They have all the features described in the above account. They have much in common with* **There's Something about Mary**.

Zygmunt Bauman on the self

According to Zygmunt Bauman (1996), in the postmodern world identity is becoming reconstructed and redefined. Bauman agrees with Foucault that identity was a modern innovation. In the modern world, the problem of identity was a problem of how to construct and maintain our identity in an effort to secure one's place in the world and avoid uncertainty. This was because in the modern world the avoidance of uncertainty was seen as an individual problem, although support was always available from various professionals such as teachers and counsellors. Modern cities are lonely places, and surrounded by so many people, it is difficult to feel part of a community in the way people may have done in the past. In a city, we are not known and so our names and identity are not fixed through relationships with other people. The modern city is a place of nothingness which modern people had to find their way through. Bauman describes this as playing the part of a pilgrim, who keeps to a narrow path in order to find salvation. It was for this reason that modern people were forced to construct an identity for themselves. This becomes a life project, and ideally it should be established early in life and be used to make sense of the various uncertainties, fragments and divisions of experience which make up the post-traditional world. In other words, by creating a fixed and secure identity we attempt to make the world more ordered and more predictable for ourselves.

In contrast, in the postmodern world the problem of identity is one of avoiding a fixed identity and keeping our options open. We now avoid long-term commitments, consistency and devotion. In place of a life project established as early as possible, and which we loyally keep to, postmodern people choose to have a series of short projects which are not fixed. The world has a feel to it of being in a continuous present. The world is no longer agreeable to pilgrims. In place of the pilgrim there are a number of other lifestyles which emerge: the stroller; the vagabond; the tourist and the player. These lifestyles are not new to the postmodern world, but whereas in previous times these lifestyles were practised by marginal people in marginal situations, they are now common to the majority of people in many situations.

The pilgrim has been replaced by four successors, which are postmodern life strategies:

- **The stroller or the *flâneur***. According to Bauman this became 'the central symbolic figure of the modern city' (Bauman, 1996:26). This identity type is very shallow and looks only at the surface meaning of things in the metropolitan environment. What one sees is that for that person, all meaning is found in appearance; there is no deeper meaning underneath the surface of anything. The shopping mall is the place where we are most likely to see the *flâneur* in the postmodern world.

- **The vagabond**. This identity type is continually 'the stranger'; in a similar fashion to the pilgrim this person is perpetually on the move, but his/her movements have no fixed itinerary. We are talking of the person who moves jobs and relationships constantly and the modern travellers who move from country to country fit the model. In the modern and pre-modern world the vagabond was unable to settle down in any one place because the vagabond was always unsettled: 'The settled were many, the vagabonds few. Postmodernity reversed the ratio ... Now the vagabond is a vagabond not because of the reluctance or difficulty of settling down, but because of the scarcity of settled places' (Bauman, 1996:29). The world is becoming increasingly uncertain and unsettled.

- **The tourist**. The tourist moves purposefully, from home to a place in search of a new experience. This could be the ambitious person who moves from job to job seeking promotion and increasingly different experiences. This is a marginal activity rather than a marginal person. In the postmodern world we are losing the need for a home, but have a greater taste for the new experience. Home may offer security, but it also has the numbing boredom of a prison.

- **The player**. For the player life is a game; nothing is serious, nothing is controllable and nothing is predictable. Life is a series of 'moves' in a game which can be skilled, perceptive and deceptive. The point of the game is to 'stay ahead' and to embrace the game itself.

Life then is developing a rather shallow feel to it; it is fragmented and is discontinuous in nature. There is no such thing as culture; there is merely a variety of lifestyles from which individuals may choose their own identity type.

Wagner (1994) also outlines the notion of self in the postmodern condition. He argues that modernity gave individuals scope to construct their own identities, in the postmodern condition there has been a superabundance of material products, cultural orientations and consumer practices which has led to a momentous extension to the range of identity constructions available. In addition, the 'enterprise culture' led directly to the 'enterprise self' – and a significant increase in individual autonomy:

> *Rather than resting on a secured place in a stable social order, individuals are asked to engage themselves actively in shaping their lives and social positions in a constantly moving social context. Such a shift must increase uncertainties and even anxieties.*
>
> Wagner (1994:165)

Modernism was a form of social organisation which attempted to refashion and control the irrational forces of nature in the interests of satisfying human need or human desire. The relationships between people in the modern world were almost always rational and logical in nature, in contrast to the unpredictable and variable nature of life under postmodernism.

Area summary

This area has attempted to look at the nature of culture and the nature of the self as a 'human agent' within a culture. All sociological theories make assumptions about the nature of the self and its relationship with the social structure. Interactionists such as Erving Goffman, and other theorists who place a great deal of emphasis on social action, argue that the self has the ability to make a difference in the world. It creates a culture made up of interactions between individuals. Feminists, Marxists and functionalists, in contrast, believe that people are the creations of their culture. They are the victims of a conspiracy to prevent them from thinking and acting autonomously. In other words, for feminists, Marxists and functionalists the self has very little 'agency' – little or no ability to make a difference in the world.

For Marxists people are pushed about by economic factors and their ideas are shaped and manipulated by ideology. For the feminist, people are pushed about by patriarchy, ideas about male supremacy which lead to sexist practice. This area has raised the question of what it means to be a woman, a man and a young person in our culture. For the functionalist, ideas are shaped by the common value system. This area looked at Durkheim who discussed the role of the collective conscience in shaping the ideas of the person. Anthony Giddens, with his theory of structuration, attempts to bring these two theories together, by arguing that individual human agents have the ability to make structures – including the class structure.

All people live within a culture. In addition, the cultures that we live in are going through a process of transition. This area has highlighted the debate about whether national cultures are going through a process of globalisation – is the world becoming a single place, with one culture? Finally, it looked at the contribution of postmodern thinkers who cast doubt on the value of notions such as human agency, culture and structure.

Definitions

Body	The physical frame which the human agent (self) inhabits
Cultural relativism	The belief that no culture is superior or inferior to any other
Culture	Common ways of living: **high culture** is said to include such things as fine art and classical music **popular culture** is expressed in such media products as soaps and tabloid newspapers.
Ethnocentrism	A belief that one's own culture and the perspectives that come from that culture are superior to any alternatives from elsewhere
Folk culture	Highly localised and created by people for their own needs
Globalisation	The world is becoming a single place: politically, economically and culturally

Human agency	The ability of individuals to make a difference in the world
Ideology	A body of ideas and beliefs, which may be true or false, imposed on a person for the purpose of manipulation
Low culture	The culture which is said to be lowbrow and less demanding, such as soaps
Mores	Informal rules which are used to keep order within groups
Norms	Accepted ways of behaving within groups
Person	A human agent, a unique individual with an identity
Self identity	How we choose to define ourselves as people in terms of our selfhood
Socialisation	An ongoing process of development in which a person becomes a member of a culture
Structuration	The process by which the human agent (self) creates structures
Values	Something which is held in high regard with a community, such as a set of principles, morals or code of ethics

Data response questions

The point is, Des McHale insists, that the ethnic joke works because it cannot be true. 'Maths helps here. Chaos theory proves there is gross simplification in any model ... The fact is that all people are unique. If it is possible to pin down some racial characteristics, not every member of the group will share them all. The fact that racial differences are perceived rather than real is what makes the joke. It's the process that is funny, not the substance.'

There is some disagreement between us here. If it's the process that is important, why do we always pick on Irishmen?

Paul Vallely, **25 September, 1995. The Independent**.

During the 17th and 18th centuries Wales became more divided socially and culturally as far as rulers and ruled were concerned. The wealthiest and most politically powerful people in Wales were the great landowners who became increasingly English in culture and language as they looked to London and the universities of Oxford and Cambridge for their education and careers. They became more anglicised as they saw England as a land of opportunity and wealth. Many were members of the Anglican Church and they supported the Tory party in politics. On the other hand the poorest sections of society, the tenant farmers and labourers who worked on the land, spoke Welsh and held on to their traditional way of life.

Wallace and Johnson (1999:1)

This is an experimental Black cultural studies site set up because of a lack of resources on the Internet around questions of ethnicity, race, and gender among populations of the African Diaspora (though there are certainly some wonderful exceptions). We certainly do not make any claims for this collection of resources as exhaustive. To begin the task, the creators of this page decided to include bibliographical information on cultural workers working in such areas as Black literary criticism, Black popular culture, Critical Race Theory and film theory. The decision was made to assemble this information under the rubric 'Black Cultural Studies', a problematic and contested term which will no doubt require some revision. By deploying the term 'cultural studies' we take as a starting principle the work of Stuart Hall and The Birmingham Centre for Contemporary Cultural Studies.

http://www.tiac.net/users/thaslett/

a Using all the items, identify four features that could be said to contribute to one's sense of cultural identity. (2)

KNOWLEDGE AND
UNDERSTANDING

b What evidence is there in item B to suggest that the cultural traditions defined as 'Welshness' are not simply related to ethnicity? (5)

IDENTIFICATION AND
INTERPRETATION

c Offer a sociological explanation which might account for the popularity of the ethnic joke in many cultures. (6)

IDENTIFICATION AND | ANALYSIS AND
INTERPRETATION | EVALUATION

d Using all the items, assess why ethnicity is such a difficult area for sociologists to define satisfactorily. (9)

ANALYSIS AND
EVALUATION

Structured questions

a What are the identifying features of the 'new lad'? (2)

> **GUIDANCE** *A variety of features would do here; you should emphasise that laddishness is a male cultural form. It is associated with male magazines and masculinism, and represents values of drinking, sex and sport.*

IDENTIFICATION AND
INTERPRETATION

b Assess the extent to which popular culture represents a rejection of middle-class values. (9)

> **GUIDANCE** *This is a complex and interesting question because you are being asked to evaluate Marxist theory, most especially the views of the Frankfurt School. Marxists are trapped by the notion of 'false consciousness' and the Marxist belief that revolution is inevitable into looking for reasons why the revolution cannot happen, or for evidence that the working classes do in fact have revolutionary potential. In this case, many Marxists have suggested that popular culture rejects the middle-class values of the bourgeoisie. This is the view taken by Willis in his study of the lads of Hammertown. There is a tone of rebelliousness in much popular culture. However, popular culture is often produced for the masses and is not spontaneously generated by them. Think of the importance of* **The Sun** *newspaper produced by Rupert Murdoch. Popular culture has typifying features which represent sexism and often racism too. It rejects intellectualism and the currency of ideas about politics.*

ANALYSIS AND
EVALUATION

c Evaluate the suggestion that there is no such thing as youth culture. **(9)**

> **GUIDANCE** *This question asks you to assess whether young people have values, norms and mores which are radically different*
>
> | IDENTIFICATION AND INTERPRETATION | ANALYSIS AND EVALUATION |
> |---|---|
>
> *from those of the culture around them. There is much evidence that they do. Functionalists have spent considerable time looking for subcultures and using youth culture to explain phenomena such as crime and delinquency among young people. At some points in the history of the twentieth century there seem to have been spontaneous developments in youth culture, which have had a dramatic impact on the politics of a generation. Consider the case of the hippies of the late 1960s and early 1970s. The influence of that youth culture on music, clothing and social attitudes lingered on even when hippie styles became something of a joke.*
>
> *There are issues with youth culture in that it depends on whether there is such a thing as a subculture. This in itself is contested by many sociologists who reject the idea that young people have a culture which is at odds with mainstream society. Marxists tend to look at popular culture rather than subculture and identify a number of characteristics of popular culture which are cross-generational.*
>
> *There is a question as to whether youth culture is generation-based or whether other factors influence it. Consider the case of black youth culture; does it, as Gilroy, Rex and Hall suggest, represent not so much a culture of youth, but a rejection of the moral values of racism implicit in our society?*
>
> *Finally, you would need to consider the case of postmodernism. Postmodernists do not see that youth culture exists, but point to a fragmentation of all cultural forms so that people are free to adopt identities which suit them or to develop social identities based on their consumption of commercial products. Refer to the ideas of Baudrillard in this context. Certainly young people are product-orientated in the matter of clothing styles and so their styles are more distinctive, but older people tend to purchase larger and more expensive items such as motor cars.*

Essay titles

1 Outline and evaluate the usefulness of postmodernism to sociologists in understanding issues of culture and identity. **(25)**

2 Assess the view that the concept of 'woman' is socially constructed rather than biologically determined. **(25)**

3 Evaluate the view that culture is created for working people in order to dominate and control their lives. **(25)**

4 To what extent are humans agents in the creation of culture? **(25)**

5 Evaluate the suggestion that traditional definitions of gender are being rewritten in contemporary society. (25)

	IDENTIFICATION AND INTERPRETATION	ANALYSIS AND EVALUATION

GUIDANCE *There are a number of elements in this question and you would be advised to look at the wording very carefully before attempting an answer to what seems a deceptively simple question.*

First, it may be necessary to prove that gender is a social and not a biological definition. This only needs a sentence or two, but you do need to make clear that gender is learned behaviour. Secondly, if your answer considers only one of the genders, and you concentrate on femininity, then you are not answering the question. If the examiner had wanted you to write about women or men only, then this would have been specified in the title.

You need to decide on what the traditional definitions of gender are. These are blurred by class distinctions so that whatever was appropriate for a 'lady' in Victorian times would not have applied to a female domestic servant.

The next question for you to consider is whether there has been a rewriting of gender. There is evidence on both sides of the debate. Feminists tend to argue that females experience deprivation and exploitation, so they would not be willing to admit to the growth of the new man. However, there is evidence that new masculinities are available, which vary from the caring and sharing man to the new lad described by Segal, who rejects this element of his personality.

Females, however, have far greater opportunities in the wider world and there is evidence that in the late 1990s, traditional feminine qualities are much admired in the world of business where negotiating skills and non-confrontational tactics which women have used as part of their social armoury are valued.

Postmodernists argue that all notions of gender are being rewritten, so that the work of Foucault and 'queer theory' are of relevance. Gender is one of a number of potential identities that people can assume and a degree of gender bending as part of a fashion statement is tolerated. However, working-class culture still tends to reject this form of social experimentation.

The conclusion which you may arrive at is genuinely open. However, you should signal the conclusion which you intend to arrive at through the whole of your essay. It should not read as a final surprise, but hinted at in the evaluations which you make in the body of the essay.

Further reading and references

Taylor, P. (1997) *Investigating Culture and Identity* London, Collins Educational. This is a fascinating and accessible book by a well-known author of texts. It offers a thorough overview and contains a variety of interesting stimulus materials.

Hodder and Stoughton produces an excellent text by David Abbott (1999) in its *Access to Sociology* series, *Culture and Identity*, London, Hodder and Stoughton. It is more theoretical than Taylor's book in that there is little discussion of media texts, but the information is clearly presented, well explained and offers a simple overview of what is needed.

Burkitt, I. (1991) *Social Selves: Theories of the Social Formation of Personality*. Sage.

Jenkins, R. (1996) *Social Identity*. London, Routledge.

Internet sites

Enter the words 'cultural studies' into any search engine and you will reveal a vast number of interesting sites which will support your studies into the sociology of the media or help you with Media Studies if you are studying that with Sociology. A site which is still developing is the black cultural studies site at <http://www.tiac.net/users/thaslett>. Cultural Studies Central is useful and has a number of excellent links to sociological theory sites as well as more traditional media sites. Find it at <http://www.culturalstudies.net/>. Sarah Zupko's popular culture site has a wonderful array of links, articles and resources. It is at <http://www.popcultures.com/>.

Another amazing site which fully explores the nature of changing gender identities in the context of theory and popular culture is to be found at <http://www.leeds.ac.uk.icstheory-r.htm>. Judith Butler, Foucault and queer theory are particularly well addressed, as is postmodernism.

See also Deleuze & Guattari at http://www.uta.edu/english@apt/d&g/d&gweb.html

Bibliography

Abbot, D. (1999) *Culture and Identity*, London, Hodder and Stoughton.

Aitchison, D. and Carter, I. (1990) 'Battle for a Language'. *Geographical Magazine* (March).

Appadurai, A. (1992) 'Disjunction and Difference in the Global Cultural Economy' in Theory, Culture and Society 7: 295–310

Barker, M. (1981) *The New Racism*. London, Junction Books.

Bauman, Z. (1996) 'Culture on Praxis' in S. Hall and P. du Gay (Eds.) *Questions of Cultural Identity*. Routledge, London.

Blanchflower, D. and Sargent, J. (1994) cited in Bovey, *The Times* 20 March 1994.

Bordua, D. (1961) *Delinquent Subcultures: Sociological Interpretations of Gang Delinquency*. Annals of the American Academy of Political and Social Science 338 (November)

Brittan, A. (1989) *Masculinity and Power*. Oxford, Blackwell.

Burkitt, I. (1991) *Social Selves: Theories of the Social Formation of Personality*. London, Sage.

Crewe, I. (1992) 'Changing Votes and Unchanging Voters' in *Electoral Studies*, Dec.

Derrida, J. (1991) *A Derrida Reader: Between the Blinds*. Hemel Hempstead, Wheatsheaf.

Devine, F. (1992) *Affluent Workers Revisited: Privatism and the Working Class*. Edinburgh, Edinburgh University Press.

Falk, P. (1994) *The Consuming Body*. London, Sage.

Featherstone, M. (1990) *Consumer Culture and Postmodernism*. London, Sage.

Foucault, M. (1977) *Discipline and Punish*. London, Tavistock.

Gans, H. (1974) *Popular Culture and High Culture*. New York, Basic Books.

Garfinkel, H. (1967) *Studies in Ethnomethodology*. Cambridge, Polity Press.

Goffman, E. (1963) *Stigma: Notes on the Management of a Spoiled Identity*. Harmondsworth, Penguin.

Goffman, E. (1959) *Presentation of Self in Everyday Life*. Harmondsworth, Penguin.

Goldthorpe, J. H., Llewellyn, C. and Payne, C. (1987) *Social Mobility and Class Structure in Modern Britain*. Oxford, Oxford University Press.

Hall, S. (1992) 'New ethnicities' in J. Donald and A. Rattansi (Eds.) *Race, Culture and Difference*. London, Sage.

Hannerz, U. (1996) *Soulside: Inquiries into Ghetto Culture and Community*. New York, Columbia University Press.

Hebdige, D. (1979) *Subculture: The Meaning of Style*. London, Methuen.

Hechter, M. (1976) *International Colonialism: The Celtic Fringe in British National Development*. London, Collins.

Held, D. (1980) *Introduction to Critical Theory*. London, Hutchinson.

Held, D. (1995) 'Liberalism, Marxism and Democracy' in S. Hall et al. (Eds.) *Modernity and its future*. Cambridge, Polity Press.

Hoggart, R. (1957) *The Uses of Literacy*. London, Chatto and Windus.

Jenkins, R. (1996) *Social Identity*. London, Routledge.

Kellner, D. (1997) 'Culture' in D. Owen (Ed.) *Sociology after Postmodernism*. London, Sage.

Kirby, M. (1996) *Sociology in Perspective*. Oxford, Heinemann.

Kluckholm, C. (1951) 'The Concept of Culture' in D. Lerner and H. D. Lasswell (eds) *The Policy Sciences*. Stanford, Stanford University Press.

Lacan, J. (1977) *Ecrits: A Selection*. London, Tavistock.

Leach, E. (1964) *Rethinking Anthropology*. London, Althone Press.

Lockwood, D. (1958) *The Blackcoated Worker*. London, Allen and Unwin.

McLeish, D. (1993) *Key ideas in Human Thought*. London, Bloomsbury.

Marris, P. (1996) *The Politics of Uncertainty*. London, Routledge.

Marsh, I. (Ed.) (1999) *Sociology: Dealing with Data*. Harlow, Longman.

Mead, G. H. (1934, 1967) *Mind, Self and Society*. Chicago, University of Chicago Press.

Mead, M. (1935) *Sex and Temperament in Three Primitive Societies*. New York, Morrow.

Miles, R. (1989) *Racism*. London, Routledge.

Miller, D. and Swanson, D. (1958) *The Changing American Parent*. New York, Wiley.

Nixon, S. (1996) *Hard looks*. London, UCL Press.

Oakley, A. (1981) *Subject Women*. Oxford, Martin Robertson.

Pfohl, S. (1992) *Death at the Parasite Café: Social Science (Fiction) and the Postmodern*. Basingstoke, Macmillan.

Robertson, R. (1992) *Globalisation*. London, Sage.

Segal, L. (1990) *Slow motion: Changing masculinities, changing men*. London, Virago.

Sharpe, S. (1976) *Just Like A Girl*. Harmondsworth, Penguin.

Sklair, L. (1993) *Sociology of the Global System*. Baltimore, John Hopkins University Press.

Strinati, D. (1995) 'Postmodernism and Popular culture'. *Sociology Review*, April.

Taylor, P. (1997) *Investigating Culture and Identity*. Collins Educational.

Thornton, S. (1995) *Club Cultures, Music Media and Subcultural Capital*. Cambridge, Polity Press.

Wagner, P. (1994) *A Sociology of Modernity: Liberty and Discipline*. London, Routledge.

Wallerstein, I. (1991) 'The Construction of Peoplehood: Racism, Nationalism, Ethnicity' in Balibar, E, and Wallerstein, I. (eds) *'Race', Nation, Class*. London, Verso.

Williams, R. (1981) *Culture*. London, Fontana.

Williams, R. (1990) *What I Came to Say*. Cambridge, Cambridge University Press.

Willis, P. (1990) *Common Culture: Symbolic Work at Play in the Everyday Lives of the Young*. Milton Keynes, Open University Press.

Young, M. and Willmot, B. (1973) *The Symmetrical Family*. London, Routledge.

Mass Media and Popular Culture

This area covers:

■ The history and significance of the mass media in our society
■ The relationship of the media with audiences
■ The relationship of the media with society.

By the end of this unit, you should be able to:

■ show some understanding of the importance of the media in our daily and cultural lives

■ make judgements about the nature of the impact of the media on individual understandings of the social world

■ understand the differences and the similarities between the Marxist and the Pluralist views of how the media represent and create the social world for us.

Key terms

agenda-setting	mass media
centrality of the media	mediation
gate-keeping	passive and active audiences
Hypodermic Syringe	Cultural Effects
Uses and Gratifications	semiology

Area 5   Contents

Introduction

The aim of this section of the text is to look at the mass of theory that has gathered around the study of the media, with reference to the role that the media play in social change. The impact of the media on society as a whole, as well as the individual relationships which audiences may form with their chosen media products, will be studied. The relationship of the media with the creation of a variety of cultural identities, including the key elements of social differentiation, will be an underlying theme of this whole area.

Many commentators, particularly from the Marxist perspective, point to the possibility of social control via media production because of the power that the mass media have over the creation of social reality. Pluralists take a more optimistic viewpoint and suggest that the media merely reflect public concerns and interests. It is necessary therefore for students to evaluate the cultural values that may be attached to media products and to understand how moral and political ideologies may underlie both the creation of and the interpretation placed on media texts by audiences. Finally, the power and wealth of media companies and their role in creating a new, postmodern and global society will be investigated.

> **HINTS AND TIPS**   *You are advised to look at Area 4 on Society and Cultural Identities to see how popular culture is defined and explained. If you are following the Popular Cultures option of the OCEAC syllabus then you are advised to look at Areas 4 and 5 with some care. Both areas are extremely relevant to the same debate because it is considered by many writers from all perspectives that popular culture is both created and spread to people by the media.*

Defining the mass media

All forms of communication that reach a large number of people can be considered as part of the **mass media**. The media are normally referred to in the plural because there are so many possible forms of communication that may be seen, heard or used by people. However, when one is referring to a single form of communication such as television or radio, this is a medium.

To understand the significance of the media in our daily lives, attempt the following exercises before progressing through the chapter.

- Make a list of different forms of mass communication.
- List all the forms of mass media to which you are exposed in the space of one month.
- Make a guess as to how much time you spend on each form of the media, in the space of a month.
- Estimate how much money people within your household actually spend on the mass media in one month.

TASK

Hypothesis – 'The mass media are very significant in people's daily lives.'

Context – This hypothesis requires interpretative and qualitative methods rather than quantitative methods because you will offer a conclusion that relates to the meaning the media have for the people you are studying. There is a variety of media forms and you may have to remind people of the differing media available as you design your questionnaires or interview schedules. It may be that your interviewees' significant media forms are very different from your own and, perhaps, do not exist any longer as the pace of technological change has been very swift.

Method – Interview a number of people who are older than you about the significance of the media in their past lives. Ask about important memories and childhood exposure to cinema, television, magazines and radio. Write a short evaluative account of what you have discovered.

Evaluation – It is probable, unless you have a firm view of exactly what you mean by 'very significant', that the project will lose direction. Are you referring to emotions, social life, political events, or time spent in the company of the media? Are all media forms equally important at the various stages of people's lives?

A completed analysis may suggest that people spend an overwhelming amount of their physical time with the media. For instance, it is quite probable that a student will spend more time with the media than with family, friends, or course of study. This concept is known as the **centrality of the media**. It should underlie all individual thinking and analysis of the mass media.

It is thought by many that we create our personal views of reality from the mass media. The outside world is brought into our homes and it has begun to replace local knowledge and awareness. This concept is known as **mediation** and is associated with the work of Marshall McLuhan, among others. Theories of mediation suggest that the media have become so important in our lives that they replace many community-based forms of social and cultural life that would have existed in the past. This idea is referred to again in the section on global media (page 280). Many people probably

know more about the intimate daily lives and relationships of the fictional characters of an Australian soap opera than of their own neighbours. The theory is rather more complex in that it is believed that the ideologies or beliefs of powerful groups can be transmitted to ordinary people via their acceptance of the media.

A C T I V I T Y KS **WORKING WITH OTHERS**

| IDENTIFICATION AND INTERPRETATION | ANALYSIS AND EVALUATION |

Within groups, discuss the impact you think it would have on society if all media forms were to disappear tomorrow.

Begin the discussion with your personal lives and expand outwards to consider the effects on the political, social and economic spheres of life.

The current debates in the media

The questions that follow are intended to offer you a rough overview of some current media debates. You are advised to consider them carefully as you read the chapter and to ensure that you have your own carefully considered sociological evaluations in place before examination.

Political

- To what extent can the media influence our political viewpoints?

- Are the media capable of mind control?

- Are the media trivialising the important political issues of the day by turning them into 'sound-bites' of three minutes' duration or by looking at the images of politicians rather than their policies?

- Do certain people employed in the media act as 'gate-keepers' in the sense that important ideas and discussion topics are kept from public awareness?

Sociological

- Do the media create our culture by influencing the way that we are socialised and perceive the world?

- Do the media create our notions of reality by offering us a simplified and one-dimensional view of the world?

- To what extent do the media create social events according to their own need for increasing sensational news items?

- Are media messages one-way or do we have an impact on what messages the media offer us?

- Are we able to reject the messages of the media and create our own realities?

- Can the media act as an agency of 'agenda-setting' by allowing discussion of only certain issues at the expense of others?

Current affairs

- Are the media implicated in the perceived rise in the violence of our society?

- Do the mass media intrude too much on the lives of the rich and famous?

- Do the media create mass emotions and reactions to certain current events through moral panics or hysterical reactions?

- Should we allow people access to sexualised and/or violent and abusive behaviour via the mass media such as television, film or the Internet?

Organising thinking about the media

There are a number of broad sociological themes apparent in the study of the media.

- *How do the media themselves create a social construction of the world for us?* The areas of discussion here relate to studies of the control of information, the ownership of media institutions and the way that ideas and social groups are represented to us

- *How do we, as consumers, understand and receive the messages that we are given?* The main ideas to consider in this debate revolve around audience reception and the impact of the media on the way that we actually behave.

- *What impact do the large media companies and their products have on our culture?* The significant areas of debate here are the extent to which the media cause social and moral change and to what extent we are able to resist the consumerist messages that they offer us.

HINTS AND TIPS   *If study of the mass media and communication is to form an examination option for you, and you have not already done so, then you should read through Area 4.*

Development of the mass media

The development of industrialised society is inextricably linked with the development of the media. The entertainment and news media form one of our society's most significant industries. Marketing and media management is part of the consciousness of virtually everyone in any form of industry involved in dealing with the public in present-day society. However, the media were not always so significant in society.

Our culture has evolved into a media-obsessed and media-literate society from the infinitely less sophisticated and more élitist society of the Victorian era. Significant factors in the development of the media are discussed in the following paragraphs and students should develop this section with their own notes and personal research.

HINTS AND TIPS   *To understand the significance of the growth of the mass media and the impact of technology on popular culture, create a brainstrom diagram to show all the changes which have taken place in the media and popular culture since your own birth. When you start to think about it, you may be surprised at what has actually happened.*

Technological developments

The impact of the mass media has been argued to have been quite small on our society before the start of the twentieth century. Popular media forms at the turn of the century were limited by the technology available. They were dominated by print forms such as picture postcards, newspapers and printed sheets of piano music, which could be played by people in their own homes.

The early and middle part of the twentieth century was dominated by the development of the radio and of cinema. These media forms were of special significance during the Second World War (1939–45) because war news was essential to those millions of people involved in the progress of the war. The government supported the cinema industry because it could be used for **propaganda** purposes. Deliberate messages of hope and victory were circulated to keep up the morale of the population, to encourage people to fight and to work in factories. This idea will be considered again later in this area (page 256).

Figure 5.1   Media forms from the turn of the century may have been replaced as newer technology supersedes the old.

After the end of the Second World War in 1945 there was a massive growth in the production and significance of popular music records and television. People had more wealth than at any other stage in the century, there were high levels of employment and companies could invest in research into technology. Working hours had fallen and many people had more leisure than before the war. Think back to ideas of mediation at this point. Consider how strongly one could argue that the growth and ownership of media technology have moved away from ordinary people into the hands of the wealthy and powerful. This is a significant debate in cultural studies.

HINTS AND TIPS *Is there a strong argument to suggest that the development of the media relies just on the growth of technology?*

What other social factors might play a part in the development of the media?

To what extent does the rise of popular culture depend on improved technology, leisure and wealth among young people?

Move from home-produced media to major budget productions

This analysis forms part of the mediation debate and was of real significance in the early study of the media. Theory suggests that, in the past, communities would create their own culture and entertainment, which would be passed down through the community by oral tradition. In practice, anyone could therefore create a **cultural artefact** such as a song, picture or a story. Even in Victorian times, media productions were part of a community tradition: people bought commercially produced sheet music, but they actively participated in music production through the playing of instruments and communal singing.

The control of the production of cultural artefacts has moved from the people to an industry. Fewer people are involved in the production of media artefacts and the control of production is in the hands of the very wealthy who can afford to bankroll a project (a film may cost hundreds of millions to produce and actors may charge tens of millions for their services). Very few independent films, programmes or collections of music,

Figure 5.2 The notion of the teenager grew up at the same time as popular music was first aimed at a teenage market in the 1950s

which are not produced by major distributors, will gain a wide hearing from the public. This stance is supported by McLuhan (1964). The Marxist view is that those who control the means of production also control the ideas that are produced about society. The notion is known as the **bourgeois hegemony** and is linked to the writing of **Antonio Gramsci**. This debate will be revisited in this area when the ownership of the mass media is discussed.

A useful concept to introduce into your thinking at this point is the notion of **resistance**. This idea is used by many sociologists working in a variety of areas of study, particularly Stuart Hall and Heidi Safia-Mirza. It should also form part of your consideration of globalisation theory. Resistance theory suggests that many groups of people reject a dominant viewpoint or ideology in some way and create their own meanings. When studying the media, the suggestion is that some

Antonio Gramsci
(1891–1937)

Gramsci was an Italian from an educated family who grew up in conditions of some discomfort and poverty, due possibly to the malice of political enemies of his father. He suffered from poor health owing to a spinal condition and grew up sickly and malformed. His whole life was an example of tremendous personal, political, and physical bravery.

He was a journalist and became important in the Italian Communist Party. This was a particularly courageous act because it made him an enemy of the Fascist dictator of Italy, Mussolini. He must have been aware of what the full consequences of his actions and writings would be for him.

Gramsci was imprisoned, denied medical treatment, and forced to do hard labour. While in prison he completed notebooks of political and social theory on toilet paper and any other scraps that came to hand. He died of a neglected illness in prison and after his death these scraps of paper were smuggled out of the country by the friend who arranged his funeral

Mass literacy

There are two forms of literacy to consider here.

Literacy

Literacy can refer to the simple ability to read. Newspapers and comics could not reach a wide audience until the price of production was such that ordinary people could afford them, and until educational standards were high enough to ensure that enough people could actually read them.

Media literacy

This is a slightly more developed concept. The ability to recognise the codes and conventions of a media form is known as media literacy. We cannot necessarily understand what we are seeing on television or on the cinema until we recognise certain key conventions. For example, in many thrillers one or more of the following unattractive features may distinguish the villain: ugliness, fatness, a scar, the fact that she or he smokes, disability or a foreign accent. This idea is revisited when considering **semiology** and the language of signs.

people reject commercial media productions in favour of small-scale independent productions. The very existence of minority papers and magazines such as *Viz, 2000 AD* and *The Big Issue* or of independent film makers and music makers suggests that the major media groups do not fully control what we see and view. The Internet has an enormous number of sites, many supported by large corporations, but others are supported by single individuals who have access to a computer, a telephone line and the relevant technology.

ACTIVITY — WORKING WITH OTHERS

IDENTIFICATION AND INTERPRETATION

Ask children to draw a picture of either a scientist or a criminal. The strong possibility is they will produce pictures of men, using conventions typical of media stereotypes.

Illustrate the exercise with samples of pictures drawn from such an exercise.

ACTIVITY — WORKING WITH OTHERS

IDENTIFICATION AND INTERPRETATION

Consider the variety of popular music forms the people in your study group enjoy. How many prefer 'cult' or 'independent' music styles to commercially produced 'pop'? How easy is it to find radio music programmes that concentrate on independent or non-commercial popular music? This analysis could extend to other media productions such as films and print-based media.

A simple quantitative survey using a simple questionnaire would probably be enough for this type of exercise.

The content of the mass media

The media have the power to create an understanding of the world for us. We may feel that we know a great deal about people, and cultures, not our own: for example the USA. How reliable is this 'knowledge'? The answer is that it is not. Two factors will affect the 'knowledge' that we have.

■ The first factor is the media forms that we choose to use. However, people are employed to select what is broadcast or written. They are **editors**.

■ The second factor influencing the knowledge that we have of the world outside our own is the choice of the editor of the media form. This last concept may be referred to as **selection**.

Gate-keeping

This idea first appeared in the work of David White in the 1950s. It lingers in importance in media debates. A **gate-keeper** is a powerful and important figure who selects the content of news production. This person will apply the prejudices of class and politics to the selection of news content. Important information may never enter public discussion because an informal process of censorship is applied. Critics of this view suggest that it implies paranoia and conspiracy theory. After all, there is a variety of sources of information available to people and the media are in competition to provide us with news.

ACTIVITY   *KS* **INFORMATION TECHNOLOGY**

KNOWLEDGE AND
UNDERSTANDING

What types of story do you feel would not be published or broadcast? Look at <www.drudgereport.com>. This site deals with the seamier side of American politics and has a reputation for considerable accuracy in its reporting. It is also somewhat coarse. Many of the stories could not be printed in regular journals.

Agenda-setting

This is a broader view of a similar process, which is related to cultural effects theory. It is often part of the discussion of the impact of the media on power and politics. It is associated with the work of Steven Lukes, neo-Marxist, in his considerations of power. It is also important to the work of the Glasgow Media Group and of Stuart Hall. The view is that the ideology of the newspaper owners and the journalists who collect the stories of news events imposes a structure on the nature of the questions they ask. The argument is that a pro-government, pro-employer line is taken in news broadcasts, which portrays critics of the official view as 'trouble-makers' or deviant.

A typical agenda-setting argument would be that, while people are arguing in the media about whether schools are 'good' or 'bad', important debates on education are ignored. They may be relegated to the broadsheet newspapers where fewer people have access to the discussion. The relationship of this view to Marxist thought and theory is clear.

Critics of the agenda-setting argument include pluralists, who suggest that the sheer variety of media productions ensures a wide coverage of all viewpoints. Television companies and the BBC are under contractual obligations to remain impartial in any debate. Critics of the reporting of the BBC come from both left and right of the political spectrum, arguing that the BBC favours the opposing political grouping to the one that they support. This, the BBC suggests, is proof that debate is impartial.

Glasgow University Media Group

Greg Philo and the Glasgow University Media Group (GUMG) have done some of the most important work in this area in a series of publications. Although the perspective used by the GUMG is broadly Marxist, the methodology was drawn from interactionism and involved detailed content analyses of news broadcasts and newspaper coverage of events.

The members of the GUMG identified in news-based texts 'codes' or patterns of thought that are typically supportive of traditional and conservative analysis. Writers and commentators are not critical of powerful groups in society. They use written and verbal language and non-verbal language and sets in a value-laden way that implies disapproval of those who are in dispute with the official line of thought. The position put forward in the first major publication, *Bad News*, was that reporters reflected the official government line because they felt that they were reflecting public debate, but that they were actually able to set the agenda. The GUMG identified trade unionists and anti-nuclear protesters as being particular victims of biased reporting and was later concerned with the degree of impartiality of coverage of the Falklands War (1982). This discussion is typical of its time, as the early 1980s were a period of great political turmoil and polarisation of viewpoint, due to the often confrontational political style of the then Prime Minister, Margaret Thatcher.

Editorial control over the content of the media

There is a central question in this debate that relates to the content of the media. Whenever accusations are made to the effect that newspapers or the television are putting out too much violence, sex or gossip the answer offered by media companies is that violence and sex is what people want. Sex and violence ensure high media profits. Many people accused the tabloid press of exploiting images of the late Princess of Wales: however, even after her death her face on a magazine cover ensures a vast increase in sales.

Many factors affect editorial decisions. Studies such as those by Galtung and Ruge (1973) and Clara (1972) offer these suggestions:

- Ethnocentricity – We like our news stories to be about events in our own areas and countries.

- Personality – We enjoy stories about people and many events will be reported from an individualistic perspective.

- Visual appeal – Stories often sell because there is a good photo opportunity.

The more popular the newspaper or news programme, the less political is the news content generally. The debate can be summarised in the most simple of terms as agreement with one of the following sociological perspectives. Your evaluation of the discussion should therefore take one of the positions below, or offer a view at some intermediate point. Together they are incompatible.

ACTIVITY   KS **PROBLEM SOLVING**

IDENTIFICATION AND INTERPRETATION

❝ News values are (unwritten) judgements that editors and journalists place upon a particular event in order to create a story about that event. For example, royal events generally have high news value. People are interested in reading about what the royal family does and thinks. More 'gossipy' stories about the royals will, however, hold less value for a quality paper; they are more likely to appear in a popular paper because they are more in keeping with the paper's housestyle.

Connell et al. (1996) *Examining the Media*

Look at the following imaginary news stories
1   Improved investment in banking means some people are more wealthy
2   A footballer and a member of the Royal Family are in a sex scandal
3   Changes in the education system in this country mean that fewer subjects are to be taught in schools

Which story would you put on the front cover of a popular or tabloid newspaper if you were trying to sell as many copies as possible?
Which story is most important in terms of effect on our individual lives?

- **Pluralistic**   The media are responding to the most base elements in public tastes by providing us with a diet of gossip and sex because that is what audiences demand.

- **Marxist**   A deliberate conspiracy is being waged by the owners and editors to debase and degrade public taste in order to stop people challenging the dominant ideology of capitalist society.

Semiology and the sociology of meaning

Semiology is a term associated with the writings of Saussure. It refers to the process of reading meaning into signs. Those involved in the creation of media products create images and rely on the audience to decode those images and create meanings. For instance, if you see a picture of the Eiffel Tower at the start of a film then you, as audience, understand immediately that the main action is to take place in Paris. This ability to read or decode signs is known as media literacy and is a concept that you have already met.

The ideas that lie behind semiology and the sociology of meaning are partly drawn from micro-sociology, especially interactionalism and ethnomethodology. Often the semiological interpretations of media texts which you read in textbooks and journals are applied forms of the analysis suitable to critical studies of literature texts, with some sociological context applied. One of the key texts used as a basis for the methodology is Judith Williamson's *Decoding Advertisements* (1978).

However, if we acknowledge that the media can create a social construct then we must understand the mechanisms by which this process takes place. The example of the Eiffel Tower was simplistic. Far more sophisticated images can occur in the media, and they are understood at a level which is not always conscious.

HINTS AND TIPS *We tend to associate physical beauty with moral goodness for all characters in media productions so that the good-looking man is also the brave hero. There is a further dimension to this simple analysis in that moral goodness is often equated with fragility, thinness, and passivity in females (think of the currently attractive females of popular TV programmes). Sexually provocative females often represent bad people.*

ACTIVITY   KS**COMMUNICATION**

IDENTIFICATION AND INTERPRETATION	ANALYSIS AND EVALUATION

Make a collection of pictures of cartoon characters from Disney films or computer games. How do you recognise characters as being good or evil? What are the key characteristics of 'good' people or 'bad' people in children's cartoons? What significance does this hold for our cultural and social interpretations of ugliness, fatness and disability?

Media and ideology

An ideology is a belief system. In the case of the media, the sociological debate is one that hinges on the idea that the media are used to influence people's ideas and beliefs about the world. The debate over media productions and ideology is an old one because the media have been used to disseminate ideas as much as to tell stories from the beginning of story-telling itself. There are two elements to the debate:

- The media contain ideas: this makes them **ideological**.

- The media can be used deliberately to sway people's opinions and manipulate them. This makes them tools of **propaganda**.

The media certainly have been used and manipulated by governments. This is most openly discussed in books on wartime propaganda. Some excellent writers and artists were employed specifically to produce propaganda through the Second World War in Britain. Although the political message of much pro-Nazi propaganda art and cinema is more than a little repugnant to modern thinking, commentators are often disconcerted at its quality.

The question of whether the government can manipulate ideas through the media alters in significance and meaning in our society. If the media are used as an effective ideological tool during times of war, when people are aware of what is happening to them, what is possible when people are not aware and the message is not so open? Are we still in the hands of the media as manipulators and conspirators to keep us silent against injustice?

- Marxists are particularly interested in this debate because it is especially associated with their concern with the covert nature of social control.

- Feminists are interested in the ideology of gender as it is presented in the media because it is so linked with the ways in which we are socialised into behaviour patterns.

- Pluralists have less interest in this debate except to refute the views of Marxists because they tend to believe that the media represent a variety of possible interests and interest groups.

This over-simplifies the discussion in many respects. It underlies virtually all writing on the media and culture. It is certainly part of the audience debate and this type of thinking underpins discussion on the significance of media ownership and representation theory.

The work of Gramsci is particularly important in this debate. He introduced the concept of hegemony to analyses of ideology. He developed Marxist theory from a simple economic control over society to the notion that ideas and values are very much part of the way in which we are controlled. We can be coerced or threatened into obeying the powerful, but we retain the ability to resist. However, if people can control our minds, we willingly accept their view of the world and are unable to resist their power over us.

The question of ideology is linked to the idea of mediation in the work of John Thompson. He seems to suggest that ideas are used to support the viewpoint of dominant groups in society and that the media are particularly effective because they are a one-way mode of communication: we cannot answer back effectively. We can only refuse to purchase.

The Glasgow University Media Group, in *Bad News* and *More Bad News*, has produced work that is relevant to most of the debates in this area. It is generally the GUMG view that an underlying ideology which represents the interests of the dominant groups in our society is offered to us under the guise of disinterested reporting.

ACTIVITY   KS COMMUNICATION

IDENTIFICATION AND INTERPRETATION	ANALYSIS AND EVALUATION

As an illustration, science fiction movies during the 1950s and 1960s often acted as a contemporary commentary on the Cold War. This was a period when the USA and the USSR were the two dominant world powers. Americans feared that Communists would take over the free world and so Hollywood films were obsessed with the idea of invasion and mind control. The imagery of popular films such as *Invasion of the Bodysnatchers* was more closely allied to the perceptions at the time of the Communists as hidden mind-controlling invaders than to ideas that were current about possible alien life forms.

Watch the 1997 film *Independence Day*. What beliefs (or ideologies) about present-day America and its relationship with other countries can you see embodied in the story? Practise semiology and look particularly at symbols of American geography, power and politics as they appear in the film and its trailers.

Popular culture

Many writers from both extreme right-wing and extreme left-wing positions have expressed concern about the creation of a mass culture by large companies for the large mass of the people. Much of the debate centres on a series of common assumptions about the quality and merit of certain types of cultural productions and their impact on the people who accept them. These assumptions are either made or challenged by academics. Reduced to their most absolute and simplistic terms, they are:

1 Cultural artefacts produced by working-class people for themselves are 'good'.
2 Cultural artefacts produced by major media companies for working-class people are 'bad'.
3 Cultural artefacts produced by educated and intelligent people are 'good'.
4 Cultural artefacts that are difficult to understand, radical or conceptual are generally 'bad' unless the creator is male and long dead or persecuted.

To illustrate the point, Steve Goodman (1997) pointed out that many media educators believe that television viewing time should be limited for children in order to promote 'good viewing habits'. Here, a critical value judgement about the nature and impact of popular television programmes on the young is being made. Could you imagine a parallel situation in which an English teacher would advocate seriously limiting reading among the young in order to promote 'good reading habits'?

Negative views of the mass culture debate	Positive views of the mass culture debate
The mass production of media products will result in the loss of originality *Hannah Arendt*	Majority culture is not always in bad taste, this view reflects the value judgements of critics *R. Williams*
There has been a loss of quality in the cultural productions of popular art *Bell*	How can we decide whether something is good or bad? It is difficult to categorise media and cultural products *Halloran*
Mass society creates the conditions for totalitarian thought to develop *Kornhauser*	People are not merely passive consumers of mass media products *Strinati*
Mass culture is an instrument of political domination *McDonald*	Popular media and art forms allow ordinary people to participate in cultural productions which once would have been the province of the wealthy *Benjamin*
Traditional British culture is being swamped by American cultural traditions *Hoggart*	There is a breakdown of the difference between popular culture and high art *Harvey*

Adapted from interpretations in Strinati (1995)

Figure 5.3 Perspectives on the popular culture debate

HINTS AND TIPS   *If we are honest, many of us prefer not to think too hard about the world and thoroughly enjoy popular cultural artefacts such as game shows or chat shows. Some people may, however, feel slight shame in admitting to popular cultural tastes and may feel that they 'ought' to enjoy political documentary and serious debate. Others of course will genuinely prefer certain types of media production over others. See the discussion of Ang's work in Strinati (1995: 47)*

Postmodernism and culture

The nature of popular culture itself is essentially a very postmodern debate. The most recent social issue is the consideration of ways in which we are defined and self-defining by consumption patterns rather than beliefs and moral stances. This discussion is well covered in this area. In terms of cultural analysis, there is the suggestion that instead of sharing cultures and values with our neighbours and communities, a global culture is developing which is ironically best described as separatist, shallow, individualistic and consumerist. We are unified across the world by our spending desires and by our collective failure to share any deep moral or social purpose.

A C T I V I T Y   KS COMMUNICATION, WORKING WITH OTHERS

ANALYSIS AND EVALUATION

Using a combination of open and closed questions, ask a sample group of respondents if they enjoy *The Sun* or *The Guardian*, enjoy *Panorama* or *Gladiators*, enjoy rock bands or opera.

Now ask members of the same sample which of the alternatives presented is 'better' or 'more valuable'.

Explore the reasons they offer for their preferred choices. How do your findings develop the impact of the media on the audience debate?

What do your findings tell you about why popular culture produced by leading media companies is so popular?

You could develop this work by considering whether focus groups or individual interviews would give you better and more reliable results.

A C T I V I T Y   KS INFORMATION TECHNOLOGY

KNOWLEDGE AND UNDERSTANDING

For a fuller discussion of the media and ideas to help you understand the conceptual side of postmodernism and semiology see Daniel Chandler's detailed and interesting Internet site at Aberystwyth University. Watch out for the little in-jokes! There are also some very useful links to other sites. The address is <http://www.aber.ac.uk/~dgc>

Moral panics, folk devils and youth culture

Media and cultural studies arguably began in this country with the seminal work *Folk Devils and Moral Panics* by Stanley Cohen, published in 1972. He concentrated on small youth culture groups: the 'Mods and Rockers' of the early 1960s. Boys from London used to congregate in seaside resorts within easy reach of the city on summer holiday and Bank Holiday weekends. There were scuffles between and within some groups which were reported in various newspapers in a highly coloured way, suggesting that seaside towns were being torn apart by rival gangs of teenage boys. The stories actually became true in later violent scenes in seaside resorts.

Cohen's analysis, much simplified, suggests that the media are under pressure to sell their products and tend to simplify and exaggerate stories because we like strong and easy story lines. They tend to aim for and appeal to 'the man in the saloon bar' as their typical reader.

A **moral panic** is an atmosphere of panic that the media can create about an issue relating to cultural and moral values which has caught the public imagination – violent children, single mothers, Saddam Hussein or certain media products and personalities. The target of the hate, worry and fear is known as the **folk devil**.

This is the spiral of amplification of deviance as applied by Cohen to the Mods and Rockers. This process is known as Reification of deviance or Self-fulfilling prophecy.

1   Problem/fashion/trigger – boys seek fun
2   Solution to trigger – go to seaside resort
3   Reaction from media – activities exaggerated
4   Moral panic – public becomes anxious
5   Reaction from law and order – authorities become confrontational to be seen to be 'doing something'
6   Isolation of deviant group – boys feel persecuted and anti-order
7   Confirmation of stereotype – people live up to their image as 'hard troublemakers'
8   Boredom with story

In cultural terms, the media can create a fashionable behaviour by condemning and criticising it. It gains significance and momentum so that people are attracted to and imitate the behaviour. A cultural form is therefore **reified** or made real through media coverage. Curiously, media forms can end up demonising other media forms and creating a hysterical moral backlash upon flimsy evidence. The popular newspapers, for instance, often criticise television and film for being too sexually explicit or too violent.

ACTIVITY   **KS COMMUNICATION**

KNOWLEDGE AND UNDERSTANDING

To develop this point, it might be useful to collect a cuttings file of stories that offer examples of sensationalised reporting of criminal cases and which represent modern folk devils as they are being created.

Ethnicity and moral panics

Much work in this area is associated with the Centre for Contemporary Social Studies at Birmingham University. Stuart Hall is the most noted personality and his analysis suggests that Marxism predicts crises in the economic state of capitalism. Eventually, there will be an enormous crisis known as the *Coming Crisis of Capitalism*, which will precipitate the overthrow of capitalism by the proletariat. However, there may be smaller crises before the big one. Hall believes that such crises have already occurred, but that the media serve the interests of the state by creating moral panics. There is a broader discussion of this work in Area 12. His analysis concerned the origin of the term 'mugging' and its association with young black men. He claimed that a racist press during the 1970s sensationalised street crime, creating a folk devil of the mugger. This effectively diverted attention away from the dire economic problems faced by the state, and the emphasis on race divided the working class, who no longer presented a unified resistance to the rule of the state. You should note the importance of resistance theory which is referred to elsewhere in this area.

The mass media and representation theory

Part of the analysis of how the media create a social construction of the world revolves around the issue of how members of minority groups in society are represented in the media. This is a particularly serious issue for the 'disempowered', who are not often a part of the organisational structure of companies producing media products.

One of the key features of the representation debate is the notion of the stereotype. This is drawn from interactional theory where the symbol is so significant. The argument is that the media must convey almost instant understanding to viewers and readers of texts. This is often done in the form of a **visual code**. These codes are instantly understood and read. Their use leads to a shallow portrayal of character in which signs and visual cues take the place of real understanding. This process can be seen at its most obvious in racist jokes. For example:

- a woman wearing a short skirt will be understood by an audience as sexually promiscuous
- a person who is to be seen as stupid or naive will be portrayed as Irish

The real significance of the stereotypical portrayal of a social or ethnic group can be seen in the films of the Nazis, where Jews were always shown as evil villains. Joseph Goebbels, the Nazi propaganda minister, was able to dehumanise Jewish people to such an extent by playing on the popular prejudices of people that the 'Final solution' or Holocaust could be put into effect. Until very recently, the 'black guy' hardly ever survived to the final reel of a Hollywood action film and never got a white girl. Mario van Peebles, the film director, suggests that this situation changed only when Hollywood became aware that Afro-Americans had become economically significant as a market for media products. Beverly Skeggs and other writers are concerned not just with how certain groups are represented but also with the way that we should consider the nature of 'other'. This is also an important question in terms of the sociology of cultural identity. For example, to claim to be Welsh or Scottish is to define oneself as not English and the English are therefore 'other' in this context.

The media often use this notion of the other to ignore or misrepresent social groupings. 'Buddy movies' offer a case in point. The hero will have a close same-sex friend whom he loves dearly, for example in the *Lethal Weapon* series. The hero must therefore be defined as rampantly heterosexual and not 'other' or homosexual, despite the nature of his love for his male friend. Heroes cannot be homosexual: homosexuals are 'other' and not heroic. There have been changes so that more positive images of homosexual men and women are available, in contrast to British films of the 1950s and 1960s, such as the *Carry On* series of films. In these, certain characters were extremely camp and overtly homosexual in their behaviour, but were shown pursuing or being pursued by women as a source of their humour. Homosexuality could not be mentioned in such films, because the act was still a crime, and men were ashamed to admit to their true feelings.

Gender and body image

Much writing on gender is female-oriented because the discussion was opened by feminists. Often it is concerned with seeing the female as a 'victim' of a mediated process, where women are reduced to mere body parts or domestic labourers. Meehan, in Trowler (1996), offers such an analysis by categorising female stereotypes on TV into a number of 'types'. In Britain in the 1970s, McRobbie looked at the socialisation of teenage girls and conventions of teen magazines and discovered that exaggerated romance was a key to much of the literature. Girls are offered an escapist fantasy, which is far removed from the reality of their own experiences but which eventually traps them into domestic life.

This type of work is still relevant today, when there is pressure on women to conform to social stereotypes or notions of beauty. It remains an issue related to questions of unattainable body image and the distorted attitude towards food that many women have. This was an area explored by Naomi Wolf in *The Beauty Myth* and Susie Orbach's *Fat is a Feminist Issue*. However, the media industry has responded to societal changes in the roles of women. Women are now visible in a variety of authoritative and dominant roles, which would have seemed impossible when the original debate was begun. Interestingly, Susan Faludi, a prominent feminist, has pointed to a process where there has been a rejection of positive images of women in the media so that the villains in films such as *Basic Instinct* are independent and assertive career women. Increasingly, there is concern at the way that males are also being trapped into a concern with masculine body image as they lose their sense of gender identity and are threatened with the rise of feminism. This idea is also associated with Faludi and is extremely well covered in Area 4 on Society and Cultural Identities.

> **HINTS AND TIPS**   *Your discussion of gender representation and socialisation under examination conditions should ideally mention the fact that there are two genders, both of which are gaining their notions of correct gender behaviour from the media. Girls may well be victims, but boys are under similar pressure from concepts of masculinity, and their response to media images may result in social handicap and criminality.*

Bea Campbell, in her book *Goliath*, is very concerned with gender issues. She points out that in many modern families there is no stable male figure with whom boys can identify. The media view of masculinity has come to take the place of a realistic role model. The process operates something like this:

- Working-class culture has long emphasised masculinity.

- In the past, masculinity was defined for many as the ability to do a day's hard physical labour.

- The hard manual labouring work in factories, which was previously done by men, has been superseded by automation and light labour. At the same time, traditional family patterns have given way to looser family structures with women at the centre.

- Boys see women as carers, so to be a man requires a sense of being 'other', which is 'not a woman' and femininity must be rejected.

- Cultural notions of masculinity are changing under these social pressures. Arnold Schwarzenegger and stars of other ultra-violent movies offer an **ideology of masculinity** which is brutal, dominant, and forceful.

- These media representations have become a masculine role model for young men in the poorest sectors of society.

Ethnicity

The question of ethnicity has a number of elements to consider. Some strands will be identified for you.

1 Ethnic minorities are invisible
2 Ethnic minorities are objects of charity
3 Ethnic minorities are stereotyped as criminals and offenders

The first dimension is that ethnic minority groups are often invisible on mainstream television. Despite a large ethnic minority community in Australia and in British inner city areas, some ethnic minority groups are rarely seen in soap opera. This is beginning to change, but good parts for black actors are hard to find. Certain ethnic groups, such as the ethnic Chinese or South Asian, are ignored by the media. Thriving cultural traditions are marginalised and, although films made in Bombay (known as 'Bollywood' films) are enormously popular, they are not generally seen in many mainstream cinemas. This may change as the Asian market grows in commercial significance. See the 'Sociology in Practice' section on page 273.

African and Asian children are often represented as being the victims of famine. This negative imagery creates a view of the peoples of developing countries as charity cases and the helpless recipients of western aid programmes. This image is shallow. It encourages a stereotypical perception of ethnicity that obscures a much deeper and more penetrating analysis. Many commentators, particularly in the development debate, see the western world as in an exploitative relationship with poorer countries. Many are paying far more in debts to western banks than they receive in development and charity aid. It could be argued that they are subsidising western economies!

A third analysis of the relationship between ethnicity and the media is the way in which racial stereotypes are encouraged and developed by the media. American blacks are often used to portray drug dealers or prostitutes, and the villain will often speak with an English accent or be played by an English actor with a false accent. This can be a very insidious process because it is sometimes difficult to recognise until it is pointed out. Better quality programmes do not use stereotypes and so commentators are forced into generalisations when discussing film and television. It is always easy to quote the exception to the rule; for

Figure 5.4 Negative imagery may show non-Europeans as victims in order to gain money through sympathy donations. They may ignore more positive aspects of the work of the charity or of the life of some people in Third-World countries.

instance the black police sergeant is also a stereotype of thrillers. Film-makers are aware of it enough to consciously tease an audience. For instance, in *Alien Resurrection* the survivors are all those who would normally be expendable in a film: the woman, the black, the cripple, and the robot!

In this context, note the work of Stuart Hall et al. in *Policing the Crisis*, where the creation of a new concept of street crime, 'mugging', was created by the media in the 1970s and was promptly associated with disaffected black youths.

Age and ability

Semiological analysis shows us that a scar, old age, ugliness or disability is often a code for wickedness, especially in children's drama. Erving Goffman, in his book *Stigma*, looked at the ways in which disabled people are defined by their disability and assumptions are made about character. This discussion is more fully developed under the heading of non-culpable stigma in Area 12. In the media, disabled people fall into two categories:

■ as victims of age or disability

■ as evil, their outward ugliness being a manifestation of inner wickedness

The first image is typical of many charity benefit shows, such as *Children in Need* or *Telethon*, where people are urged to offer money to the 'less fortunate'. Many people in radical disability groups consider this as a massive insult from an industry which employs few who do not conform to western conventions of beauty and appearance. Perhaps the media could campaign for the rights of the disabled to use public transport? They could offer wider employment to disabled actors in plots where the character is to the forefront and not the disability.

> **HINTS AND TIPS**   The Austen Powers films of the early 1990s have a great deal of fun satirising the media convention of equating evil with scars and disability with the character of Dr Evil and his henchmen.

ACTIVITY   **KS PROBLEM SOLVING**

IDENTIFICATION AND INTERPRETATION

a List notable villains in the James Bond series of films.

b How many of them are disabled, disfigured or deformed in some way?

Class

There are two elements to the discussion in this area:

■ How are different social classes depicted in the media?

■ How are media products marketed to people of different social classes?

Many of the points made about stereotypes also apply to the depiction of social class, but it is an under-researched area generally. Primarily the problems relate to the nature of defining class but social class is a major theme in British drama and a key element of British situation comedy. To illustrate this point, one need only attempt to identify the number of programmes and comedy series on television which satirise the working class or 'snobs' and 'posh' people.

There is an increasing number of analyses of the marketing of the media and audience response and interpretation. Buckingham (1993) strongly argued in favour of seeing the audience of media texts as active in the sense that a number of variables including social class will affect the interpretation that people put on what they view. Much of the work in this area has concentrated on how notions of gender are developed by the media but social class is obviously a strong variable, if only because it affects the choice of media consumed. Tabloid newspapers are consciously marketed at the working classes who are likely to be less highly educated; the market for broadsheets is generally among educated people who tend to be found among professional middle-class groups in society. This theory can be tested by listing and pricing the types of products advertised in each style of newspaper.

ACTIVITY   KS PROBLEM SOLVING

IDENTIFICATION AND INTERPRETATION

Fill in this chart in your own time. Remember that his is a matter of opinion rather than fact and you should be able to support your views. How easy was it to think of positive or negative images typical of certain social groups?

Social Category	Positive Image	Negative Image
old woman	Miss Marple	Dot Cotton
old man	Last of the Summer wine	Victor Meldrew
teenage boys		young tearaways in The Bill
homosexual men		
working class person	London's Burning	Keeping up appearances
middle class people		
women		
men		
disabled people		
black/ethnic minority people	drug dealers	the police in The Bill nurses in Casualty

The impact of the media on audiences

Having seen how the media can create notions of reality via the building-up and maintenance of stereotypes, we must now consider the impact of the media on those who view it. The debate centres on the ability of the audience as a whole to accept or reject media messages and can be defined as being between views of audience as active or passive receivers of media messages.

There are four main theories that discuss the relationship between the media and the audience.

The Hypodermic Syringe model of media reception

This view of the impact of media on audiences is very widely held and is often attractive to those who come to the analysis of the media for the first time. This point alone should make you cautious about accepting the ideas without considering their full implications.

One of the major problems of Marxism is the prediction that the working classes would rise against their oppressors and create a classless society. This has obviously not yet happened in any society. Marxists are left with the analytical problem of explaining the failure of the working classes to develop class consciousness. This dilemma, applied to the media, leads Marxists to the view that the media are a way in which the bourgeoisie can stun the working classes into submission by their domination of the creation of ideas. The media, from this perspective, are conceived as a drug which will offer shallow pleasure and stop the users from being fully aware of the world about them. Thus, the workers fail to develop their understanding of their position in the class structure and the promised revolution does not materialise: instead of worrying about their true position in a capitalist society, they are harmlessly concerning themselves about which film stars are sleeping together.

The Hypodermic Syringe model was widely held in the 1930s by members of the Frankfurt School, a group of German thinkers and writers who escaped persecution from the Nazis by moving to America. It was offered as a solution to the problem of how the Fascists had managed to gain power in Germany. Similar ideas were still current in the 1970s in the work of writers such as Hannah Arendt and Herbert Marcuse.

There are a number of widely held criticisms of this viewpoint.

- It sees audiences as passive receivers of the media.

- It ignores the extent to which people can, and do, resist the ideas and representations offered to them.

- Feminists, such as Meehan, McRobbie and more recently Naomi Wolf, often target media presentations of femininity.

- If the media are in fact a drug that induces a hypnotic inability to challenge the ideology which they offer, how are some people able to challenge these dominant perceptions?

A 'them' and 'us' perspective in the writings of Marxist academics is therefore apparent. They could be accused of patronising the very class of people who are to form the basis of the new society they wish to create.

The Hypodermic Syringe model would suggest that the media are a homogeneous group, all passing on the same message to a passive and mindlessly receptive audience. This severely underestimates the variety of media messages available and ignores the social world of those who receive the media, according to Lazarsfeld (in Gurevitch et al. 1982: 39).

Hypodermic Syringe models also fail to recognise that a great deal of social interaction takes place in and around the media. We are able to choose which media to purchase and take active steps to purchase certain products. Much social and media discourse takes place around media products so that intertextuality is significant. **Intertextuality** is the reference in one media text to another. Entire magazines are devoted to the discussion of television stories or films. Social interaction in the workplace will often centre on discussion of events on television the previous evening.

Obviously the relationship between the media and the audience is more complex than the Hypodermic Syringe model would suggest. To reject this position totally is to ignore the possible extent to which we are influenced by the agendas of media agencies.

The Two-step Flow model of audience reception

This model of audience reception is offered by writers such as Katz and Lazarsfeld, who studied social groups. They were critical of the Hypodermic Syringe model but they still see the message of the media as essentially a media-to-audience process. The smooth flow of the message from the media to the audience is filtered through the social groups to which people belong. Certain people within a community act as opinion leaders and others follow their lead.

This perspective is not often quoted in modern British texts as it is essentially psychological in its analyses and is rooted in various studies of American small-town society. It is, however, more widely discussed in American media studies texts where the ideas remain influential. It also tends to see the audience relationship with the media as passive, but it remains useful to understand the significance of the discussion of media in society and underlies the importance and significance of media criticism.

Writers, such as Katz, who work in this tradition often adopt a psychological testing approach but have failed to prove that the media do actually have an influence on behaviours in either the short or the long term. While links probably exist between behaviour and the media, it is impossible to prove conclusively that they do, given that people respond to stimuli in individual ways.

HINTS AND TIPS   You are strongly advised **not** to attempt to prove direct links between the media and certain forms of behaviour such as anorexia or violence in any direct way in coursework, as the attempt is almost certainly doomed to failure. Common sense suggests there may be a link; however, the burden is on you to **prove** the link, which is virtually impossible.

Uses and Gratifications theory

This theory offers an active view of audience interaction with the media. It is associated with the work of McQuail and Lull in particular. Audiences are not merely passive receivers of media output but actively seek media texts for specific and purposeful reasons. This theory is individualistic in that it is acknowledged that people have differing and personal reactions to media products and texts. According to McQuail (1998), our use of the media satisfies personal and social needs, the most important of these being:

- **Entertainment or diversion**   We are able to forget our daily lives and become immersed in a media product.

- **Identification**   Storylines will appeal to our personal, social and emotional needs, offering us an insight into and a parallel with our own life situations.

- **Personal identity**   Programmes are often aimed (narrowcast) at particular social groups and we gain a sense of self from our use of media products. People who form fan clubs would identify themselves in terms of their media consumption.

- **Surveillance**   People are aware of events in their communities and the wider world through media usage of local newspapers or news bulletins. Magazines such as *Hello!* might satisfy a need for knowledge of the lives of celebrities.

Uses and Gratifications theory can be simplified in terms of

- What media do I enjoy and why?
- What do I learn about myself from the media?
- What social identity do I gain from what I consume?
- What do I learn about the outside world?

ACTIVITY KS **WORKING WITH OTHERS, COMMUNICATION**

IDENTIFICATION AND INTERPRETATION	ANALYSIS AND EVALUATION

Interview other people about their own personal use of and need for media products based on the questions above. You will need to consider your interview design carefully to elicit useful information. Attempt a brainstorming session with others in your group. Can you think of any other uses that people could put the media to?

Evaluation   How useful is this approach to an understanding of wider society and its relationship to the media?

- Uses and Gratifications theory is immediately attractive and offers a clear explanation of how individuals relate to and choose media products.

- It is close to reality in that people may all be media saturated, but are by no means sharing the same experiences of the media in their daily lives.

- While it offers an explanation for people's relationships with their chosen media forms, it does not offer an over-arching theory of the impact of the media on society and is therefore psychological and individualistic in its account.

Cultural Effects theory

Cultural Effects theory is also Marxist in origin, and represents a return to the Hypodermic Syringe model of audience receptions. In the case of Cultural Effects, the analogy that one should use is not so much a syringe, as a drip feed of ideas. It is of considerable significance for those studying popular culture options.

The work is most closely associated with the Glasgow Media Group, who have produced a series of articles and books based on content analysis (the work of this group of academics has already been discussed). The idea is that one overview of society permeates all media productions and, therefore, that we are not aware of the steady reinforcement of social stereotypes and ideological perspectives. A socially constructed view of the world is offered to us, and it represents the interests of the ruling élites – the owners of media companies.

As with all research based on Marxist theory, the criticism is always levelled that it is ideologically inspired and therefore unreliable. However, the evidence of a pervading point of view proposed by many media forms is compelling. An active audience is assumed in Cultural Effects theory in that people of different social groups can and do understand (read) media texts in widely different ways. Audiences are capable of rejecting media messages and often select their media forms to reinforce their existing perceptions of the world.

All audience reception research founders on the basic problem of actually measuring the impact of the media on individuals. Common sense may tell us that we, or more often other people, are influenced by the media that we choose, but there is still no proof that our behaviour or attitudes are influenced in any perceptible or consistent fashion.

	Hypodermic Syringe model	Two-step Flow model	Uses and Gratifications theory	Cultural Effects theory
When theory was influential	1920s and 30s	1950s	1972	1980s
Effect on audience of media	Media act as drug injected into veins of audience	Opinions are formed in a social context with opinion leaders. Ideas flow from radio to leaders to rest of population	People use media to satisfy needs: Company? Social ritual of buying paper? Social prestige? Social definition?	Public consciousness is created as long-term effect of creating reality and constant repetition
Methodologies	Loboratory experiments were used – e.g. Bandura and the Bobo doll	Research into attitude change	Interviewing people about needs and relationships with media	Content analysis and attitude formation
Influential perspective	Marxist	Psychology	Two-step and interaction psychology	Neo-Marxist
Main theorists	Frankfurt School	Katz and Lazarsfeld	McQuail, Blumler and Brown, Lull	**Philo** and Glasgow Media Group
Criticisms of theory	■ Simplistic ■ Passive audience ■ Ignores our ability to reject messages we dislike	■ Media are shown to have little short-term effect on people ■ Ignores long-term effect	■ Individualistic ■ Ignores 'society' ■ Does not fully investigate the nature of the messages offered	■ How can effects be measured? ■ Accused of left-wing bias to design of research

Figure 5.5   Summary of theories of media reception

PROFILE

Dr Gregory Philo
of the Glasgow University Media Group

Gregory Philo is one of the most important British contributors to recent British cultural writing. He was brought up in Kent and gained his first degree in Sociology and Politics from Bradford University in 1971.

Philo gained his doctorate from Glasgow University in 1989 when he studied the influence of media on public belief. This work was later published as **Seeing and Believing: The Influence of Television** (Routledge, 1990).

His most significant work to date has been with the Glasgow University Media Group. You are advised to be very familiar with some of the research work that has been produced by Philo and the Glasgow Media Group, as it is relevant to most areas of debate in this area.

In the late 1970s and early 1980s, Philo's work was concerned with the nature of and collection of news. More recently, the main discussion of the GUMG is related to the way in which audiences receive and interpret media messages. Publications cover considerations of media coverage of topics as various as mental health, ethnicity, children and violence, the developing world and food and health scares.

Members of the Media Group have also written about the teaching of journalism and have been very critical of 'postmodern' trends in media and cultural studies. The most recent summary of their work is in **Message Received** (Longman, 1999), edited by Philo and in **Cultural Compliance** by Philo and David Miller (Longman, 1999).

Gregory Philo is the research director of the Media Unit at Glasgow University. The Unit has invented and developed a variety of methodological techniques to collect its data. Philo's ideas are particularly linked in this chapter with the discussion entitled 'Cultural Effects theory'.

Censorship, free speech, constraints and controls

This particular debate follows most naturally from discussion of the impact of the media on audiences because arguments in favour of controls often relate to viewpoints about the relationship of media and audience. This area of theorising also has particular relevance to sociological evaluations of the relationship between media and ideology. There are two popular views of the impact of watching violence and sex on film and television. These are common sense views in the sense that it is difficult to prove psychologically in any definitive way what the impact of sex and violence in the media has on the personality of the receiver.

> **HINTS AND TIPS**   Look in psychology texts at the work of Bandura and his Bobo Doll experiments for a view of the problems implicit in trying to establish a causal relationship between the media and actual behaviour.

Catharsis is the release of negative emotions. It is often cited as an argument to defend the free depiction of sexuality in the media. It is said that people should be able to view sexuality on screen so that they can experience emotional release in a controlled and positive fashion.

Desensitisation is the notion that we lose sensitivity to upsetting ideas and images as we see more and more of them, and is often quoted against the depiction of violence. The suggestion is that films and programmes become ever more violent as we are inured to the horrors depicted and wish for more and better effects. We are no longer upset or shocked by violent deaths but require increasingly exciting events. Violence becomes gratuitous (for its own sake) in order to provide us with thrills.

There is a great deal of common-sense evidence to support both views.

- Many people watch violence on film and enjoy it without using it in their daily lives. Watching Spielberg's *Saving Private Ryan* can be traumatising because of the extreme emotions and violence of the opening 20 minutes but there is little record of anyone attempting to invade France because of it.

- Children do imitate violence that they have seen and the Power Rangers were banned in the Scandinavian countries after a child killed a playmate by imitating a karate kick and rupturing his friend's spleen.

- Violence has become ever more acceptable so that the shocking scenes of films of 20 years ago seem quite innocuous today.

> **HINTS AND TIPS**   Attempt a small survey of friends to see how many actually feel that violence in the cinema should be limited and yet, if asked, how many also enjoy thrillers such as the **Lethal Weapon** series which rely on violence for their effects.

All societies have had some form of censorship or control over media productions. People in western society generally believe in free speech, which is the idea that you can say anything you wish in any public forum, although few would allow racists or sexually or violently abusive people the right to put forward their views. The issue actually becomes not whether we should have free speech, but who do we allow to control media output?

> **HINTS AND TIPS**   Censorship can be a tool of social control in the correct hands (consider the issues of gate-keeping and agenda-setting). History texts will also be useful for detailed information on the way that dictators such as Stalin and Hitler were able to control their populations by propaganda and restricting free speech.

Very many agencies and rules are involved in the statutory and voluntary regulation of the media. Some of these include:

- The Advertising Standards Authority, which attempts to ensure that all advertisements are decent, honest and truthful.

- The Broadcasting Standards Authority, which looks at complaints made by the public about radio and television broadcasts. Most complaints are about the portrayal of sex, violence, or bad language.

- The Radio Authority, which regulates and licenses all independent radio channels.

- The Independent Television Commission, a body that regulates independent television. It grants licences and issues guidelines.

There are also government restrictions on what may be broadcast. Among these are:

- The Official Secrets Act, which controls and limits what may be revealed by signatories about the work and interests of the government.

- The Public Order Act. This makes it an offence to publish anything that can be said to raise racial conflict.

- The D notice, which can be used to 'kill' any story that the government feels that it would not be in public interest to divulge.

Ownership and control of the media

This is an enormously important debate within the media, as some commentators believe that huge media companies have a vast influence over people's beliefs and culture. Some think that one dominant media-created Americanised culture is destroying the cultural variety and traditions of certain parts of the globe. This view is known as globalisation and associated with the ideas of Marxists such as Jürgen Habermas and the Frankfurt School.

The growth of multi-nationals and the power of media companies

A few major media companies are increasingly dominating the world. Companies such as Disney and Rupert Murdoch's News International have a global significance which make them more powerful in both economic and ideological terms than any other institutions.

Significant personalities in the ownership of the media include the following people:

- Bill Gates is probably the world's richest man and his money was made from the sale of computer

software; he owns about 20 per cent of Microsoft who run the Windows programmes. It is estimated that his personal fortune represents something over $100 billion and that he is richer than most of the world's countries. The *Sunday Times* Power List 1999 suggests that Gates is moving into cable television and is in competition with Rupert Murdoch for control over television markets.

- Rupert Murdoch is owner of News Corporation. In Britain, he owns *The Times* and The *Sun*, both highly influential papers. In terms of his real influence, however, these are small companies as he is also the owner of Sky television and has most of the Asian satellite television market as part of his company structure. He is a significant figure in Australian media. He is now moving into Internet companies. It is claimed that he is wealthy enough to be able to ensure that he pays very little tax in any of the countries in which he operates because he is multi-national and can move his money around the world.

Many commentators, particularly Marxists, view these developments with considerable concern. Giddens (1997:388) points out that the owners of the great global media empires 'are in the business not just of selling goods but of influencing opinions. The proprietors of such corporations, like Murdoch or Berlusconi, make no secret of their rightist political views, which inevitably are a cause of concern to political parties and other groups holding different political positions.

Marxism and globalisation

The case of Silvio Berlusconi illustrates many of the concerns of Marxists about the power and influence of the media. He was a major owner of a number of small Italian television channels and soon used the power of the publicity he wielded to make a bid to become Prime Minister of Italy in 1994. In the event, he lost power after a series of charges of corruption and bribery.

However, issues are raised by this ability of the media to control our information and to shape our desires. Blumler (1992) has suggested that the quality of television declines as the number of new media outlets increases, because in the competition for viewing figures, the material broadcast becomes ever more lurid and sensationally presented. Adorno worries that we develop 'commodity fetishism'. Media products are aimed solely at the market and we value them not for their intrinsic cultural quality but for their cost to us in terms of money. This is also linked to postmodern and interactional ideas, which suggest that we are so dominated by our desire to consume and possess products that we are defined by the products we consume.

Pluralism

Pluralism, because of its links to functionalism and its consensual view of society, takes a far more optimistic view of the impact of global media culture on our society and media. Pluralists claim that more variety and narrowcasting to selected audiences reduce the power of companies to control our viewing and ideologies. Companies are required to respond to our wants and to provide us with what we require. Naturally, this perspective is embraced by the media-producing companies. Murdoch points out that media production is ridiculously expensive and badly selling programmes can incur massive losses. Hollywood companies have collapsed because films have not sold at the box office.

The debate centres on the ability of media companies to shape public taste in cultures different from western capitalism and the ability of these cultures to resist the pressure. However, a further development of the debate is associated with postmodernism which suggests that culture is itself fragmenting into a form of 'pick and mix' where style is more significant than ideas.

Cultural imperialism

Imperialism

Imperialism is the domination of one nation over another. It can be based on:

- political control – e.g. England over Scotland
- military control – e.g. Britain over its empire until 1949
- economic controls – e.g. Britain over countries dependent on trade and/or aid.

Most European nations once had an empire and dominated portions of the globe for trade and military purposes. European control over these other areas was lost, often because of, or just after, the First and Second World Wars. Although direct control was lost, there remains a legacy of cultural values in these dominion areas – shown by language, dress style, legal and political systems and religion typical of the colonial empire left behind in the subject state.

Cultural imperialism

In **cultural imperialism** richer countries systematically control the cultural life of another country in order to create patterns of consumption of goods (e.g. clothes, foods, music, lifestyle products). This contributes to the decline of the culture of that nation. This view is particularly associated with the work of Schiller.

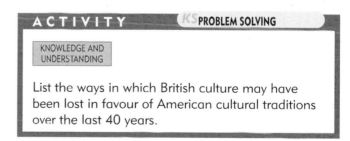

ACTIVITY   KS **PROBLEM SOLVING**

KNOWLEDGE AND UNDERSTANDING

List the ways in which British culture may have been lost in favour of American cultural traditions over the last 40 years.

Media imperialism

Media imperialism theory belongs to a mode of thought similar to the Hypodermic Syringe model of audience effects. There has been little quantifiable research to prove that poorer countries are simply abandoning their own traditions in favour of western thought. Few thinkers are willing to apply the simplistic notion of the Hypodermic Syringe model in the west, and are we to assume that people in Africa are less intelligent and more unsophisticated than we are when we apply the same theoretical thinking to their receipt of media productions? Obviously cultures are changing but the early Cultural Imperialism models may not approach the complexity of analysis required to understand these changes. It has also been found that, if offered the choice, people will prefer to watch good-quality productions from their own cultural traditions than similar American or western European ones.

TASK

Hypothesis – People prefer to watch television programmes produced within their own cultural heritage than similar imported programmes.

Context – Although the hypothesis is apparently simple, your discussion should centre on the context of resistance theory. You are attempting to discover if people resist cultural productions that may represent other cultural experience. You might need to consider how much air time is actually given over to foreign productions.

Method – Begin your study with a simple quantitative survey to discover if people around you prefer home-grown television to foreign imports. Start with simple and popular programmes such as **Neighbours**, **Home and Away**, **EastEnders** and **Coronation Street**. You will probably need to develop the idea by considering why certain programmes are preferred.

Evaluation – You might find that your results are not as clear cut as you could like them to be and are not going to offer you evidence of resistance but lead you to questions of taste or of style. Many American programmes, such as medical drama and cop shows, have higher production values and are therefore more exciting than their UK equivalents. Soap operas have different target audiences and Australian soaps tend to aim for a younger age range than British soap opera, which is more akin to drama. Programmes may actually be shown at different times of day, which will affect viewing patterns.

Small World theory

This view is more pluralistic in thought. It was identified by Marshall McLuhan in the 1960s, who said that the growth of the media had united humanity in a 'global village'. Products are truly multi-national. The world appears to be 'shrinking'. Events in the Far East affect us immediately – think of the effect of stock market crashes in Hong Kong on British share prices. There are huge global media companies such as Microsoft and Murdoch's companies.

We buy products, and we use media from, a variety of countries and as a result we absorb foreign cultural traditions into our daily modes of life. This implies that our cultures are merely changing, rather than being lost to an all-encompassing American view of the world. Is this view overly optimistic? One only has to consider the speed of loss of culture in remote areas to see how contact with the west has been devastating for 'primitive' indigenous peoples. How much more insidious might this process be in our own, more complex, societies?

Resistance theories

Resistance theories offer the view that cultures are able to resist the dominant ideologies of western media output and create their own meaning from the material they are offered. However, television personalities and pop stars are seen by a world audience and are known beyond the areas in which they have any cultural significance (examples include the late Princess of Wales and Manchester United FC). Advertising campaigns are certainly cross-cultural, particularly for youth products such as Levi's and various brands of soft drinks. Questions that have no real answer and which are the subject of enormous debate around this issue include:

- Is global satellite television more important than terrestrial communication in controlling people?
- Do all cultures, social classes and genders interpret programmes in the same way?

Evidence of cultural resistance to globalisation

British television features a variety of imported films and programmes, although they still actually amount to a small part of the schedules. Some of these foreign programmes are bought because they are cheap ways of filling air time. Most poor countries begin their television programming using American programmes because they are cheap; and eventually show their own programmes. Local populations have been shown to prefer their own programmes.

It is argued that many populations watch foreign programmes and interpret them through their own cultural viewpoints. This is supported by the observation that there are huge markets for Indian films, which dominate the entire Asian market. Hollywood frequently remakes French films for American audiences and Hollywood remakes American films for Asian populations. In American films, as a general rule, the hero is thin and the bad guy is often fat or seems old. The reverse applies to many Indian films, where fleshiness is considered more beautiful and age is respected. Also, white is the Asian colour of mourning while it suggests purity and virginity in western cultures.

The products of ex-colonies are sold to back to the old empire-building nations of Europe: Australian films, such as the *Mad Max* series starring Mel Gibson, were major hits in Britain, Brazil sells soap operas to Portugal and most Arabic programming is produced by Egyptians in preference to the output of the USA. Small independent companies in Britain are producing popular films for local markets and some have become world-wide hits – for instance *Trainspotting* and *Four Weddings and a Funeral* were extremely successful in the early 1990s. It should be added that the financing of small local films can be very problematic and budgets are often small. Despite that, independent cultural productions for the Welsh market such as the tragic story of *Hedd Wyn* (which was made in both Welsh and English language versions), while not widely known have considerable local standing.

In reaction to globalisation theory, it is suggested that cultures are able to resist Americanisation and cultural colonisation. However, they may also reject media interpretations of events. The most notable example of this is the way in which many sections of the media were able to change position from highly critical to totally laudatory with respect to their judgements of the Princess of Wales around the time of her death. This change of face may have been prompted when it became clear how strongly many members of the public had reacted to the news of the car accident.

Working at a more personal level on resistance to media interpretations of events, Paula Skidmore (1995) is a member of the Glasgow Media Group. She studied

reports on child abuse cases. She found that most media coverage was reactive (responding to cases) rather than proactive (talking about the issues and therefore creating the story). In most case-based stories, the media tended to point the finger at social workers. Parents were described as fighting for their children while wicked social workers tried to grab them. When she studied audiences, she found that many people agreed with the perceptions of the stories that they had read, however they also believed that the media in general scapegoat social workers. This suggests a degree of resistance to the perceptions and representations of media. It also contradicts Hall et al. who took the view that people did accept official versions of the truth. Interestingly, Skidmore notes that 'child abuse fatigue' has developed. The story has not gone away. Abuse continues but it is just less interesting and less likely to be reported in detail in the press unless there is a particularly shocking story.

Postmodernism

Modernism is the old idea that society is constantly progressing and improving. Many writers reject this theory and replace it with a series of suppositions and debates that are controversial and can be a little difficult to relate to initially. This type of writing and thought is usually described as postmodern. **Postmodernism** is not a single unified theory as such and therefore some of the viewpoints expressed are generalisations. Because it is open to individual interpretation, it may also be couched in extremely difficult language.

The most accessible postmodernist writer is Barthes, but other postmodernists include Derrida, Foucault and Lyotard. Postmodernism is extremely important in any consideration of culture, and therefore you should look for all the references to postmodernism in the index of this book and read what is written to support your understanding of this section.

Postmodernism embraces all forms of artistic and social expression, so architecture or music can be defined as postmodern. The basic idea about the media is that we are media saturated. The media create our culture and social reality. Postmodernism says that the old greats have no significance in terms of analysis and describes culture in terms of short-term fads and trends. Because the media are very visual and extremely short term, we have come to think and behave in that way – we value style, references, jokes, and image over any solid worth in our media. For instance, Quentin Tarantino's film *Reservoir Dogs* has been described as postmodern because it breaks or changes many of the traditional rules of film-making. It contains many references to other films and jokes for people to pick out. This is known as referentialism or intertextuality.

This is a reflection on how people are now relating to their social world. Because we have no certainties, and because we reject the strict moral codes and rigid interpretations of society (which are called **meta-narratives**), we must constantly challenge and reinvent ourselves. We have therefore started to define ourselves by what we buy and use. Clothing has traditionally been used to offer others a 'handle' to our social position, our gender and our status. For example, in postmodern society a pair of denim jeans is no longer a consciously adopted uniform of working-class American labouring men but is a style statement and could be worn ironically in order to emphasise femininity, wealth and status. In global terms, we mix and match cultural identities and products because we have lost an understanding of their cultural value and meaning. Consider the way that western pop celebrities and film stars have adopted eastern religions such as Buddhism or the way in which body piercing and tattooing (reminiscent of Maori and Celtic cultures) have become high fashion, used without any sense of their meaning and religious purpose.

	Traditional Marxist	Neo-Marxist	Pluralist	Postmodern
How do we view the world?	Our view of reality is created for us by those who control the production of ideas. These people represent the interests of the capitalist class	There are a number of ways of looking at the world, but we tend to take the dominant views that are offered to us by the media	So much occurs that no one can get a full view of events. We tend to take our ideas from the media and then process them for ourselves	Our views of the world are socially constructed. We are constantly engaged in recreating our views of the world and this process is known as a discourse. Individuals and the media are part of this discourse
Are the media ideological in intent?	Yes. The media are dominated by a capitalist class and operate in the interests of the wealthy and powerful	Yes. The media put forward a view of the world that represents the views of the dominant social class	No. The media respond to the views of the customers. All groups have equal access to the media to put forward views	No. All kinds of groups have access to the media. Postmodernists suggest that even ideologies are open to social construction
Is news a media creation?	Stories can be invented to discredit those who wish for a just and equitable society	The dominant ideology shapes what is known of the news	News values reflect the needs of the public	The news is a discourse in society. The news is constructed in the sense that all reality is constructed
Can news coverage be manipulated?	The media can be manipulated by politicians. This is seen at its most extreme in political propaganda	A particular view is constructed which reflects dominant ideologies. The media serve to maintain the *status quo*	The media offer various views of reality. The audience is educated and selects coverage that reflects rather than challenges its views	Reality is nothing more than a mental construct. The news media help to create a subjective reality
Examples	The outcome of elections is affected by direct intervention of press barons	News reporting is biased against environmental issues and ignores alternative perspectives	The news puts forward a variety of views from which people can select	Political parties concentrate on image creation because few people understand the issues. They vote for perceptions, not policies

Based on an analysis by Trowler P (1996), *Investigating the Media, 2nd Edition*.

Figure 5.6   Can the ownership and control of the media affect the way that we understand the world?

Critics of postmodernism could argue that it hovers dangerously close to New Right thinking in its insistence on individualism. However, the moralistic tone that characterises the productions of New Right writers is missing from postmodern analysis, which is generally an optimistic stance from which to look at social change (see Figure 5.6).

SOCIOLOGY IN PRACTICE

The role of the video player in maintaining cultural traditions among South Asian families in London

Indian cinema in Southall: from public pleasure to private leisure

The first 'Indian' films were shown in Southall in 1953 in hired halls and then in three local cinemas. During the 1960s and 1970s the cinema provided the principal weekend leisure activity in Southall and represented an occasion for families and friends to get together; the social event of the week.

In 1978, when VCRs came on the market, many families were quick to seize the opportunity to extend their choice and control over viewing in the home. Many Asian communities obtained them as early as 1978–9 before most other households in Britain. It is estimated that between 40 and 50 per cent of households in Britain now own or rent a VCR but in Southall the figure is held to be 80 per cent.

Most shops rent popular Hindi (also known as 'Bombay') films and although films in Panjabi and Urdu are also available from shops they lack the broad-based appeal of the popular Hindi movie. In fact the Bombay film has gained something of a cultural hegemony in south Asia and among many 'Asian' settlers across the world. To understand this one has to look to the specific evolution of the popular Hindi genre which, in order to appeal to a mass audience, had to produce films which would cross the linguistic, religious, and regional differences that exist within India, as indeed within Southall.

Many of the films combine a catholicity or universality of appeal with a careful handling of regional and religious differences. A distinctive form of Bombay Hindi, characterized by a certain 'linguistic openness' has evolved which makes most films accessible also to speakers of other south Asian languages. The distinctive visual style, often foregrounded over dialogue, combines with successive modes of spectacle, action and emotion which facilitates cross-cultural understanding. In the light of this we can understand the huge uptake of Hindi films on cassette among the diverse linguistic groups in Southall.

With the arrival of video, the adventure, romance, and drama of the Bombay film was to be enjoyed in domestic privacy. A small piece of home technology brought the cinema hall into the home, or so it appeared. A lot was gained but much was lost. The weekly outing became a thing of the past as the cinemas closed and the big screen image shrunk into the TV box and entered the flow of everyday life in the living room.

In Southall the rapid expansion of the home video market needs to be considered not only as providing an extension to an already important and dynamic film culture but also very much a response on the part of a black community to life in Britain. Southall, like many other black communities, has come into existence in the first instance as a result of racist immigration and housing policies. Such communities have developed as 'sanctuaries' against the racism they experience. The exclusion and marginalization of many people in Southall from mainstream British society, coupled with the failure to provide adequate leisure/culture facilities, has (like among the *Gastarbeiter* (guest worker) Turkish community in West Germany) contributed to the development of an important home video culture.

But the consequences of a decade of video use are perceived in contradictory ways by the youth of Southall. Many young people feel that the VCR has served further to isolate the community from mainstream British society. It is also seen to have specific effects on the lives of women: 'The video has isolated the community even more. They might as well be in India, especially the women.' Others see it as a liberating pleasure, especially for females: 'Some girls can't get out of the house that much so they can get a film and keep themselves occupied within the four walls of the house. It's an advantage for them.'

Such contradictory evaluations need to be seen in the contexts in which they originate.

Domestic viewing contexts

During the course of the study it became possible to construct a broad typology of contexts and associated texts. For the purpose of this account I shall concentrate on weekend family viewing because this situation was so frequently and consistently discussed by all interviewees, and due to the importance given to it within this cultural context.

The VCR is used predominantly at the weekend in most families. Viewing 'Indian' films on video is the principal, regular family leisure activity. Weekend family gatherings around the TV set are a social ritual repeated in many families. The VCR and TV screen become the focus and locus of interaction. Notions of togetherness and communality are stressed: 'It's probably the only time in the week that we are all together so when we're watching a film at least we're all together.'

This togetherness is by no means that of passive viewers: 'No one is silent, we're all talking through the film about what's happening here and there and generally having a chat … it sort of brings you closer together.'

The weaving of conversation through the narrative is facilitated by an impressive familiarity with films brought about by repeated viewings. The episodic structure of films which moves the spectator through the different modes of spectacle, song and dance, drama, action, and affect also provides natural breaks of talk, emotion and reflection.

With such large family gatherings the question of power and control over viewing becomes important. The interviews highlight the way in which parents actively set and maintain viewing rules which govern viewing patterns and modes of parent–child interaction.

While the father is usually seen to determine when children are allowed access to the screen by his absence or presence in the home, the mother is perceived as exercising a greater degree of power and control over the choice of what is watched. This was a significant pattern across the interviews, emphasizing the important role mothers play in socializing their children in the domestic context. It also makes clear that the relationship between family power structures and family viewing patterns is not one of simple correspondence.

There are also clear differences in the attentiveness and in the degree of salience of Indian films to various family members, which are obscured by the simple observation that the family all watched the same programme. Many young people say they sit with parents and view parts of the films just to please them, or say that their parents encourage or even 'force' them to watch.

As gender differences are important to understand parental control over viewing they are also a significant factor in understanding young people's viewing preferences and behaviour. Boys tend to experience greater freedom in deciding how they use their leisure time and spend more time engaged in activities outside the home. In contrast, girls are usually socialized to remain within the domestic realm and often participate in strong and supportive female cultures in the home where the viewing of Indian films on video frequently plays an important role. This explains to some extent the generally greater engagement with popular Hindi videos on the part of most girls interviewed. In one interview two boys rather begrudgingly claim: 'It doesn't hurt to watch an Indian film with the parents.' 'No, it kills you.'

In spite of this repeatedly expressed reluctance the way in which the screen can serve social interaction in the family tends to override individual preferences and return young people to the family situation. One boy commented to the general agreement of the group: 'Well we don't usually stay in another room while they're watching, if you've got something to yourself, you isolate yourself, don't you?' It is clear that what might be seen on the one hand as 'enforced' or 'reluctant' viewing can take on pleasurable connotations where the emphasis is on 'being together'. Parents do not have much time for leisure due to long working hours and shift work, so the time when the family is together around the TV set is often much appreciated by all concerned.

Conversely, the family audience is frequently fragmented by English and American films: 'When it's Indian films it's all of us together but when it's English films it's just me and my brother.' This fragmentation is partly due to the texts of English and American films themselves. Given parental reservations about the language, sensuality, and references to sexuality, young people may often prefer to view them on their own to escape parental censure or vigilance.

You may now have the impression that the avid consumption of VCR films falls into two neat categories. While Hindi films tend to be viewed in large family gatherings and to be celebrated by intense social interaction, British and American films tend to be consumed on their own in a more or less assertive circumvention of parental control and preferences. While viewing patterns tend indeed to correspond to this dichotomy, young people's viewing of Hindi films raises further ethnographic questions about perceptions of 'Indianness' and Britain or India and 'Britishness'.

Source: Marie Gillespie 'Technology and tradition – audio visual culture among south Asian families in west London' in Ann Gray and Jim McGuigan (1993: 148–151) *Studying culture, An Introductory Reader.* London, Edward Arnold.

1   Suggest why the ownership of a video recorder by a South Asian family could represent evidence of resistance to cultural imperialism.   **(4)**

2   How do Asian males and females relate differently to the use of the video machine? What does this suggest about the nature of audience?   **(6)**

3   Do videotape machines and tapes '*isolate the community from wider British culture*' or '*liberate and unite the South Asian community*' in Southall? Make notes to support both points of view.   **(12)**

4   How may the viewing of Hindi films create a notion of their culture for second-generation British Asian children? Outline the various processes involved.   **(10)**

Area summary

This topic is both long and complicated from a sociological point of view. There are various approaches to both the subject matter and the material. Key terms, such as popular culture, are not easy to define and the language used by many of the theorists is often inaccessible. This complexity is such that the study of the relationship between the mass media and society is becoming part of a new study area known as cultural studies.

The media are enormously significant in our lives; they entertain and inform us. More importantly, from a Marxist perspective, it is possible that they can create our notions of reality so that we become tools in the hands of those who control the media. Consumers are receiving ideologies that may lead them into blind acceptance of social principles that act against their personal interests. Pluralists point out that when we criticise the content of the media we may be criticising our own desires and tastes, because the media provide a mirror image of our interests and desires. Postmodernists may see the media as part of a process of creating a cultural world that is unified by consumerism and short-term understanding.

The one thing that all these perspectives and studies seem to agree on is that the media are very important in creating our notions of reality and in defining us as individuals.

> **HINTS AND TIPS** The most common mistake for the desperate candidate to make is to develop an account of a programme or some other **media text** in an answer to a question which is about evaluation of concepts. Although you may refer to certain media texts such as films or music, you should not attempt a detailed analysis of any particular media product. This is the concern of media studies. Your concern as a sociologist is with the relationship between the mass media and the culture of our society.

Definitions

Agenda-setting	The media are able to control what we think about and discuss
Bourgeois hegemony	The wealthy can control our beliefs because they control the production and dissemination of ideas
Centrality of the media	The media are central to our lives and we are media obsessed
Cultural imperialism	The process of one culture dominating another, causing the loss of cultural traditions, and often via the media
Cultural artefact	Any art or media creation
Culture	The beliefs, ideas, norms and values of a society, sometimes divided into 'high' (which represents the culture of the wealthy) and 'low' (which represents popular culture)
Desensitisation	An inability to feel strongly about issues, brought on as a result of over-exposure to shocking images

Dumbing down	The process of making media texts easier to understand and more popular for ordinary people by losing quality and distinctiveness
Editors	Those people who are able to select the content of a media product such as a news programme or newspapers
Folk devils and moral panics	The media create a hysterical over-reaction (moral panic) to a news item (folk devil) through over-reporting
Gate-keeping	The media can prevent news coming to us because of the editorial policies of the owners
Ideology of masculinity	Belief about the nature of masculinity
Intertextuality	The relationship between media products whereby newspapers will offer stories about film stars or cartoons will refer to famous film scenes – this a familiar form in *The Simpsons*
Imperialism	The process by which wealthy industrialised countries were able to dominate less wealthy agricultural countries in what is now known as the third world
Hypodermic Syringe	The media act as a drug to dull us into submission, to prevent real thought and understanding
Mass media	Any form of communication which reaches a huge audience around the world
Media text	Any media production – a book, poster, advertisement or film
Mediation	The media offer us a window into the greater world and are central to our interpretations of that world
Meta-narratives	A strict modernist interpretation of society which offers an overview in terms of moral codes
Modernism	The belief that society is improving and that we should seek absolute knowledge
Postmodernism	The belief that society merely changes, it does not improve and that there can be no moral absolutes because all knowledge is relative
Passive and active audiences	Passive audiences accept the media uncritically and active audiences are in a relationship with their preferred medium
Pluralist theories of media	The media reflect the demands that we make upon them and respond according to what people require
Propaganda	Media materials designed to manipulate public opinion
Reify, reification	A term used in labelling theories, where a label is made socially real through the act of being applied to someone
Resistance	The dominant ideas of the media and the culture can be rejected by audiences in a variety of ways
Selection	The process of choosing the content of a programme or text
Semiology	The media use symbols to communicate complex messages, which we learn to read
Visual code	The language of photography and drawing by which we are able to gain a message

Data response questions

Item A

To sell to this mass consuming public, the bland and standardised formulas of mass culture are developed because they can be made to appeal to everyone since everyone, every atomised person, is open to manipulation.

Strinati, D. (1995: 12) **An Introduction to Theories of Popular Culture**

Item B

It is in their interests to maintain such a system because it is the one which favours the pursuit of profit and the raising of finance through shares (among other capitalistic features). So the media owners tend to favour Conservative politics. Many British newspapers can be shown to favour this political party and/or its politics to some degree.

Burton (1990: 40) **More than meets the eye**

Item C

*It could be argued that power in the newspaper industry lies with the audience, who can decide each day which newspaper to buy. If a newspaper loses its readers to a rival it may go out of business or it may have to modify its format or style like the **Sun** did after it was acquired by Rupert Murdoch in the 1960s.*

Gration et al. (1988: 93) **Communication and Media Studies**

Item D

Publicity is always about the future buyer. It offers him an image of himself made glamorous by the product or opportunity it is trying to sell. The image then makes him envious of himself as he might be.

Berger (1972) **Ways of Seeing**

a Which sociological perspective is being described in Item A? Explain your reasoning for your answer. **(3)**

| KNOWLEDGE AND UNDERSTANDING | IDENTIFICATION AND INTERPRETATION |

b Using Items B and C and your own knowledge, suggest what social factors determine the products that media companies offer to the public. **(6)**

| KNOWLEDGE AND UNDERSTANDING | IDENTIFICATION AND INTERPRETATION |

c Sociologically evaluate the suggestion that the media are part of a conspiracy to support the views of the wealthy and powerful. **(8)**

| ANALYSIS AND EVALUATION |

d Evaluate the suggestion that in a postmodern world where the old certainties no longer apply, people must create their own realities through the use of the media. **(10)**

| ANALYSIS AND EVALUATION |

Structured question

1   To what does the term mass media refer?   (2)

> **GUIDANCE**   Note that there are two marks. Two specific elements are required in the answer to gain the marks. These are in answer to the two words in the phrase 'mass media'. 'Mass' obviously refers to the number of people who receive the message and 'media' refers to the means of communication. Any more writing is a waste of time but failure to address the two elements of the phrase will lead to loss of easy marks.
>
> KNOWLEDGE AND UNDERSTANDING

2   How might the television mediate society for its audience?   (5)

> **GUIDANCE**   The question here requires that you explain what mediation is, and then that you apply that understanding to a consideration of the theory in respect of one form of mass media. The choice of television as the media form to consider makes the question something of a gift because almost everyone has a television or some access to television. Television is now so common that some people have a television in every room of the house. Areas to consider are the ways in which television has come to replace a sense of community. People are passive receivers of information whereas once they would have been creators of entertainment. A second element of the question is the way in which television can create a reality and the extent to which that reality reflects people's own lives or the lives and ideologies of the creators and editors of the programmes.
>
> KNOWLEDGE AND UNDERSTANDING | IDENTIFICATION AND INTERPRETATION

3   To what extent do the media create our notions of ethnicity?   (8)

> **GUIDANCE**   For this question you will need to consider and define ethnicity. If you take the view that ethnicity somehow applies to people in cultural minorities, then you will have missed the point of the question. Ethnicity applies to everyone and those who come from families with longstanding roots in British culture are still members of an ethnic group and will gain their concept of what it means to be British from the media. If you consider that you are English, beware of failing to remember that there are minority British cultures, such as the Scots and Irish, who can also be stereotyped by media representations of their nationality. Having considered questions of ethnicity, you will now have to suggest a variety of ways in which ethnicity is transmitted as a cultural concept. Here are some suggestions: sporting fixtures, notions of other cultures, ethnocentricity in news reporting, representation of those from ethnic minorities. If you restrict yourself to a discussion of how notions of ethnicity are transmitted you are limiting yourself. Some examples and reference to theory are essential in this question. You should consider questions of ideology and consideration of the work of Hall and **Policing the Crisis** would give you a sound example to consider.
>
> KNOWLEDGE AND UNDERSTANDING | IDENTIFICATION AND INTERPRETATION

4   Evaluate the suggestion that the mass media are able to promote a single over-riding ideology via large media conglomerates   (10)

> **GUIDANCE**   This seems to invite you to weigh up theory, and you cannot go far wrong if you simply apply your understandings of Marxism and Pluralism to the question. Marxism tends to see the media in terms of a giant conspiracy (you might like to mention the Hypodermic Syringe model and the Cultural Effects model). Pluralism offers a view that the media simply respond to the demands of the audience and allies itself to postmodernism. You must choose between the two general positions. This, though, would gain you only a proportion of the marks
>
> ANALYSIS AND EVALUATION

because if you analyse the question thoroughly you will see that it is essential that you should show some understanding of what a large media conglomerate is and how it operates. This is a slightly different question from applying the theory to a general analysis of the media because there are questions of the extent to which a giant media conglomerate is in a position to dictate to the audience and the extent to which people can resist its message. You might need therefore to make a cursory mention of the globalisation debate in your answer.

Essay titles

1 Sociologically examine the contribution of the media to social control in western societies. **(25)**

2 Evaluate the suggestion that the view of the world we receive via the media is merely a social construction. **(25)**

3 Evaluate the extent to which audiences can be seen as passive receivers of the news media. **(25)**

GUIDANCE   This is a fairly straightforward question at first glance because you are invited to trawl through the various models of audience reception and evaluate each in turn. You would identify the passive receiver as a Marxist model and then you would look at the Two-step Flow, Uses and Gratifications theory, and finally Cultural Effects theory. In fact, if you do this well, then you are virtually assured of a fairly good mark. The approach advised, of just going through the information offered, would be unlikely to get you more than a C grade.

ANALYSIS AND EVALUATION

Consider how you would respond if you were a marker and had to read something in the order of 200 essays which simply considered the main issues in a well-trodden debate? Markers aim to be fair, but will reserve the highest marks for those who can bring some evidence of personal engagement and understanding to the discussion. The issue for a candidate is how to bring a dimension to a relatively unimaginative essay title which shows more than just an ability to repeat sections of a textbook or teacher notes. In this case, the element of the question which needs to considered, and which could be overlooked in the rush to provide a coherent response in the time allocated, is the creation and reporting of the news.

In this case, you might need to develop areas of discussion that challenge the notion of a passive audience and your debate may include thoughts on postmodernism as opposed to Cultural Effects theory. Do audiences choose news forms that support their preconceptions or do they deliberately seek out a variety of positions and choose between them? What happens if the news contradicts their own experiences – as in the case of Liverpool readers of **The Sun** in the aftermath of the Hillsborough disaster? You could look at the folk devils and moral panics debate – is this evidence of mere response to the media or are the media themselves engaging in a tacit policy of misleading people? The wider ranging your discussion, the more interesting your answer and the better marks you will achieve. Be certain, however, that in your attempt to do something interesting with a question, you remain on target and make all the discussion pertinent to the topic!

ANALYSIS AND EVALUATION

Further reading and references

Trowler, P. (1996) *Investigating Mass Media*, 2nd edition. London, Collins Educational.
The key text for most students of the sociology of the media should be Paul Trowler's book. It covers all the significant research evidence, although it is a little thin on the globalisation debate.

Strinati, D. (1995) *An Introduction to Theories of Popular Culture*. London, Routledge.
Do not be put off by the fact that this is pure text: it reads very well indeed. It summarises and discusses all the key perspectives in a systematic fashion.

Culler, J. (1983) *Fontana Modern Masters: Barthes*. London, Fontana.

Barthes, R. (1993) *Mythologies*. London, Vintage.

If you would like to develop your interest in semiology, see either of these texts. They are highly complex, but they will repay effort spent on them. You may find it useful to see Strinati's text first before graduating to this material.

Any of the various texts produced by members of the Glasgow University Media Group will repay study time, introduce you to a whole variety of new perceptions of the world of the media and develop your understanding of the nature of cultural effects.

Van Zoonen, L. (1994) *Feminist Media Studies*. London, Sage.
This offers a radical and different perspective for those who would like to consider the issue of gender in more depth.

Internet sites

http://www.aber.ac.uk/~dgc
The best source for media studies theory is Daniel Chandler's ever expanding and highly detailed site at Aberystwyth University. He has a huge amount of information which is pitched slightly above A level standard, but with which you should attempt to get to grips as a practice for higher education. Keying Media into any computer should lead to the site eventually if you follow the links. This site also has a huge number of links.

http://www.popcultures.com/
There are some good theoretical sites for the study of popular culture and cultural theory. One of the best is Sarah Zupko's Cultural Studies Center. It has some fascinating links, including one to a study of racial stereotypes in Hollywood films during the 1940s which is illustrated and well written.

http://www.soft.net.uk/cultsoc/MUHome
A completely refreshing site, which totally fails to take itself seriously, is Mick Underwood's clever and well designed cultural studies site. There is a great deal of theoretical discussion and a fair number of excellent jokes at the expense of the computer nerd.

Bibliography

Adorno, T. (1950) *The Authoritarian Personality*. New York, Harper.

Alvarado, M. and Boyd-Barrett, O. (1992) *Media Education*. London, BFL.

Bandura, A. (1959) *Adolescent Aggression*. New York, Ronald Press.

Barthes, R. (1973) *Mythologies*. St. Albans, Paladin.

Berger, J. (1972) *Ways of Seeing*. London, Penguin.

Blumler, J. (ed). (1992) *Television and the Public Interest*. London, Sage.

Buckingham, D. (ed). (1993) *Reading Audiences: Young People and the Media*. Manchester, Manchester University Press.

Burton, G. (1990) *More Than Meets the Eye*. London, Edward Arnold.

Campbell, Beatrix (1993) *Goliath: Britain's Dangerous Places*. London, Methuen.

Clara, L. (1972) *Creating the Mature Reader*, The Commercial Appeal.

Cohen, S. (1972) *Folk Devils and Moral Panics*. London, Paladin.

Connell, B., Brigley, J. and Edwards, M. (1996: 126) *Examining the Media*. London, Hodder & Stoughton.

Curran, J. and Seaton, J. (1988) *Power without Responsibility*. London, Routledge.

Galtung, J. and Ruge, M. in S. Cohen and J. Young (1981) *The Manufacture of News*. London, Constable.

Giddens, (1997: 388) *Sociology, Third Edition*. Cambridge, Polity Press.

Gillespie, M. (1989) *Technology and Tradition – Audio Visual Culture Among South Asian Families in West London* in Gray A and McGuigan A (1993) *Studying culture, An Introductory Reader* London, Edward Arnold

Glasgow University Media Group (1976) *Bad News*. London, Routledge and Kegan Paul.

Glasgow University Media Group (1980) *More Bad News*. London, Routledge and Kegan Paul.

Glasgow University Media Group (1993) *Getting the Message*. London, Routledge and Kegan Paul.

Goffman, E. (1963) *Stigma: Notes on the Management of a Spoiled Identity*. New York, Prentice-Hall.

Goodman, Steven (1997) *An Open Letter to Media Educators* at <http://interact.uoregon.edu/mediaLit/FA/MLArticleFolder/goodman.html>

Gration, G., Reilly, J. and Titford, J. (1988) *Communication and Media Studies*. London, Macmillan.

Gray, A. and McGuigan, J. (1993) *Studying Culture, An Introductory Reader*. London, Edward Arnold.

Gurevitch, M., Bennett, T., Curran, J. and Woollacott, J. (1982) *Culture, Society and the Media*. University Paperbacks, London.

Hall, S., Cutcher, C., Jefferson, T. and Roberts, B. (1978) *Policing the Crisis*. London, Macmillan.

Hartley, J. (1982) *Understanding News*. London, Methuen.

Hood, S. (1983) *On Television*. London, Pluto Press.

Ingham, B. (1991) *Kill the Messenger*. London, Fontana.

Katz, S., Vesin, P. (1986) *Children and the Media*, Los Angeles, Children's Institute International.

Katz, E. and Lazarsfeld, P. (1955) *Personal Influence: the Part Played by People in the Flow of Mass Communications*, Glencoe Illinois, Free Press.

Lull, J. (1988) *World Families Watch Television*. London, Sage.

Lull, J. (1995) *Media, Communication, Culture: A Global Approach*. Cambridge, Polity.

Lyotard, J. (1984) *The Postmodern Condition*. Manchester, Manchester University Press.

Marcuse, H. (1964) *One Dimensional Man*. London, Routledge.

Masterman, L. (1985) *Teaching the Media*. London, Routledge.

McLuhan, M. (1964) *Understanding Media*. RKP London.

McQuail, D. (1972) *The Sociology of Mass Communications* Harmondsworth, Penguin.

McQuail, D. (1998) *Mass Communication Theory: An Introduction (3rd ed)* Sage.

McRobbie, A. (1991) *Feminism and Youth Culture*. London: Macmillan.

Meehan, D. (1983) *Ladies of the Evening: women characters of primetime television*, Metuchen, NJ, Scarecrow Press.

Orbach, S. (1988) *Fat is a Feminist Issue*, London, Arrow.

Philo, G. (1990) *Seeing and Believing*. London: Routledge.

Root, J. (1986) *Open the Box*. London: Comedia.

Schiller (1977) *Advertising and International Communications* in *Current Views on the World Information Order*. Prague: International Organisation of Journalists.

Sharpe, S. (1976) *Just Like a Girl*. Harmondsworth: Penguin.

Skeggs, B. (1990) *Formation of Class and Gender*. London: Sage.

Skidmore, P. (1995) *Just Another Moral Panic: Media reporting of child abuse*. Sociology Review Volume 5:4.

Sklair, L. (1991) *Sociology of the Global System*. Hemel Hempstead: Harvester Wheatsheaf.

Strinati, D. (1995) *An Introduction to Theories of Popular Culture*. Routledge, London.

Thompson, J. (1995) *The Media and Modernity: A Social Theory of the Media*. Cambridge: Polity Press.

Trowler, P. (1996) *Investigating the Media 2nd Edition*. London: Collins Educational

Van Zoonen (1994) *Feminist Media Studies*. London: Sage.

Wall, I. (1990) *Reading Movies*. London: Film Education.

Watson, J. and Hill, A. (1997) *A Dictionary of Communication and Media Studies*. London: Arnold.

Whale, J. (1977) *The Politics of the Media*. London: Fontana.

White, D. M. 91950) *The Gatekeeper: a Case Study in the Selection of News*, Journalism Quarterly, 27.

Williamson, J. (1978) *Decoding Advertisements*. New York: Marion Boyars Publishers.

Wolf, N. (1992) *The Beauty Myth*. New York, Anchor.

Families and Households

This area covers:

■ The history and ideology of the family in our society

■ Considerations of the nature of the changes that have taken place in families

■ The nature of the relationship between family, the law and wider society

By the end of this area you should be able to:

■ show some understanding of the importance of the family as an institution in our society.

■ recognise the nature of the many changes that have taken place in family structure and organisation.

■ identify factors that may contribute to family change and organisation in modern Britain.

■ identify ideologies of the family and family structure and recognise when those ideologies become the basis for legislation.

Key terms

family	household
monogamy	nuclear family
polygamy	extended family
divorce	reconstituted family
conjugal role	symmetrical family

Area 6   Contents

Introduction

This area will look at the structure and organisation of families in our culture. This is an increasingly controversial area of sociology as rapid changes in the nature of families and family units are taking place.

What is a family?

A **family** is a religious, moral, social and legal institution and as such it is enormously difficult to define. People may count distant and non-blood relatives as family and yet feel no sense of kinship with close relations who can be ignored for years and contacted only for weddings and funerals. The English language has relatively few words to express family relationships, but other languages can express family relationship in precise detail, and people can offer lists of their ancestors over a variety of generations. In Britain, we would probably tend to define families as people we care about or feel some sort sense of duty towards, but this is of little use sociologically because sociology is concerned with social patterns.

One of the earliest writers in the functionalist tradition, George Murdock, suggested that a family consists of a social group which includes sexually cohabiting adults and their children. He used an anthropological process to test the claim that the **nuclear family** is universal in all societies. He suggested that no matter how far from our own cultural norms the family arrangement was, there would be at its core two sexually active adults (a man and a woman) and their children. This is a controversial position to hold nowadays, and few people would limit themselves to Murdock's definition of family. However, he makes a number of points that remain valid for discussion:

- Families appear to develop social structures that suit their physical environment. Family form can vary enormously from culture to culture.
- Families are linked by **kinship** ties, duties of obligation and rules which must be observed.
- Families offer social support to the mother and her children.

Anthropologists have supported the view that family structure reflects geography, so that nomadic cultures in difficult geographical regions are often **monogamous** (having only one partner in marriage), and farming communities in areas where child mortality is high are more likely to be **polygamous** (having multiple partnership arrangements). This is functional for the social group because monogamous family arrangements reduce the number of children born, whereas polygamy increases population growth, as there is no surplus of unwed and non-child-bearing women in a polygamous population. The conclusion that you should draw from this short section and from the activity below is that families are defined in very different ways, according to culture, and that there is variation in family structures around the world.

ACTIVITY

KNOWLEDGE AND UNDERSTANDING

Make up a project to develop your class notes. Get members of the group to find out more about the various family forms that exist in cultures around the world. Use the Internet to look up variations in family form using some of the following key terms or words from the list of family structure analysis:

- concubine
- polyandry

- polygyny
- polygamy (sites linked to Mormon religious groups may offer an explanation of how this works in the USA).

Anthropology and historical sites are a source of information. When you have discovered useful information, make multiple copies and share it with other people in your class.

The terminology of family structure analysis.
Note that these definitions are rather general in nature because there is debate as to their precise meaning. Use a dictionary to check how each term is defined in detail. The terms will be used without further explanation throughout this area and you will be expected to understand them.

Cohabitation   People who live together as married partners but who have not undertaken a legal marriage ceremony.

Extended family   A family consisting of a variety of generations who live together or close by each other and have close social interaction. An extended family can be horizontally extended, with aunts and uncles actively participating in social arrangements.

Gay family   Adults of the same sex who share the rearing of children.

Household   People who share a common residence, some of whom may be unrelated to each other (for example, students in a flat share, a live-in nanny or servant).

Illegitimacy/illegitimate child   Children who are born to parents who are not legally married.

Kinship   People whom you regard as family by reasons of blood or marriage and to whom you owe obligations.

Marriage   A legal status where people have publicly made promises to each other about their future relationship.

Matriarchy   A society dominated by the needs of women.

Monogamy   An exclusive marriage arrangement between two partners, usually one man and one woman, although gay couples have been known to describe themselves as monogamous.

Nuclear family   A family of two adults and their children.

Patriarchy   A society dominated by the needs of men.

Polyandry   A social arrangement of multiple husbands.

Polygamy   An arrangement of multiple marriage partners.

Polygyny   An arrangement of multiple wives.

Reconstituted family   Parents have remarried and there are children from more than one marriage in the home.

Serial monogamy   Having a number of partners, but only one at a time.

Single parent   One adult and his or her children. This can arise from choice, divorce or widowhood.

Ideology of family in our society

Our society has a clear ideology of family that is apparent wherever you look. This ideology often bears little relationship to the realities of family life and may even seem a little old-fashioned. Yet, as will be seen later in this area, it influences political and social decision-making in Britain. The dominant ideology of family life is Christian and linked with religious and moral belief – and particularly with sexual behaviour. In our society, family ideology tends to be patriarchal: the man provides financial and moral support for his wife and children. However far this may actually be from most people's lives, it is an assumed relationship which can be seen in all forms of cultural expression, such as advertising or television (one has only to look at the cartoon section of a tabloid newspaper to see examples of such assumptions in the stories). Furthermore, sexual behaviour is in theory limited to married **couples** only, and its purpose is for the procreation of children and the satisfaction of the male.

You should consider the dominant ideology of the family because it underlies political thinking and policy-making. Many writers and thinkers have such an overwhelming belief in an ideal of family life that they feel that the changes taking place in the structure of families in our society may lead to a general breakdown in law, order and morality. This ideal is closely related to the sociological expression '**the cereal packet norm**': a family group consisting of mother, father and various children of both genders.

Almost all the theories considered in the next section seem to share this overview of family and gender relations. They see males as dominant in the domestic arena and women as subordinate to the needs of men. This perception has not been significantly challenged by western families. The different perspectives offer analyses of the causes and reasons for the division in the roles of husbands and wives that are remarkably dissimilar.

A C T I V I T Y　KS　**PROBLEM SOLVING, COMMUNICATION**

IDENTIFICATION AND INTERPRETATION

Brainstorm a list of visual images of the family that you can see in the mass media. Go into a local branch of a popular newsagent and look for images, such as those on Christmas cards and magazine covers. Use your local supermarket and investigate the images of family life on the packaging of products we buy and the advertising we see. What images of family life recur over and over again?

Contemporary issues raised by the study of the family

Look at the questions below. They should frame some of your thinking on family analysis, and they reflect many modern debates. These questions may be social and moral concerns, but you must use sociological theory and fact to inform your answers. If you do not, you will be applying common sense, and in sociology, common sense is another term for ignorance.

Family structure and form:

1　Are all forms of family arrangement, including gay families, equally valid?
2　Is it a person's right to have a child?
3　Is sex before marriage acceptable?
4　Is marriage for life?
5　Should divorce be more difficult to obtain?
6　Should marriage be made more difficult?

Gender and family:

7　Why marry? Are there different reasons for marriage for men and for women?
8　Is love and mutual sexual desire a good reason for a couple to marry?
9　What do men gain from marriage?
10　What do women gain from marriage?
11　Is it wrong for people of the same gender to marry each other?
12　Is sex less important or valid if it is based on the need to gratify a physical desire rather than as an expression of emotional need?

Children and families:

13　Do children need fathers?
14　Do children need mothers?
15　Do fathers have rights over their own children?
16　Should mothers have rights over children?
17　How important is the grandparent/grandchild relationship?
18　Is a biological parent more important than an adoptive parent?

The family and social responsibility:

19　Is it the responsibility of the family or of the state to look after the disabled, the sick and the frail elderly?
20　Is institutional care of the elderly necessarily a bad thing?
21　What responsibilities should children have for their elderly parents?
22　Should families or schools teach morality and values to children?
23　Are parents responsible for the behaviour of their children?
24　Has the state the right to remove children from people who it considers to be poor parents?
25　Who does the housework?
26　Who makes the important decisions in a household and how are these decisions reached?

Theories of family

Functionalism

The writer most closely associated with functionalist analyses of family was the American Talcott Parsons. Parsons, as a functionalist, was a **consensus** theorist. His view of society stressed order, conformity and organisation. You will note the similarity between his ideas and those of Murdock discussed earlier. Parsons said that the modern family fitted the needs of modern industrial society. This idea is known as the **fit thesis**. Families, he argued, offer females an **expressive** and emotional role through satisfaction as housewives and mothers. Males, on the other hand, have an **instrumental** work role, providing for their families. This means, in simple terms that *women feel* emotions, but that *men do* things. There is no strain in such a relationship because females are not in competition with male breadwinners. As a point of evaluation, these views must be challenged because they ignore power inequalities between men and women.

- Women and men are seen as different and unequal.
- Women's paid work is seen as unimportant and is ignored.

Parsons felt that the family has two basic functions:

- it socialises children
- it stabilises adult personalities

and a number of subsidiary functions.

ACTIVITY   **COMMUNICATION**

IDENTIFICATION AND INTERPRETATION

Watch Walt Disney's *Lady and the Tramp* for an extremely clear illustration of the functionalist view of marriage and family. What do you learn about Disney's ideology of gender relationships and assumptions about male and female behaviour from that film? This offers an extremely clear example of how the love of a good woman (such as the naïve Lady) will tame the wild sexuality of the male Tramp and stabilise him into a house dog. The love of a bad and sexually active female such as the Pekinese from the Dog Pound only leads to disappointment for the female.

Other functionalists, such as Murdock, add the following list of functions to the family:

- sexual control
- economic support
- creation of children
- socialisation of children
- sense of name and belonging.

ACTIVITY   **COMMUNICATION**

IDENTIFICATION AND INTERPRETATION | ANALYSIS AND EVALUATION

Read and analyse the words of the formal church wedding ceremony. What ideologies about the purpose and nature of family can you see in the service? To what extent do these ideas tie in with the functionalist perspective on family?

Parsons' fit thesis suggested that:

- Families are becoming nuclear so that people are geographically mobile and can move around for work.
- Family life must offer people a sense of solidarity because this has been lost as society has become more fragmented and less community oriented.
- Many traditional roles of the family have been taken over by the state. Most notable among these are health and educational functions, which now belong to schools and hospitals.

■ A woman's role in the family is determined by her biological and nurturing functions.

The fit thesis, with its focus on the internal structures of family life, is generally agreed to be hopelessly optimistic. Criticisms of the functionalist view of family come from a variety of directions.

Historians

Historians, such as Laslett and Anderson, suggest that families were never extended in the past in the way that functionalists describe. The land, farms and farming methods could not support large populations and family structures had the effect of limiting population. People married late and died relatively young. People generally recognised that a serious illness would result in death. As evidence, wills were usually written within the days preceding death and people rarely wrote more than one version of a will. Conception could be controlled through breastfeeding, which limits female fertility, and other methods must have been known as there was often a regular gap of some years between registered births. Child mortality rates were very high and so, although a number of children could have been born to a family, it would be expected that only one or two would survive in normal circumstances. The study of pre-industrial society through wills and parish records suggests that families were generally nuclear because so few children survived to adulthood. Those who did delayed marriage till the death of their own parents. Farms were not run by families alone but included a variety of household servants, generally the children of equals who were waiting to inherit their own property so that they could marry. Childless couples would adopt the orphaned or surplus children of neighbours and relations.

Feminists

Feminists such as Oakley suggest that the functionalist view of the family ignores the significance of the experience of women and in fact offers a justification for their oppression in that functionalists think it to be good for society.

Radical psychiatrists and psychoanalysts

Radical psychiatrists and psychoanalysts such as Laing and Cooper suggest that much mental illness is caused by the strain of family life on individuals. This view is also known as anti-psychiatry and is more of the 1960s and the 1970s than the present day. It still influences some perspectives such as feminism, where a woman's mental instability and misery can be explained in terms of family and patriarchy.

Marxism

Marxist analyses of family life stress the way in which family reinforces existing social inequalities. The family has become a **unit of consumption**, existing to buy goods, rather than a **unit of production**, which it was in pre-industrial society.

> **HINTS AND TIPS**   It is very easy to dismiss functionalism because of its idealistic and somewhat dated view of family relationships. However, you should also recognise that many people are happy to run their lives in a family unit that is very like the one described by Parsons and they gain satisfaction from that lifestyle.

Marxism

Marxist theory of the family begins with the work of **Friedrich Engels**, and existed well before Parsons' analysis. However, it offered a deeply critical analysis that was exciting and well ahead of its time, though it is mainly historical in content. Engels published *The Origin of Family, Private Property and State* a year after the death of his friend Karl Marx in 1884.

Engels saw the development of the family in evolutionary terms, much as he and Marx had described the evolution of capitalist society. He suggested that the first human society was promiscuous and that marriage and the family evolved along with the concepts of private property and inheritance. In crude terms, women can be proved to be the mothers of the children they bear, as witnesses are present at the birth. However, there are usually no witnesses to conception and a man has no certainty that the children a woman bears are his – he must take her word for it. Blood testing and genetic analysis has altered that, but these are very recent technologies. To ensure that the children to whom he intends to leave property are his own, the man must own his wife and restrict her freedom. Monogamous marriage, according to Engels, is the solution to controlling female sexuality and ensuring continuity of male family lines. Although the evidence for prehistoric promiscuity is fairly limited, Engels' broad outline does seem to have validity.

Engels' work here is important for the following reasons:

- he described the way in which family structures change in response to changes in broader society (note the similarity to functionalism here)
- his analysis links the position of women in society to their ability to control property and wealth.

PROFILE

Friedrich Engels
(1820–1895)

Friedrich Engels was born into a wealthy family in the Rheinland (now part of Germany). He rejected the ideas of his conservative family and became a close friend and working partner of Karl Marx (1818–1883). The contribution that Engels has made to social theory would be far more recognised if he were not so overshadowed by the towering figure of Marx.

In the earlier part of the nineteenth century he became involved in revolutionary and political activity and he and Marx moved to England in exile after 1848. Engels worked for the family business in Manchester and was able to support Marx with gifts of money. He wrote many books and pamphlets on his own behalf, as well as with Marx. After Marx's death, Engels prepared the two unpublished sections of **Das Kapital** for publication.

The first work that Engels wrote was his 1844–5 study. **The Condition of the Working Class in England** can be considered as pioneering social research. It was based on his experience of the industrial revolution in Lancashire and contains a class war analysis of relationships between workers and mill owners.

Eli Zaretsky developed Engels' analysis further by suggesting that families prop up capitalism because they reproduce on a small scale the power relationships of broader society. Males earn the money and create patriarchal families. Females have no economic power and yet they do much of the work of the family. Although the work of Engels and other Marxists was in print and known about, it did not really gain recognition until the middle of the twentieth century when feminists drew on these ideas to develop their own distinctive analyses.

ACTIVITY   KS COMMUNICATION

KNOWLEDGE AND UNDERSTANDING	IDENTIFICATION AND INTERPRETATION	ANALYSIS AND EVALUATION

Plan a short answer to the following question as though it were a 12-mark part of a stimulus question. You can then practise the skill of selection of evidence.

Evaluate the contribution of Marxist thought to an understanding of the development of the family.

HINTS AND TIPS   Marxism offers a critical analysis. It links social change with family change. It offers a valid interpretation of and reasoning for the development of social attitudes, which see women as the property of men. It makes a clear link between economics and family life. It is also of value as a starting point for feminist analysis.

Prominent theories based on Marxist analyses of family include the following.

- Gittins suggests that family life is often seen as a microcosm (or small version) of society to illustrate its workings.
- Althusser said that the norms and values of family life are part of the ideology of capitalism and identifies them as part of an ideological state apparatus.
- Feeley suggested that authoritarian families teach people to accept social structures without questioning their validity.

Feminism

Feminism gathered momentum throughout the twentieth century. Early feminists were concerned with practical issues such as knowledge of birth control and the acquisition of voting rights. By the early 1960s, many of the first battles had been fought and won.

Attention was then focused on the lives and experiences of ordinary women.

Phenomenologists Janet Moss and Scarlet Friedman, writing in the feminist tradition in the 1960s and 1970s, suggested that:

- Femininity is defined for women in our culture through the ability to do domestic work.

- There is strong pressure on women to become wives.

- Women see marriage as a status gain.

- Marriage actually means loss of status and power.

- Women seek fulfilment in the home, but the domestic role is subordinated to the needs of the man.

- Women learn to subordinate themselves to the needs of others and lose their sense of individuality.

- Women's careers and time are subordinate to the needs of their male partners.

This list illustrates a valid point that the sociology of the family is bound up totally with the sociology of gender. This was even truer of its beginnings than in the present.

Feminism has broken itself down into occasionally vicious political and sociological debates based on perspectives, which are listed below. You should note that these divisions act merely as a rough guide. there are debates within debates!

- **Radical feminists** such as Ann Oakley, Kate Millet, Andrea Dworkin and Shulamith Firestone suggest that the most significant inequality is that which women face from men. Some radical feminism can be extreme, more so in its early days than in the present. There is sometimes, but not always, a link with the politics of lesbianism.

- **Marxist feminists** such as Juliet Mitchell, Nancy Chodorow and Bea Campbell see a link between patriarchy and capitalistic society. Generally they suggest that female oppression is linked to ideological and/or economic domination.

- **Liberal feminists** such as Sue Sharpe and Rosalind Delmar have a broader agenda because they are concerned with the impact of gender divisions

within society. They are prepared to concede that males are also the victims of gender socialisation and they tend to seek legislative change to ensure equality for men and women.

PROFILE

Simone de Beauvoir
(1908–1986)

Simone de Beauvoir is one of the heroines of modern feminism. She was born in Paris in 1908 into a relatively well off, though not wealthy, family. She was very well informed and her analyses included sociology, literature, philosophy, and history. Her writings (novels, fiction and academic studies) concentrated on the role of women's experiences, which she saw as being separate and very different from those of men.

She had a longstanding relationship with the existentialist philosopher Jean-Paul Sartre, with whom she refused to have any form of conventional marriage arrangement. While it would be insulting to many people to define them by their companions, in this case the relationship was also a partnership involving exchange of ideas. Sartre is widely considered to be one of the leading thinkers of modern European philosophy

De Beauvoir was a prolific writer, but her most famous work is the enormous volume **The Second Sex**. This text considers the social and political impotence of women who, she argued, are forced to depend on males for experience and action. It would be a long project to read such a large book, but many people regard it as an extremely worthwhile experience and have gained a great deal from the exercise.

De Beauvoir was extremely influential among academics and Shulamith Firestone's **The Dialectic of Sex** (1979) was dedicated to her. She was widely read by women in the early feminist movements of the 1970s. She nursed Sartre until his death, wrote a book about the experience, which she published when she was in her seventies, and died in 1986.

In terms of feminist studies of the family, there are three basic issues underlying research and debate:

- domestic labour and housework
- power relationships within the family
- the socialisation of young women into domestic roles

These strands are deeply interwoven, and few studies will fit neatly into one of the above categories. However, they do illustrate the concerns that feminists have raised in their discussions. More recent work, such as that by the well known journalist and commentator Bea Campbell, has begun to look at the socialisation and rearing of young males.

ACTIVITY KS WORKING WITH PEOPLE

KNOWLEDGE AND UNDERSTANDING	IDENTIFICATION AND INTERPRETATION	ANALYSIS AND EVALUATION

Use the following questions as a guide to discussions within your group.
1 What general differences are there between the three main feminist perspectives?
2 What criticisms can you make of feminism as a sociological perspective?
3 What does feminism add to the study of sociology that would not be considered otherwise?
4 Do we take feminism too seriously?
5 Can a man be a feminist?

TASK

Hypothesis – Women remain responsible for the bulk of domestic labour in the home.

Context – This is a question which will support your study in a significant part of the syllabus.

It is a significant feminist debate because housework remains a symbol for many of the oppression of women and their relegation to the domestic sphere. There is also a functionalist argument as to the extent to which men are now participating in housework, if only to support their working wives. You will be investigating **conjugal role** and some of your conclusions might be related to power relationships within the home. A lot has been written on this debate and so your review of literature in the context should be significantly easier than with some other studies.

Method – Identify a number of domestic tasks. Ask a sample group of men and women which of these tasks they undertake in the home and how many hours they devote to those tasks. You might also need to ask if people have paid employment and how many hours

they work. A non-working partner could reasonably be expected to do more in the home than a working partner does.

Make sure that the domestic tasks include car maintenance and other more 'masculine' jobs. You will then be able to quantify the amount of domestic labour that each partner contributes to the family.

Evaluation – There is no certainty of unanimity between men and women as to how much each contributes. Men are likely to over-estimate their contribution and women to devalue the male contribution. This provides you with an excellent discussion on the value and meaning of answers to empirical questions for the evaluation section of your work. Some tasks are likely to be gendered, such as lawn mowing or toilet cleaning. You may well therefore discover that housework does not simply represent a power relationship between couples, but illustrates a more complex set of meanings as to the nature of gender itself.

Changes in family structure

We have very little formal knowledge of how many marriages, irregular liaisons and separations took place in the past before **divorce** and separation laws made

such phenomena something that can be measured. Parish registers and some historical records such as Le Roy Ladurie's fascinating descriptions of medieval French village life in his classic book, *Montaillou* (1978), offer an insight into some communities. A detailed check of many family histories may reveal patterns of separation or marital unhappiness that were concealed from neighbours and even some relatives. Much family history could be extremely complex and little of it would have been obvious in any official record, as these were often knowingly falsified or irrelevant. We know that families would pass off illegitimate children of daughters as belonging to the grandmother and that abortion, if not commonplace, certainly was practised. We do not know if marriages are happier or unhappier now than in the past. Women's aid groups will offer hearsay evidence of very elderly women, even some of 80 years or more, coming forward for the first time to reveal habits of domestic violence from their partners which have stretched over entire lifetimes.

Given the above, sociologists have still made detailed assumptions about both the nature of family relationships and the structure of families. They have made specific claims about how families and their structures have changed – and within Britain this is a debate that falls neatly into two sections.

Since the end of the Second World War in 1945, there have been dramatic changes in the nature of British society. The first part of the debate centres on work that was accomplished and challenged in the 1960s and 1970s. The second part has to acknowledge what has happened in British society since the 1980s. There is a useful German word – **Zeitgeist**, or spirit of the time – which offers a view of how people lived and what ideas they had. Figure 6.1 attempts to provide you with a rough overview of family structure and debate, taking into account the Zeitgeist.

> **HINTS AND TIPS**   To get a good overview of events and ideas, talk to people who are older than yourself about the kinds of attitudes that they had when they were younger. You will realise the radical changes in morality and behaviour that have taken place in our society.

Historical – British empiricism

Some of the most important work on family structure and organisation was carried out during the 1950s and 1960s in a series of studies of the working-class community of Bethnal Green, which has long since disappeared under what is now Tower Hamlets. Bethnal Green was a London dockland community

where people, serving in heavy industrial work, had been settled for a long time. The community was extensively surveyed by sociologists working from the London School of Economics and different authorial teams considered various elements of family life. The best known among these is probably Young and Willmott.

There is an irony in that the community was being studied as it was disappearing. The old poor-quality and badly built Victorian terraces were being knocked down in slum clearance programmes. Sociologists such as Young and Willmott described a traditional working-class community that looked after its own, with **extended families** and different lives for men and women. Social relationships were held together by the women and, although men earned the money, it was likely that many women actually controlled the daily spending. The books produced as part of this sequence of studies are still extremely interesting and accessible to read, although they describe a life pattern that is much less common than it was.

The breakdown of the community and the growth of slum clearance meant that families were split up. They were re-housed in estates in Essex and throughout the outskirts of the London area with little regard for community patterns. Willmott and Young, who had studied Bethnal Green, now looked at the new working-class families who had lived in the new estates. They produced their influential book *The Symmetrical Family* in 1973 and triggered a debate that continued for a long time and which fuelled the anger of early feminist sociologists.

They suggested a four-stage development of the structure of the modern family, which owes more than a little to the work of Talcott Parsons and the fit thesis (Figure 6.2).

This thesis had been superseded, but can still be found in some early GCSE textbooks presented as a factual analysis:

- Feminism pointed out that the questionnaire Willmott and Young used asked only whether men helped their wives in the home. This question itself displays patriarchal belief, and gave false positives. Cooking breakfast once a week was taken as evidence of helping in the home! One of the most significant pieces of work with reference to this

Time scale	Events and changes in society	Research emphasis
Post-war period and 1950s	Birth rate rose after the war. City centre slum clearance programmes took place. Movement into new estates outside cities. New industries, such as car building, grow. Traditional industries, such as coal and docks, are in trouble. Commonwealth immigration of Asians and West Indians begins in 1948	Sociologists were interested in describing and documenting the lives of the working class and looking at the changes taking place in family structure and organisation
1960s	City centre slum clearance programmes continue. Development of city centre high rise blocks. New technological and service sector work gains importance as traditional industries are in serious decline. Towards the end of the decade, there is a spirit of youth rebellion, leading to protest movements. Birth control pill invented	Embourgeoisement thesis – the suggestion that the working classes are richer and therefore more like the middle classes is investigated and rejected. Families are described as 'home-centred' and 'privatised'. Symmetrical Family thesis developed and rejected by early feminists
1970s	Tower blocks are rejected as costly mistake. Crime grows in new outer city estates. People reject traditional values and experiment with alternative family styles. Divorce made easier. Gender equality legislation passed in 1978. Women are more likely to have career jobs. Cohabitation becomes acceptable but seen as 'trial marriage' rather than marriage alternative. Liberalisation of homosexuality laws	Critical analyses of family developed. Feminism begins as very angry writing. Marxist and radical theories developed and more widely disseminated. Advent of theory of 'New Man'
1980s–mid-1990s	New Right political agenda comes into play. This takes little account of the reality of people's lives. Divorce rates rise. Single parenthood more common. Marriage is less popular and freer moral stance is taken with regard to sexuality. Fatherhood given status and Child Support Agency comes into being with aim of reducing benefits by making fathers responsible for children. More women choose single parenthood as a positive option	Feminism still angry, but looks at reality of working-class life. Feminism turns towards suggesting that working-class notions of masculinity are the real problem. University research becomes more geared to the needs of funding organisations and therefore moves away from 'pure' research and into problem-based approaches
mid-1990s	Change of government to Labour party had meant little real change of policy by 2000	

Figure 6.1   Timeline summary of changes in British society

Stage one: The pre-industrial family	The family is a unit of production. People live in extended or nuclear families working on farms. Family relationships are not that close and marriage is for economic reasons
Stage two: The industrial family	Family members are now employed in factories. Extended families develop in parts of cities and members of such families protect each other. Families are female-centred in matriarchal households. Men work and women are at the centre of domestic life
Stage three: The modern family	Families are symmetrical and home-centred. Husbands and wives share the burden of domesticity equally. Family relationships are privatised and child-centred. Families are not so reliant on distant kin and extended families. The working classes are more like the middle classes (this last suggestion is known as the **Embourgeoisement** thesis).
Stage four: The future family	Workers will become increasingly like the middle class. Men of the family will become more work-centred and women will return to the home.

Figure 6.2   Four-stage development of the modern family

was Hannah Gavron's *The Captive Wife* (1966), which painted a picture of women who were emotionally and financially dependent on men. This point is of particular significance in the gender role and domestic labour debates that are central to critical and feminist analyses of the family.

- The idea that the working class would follow middle-class behaviour patterns as they became wealthy and earned more had already been comprehensively rebutted by Goldthorpe and Lockwood's 1969 studies of *The Affluent Worker* of the car plants in Luton. This work suggested a pattern of privatised families but very different social class-based lifestyles.

The debate that ensued was a fierce one and centred largely on female domestic labour. This is a very serious point indeed because underlying the question of who washes the dishes are much more important issues of gender power relationships.

- Who makes the decisions within the home? This raises a profoundly critical analysis of families which takes in male violence against women and their children and emotionally abusive relationships.

- Who earns the higher pay in society? Women's labour in the workplace tends to be low paid. It also reflects the type of work that is done in the home. Feminised work is cooking, cleaning and childcare. This extends into the professions, where women teach and nurse. Both forms of work, it is argued, are relatively poorly paid in comparison with male professions. This is still an issue of serious debate, particularly as women often retain financial responsibility for the children if a relationship ends, and daughters tend to take care of their elderly parents.

Despite the picture that feminists painted of domestically overburdened wives and husbands who maintain exploitative relationships, many men do play far more of a domestic role in the home than would have seemed possible for working-class men in the past. Through the 1970s and 1980s, there was much discussion surrounding the existence of the **New Man**, who was taking on a caring, sharing role within families and who challenged the old male stereotypes. Many women would argue that it is probable that reports of the New Man were exaggerated. Evidence collected by feminists such as Ann Oakley and Sue Sharpe suggested that men may do more in homes but rarely participate equally in domestic chores, which remain the province of women. They also have a tendency to do the 'fun' jobs such as playing with the children rather than the unpleasant and dirty work.

HINTS AND TIPS   *Research into the existence, or not, of New Men is an extremely profitable area for coursework study. You might also consider whether adolescent females and adolescent males are expected to contribute equally to housework. Questions of the kind of domestic labour that each gender is actually prepared to undertake often produce interesting results, with men being delighted to participate in childcare, but less willing to undertake unpleasant tasks.*

Arguments about the role and nature of partnerships within marriages were overtaken by fundamental shifts in public morality. By the mid-1980s it was no longer expected or felt necessary to have a wedding certificate in order to have a publicly acknowledged sexual relationship. This is, of course, a broad generalisation, but the wedding ceremony and marriage itself took on a new and very different order of social meaning.

Modern family structures

Many of the following changes in the structure of the family will be returned to later in this section and you should relate this material to the discussion on The Death of the Family debate (page 321). Here you should note the following rough guide to statistical changes in family structure (see data in *Social Trends* each year). Other books of statistics are published and will offer more detailed figures for you to analyse.

- Divorce is more frequent.

- There is remarriage after divorce. Many children live in reconstituted families.

- People live longer and marriage is more likely to end in divorce. In the past, marriages had a much shorter duration and ended in the death of a partner.

- Children are less likely to be born to married couples, although often the partners are in a stable relationship.

- Single parenthood is typical of younger people.

A C T I V I T Y

KS **WORKING WITH OTHERS, INFORMATION TECHNOLOGY**

KNOWLEDGE AND UNDERSTANDING	ANALYSIS AND EVALUATION

Collect as many tables and charts from as many sources as possible to support the above analysis. You should look at *Social Trends*, Home Office data on the Internet and at CD-ROMs to gather supporting evidence. When you have discovered a

table or some statistical evidence, copy it. Practise the skill of turning the numbers into a written explanation of what you have learned by looking at them. Share this material with your study partners.

- Very wealthy and very poor women are less likely to see the need for a long-term male partner to share parenthood.

- People live together before marriage. Frequently they have already expressed commitment by undertaking joint house purchase.

- People may choose never to undertake a wedding ceremony although they may remain in a monogamous family relationship with each other for many years.

- People in stable partnerships may not even share an address.

- There is some evidence to suggest that men may take on father roles with the children of their partners rather than with their own biological children.

- Traditional gender patterns of domestic labour and roles appear to be changing, although this remains a matter for debate.

Variety of family structure

In this section we consider the complexity and variety of family structure in modern Britain. In examinations, students are often asked to consider whether the nuclear family is typical of modern British society. In practical terms, the answer to such a question is a guarded 'yes'. This material also relates to discussion, which centres on debates linked to 'Is the family a dying/redundant institution?' Although most people do live in a variant of the nuclear family, there is still plenty of evidence to suggest that it is only one of the many family forms that can be found in our society.

Households and communal living

Many people share homes. This pattern is typical of students and young people in their first jobs. These home-sharers are not families and the arrangement is based on economics and friendship patterns, so they can therefore be classified as a **household**. In the 1970s, and still in some rural areas of Britain today, people experimented with other forms of communal living and house-sharing.

Ethnic minority families

Those British whose parents or grandparents were born in other countries may also have strong links with cultures whose traditions are very different from westernised Christian tradition. Islamic law, for instance, will allow a man to have more than one wife: this is illegal in Britain and classified as the crime of bigamy, but cases have been reported.

HINTS AND TIPS *Two immigrant community patterns are described below, but remember that there is a variety of patterns even within groups.*

Generalisations that can be made would suggest that among communities from the Asian subcontinent family is a very significant concept. They are likely to be extended, with members of families sharing homes or living very close to each other. However, Asians live within communities as well as families and the significance of extended family within the Asian community can sometimes be overstressed. Anwar (1979) studied the Pakistani community in Rochdale and discovered that family members supported each other with house loans, job-hunting, form-filling and accommodation. This help was not merely friendly, but also helped to maintain the honour of the whole community. Weddings and family festivals took on enormous social significance.

The 1984 survey *Black and White Britain* found high patterns of single-parent or female-dominated families and a tradition of absentee fatherhood, which had developed in the Caribbean and carried on in Britain. The role of marriage as an institution is less significant in the Caribbean and it is suggested that this is a remnant of slavery. There are two possible ways in which slavery affected the culture of the Caribbean with regard to marriage:

■ Under slavery the children were the property of the owner of the mother. Families were frequently broken and marriage between slaves was, in any case, illegal.

■ When slavery ended, men were unable to find work. They formed migrant labouring communities and could not take on the responsibility of fatherhood. Mothers took on the role of primary family support and women looked after each other.

Once in Britain, many Caribbean immigrants experienced racism and were unable to obtain highly paid work. If they became unemployed, then it was inadvisable for them to marry. The benefit system discouraged marriage and cohabitation, as couples gain less from the state than they do as two separate individuals. Nevertheless, most West Indians did in fact live in married or cohabiting two-parent families. It should also be noted that there is a high and increasing rate of intermarriage and cohabitation between the Afro-Caribbean and white communities. It could be argued that the ethnic distinctions between the two groups – which have always been fairly loose in dockland areas, where intermarriage was not uncommon even at the turn of the century – have lost some of their significance in modern British society.

Gay families

Like some heterosexuals, some homosexuals are promiscuous or do not form long-term relationships. They may even engage in heterosexual marriage partnerships but satisfy their homosexual desires outside the marriage or deny them altogether. However, others form longstanding emotional bonds with patterns echoing those of traditional marriage and family partnerships. Plummer (1978) identified a variety of homosexual relationship patterns. This research was conducted when tolerance of homosexuality was not common and had only recently been legitimised in law. It does not therefore acknowledge lesbianism and so Plummer talks of men only.

■ The couple may adopt heterosexual marriage patterns with a dominant partner and a ritualised form of marriage.

■ There may be an equal boyfriend relationship where the partners live apart. They may even disguise the nature of their friendship from all but their closest friends.

■ The partners develop a personal relationship with understood rules and a lifestyle arrangement.

There is a grave danger in generalising about homosexual relationship patterns: people develop the relationships they require to suit their beliefs and needs, regardless of their sexuality. You should note that same-sex partners are not allowed a legal status equivalent to marriage in terms of legal rights and duties. This is very significant, as a same-sex partner cannot be next of kin as a marriage partner is, and may be excluded from funeral arrangements and inheritance by a disapproving family.

There are few accurate figures on the number of homosexual couples who have chosen to bring up children. This is an extremely sensitive subject as many people have strong moral and ideological objections to the idea that non-heterosexual couples should be allowed to have parental rights. The area is a minefield of high emotion and popular prejudice. Lesbian

---

ACTIVITY   KS **WORKING WITH OTHERS**

KNOWLEDGE AND UNDERSTANDING	IDENTIFICATION AND INTERPRETATION

Be tactful and polite, but if you or members of your teaching or study group originated in ethnic minority groups, then you or they may be willing to explain something of that culture's family structure and significance to all. Remember that you *must* respect people's right to refuse what they may feel is intrusive inquiry into a private area of their lives.

couples may have fewer problems with the acquisition of children if they are willing to participate in heterosexual relations or can find a sperm donor willing to help, but gay men have also taken on parental roles. Hospitals have shown themselves unwilling to help with conception if lesbian partners have fertility problems. The evidence is limited, but if you wish to pursue enquiries, then you could perhaps contact self-help groups and welfare organisations for information.

HINTS AND TIPS *Use a telephone directory to obtain addresses of gay and lesbian organisations but make contact by a courteous letter if your research is sociological rather than personal in intent. If you wish to develop your independent study then write from your home address. If you name your school or institution then you must show the letter to a teacher. Note that teachers are in a difficult position over the question of homosexuality, regardless of their personal views. Government guidelines for personal and social education emphasise the point that students must be taught that homosexual behaviour is 'abnormal'. This might be a point that you should consider when thinking about the significance of family ideology.*

SOCIOLOGY IN PRACTICE

Like most first-time dads, Barrie Drewitt and Tony Barlow are eagerly awaiting the arrival of their babies. They've bought cots and prams, decorated the nursery and even decided on names.

The difference, of course, is that Barrie and Tony are a gay couple from Essex — and their 'twins' will be born to a surrogate mum they found in America. Not the most conventional set-up, you'll agree, but everyone involved in this bizarre baby-making arrangement is delighted.

For Barrie and Tony, the twins' birth in December will mark the end of years of heartbreak as they tried to make their dreams of parenthood a reality.

'We've been to hell and back in the past couple of years,' says Barrie, 30, a former nurse. 'I'd always wanted a child. We both come from big families, and seeing our relatives popping them out all over the place made it worse.

'First we tried to adopt. Essex County Council told us we might be able to adopt a child with Down's syndrome. We were introduced to one child but just as we were getting to know each other, they turned us down. And, of course, that was upsetting. Then we tried artificial insemination with a female friend, but it didn't work.'

So instead, the couple, who've been together for 11 years, turned to surrogacy. They had to go to America, where the laws are more relaxed than in the UK, to find a surrogate mum.

The procedure was an expensive one, costing about £200,000, but Tony and Barrie are well off. 'Luckily, we can afford it but we'd have re-mortgaged our home to have these children if we'd had to,' says Tony, 35, a dermatologist.

They recently sold their clinical testing company, which tests drugs, toiletries and cosmetics on humans, for £4 million — and still collect salaries from managing it full-time.

And, as both men grew up on rough estates in Manchester, they want to give their kids all the luxuries they never had, like piano lessons and holidays.

Tony and Barrie's first step towards realising their dream came in 1997, when they registered with a Californian agency which introduced them to one woman who'd donate her eggs, and another who'd be the surrogate and carry the child. Using a separate donor ensures that the surrogate has no claim on a child once it's born.

When the agency introduced them to Rosalind Bellamy, a new surrogate mother, everything just fell into place.

'We got on really well with her and her husband Chris, and I felt we were in safe hands because Rosalind had already been a surrogate,' says Tony.

'We were looking for people who'd be interested in the children and be part of an extended family,' adds Barrie. 'We've got a house in Beverly Hills, so we'll take the children on holiday there every year. We want them to know where they've come from.'

Barrie and Tony, who share a home in Chelmsford, Essex, have already invited the donor and her family on holiday to Britain.

The surrogate's story

This will be Rosalind's second surrogate birth – and her second set of surrogate twins. She and husband Chris, a 33-year-old flooring contractor, already have four sons of their own, aged between eight and 15.

'This time, I wanted to be more involved and Barrie and Tony are keen for us to be part of the family.' Rosalind, Chris and their children recently visited Tony and Barrie in England so they could get to know each other better.

Chris says that the whole family has made sacrifices. 'Sometimes Rosalind misses a school concert or a sports day because she's going to the doctor, but it's worth it,' he says.

'We feel so strongly about what we're doing that if people are negative about it, we just get more positive,' says Chris.

Rosalind adds, 'I tell people to ask themselves what they'd do if they couldn't have kids. Does God get upset if we give someone a new heart?'

Source: Adapted from *A Family* by Fiona McNeill, *Woman's Own*, 6 September 1999:10–11.

1 What is a surrogate mother? **(2)**

2 Why is it necessary for Barrie and Tony to use a surrogate mother to have their children? What other methods of acquiring a child did they attempt? **(4)**

3 Why was it legally necessary for Rosalind to be implanted with eggs from another woman for the purposes of the surrogacy? **(3)**

4 What arguments are there for and against the suggestion that Barrie and Tony should be regarded in the same way as a legally married couple? **(6)**

5 Can Barrie, Tony, and their children be regarded as a family in sociological terms? **(3)**

6 What advantages and disadvantages will the children of the surrogacy experience as they grow up? Make a list of different ideas. **(6)**

7 Sociologically evaluate the functionalist suggestion that it is necessary for children to be brought up by both a mother and a father, with reference to the article and other information. **(8)**

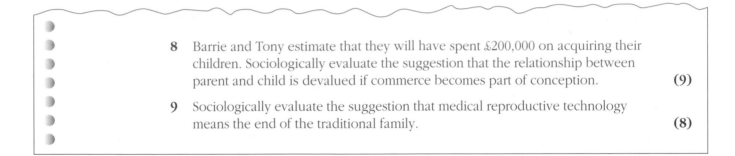

8 Barrie and Tony estimate that they will have spent £200,000 on acquiring their children. Sociologically evaluate the suggestion that the relationship between parent and child is devalued if commerce becomes part of conception. **(9)**

9 Sociologically evaluate the suggestion that medical reproductive technology means the end of the traditional family. **(8)**

Single parenthood

Generally the evidence suggests that women are more likely to be single parents than men. Census data from 1991 suggests that lone parents head about 10% of all households and that women head the majority of these households. Approximately one in five families with children is headed by a lone mother. Lone fathers consist of fewer than 2% of all households.

The possible reasons for single parenthood are simple:

■ death of a partner

■ divorce

■ choice

There has been a very significant rise in the number of children born outside a formal marriage agreement. Currently the figures are running at about 30% and rising. In fact, many of these children are born to parents who cohabit. Ann Condy (1994) suggests that 50% of children born outside formal marriage are registered by couples who share an address. The number of children born to single teenage mothers has steadily fallen, but the British rate remains one of the highest in Europe and is the subject of regular **moral panics**. Moral panics are more fully discussed in Area 5 and refer to a state where newspapers and politicians fuel public hysteria.

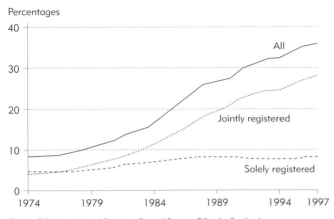

Percentages

Source: Office for National Statistics; General Register Office for Scotland

Figure 6.3 Births outside marriage as a percentage of all live births (Great Britain).

Single parenthood – the public debate

A number of strands to the arguments and public debates surrounding single parenthood can be identified:

■ Are women choosing to be single parents?

■ Should the state subsidise the children of women who choose to be unmarried?

■ Are men reneging on their responsibilities to families?

■ Should men be forced to contribute financially to the support of children that they father, especially given the fact that the male contribution to the act of conception can be both extremely casual and short-lived or even forced on a woman against her will?

■ Who should take financial responsibility in the dual event of the failure of contraception and the unwillingness of a woman to abort?

■ Are very young women taking on motherhood while still too immature to understand the full consequences?

■ Are very young women becoming mothers for the 'wrong' reasons, such as for housing or benefits?

Reconstituted families

Recent statistical evidence suggests that reconstituted families are becoming more common, although the evidence is inconclusive. Certainly, many people remarry after divorce (often within four years), and it has been estimated by Condy that over 8% of families with children contained stepchildren. These stepchildren mainly consisted of the mother's children by previous relationships, but 6% of families contained children by the father's previous relationships. In 6% of cases, both partners had brought children to the marriage. Factors which could affect the accuracy of the figures include the possibility that parents may marry after the birth of their children or that men may, knowingly or unknowingly, accept children they have not fathered as their own.

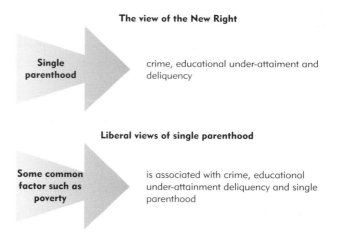

Figure 6.4   Comparison of impact of single parent on society: New Right vs Liberals

Changes within the family

Here the debate moves to a consideration of the nature and significance of changes in family relationships and the impact they have had on public debate. We will return to previously considered issues in order to develop the discussions more fully.

Single parenthood and the gender debate

This is a very complex and emotional area of study, often because there is a conflict of interest between women who are single parents and those who have a rigid ideological belief in the idea that all families should consist of two parents (this is discussed more fully later in this section). The problem is that there is an extremely clear link between single parenthood and poverty. This connection becomes exaggerated when the single parent is a young adolescent; and the children of young teenagers who were raised in

poverty are likely to become young or underage mothers themselves.

There are less well understood links between single parenthood and other deprivation-related phenomena such as crime, emotional and behavioural disturbance, and poor educational attainment (Figure 6.4).

The debate about single parenthood is taking place in the political arena as well as in academic sociological circles. Few people would condemn those forced to live as single parents because of death, but there has been an element of condemnation of the other two causes of single parenthood. For instance, in 1995 John Redwood MP, a notable member of the New Right, who was then a serious contender for the leadership of the Conservative party (which was in government) said that teenage single mothers should put their children up for adoption before accepting state benefit. He was widely supported in his comments by a number of MPs. The supporters of John Redwood suggested that:

- young girls should consider education more important than motherhood
- single motherhood is innately bad because children need parents of both genders
- there are incentives in the benefit system which lead girls to feel that motherhood is somehow going to get them an income and housing

KNOWLEDGE AND UNDERSTANDING	IDENTIFICATION AND INTERPRETATION	ANALYSIS AND EVALUATION

Read the following quotation:

> ‘ *Why the denial? Why should the suggestions (for what to do about the 'problem' of teenage mothers) not be punitive? Why should social policy not use stigma? Lone parents cost the taxpayer some £9 billion a year (I refer to unmarrieds and divorcees, not the bereaved). Taxpayers include poor married couples struggling to bring up children and pass on to them their own values of respectability. The Government, Mr Redwood and perhaps even Tony Blair want to cut this subsidy and encouragement to unrespectable (sic) behaviour. Why not use shame to do so? The Victorians did.*

Digby Anderson *The Times*, 15 August 1995

1 Find out how Victorian single mothers were treated. How different is it from the treatment that single mothers in our society receive?
2 In what ways does society support single parents? Make a list of possible benefits that they may receive.
3 How might a feminist sociologist respond to this assessment of the problem of teenage motherhood? Suggest a number of responses.
4 Sociologically evaluate the suggestion that single motherhood is a problem for our society.

In response to this attack, Dr Nona Dawson of Bristol University pointed out in *The Times* of 15 August 1995:

- approximately 4,000 schoolgirls have babies each year
- middle-class teenagers were more likely to terminate an unwelcome pregnancy
- only a third of teenage mothers are able or willing to stay on in school and few schools could offer support in terms of childcare
- those who did stay on in school often lacked support from their friends
- families could not look after a teenager's baby easily because grandmothers often had jobs

- many teenage mothers become pregnant after only one experience of sex
- many teenage mothers themselves are from lone-parent families
- many teenage mothers who rely on the state live in poverty and with very poor living conditions

HINTS AND TIPS You can find out about what benefits are available to lone parents from your local Post Office, your local Citizen's Advice Bureau or direct from Social Security.

A number of other issues were raised by the debate:

- There is a suggestion that by making single mothers a problem, a dual morality is in operation – men may abandon families but escape the stigma of single parenthood.
- It is only poor women who are targeted by the New Right. Rich women remain free to bear children as they wish, as long as they do not claim benefit.
- The poverty associated with single parenthood can be alleviated with cheap or subsidised childcare and improved pay and conditions for women.
- If women separate from their husbands, they are far more likely to experience a severe fall in income, but they are still willing to leave unhappy marriages.
- Women are more likely to ask for a divorce than men. Allegations made in court imply many men have systematically abused and neglected their families.

HINTS AND TIPS Consider a coursework study into attitudes towards parenthood, pregnancy, divorce, and marriage based on comparisons of class and/or gender groups among young teenagers.

Role of women

The role of women within the family has changed alongside shifts in personal morality as it applies to women. At the turn of the century women lived shorter lives, had more children in marriage, few legal or social rights and responsibilities and were relegated to a domestic role. They could not divorce or vote. They had to accept beatings. Sexual misdemeanour or an illegitimate child could mean a spell in prison or mental

TASK

Investigation – Single parents experience many difficulties in our society.

Context – This type of study would best be conducted with some degree of qualitative research methodology because there are many single parents in our society and it will be difficult for you to find a sample that can represent all single parents. Many are likely to experience poverty and live on benefit, and so have difficulties in relating to their status as welfare claimants but this is by no means certain. After all, some members of the royal family are single parents but they do not live on benefit and cannot be claimed to suffer material deprivation.

Single parents will have a variety of problems depending on the age of their children, their gender, their age, their occupations and their income. Not all their perceived problems will be related to finance because some may feel isolated if they are not in a relationship. Again, do not assume all parents see single parenthood as a negative state. People may actually be thrilled and delighted at the freedom that isolation offers. You will be best to rely on the experiences of family and friends and to keep your sample extremely small. By doing this your work will be unrepresentative but you can acknowledge this in the evaluation.

Method – Revise qualitative study carefully. You will see that interviewing is probably the best methodology to use. You will have problems with sampling if you try to use any representative methods such as random or quota sampling. Snowball sampling is most sensible, but you will have to acknowledge in your evaluation that your sample is skewed.

Be sensitive in your questioning. You are looking at a complex area of someone's life and you must therefore ask permission before pursuing any line of questioning. Take advice from your teacher before any approach to a possible respondent. As a rough guide, do not tackle the question of why the marriage or partnership failed – you will get only a one-sided view anyway.

Evaluation – Your results will certainly show bias depending upon your sample. You will have a valid piece of research, but you might not have a *reliable* piece of research so do not draw too many conclusions about all single parents on the basis of what you have done. You will have gained considerable understanding of the meanings of the lives of some single parents, but only numerical data can be claimed to offer a national picture of how people actually live.

---

hospital as a punishment for moral transgression, even though many women were completely ignorant about sex and children may well have been the result of rape, seduction or **abuse**.

It is often claimed that few women worked outside the home after marriage. While this is possibly true of middle-class women, who would have been expected to give up paid work on marriage, working-class women have probably always had to work, but little of it would have been official in any capacity and there would be little statistical evidence of their activity. Working-class women have probably always cleaned, cooked, looked after other people's children or taken in domestic work such as washing and ironing for small cash-in-hand sums.

There are many reasons for the changes that have taken place with regard to women's position in the family. A few are suggested in Figure 6.5. It should be noted that, although women's lives are considerably improved over those of their great-grandmothers, women still earn less than their male counterparts and may experience male violence or domination in many areas of their lives.

ACTIVITY   WORKING WITH OTHERS, COMMUNICATIONS

IDENTIFICATION AND
INTERPRETATION

Interview women who are much older than you about changes that have taken place in the lives of ordinary women. Ask about how they were treated in the home, the chores they did, and the expectations they had of careers and the future. Ask them to reflect on whether women today have a better experience of life than they themselves had. You may be surprised at some of the answers you receive. If you are in a mixed group, you may find that males and females will gain different answers to the questions.

Cause of family change	Possible impact on family structure and women's lives	But
Effective contraception	Families are smaller. Women can control their own sexuality. Childbirth and pregnancy are matters of choice. Women can work. Female health has improved	Women may be sexually exploited by unscrupulous men and girls still run the risk of a reputation as a 'slag' if they do and 'frigid' if they don't
Women work	Families are smaller. Women are no longer socially, emotionally and economically dependent on men. Women may gain self-respect and esteem through work	Some women may work and do all the housework as well. Women tend to earn less in paid work than men do
Technology has changed	Child mortality rates have dropped so women are under less pressure to be regularly pregnant. Homes are warmer and more comfortable. There is domestic equipment which makes life easier for women. There is medical reproductive technology	Standards of cleanliness and domestic order are probably higher. Children are seen as a right and people are placed under pressure to have babies
Equality movements and legislation	It is illegal to discriminate on grounds of gender so women have recourse to the law if abused. Women can exercise power in the workplace. Younger women can have high expectations of careers	Women are raised to a 'have it all' culture and those who would prefer domestic lives may be pressured to work and be high achievers. Some men seem to feel threatened by successful women
Morals and values have changed	Divorce has become morally acceptable and even common. Divorce laws have been relaxed. Sexual behaviour and marriage are not necessarily linked. Never-married motherhood is acceptable and even common	Many women remain totally responsible for children and are under pressure to bring up families single-handed

Figure 6.5   Impact of social change on lives of women.

Domestic labour

There has been much controversy based on the arrangements within families in relation to responsibility for domestic labour. It is well documented by writers such as Roberts, who described Salford slum life at the turn of the century, that working-class men at that time paid little or no attention to domestic chores. Traditional working-class husbands and wives would boast that the husband did not know where to find the kitchen.

HINTS AND TIPS   *Revise the discussion of the work of Young and Willmott earlier in this area.*

Elizabeth Bott noted the start of a change in 1957 when she described two patterns of domestic role sharing:

■ Segregated conjugal roles exist when men and women have markedly different patterns of tasks and roles within the family.

■ Joint conjugal roles suggest a number of shared activities take place between husband and wife.

She suggested that the pattern of the new emerging working class tended towards role sharing. Functional sociologists such as Young and Willmott had also shown that a breakdown in traditional labour patterns had taken place with the development of the privatised family. Students should refer back to that argument in any discussion of domestic labour and domestic roles.

The tenor of the research changed sharply when Oakley, a feminist, in 1974 argued that all domestic labour was a feature of **patriarchal** exploitation. The debate moved to an investigation into whether there is such a thing as a 'New Man', who is willing to take on a more caring, sharing and nurturing family role. Hearsay evidence will suggest that many men do, in fact, contribute a great deal to family arrangements. Rutherford (1988), for instance, suggested that the rise of feminism has created a need for men to reappraise their position within society and the family. Working-class men in particular have been threatened as traditional male employment gives way to more feminine working practices. He claims that men have responded to this threat in a variety of ways.

Some have tried to reclaim their masculinity through expressions of overt rejection of femininity, but the 'New Man' is adaptive and takes on a different family role which involves active participation in parenting and domestic labour. Certainly, men have been actively encouraged to participate in areas that would once have been the sole domain of females and of professionals, such as childbirth, and the comedian Ben Elton has a television comedy routine based on the experience of a cervical smear test.

Sheeran (1993) suggests that, although men do take on more caring social roles within families, women still provide the bulk of childcare and domestic work. Women's employment tends to be secondary to male work roles – this may, however, be pragmatic rather than an expression of male superiority within the home: men are more likely to earn higher incomes or be promoted. Morgan (1994) points out that the issue of domestic labour is likely to gain significance as the provision that the Welfare State is able to offer is eroded by cost cutting and 'care in the community' initiatives. Women are often the family members expected to take responsibility for the elderly and the sick. Once they were confined to the home to bear and care for children; now they may be forced back into the home to support the elderly and long-term sick.

Domestic abuse

There is a very dark side to human relationships, which is identified and discussed by interpretative approaches to the analysis of family relationships. Literature has recognised how intense and unpleasant family life can be for some members over the generations and sociologists are working in an area that many

> **ACTIVITY**   KS **WORKING WITH OTHERS**
>
> ANALYSIS AND EVALUATION
>
> Conduct a small survey into people's attitudes towards smacking as a punishment for small children. How many people would accept smacking as acceptable? Find out if parents who generally disapprove of smacking have actually smacked or hit children.
>
> Evaluate your work by deciding if smacking suggests that abusive attitudes are prevalent in our society.

understand and have experienced. The problem for sociologists is that abuse can be difficult to define in any clear-cut terms. Many codes of law, including the medieval Welsh Codes of Hywel Dda (Hywel the Good), which were renowned in their time for wisdom and fairness, accept that husbands may beat their wives as long as they do no permanent damage. In the present day, all violence against children is considered totally inappropriate in Norway and smacking is not only frowned upon but also illegal. Norwegian people consider the British to be abusive parents.

Even sexual abuse may be open to some degree of interpretation, so pragmatic definitions are probably the best ones to adopt. It is not the act but the emotion which defines if an act is acceptable: if it offends or hurts the victim and gives satisfaction to the perpetrator, then as a rule of thumb, it is probably abuse. A variety of forms of abuse are recognised by the NSPCC which categorises:

■ sexual abuse

■ emotional abuse (which includes neglect as well as positive actions of cruelty)

■ physical abuse

Any person may be an abuser. Children may abuse parents and their own siblings. Women may abuse. Bullying behaviours are abusive.

> **HINTS AND TIPS**   *Be warned. This is not a suitable area for you to study for coursework. You have not been sufficiently trained and may unintentionally be led into unethical areas of debate.*

In the 1970s, psychoanalysts such as Laing and Cooper, building on the work of Freud and Jung, suggested that mental illness was a sane reaction to an insane family relationship. In the 1980s, feminists such as Barnard went so far as to say that marriage itself makes women mentally ill. There is evidence to support this view and it is a growing area for research. More recently, people have taken a medical approach to mental instability, seeing it as an illness rather than a state of mind. However, it is clear that emotional abuse can create situations in which extraordinary acts of violence may occur. Recent case studies by Gitta Sereny of the child murderer Mary Bell and of the very young killers of the toddler James Bulger offer a view of how a disturbed and abusive childhood can result in human tragedy. These cases are isolated and thankfully rare, however, and do not offer a comprehensive sociological overview.

Of more significant sociological interest is the study of domestic violence. This is because it offers a view of gender relationships in our society. Male violence against women was not seen as a crime or a problem until relatively recently. Rape within marriage was only acknowledged as a crime after a particularly vicious and drunken sexual attack by a husband and his friend on a wife who had lived apart from him for some time. The friend was gaoled but the husband could not be charged with an offence. In 1979, Dennis Marsden and David Owen studied a group from a women's refuge in Chiswick and reported on a study of a sample group of 19 marriages, suggesting that even such a small sample justified publication because there was so little known about violence in marriage. They estimated that 1% of marriages are violent. Women's Aid groups feel this to be a serious underestimate and suggest that only 2% of violent incidents are ever reported officially, with an average wait of seven years between the first incident and a female application for help from the police, a refuge or social worker.

Dobash and Dobash in 1979 suggested that most violence in society is directed by males against females and that children are the witnesses. The argument has been developed by more recent studies. Kelly for instance, in 1988, suggested that male violence is the source of female subordination. Pahl, in 1989, pointed out that boys are often trained in power relationships within the family situation. Indeed, Marsden and Owens's original study in 1979 suggested that violent incidents were often triggered by very minor events and that often the violence represented efforts at male authority, control and domination of the female in what could otherwise be sexually and emotionally satisfying

---

How not to be an abused woman

- Don't dress up when his friends come round. He'll say you are making up to them.

- Don't look a mess when his friends come round. He'll say you are trying to show him up.

- Don't ask your friends around. He won't want the house full of chattering females.

- Don't not ask your friends around. Are you ashamed of him or something?

- Don't have supper on the table when he gets in. He'll think you are getting at him for being late.

- Don't let supper be late. The least he deserves after a hard day's work is to have his supper ready on the table.

- Don't let the children stay up until he gets home. He'll be too tired to bother with a lot of screaming kids.

- Don't send them to bed before he gets there. Do you want them to forget their father?

- Don't ask him what kind of day he's had. You should be able to see by looking at him that it has been dreadful.

- Don't forget to ask him how his day was. A woman should show some interest in what her man is doing.

- Don't tell him about your day. He doesn't want to hear a lot of complaints when he has just got in from work.

- Don't forget to tell him about your day. Are you sulking or what?

- Don't put on a sexy negligee at bedtime. You look ridiculous and anyway, whose money are you spending?

- Don't go to bed in your pyjamas. It would be nice if a man had something attractive to sleep with occasionally.

- Don't put your arm around him in bed. When he wants it, he'll ask for it.

- Don't turn away and go to sleep. Are you frigid or what?

And lastly ...

When he hits you, don't fight back. You'll make it worse. And don't, whatever you do, cower away. It'll make him feel guilty so he'll hit you more. That's it then. If you follow these few little tips, you'll never get battered again. Unless of course, you ask for it ...

Source: Welsh Women's Aid – unattributed.

relationships. Little has been written to challenge this view of violence. As a counter to this, some recent research for television programming has uncovered evidence of violence directed by women against their male partners, violence which men are unwilling to report because of current expectations of male behaviour. Bullying in any form would seem to be linked with humiliation, power and control.

> **HINTS AND TIPS** *The domestic violence debate should be linked with any discussion of patriarchy within the family and bears directly on Marxist and Marxist-feminist analyses of family relationships.*

> **HINTS AND TIPS** *Most Women's Aid groups see education as a powerful weapon against the acceptance or tolerance of domestic violence. Contact them through your local telephone directory (though not, of course, through their Helpline number) and ask if they would be willing to speak to your group about their work and their experiences.*

Divorce

Divorce rates have risen dramatically over the last 100 years. Read without further knowledge or commentary they represent a massive social upheaval in family structure and patterns of gender relationships in our society. For many people of the prewar and postwar generations who were brought up with the view that divorce was shocking, immoral and possibly an offence

> **ACTIVITY** KS **WORKING WITH OTHERS**
>
> IDENTIFICATION AND INTERPRETATION
>
> Talk to people who are much older than yourself and ask about the attitudes to divorce that were typical of the 1940s and before. How many express views representative of disapproval or shame?

> **HINTS AND TIPS** *Remember, as a sociologist, you are not interested in why individual marriages break down. The reasons will probably be as unique as the people involved. Your concern is with general patterns of social behaviour.*

against God, the prevalence of divorce is also evidence of a serious moral breakdown in society. This argument will be examined from two different points of view. It is necessary to understand the following two debates:

- Why have divorce statistics increased so dramatically?
- Does this change represent a major change in morality, with people rejecting families altogether? Is it merely a broader shift in patterns of **pair-bonding** or formation of couples?

Divorce: patterns and causes

Divorce rates have risen for the following reasons:

Divorce is easier to obtain than it once was because of legal changes

A history of legislative changes in family law make the process simpler and easier than in the last century where people had to take out an Act of Parliament. Each change in divorce law has resulted in a massive increase in the numbers applying for legal ends to marriage. This certainly applied after the Matrimorial and Family Proceedings Act of 1984, which reduced the minimum period for petitioning for a divorce to one year from three. The very poor and the very rich are more able to obtain divorce as the poor can qualify for legal aid payments and the very rich can afford the services of lawyers. The moderately well off will find divorce a costly business. There was a slight backlash against the perceived ease of divorce with the Family Law Act of 1996, which came into force in 1998, where the amount of time before a divorce can be granted was extended to 18 months. Couples are also now required to seek counselling.

Changes in religious practice and belief (secularisation) mean divorce is acceptable

Divorce has always been considered a sin in Christian doctrine. The traditional marriage ceremony states 'those whom God has joined together, let no man put asunder'. Stricter elements of the Greek Orthodox church will not even allow the bereaved to remarry because they will then have two marriage partners in heaven. There were ways of ending bad marriages but

Divorce: by duration of marriage (United Kingdom)

Percentages

	1961	1971	1981	1991	1993	1996
0–2 years	1	1	2	9	8	9
3–4 years	10	12	19	14	14	13
5–9 years	31	31	29	27	28	28
10–14 years	23	19	20	18	18	18
15–19 years	14	13	13	13	12	12
20–24 years		10	9	10	10	9
25–29 years	21	6	5	5	5	6
30 years and over		9	5	4	4	5
No. of divorces in thousands	27.0	79.2	155.6	171.1	180.0	171.0

Source: Office for National Statistics; General Register Office for Scotland; Northern Ireland Statistics and Research Agency

Figure 6.6   Divorce by duration of marriage

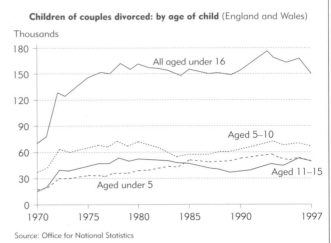

Children of couples divorced: by age of child (England and Wales)

Source: Office for National Statistics

Figure 6.7   Children of couples divorced: by age of child

1 In which year was the divorce rate per thousand highest?

2 In which year was the divorce rate lowest?

3 Suggest one reason why there was an increase in the divorce rate after one year of marriage between 1981 and 1991.

4 At which point in a marriage are couples most likely to obtain a divorce?

5 How many children were affected by divorce in 1997?

6 What implications do the graphs have for the government in terms of social policy with regard to
- the provision of benefit for single parents?
- housing provision and housing stock?
- employment and taxation laws for single parents?

these involved claiming that the marriage had not taken place correctly and made any children illegitimate. Fewer people accept these doctrines today and many people do not subscribe to any religious groupings or belief. Some liberal religious groups will even allow divorced people to remarry in church.

Changes in the role of women have affected divorce patterns

In the past, many women would have accepted a poor marriage as bad luck. It was their religious duty to be a good wife. Few women in modern society would accept this view, although many wives will attempt to hold together marriages where they are abused for some considerable time before giving up. Oakley has pointed out that women are not financially dependent on their men if they work and, whereas in the past they would have lost their children, now it is men who will stand to lose touch with their offspring if the relationship ends.

Demographic changes have taken place in society

People live longer. This affects marriage where people can regularly expect to live up to 60 years together. It has been suggested by historians such as Anderson that the average marriage in the past was nearer to 15 years in length. Death in childbirth shortened women's lives but those who survived their childbearing years could expect a near-normal life expectancy. However, in Tudor times, childbirth was so dangerous that wealthy women would often have their portraits taken and write their wills before the births of their children. People did not expect to experience marriage for long enough to become seriously disillusioned and, according to Young and Willmott, may possibly have expected less from the relationship in the first place.

Modern life puts stress on family relationships resulting in divorce

This is, in essence, a functionalist and interpretivist point of view. Work of writers such as the psychoanalysts

Cooper and Laing have already been discussed briefly and consensual writers will tend to argue that increasing divorce is evidence of a breakdown in society.

The death of the family?

There are two views to this discussion and any questions need to be examined in terms of the broader sociopolitical debate.

■ The New Right view is very much that family structure is breaking down as a result of the pressure of divorce and that social policy needs to support families in order to support the basic structures of society. Families are seen as the setters and upholders of morality and if they collapse then morality collapses. This view was endorsed by the Labour Chancellor of the Exchequer, Gordon Brown, when discussing changes to tax laws as they apply to families in March 1999.

■ Critical analyses of the family would tend to follow a line of thought that suggests that there is massive change in family structure and this reflects a new freedom that people have to express themselves. The value judgement that they would make is that families are changing and that our choices as to whom we count as kin are individualised and personal. Generally they suggest that this is a good thing for individuals. Critical feminists such as Bea Campbell though would add the caveat, or afterthought, that things have not travelled as far as they might and that patriarchy and masculinity still impact in a negative way on the daily experiences of women, particularly in working-class areas.

Divorce statistics show an inexorable rise in the breakdown of marriage throughout the twentieth century. Even Roman Catholic countries are accepting the reality of divorce, though this runs against the deepest and most sincere Roman Catholic belief. In addition, there is a rise in the number of **never-marrieds** and people who have actively chosen **singlehood** as a lifestyle option. These changes and social options, which were not previously possible, have led many commentators both from the right and the left of the sociological and political spectrum to claim that the traditional family is dead or dying. Any discussion under examination conditions should consider the death of the family in the broadest terms

in the light of the rise in single parenthood, gay pride and actively single people.

Statistical analysis is far from clear-cut and can be used to support both the view that family structures are changing and that the traditional family is dying out. *Social Trends 1999* showed a rise in the number of people living alone from 14% in 1961 to 28% in 1998. When this takes into account the fact that the number of households has increased from 16.3 million to 23.6 million, then the increase in the actual number of people living alone becomes very significant. There has also been a fall in the average household size from 3.1 in 1961 to 2.4 in 1998. However, these demographic changes may be a reflection of the fact that people have longer lives and many experience widowhood. Many couples are actively choosing to remain childless. In 1998, married couples with no children represented 28% of all households. These statistics may exaggerate the number of deliberately childless people, as some couples will have adult children who have left home.

ACTIVITY — INFORMATION TECHNOLOGY

KNOWLEDGE AND UNDERSTANDING

Use any of the search engines under the following key words 'Roman Catholic' and 'family' to find a variety of American Internet sites which present pro-family and pro-life views. 'Divorce' and 'family breakdown' will offer a variety of interesting sites including a strong American lobby for the rights of fathers to have custody of children in the event of divorce.

Is there real evidence of a breakdown in marriage?

Traditional commentators both here and in the USA suggest that there is a serious breakdown in marriage and they link it with resultant catastrophic effects for society, such as a rise in juvenile crime and a breakdown in public morality. For this type of discussion, use the Internet to collect data and opinions. The terms 'alternative' and 'family' will lead to a number of interesting and bizarre sites, though school and educational computers may censor some of the material available and sociologists should use their discretion as to which sites are serious and which are merely prurient or sensationalist.

However, is the case proven that the traditional family is dead? Divorce and family breakdown are typical of poverty, as are crime, ill-health and poor housing. Juvenile criminals may come from families that have broken up as is suggested by early commentators such as John Bowlby in the 1940s. Can it really be claimed, as so many of the New Right do, that this is a causal relationship? Could it be that divorce and criminality are merely linked as common symptoms of the deprivation from which young delinquents may suffer?

Do divorce and family change statistics merely represent a shift in patterns of family style and formation, with family remaining a popular lifestyle choice?

The statistical evidence is not clear in any direction. However, it would suggest that people remarry fairly quickly after divorce, with the average length of single parenthood being about four years. The General Household Survey of 1991 suggests that most people who divorce before the age of 35 will remarry within 10 years. Despite the trauma of divorce, many marriages are remarriages of divorced people. Single mothers will usually register a father for their babies even though there is a disincentive for them with the advent of the Child Support Agency and the Children Act (which are discussed more fully later). The implication is that although people may reject individual marriage, they do not necessarily reject marriage or partnerships as institutions. Family relationships remain: they just get more complicated with the addition of extended kinship relationships and step-families.

For a discussion of the changing nature of the family, refer back to page 304, where there is a description of the various types of family and household present in contemporary Britain.

ACTIVITY KS **COMMUNICATION, PROBLEM SOLVING**

KNOWLEDGE AND UNDERSTANDING	IDENTIFICATION AND INTERPRETATION	ANALYSIS AND EVALUATION

Collect evidence both for and against the suggestion that the family is in decline. Does the evidence of an increasing variety of family form in modern Britain represent a change in or a collapse of family life? Attempt a brief overview to support your personal point of view.

Childhood and Old Age

The most important notion here is that age in our society is a **social construction**. A social construction is something which is considered and treated as a fact, but which is actually invented and agreed by most people in the culture. For instance, what actually *is* an 'old' person? We have an agreed view of old age, which involves wrinkles, grey hair and physical weakness; however, someone from another culture may consider old in terms of wisdom, maturity and spirituality.

In many societies, there is a specific age at which a child can be said to transform into an adult. Often a ritual at or about puberty signals the change in status, and anthropology texts will have many examples of sometimes enormously dangerous rites of passage, which involve the killing of an animal or elaborate body art and tattooing. Within our own society, the situation is not clear-cut and we have various anomalies, especially with regard to sexuality. People may have sex at 16 years of age, but must wait two more years before they are allowed to watch a video portraying a sexual act. Even the age at which young women may marry is a cultural variable, with some states of the USA accepting the marriage of 14-year-olds as legally acceptable and binding. In our society the situation is so ambivalent that we have a specially coined term, first used in the 1950s to describe a transitional stage between child and adult, the **teenager**. We also use the technical terms **adolescence** and **youth** to describe this period of a person's life.

Childhood

The view that we have of childhood colours our laws and our behaviour towards young people. To develop the point, many people are profoundly shocked and desperately upset by the notion of children killing other children. Given the violence that young humans are capable of expressing towards each other in play situations, and the cruelty of bullying, it is possibly surprising that the death of children at the hands of other children is not more common, though this is a controversial view! Many children will have been the victims of angry and abusive attack from brothers and sisters and these are seen as part of the normal discourse of family life. This is a very under-researched area and much work on children has not been exploring childhood as such, but looking at the problems that children experience as a result of poverty or abuse. The perception is that children are the victims of adults.

The debate as to the nature of childhood was probably triggered by the French historian Phillipe Aries (1962) in his seminal text, *Centuries of Childhood*. In a very academic, but fascinating, argument using some graphic accounts of children in medieval and early modern society, Aries was able to suggest that childhood itself is a modern concept. In the past, poor children worked and rich children were dressed as and expected to behave as miniature adults. A practical view of things was the norm. Even the Victorians, who sentimentalised pretty and wealthy children in portraiture and literature, had few difficulties about allowing the offspring of the poor to work in the most disgusting and degradingly inhuman conditions in coal-mines, factories and sweeping chimneys. Aries' argument is that the modern childhood, as a distinct and separate state from adulthood, probably dates to early modern times and that it is socially constructed.

ACTIVITY   **COMMUNICATION**

IDENTIFICATION AND INTERPRETATION

Ask people to freely associate and to write down the first 10 words that come into their heads when asked to think about childhood. How many shared ideas do you discover? Look at magazines and newspapers. What adjectives are used to describe children? You will find certain ideas such as 'innocence' or 'playing' repeated time after time. These words will represent the social construction of childhood in our society.

There is also a historical debate as to the nature of the relationship that parents had with their children. It has been suggested that child mortality rates were so high in the past that parents did not grow to love their children as they do now. This seems fallacious – historical evidence, diaries and documentation show that, despite the fact that so few children survived, parents felt the same love for their offspring as do modern people. Their expression of that affection could be somewhat unusual to modern eyes: for instance, Victorian parents would have photographs taken of their dead babies in coffins made into postcards to be sent to relatives!

Studies of the lives and experiences of children in families have been conducted, but these are few and far between due to the expense and difficulty of such work. The most famous studies were carried out in the 1970s by John and Elizabeth Newson, who discovered clear and statistically supported evidence of major differences between social classes in child rearing practice after interviewing quite large samples of parents. Similar findings were made by Davie et al. (1972) in their famous longitudinal study *From Birth to Seven*. Despite the fact that parents are very likely to attempt to impress the interviewer and that their stated and actual practices may vary, a number of variations are noted:

- Middle-class parents tend to talk through problems and issues such as misbehaviour, whereas working-class parents may use physical force and restraint on children.

- Middle-class parents were likely to have liberal attitudes to sexuality and sexual expression so that the children were likely to have seen their parents naked.

- The use of dummies and soothers for babies was more prevalent in working-class households. Middle-class parents who used dummies displayed shame and discouraged the use.

- Middle-class mothers were more likely to breast-feed.

The studies discussed were concerned with the impact of wealth and poverty on families and disturbing differences in health and educational attainment were noted, including relationships between class and poor reading skills (Davie et al., 1972: 102) and physical height and weight (Davie et al., 1972: 82ff). The lower social classes were very much the losers in each case.

Another element of family discussion that should be noted, if only to underline later social policy debate, is that many parents consider their children to be possessions, merely extensions of their parents rather than autonomous beings. As such they are extremely vulnerable to abuse by parents and closely related adults around them. Families can be very dangerous places for many children and, shockingly, the single largest category of murder victims is babies under one year old, by their parents or adults who have care of them. Marxists and feminists would also argue that the patriarchal or male-dominated attitudes of many families can lead to pressures on children to succeed or fulfil parental ambitions.

> **HINTS AND TIPS**   *There are cultural variations in the way that people respond to and bring up children. To develop the point, ask those among you with experience of other cultures if they share the same social construction of childhood as we do in Britain. Ask parents who have been on holiday with children if they have experienced differences between the attitudes of the British and of other cultures to their children.*

Old age

The age at which one becomes 'old' varies culturally. In the past, very few people would have lived to see their 70th birthday, whereas in our culture this is the norm. Our society is largely youth-fixated. For instance, the notion that we have of beauty for a woman is actually more typical of early youth or even pre-pubescence than full physical maturity; we admire the hairless body, extreme thinness, slim hips, small chest and a wide-eyed appearance. We often see old people in terms of objects of derision (as 'wrinklies') or of victim-like dependence ('sweet little old ladies').

This derogatory attitude towards elderly people is by no means a cultural universal. Anthropologists would point out that many cultures value their old for two reasons:

- They are the repositories of the wisdom and experience of the people and a source of knowledge.

- Many cultures have some form of ancestor worship and their veneration for their own dead leads them to respect and honour those who either knew the dead or are likely to be dead in the near future.

Old age is beginning to be a problem for society as a whole, however, because demographic changes mean that far more people are surviving to experience advanced old age. Many are unhealthy or disabled because they have survived medical conditions such as strokes or heart complaints that would have killed them in the past. Often they cannot rely on overburdened children to take on their care. This is a point of significance in Area 10.

> **HINTS AND TIPS**   *This is a seriously under-researched area and would therefore be a fascinating and fruitful area for further study as a coursework project. You could interview the old themselves or talk to younger people about how they view people who are beyond retirement age. Alternatively, find out more from secondary sources about the problems of the elderly – perhaps problems that they experience in terms of poverty or disability.*

ACTIVITY   KS **WORKING WITH OTHERS**

KNOWLEDGE AND UNDERSTANDING	IDENTIFICATION AND INTERPRETATION

You could imitate some of the physical difficulties that elderly people experience through attempting the following exercise and making notes on your own reactions. You are advised to spend a day with one or more of the following simulated age-related disabilities. If you go shopping, take a friend to ensure that you do not put yourself in danger.

- Wear sunglasses smeared on the inside with Vaseline to simulate cataracts. You could also buy some ordinary prescription magnifying glasses from any good chemist; these will blur and distort vision.

- Fold aluminium foil into a ball and put it inside a shoe to simulate the pain of arthritis.

- Wear thick gloves to dampen sensation to the hands.

- Use a pair of earplugs to limit sound penetration.

Family and social policy

You must be aware of recent legislation which has had an impact on families and family structure.

> **HINTS AND TIPS** *For further information on benefits, legislation and allowances, contact the local Citizen's Advice Bureau, the Social Services Department and the Post Office where leaflets will be available for you to add to your folder. You could invite a guest speaker from Social Services or Barnardo's to talk about legislation and the family.*

Child benefit

This is a universal benefit. All parents, whatever their income, receive child benefit. This is a matter of some controversy because some families who do not appear to need the money are in receipt of the payment.

Arguments against universal child benefit:

- If the money was targeted at poor people, then more money could be given to people in need.
- It is the responsibility of the family to pay for children.

Arguments for universal child benefit:

- It is cheaper than giving tax relief for children.
- The money goes to the mother. If it went to the father he might not spend it on children.
- If people had to claim the money, some would fail to get it for reasons such as low literacy and families would be short of money.
- Children are very expensive and this money clearly does not go any way towards the full cost of a child.

The Children Act 1989

This act was an attempt to rationalise piecemeal legislation affecting children which had been passed over the years. It acknowledged that children are vulnerable but that they have certain rights. The main provisions of the Act came into force in 1991, and it defined the roles and rights of children, parents, and local authority social services departments.

It made the interests of the child the most significant factor in any legal actions with regard to that child's future. It overturned a previous supposition that parents know best about what is good for their children, unless proved unfit. Courts are allowed to overrule parental decisions about medical treatment, for instance, and can make decisions about how capable parents are of caring for a child. This resulted in a number of court actions, for example where children chose to live with someone other than a biological parent and were able to take their cases to law. Many of the provisions are detailed reorganisations of legal structures and procedures governing care orders and residence laws.

The underlying ideology of the Children Act was, however, to offer support to the family – and it is clear that parents have primary responsibility for children until they are 18 years old. The shift in emphasis has been to acknowledge the rights of children as individuals rather than to challenge the primacy of family or family relationships.

The 1991 Child Support Act

This very controversial legislation required lone parents who receive Income Support, Family Credit or Disability Allowance to give information about absent parents. The Child Support Agency (CSA) would then contact the missing parent in an attempt to force payment of a contribution to the costs of caring for the child. The amount would vary according to the income of the absent parent. Previously, it would have been the responsibility of the parent with care responsibility to obtain money via the courts. Some men claimed that the CSA had levied punitive sums of payment on them and there were instances of suicide by men who felt unable to meet their financial obligations. A number of pressure groups grew up among fathers to challenge the terms of the Act and the Child Support Agency was modified in response to public pressure. Women also often objected to the Act, especially those whose marriages had collapsed through sustained domestic violence and who kept their whereabouts secret from their estranged partner.

Marsh et al. (1996) suggested that the CSA was under such pressure to recoup money for the state from absent fathers that it was targeting fathers who were making regular payments to their families rather than attempting to locate and obtain money from those who never paid anything.

HINTS AND TIPS   What ideology do you feel underlies the Child Support Act? Many writers feel that it reflects the ideology of the New Right. You can find the CSA website at http://www.dss.gov.uk/csa

Area summary

You should have realised that the family, and concepts of the family, are deeply embedded in our culture and beliefs. Discussion surrounding the family is political, sociological and even religious. Ideological beliefs and concepts of family underlie many of the social structures of society, and include the financial and moral considerations of who should take care of the weaker and non-productive members of society.

More significantly, it is difficult to separate study of the family from deep-seated issues of gender politics because it is in the family that we learn our gender roles – and, arguably, learn to exploit each other.

The family is a radically changing institution and the beliefs and social understandings of the past no longer bind us. This has given rise to emotional debate about the nature of sexual morality, which is central to our social construction of what the family is and should be. This debate has had a profound impact on many of the institutions of our society: politics and government, the social security system and the education system are all affected by public debate and belief about the nature and meaning of family.

There is a clear and deep gulf between our ideological beliefs of the nature of family relationships and the reality of family experience. Human social behaviour is a far more shadowy and messy business than we would like it to be. Our religious ideology presents the family as a haven and a safe place but the reality is that many people are more at risk of physical and emotional abuse or neglect from those who should protect them than they are from random strangers. However, this reality has had little impact on our legislators, who still feel that the family should be supported in its narrowest Christian form – regardless of whether this particular format works for many people or whether they are gradually abandoning the narrowest definitions and adapting their family forms to suit their lifestyles.

Definitions

Abuse	Behaviour that satisfies the person who is acting, but which the person receiving hates. This can be emotional, sexual or physical abuse
Adolescence	Those who have recently entered or passed through puberty
Bigamy	The illegal marriage of a person to more than one person at any given time
Cereal packet norm	A view of family life which suggests that a family consists of an employed father, a domestic mother and their children
Couple	A pair of adults who share a home and/or an emotional or sexual relationship
Conjugal role	The roles of the partners in a marriage with relationship to domestic duties
Consensus	The idea that society exists because we all agree with a set of shared values
Divorce	A legal process ending a marriage

Embourgeoisement	The view that working class people are becoming more like middle-class people
Expressive role	Refers to the emotional support offered within a family
Extended family	A family consisting of a variety of generations who live together or close by each other and have close social interaction
Family	Those to whom we owe obligations of affection and duty by reason of ties of kinship of marriage
Fit thesis	The view that families evolve to fit the needs of society
Gay family	Adults of the same sex who share the rearing of children
Household	A group of people who are not all necessarily related who share a house
Instrumental role	The role concerned with purpose and action so that males are seen as working for money for the family
Kinship	People who you regard as family by reasons of blood or marriage and to whom you owe obligations
Monogamy	A single-pair marriage partnership
Moral panic	When people seem to get upset by a fashionable issue. The term was coined by Stanley Cohen to describe a media-fuelled panic about a given topic
New Man	A man who has rejected traditional masculinity and who is willing to participate in domestic chores
Never-married	Those who remain unmarried through choice
Nuclear family	A family of two adults and their children
Pair-bonding	When two people have intimate relationships with each other which exclude other people
Patriarchy	A society dominated by the needs of men
Polygamy	Arrangements involving multiple partners in a marriage bond
Reconstituted family	Families which consist of a married couple who have children from more than one partnership in the home
Serial monogamy	Having a number of marriage partners, but only one at a time
Singlehood	The state of being single and without a partner
Single parent	One adult and his or her children. This can arise from choice, divorce, or widowhood
Social construction	A phenomenological term describing the way that socially we construct meanings for certain conditions or behaviours and attach significance to them
Symmetrical family	A family where both partners play equal roles within the family
Unit of consumption	Families buy and use things together, e.g. cars come in family sizes and food is sold in family packs
Unit of production	Families make things for sale and their own consumption
Youth	The state of being young, or alternatively – a young male
Zeitgeist	The spirit of the age

Activity

Use this area to make notes on the following debates:

1   Give sociological reasons why divorce is more common today than in the past.

2   Define the term *social construction* and apply it to childhood, old age, marriage relationships and any other areas of the family which you consider could have been socially constructed.

3   Summarise the ways in which family structures have changed since the Second World War.

4   Suggest ways in which the role of women within families has changed since the beginning of this century.

Survey techniques

Practise survey techniques by attempting some of the following small-scale projects in order to develop your understanding of families and family relationships. Any of them could be developed into a coursework project because the link between the question and the method chosen is clearly defined.

1   Speak to a number of parents to find out what they consider to be the greatest challenges facing anyone bringing up a family in modern Britain.

2   Ask people for the reasons why they chose their current marriage or relationship partners. Where did they meet and what made this person a suitable partner for a long-term relationship?

3   Find out reasons for and against the practice of arranging marriage partnerships for children. Why does the tradition survive and why is it so common?

4   What expectations do young people have of their future lives? How significant is marriage in those plans?

5   What do single parents feel are the biggest problems that they have to deal with in order to bring up their children?

6   Do males and females have differing expectations of marriage relationships?

Data response questions

Item A

In conclusion, it can be said that although the middle class mother may encounter psychological difficulties concerning her role as an individual with her first baby, she very soon makes a deliberate effort to assert her own rights as an individual. The working-class mother who sees motherhood as inevitable is in fact far less prepared for the ties of children and is less able to cope with the isolation that follows.

H. Gavron (1966: 89) *The Captive Wife*. **London, Pelican**

Item B

Deep in the Jewish girl's unconscious, from the earliest childhood, the idea was embedded that the good daughter is the one who grows up to be a good mother. She is the daughter who repays the mother's outpouring of love by giving her a grandchild. And at this, the daughters rebelled.

B. Bettelheim (1971: 39) *Children of the Dream*. **London, Paladin**

Item C

Cooking and preparing meals for men and children is, according to family ideology, a central part of a woman's role within the home; it is fundamental to her role as wife and mother. This view was clearly expressed by many of the women we spoke to and they linked cooking to the importance of sharing meals as a family …Women cooking is therefore seen as central in terms of creating a family and is justified with reference to a gender division of labour which defines men as bread-winners and women as home-makers.

Charles, N. (1990: 59) 'Food and family ideology' in: C. C. Harris *Family, Economy and Community*. **Cardiff, University of Wales Press**

Item D

A feasible conclusion is that biological parents are considered better equipped with traditional parental characteristics than are step-parents for assuming the parenting role. Even in the educational system an unbiased view of step-families is sadly lacking. Of the 28 most widely used texts in U.S. college courses dealing with family living, none includes the possible strengths associated with the step-family structure; all delineate only the potential problems.

Burrell, N. (1995: 293) 'Communication patterns in step-families' in M. A. Fitzpatrick and A. L. Vangelisti *Explaining Family Interactions*. **London, Sage**

a   Explain the term 'ideology of the family' in Item C.   (2)

> KNOWLEDGE AND
> UNDERSTANDING

b   Using the items and other sociological knowledge, suggest two ways
in which daughters may be socialised into an acceptance of the role
of motherhood from an early age.   (6)

> IDENTIFICATION AND
> INTERPRETATION

c   Evaluate the suggestion that marriage is an institution for the
domination and control of the female gender.   (9)

> ANALYSIS AND
> EVALUATION

d   Assess the view that suggests that biological parents provide a more
satisfactory up-bringing for children than other loving adults.   (9)

> **GUIDANCE**   Question d is consciously testing your ability to take sociological   ANALYSIS AND
> knowledge and apply it to debates, which have been discussed but not actually   EVALUATION
> signposted in the Area you have just completed. If you recognise the view that biological parents are
> somehow 'better' as being associated with a 'New Right' or conservative view of family relationships,
> you can then challenge those assumptions from a Marxist or feminist view point by using the
> patriarchy, abuse and violence debates. You must remember that children have two biological parents
> and that any answer that fails to consider fatherhood is failing to address the full complexity of the case.

Structured questions

a   Suggest two ways in which families can come to be headed by a single
parent.   (2)

> **GUIDANCE**   Question a represents a fantastic give-away of two marks. You should   KNOWLEDGE AND
> never ignore these simple questions as two marks could well represent the   UNDERSTANDING
> difference between one grade boundary and another.

b   Why has the social phenomenon of lone parenthood increased so rapidly in
recent years?   (6)

> **GUIDANCE**   Question b is related to a variety of factors, including   KNOWLEDGE AND   IDENTIFICATION AND
> divorce and the changing role of women in our society. However, if   UNDERSTANDING   INTERPRETATION
> you apply and adapt your understanding of the factors that contribute to the rising divorce rate you
> have most of your six marks. You will of course need to refer to theory and sociological knowledge.

c Sociologically evaluate the suggestion that the increase in the number of lone parents is a matter for political and social concern. **(8)**

> **GUIDANCE**   This is a little more testing. The argument asks you to think about the death of the family debate and to consider:
>
> ANALYSIS AND EVALUATION
>
> **a** if the family is really dying out with consequent problems for society
> **b** if the meaning of marriage is changing.
>
> A more sophisticated answer may also point out that there are problems for society because single parenthood is not a very positive life change for a woman, related as it often is to poverty and lack of status, support or adequate childcare. It is these factors that may influence the life chances that their children experience.

d To what extent can it be argued that criticisms of lone parenthood mark an ideological concern related to the freedom of women from traditional sexual morality? **(9)**

> **GUIDANCE**   Question d probably seemed very complex at first sight, but if you break down the argument into its component parts, you will note that it is asking you to consider a critical analysis of the views of the New Right. The prompt words that give you the clue are 'ideology' and 'sexual morality'. If you refer to feminism, Marxist and perhaps, post-modernism, then you will have the cues to suggest that the hostile reactions that many have to single parenthood is because it suggests that females are choosing to remain unmarried and without male partners. It is a challenge to patriarchy and functional views of the dynamics of family life.
>
> ANALYSIS AND EVALUATION

Essay titles

1   Assess the value of functionalist theory to an understanding of family structure and development.   **(25)**

2   Evaluate the suggestion that feminist writers have an unnecessarily pessimistic view of family relationships.   **(25)**

3   To what extent can it be argued that the male role within the family has been eroded or lost over the last century?   **(25)**

4   'The experience of childhood in our society is problematic for adults and for children.' Use sociological knowledge and evidence to assess the above statement.   **(25)**

GUIDANCE   *This question is very open and there are a number of concepts for you to consider in the essay. It may be that you will have to be selective in your ideas. Here are some points to guide you in your note taking: legal definitions, child abuse, children's rights, adolescence, social constructs, child rearing, socialisation, norms and values, feminism, experiences of children, divorce, single parenthood*

As the question is so very open you really do have room for some freedom of thought. Consider what your general conclusion is likely to be.

Choose from one of the following positions

■   *Yes, there is a problem for adults and for childhood as we have confused and conflicting expectations of what children should be.*

■   *No, there is no problem in our society for either adults or children. This is probably the most difficult position to argue.*

■   *Maybe it is problematic for some adults and children, but the majority of people experience children and childhood as a positive and productive experience.*

You may need to think about some of the following ideas, for instance, how do we define childhood in our society? Our social constructions of childhood for instance are affected by social class and the age which created the idea. You may need to think about child abuse and family break-up. Child abuse appears to be endemic in our society and yet children are considered to be safer at home than elsewhere. We reject physical abuse of children and are also likely to be shocked at it, and yet smacking is condoned as a punishment. Mothers are encouraged to stay at home with their children, unless of course they are single parents when they are encouraged back into the workplace. Both males and females are encouraged to work long hours even when they have small children. You may need to think of the impact of divorce on families and on the relationship between children and their fathers. Finally you will need to discuss the ideologies of the New Right, and also consider their impact on family and social policy in Britain today.

Further reading and references

Episodes of chat show programmes such as Jerry Springer and Oprah Winfrey offer very different views of the reality of family life. Despite their sensational and obvious freak show qualities, these shows demonstrate that traditional ideologies of family life may appear in the value systems of people, but that many live their lives to a quite different set of rules. Another source of interesting data to consider might be the cheaper women's magazines such as *Bella*, *Chat* and *Best*, which specialise in human-interest stories.

For critical views of the family it is necessary to turn to feminism and to critical analyses of family in gender studies sections of libraries. Ann Oakley is particularly well known for her work in this area and you should look for *Housewife*, *Subject Women* and *The Sociology of Housework*. Be warned, however, that because of Oakley's pre-eminence in this field, it is easy to forget that other writers have also looked in a critical way at family relationships. One of the other best known texts is Barret and McIntosh (1982) *The Anti-social Family*, which offers a devastating critique of the role of the family in modern society.

Internet sites

For a view on the distribution and causes of divorce, you should look at Nicky Hart's *When Marriage Ends*. Her analysis draws on Marxism, feminism and interactionalism and offers an alternative to traditional views of family life.

Nik Jorgensen's *Investigating Families and Households*, in the Collins Sociology in Action series, offers an extremely detailed and interesting overview of a number of debates in this field and provides a useful support for students.

The Internet is a fascinating resource for the study of the family because the strength of the traditional ideology of the family and its links with organised religious belief in the USA mean that there are a vast number of sites. Many of these support New Right thinking and some are subsidised by entertainment corporations such as Walt Disney, which supports a very cosy image of family and family relationships. Key in the search word 'family' and take your pick.

Bibliography

Anwar (1979) *The Myth of Return: Pakistanis in Britain*. London, Heinemann.
Ariès, P. (1962) *Centuries of Childhood*. London, Jonathan Cape.
Barrett, M. and McIntosh, M. (1982) *The Anti-social Family*. London, Verso Editions.
Bethke, E. J. (July 1995) *Center of the American Experiment WebPage*
     http://www.amexp.org.
Bettelheim, B. (1971) *Children of the Dream*. London, Paladin.
Bott, E. (1957) *Family and Social Network*. London, Tavistock Publications.
Bowlby, J. (1969) *Attachment Loss*. New York, Basic Books.
Bradshaw, J. and Millar, J. (1991) *Lone Parent Families in the UK*. London, HMSO.

Brown, C. (1984) *Black and White Britain: The Third PSI Survey*. London, Heinemann.

Burrell, N. (1995) *Communication Patterns in Step-families* in Fitzpatrick, M. and Vangelisti, A. *Explaining Family Interactions*. London, Sage.

Campbell, B. (1993) *Goliath: Britain's Dangerous Places*. London, Methuen.

Chang, J. (1991) *Wild Swans: Three Daughters of China*. London, Flamingo.

Charles, N. (1990) *Food and Family Ideology* in Harris, C. C. *Family, Economy and Community*. Cardiff, University of Wales Press.

Condy, A. (1994) *International Year of the Family Factsheet 1: Putting families on the map*. London, United Nations IYF.

Corbin, M. (ed) *The Couple*. Harmondsworth, Penguin.

Davie et al. (1972) *From Birth to Seven*. Harmondsworth, Penguin.

de Beauvoir, S. (1979) *The Second Sex*. Franklin Center, Franklin.

Deem, R. (1990) *Women and Leisure – All Work and No Play* in Sociology Review March 1990.

Dobash, R. E. and Dobash, R. P. (1979) *Violence against Wives*. London, Open Books.

Engels, F. (1968) *The Origin of Family, Private Property and State* in Marx, K. and Engels, F. *Selected Works in One Volume*, London, Lawrence and Wishart.

Firestone, S. (1970) *The Dialectic of Sex*. New York, Morrow.

Fitzpatrick, M. and Vangelisti, A. (1995) *Explaining Family Interactions* London, Sage.

Fletcher, R. (1966) *The Family and Marriage in Britain*.

Frean, A. (1997) *Why parents are £50,000 out of pocket* in The Times (10th July 1997).

Gavron, H. (1966) *The Captive Wife*. Harmondsworth, Pelican.

Goldthorppe, J., Lockwood, D., Bechofer, F., Pialt, J. (1968) *The Affluent Worker in the Class Structure*. Cambridge, C.U.P.

Green, G. (1970) *The Female Eunuch*. St Albans, Paludin.

Hart, N. (1976) *When Marriage Ends*, London, Tavistock.

Hudson, F. and Ineichen, B. (1991) *Taking it Lying Down: Sexuality and Teenage Motherhood*. London, Macmillan.

Jorgensen, N. (1996) *Investigating Families and Households*. London, Collins Educational.

Jorgensen, B., Heyhoe, R., Savvas and Best (1997) *Sociology: An Interactive Approach*. London, Collins Educational.

Le Roy Ladurie, E. (1978) *Montaillou*. London, Scolar.

Maclean, Mavis (1991) *Surviving Divorce: Women's Resources After Separation*. Basingstoke, Macmillan Education.

Marsden, D. and Owen, D. (1975) *The Jekyll and Hyde Marriages in New Society*. IPC Magazines 8/5/75.

Marsh, I., Keating, M., Eyre, A., Campbell, R., McKenzie, J. (1996) *Making Sense of Society*. Harlow, Addison Wesley Longman.

McAllister, Fiona (1995) *Marital Breakdown and the Health of the Nation 2nd Edition*. London, One plus One Charity.

Morgan, D. (1994) *The family* in Haralambos, M. ed. *Developments in Sociology vol. 10*. Ormskirk, Causeway Press.

National Council for One Parent Families (1995) *Splitting Up*. London, NCOPF.

Newson, J. and Newson, E. (1965) *Patterns of Infant Care in an Urban Community*. Harmondsworth, Penguin.

Oakley, A. (1974) *Housewife: The Sociology of Housework*. London, Martin Robertson.

Oakley, A. (1986) *From Here to Maternity: Becoming a mother*. Harmondsworth, Penguin.

Oakley, A. (1981) *Subject Women*. Oxford, Martin Robertson.

Office of Population Censuses and Surveys (annually) *Social Trends*. Harmondsworth, HMSO.

Pahl, J. (1989) *Money and Marriage*. London, Macmillan.

Pizzey, Erin (1974) *Scream Quietly or the Neighbours will Hear*. Harmondsworth, Penguin.

Plummer, K. (1978) *Men in Love: Observations on Male Homosexual Couples* in M. Corbin (ed) *The Couple*. Harmondsworth, Penguin.

Roberts, R. (1973) *The Classic Slum: Salford Life in the First Quarter of the Century*. Harmondsworth, Pelican.

Sharpe, S. (1976) *Just like a girl: how girls learn to be women*. Harmondsworth, Penguin.

Sheeran, Y. (1993) *The Role of Women and Family Structure* in Sociology Review. April 1993.

Tinker, A. (1981) *The Elderly in Modern Society*. London, Longman.

Tischler, H. L. (1996) *Introduction to Sociology*. Fort Worth, Harcourt Brace.

Young, M. and Willmott, P. (1973) *The Symmetrical Family*. Harmondsworth, Penguin.

Young, M. and Peter, W. (1973) *The Symmetrical Family: A Study of Work and Leisure in the London Region*. London, Routledge and Kegan Paul.

Zaretsky, E. (1976) *Capitalism, the family and personal life*. New York, Harper Row.

Area 7

Work, Organisations and Leisure

This area covers:

- The sociological literature on work, organisations and leisure
- The relationship between work and other aspects of a person's life
- A consideration of the sociological debates about what it means to work, the nature of work people do and the types of organisation in which they do it

By the end of this area you should be able to:

- understand the nature of work, organisations and leisure.
- understand the arguments surrounding the transition from Fordism to post-Fordism.
- identify what a range of sociologists have said in the debates about these topics.
- identity and evaluate the differing conceptions of the organisation.
- understand the notion of McDonaldisation.
- successfully attempt examination questions in this area.

Key terms

work
formal economy
informal economy
bureaucracy
leisure

finance capitalists
property for use
property for power
contingency theory
adhocracy

Area 7 Contents

Introduction

This area is about the nature of work and the transition from ways of working which were said to be **Fordist** in nature to ways of working which are said to be **post-Fordist** in nature. For many writers, such as Crook (1992), this transition is part of a greater process of postmodernisation in which the world is becoming a much more uncertain place. Henry Ford (1863–1947) was one of the first capitalists to make use of the assembly line to mass produce a standardised product. Ford made extensive use of the principles of scientific management developed by Frederick Taylor (1856–1915) to make the most efficient use of the resources available in order to maximise profits.

Fordism was said to have described a form of society and ways of working within advanced industrial societies for most of the twentieth century. According to Robin Murry (1989), Fordism was based upon four principles:

- **standardisation** – each task was performed in the same fashion and at the same pace, as specified by management

- **mechanisation** – machines were used where possible to replace the work of people

- **scientific management** – forms of management based upon the work of Taylor (1911)

- **flowline production** – products were on a line which flowed past the worker

Moreover, under the influence of economist John Maynard Keynes, the effect of Fordist ideals spread beyond places of work to other areas of social life. Increases in wages were used to buy the expanding production of 'massified' products such as cars, televisions and other consumer durables. This would strengthen the power of capital in society, as workers were dependent upon employers to provide employment and wages needed to buy into the consumer lifestyle.

However, Fordism had its limits. Work on the production line was often monotonous. In addition, workers would attempt to assert some control over their work environment by taking industrial action or by forms of industrial vandalism or cutting corners. Moreover, the inflexibility of the bureaucratic work

organisations and the work practices that went on within them were slow to respond to changes in consumer taste and fashion. By the early 1980s the Fordist cycle of increasing wages, consumer demand and production was broken. As Michael Piore and Charles Sabel (1984:189–191) explain, capitalist societies expressed a 'second industrial divide'. Taking the lead from the 'just in time' systems first used in Japan, by the early 1980s new forms of flexible work practices with fewer full-time, permanent workers and more part-time, temporary or subcontracted workers were thought to be more profitable as they were much more responsive to changes in consumer taste and demand. In order to enhance profits workers needed to be multi-skilled, versatile and to work in teams. Post-Fordism, according to Lash and Urry (1987), signalled the end of 'organised capitalism'; employment is both less secure and more fragmented. Post-Fordism brought 'flexible firms' (Figure 7.1) which operate 'flexible production' for 'niche' markets.

Conjunctural Causes	Outcomes
Weak trade unions	Primary labour group
Unemployment	Functional flexibility
	(variability of tasks)
	FLEXIBLE
⇒	EMPLOYMENT ⇒
	PRACTICES
	Secondary labour group
	Numerical flexibility
	First peripheral group
	Short-term workers
Greater competitive pressure	Second peripheral group
	Part-timers
Greater vitality and uncertainty	Temporary workers
	Casual workers
Technological change	
	Distancing, i.e. subcontracting
	Pay flexibility

Figure 7.1   The flexible firm

The effects of these changes for young people have been outlined by Gary Pollock (1997). Drawing upon longitudinal data from the Bureau of Health Protection Services study of 10,000 people every year since 1991, Pollock shows that for people aged between 20 and 24 the labour market trend is for lower levels of work for men, and an increasing number staying on in education. For women there was an increase in labour market participation but this trend had levelled off by

IDENTIFICATION AND INTERPRETATION	ANALYSIS AND EVALUATION

Read the following passage:

' *Fordist firms retained a permanent staff of salaried, full benefited personnel and maintained a relatively permanent workforce of production workers who 'clocked in' on a daily basis. By contrast, flexible firms rely on a spatially dispersed network of workers, many of whom maintain very weak ties with the parent firm. Benetton, the Italian fashionwear company, for instance, does not even own its own stores. The full cost of setting up shop must be borne by the operator although s/he must operate within the rules of Benetton's shop organisation, that is, no backroom stockholding, a particular interior design and selling only Benetton products. Benetton's production facilities employ only about fifteen hundred workers, whose efforts are complemented by two hundred subcontractors, each employing thirty to fifty workers. Commenting on such trends, The Economist (11 June 1994) had remarked on the difficulty of trying to decide whether firms such as Benetton or Nike are 'big' or 'small'. Judged in terms of their core workers, both firms are small local operations; judged in terms of contract workers, however, they are sprawling multi-nationals. Indeed, organisations such as this are not so much single entities as fluid networks, adding value by co-ordinating activities across geographical and corporate boundaries. In other words, the best firms are both 'big' and 'small', depending on what they are doing.*

Source: adapted from Ashley (1997:108–109)

1 Outline what you think are the advantages for Benetton of having a network of subcontractors rather than employing a large workforce directly.

2 Outline what you think are the advantages/ disadvantages for the consumer of Benetton having a network of subcontractors rather than employing a large workforce directly.

3 Outline what you think are the advantages for the subcontracted workers of Benetton having a network of subcontractors rather than employing a large workforce directly.

1997. However, the increase was associated with part-time work and short-term contract work. Many sectors of the labour market are becoming unavailable to young people and young people find it difficult to predict what jobs they will do in the future as the supply of labour is greater than the demand. Pollock describes the employment market for young people as 'a risk fraught system of flexible, pluralised, decentralised underemployment' (Pollock, 1997:616).

Later in this area we will look at the Labour government's 'New Deal', which is a welfare-to-work scheme aimed at reducing levels of unemployment. First, let us look at the emergence of the Fordist system, and the debates during the Fordist era.

Ownership and control

According to Peter Sanders, since the nineteenth century the capitalist class has fragmented. Most notably there has been a division between the ownership of the means of production and the control of the means of production. Many millions of people place their money in pension funds, endowment mortgages etc., which provide a source for investment in capitalist enterprises. Yet the mortgage payers do not control the means of production that they have indirectly bought.

This fits into a New Right view of the world: the fragmentation of the capitalist class has brought about a property-owning democracy with the mass ownership of houses and share ownership, encouraged by privatisation.

Control of these assets is in the hands of managers, who do not own the means of production. A number of commentators have referred to this as a managerial revolution.

In contrast, making use of Marxist, elitist and Weberian concepts, John Scott (1997) argues that a coherent capitalist class still remains as a powerful economic and political bloc. Scott makes a distinction between **property for use** and **property for power**.

Individuals who pay mortgages and pay into pension funds do so in order to improve their lifestyle.

However, they do not control how the money they have paid is used even though they, the individuals who make contributions, would suffer if the investments made on behalf of their pension funds were to crash. Investment decisions are in the hands of **finance capitalists** or fund managers. Managers and directors are salaried employees: in 75% of the top 250 British companies they own less than 5% of the shares. However, even if the fund manager is an employee, the decisions he or she makes must be in the interests of the capitalist class, otherwise they may lose their jobs. Consider the activities of Nick Leeson, whose ill-informed or ill-judged investment decisions in the Far East brought down Barings Bank and resulted in Leeson's imprisonment.

Within capitalist society, Scott argues, the power bloc is a 'tightly integrated group with numerous overlapping business activities'. Many of these people went to the same public schools and universities and are friends. In other words, there is what Anthony Giddens (1984) has called a high degree of 'closure' at the top of the class structure. People not only attempt to gain advantages for their children by buying them places at private schools etc. but family and friends prevent individuals from dropping out of the top classes and do not allow individuals from lower positions into the top class.

Theories of management

According to Frederick Taylor in *The Principles of Scientific Management* (1911), nineteenth-century management had little or no understanding of the techniques or skills needed, or the time it took, to produce a product. Managers were generally unpleasant to people who looked as if they were not busy. Taylor termed this form of management 'ordinary management' and workers attempted to undermine ordinary management by:

- **Natural soldiering** – Taylor assumed that people are naturally lazy and, as such, that all individuals have a tendency to do as little as possible.
- **Systematic soldiering** – Work groups put pressure on individual members to conform and work to an

agreed speed. Workers work together at a speed they find acceptable: individuals who want to work faster are discouraged from doing so.

Scientific management empowered the manager, by giving him a full understanding of all aspects of the production process. This allowed management to select the right people for the job. Production could be broken down into the simplest of tasks, which a worker could learn in a very short period. Management would measure how much time was needed to perform each task and individual workers would be given financial incentives to work as quickly as possible. This management style was most vigorously adopted by Henry Ford in his production of the model T car, and became known as 'Fordism'.

Human Relations

In the 1920s and 1930s, during the economic slump, Elton Mayo and his team carried out a series of investigations at the Hawthorne plant of the Western Electric Company. Very much influenced by both Durkheim and Parsons, with their ideas of solidarity and anomie, Mayo and his team feared that during the slump workers were more likely to experience the sense of normlessness which Durkheim had termed **anomie**. Mayo observed that this anomic uncertainty led workers to form informal organisations (compact social groups) at work to give their lives a degree of certainty.

In contrast to the ideas of Taylor, people could not simply be motivated by money. Management had to take into account the deeper psychological motives of workers, and had to gain an understanding of these motives in order to manage efficiently. It is important to note that Human Relations was still Fordist in nature, as its aim was to enhance management control and increase productivity.

Human Relations assumes that:

- a work organisation is a social system, which has norms and defined roles
- workers' behaviour is influenced by feelings and sentiments
- the informal work group affects the individual performance of workers

- management should be democratic
- satisfied workers show higher productivity
- organisations should have opportunities for participation by workers and open channels of communication
- the manager needs competent social skills

However, according to Rose (1978:170), by the 1940s Mayo's Human Relations School of Management had been criticised on a number of grounds.

- Mayo and his team neglected the role of trade unions in empowering workers.

- The managerial bias of the Human Relations approach is unstated. In the last analysis Human Relations is, like Taylorism before it, about making management more effective and workers more productive.

- Within the Human Relations approach there is an acceptance that the manipulation of workers' ideas is an acceptable managerial tool.

- The causes of industrial conflict are not fully or clearly stated.

- There is a failure to relate the social relations factory to the wider social structure. Conflict may be a product of class conflict in the wider society.

- Mayo and his team had a fear of anomie and its possible consequences in bringing about social change. In the last analysis, the Human Relations approach is about preventing change and maintaining the social relations within capitalism.

In some areas of industry, by 1970 the ideas of Mayo did provide the basis for schemes of 'job enrichment' or 'job enlargement'. Often this involved greater decision-making within teams at work – for example, team working at Volvo was designed to enhance the workers' motivation and give them a greater sense of identity.

Post-Fordism

In the 1990s many researchers, for example Lash and Urry, described capitalism as having a 'disorganised' feel to it. Employers demanded greater flexibility from their workers, often employing only a small core group of permanent staff, with the rest on short fixed-term and highly flexible contracts. This type of management practice can be described as post-Fordist and has a postmodern feel to it.

David Ashley (1997) summarises post-Fordism thus:

- A shift to new 'information technologies'.

- Emergence of a more flexible, specialised and decentralised labour force, together with decline in the old manufacturing base and the rise of, computer-based, hi-tech industries.

- A contracting-out of functions and services hitherto provided 'in-house' on a corporate basis.

- A leading role for consumption and a greater emphasis on choice and product differentiation, on marketing, packaging and design, on the 'targeting' of consumers by lifestyle, taste and culture.

- A decline in the proportion of the skilled, male manual working class and a corresponding rise in the service and white-collar class.

- More flexi-time and part-time working, coupled with feminisation and ethnicisation of the workforce.

- A new international division of labour and an economy dominated by multi-nationals.

- Globalisation of the new financial markets.

- Emergence of new patterns of social division – especially those between 'public' and 'private' sectors and between the 'new poor' and underclasses of the one-third that is left behind.

Adapted from Ashley (1997:95–96)

HINTS AND TIPS *Typical examination questions in the past have included:*

- *Has there been a 'managerial revolution' in which people are seen to be more important than profit?*
- *Assess the impact of Taylorism on the way in which work is organised.*

In order to answer these questions fully you will need to be aware of the Marxian arguments surrounding the concept of 'de-skilling', which can be found in the work of Harry Braverman, but always remember to set the theoretical scene by outlining and evaluating the Fordist assumptions that Taylorism and Human Relations theory make.

Work satisfaction

According to Marx people have an inbuilt need and desire to be creative; this is part of what Marx termed our 'species being'. However, within capitalism work can often be dull, boring and monotonous. Many occupations within capitalism do not give people the opportunity to express their natural creativity, and the feeling we have when our creativity is suppressed is what Marx terms alienation.

For Marx, the overthrow of alienation requires termination of capitalist relations of production. The exploitative relationship between the bourgeoisie and the proletariat should be abolished.

In *Alienation and Freedom* (1964), Robert Blauner outlines a non-Marxist but technologically determined view of alienation. He explains that the 'most important single factor that gives an industry a distinctive character is its technology.' (Blauner, 1964:6). He goes on to explain that alienation is 'a general syndrome made up of a number of different objective conditions and subjective feeling states.' (Blauner, 1964:15).

A work situation can cause four kinds of deprivation, which are to be found within the alienated condition:

1 **Powerlessness** – This can be measured by looking at the extent to which workers can manipulate their conditions of employment, for example by regulating the speed at which they work.
2 **Meaninglessness** – Some products that workers make clearly have a meaning for them: shoes are clearly meaningful for the people who make them, although parts for jet engines may not be.

3 **Isolation** – This is concerned with the 'absence of a sense of membership in an industrial community' or the absence of a supportive work group.
4 **Self-estrangement** – This is where work plays only a limited role in people's self identity, usually because they treat work as a means to an end; they have in other words an instrumental attitude towards work.

Print workers have a very low level of alienation, according to Blauner, but mass production workers have high levels. This may well be because these people have low levels of control and meaningfulness together with high levels of isolation, all of which limits their self-actualisation.

Studies similar to Blauner's were conducted by Michael Fullan (1970) in his work on printing, car production and the oil industry in Canada, and Trist and Banfold did a study of the British coal industry in 1951, which came to similar conclusions.

Blauner's picture of the future of work is still a very optimistic one, because **technological determinism** has taken the form of an 'inverted U curve' (see Figure 7.2). Before industrialisation, craft workers had low levels of alienation. This was replaced by machine minding, which has high levels of alienation. In future years, when work is more fully automated, people will have much more enriched jobs servicing the technology, diagnosing its problems and dealing with its breakdowns.

Blauner's analysis is, however, rather limited: alienation is simply deprivation at work. His analysis does not address wider socio-economic issues outside

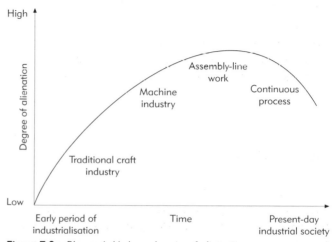

Figure 7.2   Blauner's U-shaped curve of alienation

the workplace, most notably class relations. In addition, Blauner undervalues the role of the human agent. In other words, he assumes that people are pushed about by forces outside their control. We need to take into account how workers give meaning to their work.

Stoppages, workers involved, and working days lost in 1993 and 1992

	1993	United Kingdom 1992
Working days lost through stoppages		
In progress in year	649,000	528,000
Beginning in year	566,000	471,000
Workers involved in stoppages		
In progress in year	384,800	147,600
Of which: directly involved	383,100	140,100
indirectly involved	1,600	7,500
Beginning in year	382,700	142,300
Of which: directly involved	381,000	139,700
indirectly invovled	1,600	2,600
Stoppages		
In progress in year	211	253
Beginning in year	203	240

Source: *Employment Gazette*, June 1994 page 200

Figure 7.3 Labour disputes

ANALYSIS AND EVALUATION

Do you agree that Blauner was right about the future of work? Your answer could be used to good effect in the following exam question from the AEB Summer 1995 paper:

■ Evaluate sociological explanations of the ways in which automation affects workers' attitudes to their work. **(8)**

To get a good mark, you should compare the determinism of Marx and Blauner with the way that Weberians look at the meanings workers give to their situations. However, as in Hints and Tips on page 342, in order to answer these questions fully you will need to be aware of the Marxist arguments surrounding the concept of 'de-skilling' – but always remember to set the 'theoretical scene' by outlining and evaluating the Fordist assumptions that Taylorism and Human Relations theory make.

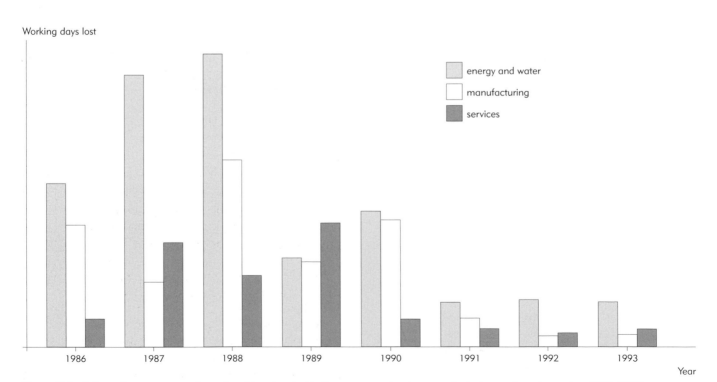

Working days lost

- energy and water
- manufacturing
- services

Year

Figure 7.4 Labour disputes: comparison of working days lost in the energy and water; manufacturing; and service sectors 1986–1993

Industrial conflict

As Figures 7.3–7.5 show, the number of days lost due to industrial action fluctuates widely from year to year. The peaks in the figures were due to major disputes in large industries. The 211 stoppages in 1993, fewer than in any previous year since records began in 1891, included 83% of days lost due to just 18 prominent strikes, and 42% of all workers on strike in 1993 were involved in the civil servants' strike, which was over market testing, privatisation and cuts in service.

Why are some industries more prone to strikes than others? Newspapers often point to agitators as a major cause of strikes in particular industries: for example, miners' leader Arthur Scargill in the 1980s. The suggestion is always that agitators do not have genuine grievances.

Poor communication between employers and employees is also often suggested as a possible cause of strike action. However, Daniel and Millward's 1972 study of workplace industrial relations in Britain found that companies which had an accepted negotiating procedure were more likely to face industrial action.

The organisation ACAS was established to improve negotiations between the two sides of industry and facilitate better communication.

According to Clark Kerr and Abraham Siegel (1960), community solidarity can also be a key factor in strike action. Working-class communities that are geographically isolated, like coal-miners, deep sea fishermen and some workers in heavy industry, have had in the past higher levels of strike action. This is possibly because if a community is dominated by one employer then grievances at work are more likely to become grievances within the community.

Richard Hyman (1972) argues that the explanations of strike action outlined above underestimate the role of the human agent. In other words, the explanations assume that people are pushed about by forces outside their control. Hyman says that to explain strike action we need to look at how the workers 'define the situation'. The concept of the 'definition of the situation' is concerned with how people interpret the activities and events around them, together with an assessment of how, as individuals and as a collectivity, people might bring about or (if they so wish) prevent change.

Year	Working days lost (000s)	Working days lost per 1,000 employees	Workers involved (000s)	Stoppages
1974	14,750	647	1,626	2,946
1975	6,012	265	809	2,332
1976	3,284	146	668	2,034
1977	10,142	448	1,166	2,737
1978	9,405	413	1,041	2,498
1979	29,474	1,273	4,608	2,125
1980	11,964	521	834	1,348
1981	4,266	195	1,513	1,344
1982	5,313	248	2,103	1,538
1983	3,754	178	574	1,364
1984	27,135	1,278	1,464	1,221
1985	6,402	299	791	903
1986	1,920	90	720	1,074
1987	3,546	164	887	1,016
1988	3,702	166	790	781
1989	4,128	182	727	701
1990	1,903	83	298	630
1991	761	34	176	369
1992	528	24	148	253
1993	649	30	385	211

Source: *Employment Gazette*, June 1994, page 200

Figure 7.5   Work stoppages in progress, 1974–1993

ACTIVITY   **PROBLEM SOLVING**

KNOWLEDGE AND UNDERSTANDING	IDENTIFICATION AND INTERPRETATION

This activity is to help you attempt the following exam question.

■ Assess sociological contributions to an understanding of strikes.   (8)

Take a look at the data on the number of working days lost due to strike action from the most recent edition of *Social Trends*. Identify which industries lose the highest number of days through strike action, which regions lose the highest number of days through strike action, and any other defining characteristics of the number of days lost. Also, is the trend in the number of days lost increasing or decreasing? This information will provide you with up-to-date information that you can use to evaluate any theory or opinion about strike action.

Work and leisure

ACTIVITY KS **WORKING WITH OTHERS, COMMUNICATION**

IDENTIFICATION AND
INTERPRETATION

This activity will help you draw upon your own personal experience when answering questions about leisure.

Can you define the time spent on the following activities as work or leisure?
1 Sleeping
2 Washing and feeding youself
3 Washing and feeding your baby
4 Feeding and walking the dog
5 Walking to work
6 Cutting the lawn
7 Reading a trade magazine about your own area of paid work, at home

Which of the above activities fit into the following categories:

■ time spent on our own physiological (bodily) needs
■ work obligations
■ non-work obligations, childcare and home maintenance
■ a chosen use of discretionary or free time, time which is left over for our use as leisure.

According to Keith Grint in his book *The Sociology of Work* (1993) there is 'no unambiguous or objective definition of work'. Grint goes on to explain that work is a 'socially constructed activity that transforms something'. The simple definition of work as 'paid employment' does not do justice to the complexity of the labour market, or to the meaning of work for individuals. As Grint explains, work becomes part of our identity, giving status, economic reward and the prospect of accomplishing our possibilities. As Ulrich Beck (1992) says, when we are asked 'What do you do?' we are expected to explain our occupation.

Gershuny and Pahl (1980) make the distinction between the **formal economy**, which is recognised employment that contributes to the nation's gross national product, and the **informal economy**, which they divide into three parts:

1 The black economy – any form of 'undisclosed income', work which is done for 'cash in hand'. This can include such diverse types of employment as 'baby sitting' and individuals working while claiming benefit.
2 The household economy, which includes things such as housework.
3 The communal economy, which might include activities such as volunteer work on hospital radio or working for St John's Ambulance. Many of these activities would not be described as fun, even though they may be done in our 'leisure time'.

Rosemary Deem further subdivided the 'black economy' into:

■ Crime-related, which involves both time and effort, and for which people are motivated by financial gain. This could involve activities such as prostitution and drug dealing.
■ Moonlighting by the 'unemployed' – in other words, not declaring income.
■ Stealing from employers.

Deem also divides the informal sector into domestic work and communal work.

ACTIVITY KS **COMMUNICATION**

IDENTIFICATION AND
INTERPRETATION

Are you involved in the 'black economy'? Ask fellow students what work activities they are involved in. This will give you some insight into the nature of the 'black economy' in your area.

What people do in their work time may directly affect their non-work time or leisure time. Stanley Parker has outlined three distinct patterns of leisure, which he claims are developed as a reaction to the experiences people have at work. People:

■ continue their working life into their leisure hours – **extension**
■ develop leisure patterns which are clearly in opposition to their work – **opposition**
■ display neutrality about the type of leisure activity they are involved in; leisure may be separate from work but this might not be planned – **neutrality**

By way of criticism, we could argue that Parker assumes that leisure time activities are determined by work activities. In other words, Parker undervalues the role of the human agent and does not take into account individual choices or individual pleasure.

Technological change

In attempting to understand the possible effects of technological change on the labour market, it is possible to identify two contradictory views: a pessimistic view and an optimistic view.

Harry Braverman's Labour Process Theory argued that the introduction of new technology is an aspect of class relations; a tool which can be used by management to exercise greater control over the workforce. It leads directly to further proletarianisation, in particular by:

- Deskilling – new technology makes people's skills and their personal initiative redundant. Individuals experience downward mobility as they are replaced by machinery.

- Proletarianisation of places in the class structure – new technology can be used to undermine the skill of professional groups, leading to downward social mobility of whole occupational groups.

Graeme Salaman (1987:32), however, suggests that this view

> *is theoretically unnecessary and empirically inaccurate. In theory, the relationship between capitalism, technology and work design does not need to take the form of a universal tendency towards deskilling, but simply of the long term dominance of competitive levels of profitability.*

In addition, Salaman challenges the assumption that millions of people will lose their jobs because of new technology. For example, Jenkins and Sherman had claimed in 1979 that by the end of the 1990s unemployment caused by the introduction of new technology would be 5.2 million people. Salaman suggests that

- new technology creates as well as destroys jobs

- profitability and employment can be maintained by improvements in quality

- companies reduce staff by 'natural wastage' rather than mass redundancy

Goldthorpe and Payne, making use of the data from the British Election Survey, found that individuals in the middle of the class structure, notably routine white-collar workers, claimed that they had not experienced either deskilling from new technology or a loss of independence at work. It was people at the bottom of the class structure who were most likely to say they had experienced deskilling.

Again, in contrast to Braverman, we could argue that new technology can help to bring about what Anthony Giddens has referred to as a post-scarcity

'Fordist' old	ICT new
Energy-intensive	Information-intensive
Design and engineering in 'drawing' offices	Computer-aided designs
Sequential design and production	Concurrent engineering
Standardised	Customised
Rather stable product mix	Rapid changes in product mix
Dedicated plant and equipment	Flexible production systems
Automation	Systemation
Single firm	Networks
Hierarchical structures	Flat horizontal structures
Departmental	Integrated
Product with service	Service with products
Centralisation	Distributed intelligence
Specialised skills	Multi-skilling
Government control and sometimes ownership	Government information, co-ordination and regulation
'Planning'	'Vision'

Figure 7.6   Change of the techno-economic paradigm

society, in which all people can enjoy higher standards of living.

In more recent years Freeman and Soete (1994) have suggested that the further introduction of computerisation could lead to a severe decline, not only in the numbers of people employed in manufacturing but also in professional and white-collar areas such as banking. Mass unemployment, they claim, can be avoided only by cutting the hours worked by people in these sectors and by making work more flexible. In many respects Freeman and Soete are echoing Jenkins and Sherman.

We might respond to this by pointing out that dire predictions have been made before about the effects on employment of new technology. We should not accept uncritically that information technology leads to mass unemployment. Other factors are also in play: employes do not always replace people when they leave; recruitment cutbacks also affect employment statistics. Redundencies are not inevitable and new technology is not always to blame.

Patterns of unemployment

The economic recessions of the early 1980s and early 1990s were both followed by a rise in unemployment. Unemployment for men rose far less steeply than for women.

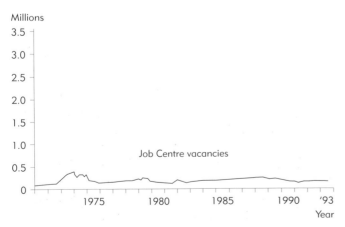

Millions

Job Centre vacancies

Source: Department of Employment, in *Social Trends* (1994), page 55

Figure 7.7 Claimant unemployment, 1971–1993

Sociologists argue that the way in which unemployment is measured underestimates the true number of people who are without work. Madry and Kirby outline the changes which governments have made to the way in which unemployment statistics are calculated (Figure 7.8).

Unemployment amongst women and ethnic minorities

Unemployment is not evenly distributed in the population. The Department of Employment in 1994 claimed that there were 2,101,300 men unemployed and 633,100 women. However, most married women are not eligible for a wide range of benefits and therefore do not appear on the unemployment register, even though they may be out of work and actively seeking employment.

In 1984 Martin and Roberts claimed that 50% of women who were actively looking for a job were not classed as unemployed.

There is also clear data which shows that ethnic minorities are more likely to be unemployed. One possible reason for this is open racism. Richard Jenkins (1986) carried out a study of the procedures used by managers when selecting people for employment. He identified two selection criteria:

1 suitability – concerned with the applicant's qualifications and experience
2 acceptability – whether the applicant would 'fit in' with the other employees

This latter criterion is often racist in nature, and prevents many people from entering employment.

Young people

Young people are also much more likely to be out of work. One possible reason for this is that the education system may not provide an education or training that prepares them for the labour market. In an effort to make young people more employable the Manpower Services Commission (MSC) was created in 1973 to provide training. The MSC was responsible for a range of job creation programmes and work experience programmes. In 1978 the MSC launched the Youth Opportunities Programme (YOP), which was initially a

Date	Change	Estimated effect on monthly count
Oct 79	Change to fortnightly payment of benefits	+20,000
Oct 79	Compensating adjustment to seasonally adjusted total	–20,000
Feb 81	First estimate of special employment and training measures	–495,000
		(by Jan 86)
Oct 81	Compensation to seasonally adjusted totals for emergency measures taken during DHSS industrial action	–20,000
July 81	Unemployed men over 60 given option not to register for work	–30,000
		(by May 82)
Oct 82	Change in definition and compilation of monthly figures from clerical to computer count	–190,000
Apr 83	Men over 60 no longer required to sign on	–107,400 (by June 83)
June 83	All men over 60 allowed long-term supplementary benefit rate	–54,400
		(by Aug 83)
Oct 84	Change in Community Programme (CP) eligibility	–29,000 (by Jan 86)
July 85	Computer reconciliation with Northern Ireland DHSS records	–5,000
March 86	Introduction of two-week delay in publication of monthly totals	–50,000
June 86	New method of calculating unemployment rate, using larger denominator	–1.4 percentage points
Oct 86	Abolition of the right to claim either half or three-quarter unemployment rates	–30,000 (by Oct 88)
Oct 86	Voluntary unemployment deduction from unemployment benefit increased from 6 to 13 weeks	–3,000
June 88	New, larger denominator used in calculating unemployment rate	–0.1 percentage point
Sept 88	Benefit removed from all 16 and 17-year-olds, removing them from the register	–120,000
Oct 88	Social Security Act contribution amendment	–38,000
Apr 89	26,000 redundant ex-miners no longer required to sign on	–26,000
Oct 89	1989 Social Security Act requires that all claimants must be able to prove that they are actively seeking work, or have not refused work because of the low wages offered	–50,000
Dec 89	Changes to effect of earnings on Unemployment Benefit. Some casual or part-time workers denied benefit	–30,000

Source: Adapted from Taylor (1990), Appendix 1

Figure 7.8   Recent changes in published unemployment statistics

one-year voluntary programme for unemployed school leavers. YOP trainees were given on-the-job training and one day per week training out of the work environment, usually in a local further education college. YOP trainees were given a training allowance, which was marginally above what they could claim in benefits; however, employers could 'top up' the allowance if they wished. In 1983 the Youth Training Scheme (YTS) was introduced, and in 1986 it became a two-year programme. Because of changes to the social security system, the YTS had more of a compulsory feel to it, as young unemployed people were no longer allowed to claim benefits. On leaving school a young person had essentially three choices: get a job, go into full-time further education or training, or join the YTS.

Dan Finn (1987) did a study of the YTS in Coventry and Rugby. He found that, contrary to the beliefs of the MSC, which administers it, most young people had at least one part-time job and hoped to transform this into full-time employment when they left school. However, it was cheaper for employers to take on the YTS trainees than full-time staff, and this suggests that the YTS may have helped to create more youth unemployment rather than make young people more employable.

According to the Department of Employment, in 1994 47% of YTS trainees got jobs when they had completed their training.

Unemployment is also related to geographical region. People in Scotland, Wales and the north of England are more likely to be out of work, mainly because in the past northern regions were more dependent upon heavy industry, which has shown the steepest decline since the 1970s. However, we must not overlook the fact that in the south-east, particularly in Greater London, there was a significant decline in the number of manufacturing jobs.

New Right theorists are more likely to point to the Welfare State as a cause of increased unemployment amongst the above groups: they consider that benefits are too high and people have no incentive to find work. The Welfare State has created a dependency culture amongst some sections of the population.

Effects of unemployment

In our society, a person's occupation is a key factor in his or her identity. It also affords a sense of worth and self-esteem. As Brendan Burchell (1994) explains, it is not surprising that unemployment can have damaging psychological effects – for example, isolation.

As Glyptis (1989) points out from a case study of 60 unemployed people in Nottingham, many unemployed young men aged between 16 and 24 become 'home bound', spending between 17 and 33 hours per week indoors and mainly alone.

Physical health can also suffer during periods of unemployment. Harvey Brenner (1979) suggests that if a country has one million people unemployed for over five years there are likely to be 50,000 more deaths from general illness.

In 1981 Fagin and his colleagues carried out a series of in-depth interviews with 20 families where the chief male wage earner had been out of work for 16 weeks or more. Fagin concluded that:

■ unemployed men's wives who had previously had ill health suffered from relapses; often this was associated with feelings of insecurity

■ men who had suffered from ill health at work showed some improvement in their health when initially unemployed

■ unemployment can bring about psychological changes in men, including clinical depression, insomnia and suicidal thoughts

■ physical symptoms also show themselves: for example, asthma, psoriasis and headaches

■ unemployment can also affect children's health: accidents, sleeping difficulties and behaviour problems are more common in children of the long-term unemployed

Richard Lampard (1994) has shown that unemployment can have an adverse effect upon marriages: often the lowering of living standards which comes with unemployment can be a major cause of marriage break-up.

Finally, some researchers have suggested that there is a link between unemployment and crime. David Dickinson (1994) has suggested that as the level of unemployment increases the number of young unemployed men

---

HINTS AND TIPS   In the AEB Winter 1995 exam the following question was asked:

■   *Evaluate sociological contributions to an understanding of the experience of being unemployed.*   **(7)**

There is a number of ways in which this question can be attempted. One approach would be to distinguish between the life experiences of young and old, male and female, skilled and unqualified, isolated individuals and whole communities suffering from mass redundancies. This approach, investigating the social distribution of unemployment, might be compared with a psychological perspective. You could also explore the ideas of youth subculture or dependent/underclass welfare claimant culture among the long-term unemployed.

HINTS AND TIPS

■   *To what extent do sociologists agree that new technology will lead to higher levels of unemployment?*   **(8)**

■   *Evaluate the argument that the increase in advanced technology will lead to growth in the skilled workforce and a decline in unskilled labour.*   **(9)**

In both these questions there is an opportunity to discuss the New Deal, which the government claims will enhance the employability of people who are currently unemployed.

convicted of crime increases. There is also a possible link between rioting and unemployment, which was identified by Gallie, Marsh and Vogler (1994).

The New Deal

In Area 14 we will give a full outline of the New Labour–Third Way philosophy and its communitarian assumptions. However, this is also relevant to the area of work. The New Deal was one of Labour's 1997 election pledges: its intention was to reduce 'youth unemployment' through a programme of 'welfare-to-work'. The principal aim was to assist the transition from benefit to work for 18–24-year-old people who have been in receipt of benefit for over six months. After an initial interview, the young unemployed person would be invited into the 'Gateway': a four-month period of personal assessment which is used to determine what the individual is already capable of, and what type of occupation is suitable to his/her needs. The Gateway is also a stage where difficulties such as literacy can be dealt with, any personal problems (such as drug or alcohol abuse) can be identified and rehabilitation, often with the use of mentors, can be provided.

After the Gateway there are four options:

1   work in the private or public sector
2   work in the voluntary sector
3   work with the Environmental Task Force – cleaning rubbish from rivers, cleaning graffiti, etc.
4   full-time education or training.

If the young person goes into full-time work, the employer will receive a subsidy of £60 per week plus £750 training expenses, to allow the young person to receive one day a week training over a six-month period. If the young person chooses one of the other options, he/she will receive an extra £15 per week in addition to benefits.

It is commonly assumed by people on the Right that the benefits system created a dependency culture and that reform of the benefits system had not broken the cycle of dependency. The New Deal involves investing in individual people through training and increasing their employment skills. As a consequence, employment opportunities are gained by the individual, and this, in turn, creates economic prosperity and competitiveness in the global market. The communitarian edge to this policy is that for a person to take from the community they must give something back. Hence, citizenship rights are earned via work. As Raymond Plant (1998:30) explained:

> *The ideas of reciprocity and contribution are at the heart of this concept of citizenship: individuals do not and cannot have a right to the resources of society unless they contribute to the development of that society through work or other socially valued activities, if they are in a position to do so.*

Tony Blair himself explained in a party political broadcast: 'Everybody who has a contribution to make can.'

The Labour government claims that it is committed to eradicating social exclusion. As David Muligan, director of Demos (a Third Way think tank), has explained, the unemployed 'are more properly defined as excluded because they live outside the worlds of work, of education, of sociability itself' (quoted in Lloyd, 1997:14).

But why do we still need the work ethic when the number of full-time jobs is seen to be declining?

In *Work, Consumerism and the New Poor* (1998), Zygmunt Bauman questions the common assumptions concerning the moral defectiveness and criminal intent of the poor, who he says are now viewed by taxpayers as the outright enemies of society. People on welfare are seen as 'the natural catchment area for criminal gangs', and 'keeping people on welfare means enlarging the pool from which the criminals are recruited' (Bauman, 1998:77). Bauman traces the history of the work ethic from the early years of the industrial revolution, when enterprising people were needed to create opportunities for themselves and others, providing the newly emerging working class with meaning for their lives as factory employees and a sense of purpose in work. In the early post-war period, government policy, under the influence of the Beveridge Plan, viewed the poor as a 'reserve pool of labour', which needed to be given skills and abilities through state-financed education and training and adequate health and social security systems to keep the potential workforce fit, able and ready to work. However, at the start of the twenty-first century, the 'reserve pool of labour' is no longer needed. In contrast to the Marxian analysis of class, companies have found ways of generating profits from low-cost products which do not require large numbers of workers to produce them. Hence, we have a growing section of the population who are classed as 'poor'. The work ethic is still with us but is now used to class the poor as people who 'simply lack the competence to appreciate the advantages of working; they make wrong choices, putting "no work" above work.' (Bauman, 1998:71). In other words, the work ethic is used by the non-poor to define the poor as people who lack wits, will and effort.

Bauman argues that we should change our perception of the poor. In a nutshell we, as individuals, should be both with the other and for the other (it is the poor who are cast as the other). The difference between *being with* and *being for* the other is about the level of commitment that we have for the other, about having an emotional engagement with them. This involves regarding the other not as a type or a category but as a unique person, that is:

- rejecting indifference towards the poor
- rejecting stereotyped certainty towards the poor, the view that 'they always behave like that'
- viewing the poor in a manner which is free from sentiment

The moral stance means assuming some responsibility for the poor; acting on the assumption that the well-being of poor people is a precious thing, calling for our effort to both preserve and enhance it.

What is Bauman's solution to this interesting question? He argues that we should see the work ethic for what it is, as something which generates a 'moral economy' filled with 'concentrated and unchallenged discrimination'. In its place we should have an 'ethics of workmanship' which recognises the value of unpaid work, which currently is classed as non-work. In addition, we should consider 'decoupling income entitlement from income-earning capacity' (Bauman, 1998:97). This is an interesting choice of words, but it cannot hide the stale, old message of 'Let's bring back socialism'. What Bauman is saying is the same as Marx did in the nineteenth century: 'From each according to his abilities, to each according to his needs.' Not only has socialism been rejected fully and comprehensively by almost everybody, but there is a flaw in both Bauman's analysis and socialism. When we take responsibility for the other, we run the risk of imposing our will, which can lead to cruelty. Bauman fails to take into account the ability of people to take responsibility for their own lives and actions. People are not pushed about by forces outside their control – some lone parents spend a lifetime on welfare, others make successful lives. The contemporary world is a world of choice and we are all choosers.

TASK

Hypothesis – Child labour is common in Britain.

Context – It is commonly assumed that child labour exists in the Third World but not in Britain. However, next time you go into a shop, a fast food outlet, leisure centre, garden centre, etc., look at who is serving you. The terms and conditions of employment of children and young people are very often poor compared to those of adults who do the same job. In addition, many children are working illegally, for example in bars and restaurants, and almost always without trade union representation or adequate health and safety provision. For example, there is a legal limit on the weight that an employee of the Post Office is allowed to carry, but not for a boy or girl doing a paper round. Child labour is almost always in the black economy.

Method – This type of investigation is most suited to a qualitative research strategy. As no obvious sample frame is available, you can never be sure of the representativeness of your sample. Select a group (for example, a class of schoolchildren), find out how many work, what is the nature of that work, how much time they spend at work, and if their pay and conditions differ from those of any adults who do the same tasks.

Evaluation – Did you find that most children work? Did you find that a number had several occupations, even though some may not be classed as 'real work' – for example minding younger children in the family? This fairly simple task can raise a whole range of ethical problems for you as the researcher. What do you do if you find out that an under-age person is working? That someone is working excessively long hours? Or that a young person is doing an unsafe job?

Organisations

Organisations can be defined as social units that aspire to achieve particular objectives or ends which they are structured to promote. In other words, organisations have been deliberately put together to carry out a specific task. They are bureaucratic in nature and they usually carry out their function rationally.

All organisations are said to be bureaucratic in nature, which Martin Albrow (1970) defined as:

> *Social units in which individuals are conscious of their membership and legitimise their co-operative activities primarily by reference to attainment of impersonal goals rather than moral standards.*

In addition, organisations can be divided into a number of types depending on what they do.

- **Total institutions** – This is a term defined by Erving Goffman to describe five distinct types of institution in which people live and work within a closed community, under fixed supervision, together with a rational plan which points towards a fixed number of goals. Examples include such diverse organisations as barracks, boarding schools, prisons, mental hospitals and leper colonies. When people enter these institutions they are subject to 'rituals of degradation' in which both the staff and the inmates attempt to destroy the individual self of the newcomer, to take away his/her individuality. This makes all the inmates appear as a 'batch' to the outside observer.

- **Voluntary associations** – These provide a setting for people who share common interests. Again, there are diverse examples to draw from: political parties, new social movements, local sports teams. According to Robert Michels (1876–1936), all organisations are inevitably oligarchic. In other words, within any organisation we will find a few people who make the key decisions and the rest of the membership is powerless. Michels termed this the 'Iron Law of Oligarchy', by which he meant that no organisation could ever be democratic or allow true participation in decision-making by its members. For a fuller outline of the assumptions upon which élite theory is based you need to read Area 14.

However, in a post-Fordist world, which has an uncertain or postmodern feel to it, new forms of pluralistic or non-hierarchical organisation are possible. People can work within quality circles, in which workers are not constrained and powerless, as they would be under some form of Tayloristic scientific management. They are not 'deskilled' as Braverman would suggest, but work within structures that empower individuals by allowing democratic participation in decision-making.

ACTIVITY **PROBLEM SOLVING**

KNOWLEDGE AND UNDERSTANDING	IDENTIFICATION AND INTERPRETATION	ANALYSIS AND EVALUATION

Look at the following exam questions, and identify the key theory and key theorist you think you are expected to discuss. For example, the concept of 'total institution' was developed by Erving Goffman who was a symbolic interactionist.

- Critically examine the view that the 'Scientific Management' and 'Human Relations' approaches to study are biased in favour of management.

- Assess the usefulness of the concept of 'total institutions' to our understanding of behaviour in organisations.

- Is there a conflict between organisational needs and democratic participation by individuals?

- Are organisations inevitably undemocratic?

HINTS AND TIPS *Examiners always look for an account and an evaluation of different approaches. A good starting point is always to identify whether the main theory the question is about is functionalist, Marxist or interactionist in nature. Once you have identified the main theory, outline its key assumptions and evaluate them. This could involve challenging the modernist nature of any assumptions you can identify.*

Bureaucracy

According to Max Weber (1864–1920), **bureaucracy** is both the most rational and the most efficient of all forms of administration. All forms of bureaucracy need rules. Present-day organisations make use of quality assurance programmes or systems which are rational in exactly the way that Weber described them. Examples include BS 5750, ISO 9000 and Investors in People, which all involve the establishment of systems that attempt to guarantee that procedures are carried ou. Quality is understood as making sure that the formal rules are followed.

Weber's ideal type of bureaucracy

Weber's ideal type of bureaucracy is more fully developed in Area 14. It is a useful model by which to measure other forms of administration. This model contains the following characteristics:

- the organisation is in the form of a hierarchy
- its operations are governed by a system of abstract rules
- the ideal official conducts tasks without friendship or favour to any clients
- all bureaucrats have a fixed number of recorded duties
- employment in bureaucracy is based upon qualifications
- from a purely technical point of view, this form of administration has the highest degree of efficiency

For Weber, bureaucracy was precise, soulless and machine-like, a technical instrument for achieving preconceived goals. However, bureaucracy has an inherent tendency to exceed its function, and to become a separate force within society. The source of power for the bureaucracy is based upon knowledge, and by this Weber understood technical expertise, which is protected by secrecy.

Most of the critiques of Weber's work in this area fail to take into account the nature of an ideal type. The ideal type is a model, made up of a list of characteristics which the researcher considers to be the most significant. Construction of the model is on the basis of what Weber termed **value relevance**, which means the informed personal opinion of the researcher. From this starting point the researcher goes on to evaluate real bureaucracies. Individuals who criticise Weber's ideal type of bureaucracy could be said to have different informed opinions about the nature of bureaucracy.

However, many sociologists could argue that Weber's conceptions of power, authority and legitimacy are too restricted in their focus. In contrast to Weber, Steven Lukes (1974) argues that power has three dimensions or appearances:

1 Decision making, which is concerned with the activities of the decision makers.
2 Non-decision making, which is concerned with the way in which power is used to limit the range of decisions from which the decision makers can choose.
3 Shaping desires, which is concerned with the ways in which individual attitudes and beliefs are manipulated to make them accept a decision which is not in their own interests.

In contrast to Weber's view, all organisations have both formal and informal aspects. The **formal organisation** contains strictly laid-down patterns of authority, rules and procedures. It has a high degree of rationality and makes the most efficient use of the resources available. It aims to produce maximum predictability. The **informal organisation** includes friendships or personal relationships, the unofficial way of doing things.

A formal organisation has:

- a well defined, durable and inflexible structure
- a well planned hierarchy
- clear channels of communication
- a specified job for each member
- well defined objectives

Informal organisations have

- a loosely organised, flexible, ill defined structure
- no defined goals or objectives
- no clearly defined relationships

The goals of organisations are difficult to measure: long-term goals may have to change while short-term goals may compete with each other. In this sense, it might be better to have an organisational structure that is less durable but which can change to meet the needs of its stakeholders. This idea formed the basis of what came to be known as **contingency theory**.

Contingency theory is an approach to organisations that has none of the abstraction of general systems theories. It is a pragmatic approach to management, in which the manager must be flexible and have an intuitive sense of the situation.

Henry Mintzberg, in contrast to Weber, argued for what he called the **adhocracy**, which literally means that managers make it up as they go along, without universal principles. This is a fluid and flexible administration based upon teams which, from their own rules, prefer informal organisation standardisation of the activities of members. The adhocracy has the advantages of the informal organisation's flexible search for better ways of working in the face of new circumstances and innovative team work. These may take the form of quality circles, which give individuals opportunities to develop their skills in a number of different areas.

However, many researchers have shifted from these Fordist notions of organisation to industrial systems that are post-Fordist in nature.

ACTIVITY   KS **COMMUNICATION**

KNOWLEDGE AND UNDERSTANDING	IDENTIFICATION AND INTERPRETATION	ANALYSIS AND EVALUATION

Is bureaucracy necessarily the most efficient form of large-scale organisation?

The argument here is to explain how post-modern organisations may try to encourage initiative, autonomy, flexibility, multiskilling, decentralisation, flatter hierarchies yet retain a core of detailed rules and procedures, with a centralised overall structure of control, with careful monitoring of performance

---

HINTS AND TIPS   *In most questions about work relations and work organisations it is important to discuss the organisational background to any research you are discussing. It is useful to have in mind an answer to the question 'Evaluate the contribution made by Weber to an understanding of power and authority of society'.*

McDonaldisation

According to George Ritzer (1993) the process of McDonaldisation is about applying the production line approach (which has been common in a number of industries for many years) to the hospitality industries. Ritzer views this process as a bad thing because it is seen as reducing both diversity and choice. McDonaldisation has four key components:

1 **Efficiency**, which involves 'choosing the optimum means to a given end' (Ritzer, 1993:36). This efficiency is defined by the organisation rather than the individual and is in effect imposed upon the individual.

2 **Calculability**, in which there is 'an emphasis on the quantitative aspect of products sold (portion size, cost) and service offered (the time it takes to get the product)' (1993:9).

3 **Predictability**, in which there is a 'discipline, order, systemization, formalization, routine, consistency and methodical operation. In such a society, people prefer to know what to expect in most settings and at most times' (1993:79). The experience is the same for the consumer in every shop and work becomes very routine for the workers.

4 **Control**, where management have a need to control both the workers and the customers in an effort to reduce the level of uncertainty within the organisation.

These processes have their own irrational outcomes, which Ritzer describes as follows: 'Rational systems inevitably spawn a series of irrationalities that limit, eventually compromise, and perhaps even undermine their rationality' (1993:121).

The inefficiencies generated by these rational processes include:

■ longer waiting times and more work for the customer – having to make your own salad in the salad bar, or pour your own drink in the fast food restaurant

■ dehumanisation of the worker and of the customer

■ the emergence of unforeseen anomalies, things that go wrong without being planned for.

Area summary

In this area we have looked at the changing nature of work from the nineteenth century to the present. This has involved looking at the development of what came to be know as Fordism to what is known as post-Fordism. This was seen to be part of a more general transition from modernity to more post-modern forms of work practice and forms of organisation. We ended with a discussion of McDonaldisation. In the early years of the twentieth century, the nature of the work that most people did was strongly influenced by Taylorism, with its emphasis on standardisation, mechanisation, scientific management and flowline production. Many of us now work in groups which have very different organisational principles, what we referred to in the area as 'flexible firms'. On the way to the flexible firm we looked at the human relations school of management which had a great influence on work practices in the 1950s and 1960s. There is still industrial conflict and we still have unemployment, and we looked at the way in which the Blair government attempted to deal with the nature of unemployment by introducing the New Deal. According to Zygmunt Bauman, the new poor are seen as a major threat to our social life. New Deal is meant to resolve any such treat to our everyday lives. We also traced the changing nature of ownership and control of places of work, which has had a significant impact on a number of sociological perspectives. How can Marxism still be relevant today if we have no bourgeoisie?

Definitions

Adhocracy	An organisation characterised by adaptability and responsiveness with a focus on the task at hand
Anomie	A state of normlessness, in which a person loses sight of the accepted ways of behaving within a community
Bureaucracy	A form of administration which is a rational system of offices in the form of a hierarchy
Contingency theory	An organisational theory developed by Fremont E. Kast and James E. Rosenzeig in *Contingency Views of Organisational and Management*, Palo Alto, California (1973), which focuses upon the variables and subsystems within any structure which a manager must balance in an effort to make the organisation run efficiently
Finance capitalis	A class of people who make money from their ownership and control of financial assets
Fordism	A form of organisation of work and work practices which is rational, formal and takes control away from the workers
Formal economy	The legitimate economy, in which people have contracts of employment and pay taxes
Formal organisation	An association or group with a form of rigid rules and clearly defined structure, for example a work organisation

Informal economy	The illegitimate economy, in which people do not have contracts of employment, do not pay taxes and are often claiming benefits whilst working
Informal organisation	An association or group with no rigid rules and no clearly defined structure, for example a friendship
Leisure	Often pleasurable activities which people choose to participate in during their non-work time
Post-Fordism	A form of organisation of work and work practices which is not rational, informal and can empower the workers
Property for power	Exercising power over others by the use of property and other assets
Property for use	The use of property for the purpose of living rather than for purposes such as making profit
Technological determinism	The argument that technology has a central role to play in social change, that the culture and social structure reflects changes in technology
Value relevance	A term used by Max Weber to describe the initial phase in the process of constructing an ideal type; in which a researcher selects a number of characteristics which they consider to be the most significant on the basis of their informed opinion
Work	An activity which is carried out usually for money and with an element of obligation

Data response questions

Item A

You have described the McDonaldised society as a system of 'iron cages' in which all institutions come to be dominated by the same principle. So what sort of world would you like us to be living in?

Well, obviously [laughter] ... a far less caged one. I mean the fundamental problem with McDonaldised systems is that it's other people in the system structuring our lives for us, rather than us structuring our lives for ourselves. I mean, that's really what McDonald's is all about. You don't want a creative person clerk at the counter – that's why they are scripted. You don't want a creative hamburger cook – you want somebody who simply follows routines or follows scripts. So you take all creativity out of all activities and turn them into a series of routinised kinds of procedures that are imposed by some external force. So that's the reason why it is dehumanising ...
I'd like to see a society in which people are freed to be creative, rather than having their creativity constrained or eliminated.

Interview with George Ritzer, at
http://www.enviroweb.org/mcspotlightna/people/interviews/ritzer_george.html
author of The McDonaldization of Society

Item B

Unlike the pre-Thatcher era, when Britain's labour market was more regulated and highly unionised, employers in 1993 were more able to 'hire and fire' staff. More pressure was also put on unemployed people to actively seek work. In such a 'flexible' labour market, employers found it easier to adjust employee numbers in line with their requirements. Employers are quick to shed jobs when business outlook is depressed – which may explain what has been described as 'oversacking' in the summer and autumn of 1992, when job shedding reached record levels. But employers are quick to create jobs once prospects recover (and find that unemployed people are prepared to take them).

Philpott, J. (1994:114) The Labour Market. Deddington, Phillip Allan.

Item C

New Deal is a key part of the Government's Welfare to Work strategy. New Deal has been created to help unemployed people into work by closing the gap between the skills employers want and the skills people can offer. It's ambitious, it's different, and it's a real opportunity to get people off benefits and into work. The step-by-step guides for employers, 18–24 and 25 plus will show you how New Deal works from start to finish.

New Deal is just that – a genuine deal because everyone gives something

■ *Employers offer people a chance to show what they can do*
■ *People provide abilities and potential*
■ *The Government is committing up to £3.5 billion over four years*

And everyone gets something in return

■ *Employers get new talent for their business*

■ *People get new skills, new opportunities and a new start*

■ *We all benefit from a more successful economy and a vibrant community*

Who is it for?

■ *New Deal for young unemployed people is for 18–24 year-olds who have been claiming Jobseeker's Allowance for six months or more (including those getting NI credits only). Some people can join New Deal sooner – ask your Jobcentre*

■ *New Deal for Lone Parents is for anyone who is looking after at least one school-aged child on their own, and claiming Income Support. If you're a lone parent aged between 18 and 24 and are currently claiming Jobseekers' Allowance, you'll be invited to join New Deal for 18–24.*

■ *For information on the options available for New Deal participants aged 18–24, go to Full-time education and training, The employment option, The Environment Task Force or The voluntary sector. New Deal can also help young people who want to work for themselves. To find out how, go to Self-employment.*

■ *New Deal for people aged 25 plus is for jobseekers 25 or over who have been unemployed for two years or more.*

■ *New Deal offers people with disabilities the same opportunities as any other jobseeker.*

■ *New Deal Jobseekers with Disabilities sets out what JSA claimants with a disability or health condition can expect from New Deal. In some pilot areas, New Deal for Disabled People is helping people claiming Incapacity Benefits to get into work.*

Source: http://www.newdeal.gov.uk/homesubl.asp

Item D

Orientation	Meaning of work	Involvement in organisation	Involvement in work	Relationship between work and non-work life
Instrumental	Work as source of income	Calculative only	Work not a central life interest	Sharp separation
Bureaucratic	Service to organisation in exchange for career	Moral obligation to organisation	Career a central life interest	Social aspirations and status related to career
Solidaristic	Work as a group activity	Identification with enterprise or work group	Work a central life interest	Strong occupational community

Source: adapted from Goldthorpe and Lockwood et al. (1968a: 38–41)

Figure 7.9   Attitudes to work

Item E

How to achieve instant employability, if not a job:

OK, so what exactly is the New Deal?
In its ur-form, it was one of Labour's "five early pledges": a promise to get 250,000 under-25s off benefit and into work, paid for by a windfall tax. Small hitch/windfall benefit: those eligible (six months on the dole is the qualifying period) have fallen to 118,000 post-election. But a promise is a promise: as ministers are fond of pointing out, when David Blunkett was 18 (that's 1965), youth unemployment was 5,500.

Whose idea was it?
Gordon Brown's. His press secretary Charlie Whelan claims to have thought up the name – though for some reason F D Roosevelt lurks around the back of one's brain ...

What do the unemployed get out of it?
Let's stick for a moment with 18–24 year olds. They start off with four months in a "Gateway" – not a supermarket but a personally supervised assessment period, to help with job search and problems such as literacy. Up to 40 per cent are likely to get jobs anyway during this time, as part of normal labour market turnover. The rest can then choose:

a)   a public or private-sector job (Blunkett wondered if the Tories might like to take on someone at Central Office);

b)   full-time education and training;

c)   a place on an "Environment Task Force", clearing inner-city graffiti, weeding large fields or building a playground;

d)   voluntary sector work.

And the pay?
Those who take on work should get "the rate for the job". The carrot for employers is a £60-a-week subsidy, plus £750 to cover one day's training a week for six months. In the ETF and voluntary sector, it's benefit plus £15 a week; in full-time education or training, benefit plus expenses.

So it's really just another youth training scheme?
Wrong, wrong, wrong. It's different and new, because of:

a)   long-termism. Funding is committed until 2002, so cannot be messed about with or cut;

b)   multiple ownership. Councils, chambers of commerce and TECs will be involved in local schemes. In ten districts, the New Deal will be run by the private sector;

c)   the Gateway, which will help those with drug or drink problems, offering "mentoring" schemes, which have a good record of success in the United States.

Sounds too good to be true. Let's hear the downside...

Anyone who refuses the options they're offered will have their benefit cut, although none of the 15,000 who've started have yet been penalised in this way.

Employers don't have to keep their New Dealer on after six months – they can simply swap them for another one, who comes complete with subsidy.

Unions are worried about the quality of training and whether the "rate for the job" will really materialise for most of the youngsters.

There are worries that young blacks will opt out. In London, ethnic minorities are a third of the New Deal target group.

What about the rest of the jobless?

The government has belatedly bowed to pressure to extend the scheme to the 216,000 older long-term jobless. But they're getting £450 million of windfall tax, compared with £2.6 billion for the under-25s: that's £22,000 per junior and £2,000 per senior. Pilots start in November, and it'll probably be called the Return of the New Deal. There will also be pilots for extra help for out-of-work over-50s. That's most likely to be called the New Deal Strikes Back.

How many New Deals can we stand?

You haven't heard the half of it. You may have heard of...

a) the New Deal for lone parents, a Harriet Harman special;

b) the New Deal for people with disabilities, a voluntary programme starting in the summer;

... but did you know about:

c) the New Deal for 300,000 partners of the unemployed?

d) the New Deal for disadvantaged communities, which will channel £15 million to Britain's worst council estates?

e) the New Deal for schools: £1.3 billion to pay for repairing and replacing Britain's most run-down classrooms?

As Humpty Dumpty said, the New Deal means whatever I choose it to mean (or whatever Gordon chooses it to mean, until the windfall cash finally runs out).

a   What do you understand by the term 'flexible labour market'?   **(1)**

b   What do you understand by the term 'McDonaldisation'?   **(1)**

c   How important is technology in the rise and fall of occupations within the labour market?   **(5)**

d   Using information in the items and elsewhere, assess the relative importance of technology as a factor in the deskilling of the labour force.   **(9)**

e   To what extent do you think that the New Deal will make it easier for young people to gain access to the labour market?   **(9)**

Structured questions

a What is post-Fordism? (1)

b Suggest two reasons why some sociologists may reject the conception of post-Fordism. (4)

c To what extent can it be argued that technological change has had a significant impact on levels of unemployment? (10)

d What impact have postmodern ideas and argument had on the way in which sociologists look at issues of work and leisure? (10)

Essay titles

1 Evaluate the arguments sociologists have offered for the transition from Fordism to post-Fordism. (25)

2 Outline and evaluate the significance of McDonaldisation to our understanding of work. (25)

3 'New Deal provides opportunities for people to work by enhancing their skills and abilities' To what extent can sociological arguments and evidence be used to support this view? (25)

So you want to be a citizen?

The welfare state is about to undergo substantial reform and it is important that we establish the underlying vision that should inform that process, rather than making changes incrementally and without any clear indication of how they fit into a larger picture.

Over the years the British welfare state has embodied two contrasting, and in many respects contending, notions of citizenship. The first sees citizenship as a status that is not fundamentally altered by the virtue (or lack of it) of the individual: it does not ask whether the citizen is making a recognised contribution to society. This form of citizenship comes through membership of a particular political community and implies two sorts of rights: rights not to be interfered with (that is, negative rights), and positive rights to the economic and social conditions of citizenship – health, education and welfare. You should thus be able, as a citizen, to claim benefits even if your way of life is disapproved of by others (so long as you are not interfering with them) and even if you are not discharging what others may regard as your proper obligations to society.

The second, and alternative, view of citizenship places much less emphasis on rights, and focuses instead on obligation, virtue and contribution. On this view citizenship is not a kind of pre-existing status, but rather something that is achieved by contributing to the life of society. The ideas of reciprocity and contribution are at the heart of this concept of citizenship: individuals do not and cannot have a right to the resources of society unless they contribute to the development of that society through work or other socially valued activities, if they are in a position to do so.

It is very clear that the present government wishes to develop welfare reform in terms of the second paradigm, using an obligation-based notion of citizenship.

The history of welfare, however, is more complex than this suggests. Professor Jose Harris, the biographer of William Beveridge and our leading historian of the welfare state, has argued that, "contrary to its reputation for stigma, discretion and selectivity, the English Poor Law had been available for several centuries as a system of relief based not on contribution or contract but on mere membership of the community."

By the time Beveridge came to work on his report, the two approaches to citizenship were becoming more clear-cut. One was based on status, paid for out of tax revenues, non-contributory but means-tested; the other was based on contribution, often involving insurance payments by the individual and calculated to promote saving and thrift. During the 1930s, with the notable exception of Harold Laski, its chief intellectual, the Labour Party had come to favour benefits paid for by general taxation rather than insurance, and thus had endorsed the status view of citizenship.

Beveridge, however, set his face against this view, and his whole report is a clear endorsement of the insurance-based approach: that is to say, one based on contribution and reciprocity. Security was to come through participating in the labour market and paying insurance contributions when in work. Thus economic and social citizenship had to be earned.

He rejects of the idea of a citizen's right to an unconditional benefit. A central distinction was drawn between insurance and assistance. Far from the status of citizenship creating rights, for Beveridge it was insurance and contribution to the labour market that did so. Work and contribution were the passports to citizenship rights.

By the 1970s the Labour Party had begun to argue that public expenditure on welfare could be an instrument of greater social and economic equality. If this was to be the case, however, then general taxation was going to have to play a much larger role than insurance contributions in securing benefits.

Finally, the emphasis on universality and the need to avoid stigma (not judgmentalism again) argued in favoured at least blurring any sort of sharp distinction between insurance-based and other sorts of benefit.

The government has made it clear that it wishes to move the UK back to at least some of the principles that underlie the Beveridge report, with a major emphasis on the notions of reciprocity and contribution and an obligation-based view of citizenship, and particular stress on the idea that work is a major component of citizenship. The government is concerned about dependency – the ways in which recipients of benefits become cut off from the disciplines and sociability of the labour market.

Second, it fears that the moral hazard of an entitlements approach to benefits will foster habits of mind that trap individuals in poverty and outside the labour market.

Third, this leads to a wider concern with free-riding, where non-contributory benefits are funded out of general tax revenues, raised largely from people who have to work. Many of them pay substantial tax on wages from low-paid jobs.

Fourth, even if an entitlement view of welfare on a non-contributory basis were considered legitimate in moral or philosophical terms, tax-payers would not be prepared to fund benefits at a level that would lift people out of poverty.

Finally, tax-payers are right to resist such levels of payment on economic grounds, because the UK has to operate in an intensely competitive global market in which other countries have lower costs.

Hence the proposals to reform the welfare state.

But what about the New Deal and the general strategy of welfare-to-work? Today I can see two major pitfalls.

The first has to do with work itself and the place it is given in new Labour's scheme of things. If work is to be the passport to social and economic citizenship, then we must expect to see pretty stringent tests, particularly on groups such as the disabled to discover whether (in their case) the degree of disability does preclude a person from entering the job market. If, however, the unemployed or those on disability benefit are to be encouraged to return to the labour market, employability will be central.

That is to say, those who are currently outside the labour market must be equipped with the skills that employers want. Now, this is not a straightforward task because we are also told, with increasing frequency, that there is a smaller and smaller market for those with low skill-levels. If this is true and if the young unemployed are to be got back to work with a chance of lifetime employability, if the long-term adult unemployed are to be got back to the labour market and if the abilities of the disabled are to be capitalised upon, then the skilling level is going to have to be quite high and sustained over a long time. This will be extremely expensive.

If we are to have a radical overhaul of unemployment benefit and the disability benefits in favour of work-oriented schemes, these changes have to be sustainable in the long term without, windfall cash. At the moment, there is no clear indication how this longer-term welfare-to-work strategy, coupled with the delivery of employability skills, is to be sustained.

This brings me on to my second point about work, which is the availability of jobs. If the jobs are not there, the government is willing the end and not the means. It wants welfare to be replaced by welfare-to-work and status citizenship to be replaced by supply-side or contribution-based citizenship; but while it can organise the supply side (and has done so in a very impressive way since the election), the question of whether there are jobs for those equipped with supply-side skills to go to is another question altogether.

The true logic of the government's position, that work is the passport to social and economic citizenship and the way out of social exclusion, is for the state to become the employer of last resort. Consequently, it is emphasising contribution and reciprocity as central conditions of citizenship without being able to guarantee that society can, in fact, keep its side of the bargain. I do not think the government can insist on a welfare-to-work strategy without also having a strategy for jobs, which, to be fair, would imply that it will become the employer of last resort.

An equally difficult question is what to do about those who will have to live on benefits because they cannot be active in the labour market.

We surely cannot go down a road that would lead us to a position which, however inadvertently, stigmatises those who cannot meet the conditions of being active and contributing citizens. During a recession there are going to be many who have to be back on unemployment benefit for long periods, unless the government becomes the employer of last resort.

The new approach to benefits presents lots of opportunities for the voluntary sector, as the most articulate defenders of many of those who are unlikely to be able to enter this new circle of opportunity.

Source: Raymond Plant, *New Statesman*, 6 February 1998.
Based on an address by Lord Plant to the National Council of Voluntary Organisations.

1 How does the author suggest that we make people '*want* to get off welfare'? **(4)**

2 What is the value of people 'pooling their entitlements'? **(4)**

3 What is the role and the purpose of the Consortia? Do you believe that it would reduce welfare dependence and get people back to work in Britain? **(8)**

4 What are 'social entrepreneurs'? **(6)**

Further reading and references

Del Roy Fletcher (1997) 'Evaluating special measures for the unemployed: Some reflections on recent UK experience' in *Policy and Politics* 25, 2.

Waters, W. (1997) 'The "Active Society": new designs for social policy' in *Policy and Politics* 25, 3.

Compston, H. (Ed.) (1997) *The New Politics of Unemployment*. London, Routledge.

Internet sites

What is New Deal? http://www.newdeal.gov.uk/homesub1.asp
www.abacom-com/sociology/soclinks/politics/html
www.stile.lot.ac.uk/~gyobs/GLOBAL/t0000006.html
Global Observatorys Resource Information
An excellent outline of new social movement with a good range of links.

Bibliography

Albrow, M. (1970) *Bureaucracy*. London, Pall Mall.
Ashley, D. (1997) *History Without a Subject*. Boulder, Westview Press.
Bauman, Z. (1998) *Work, Consumerism and the New Poor*. Milton Keynes, Open University Press.
Beck, U. (1992) *The Risk Society*. Cambridge, Polity Press.
Blauner, R. (1964) *Alienation and Freedom*. Chicago, University of Chicago Press.
Braverman, H. (1974) *Labour and Monopoly Capital*. New York, Monthly Review Press.
Brenner, B. (1979) 'Mortality and the National Economy'. *The Lancet*, September.
Burchell, B. (1994) 'The Effects of Labour Market Position, Job Insecurity and Unemployment on Psychological Health' in D. Gallie, C. Marsh and C. Vogler (Eds.) *Social Change and the Experience of Unemployment*. Oxford, Oxford University Press.
Crook, S., Pakulski, J. and Waters, M. (1992) *Postmodernisation*. London, Sage.
Daniel, W. W. and Millward (1972) *The Right to Manage*. London, MacDonald.
Deem, R. (1988) 'Women and Leisure'. *Social Studies Review*, 5, 4.
Department of Employment (1994) *Labour Force Survey*. London, HMSO.
Dickinson, D. (1994) 'Criminal Benefits'. *New Statesman and Society*, January.
Durkheim, E. (1938, first published 1893) *The Division of Labour in Society*. Glencoe, Free Press.
Fagin, D. (1986) *Unemployment and Health*. London, HMSO.
Finn, D. (1987) *Training Without Jobs*. London, Macmillan.
Freeman, C. and Soete, L. (1994) *Work for All* or *Mass Unemployment*. London, Pinter.
Fullan, M. (1970) 'Industrial Technology and Worker Integration in the Organisation'. *American Sociological Review*, December.

Gallie, D., Marsh, C. and Vogler, C. (Eds.) (1994) *Social Change and the Experience of Unemployment*. Oxford, Oxford University Press.

Gershuny, J. I. and Pahl, R. E. (1980) 'Gritain in the decade of the three economies'. *New Society*, January.

Giddens, A. (1984) *The Constitution of Society*. Cambridge, Polity Press.

Glyptis, S. (1989) *Leisure and Unemployment*. Milton Keynes, Open University Press.

Goffman, E. (1961) *Asylums: Essays on the Social Situation of Mental Patients and other Inmates*. London, Penguin.

Goldthorpe, J. and Payne, G. (1986) 'Trends in Intergenerational Mobility in England and Wales.' *Sociology*, Vol. 20.

Goldthorpe, J. H. and Payne, G. (1983) 'Women and Class Analysis: In Defence of the Conventional View' in *Sociology* 17: 481.

Grint, K. (1993) *The Sociology of Work*. Cambridge, Polity Press.

Hyman, R. (1972) *Strikes*. London, Fontana.

Jenkins, C. and Sherman, B. (1979) *The Collapse of Work*. London, Eyre Methuen.

Jenkins, R. (1986) *Racism and Recruitment: Managers, Organisations, and Equal Opportunity*. Cambridge, Cambridge University Press.

Kerr, C. and Siegel, A. (1960) *Industrialism and Industrial Man*. Cambridge, Mass., Harvard University Press.

Lampard, R. (1994) 'An examination of the relationship between marital dissolution and unemployment' in D. Gallie, C. Marsh and C. Vogler (Eds.) *Social Change and the Experience of Unemployment*. Oxford, Oxford University Press.

Lash, S. and Urry, J. (1987) *The End of Organised Capitalism*. Cambridge, Polity Press.

Lloyd, J. (1997) 'New Deal'. *New Statesman and Society*, February.

Lukes, S. (1974) *Power: A Radical View*. London, Macmillan.

Mandry and Kirby (1996) *Investigating Work, Unemployment and Leisure*. London, Collins Education.

Martin, J. and Roberts, C. (1984) *Women and Employment: a Lifetime Perspective*. London, HMSO.

Mayo, E. (1933) *The Human Problems of an Industrial Civilization*. New York, Macmillan.

Michels, R. (1911) *Political Parties*. New York, Free Press.

Michels, R. *Political Parties: a Sociological Study of the Oligarchical Tendencies of Modern Democracy*. This study was first published in Germany in 1911. The first English translation was published in 1915.

Mintzberg, H. (1979) *The Structure of Organisations*. New Jersey, Prentice Hall.

Murry, R. (1989) 'Fordism and Post-Fordism' in S. Hall and M. Jacques *New Times: The Changing Face of Politics in the 1990s*. London, Lawrence and Wishart.

Parker, S. (1967) 'Work and Leisure' in Butterworth and Weir *Sociology of Modern Society*, Harmondsworth, Penguin.

Parsons, T. (1951) *The Social System*. Glencoe, Free Press.

Philpott, J. (1994) *The Labour Market*. Deddington, Phillip Allan.

Piore, M. and Sabel, C. (1984) *The Second Industrial Divide: Possibilities for Prosperity*. New York, Basic Books.

Pollock, G. (1997) 'Uncertain Futures: Young People in and Out of Employment since 1940' in *Work, Employment and Society* vol 11, No 4: 615–38.

Plant, R. (1998) 'Citizenship'. *New Statesman and Society*, February.

Ritzer, G. (1993) *The McDonaldization of Society*. Thousand Oaks, Pine Forge Press.

Rose, S. (1978) *Science and Politics*. Harmondsworth, Penguin.

Salaman, G. (1987) 'Information technology and the debate about work'. *Social Studies Review*, May.

Sanders, P. (1988) 'Race in the UK' in Blackstone, T. ed. *Race Relations in Britain: Developing an Agenda*. London, Routledge.

Scott, J. (1997) *Corporate Business and Capitalist Class*. Oxford, Oxford University Press.

Taylor, F. (1911) *The Principles of Scientific Management*. New York, Harper and Row.

Taylor, F. W. (1990) *Scientific Management*. New York, Harper and Row.

Trist, E. L. and Banfold, K. W. (1951) 'Some Social and Psychological Consequences of the Longwall Method of Coal-getting'. *Human Relations*, February.

Weber, M. (1922) *Economy and Society: an Outline of Interpretive Sociology*. Berkeley, University of California Press.

Education

This area covers:

- The political and social significance of formal education systems within the UK
- The relationship of the formal education system to pupil achievement
- A consideration of processes within and outside the education system which can affect the structure and organisation of the system and pupil achievement.

By the end of this area you should be able to:

- recognise why education is such an important policy area in the political arena
- identify factors within schools and within society that can affect pupil attainment
- identify the wide variety of ideologies and social theories which underlie educational planning and practice
- understand something of the social and historical factors which have contributed to the development and organisation of our current education system.

Key terms

vocationalism	local education authority
compensatory education	state maintained schools
meritocracy	independent education
egalitarianism	grant maintained schools
libertarianism	curriculum

Area 8   Contents

Introduction

This area will look at the role and structure of educational practice in our society. You will examine educational theory and the consequent social policy, which affects the structure and organisation of our education system. You will consider the impact of that policy on children and their subsequent life chances.

This is one of the most significant and political areas of study within the field of sociology. The aim of this section is to examine some of the social and political theory related to education and to see how that theory has affected the structure of the education system in the UK. We insist that our children experience a minimum of 11 years of compulsory education and it has been the role of sociologists to consider how this experience has affected our children and our society.

The government spends billions on education. Government targets in 1999 for spending on education across the UK in 2001–2002 were set at £47.9 billion, yet many still claim that it is badly underfunded. Huge numbers of people are employed in colleges and schools. There are hundreds of different interest groups, all of whom have extremely strong opinions on how best to develop people's minds. Education can also be seen to have a significant effect on the way individuals organise their daily lives because it has such a great impact on their earning potential. Educational success can be seen to underlie the social values we place on other people. It is also one of the most highly researched topics in sociology so many books, journals and newspaper columns are devoted to discussions of education. Students must therefore develop their own sociological overview of the various ideologies of the nature and purpose of education. They should also recognise that many of these views are contradictory.

Even within perspectives there can be conflicting understandings. For example, Marxists and left-wing thinkers may view educational systems either as a system of gaining mind control over young children or as a liberating influence on them. Meritocrats see education as a way of preparing clever students for the best jobs, but may also admire the social divisiveness that can result from selection of students. All are

agreed, however, that education can be one of the most significant life experiences of any individual and are united in striving for the very best education for all children.

The sociological argument therefore centres on the following debates:

■ What is the nature and purpose of education?

■ What do we need to know to survive as social and economic beings?

■ How does the process of learning affect our understanding of the social world and our position within it?

■ How best can the very expensive educational institutions and structures within our society serve the needs of that society?

Defining education

We learn continuously. From the moment of birth to the point of death we must adapt our behaviours to changing social situations. Any learning could theoretically be described as a part of our education. However, this definition is far too broad to be of any use in terms of study and therefore general social learning is more usually thought of as **socialisation** by sociologists – you may have already met this idea in Area 4.

In sociological terms, education is usually seen as the process of acquiring certain skills or knowledge within an institution designed for that purpose. The technical terms offered by functionalists to cover the various

HINTS AND TIPS   Be ruthless in your use of teachers, who should become a primary resource for information about the education system. Engage them in as much discussion as possible about their work and their perceptions of the education system itself. Most are compulsive talkers about their work and will welcome a willing listener. You will also gain a great deal from talking to people older than yourself such as your parents and grandparents or people who have been to different schools and have different experiences. You may even wish to visit schools of different types in your neighbourhood. Most will be very supportive, especially private schools.

types of learning that we undertake are identified below.

- **Formal education** is the process of being educated in a school or institution by trained personnel.

- **Informal education** is learning acquired at home.
- **Non-formal education** is offered in a formal social context such as a club or youth group where skills and knowledge are passed on.

Current issues in education

Most of the following discussion points centre on the idea that ideology, economics and political expediency underlie much educational policy decision-making in our society.

You should test the current belief that encouraging competition between schools for the best students, between parents for the best schools, between teachers for higher pay scales and between pupils for the best facilities is the best way to raise standards of education for all children in this country.

Return to these questions when you have finished studying this area and see if your personal views have changed once you have acquired some sociological understanding of the issues.

Use these questions and ideas to help your discussions:

Schools and pupils:

- Will competition between pupils encourage a cultural change in our society that emphasises success?

- Are all schools equally placed to attract clever and well motivated pupils?

- Could successful schools become overcrowded?

- Is it fair that some schools should have poorer facilities because they cannot attract students?

- What kind of children will schools reject from their lists?

- Will schools want to take the badly behaved and the lowest achievers?

- What happens to the students that no one wants in their school?

- Is it fair to the intelligent and well motivated to have lessons disrupted by those who are badly behaved and less motivated?

Schools and community:

- Do parents know better than teachers what is best for their children?

- Is a school's public reputation a fair assessment of the quality of teaching and the learning that is taking place in the institution?

- Is it sensible in a small town to have two schools in competition with each other?

- Will schools be encouraged to sell their services to pupils?

- Would it be acceptable for schools to pay clever children to attend so that the results would look better in the league tables?

- Should schools pay out large sums of money on 'selling the school' and marketing it to the local community?

- Can schools be trusted not to exclude from their lists before examination children who are likely to get bad results?

- Will teachers put pressure on the most able students to take lots of subjects or *their* subjects just to improve the results?

- Are some schools complacent because they have no competition and no incentive to improve the service they offer?

Social and moral debates:

- Should teachers of 'rarity' subjects or subjects such as science be paid more than teachers of popular subjects?

- Money is placed in school budgets for those with special needs such as physical disability. Should intelligent and gifted children also receive extra funds to develop their talents?

- Does a sense of competition encourage well motivated students?

- What type of parents will benefit from a selective education system?

- Is it good for society to have a large gap between rich and poor, educated and uneducated?

Contrasting theories of the education system, including its role in socialisation

Educational philosophies

Education has a far wider set of meanings and ideologies, or beliefs, than sociology offers. Many of these beliefs and understandings predate the development of sociology as a subject discipline and are better described as philosophies or ideologies. These include the following terms and you should ensure that you fully understand the meanings before progressing through this area.

Compensation

This is the belief that education can correct some of the problems and evils of society. This philosophy can take two forms, in that Right realist thinkers suggest that schools should teach morality and Left-wing thinkers will want schools to support the poorest children in society so that the disadvantages they suffer because of poverty will not affect their learning.

Comprehensivisation

This is the suggestion that all children should attend the same schools and that schools should make equal provision for all. Differences of gender, race, ability and social class in particular should be disregarded so that all children have equal access to what the school has to offer.

Egalitarianism

This means that if 50% of the school population is female, then 50% of those who achieve top grades will be female, as will half of all those who leave school without qualifications. Sociologically, this view is often associated with Marxism or feminism. Marxists study class differences and feminists argue that education systems reinforce and consolidate gender inequalities.

Libertarianism

This is a somewhat dated view of education, although many of your older teachers may have been trained in this tradition. It suggests that education should allow people to deconstruct knowledge, to understand and thereby control their lives by studying. The principle still underlies much educational practice although the underlying theory has been rejected by many.

Meritocracy

Meritocrats believe that education should provide a ladder of opportunity for the brightest and the best among us. Meritocratic arguments are often used to support selective education. This is generally a functionalist perception of the purpose of education.

Vocationalism

This is the belief that the purpose of education is to prepare students for future life/career/place in the workforce. This is likely to be associated with functionalism and forms an element of the theories of the New Right. Unsurprisingly, this is a view put forward by employers and industrialists.

Lifelong learning

This is a newer philosophy associated with the Labour government of the late 1990s. It supports the idea that technology and society are moving so fast that the workforce needs to be able to develop a flexible approach to learning new skills. People must be trained to learn for themselves and to adapt to new ideas – hence the emphasis on key skills which forms part of this text.

HINTS AND TIPS   *Create an A3 size poster with these words and simple explanations to put up in your study area as a constant revision aid. Add these words to any glossary that you may be keeping. These words will be used constantly throughout the area without further explanation.*

Structural functionalism

Structural functionalism was the dominant social perspective in education in the 1960s and 1970s. Taking the ideas of Durkheim as a starting point, structural functionalists have a consensus view of society and talk of shared values and meanings. They are concerned with the purpose of institutions within society and see education as one of the most significant because it forms part of socialisation and is a mechanism for passing on the culture of a society. The American sociologist Talcott Parsons suggests that there are two questions that should concern the sociologist:

1 What purpose does the education system serve for society as a whole?
2 What value or purpose does the education system have for the individual?

Parsons claimed that the education system exists as part of a cultural **meritocracy** and that the most able people will rise through the education system and be in a position of power within a country where they will use their gifts to support the rest of us. Most people would recognise that this view, although it has some resemblance to the aims of the education system and to popular belief, is hopelessly idealistic and unrealistic.

There are two main forms of argument against the structural functionalist view.

The British response to structural functionalism

In Britain, the criticisms made of this view were generally statistical and tied to the debate about the structure of the education system set up by the 1945 Education Act. Much work was linked to studies of social class and proved beyond doubt that children did not succeed according to merit: a major determinant of success is the social class of the father. The best known study was part of the Oxford Mobility Study and was conducted by Halsey et al. (1980). Their study, *Origins and Destinations*, offered a devastating critique of the claims that the British education system was meritocratic by proving conclusively that boys from the highest social classes had far better chances of benefiting from education than those from the lower classes. Halsey's research was actually conducted in the early 1970s and few of his respondents would have attended comprehensive schools, but it is unlikely that the situation has changed dramatically. A major flaw in this quantitative work was that it did not consider the experiences of girls because it was attempting to replicate earlier work by David Glass.

The American response to structural functionalism

In the USA in the early 1970s, Alvin Gouldner offered a theoretically based critique of structural functionalism

and, although his argument was with that theory, it affected the study of education in particular. His key texts were *The Coming Crisis of Western Sociology* and *For Sociology*. He claimed that structural functionalism is untenable for two reasons:

1 It is not value free, but offers a deeply conservative view of society.
2 The theories of structural functionalism do not come true.

Gouldner is best understood by learning something of the politics of the late 1960s, when radical changes were taking place throughout western society. Student riots were taking place in cities all over Europe and the USA and, although many centred on opposition to the American war in Vietnam, others were linked with embryonic but powerful civil rights movements such as women's liberation, gay liberation and black power. Youth culture embodied a spirit of rejection of authority and the idea that a new order of liberation and equality would come into being.

Gouldner's argument, which is very much of the 1970s, can be summarised in this form:

- Structural functionalism suggests that we are socialised into roles by education.
- Education is meritocratic and the best people will get the best jobs.
- A deviant from this system will, therefore, according to functionalism, be mad or bad.
- How is it that the brightest and best student minds are rejecting the education system in their thousands throughout the western world? This points to an underlying contradiction, to which structural functionalism can offer no coherent or reasonable response.

The impact of this work was considerable at the time, and the stranglehold that functionalism had over American thought in particular was lost. There was more room for analyses that were critical of American society. These had always been present but not given due regard. Other well known American writers, such as C. Wright Mills, started with a position nearer to that followed in Britain. Mills pointed to the way that top professionals were able to control entry to their ranks, so that their own children could benefit from the high status that this work offered.

There were a number of sociological responses to the rebuttal of functionalist analyses of education dating from the 1970s. These are considered below.

> **HINTS AND TIPS** It is often tempting to reject functionalism outright because it seems overoptimistic and unrealistic. This is to ignore the fact that education actually does provide a ladder of opportunity for many people. You will discover that many of your teachers have come from working-class households. Education has traditionally been a route to middle-class work for ambitious working-class people, especially those from the old coal-mining areas, and in Scotland and Wales.

Marxism

Marxism has always offered an alternative mode of thought to functionalism. Early Marxists made a number of observations about the education system that offered a more satisfying explanation of the social inequalities that seem to form part of the structure of the system. These theories underlie the more detailed explanations of the unequal performance of social groups that follow later in this area.

One of the themes of neo-Marxism is the analysis of the failure of the working classes to achieve class consciousness and overthrow the dominant ideologies of the bourgeoisie. This thought underlies Marxist analyses of both family and the mass media. In education the analysis is simple: children accept the knowledge that is offered to them at school and so are trained into conformist acceptance of the present system. This position later develops into a major debate about the social construction and nature of knowledge.

The French sociologist Althusser (1965), for instance, claimed that the education system existed as part of the structure of the state. It is largely run in order to socialise children into an acceptance of their subordinate class position. Bordieu (1984) suggested that schools are middle-class institutions organised in such a way as to benefit the offspring of the middle classes. He claimed that the children of the middle classes benefit from **cultural capital** because the trade of school is not just knowledge but also cultural understandings. Cultural capital can be seen as the mode of thought and values typical of the wealthy classes. These may seem alien to children from working-class backgrounds, who will under-achieve even if they have intelligence levels similar to those of the children of the middle classes. Middle-class children, however, can use these values and ways of behaving to trade on, because they know and understand the system.

The major American writers in the Marxist tradition were Bowles and Gintis who argued that education systems exist to reproduce the workforce needed by the capitalist classes. They described the **hidden curriculum**, a key idea that underlies much later thought in this area. What schools intend to teach is known as the **curriculum**, but they also teach skills and ideas that are not intentional or readily obvious – the hidden curriculum.

> **ACTIVITY** **KS PROBLEM SOLVING**
>
> **IDENTIFICATION AND INTERPRETATION**
>
> One of the most important lessons we learn is to tell appropriate lies to people in positions of power. For instance, list the various excuses that people make to avoid telling the teacher that they have not done homework. Why is it necessary to lie to your teacher in this situation? In the past, school uniform often consisted of a stiff collared shirt, a tie, black laced shoes, and a tailored jacket. In many schools it still does. What hidden curriculum message could this particular choice of garments be passing on to working-class boys or to girls?

Bowles and Gintis (1976) suggest that capitalism affects the ideology and organisation of schools in the following ways:

- Schools value conformist and passive pupils.
- Schools operate on hierarchies and teach children to accept authority.
- Schools ask children to work for rewards, which follow later in a form of exchange – 'Work now and pass your exams later.' This prepares them for work.
- Schoolwork is often boring and children are encouraged to work not for their own satisfaction but for rewards.
- The division of schoolwork into subject areas causes children to accept a division of labour rather than to see education as an organised and organic whole. This reflects the divide and rule policies practised by employers in the workplace.

In Britain, the most highly praised and interesting work is that of **Paul Willis** (1977) in his book *Learning to Labour*. He starts with a central puzzle which is that, given that working-class work is boring, badly paid, causes ill health and is insecure, why do working-class children behave in such a way as to ensure that this is the only kind of employment they will obtain?

Willis carried out an ethnographic study of 12 'lads' from a Midlands school over a period from their last year in school to their first months of paid employment. The culture he describes is masculine, rebellious, and physical. His answer to the puzzle is that the culture the 'lads' adopted was a preparation for their future work and represented a working-class rejection of the middle-class values of their school. The 'lads'' rejection of school makes them the victims of a system where their labour will be exploited in the workplace. He suggests that his cohort shows potential for the development of resistance to the bourgeois values of society. They see schooling as irrelevant to their future lives and resist the ideology of the school.

There has been criticism of the methodology that Willis uses, most notably by Blackledge and Hunt. They state that Willis draws grand conclusions from a small sample and ignores other cultural groups within the study school. He appears to share sympathy with the 'lads' in their rejection of British society and admires some of their rebellion. He uses their social definitions and refers to the conformist pupils as 'ear'oles', for instance. This attitude may affect his conclusions. Willis also notes that the 'lads' are sexist and fiercely racist and is rightly critical of them. He points out that they feel threatened by their belief that West Indian boys are 'well endowed' sexually. However, it is possible that Willis, in his desire to discover a form of left-wing class consciousness in their culture, may underplay the possibility of a dangerously fascist tendency in many of the views that the 'lads' express.

PROFILE

Paul Willis

Paul Willis has been an extremely influential figure in cultural studies. He was brought up in Wolverhampton and gained his first degree in English Literature from Cambridge University in 1966.

Willis gained his doctorate from The Centre for Contemporary Cultural Studies at Birmingham University in 1972, when he made ethnographic studies of the local biker and hippy cultures. This was published as *Profane Culture* (1978, Routledge). He was a member of the Centre for Contemporary Studies as a student then research fellow between 1968 and 1981. Currently Willis is Professor of Social and Cultural Studies and Head of Media and Cultural Studies at the University of Wolverhampton.

He has written widely on issues of culture and social class, generally from a broadly neo-Marxist or Cultural Effects stance. *Learning to Labour*, the text discussed in this area, was published in 1977, and by 1978 had been reprinted twice. It remains a classic in the field.

The methodology with which Willis is most commonly associated is ethnography and includes the use of observational technique, diaries and interviews. Currently he is working on forms of the situated and creative reception of the cultural media and on other aspects of contemporary change in working-class culture.

HINTS AND TIPS *The understanding that some Marxist theorists may have a political desire to prove Marxist theory correct should form part of any evaluation that you make on Marxism as sociology.*

ACTIVITY KS COMMUNICATION, INFORMATION TECHNOLOGY

IDENTIFICATION AND INTERPRETATION	ANALYSIS AND EVALUATION

Ask a wide variety of teachers to suggest four words that would sum up some of the characteristics of their perfect pupil. Put these words into categories and then use a spreadsheet program to draw graphs and pie charts of your results.

- ■ To what extent are teachers describing a conformist style of student?
- ■ How far does your research support the views of Bowles and Gintis?
- ■ Show your results to some teachers; are they surprised by your findings?

Interactionalism

Notable contributions to educational thinking have been made from a variety of American and British writers using the interactional perspective. Interactional thought is somewhat difficult to separate from research based on other theoretical perspectives because Bowles and Gintis, Willis and feminist writers draw on the methodology of interactionalism.

Interactionalism begins with the position that we develop a sense of who we are, or *self*, through our interactions with other people. Given this, our sense of self may develop from some *significant others* in our lives: our parents, our friends, our teachers. Education therefore is enormously important because it is from teachers that we learn a whole range of social definitions, which we can apply to ourselves.

An influential book in its time, Rosenthal and Jacobsen's *Pygmalion in the Classroom* (1967), suggested that the attitude of teachers to children could affect their measured level of intelligence. Students in a poor school were tested for intelligence levels. Teachers were told that the test was actually a predictor for very sudden increases of ability. Names were given at random to the teachers, who were told that these particular children would show significant improvement in ability over a six-month period. The children were then retested and it was claimed that the children whose names were given to the teachers as 'bloomers' or improvers showed improvement. However, the teachers themselves could not remember which children had been predicted as 'bloomers'. The methodology has since been largely discredited for a number of reasons:

- The work was entirely based on a little-known and inaccurate intelligence test.

- Student study groups were subject to change of people and were not static.

- The statistical evidence did not always support the interpretations that were placed on the findings.

- It presupposed that teachers actually believed what they were told by psychologists – and the story that was manufactured for the teachers as a pretext for the work was more than a little far-fetched.

There are also claims that the research was unethical in design because it encouraged teachers to perceive certain pupils as somehow different and worthy of extra attention. There is, however, a common-sense appeal to the idea that caught the imagination of teacher trainers at the time.

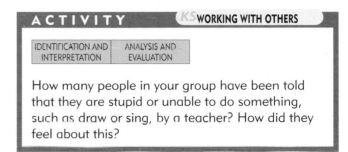

ACTIVITY   KS **WORKING WITH OTHERS**

IDENTIFICATION AND INTERPRETATION	ANALYSIS AND EVALUATION

How many people in your group have been told that they are stupid or unable to do something, such as draw or sing, by a teacher? How did they feel about this?

The key theme to interactional sociology is that teachers and school processes label pupils as intelligent or not able, and pupils then behave to those perceptions. This process was defined as the **self-fulfilling prophecy**. Although Rosenthal and Jacobsen were by no means the first to make claims about the nature of the interaction of pupils and school, this particular work was extremely popular. A whole sequence of more reliable and valid studies into various aspects of interaction followed.

David H. Hargreaves

Hargreaves is associated with a variety of interactional studies of classrooms. He was interested in the way that teachers began to 'know' or to label pupils. He suggested that a three-stage process occurred, in which teachers typified pupils on the basis of appearance and behaviour, these first judgements were confirmed or rejected and then the teacher arrived at a judgement by which all future acts would be assessed. In evaluating interactional theories, the following points should be considered.

- Teachers might be justified in this evaluative process. They are very experienced and may well be able to recognise certain signals. Are teachers to be faulted for recognising signs?

- Where do the labels originate? Pupils can often signal rebellion and rejection of school to their teachers at an early stage. In this case the labelling process surely starts with the student and not the teacher or the school.

- Working in the USA, Cicourel and Kitsuse suggested that factors that affect teacher assessment of students could be appearance, manners and clothing. These are all identifiers of social class. This work has been supported by much research. It is probable that teachers *do* evaluate children on the basis of their social class and on features other than ability.

- This process seems too deterministic. It implies that once a child is labelled then he or she will reject school, thus enacting the self-fulfilling prophecy. However, negative labelling can cause students to reject the judgements of the teacher, and some students will work hard and pass examinations to 'spite' their teachers. Feminists such as Heidi Safia-Mirza found that black and Asian girls were able to reject labels and educational success became part of their process of **resistance** to teacher labelling.

The key issue with interactionalism is always that it does not consider fully the issue of how labels arise. The focus is on the person in power, who labels, and then the impact on the 'victim'. This ignores the possibility that the victim may initiate the process. There is also lots of evidence to show that labels, if applied, can be resisted.

> **HINTS AND TIPS** *Although it is superficially attractive to many as a project area, you are advised to leave teacher-labelling theory alone. Most teachers are far too well trained and experienced to make very obvious mistakes for you to concentrate on. However significant labelling may be, it is far from a proven cause of school failure.*

Feminism

Politically and socially, feminism arose out of a direct challenge to the orthodox truths of the late 1950s and 1960s, which suggested that women were different from men because of their biology. This is a view known as sociobiology. Even in the 1960s, government reports in education such as The Newsom Report of 1963, published under the title *Half our Future*, would support notions of male and female differences in mind set and understanding. Implicit in much of this thinking was the suggestion that females were somehow also inferior and domestic, emotional and shallow, unscientific and generally unsuited for work or training. Girls clearly did less well at school at the age of 16, but this was not a

problem because they were all going to marry and bear children and would gain satisfaction from that.

Many women over the years had issued personal challenges to that patriarchal view and the history books are full of women who provided positive examples of achievement and success. Often though, these women were wealthy and single or had husbands who would support their ambitions. The first shots were fired in the battle for ordinary women in the early 1960s by the influential American writer Betty Friedan in *The Feminine Mystique*. Within 20 years, the sociology of education was full of research that proved beyond a doubt how schools reinforced notions of gender through organisational and interactional patterns, which constantly supported the myth of male superiority and higher intelligence.

Although feminism begins with a conflict view of society and is often linked with Marxism, the methods that were used by feminists in schools often drew on interactional techniques of observation. A large number of female academics became engaged in this type of research, but not all the work is female in origin. A brief summary of some of the most important work, which offers conclusions relevant to gender issues, is given in Figure 8.1.

ACTIVITY KS **COMMUNICATION**

KNOWLEDGE AND UNDERSTANDING	IDENTIFICATION AND INTERPRETATION	ANALYSIS AND EVALUATION

Using Figure 8.1 as your starting point, attempt the following activities.

1 Use this textbook to revise what you can about the three main forms of feminism: Marxist feminism, Radical feminism, Liberal feminism.

2 Summarise the contribution of writers on gender and inequality to the debate about the relative success of females and males within the education system.

3 Attempt to bring the table up to date by looking in back issues of *Sociology Review* and *S: the Sociology Magazine*. You might find that research is also carried in newspapers. The *Education Guardian* on a Tuesday is useful to you here.

4 Assess the feminist contribution to the debate about differential achievement on gender lines.

Sue Sharpe (attitude survey)	*Just like a girl* (1976)	Girls' priorities are family and domestic life leading to low-status work
Nilsen	1975	Analysed award-winning picture books and found domesticated, passive females and active, aggressive males
Sue Lees (attitude survey)	*Losing out* (1986)	Based on Sue Sharpe, found out girls are more career-oriented but still expecting to become domestic workers
Kelly	1980s	Boys dominate science lessons through physicality and taking control. This reflects patriarchal society
Rosemary Deem	1980s	Teachers encourage boys in physical activities such as lifting. Knowledge is itself patriarchal and sexist
Belotti	1982	Children's schoolbooks and fairy-tales emphasise the active nature of the male and the passive nature of the female
Michelle Stanworth (observation)	1983	There is a hidden curriculum of gender in schools and unruly behaviour is typical of boys
Samuel (content analysis)	(1983)	Textbooks in traditional male subjects use masculine examples and rarely depict women
Lobban (content analysis)	(1970s)	Books in school are sexist. Males take adventure roles and females are domestic
Pierre Bordieu (theoretical)	(1990)	Schools serve to legitimise the success of males

Figure 8.1   Some research findings related to education: this may serve as a model for note taking

> **HINTS AND TIPS**   *You should note how significant the Marxist concept of the hidden curriculum is in feminist research. While much discrimination against girls is overt and can be seen clearly, more is covert and therefore difficult to resist or reject. This type of thinking shades into Cultural Effects theory where it is believed that the impact of continually repeated ideas can create false notions of truth and reality.*

It is interesting to note here an idea that we will return to in more detail later in the area. Much of the research that is reported in Figure 8.1 has been overtaken by changes in society. Currently, girls are achieving much better than boys at GCSE level and it is expected that they will overtake boys at 'A' and degree level in the near future. This is now a 'problem', which must be addressed by schools. For example, the Sackville School Sociology Group, in its Internet site http://homepages.enterprise.net/sackville/ (which was still current in 1999), reports that boys generally do not make such good relationships with teachers as girls and that they are more likely to blame the teacher than themselves for poor achievement.

	Popular theories	**Critical theories**
Thinking	Functionalism and the New Right	Marxism and liberation theory
Work	To select people for the right jobs in society	To ensure that the children of the wealthy and powerful get the best jobs
Ideas	Education offers people morals and values	Education trains people to accept a view of the world that is conformist and passive so that poorer people can be exploited
Socialisation	People are trained in skills for future life	People learn not to question authority and are offered an education which limits them to specific workplace roles
Curriculum	People are given the curriculum that they will need to do well in society	The curriculum is tailored to the needs of those in power and reflects ideological beliefs
Social mobility	Education exists to provide a route up through society for the most able	Education serves to keep most people in their place

Figure 8.2   What is the purpose of education? An overview of educational theory

The history and structure of the current system of education

The constant debate between the various educational philosophies, outlined in the previous section, has most informed the current structure of the system that has

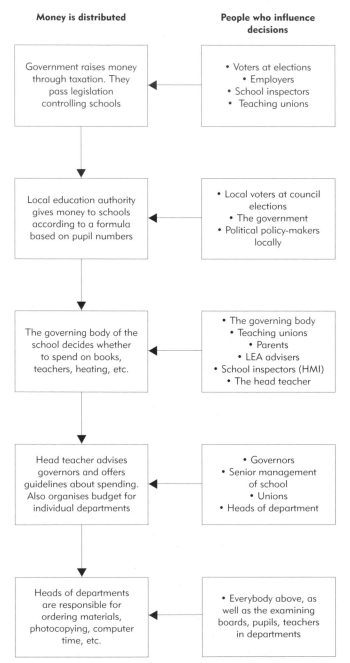

Money is distributed

People who influence decisions

Government raises money through taxation. They pass legislation controlling schools

- Voters at elections
- Employers
- School inspectors
- Teaching unions

Local education authority gives money to schools according to a formula based on pupil numbers

- Local voters at council elections
- The government
- Political policy-makers locally

The governing body of the school decides whether to spend on books, teachers, heating, etc.

- The governing body
- Teaching unions
- Parents
- LEA advisers
- School inspectors (HMI)
- The head teacher

Head teacher advises governors and offers guidelines about spending. Also organises budget for individual departments

- Governors
- Senior management of school
- Unions
- Heads of department

Heads of departments are responsible for ordering materials, photocopying, computer time, etc.

- Everybody above, as well as the examining boards, pupils, teachers in departments

Figure 8.3   Who runs a local authority maintained school?

Organise a discussion on the following topic:
- To whom should schools be answerable: governors, parents, teachers or students?

You may wish to collect opinions from some of these people before you begin your debate in order to get as wide a perspective on the issues as possible.

been created in British society. Note that our current system is by no means uniform throughout the country: the structure you have experienced may not be typical of what occurs in neighbouring counties. Scotland already has a different educational structure from England and Wales. Not all recent English legislation applies in Wales and it is probable that, after the full development of the National Assembly of Wales, there will be increasing variation between the various home countries and districts.

HINTS AND TIPS   *Although the origins of the British educational structure lie in legislation passed in the 1940s it is essential that the most recent educational debate is considered in your examination answers. Be certain that you are fully up to date with recent educational policy and thinking by looking at the supplements of broadsheet newspapers or past copies of the* **Times Educational Supplement**, *which your teachers can pass on to you. If you are planning to teach as a career, then this advice is essential.*

The 1944 Education Act

Before the 1944 Education Act, education could be very poor, with teachers concentrating on only the basics of reading, writing, and arithmetic. Children attended primary schools until they left education altogether at 14 years. Some children would be removed from primary schools at 11 to attend an academic and high-status **grammar school**, but most received only a rudimentary education that depended on the skills and interests of the class teacher.

The 1944 Act, which is often known as the Butler Act, was devised during the bleakest moments of the Second World War and was partially a morale booster. It was idealistic and **egalitarian** in intent because it offered all children secondary education. Underlying the act was a meritocratic philosophy in that children were to be given the secondary education that best suited their needs. Their needs were to be assessed at age 11 on the basis of a single examination known as the *11 plus* (11+) which was a test of English, mathematics, and intelligence. Older people may refer to this examination as the '*scholarship*'.

In practical terms, whatever the noble intentions of the Act, the secondary schools that resulted tended to reflect the class structure, beliefs, and class mix of society at that time.

- Children who did well in the 11+ attended grammar schools, which concentrated on academic skills and led to higher-paid middle-class occupations. Grammar referred to a curriculum composed of academic subjects such as history, mathematics, and languages. Depending on the area in which children lived, between 20 and 25% of children went to grammar schools. **Local education authorities** controlled the number of places available and these could be allocated on an arbitrary basis.

- Children who did less well in the 11+ (and who were seen as 'failures' by many) were taught at a lower level. They were offered a practical curriculum consisting of subjects such as woodwork and gardening. This would lead to low-paid manual work. Depending on the area in which they lived, they would attend either a **technical grammar school** or a **secondary modern school**. Few technical schools were built, so roughly 80% of the population attended secondary modern schools.

It can be argued that this structure illustrates or reflects snobbery about the value of practical knowledge and skills, which still can be seen in some areas of our education system today. It was clear from an early stage that grammar schools filled with the children of the middle classes and that the working-class children who attended them often felt out of place (Douglas, 1964). Nevertheless, many adults from working-class origins have very good cause to be grateful to the grammar schools because they offered a route out of poverty. Conversely, middle-class children who failed the 11+ could still experience a grammar school curriculum because a variety of small independent schools grew up to take on this sector of the educational market.

ACTIVITY KS **WORKING WITH OTHERS, COMMUNICATION**

KNOWLEDGE AND UNDERSTANDING	IDENTIFICATION AND INTERPRETATION

Ask people who experienced the 11+ what they remember of it. In some areas of the country you will have to speak to people in their 40s and 50s, but the exam still exists in other places and your respondents could be younger. For many it will have been a very significant experience of their childhood. Find out if they passed or not, and what the consequences of passing or failure were for them. Be sensitive in your questions.

Circular 10/65

In the early 1960s it was recognised by many, including supporters of the grammar school tradition, that the 1944 Act had not succeeded in its intent of egalitarianism. In 1965, the Labour government sent out an Education Department Circular known as *10/65*. Local education authorities were instructed to plan for comprehensive reorganisation. Schools were to accept all children on an equal social basis, though not necessarily on the grounds of gender. This led to a variety of schemes. Even within local authorities there may be a variety of school organisations loosely termed as comprehensive. Many education authorities, such as Kent and Worcester, never became comprehensive because they submitted impractical plans year on year – possibly deliberately to avoid changing their local systems.

Comprehensive schools were never fully popular in some sections of the community because grammar schools were seen as bastions of achievement. This is ironic for a number of reasons:

- Historical research suggests that grammar schools managed to fail their lower or C-stream pupils, who were seen as failures within the context of the institutions (Lacey, 1970). Examination results have improved considerably since the days of grammar schools, though some people feel that standards have dropped.

- Middle-class parents objected to grammar schools in the 1940s because they suggested that social mixing would occur. They then used the same arguments against comprehensive schools.

Arguments in favour of comprehensives	Reasons for their unpopularity
Comprehensive schools offered economy of scale. More subjects could be offered within one institution and without unnecessary duplication of staff	The resulting schools were often enormous and anonymous. Some were on more than one site
Comprehensive schools could offer equality in that all social classes could mix	Middle-class parents often did not want their children to mix with poorer or less well disciplined children
All children were offered equality of access to the curriculum and were not forced into a specialist curriculum at 11	It was believed by many that clever children might be held back by working at the pace of the slowest
Children were not doomed to feel failures on the basis of an examination taken when they were 11	Many parents were thrilled with the social status gained from having a child at the grammar school. Comprehensives lacked the same social cachet

Figure 8.4   The comprehensive school debate

ACTIVITY KS **COMMUNICATION, WORKING WITH OTHERS**

IDENTIFICATION AND INTERPRETATION	ANALYSIS AND EVALUATION

Many people will argue in favour of the return of grammar schools; very few suggest that secondary modern schools deserve to be resurrected. Is this because most people who are in favour of grammar schools feel that their children would have attended one? The proportion of grammar school entrants to secondary modern school entrants was generally about 1:5.

Ask a variety of parents these questions:
1   Do they think that their children would have passed or failed the 11+ if it were still used?
2   Would they like to see the return of grammar schools?

Evaluation question: Is there a difference between the number of passes and parental beliefs about the intelligence of their offspring?

Reasons for the 'failure' of the comprehensive dream

There has been much sociological evidence to suggest that comprehensive schools, at their best, can be highly successful in giving children a social mix and equal access to the curriculum. They seem to be able to do well by students of all abilities.

■ More students achieve examination passes in modern schools than in the past. The results have been steadily rising year on year.

■ The National Children's Bureau studied 16,000 children born in one week in 1958. Its work suggested that children in the top intelligence range did equally well irrespective of which type of school they attended.

■ Rutter, in *15000 hours*, suggested that among a number of factors that made a school good was a reasonable spread of ability among the intake, and that the spread of ability was more significant than class.

■ Ball (1981) found that when mixed-ability teaching was introduced in his study school, Beachside Comprehensive, many behavioural problems disappeared. However, he noted that stratification still occurred within classrooms.

■ Local authorities tended to allocate high funding to grammar schools and low funding to secondary moderns (Byrne, 1975). This disparity did not persist into comprehensivisation – in theory.

However, not all comprehensive schools are equal and the policy was never fully implemented. Very few schools ever approximated the dream school of a mixture of abilities and social classes working together, each to the best of his of her ability level.

■ Not all schools were fully comprehensive because in the early days many retained a different curriculum for the better students. Grammar school streams remained, even though children were taught in the same building.

■ Not all schools were comprehensive because they served different geographical areas. Can a large school serving a council estate in a deprived area really be considered in the same light as one serving a small middle-class dormitory town? Middle-class parents will move house to be in the catchment area of a school with a good reputation.

- Benn and Simon found in 1970 that many comprehensives restricted access to subjects on the basis of gender, sometimes because of limited access to facilities. In theory this should no longer happen as a result of the implementation of the National Curriculum, but some anomalies remain.

- Many schools had bad reputations for bullying. Some of this bullying may well have been mythical (Measor and Woods, 1984:16ff) but it would cause parents to distrust neighbourhood schools. Over 6% of parents have their children educated out of the state sector and bullying is often cited as a reason for this choice (Walford, 1991).

- Buildings from the early stages of comprehensivisation were often very hurriedly built, cheaply constructed and poorly designed. This affected facilities, access, and children's behaviour in public areas.

- Many schools were comprehensive, but the best or wealthiest students were 'creamed off' by attending a local independent school, a church school or a local grammar school, many of which survived in tandem with the state system.

The conclusion to this consideration of comprehensive schooling must be that even if schooling could correct the massive inequalities of wealth and power in our society (and many doubt that it can), policies need to be implemented in an organised, well funded and structured manner. The Labour governments of the 1970s offered none of these supports to their ideological – and at that time controversial – policy while Conservative governments were actively hostile. Circular 10/65 was even suspended for a short period. Pupils, schools and teachers found themselves in an educational situation that was set the enormous task of changing British society for the better, but without the goodwill of the teachers or the support and understanding of parents. Given the circumstances, comprehensives enjoy considerable success and many teachers, parents, and educationalists now offer wholehearted support to the concept of comprehensive education.

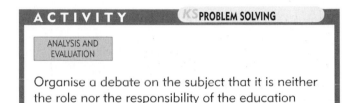

ACTIVITY KS **PROBLEM SOLVING**

ANALYSIS AND EVALUATION

Organise a debate on the subject that it is neither the role nor the responsibility of the education system to change society. Make notes both for and against the proposition.

The great debate

James Callaghan, the Labour Prime Minister, is often credited with initiating this debate in 1976 in a speech to Oxford University staff and students. Callaghan said that the key to economic success in Britain was improvement in the quality of manufacturing and that we were not producing people with the skills to be good workers. He voiced a growing concern that education was not serving the needs of the community, and this triggered a movement towards **vocationalism** in education. His speech may also have initiated a critical and dissatisfied view of teachers and the education system itself that is still clearly apparent in political and media debates.

Schools were instructed to move towards educating children for work, and this is still a primary aim of much of what happens within them. There was an expansion of careers education and skills training which moved naturally into the philosophies put forward by the Conservative government of 1979.

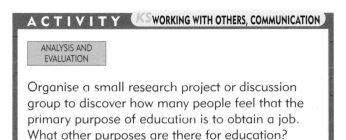

ACTIVITY KS **WORKING WITH OTHERS, COMMUNICATION**

ANALYSIS AND EVALUATION

Organise a small research project or discussion group to discover how many people feel that the primary purpose of education is to obtain a job. What other purposes are there for education?

The next significant changes to the education system were instituted under the Conservative governments of Margaret Thatcher. During this period there was a regular changeover of Secretaries of State for Education, so policy rather than single individuals probably guided the reforms.

ERA 1986 and 1988

These Acts resulted in a far-reaching and radical reform of the education system, and there is a great deal of debate about the implications of these changes. Their underlying ethos was New Right, which is typified by individualism and a fixed belief in the benefits of a free market. It is a common belief, but not one that is supported by research evidence, that **independent schools** are somehow 'better' and more efficiently organised than state sector schools (Walford, 1991). It was felt that making state-funded schools responsive to market forces, and therefore like independent schools, would encourage good practice and a more efficient education system.

The main provisions of the Educational Reform Act of 1988 were

■ the National Curriculum
■ local management of schools (LMS) – a change in school financing
■ opting out of local education control

National Curriculum

There are three core subjects: English, mathematics, and science. All students study these until the age of 16. Other subjects must be taught to all children until the age of 14. These foundation subjects are technology, history, geography, music, art, PE and (at secondary school) a modern foreign language. In addition, children in Wales who are not taught in Welsh are given compulsory Welsh language teaching until the age of 16. The core subjects are tested at 7, 11, 14 and 16 as Standardised Attainment Tests. Many of you will have taken such tests. The content of the National Curriculum has been altered significantly due to teacher concerns about the practicality of implementing the Dearing Report which initiated the Curriculum in schools.

LMS and governing bodies

Schools were given far more control over the spending of money. Control over school budgets was in the hands of local education authorities, who would have education policies covering small regions. The control of budgets and spending has passed into the hands of the individual governing body of a school. This is a

move away from centralised educational planning within a local area towards competition between local schools.

The governing body consists of a variety of individuals (many of whom are not education professionals) with considerable power within a school. A strong governing body might be able to act as a neutral body supervising a school but a weak governing body may simply act as a 'rubber stamp' to the powers of the head teacher.

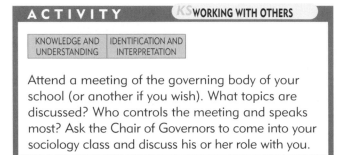

ACTIVITY   **KS** WORKING WITH OTHERS

| KNOWLEDGE AND UNDERSTANDING | IDENTIFICATION AND INTERPRETATION |

Attend a meeting of the governing body of your school (or another if you wish). What topics are discussed? Who controls the meeting and speaks most? Ask the Chair of Governors to come into your sociology class and discuss his or her role with you.

Opting out

Some schools have severed all links with their local education authorities. They take their funding directly from central government rather than from local education authority funds. Schools were offered considerable financial incentives to opt out of LEA schemes and you will recognise such schools by the term **grant maintained** in their names. Many schools in England became grant maintained or **state maintained**, but the policy was far less popular in Wales and Scotland.

More recent developments

Since the election of the 'New' Labour Party in 1997, there has been a continuation of many of the policies of the Conservative Party. The government has declared educational improvement to be at the core of its social policy, and you should be aware of some of the declared policies.

The creation of a new pay structure for teachers

This is likely to be very contentious and create considerable debate within the profession. There is a crisis in recruitment and retention of teachers, which the government intends to solve by creating a new 'super-teacher' status with higher pay.

The literacy hour

Primary schools are to encourage literacy by spending an hour a day teaching reading. Some teachers, who feel that the rest of the National Curriculum may not receive full attention, have seen this as problematical.

Reform of post-16 education

A level has been seen as both overly academic and limited in terms of what could be studied. The structure of examinations has been changed to enable students to experience a broader curriculum, whilst at the same time developing key skills which are cross-curricular – that is, transferable from subject to subject.

> **HINTS AND TIPS**   *The text of this book was written and revised during 1999 when it was fully up to date. It may be that, by the time you use it, further changes have taken place in the education system. Be aware of the changes and be aware of all legislation and reports that affect schools. Read broadsheet newspapers such as* **The Independent** *and* **The Guardian** *regularly.*

TASK

Hypothesis – Teaching is an attractive career.

Context – This hypothesis is very open because the terms 'attractive' and 'career' are relative, subjective and personal. Schools are not all the same, and people's views of their work are affected by their management structure. A variety of methods could be used and the topic lends itself to imaginative selection of sample populations.

Consider your sample first. You could speak to serving teachers about their views of teaching as a career. This might, however, be inadvisable within your own institution, as teachers are often circumspect in what they will tell pupils about their conditions of work. Teachers at another school may be happier to be open about their feelings about pay and conditions of service.

Method – Talk to students about their perceptions of teaching as a career. Why might they be attracted to or reject a career in teaching? Ask about their future plans and whether teaching could offer them the satisfaction they might require. Have teachers actively attempted to dissuade good candidates from the job?

Look at teaching union literature and current debates in the *Times Educational Supplement*, the main newspaper for teachers.

If there are student teachers at your school, you might wish to interview them informally about what made them choose teaching. You might even ask them how teachers in post have advised them informally about the work and their career prospects. You may be a little surprised by what you learn.

Evaluation – This should consider the question of the pay and career structure that the government has offered and future developments within education. If it does not, you will have missed an excellent chance to make your research relevant to recent social policy. Your evaluation should rest on public perceptions of how people view the work of teachers.

ACTIVITY

KS WORKING WITH OTHERS, INFORMATION TECHNOLOGY

KNOWLEDGE AND UNDERSTANDING	IDENTIFICATION AND INTERPRETATION	ANALYSIS AND EVALUATION

Develop your understanding of the factors that influence the development of educational organisation within a culture. Find out what you can about how educational structures can vary from country to country. There are two possible methods:

1 Your foreign language teachers will be able to offer a very brief overview of some European systems and philosophies. Be prepared to recognise that, even in western cultures, there can be considerable variation.

2 Browse the Internet and make contact with a school in another country.

Decade	Philosophical debates	Key events and prevailing politics
1940s	Egalitarianism	All children should have access to secondary education. Secondary education should be suited to the intellectual needs of each child. That provision to be decided on the basis of a single examination known as 11+
1950s	Butskellism – a consensus view from both political parties that all is generally well in education	Education provision is expanded to meet the needs of growing population born after war. Schools are highly gendered in their provision as they are designed to suit perceived social needs of children. Increasing concern among left wing and libertarians about secondary education, which is proven to be socially divisive, as middle classes go to 'better' grammar schools and working classes go to less well equipped and vocational secondary modern schools
1960s	Grammar *versus* comprehensive	Universities are expanded and newer colleges known as polytechnics set up as a result of the Robbins Report to train more students to degree level. Labour party asks all local education authorities to convert existing education provision to comprehensive provision. Many resist. Others create a variety of schemes
1970s	Grammar *versus* comprehensive: the great debate	There is concern that the new comprehensives are not doing their job. This is sometimes a failure of schools to integrate social classes. Many schools retain grammars and secondary moderns within one building. Other comprehensives are very large and split site. Social values of society are changing and teachers are abandoning old disciplinary techniques. Some of these were seen as very brutal, such as the cane. Teaching strategies are not in place to monitor and moderate behaviour. Comprehensives have a poor reputation not always supported by the evidence of social research. Vocationalism is introduced into schools
1980s	The New Right and Thatcherism Market values Consumer values	Market forces can be applied as a political solution to all problems so control of education is taken from local authorities and put into a combination of state regulation and dictation with control by community. Some school selection of pupils allowed. Parental selection of schools also permitted. National Curriculum and SATs League tables Governing bodies Parental choice and school selection of pupils Inspection on a regular basis Schools control more of their own money via LMS Grant-maintained schools and city technology colleges Polytechnics become 'new' universities Colleges of further education become independent bodies
Mid-1990s	Thatcherism gives way to New Labour, which is a modification but also a continuation of new values. Introduction of philosophy of 'lifelong learning'	New pay deals for teachers. 'Super-teacher' status. Recruitment crisis in key subjects. Skills training emphasised. Reorganisation of A level. Schools adapt modern management systems for organisation with target-setting and skills-based training systems for education

Figure 8.5   An overview of the structure of the education system in the UK from 1945 to the present day

Cultural transmission and reproduction

This is a debate that raged throughout the 1950s and 1960s and which lost significance only in the 1970s with the dominance of New Right thinking and Thatcherism. This discussion centres on the suggestion that the clear failure of working-class children to achieve the same results as middle-class children is something to do with the homes and culture of the working classes themselves.

There are three threads to the argument:

1   material poverty
2   cultural deprivation theory
3   linguistic deprivation theory

Material deprivation

Material deprivation means that people suffering from poverty are deprived of the materials of acceptable living. There have been many studies into the impact of poverty on families and this is more fully discussed in Area 10.

This was a cornerstone of cultural theory, accounting for the variable levels of achievement of children in various social classes. The principle is that if children lack the basic necessities of good living they cannot be expected to succeed in the education system. This type of theorising dropped from the agenda during the years of Conservative government beginning in 1979, but as New Labour seemed to be unwilling to address this particular debate (1999), it began to reappear in educational journals. Each new generation of researchers discovers that people in their society are desperately poor and deprived and are shocked to discover the extent of inequality experienced.

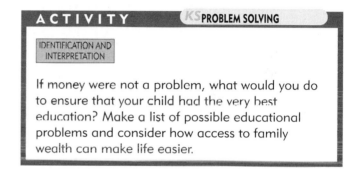

ACTIVITY   KS **PROBLEM SOLVING**

IDENTIFICATION AND INTERPRETATION

If money were not a problem, what would you do to ensure that your child had the very best education? Make a list of possible educational problems and consider how access to family wealth can make life easier.

J.W.B. Douglas published a sequence of research findings based on a longitudinal study of children born in the first week of March 1946. Douglas found a direct

	Home and cultural explanations	School and institutions
Language	Students are taught a language at home which is at odds with the one spoken in school	Teachers identify with those who speak in the same way and misinterpret the meanings of children who do not
Gender	Children are taught in the home to behave along gender role patterns and bring this to school	Children are taught gender in school because of gender-differentiating behaviours of staff
Economics	Poor children will do less well because they lack many basic necessities for health and education	Schools serving poor areas lack many of the basic necessities and have poor facilities
Knowledge	Students have a home culture which does not value the same knowledge as teachers and schools	Teachers impose a set of alien moral values and do not recognise the cultures of the children they serve
Ethnicity	Children are disadvantaged by lack of language and a sense of alienation from western cultural values	Schools and teachers are both intentionally and unintentionally racist
Parental involvement	Parents do not take, or are unable to take, an interest in their children's education	Schools are inefficient and badly run. They are run for the needs of the staff and not the children
Interaction	Children behave in such a way as to trigger teacher responses	Teachers label children and then act according to the labels they have accorded to children

Figure 8.6   An overview of theory: why do pupils fail?

link between social class and educational achievement (or lack of it). He was critical of a variety of elements of working-class culture, which he claimed contributed to the failure of working-class children. These included the following:

- The failure of working-class parents to visit schools and take an interest in the work of their children.

- The 'inferior' child-rearing patterns of the working classes.

- The failure to provide a stimulating environment for children.

Douglas also pointed out that the cause of many of these defects could be discovered in the conditions in which poor children lived. They shared beds because of overcrowding and their health was not reliable. They could not concentrate in school if they were hungry, ill and tired. They attended poorer schools near to their homes, whereas the middle classes could afford to be selective in the choice of school as they had a family car for transport. Douglas also brought attention to the fact that many schools were in an appalling physical state in poor areas, lacking basic heating, lighting, and sanitation. Douglas made the further observation that children seemed to be streamed on the basis of personal hygiene. Wedge and Prosser, in their 1973 study *Born to Fail*, made a similar strong statistical argument to show how poverty could be a negative influence on achievement.

Recent personal accounts of how poverty and deprivation can affect the education of children can often be seen in anecdotal form in newspapers such as the *Times Educational Supplement*. Many serving teachers will have their own favourite horror stories.

Cultural deprivation theory

Cultural deprivation theory is not now so significant, but it still justifies some thought. It begins with the understanding that the cultures of working-class people and middle-class people are different. It then notes that working-class people do less well in education. Some theorists then make a causative link between the two ideas and suggest that working-class people do less well because their culture is somehow inferior. This is a hugely political view as it is so critical of working-class culture. It points out that the working class does less well and then moves on to blame the victims for their own failure. However, there is an element of attractive common-sense appeal to the idea. There are two questions to be considered here:

- Is there a culture or cycle of disadvantage?

- Is the culture of working-class people different or deficient?

Melvin Kohn tested families in Washington DC in the 1940s and 1950s and discovered that there are class differences in culture. He described middle-class parents as desiring independence of mind and working-class parents as valuing obedience. John and Elizabeth Newson (1963) in Britain made similar findings in their study of families in Nottingham. They further claimed that poverty led to irritability among mothers.

Oscar Lewis in the late 1950s introduced the idea of the **culture of poverty**. He claimed that poor people developed distinct subcultural values, which enabled them to survive poverty but which disadvantaged their children in school. At an individual level, people grow to feel helpless and unable to change their circumstances. By the age of six or seven, children have absorbed the values of their culture and cannot take advantage of opportunities.

> **HINTS AND TIPS**   *If you consider whether there is a culture of failure, consider also whether a culture of success may have a distinctive value system, which is in some way 'better'.*

The level of the debate was raised by growing awareness of the theorising of the Marxist, Bordieu, who has already been discussed briefly in this area. Bordieu describes a situation where cultural knowledge reflects the interests and concerns of the dominant classes – cultural capital. Bordieu discusses in detail a whole variety of behaviours, which form part of a **habitus** or preferred mode of thinking, acting and perceiving. Those individuals who possess the dominant culture are recognised in schools, and supported by teachers who possess the same cultural background.

Similar to this is C. Wright-Mills' concept of **élite self-recruitment**. Members of the highest sectors of society can prevent educational failure and protect their interests (and those of their children) by sending their children to the best **public schools**. This gives the child a chance to acquire the social skills and background to rise to the best and most powerful positions.

Linguistic deprivation theory

This is a major area with links to philosophy, linguistics, and psychology. The suggestion begins with the observation that people from different social groups speak and use language in different ways. This initiates the question, 'Does the language we use limit the possibility of certain kinds of thought?', among others. To illustrate this point, the Romans were not able to do complex or abstract mathematics because their numbering system was complicated and they did not have the concept of zero. They were limited in the possibilities of thought by the limitations of their mathematical language. It was commonly believed that working-class people suffer **linguistic deprivation** because they do not speak in the rhythms and vocabulary of the educated middle classes. Their thought was limited by lack of linguistic skills.

This is a highly debatable point and the research is by no means conclusive. Although the meanings of all conversations remain similar, there are differences of:

- semantics (precise meaning of words)
- syntax (grammar used)
- lexicon (vocabulary)

One of the most controversial figures in the debate in educational sociology is Basil Bernstein, who is probably more well known for what people have *claimed* he said than anything he *did* say. His writing style is both opaque and complex and he appears to have shifted position during his career. He suggests that social relationships affect speech habits and that speech habits can impact on social relationships. Language is one way in which we perceive the world because it gives us the symbols for interpretation.

Education texts of the 1970s claim that Bernstein suggests that people have an ability to perceive the world which is limited by their habits of speech and thought. He is said to suggest that working-class people speak in a restricted code of language, which is familiar and has certain repetitive patterns; they are unable to hold complex ideas. Middle-class people use an elaborate code, which is individualistic and abstract. This led to much language-based work in schools to 'correct' working-class habits of speech and thought. Bernstein now claims he was arguing a different and more complex case about the way in which people use language socially and how working-class children may be disadvantaged because they do not comprehend the social patterns and codes used in schools.

Evaluative points include the following issues:

- It would be difficult to establish whether patterns of speech are elaborate or restricted, and little practical work has emerged from this debate.

- Rosen points out that the work is misused by teachers, who can legitimise a labelling process (and resulting low expectation) of working-class children.

- Labov, who studied American Non-standard Negro English, says that it is more suited to complex thought than the wordier style of middle-class English.

- Many children consciously adopt two different patterns of speech, which they will use in the appropriate social circumstances, just as they can adopt two completely different languages if brought up using both in normal social situations. Consider the British children of immigrant parents who often move in three or four language traditions with very little problem.

ACTIVITY   KS **COMMUNICATION**

IDENTIFICATION AND INTERPRETATION	ANALYSIS AND EVALUATION

What difficulties would you face if you attempted to prove that language affects your ability to think?

Does the fact that the scientific evidence to support or disprove any linguistic deprivation theory is difficult to obtain invalidate the observations?

HINTS AND TIPS   *The questions asked of you about the work of linguistic deprivation are highly theoretical; it might be an issue for you to think about and return to on a regular basis. Do not expect to have ready or easy answers.*

Do schools really fail pupils?

There is a growing body of evidence to support the view that schools are the major factor in the achievement of children. If we concentrate on how pupils fail schools, we may well overlook the fact that schools can be disorganised, unstructured and bad places in which to learn. This point has been made by sociologists from a number of perspectives and underlies much recent thinking, especially that of the New Right. Nell Keddie pointed the finger at schools from a feminist perspective in the 1970s. Michael Rutter supported this view in his influential text *1500 hours* when he suggested that school ethos is a major factor in educational achievement. A large number of commentators have emphasised the role of teachers and school efficiency in school success and this view has influenced public policy on education.

However, to provide balance to the politically led swing against home and cultural explanations of failure, there are genuine issues that need to be considered.

■ Schools defined by Ofsted (Office for Standards in Education) as failing are almost always in poor areas.

■ Parental involvement in schools is often lower in deprived areas. Working parents may have unsociable hours or be employed on an hourly rate. Transport is likely to be problematic.

■ The parents of children who live in deprived areas are likely to have had extremely negative experiences of school and education themselves because they will have experienced secondary modern schools or the early and confused changeover that marked the beginnings of comprehensivisation.

■ Schools in poorer areas are more likely to be targets of vandalism, graffiti and theft.

■ It is easier for politicians to blame schools and teachers for failing children than to point the finger at voters for their attitudes towards their children's education.

■ Teachers know that some schools are 'rough' and have a reputation for difficult pupils. There are higher rates of violence against teachers. Teachers in such schools are more likely to suffer stress-related illness. Many will therefore avoid working in those schools. Staff turnover may be high and morale low.

■ Schools serving poor areas will have a higher proportion of special-needs pupils, more pupils whose first language is not English and higher rates of exclusions.

■ Sometimes schools in poorer areas will have higher rates of '**value added**' than schools in wealthy areas. Value added is the term for an adjusted score for actual pupil achievement against predictions of achievement based on reading ages and SATs scores.

■ Immigrant parents may feel the need to take children out of school while they visit family in their country of origin. This can affect attainment.

■ Attendance problems and truancy rates tend to be higher in schools serving the poorest communities.

A C T I V I T Y   KS**COMMUNICATION**

IDENTIFICATION AND
INTERPRETATION

When the studies into home and cultural reasons for failure described above were undertaken, the arguments were about the relative under-achievement of working-class boys. Go through the previous section and see how well the points made can be applied to ethnic minority groups, the physically or mentally disadvantaged or to girls.

Compensatory education – policy and debates

Go through these notes in your library or learning resource centre and develop them by looking up the terms and making brief notes on the words or terms that are marked in bold.

KNOWLEDGE AND UNDERSTANDING

In the USA in 1964, President Johnson opened the 'War on Poverty' because people were shocked to discover that 50% of men called for military service were educationally or physically unfit as a result of poor homes. The underlying philosophy of his policy was that poverty could be cured through education in the correct attitudes and values for success. The poorest people are 'culturally deprived' and trapped in a 'cycle of poverty'.

Compensatory education could offer very young poor children some of the educational advantages of the richer child and change their attitudes and values. It was claimed that, through education programmes, children's IQs could be raised by 20 points! The most comprehensive programme was Head Start. It involved health care, social services and education. Parental involvement was a key component, so parents and children were taught together.

By 1970, Project Head Start was being deemed a failure because it was not raising IQ levels and educational standards. This criticism ignored the wider aims of resocialising children and communities. The projects initiated under Head Start have begun to change and there are funding problems. However, Liberal educationalists rate it very highly as a scheme.

In Britain, the ideas of Head Start came later in the decade. A.H. Halsey asked for positive discrimination for schools in poorer (deprived) areas. Geographical areas were designated Educational Priority Areas and teachers were paid more to work in schools in these areas. Local educational authorities will still consider social need as a reasonable argument when deciding where to allocate funding for nursery schools.

The thinking was that good schools in poor areas could compensate for 'bad' socialisation and 'bad' parenting. Basil Bernstein criticised the idea of compensatory education by suggesting that schools reflect inequalities in society. He wanted the emphasis changed from under-fives to the whole education system. Rutter in *15000 hours* suggested that schools vary in quality, some schools being successful because they have a better ethos than others.

The push for improving conditions in poorer areas came from thinkers with a Marxist or socialist philosophy. This type of thought was unfashionable in educational administration after the change in government in 1979 to Conservatism and the New Right. The criticism was that there were few obvious changes as a result of the money that was spent in poor areas. The new philosophy was not to 'throw money at it' but to obtain better value from that money. Market forces should be used in the provision of education services to make the poorer schools come up to the standards of the best schools.

Compensatory education as an issue is probably dead. The debate has nevertheless fuelled much current thinking in education and has had an impact on current educational organisation in the UK.

Questions:

1   Which underlying philosophies did the notion of compensatory education draw on?

KNOWLEDGE AND UNDERSTANDING

2   Sociologically evaluate the notion that schooling can compensate children for deprivation experienced in their early lives.

ANALYSIS AND EVALUATION

3   Sociologically assess the claims that were made that compensatory education could 'cure poverty'.

ANALYSIS AND EVALUATION

Factors shaping the curriculum, and the social construction of knowledge

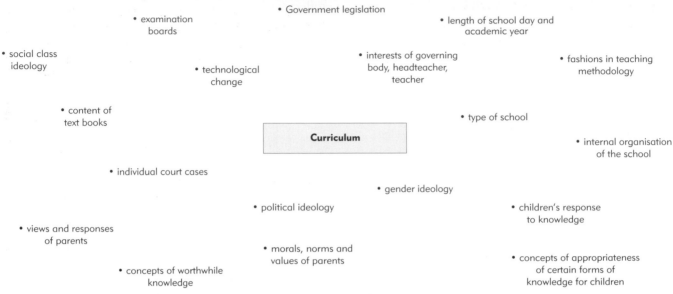

Figure 8.7 Social, political, and practical factors which may shape the curriculum

National Curriculum

Everything that you are knowingly and deliberately taught in school is written down somewhere in a scheme of work. This is the curriculum. It is what your school or college sets out to teach you. The curriculum seems a straightforward idea but, as many sociologists have pointed out, knowledge is a social construction. We value certain forms of knowledge more than others. Consider, would most teachers prefer students to know about sport or politics? Would

schools be able to place significant value on culturally specific knowledge such as certain forms of cooking traditions? The sociological debate has two elements:

- What is the National Curriculum and how should schools implement it?

- What knowledge is embodied as significant in the National Curriculum, and does it have an underlying social and political ideology which is presented to children as fact?

ACTIVITY

KS WORKING WITH OTHERS, COMMUNICATION, PROBLEM SOLVING

IDENTIFICATION AND INTERPRETATION	ANALYSIS AND EVALUATION

What is the most useful knowledge you have? Make a list of the things that you know which have been most important or emotionally and socially significant to you. How much of this important knowledge was deliberately taught to you in school?

If you had complete control over the education system and could choose what children learn, what

subjects would you include in the curriculum? What, if anything, of what you are currently learning would you leave out?

Draw up a plan for a national curriculum with others in your group. Evaluate it by considering whether your students would be good workers, have good social skills, know more, or analyse more. Would your curriculum be appropriate for children of all social backgrounds?

There is a practical outline of the institution of the National Curriculum in the discussion on educational changes (page 366). We will consider the second question in this section.

In practical terms, the institution of the National Curriculum was a good way of ensuring that schools are forced to make equal provision for all children, especially with relation to gender: subjects which *must* be studied cannot be seen as either 'male' or 'female'. However, it is also argued that the Thatcher government embodied a degree of anti-feminism (Segal, 1983) – many politicians spoke of a return to Victorian values and the implicit understanding was that women should return to the home. Could these values have affected the content of the National Curriculum instituted by that government?

Political nature of the curriculum

Liberation theory and radical approaches point to the political nature of schooling. Ivan Illich, in his famous text *Deschooling Society* (1973), suggested that schools kill creativity, insist on conformity, and offer indoctrination into capitalistic society. Children learn to accept authority unthinkingly and this leads them to accept government dictates in the same way. Illich differs from Bowles and Gintis, who are Marxists, by blaming schools for the evils of society. Their view suggests that society carries responsibility for the inadequacy of schools.

> **HINTS AND TIPS**   *You will recall that Bowles and Gintis have already have been introduced in the section on Marxism. Their contribution to this debate was the notion of the hidden curriculum. The contribution of Bordieu and others to this debate is obvious, and you should return to those sections of this area to reinforce your understanding.*

Points of evaluation here could include the following:

- Children actually ignore much of what happens in school. The content of what they learn is not especially relevant and is not a factor that shapes their lives. Paul Willis illustrates this with his analysis of the 'lads'.

- The issues raised by the Great Debate suggest that the curriculum does not serve the needs of

ACTIVITY   KS **COMMUNICATION**

IDENTIFICATION AND INTERPRETATION

The Welsh Joint Education Committee produced some otherwise excellent booklets for Childcare Certificate of Education, which were widely used in the early 1980s. It was suggested that curry and spiced food was inappropriate for pregnant women. How might children from Asian or West Indian families read that 'fact'?

Is any of your teaching group aware of any other examples where dominant cultural ideas are presented as fact in children's texts? Primary school learning books and children's stories may offer examples. Encyclopaedias and general advice books dating from before the Second World War offer very blatant sexism and racism. An edition of Arthur Mee's children's encyclopaedia dated 1938 (Volume 5:3183) describes the population of South Africa before the arrival of the Europeans as 'mostly uncivilised, but capable of bringing to the coast things which civilised people desired, particularly gold dust and ivory'. Later in the same article it is claimed that 'peaceful industries are taught (to the natives), knowledge is steadily spread and superior conceptions of right and of happiness raise … the standard of human life'.

Although difficult to obtain, except perhaps in second-hand bookshops and jumble sales, such books are worth the effort of discovering, and are unintentionally hilarious in the quite appalling social attitudes that they reveal.

employers and the bourgeoisie but rather reflects the cultural values of teachers. This may no longer be true since the advent of the National Curriculum and the point is worthy of some thought.

The 'new' sociology of knowledge

This type of thought is no longer new, as it is associated with the work of Michael F.D. Young in the early 1970s. Young, and others such as Nell Keddie, pointed out that children in lower streams in school are denied access to high-level knowledge. This is not a new observation: it was made about the relationship between secondary modern schools and grammar schools. Young said that those in power define knowledge. They will point out that their knowledge is superior and use this knowledge to maintain powerful and privileged positions in society. Professional people, such as doctors and lawyers, can define and test the acquisition of knowledge. Specialist language is not an aid to understanding but a barrier to those who do not have access to the privilege of knowledge.

ACTIVITY KS COMMUNICATION

ANALYSIS AND EVALUATION

You will find that sociology books printed in the USA are different from British books, not only in style, but also in content. Texts produced in the USA tend to underplay Marxism – and it is not even mentioned in texts produced before 1970s. To prove the point, go to any major bookstore (not a stationery shop) and look at the range of texts. Now consider – who defines what sociology should be in your institution and in this country?

In order to evaluate Young and the **sociology of knowledge**, note that:

- Young is correct in underlining the fact that knowledge is a social construction. 'Facts' from the past included the clear knowledge that the Earth was flat, that the Sun rotated around the Earth and that educating women would cause them to lose the ability to bear children.

- Professional people use knowledge in a powerful way to deny other people access to and control over certain areas of their lives. Think about the language lawyers use, for example.

- Having made these points, this area of thought becomes something of a dead end because it is difficult to begin from a standpoint that denies the validity of knowledge and go on to produce reliable and quantifiable research.

- If there is no such thing as reality or fact, because knowledge is a social construct, then this work carries no more significance or weight than any other comments on education because the same reasoning should apply.

'Malestream' knowledge

Feminist researchers have taken the arguments related to the curriculum a step further by pointing out that not only is there a dominant knowledge that informs the curriculum but it is a male knowledge which they call **malestream** thought. They suggest that malestream thought is so pervasive within schools that often it is unchallenged. Much professional literature has grown up on the point.

It is claimed that male dominance has a considerable impact on girls. Certain subjects are feminised and low status, others are masculine and higher status (Kelly, 1985). The male subjects are the ones that lead to better-paid jobs. Even now, in some courses it is necessary to study art, music or literature produced by men. Within sociology, classical theory is male theory and females and feminism are sometimes presented as an afterthought to discussion. Comprehensive schools were instituted to create class equality, but gender equality was not an issue.

> *HINTS AND TIPS* Look at the discussion of female achievement on page 379 for ideas to develop an observation study. An abbreviated summary of feminist research in education can be found in the theory section. Refer back to your notes.

Teacher–pupil relationships and pupil subcultures

This is an area in which most of the work was completed in the 1970s and 1980s. It is linked with the debate that centres on selection of pupils on the basis of ability. The underpinning theory was interactional in that it was assumed that pupils would respond to teacher labels, reject schools and form an anti-school culture if they were labelled as of 'low ability'. The dominant methodology used was observational.

Hargreaves (1967), Lacey (1970) and Ball (1981) all provide overwhelming evidence that ability grouping of pupils can contribute to the formation of anti-school cultures. Pupils will appear to reject the school that has devalued them and can form subversive and difficult classes to teach. Your considerations and evaluations of these views should refer to the theoretical discussion of interactional perspectives on education because they have the same faults. Consider also the possibility that students are placed into ability sets not on the basis of ability but on the basis of their relationships with their teacher. If this is so, perhaps the anti-school behaviour was evident before the ability setting: this is a view supported by the work of Willis (1977). A more interesting question that has been posed by educationalists and sociologists is 'Why do pupils conform?'

ACTIVITY   KS **WORKING WITH OTHERS**

ANALYSIS AND
EVALUATION

Ask teachers, including older or retired ones who come into your school for supply work, what they feel are the advantages and disadvantages of mixed-ability teaching.

Private and public schools

This is a desperately under-researched area and much of the debate is in the political rather than the sociological arena, although sociologists such as Geoffrey Walford have struggled to open the debate. In Britain, children may attend privately funded institutions, known as **'public' schools** if they are very expensive and 'private' or 'independent' schools if they are at the lower end of the market. The terms are often blended as though the sector was one; this is a profound misunderstanding – Harrods and the corner shop are both retail outlets but one offers a very different service from the other. These schools may exist as part of a charitable foundation, to provide an alternative form of education to that provided by the state or simply to make money. Parents have already paid for education through the state and now pay again in the form of fees, which can be very high indeed. The best known schools are often located in rural areas with large grounds. The lower end of the sector will probably be found in large Edwardian villas near city centres. Even this is a generalisation; some towns, such as Malvern, are famous for the number of private schools.

A number of issues should be raised with regard to independent schools.

- The number of children attending independent schools at any one time varies but usually it is about 4–7% of the school-age population. There is some variation in the density in the independent sector – cities tend to have a large number of such schools, but the regions may not have as many.

- It is extraordinarily difficult to gain information about the sector as a whole because no comprehensive list of such schools exists. Some of these schools can be quite short lived. It is best to approach schools directly for information.

- Independent schooling should never be considered as a uniform sector. There is huge variation between schools. They may cater for the educationally disadvantaged, the profoundly rich, the moderately wealthy but aspirational and those who wish for a religious education that is not provided for by the state.

- There is an automatic assumption that such schools are superior (Griggs, 1985) but the case is not proven. Many have good facilities and others are very poor indeed. Some may attract good teachers, but others offer no ongoing training and even pay below the going rate or on an hourly basis.

- Many egalitarians object vigorously to the existence of such schools. Some European countries have no such sector. The argument is that if parents were forced to send their children to state schools, then their wealth and concerns would be directed at state education. Conservative politicians were regularly accused in the past of undervaluing the state sector because they could be secure in the knowledge that they and their children would never set foot in a state school.

- Independent schools are effectively subsidised through the state (Griggs, 1985) by favourable taxation and charitable status laws. In 1967, over half of all independent and all the public schools were charities. There used to be some subsidy of places at independent schools for the children of the less well off, through the Assisted Places scheme which was abolished in 1997. Some independent schools offer scholarships, but in practice very few genuinely poor children will attend such schools.

- There is a tendency for many schools to be male-oriented. Figures produced by Griffiths (in Walford, 1991) suggested an approximate two-thirds/one-third split. Again this is unreliable evidence because the figures are not easily available.

- The political argument against public schools is that they offer an unfair advantage to the children of the wealthy and the powerful. That an advantage of some form is offered cannot be denied, or why would such schools exist? Tessa Blackstone has pointed to the '**old boys' network**', which means that social advantages exist for the ex-pupils of public schools. C. Wright Mills has already been mentioned in relation to élite self-recruitment where he suggests that those in power are able to promote the interests of the children of the powerful and wealthy. This is supported by the fact that parliament and the professions are full of the products of public schools. However, most informed commentators are agreed that the educational advantages (over and above improved facilities, smaller classes, and social exclusivity of such schools) may well be spurious. Even the smaller classes and improved facilities may be false claims in the case of some of the less wealthy schools.

ACTIVITY KS COMMUNICATION

IDENTIFICATION AND INTERPRETATION	ANALYSIS AND EVALUATION

Write to as many of the private and public schools in your area as you can find addresses for and ask for a brochure for parents from each. Look carefully at these prospectuses and identify what the schools are attempting to sell.

Differential educational attainment

Class

There is a clear and unarguable connection between the social class of your family and your probable educational attainment: children from poorer homes will achieve less well in school than children from wealthier homes. This is not to say that children from poor homes cannot achieve high academic honours – many do – but they will struggle against a system which generally favours the middle class. This pattern of educational attainment will go on to further disadvantage the poorer people in our society. They may well have problems in the job market and are likely to be disempowered if they come into conflict with the criminal justice system, the benefit system, or any other institutions.

ACTIVITY KS COMMUNICATION

IDENTIFICATION AND INTERPRETATION	ANALYSIS AND EVALUATION

To understand the point fully, go through your study notes on this and other areas again, and identify all the probable causes for the known pattern of lower working-class educational attainment, referring to social theory.

You should identify factors in the following areas:

- home and cultural environment
- school environment
- the overall structure of society
- institutions of education.

If your list is not a long and complex one, then you should try again because you have not been thorough in your work.

HINTS AND TIPS Are poor people less intelligent than richer people? The evidence lies in favour of the idea that intelligence tests themselves can be culture-bound and that psychologists are by no means agreed on a definition of intelligence.

Glass, in 1954, was one of the first to raise the issue of social class and did so in the context of meritocratic and egalitarian arguments of the 1950s. He pointed out that children could move up the social scale, but were unlikely to drop back from professional to manual work. Halsey et al., in *Origins and Destinations* (1980), supported this finding. You should refer to the area on social class and mobility for a more detailed discussion. More recent work by Gillborn and Gipps (1996) supports the view that, whatever the nature of other social differentiations (such as ethnicity and gender) that can affect achievement, class underlies them all.

There has been a tendency among politicians, the schools inspectorate and media pundits to move away from the idea that social inequality is the cause of low attainment (this shift in perception has been signposted throughout this area). The currently held view of those with political power is that schools are to blame and are failing our children (Chris Woodhead, currently (1999) Chief Inspector of Schools in England, has firm views on this point). Sociologists, however, are beginning to argue more strongly that class needs to be raised again as a political issue. This is a point made by Mac an Ghaill (1996).

The middle classes have known strategies for arranging advantage for their children, and there is a great deal of anecdotal evidence to support the list below. The impact of these measures is to ensure that middle-class children do not have to be in the same classrooms as working-class children. You might be able to add ideas of your own to this list.

- Applying to selective or specialist music schools for their children.

- Changing address so that they can move to a school with a socially selective catchment area.

- Falsifying addresses to pretend to live in the catchment area of the school of their choice.

- Arranging for coaching for selective school entrance examinations.

- Paying for education or applying for scholarships to private schools.

- Attending church to go to religious denomination schools.

- In Wales, parents will arrange for Welsh-language provision schools.

- Arranging coaching and helping with coursework elements of GCSE and A level.

ACTIVITY   KS **PROBLEM SOLVING**

IDENTIFICATION AND INTERPRETATION

If you were rich and professionally successful, why might you be nervous of allowing your child to mix with children from run-down and inner city estates? Are all your fears likely to be realistic? What could you do to avoid having to send your child to the same school as poor and deprived children?

Gender

The situation with regard to gender is by no means as clear-cut as with social class. Most research was completed when the under-achievement of girls in school was absolutely clear. Now the pattern of gender attainment has changed (you have already been introduced to this idea). An overview of statistical evidence produced by Ofsted and the National League tables suggests the following patterns:

- Girls achieve better grades at GCSE than boys, and are gradually repeating the pattern at A level.

- Class is still a factor in attainment, with middle-class boys achieving better than working-class girls.

- Boys' attainment is improving slowly but girls are overtaking them rapidly at GCSE.

- Among ethnic groups, Afro-Caribbean girls out-perform boys but Bangladeshi and Pakistani girls achieve less well than boys.

- All other factors being equal, girls in single-sex schools tend to achieve far higher results at GCSE than do girls in mixed-sex or boys in single-sex schools.

The debate has become tied in with the political agenda of feminism and the suggestion that, while mixed-sex schools are generally better for boys in raising their attainment and general behaviour patterns significantly, girls will do better in single-sex education. Many schools are very concerned with the failure of boys to make the same rate of progress as girls at GCSE and strategies are being put into place to deal with this. Suggested reasons for the failure of boys to increase their attainment in line with girls include the following:

- Cultures of masculinity have grown up among working-class boys, which cause them to reject education as female. Askew and Ross in 1988 found that boys develop less positive attitudes towards education, and this is manifested in poor behaviour patterns and high truancy rates. This view is supported by the Sackville School, whose own research into attainment levels at GCSE has formed part of its website. Bea Campbell points to the many male role models that suggest that masculinity is action-based. This is in direct contradiction to the needs of schools which value conformity. In contrast, girls see more opportunities opening up for them and expect to have careers *and* families. Girls acknowledge that education offers them the opportunity to make positive choices so that they do not need to be economically dependent on men.

■ There has been a suggestion that schools and the government, in introducing equality polices to correct the failures of the past, have caused the pendulum to swing against boys so that they no longer feel that school caters for their needs. Many primary-age reading books offer a model of a mother and child, and the father is not a visible presence. GCSE now includes coursework which appears to favour the more consistent work patterns of females, who are noted as being more conscientious. Curriculum materials include feminine examples and girls are actively courted by groups such as Girls into Science and Technology, which encourages them into male-dominated professions. Teaching has become a gendered (and female) occupation at primary level. There is a suggestion that boys no longer have positive male role models in early education. The effect of this is compounded by the shortage of male role models in the home due to the growth of single-parent families. Recent government policy is directed at attracting men into primary teaching.

There is a further significant element to the debate, which is that, although girls appear to be achieving rather better than boys at GCSE, beyond the point where the National Curriculum ends boys and girls choose courses and training on stereotypically gendered lines. This is of significance because subject choice can influence career choice, and women tend to be found in the lower-paid jobs and professions. All research previous to National Curriculum and GCSE analysis tends to show that, whereas boys achieve well in sciences and mathematics, girls tend to gravitate towards language-based subjects. In 1995–6, the Welsh Funding Coucil for Higher and Further Education found that men preferred to study engineering and science or maths at higher education and that women selected courses in business,

Observing a classroom for equality of gender treatment

If you study education as one of your key areas, you are advised to spend time observing classes in primary schools. Observation is more effective if you structure your ideas of what exactly you will look for in advance, as no teacher deliberately sets out to label or stereotype. All schools have an equal opportunities policy and most teachers observe it very carefully.

There are things to look out for when observing whether gender stereotyping occurs in schools. You will be looking for unintentional and institutional gender stereotyping, which will be difficult to spot and has been overlooked by the staff of the school themselves. You could adapt this mode of thought to address issues of ethnicity or social class. Look for hints of all of the following but concentrate on the signs that you find significant.

1 How are the pupils arranged in the classroom? Is gender significant?
2 Are girls and boys asked the same number of questions? Are they given an equal amount of attention? Are they told off equally? Are they praised equally?
3 Are there differences in terms of punishments meted out? Is the tone of voice in a reprimand the same for a girl and a boy?
4 Do boys and girls attempt to get teacher attention in the same way? What techniques do the children use? Which techniques appear to be successful?
5 Are boys and girls encouraged to play sports traditionally associated with the other gender or to have mixed teams?
6 Is there equal access to books and computers? Are girls and boys using this equipment equally?
7 Are girls and boys given different tasks in the classroom or identified by gender in other ways, such as on registers?
8 What is the gender arrangement of the staff? Look at the key posts. Do members of one gender occupy them more than the other? Which gender do you tend to see in positions of authority?

management and health. A QPID report (published at http://www.dfee.gov.uk/skillnet/q_71.htm) discovered that 65% of the women who took up modern apprenticeships were concentrated in business and administration, hairdressing, retailing and care. Men undertook apprenticeships in engineering, the motor industry and construction. The report went on to point out that employers often expressed a preference for candidates of one gender. One of the most significant findings was that by Year 11, students had very 'entrenched gender attitudes'.

Issues which could be raised in evaluations of the above types of theorising include the following points. While patterns of attainment may be changing at GCSE and perhaps at A level, this severely over-estimates the amount of change that is taking place in broader society where women are still less well paid and often combine work with family duties. Feminists argue that while girls are attaining higher grades, boys are still the focus of attention among educationalists. Postmodernists have also pointed out that, by looking at gender patterns alone, the debate is being over-simplified, because a number of factors including class and ethnicity may also affect results. This can be seen from the summary of Ofsted findings offered previously.

> **HINTS AND TIPS**   *This would be a particularly interesting and simple area to use as the basis for coursework. Sociology seems to be a gendered subject, in that approximately 80% of students are female. Can you suggest reasons why this is so?*

Ethnicity

Culture and ethnicity is a very complex area to study and most research in this area is blunted by the problems that are inherent in defining a person's ethnicity. Britain has been a multi-cultural society for a long time. This means that racial and ethnic types have become blurred – and in dockland areas in particular, they are not clear-cut. While sociologists refer to ethnicity in cultural terms, the general public may still react to visual cues such as skin colour so

that all subcontinental Asians may be subject to abuse as 'Paki'. This single factor will obscure differences of language, culture, religious observance, educational attainment, social class, political belief and moral values. However, there are still issues to be discussed in terms of ethnicity and educational attainment.

> **HINTS AND TIPS**   *Questions that hinge on the difficulties of defining a person's ethnic group (or in defining ethnicity at all) crop up in all areas of the paper. You would be well advised to address this issue carefully and be certain that you have understood it.*

General patterns relating to ethnicity and attainment suggest that children from ethnic minorities tend to experience a negative image in school because the curriculum tends to be geared towards the needs of Europeans (Croard, 1971). Very little 'black' history is on offer, for instance. However, all schools have an equal opportunities policy. If racism occurs within an institution it is likely to be covert and institutional rather than overt. This is a marked change over 30 years, from a situation in which very clear examples of racist language and opinions could be discovered in many school texts.

The evidence is by no means clear-cut despite an abundance of statistical data. Evidence from the Swann Report of 1985 suggests that children from ethnic minority backgrounds do less well in school than White children. West Indians tend to be under-represented in higher education and Tomlinson (1980) points out that they are over-represented in special-needs education. Certain Asian groups, such as the Bangladeshi community, seem to do poorly in school whereas others, such as Pakistanis, Chinese and Hindus, tend to be over-represented in university.

> **HINTS AND TIPS**   *Should you choose to study this area in coursework, it would be advisable for you to consider your own motives with some care. A white person may be seen as patronising by the study group, but one who is from a visible ethnic minority might be seen as having an axe to grind and is therefore threatening to people. Comparisons in attitudes towards education between two different ethnic groups will yield interesting results in coursework.*

ACTIVITY

KNOWLEDGE AND UNDERSTANDING	IDENTIFICATION AND INTERPRETATION	ANALYSIS AND EVALUATION

(Great Britain)

Percentages

	Degree or equivalent	Higher education qualification[3]	GCE A level or equivalent	GCSE grades A to C or equivalent	Other qualification	No qualification	All
Males							
Indian/Pakistani/Bangladeshi	18	5	16	14	25	22	100
Black	14	6	22	18	24	16	100
White	14	8	32	18	14	15	100
Other groups[4]	20	5	17	15	27	15	100
Females							
Indian/Pakistani/Bangladeshi	9	5	11	18	25	33	100
Black	9	12	14	27	22	16	100
White	11	9	16	29	15	20	100
Other groups[4]	12	8	15	17	33	15	100

[1]Men aged 16 to 64, women aged 16 to 59
[2]Combined quarters: Spring 1997 to Winter 1997–98
[3]Below degree level
[4]Includes those who did not state their ethnic group

Source: Department for Education and Employment from the *Labour Force Survey*

Figure 8.8   Highest qualification held[1], by gender and ethnic group[2], 1997–1998

Answer the following questions.

1   Which ethnic group has the highest percentage of people with a degree or equivalent qualification?
2   What sociological problem in identifying ethnicity does this pose for researchers?
3   Among groups identified as black, are males or females more likely to hold a higher education qualification?
4   What percentage of white males has a GCE A level or equivalent?
5   Are males or females more likely to obtain a degree or equivalent qualification?

6   Among the Indian/Pakistani/Bangladeshi community, are males or females more likely to remain unqualified?
7   Among the Indian/Pakistani/Bangladeshi community, are males or females more likely to have GCSE passes at C and above?
8   Which ethnic community has the highest percentage of unqualified people?
9   How reliable do you consider this data to be?
10 How useful is this information to a sociologist?

Profession and institutions

HINTS AND TIPS   *Remember that much of the work that you did on the development of the education system also fits into this particular area of discussion. You are advised therefore to return to that area for revision purposes and to refer to it in examination questions.*

What makes a good teacher?

Most of us have met people we feel to be 'good' teachers. However, few of us can agree on which teachers fit the description. Politicians of the New Right constantly emphasise traditional teaching methodologies and Chris Woodhead, Chief Inspector of Schools in England, is famed for his promotion of 'whole class' teaching. He claims that the popular teaching styles of group work and child-centred learning lead to poor learning skills. A huge amount of research is currently taking place, which is devoted to discovering what methods of teaching work. There is a conflict between those who emphasise the personal characteristics of the teacher and those of the New Right who emphasise teaching methodologies and outcomes.

SOCIOLOGY IN PRACTICE

Bad teachers are main cause of pupil failure

The most comprehensive survey of performance in schools has revealed that pupils fail because of their teachers, not because of their social background. In the worst cases, 14 year-olds from similar neighbourhoods who attend different schools show gulfs in academic achievement equivalent to six years of study.

Until now many education experts had believed that schools and teachers were less important to a child's performance than factors such as wealth and home life.

John Marks, author of the report for the Social Market Foundation, a leading policy think tank, said: "There are enormous differences between schools. These start when pupils are young and become so large as they grow older that we must now question the quality of teaching in a third of the schools in the country."

Marks's findings, published this week, are based on the results of tests and exams taken by 2.4m primary and secondary pupils in 23,000 schools across England last year.

Chris Woodhead, the chief inspector of schools, said: 'The report confirms the messages that have emerged from inspections that poor performance in some schools cannot be explained away in terms of social circumstances. What matters is the quality of teaching and leadership."

Marks, a former member of the School Curriculum & Assessment Authority and of other government watchdog bodies, found that differences in performance emerged in the first years of schooling, with pupils at the worst primaries trailing those at the best by nearly 2.5 years by the age of seven – even when they came from similar social backgrounds. In the worst schools, up to 90% of seven-year-olds were unable to do basic sums such as multiplying 2 × 5, something an average child should be able to do by the age of six.

Previously, experts believed that such differences narrowed as children grew older but Marks's study shows the reverse is true, so that at the age of 11 there is a difference of nearly four years among schools whose pupils come from similar backgrounds.

The gap increases further when such youngsters move to secondary school. By the age of 14 the difference between schools can reach five years in mathematics and more than six years in English. The variations are reflected in GCSE exam results which show that 16-year-olds from a good school can achieve average exam results five times better than close neighbours who went to a bad one. The report warns: "The spread of standards between schools may even be increasing because, while good schools are improving, poorer schools are not."

In Barnsley, where GCSE results make it one of England's worst 10 education authorities, the variation between 14-year-olds at schools with similar types of pupils was 3.5 years in English and mathematics. In some schools more than 30% of pupils obtained no GCSE passes at all.

In Milton Keynes the picture was similar, with standards in English and mathematics among 11-year-olds varying by up to five years between schools with the same type of catchments.

"In English schools, standards are perilously low and disastrously variable," Marks concludes.

Nigel de Gruchy, general secretary of the National Association of Schoolmasters and Union of Women Teachers, blamed the variation in standards on the shortage of high-calibre teachers. "We need dedicated high flyers prepared to go into the difficult schools," he said.

Source: Judith O'Reilly *Sunday Times* 6 September 1998

1 Who is the author of the report discussed in the article? **(1)**

KNOWLEDGE AND UNDERSTANDING

2 Who commissioned the report discussed in the article? **(1)**

KNOWLEDGE AND UNDERSTANDING

3 Why is it relevant for a sociologist to know who has paid for data to be collected? **(2)**

KNOWLEDGE AND UNDERSTANDING

4 What tests and examinations are probably referred to in the third paragraph of the article?

KNOWLEDGE AND UNDERSTANDING | IDENTIFICATION AND INTERPRETATION

5 What position of authority did Chris Woodhead hold when this report was written? **(1)**

KNOWLEDGE AND UNDERSTANDING

6 With what social and political perspectives is Chris Woodhead generally associated? **(4)**

KNOWLEDGE AND UNDERSTANDING

7 What problems with the sociological reliability of the data on which the report is based might a sociologist be able to point out? **(6)**

IDENTIFICATION AND INTERPRETATION

8 Suggest a variety of possible alternative explanations to the 'bad teacher thesis' for the findings reported in the article. **(6)**

IDENTIFICATION AND INTERPRETATION

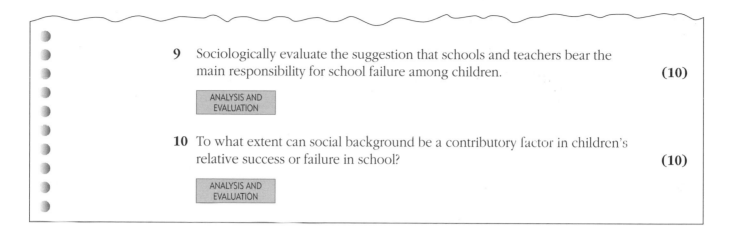

9   Sociologically evaluate the suggestion that schools and teachers bear the main responsibility for school failure among children.   **(10)**

ANALYSIS AND EVALUATION

10 To what extent can social background be a contributory factor in children's relative success or failure in school?   **(10)**

ANALYSIS AND EVALUATION

This is an extremely significant political debate because the government intended (1999) to introduce different and higher pay scales for teachers considered to be better than the average. In a sequence of proposals, which have not been welcomed by teaching unions, it has been suggested that certain individuals can apply for 'super-teacher' status and accelerated promotion prospects in return for an increased workload and shorter holiday time.

Interestingly, the government Green Paper, which embodied proposals for changes in the structure of the teaching profession, evaded the issue of what is a good teacher. Many teachers fear there will be a link to pupil examination performance. Given the clear relationship between social class, gender and examination results, those who teach in single-sex girls' secondary schools serving middle-class areas will probably also prove to be the 'best' teachers.

TASK

Hypothesis – A good teacher is one who makes children pass examinations.

Context – This hypothesis is closed. The question that you are to test is one that lends itself to quantitative analysis of people's responses to a key question about the purpose of teaching. You should revise quantitative methods.

You will achieve the most interesting results if you compare and contrast a variety of sample groups. Do people of different ethnicities have the same view of the hypothesis? Will your respondents' class, age, occupation, or experience of education affect the responses that you obtain? Many people will agree with the hypothesis, so you might need to suggest other characteristics of a good teacher and see if people feel that elements other than the ability to pass examinations form part of the equation. It might be interesting to consider whether teachers and pupils share perceptions of what makes a good teacher.

Method – Design a simple questionnaire with closed questions. Ask people what characteristics they rate as important in a teacher. You might ask respondents to rank those characteristics or to offer a mark out of five depending on degree of agreement. You should compare two different social groups to get the fullest picture.

Evaluation – Do you trust your results to be reliable? What factors can influence people's responses? Would people have answered differently if your questionnaire design had been different? If you wish to work with other people, then maybe you could try a variety of questionnaire designs on the same sample groups and compare the results.

Use a spreadsheet programme such as Excel to analyse your results and then make a variety of graphs.

Teaching as a personal style	Teaching as a matter of results
A good teacher makes children feel good about themselves, recognising that they are individuals and need individual attention. Roger Smith, 1994	*... demonstration by the teacher of proven and sustained high quality teaching resulting in positive outcomes for pupils.* Welsh Office, 1999

PROFILE

Ted Wragg

Ted Wragg is a very important figure in the study of education, and in particular in research into classroom teaching and learning processes. He was brought up in Sheffield and gained his first degree in German from Durham University in 1959.

Wragg gained his Master's degree from Leicester University in 1967 and his doctorate from Exeter University in 1972. Both his theses involved the study of student teachers and teacher–pupil interaction in the classroom.

He has written widely, both popular and academic work, and is the author of over 40 books on education. His realistic approach is obvious in regular articles in the **Times Educational Supplement**. Many teachers regard him as a voice of sanity and good humour. He currently works at Exeter University – you can visit its website to learn more about its department of education.

His work has been particularly concerned with what makes an effective school and an effective teacher. He has argued against rigidly formulaic answers to current educational problems and this has brought him into conflict with the ideas of the New Right (discussed throughout this area).

The methodology with which Wragg is most commonly associated is live observation of classroom events and a mixture of qualitative and quantitative methodology. Currently he is working on a research project studying teaching competence, which includes the largest study of teachers alleged to be incompetent ever undertaken in Britain.

Lifelong learning

It is clear that modern industrial society requires a well qualified workforce. There are fewer unskilled jobs than in the past because of the significance of machines, and this work is mostly feminised production-line work, supermarket work or cleaning.

The big new philosophical movement, which is underlying much work in schools, is the idea of skills-based learning. Students are expected to acquire transferable skills and to prove levels of expertise. This idea has underpinned the GNVQ movement and is a now a factor in A level training. The motivating belief behind these changes is the idea of learning as a skill which people can be trained to acquire. Having acquired key skills people can apply their understanding to any area of their lives. This ensures a flexible workforce who can adapt to social, industrial and commercial changes.

The key skill areas are:

- communication
- numeracy
- information technology

There are personal skill areas too:

- working with people
- problem solving
- learning skills

HINTS AND TIPS *Develop your evaluation skills by thinking about the following questions. Why do you think that the government chose these skills and not others to develop? What skills do people in your group feel that they need to succeed in life? How can you test people's abilities in these skills? You may need to revise and consider both ideology and vocationalism to address these issues.*

ACTIVITY

KNOWLEDGE AND
UNDERSTANDING

Use this area to write a short explanation of each of
the following:
1   The 1944 Education Act
2   ERA 1986 and 1988
3   Compensatory Education and Head Start schemes
4   Elaborated and restricted language codes
5   Cultural deprivation
6   Material poverty
7   'Super-teacher' status
8   Key skills and transferable skills
9   Old boys' network
10 National Curriculum

Area summary

The education system that we experience is a fundamental factor in our development as individuals. It can affect our earnings, morality, self-belief and understanding. A wide range of philosophies and value systems has impacted on the development of our educational structures and therefore on the lives of our children. Some of these philosophies are not strictly sociological in origin, but they have affected sociology as a discipline. It is an accusation made by sociologists such as Ted Wragg that educational change is often based on ideologies and not on research evidence, so that sociological research has a tendency to follow where political and moral ideologies have led.

There are clear and basic inequalities in the outcome of education which are precisely documented in the case of gender and class. Working-class children continue to do less well in the system despite all the changes that have been made to improve their position. Gender attainment patterns are changing rapidly in favour of girls, from the youngest age groups upwards, and this reflects quite dramatic changes in the nature of the relationship between the sexes in broader society. Research on ethnicity is always hampered by the difficulties of clearly allocating or defining culture, so the evidence is less clear-cut. It still points to the fact that our education system is geared to the needs of the white majority, despite a genuine desire for multi-culturalism and anti-racism on the part of many teachers.

The finger of accusation has been pointed at both schools and at pupil cultures in order to explain differential achievement. Early home and cultural theories stress poverty and deprivation in the home. School theories begin with accusing schools of reinforcing structural inequalities in society. Interactionalists suggested that teachers express prejudice and label children. Marxists and feminists point to institutional inequality and the hidden curriculum. However, the New Right, which is the dominant political force even in the present Labour government, now suggest that schools bear the full responsibility because they are simply not competent.

Definitions

Compensatory education	Belief in and practice of attempting to make up for bad parenting through the education system
Culture of poverty	The idea that poverty encourages people to behave in a way that will actually keep them poor and disadvantaged. They develop a culture which adapts to poverty and they find it difficult to fight this culture
Comprehensive school	A school that accepts students in the same proportions as they appear in the community
Cultural capital	The knowledge of morals, values and modes of behaviour which upper and middle-class people can pass on to their children

Curriculum	All that is taught in schools
Egalitarianism	Belief that children should have equal access to education and should have equal chances of success and failure while experiencing education
Élite self-recruitment	The children of the élite groups are able to use social contact and educational knowledge to join the élite themselves
Grammar school	A school that teaches a formal academic curriculum. This may or may not be geared to the needs of the most able pupils, though under the terms of the 1944 Education Act some form of academic selection was required for entry to state-funded grammar schools (but not to private grammar schools)
Grant maintained schools	These receive money directly from central government and not via the LEA
Habitus	A preferred mode of thinking, acting and perceiving
Hidden curriculum	Children are taught things by a school that the school neither intends nor expects. Generally these reflect social expectations and understandings
Independent school	Run as a commercial enterprise or as an alternative to the state system
Libertarianism	Belief that education can liberate a child from the false consciousness imposed by capitalism by freeing the child to experience alternative points of view
Liberation theory	Education should free the mind and open up possibilities for alternative belief and thought
Lifelong learning	Schools should train children in learning skills so that they will continue to learn and be receptive to further training throughout their adult lives
Linguistic deprivation	Poor children are deprived of the language skills that are needed for success in school
Local education authority	Usually referred to as the LEA, this is the local council which administers and funds schools centrally providing services and allocating monies to schools
Malestream	Belief that the knowledge which is valued in society is masculine knowledge
Meritocracy	Belief that education should be geared to the needs of the best students to enable them to progress through society
Public school	An educational foundation for the children of the very wealthy, which charges high fees
Resistance	Children can reject the message they are given at school
Secondary modern schools	These were intended for the least able children to train them for work and basic skills
Self-fulfilling prophecy	The idea that teachers mould children through their expectations of their performance
Socialisation	The process of learning how to behave in a way that is appropriate to society

Sociology of knowledge   The study of the social value which is attached to certain types of knowledge

State maintained schools   These receive money directly from central government and not via the LEA

Technical grammar schools   Few of these were built after 1944 when they were instituted. They were vocational schools intended to train children for skilled manual work.

Value added   This refers to data collected by schools. It assesses children's performance at SATS and then predicts grades at examination for those children. Schools which achieve better grades than predicted are said to have high value added scores

Vocationalism   A belief that education should serve the needs of the workforce, the economy and employers

Data response questions

Item A

In Playgroup

Boys make straight for the construction toys or the bikes while the girls are playing in the home corner, doing a drawing or talking to an adult. Children have already developed clear ideas of what boys do and girls do.

Donald MacLeod (17 June 1997:3) **The Guardian**
Education supplement.

Item B

Inspectors have discovered that boys are finding it impossible to keep up with girls in school exams.

They looked at 250 school inspection reports and found that many more girls are achieving top grade GCSEs.

About 43% of girls gained five or more top grade GCSEs across Britain compared to just 34% of boys.

There has always been a difference between the results, often put down to girls' greater maturity and willingness to work.

Margaret Reilly **Western Mail**

Item C

The heroes of today's male teen culture, what defines you as cool, are more likely to be gangsta rappers than Take That. And of course drugs are now widely available in most secondary schools. In other words the nineties construction of masculinity, one which is endorsed everywhere we look – including by the middle classes who have shaped their own version of it in the form of lad culture – has hardened into a limited and limiting selection of macho attitudes.

Linda Grant (11 March 1996) **The Guardian** Women's section.

a Explain briefly the relationship between GCSE results and gender. (2)

> KNOWLEDGE AND
> UNDERSTANDING

b Outline one sociological explanation of the differential between boys' and girls' results at GCSE. (5)

| KNOWLEDGE AND UNDERSTANDING | ANALYSIS AND EVALUATION |

GUIDANCE   The stimulus passages offer suggestions for you to develop. There is a home and cultural explanation in Item A, a cultural explanation in Item B and a feminist cultural explanation in Item C. Note that none of the items suggest that schools carry responsibility, but this is also a possibility for you to discuss.

c   Evaluate the contribution of feminism to an understanding of differences in gender performance in schools. **(10)**

> **GUIDANCE**   *The question asks for a judgement of the work of feminists rather than for explanations*
>
> | KNOWLEDGE AND UNDERSTANDING | IDENTIFICATION AND INTERPRETATION | ANALYSIS AND EVALUATION |
> | --- | --- | --- |
>
> *of why there is different gender performance. Your conclusions should suggest something to the effect that feminism has helped us a great deal, a little or not at all.*
>
> *You must be careful to concentrate on feminism as a research process rather than its equally significant role as a social and political movement. It is easy to confuse the two and to lose marks considering the impact of feminist thought rather than the sociological implications of its conclusions. Explanations of feminism should be short. Consider what this perspective has offered to our understandings of socialisation and the interaction between students and teachers. This means that you will have to acknowledge the debt that feminism owes to other analytical traditions. Do not forget that early feminism tended to suggest that females were the victims of an educational process. This case is more difficult to argue now at GCSE level, although there is a clear case to answer at higher levels. More recent feminism has concerned itself with notions of gender and masculinity.*

Structured question

1   What is the National Curriculum? **(1)**

2   Suggest two reasons why the introduction of the National Curriculum may be considered to contribute towards social equality in Britain. **(4)**

3   What impact have the educational reforms of the Conservative government (1979–1997) had on schools and the education system of Britain? **(10)**

4   To what extent can it be argued that the British education system reflects inequalities in society? **(10)**

Essay titles

1   Evaluate the usefulness of home and cultural explanations to account for school failure. **(25)**

2   Does sociological research support the notion that 'market forces' should determine the provision of education? **(25)**

3   Evaluate the suggestion that knowledge is a social construction. Make reference to the National Curriculum in your discussion. (25)

KNOWLEDGE AND UNDERSTANDING	IDENTIFICATION AND INTERPRETATION	ANALYSIS AND EVALUATION

GUIDANCE   *This is a really interesting question because it opens the door to theoretical discussion, but you are also required to consider recent educational change and practice. It is probably not as difficult as it looks at first. You need to consider the question of whether knowledge is socially constructed. The answer cannot be 'no'. You have a choice between 'yes' and 'maybe' because the evidence so clearly supports the phenomenologists in this particular debate. The reasons for that make up the body of the essay.*

You must consider the question of whether there is such a thing as 'pure' knowledge. You could refer back to the questions of whether sociology is a science for some pointers in this direction. Max Weber and many functionalists certainly seemed to think that knowledge could be value-free, and even felt that sociology could be value-free. However, this is a distinctly difficult position because any study of culture will show that certain forms of knowledge are considered more valuable than others. You will need to refer to questions of the sociology of knowledge and the work of Michael Young, which are considered in this area.

The issue of the National Curriculum is an interesting one because it has been such a controversial and sometimes unpopular policy in schools. You will need to provide some background to that debate and to locate the policy in the moral and political philosophy which led to its creation. Having done that you can now fully address the question of whether knowledge is socially created and the following questions give you an overview of the plan to that essay.

■   *Is knowledge value-free?*

■   *Why do we have a National Curriculum?*

■   *What political values are placed on knowledge? To what extent is knowledge ideological in content? Who dictates the content of the National Curriculum?*

■   *What moral values are placed on knowledge? Whose knowledge is of most value? What knowledge do we reject? Is there a moral content to the National Curriculum?*

■   *What social and economic values are placed on knowledge? What knowledge do we insist is important enough to pass on to our children via the medium of schools? Who benefits from the training that children receive?*

Other ideas that you could consider include notions of the hidden curriculum, malestream knowledge, the role of education in creating ideologies, the role of education in socialisation and social control.

Further reading and references

You should look for education supplements of the major broadsheet newspapers such as the *Independent* and the *Guardian*. Ask teachers to give you copies. Do not be put off if they are difficult to start with, you will soon get into the swing of things.

Read the *Times Educational Supplement* (*TES*). Again, teachers will be a good source of this newspaper. The letters and opinion pages will tell you a great deal about recent research and government policy. The *TES* has a Website, which you can access. Teachers' unions also produce papers and journals and you are advised to get copies from staff in your school.

Current data on education and training is available each year in *Social Trends*, published by HMSO. Copies of this publication are kept in major libraries and some schools or colleges may have copies on CD-ROM.

The Open University offers many reliable texts on educational research. See Potts et al. (1995) *Learning, Teaching and Managing in Schools* or Moon and Mayes (1994) *Teaching and Learning in the Secondary School* (Open University, Routledge and Kegan Paul) for an overview of recent concerns and educational issues.

To learn more about the independent sector and public policy, look at Salter and Tapper (1985) *Power and Policy in Education: The case of independent schooling*, published by Falmer Press.

Internet sites

Collect data about individual schools in England by accessing the official government Website www.open.gov. uk. Once you reach the site, search under 'education', 'DFEE' or 'Ofsted'. You can also go directly to http://www.dfee.gov.uk where there is a variety of succinct reports and articles that could support coursework and give it some recent empirical findings to quote. The *TES* has a Website, http://www.tes.co.uk that you can access. Although this is designed for education professionals, it is an absolute gold-mine of research findings and recent political debate. The appropriate sites in Wales and Scotland are not as reliable currently, but given the speed of technological change, the situation may improve.

Many schools have Websites and you should try and access as many of these as possible.

Bibliography

Althusser, L. (1965) *For Marx*. Harmondsworth, Penguin.

Askew, M. and Ross, S. (1988) *Boys Don't Cry: Boys and Sexism in Education*. Milton Keynes, OUP.

Ball, S. (1981) *Beachside Comprehensive: A Case-study in Secondary Education*. Cambridge, Cambridge University Press.

Bangaw, (CSV Media) *Out of School Advice Leaflet*. (1994) Cardiff, HTV Wales, Culverhouse Cross.

Benn, C. and Simon, B. (1970) *Halfway There*. London, McGraw Hill.

Bernstein, B. (1971) Class, Codes & Control. Vol. 1. London, RKP.

Blackledge, D. and Hunt, B. (1989) *Sociological Interpretations of Education*. London, Routledge.

Blackstone, T. in Lodge, P. and Blackstone, T. (1982) *Educational Policy and Educational Inequality*. Oxford, Robertson.

Bourdieu, P. (1984) *Distinctions: A Social Critique of the Judgement of Taste*. London, Routledge.

Bowles, S. and Gintis, H. (1976) *Schooling in Capitalist America*. London, Routledge and Kegan Paul.

Browne, K. (1992) *An Introduction to Sociology*. Cambridge, Polity.

Burgess, R. (1985) *Education, Schools and Schooling*. London, Macmillan.

Byrne, D. S., Williams, B. Fletcher, B. (1975) *The Poverty of Education*. London, Robertson.

Cicourel, A. and Kitsuse, J. (1963) *The Educational Decision Makers*. Indianapolis, Bobbs-Merill.

Coard, B. (1971) *How the West Indian Child is Made Educationally Subnormal in the British School System*. London, New Beacon.

Cole, M. ed. (1989) *The Social Contexts of Schooling*. London, Falmer.

Douglas, J. W. B. (1964) *The Home and the School*. London, Macgibbon and Kee.

Fullan, Michael G. (1991) *The new meaning of Educational Change* London and New York, Cassell

Freidan, B. (1965) *The Feminine Mystique*. Harmondsworth, Penguin.

Giddens, Anthony (1997) *Sociology 3rd Edition* Cambridge: Polity.

Gillborn and Gipps (1996) *Recent Research on the Achievements of Ethnic Minority Pupils*. London, HMSO.

Glass, D. ed. (1954) *Social Mobility in Britain*. London, Routledge and Kegan Paul.

Gouldner, A. (1971) *The Coming Crisis of Western Sociology*. London, Heinemann.

Gouldner, A. (1975) *For Sociology*. Harmondsworth, Penguin.

Griggs, C. (1985) *Private Education in Britain*. London, The Falmer Press.

Hall, S. and Jacques, P. eds. (1983) *The Politics of Thatcherism*. London, Lawrence and Wishart.

Halsey, A., Heath, A. and Ridge, J. (1980) *Origins and Destinations*. Oxford, Clarendon Press.

Hargreaves, D. (1967) *Social Relations in a Secondary School*. London, RKP. *Social Trends 27 and 29* (1999). London, HMSO.

Illich, I. (1973) *Deschooling Society*. Harmondsworth, Penguin.

Keddie, N. ed. (1973) *Tinker, Tailor*. Harmondsworth, Penguin.

Kelly, A. (1985) *The Construction of Masculine Science. British Journal of Sociology of Education*, Vol. 6, 133–54.

Kohn, M. (1969) *Class and Conformity*. Homewood, Ill., Darsey Press.

Labor, W. (1972) *Language in the Inner City Philadelphia*. Penn., University of Pennsylvania Free Press.

Lacey, C. (1970) *Hightown Grammar*. Manchester, Manchester University Press.

Lewis, O. (1966) *LaVida* New York, Random House.

Lewis, O. (1961) *The Children of Sanchez*. New York, Random House.

Mac an Ghaill, M. (1996) *Sociology of Education, State Schooling and Social Class: Beyond Critiques of the New Right Hegemony* in British Journal of Sociology of Education, Vol. 17, No. 2, June.

Mac an Ghaill, M. (1988) *Young, Gifted and Black*. Milton Keynes, Open University Press.

Marsh, I. (1996) *Making Sense of Society*. London, Longman.

Measor, I. and Sikes (1992) *Introduction to Education: Gender and Schools*. London and New York, Cassell.

Measor, I. and Woods, P. (1984) *Changing Schools: Pupil Perspectives on Transfer to a Comprehensive*. Buckingham, Open University Press.

Meikle, J. *Asian Pupils Doing Better than English Classmates*, in The Guardian, 16 February 1991.

Ministry of Education (1963) *Half Our Future: A Report of the Central Advisory Council for Education* (England). London, HMSO.

Moon, B. and Mayes, A. (1994) *Teaching and Learning in the Secondary School*. London, Routledge in association with OUP.

National Union of Teachers, *The Teacher*, (journal of NUT).

Newsom Report (1963) *Half our Future*. Central Advisory Council for Education, London, HMSO.

Newson, J. and E. (1965) *Patterns of Infant Care in an Urban Community*. Harmondsworth, Penguin.

Parsons, T. (1973) *The American University*. Cambridge, Mass., Harvard University Press.

Potts, P., Armstrong, A., Maskerson, M. eds. (1995) *Equality and Diversity in Education 1: Learning, Teaching and Managing in Schools*. London, Routledge.

QPID (1999) *Modern Apprenticeships and Gender Stereotyping* <http://www.dfee.gov.uk/skillnet/q_71.htm>

Rosen, H. (1974) *Language and Class*. Falling Wall Press.

Rosenthal, E. and Jacobsen, L. (1968) *Pygmalion in the Classroom*. London, Holt Rinehart and Winston.

Rutter, M., Maughan, B., Mortimore, P. and Ouston, J. (1979) *Fifteen Thousand Hours*. London, Open Books.

Salter, B. and Tapper, T. (1985) *Power and Policy in Education: The Case of Independent Schooling*. Lewes, Falmer.

Segal, I. (1983) *The Heat in the Kitchen* (in Hall, S. and Jacques, P. eds. *The Politics of Thatcherism*). London, Lawrence and Wishart.

Spender, D. (1983) *Invisible Women: The Schooling Scandal*. London, Women's Press.

Stanworth, M. (1983) *Gender and Schooling*. London, Hutchinson.

Swann Report (1985) *Education for All: Report of a Committee into the Education of Children from Ethnic Minorities*. London, HMSO.

Tomlinson, S. (1983) *Ethnic Minorities in British Schools*. London, Heinemann.

Tomlinson, S. (1980) *Educational Subnormality: A Study in Decision Making*. London, Routledge.

Walford, G. ed. (1984) *British Public Schools: Policy and Practice*. London, Falmer.

Walford, G. ed. (1992) *Private Schooling: Tradition, Change and Diversity*. London, Paul Chapman Publishing.

Warnock Report (1978) *Special Educational Needs: Report of a Committee of Enquiry*. London, HMSO.

Wedge, P. and Prosser, H. (1973) *Born to Fail*. London, Arrow Books.

Westergaard, J. and Resler, H. (1976) *Class in a Capitalist Society*. Harmondsworth, Penguin.

Wright Mills, C. (1954) *Mass Society and Liberal Education*. Chicago, *Center for the Study of Liberal Education for Adults*.

Wright Mills, C. (1959) *The Power Elite*. New York, OUP.

Young, M. F. D. ed. (1971) *Knowledge and Control: New Directions for the Sociology of Education*. London, Collier MacMillan.

Religion

This area covers:

- The history and nature of the study of religious faith
- Contrasting theories of the nature of religious expression
- A consideration of the links between religious ideology, social control and social change
- The role of religious belief in modern society
- The various forms of religious institutions within our society.

By the end of this area you should be able to:

- show some understanding of the importance of religious and magical belief in our daily lives, even to the extent that we will define ourselves as individuals through the expression of our religious beliefs

- recognise the relationships between religious belief and the ideologies of the nature of society

- recognise the complexities of the relationship between religion as a force for conservatism and religion as a force for social change

- recognise the multi-cultural and multi-faith nature of our society

- understand the variety of institutions and forms that religious practice can take

- understand the secularisation debate.

Key terms

secularisation	church
denomination	magic
sect	superstition
religion	ideology
cult	new religious movements

Area 9   Contents

Introduction

The study of religious belief is at the heart of the development of sociology as an academic discipline. The early sociologists grew up in an age of strong religious conviction where deep belief and daily religious practice was part of the structure of life, but where people were also finding the moral courage to question the conventional truths of the time. It is probably not a coincidence that the founders of two major structural perspectives – Marx and Durkheim – came from traditional religious Jewish backgrounds, even if they themselves did not practise. Sociology grew from the first questioning of the 'fact' of religious faith. It was the ability of people to question their religious tradition that handed them the clue that if society was not the creation of God, it was possibly therefore the creation of humans and a suitable area of study. Sociology does not have a great deal to say on the existence or non-existence of God/s: this is a matter of individual conscience and of little relevance to this area of study. However, belief in God can give certain people a sense of higher moral authority, which they can then impose on others, and this *is* the proper concern of sociologists. Religion and religious belief are a source of control in society because they give us our norms, morals and values. Our religious tradition is at the core of our culture. However, it can also be a major source of resistance to a status quo and a source of social change.

There are many forms of religious belief. What is the difference between superstition and faith? Is one form of belief more valid than any other? Because forms of religious belief are different, there are also serious questions as to the organisation of formal religious structures. The Roman Catholic Church, for instance, operates a vast bureaucracy and has a phenomenal legacy of wealth in the form of art treasures and religious architecture which it cannot use and which it must support. Other forms of religious organisation happily operate from the living rooms of the people concerned.

Religious belief has given us some of the most significant cultural expressions of the human spirit in terms of art, music and architecture but it continues to give people justification for the most appalling acts of cruelty and barbarism.

Time scale	Locality of origin	Religion	Founder	Splits and schisms
Before 1000 BC (Christian calendar)	Middle East	Judaism	Moses	Influences Christianity (0 BC) and Islam (AD 600)
Before 1000 BC (Christian calendar)	Indian subcontinent	Hinduism		Influences Jainism (500 BC), Buddhism (500 BC), Sikhism (AD 1600)
500 BC	China	Confucianism	Confucius Lao Tse	Confucianism and Taoism in China and in Japan. Some considerable difference in practice and belief, but basic precepts similar
500 BC	Iran and Iraq	Parsi	Zoroaster	Survives in India
500 BC	India	Jain		Variant of Hinduism
400 BC	India	Buddhism	Guatama (or the Buddha)	Variant forms in many Far Eastern Nations, gaining popularity as a world religion. Becomes Zen Buddhism in Japan
0 BC	Israel	Christianity	Jesus Christ	Splits into Eastern Orthodox Christianity and Roman Catholicism (AD 1000). Catholicism later splits into Roman Catholic and various Protestant groups (throughout Middle Ages and beyond). Protestantism subject to further schism in modern times
AD 600	Middle East	Islam	Muhammad	Has a huge sphere of influence due to notion of *Hezbollah* or Holy War. Cultural variations exist. Also subdivision between Sunni and Shia
AD 1600	Punjab	Sikh	Guru Nanak	Absorbs ideas from Islam and Hinduism

Note that the dates offered are merely a general indication of when changes occurred

Figure 9.1　A time scale of the development of world religions

HINTS AND TIPS   Keep simple notes or carry out basic research into the main religions of the world and try to understand the variation of belief between each of these religions. Use CD-ROM or the Religious Studies section of your local library. You could share notes within your group. Suggested religions and religious groupings include:

Buddhism, Christianity, Confucianism, Hinduism, Islam, Jainism, Jehovah's Witnesses, Judaism, Mormon, Parsi (Pharsee), Sikhism. You may think of others.

Organising your ideas about the sociology of religion

The sociology of religion is concerned with key themes. These are as follows:

What is the role of religion in society?

Religion plays an enormous part in society. People are willing to die for it, and – more importantly – are happy to kill other people on religious grounds. The history of western European Christianity, for instance, is also one of intolerance, torture and bloodshed, despite the fact that many insist Christianity encourages love and tolerance. Religion fulfils a variety of functions for society and sets a pattern for all our social behaviour.

How does religion help us make sense of our world?

There are a number of ways of understanding and interpreting the world: science offers us an understanding, as does common sense. However, there are questions which trouble many of us, and yet which have no obvious answer – Why do we die? Why do we live? Why do bad things happen to us? This range of questions, which cannot easily be understood through science or common sense, finds its answers in religious doctrine. Most religions exist as a series of answers to difficult philosophical questions and these answers are a matter of belief. Many sociologists refer to religions as **belief systems**. Note that belief systems are also

ideologies, or sets of ideas about the world, which embody morals and values.

Are people and societies becoming less religious?

This is a serious debate, known as the **secularisation** debate, and is raised as an issue throughout this area. Many commentators claim that people in western society are becoming secularised. This means that they no longer all believe in the formal structures of religion, as they once appear to have done. Certainly, far fewer people attend church on a regular basis but, on the other hand, there has been a growth of interest in other forms of spiritual and superstitious belief such as astrology and New Age ideas.

HINTS AND TIPS   Much sociological analysis of religion is done from broadly western social perspectives or using Christian examples. As a result, some of the language used, such as 'church' to describe a formal religious organisation, is terminologically inexact! There is room for more work in this area using other faiths as a starting point.

If you or your family practise a religion other than Christianity, you should try to evaluate the ideas that you encounter throughout this area in the light of your knowledge and understanding of this religion. Share your perspectives with your teaching group, who will benefit from your insight.

What is the nature of religious belief?

We can infer that the earliest humans had religious belief although we have very little other information about them. Very early human groups buried their dead according to rituals and with grave goods and offerings such as food. It is believed that cave art had religious or magical significance for the people who created it. Although it is a strong and almost universal impulse in people, religious belief is very difficult to define in a practical sense. We know what it is when we experience it ourselves, but how can we define others' beliefs and behaviour as religious? Many people experience their belief as intellectual faith, others experience emotional

	Formal Christianity, such as Roman Catholicism or Church of England	**Islam**
Belief	There is only one God. Jesus was his son	There is only one God. Muhammad was his prophet
Practice	Attendance at Eucharist once a week, on Sunday	Attendance at prayer on Friday and regular prayer during the day
Experience	The Christian Eucharist is supposed to offer a deeply spiritual emotion of sharing and closeness to God	A visit to Mecca offers deeply spiritual experience and closeness to God
Knowledge	Christians need to know portions of the biblical story, the Ten Commandments and some portions of the divine service such as the Creed, or statement of belief	A good Moslem would need to be very aware of the Qu'ran and might even know portions of the text by heart
Consequences	There are remarkably few for a Christian. For strict believers certain foods, including meat and eggs, should be avoided during the Lenten fast and sex should take place only after a formal religious marriage	There are strict rules in application, including the circumcision of boy babies, dietary restrictions, clothing codes and fasting during the lunar month of Ramadan

Note that this is intended as a rough guide only and that there are variations within Formal Christianity and Islam

Figure 9.2   Dimensions of religious behaviours

reactions, and yet others view religion as a form of supernatural insurance policy that will gain them a pleasant experience after their death. To complicate the issue, there are people who have personal creeds and beliefs drawn from a variety of sources and yet who reject any form of structured religious organisation.

Glock and Stark (1968) identified five elements of religiosity:

1   **Belief** – the core beliefs of any religious sect or grouping.
2   **Practice** – the formalised acts of worship.
3   **Experience** – the idea that religion can help one have some personal experience of God or the transcendental.
4   **Knowledge** – understanding of the basic beliefs or tenets of one's own religion
5   **Consequences** – the way that religious belief extends into one's experience and practice of daily life.

> **HINTS AND TIPS**   You would gain a great deal from attempting to develop the exercise in the table above with reference to others' religions which you are aware of within your group.

What is religion?

Religions can differ from one another in a whole variety of dimensions. Here are some technical terms and ideas:

- **Theism** means a belief in a god
- **Monotheists**, such as Jews and Christians, believe in one god
- **Polytheistic** religions such as Hinduism have several gods
- **Buddhism** is non-theistic in that it is a religion without a god, although it sets a series of moral standards and codes
- **Atheism** is a rejection of the notion of a god
- **Agnosticism** is the maintenance of an open mind as to the existence/non-existence of god
- **Humanism** is a belief that the values which derive from human experience are more valid than claims derived from a religious source
- **Totemism** is the belief that objects or animals hold a spiritual significance and that they should be revered as representatives of the god or spirit contained within them
- **Magic** is the attempt to control supernatural forces, gods and spirits and to force them to do your bidding
- **Superstition** is the belief that certain actions and events can ward off evil, result in, or prophesy, misfortune
- **Supernatural** refers to any event that cannot be accounted for through normal everyday or scientific understandings

The situation is by no means clear-cut, however. Christianity is monotheistic, but some Roman Catholics may venerate a series of lesser spiritual figures, such as the Virgin Mary or Saints, who will intercede on their behalf. A few Catholics may even be totemistic and venerate religious relics as having sacred power. It has also been claimed that some forms of political belief are religious in significance, and that a type of worship of a political figure forms part of the state in North Korea and existed in the cult of Lenin in the USSR before the death of Communism. Belief in various astrological formulae formed part of many ancient religious systems, though perhaps few would consider that the daily checking of a newspaper horoscope today is in any sense a religious observance.

HINTS AND TIPS *You will see as you progress through this area that the definition of a religion or religious belief will vary according to the perspective of the researcher or writer, and according to the individual.*

ACTIVITY KS **WORKING WITH OTHERS, PROBLEM SOLVING**

| IDENTIFICATION AND INTERPRETATION | ANALYSIS AND EVALUATION |

Design a small survey of your friends and other students. Ask if they feel themselves to be religious or if they have spiritual feelings. Develop the study by asking what forms their religious belief takes and how they practise their religion. Ask how many wear symbols of religious belief such as St Christopher medals or a Star of David. Use Glock and Stark's typology of religiosity as your starting point for questionnaire or interview design.

What do you learn about the varieties of religious belief and practice within your small sample?

What problems does this variety of belief systems create for sociologists?

Religion as social control

Early sociologists pointed to the way that religion forms part of the social control mechanisms of society. This is part of the social analyses of both functionalism and Marxism and happens in a number of ways.

Religion validates social structures, which could be seen as divisive and unfair

The classic example is Hinduism, which uses doctrines of **karma** and **dharma** to validate a very rigid and closed system of social stratification known as **caste**. If a person is born to a position or role in life, then he or she must become part of that occupation, marry within it, and teach the children to do the same. People accept these limitations on their lives, as they believe that they will be reincarnated to a better life.

- Kharma can be seen as similar to the concept of 'fate'. This life is a punishment or reward for the actions of a previous life.
- Dharma is a form of 'acceptance'. Be good in this life and the next will be better!

Christianity has been used to validate anti-semitism and slavery at various times in its history. The biblical story of Eve tempting her husband Adam into evil actions has been used to explain the oppression of women throughout history.

Religion offers an appeal to a higher authority

This idea is known as **legitimisation** and it is a Weberian concept. If God makes laws, then breaking these rules is far more serious than breaking rules made by humans. Much of the legal system has an air of religiosity about it: ritual, costumes and exaggerated formality provide examples. Rules governing family behaviour often reflect the religious beliefs of a culture. British society allows only single-couple heterosexual marriage, which reflects Christian religious belief.

Most religions offer a model of correct conduct based on moral values

There is a person or being whose behaviour sets an example for others to follow. This person behaves according to a set of moral values embodying social rules and sets rules for others to follow. There may also be a set of written rules, such as the Ten Commandments, which should be followed by all Christians and all Jews.

Religion brings people together and sets prohibitions

Religion is an expression of the collective belief of a society. This is very much a functionalist idea in that people are united in a set of common beliefs. However, there is a further dimension to this collective activity and belief in that people are united in their condemnation of certain acts. So religion can set prohibitions. You will note that many of the Ten Commandments of Moses are expressed in terms of the things that one is *not* allowed to do.

Religion is used to control human sexual expression

Often the moral lessons of religion are related to the control of human sexuality. Many of the points made previously in this section on control can apply to the control and organisation of sexuality, and questions of personal morality certainly apply to questions of sexuality. Not all religions are equally controlling of sexuality, and some actively celebrate the sexual act as an act of worship. However, within many religions there are rules to regulate the number and the nature of sexual partners and these are intimately tied up with religious ritual. Christianity, for instance, uses a very coded language in the marriage ceremony to describe sexuality, but the references to sexual behaviour and practice are clear and explicit if you look carefully at the wording of a ceremony. Indeed, a Christian marriage is not complete until the sexual act has taken place. Fundamental Islam sanctions the stoning to death of women who have committed adultery. Feminists point to the religious rules that govern sexuality as being forms of direct control of women: for instance churches would chastise unmarried mothers, but would not apply the same sanctions to unmarried fathers.

HINTS AND TIPS Strictly orthodox Jewish ritual dealing with sexuality and sexual practice provides an excellent example of the way in which religions choose to control and regulate the intimate practice of couples. There are clear rules governing when, how and why sex should take place between marriage partners. Do not ask an orthodox Jew directly, as he or she may find it extremely embarrassing. See what you can discover from texts and religious books.

There is a link between religion and state

In Britain, for example, the head of State is also head of the established Church of England. In historical times, the monarch's religion was the state religion and to worship in any other form was considered an act of treason, for which people were tortured and executed. A notable example is the executions of the Oxford Martyrs. The Archbishop of Canterbury (Cranmer) and bishops Ridley and Latimer were burned in the reign of Mary I for expressing Protestant belief. They died with notable courage and this remains one of the significant moments of British history.

Religion invests everyday social order and activity with additional meaning

The phenomenologist Berger (1969) noted the existence of a **sacred canopy**, where ordinary activities become invested with extra meaning because they form part of religious obligation. Sacred canopy suggests a cover of spirituality, which make any actions especially significant because they are a form of worship. As Fulcher and Scott (1999) point out, people conform to the rules of their society because of a sense of higher order and larger purpose.

ACTIVITY KS **WORKING WITH OTHERS**

ANALYSIS AND EVALUATION

How does religious belief affect people's daily lives? Even if you are not personally religious, religion and the religious belief of your culture may affect your ideas. Be imaginative in this exercise. Consider the following list and add your own ideas to it: the food you eat, the structure of your family, your moral ideas of right and wrong, the clothing that people feel is appropriate for you to wear, the relationship that you have with your parents.

Social theories of religion

A number of writers in the early nineteenth century suggested that religion was simply superstition based on ignorance. One of the earliest writers on the nature of religion was Auguste Comte, who suggested that religion was undermined by the growth of science. Religion, he felt, was abstract, but science was testable and offered reality. He went so far as to offer the view that sociology, the science of society, could come to replace traditional religious belief.

> **HINTS AND TIPS**   All through this area, you should note your own evaluations regarding the following three sets of ideas:
>
> ■ What is the link between religion and social ideology?
>
> ■ Is religious belief a force for social change or for social order?
>
> ■ Many people see scientific practice and religious belief as fully compatible. Find arguments both for and against this view.

Durkheim

Durkheim felt that something that was as central to social life as religion could not be explained away as ignorance, but must have its roots in some form of social need. It fulfilled a purpose for society. He took a very broad definition of religion and saw it as a unified system of beliefs about the nature of sacred things. One of his central ideas was an analysis of the **sacred** and the **profane**. Profane refers to the non-sacred or daily life, but sacred things are made special by the meanings attached to them. Sacred objects could be

■ times (Christmas, Divali)

■ places (Mecca, Amritsar)

■ events (marriage, death)

■ objects (cross, candles, icons)

Durkheim agreed with Comte that shared religious belief lay at the heart of social consensus because it

■ set the rules for social interaction

■ offered social solidarity

He also predicted that traditional religious belief would die away in the face of scientific understandings of how the world worked.

> **HINTS AND TIPS**   Develop this idea for yourself by listing the ways in which science and religion offer very different views of the world. To ensure that you really understand, suggest some ideas why science and religion are not compatible belief systems.

Durkheim's ideas on the nature of religion were fully developed in his famous study, *The Elementary Forms of Religious Life* (1912). Here, Durkheim added a new dimension to the debate. He suggested that we worship our own society in our religion because our religion embodies the ideas, morality and culture that we share. This is a less complicated idea than it may at first seem. Take Islamic and Jewish religious food laws, which ban the eating of pork. This rule is one of survival in a desert climate (the Middle East) where the religions developed: pigs carry human parasites and the meat will go bad very quickly. However, a law that helps people's health has become part of the ritual and religious practice of the culture.

For Durkheim, religion held society together because it grew out of social and cultural beliefs. Tribal cultures were unified by their acts of collective worship. In our own society, religion has a number of functions:

■ Shared religious belief unifies people.

■ Religion offers people a sense of belonging to their society and gives them identity.

■ Religion forms part of the collective conscience in that people are united in their sense of morality and values.

To evaluate Durkheim's views you will need to consider the following points:

■ Durkheim fails to account for the development of new religions, some of which actually represent a rejection of the norms and moral values current at the time.

■ Religious symbolism may not reflect a social view, but reflect a spiritual belief. For instance Kingsley Davis suggests that a crucifix represents a hope of life after death.

■ Weber points out that religion can be a potent factor in social change. Recent examples include the mobilisation of the black religious community by Martin Luther King that gave rise to emancipation movements in the USA.

■ Religious belief is not always a force for social integration. For example, in Northern Ireland or the former Yugoslavia religion challenges social order and cohesion.

■ In support of Durkheim, some religious movements seem to grow out of **anomie**, which is a sense that people have of not belonging to society. In these cases, there is a strong urge for people to return to the religious values of the past. The Industrial Revolution in Britain, for instance, was marked by a series of **revivalist** movements, such as Methodism and Presbyterianism.

- Bainbridge and Stark argue that people have a perpetual need for religion and that new movements spring up to fill the place left by those that no longer suit the needs of people.

ACTIVITY KS **IMPROVING LEARNING**

ANALYSIS AND EVALUATION

Make a list of the good and bad things that religion has done for society. You may enlist the help of a history teacher or some history students for this exercise. Make sure that your ideas are wide-ranging. Do not criticise any given religion but look at the impact that it has had on people's behaviour.

Parsons

When we are faced with situations that frighten or shock us, such as an accident or illness, we often want to know why this appalling thing has happened to us: 'Why me?' Talcott Parsons suggested that we answer this question through religion. He developed Durkheim's analysis of religion as a force for social cohesion and agreed that it was an embodiment of the values of society. He felt that religion had one main function, that of maintaining social order. It does this in two ways:

- by giving people comfort when they are faced with situations that cannot be predicted
- by giving people a sense of a higher purpose

Religion offers people answers to the big questions, in that people believe that the frightening and unhappy events in people's lives are simply the will of God.

Malinowski on *Magic, Science and Religion*

Bronislaw Malinowski (1954), operating from within a functional tradition, conducted a famous study of **religion** and **magic** among the Trobriand islanders. He observed that the islanders had great understanding of their environment, being experts at fishing and farming. They recognised that skill played a part in the success of their efforts but they relied on the use of magic and never failed to carry out the prescribed rituals, believing that to fail to would bring disaster. Malinowski further noted that if good results were guaranteed from certain actions, such as lagoon fishing, no magic rituals were used. However, if the islanders went deep sea fishing, which was dangerous and unreliable, a whole series of rituals was used.

He suggested that religion and magic are both used as solutions to stress and fear. They differ in the following ways:

- Magic is used for practical purposes in order to alter events. It is instrumental in that it has a purpose. Magic is used to prevent death in childbirth where the outcome is uncertain.
- Religion is expressive of a community feeling. It is used to celebrate the birth of a child and to unite the community.

To evaluate Malinowski you may need to consider the following points:

- Radcliffe-Brown suggested that the rituals could be self-defeating in that they give rise to fear.

Points to support functionalist analysis	Criticisms of functionalist theory
Functionalism does seem to offer an account of the personal attraction of religious belief in that people do seek reassurance when things go wrong, and seek it in God	Religion has been used to justify the most appalling social barbarism such as the recent wars in former Yugoslavia, which have some foundation in religious intolerance
Personal pain and grief can be made meaningful if people gain comfort from religion	The comfort offered by religion can lead people to accept terrible injustice and inequality because they are taught that they will be rewarded in an after-life
Religious practice and ceremonial at times of social stress such as bereavement offers the participants a sense of comfort and unity	These observances can be mere ritual, obscuring people's sense of social reality

Figure 9.3 An evaluation of functional analysis of religion

- Homans suggested that Malinowski was correct because if the ritual is carried out correctly people are reassured.

- Malinowski, as with other functionalists, tends not to consider what the nature of the religious experience actually is for the individual.

- Haralambos and Holborn (1995) point out that, although Malinowski considers certain rituals to be religious and others to be magic, this is in fact his own interpretation of events.

- Bainbridge and Stark (1985) suggest that magic and science are related in that the popularity and acceptance of one is linked to a decline in trust in the other.

> **HINTS AND TIPS** *Magical behaviour is by no means limited to the Trobriand islanders or to 'primitive' tribes. How many people in the class have little personal rituals or sayings to ensure success in examinations or to bring their teams good luck?*

Marx

Marx did not write a great deal on the subject of religion, but his ideas seem to be similar in some respects to those of Durkheim. He agreed with Durkheim that religion would die away and that it embodied the values of society. Religion is a social construction for both of them, although neither would have expressed the ideas in those terms. The difference between them arises because, whereas Durkheim is essentially **consensual** in his analysis and looks for the things that bind society, Marx believed in social conflict and was aware of the things that divide society. His view was that the capitalist classes control society

because they have the monopoly on wealth and power. The relationship between rich and poor is essentially exploitative. The rich are able to maintain their position of superiority because they can impose an ideology, or set of beliefs, on the poor.

> **HINTS AND TIPS** *This concept of mind-control and ideology is explored in Areas 5 and 8. It is a theme that links most of the sociological topics which you will study.*

One way in which the powerful maintain their hold on the poorest people in society is through the interpretation and maintenance of religious feeling. The poor are discouraged from seeing the reality of their lives and their oppression within the class system. They are taught that they cannot change society because it is a creation of God, and they do not appreciate that society can be changed. Instead, they are led to believe that they will receive their reward for their suffering in an after-life. Traditional Christian doctrine, hymns and **liturgy** (the words of the religious services) are full of examples of such ideas. For example, Jesus is quoted in one of the Gospels as saying that it is as easy for a rich man to go to Heaven as for a camel to pass through the eye of a needle (refer back to the Hindu concepts of kharma and dharma). More recent theory stresses the role of religion as a form of social control and students should refer to the ideas of Althusser, who considered religion to be an apparatus of state control over the masses.

> **HINTS AND TIPS** *Ask someone with a good knowledge of the Christian Gospels or religious practice to point out other examples of places where Jesus preaches acceptance of how things are because a reward will follow in Heaven for the good people.*

Points to support Marxist analysis	Criticisms of Marxist theory
There is a connection between religion and the state which is apparent in such historical ideas as 'the divine right of kings'	Many religions originate among the poorest sectors in society and some are actually revolutionary
Religion has been used to justify the most appalling oppression, such as slavery and apartheid	There is a tradition of 'radical' theology, particularly in places such as Latin America and Nazi Germany, where priests opposed totalitarianism and oppression
Religious belief is often at its strongest among the poor and oppressed, especially among women, who are the least powerful in society	Marxism is itself seen as a religious form, especially in China where there was a cult of Mao Zedong, the first Communist leader, and in North Korea with the cult of Kim Il Sung

Figure 9.4 Evaluating Marxist theories of religion

ANALYSIS AND
EVALUATION

Marx and Engels famously described religion as 'the opiate of the people', implying that it is a drug which anaesthetises people against the ills of the world and dulls their ability to think for themselves. Organise a class discussion on this subject and then suggest points both for and against this view in essay form. You may wish to look at The Communist Manifesto, where these words occur, before your discussion. If well translated, this is a short book and really quite straightforward to read.

Curiously, Marxism has actually inspired religious action and belief in a philosophy known as **liberation theology**. Many Latin American countries, where Roman Catholicism is the dominant religion, have experienced periods of dramatically cruel and vicious dictatorship. Priests such as Oscar Romero, the Archbishop of San Salvador in El Salvador, preached justice and equality, knowing what the probable outcome would be. He died on 21 March 1980 in a burst of gunfire while celebrating Mass in his own cathedral. In 1979, many Catholic revolutionaries supported the *Sandinistas* against the government of Nicaragua. In the light of this it is necessary to consider whether the Marxist view of religion as a force for capitalism is in fact justified. A more recent neo-Marxist writer, Maduro, suggests that the church can be independent of the state to become a force for justice and change. If people are unable to express their suffering formally then they will call for help from individual priests. The formal organisation of the church may not always respond, but brave people will.

Weber

Although Max Weber has not given rise to a sociological perspective in the same way that Marx or Durkheim did, he still remains one of the great theoreticians. It is sometimes easy to overlook his contribution to some debates, but his ideas are crucial to an understanding of the relationship between society and religion. Although Weber is a structuralist and therefore interested in the structures of society, he also understands that social meaning and individual interpretations play a part in social behaviours. He shares some ideas with Durkheim when he suggests that people attempt to make sense of the world, and when he points out that ideas must meet the needs of society and of people if they are to survive. However, his contribution to the debate is to point out that religion can itself be a source of major social change through the intervention of significant ideas or significant people.

Weber was highly prolific despite periodic bouts of ill-health, possibly depression. He was in many respects an unusual character and he is certainly worthy of further research and note-taking. His best known work in this particular area was *The Protestant Ethic and the Spirit of Capitalism*, which has remained highly influential partly because it offers an alternative view of the rise of capitalism to the one suggested by Karl Marx. Although Weber was interested in the rise of capitalism, the key to an understanding of his work is the appreciation that his real concern was with the relationship between ideas and society. He was fascinated by the idea of rationality and order and how these concepts have given rise to the society that we know and understand. There are two main debates in this area to which Weber has made a significant contribution.

Weber: religious ethics and social change

Many of the inventions that gave rise to the Industrial Revolution were not so much inventions as reinventions. The Romans knew how to harness water power and the Arabs had invented an early steam engine in the sixteenth century, but neither of those cultures went on to develop industrial societies and the inventions remained no more than amusing toys. What, Weber asked himself, was different when these technologies appeared in western societies and triggered the substantial changes known as the Industrial Revolution? He suggested that other societies did not have the values necessary for the development of capitalism.

Although religion was only one of a number of factors which gave rise to the massive social change known as the Industrial Revolution, in Weber's view it was the most significant. Many of the people in the industrial north of Europe were Calvinists. This seems a rather bleak religious viewpoint, because Calvinists believe in **pre-ordination**, or predestination. This doctrine suggests that people do not have free will to make their own choices, but are allocated places in Heaven in advance. Those who will go to Heaven are 'the elect'. However, to be sure of their place among the elect, people should live sober, hard-working and worthy lives. If God has allocated a place in Heaven to a person, then he will favour that person in life.

Weber suggested that this type of religious belief naturally gave rise to capitalism because:

■ it made it possible for people to accumulate wealth and to reinvest it

■ it saw poverty as a sign of moral degradation so people were under no obligation to look after the poor

■ people did not enjoy their wealth by spending it but put it to work, making more money

■ accumulation of money and property was a sign of favour from God

Weber and the legitimisation debate

According to Weber, state religions offer **legitimacy** and power to government. This is a point of view that he shares with Marxists and it is known as the legitimisation debate. This idea is very important in the understanding of government and politics. Weber argued that there are three types of authority:

1 **Rational legal authority** – people follow rules because they see that it makes sense to do so.

2 **Traditional authority** – people obey because they always have and they do not question the right of the leaders to rule.

3 **Charismatic authority** – people obey because they are hypnotised by the powerful personality of the leader.

Weber suggested that much social change has occurred because charismatic leaders arose and people followed. Many religions have a single prophet and there are any numbers of charismatic leaders who have influenced people's religious belief in modern times. Indeed, there is a branch of non-conformist religious practice known as **charismatic**, which is noted for the beauty of speech of the preacher – who can sway a congregation by the power of language. John Wesley, the leader of the Methodists of the late eighteenth century, was a noted charismatic and reduced congregations to tears and even to epileptic fits.

ACTIVITY KS **COMMUNICATION**

KNOWLEDGE AND UNDERSTANDING

Make a list of charismatic religious leaders who have influenced social events or people's beliefs. Ask people to name significant religious leaders for you and then look them up in CD-ROM, encyclopaedias, and the Internet. If you can, try and look out for film or tape of Martin Luther King's 'I have a dream' speech which is almost guaranteed to bring a person to tears. You can hear a portion of this on *Encarta* if you have access to the CD-ROM.

Analyses in favour of Weberian thought	Analyses critical of Weberian thought
He provides the best challenge to Marxist thought on the development of capitalism which is sometimes a little simplistic in that Marx considers economic factors alone	There is not quite such a clear-cut relationship between Calvinism and capitalism as Weber claims. Some Calvinist areas did not develop capitalism while other areas, which were not Calvinist, did
Weber sees religion as a positive force for social change whereas both Durkheim and Marx offer a passive view of religion arising out of society	Extreme Protestants were barred from a variety of professional occupations and so they were forced into business
Weber offers us an understanding of the meaning of religion in people's lives	Weber's concern with meaning also leads to the suggestion by some writers that Weber tended to 'over-play' the evidence in favour of his own theorising

Figure 9.5 Evaluating Weber

Religion as a source of identity: Weber versus Marx and Durkheim

This is an area that is discussed in Area 4, where it should be absolutely apparent that we draw our sense of self identity from our culture, and that religion is at the core of culture. You should consider this in detail because it is clear that the combination of religious belief and nationality can be a source of great pride to people. Historically, this combination was the flame that lit the gas ovens of the Holocaust and sparked the bombings in Northern Ireland. The case could be argued with reflections on the extent to which Marxist and Durkheimian concepts of the unifying force of religion as a factor for social cohesion compares with Weberian notions of religion as a source of social change. For example, the case could be argued with reference to Islam as a force for resistance against western global culture, the link between the Welsh language and religious non-conformity and discussions of American black Evangelism and the Jamaican cult of Ras Tafari which rejects the values of western capitalism. This argument closely parallels a later discussion in this area on the relationship between religion and social class.

> **HINTS AND TIPS**   It is often easier to see Marx and Durkheim as opposite ends of a spectrum in all things, but this is occasionally misleading. As theoreticians, they have many things in common. The point of difference is that Marxists tend to see society as being run for the benefit of the wealthy whereas Durkheim sees it as being run for the good of all.

Phenomenology

Berger and Luckmann are most noted for their view that people need to give meaning to their lives. This has led them into an analysis of religion that is similar to the views expressed by the functionalists, despite the very different origins of their theory. Religion is one of a number of social creations (or constructions) which serve this purpose. Each society has a sense of higher knowledge about the meaning of life and religion is created to help build, maintain and legitimise meaning. In a sense, this translates as an explanation of 'higher truths' being developed to give people the sense that their lives have purpose. Obviously this process is very

personal. The impact of this on society, however, is to unite people. The link between phenomenological analysis and the functionalist view is in the suggestion that religion unites society because it gives a sense of higher meaning and shared belief. Phenomenologists actually approve of religious belief because they feel that, if we lose our sense of shared religion, society will lose its sense of purpose, and we will lose our sense of morality. This type of thinking has reference to the beliefs of the New Right (this is a point that will be returned to in a consideration of the secularisation debate).

It has been suggested that Berger and Luckmann have failed to take account of religion as a force for social disruption and change. Phenomenology does not consider modern societies where people are uninterested in formal religious practice and there is fragmentation of belief. As with much phenomenology this is a difficult set of ideas to test, concerned as it is with the nature of meaning.

Feminism

Many early religions perceived the supreme deity to be female. There are a number of Earth goddesses – such as Athene (Greek), Diana (Roman) and Rhiannon (Celtic) – associated with the moon and night, often with owls. These goddesses survive in myths about witchcraft and in the Earth Mother cults such as the intense interest in Gaia, which is typical of New Age religions. The worship of femininity as symbolised by night is clearly linked to fertility belief because the phases of the moon reflect the phases of the menstrual cycle. Even today, Islamic tradition is based on a lunar calendar, which probably pre-dates the Prophet. The moon is also significant in dating Easter and Passover. These religious ideas may come from a failure to understand the role of the male and of the sexual act in human reproduction. This is not quite as ridiculous as it seems: Ancient Greeks appear to have believed that their horses were impregnated by the wind.

Most modern world religions, however, are **patriarchal**, or masculine in nature. God is seen as a man, as a father figure, and the manifestations of his wisdom on Earth are through the agencies of men. The Roman

Catholic cult of the Virgin Mary is an exception, but she does not represent power or action as she is a passive figure who exists to weep over the death of her son. You should also note that there is a dimension of sexual control in this image; Mary is a perfect woman, and she has been able to bear a child without recourse to tempting a man into a sexual relationship. There is a religious logic to this; only men had the power in the various cultures to make the revelations that become the foundation of religious doctrine.

Feminists point out that religion is a tool in the oppression of women. Many writers have suggested that there is a fundamental hatred of women expressed in the Judaeo-Christian tradition that sees women as 'unclean' and the possessions or the temptresses of men. Expressions of this patriarchal ideology can be seen in all forms of religious tradition and practice. Women are 'churched' (made holy again) in a special ritual after the births of their babies. Even the traditional wedding ceremony sees the woman as a possession of a man: the nearest male relative of a bride is asked to 'give her away'. Some Islamic traditions require females to experience genital mutilation despite there being nothing in the Qu'ran to support this act. Women are required to conduct themselves in a way that protects men from their own lust. The belief in male divinity is therefore a social expression of an idea that is used to repress and confine women, to suppress their sexuality and to control their actions, and to give them the status of possessions.

> **HINTS AND TIPS** It is easy to consider that feminism is one perspective, but this is incorrect, because feminism is one of the most vigorous current debates within sociology. As a result there are a number of perspectives that can be taken by writers in this tradition. Make sure that you are aware of some of the debates by looking at Area 1.

What are the main concerns of feminism?

Organised religious institutions are masculine

It should be noted that, while the bureaucracies of churches are masculine, women are the ones who actually go to church. The domination of religious institutions by men is a hegemony that is challenged from within the organisations. The challenge often comes from those who attempt to combine feminism with religious orthodoxy, such as Christine Odone, a past editor of the *Catholic Herald*. The political implication of this in recent years has been the move to ordain women in the Church of England: a bitterly fought battle. The process is by no means restricted to Christianity: a woman has recently reached high office among the Sikhs.

Religious belief is used to underline a strict interpretation and ideology of the family

This is particularly relevant to considerations of the role of the family and the political ideologies of the New Right, which has upheld the view that the strict Christian interpretation of family life is the 'correct' form of family.

Masculinity is raised to a semi-divine status, which has reduced femininity to a second-class status

If your god, or his representative, is male, then oppression of females because of their inferior biology is justified.

> **ACTIVITY** *WORKING WITH OTHERS*
>
> ANALYSIS AND EVALUATION
>
> Discuss with people of various faiths what the teaching of their religion is with regard to the role of women and the importance of family life. You could also look in textbooks in the Religious Education section of your library. Do you find evidence in support of or counter to feminist ideas? Moslems, for instance, claim to see women as separate but equal in status. Their young males, however, have more freedom in their behaviour.

However, feminist research has also looked at the issue of female interest in worship. A number of recent writers such as Simon and Nadell (1995) point to the link between femininity and caring. Some have even suggested that males and females experience different notions of God.

Hypothesis – The notion of God is a gendered interpretation.

Context – There are two ways of interpreting this argument:

■ God himself is a gendered interpretation shared by both males and females

■ Males and females have separate and gendered interpretations of the notion of God and of religion

You would be looking at a lot more than religious belief with such a study because the key to the investigation is whether males and females have different social constructions of the world and the meaning of spirituality. You would also be looking at patriarchy and patriarchal ideology in the intimate sphere of people's personal beliefs.

Method – Design a simple qualitative survey and ask a variety of people for a definition of God and about the attractiveness of belief in God. You would be best to ignore their personal religious beliefs. Do not restrict yourself to the faithfully religious because your question is about gender and you do not want to introduce other variables. Do not use sociological terminology such as 'gendered interpretation' in your questionnaire as people will not understand what you are asking. You will get silly or irrelevant responses.

Your sample frame is not so significant in this question because interpretative studies such as this question meaning. Make sure that you ask an equal number of males and females. Even though you are asking about meaning, and using an interpretative style of question, you would be better to keep your questionnaire extremely short and to extend the number of respondents to ensure a wide range of response.

Evaluation – Did you discover that notions of God and religion vary between the genders? To what extent did females emphasise caring? If you discover that females and males *do* share a notion of God, you might have to consider whether the notion itself or the research design was at fault. You would also have to look deeply at people's understandings of God to see if they are patriarchal in nature.

However, if you discover that there are different notions of God, then you may have to consider some interesting questions about the relationship between religion and patriarchal ideology. In either case, this could be an interesting study because you would have to combine research design techniques that draw on interpretivism with quite scientific and empirical questions about the number of variables that you can introduce into your study.

Postmodernism

Modernism is a term used to describe a search for a set of absolutes, for the 'truth'. It is linked with a theory known as **march of progress**, which implies that everything is getting better all the time. In sociology, modernism is strongly associated with empiricism, or the application of science, so it unites both Marxism and functionalism. However, **postmodernism** is a more recent set of principles that can be looked at in the study of religion in the following ways:

■ For some writers postmodernism is actually a description of the current state of society. This is significant in the secularisation debate, where postmodernism is used by some commentators to account for the importance and significance of the New Age.

■ For other writers, postmodernism is a new form of theory about society. Again, this is relevant to a discussion of religion, because postmodern analyses can be applied to considerations of the nature of belief itself.

> **HINTS AND TIPS**   You should also be cautious of embracing any profoundly popular or fashionable theory in sociology because inevitably, as with any fashion, the backlash is extreme. To use an analogy, consider any very high-fashion clothing styles, such as shell suits, which were popular between 1987 and 1992. Could you wear them now? Currently postmodernism is growing in popularity, but to totally adopt it as a stance is to miss the value in other sociological positions. The same point applies to complete rejection of unpopular positions such as functionalism.

As postmodernism applies to religion, the following positions are significant:

- People no longer believe in the old 'truths' such as religion or political ideology. People create society as they go along so there is no permanence. This also means that people can embrace all possibilities – for example they can now mix and match religious beliefs to create individual realities.

- Society and individuals have become 'de-centred' in that they share no great sense of purpose. This is in contrast to the views of Marxists and functionalists, who are structuralists.

- Fashion and trend have come to matter more to people than values and morality. This is of significance in causing them to reject the absolute moralities of religion.

- The media dominate and define cultural terms. Each belief and debate is short lived and holds significance only until it is replaced by the next. This is in opposition to religious belief where truths are held to be absolute and permanent.

HINTS AND TIPS   Postmodernism claims that all truths are relative. If all theories are relative, postmodernism is no better than any other theory, which operates as an overview of how society works. It has argued itself out of credibility. However, postmodernism could still be a good description of how society is beginning to operate. Decide for yourself.

Postmodernist processes have had a number of effects on religion and society:

- Many people now believe in forms of relativism. People can individualise their religious belief so that Christians can profess belief in reincarnation or astrology. In the past this would have been a highly dangerous thing to do and would have resulted in social outcast status at best, and probably in a very painful death.

- Morality itself has become relative. It is no longer wrong to steal because a god said so; people will make fraudulent claims on insurance companies or shoplift 'because the companies can afford it'. Many such people would describe themselves as basically honest.

- People are aware that religious belief changes so they will pick and choose from within their own tradition. For example, some Roman Catholics will use birth control despite its being banned by the Church.

Arguments in support of postmodernism	Points of criticism
Fewer people attend church or any other form of religious building on a regular basis and the churches have had to respond by making a direct appeal to congregations and attempting to graft popular songs and dance into worship	It is mistaken to ignore the old social realities because they still govern the lives of many people. So, although fewer people would profess themselves to be Christian in our society, Christian morality is still a power to be recognised
New Age beliefs are common and these consist of a whole range of practices drawn from a wide variety of traditions, including western herbalism and Chinese feng-shui, applied with little understanding of the cultures from which they are drawn	Habermas, a critic of post modernism, and others who are influenced by Marxism, feel that postmodernism is an attack on one of the principal aims of sociology, the gathering of evidence that leads to understanding
People no longer turn to religion for comfort and help in times of trouble and stress but use therapists, counsellors, psychics and suchlike to come to terms with their difficulties	Many people are turning towards formal and rigidly orthodox practice and belief such as Islam and fundamental Christianity because they *do* believe that there are moral absolutes, which define right and wrong

Figure 9.6   Evaluating postmodernism

Knowledge, power and ideology

Given the various perspectives, the discussion needs to be widened into application of the theories as they apply to elements of contemporary society. There needs to be serious consideration of the ideologies of religion and the uses to which they are put. Although no-one would claim that *all* who subscribe to fervent religious belief are either self-righteous or bigoted, religious belief has been used to justify very cruel and inhuman behaviour.

Humans have a remarkable ability to delude themselves and to find reasons why they should behave as they do, so intolerance of others can be a feature of religious practice even though most Holy Scriptures of most world religions would argue against it. To develop the point, Christ is reported to have said, 'Love thy neighbour as thyself' and to have preached a doctrine

	Legitimisation	**Ideology**	**Collective consciousness**
Durkheim	Shared religious belief ensures social consensus and embodies our values, morality and culture	We worship our society and our culture in our religious forms	Religion offers a unified set of beliefs about the nature of sacred belief
Parsons and functionalists	Religion maintains social order	Religion embodies the higher morals of our society and is an ideal to which we aspire	Religion gives people a sense of higher purpose
Marx and neo-Marxism	Shared religious belief legitimises the power that the wealthy have over the working classes and is a tool of oppression	Religion embodies the morality of the wealthy and the poor are taught to believe that the wealthy have a right to rule	Religion causes people to accept a false consciousness of their position in society and, though it offers comfort, it prevents them from accepting the realities of their economic systems
Weber	Religious belief is one of a number of forms of power. People accept the legitimacy of those who claim power through the force of religion because it is a form of tradition. Religious belief can also contribute to people's personal charisma	Ideas must meet the needs of society if they are to survive and this can happen through the medium of religious belief. Religion can be a source of social change	Shared social meanings are embodied in religion
Feminism	Shared religious belief legitimises the power that males have over females and is a tool of oppression	Religion embodies the morality of males. Women are taught to believe that the men have a right to control their lives and their sexuality in the way they do	Religion offers comfort to women and gives them a way of accepting the realities of their oppression
Postmodernism	Religious belief is one of the old certainties and moral absolutes that are rapidly disappearing from culture	Religion is one of a number of belief possibilities	There is no such thing as a collective consciousness because people can pick and choose their belief systems

Note: The headings above are all drawn from perspectives. Legitimisation is Marxist and Weberian, whereas collective consciousness is functionalist

Figure 9.7 A summary of the main perspectives of the sociology of religion

of trust, respect, honour, and love but that does not seem to have prevented Christians from slaughtering millions of people of their own religions (and of others) over the centuries in the name of their leader. Indeed, it can fairly be said that large portions of the history of western Christianity are written in blood. It is this anomaly that the sociology of religion seeks to address: how can religion be abused by people to support their own moral philosophies and to justify their own cruel behaviour?

Most religions share the belief that the people who subscribe to their creeds

■ are in receipt of a knowledge or understanding that will bring them benefit in this world or the next

■ have been 'chosen' to receive this specialised set of philosophies, which will 'save' them from harm, either in this world or the next

■ are in some way correct, which can also imply to some that those who do not share their beliefs and

moral practices are incorrect and even morally inferior or suspect

■ should have belief without the benefit of proof that the ideas are correct – this is known as faith

■ should try to bring those who do not subscribe to their belief systems to an understanding of the benefits that the beliefs bring. This process is known as 'missionary work' in Christianity.

HINTS AND TIPS *You can easily gain a flavour of the ideological and religious content of the various Christian denominations by listening to Church services on BBC Radio 4 on a Sunday morning. There is also a service every morning on Radio 4 long wave at 9.45 a.m. These services repay systematic content analysis. The timings and the denominations are in TV listing pages. Note, too, that you can listen only to Christian services: other religions are not catered for in the same way. If you are not Christian, this exercise should be extremely interesting to you and will allow you some understanding without the embarrassment or sacrilege of attending a service.*

Not all religions are under the same obligation to gain converts: some sects and cults are often strongly under this rule and some, such as the 'Children of God', have even resorted to asking young women believers to prostitute themselves in order to gain new members.

The state and the Church of England

There is an organised link between the British state and the Church of England, and the movement to remove this link is known as **disestablishmentarianism**.

■ The head of state, the monarch, is also the head of the Church of England and carries the title *Fidei Defensor* ('Defender of the Faith'). This title is on coins, where you will see the letters FD next to the name of the monarch.

■ Bishops of the Church of England have seats in the House of Lords.

■ All schools are legally obliged to hold religious services daily and to teach Christian values and morality.

■ The Church of England is wealthy; it has holdings in land and property.

■ The BBC must broadcast a given amount of religious and moral material. Religious groups can speak on *Thought for the Day* on Radio 4, but non-religious moral groupings such as the Humanist organisation are not allowed this time.

Racial ideology

There is a historical association between the ideology of religion and the sense that those of different ethnicity are somehow inferior or not quite fully human. The medieval Christian church linked the idea of Satan, who is evil, with blackness. Wall paintings show him personified as black-skinned. This made it possible for many people in historical times to see black people as being in need of the saving words of Christianity and was one of the main justifications for the continuation of slavery and the slave trade. You will find a little more on slavery in Area 3. Slaves were baptised and, although their earthly lives were full of pain, they had the knowledge that they would

experience Heaven. It should also be noted that the movement against slavery developed earlier in Britain than in many European nations, or the Americas, and was led by devoutly Christian social reformers such as William Wilberforce. There is a lavish memorial to the ending of slavery quite near to the House of Lords.

ACTIVITY KS COMMUNICATION

KNOWLEDGE AND UNDERSTANDING	ANALYSIS AND EVALUATION

Learn what you can about the slave trade in Britain and in the Americas. History GCSE books will be very good on this topic. Discover what moral justification people gave at the time for the continuation of slavery. Evaluate the evidence by asking yourself whether people were slave traders because it made them rich or because they really believed that it was their moral duty to convert Africans to Christian belief. Remember that the answer is never as simple as it might first appear.

The New Right and the decline in moral standards

There is a strong link between the political philosophies of the New Right and Christian moral belief. This is well covered in Area 14 and is also referred to in Area 6. The Christian perspective impacted in a significant way on the political structures and the legal systems of our society under the policies of Margaret Thatcher and the Conservatives from 1989.

■ Those who do not hold the moral beliefs of Christianity with regard to sexual behaviour, such as never-married mothers, tended to be seen as the authors of their own misfortune and poverty rather than as the victims of a social structure which devalues women and alienates the poor.

■ The problems of British society were seen in terms of the decline of moral standards and there was an emphasis on the teaching of moral values in schools. An authoritarian line was taken with regard to crime and punishment, so criminals were to be punished for their wrong actions.

HINTS AND TIPS *The analysis of religious belief offered above suggests that those who do hold strong belief in the morality of their religion are interested in the control of the behaviour of others. Can you attempt to identify ways in which Christian morality has affected our social ideas relating to families and family structure? Think of monogamy for a start.*

The rise of fundamentalism

Fundamentalism and fundamental belief is a significant part of the study of religion because arguments rage as to its significance. Fundamentalism is common to a number of religious groupings around the world, and fundamentalists argue for a return to a 'purer' form of religion and the moral values of the past. In practice, this usually requires strict observance of scripture as the direct 'word of God', rather than as a document which is open to interpretation, and the adoption of strict and extremely conservative moral values. Fundamentalist groups are often led by a charismatic preacher and have much in common with cults or sects, so the discussion which is relevant to those analyses later in this area also applies to fundamental religious groups.

In practical terms, fundamentalism can also represent very significant social feeling because, in the west at least, fundamental Islam can be seen as a rejection of the prevailing morality of western capitalism. Fundamentalism is common among immigrant groups so West Indian Christian Pentecostalists are seen to be seeking relief from social and economic oppression. Bruce describes fundamentalism as a form of **cultural defence**.

American evangelism

American society has its roots in religious intolerance in Europe throughout the sixteenth and seventeenth centuries, when many people fled from persecution in their home countries and settled in what is now the USA. The American constitution was written in such a way that America is a secular state, but with religious foundations, and people have the freedom to practise their religion in any way they choose. America is a multi-faith society, with hundreds of different major religious groupings, such as Judaism, Jehovah's Witnesses, Mormons, Roman Catholics, Protestants, and thousands of sects and cults.

The Christian Evangelist movement is important in the USA. Members take a literal view of the Bible and believe that it is the true written word of God. This is clearly linked with fundamentalism. The Bible is not seen as a matter for interpretation. At their most extreme, some evangelists believe it to be their duty to initiate the end of the world to encourage the Second Coming of Christ. Cameras have been mounted in Jerusalem to capture this on video. This movement is an extremely powerful political lobby, which raises millions of dollars for right-wing political causes, and some evangelists are very open about their politics. The movement was able to donate money to support the presidential candidature of Ronald Reagan, who supported the New Right during his presidency in the 1980s. It is able to raise huge sums of money through television evangelists, who beg for contributions. The Christian evangelical movement is wealthy enough to run theme parks and holiday centres for members of its churches, despite the fact that it is supported by some of the poorest people. The 'televangelist' movement has access to American cable channels and is now beginning to target a European market.

The Ku-Klux-Klan originated in what is known as the Bible Belt of the southern states of the USA and uses a burning crucifix as its symbol. Although this group has lost some status and power since the 1930s, remember the link between their religious extremism and their racism.

HINTS AND TIPS
- *American sociology textbooks, such as Tischler's (1996)* **Introduction to Sociology** *and Newman's (1995)* **Sociology: Exploring the Architecture of Everyday Life** *note, but fail to explore, the significance of the Christian lobby in their own society.*
- *Not all evangelists are necessarily right-wing in politics. Noted civil rights workers in the field of race relations in the USA, Jesse Jackson and Martin Luther King, rose to prominence through black evangelical movements.*

The rise of Islam

Several commentators have pointed to the idea that modern society is becoming globalised. This idea is attributed to Professor Anthony Giddens of the London School of Economics and the postmodernists, who suggest the following points about our culture:

■ We are beginning to share cultural ideas in a sort of cultural 'mix-and-match'.

■ Cultural ideas tend to be westernised and associated with Americanisation. This process has been variously called McDonaldisation (after the hamburger chain, where it is used to refer to work practice; see Area 7), and Disneyfication (after the media empire).

Many cultures are able to reject absorption into a global culture by practising culture or allegiance that is at odds with western society. The practice of religion is used as a form of social resistance to the loss of cultural ideas. For example, the wearing of the 'hijjab' (or scarf to cover the face and hair) by many Islamic women is a cultural and political statement, and has actually been seen as threatening to many in the west. Islamic fundamentalism, which is a strict interpretation of the words of the Qu'ran, is an attempt to turn away from the decadence of western cultural influence. Many African Americans, possibly nearly a million, have joined Nation of Islam, which is rather different from traditional Middle Eastern Islamic belief. This is seen as a statement against white domination, which imposed Christianity upon the slave populations.

ACTIVITY   KS **COMMUNICATION**

IDENTIFICATION AND INTERPRETATION	ANALYSIS AND EVALUATION

Organise a class debate on the question:

■ Is strong religious belief a force for good in society?

Make sure that both sides of the argument are fully explored. You might need to do a great deal of research to find examples and evidence to quote from. Remember that your comments should also be made with reference to the sociological theories that you have studied.

Religion and nationalism: a historical case study

This is a historical as well as a sociological debate and one significant study in this field is that of Gwyn Alf Williams – *When was Wales* (1985). In Wales the growth of nationalism was tied closely to extreme Protestantism, known as non-conformity (this means non-conformity to the Church of England). The major types of non-conformist sect are Methodists and Presbyterians (chapel attenders rather than church attenders). Williams identifies several characteristics of non-conformist religions:

■ they are not the state religion

■ services are very simple because there is no priest to intercede between man and God

■ reliance is on the direct word of God made manifest in the Bible

■ the religious practice is a return to the 'pure' forms of the early church

■ there is a tendency to split and factionalise over tiny points of doctrine

■ revivalism, ecstasy states, missionary zeal and concern for the individual soul are typical of religious worship

■ often, though not always, there is extreme rigour and high-mindedness on matters of sex, role of women, language, and alcohol

The position in Wales during the growth and flowering of the Industrial Revolution was that 50% of the population were dissenters from the Church of England – that is, they were non-conformists. These people were Welsh speakers. They were able to read their language, though many could not write it, and the main primer for learning to read was the Welsh translation of the Bible. Children were taught to read in the chapels on Sunday because they were working on the other six days of the week.

Non-conformists tended to live in very isolated rural communities or the new industrial towns of the coal-mining areas. Life was very hard (75% of the death rate in the 1850s in mining communities was of children under the age of five). People were fervent in religious practice, which was linked to singing and music, so that nationality and religion became linked. Myths of Wales as the 'land of song' tend to originate in this era and persist in the singing of hymns in Welsh at rugby matches. Even dissenting politics such as Chartism (a worker's voting movement popular in the whole of the UK) had a particularly nationalistic and religious dimension in Wales.

The upper echelons of society were playing at Welshness with a romantic and distinctly sentimental view of what being Welsh meant. However, non-conformity was linked to Liberal political action (in 1916, David Lloyd George became Liberal Prime Minister) and the growth of the Labour Party. Before Lloyd George became Prime Minister and actively involved in the First World War, his greatest political achievement was to disestablish Wales from the Church of England, a battle that was fought from 1912 to September 1914. Disestablishment came into force 31 March 1920. The Church of England is now one of many sects in Wales rather than a state religion as in England. This cost the Church of England some taxes (tithes) and endowments and the Church of England was renamed Church in Wales. Note the difference in relationship pointed to by the change of 'of' to 'in'!

Institutions of religion

Religions are a shared institution in society. Personal beliefs do not form part of the analysis below because they have little social reality. Religious institutions, however, are deeply significant because they have social, political and economic power. They can also legitimise actions because they represent a higher order of reality than the secular. No one would argue against the view that, regardless of the actual man who holds the position, the Pope is an enormously powerful person.

> **HINTS AND TIPS** At this point you should return to Weber's analysis of power, which has been described in this area and which is also discussed in Area 14.

Very few religions are unified into one all-encompassing set of beliefs that all members subscribe to. Christianity has a tradition of splitting (schism) so that there is a huge variety of religious positions that can broadly be described as Christian. Schism can be related to fundamentalism and rejection of the worldliness of state religions. Sometimes these groups can be very hostile to each other: for example, the Roman Catholics and Protestants in Northern Ireland. Islam has two major groupings (Shia and Sunni), which have differences of practice and have also subdivided into smaller groupings known as sects. These can also sometimes be intolerant of each other's belief and practice.

Because the analysis of the religious groupings has taken place within a Christian academic tradition, the terms used are specifically Christian, but the analysis nevertheless applies to all religious groupings. Selfe and Starbuck also point out that this work has been criticised on the basis that, although people have tried to create typologies (or defining lists) of religious groupings, it is actually quite difficult to assign certain religious groups to each of the definitions on offer.

ACTIVITY KS **COMMUNICATION**

KNOWLEDGE AND UNDERSTANDING	IDENTIFICATION AND INTERPRETATION	ANALYSIS AND EVALUATION

Choose a major world religion that has groupings within it, such as Sunni and Shia or Catholic and Protestant. Attempt some basic research into the following historical elements:

- What are the differences in belief that caused the two groups to split?

- What were the political dimensions of the split at the time that it occurred?

- Was the split between the two groupings peaceful and tolerant or was it accompanied by war, bloodshed and violence?

- What have you learned about the significance of belief in people's lives?

A historian might be a good source of information, but explain that you need only a fairly simple overview as some of these arguments, which led to what is known as 'religious schism' or religious division, are fairly abstract and difficult unless you understand a lot about the religion.

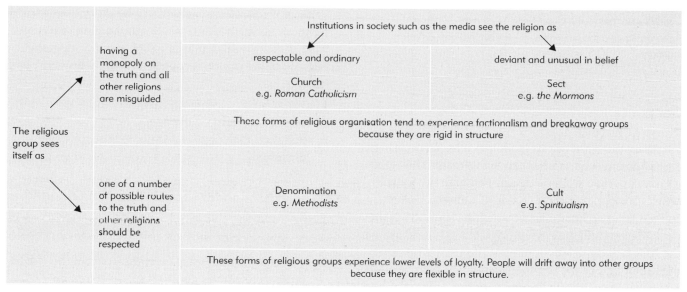

Figure 9.8   A typology of religious organisations based on the work of Roy Wallis (1976). Adapted from Bruce (1995)

Ecclesia

An **ecclesia** is an official or national religion. Many states have a religion, which is identified with the needs and ethics of the state. Eire is so identified with Roman Catholicism that abortion and divorce are not allowed by the state. The Catholic Church bans them, so non-Catholics in Eire are also prohibited from these practices. Islam in Saudi Arabia is an ecclesia and so non-Moslems are prohibited from drinking alcohol.

> **HINTS AND TIPS**   The term **ecclesia** is used by Max Weber. It originated in historical discussion of the role of state and religion, before the growth of secularisation, during the Middle Ages, when people had no choice as to their religious affiliation.

Church

A **church** is a broader term, referring not only to the buildings in which people worship but also to a moral community that unites all believers. It is similar in idea to an ecclesia, and often the two terms are used indiscriminately. A church, however, may not be as fully linked to the state as an ecclesia. Yinger (1970) suggests that people may be united by a church, but can reject an ecclesia because of the role of the state in its formation.

Denomination

This is a smaller group than a church and tends to be limited to a particular group of people within society. Yinger suggests that denominations become involved in secular society and may even comment on political events. Yinger claims that they are more tolerant of other religious groupings and some become involved in the **ecumenical** movement, which is an attempt to join religious groupings in shared worship. The ecumenical movement is stronger in the USA than in Britain, possibly because the USA has no official state church and is a denominational society.

A number of features make a **denomination** smaller than a church, and these are related to the point that a denomination is usually seen as a subset of a larger church movement. One of the most studied denominations is Methodism, which broke away from the Church of England in the eighteenth century. According to analysts, denominations tend to have less bureaucracy and are not as formal. They frequently dispense with the ritualism of the church but replace it with a powerful and personal sense of God and community which is related to fundamental belief. Various Christian denominations require people to choose baptism as adults, for instance, although the Church of England baptises babies. The argument among the denominations is that babies cannot make binding promises of personal faith, whereas adults can.

HINTS AND TIPS   You should refer back to the study of non-conformity and the work of Gwyn Williams to support this debate.

Sects

These are smaller religious groupings than denominations and often are seen as less than mainstream. They tend to attract people who are dissatisfied with the formal religious groupings of their culture and who prefer to be in smaller communities of worship. They attract the deep thinkers and the devout. Typical sects could include the Amish and the Mennonites of the USA, who reject the technology of the twentieth century as being worldly and evil and who therefore live very simple lives.

*HINTS AND TIPS   You may find watching the film **Witness**, which stars Harrison Ford and Kelly McGillis, of particular interest, as it is a thriller set among the Amish community of North America.*

A C T I V I T Y   **KS PROBLEM SOLVING**

IDENTIFICATION AND INTERPRETATION	ANALYSIS AND EVALUATION

Sects are often very small groupings and are of considerable interest to sociologists. What difficulties might you experience if you were to attempt a sociological study of a sect?

Cults, sects and new religious movements

HINTS AND TIPS   This is a complex area of sociology and many writers attempt to create analytical structures. This is virtually impossible because of the variety of belief and complexity of behaviour of sect, cult and new religious movements. You might need to read this section more than once to understand the debate.

Sociologists sometimes use '**cult**' and '**sect**' interchangeably, because few religious organisations fit neatly into one of these categories. Look at the defining features of a cult described by Hassan (1988) (below). You will note that his definition of a cult is very much at variance with Figure 9.8, which is drawn from the

work of Wallis. Hassan appears to be describing what we more normally think of as a cult religion, but this is what Wallis would define as a sect. Hassan suggests that cult belief can be recognised by the following eight features:

1   There is no possible alternative point of view to the one put forward by the cult.
2   Religious faith is put into simple terms: usually a **dichotomy**, or two-part split, often between good and evil.
3   Members of a cult are the chosen. They have an élite mentality.
4   The personal must take second place to the needs of the cult.
5   The cult member must meet the goals of the cult in order to retain the goodwill of the community.
6   The cult member can be manipulated through insecurities. There is constant fear of temptation and a failure to be good enough.
7   The cult member lives in the present and in his or her life as member of the cult. The future is a time of reward and the past was a time of negativity and lack of enlightenment.
8   The cult will not allow a person to leave, stressing the terrible things that will result.

HINTS AND TIPS   Many sects and cults have extreme beliefs and some are led by a single charismatic leader. There has been a history of group suicide among sect members (you may have heard of David Koresh and the Branch Davidians). A more recent newsworthy grouping was the Heaven's Gate sect of California, members of which believed that they would be taken to Heaven by spaceships hidden by the Hale Bopp comet. You are strongly advised to research these types of groups through collections of press cuttings or on CD-ROM in a public library rather than to attempt direct contact.

Three varieties of cults can be identified.

■   **World-affirming cults** may be loosely structured and non-authoritarian. Quakerism follows this pattern as there is no set religious ritual and individuals may believe and worship as they please within a general shared ideology of peace, friendship and tolerance.

■   **World-rejecting cults** fit the popular stereotype of a cult, and are probably more properly described as sects. More generally these cults are total institutions, controlling all aspects of their members' lives. They are often accused of 'brainwashing' and may use psychological techniques of isolation and reward on followers. Examples are the Children of God or the Branch Davidians.

- **World-accommodating cults** seem to be able to follow a middle ground between rejection of the secular world and the affirming position. These seem to survive well and are relatively stable. Spiritualism and Scientology are examples.

There has been a tradition of the development of **new religious movements** and cults throughout western history.

- Some cults are mild variants of traditional religions. Some of the cults of the Middle Ages fitted this pattern.
- Cults such as Rastafarianism can be wildly unusual and offer a radical break from all previous belief.
- Other cults, such as the Shakers, refer back to the 'purer' beliefs and practices of the past.

Many new religious movements and cults are **millenarian**. This means that they believe that the end of the world is close. In 1999, many Americans preparing for **the Rapture** which, they believe, were will absorb them into the body of Christ in the almost immediate future. Christianity itself began as a millenarian religion as its earliest followers believed that they would see the Second Coming of Christ within their own lifetimes. The Book of Revelations in the Bible, which prophesies the end of the world, should be seen in this light.

HINTS AND TIPS   The word 'mille' is Latin for 'one thousand'. Many early Christians believed that the world would come to an end one thousand years after the birth of Christ. Any belief structure that suggests that the end of the world is coming soon is therefore described as millenarian. Be careful not to confuse **millenarian** with **millennium**.

Note that the millennium is a Christian concept. Other religions follow other calendars and do not attach the same significance to dates and to mathematics as Christianity, which draws this element of its belief from Jewish Cabalism. Cabalism and early Christian neo-Platonism held that God is to be found in the analysis of number and pattern, hence the significance of the millennium and of other sacred or superstitious numbers such as 666 or 13 to some Christians.

Peter Worsley, in the readable *The Trumpet Shall Sound* (1970), discussed the origin of cargo cults in the Pacific. Cargo cults developed when people from tribal cultures met western people for the first time and attempted to understand what they were seeing. Westerners had access to all forms of technology and machinery, but the native peoples often lived in primitive agricultural conditions. In New Guinea the tension resolved itself in religious ideas that suggested that westerners were ancestors and gods. They would return with cargo for all. This is echoed in the Ghost Dance cult of the native Americans of the nineteenth century, who, when faced with the slaughter of the buffalo upon which their lives depended, resorted to a millenarian cult which prophesied the end of the world. See *Bury My Heart at Wounded Knee* by Dee Brown (1975).

Jean Ritchie suggested that many modern western cults and sects treat women particularly badly. She cites Krishna cults, the Children of God and the Central London Church of Christ in particular as being guilty of treating female converts as less worthy than males. The Mormons, for instance, believe that a woman cannot go to heaven on her own merits, but is called by her husband. Ritchie claims that the most common cult recruit is a white, middle-class man who is looking for a spiritual dimension to his life. She does, however, note that a number of cults – such as the Spiritualists and the Christian Scientists – have actually been initiated by women. **Eileen Barker**, who points out that cult membership is often disproportionately from the middle or upper classes, echoes this view. Often the members have better than average education although there are exceptions, such as the Rastafarians, who attracted dispossessed black youths. Incidentally, Christianity began among the poor and dispossessed of the Roman Empire, and for a long time was a slave cult.

Bainbridge and Stark identify three types of cult:

- **audience cults**, where there is little contact between members. People may have mild belief in UFOs or astrology
- **client cults**, where there is a service to followers such as relaxation or something more specific
- **cult movements**, where the cult is all things to the member

To the non-believer, cults have extraordinary beliefs, but they exert significant power over the lives of members. Cult beliefs often echo the concerns of the time: in the nineteenth century revelations from angels or the dead were common. In the twentieth century, there was a strong tendency for beliefs to involve aliens and space creatures. There was also a movement towards the adoption and adaptation of beliefs from non-western religious movements. As a final point, it should be noted that the world religions are generally descendants of cults and sects. The ideas of Bainbridge and Stark (1979) are particularly interesting because they suggest that there are three models of the formation of new religious movements.

■ **Psychopathology model** People tend to follow someone who is mentally or emotionally unstable and who makes grand claims originating from delusions. These people will claim divine inspiration and that they hear directly from God. The cynical non-believer could look at the claims of the origins of the Book of Mormon and the Jehovah's Witnesses in such a light.

■ **Entrepreneur model** People aim to make money from their religiosity. For example, Gurdjeiff in the 1930s was open about his career as a con man before targeting the wealthy. Other cult leaders have become extremely rich from their work; for instance Jim Bakker, a televangelist in the USA, was jailed for fraudulently spending donations despite the fact that he was already a millionaire.

■ **Evolution model** Groups of people with a similar view of the world come together to develop a religious movement that is at odds with or different from already existing practice.

ACTIVITY KS WORKING WITH OTHERS

ANALYSIS AND EVALUATION

Suggest why you think that people might find cult membership attractive. Look at one particular cult such as Jehovah's Witnesses, Seventh-Day Adventists or Mormonism if you wish. This could form the basis of a class discussion.

HINTS AND TIPS   *There is disagreement among various sociologists about the definition of cult and sect. Some of Wallis's cults would seem to be more like New Age religions for instance, so you might wish to consider Figure 9.8 as a working rule of thumb rather than a hard and fast guide to the possible forms that religions can take.*

	Church	Denomination	Sect	Cult
Structure	Large hierarchical religious organisation	Large formal religious organisation	Small voluntary group	Small group
Organisation	Based on priesthood and rituals	Based on priesthood and **lay** (or non-official) members	Charismatic leadership and authority	Charismatic leadership
Relationship with secular society	Generally recognises state and accepts norms and values of society	Usually recognises value of state and shares most norms and values	Critical of mainstream society	Often reclusive and withdrawn from society with differing prevailing norms and values
Relationship with members	Little formal commitment required from members	Stronger commitment of members following rules such as teetotalism or non-gambling	Exceptional commitment of members	Flexible commitment, but exceptional while in place
New members	Children join at birth	Adults join, but children inducted early	Members converted, though some second-generation membership. Members can be expelled	Membership is flexible and movement between cults can take place. Expulsion possible
Time scale	Often developed over centuries	Often more than a hundred years of development	Can continue beyond death of leader, but generally have a discernible life span. May evolve to denomination status	Often short-lived and die with the leader

Figure 9.9 Typology of religious organisations

Eileen Barker

Eileen Barker will already be familiar to many students, as she has contributed to many A level conferences and she is an active and exciting speaker. She is one of the leading figures in the contemporary sociology of religion and the sociology of new religious movements. She is Professor of Sociology with special reference to religion at the London School of Economics.

She was born in Edinburgh, but since the age of 11 has spent most of her life in England. She gained her first degree in Sociology from the LSE in 1970 and gained her doctorate from LSE in 1984 with a thesis later published as *The Making of a Moonie: Brainwashing or Choice?*

She has over 160 publications, including *New Religious Movements: A Practical Introduction.* Her work has been concerned with the role of religion in the modern world, with particular reference to minority religions and cults. She is interested in the variety of forms of religious experience and behaviour. Currently she is working on changes occurring in new religions, religion in eastern Europe and the former Soviet Union, and religious and moral pluralism in Britain.

New Age religions

The '**New Age**' is a term that has come to significance relatively recently, although it first appeared as a concept in the late 1960s and early 1970s. It is a blanket expression that covers all kinds of beliefs and behaviours, which are linked by spiritual concerns and a rejection of scientific and rational logic. Not only is modern thought rejected, but mainstream religious belief and formal worship also tends to be rejected. Typical New Age practices include swimming with dolphins, clairvoyance, a belief in the healing power of crystals and spirituality of various forms. Truth is a relative and personal phenomenon. It is possible to find New Age discussions, particularly debates by believers in Gaia, in many of the religious chatlines on the Internet. These seem to combine mysticism with lack of awareness of, or rejection of, mainstream knowledge and methods of analysis.

HINTS AND TIPS You may be very interested in some of the pagans who advertise themselves on the Web. Use any search engine and ask for 'Druid', 'Celt', 'Pagan', and 'Webring' to find an immense amount of material from various groups. You will find rituals, photographs of members, and other detailed explanations of belief. Note that, although these groups are almost exclusively very high-minded North Americans, they draw on (sometimes very inaccurately) and blur together religious cults and myth of long-dead European religions.

ACTIVITY KS **COMMUNICATION, WORKING WITH OTHERS**

IDENTIFICATION AND INTERPRETATION	ANALYSIS AND EVALUATION

List all the various forms of New Age belief and practices that you can think of as a group. How many people subscribe to them, even half-heartedly, and how many buy products associated with the New Age? Be imaginative and consider a whole variety of cultural expressions such as fashion, leisure, music and interior décor.

New Age belief can be seen in the commercial and business world; some management consultants are said to employ graphologists (handwriting experts) to assess the personal characteristics of candidates. Former England football manager Glenn Hoddle displayed many New Age elements in his control of his team. He claimed devout Christian belief, which offers us a view of a single life with salvation at the end, and yet he was able to combine this with the Hindu doctrine of reincarnation and faith in a spiritual adviser. He finally lost his post in 1999, when he seemed to suggest that disabled people bore the responsibility for their

ACTIVITY KS **COMMUNICATION**

IDENTIFICATION AND INTERPRETATION

Assess the popularity of New Age beliefs and the considerable market that they have by looking in the reference sections of the major bookshop chains. Look at the variety of religious books, the psychology section and the self-help areas for clues as to the nature and volume of the market. You could also look at the list of best selling books in some of the newspapers and identify how many are New Age.

handicaps because of faults in a past life, an enormous heresy. It was, however, pressure from the disabled, and not from Christians, which forced his dismissal.

New Age belief can also be seen in a rejection of the modern world in the eco-warrior movement and with the tepee people of mid-Wales. The New Age does not reject capitalism in any over-reaching fashion but is a lot more about personal salvation and self-expression.

Steven Bruce (1992) points out that there is a 'consumerist ethic' in religious belief, so that people may belong to cults for only a short time before moving to the next stage in their personal journeys. In his view it is this that makes the New Age of less social significance than Methodism in the late eighteenth and early nineteenth centuries, because there is no unity of belief or practice among the New Agers. Paul Heelas (1996) suggests that New Age beliefs offer:

- **Utilitarian individualism**, in which people are concerned with their personal happiness and success in the material world of work. They resort to New Age beliefs to help control their personal destinies. *Feng shui*, for instance, suggests that people can gain power and control of their lives by harnessing the power of their interior furnishings, toilet seats and pot plants.

- **Expressive individualism**, which is more of an expression of dissatisfaction with the self. Our culture is critical of the less-than-perfect and feminists have pointed out that much consumer culture, especially that directed at women, is about becoming 'better', 'thinner', 'more sensual' and closer to perfection. New Age practices offer insights into the self to help with the quest to become a better human being.

HINTS AND TIPS *You are advised to read and revise your notes on postmodernism at this point because the New Age and postmodernism are often linked in examination questions.*

Writers have suggested that the New Age is linked to postmodernism but both Heelas (1996) and Bruce (1995) seem to see it as plugging the gap that secularisation and loss of community have brought to many lives. Bruce points out that many New Agers are professional and educated middle-class people who work in human-based professions and who have a

TASK

Hypothesis – New Age practice and belief is extensive in modern society.

Context – You will have to list a variety of New Age beliefs and practices, and attempt some form of definition of New Age belief before beginning your study. You will also need to work out a narrower context for your study than modern society. If you choose to work to the broadest definition, then a supermarket study would be the best way to get a variety of answers, but the quality of the responses will range from completely irritated to the frankly silly. Talking to strangers about religion will provoke in them the suspicion that you are attempting conversion or could engage you in a philosophical debate about religious belief that was not your intention.

A limited population frame of people in your college or school will be more satisfactory and then you could link the New Age with gender or other social variables to deepen the scope of your study.

Method – Your best method is to ensure that your questions are closed. You are strongly advised to limit possible responses to 'yes', 'no', 'sometimes', or 'don't know'. Ask if people believe in UFOs, astrology, reincarnation, the power of crystals and if animals can cure autism. It may seem strange to use quantitative methods to understand and interpret the nature of belief, but the results will be far easier to process than the rambling narratives that may follow open-ended questions on a topic such as this.

Evaluation – There is a tension between method and theory in this research design which relates to the application of scientific sociology to help you understand how people construct social meanings. This means that you will have a great deal to discuss about the methods that you use. It is easy, when conducting a research project to become so heavily involved in the analysis of results that the purpose of the exercise, which is to test method, is lost. However, this research will yield interesting results although the focus is more naturally on the processes used to gain the results.

training in searching for a higher self or a higher knowledge. These are people who have been trained to be sceptical of authority and who have therefore developed individual philosophies and creeds. Heelas suggests that New Agers are not postmodern because postmodernism is characterised by the short-lived and ephemeral. New Agers are deeply serious and often see their efforts as a return to or retrieval of lost religious wisdom and knowledge.

SOCIOLOGY IN PRACTICE

The barefoot cosmic doc will see you now

He describes himself as a "spiritual yob" and "cosmic lad about town" – and celebrities can't get enough of him. Known as the Barefoot Doctor, 44-year-old Stephen Russell has star followers said to include Madonna, Tom Cruise, Nicole Kidman, Christy Turlington and Robert De Niro and Jamie Catto from Faithless.

I follow the smell of sandalwood joss sticks into his consulting room. He is barefoot (well, that's the gimmick), and wearing a white Ralph Lauren shirt, well-cut khaki trousers, and almost immediately freaks me out by suggesting that I need to go to the toilet (my vibes were giving it away, apparently).

Russell has no formal medical qualifications, but is an associate of the British Acupuncture Association. He uses treatments such as hands-on healing, massage, acupuncture, hypnotherapy, martial arts, music therapy and Taoist philosophy. The diagnosis starts when a patient rings the bell – the BD says he can detect many problems simply by the way callers stand on the step. "I ask a few core questions to determine which organs are doing what, then I take the pulses [in Chinese medicine there are six] and get them on the table".

What causes disease, he says, is energy blocked in the body: "I can unblock it," he says. "In the first part of the session, I break down all the dodgy energy – in other words, I release tension. Then I build it back into a balanced, strong state." Patients also experience his own "wayward Taoist healing" which transmits "energy" from his hands to the patient. Russell says he acts as a conduit for spiritual forces, focusing energy over points in the body believed to link up to internal organs.

He claims his healing hands have cured advanced cervical cancer, hepatitis C and psoriasis – and boosted one woman's bra size. And he has unshakeable faith in his abilities, plus the charisma to convince others.

Russell had his first spiritual experience at the age of four. "Suddenly, the whole universe was filled with this incredible sound of 'om'. I knew it was the Tao, or great spirit, talking."

Convinced that a nuclear bomb would wipe out Britain, he scoured the USA looking for a Hopi Indian chief, who he hoped would offer salvation. After four years, he found one: "He said, 'There won't be a war. Our prayers will stop it. You need to go away and heal yourself. Then you can heal other people.'"

So he studied Chinese medicine in the US for three years, returned to London, and set himself up as an acupuncturist. Twelve years ago, he adopted the Barefoot Doctor sobriquet, which refers to his disaffection with footwear and also to the "barefoot doctors" who travel around China.

His clients come from a broad spectrum: "On one extreme, there are multi-zillonaires. On the other, care in the community sort of characters. I don't even let them take their shoes off, because it would make too much smell."

The doc doesn't have set fees. In return for a half-hour session, he might get £40, a scented candle, or a trip to the other side of the world to help a client relax before a party or premiere. Stars are told their wealth and privileges are spiritually enriching. "Fame and fortune is just a great opportunity for networking yourself around, spreading your love, and connecting with the spirit."

Many would see fame and fortune as incompatible with spiritual fulfilment, but the doctor thinks otherwise: "Once you've dedicated yourself to a spiritual path, you can choose it any way you want. You can renounce all comforts and get your lessons by sitting and being with yourself inwardly. But, generally, people are attracted by the glitz of the material world. If you follow that path, you'll get just as many lessons."

Russell is so convinced about the benefits of his approach, and of attaining fame and fortune, that he has written a book, The Barefoot Doctor's Handbook For Heroes, on how to become a superstar. My favourite tip for general spiritual welfare is "chanting 'om' to yourself (quietly) while standing in line at the cashpoint".

In three months, Russell claims, the book will bring you fame and fortune: "It could be fame within your workplace, or within your industry. And you will increase the amount of money you have coming in."

And if it doesn't work? Read page five: "This handbook is a complete con and the author an out-and-out con man." It's a joke. But you have been warned.

Source: Catherine Bassindale (4 May 1999:16) *The Guardian*

1 Identify three beliefs that the 'barefoot doc' expresses which are typical of New
   Age belief.   **(3)**

   | KNOWLEDGE AND |
   | UNDERSTANDING |

2 What elements of the barefoot doctor's character, as described in the article,
   suggest that he would make an attractive cult leader?   **(2)**

   | KNOWLEDGE AND | IDENTIFICATION AND |
   | UNDERSTANDING | INTERPRETATION |

3 Can the New Age be better described as a cult or a sect?   **(4)**

   | KNOWLEDGE AND | IDENTIFICATION AND |
   | UNDERSTANDING | INTERPRETATION |

4 What evidence of globalisation can be discovered in this article?   **(6)**

   | IDENTIFICATION AND |
   | INTERPRETATION |

5 Using the article, suggest why wealthy and educated people would be attracted
   to this type of belief in particular.   **(6)**

   | IDENTIFICATION AND |
   | INTERPRETATION |

6   What powers are credited to prayer in the passage?   **(4)**

> IDENTIFICATION AND
> INTERPRETATION

7   Evaluate the suggestion that New Age beliefs do not constitute a religion in any true sense.   **(10)**

> ANALYSIS AND
> EVALUATION

8   Assess the extent to which the current popularity of New Age beliefs provides evidence to support the postmodernist position.   **(10)**

> ANALYSIS AND
> EVALUATION

Secularisation debate

This is an extremely significant debate in sociology and is the subject of public discussion on a regular basis. Many commentators deplore the apparent lack of religious faith and church attendance in our society, linking it with a general social and moral decline. There is a commonly held view that people are not as religious as they once were and that the evidence of this is a fall-off in church attendance. To look at this systematically, we need to consider the following problems associated with the sociological analysis of religious belief:

- What is religion?
- How do we measure religious commitment?
- How do we compare religious belief now with that of the past in order to prove or disprove secularisation?
- How do we interpret the social significance of religion in modern society?

To prove secularisation is actually taking place, a commentator needs to prove that religion has less significance now than in the past or that people are less religious in Britain than in other societies. Robertson has pointed out that religion can be seen in two ways:

HINTS AND TIPS   *You are advised to look for media articles about the decline in spiritual values and church attendance around the major Christian religious festivals such as Christmas and Easter. Experts are frequently asked to comment about the 'real' meaning of Christmas or Easter. The most cynical view is that these articles are traditional stand-bys to fill column inches, but there is little doubt of the sincerity of the writers and you will learn much about traditional Christian ideology from reading this type of work. You may also discover some useful statistical analysis and research evidence in the discussions produced by the more serious newspapers.*

1   it is an activity, such as going to church
2   it is a set of cultural attitudes

If religious belief is defined solely in terms of church attendance, then it has suffered a significant decline in Britain. But attendance at church is not necessarily a good signifier of spirituality. There are those who have no particular belief, but who value their church for practical or social reasons, as a form of social club. Many parents will attend Church of England services in order to secure places at church schools, which may have more social and educational standing than the local comprehensives.

The evidence that people were more religious in the past is limited. Certainly people at various stages were more informed about religion, but the only reading matter available to most people was the Bible. Engels,

writing in the 1840s, is noted for pointing out that
working-class people lacked interest in religion.
Regular attendance at church was not particularly high,
despite the fact that people would have been expected
to attend church for social reasons and that much social
life centred on the church. Victorian writers such as
Dickens, George Eliot and Samuel Butler were not
above poking gentle fun at the hypocrisy of those who
were important in the church but who were morally
unpleasant and intolerant in their private lives. Bruce
(1992) points out that in many areas during the
Industrial Revolution religion was the property of the
wealthy and the landowners. There was a falling away
from, and even a positive rejection of, state churches
among the industrial working class. This view supports
the analysis made by Gwyn Alf Williams of the social
significance of non-conformity in Wales, which was
discussed earlier in this area. People became able to
choose the religious ideologies that appealed to their
perspectives. This impacted on the significance of the
state religions in society, because religious observance
became fragmented.

> When a society is divided into competing religions, the
> democratic state cannot support any one of them. The
> Church of England may retain the odd bit of
> flummery but it can no longer rely on the state to
> punish those who prefer to avoid its offices.

(Bruce, 1992:12)

As a point of evaluation, you should note that many
writers probably over-estimate the significance of the
church in the past. Those writing from a traditional
Christian or New Right perspective could possibly even
be accused of having a vested interest in proving a
decline in religious practice.

Study of modern society seems to both support and
reject the secularisation thesis. So what is the position
of religious faith in contemporary western society?

- Most people seem willing to profess belief in a god,
  but not all pray regularly

- Very few people attend a church or a service on a
  regular basis, but this may reflect a decline in the
  faith in institutions rather than in religion (Bruce,
  1995).

- Christians and members of other faiths can be a
  powerful political lobby. Consider the case of
  Victoria Gillick, who took a strongly Christian moral

line over the teaching of sex in schools and forced
the government into a position where children
could be withdrawn from sex education lessons,
even up to the age of 18.

- There has been a general decline in the number of
  clergy. However, they are often better trained and
  educated than they once were. The church is no
  longer an escape route for the younger sons of rich
  families, who would take pay but fail to minister to
  people.

- Many chapels and churches have closed through
  lack of congregations. However, the number of
  people who watch or listen to broadcast services or
  the media or who buy religious magazines and
  papers has grown.

- Women tend to attend church more frequently than
  do men.

- In the USA there has been a growth in new religious
  movements, although many have also died away.

- Certain denominations have been more affected by
  falling numbers than others.

- Most observers note that few people have any
  general knowledge about the Bible.

- Sunday was once a day that was theoretically devoted to religion. In the Celtic fringes of Scotland and Wales, it was even difficult to buy alcohol in the past, but Sunday is now more usually devoted to leisure and shopping.

ACTIVITY KS **WORKING WITH OTHERS, COMMUNICATION**

IDENTIFICATION AND INTERPRETATION	ANALYSIS AND EVALUATION

Find the most knowledgeable about religious matters among you and devise a religious knowledge test for as many people as are willing to answer the questions. Assuming that your test is devised by an RE teacher or student, it will probably reveal significant lack of awareness of even the most basic tenets of religious knowledge. Are regular church attendees more knowledgeable than non-believers? What light does this exercise throw on the value of the compulsory hour of RE in all schools?

Arguments for the secularisation thesis	Arguments against the secularisation thesis
Geographical mobility means that people no longer centre their social lives around church, chapel and community as they once did	Religion is not less significant Traditional churches have lost their hold on populations
In the past, it was necessary to go to church to be married, baptised or buried. The state has taken over these roles	These ceremonies are still carried out in churches. They are seen as desirable and many people will even attend church on an occasional basis
People do not go to church and therefore they do not pass the habit on to their children. The process becomes self-continuing	There can be strong outpourings of religious emotion at times of public emergency – and millions watched the funeral of Diana, Princess of Wales
People are more exposed to different religions as we are in a multi-cultural society and see that there are alternative beliefs	The state and the church are still very strongly linked so that collective worship is compulsory in schools. It often has a Christian flavour

Figure 9.10 Overview of secularisation

Writers that you may need to consider in any debate on secularisation:

- **Will Herberg** (1956), as an American takes a functional view of religion and considers it from the perspective of purpose. His view is that religious practice is an expression of community belief and practice as opposed to individualism.

- **Robert Bellah** (1965) suggested that religion is a personal and spiritual activity.

- **Bryan Wilson** (1966) takes the view that religion is giving way to scientific thought so that religious practice is declining in western societies. This position is very much in the tradition of Durkheim and Comte.

- **Bryan Turner** (1983) suggested that secularisation has come about because the nature of capitalism has changed. It is no longer in the hands of individuals, but belongs to corporations. This has led to changes in the way in which the wealthy can dominate society and ideology. As a result, religion is less significant as a moral and social power than it once was. This is clearly a neo-Marxist position.

- **Peter Brierly** (1991) argues for the increasing and incremental loss of religious practice but also suggests that religious belief is not changing markedly.

- **David Martin** (1990) regards the debate as being based on a number of untestable suppositions about the past. The term secularisation is difficult to define and he is extremely critical of it, because he feels it belongs to the strand of sociology that claims that religion is dying out. Martin considers that the role of religion has changed in society and that, whereas once it was institutional, now it is a private concern.

- **Ernest Gellner** (1992) takes the view that the failure of Islam to secularise is related to its rejection of western perceptions.

- **Steve Bruce** (1995) provides evidence to suggest that the decline of religious practice is not universal, but that there is a strong cultural element to it. This is covered in the next section.

Multi-culturalism and faith

HINTS AND TIPS *A detailed discussion of this topic is to be found in Bruce (1995).*

This particular topic is a significant part of the secularisation debate because it is suggested that although the Church of England and the state are combined and closely linked they are no longer the same thing. Prince Charles, as heir to the throne and presumed inheritor of the title Defender of the Faith, and as Head of the Church of England, cannot marry a Roman Catholic. It could be argued that few people beyond those in the Church would really care if he did or not. The claim is that nowadays the Church of England is actually a denomination because it has lost its pre-eminence. Britain has been home to a variety of faiths and ethnicity throughout history, each of which has left a legacy to our culture. It is therefore necessary to look at some of the many faiths in modern Britain and to consider their political and social importance.

The Jewish community

Jews have been present in Britain since the Middle Ages and the evidence for their social significance is the unhappy fact of occasional massacres and popular uprisings. The Jews of York suffered a famously brutal attack and siege in the eleventh century. In the present day, Jews may be united by religion but they are an ethnically diverse community originating in a variety of European nations and having arrived at different stages in history. Judaism perceives itself as not just a religion but also an ethnicity. A person can be Jewish but refuse to follow the tenets of the faith. There is also a variety of traditions, with degrees of practice varying between extreme orthodoxy and liberalism. Jewish populations survive in many of the major cities: Manchester, Cardiff, and Glasgow support large communities. Most live in London. There has been a decline in the strength of the community due to emigration to Israel and some marriage out of the faith. For Jews, a person is Jewish only if his or her mother was Jewish.

The Islamic community

This has many of the characteristics of the Jewish community, and the religions are very similar in many of their practices despite some degree of mutual intolerance. The various Islamic groups are ethnically and culturally very diverse and traditions vary between cultural communities. Most Moslems are found in the major industrial centres around London, Birmingham, and the north of England. There is a large population of middle-class professional Moslems who generally derive from Kenyan Asian groups and from India. Most Moslems in Britain were born here. The various Moslem groups appear to be more tolerant of each other's faiths than do Christians. However, Moslems tend to guard their religious traditions with some care; this is possibly related to their position as immigrants who have experienced racism (Bruce, 1995). It should be noted that there have been western converts to Islam, most notably a pop star of the 1960s, Cat Stevens, who is now an imam (Moslem priest).

West Indian Pentecostalists

These communities derive from the immigration from the West Indies, which began in 1948. They are found around ports such as Bristol and in London. These people tend to have a significantly higher rate of church attendance than do the general population. Many experienced considerable racism and intolerance in the formal church services of the 1950s so they formed their own communities with extremely strict rules of conduct and morality. Services may enable members of the congregation to experience ecstatic states induced by music and dancing. West Indian Pentecostalists are popular on religious programmes such as *Songs of Praise*, probably because of their exciting tradition of gospel singing.

Hinduism

This derives from the Indian subcontinent although many of the British Hindu population arrived after being expelled from Africa in the 1960s. Hinduism is a pantheistic religion with a variety of gods and beliefs. There is a strong element of spiritual and philosophical tradition and this has attracted many western converts. There is a variety of ethnicities and language groups among Hindu populations. Temples are now being built in many cities where Hindus live.

Sikhs

Sikhism originated in the Punjab, and developed from Hinduism. It is less tolerant of the caste system and is monotheistic, however. Sikhs have settled in London and most other metropolitan centres. Sikhism stresses the significance of community tradition and belief and is tolerated in Britain to the extent that representatives are asked to speak on BBC Radio 4's *Thought for the Day* (at about 7.50 each morning). Sikhs may occasionally be hostile to, or feel threatened in a political sense by, the Hindus, and this is related to political pressure for a separate homeland. The Punjab is a spectacularly beautiful area in the northern part of Pakistan, with access to plentiful water. The Sikhs and India all lay claim to this region.

A number of other issues should be noted with regard to non-Christian religions:

- The religious communities described are not protected in Britain by laws against sacrilege or offence against their religion, as Christianity is.

- While church attendance has been declining in Britain, there has been little evidence that the minority religions have experienced similar significant loss of congregation, with the exception of the Jewish community.

- Many run their own schools or offer supplementary schooling to children from the community.

- For many of these people, religion is more than a matter of belief because their faith is inextricably bound up with their culture and identity.

- For some groups, the faith has been a support against the racism of the host community.

- Anecdotally, some of these religious groupings are more traditional in Britain than in the countries of origin where there is less of a threat from loss of faith among the children.

Religion as stratification

There is debate as to the extent to which religion originates in poverty and deprivation or represents social class interests. It will take very little imagination to realise that this is a debate that is drawn from and tests Marxism. You should draw your examples and sociological theories from the previous discussions in this area; however, Figure 9.10 will support your understanding.

Religion represents the poor and disaffected?	Religion is a tool of oppression?
In the USA, black evangelical religious leaders tend to be liberal and to support social equality movements	In the USA, white evangelical religious groups tend to support the Right and forces for tradition
Cults such as Rastafari originated among the poor and disaffected black peoples of Jamaica and have become demonised by the media for their beliefs and their behaviour (Barker)	Catholicism in particular, but Christianity in general, has been used in many countries in the past to justify oppression against minority groups such as the Jews
There is a tradition in South American countries in particular of the radical priest, who represents the interests of the poor and oppressed. This movement is known as liberation theology	Often these priests have had problems with their church authorities. Cases documented include that of Bolo Hidalgo (Torres 1973)
In the 1980s, the Church of England criticised the government for allowing poverty	Many writers have suggested that the church should not involve itself in the politics of daily life
The Ghost Dance and cargo cults arose in communities that were disrupted and even at the point of being killed by the arrival of western Europeans among peoples who had been defeated (Fallding)	The religion, morality and values of the ruling classes and the conquerors may sometimes be imposed on the vanquished and defeated. In other cases the defeated will convert to the conqueror's religion in order to gain social prestige (O'Dea and O'Dea Aviad 1997)
Lower-class Afro-Caribbeans tend to support pentecostal and evangelical groups of extreme faith (Pearson)	Upper-class Caribbean blacks will tend to belong to more mainstream churches (Pearson)
Christianity represents the interests of the poor and the Bible is critical of the wealthy	It was these creeds that the wealthy have been able to use to keep the poor and the enslaved in their place (Marxism)
Many cults have originated among the poorest people in society	Many of the people who become cult and sect members are from wealthy or educated backgrounds (Barker)

Figure 9.11   Religion as stratification

Area summary

By now you should have appreciated just how important the study of religion is to the development and understanding of sociology. It marks the first realisation that culture and belief are what make humans as they are and underlines the point that whatever the nature of your faith, your behaviour is determined by your ideology. You will note that structuralists such as Marx and Durkheim share many ideas but that their understandings of the purpose of religious practice for society are different. They see religion as unifying, whereas Weber sees it as a potent force for social change triggered by both single charismatic individuals and the power of ideas. Religious belief can be liberating both personally and emotionally, offering individuals such support that Bainbridge and Stark believe it will always remain at the core of society. However, in the most contradictory of ways, religion can also be a power for great social evil, repression and oppression because it can be used to validate cruelty and violence against others.

The forms that religious belief can take are extraordinarily diverse. In some cases the state and the church are linked in such a way that they cannot be separated. Many other religious groupings are informal in the extreme and perhaps even barely recognisable as such, even to the practitioners. It becomes difficult to define religion at all, given that elements of magic and superstition can also be involved in religious belief. There can be fluidity in practice so that people will revert to churches in times of crisis and great joy but ignore their existence at all other times. The ritual of formalised religion lies at the core of our culture and so many of the key events in our lives are marked by religious observance: birth, marriage and death.

There has been a break with the uniform religious belief and practices of the past so that people are now free to seek their beliefs where they will. This raises serious questions for the sociologist about the attractions of cults and new religious movements, some of which may seem extremely bizarre to the non-believer but hold such a power and fascination for believers that they will willingly take their own lives and the lives of others.

Finally, it is important to understand that Britain is a multi-faith society and that diversity of culture and tradition is very significant. Do these changes mean that religion is dying away in our society? Are we merely changing the nature and patterns of our faith by seeking something that is more appropriate to our personal and social needs at the start of a new Christian millennium?

Definitions

Anomie	A sense of not belonging to or understanding the rules of society. The term was coined by Durkheim
Belief systems	This is a way of referring to a set of religious or political beliefs or ideas

Cargo cults	Tribal societies in remote areas respond to their first contact with western culture with the belief that their ancestors or gods will return bearing cargo or gifts. This becomes a new religious movement in the form of a cargo cult
Caste	A closed form of rigid social stratification based on birth, status and occupation, found in India before 1949 and in other societies
Charisma	The power of a personality to affect others, typical of certain religious leaders
Church	A structured belief system that has become part of the machinery of the state
Consensual	This refers to agreement and to shared values
Cult	A small religious grouping of looser structure than a sect
Cultural defence	The need for a society to protect itself from unwelcome change
Denomination	A religious group that is large, formalised and yet not truly part of the state
Dharma	In Hinduism, the belief that if you are good person, then you will be reincarnated to a higher caste in a future life
Dichotomy	This is a Marxist term and refers to a way of viewing society in terms of opposites or two diametrically opposing parts
Disestablishment	The separation of church and state
Ecclesia	A form of religious organisation described by Weber where church and state seem virtually indivisible
Ecumenical	The movement which attempts to unite differing forms of religious belief
Fundamentalism	The desire to return to a 'purer' form of belief and religious practice
Ideology	A belief system
Karma	In Hinduism, the belief that your present caste position is a reward or a punishment for virtue or sin in a previous existence
Lay	Not of the church
Legitimacy	The way that a belief or idea can give power to ideas to make them correct
Legitimisation	This is the idea that religion makes the orders and laws which come from other people in society seem as though they come from a higher authority, which gives those rules a sense of being highly significant
Liberation theology	This is a blend of Marxism and religion and it suggests that people can be freed from domination and exploitation. It tends to side with the poor against the powerful and is typical of South America
Liturgy	The words of a religious service
Magic	The attempt to influence events via supernatural agencies
March of progress	A similar term to modernism it is the belief that society is always improving thanks to advances in technology and science
Millenarianism	The belief that the world is coming to an end in the near future

Modernism	This is the belief that society is improving and that there are ideals such as freedom and justice which we should all seek
New Age	A rejection of traditional science and an attempt to understand the nature of personal spirituality by harnessing the knowledge and beliefs of different and older cultures
New religious movements	Cults and sects which have developed recently
Patriarchy	A description of a society ruled and dominated to serve the needs of men
Postmodernism	The suggestion that society is fragmenting and that people no longer believe in absolutes because everything is relative
Pre-ordination	The belief that your life is mapped out for you before your birth
Profane	To do with the daily, non-sacred life
The Rapture	A belief common among some fundamental Christians that they will be taken to heaven in bodily form at the Apocalypse where they will experience the joy of being united with Jesus
Religion	A belief system
Revivalist	This refers to a form of religion which is fundamental in form and encourages people in the belief that they are returning to the religious rules of an earlier and 'purer' time
Sacred	To do with religion and the worship of god/s
Sacred canopy	Activities have meaning because they are part of religious obligation
Sect	A small religious grouping of fierce belief which separates itself from the aims and values of mainstream society
Secularisation	The process of a society becoming less religious
Superstition	Illogical belief that presupposes cause and effect between an act and its aftermath

Data response questions

Item A

Some people have had difficulty in obtaining reliable information about the beliefs and practices of an unfamiliar religious or spiritual group that a relative or a friend has joined.

Politicians and clergy have been besieged with requests to do something about some of the groups which give particular cause for concern, but have often found difficulty in knowing what it was that they were meant to be doing something about, or how to set about getting information.

Leaflet from **Inform**

Item B

Evara (an elderly man) prophesied the coming of a steamer, carrying the spirits of dead ancestors on board, who would bring with them the 'Cargo'. In the initial stages, rifles were included among the expected goods ... Later teachings stated that the Cargo was to be allotted to villages by the signs of identity on the crates. The spirits had revealed that all the flour, rice, tobacco and other 'trade' belonged to the Papuans, not the Whites. The latter would be driven away, and the Cargo would pass into the hands of its rightful owners, the natives. To obtain these goods it was necessary to drive out the Whites.

Worsley, P. (1970:91) **The Trumpet Shall Sound**. London, Paladin.

Item C

In the Netherlands and Italy the parties of the left and (a minority) of religious groups opposed the installation of nuclear missiles and local government bodies and official agencies lent their support to the protest in a variety of ways ... religious groups introduced a series of intensely emotive forms of action ...

Della Porta, D. and Diani, M. (1999:188)
Social Movements: An Introduction. Oxford, Blackwell.

1   What is a Cargo cult (Item B)?   (1)

> KNOWLEDGE AND
> UNDERSTANDING

2   *Inform* (Item A) is a charity dealing with new religious movements.
What is a new religious movement?   (1)

> KNOWLEDGE AND
> UNDERSTANDING

3 Identify two characteristics of a new religious movement. **(4)**

> KNOWLEDGE AND
> UNDERSTANDING

4 Using the items and other knowledge, suggest reasons why authorities can
sometimes fear the activities of new religious movements. **(6)**

> IDENTIFICATION AND
> INTERPRETATION

5 To what extent can it be argued that religion is a source of social change? **(9)**

> ANALYSIS AND
> EVALUATION

6 Evaluate the suggestion that cults are a danger to the cohesion of society. **(9)**

> ANALYSIS AND
> EVALUATION

Structured questions

1 How might a sociologist identify a belief as an example of New Age
practice in Britain today? **(2)**

> **GUIDANCE** The two marks available should suggest to you that two separate
> elements of New Age practice are required. A number of elements should suggest
> themselves to you and this might be a good classroom exercise, to brainstorm and then to develop a
> typology of New Age beliefs.
>
> KNOWLEDGE AND
> UNDERSTANDING

2 Identify two variant forms of New Age practice. **(4)**

> **GUIDANCE** At first glance, this is the same question as the one above, but if you
> look carefully, question 1 was asking about characteristics of New Age belief, and
> this question asks you about what people do. In this case, you could point out that they 'mix and
> match' religious beliefs, or that they absorb elements of other cultural traditions into their behaviours or
> that they do not identify themselves with formalised groupings. As there are four marks available, note
> that you should identify a form of practice and then develop the answer with an example so that 'mix
> and matchers' may try and reconcile Christianity with Buddhism.
>
> KNOWLEDGE AND
> UNDERSTANDING

3 Why have some sociologists seen the New Age as typical of postmodern
   thought? **(6)**

> **GUIDANCE**   *For a question such as this a fairly systematic*
> *approach is required. New Age beliefs should be identified in the*
> *very briefest of terms. Postmodernism needs a sentence or two, and then you should identify at least*
> *two reasons why New Age practice is proof of postmodernism. Suggestions include the rejection of old*
> *values and the individualism of postmodernism and New Age thought, the other is the tendency to*
> *create references.*
>
> KNOWLEDGE AND UNDERSTANDING | IDENTIFICATION AND INTERPRETATION

4 To what extent can it be argued that British society has become more
   secularised? **(10)**

> **GUIDANCE**   *This could be a full essay title worth 25 marks and it would be easy to*
> *panic and attempt to write a full answer. However, this would be a mistake, as the*
> *question is not just testing your ability to evaluate but is also testing you in the academic skill of*
> *selection. Can you write a sensible overview, with some reference to theory, in 20 minutes? If not, then*
> *perhaps you could practise this with other questions that appear in the other areas in this book as well*
> *as here. You will need to have your conclusion clearly in mind before you begin your answer. Is British*
> *society secularised? The available answers are 'yes', 'no' and 'maybe'. The choice of conclusion is your*
> *own and the skill of evaluation is your ability to argue for any one of the possible answers. It would be a*
> *useful exercise in evaluation to plan possible answers leading to all three conclusions. However, in a*
> *broad question such as this, the 'maybe' option is by far the safest. Offer evidence for and against*
> *secularisation and refer to actual research evidence. For your conclusion, suggest that although the*
> *nature of religious belief may have changed and the role of the institutions of religion has changed,*
> *there is little evidence to support the view that society is less religious.*
>
> ANALYSIS AND EVALUATION

Essay titles

1 The main purpose of religion is to integrate society. Evaluate the previous
   statement in the light of your sociological knowledge. **(25)**

2 To what extent should we distrust religion and the motives of the religious
   in our society? **(25)**

3 Evaluate the suggestion that a church is merely a sect that has grown up. **(25)**

4 Is the Church of England merely a denomination in modern Britain? **(25)**

KNOWLEDGE AND UNDERSTANDING	IDENTIFICATION AND INTERPRETATION	ANALYSIS AND EVALUATION

GUIDANCE *Because the wording of the question does not emphasise the term 'sociological' it will be tempting to present a rambling and marginally politicised account of the role and power of the Church of England. This is an obvious trap for the unwary and the apparent simplicity of the wording hides a complex sociological analysis. The question is a great deal wider than it first appears and will enable the knowledgeable to draw on a number of strands in the sociology of religion.*

There is little reason for you to know a great deal about the Church of England and its role in the British state though some reference to it is necessary. This is sociology and you are being asked to consider theory and research as applied to a consideration of modern British society. It is necessary to define the term 'church' and then to consider the nature of a 'denomination'. What are their typifying features? How do these two separate forms of organisation differ in their relationship to broader society? You must take a far broader view and look at the role of a state religion in a secularised, multi-faith and postmodern society.

You are also being asked to consider to what extent the state and the church are linked and you will therefore have to consider arguments both for and against the suggestion that the Church of England legitimises the state. You may need to consider the functions of religion from both a Marxist and a Durkheimian perspective.

This is one of those questions which has a genuinely open-ended answer. You can agree, disagree, or compromise in your response to the terms of the question. You must, however, be sure to draw a firm conclusion in whatever line you take and be certain that your overall evaluative conclusion is generally apparent from the first paragraph.

Further reading and references

Bruce, S. (1995) **Religion in Modern Britain**. Oxford, Oxford University Press.
An excellent and well-priced little book for the advanced student or undergraduate.
It is extremely well written and contains a mass of relevant data, particularly relating
to the nature of belief.

Selfe P. and Starbuck, M. (1997) *Religion*. Access to Sociology Series. London,
Hodder & Stoughton.
Another inexpensive little text which is written to a level more appropriate for A
level. It is particularly good on theories of religion and contains many little features,
which will advance your understanding of the topic and supplement the work in this
text.

Lurie, A. (1998) **Imaginary Friends**. New York, Henry Holt.
A fictional account of two sociologists attempting an observation of a New Age
religious cult. It deals with questions of truth and reality – and for the
knowledgeable there are a few excellent jokes at the expense of sociology. It also
raises many issues to do with the problems of interactional methodology. Novel
reading is a highly recommended way of revising without pain.

O'Rourke, P. J. (1988) *Holidays in Hell*. New York, Vintage Books.
Those among you who are completely insensitive might be interested in this
collection of P. J. O'Rourke's journalism. Others are advised to avoid this work as
O'Rourke practises 'gonzo journalism' which is highly calculated writing, deliberately
designed to be totally offensive to everyone irrespective of gender, age and political
perspective. In this book, which to some is extremely funny, there is a politically
incorrect account of a visit to an evangelical Christian holiday camp in the southern
states of the USA, which will provide an observational account of how family
ideology, religion, and social control are linked.

Inform is a charity dealing with and providing information about new religious
movements. It can be contacted at Inform, Houghton Street, London, WC2A 2AE.

Internet sites

You are advised to use the Internet to find out more about cults, new religious
movements and more established religions such as Jehovah's Witnesses or the
Mormons. Many of these groups maintain excellent Websites, although you will also
find sites that are very critical of them. You are advised, as sociologists, to be certain
that you are aware of the dangers of becoming too closely involved with some of
the groups, who will certainly regard a direct personal contact as an invitation to
attempt conversion or at least to mission to you. Do not offer your e-mail address to
these groups and make it clear in all of your correspondence that your interest is
merely academic and that you are not a potential convert.

Bibliography

Althusser, L. (1984) *Essays on Ideology*. London, Verso.

Bainbridge, W. and Stark, R. (1979) *Cult formation: Three Compatible Models. Sociology Analysis*. No. 40.

Barker, E. (1984) *The Making of a Moonie*. Oxford, Blackwell.

Barker, E. (1995) *New Religious Movements: A Practical Introduction*. London, HMSO.

Bellah, R. (1965) *Religious Evolution* in Lessa, W. and Voight, E. *Reader in Comparative Religion: An Anthropological Approach*. New York, Harper Row.

Bellah, R. (1966) *Civil Religion in America*. New York, Daedalus.

Bellah, R. (1970) *Beyond Belief*. New York, Harper Row.

Berger, P. and Luckmann, T. (1967) *The Social Construction of Reality*. New York, Doubleday.

Berger, P. L. (1969) *The Social Reality of Religion*. London, Faber and Faber.

Brierly, P. (1991) *'Christian' England*. London, MARC Europe.

Brown, D. (1975) *Bury my Heart at Wounded Knee*. London, Picador.

Bruce, S. (1995) *Religion in Modern Britain*. Oxford, Oxford University Press.

Bruce, S. (1992) *The Twilight of the Gods: Religion in Modern Britain* in *Social Studies Review*, November 1992.

Bruce, S. (1996) *Religion in the Modern World: From Cathedrals to Cults*. Oxford, Oxford University Press.

Bruce, S. (1999) *Choice and Religion: A Critique of Rational Choice Theory*. Oxford, Oxford University Press.

Davis Kingsley (1949) *Human Society*. New York, Macmillan and Co.

Della Porta, D. and Diani, M. (1999) *Social Movements: An Introduction*. Oxford, Blackwell.

Durkheim, E. (1912) (trans 1961) *The Elementary Forms of Religious Life*. London, Collier Books.

Durkheim, E. by Pickering, W. (1994) *Durkheim on Religion*. Atlanta, Ga, Scholars Press.

Fallding, H. (1974) *The Sociology of Religion: An Explanation of Unity and Diversity in Religion*. London, McGraw Hill.

Fulcher, J. and Scott, J. (1999) *Sociology*. Oxford, Oxford University Press.

Gellner, E. (1992) *Post-modernism, Reason and Religion*. London, Routledge.

Haralambos, M. and Holborn, M. (1995) *Sociology: Themes and Perspectives 4th Ed*. London, Collins Educational.

Hassan, S. (1988) *Combating Cult Mind Control*. Rochester, VT, Park Street Press.

Heelas, P. (1996) *The New Age: Celebrating the Self*. Oxford, Blackwell.

Herberg, W. (1956) *Protestant, Catholic, Jew*. Garden City NY, Doubleday.

Homans, G. (1950) *The Human Group*. New York, Harcourt Brace and World Inc.

Luckmann, T. (1978) *Phenomenology and Sociology: Selected Readings*. Harmondsworth, Penguin.

Lurie, A. (1998) *Imaginary Friends*. New York, Henry Holt.

Maduro, O. (1982) *Religion and Social Conflicts*. New York, Orbis.

Malinowski, B. (1954) *Magic, Science and Religion*. New York, The Free Press.

Martin, D. (1976) *A General Theory of Secularisation*. Oxford, Blackwell.

Martin, D. (1990) *Tongues of Fire*. Oxford, Blackwell.

Martin, D. (1978) *A General Theory of Secularisation*. Oxford, Blackwell.

Newman, D. (1995) *Sociology: Exploring the Architecture of Everyday Life*. London, Pine Forge Press.

O'Dea, T. and O'Dea Aviad, J. (1997) *The Sociology of Religion 2nd edition*. New York, Prentice-Hall.

O'Rourke, P. J. (1988) *Holidays in Hell*. New York, Vintage Books.

Radcliffe-Brown A. R. (1938) *Taboo*. Cambridge, Cambridge University Press.

Ritchie, J. (1991) The Secret World of Cults: Inside the Sects That Take Over Lives. London, Angus and Robertson.

Robertson, R. in Bromley, G. ed. (1991) *New Developments in Theory and Research*. Greenwich, CONN, JAI Press.

Robertson, R. (1978) *Meaning and Change: Explorations in the Cultured Sociology of Modern Societies*. Oxford, Blackwell.

Selfe, P. and Starbuck, M. (1997) *Religion*. London, Hodder and Stoughton.

Simon, R. and Nadell, P. (1995) *In the Same Voice or is it Different? Gender and the Clergy: Sociology of Religion*, Vol. 56 No. 1.

Stark, R. and Glock, C. (1968) *American Piety: The Nature of Religious Commitment*. Berkeley, University of California Press.

Stark, R. and Bainbridge, W. (1985) *The Future of Religion: Secularisation, Revival and Cult Formation*. Berkeley, California Press.

Tischler, H. (1996) *Introduction to Sociology 5th Edition*. Fort Worth, The Harcourt Press.

Torres, C. (1973) *Revolutionary Priest*. Harmondsworth, Penguin.

Turner, B. S. (1983) *Religion and Social Theory*. Atlantic Highlands, NJ, Humanities Press.

Wallis, R. (1984) *Elementary Forms of the New Religious Life*. London, Routledge.

Weber, M. (1958) *The Protestant Ethic and the Spirit of Capitalism*. New York, Scribner's Sons.

Weber, M. (1996) *The Protestant Ethic and the Spirit of Capitalism*. (trans. Talcott Parsons). Los Angeles, CAL, Roxbury Publishing Co.

Williams, G. (1985) *When was Wales*. Harmondsworth, Pelican.

Wilson, B. (1966) *Religion in a Secular Society*. London, C A Watts.

Worsley, P. (1970) *The Trumpet Shall Sound*. London, Paladin.

Yinger, J. (1970) *The Scientific Study of Religion*. London, Macmillan.

Wealth, Poverty, Welfare and Social Policy

This area covers:

- A survey into theories of poverty and wealth distribution with particular reference to the United Kingdom
- A review of some of the sociological literature which has attempted to understand the impact of poverty and vulnerability on poor people
- A history of the development and structure of welfare provision in modern Britain since 1945
- A view of the political theorising that underlies legislation and legislative change
- A consideration of the question of who takes responsibility for the vulnerable people in our society.

By the end of this area you should be able to:

- recognise that there is a variety of ways of measuring poverty, which can relate to social inequality as well as lack of basic necessities
- understand why, despite the best efforts of politicians and welfare services, poverty still persists in our society
- show that you understand that there is a variety of formal and informal agencies which take on responsibility for the vulnerable people
- understand something of the history, the development and the structure of the care and welfare services in our society.

Key terms

poverty	collectivism
wealth	individualism
welfare	community care
equality	institutional care
underclass	client groups

Area 10 Contents

Introduction

This area considers the problem of poverty and inequality in British society and the various sociological theories to account for the existence of the poor. It also considers social policy making and the development of the welfare state in Britain. This is significant to sociology because it affects the way in which we structure and organise our society.

This area is significant in sociology and social administration because it develops out of a huge religious, political and social debate in our culture. There are philosophical issues to consider in that many people think it is immoral for some people to be extremely wealthy while others are without the basic necessities. Much of the research into poverty and the theorising that led to the development of the welfare state originated in a strong sense of moral outrage at the existence of poverty. Other writers and thinkers feel that the wealthy have a right to enjoy the privileges that they have earned because people who are poor lead lives that lead to misfortune and poverty. This type of thinking leads to a discussion of Marxism, where sociologists would argue that some people are wealthy because other people are poor. Marxists would claim that the relationship between the wealthy and the poor is one of exploitation and social control. Marxists and socialists suggest that the poor are made to feel either that they should be grateful for poverty because it will bring them salvation in the next world or that their poverty is justified because they are neither as clever nor as hardworking as the rich.

Attempts are made by society to support the poor and yet poverty persists. The budget for welfare payments in Britain is enormous; there is a debate as to which sector of society should provide the money. It is claimed that people dislike direct taxation and yet it is through taxation systems that we can afford to support the weakest in our society. Statistics suggest that poor people live shorter and harder lives than wealthy ones and that poverty is a grinding and grim reality for a large proportion of people in modern Britain. Is this because poor people are feckless and selfish? Are they poor because they will not face the consequences of mistakes they have made? Do they choose to depend on the charity of others rather than help themselves? Some functionalists, for instance, argue that poverty can induce a state of mind in which people become helpless and unable to rescue themselves from the poor quality of life that they experience.

There is also the question of who should bear responsibility for the vulnerable and the weak. Can our society afford to support the non-productive through welfare systems? Is it possible that some perfectly healthy people actively choose to live on welfare benefits rather than work? Many people who are surviving on benefits would prefer to work, but if they have a disability or family responsibility then the work that is available to them is not tailored to their needs and does not pay enough. How can those who are completely unable to provide for their own needs be best cared for? Should they live among us or be placed in institutions geared to their care? If the weak and the disabled are to be cared for in the community, who should that community consist of? Families can be overwhelmed by the huge amount of work involved in caring for a confused elderly person, a severely handicapped and sick adult, or a developmentally delayed child. Are these people the responsibility of those who are related to them or do they belong to all of us?

Defining wealth

> **HINTS AND TIPS**   *To understand wealth properly as an issue on its own, it is essential that you read through the discussion of stratification and class in this text. A literary study of wealth is Scott Fitzgerald's masterpiece* The Great Gatsby.

Much of the material in this area is linked with ideas considered in Area 3, which discusses social class. Refer back to Area 3 for more detailed understandings. The real focus of this area is not so much wealth as inequality. It is **wealth** in relationship to **poverty** that is the point of discussion. We actually know very little about wealth in this country and there is little sociology of the rich.

Ways in which people can become very wealthy include:

- ■ **Inheritance, especially of land and property**. The Duke of Westminster is one of the most commonly quoted figures in this context and it is estimated that he is one of the 10 richest people in

Britain. He owns land in London, Scotland, the USA, Canada, Ireland, and Cheshire, and commutes to work by private jet.

ACTIVITY KS **WORKING WITH OTHERS**

IDENTIFICATION AND INTERPRETATION

While many people would probably enjoy the chance of some participant observation in this field, the wealthy themselves are very wary of study. Suggest reasons why this may be so.

ACTIVITY KS **COMMUNICATION**

IDENTIFICATION AND INTERPRETATION

Look at back copies of Hello! and OK magazines. In what ways are the lives of wealthy celebrities different from our own? Remember that these magazines exist as promotional materials for actors and pop stars. Look at the norms and values that are expressed in these magazines.

■ **Business and management**. The creation of successful businesses can make people extremely wealthy. Examples include the Sainsbury family, Rupert Murdoch, Richard Branson. Bill Gates, who owns Microsoft, is estimated to be the richest man in the world. Note that very few of these people began from a family position where they were extremely poor – most were comfortable if not as wealthy as they are today.

■ **Entertainment**. Stars of pop and sport can become wealthy, especially if they invest their income in property and businesses. Examples of such wealthy people include Hollywood film stars, directors such as Steven Spielberg and singers such as Elton John and Rod Stewart. More recent examples are Posh Spice and David Beckham.

The most commonly used definition of wealth is money, or property, which is surplus to one's actual needs. If you own just one house, it is not usually counted as wealth by taxation systems, even if it is a mansion, because you need somewhere to live. Wealth is the property a person can own and turn into money

through sale. *Social Trends*, a good source of information on wealth, suggests that since 1976, over 90% of the wealth of Britain has been owned by 50% of the population and that the most wealthy 10% of the population own approximately half the wealth. The figures have changed a little over the last 20 years, with some distribution of wealth throughout the rest of the population. However, if some people are so very wealthy, it requires little imagination to realise that the remaining people may have very little of the wealth of the country to share between them.

HINTS AND TIPS   Social Trends *is based on government data. This implies that its findings, especially with regard to wealth, will be a serious underestimate because the very wealthy can afford tax accountants whose business it is to ensure that they pay as little tax as possible. Can you suggest ways in which the very wealthy, such as Rupert Murdoch, can legally minimise payment of tax in Britain?*

ACTIVITY KS **APPLICATION OF NUMBER**

IDENTIFICATION AND INTERPRETATION

Use Figure 10.1 to identify a variety of trends in relative wealth and poverty over the period between 1971 and 1996. Note that median means average.

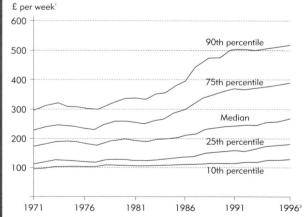

Real¹ household disposable income² (United Kingdom)

£ per week¹

- 90th percentile
- 75th percentile
- Median
- 25th percentile
- 10th percentile

¹ Before housing costs adjusted to January 1998 prices using the retail prices index less local taxes
² Equalised household disposable income has been used for ranking the individuals.
³ Data from 1993 onwards are for financial years

Source: Institute for Fiscal Studies

Figure 10.1   Real household disposable income, UK

Inequality and wealth

Many commentators have argued that the welfare state has helped to limit the effects of poverty in Britain and this argument underlies the entire debate in this area of study. Writers from a Marxist tradition, such as Westergaard and Resler or Le Grand, suggest that the wealthy benefit more from welfare provision than the poor do. Others have suggested that the poor have become more powerless. Certainly, since the 1980s there have been changes to taxation and **benefit** systems. A number of factors seem to point to an increase in the degree of inequality of wealth that we experience in Britain.

Taxation systems

Income tax was cut at the highest rates so that the wealthy pay a smaller proportion of their income to the state.

Employment changes

Many high-employing traditional industries such as coal-mining were contracted. Certain areas have experienced very high unemployment, so wages remained low as people were prepared to take work at any rate of pay.

Benefit changes

Certain people became ineligible for state support and benefit. For example, young people can no longer claim benefit before the age of 18. It has been claimed that benefits have not kept pace with average changes in income or inflation so that they are worth less in real terms than they once were. Many pension rises appear to offer an increase in actual money received, but in practical terms have been cuts in income because they do not keep up with inflation and cost of living increases.

Income support

The numbers of people who receive income support are increasing. This is a benefit for those whose earned income falls below a point at which the government defines you as poor. This is known as the **poverty line**. It could be argued that it is in the interests of the government to draw the poverty line as low as acceptable. In 1993, 5.6 million people received this benefit. This is just below 10% of the population.

Child health

There has been an increase in diseases such as asthma and eczema among children. These illnesses can be triggered by environmental factors such as stress, pollution, and poverty. The children of the poor are more likely to experience poor health than the children of the rich are. Many studies have shown that the children of the poor have a slightly lower average height and that they are more likely to experience weight problems associated with poor diets.

Using Figure 10.2 you can see that family status and age are significant variables in people's disposable income. Pensioner couples tend to be in the bottom

Percentages

	Bottom fifth	Next fifth	Middle fifth	Next fifth	Top fifth	All² (=100%) (millions)
Pensioner couple	23	29	21	15	12	5.1
Single pensioner	25	33	21	13	7	4.1
Couple with children	19	17	24	22	17	17.2
Couple without children	10	11	16	26	38	10.5
One adult with children	42	35	14	6	3	4.6
One adult without children	18	17	19	22	24	8.2
All individuals	20	20	20	20	33	49.7

¹Equivalised household disposable income, before housing costs, has been used for ranking the individuals into quintile groups. See Appendix, Part 5: Equivalisation scales.
²Figures are grossed to population totals

Source: *Family Resources Survey*, Department of Social Security

Figure 10.2   Distribution of equivalised disposable income¹: by family type, 1996–1997

two-fifths of the population in terms of disposable income and single pensioners are even more likely to find themselves in the low-income category. Couples without children have far more chance of being in the top-income brackets. This suggests that there is a life cycle in terms of income, with people being vulnerable to poverty if they are old or have children. The risk of having a low income increases if a person becomes a single parent. *Social Trends* 29 (1999) page 95 points to gender differences in terms of disposable income and suggests that 'men are more likely to live in households at the top of the income distribution'. It also points out that children are more likely to live in households that have low incomes.

Ethnicity and poverty

There is a general assumption that people of ethnic minorities are more likely to experience poverty, but this hides a great deal of variation in the social composition of ethnic minority communities. Recent research carried out by Platt and Noble (1999) in Birmingham and published by the Joseph Rowntree Foundation found considerable evidence of low income and poverty among ethnic minority communities. This is probably due to the age distribution of the immigrant population, which generally tends to be younger than the resident population. Black Caribbean single parents are more likely to be working than lone parents from other ethnic groups, but they tend to be concentrated in low-paid jobs. Later in this area it will also become apparent that some ethnic communities are reluctant to claim benefits to which they are entitled for religious and moral reasons. This increases their vulnerability to poverty.

The most recent picture

John Hills (1999), for the Joseph Rowntree Foundation, summarises the recent pattern of income distribution:

- Average incomes grew by about 40%, but for the richest they grew by 60–68%. The poorest 10% of the community experienced a growth in income of between 8 and 10%.

- Income inequality in the 1990s was greater than at any time since the 1940s and the UK experienced a large and rapidly increasing differential between rich and poor, almost equalling that of the USA.

- Poor people tend to move in and out of poverty because there is a degree of social mobility among people who work.

In 1994–5, the poorest people in our communities were:

- pensioners – although pensioners are still poor, they do not provide as large a proportion of the poor as they did in the 1960s

- lone parent – 75% of lone parents are among the poorest 40%

- ethnic minorities – the Pakistani and Bangladeshi community are particularly vulnerable to poverty though it is less frequently experienced by members of the Indian community

- people in social housing – those who rely on social housing such as council housing and housing authority provision remain poor

Defining poverty

There are three active definitions of poverty that we can use. These are outlined in Figure 10.3. Each has its limitations and so, in any debate on poverty, the definition being used is of real significance.

Poverty and social research

One of the most famous figures of social research into poverty was Seebohm Rowntree. He conducted three studies of poverty in York in 1899, 1936 and in 1950. His method was to use a nutritionist to draw up a family shopping list, which contained items that would satisfy basic human food needs. On the basis of this, Rowntree defined the absolute minimum amount of money on which any person could live. Anyone found to have an income below this sum was declared to be below the poverty line. His definition of poverty was therefore absolute as it did not include sums for

Terminology	Definition	Evaluative points
Absolute poverty	A person lacks the income to provide basic human needs of food, shelter and clothing	Physical needs vary from person to person: food requirements are higher for a manual labourer than someone who is elderly and immobile. Need for shelter varies with climatic conditions – one can survive a summer in Britain without a home, but winter could kill. One can merely survive on a very minimal income, but we expect a certain quality of life in our society and poverty can be about cultural expectations
Relative poverty	A person has a standard of living that is lower than that of those around him or her	This is a notoriously vague concept because relative concepts always involve notions of time and place: **Time** – In the early 1960s, houses were heated by open fires and very few people had access to a motor car. We might consider these to be features of extreme poverty today **Place** – people outside major cities might expect to have access to some garden space and to have better housing conditions than would be normal for those who live in urban areas where people are more likely to occupy flats
Subjective poverty	People feel poor compared with those around them	Expectations vary: a wealthy person among millionaires is poor, but can hardly expect the state to supplement his or her income. We may have false concepts of others' wealth and expectations – TV advertising operates through implying that most people are wealthy and can afford luxury items

Figure 10.3   Definitions of poverty

ACTIVITY

KS APPLICATION OF NUMBER

ANALYSIS AND EVALUATION

- Make a list of the absolute and bare necessities of life. Decide on an approximate costing per week or per month for these items.

- Make a second list of the things that you feel that you need to maintain an acceptable but not extravagant standard of living in our society. Decide on an approximate costing per week or per month for these items.

- Make a third list of the things that you feel that you would require for a very pleasant and comfortable lifestyle. Decide on an approximate costing per week or per month for these items.

1 What do you notice about the differences between the sums that you require for each of the three standards of living?
2 Is absolute poverty an adequate concept to use in order to define poverty in our society?
3 What will you have to earn to live in the lifestyle to which you feel that you would like to have? Is this a realistic possibility for you?

luxuries or allow people the possibility of occasional bad money management. Despite drawing the poverty line as low as it could possibly be, Rowntree still

discovered that, in 1899, 33% of his sample were living below the poverty line. In 1936, the figure had dropped to 18% and by 1950 only 1.5% of his population were below the poverty line. On the basis of this discovery, Rowntree concluded that **primary poverty** was disappearing. It is interesting to note that the causes of poverty in his study appeared to change from poor wages in 1899 to old age in 1950, despite the development of the state pension.

> **HINTS AND TIPS**   By using an absolute definition of poverty, Rowntree was almost certain to discover that poverty was disappearing. Would he have been able to draw the same conclusions if he had been using a relative definition of poverty?

To evaluate Rowntree's work you may need to consider the following points:

- The shopping list was nonsense. Ordinary people do not know the nutritional value of food and cannot shop to find the cheapest produce. Before refrigeration in shops was common, farm produce came in and out of season and varied in price and quality with the time of year.

- Rowntree used 1899 definitions of poverty and standard of living and applied those definitions to people who were living in the 1950s when standards of living for ordinary people had risen. He did not take **secondary poverty** or relative concepts of poverty into account and standards of social life had improved considerably. In 1899 heating and lighting were luxury items, for instance, but not in 1950.

> **HINTS AND TIPS** *For an insight into the lives of the very poor at about the time that Rowntree was considering the poor of York, look at Robert Roberts' account of society in Salford in his childhood in* The Classic Slum.

ACTIVITY KS WORKING WITH OTHERS, COMMUNICATION

IDENTIFICATION AND INTERPRETATION	ANALYSIS AND EVALUATION

Interview people of various ages about the conditions in which they lived when they were young. Guide the talk by asking about food, furnishings, domestic chores, clothing, entertainment, income, lighting, and heating. You may need to take account of their social class because there was considerable inequality of wealth. Remember too that some elderly people may be tempted to paint a rosy picture for reasons of their own, so you will need to listen beyond their emotions about their childhoods to gain an accurate account of the physical conditions in which people lived. You may need to consider whether you are sentimental about the past too; try hard to empathise fully with your respondent's experience to understand how difficult life could be. Pool your findings with others in your group.

- Evaluate your work by considering whether general standards of living have improved for most people.

- Were you shocked or surprised by anything that you discovered? Why?

- Which generation do you feel experienced the most difficult physical conditions?

- If you discover someone who experienced genuine poverty *by the standards of the time in which they lived*, then make a special note of the findings and be certain to make sure that people in your group are aware of what you have discovered about that respondent's experiences of childhood.

Peter Townsend, one of the foremost writers on poverty, used a different measure of poverty when conducting his 1979 survey, *Poverty in the United*

Kingdom. He talked in terms of **indices of deprivation**. He identified a number of factors that he claimed indicated poverty; these include:

- not having had a holiday over the last 12 months

- inability to have meat regularly in the week or a cooked joint of meat on a Sunday

- lack of a cooked breakfast

- lack of private family access to a toilet, a sink and cold tap, a bath or shower or a gas or electric cooker.

Some of his indices of poverty seem very reasonable, but others – such as not entertaining friends or family to a meal – could well be a matter of culture or social habit rather than poverty. Nevertheless, despite many deeply held reservations with this method of assessing individual poverty, people still often use it as a way of working out the level of deprivation people experience.

ACTIVITY KS WORKING WITH OTHERS, COMMUNICATION

IDENTIFICATION AND INTERPRETATION

In groups, identify 10 factors that you feel indicate that a person is living in poverty. Do all your groups have the same 10 indices?

Can anyone think of a better way of assessing a person's level of secondary poverty?

The experience of poverty

Coates and Silburn (1970) in *Poverty: The Forgotten Englishmen* studied the experience of poverty as a subjective condition in a vivid and very shocking text, which was widely reprinted throughout the early 1970s. They looked at a poor area of Nottingham, St Ann's, and discovered that many people were living lives of quiet desperation as a result of low wages or dependence on benefit. Many of these people had dependent children. Some had very large families, but the norm was for only two or three children. They identified a series of commonly held myths about the poor:

- the poor spend their money unwisely

- the poor have more than enough money but spend it on gambling and drink

- the poor 'bring it on themselves'

TASK

Hypothesis – The media do not present a realistic view of poverty.

Context – You are far safer to consider fictional poverty than to ask people about their personal experiences of poverty. However, this title is far too wide and you will need to make your focus a television programme or genre of programmes. Film directors such as Ken Loach attempt to portray a realistic picture of the lives of the poor and disadvantaged, but in general the media often glamorise the lives or the problems of poor people. The best type of programme to consider might be 'social realism' type soap operas such as Coronation Street or Eastenders, which are set in communities where poverty is, in theory, common.

Method – You will need to use some form of systematic content analysis or you will tend to generalise about what you see, and this could lead to descriptive writing which carries few marks. Use a pencil and paper as you watch your chosen programmes or read your specific text. Look for actual signifiers of poverty – the signs and indicators that people are poor. Do people in the programmes appear to be without the things that we consider necessary for a decent style of life? Do they suggest that they cannot afford any of the necessities of life?

How often does lack of money appear to be a storyline even for characters who appear to be living on a low income in the stories? Are there scenes where people have trouble with their benefits or their allowances? Do they refer to having to do without heat, light, or water because of bills? Is there mention of acquiring items of clothing in charity shops or any other form of having to make do and mend? Create a tick list and note how often you see any of these indicators of poverty in the programmes.

As a triangulation, ask people if the characters in your chosen television programme seem realistic. You might also consider whether some people are seen to bring their money troubles on themselves in soap opera.

Evaluation – This is an interesting area to study because we often draw our ideas of other people's experience from the media. Many people consider it bad manners to discuss personal finance and so they may have to draw their concepts of poverty from the media rather than from a more real experience. With this study, you are investigating the origins of those perceptions. You will need to consider how useful content analysis is as a method of understanding how we gain our ideas. You will need to look at **Cultural Effects theory** (Area 9) and **content analysis** (Area 2).

They countered this type of thinking in a closely argued account which suggests that many people were living below any definition of the poverty line. They stated that the poor tend to be ghettoised in areas of low rent and poor-quality housing, where they are away from the rest of society. They also pointed out that much poverty is discreetly hidden so that people may wear good-quality second-hand clothing or cast-offs from wealthier friends. As they pointed out, a child's shoes might be of leather, but they may not fit properly.

A number of similar studies, such as Wedge and Prosser's *Born to Fail*, were produced at the same time and pointed to evidence that, despite 30 years of the welfare state, large numbers of people were living in poverty and deprivation. This tradition of the exploration of poverty has tended to die away in modern sociology, possibly because of the increasing dependence on universities for outside funding. Poverty is an issue for the poor and, as Coates and Silburn pointed out, the rest of us would rather ignore it.

HINTS AND TIPS   *American television programmes are very careful not to present too grim a view of life and will rarely attempt to portray poverty realistically even in 'gritty' programmes set in police stations and hospitals. Poverty is a backdrop against which the hero can be seen to be noble rather than forming part of the structure of the programme. 'Poor' characters may be inappropriately well dressed or live in huge homes crammed with material goods.*

Who are the poor?

In our society a number of factors seem to predispose people to poverty:

- unemployment
- low pay or lack of skills

- membership of certain ethnic minorities
- single parenthood
- dependency on benefit because of ill health, disability or retirement

In social work terms, these are groups of people that are often described as **client groups**. None of the factors listed above is absolute proof of poverty – members of the Royal Family are retired, in debt or are single parents, but no one is seriously concerned about poverty or deprivation among titled people and the landed gentry. It is those without any source of income beyond the state or their employment who become the poor.

ACTIVITY KS PROBLEM SOLVING

KNOWLEDGE AND UNDERSTANDING

See what you can discover about the benefits and welfare payments people are entitled to if they are:

- unemployed
- receiving low pay at work
- single parents
- dependent on benefit because of ill health, disability or retirement

You can probably discover this in the following ways:

- Ask people what they receive if they fit into one of the above categories and how they feel about their income. Be cautious, however; this is extremely personal and you may receive rude responses!
- Visiting the Citizen's Advice Bureau for leaflets.
- Picking up leaflets in a Post Office or a Benefit Office.
- Visiting a government Website for advice – this can be time-consuming, however.
- Ask Social Services for a leaflet.

In your evaluation of this exercise, consider how easy it was to obtain relevant information. How easy would it be if you were poor, sick, had children with you or had sensory or physical problems?

Certain groups are particularly vulnerable to poverty and deprivation for a number of social reasons (this was discussed with regard to disposable income on page 469). Illustration of this point is offered below for gender and employment, but the arguments and analyses can be applied to any of the client groups listed as being vulnerable to poverty.

If you look at Figure 10.4, you will see that certain groups are particularly likely to be poorly paid. Younger workers receive low wages, but are less vulnerable after the age of 21. Taken overall, women are more likely than men to be among the lowest paid, but this is due to the fact that they are more likely than men to be low paid as full-time workers. Interestingly, there is little gender difference in the percentage of men and women who are low paid and in part-time work but, in practical terms, you should note that far more women than men are part-time workers. This is a point which is particularly relevant when you consider that women are more likely than men to have family responsibilities as single parents. It is also interesting to note that *Social Trends* points out regional differences among low-paid people, with workers in the north east, Wales and Northern Ireland being more likely to be low paid.

Gender

Women are vulnerable to poverty for a number of reasons:

- They have a less powerful position in the labour market and therefore have lower incomes.
- Women are more likely to take on the burden of care for a vulnerable adult or for a child.

(United Kingdom)

Thousands

	Lower estimate	Central estimate	Upper estimate	Percentage[1]
Age				
18 to 21	201	221	241	14.0
22 and over	1,513	1,683	1,852	7.8
Male employees				
Full time	310	357	403	3.2
Part time	201	211	221	20.5
Female employees				
Full time	270	335	398	5.6
Part time	932	1,001	1,070	19.7

[1] Based on the central estimate

Source: *Labour Force Survey* and *New Earnings Survey*, Office for National Statistics

Figure 10.4 Estimated numbers of people earning less than the national minimum wage, by age and employment status, spring 1998

- Women lose their rights to benefits accrued by their husbands' employment on divorce.

- Some women have never worked because this was not expected of them until the last 20 years or so. Women currently in their eighties probably gave up work on marriage or may never have worked outside the home at all. They are entitled to only the most basic of benefits because they have not contributed to the National Insurance Scheme.

Employment and poverty

The unskilled and the working classes are very vulnerable to poverty because these are people who may drift in and out of employment or take on part-time employment. These people are eligible for only the lowest level benefits because in the UK eligibility for benefit is often assessed on contributions that are made while the person is in full-time work. This leaves those who are nearing retirement very vulnerable because base rate pensions are acknowledged to be very poor indeed. Other unskilled people may be forced into the black economy or fraud; they work in low-paid jobs and also claim benefit. They risk being caught and sent to prison or fined, or are prey to loan sharks if they need to borrow money for material goods such as household equipment.

Those with learning, sensory or physical disability are at particular risk of poverty because the acquisition of skills for employment can be more of a problem to them. They face discrimination from employers and may have experienced a poor education. Their work attendance records may be affected for reasons connected to their conditions. There may be additional hidden costs that relate to the disability. Good quality prosthetic limbs for amputees cost many thousands of pounds, and those with defective vision may need to use unreliable public transport systems. The National Health Service or the Social Services provide only the most basic of aids to normal living and independence.

The 'problem' of the continuation of poverty

Despite the fact that in Britain there has been a welfare state which should look after all its citizens and which

Theoretical perspective	Overview of theory	Associated writers
Marxist	Poverty is caused by capitalism. The rich are rich because they can exploit the poor as they hold power over the social system	Marx and Engels
Neo-Marxist	While no one can argue against the view that the working class tends to be poorer than the bourgeoisie, even within the working class, certain groups are more vulnerable than others. They are weak because they have little power in the market place	Peter Townsend
	Society is unequal along a number of dimensions. Poverty is one of these	Lukes, Halsey
Functionalist	It is necessary to have inequality. The rewards in life go to those who are stronger, fitter, and more useful to society. The best people need to be paid more so that there is competition for the best jobs and the most talented will get them	Parsons, Moore, Gans
Structural theory	The poor are the victims of the structure of society, which traps people into a position where they have to develop behavioural strategies and cultures in order to survive	Robert Merton
New Right	The poor are poor because they have a culture of poverty, which is typically masculine and fatalistic. They live in the present and are unable to plan for the future	Oscar Lewis, Banfield
New Individualism	People are trapped in poverty by the operation of the welfare state. They have lost the ability to control their own lives. The solution to poverty is to get people into work and to educate them for work through skills training	Melanie Phillips, Frank Field

Figure 10.5   Social theories to account for poverty

was designed to alleviate poverty, poverty still persists and the evidence is clear to all of us. The concept of poverty varies according to social perspective and individual ideology. There has been evolution and change in the ideas of what causes poverty and Figure 10.5 offers an overview of the debate that follows.

Victorian people would often use the concept of **deserving** and **undeserving poor**. They thought that some people were poor despite themselves and therefore were deserving of help and charity. The undeserving poor were those who spent their money unwisely, on drink and gambling. Their poverty was seen as the result of immorality. Although the concepts and the expression now seem dated, the thinking behind these concepts can still be found. Underlying the next debate therefore are two totally different perceptions of poverty:

1 The poor are responsible for their own condition because of some failure within their lives or their culture, which leads them to experience deprivation. This type of thought is associated with functionalist or New Right analyses.

2 The poor are the victims of a society which is unequal, greedy, and exploitative. This is generally a Marxist analysis.

Poverty seems to be an inherited condition in that many of the poor people in our society come from poor homes. This is not an argument to say that poverty is genetic in origin, although that case has also been argued by sociobiologists. During the 1930s, for instance, the lack of height of city children was explained in terms of poor genetics. It was not until the rationing of the Second World War improved the diet of the poorest families that the link between quality of diet and adult height was established. The question is one of why, if life is so difficult for the poor, do so many children of poor families seem unable to alter their own lives to ensure that they do not experience poverty for themselves? A number of strands of thought can be seen in this debate.

Cycles of poverty

Many people have identified what is commonly known as a **cycle of poverty**. Children who grow up in material poverty experience innate disadvantage in life

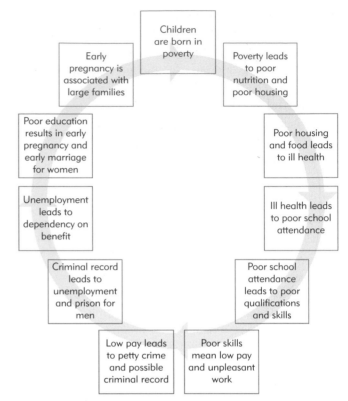

Figure 10.6   The cycle of poverty

and become poor themselves. Implicit in this description is an understanding that the working classes are most vulnerable to poverty because they experience unsteady employment and poor education. This belief is widespread and so sensible that it has not really been challenged. It is also the type of thought that has influenced the development of the welfare state in that provisions of the welfare state can often be seen as interventions to break habits and patterns of the cycle. This is best shown in diagrammatic form (Figure 10.6).

HINTS AND TIPS   Some welfare interventions have been identified in Figure 10.6 but there are many others. As a group you should identify as many as possible that have been attempted and add them to your own versions of the cycle of poverty.

Culture of poverty

Oscar Lewis (1961) associated poverty with a culture of **fatalism**. Fatalism is an idea that suggests that it makes no difference whatever actions you take because everything is already decided. After studying poor

Spanish Americans (Hispanics) in Puerto Rico and Mexico, Lewis suggested that the poor remained in poverty because they developed a culture of fatalism and despair, which he called a **culture of poverty**. They believed themselves to be helpless and inferior, the victims of bad luck and a malign fate.

- *Family life* is typically unsteady, with changes of partner, abandonment of children, and female-centred families become the norm.

- *Community life* is likely to be lacking. The poor do not associate themselves with self-help groups, unions or social groups. They are marginalised from society and survive on its edges. They reject the support of welfare agencies and mistrust the police.

- *Education and work* – the poor have low levels of literacy and education. They do not join trade unions or political parties and do not push to improve their position in life. Again, there is an understanding that the poor are the working class in this analysis.

- *Personal beliefs and behaviour* – the poor tend to look for immediate pleasure rather than waiting and working for the future. They have little sense of history or place. They tend to have highly masculine cultures and are impatient of females.

Lewis saw the poor as taking on this way of life as a sensible response to the circumstances in which they found themselves. However, it is precisely those defensive responses which keep the poor in such conditions because they pass on their culture to their children, and the process becomes self-perpetuating. If opportunities are presented to people who have developed a culture of poverty, they cannot act on them because of their values and morality. This point of view was highly popular in the USA in particular and underpins many of the social welfare programmes that have been developed. It has also influenced the thinking of the modern commentators on welfare who are allied to the Labour party of Tony Blair, and who can best be described as New Individualists despite their self-professed position of 'New' Labour.

To evaluate the culture of poverty theory it is necessary to include some of the following ideas.

- Poor people can, and do, escape from poverty. Education often provides an escape route. Refer to Area 3, which discusses social mobility.

- Schwartz among others points out that poor areas of many Third World slums, such as the *favelas* and *barrios* of Latin America and the shanties of Africa and India, have thriving cultures and innumerable self-help groups, often run by women.

- It is difficult to identify a 'culture' as such. The concept of culture implies that people have acquired a set of social rules that they cannot break, but this is arguable. Can we assume that all poor people have exactly the same view of the world?

- There is evidence of resistance to the accepted norms of society as described by functionalists in that poor people do not seem to recognise their culture as in any way inferior to that of the rich. It would be patronising to argue anything different.

ACTIVITY KS **COMMUNICATION**

IDENTIFICATION AND INTERPRETATION

As a class discussion exercise, carry out a small empathy exercise and put yourself in the position of someone who is very poor. You have been invited for a job interview in a city far away from home. It offers extremely good prospects and the organisation seems keen to have you. What practical and social barriers stand in the way of your taking up this amazing opportunity?

Social realism

In direct contrast to the culture of poverty debate is a set of theories which point out that it is not culture which prevents poor people from having the same opportunities as the wealthy. It is poverty itself which is the enemy of the poor. Hylan Lewis saw the same behaviours as Oscar Lewis, but suggested that the poor are behaving in a realistic and sensible fashion when they respond to the moment rather than engaging in practices such as saving for the future. The argument can be illustrated in the following fashion:

- **Culture of poverty** assumes that poor men are irresponsible and so they drink in pubs. They spend their money and are trapped in poverty.

- **Social realism** offers the view that if one's home is unpleasant, cold and damp, then a pub is warm, attractive, and social. Men drink to avoid unpleasant housing. This is expensive, but not as expensive as heating a home well.

ACTIVITY   KS PROBLEM SOLVING

IDENTIFICATION AND INTERPRETATION

During a piece of coursework, a student discovered that a poor family normally living on benefit had spent £8000 it inherited on a holiday and expensive consumer goods such as a satellite dish and designer clothing in the space of two weeks.

- Account for this apparently illogical behaviour, applying both the culture of poverty thesis and the social realism thesis. Consider the impact of the inheritance on entitlement to benefits.

- How would a wealthier family have treated the same £8000 inheritance?

- Why would its behaviour probably be different?

- How might the wealthier family view the behaviour of the poor family?

You will find this analysis much easier if you try to empathise with the poor family and the wealthier family.

An American researcher, Elliot Leibow, conducted observations among poor black Americans. He discovered that families often broke up through the pressure and stress of poverty. Rather than admit the reality of the situation, poor men had to protect their self-esteem through offering romanticised notions of masculinity as the cause of marital breakdown. They did this to avoid the truth, which was that they could not achieve the wealth and status to which they aspired. The behaviour of the poor, which could be seen as creating problems, may actually be a logical response to their situation.

Underclass debate

It is not uncommon in the human psyche and throughout Christian and other religious belief systems to argue that the victims of misfortune are themselves to blame. This can be seen in rape cases, where 'she

was asking for it' is often used as a defence. Applied to the poverty debate, the same mode of thought appears as the suggestion that the poor have brought their poverty upon themselves. This is a very popular belief and has its roots in theorising from the nineteenth century. The eminent philosopher and thinker Herbert Spencer argued that poverty was good for society as it encouraged people to work in order to avoid being poor. The poor themselves deserved to suffer poverty because of their lack of morality.

Those living on benefits today are often seen as lazy, and the term 'dole scrounger' was frequently employed by the tabloid press to describe people dependent on benefits in the 1970s and 1980s. This particular debate should be taken in the context of the popular political climate of the time, which resulted in the election of Margaret Thatcher in 1979 and the subsequent dominance of the thinkers of the New Right. In terms of poverty and welfare, you might like to note that the New Right suggested the following ideas about poverty:

- People are often lazy and selfish so they must be encouraged to work by making welfare payments low enough to make life uncomfortable.

- People who live in areas where few work will develop a culture that encourages laziness.

- People get used to relying on others if life is made easy for them and all their self-will and self-reliance is lost. They must be encouraged to take control of their own lives, by punitive methods such as having their benefits cut if necessary.

This belief is also known as the **culture of dependence** theory. The idea suggested was that if people can have benefit easily, they lose the incentive to work. Critics pointed out throughout the 1980s that it was all very well for the government to tell people to go and look for work, but unemployment levels were so high in some areas that the search was a lost cause before it began.

David Marsland (1989) went so far as to argue that the welfare state actually created poverty. His suggestion was that people had come to expect that they could survive on benefit and so developed a dependency culture. To illustrate the point, he suggested that women no longer needed to rely on men to support their children and that the state and benefit system had actually taken something away from the role of the father. Women then felt that they could have children with no support from a man and became single parents through choice. He made a strong case for targeted benefit, which should go only to the very deserving and to the poorest people. The Labour government of the late 1990s adopted many of his ideas in their thinking about the welfare budget. Harriet Harman, then Secretary of State for Social Security, writing on the 50th anniversary of the creation of the welfare state on 5 July 1998, stated that the purpose of the welfare state is to 'provide active help and encouragement to get back into work. It makes sure that work pays.'

Charles Murray, an American, claimed in the late 1980s that Britain was developing an **underclass**. He defined the underclass in very much the same terms as the Victorians described the undeserving poor. These people, he claimed, were those who were happy to live off the state. He identified particular groups of people, such as the unemployed who were unwilling to take jobs, the women who had children but did not marry and the criminal sector of the community, as belonging to the underclass. He adopted many of the ideas of the culture of poverty theory, but offered the radical solution of putting community power into the hands of local people who would then impose moral values on the poor. His more recent (1994) book, entitled *Underclass: The Crisis Deepens*, claims that the underclass is growing. David Green (1998) claims that there has been a decrease in poverty, but the fact that dependence of people on benefit has increased dramatically supports Murray's thesis.

TASK

Hypothesis   Many people support the view that the poor are victims of their own bad behaviour.

Context   If you ask people directly, very many will disagree with the hypothesis, some of them strongly. However, with this survey, you are testing unspoken (and possibly unknowing) attitudes that people have to the poor. Just as people who tell racist jokes may be shocked if accused of racism and deny it vehemently, then many people will not recognise the significance of their own attitudes to the poor. They do not need a novice sociologist pointing this out to them either, so be guarded in your approach.

You will need to be subtle in your questioning and survey design so that you can understand something of people's views without revealing the exact purpose, which is to discover to what extent people actually do condemn the poor for their poverty. Explain that you are conducting a survey into attitudes to poverty.

Method   The simplest method to use is one that asks people to what extent they agree or disagree with a list of statements. These can vary from the very provocative such as, 'The unemployed are a bit lazy' to the rather more subtle 'Poor people should be helped to work for their money' or 'Is it acceptable for people on benefit to smoke cigarettes?' Statements or questions should be composed so that they are extremely simple and do not contain too many ideas.

As this is quantitative research, ask as many people as you can to improve the quality and reliability of your results. A shopping centre survey would be a useful way of acquiring all the data that you need in one day. Remember that a number of the people you approach may in fact be unemployed, so you need to consider whether questions about work status are needed. You may also need to explain the purpose of your work to strangers with rather more care than you do to people who know you and trust your motives.

Evaluation   You will possibly find your results difficult to analyse with any precision. Do not let this put you off, as the purpose of the coursework section of the paper is to test your awareness of the problems attendant on social research. You may find a number of points to consider when assessing what your figures show you.

People may well be remarkably inconsistent even within one survey and this is something for you to note in your work. However, the probable outcome is one that will show that while people will not agree with the most extreme of your comments, most will show a tendency to agree strongly with the milder suggestions. When evaluating your research, consider whether you would have had the same pattern of responses in a dole office queue or in a factory. Are there gender or age differences in patterns of response? Do people remark on or consider the position of the less able and the old when talking about their views on poverty?

Critics of the New Right and underclass theories make the following points:

- The arguments are not well supported by statistical evidence. For instance, single parents are just as likely to be widowed or divorced as never married. Many were in stable, if not married, relationships when their children were born.

- Official statistics should always be treated with the utmost caution because they are generally unreliable.

- There is a moralistic and judgemental undertone to the argument – poor single mothers are bad, but wealthy single mothers seem not to be an issue.

- Anthony Heath found that many unemployed appear to want work. The problem is not one of working, but of finding a job that pays enough for them to survive. Frequently, the jobs that are available for the least skilled would leave people worse off if they took them than if they remained on benefit.

> **HINTS AND TIPS**   You should note that, although the underlying philosophies of the New Right (who believe in market forces) and the New Individualists (who reject planned socialism and old-style Labour thinking) are very different, the practical applications of their views result in broadly similar policy making.

In contrast to the above theorising is the extremely well known writer and Labour party politician, Frank Field. Field argued that the very poorest who formed the underclass were the victims of an unequal and unjust society. He claimed that state benefits are too low and that certain groups were particularly vulnerable: the long-term unemployed, the elderly, and long-term single parents. The unskilled working classes seem to be the ones at most risk of joining the underclass due to their lack of power in the employment market. In the 1980s, when in opposition to the Conservative government, he proposed raising benefits, supporting training and helping the poor through social engineering schemes such as locating factories and civil service jobs in areas of unemployment. When in office, while some of the above schemes became part of policy, Field also supported legislation to target benefits at the vulnerable and to stop welfare payments to those who refuse jobs or training.

Theories of welfare

There is a clear link between theories of poverty and theories of **welfare**. You should refer back to the notes on the theory of poverty in this area before proceeding to the debates surrounding the solutions to the problems of poverty. Theories of welfare offer an interesting perspective on the poverty debate because the arguments become much more political in the broadest sense. People's ideology will affect the legislation that they create. The argument therefore moves into a more complex series of issues, not just about poverty but also about equality and the impact of the **welfare state** on various sectors of society.

Marxism

Marxists tend to see welfare as a way of reinforcing the *status quo.* They are deeply suspicious of the motives of capitalism and in their view welfare provision is a way of postponing the development of class-consciousness among the working classes without actually addressing any of the gross inequities in society. Welfare provision puts a brake on the arrival of the post-revolutionary Utopia.

Welfare state provision is necessary to capitalists because they need a healthy and reasonably well educated workforce. In Britain, and in other countries, capitalists do not even fund welfare systems because the workers pay for it through direct taxation. They are paying for their own health. Poor people, it is argued, carry far more of a tax burden in real terms than the wealthy because the cost of indirect tax such as VAT on items such as beer and cigarettes takes a larger proportion of their income. Writers such as Westergaard and Resler suggest that the wealthy benefit more from the welfare state than do the poor. The example they offer is that of tax relief on mortgages, which effectively cost the state more than the cost of subsidised council housing. Note that the Labour Government elected in 1997 abolished this tax relief, but also that there are fewer houses in the ownership of local councils as housing associations have taken over the role of providing housing for the less well off.

This is perhaps an over-simplification, but O'Connor points out that in American cities welfare provision and the social services can be seen as a measure of social control rather than of alleviating poverty. People do not receive benefit or support unless they fulfil certain conditions such as availability for work. Certainly, there is often a clear difference in culture and values between social workers, teachers, probation officers and their client groups. Welfare has provided a professional role for ambitious and upwardly mobile members of the working classes in low-paid but relatively high-status occupations.

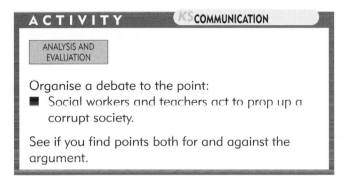

ACTIVITY   KS **COMMUNICATION**

ANALYSIS AND EVALUATION

Organise a debate to the point:
■ Social workers and teachers act to prop up a corrupt society.

See if you find points both for and against the argument.

Socialism

Socialist thought in the UK has often been linked with academic writing and socialists have been influential in the development of the welfare state. There is often a religious motivation in the thought of socialists such as Tawney and Titmuss, which is linked to deeply held religious or moral beliefs. Socialist writers can be identified because they tend to argue in terms of community values and have little of the hostility towards welfare provision that distinguishes Marxist thought.

Socialists argue that the welfare of individuals is the responsibility of the state. They argue for redistribution of income through taxation so that the rich can fund the welfare of the poor. They differ from liberals because they wish to change the structure of society to benefit the poor and equalise the differences between rich and poor. J. K. Galbraith, for instance, talked of a 'balanced society' although he is more often identified as a liberal thinker than a socialist. Socialists tend to argue in favour of universal access to welfare and are

generally opposed to targeting of benefits because then it is necessary to ask people about their entitlement to state support through a system known as **means testing**. Means testing is known to put many people off applying for benefit because of the complexity of the forms and the humiliation of having to ask for help. Those students who have applied for subsistence grants for college will understand this process.

Liberalism

Liberalism is often, but not always, associated with the views of people who regard themselves as highly civilised, and with privileged people who feel that it is morally wrong to allow poverty to exist alongside wealth but who have no desire fundamentally to change the system. There is a Christian element to the beliefs of liberalism. This is a perspective which was important in the development of the welfare state and which is gaining in significance with the re-emergence of the Labour party. (This should not be confused with the political party of the same name, because it is a philosophical and moral stance, although there is an overlap in viewpoint.) People who are liberals have been members of both the Conservative and the Labour parties. The state is seen as balancing the needs of all of the population by attempting to moderate the worst excesses of capitalism and create a better society for all people. Welfare is needed to support capitalism and to support the weak.

HINTS AND TIPS   *Giddens is strongly linked with the Labour Party of Tony Blair, and is regarded as his favourite academic.*

More recently, writers who support 'the middle way', such as Anthony Giddens, suggest that the state cannot leave some problems to market forces to solve, because these problems are too big or too complicated. Liberals tend to be pragmatic – they sort out problems as they arise without either looking for them or allowing any rigidly held viewpoints to influence an essentially common-sense view of events. William Beveridge, who was largely responsible for the institution of the welfare state in 1946, saw himself in terms of being a 'practical' and 'common-sense' person. He was less interested in social theory than in science and saw himself primarily as a social scientist.

Feminism

The link between the development of feminism and Marxist analyses should be clearly understood by anyone with an interest in sociology. Functionalism and consensus theories of society assume that people share values, and yet this is clearly an unwise assumption when applied to the politics of gender.

Feminism offers a number of fascinating insights into the welfare systems of western society. In general, feminists tend to argue for a radical reorganisation and re-think about the nature of state support for the weak members of society. They suggest, and this is recognised as being a fair point by the Department of Social Security, that when the system we experience in Britain was devised it had a conservative view of the role of women. Women were seen in the role of domestic labour and so benefits tended to be geared to the needs of working men. For instance, maternity leave is a right for women, but new fathers have no such privileges even if they lose their wives in childbirth and become single parents. Modern feminists take the view that the welfare state should be looking at the needs of modern women. Adequate funding or tax relief for childcare would enable single parents to join the workforce if they wished.

The various feminist groups tend to unite in their desire for anti-discrimination laws, but they have differing views according to their perspective on the role of the welfare state. Liberal feminists believe that society can adapt, Marxist feminists share many of their positions with Marxists, and radical feminists take the view that separate services should be provided for women to take into account their special and particular needs.

Some recent writing is also interesting, because black feminists point out that the welfare state embodies cultural values, which act against the interests of ethnic minority groupings. Disabled feminists develop this issue with reference to the views of the disabled.

All feminists agree about the following two points:

1 The welfare state exploits women as carers and supporters. Gaps in provision are selflessly filled by neighbours, daughters and mothers, often at great personal cost.
2 The state also targets those women who are the receivers of benefits – so, for instance, young single

mothers are folk devils and seen as a source of bad parenting and crime in society. They become the victims of the analyses of the New Right.

> **HINTS AND TIPS** If you know well anyone who is a carer, and if he or she is willing to talk openly with you, ask about the amount of time that the caring takes. What does it cost the family in terms of emotions, finances? What impact has caring had on their lives? If you have a family member with special needs because of age or disability, you may be able to help the rest of the class to think about the impact of caring on people's lives.
>
> All students should be careful how they handle this topic, as this is a very sensitive subject which could touch very raw emotion. Remember too that there are cultural variations in what people can expect from family members so that some Asian cultures would have difficulty understanding the perspectives of some western family groups, particularly with reference to the care of the elderly.

ACTIVITY KS WORKING WITH OTHERS

ANALYSIS AND EVALUATION

John Redwood, a noted New Right politician, suggested in 1996 that the children of young single mothers should be adopted or looked after by the grandparents rather than the mothers receiving benefit. The mothers should then continue with their education or training for work.

Make a list of points both supporting and rejecting these views. If you wish, you could survey people to see what their opinion of John Redwood's suggestion is. Note differences of income, gender and age to see if responses vary according to the possibility of the person becoming a single parent or if the person is paying taxation bills.

The New Right

The views of the New Right about the origins of poverty have already been discussed. Norman Dennis (1993), for instance, argues that single parenthood is far more significant than poverty as a cause of poor school performance and delinquent attitudes.

Thinkers of the New Right are as opposed to the development of the welfare state as Marxists. However, their rationale is that the welfare state is inefficient because it depends on taxation. High taxation acts as a disincentive to people to earn lots of money because if they are taxed they cannot benefit from the money they have earned.

HINTS AND TIPS   *The above analysis of the New Right offers an interesting perspective into their views on human nature and social psychology. Rich people need rewards to work well; poor people need fear of deprivation to make them work!*

PROFILE

Fredrick von Hayek

(1899–1992)

One of the most influential thinkers in the development of the New Right, the Austrian economist Fredrick August von Hayek studied law and political science, but his main writings were in economics. He taught at the London School of Economics in the 1930s and later at the University of Chicago until the 1960s. His writing was abstract and theoretical before his retirement, but became more political as his influence on social policy in Britain and the USA grew.

His most famous work, **The Road to Serfdom**, was published in 1944, and in it he criticised the idea of state intervention in economic life. He was awarded the Nobel Prize for Economics in 1974. However, his real and significant influence on politics came at the end of his life when the New Right took up his ideas.

In essence, he held the view that there is no such thing as society (a position he shares with Interactionalists) but this basic position led him to a far different set of conclusions. He suggested that people make rational decisions based on their own estimations of their own needs. He considered that the government should not intervene in the economy to support workers because the welfare provisions offered by the state become politicised and have to take over more elements of individual lives. This leads to totalitarianism and the loss of freedoms. His views have been used to provide an intellectual basis for controversial social reforms and the full impact of these on our society has yet to be understood.

The New Right suggests that the state employs a huge number of people in the provision of the welfare state, people who would be better employed in creating wealth through proper work in the private sector. Welfare provision undermines people's freedom to pay for the service that they require in the form that they require it. For instance, the wealthy must pay twice for education, once through taxation to the state system and again in fees for their children to attend privileged independent schools.

The New Right, when in office under Margaret Thatcher in the 1980s, highlighted a number of serious issues for the electorate and affected the nature of the debate on social provision. It argued in favour of efficiency and the streamlining of services. It also suggested that the government could not afford to keep pouring huge sums of money into the welfare state and highlighted the very high cost of benefits to the working population.

ACTIVITY   KS**COMMUNICATION**

ANALYSIS AND EVALUATION

Compare and contrast Marxist views of welfare provision with those of the New Right. What similarities and differences can you note?

Social policy and welfare – the origins of the welfare state

HINTS AND TIPS   *Although the following analysis tends to be historical in description, you should have the theoretical positions on the origin of poverty and the purpose of welfare provision at the front of your mind to offer you an understanding of events and to give depth to the debate.*

The first laws to deal with the poor originated in Tudor times (1601) when thieves and beggars were seen as a threat to social order and the state. Society and social order was organised around the parish, or small area centring on a single church. The people of each parish were held to be responsible for their own poor so local taxes were levied to support the poor people of the parish. This system broke down as a result of industrialisation when some parishes grew to hold populations of poor labouring people that were too large to be supported through local taxation systems. It was felt that the best way to discourage people from becoming poor was to ensure that people who become poor were fed and looked after, but in conditions that were so punitive and unpleasant that no one would want to experience poverty. Workhouses were set up and the poor and orphaned were forced to work for their food.

> ***HINTS AND TIPS*** *Charles Dickens campaigned against the workhouse system through his novels, in particular* Oliver Twist. *For a flavour of the system, you should read* Oliver Twist, *or obtain a video copy of the musical film* Oliver. *When watching the film, remember that the reality of conditions for the poor in Victorian Britain were far worse than could be acceptably written about in a popular novel or portrayed in a popular film. A later social protest novel was Robert Tressell's moving story* The Ragged Trouser'd Philanthropists *(1914), which is a fairly straightforward description of Marxist theory as well as a story.*

At the beginning of the twentieth century, social reformers such as Joseph Rowntree and novelists such as Dickens had begun to point out that many of the poor could not be held responsible for their condition. Members of the government were shocked at the poor physical condition of the nation when attempting to recruit soldiers for both the Boer War and the First World War and an appreciation of the need for state strategies to deal with poverty developed. A number of laws came into operation, including the Old Age Pensions Act of 1908 and the National Insurance Act of 1911. These were seen at the time as short-term solutions but they were significant because the state had taken on responsibility for poverty and ill health.

> ***HINTS AND TIPS*** *Look at Area 8 to note that the link between the poor health and literacy of men drafted for the Vietnam War in the 1960s shocked the USA government into attempting to alleviate poverty via compensatory education schemes.*

The origins of the welfare state as we know it today lie in one of the most significant documents of the twentieth century, the Beveridge Report of 1942, which is correctly known as *The Report on Social Insurance*

ACTIVITY KS**INFORMATION TECHNOLOGY**

> KNOWLEDGE AND UNDERSTANDING
>
> Go to the DSS Website (http://.dss.gov.uk/50years/index.htm) and explore the history, development and aims of the social security system in Britain today. This is an extremely good site: well set out, interesting and detailed. It is easy to understand and will give you as much as, or more than, you will need for the examination. There is a list of the main changes since 1948 and there are quotations from a number of writers, politicians, and philosophers.

and Allied Services. In this report, **William Beveridge** identified five 'giants' which he said it was the duty of the state to wipe out (Figure 10.7).

Underlying Beveridge's planned reforms were three basic principles:

- **Adequate rates of support** – the benefits provided by the state were to be high enough that people could be free of poverty.

'Giant'	Later government strategy
Idleness	By this, Beveridge meant unemployment, which was to be targeted by government policies that would defend jobs. This was later translated into action through the nationalisation of major industries such as coal-mining, the railways and docks. All these industries were major employers and were also facing decline as competitors such as oil and car manufacture became more significant to the economy
Ignorance	This referred to the expansion of secondary education through the Butler Act of 1944. You will learn more about this in Area 8
Squalor	This was to be targeted by massive slum clearance and housing re-build programmes, which were a feature of the 1950s and 1960s. This is referred to in Area 6 because it had such an impact on family life and structure
Want	This is what we know as poverty and it was to be eliminated through the benefit system of social security payments to the unemployed, the old, and the sick
Disease	This was to be tackled by the founding of the National Health Service and free medical provision on the basis of need and not wealth. You will learn more about this in Area 11

Figure 10.7 The 'giants' in the Beveridge Report

A C T I V I T Y   KS **COMMUNICATION**

ANALYSIS AND
EVALUATION

Organise a debate to the effect that Beveridge
had set an impossible and idealistic task which all
future governments were bound to fail. Make sure
that you have suggestions both for and against the
discussion point.

■ **Flat rates** – the contributions and the benefits were
to be paid at a flat rate by and to everyone, regardless
of income. Beveridge was in deep disagreement
with the Labour government in 1949 over the
introduction of fees to cover some dental costs.

■ **Comprehensive coverage** – the planned schemes
were to cover as many people as possible.

To tackle poverty specifically, everyone was to pay into
a special fund known as **National Insurance**. This was
originally recorded as a stamp on a card, and older
people may still talk of their contributions to National

PROFILE

William Beveridge

(1879–1963)

William Beveridge came from a well-to-do family
and was educated at Charterhouse School and
Oxford University. Although he had planned a
career in law, he became interested in social
research in his early twenties and studied
unemployment.

He worked as a civil servant and as a journalist
before returning to an academic life as Director of
the London School of Economics. He served on a
variety of public committees throughout the
1920s and 1930s.

At the outbreak of the Second World War in 1939,
Beveridge was sidelined into chairing what was
then seen as a small governmental committee,
which was researching insurance and welfare. His
report, published in 1942, became the triumph of
his career and the foundation of the welfare state.

He was by principle a member of the Liberal party
and even served as an MP for a very short time. He
became a member of the House of Lords in 1946.

Insurance schemes as 'paying their stamps'. Employers,
employees, and the government all contributed to the
scheme. If people became unemployed or retired from
work then they would be paid benefit automatically.
Those people who had never contributed to National
Insurance, such as the long-term sick and disabled,
would receive National Assistance. However, this was
not an automatic right; this benefit was to be means
tested, which means that people would be assessed for
their eligibility on the basis of their income.

To evaluate Beveridge and the impact of his reforms on
the welfare state you may need to consider the
following. Poverty before the Second World War had
been extreme and widespread, and Beveridge hoped to
ensure that no one experienced the same again.
Beveridge fully expected that the demands on the state
for benefit would be low. He believed that
governments could ensure high employment and that
the National Health Service would limit the amount of
severe illness in society. The system that Beveridge
created was ideological in that he did not foresee
changes in family structure and employment patterns.
He based his system on the assumption of a male
breadwinner and a domesticated wife working within
the traditions of the industrial structure of the 1930s. He
did not foresee the impact of the new consumer society
that developed after the Second World War.

Areas of life that had previously been the concern of
individuals, such as health care and, from that, the health
of the nation, were now seen as the legitimate business
of government and the expansion of government
interest into other spheres of private concern
developed exponentially. There was a major change in
attitudes: benefit was seen as a right to everyone and
people should feel no shame in receiving their rights.
This was in marked contrast to what had gone before
where people were offered charity and felt humiliated
and patronised when needing financial assistance.

However, some low-paid work offered less money
than state benefits so people could be better off
unemployed than in work. Money that was paid into
the system was always paid out again immediately so
that people who were investing in National Insurance
schemes were paying into a promise. There was no
invested money, so if employment dropped the
employed would have to pay more into the system to
make sure that all the unemployed could have benefits.

In times of high unemployment this was seen as a burden for tax payers and the low paid would actually be better off unemployed than experiencing low pay and high taxation.

As society changed, new benefits were introduced and changes were made to the system in an *ad hoc* fashion. The system grew so complex and unwieldy that few people really understood it, whether claimants or administrators. This meant that the most vulnerable were unable to claim their entitlements. In the 1970s, there were claimants' unions dedicated to help people navigate the system. It has become extremely expensive to administer the welfare state and the Department of Social Security is one of the largest employers in the country. Both the Conservative government of the 1980s and mid-1990s and the following Labour government pledged to reform and rationalise the system. The changes that they instituted are considered in more detail in the next section,

because they are part of a profoundly serious debate about the following two issues:

- What is the relationship of the government to welfare provision?
- How should welfare provision be funded?

The state, poverty and welfare provision

Beveridge set up the welfare state under the principle of universalism: all those who needed should receive. However, Beveridge assumed that need would decline because the welfare state would eliminate need and want in society. He was sadly misguided in this idea and could not have predicted many of the subsequent changes in society. Between 1945 and 1979, the main debate for social administrators and politicians centred on an argument between **universalism** and **selectivism** about who should receive benefit.

- **Universalism** is the notion that all who qualify should gain benefit. The advantages are that benefits such as Child Benefit become cheap to administer but the disadvantage is that the bill for such benefit is high. There is some discussion of this in Area 6, where social welfare policies and their implications are discussed. This principle is related to the notion of **collectivism** which is a socialist belief that the whole of society is responsible for those in need.

- **Selectivism** is the notion that benefits should be targeted at those in most need. The advantage for government is that many people do not apply. Selective benefits rely on means testing, which is another major political debate. Means tests are

Collectivism	Individualism
Associated with the idea that we should all care for each other as part of a concept of community	Associated with the idea that we should take responsibility for our own lives and destinies
Believe in universal benefits and claw back through taxation	Believe in targeted benefits and privatised provision of services. Support means testing of benefits
The welfare state should be paid for by those who can afford to subscribe and through taxation schemes and redistribution of income	The welfare state is an expensive luxury and people should provide for their own needs and welfare
The poor should be given the means to live to an appropriate standard for society	We need the rich to create wealth and high taxation means that the wealthy will have no incentive to work
Marxists, socialists, some liberals, feminists	The New Right, functionalists and some liberals

Figure 10.8   Principles underlying welfare provision in Britain

---

ACTIVITY   KS INFORMATION TECHNOLOGY, WORKING WITH OTHERS

KNOWLEDGE AND UNDERSTANDING	ANALYSIS AND EVALUATION

Using a social welfare textbook or the Department of Social Security Website, make notes on the main changes in welfare provision in the UK. Do not

simply download or copy – you should process this information by suggesting ideological and practical reasons why you think that each of these changes was instituted. This might be an exercise where you benefit from working with a partner.

administered by complicated application forms, which ask questions about your income (or means) and your eligibility for benefit. Means testing depends on the efficiency of bureaucrats in administering the testing procedure and many people find means tests complicated and do not ask for the benefits to which they are entitled. This is linked to **individualism**, in which individuals should be responsible for their own care.

Varieties of benefit	Examples
Contributory benefits: People pay towards these benefits throughout their working lives and draw on them as they need them	Sick pay Incapacity allowance Maternity allowance Widow's benefit Retirement pensions
Means-tested benefits: People are tested on their income and if it is low enough they qualify for the benefit	Jobseekers' allowance Disability working allowance Social fund Income support Family credit Housing benefit
Non-contributory benefits: These are usually targeted at specific needs or groups of people	Child benefit Attendance allowance Disability living allowance Invalid care allowance One parent benefit

Note that these allowances are subject to frequent change and alteration by the government.

Figure 10.9   Forms of benefit in UK

ACTIVITY — PROBLEM SOLVING

ANALYSIS AND EVALUATION

Your child has a disability and you have been told that specialised and privately designed computerised systems would help that child's development. These cost £10,000 each and you have a limited income. Consider the following questions.

- Is access to support for this child your right or a privilege to which you should expect to make a significant contribution, thus depriving your other children of things that they need?
- Will it benefit the child if you make him or her an object of local charity and ask for donations?
- Should the child benefit as an individual or should the money be given to a school so that all children who need the equipment have equal and very small shares of the equipment?

The issues that this section is concerned with rely on a broader consideration of the practical and ideological lessons that politicians and planners have learned from the great social and political experiment that is the welfare state.

- Poverty is relative. Even if people's physical needs are met, they have social needs for certain goods and services, and as the general standard of living increases so these needs increase.
- Certain events that affect welfare services cannot be predicted or budgeted for efficiently. Certainly no one predicted the impact of HIV or the development of fertility treatments on the provision of health care. More recently, the drug Viagra has been the subject of debate in terms of health care. Do men who suffer from sexual dysfunction have an automatic right to an expensive drug, paid for by the rest of society?

- It is difficult to predict the impact of or demand for services. When old-age pensions were introduced, it was assumed that people would die soon after retirement. Life expectancy has increased dramatically and over 15% of the population now qualifies for age-related pensions.
- People did not expect or predict the amount of abuse of the system that developed. The black economy of people doing casual, low-paid work for cash and still drawing benefit is assumed to be enormous but there are no accurate figures. In some ways, the system encourages this behaviour because the rules about doing paid work while drawing benefit are complex.
- The welfare bill for this country is huge. In 1997–1998, social security cost £100 billion, education £38 billion, and health and social services £53 billion. These three departments accounted for approximately two-thirds of the income of the country. People still complain that these services are underfunded, and the evidence that they are short of money is all around us. It is not surprising that governments wish either to limit the welfare budget or ensure that the money is well spent. Tony Blair, when elected Prime Minister in 1997, told the European Council of Ministers that welfare reform to reduce the budget was one of the main priorities of his government. Note, however, that a comparison of EU member states shows that the

UK has one of the lowest expenditures per head of population (Figure 10.10).

■ Welfare is paid for through direct taxation, which comes out of people's pay packets, and through indirect taxation such as VAT, which is levied on consumer goods. Many people dislike paying tax and a promise to cut taxation was one of the key features of the political campaign that resulted in the election of the Conservative government of 1979.

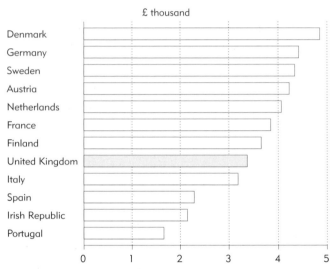

£ thousand

¹Before deduction of tax, where applicable. Figures are Purchasing Power Parities per inhabitant
²Data for Belgium, Greece and Luxembourg are not available

Source: Eurostat

Figure 10.10 Expenditure¹ on social protection benefits per head: EU comparison², 1996

ACTIVITY KS **WORKING WITH OTHERS**

ANALYSIS AND EVALUATION

Imagine that a simple cure for obesity has been discovered. It costs £250 for a month's supply. The drug must be taken throughout that person's life to keep him or her at natural body weight. Organise a class debate centred on these two questions:

■ What are the benefits to society of such a drug?

■ What are the implications for the health and welfare budgets of our society given that approximately 1 in 5 of the population is clinically obese?

HINTS AND TIPS *The real thrust of the argument is to consider who should pay the bill for the welfare state.*

■ *Individuals should provide for themselves.*
■ *All tax payers should contribute because they are all possible claimants.*
■ *Wealthy tax payers should support the poor because they can afford to.*

Policy and politics

Each political party has a particular stance on the welfare debate and you should be aware of how the ideology of each can affect the direction and structure of welfare provision.

HINTS AND TIPS *Write to the various political parties to ask for information about their policies with regard to welfare provision and poverty. During the run-up to an election, you will receive a huge amount of literature through the door. Save these pamphlets to understand the general principles along which the parties operate. You may find Website information on political parties to support your research.*

Conservatism

Conservatism has always stood for individualism, which is the idea that the state should not interfere in the lives of the people. Policy during the years of Conservative administrations saw governments applying market principles to the provision of services in the view that this made them more efficient. You will understand the impact of this on education in Area 8 and in health provision in Area 11. The Conservative conception of the welfare state is that people should organise their own provision and that the state should act as a safety net for those who are weakest and most vulnerable. There was also, however, a paternalistic strand in traditional conservative thinking which viewed the state as a 'good father', someone who knew better than you what was good for you and who could be relied on to have your interests at heart even if you did not like the consequences. This was allied to ideas of the working-class Conservative voter as being **deferential**; some poor people in the past regarded the wealthy and powerful as having the right to rule because of their education and class. In return the wealthy and powerful felt they owed a duty of charity to the poor. This view of the world was at odds with the 'realism' of conservatism under Margaret Thatcher, which is often referred to as the New Right. Thatcherism denied the impact of social class on politics and saw economics as being the most powerful influence on social relations. The emphasis on economics is something that the New Right shares with Marxism.

The New Right and Thatcherism

The impact of the New Right on the welfare state was to remove one of the core principles of Beveridge's original conception, which was universalism. To be fair to the New Right, this principle was not as strongly held in the 1970s as in the 1940s, but the contraction of benefits was notable throughout the 1980s. The main piece of legislation was the Social Security Act of 1986. This had the effect of introducing the following elements into the welfare system:

- **Prescription charges** were introduced. These have risen dramatically since 1979 when the cost of a prescription was 20p.

- **Care in the Community** became policy and mental hospitals and long-term institutions were closed down. This is a contentious issue: although people have undoubtedly benefited from being placed in private homes, other mentally ill people have found themselves homeless and unsupervised.

- **Hospital and Health Care Trusts** were set up to provide care. These are effectively Quangos (Quasi-autonomous non-governmental organisations). They try to run on the principles of a business, but their funding and money comes from government grants rather than from local government.

- **Housing** was once provided by local councils in order to help people who could not afford their own property or mortgages. The government aimed to encourage councils to sell their stock to tenants or to housing associations to manage privately.

Who claims?

There are clear differences between certain social groups in their take-up of welfare benefits and the

cost they represent to the state. There are also differences in attitudes towards benefit claims among social groups.

The main cost to government of welfare is social security payments to the elderly, sick and disabled. These are not separate groups; there is considerable overlap. As people live longer, they also experience a high risk of disability through ill health and disabling physical conditions. Many children are surviving conditions that might once have killed them in early infancy but, with advanced medical technology, they are going on to live full and active lives. One of the largest areas of cost to the state is an increase in lone parents: *Social Trends* 29 (1999) points out that 55% of all government spending on the family goes to lone parents.

Law et al. (1999) in their research at the University of Leeds discovered that there is considerable variation among ethnic groups in their attitudes towards

(Great Britain)
£ billion at 1997–98 prices[2]

	1981–82	1986–87	1991–2	1997–98
Elderly	29.7	35.1	37.2	42.8
Sick and disabled	7.7	11.4	15.9	24.0
of which: short term	1.5	1.7	1.6	1.2
long term	6.2	9.7	14.3	22.9
Family	10.1	12.5	13.6	18.6
of which: lone parents	2.2	4.3	6.7	9.9
Unemployed	7.8	11.6	8.9	6.3
Widows and others	2.0	2.0	2.2	2.0
Total	57.2	72.6	77.7	93.7

[2]Adjusted to 1997–98 prices using the GDP market prices deflator

Source: Department of Social Security

Figure 10.11 Social security benefit expenditure in real terms by recipient group

Questions

- How much money was spent on welfare benefits in 1997–1998?

- Which social group was most expensive in real terms in 1997–1998?

- Account for the increase in payment in real terms to single parents and the elderly between 1981 and 1997.

- Which social group has experienced a fall in payments since 1981? Suggest reasons why this may be so.

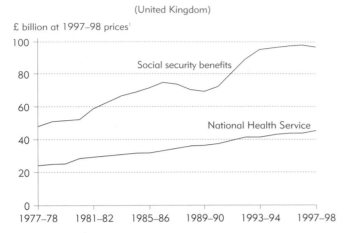

(United Kingdom)

£ billion at 1997–98 prices[1]

'Adjusted to 1997–98 prices using the GDP market prices deflator

Source: Department of Health; Department of Social Security; Departmentof Health and Social Services, Northern Ireland

Figure 10.12 Real[1] growth in social security benefits and National Health Service expenditure

claiming and the benefits system. They found that the Chinese and Bangladeshi communities had negative perceptions of claiming and delayed claiming, or did not claim, benefits to which they were entitled. Some members of the Afro-Caribbean and Asian communities found that benefits were not well administered and some stated that they were patronised and insulted by staff. Afro-Caribbeans were more likely to see benefits as a right than members of other ethnic communities such as the Asian Moslems, who tended to see benefit as being a charity for the poor and whose religious scruples made it difficult for them to claim. They also point out that there is little official monitoring of services to members of ethnic minority communities and so there is a lack of significant official data on which to base research.

The actual impact of these policy changes can be seen in the above graph which shows in adjusted figures a general pattern of significant increases in social security benefit payments and health service funding between 1977 and 1991.

The Labour party

The Labour party underwent a significant change of position with regard to welfare during the long years between 1979 and 1997 when it was out of power. The 'old' or traditional Labour party saw the provision of

welfare rights as part of its duty to the population. It operated on notions of equality and was associated with heavy taxation burdens for the wealthy to pay for the welfare state.

The Labour Government of Tony Blair

After the return of the Labour party to power in 1997, a new perspective was on offer, which we have called New Individualism in this area. A group who defined themselves as 'New' Labour and who dominated the Labour party came to hold power under the leadership of Tony Blair. The 'new individualists' reject market forces as organising society, but also reject the forms of socialism which imply planned economies and centralised governments. They claim to support the welfare state but feel that the wealthy should support themselves as far as possible and have supported private pension schemes and targeted benefits. The language of New Labour includes such terms as:

- **Mutualism** – the idea that companies, trade unions and co-operative groups could provide welfare benefit for people who could pay in small sums. The idea harks back to the 1930s when workers set up mutual benefit societies for themselves in a form of non-profit-making insurance against ill health and bad luck.

- **Stakeholder society** – it is thought that people need to feel in control of their own welfare provision. People could build up individual accounts with National Insurance. If they want to add more investment to their fund they can, and will then receive pension payments above the basic minimum.

Care provision in the UK

Welfare pluralism

This term refers to the idea that there are several care-providing organisations within our state. Although in theory the state provides care for everyone, in practice this is far from the case. Many of the vulnerable would be in very grave difficulties without the groups who support people who find it difficult to support themselves. Figure 10.13 illustrates the main forms of care, which are expanded by further discussion.

Informal voluntary care is the care provided by relatives or community members who carry the burden of supporting a family member with special needs due to age or infirmity. Feminists such as Finch and Groves (1983) point out that this burden often belongs to women who provide unpaid domestic labour, often giving up their own chances of a career or social life. The **Care in the Community** initiative was criticised because in many cases the sick were placed in the care of their own families. The adult infirm were sometimes placed with parents who were themselves elderly, sick or unwell.

Increasingly people are turning to the independent or non-governmental sector for welfare provision. Two forms of provision are available: voluntary (or non-profit-making) bodies or **charities** and privately owned businesses.

Charities

Charities have a number of functions, including awareness raising, fund raising and social and moral support for members. Some are very efficient at helping the vulnerable, and children's charities – such as Barnardo's – are efficient and well-run organisations supporting social services and receiving grant aid for their work. Some charity groups find it necessary to operate on very small budgets and to depend on very hard-working volunteers because of the nature or rarity of the specific problem that they wish to tackle. Children and animals are likely to be better funded through voluntary donations than less attractive or rare disabilities and medical problems. However, other sources of funding for voluntary groups include:

- grants from the government or council

- earnings from investments and charity shops

- requiring people to pay a fee for some services provided

Provider	Form of provision	Forms of care provided
The welfare state	Central government (often as a funding agency)	Social security benefits and pensions Health Service Employment services and schemes Home Office – prisons, probation and police Education
	Local government (often as a service provider)	Social services Schools and nurseries Housing departments Leisure services
The community	Variable and personal, from family members, agencies, neighbours and concerned others	Variable, depending on the need of the receiver and willingness of those who offer help. Can be related to wealth and opportunity of family and of local authority services and charities
The voluntary sector (charities, self-help and campaigning groups)	Support from charitable organisations. Support from concerned individuals, many of whom donate time, money and effort to a cause or organisation	Can be related to wealth and purpose of the charitable organisation. Can be help to individual organisations such as schools and hospitals by volunteers. Can be grant aided funding of major projects. Some charities provide services to local authorities on a support or contractual basis. Provides individuals with a sense of purpose as helpers
The private sector	Private schools Nursing homes Nurseries Hospitals Private care services in home Residential homes for sick and elderly	Any form of care or service which individuals are willing to pay for. Sometimes this can be a personal and private arrangement for nursing care in home; often it can be institutional. Some support of the local authorities may be offered, but this support is paid for. There can be an overlap between charity and private, in that charities may run facilities such as holiday respite homes for which they expect people to pay

Figure 10.13   Forms of social welfare provision

- support from the National Lottery
- donations from individuals and businesses

One particular issue needs to be raised carefully. Some charities raise money by making disabled people objects of other people's pity. Disablement groups often feel that what they really require are social rights such as access to buildings.

Agencies and business groups

Such groups have always been working parallel to the welfare state in the form of private clinics and residential care homes. Since the 1990s these have proliferated. Between 1986 and 1990, care was provided by an agency, funded by social security benefits, but this became expensive as costs rose and the government capped LEA budgets with the Community Care Act 1990. Currently, the more usual scenario is for elderly people to be cared for in their own homes, but for the Social Services to contact care-providing agencies for clients. People can also initiate the contacts themselves. These groups are selling a service and expect to make a profit.

> **HINTS AND TIPS** How might the profit motive affect the quality of the services provided by health and welfare care agencies? You might be advised to consider the case carefully at this point. Do not be overly critical or overly positive, but attempt to see both sides of the argument.

Access to care

Access to care can be severely limited in a number of ways. Some of these are institutionalised into care organisations whereas others are cultural or accidental. There is some overlap between the services offered and people can fall into the gap between services. This happens to children who attend special schools – is speech therapy a medical or an educational need? Neither the Health Service nor the Education Authority is willing to pay and access may be limited as a result. Speech therapy may be offered not just on the basis of need but also on the ability of the parents to demonstrate that their child has a particular need or to take a local authority or health service to court. Note therefore that those with more money, influence and power can have

access to more services and support than the poorest and most defenceless.

Research conducted by Dobson and Middleton (1999) highlighted the very real costs of disability and the difference that adequate support and welfare provision can make. In a study using focus groups and looking at the problems experienced by the parents of severely disabled children, they discovered that benefits were wholly inadequate for the support of a child. They estimated that a child with a severe disability cost an average of £7000 each year to support and that benefits would need to be increased by 20–50% to meet the real costs of a minimum budget. They also discovered that parents were not made aware of entitlements and many did not receive support. Parents reported continuous stress from battles to obtain services and support, while at the same time struggling to maintain employment, care for the needs of their child and suffering from the lack of provision of adequate childcare.

Provision for the elderly

It should already be apparent that elderly people in our society are more likely to experience chronic poverty, and their problems of lack of finance are also likely to be compounded by social isolation brought on through age and disability. This is a serious problem for the government because already nearly 20% of the population is over the standard retirement age and drawing benefit, and the numbers will increase as a result of demographic changes.

State pensions are set at a very low level and the government has done little to increase their real value. This is a social class and gender issue as well as an issue of age, because those who survive on state pensions are unlikely to have paid into an occupational scheme. These people tend to be women, members of certain ethnic minorities, the sick and disabled and the working class. In addition, women currently have a longer life expectancy than men, although this might change as smoking becomes increasingly a female habit. Both the Conservative government of the 1980s and the Labour government of the 1990s have encouraged people to pay into private schemes to top up their pensions through tax incentives. The most

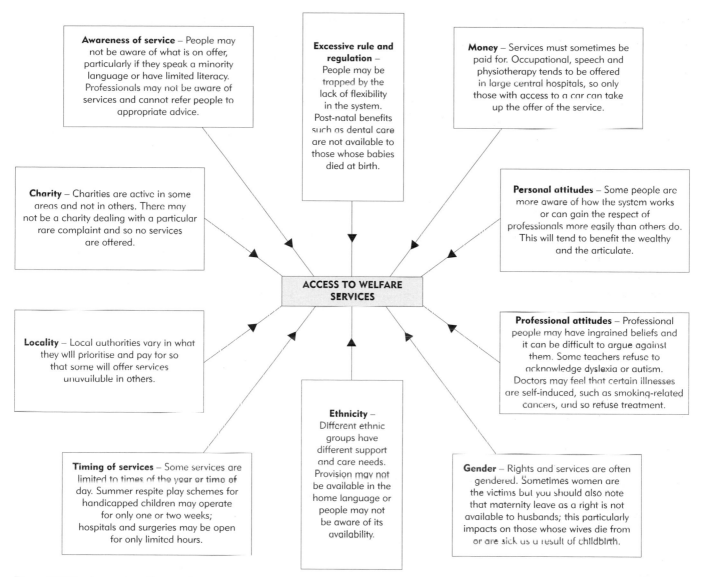

Awareness of service – People may not be aware of what is on offer, particularly if they speak a minority language or have limited literacy. Professionals may not be aware of services and cannot refer people to appropriate advice.

Excessive rule and regulation – People may be trapped by the lack of flexibility in the system. Post-natal benefits such as dental care are not available to those whose babies died at birth.

Money – Services must sometimes be paid for. Occupational, speech and physiotherapy tends to be offered in large central hospitals, so only those with access to a car can take up the offer of the service.

Charity – Charities are active in some areas and not in others. There may not be a charity dealing with a particular rare complaint and so no services are offered.

Personal attitudes – Some people are more aware of how the system works or can gain the respect of professionals more easily than others do. This will tend to benefit the wealthy and the articulate.

ACCESS TO WELFARE SERVICES

Locality – Local authorities vary in what they will prioritise and pay for so that some will offer services unavailable in others.

Professional attitudes – Professional people may have ingrained beliefs and it can be difficult to argue against them. Some teachers refuse to acknowledge dyslexia or autism. Doctors may feel that certain illnesses are self-induced, such as smoking-related cancers, and so refuse treatment.

Timing of services – Some services are limited to times of the year or time of day. Summer respite play schemes for handicapped children may operate for only one or two weeks; hospitals and surgeries may be open for only limited hours.

Ethnicity – Different ethnic groups have different support and care needs. Provision may not be available in the home language or people may not be aware of its availability.

Gender – Rights and services are often gendered. Sometimes women are the victims but you should also note that maternity leave as a right is not available to husbands; this particularly impacts on those whose wives die from or are sick as a result of childbirth.

Figure 10.14   Access to welfare services

vulnerable members of our community are those who have the least ability to secure for themselves a comfortable old age.

The chronically sick and the disabled

Disability and sickness can strike suddenly or can be as a result of a lifelong condition. Estimates of the number of people who are registered as sick and disabled vary, but probably over 10% of all adults and under 5% of all children experience long-term sickness or disability. Obviously conditions vary in the extent to which they incapacitate people, and many long-term

sick and disabled people are also elderly but employment prospects for those who might choose to work are very limited. It should be clear from the study of this area that disability has profound effects on a person's lifestyle and can be extremely expensive if someone requires special adaptations to live independently. Disabled people may well experience discrimination in education and employment, so it comes as little surprise to realise that over half of all disabled people are in low-paid jobs or unemployed. In addition, if the disability is severe, family members may be required to take on the care and support of the affected person, which limits their own ability to maintain a job.

Residential care versus care in the community

Throughout the 1930s and later, disabled people were often seen as a source of shame and embarrassment to families. This meant that they would be taken to hospitals and institutions away from the rest of society, known as **asylums**. Those parents who did not particularly subscribe to that view would have to fight very hard against the authorities, who would try and place children in care institutions 'for their own good'.

Huge asylums were built, housing hundreds of people, often in pleasant country areas and well away from the population centres. These were **total institutions** in that people lived the whole of their lives in the institution, which provided total care. These were closed communities and had virtually no contact with outsiders. The architecture was often forbidding: grey concrete and castle shapes were particularly popular. If people were sent to a prison, there was a limit to their sentence and they would know that they would eventually be released. There was no such possibility for people in asylums, who could be imprisoned for the whole of their lives. In addition, there was often confusion between physical and mental disability so that people with cerebral palsy, who often had communication problems, were labelled as mentally disabled and placed in situations where they were powerless and lacked stimulation. Definitions of mental instability were not necessarily ones that people would agree with today – for example, moral codes were used to define unmarried mothers as mentally ill.

> **HINTS AND TIPS**   Older people may well know of the location of such hospitals. They tended to enter local folklore as bad places and many people had a horror of them. Common slang for asylums called them 'bins' or 'loony bins'. What does this tell you about attitudes that people had to those with special needs? Are you aware of local asylums and mental hospitals? Ask older relatives about their memories of how people talked about disability and mental illness.

Throughout the 1970s pressure increased on government to close the large asylums and to bring people with special needs back into the community. The reasoning behind this was very much prompted by the influence of the interactionist Erving Goffman's

> **ACTIVITY**   **KS COMMUNICATION**
>
> ANALYSIS AND EVALUATION
>
> Read Ken Kesey's *One Flew over the Cuckoo's Nest* or watch a video of the film starring Jack Nicholson. Both the film and the book are classics: a grim story told with genuine humour and with a slightly hopeful ending. As a group, analyse the relationships between the care staff and the inmates of the asylum. To what extent is the institution an instrument of social control?

(1968) seminal text *Asylums*. This has been reprinted regularly since it first appeared. Goffman described a situation where people are stripped of identity and forced to see themselves in terms of being an inmate. People become institutionalised and cannot conceive of themselves as individuals without the institution. They are characterised by passive behaviour and rely on the routines that the institution has established for their security and serenity.

The argument against institutional care is summarised below.

- Many inmates become institutionalised and lose all sense of self or purpose.
- Institutions are often run for the benefit of the staff, not the inmates.
- Other people in the community learn to fear the disabled or sick, seeing them as a danger to the community because they need to be locked away.
- Institutional care can be very expensive.
- Once people entered institutions they were seen in terms of their institutional self and it became almost impossible to be released, no matter what the grounds for the original institutionalisation. Note that this often included physical disability and moral incapacity (girls having sex before marriage).
- There have been many serious cases of mistreatment and abuse of vulnerable patients at the hands of staff.

> **HINTS AND TIPS**   Erving Goffman's book is a relatively easy read and his work is absolutely fascinating. It will repay the time that you spend on it. See what else you can find in the library to look at.

Nurses suspended for 'sadism' to elderly

Eight nurses have been sent home for alleged cruelty to patients in the largest mass suspension from an NHS hospital.

The suspensions follow claims made by student nurses on a five-week attachment to a 25-bed unit treating elderly mentally ill people.

The two women, one of them a mature student, recorded more than 30 examples of alleged sadistic and inhumane treatment. In one instance, they claim a woman in her seventies was force-fed scalding hot food, burning her mouth. They also claim patients, mostly in their seventies and eighties, were bruised by rough treatment, taunted with abusive names, left naked or semi-clothed for prolonged periods, or were forced to sit neglected in cold corridors.

One elderly woman, in the group of 19 patients allegedly mistreated in April and May this year, has since died. All are said to be suffering from Alzheimer's disease and other forms of dementia, and none is believed capable of being interviewed.

The suspensions from Tolworth hospital in Surbiton, Surrey, originally built as an isolation hospital, are not the only cause for concern. In another investigation, St. Ebba's hospital, Epsom, a few miles from Tolworth, has suspended seven nurses since July. The hospital confirmed that the suspensions involved similar allegations of mistreatment of elderly patients. "We take complaints of this nature seriously and we are following normal procedure of suspending staff involved pending an investigation," said the hospital.

Nurses suspended at Tolworth, who include the ward manager, other senior nurses and some unqualified assistants, have reacted angrily to the allegations. They maintain hospital managers failed to deal with staff shortages which sometimes meant only two nurses, one of them unqualified, were left in charge of up to 25 incontinent, demented people, most of whom had to be spoon-fed.

Claire Burroughs, a spokesman for the hospital, admitted there were five vacancies in the 18-strong workforce meant to cover the affected ward, but said it was up to senior staff to raise concerns about patient care and arrange extra temporary help.

"After preliminary investigations, we decided these staff should be suspended," she said. "The investigation will produce a public report by the end of the year."

Elsewhere there have been reports of elderly people drowning in hospital baths, being starved or given the wrong drugs.

Lisa Mahoney, 36, who works for the charity Age Concern in Harlow, Essex, lost her 71-year-old father after weeks of inadequate nursing care. Bill Mahoney was admitted to hospital unable to speak after a stroke. He received insufficient feeding, bathing and an overdose of the drug insulin.

The family received some compensation from the local Princess Alexandra hospital, but Mahoney said: "Nobody should be treated like that. People are still people, however old and infirm they are."

The number of qualified nurses removed from the national register because of cruelty to elderly patients is running at more than 40 a year. Charities and pressure groups campaigning for better care for the elderly say increasing reliance on care assistants and temporary staff provided by agencies is worsening the problem.

The Department of Health said it plans to tackle the lack of protection for patients in the care of unqualified healthcare staff. There are more than 116,000 such care assistants working in the NHS compared with 332,000 trained nurses.

"We are planning to review their role with a vew to producing a report next April," a spokesman said.

Lois Rogers (19 September 1999) *The Sunday Times*

1 How many nurses were suspended for cruelty to elderly patients last year? **(1)**

2 What is the proportion of untrained staff to trained staff working in National Health hospitals? Offer a rough figure. **(1)**

3 Find reasons that are offered in the article to account for the alleged cruelty. **(3)**

4 What reasons make it difficult for the hospital or the patients to bring a criminal charge against people who are cruel? **(3)**

5 Suggest reasons why it may be necessary to place disordered elderly people in hospital, even if they have no specific physical problems. **(4)**

6 How could elderly people be supported in their own homes? **(4)**

7 What problems would caring for the seriously disordered cause for local authorities and for families? **(5)**

8 On what grounds could you suggest that the number of cases of the maltreatment of the elderly might actually rise over the next decades? **(6)**

9 Can you suggest what the article tells us about social attitudes towards the elderly in our society? **(8)**

10 Suggest reasons why the care of the elderly in our society could be described as a feminist issue. Do you agree with this position? Give sociological reasons for your views. **(9)**

There was very strong pressure from a number of concerned groups throughout the 1970s to end the great Victorian asylums, but the real impetus for change came with the arrival of the Conservative government of 1979. When Care in the Community came, considerable distrust of the motives of government was expressed – was this a genuine desire to help the disabled or a cost-cutting exercise? (Note that although the term '**community care**' is used, in most cases family members provide this care.) Many writers suggest that community has broken down and that very few people experience community life in Britain. Housing associations and disabled charities often experience considerable hostility when planning new housing schemes for the disabled or the mentally infirm.

Curiously, there has been some pressure to increase residential and institutional care for certain forms of mental disability, such as schizophrenia or depression, where people feel more secure in a structured environment.

HINTS AND TIPS   *There have been cases of mental patients harming members of the public because they have not been supervised and have not taken medication. Whilst not minimising the danger and anguish that relatives and strangers may have felt in these situations, you should note that most mental patients are more likely to harm themselves than strangers.*

Care in the community and the family

Most provision of care is by families, especially women, although men are also carers. The Equal Opportunities Commission suggested in 1990 that two-thirds of carers are female. Caring can be a desperate and difficult task, resulting in loneliness and isolation for the carers. Money may be in short supply for carers if they are relying on benefits and some individuals require 24-hour supervision. Research by George in 1992 showed that 50% of carers were themselves receiving old-age pensions and that 55% of carers were under significant stress due to their fears for the dependent relatives after their own death. The problem is very acute for those who have a disabled child, who may live for a long time after the death of the parent. Problems are likely only to increase as the population is living longer. The proportion of elderly people in the population is growing and as families are tending to be smaller than in the past, the burden could fall on one child to care for two elderly or demented parents over long periods. There may well be considerable and increasing pressure on government to provide more support for carers in terms of services or residential provision over the next 30 years.

Points in favour	Concerns and criticisms of the practice
Asylums were terrible places to be	The weak and destitute mentally sick are often housed in poor areas where there is little in the sense of community. There is evidence that some people in prison are those who would formerly have had psychiatric help. Some communities are unwilling to accept the unusual
Community care is cheaper than residential care	Not if it is done properly by health care professionals and paid workers. Currently it depends on families and volunteers. There is little aftercare service for some patients
A wide range of welfare provision is available to support people in their own homes	These are variable and depend on a number of factors, including the general wealth of the local council. Some are voluntary and therefore subject to cuts
Abuse was noted in some institutions	The vulnerable are also subject to abuse in the community. There has been evidence of unscrupulous practice by private welfare agencies, who charge high rents but do not provide the service that they are paid for. Overstretched social workers are unable to monitor the situation
Many psychiatric drugs have long-term effects that aid the patient	Patients can forget doses and do not realise that they are losing control over their own lives. The most disturbed are the least likely to recognise their own need and there have been cases of self-harm and of violence against strangers (even murder)

Figure 10.15   Care in the Community – the debate

Area summary

Working through this area you should have gained an appreciation of the significance of wealth to the whole of our culture and way of life. Our society is affluent and yet there are wide differences in the quality of life between those who are wealthy and those who are poor. We have to ask ourselves some serious questions about the relationship between wealth and poverty. Poverty obviously involves a lot more than lack of money, associated as it is with deprivation that can span the generations and produce shortened and stunted lives. Are those who are poor exploited by the wealthy or do they create their own misfortune and deprivation? Are some people more worthy of our sympathy than others? It is commonly stated that wealth cannot bring happiness, so perhaps the benefits of wealth are over-stated and Karl Marx was incorrect, the poor should be grateful for what they have rather than concentrating on what they lack.

Whose task is it to care for the weaker members of our society? Is it the responsibility of the wealthy to look after the poor? Many people argue that there is very little redistribution of income in our society, and that it is not actually the rich who fund the welfare state but the poor themselves, through taxation on luxuries. Do we, as functionalists claim, need poverty in our society to act as a salutary reminder to the hard-working among us what will happen if we become lazy and irresponsible?

Our society has had a welfare state for something over 50 years. It was created with the express intention of solving the problem of poverty and deprivation. To what extent has it been successful? It is extremely expensive to our society and we each contribute huge sums of money towards it. Can the welfare state be trusted to actually look after us when things go wrong? If we become incapacitated for any reason, how should we be cared for? Families will take on care, but often at the cost of the pride of the vulnerable and the health of the carer. As many of us come from small families and have no living relatives willing to care for us, how will our care be provided? Is institutional care better than being left unsupported? To what extent is the notion of 'care in the community' a myth, given that so few of us live in anything that could be described as a community in modern Britain?

Definitions

Asylum	An institution for the care of the sick and infirm
Absolute poverty	A condition in which a person is without some of the essentials for survival such as food or heat; sometimes referred to as primary poverty
Benefit	Payments from the state
Care in the community	This is a vague and general term used to cover a variety of systems whereby people are no longer cared for in institutions but must learn to cope with or without support in local communities

Charity	An organisation funded primarily by volunteers, grants and donations which seeks to educate people about, look after certain sections of, and to act as a political mouthpiece for, a sector of the community
Client groups	The people who qualify for help and support
Collectivism	The notion that we are all responsible for the poor
Community care	A welfare policy that suggests that the sick and disabled should live in the general community
Culture of dependence	This is similar to culture of poverty but claims that people grow to depend on state handouts rather than contributing to society in a more positive way
Culture of poverty	It is suggested that poor people develop a culture which helps them to survive poverty but which also prevents them from helping themselves out of poverty
Cycle of poverty	The belief that poverty occurs in cycles and can pass on through the generations
Deferential	The idea that people of lower status and social standing should give way to those with more prestige than they
Deserving poor	These are people who are poor through no fault of their own
Equality	A state where there is little difference in wealth or status between citizens
Fatalism	A belief that you cannot change events
Indices of deprivation	These are the various signs that a person is experiencing poverty such as poor housing, inadequate clothing or lack of food
Individualism	The idea that we should take personal and individual responsibility for our own lives
Informal voluntary care	This is provided on a friendship or family basis; people look after each other
Institution care	To be cared for in a place designed for the purpose of caring such as an asylum or hospice; people are employed to care
Means test	A test to decide if a person is eligible for state help
Mutualism	The idea that people and the state should work together
National Insurance	People pay money into a state scheme known as National Insurance; if they fall upon hard times, they can then claim benefits
Poverty	A lack of basic necessities or the wherewithal to buy what is needed
Poverty line	A point or sum of money said to divide the poor from the non-poor
Primary poverty	Lack of the basic necessities of life; also called absolute poverty
Relative poverty	Poverty that is related to lack of the things that others consider necessary for a decent standard of living; sometimes referred to as secondary poverty
Secondary poverty	Poverty that is related to lack of the things that others consider necessary for a decent standard of living
Selectivism	Benefits should be targeted at those most in need of help
Stakeholder society	This is the idea that people will work harder for the benefit of all if they can also feel that there is a personal benefit to themselves

Subjective poverty	A sense of being poor when measuring oneself against others in a peer group
Total institution	An institution that takes over all the decisions of a person's life
Underclass	People who are at the very bottom of society and who have little desire to improve their status or condition, according to theorists of the New Right
Undeserving poor	A Victorian term used to describe people who contributed to their own poverty through drinking or other 'bad' habits
Universalism	The principle that everyone should receive benefits to which they are entitled
Wealth	A surplus of the things that you need for living and which can be sold to raise additional funds
Welfare	The idea or the practice of supporting the needy in society through payment of benefits or provision of services such as education or health
Welfare state	Organisations of government to look after the health and welfare of the population

Data response questions

Item A

A serious argument ... has been mounted by William Julius Wilson (1987) and it centres on the causation of welfare problems through the unavailability of work. His argument is important because it does not depend on the familiar explanations for the plight of the underclass and the disadvantages of minorities (especially the black population) in the USA in terms of discrimination ... His explanation of the inner city problem is that there has been a dramatic reduction in employment opportunities for disadvantaged people. The old manufacturing jobs that used to be located in the inner cities have largely disappeared.

Barry, N. (1999:191) **Welfare** 2nd edition. Open University Press.

Item B

It is no exaggeration to regard (John) Rex as the founding father of the theoretical study of race and ethnic phenomena in the UK despite the many criticisms, some unjustified, of his work. He was able to identify racist exclusions as central and malignant forces in modern industrial societies, and linked them to economic and political inequalities more generally. He was also less than optimistic about the capacity of the liberal democratic and welfare state to deliver society from the inequalities that reproduced racist ideas and actions; hence the enormous weight he gave to class and ethnic mobilisation as forms of struggle.

Flora Anthias (1995:331) in George, V. and Page, R.
Modern Thinkers on Welfare. Prentice-Hall.

Item C

Ethnic minority households are four times more likely than White households to become homeless. Of the young homeless, a study of a number of London boroughs found that young Blacks were disproportionately represented. For example, in Newham (east London) over 50% of referrals to hostels for the homeless were for Black single people ... This Act (Race Relations Act 1976) made it illegal to discriminate directly or indirectly in the provision of goods or services to the public or in the areas of employment and housing. It also became illegal to incite racial hatred.

Moore, S. (1998:385) **Social Welfare Alive**, 2nd edition. Stanley Thornes.

a   Which Act of Parliament made it illegal to discriminate against people on the
    basis of race? (Item C)   (1)

KNOWLEDGE AND
UNDERSTANDING

b Summarise Wilson's views on the causes of welfare problems (Item A). **(2)**

IDENTIFICATION AND
INTERPRETATION

c Identify and explain two possible causes for the disproportionate amount of poverty among ethnic minority families in the UK. **(4)**

IDENTIFICATION AND
INTERPRETATION

d Using the items and other knowledge, suggest reasons why it is difficult to identify the causes of poverty in our society. **(8)**

IDENTIFICATION AND
INTERPRETATION

e Evaluate the suggestion (Item A) that a major cause of poverty is the lack of acceptable work. **(8)**

ANALYSIS AND
EVALUATION

f Using the items and your own knowledge, evaluate the suggestion that the social welfare system is a source of social change in Britain. **(12)**

ANALYSIS AND
EVALUATION

Structured questions

a Identify two characteristics of a total institution. **(2)**

> **GUIDANCE**   *This question is one of pure knowledge, and you should refer to Erving Goffman's work. Total institutions have complete power over an individual, so any of the implications of that power relationship will offer you a characteristic of a total institution. Think of a prison.*
>
> KNOWLEDGE AND
> UNDERSTANDING

b In Britain, we experience 'welfare pluralism'. To what does this term refer? **(1)**

> **GUIDANCE**   *This is simple and if you do not know the answer then you need to spend more time learning the vocabulary of this section. Pluralism means that there is more than one way in which we can receive welfare benefits and a number of different forms of agency are involved in welfare provision.*
>
> KNOWLEDGE AND
> UNDERSTANDING

c   Summarise the ideologies of the 'New Right' as they apply to the provision of welfare services.   **(1)**

> **GUIDANCE**   You should make sure that you fully understand the thinking of the New Right. Refer to market forces, individualism, and the need for moderation of spending on welfare services. If you recognise the link between the New Right and the politics of conservatism you will gain marks. To gain the full marks for this question some reference to actual legislation might be necessary, so refer to changes in British Welfare provision between 1979 and 1996.
>
> IDENTIFICATION AND INTERPRETATION

d   Why do some sociologists consider that the welfare state may be part of the institution of social control in our society?   **(8)**

> **GUIDANCE**   This question actually asks you to provide a Marxist analysis of the workings of the welfare state. The clue is in the words 'social control'. You need also to provide evidence of knowledge of the welfare system. For instance, there is a strong work ethos in the current welfare state, and social security payments are linked to the search for work. There is very little imposition on employers by government to ensure that the work offers acceptable conditions of employment, is well paid or secure. It is not necessary for you to offer a view as to the correctness of Marxism because you are simply applying an analysis derived from a perspective, which you should understand thoroughly, to a social system.
>
> IDENTIFICATION AND INTERPRETATION

e   Evaluate the suggestion that the 'care in the community' policy is a feminist issue above all.   **(12)**

> **GUIDANCE**   Here you must make a deliberate choice of position while planning an answer. Is care in the community a feminist issue? There is a very strong case to be made for this view of the situation. With a breakdown of community, care is usually provided by women and as primary carers, they may experience little in the way of support. To develop the case, they may lose their jobs and work long hours to support a family member. Carers may even suffer a breakdown in their own health as a result of the stress of the situation. A strong criticism of the practical workings of the community care system could well be indicated. However, to balance that view, the experience of disability and sickness is not gendered and the victims of the community care schemes that are not successful are not only female. Men may also be failed by lack of facilities and while primary carers are female, they may well be members of families who are affected by the caring. There is no monopoly on care by women either, men **do** act as primary carers. In terms of childcare, because there is an assumption of some particular bond between women and children, men may not have the same welfare rights or support even if they do find themselves as sole carers.
>
> ANALYSIS AND EVALUATION

Essay titles

1 Evaluate the suggestion that the provision of welfare benefits has created poverty in the UK. (25)

2 Assess the evidence to suggest that poverty has decreased in modern Britain. (25)

3 Is poverty functional for society? (25)

4 Evaluate the suggestion that there is no such thing as poverty in our society, there is merely inequality. (25)

5 Evaluate the suggestion that the poor develop a culture of poverty. (25)

6 The welfare state cannot solve the problems of inequality in Britain. Discuss. (25)

GUIDANCE *Although this is basically a simple question which asks for an overview of the*

KNOWLEDGE AND UNDERSTANDING	IDENTIFICATION AND INTERPRETATION	ANALYSIS AND EVALUATION

debate, there is an opportunity for the best among you to shine. Both Marxists and the New Right would agree with the basic position and argue that the welfare state cannot solve problems of inequality, but Marxists suggest that the welfare state is merely part of the problem in that it papers over grave inequalities and is a tool of oppression. The New Right argues that the welfare state has created a culture of dependence where people have lost their initiative.

Socialists and liberals believe fervently in the welfare state and feel that it is not the principle itself that is flawed, but that the system needs to be adjusted to become the best that it can be. This is an opportunity for you to refer to functionalism and the view that, once material needs are satisfied, there is no need for equality as people need inequality as a spur to improve themselves. Inequality, as such, is not a problem.

Given the above, your safest strategy is merely to offer an overview of the debate, mentioning the principles of universalism and selectivism along the way, and then offer a conclusion which agrees, disagrees or takes a middle path between the two positions. A clear, well written answer with plenty of evaluation will score well in the marking. However, there are possibilities for the brave to show that they have evaluative skills, and to produce a more interesting answer.

This question opens up a range of possible answers if you choose to use one of the above perspectives as your starting point and apply that analysis to take a critical look at other views. For instance, there is a critical line of thought that can be applied to the question and which derives from Marxism and feminism. This position points out that the provision of the welfare state is not itself equal and that some benefit more than others. Access to the services is not equal and the poor can become victims of their vulnerability because they have fewer means at their disposal to argue for their rights and needs. You can offer an overview of the Care in the Community debate and question whether it was developed as a genuine attempt at reform or a cost-cutting exercise. You might also look at the question of the existence of a private and charity care sector.

Whatever you attempt with this question, you must remember that your answer should be sociological in intent and refer to theory and to actual examples. A common-sense answer will not be effective under examination conditions.

Further reading and references

George, V. and Page, R. (Eds.) (1995) *Modern Thinkers on Welfare*. Prentice-Hall. An excellent little textbook which is perhaps more suitable for those on higher level social administration courses than for A level Sociology. It offers an essay by a major writer on each of a number of theorists and places each within the context of the broader political debate. The essays themselves may be detailed for some but the introductions to each type of thought offer a simple overview.

Moore, S. (1998) *Social Welfare Alive*, 2nd edition. Stanley Thornes.
For an overview of the welfare system itself, you would be well advised to look at this book. It is probably more appropriate to Health and Social Welfare courses than for A level Sociology in that it contains little consideration of the poverty debate but it is interesting and contains a good overview of the welfare services as they relate to benefits and social services. There is an excellent list of addresses of organisations at the back.

Bruce, M. (1965) *The Coming of the Welfare State*. London, Batsford.
This traces the early history of the welfare state. It is very interesting and will give you an overview of some of the philosophical and moral positions underlying the creation of the welfare state. For examination, however, you would be advised to focus on more recent materials.

Trowler, P. (1996). *Investigating Health, Welfare and Poverty*, 2nd edition. London, Collins Educational
Paul Trowler's contribution to the Sociology in Action series offers a highly detailed view of the debates.

Internet sites

The Department of Social Security Website (http://.dss.gov.uk/50years/index.htm) explores the history, development and aims of the social security system that exists in Britain today. This is an extremely good site, well set out, interesting and informative. The home page of the site can be found at http://www.dss.gov.uk and this has a range of links to other agencies and will be useful to you in your studies.

There is a vast amount of useful data on the Joseph Rowntree Foundation Website, which carries research findings from a variety of academics presented in a simple and succinct way. It can be found at http://www.jrf.org.uk

Bibliography

Abel Smith and Townsend, P. (1965) *The Poor and Poorest*. Harmondsworth, Penguin.
Barrett, M. and McIntosh, M. (1991) *The Anti Social Family*. London, Verso.
Barry, N. (1999) *Welfare 2nd Edition*. Milton Keynes, Open University Press.
Begum, N. (1992) *Disabled Women and the Feminist Agenda*. Feminist Review, No. 40.

Bruce, M. (1965) *The Coming of the Welfare State*. London, Batsford.

Coates, K. and Silburn, R. (1970) *Poverty: The Forgotten Englishmen*. Harmondsworth, Penguin.

Dennis, N. (1993) *Rising Crime and the Dismembered Family*. London, *The Institute for Economic Affairs*.

Dobson and Middleton (1999) *Paying to Care: The Cost of Childhood Disability*. Joseph Rowntree Foundation.

Field, E. (1982) *Poverty Politics*. London, Heinemann.

Field, F. (1989) *The Emergence of Britain's Underclass*. Oxford, Blackwell.

Finch, J. and Groves, D. eds. (1983) *Labour of Love: Women, Work and Caring*. London, Routledge and Kegan Paul.

Finch, J. (1989) *Family Obligations and Social Change*. Cambridge, Polity.

Galbraith, J. K. (1960) *The Affluent Society*. Boston, Houghton Mifflin.

George, V. and Page, R. (1995) *Modern Thinkers on Welfare*. London, Prentice Hall.

Giddens, A. (1995) *Affluence, Poverty and the Idea of a Post-Scarcity Society*. Geneva, Switzerland, UNRISD.

Goffman, E. (1968) *Asylums*. Harmondsworth, Penguin.

Green, D. (1998) *Benefit Dependency: Law Welfare Undermines Independence*. London, IEA Health and Welfare Unit.

von Hayek, F. (1986) *The Road to Serfdom*. London, Ark Paperbacks.

Heath, A. (1992) *Understanding the Underclass*. London, Policy Studies Institute.

Hills, J. (1999) *Income and Wealth: the Latest Evidence*. Joseph Rowntree Foundation Website.

Law, I., Hylton, Karmani and Deacon (1999) *Racial Equality and Social Security Service, University of Leeds Departmental Working Paper No. 10*. Leeds, University of Leeds.

Le Grand, J. (1982) *The Strategy of Equality*. London, Allen and Unwin.

Leibow, E. (1967) *Tally's Corner*. Boston, Little Brown.

Lewis, H. (1955) *Blackways of Kent*. Chapel Hill: University of North Carolina.

Lewis, O. (1961) *The Children of Sanchez*. New York, Random House.

Lewis, O. (1966) *LaVida*. New York, Random House.

Marsland, D. (1989) *Universal Welfare Provision Creates Dependant Population* in *Social Studies Review*.

Mead, L. (1985) *Beyond Entitlement*. New York, Basic Books.

Middleton, L. (1999) *Disabled Children: Challenging Social Exclusion*. Oxford, Blackwell Science.

Miles, R. (1989) *Racism*. London, Routledge.

Moore, S. (1998) *Social Welfare Alive 2nd edition*. Cheltenham, Stanley Thornes.

Murray, C. (1984) *Losing Ground*. New York, Basic Books.

Murray, C. A. (1994) *Underclass: The Crisis Deepens*. London, Institute of Economic Affairs.

Murray, C. A. (1990) *The Emerging British Underclass*. London, IEA Health and Welfare Unit.

Murray C. A. (1988) *In Pursuit of Happiness and Good Government*. New York, Simon and Schuster.

O'Connor, J. S. (1999) *States, Markets, Families: Gender, Liberalism and Social Policy in Australia, Canada, Great Britain and the USA*. Cambridge, Cambridge University Press.

Offe, C. (1976) *Industry and Inequality*. London, Edward Arnold.

Oppenheim, F. (1993) *Poverty: The Facts*. The Child Poverty Action Group.

Pierson (1991) *Beyond the Welfare State*. Cambridge, Polity.

Platt, L. and Noble, M. (1999) *Race, Place and Poverty*. York, YPS.

Rex, J. (1988) *The Ghetto and the Underclass*. Aldershot, Avebury.

Roberts, R. (1973) *The Classic Slum: Salford Life in the First Quarter of the Century*. Middlesex, Pelican Books.

Schwartz, A. (July 1975) *A Further Look at the Culture of Poverty: Ten Caracas Barrios* in *Sociology and Social Research*.

Tawney, R. H. (1961) *The Acquisitive Society*. London, Collins.

Titmuss, R. (1967) *Choice and the Welfare State*. London, Fabian Society.

Townsend, P. (1979) *Poverty in the United Kingdom*. Harmondsworth, Penguin.

Townsend, P. (1963) *The Family Life of Old People*. Harmondsworth, Penguin.

Tressell, R. (1991) *The Ragged Trouser'd Philanthropists*. London, Paladin Grafton Books.

Trowler, P. (1996) *Investigating Health Welfare and Poverty, 2nd Edn*. London, Collins Educational.

Wedge, P. and Prosser, H. (1973) *Born to Fail*. London, Arrow Books.

Westergaard, J. and Resler, H. (1975) *Class in a Capitalist Society*. Harmondsworth, Penguin.

Health

This area covers:

- The sociological literature on health, illness and mental illness
- The relationship between health and the social structure
- A consideration of the sociological debates about health inequality.

By the end of this area, you should be able to:

- understand health, illness and mental illness
- identify what a range of sociologists has said about health, health inequalities, mental illness and its relationship to the culture/society that we live in
- identify and evaluate the differing conceptions of health
- successfully attempt examination questions in this area.

Key terms

health	medical nemesis
illness	situational improprieties
disease	total institution
medical model	sick role
iatrogenesis	institutional psychiatry

Area 11   Contents

Introduction

This area will look at the nature of health, illness and disease. Some sociologists argue that poor health is created by the society or culture that we live in, for example by economic factors, ideology or language. In contrast, many doctors argue that the self is an 'agent' which has control over its own body and creates levels of poor health in society through working conditions and eating and drinking habits.

Health is a physiological state, a psychological state and a social state. Our understandings of what it means to be 'sick', 'dependent' or 'disabled' are specific to the culture in which we are brought up. In addition, the meaning of 'health' is relative; it changes over time and from place to place. In other words, what it means 'to be healthy' is open to a wide range of individual, social and cultural interpretations.

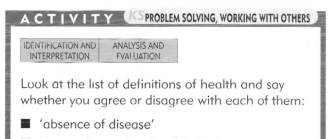

ACTIVITY   KS PROBLEM SOLVING, WORKING WITH OTHERS

IDENTIFICATION AND INTERPRETATION	ANALYSIS AND EVALUATION

Look at the list of definitions of health and say whether you agree or disagree with each of them:

- 'absence of disease'
- 'a complete state of well-being'
- 'not being ill'
- 'the ability to function normally'
- 'a state of fitness'

These definitions of health fall within a **medical model** of health or, as it is sometimes referred to, the bio-mechanical model. In contrast, the World Health Organisation has a much broader definition of health:

> *'Health is not merely the absence of disease, but a state of complete physical, mental, spiritual and social well-being.'*

WHO (1974)

Illness is even more subjective, as it is about how you 'feel'; **sickness** is reported illness, and **disease** is an unhealthy condition of our body or our mind. In other

ACTIVITY   KS PROBLEM SOLVING, WORKING WITH OTHERS

IDENTIFICATION AND INTERPRETATION	ANALYSIS AND EVALUATION

- According to the WHO definition, is 'good' health ever possible?
- Can a person with a 'disability' be healthy?
- Could a person with a cold, period pain, back-ache or asthma be regarded as healthy?

words, health, illness and disease are social products. The state of our health reflects our lived experiences as people from distinct classes, races, gender, ages and disabilities. Once we have come to a definition of health, we have problems about how to measure it. The three most common ways to measure health are:

- **life expectancy**, calculated from mortality (death) rates
- **potential years of life lost** (PYLL), which makes use of mortality rates
- **standardised mortality ratios** (SMR), which measure relative chances of death at a stated age

The National Health Service in Britain

Since its creation in 1948 the NHS has changed its administrative structure several times. However, the principles and underlying aims are said to have remained the same.

- **The Collectivist principle** – the state had a responsibility for the health care of its citizens, providing an optimum standard of service via hospitals, family practitioner services (GPs, dentists, etc.)
- **The Comprehensive principle** – all the health care needs of the population are catered for
- **The Universal principle** – the full range of health services are provided for the whole population, and

there is what many people believe to be a set of health care rights

- **The Equality principle** – equal access to the service, services relevant to the needs of the people, services should be easy to use
- **The Professional Autonomy principle** – doctors are free to prescribe whatever is appropriate for their patients, free from government interference

---

A C T I V I T Y KS **PROBLEM SOLVING, WORKING WITH OTHERS**

IDENTIFICATION AND INTERPRETATION

Compare the two quotes below and identify any differences between them.

❛ *All the service, or any part of it, is to be available to everyone in England and Wales. The Bill imposes no limitation on availability – e.g. limitations based on financial means, age, sex, employment or vocation, area of residence, or insurance qualification.*

Ministry of Health (1946: 3) *The National Health Service Bill* London, HMSO.

❛ *The purpose of the NHS is to secure through the resources available the greatest possible improvement in the physical and mental health of the people of England by: promoting health, preventing ill health, diagnosing and treating disease and injury, and caring for those with long term illness and disability.*

The NHS Executive's priorities 1995/96, cited in *1996/97 NAHAT NHS Handbook.*

With the election of the Thatcher governments in the 1970s and 1980s the NHS experienced movement towards marketisation. By 1990 Britain had:

- self-governing hospitals
- GPs who managed their own practice budgets
- measures to restrict the NHS drugs bill, with GPs having to justify their spending habits, and more audit arrangements
- a reformed management in which hospitals would be run by executives who would be expected to make more use of consultants

---

A C T I V I T Y KS **PROBLEM SOLVING, WITH OTHERS**

IDENTIFICATION AND INTERPRETATION	ANALYSIS AND EVALUATION

❛ *In 1993 Wythenshawe Hospital staff decided not to perform a coronary artery bypass graft operation on Mr Harry Elphick because he was a smoker. Mr Elphick died before other treatment could be arranged. The decision was attacked as victim-blaming by some and defended by others for signalling that we are all responsible for helping to maintain our own health.*

Source: Sheaff (1996: 83)

- Do we still provide health services on the basis of need? Did Mr Elphick have a real need?

- above all, funding arrangements in which there would be an internal market for health care in the NHS and the money would follow the patient

A central element to the changes that the Thatcher governments introduced was a new contract for GPs. Since 1990 GPs have had to be more active in health promotion, providing health checks every year for people over 75, and every three years for those of 16–74. GPs would be given targets – for example, for immunisation, cervical cytology. GPs are rewarded if they meet their targets and are given additional money for running Health Promotion Clinics, such as well person, diabetes, heart disease, anti-smoking, alcohol control, diet and stress management. GPs would have to provide practice leaflets with information about the doctors and their qualifications, together with consumer surveys and annual reports. Taken together these measures were intended to give the patient greater choice and information, while at the same time more closely monitoring GPs.

It was suggested at the time that GPs would be reluctant to accept patients who would be a drain on their budgets and that care for the people who needed it most would thus suffer.

Before we investigate if the NHS has fulfilled its aims and objectives, let us look at the sociological perspectives of health. We will start with the medical model.

ACTIVITY KS PROBLEM SOLVING, WORKING WITH OTHERS

IDENTIFICATION AND INTERPRETATION	ANALYSIS AND EVALUATION

What do you consider to be the key elements of a just health care system?

Consider the following list, and state if you agree or disagree:

- universal access
- access to an 'adequate' level of care
- access without excessive burdens
- fair distribution of the financial costs of ensuring universal access to an adequate level of health care
- fair distribution of the burdens of rationing care
- capacity for improvement toward a more just system
- education and training of appropriate numbers and types of health care providers
- effective pursuit of high-quality biomedical research
- cost-effective use of results of biomedical research

Source: Solomon R. Benatar (*BMJ* January 1997)

The medical model

The medical model is based upon three key assumptions:

1. The causes of ill health and illness are mainly biological in origin.
2. Medicine is a science.
3. Rational scientific medicine is the only viable method of saving people from illness and disease.

As Thomas McKeown (1971) made clear, the medical model is very much an 'engineering' approach:

> *Medical education begins with the study of the structure and function of the body, continues with examination of disease processes, and ends with clinical instruction on selected sick people; medical service is dominated by the image of the acute hospital*

where the technological resources are concentrated; and medical science reflects the mechanistic concept, for example in the attention given to the chemical basis of inheritance and the immunological response to transplanted organs. These researches are strictly in accord with the physical model, the first being thought to lead ultimately to control of gene structure and the second to replacement of diseased organs by normal ones.

(McKeown 1971: 30)

The medical model restricts the 'health field' which, according to Lalonde (1974), should include environmental, behavioural and biological determinants (Figure 11.1).

The medical model

- Health is predominantly viewed as the 'absence of disease' and as 'functional fitness'.
- Health services are geared mainly towards treating sick and disabled people.
- A high value is put on the provision of specialist medical services, in mainly institutional settings.
- Doctors and other qualified experts diagnose illness and disease and sanction and supervise the withdrawal of patients from productive labour.
- The main function of health services is remedial or curative – to get people back to productive labour.
- Disease and sickness are explained within a biological framework that emphasises the physical nature of disease: that is, it is biologically reductionist.
- It works with a pathogenic focus, emphasising risk factors and establishing abnormality (and normality).
- A high value is put on using scientific methods of research (hypothetico-deductive method) and on scientific knowledge.
- Qualitative evidence (given by lay people or produced through academic research) generally has a lower status as knowledge than quantitative evidence.

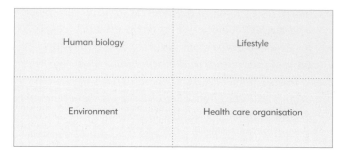

Human biology	Lifestyle
Environment	Health care organisation

Figure 11.1 The health field concept of Lalonde

Underlying assumption:
- That society has an independent existence and that social facts (phenomena) about a society can be observed at a societal level
- That the *laws* governing the rate of suicide can be discovered by using a social science method

Lines of research:
- Definition of suicide: 'every case of death resulting directly or indirectly from a positive or negative act performed by the victim himself which he knows will produce this result' (Durkheim)
- Definition of his concept of *social integration*: degree to which individuals share the norms, values, attitudes and beliefs and follow the prescribed rules of behaviour in their group

Statistical analysis to demonstrate that:
- The suicide rate is constant over time within single societies
- The suicide rate varies between different societies
- The suicide rate varies between different groups within the same society and cannot be explained by reference to the mental states of individuals: no significant correlation between number of suicides and individuals' mental states can be found

Examples of statistical patterns of variation:
- city dwellers tend to have a higher suicide rate than rural dwellers
- male suicide rate is higher than female
- unmarried is higher than married

Hypothesis building from statistical correlations:
Suicide varies inversely with the degree of integration of
- domestic society
- religious society
- political society

General hypothesis:
Suicide varies inversely with the degree of integration of social groups of which the individual forms a part

Conclusion:
Social phenomena beyond the level of the individual and the degree of social integration of the individual do influence the rate of suicide

Figure 11.2 Durkheim's research into suicide

The medical model is then a very 'mechanistic' model of the relationship between people and disease. It considers people to be 'machine like': if medical experts maintain the body it will function smoothly. This model also undervalues 'folk models' of the relationship between people and disease. In contrast, as Linda Jones (1994) argues, a sociological model of poor health would look more like Durkheim's study of suicide (Figure 11.2).

The functionalist approach

For Talcott Parsons (1951), good health is one of the key functional needs of every individual member of society. Illness prevents people from effectively performing their social roles. Parsons considers high incidence of illness dysfunctional for the social system. Being sick is not simply a 'condition', for Parsons it is a social role. Parsons outlines a set of 'institutionalised expectations and corresponding sentiments and sanctions' (Parsons, 1951: 431) which constitute the 'sick role'. The **sick role** describes the appropriate behaviour for an individual who has *chosen* to be ill:

- If people are sick they are exempt from their normal social responsibilities. This is, of course, relative to the severity of the condition. If a person undergoes open heart surgery he or she will not be expected to cook and clean at home or to be involved in paid work, but if a person has a hangover he or she will be expected to fulfil most of these normal roles.

- The sick person cannot get well by an act of will. He or she must be taken care of.

- Being sick must be regarded by the person as undesirable: the person must want to get well.

- There is an obligation to seek help from a doctor and the primary responsibility of the doctor is to 'do everything possible'.

If a person refuses to follow these four characteristics the sick role may be taken away. This is a very important point and a very useful insight. Parsons was the first sociologist to look at 'being sick' as a possible form of deviance. The role of the doctor is to perform a social control function, deciding by rational scientific means who is sick and who is not. As Parsons explains: '… the sick role not only isolates and insulates, it also exposes the deviant to reintegrative forces.' (Parsons 1951: 313). This view of medicine as an agent of social control is found in most sociological accounts of medicine and mental illness.

There is surprisingly little critique of Parsons' notion of the sick role. According to Doyal and Pennel (1982), Parsons' discussion has to be understood against the background of his broader functionalist position. Parsons assumed that capitalist societies are basically sound and progressive. He is aware that the social system will experience stresses and strains but is less concerned with how these conditions emerge than with the effectiveness of the medical system in preventing potential disruption to the social system.

Medical nemesis: the limits to medicine

One of the most original critiques of medical practice and the medical model is found in the work of Ivan Illich (1974). From his distinct phenomenological perspective, Illich is concerned with the **medical nemesis**: the effect that medical practice has on individual perceptions and on our ability to control our lives. For Illich, medicine is a 'moral enterprise'. Medicine is used to define what is normal, proper and desirable. In a similar fashion to the priest, who

informs us as to what is holy and who has broken taboo, the doctor uses inquisitorial powers to decide what is a symptom, which pain is 'merely subjective' and who is malingering.

For Illich, all deviance has a medical label. He argues that it is doctors who decide who may drive a car, who may stay away from work, who must be locked up, who may become soldiers, who may cross borders, who may not run for Vice-President of the United States, who is dead, who is competent to commit a crime and who is liable to commit a crime. Every person is given a medical status which will exempt him or her from doing some things. Doctors also have the right to encroach on the freedom of others by putting them in mental hospitals and giving them medication against their consent.

Illich argues that professional health care systems are themselves sickening. Professional health care produces clinical damage; it obscures the conditions which make people in society sick and takes away power and responsibility of people to heal themselves and shape their environment. Modern medicine is not only ineffective but physically harmful. Medicine is an epidemic and more people die by coming into contact with doctors than from any other single cause, with the exception of malnutrition. Yet doctors are increasing their control over our everyday lives by making more and more issues in our lives medical problems.

Illich's analysis is built upon three categories of **iatrogenesis** – the damage caused by doctors – in modern industrial societies:

■ **Clinical iatrogenesis** – the physical damage caused by doctors in their attempts to cure people.

ANALYSIS AND
EVALUATION

❛ *Extra therapy of the kind now offered adds to the total negative impact which the poor environment has on the health of the poor. Less access to the present health care system would, contrary to popular rhetoric, benefit the poor.*

Illich (1975: 73) *Medical Nemesis: The Expropriation of Health.*

■ Outline three reasons why you accept or reject this point.

An example is the hospital 'superbug', multi-resistant *Staphylococcus aureus*, which is immune to antibiotics and developed in hospitals as an unforeseen consequence of attempts to cure people using antibiotics.

- **Social iatrogenesis** – giving people unneeded medical care as a solution to all their problems. For example, some women who do not like their role as housewives visit the doctor and seek help for depression although the problems they have are not medicinal but social in nature.

- **Structural iatrogenesis** – the destruction of patients' independence, taking away their responsibility for their own health care. People have lost the skills, ability and confidence to heal themselves; we have become dependent upon doctors.

Illich maintains that, if we measure the positive effects of medicine against the negative effects, we would be better off without modern health care. In other words, we should disestablish organised health care so that people can take responsibility for their own health rather than being dependent on doctors. This process of abolishing modern medicine should be associated with a general de-bureaucratisation and de-industrialisation of modern society.

ACTIVITY   KS **PROBLEM SOLVING, WORKING WITH OTHERS**

IDENTIFICATION AND INTERPRETATION	ANALYSIS AND EVALUATION

What are the problems with Illich's analysis? Look at the criticisms of Illich from Doyal and Pennel below. Simply state if you agree or disagree with the point made and give a reason for your answer.

- Illich ignores the positive effects of modern medicine and concentrates on the negative effects, such as adverse drug reactions and unnecessary surgery.

- Illich talks about industrial society not capitalism. Doyal and Pennel argue that it is capitalism which is bad for health rather than industrialism.

- Illich gives no guidance as to how his commitment to change is likely to come about.

A Marxist analysis of medicine

For the Marxist the capitalist system creates a contradiction between health and profit. For example, commodity production is bad for the health of the workers: shiftwork, deskilling, overtime and the use of dangerous chemicals are all possible causes of poor health. Commodity production can also cause environmental problems, because of pollution. Finally, the commodities themselves can be bad for health – there are risks associated with the consumption of red meat, sugar and alcohol, to name but a few.

Taking a long historical perspective, which includes looking at smallpox and cholera epidemics and the incidence of tuberculosis in the nineteenth century, Doyal and Pennel (1980) argue that health is usually defined as the absence of incapacitating pathology. This involves looking at workers in 'functional terms': the capitalist system views people primarily as producers and has no concern with pain, suffering or anxieties unless they damage profit margins. They argue that all ill health in the contemporary world can be traced to the capitalist mode of production, and that the crisis in health care is caused by the contradictions within capitalism.

One of the key functions of the health care systems in capitalist societies is labour. Organised health care helps to maintain the physical fitness of labourers so that the amount of surplus value extracted from the workers can be maintained at a high level.

The other major function of the health care systems within capitalist societies is ideological. Health is defined in individualistic terms within capitalism: individuals become sick often because of their own moral failings rather than due to socio-economic or environmental factors, which are possible causes of ill health. At the same time the provision of the National Health Service allows the state to present a benevolent image of itself to the workers. Doyal and Pennel argue that the enactment of social legislation is the best strategy for stopping the spread of socialism. They quote Balfour, Prime Minister in 1895: 'Social legislation is not merely to be distinguished from Socialist legislation, but it is the most direct opposite and its most effective anti-dote.'

Doyal and Pennel also attempt to show that scientific activity – such as medicine – reflects the dominant economic interests within the society which produced the science. Medical science reflects the dominant ideology within capitalism.

The Marxist approach to medicine is then 'functional' and 'teleological' in nature. It argues that the medical system is performing functions for the capitalist system as a whole and explains its purpose in terms of goals rather than causes. We have a health service not to support the future of capitalism but because we have always had a problem of poor health in the population.

Is capitalism bad for your health?

According to Nikki Hart (1982) over the last 200 years there has been an excellent improvement in human health: a significant fall in mortality and a momentous decline in infective and parasitic diseases. This can be seen in the extension of the human lifespan and the general improvement in our physical welfare. Other improvements listed by Hart include the following:

- Extensive improvements in the sufficiency and variety of our diet.

- Sanitisation of human existence, brought about by public control of the supply of clean water and disposal of sewage.

- A transformation in average housing standards.

- A revolution in the process of biological reproduction, which has greatly extended human control over bodily processes and has important implications for sexual freedom and gender equality.

- Real progress in medical knowledge and technique – notably reducing the impact of congenital and non-congenital deformity and disability.

In contrast to Doyal and Pennel, Hart argues that capitalism has revolutionised human health and that Marxists cannot show in any conclusive way that the

capitalist mode of production is the root cause of even one major degenerative disease today. Also in contrast to the Marxist view that human health would improve under socialism, Hart argues that if the capitalist mode of production were to disappear then so would good health. Doyal and Pennel do not tell their readers how it is possible to bring about a socialist medical system. Finally, the points that Marxists made about the ideological nature of science and scientific activity are highly relativistic.

Postmodernism and medicine

In health care, many of the key aspects of orthodox views of medicine have been rejected. People no longer believe the views and opinions of their doctor without question. People also look to non-biological factors as causes of ill health, such as dissatisfaction with lifestyle or body shape. Alternative New Age medical techniques are increasing in popularity. What appear to be essentially postmodern health problems have come about because of specific lifestyle choices (for example AIDS), are human creations not found in nature (for example CJD), or are directly related to dissatisfaction with self (Koro syndrome and Capgras' syndrome are examples). Capgras' syndrome, or Capgras' symptom as it sometimes known, has been described as

> The delusion that others, or the self, have been replaced by impostors. It typically follows the development of negative feelings towards the other person that the subject cannot accept and attributes, instead, to the impostor.

Source: http:// www. ncf. carleton. ca/-ah 787/Home Page. Capgras.html

If you wish to find out more about Koro syndrome see http://members.gnn.com/lono/psychosis/muyloco/koro.htm

This cynicism affects not only medicine: in the postmodern world people have also lost faith in science and scientific rationality. Postmodernists believe that scientific rationality is just one perspective amongst many. It is the disappearance of our belief in the truth

IDENTIFICATION AND INTERPRETATION	ANALYSIS AND EVALUATION

Postmodernism casts doubt on the notion of medicine as a 'scientific' vocation, as GP James Harrison suggested: 'To speak of having a vocation in today's postmodern world is risky.' (*BMJ*, 28 December 1996). However, within medicine one response to postmodernism has been to emphasise the rational/scientific knowledge basis of medical practice, which promotes certainty.

According to Paul Hodgkin, a GP adviser at Sheffield School for Health and Related Research, there are two reasons for not dismissing postmodernism on these grounds:

‘ *Firstly, until now medicine has been glued together by a set of myths that everyone subscribed to: doctors battled against death and disease, we lived under the one true church of the NHS, and Science lit the way to a world of health for all. Today these comforting narratives are less believable. In a very postmodern way, doctors have to juggle competing ways of seeing the same situation. Clinical reality as perceived by clinicians has to be reconciled with patients' beliefs, resources have to be balanced against individual patient need, and ethical dilemmas spring hydra-headed from medical advance …*

Secondly … It is not only Marxism and the Enlightenment which is dead; utterly unquestioned biological givens are disintegrating all around us: the stability of the climate, the immutability of species, a life span of three score years and ten, the unchanging genetic make up of one's unborn children …

As technology expands the bounds of what it is possible to do, it seems inevitable that clinicians will become agents of the postmodernism that they have so far ignored. Medical technologies will increasingly be used for non-therapeutic ends. Recreational drug use may come to be matched by 'recreational surgery' … Doctors will no longer be able to comfort themselves with the hard edged certainty that their work is 'fighting disease'. Instead they will have to become purveyors of choice within the plastic limits of the flesh … we are no more immune than the Amish or the makers of Betamax …

Source: Paul Hodgkin 'Medicine, postmodernism, and the end of certainty: Where one version of the truth is as good as another, anything goes' (*BMJ*, 21 December 1996)

■ According to these items, what is the significance of postmodernism for modern medical practice?

of science, politics and religion, together with the corrosive impact of doubt, that marks clearly the transition from a modern to a postmodern mentality: 'In practice, it means constant exposure to ambivalence: that is, to a situation with no decidable solution, with no foolproof choice, no unreflective knowledge of "how to go on".' (Bauman, 1992: 244–5).

Inequalities in health

In most textbooks about inequalities in health, the discussion centres on social-class inequalities, gender and racial inequalities. However, it is important to note that there is a range of inequalities in health and that many of the now 'traditional' explanations for health

inequalities, such as the **Inverse Care Law**, apply to a range of possible groups.

The Inverse Care Law

Simply expressed this 'law' states that the people who need health care the most are the least likely to get it (Tudor-Hart, 1971). People living in poor working-class communities tend to have the worst health care facilities and the doctors who treat them would prefer to live and work amongst professional people in the suburbs. Hence the poorer the person, the poorer the standard of service provided by the NHS and so rates of mortality and morbidity are higher amongst working-class people. In 1985 Tudor-Hart introduced the idea of the 'iceberg' or the 'rule of two halves': i.e. approximately half the people who need health care do not get it.

The health needs of gay men

In their review and evaluation of the literature, Taylor and Robertson (1994) argue that gay men anticipate anti-homosexual sentiments from doctors. Paroski (1987) found that some gay people feared that a homophobic doctor would physically harm them. In addition living with homophobia can cause high levels of stress, which are associated with parasuicide, psychiatric disorders, depression and a higher incidence of substance misuse. Gay men also have a higher incidence of hepatitis, HIV infection and some other sexually transmitted diseases. When gay adolescents are in the process of forming their identity the environment in which they are growing will be largely hostile to their emerging sexual orientation. Some researchers have suggested that the lack of support to gay adolescents may explain the high level of morbidity and mortality amongst them. Mental health care professionals also have limited knowledge of gay issues. Taylor and Robertson (1994) suggest the following deficits in mental health training:

- Lack of information about sexual orientation, gay lifestyles and community resources

- The encounter with the gay client, his sexuality and the effects of living in a homophobic society

- The relationship between the attitudes, feelings and sexual orientation of the health care professional and the service user.

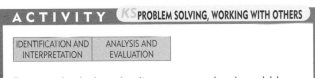

ACTIVITY   KS **PROBLEM SOLVING, WORKING WITH OTHERS**

IDENTIFICATION AND INTERPRETATION	ANALYSIS AND EVALUATION

Do you think that the 'inverse care law' could be used to explain some or all of the health care needs of gay men?

You might want to attempt a search for health needs of gay women.

Social class inequalities in health

A range of direct health effects are linked to occupational inequalities. Some occupations have lower pay, lack of job security, poor conditions of service and unsociable hours. Such occupations also have higher rates of sickness, stress, respiratory problems, back problems and risk of accidents at work. The pattern of social class inequalities in health was thoroughly documented by Sir Douglas Black in the Black Working Party (1981). Drawing upon evidence from the 1970s Black found that all the major killer diseases were more likely to affect poor people than richer people. Black examined four possible explanations for the social class inequality in health:

1   The *artefact* explanation, which states that health inequalities are not real. Health inequalities are a product of inadequate or faulty measurement devices.

2   The *natural and social selection* explanation, which states that it is health that determines social class rather than social class that determines health. In other words, there is a drift of people with poor health towards the bottom end of the class structure.

3   The *cultural/behavioural* explanation which states that poor people bring ill health on themselves by leading an unhealthy lifestyle; poor people are more likely to drink and smoke and are less likely to eat a healthy diet. This explanation has a great deal in common with the 'culture of poverty thesis' which was outlined by Oscar Lewis in the 1960s.

4   *Materialist or structuralist* explanations. The view here is that poor health is primarily caused by material deprivation. Factors like poor living and working conditions cause poor health. These are favoured by the Black Report.

Moreover, claims the Black Report, inequalities in health had widened since the 1950s. There had been a significant decline in death rates of all social classes in the 1970s, but the decline for professional people was much greater and the social class mortality gap was still wide.

The Health Divide (1987) also made clear that the occupational class gradients were becoming steeper for a range of diseases in the 1980s and that material deprivation was the most important consideration when trying to account for this. However, perhaps surprisingly, class inequality in health was not mentioned in *The Health of the Nation* report published by the Department of Health in 1992.

In 1995 the Economic and Social Research Council and the Medical Research Council announced that they were making health inequalities a research priority. Also that year the Department of Health published the finding of another working group into the issue. That report (the *NAHAT NHS Handbook*, 1997) suggested that health authorities should commit themselves to improving the health of deprived communities by:

- building people's self-confidence and self-esteem
- understanding people's beliefs
- offering practical support
- promoting a positive holistic view of health
- promoting opportunities for social integration
- advocacy for individuals and communities
- facilitating access to services and benefits

The term **holistic** has been fully explored by Nagai-Jacobson and Burkhart (1989) to mean that

- people should live in healing ways within themselves and with others
- people should experience their own spirituality if they are to live a healthy life

In the late 1990s Margaret Whitehead and Frances Drever returned to the issue of inequalities in health by looking at a range of nationally representative data sources.

They found that there were still significant socio-economic differences in mortality and morbidity. For example, data on the full range of national deaths for 1991–1993 shows that standardised mortality ratios for men aged 20–64 were almost three times higher for unskilled manual workers than for professional men. The figures for women show a slightly shallower gradient, but it is still significant. The gap in life expectancy between social classes 1 and 2 and other classes widened over the 1980s. For men the gap in life expectancy at the age of 15 widened from four to five years, whilst for women the figures show an increasing gap from two to three years.

Whitehead and Drever argue that there are two possible explanations for the increasing inequalities in health:

1. A general improvement in mortality rates for all groups, but the pace is more rapid for social classes 1 and 2.
2. The gap could be a result of worsening mortality rates in the lower social classes.

Whitehead and Drever are keen to point out that the differences in health are not caused by 'behavioural risk' factors such as drinking, smoking and lack of exercise:

' *The data on health-related personal behaviour … showed some diversity. Often, but not always, the socio-economic gradients in health-damaging and health-promoting behaviour went in the same direction as the socio-economic trends in morbidity and mortality. So, for example there were progressively higher rates of smoking, poorer diet, and lower incidence of breast-feeding with declining socio-economic group. On the other hand, there was a higher prevalence of alcohol drinkers among professional and managerial socio-economic groups. The pattern of physical activity was complex. When only leisure time activity was counted, there was decreasing activity with decreasing socio-economic group. When work-related and domestic activities were also included, there was a higher prevalence of regular activity of a moderate intensity among men in all three manual social classes and very little variation in activity levels among women across the social scale.*

Source: Whitehead and Drever (1998: 230)

According to Richard Wilkinson (1998), most of the research is concerned with attempting to understand health differences between individual people. However, this approach does not necessarily provide us with a guide to the cause of health differences between larger groups of people in the population.

The epidemiological transition

When we compare rich countries with poor countries, living standards are a key factor. Coronary heart disease, angina, myocardial infarction and a range of other cardiovascular diseases, infections and respiratory disease are related to income distribution – as are 'social' causes of poor health, suicide, homicide, accidents and alcohol-related deaths. However, Wilkinson argues, there is a threshold level at which an 'epidemiological transition' has taken place. This transition takes place when most of the population have the minimum material standard of living to have good health. In these societies infectious diseases decline and cancers and degenerative diseases become the main causes of death. The question then becomes: Why do people in Greece, Japan, Iceland and Italy have a longer life expectancy than those in richer countries such as the USA and Germany?

To support his argument, Wilkinson made use of data from Britain during the war years, from Roseto in Pennsylvania (which has better health than neighbouring towns), from Japan and various regions in Italy. In all cases social values are dominant, rather than market values. Wilkinson argues that in the developed world it is the most egalitarian societies which have the best health, not the richest. In other words, claims Wilkinson, the societies with the narrowest inequality have the best health. An important characteristic of such societies is 'social cohesion': a strong 'community life'. Individualism and the values of the market are restrained by forms of 'social morality'.

> *People with more social contacts and more involvement in local activities seem to have better health, even after controlling for a number of other possibly confounding factors ... there is increasing evidence of the physiological channels through which chronic stress can effect endocrine and immunological processes. There is even evidence showing that stressful social hierarchies predispose to poorer health amongst troops of baboons as well as in human societies.*

Source: Wilkinson (1998: 5)

Wilkinson's conclusion is that life expectancy in different societies is significantly improved when differences in income are smaller and societies are socially more cohesive.

Gender and health

Health issues and health care needs are different for women and men. Women and men are seen to have different health and life chances. If we start from a postmodernist position, we need to look at the body as a creation, and medicine and psychiatry influence people in how they both view and construct their bodies. For the postmodernist there can be no simple biological male and female. Our ideas of masculinity and femininity may influence our perceptions of health as well as the diagnoses of the medical profession.

ACTIVITY   KS **PROBLEM SOLVING, WORKING WITH OTHERS**

IDENTIFICATION AND INTERPRETATION	ANALYSIS AND EVALUATION

The mortality rate for males is higher at all ages than females in the UK. The morbidity rate for males is also higher in a number of major diseases. Look at the data below and

1 Describe the differences in male and female mortality and morbidity.
2 Outline some possible reasons for the differences in male and female mortality and morbidity.

You might want to consider if men are more likely to be involved in behaviour which could damage their health. If you wish, visit your local library and look at *Social Trends*, which provides information on rates of smoking, drinking, road accidents, and suicide, for example.

Epidemiological evidence shows that there are different disease patterns for men and women. Men and women appear to have different symptoms and define illness in different ways. Women's experiences as patients, and the way they are presented in medical textbooks, are very different. Women are also treated very differently as employees by health care organisations. Two basic ideas appear to be central to the medical ideology of women:

- Men are normal and women are abnormal
- Female abnormality comes from the belief that the 'natural' role of women is to have children (see Figure 11.3)

Male doctors have often very entrenched attitudes about women. Lennane and Lennane (1973) and Turner (1987) argue that male doctors assume that women are unable to control their behaviour, even to the point of viewing pain in menstruation and childbirth as 'psychogenic' in nature. Similar views to this can be found in Miles (1991) and Graham and Oakley (1981). Little attention is given to specific female problems in medical textbooks, unless the problem is directly related to pregnancy. Women's health problems are given a low priority in the allocation of research funding. Hence many specific health problems are labelled as psychological in nature, fitting into a stereotype of women being 'more

'Normal' women should be:	'Deviant' women:
Naturally maternal and home-centred Caring for/about families and men	Reject/find caring and maternal role difficult: carrier-oriented
More controlled by their bodies than men are	Do not accept 'natural' limits
Inferior to men	Do not accept inferior position, demand equality
Deferential/submissive	Are aggressive, over-assertive
More emotional than men	Are unfeminine, cold
'Normal' mothers are:	**'Deviant' mothers:**
Slaves to their bodies, cannot control their bodies	See childbirth as a physically stressful, life-changing event
Emotionally unstable become essentially 'childish' and present-oriented	See child rearing as emotional and exhausting experience, requiring new skills and hard labour, often with little support
Nest-builders, have caring urge	Reject social pressure to give up past life and see motherhood as primary role; demand partner shares responsibility

Drawn from: Roberts, H. (Ed.) (1981) *Women, Health and Reproduction*; Oakley, A. (1980) *Women Confined*.

Figure 11.3 'Normal' and 'deviant' women

emotional' than men. The high rate of psychiatric illness amongst women may simply be a reflection of this lack of research into the physical causes of women's health issues.

A number of studies suggest that male and female doctors treat their patients differently. Miles (1991) argues that female doctors are more likely to be open and democratic with the patient. In contrast, male doctors are more likely to take control of the relationship, assuming that women are passive by nature and need to have decisions made for them. However, Miles also found that some women consider female doctors to be 'unsympathetic'.

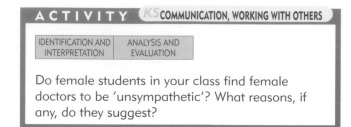

Do female students in your class find female doctors to be 'unsympathetic'? What reasons, if any, do they suggest?

The Brighton Women and Science Group (1980) suggests the following social and medical explanations of women's health:

■ Women suffer from greater vulnerability to hormonal stress, which results in a higher incidence of illness, but has no real effect on mortality rates. One of the best known pieces of research in this area is Katherina Dalton's study *The Menstrual Cycle* (1969), in which she argues that statistically women are more likely to make suicide attempts, be admitted to psychiatric hospitals, have accidents and take time off work in the 10 days before their period starts. However, as Ann Oakley (1985) points out, 'maleness' or 'femaleness' cannot be established from a hormone count.

■ Women have more illness than men because their assigned social roles are more stressful. Marriage in particular makes great demands upon women. Married men are much less likely to suffer from stress than single men, whereas married women are much more likely to suffer from stress than single women. However, as Whitehead and Drever (1998) point out, women working in non-manual jobs experienced large declines in death rates between 1981 and 1985 and again between 1986 and 1992, irrespective of marital status. By contrast, female manual workers who were not married fared worse than married women as their death rates rose in 1981–1985 and 1986–1992.

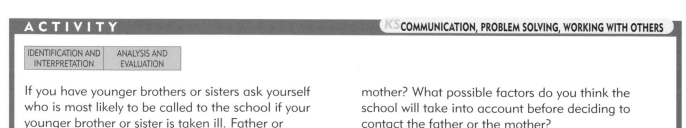

If you have younger brothers or sisters ask yourself who is most likely to be called to the school if your younger brother or sister is taken ill. Father or mother? What possible factors do you think the school will take into account before deciding to contact the father or the mother?

Figure 11.4 Mortality rate ratios (RR) by social class, women aged 35–64.
Source: 1971 LS cohort, England and Wales, 1976–92.

Social class	1976–81[1]		1981–85[1]		1986–92[1]	
	RR	**Deaths**	**RR**	**Deaths**	**RR**	**Deaths**
I/II	0.72[2]	428	0.87[2]	405	0.76[2]	450
IIIN	0.79[2]	267	0.98[2]	248	0.86[2]	294
IIIM	1.00	759	1.00	617	1.00	783
IV/V	1.09[2]	633	1.12[2]	466	1.17[2]	558
Manual v non-manual	1.38[2]	2,087	1.15[2]	1,736	1.35[2]	2,085

[1]1981 refers to census day in first time period and post census day in second time period
[2]rate ratio differs significantly from 1.00

Figure 11.5 Age-standardised death rates per 100,000 people, by social class, women aged 35–64.
Source: 1971 LS cohort, England and Wales, 1976–92.

Social class	1976–81[1]	1981–85[1]	% change[2]	1986–92[1]	% change[3]
I/II	338	344	2	270	–22
IIIN	371	387	4	305	–21
IIIM	467	396	–15	356	–10
IV/V	508	445	–12	418	– 6
Non-manual	355	366	3	287	–22
Manual	488	421	–14	387	– 8

[1]1981 refers to census day in first time period and post census day in second time period
[2]between 1976–81 and 1981–85
[3]between 1981–85 and 1986 92

Figure 11.6 Life expectancy by social class, women, selected ages
Source: 1971 LS cohort, England and Wales, 1976–92.

Life expectancy at birth (years)

Social class	1972–76	1977–81	1982–86	1987–91
I and II	77.1	78.2	78.7	80.2
IIIN	78.0	78.1	78.6	79.4
IIIM	75.1	76.1	77.1	77.6
IV and V	74.7	75.7	76.8	76.8
Total	75.1	76.3	77.1	77.9

Life expectancy at age 15 (years)

Social class	1972–76	1977–81	1982–86	1987–91
I and II	63.0	64.1	64.3	65.8
IIIN	63.8	64.1	64.3	65.3
IIIM	61.6	62.2	62.9	63.2
IV and V	61.9	62.0	62.7	62.5
Total	61.6	62.4	62.9	63.6

Life expectancy at age 65 (years)

Social class	1972–76	1977–81	1982–86	1987–91
I and II	17.3	17.9	18.0	18.7
IIIN	17.8	17.6	18.0	18.3
IIIM	16.3	16.9	16.8	16.8
IV and V	16.7	16.6	17.0	16.7
Total	16.2	16.7	16.9	17.2

■ The greater amount of illness among women is directly related to 'severe' life events such as sudden unemployment, eviction, death of a partner. This was explored in detail by Brown and Harris (see the Sociology in Action section below).

■ Women report more illness than men because it is socially more acceptable for them to do so.

■ The sick role is more compatible with women's other role responsibilities. As Oakley (1985) has pointed out, women are more likely to be the carers within families, are more likely to see themselves as responsible for their children's health and are more likely to take their children to the doctor than their male partners. Hence men are much less likely to come into contact with doctors.

■ High illness rates, particularly for depressive conditions, reflect women's over-socialisation and

---

ACTIVITY KS PROBLEM SOLVING, WORKING WITH OTHERS

IDENTIFICATION AND INTERPRETATION	ANALYSIS AND EVALUATION

Feminist health care is based upon concepts very different from the orthodox view of medicine looked at above. As Christine Webb (1986) points out:

‘ *It sees people's health problems not as individual pathologies but as shared outcomes of the kind of society we live in. For women, this means acknowledging that sexist ideas and behaviour can make you sick, and therefore that in order to be healthy these ideas and behaviour must be changed. Sharing knowledge and power between practitioners and clients, breaking down the barriers of unequal relationships, and supporting people as they take decisions and make their own health choices are ways in which feminists work towards change.*

Source: Webb (1986: 186)

■ What do you understand by the term 'feminist health care'?

■ What criticism is Webb making of scientific medicine?

■ Do you accept or reject the ideas that 'feminist health care' is expressing? Outline three reasons for your answer.

TASK

Hypothesis – Many young women are said to suffer from anorexia nervosa because of 'oppressive' images of femininity. Women accept that slimness is a form of beauty.

Context – It is commonly assumed that dieting, and the weight loss that goes with it, allows women to fulfil the cultural ideal of what a woman should look like. However, Orbach (1989) described anorexia as a 'hunger strike' against accepted femininities, rather than an attempt to achieve attractiveness. There would be ethical problems in looking at the reasons that non-anorexics and anorexics have for dieting. However, we could look at the question of whether young women are socialised into the acceptance of cultural images of slimness as a form of beauty.

Method – Take a number of pictures of women from newspapers and magazines. Make sure that these pictures are of women with different body shapes. Ask a sample of young women which body shape they prefer and why. This question should allow you to make generalisations about the motives that young women have for wanting to lose weight.

Evaluation – You will probably find that your results are difficult to analyse with any precision. In particular, it is one of the standard criticisms of qualitative research methods that it is not possible to generalise from the findings. However, there are two distinct forms of generalisation in the social sciences. On the one hand, there is **empirical generalisation**, which suggests that all cases are similar to the one that you have looked at: in other words, that your cases or subjects are typical of all cases or subjects in the area. It is unlikely that you could make generalisations about all young women from your sample. The second type of generalisation in the social sciences is the **theoretical generalisation**. This form of generalisation was used to very good effect by Freud. In this form of generalisation we start with a theory or hypothesis: such as media images are a factor in the motivation of young women to lose weight. Every case, or individual, who chooses to lose weight because of the effect of media images adds to the validity of the theory. In addition, when evaluating your research, you might want to consider if the responses of the subjects reflect the body shape of the respondent. You may find that slim women feel that they are overweight, and might want to comment on such a finding.

over-playing of the feminine role. This is normally related to the way in which women are portrayed in the media. Women who do not fit the stereotype of how a woman should look and behave are likely to suffer from a range of psychiatric disorders.

One of the most popular questions that students attempt for their coursework is about the **moral career** of the anorexic, or why some young women become anorexic. However, this research topic is full of problems of an ethical, practical and methodological nature.

The health care needs of blacks and minority ethnic groups

Since the 1970s a great deal of knowledge has accumulated on the health problems of ethnic minorities. Ethnic groups have different patterns of morbidity and mortality. *The Health of the Nation* listed a significant number of health concerns for ethnic minorities:

- coronary heart disease is higher for both men and women of Indian origin

- strokes are significantly higher for people of Caribbean and African origin: 76% for men and 110% for women

- the incidence of cervical cancers is rising for women of Caribbean origin

- incidence of schizophrenia is higher for people of Caribbean origin

- incidence of HIV infection and AIDS is higher in people of Caribbean origin

- suicide rates are significantly higher for females of Asian origin

- incidence of diabetes is more common in people of Caribbean origin than in the white population and is 4–5 times higher for people of Asian origin

- people of Caribbean and Asian origin are more at risk of diabetic renal disease, perinatal mortality and congenital malformations

---

ACTIVITY   APPLICATION OF NUMBER, PROBLEM SOLVING, WORKING WITH OTHERS

| IDENTIFICATION AND INTERPRETATION | ANALYSIS AND EVALUATION |

Read the information in the box and identify any significant differences in the health problems of different ethnic minorities. To what extent is social class a significant factor?

Black and minority ethnic groups: explanations for inequality

Most of the research in the area suggests that racial disadvantage places many ethnic minorities at the bottom end of the social ladder. Like all people in this position, they are more likely to face inequalities in health care provision, have lower life expectancy, higher infant mortality and face poorer social conditions. Karaeras and Hopkins argue that the NHS needs to adapt its services to fit the needs of cultural values of many ethnic minorities. Donovan (1986) and Thorogood (1990) said that both Afro-Caribbeans and Asians had concerns about the ways in which GPs both examined and prescribed for their patients. The way in which the NHS offers contraceptive advice is often cited as inappropriate for the needs of women of Asian origin. Mares et al. (1985) reported discriminatory treatment against Asian women in family planning clinics.

Infant mortality for children born of white British parents is usually associated with prematurity; however, the children of parents of Asian origin are more likely to die from intra-uterine growth retardation (IUGR) and malformation. IUGR is associated with poor nutrition, and in a comparison between Asian women in Birmingham and Islamabad, Karaeras and Hopkins claim that women in Birmingham eat less well. Congenital abnormalities, thalassaemia and IUGR are also associated with intermarriage between people within family groups.

Drawing upon data from the *Health and Lifestyle Survey*, Howlett (1991) reported that ethnic minority respondents were more likely to report health as a 'matter of luck' or 'a divine purpose' than did the white population. This fatalistic approach was widely shared.

Mental illness

What is mental illness? As we saw at the start of the area, definitions of health and illness are contentious. However, in the case of mental illness we have a legal definition:

' *In this Act 'mental disorder' means illness, arrested or incomplete development of mind, psychopathic disorder, and any other disorder or disability of mind; and 'mentally disordered' shall be construed accordingly.*

1959 British Mental Health Act para 4(1).

ACTIVITY KS **PROBLEM SOLVING, WORKING WITH OTHERS**

| IDENTIFICATION AND INTERPRETATION | ANALYSIS AND EVALUATION |

In your opinion, what does the legal definition of 'mental disorder' given above mean? Whatever definitions you may come across, mental illness is a behavioural disorder. It is about people behaving in ways that the rest of us find unacceptable. In the USA, *DSM-3* is the official list of characteristics for mental illness. It contains factors such as hearing voices, feeling the presence of another, ESP, etc. (Note that in special circumstances, for instance if a close relative has just died, a person may suffer from these symptoms but still be classed as sane.) Most mental illness cannot be diagnosed by looking down the microscope. This was most clearly brought to our attention by Thomas Szasz.

Thomas Szasz

In 1961 Thomas Szasz published the first edition of *The Myth of Mental Illness* (1972). For a practising psychiatrist Szasz came to the interesting conclusion that there is no such thing as 'mental illness'. Mental illness is a metaphor, a label phrased to resemble a medical diagnosis.

It would appear that, for Szasz, people have a need for explanation. It is impossible for people to say of others 'Your behaviour is unacceptable, you are a danger either to yourself or to others. We do not understand why you behave in the way that you do, but we are

---

ACTIVITY KS **PROBLEM SOLVING, WORKING WITH OTHERS**

| IDENTIFICATION AND INTERPRETATION | ANALYSIS AND EVALUATION |

Look at the quote below, and identify the reasons why you think there is such a 'thing' as mental illness:

' *… bodily illness stands in the same relation to mental illness as a defective television stands to an objectional television programme. To be sure, the word 'sick' is often used metaphorically. We call jokes 'sick', economies 'sick', sometimes even the whole world 'sick' – but only when we call minds 'sick' do we systematically mistake metaphor for fact; and send for the doctor to 'cure' the 'illness'. It's as if a television viewer were to send for a TV repair man because he disapproves of the programme he is watching.*

Source: Szasz (1972: 11)

---

going to lock you away because of it.' As humans we need to form a rational basis for why people behave in the way that they do.

For Szasz, people who are evil or undeserving should not be treated as ill but should be punished. This process has three stages:

- Stage 1: Behaviour which is seen to be unacceptable.
- Stage 2: Explanation for the behaviour which is seen to be unacceptable.
- Stage 3: Social control of the behaviour which is seen to be unacceptable.

Szasz considers that mental illness is not merely a medical label attached to people with strange behaviour and states that psychiatry is an 'immoral ideology of intolerance'. He compares the belief in witchcraft, and the persecution of witches, with the belief in mental illness and the persecution of mental patients. Moreover, because mental patients have a supposed incapacity to know what is in their best interests, they must be cared for by their families or by the state, even if that care requires imposing intervention upon the patient against their express wishes. There has been a gradual replacement of a theological model with a medical model. This has resulted in the transformation of a religious ideology into a scientific one. Both are equally unacceptable for Szasz, as both are crimes against humanity.

Szasz divides the practice of psychiatry into two:

- **Institutional psychiatry** – involuntary incarceration in mental hospitals with the employed physician as an agent of social control rather than of the patient's welfare.

- **Contractual psychiatry** – this is Szasz's preferred form of psychiatry and is the opposite of institutional psychiatry. Contractual psychiatry is based upon an informed consensus between two freely choosing individuals, one the therapist and the other the client. The therapist provides a service, requested by the client, in return for a fee. This form of psychiatry is said to be safe and presents no serious ethical problems for either the therapist or the client because in the last analysis it is a free exchange between equal partners. At any time the arrangement can be broken by either partner. Unlike institutional psychiatry, which is dangerous, based upon coercion and the tool of an oppressor, contractual psychiatry poses no threat to liberty.

There are a number of theoretical assumptions in the work of Szasz. As we have seen, he believes that the market can be used to resolve social problems, unlike the intervention of the state which is likely to be coercive. In terms of perspective, Szasz shares a great deal with symbolic interactionists.

ACTIVITY KS **WORKING WITH OTHERS, PROBLEM SOLVING**

| IDENTIFICATION AND INTERPRETATION | ANALYSIS AND EVALUATION |

Look again at the sections in Area 1 on symbolic interactionism and compare your findings with the quote below from Szasz. In your view is the statement one which a symbolic interactionist could agree with? Give a short justification for your answer.

Personal conduct is always rule-following, strategic and meaningful. Patterns of interpersonal and social relationships may be regarded and analysed as if they were games, the behaviour of the players being governed by explicit or tacit game rules.

Szasz (1972: 275)

Szasz also views mental illness as a semiological exercise (1972: 20).

Psychiatry, using the methods of communication analysis, has much in common with the sciences concerned with the study of languages and communicative behaviour. In spite of this connection between psychiatry and such disciplines as symbolic logic, semiotics, and sociology, problems of mental health continue to be cast in the traditional framework of medicine.

Szasz takes as his starting point Reichenbach's *Elements of Symbolic Logic* (1947). All semiologists differ a little in the concepts they use. However, semiology is the study of signs, and is principally concerned with how meaning is generated in 'texts'. For Szasz, mental illness is a 'text'. The essential breakthrough of semiology was to take linguistics as a model and apply linguistic concepts to other phenomena – in this case madness, and to treat psychiatry and madness as being like languages.

Szasz's use of semiology as applied to mental illness is based upon two assumptions:

1 Mental illness is a cultural phenomenon, an object or set of events with meaning. In other words, mental illness is made up of 'signs'.

2 Mental illness does not have a basic nature in itself, but is defined by a network of social relations. Mental illness has no meaning in itself.

Reichenbach identified three types of sign:

1 **Indexical signs**: 'signs which acquire a function through their causal connection between object and sign' (Szasz, 1972: 111). In other words, some types of behaviour indicate madness.

2 **Iconic signs**: 'signs that stand in a relation of similarity to the objects they designate: for example, the photograph' (Szasz, 1972: 112). Certain behaviours are symbolic of madness.

3 **Conventional signs**: 'signs whose relation to the object is purely conventional or arbitrary' (Szasz, 1972: 113). Szasz gives the example of mathematical symbols: there is no natural link between the sign and what it is meant to represent.

The following quote from Szasz (1972: 114) should show how he makes use of these concepts:

> When ... one's love object fails to listen and respond to verbal complaints or requests, one will be compelled, or at least tempted, to take recourse in communication by means of iconic body signs. We have come to speak of this general phenomenon, which may take a great variety of forms, as 'mental illness'. As a result, instead of realising that people are engaged in various types of communications in diverse communicational (or social) situations, we construct – and then ourselves come to believe in - various types of mental illnesses, such as 'hysteria', 'hypochondriasis', 'schizophrenia', and so forth.

An example of what Szasz is saying would be if your girlfriend or boyfriend no longer wanted to see you, but would not give you any reason for this decision. You might ask for a reason in a fairly polite fashion, but if they continually refused to give you a reason you might start to shout, cry or adopt more and more bizarre forms of behaviour, whilst continuing to request information. This behaviour could be classified as mental illness. What we believe to be mental illness may be a form of distorted communication.

PROFILE

Erving Goffman
(1922–1982)

Born in Alberta, Canada, Goffman studied at the Universities of Manitoba and Toronto before doing his PhD on 'Communication Conduct in an Island Community' at the University of Chicago. However, the fieldwork for his dissertation was done in the Shetland Islands. The themes developed during this fieldwork are to be found in a number of his key texts: *The Presentation of Self in Everyday Life*, first published in Edinburgh in 1956, *Asylums* (1961), *Behaviour in Public Places* (1963), *Stigma* (1963). In these texts Goffman developed a number of themes in relation to self and others within a symbolic interactionist perspective. However, from 1974 onwards his work developed a more structuralist slant when he developed the notion of 'frame', which was very much influenced by semiology, and applied this to *Gender Advertisements* (1979) and *Forms of Talk* (1981). Goffman died in 1982 in Philadelphia.

In an informed critique of Szasz, R.D. Laing (1979) argues that Szasz's point that mental illness is really a form of 'illness-imitative behaviour' is in a number of cases wrong. Laing gave the examples of compulsion neurosis and psychoses. In addition, Szasz has no analysis of the structures of power or knowledge in which mental illness emerges. This is unlike the work of Foucault, whom we studied in Area 4. Finally, the notion of contractual psychiatry is in essence what most people are involved in, even if the bill is paid for by the state.

It could be argued that only the mildest forms of mental disorder could be dealt with by the framework of contractual psychiatry: people who need therapy, but who are well enough to hold down jobs. In Szasz's vision the only people with access to psychiatric help would be those who needed it least. The people who need help the most would be least likely to be in a position to afford such therapy. Even if the state were to introduce a form of voucher system, the most ill people would be the least likely to be able to shop around.

Erving Goffman

In Area 4 we looked at the work of **Erving Goffman** on 'the self'. It is important that you look again at this section before reading on. For Goffman mental illness is a stigma, which emerges through a process of labelling; it is not a medical condition. Before we can understand fully Goffman's account of mental illness, we need to look at his conception of the social order.

In Goffman's 1963 text *Behaviour in Public Places* he outlines a model of the social order which he defines as: '... the consequences of any set of norms that regulates the way in which persons pursue objectives' (1963: 8) There are several types of social order, including a legal order and an economic order. However, the social order which Goffman is interested in is where people meet others face to face. Communicative behaviour has two forms for Goffman:

- **unfocused interaction**, in which individuals make a first assessment of the other
- **focused interaction**, where individuals gather to sustain a focus of attention, such as having a conversation

Goffman is concerned with how the social order is maintained. The social order has rules, which he terms

situational proprieties. This is a moral code which will be found in any social gathering. In addition, individuals present an image of themselves – a personal front – to show that they are willing to accept the rules: in Goffman's language to show that they are **situationally present**. To break a rule, to not live up to the personal front, is to break the moral code, which in Goffman's language is to cause a **situational impropriety**. The person who does this will be labelled, and one possible label is that of 'mentally ill'. As Goffman (1963: 47) explains:

> *... it may be permissible for a child on the street to suck his thumb, or lick a sucker, or inflate chewing-gum bubbles until they burst, or draw a stick along a fence, or fully interrupt his main line of activity to take a stone from his shoe. But the adult mental patients in Central Hospital who were observed conducting themselves in some of these ways were felt by staff to be acting 'symptomatically'.*

Situational improprieties are the start of the moral career of the mental patient, the stages that a person goes through, or the progression through a number of social roles, in order to become a mental patient. The social beginning of a person's career as a mental patient begins with a complaint about behaviour, this is the first stage on the road to hospitalisation, the application of a label. The **atrocity tales** – Goffman's term for the description of the behaviour of the labelled person – form what Goffman refers to as career contingencies. At this point we have what Goffman terms the **circuit of agents**; doctors and other professionals are requested to supply information and participate in the individual's passage from civilian to patient. In other words, the self becomes redefined.

In *Asylums* (1961) Goffman traces the ways in which hospitalisation shapes an inmate's moral career. When a person enters the total institution of the mental hospital they are subjected to **rituals of degradation**, in which staff and inmates humiliate the new inmate in an attempt to break the self-identity that he or she may have had in the outside world.

Total institutions

Total institutions are institutions in which people live and work in a closed community, under a single authority, according to a rational plan, which is attempting to achieve a number of approved goals. Goffman divides total institutions into five basic types, including such diverse institutions as ships, boarding schools and leper colonies. All total institutions have the same basic structure in Goffman's eyes. There is a strict staff or inmate status, with no social mobility between the two. Staff normally work an eight-hour shift and, unlike the inmates, are fully integrated into the wider community outside the institution. Both the staff and the inmates view each other through a range of narrow stereotypes: the inmates view the staff as oppressive, patronising and mean, the staff view the inmates as resentful, circumspect and generally not to be trusted.

Goffman's five types of total institution are:

- Institutions established to care for persons felt to be incapable and harmless – for example, homes for the aged.

- Institutions established to care for those who are felt to be incapable and a threat to the community, – for example, mental hospitals, leper colonies and TB sanitoria.

- Institutions established to protect the community from intentional dangers, and where the welfare of the inmates is not the primary objective. Examples include jails and concentration camps.

- Institutions established for instrumental reasons, principally to perform some work task – such institutions include barracks, boarding schools, ships and oil rigs.

- Institutions established as retreats from the world. Most examples given by Goffman are training centres for religious life: monasteries, convents, etc.

One of the key strengths of Goffman's work is that in his observation in *Asylums* of Central Hospital, Goffman attempted to show that the behaviour of inmates was not as irrational as the hospital staff would have us believe. Goffman attempted to find rationality in what appeared to be irrational behaviour. Hoarding behaviour was, at the time Goffman was writing, regarded by the hospital staff as an indicator of mental illness: 'normal' people do not keep all their possessions on their person. However, in the irrational situation of the mental hospital, where the inmates had no secure place to keep their possessions, the rational thing to do was to keep their possessions with them at all times.

Although not stated in *Asylums*, most of the inmates of Central Hospital were black Americans. What, if anything, is the significance of this observation?

Critique of Goffman

One of the most interesting critiques of Erving Goffman's work was published by Alvin Gouldner in his essay 'The sociologist as partisan: sociology and the welfare state.' Goffman takes up the point of view of the underdog in society, such as the mental patient and others with stigma; he speaks on their behalf, because underdogs tend not to have access to the media. Gouldner is highly critical of the partisan nature of Goffman's sociology. He claims that Goffman's work is characterised by sentimentality and that Goffman produces 'essays on quaintness':

' *The danger is then, that such an identification with the underdog becomes the urban sociologist's equivalent of the anthropologist's (one time) romantic appreciation of the noble savage.*

(Gouldner 1974: 37)

Gouldner goes on to argue that Goffman's sociology:

- is historical – Goffman does not take into account the history of mental illness
- fails to confront the matter of hierarchy
- ignores power relationships

However, according to Mary Rogers (1981), there is a theory of power within Goffman's work, although he is not particularly interested in the nature of power that we find in, for example, a Marxist analysis. For Goffman, power is about the ability of one person to change the behaviour of another person. People can exercise power by drawing upon two forms of resources:

- **instrumental resources**, which include interpersonal skills such as character, presence of mind, perceived fateful circumstances, knowledge and information control

- **infra resources**, which are concerned with perception, the skill that people have at changing the definition of the situation, use of negative stereotypes, labels and stereotypes.

It would appear that for Goffman power is a form of 'collusion' between people who have only a minimal stigma and who can 'pass' as normal against others who for a variety of reasons are unable or unwilling to accept the definition of the situation. As Goffman comments:

'We must all carry within ourselves something of the sweet guilt of the conspirators' (1959: 105).

If you have access to a library well stocked with Goffman's books you can read for yourself Goffman's theory of power. Look at the following Goffman texts and write a short report about Goffman on power: 1959: 3–4, 105, 142; 1961: 211–212; 1967: 216. You might want to compare this with Gouldner's *The Coming Crisis in Western Sociology*, p. 378–390 and *For Sociology* p. 347 onwards.

HINTS AND TIPS *If you are writing a more general critique of Goffman's work you might want to look at his research methods. In* **Asylums** *he makes use of participant observation and case studies.*

R.D. Laing

There are three key influences upon the work of R.D Laing:

- phenomenology
- Marxist theory of power and ideology
- Freud

Laing was a practising psychiatrist and one of his first patients was an 18-year-old man who believed that he was Julius Caesar. Laing talked to the young man at great length, sharing his fantasies. In his book *The Divided Self* (1960) Laing developed this technique of sharing the fantasies of patients. He argued that psychosis had a lawful shape which the patient developed to cope with a threatening personal environment. People suffered from **ontological insecurity**, in which they were uncertain about the boundaries between themselves and the world. The behaviour of the mad person should be seen as meaningful rather than odd or irrelevant. In addition, mad people had a career: madness develops through a number of distinct phases. The final chapter of *The Divided Self* was about a single schizophrenic patient named Julie. Laing investigated her family background and found that she had gone through a three-stage progression, from 'good girl', to 'bad girl' who rejected the instructions of her parents on how to behave, to 'mad girl' who was blamed for all the problems of the family. In his later works this became the **doublebind** theory of schizophrenia. In the doublebind family, all the family's problems are blamed on one single person, usually the youngest female. From the mid-1960s onwards, in place of traditional psychiatric techniques, Laing started to view schizophrenia as a healing process rather than a psychiatric problem. Schizophrenic patients are engaged in a lonely voyage through the inner space of their mind.

> **ACTIVITY**   KS **WORKING WITH OTHERS, PROBLEM SOLVING**
>
> | IDENTIFICATION AND INTERPRETATION | ANALYSIS AND EVALUATION |
>
> For Laing, families are dangerous places. Look at the conception of the family that Talcott Parsons presents. Which one do you find the most convincing? Give three reasons for your answer.

Women and mental illness

Coleman (1993), in his review of the literature, attempted to identify the factors which are responsible for the high level of depressive conditions diagnosed amongst females. He found that some 86% of menopausal women suffered from psychiatric conditions (Sutherland, 1990; Atkinson et al., 1990) and a significant number of these were diagnosed as 'clinically depressed'. In addition, the highest number of female suicides is amongst women in their 50s (Hinchliff and Montague, 1988). Coleman (1993) shows that a number of severe life events occur during middle age, such as children leaving home (Gulledge, 1991).

Women find the loss of parental role depressing (McGhie, 1979).

Physical changes to the body may also play a role in bringing about depression: loss of athletic skills and gaining weight (Bevan, 1978); tendency to tire more easily (Sutherland, 1990, Martinson, 1990). In addition, the meaning of the menopause has to be understood within a social and cultural context. Women may see it as signifying a loss of feminity (Houston et al., 1979), although post-menopausal women in Indian society have improved social standing, freedom and self esteem (Flint, 1975). Arab women in Israel also had positive attitudes to the menopause (Maoz et al., 1970). In Western society people place value on having a child (Sutherland, 1990) and on youth (Ballinger, 1990).

All medical procedures take place within such a social and cultural context. Many women suffer from painful periods and many women suffer from premenstrual tension. In British culture menstruation has a very negative image and is considered slightly shameful, hence until the late 1980s television companies were not allowed to show advertisements for tampons, and until the mid-1990s the product had to be shown in a box or a wrapper and no discussion of the advantages of one product over another was allowed. We have to remember that menstruation is a natural healthy process.

One of the most interesting studies to illustrate the interface between culture and medicine is Oberle and Allen's (1994) study of the reasons why women choose to have surgery to increase their breast size.

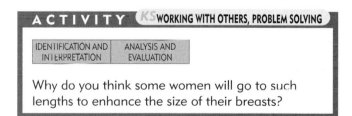

> **ACTIVITY**   KS **WORKING WITH OTHERS, PROBLEM SOLVING**
>
> | IDENTIFICATION AND INTERPRETATION | ANALYSIS AND EVALUATION |
>
> Why do you think some women will go to such lengths to enhance the size of their breasts?

Oberle and Allen's argument is that women do this to enhance their self-esteem and self-confidence. Small-breasted women feel inadequate about their breasts. There is a history of research which supports this view (Baker et al., 1974; Clifford, 1983; Goin, 1983). In addition, small-breasted women have a degree of sexual inhibition (McGrath and Burkhardt, 1984). Oberle and Allen report that women who have had breast enlargment surgery report improved self-confidence, enhanced femininity and enhanced sexuality.

Mental illness and ethnicity

During his time at Nottingham University Hospital, Glynn Harrison did extensive research on the high incidence of schizophrenia amongst the black population. Although his work can be challenged on methodological grounds – notably that he had problems estimating the size of the black population – Harrison explored some of the possible reasons for the differences.

One possibility is misdiagnosis. There is always a danger that physical symptoms will be believed to be psychological in nature, when there is a real physical cause. For example haemoglobin E disease can generate symptoms which may be classed as mental illness.

Labelling can also be a factor. Ways of behaving which are both common and acceptable in the Caribbean, for instance, may be treated with hostility in Britain. For example, within most cultures of the Caribbean there is a tendency to always stress the positive whilst speaking and not to mention any negative words, but such neologisims could be defined as symptoms of mental illness in a different culture.

It is also possible to extend R.D. Laing's theory of the doublebind family to cover the whole of the host society in an effort to explain mental illness of ethnic minorities. Immigrants were invited to live and work in Britain after the Second World War; however, once they settled here they experienced racism. Such contradictory messages, and the culture shock that comes with this, are a possible cause of mental illness.

Possible health developments in the UK

The National Health Service is currently going through more significant changes. The Labour government outlined its plans for the NHS soon after the 1997 general election. These plans include:

- Abolition of the internal market for health care that the Conservative government had introduced.

- Transferring the savings from the reduction in bureaucracy to patient care, especially to new services for children and screening for breast cancer.

- Establishment of an agency to reduce fraud in the NHS.

- Introduction of the Private Finance Initiative into the NHS to bring in private sector investment.

- Introduction of the Health Action Zones to improve links between the NHS and the local community.

Area summary

Definitions of health and illness are problematical. In this area we have looked at a number of sociological theories of health, and contrasted them with the medical model of health. Functionalists such as Talcott Parsons argued that being sick constituted a 'sick role' which contained a set of expectations on how to behave if a person claimed to be ill. If a sick person chose not to fulfil the expectations of the sick role, then they may be classed as a malinger. Parsons' view fits neatly into the 'medical model'. In contrast to Parsons' view we looked at Ivan Illich's argument that more people die by coming into contact with doctors, because of iatronogenic disease, than by any other cause except starvation. Marxists also cast doubt on the medical model, claiming that the role of the health service is to maintain capitalism. Marxists and others have looked in some detail at inequalities in health, and we have evaluated the research on class, race and gender inequality in health. In addition, post modernists reject the idea that medicine is a science, which underpins the medical model. The range of writers on mental illness – Szasz, Goffman and Laing – also cast doubt on the medical model as it is applied to mental health issues. There is evidence that in relation to gender and race, there is a significant measure of misdiagnoses, which reflects the prejudices of health care professionals.

Definitions

Atrocity tale	A commonly held belief about an evil event which may be a myth
Circuit of agents	A group of human agents (people) who share information and ideas
Contractual psychiatry	A term devised by Thomas Szasz to describe a form of psychiatry which is based upon a non coercive relationship between a doctor and patient
Disease	A physical problem with the body
Doublebind	A form of family in which contradictory pressures are brought to bear on the youngest female which R. D. Laing argued can cause mental illness
Focused interaction	The central reason or intention that people have for behaviour to take place
Health	A disputed term but usually regarded as the absence of disease
Holistic	The medical study of the whole person
Iatrogenesis	Doctor-induced disease
Illness	A both vague and disputed term, but generally regarded as a feeling of being 'unwell'
Infra resources	Resources that a person can draw upon to improve their standing within any given situation, such as their perception and skill of changing the definition of the situation
Institutional psychiatry	A term used to describe psychiatry which makes use of involuntary medication and incarceration

Instrumental resources	Resources that a person can draw upon to improve their standing within any given situation, such as character and presence of mind
Life expectancy	The average age that a population within a locality might be expected to live
Medical model	A way of approaching patients which involves the identification of pre-determined symptoms for a given condition and use of the appropriate medical intervention to cure the problem
Medical nemesis	A term invented by Ivan Illich to describe the attempt by doctors to control human behaviour
Moral career	The stages that a person goes through after the initial label. For example, the 'moral career' of the mental patient is concerned with the stages that a person goes through in order to become a mad person
Ontological insecurity	A situation in which individual people feel that they are losing touch with reality
Potential years of life lost	The number of years that a person's life falls short of their life expectancy
Ritual of degradation	A term used by Erving Goffman to describe a systematic form of humiliation imposed upon a person when entering a total institution
Sickness	A feeling of being unwell with a condition recognised by a doctor
Sick role	A term used by Talcott Parsons to describe the expectations imposed on a person who is claiming to be sick
Situationally present	A situation in which an individual accepts and follows the given situational proprieties
Situational improprieties	Behaving in an inappropriate way in a public place, and labelled as such, often the first stage in a moral career
Situational proprieties	A term used by Erving Goffman to describe appropriate ways of behaving in any given situation
Standardised mortality ratio	The life expectancy of one group in the population calculated against one other given group in the population
Total institution	An institution in which people live and work in a closed community, according to a rational plan
Unfocused interaction	Forms of behaviour that people engage in when they are making some form of assessment of another person

Data response questions

Item A

Goffman's analysis of total institutions differs from previous approaches to organisations because of its emphasis on understanding in terms of meaning.

Haralambos M. and Holborn M. (2000), **Sociology: Themes and Perspectives**, London, Collins.

Item B

Goffman's study focused on the activities that were undertaken by staff to manage the lives of their patients. The staff included not only the doctors and the nurses, but also cleaners, porters, administrators, athletics instructors, therapists, and many others. When in hospital, Goffman argued, patients must conform not only to the medical definition of their 'case', but also to the demands of the organisational routines on which staff work activities depend ... The hospital – like any other organisation – is a negotiated order, a stable system of recurrent relationships and interactions that result from conflict, bargaining and compromise among the various participants.'

Fulcher J. and Scott J. (1999), **Sociology**, Oxford, Oxford University Press.

Item C

Central to Laing's ideas is a radical critique of psychiatry. He generally opposed solitary confinement in mental hospitals and drug treatment of mental disorders. He believed that in confining people in mental hospitals, psychiatrists were functioning as agents of a repressive society. As a political libertarian, Laing thought everyone, even psychotics, must be free to decide where, how and with whom they spend their time. Once, at a formal meeting of Irish psychiatrists, he said that people were put into mental hospital not because they were suffering but because they were insufferable. It was not received well.

Fulcher J. and Scott J. (1991), **Sociology**, Oxford, Oxford University Press.

a   Goffman and Laing were described as anti-psychiatry. Drawing on information in the items and elsewhere, what criticisms did anti-psychiatrists such as Goffman and Laing make against traditional psychiatry?   **(7)**

KNOWLEDGE AND UNDERSTANDING	IDENTIFICATION AND INTERPRETATION	ANALYSIS AND EVALUATION

b   Outline Goffman's concept of the 'total institution'.   **(4)**

KNOWLEDGE AND UNDERSTANDING

c Describe the key elements of Goffman's distinctive approach to sociology. **(5)**

> IDENTIFICATION AND
> INTERPRETATION

d What do you consider to be the theoretical and methodological problems involved in the sociological study of mental illness? **(9)**

> | KNOWLEDGE AND UNDERSTANDING | IDENTIFICATION AND INTERPRETATION | ANALYSIS AND EVALUATION |

Structured Questions

1 What is iatrogenic disease? **(2)**

> **GUIDANCE** Your answer needs to explain that iatrogenic disease is doctor-induced disease. That is, disease that people get by coming into contact with doctors.
>
> | KNOWLEDGE AND UNDERSTANDING |

2 To what does the term 'health' refer? **(5)**

> **GUIDANCE** The question requires you to demonstrate that the concept of health is problematic. You need to outline some of the competing definitions of health, for example the WHO definition, which takes into account spiritual well-being, with a biological definition such as the 'absence of disease' found in the 'medical model'.
>
> | KNOWLEDGE AND UNDERSTANDING | IDENTIFICATION AND INTERPRETATION |

3 'The people who need health care the most are the least likely to get it.' Explain this statement. **(8)**

> **GUIDANCE** The statement is based upon the 'inverse care law' first outlined by Julian Tudor-Hart in the 1970s. Tudor-Hart's own research was concerned with the barriers preventing people living in working class communities from obtaining health care resources. You need to explain fully this theory. In addition, you might also want to explain that this theory is based upon the 'medical model' and assumes that health care is a good thing, but there is not enough of it. However, Ivan Illich (1974) would suggest otherwise, with his notion of iatrogenesis. Which model do you find the most convincing and why? You might also want to discuss if the 'inverse care law' may also apply to other groups in the population, for example, the health care needs of women, ethnic minorities and the alternative sexualities.
>
> | KNOWLEDGE AND UNDERSTANDING | IDENTIFICATION AND INTERPRETATION | ANALYSIS AND EVALUATION |

4   Evaluate the contribution that Functionalists have made to our
understanding of medicine.   **(10)**

> **GUIDANCE**   *This question gives you the
> opportunity to outline and evaluate the*
>
> | KNOWLEDGE AND UNDERSTANDING | IDENTIFICATION AND INTERPRETATION | ANALYSIS AND EVALUATION |
> |---|---|---|
>
> *contribution of Talcott Parsons (1951). Is Parsons' concept of the 'sick role' useful for understanding
> the nature of illness and disease? Do you accept or reject the assumptions that Parsons made about
> medical practice? Parsons assumes that:*
>
> ■   *Medicine is a value-free science. Do you accept this view? Or are doctors influenced by widely
> held beliefs and prejudice, such as racism and sexism?*
>
> ■   *Medicine is the only viable way of mediating between people and disease. Again do you accept or
> reject this assumption? Are 'alternative' or 'complementary' therapies of any value?*
>
> ■   *The causes of ill health are biological in nature. Do you accept this assumption or are 'social'
> factors, such as race, gender, class and sexual orientation significant?*
>
> *Although Functionalism has come under considerable criticism over the decades since Parsons wrote
> The Social System, there are some valuable aspects to Parsons' account. For example, he looks at ill
> health as a potential form of deviance, which is policed by doctors.*

Essay titles

1   Le Grand, in *The Strategy of Equality*, states: 'Despite the provision of
free medical care and despite all the advances in medical care of the
last half century being made available to everyone, inequalities in
health remain as firmly entrenched as ever.'

Discuss, illustrating your answers with appropriate evidence.

(25)
(AEB, November 1993)

2   What is a 'total institution'? Does this concept enhance our understanding
of mental hospitals?   **(25)**

3   Evaluate sociological approaches which have challenged medical
explanations of the social distribution of health.   **(25)**
(AEB, June 1997)

Further reading and references

Green, J. and Thorogood, N. (1998) *Analysing Health Policy: A Sociological Approach*. London, Longman.

Jones, L. J. (1994) *The Social Context of Health and Health Work*. London, Macmillan.

Internet sites

http://www.medcocbsa.swan.ac.uk/
The website for the Medical Sociology Group, which is a study group of the British Sociological Association

http://www.who.int
The World Health Organisation

http://www.abacon.com/sociology/soclinks/med.html
Allyn and Bacon Sociology Links to a range of interesting medical sociology sites

Bibliography

Atkinson, R. L., Atkinson, R. C., Smith, E. E., Benn, D. J. and Hilgard, E. R. (1990) *Introduction to Psychology* 10th edn. Orlando, Florida, Harcourt Brace Jovanovich.

Baker, J. L., Jr Kolin, I. S. and Bartlett, E. S. (1974) 'Psychosexual Dynamics of Patients Undergoing Mammary Augmentation.' *Plastic and Reconstructive Surgery* 53, 652–9.

Ballinger, C. B. (1990) 'Psychiatric Aspects of the Menopause'. *British Journal of Psychiatry* 156, 773–87.

Bauman, Z. (1992) *Intimations of Postmodernity*. London, Routledge.

Bevan, J. (1978) *A Pictoral Handbook of Anatomy and Physiology*. London, Mitchell Beazley.

Black, D. (1981) *Inequalities in Health*. Harmondsworth, Penguin.

Brighton Women and Science Group (1980) *Alice Through the Microscope*. Basingstoke, Macmillan.

Brown, G. W., Nibrolchain, M. and Harris, T. (1975) 'Social Class Psychiatric Disturbance Among Women in an Urban Population'. *Sociology* 9 (2), 225–4.

Clifford, E. (1983) 'Augmentation, Reduction, and Reconstruction: Psychological Contributions to Understanding Breast Surgery', in Geogiade N. G. (Ed.), Williams and Wilkins *Aesthetic Breast Surgery*. Baltimore, Maryland.

Coleman, P. M. (1993) 'Depression During the Female Climateric Period'. *Journal of Advanced Nursing* 18, 1540–6.

Coleman, D. and Salt, J. (1992) *The British Population: Patterns, Trends and Processes*. Oxford, Oxford University Press.

Dalton, K. (1969) *The Menstrual Cycle*. London, Routledge.

Department of Health (1992) *The Health of the Nation*. London, HMSO.

Donovan, J. L. (1986) *We Don't Buy Sickness: It Just Comes – Health, Illness and Health Care in the Lives of Black People in London*. Aldershot, Hampshire, Gower.

Doyal, L. and Pennel, I. (1982) *The Political Economy of Health*. London, Pluto.

Drever, F. and Whitehead, M. (1998) *Health Inequalities*. London, Office for National Statistics.

Flint, M. P. (1975) 'The Menopause: Reward or Punishment'. *Psychosomatics* 16, 161–3.

Fulcher, J. and Scott, J. (1999) *Sociology*. Oxford, Oxford University Press.

Goffman, E. (1959, first published 1956) *The Presentation of Self in Everyday Life*. Harmondsworth, Penguin.

Goffman, E. (1961) *Asylums: Essays on the Social Situation of Mental Patients*. Harmondsworth, Penguin.

Goffman, E. (1963) *Behaviour in Public Places*. New York, Free Press.

Goffman, E. (1963) *Stigma*. Harmondsworth, Penguin.

Goffman, E. (1970) *Gender Advertisements*. New York, Free Press.

Goffman, E. (1981) *Forms of Talk*. Harmondsworth, Penguin.

Goin, M. K. (1983) 'Psychological Aspects of Aesthetic Surgery of the Breast', in Geogiade N. G. (Ed.), Williams and Wilkins *Aesthetic Breast Surgery*. Baltimore, Maryland.

Gouldner, A. (1974) *For Sociology*. Harmondsworth, Penguin.

Gouldner, A. (1970) *The Coming Crisis in Western Sociology*. London, Heinemann.

Gouldner, A. (1974) 'The Sociologist as Partisan: Sociology and the Welfare State', in *For Sociology*. Harmondsworth, Penguin.

Graham, H. and Oakley A. (1981) 'Competing ideologies of reproduction' in H. Roberts (Ed.) *Women, Health and Reproduction*. London, Routledge.

Gulledge, A. D. (1991) 'Depression and chronic fatigue'. *Primary Care* 18, (2) 263.

Haralambos, M. and Holborn, M. *Sociology: Themes and Perspectives*

Harrison, G. and Mason, P. (1993) 'Schizophrenia – Falling Incidence and Better Outcome'. *British Journal of Psychiatry* 163: 535–41.

Hart, N. (1982) Review of Doyal, L. and Pennel, I. 'The Political Economy of Health.' *British Journal of Sociology*.

Hart, N. (1985) *The Sociology of Health and Medicine*. Ormskirk, Causeway Press.

Hart, N. (1988) *The Sociology of Health*. Ormskirk, Causeway Press.

Hinchliff, S. and Montague, S. (1988) *Physiology for Nursing Practice*. Oxford, Bailliere-Tindall.

Houston, J. P., Bee, H., Hatfield, E. and Rimm, D. C. (1979) *Invitation to Psychology* (international edition). London, Academic Press.

Howlett, (1991) *Health and Lifestyle Survey*. London, HMSO.

Illich, I. (1975) *Medical Nemesis: The Limits to Medicine*. London, Marion Boyars.

Jones, L. (1994) *The Social Context of Health and Health Work*. London, Macmillan.

Laing, R. D. (1960) *The Divided Self*. Harmondsworth, Penguin.

Laing, R. D. (1979) Review of Szasz 'Schizophrenia'. *New Statesman*, February.

Lalonde, M. (1974) 'A New Prespective on the Health of Canadians' in C. Webb (Ed.) *Feminist Practice in Women's Health Care*. London, Wiley.

Le Grand, J. (1982) *The Strategy of Equality*. London, Allen & Unwin.

Lennane, J. K. and Lennane, R. J. (1973) 'Alleged psychogenic disorders in women – a possible manifestation of sexual prejudice' in Whitelegg and Beechey, V., *The Changing Experience of Women*. London, Martin Robertson.

Maoz, B., Dowty, N., Antonosky, A. and Wijsenbeek, H. (1970) 'Female Attitudes to Menopause'. *Social Psychiatry* 5 (1) 35–40.

Mares, A., Henley, A. and Barker, C. (1985) *Health Care in Multi-Racial Britain*. London, Health Education Authority.

Martinson, E. W. (1990) 'Physical Fitness, Anxiety and Depression'. *British Journal of Hospital Medicine* 45 (5), 301–2.

McGhie, A. (1979) *Psychology as Applied to Nursing* 7th edition. Edinburgh, Churchill Livingstone.

McGrath, M. H. and Burkhardt, B. R. (1984) 'The Safety and Efficacy of Breast Implants for Augmentation Mammaplasty'. *Plastic and Reconstructive Surgery* 74 550–60.

McKeown, T. (1971) *The Role of Medicine*. Oxford, Blackwell.

Miles, N. (1991) *Women and Medicine*. Milton Keynes, Open University Press.

Miles, R. (1993) *Racism after Race Relations*. London, Routledge.

Nagai-Jacobson and Burkhart (1989) 'Spirituality: Cornerstone of Holistic Nursing Practice'. *Holistic Nursing Practice*, 3, 3.

National Association of Health Authorities (NAHAT) (1989) Connah, B. and Lancaster, S. (Eds.) *NHS Handbook*. London, Macmillan.

Oakley, A. (1984) *The Captured Womb: A History of the Medical Care of Pregnant Women*. Oxford, Blackwell.

Oakley, A. (1985) *Sex, Gender and Society*. London, Temple Smith.

Oberle, K. and Allen, M. (1994) 'Breast Augmentation Surgery: A Woman's Health Issue'. *Journal of Advanced Nursing*, 20.

Orbach, S. (1989) *Fed Up and Hungry*. London, Women's Press.

Paroski, P. A. (1987) *Health Care Delivery and the Concerns of Gay and Lesbian Adolescents. Journal of Adolescent Health Care*, 8.

Parsons, T. (1951) *The Social System*. New York, Free Press.

Reichenbach, H. (1947) *The Elements of Symbolic Logic*.

Rogers, M. (1981) 'Goffman on Power' in *The View from Goffman*. London, Macmillan.

Sheaff, R. (1996) *The Need for Healthcare*. London, Routledge.

Sutherland, F. N. (1990) 'Psychological Aspects of the Menopause'. *Maternal and Child Health* 15 (1) 13–14

Szasz, T. (1972, first published 1961) *The Myth of Mental Illness*. New York, Paladin.

Taylor, I. and Robertson, A. (1994) 'The Health Care Needs of Gay Men: A Discussion of the Literature and Implications for Nursing'. *Journal of Advanced Nursing*, 20, 3.

Thorogood, N. (1990) 'Caribbean Home Remedies and Their Importance for Black Women's Health Care in Britain' in Abbot, P. and Payne, G. (Eds.) *New Directions in the Sociology of Health*. Basingstoke, Falmer Press.

Tudor-Hart, J. (1971) 'The Inverse Care Law'. *The Lancet*, February.

Turner, B. S. (1987) *Medical Power and Social Knowledge*. London, Sage.

Webb, C. (1986) 'Women as gynaecology patients and nurses' in C. Webb (Ed.) *Feminist Practice in Women's Health Care*. London, Wiley.

Whitehead, M. (1987) *The Health Divide*. London, Health Education Council.

WHO (1974) *Alma Ata Declaration*. Geneva, WHO.

Wilkinson, R. G. (1998) *Unhealthy Societies: The Afflictions of Inequality*. London, Routledge.

Crime and Deviance

This area covers:

■ The processes within society which contribute to social control and their relationship to crime prevention strategies and law-enforcement agencies

■ The various social perspectives and the contributions they make to an understanding of the origins of crime and deviant behaviour

■ The distribution of crime in our society with relationship to age, gender and ethnicity

■ The political and social significance of crime data collection in the UK

■ Case studies of deviant behaviours, such as youth culture and delinquency, and of suicide.

By the end of this area you should be able to:

■ suggest why it is difficult to define the nature of crime or deviance and understand that these are in fact socially determined constructions

■ recognise why crime and deviance play such an important role in public consciousness and consider the impact of crime on the victims

■ identify factors within society that predispose certain people to criminal behaviours or to conviction for criminal behaviours

■ understand something of the social factors which have contributed to the organisation of our current judicial and law-enforcement system.

Key terms

alienation	deviance
anomie	policing
crime	sanctions
dark figure of crime	social control
delinquency	stereotyping

Area 12   Contents

Introduction

The study of crime and deviance is socially very significant and a highly politicised area of sociological debate. The aim of this area is to examine some of the theory of social control and to recognise that crime and deviance are political definitions which conceal some of society's darker aims of control. Features such as the law and the criminal justice system, which are a significant part of our experience of a safe society, can, in the wrong hands, be tools of oppression and suppression.

Even the extent and nature of crime become areas of serious debate because the person who can define what is criminal and what is deviant holds tremendous power over people's ability to express themselves. Can we trust the figures that society collects on the nature and extent of crime? Debates relating to definitions of crime and the methods which should be used to study it illustrate much of what is at the core of the subject of sociology as a discipline. Even though we may be uncertain as to how much crime occurs and what forms crime may take, there are issues about those who are most likely to be perceived as criminal. Our prisons are full of young working-class men. Is masculinity itself or is class victimisation the problem? Is society at fault for labelling these young men and limiting their social choices? Are they perhaps the victims of a cruel and unjust system that uses them as scapegoats to mask far more serious and terrifying legal injustices, which escape the attentions of law-enforcement agencies? Are those who make the laws protecting their own interests?

Despite these questions, crime is a major social reality, impacting in untold ways on our daily lives and the organisation of our society. There are people who are very likely to be the victims of crime and these people are often the poorest and least able to cope. Women, in particular, may feel forced to limit their activities because of the fear of crime. Are their fears real? Could they be reacting to cynical manipulation by media agencies who fuel fears and insecurities in a blatant attempt to draw attention away from graver social inequality, or are their fears realistic and understandable given the nature of social inequality and organisation?

This area will address these questions, but the evaluations and answers will have to come from the reader's own understanding of the issues involved.

Defining crime and deviance

Deviance

The rules for each society vary; this is a basic sociological and anthropological concept known as **cultural relativity**. A **deviant** is a person who breaks the rules of society, the norms, mores and values the culture holds important. This makes it almost impossible to define any act as deviant; definition of deviant will depend upon the following cultural variables:

- what was the act? (action)
- when did it take place? (location in time)
- who committed the act?
- where did it take place? (location in geography)

An act that is considered absolutely normal in the privacy of the home, such as removing one's clothing, becomes deviant at a wedding party or in the high street. An act that is considered normal in today's society – such as bearing a child outside conventional marriage – would once have been good reason for assuming the woman to be either insane or criminal. At the same time, men have rarely been punished for fathering children outside marriage. It is a safe guideline to suggest that anything that in our society which we consider to be disgusting, illegal and morally repugnant is, or has been, legal in another society at another time. The proposition holds true of things that we value in our society; other societies might consider them to be proof of insanity or criminality. The widest variations in criminal codes are often in areas that are personal; for example, rules governing sexual behaviours are radically different from country to country. The age of sexual consent in the Netherlands is 12, for instance, and many American states consider certain sexual practices, even between husband and wife in the privacy of their own home, to be illegal.

Crime

Criminality is far easier to define. If a person breaks the formal code of laws of a society, that person is a **criminal**. This point raises issues of who actually makes the laws and how they are applied. However, these are debates to which it is necessary to return in more detail later in this area. The breaking of a **criminal code** or **law** will, in theory, result in a **formal punishment** from an institutional organisation in society such as a court of law. Punishments could include time in mental hospital, or prison, community service or a fine. You should note that what is defined as a **crime** can vary: the use of cannabis in many Arab states is perfectly legal while alcohol use is a serious crime. The opposite rule applies in Britain.

Social and criminal codes

A **social code** refers to the unwritten rules that most people in society would agree are generally correct. These consist of norms, values, and mores.

- **Norms** are the rules of normal behaviour.
- **Values** are the principles that lie behind moral behaviour.
- **Mores** are people's ideas of what is right or wrong.

People who break social codes regularly are liable to find themselves defined as socially unacceptable or nasty, or to be labelled as insane. They are likely to be punished in a socially agreed way, through the application of **informal sanctions** or punishments such as mockery or social rejection. The person concerned may, at worst, be defined as insane and be placed in a mental hospital. In this case, the imprisonment will not be perceived as punishment, except perhaps by the deviant personality, but as an attempt at a 'cure'.

It is actually quite difficult to sort out the moral debates surrounding crime and deviance, given that deviance is a cultural and social variable. It is, for instance, criminal to speed on a motorway but very few drivers actually keep to any of the limits and to do so at certain times can actually be dangerous. A speeding driver is breaking a **legal code**, but is he or she breaking a social code?

You will find that many people will happily break criminal codes if they feel that the act is trivial and does not break a moral code. It may sometimes be necessary to break a social code, especially if the motive is one that is good, such as to protect a person's feelings.

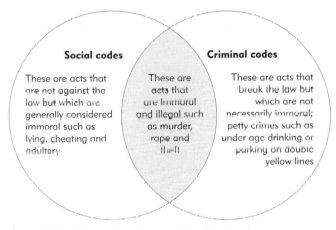

Figure 12.1   The overlap of social and criminal codes

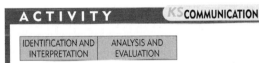

Social codes — These are acts that are not against the law but which are generally considered immoral such as lying, cheating and adultery

These are acts that are immoral and illegal such as murder, rape and theft

Criminal codes — These are acts that break the law but which are not necessarily immoral; petty crimes such as under age drinking or parking on double yellow lines

ACTIVITY   KS **COMMUNICATION**

IDENTIFICATION AND INTERPRETATION	ANALYSIS AND EVALUATION

Many people will have heard of Oscar Schindler from the film *Schindler's List* or the book by Thomas Keneally, *Schindler's Ark*. Schindler was undoubtedly deviant – he was certainly criminal. Was he correct to save the lives of Jews? Write down your reasons for considering whether Schindler, who risked his life for those of others, was correct in breaking the law.

To understand the true complexity of the debate, you should now consider the case of someone in our society who disagrees strongly with racial equality. Would that person *also* be correct to break the laws of the land? Apply the thinking that you applied to the case of Schindler and see how many of the points that you made remain valid in this morally unpleasant scenario.

More debatable, but of interest to sociology, is the breaking of a criminal code for reasons that are honest, good and morally unimpeachable because it is genuinely believed that the law itself is wrong and unjust. Germans who resisted the laws put in place by Hitler were theoretically criminal, and ran terrible risks, not only to themselves but to their families as well. Would we consider these people criminal or heroic?

Non-culpable stigma

Certain people in our society can be considered to be deviant in the sense that they are seen as somehow different (and inferior) for something that is beyond their ability to control. They are not **culpable** or guilty in the sense of having actively broken social laws but they have a **spoiled identity** or a deeply discreditable characteristic which prevents full social participation. This characteristic, or defect, is known as a **stigma**. You will find further discussion of this in Area 4. A stigma is not a characteristic of the perceived defect, but of the impaired social reactions that other people have to it. Erving Goffman (1963), an influential researcher in the interpretative tradition, identified three forms of stigma in his seminal work *Stigma*:

- defects of the body, such as a visible impairment, scar, or disability

- defects of the character, such as a record of mental ill health

- defects that relate to membership of an ethnic group which is devalued in society

Not all stigmatising characteristics are equally undesirable. An inability to see clearly without an aid (wearing glasses) is not as socially awkward as an inability to walk without an aid (using a wheelchair). Interactions between people who are stigmatised by an undesirable social characteristic and those who are not can be very uncomfortable. Non-stigmatised people often impose negative judgements. The BBC called its Radio 4 magazine programme on disability issues *Does he take sugar?* in recognition of the fact that people will ignore a disabled person to speak to an able-bodied companion as though an inability to walk well also implies an inability to understand even the simplest requests and instructions. It is the stigmatised individuals who must adjust their reactions and

behaviour to put the non-stigmatised at their ease. They use a variety of coping strategies.

- rejection of the stigmatising label and over-achievement in an area considered to be difficult or impossible for the person concerned

- the use of social props which identify the stigmatised as otherwise a very high achiever

- the joining of self-help groups to counter prejudice and social oppression

- the development of a self-deprecating humour which draws attention to the stigma and relieves the tension for the non-stigmatised

HINTS AND TIPS   Physical impairment of itself is not handicapping, if society can adjust to cope with the special needs of those who do not have the full use of body, senses or mind. Once people can learn to look beyond the stigmatising characteristic and recognise the individual, then those who do experience physical or mental difficulty can play a full part in society. It is a sad reflection on society that those who experience problems are also the ones to carry the full burden of the fact that the rest of us may find disability difficult to cope with.

ACTIVITY   KS **COMMUNICATION**

| KNOWLEDGE AND UNDERSTANDING | IDENTIFICATION AND INTERPRETATION |

Goffman's *Stigma* is a fascinating text and certainly accessible to the average student if you are persistent. You are advised to attempt to read some of it for the insight that you will gain into those who are excluded from full social participation for reasons that are not of their own making.

Social control and law enforcement

This debate has a number of elements to it. Each sociological tradition has created its own view of the nature of crime and the purpose of laws. All have one view in common: they agree that it is easier to control people through the imposition of morals and values than through the enforcement of power. If one can make people behave because they can see that it is in their own interests to do so, or because they believe it is morally correct to do so, then there is no need to force them to act in the way that you wish. The history of the twentieth century shows that if people's sense of right and wrong can be controlled they are capable of any act, no matter how brutal, fundamentally wicked or unpleasant that act is.

A C T I V I T Y   KS **COMMUNICATION**

| KNOWLEDGE AND |
| UNDERSTANDING |

To develop this idea there are two forms of activity to undertake:

1   Find out about Stanley Milgram's famously frightening (1974) study of the authoritarian personality.
2   Find out what you can about totalitarian governments such as those of Stalin in the USSR or Hitler in Germany or Pinochet in Chile and how they operated against people who dissented from the values of the state.

What lessons do you learn about the nature of social control?

The differences between the main sociological perspectives are related more to the social values of the researchers and their considerations of the purpose of social control than to the mechanisms of **social control**. Mechanisms of social control include the organisations of society and of the state, such as the family, education, the police, the law, religion, political structures, justice systems and punishment systems. Note that these are also agencies of socialisation.

Functionalism

Functionalism draws on **consensus theory** suggesting that society exists because we generally agree about its main purposes. The main theorist in this tradition is Travis Hirschi (1969), who looked at the mechanisms of why we conform, taking the viewpoint that control is necessary and valuable to society. Hirschi suggested that the absence of social control creates deviance – people violate norms if they lack the normal control mechanisms in their lives.

Hirschi begins with the eminently sensible view that all of us have the potential to commit deviant acts. He is interested in our failure to break social norms and values, which is a refreshing perspective from a

	Values of researchers	Purpose of social control	Nature of crime
Marxists	Marxist writers tend to agree that social control is oppressive and limits freedom to differ from the needs and wants of the state	The purpose of social control is so that the rich can order society to suit their own needs and satisfaction and limit the class consciousness of the poor	The poorest people are criminal because they are the victims of the legal system, which operates in favour of the wealthy and which ignores their anti-social behaviour. Crime may be an act of rebellion
Functionalists	Functionalist writers see social control as necessary for the maintenance of order and the organisation of the state	The purpose of social control is to give people a sense of belonging to and ownership of the state so that they can safely go about their business	People commit crime because they are inadequately socialised into the norms of the community or they do not accept or understand the rules which bind us all
Interpretivists	There is no such thing as society, therefore all behaviour is socially constructed	Interpretivists tend to see social control as operating at a personal level via the mechanisms of labelling of individuals as deviant	Crime is socially constructed and is a relative concept depending on variables such as time, place and the meaning that others place on the act
Feminists	Feminists suggest that society is patriarchal	The purpose of social control is to protect the interests of the ruling groups in society, particularly males	Crime is committed because it suits the needs of the person who commits the crime. It can be an expression of power and masculinity

Figure 12.2   Social perspectives and social control

discipline that tends to concentrate on crime from the perspective of rule breakers. He suggests that we fail to commit deviant acts for the following reasons:

- **attachment to others**, who display conventional attitudes and behaviours
- **commitment to conformity** – we gain status through conventional activities, invest time and effort in them and therefore value them
- **involvement in conventional activities** – we are so busy being conventional that we do not have time to consider or commit deviant acts
- **a belief in morality and validity of social rules** – individuals have a strong moral belief that they should obey the rules of conventional society

If the above four elements are strong then people do not commit crimes or deviant behaviours; if they are weak people do show deviant tendencies. When evaluating this theory there are a number of issues to bring into your discussion.

- *Does this theory account for morally motivated behaviours such as direct political actions by road protesters and Greenpeace activists?* In general, it does not give justice to those who become deviant from a genuine and heartfelt desire for moral reform.
- *Is it true that people **do not** commit deviant acts?* This is a questionable assumption at the best of times. Certain forms of deviance, such as violence within the home, are widespread. The delinquent activities of young people, such as forms of drug abuse, tend to cut across boundaries of social class and would seem generally to be age-related. Parking on double yellow lines or over pavements is almost a norm in some places.
- *Is deviant behaviour the same as criminal behaviour?* This is certainly an issue for deep consideration and is well covered in this area. You have been introduced to this debate already.
- *What types of crime are easy to commit and what types difficult to commit?* Many people are deviant because it is pleasurable and fun; for instance, many young people will be tempted to speed dangerously in their cars. They will weigh up the possible consequences of the act against the possible pleasure and choose in favour of the

dangerous and silly. However, they will not necessarily break other more serious rules with the same abandonment to the fun of the moment.

ACTIVITY   KS **WORKING WITH OTHERS**

IDENTIFICATION AND INTERPRETATION

Conduct a small-scale survey of people's law-breaking habits within your own school or college. Ask people under the age of 18, but who are preferably over 16, if they had committed any of the following acts in the last week or the last year. Make a note of gender, or any other social variables which might affect the results, such as ethnicity or religious affiliation.

- Opening mail addressed to other people
- Drinking under-age
- Failure to pay bus or train fare
- Making personal use of paper or any other items from college or from work
- Speeding or illegal parking (if they have cars)

How many people had done any of these? What do you learn about people's ability to break laws? Did you note any patterns of willingness to break law based on gender or another social variable? Did some people find they were able to break laws because they regarded them as trivial, but would feel considerable concern about breaking other laws?

Recent issues in social control

This is a developing area in the sociology of social control and students are advised to gather notes and ideas. Newer research and analysis, particularly from a postmodernist or feminist perspective, tends to point to the way that social control has become so institutionalised in society that we barely recognise its operation and accept it as a fact of life. Unless we are directly affected by the restrictions or have a deep-seated concern with civil liberties, we tend to welcome social control imposed on us as a society as a limit to the activities of the dubious and law-breaking 'others'.

HINTS AND TIPS   *You should bear these ideas in mind when considering the role of the police in our society.*

Closed Circuit Television

There has been an enormous proliferation of CCTV camera use in Britain to reduce the opportunities for crime and thereby control behaviour. This raises issues of privacy, the intrusion of the private sector into social control and the reliability and accuracy of such evidence, given that the images produced are sometimes fleeting and often of unreliable quality. A further area of concern becomes the displacement of crime to areas not covered by CCTV.

Crowd control and social control as part of the structure of social life

This draws on the work of Foucault, a prominent post-modernist, who suggested that social control is rapidly becoming a form of mind control with deviance being seen as a mental state. Stanley Cohen (1985) pointed out that more people are becoming subject to social control, and that informal social control is penetrating into the routines of existence. Schools, families and community groups are all encouraged to ensure that people conform to the rules of society. Shearing and Stenning (1985) illustrate this by considering the case of Disneyworld, where control systems are not overt but are still apparent from the moment of entering the park. Crowds are directed and controlled by co-operative and subtle means and supported by technology.

> **HINTS AND TIPS**   *What technologies and control strategies are used by your own institution? A quick survey of a shopping centre or your college would help you develop your understanding of how social control can operate on an informal and privatised basis. Those of you who have been through an airport recently will be familiar with the way that large groups of people can be controlled and moved without being made aware of the processes involved in crowd control.*

ACTIVITY   KS INFORMATION TECHNOLOGY, COMMUNICATION

IDENTIFICATION AND INTERPRETATION

Find out more about the work of Neighbourhood Watch or any other crime prevention schemes and make notes about the way that these schemes operate. The Internet has a number of American sites devoted both to personal safety, including quite aggressive home safety devices, and to guard schemes.

Criminal justice

This provides an understanding of the nature of formal social control in our society. There are a number of points for consideration:

- Who makes the laws which all of us must obey?
- How does the criminal justice system work?
- Is the criminal justice system equally fair to all people?

> **HINTS AND TIPS**   *The first two questions reflect the skill domains of knowledge, but the last one is an evaluation, which you must make on the basis of knowledge and analysis. It could be a plausible examination question so be certain that you have a view on this point.*

Who makes the laws?

Laws are made in the following ways:

- They can be passed as Acts of Parliament through a complex process, which is discussed in Area 14.
- Laws can be made through common practice over the years.
- Judges and lawyers can create law through precedent, or by interpreting the words of Acts of Parliament.

In theory, law is impartial and protects everyone in society equally. However, laws are made by human beings, legislators and politicians: who are these people in reality? In Britain, they tend to be middle-class, middle-aged, white men who have received a public school education. This is, of course, a very broad generalisation but it underscores a point made by critics of the political and judicial system such as Marxists and feminists, who suggest that law tends to protect the vested interests of the people who make the laws.

> **HINTS AND TIPS**   *Watch the Parliament channel on cable or satellite if you have access. What kind of people are our law-makers? Those of you without cable might like to watch* **Prime Minister's Question Time**, *which is transmitted on BBC 2 when Parliament is in session.*

The criminal justice system

This refers to the formal structures for controlling and then punishing the perpetrators of crime. One of the main writers in this area, Emsley, notes that in the early days of the British state this process would have been local and informal. From the mid-eighteenth century, this role was gradually taken over by the state so that it now amounts to a major employment sector in our society.

HINTS AND TIPS *If a person in our society is charged with a crime by the police, the decision whether or not to take that person to court is made by the Crown Prosecution Service. You can visit its excellent Website at http://www.cps.gov.uk. The CPS provides useful information packs. Write to 50 Ludgate Hill, London, EC4M 7EX.*

Gelsthorpe (1996) raises a number of issues relating to the criminal justice system and court processes:

■ **Is access to law processes equal?** The answer to this question is that it is not. Lawyers' fees are extremely high and only the very wealthy or those

You are advised to spend a day in a court of law. This is easy to arrange as courts are obliged to be open to the public. As a courtesy you should write to the Clerk of the Court for permission to observe and make notes. These people are extremely busy, but generally very obliging and helpful to students. Magistrate's Courts will be found in most small towns, but you may need to go to a local city to observe a Crown Court in action.

eligible for legal aid can face a lengthy court case without fear of bankruptcy.

■ **Is sentencing similar for similar offences?** There is some variation in sentencing depending upon the judge before whom the defendant appears, and depending where in the country the crime was committed. This is because the court can take into account the circumstances of the defendant. Magistrates' courts are notorious for

Type of court	What happens?
Youth courts	These are for defendants who are aged between 10 and 17. It is believed that children under the age of 10 cannot commit a crime because they are not deemed fully to understand the concepts of right and wrong. Children in youth courts are given special treatment because of their age: they are not to be named in newspapers, for instance
Magistrates' courts	These are for minor offences. People charged with crimes are tried before magistrates, who are generally volunteers. Magistrates are people who are respected in the community and who are asked if they would like to 'sit on the bench'. These people are known as Justices of the Peace or JPs. The Court is generally informal and solicitors may speak for clients. People who plead guilty to minor offences can be sentenced to a light punishment such as a fine, or a very short prison sentence. Trials are short. If you plead not guilty to an offence in a Magistrates' court, or if the crime is serious, then you are referred to a Crown Court
Crown courts	These are for serious offences. People are tried before a judge and a jury. The court is run by legal professionals such as barristers and judges who wear the traditional clothing of wigs and gowns. The Crown court is very formal and barristers represent clients. If a person is found guilty, even of a fairly minor offence, he or she can expect a serious punishment reflecting the time and expense of a trial process. Trials generally last days. There are levels of Crown court including Courts of Appeal where people can argue against the judgment of an original judge and jury if they believe there has been a miscarriage of justice
The House of Lords	This is the highest court of the land and is an appeal court. Once a case has gone to the House of Lords then the next stage is the European courts. It is enormously expensive to go to the House of Lords for a court case and few people will do this.

Figure 12.3 The courts system

regional variations in sentencing. Magistrates are selected carefully and generally they do attempt to be fair to all people. There are claims that different social groupings can be treated differently before the courts. It should also be noted that magistrates tend to be white, middle-class and middle-aged. More women are now nominated to magistrates' benches, but judges are almost universally men. In addition, they tend to be older, with a public school education and an élite university background.

■ **Can juries be trusted?** Trial by jury is one of the oldest elements of the legal system, being one of the terms of *Magna Carta* (1215). A jury consists of 12 members of the public over the age of 18 whose names are taken at random from the electoral register. They simply judge guilt and do not sentence the offender: sentencing is the role of the judge. However, there is no check to see that juries can understand the complexities of the cases before them or training in committee procedures. Opinion is divided as to their use and some juries have given notoriously unexpected verdicts. As juries are

HINTS AND TIPS *See if you can find out about the National Council for Civil Liberties for ideas and information about the criminal justice system. You can write to 21 Tabard Street, London, SE1 4LA. The Citizen's Advice Bureau will be able to offer you an address and has a Website under construction (1999).*

ACTIVITY KS **COMMUNICATION**

| KNOWLEDGE AND UNDERSTANDING | IDENTIFICATION AND INTERPRETATION |

Do some individual research to discover what you can about notorious cases of miscarriage of justice. The Internet will be able to offer information. You will also find material in old newspapers, books and on CD-ROM.

Famous cases have been made into films. These may be available on video. Do not take film versions as being perfectly truthful: stories have to be altered to suit the needs of the film-makers and to make them more interesting to viewers. Examples include:

■ Derek Bentley – *Let him have it*
■ Ruth Ellis – *Dance with a Stranger*
■ The Birmingham Six – *In the Name of the Father*

---

made up of members of the public, they are likely to reflect the attitudes and beliefs of the general public, with all that implies in terms of prejudice and discrimination.

Policing

In terms of social control, the police have a dual role to fulfil, and these roles are in total opposition to each other. The police must protect the public and act as authority figures, yet the criminals and the public are the same people! The relationship between the police and society is considered more fully later in this area, but for the moment the discussion will centre on the role that the police fulfil as agents of social control. Considerable anxieties have been expressed about the way the police have handled their situation in recent years, with accusations of institutional racism and incompetence on the one hand and complaints that they no longer represent community concerns on the other.

Writers such as Scraton and Gordon have suggested that Britain is dominated by a class-based system of criminal justice and social control. The police are not accountable democratically because they represent the interests of government. This is generally a position derived from Marxist understandings. However, writers from a more consensual position have made a similar point. For instance, Alderson (1979) and Moore and Brown (1981) suggest that the police should relate more to their communities and become part of consensual social groupings. Writers as important as Lord Justice Scarman (1981) and Reiner (1985) both suggest that the police need to improve their performance and become more professional in order to gain legitimacy. Kinsey, Lea and Young have developed this by suggesting that the police must change their relationship with the public, which has been mismanaged.

ACTIVITY KS **PROBLEM SOLVING**

| IDENTIFICATION AND INTERPRETATION |

Watch a police drama such as *The Bill* on television. Attempt to identify forms of social control that you can see depicted in the relationship between the police and the public. Remember, however, that the programme is a fiction devised by screenwriters.

Crime distributions

One of the most significant approaches to the study of crime and deviance is the positivist approach, which draws heavily on the analysis of statistics. Statistics are gathered by the Home Office, the police and many other organisations and seem to show a steady rise in criminal activity with a very slight recent downturn in the figures. We know a great deal about who is *punished* for criminal offences and who appears in court but the question for sociologists and criminologists is, do these figures actually tell us a great deal about who *commits* crimes in our society?

Crime statistics and the age of the offender

All the information we have tends to suggest that young people commit crime. In British law, children under 10 years were assumed to be under the age where the law can be said to apply to them because they are too young to understand the implications or the meaning of right and wrong. The Crime and Disorder Act of 1998 changed this view.

Statistics show that of those receiving criminal convictions, most will be between 14 and 24 years of age and that the favoured crimes are theft and handling stolen goods. Adolescents are highest in virtually all criminal categories.

Data analysis exercise – offenders as a percentage of the population by gender and by age.

People convicted[1]: by gender, age and number of previous convictions, 1996 (England and Wales)

Percentages

	Number of previous convictions					All people convicted
	0	**1**	**2**	**3 to 9**	**10 or more**	
Males						
10–17	48	20	11	20	2	100
18–34	29	13	9	31	19	100
35–54	31	13	8	24	25	100
55 and over	53	13	7	15	11	100
All males aged 10 and over	32	13	9	28	18	100
Females						
10–17	60	25	7	8	–	100
18–34	51	14	8	19	8	100
35–54	58	12	7	16	7	100
55 and over	71	7	6	13	3	100
All females aged 10 and over	54	14	8	17	7	100

[1]Based on a sample of people convicted in the first 15 days of March and November 1996 for standard list offences only. For a definition of standard list offences see Appendix, Part 9: Types of offences in England, Wales and Northern Ireland.

Source: Home Office

Figure 12.4

Offenders[1] as a percentage of the population: by gender and age, 1997 (England and Wales)

Percentages

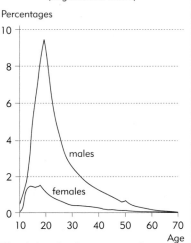

[1]People found guilty or cautioned for indictable offences in 1997

Source: Home Office

Figure 12.5

1 What percentage of the female population aged 20 years were convicted of or cautioned for an offence in 1997?
2 At what age were male and female rates of offending most similar in 1997?
3 What proportion of the male population aged 20 were convicted of or cautioned for an offence in 1997?
4 There has been a steady rise in the age of peak offending among males and females, from age 14 in 1972 to age 18 in 1997. Suggest sociological reasons why this may be so.
5 What is the proportion of male to female crime at age 19?
6 What is the proportion of female crime at age 60?
7 What was the peak age for both male and female offending in 1997?
8 Can you suggest sociological reasons for the patterns that you have described in answer to questions 5, 6 and 7?

There are a number of evaluation points which can be raised here, but all are open to argument and discussion:

- *Social Trends 29* suggests that the most common conviction for young people under the age of 17 is for theft from a shop.

- Young people *do* commit most crime. The figures are an accurate reflection of reality and the reasons are subcultural or cultural.

- Self-report studies show that the figures under-represent youth crime, suggesting that most young men have been involved in criminal activity.

- Young people are more likely to consume alcohol in public places and much crime is alcohol-related.

- Young people are more likely to be caught if they commit crimes because they are inexperienced.

- Young people experience a very significant amount of social control from a number of agencies and the police may actually target them.

- Adult crimes tend to be hidden: domestic violence, tax evasion and insurance frauds are far less likely to be reported or detected by the police.

Gender

Crime is overwhelmingly a male activity, according to the statistics. By far the largest number of prisoners are men and men are seven times more likely than women to be convicted of crime in a Crown court. Men are 10 times more likely than women to be convicted of violent and sexual offences, burglary and robbery, criminal damage and motoring offences. Recent statistics have suggested that the amount of female criminal activity is rising, particularly with regard to violence. The relative figures are so small that an increased female participation in a few crimes may imply a very serious change in society.

HINTS AND TIPS *It may be tempting to assume that because women are less likely to be criminal than men, they cannot be criminals. This is nonsense. Women have been charged and convicted of all crimes, including serious sexual abuse and murder. You should try to add data about female crime to your folders, and you might also consider if the reporting of female crime is qualitatively different from the reporting of male crime, with more reference to mitigating circumstances such as the need to feed and clothe children.*

There are two issues to raise:

1 Do men commit more crime than women?
2 If so, why do women seem to commit less crime than men?

In evaluating female crime rates you should consider the following points.

- Do the police treat women and girls differently from the way that they treat boys and men? If so, they will be less likely to appear in the crime statistics.

- Are the figures an accurate reflection of the relative amounts of male and female crime?

- Women are more likely to experience social control and do not have the freedom of the streets at night. They have less opportunity to commit crime.

- Is it possible that women are imitating male aggressive behaviour because males have a higher status in society and they are attempting to gain masculine status?

- Are women less likely to be caught than men? It may be that they do not participate in group crimes and gang behaviours and so are under less pressure to misbehave in circumstances where they will be caught.

- Women are more likely to be the victims of certain types of crime such as abuse and violence.

- There is circumstantial evidence to suggest that women are less likely to find themselves in the criminal justice system, but that if they do they are treated more harshly.

A significant debate in sociology has been the **chivalry thesis**. There is a common belief, which originates with Mannheim, that the police and courts, because they are male-dominated, are somehow easier on women. Campbell in 1981 reported that males were more likely to be prosecuted, whereas females are cautioned. Box, using self-report studies, however, suggests that women feature in criminal statistics in a broadly similar proportion to their actual participation in crime. More recent feminist research offers the view that women may be less likely to appear in criminal court processes than men, but that if they are convicted they are likely to be penalised more severely because their behaviour is seen as unfeminine. Hood (1989), who suggested that females in Crown courts in the West Midlands were a third less likely to be sent to prison, however, does not support this. Because of the differences in the number of males and females who reach courts, and because of gender differences in criminal activities, the case has yet to be proven.

The concern of much recent feminism has been with women as the victims of crime and the way in which fear of crime can limit their lives. There is some discussion of domestic violence in Area 6, and you should refer to that to develop a fuller understanding of the issues. Women are known to under-report crimes, particularly domestic violence and sexual offences. It can be difficult to obtain a conviction for rape and some offenders have been cleared of a significant number of charges of rape brought by different women. While some judges are famed for their view that victims of sexual offences held a degree of responsibility for the attacks due to their own behaviour, many commentators have a different view. Dobash and Dobash suggested that domestic violence in particular is not usually a sexual offence as such: they consider it to represent an attempt at control, domination, and humiliation. Stanko points out that the popular ideology of the home as a safe haven obscures the fact that for many women the domestic environment is an extremely dangerous place indeed.

Social class

There is a clear and unarguable link between people's social class and the likelihood that they will be convicted of a crime. Prisons and law courts are full of people of working-class origin. This debate pervades the whole of the rest of this area because the view that the working class is inherently more criminal underlies the assumptions of functionalist writers. The criticisms that are made of functionalism and subcultural theories all show ways in which the working classes can be the victims of social pressures, criminal justice systems or labelling processes which make them the victims of a biased and unjust social system. Only feminism and Left Realist perspectives support the view that working-class males actually are more violent and aggressive than others. This is because they are concerned with the perspectives of the victims of criminal behaviours, who are likely to be even more deprived than those who are convicted of crime.

The arguments can be summarised as follows:

- Are working-class people more criminal than middle-class people?
- If the working class is more criminal, why?
- Does the justice system operate in favour of the middle classes?

HINTS AND TIPS *You might like to consider the following ideas in class discussion:*

- *How do people feel they would recognise a criminal person or someone who was not to be trusted?*
- *Are the signs that they note or observe actually signals of class in our society? Think for instance of the way that those with criminal tendencies are portrayed on programmes such as **EastEnders** or **The Bill**.*

When evaluating the debate you should consider the following issues:

- Prisons are full of people who have been accused and convicted of crime. We know little about their guilt and we know little about those who have not been caught.
- Marxists might argue that working-class activities are more likely to be labelled as criminal than middle-class activities – **corporate crime** pollution by industrialists is not necessarily criminal but vandalism is.
- Middle-class crime such as tax evasion is less likely to result in a conviction than benefit fraud. This is a Marxist position.
- Hooliganism by football supporters may result in conviction, but middle-class disorder may be seen and interpreted in a different light. This view is interpretivist.
- There is evidence that middle-class people tend to know how to work a system in their own favour.
- Poorer areas of towns and cities are more likely to be heavily policed than middle-class suburban areas.

Ethnicity

This is an enormously difficult area to study, if only because there are few clear-cut divisions and categories into which people fit. The word Asian may be applied to people of a variety of religions, cultures and language groups. In addition, many areas have a tradition of mixed-culture marriage so that children may be cross-cultural in the physical sense of having parents of different cultures or cross-cultural in the sense of having parents from a different culture but belonging to British culture. Because of these problems, all data relating to ethnicity must be treated with some degree of suspicion. However, in Britain, approximately 6% of the population feel that they belong to an ethnic minority.

Figures tend to suggest that Afro-Caribbeans are over-represented in the prison population and that Asians are under-represented. There are two ways to look at the causes of this:

1   Afro-Caribbeans commit more crime.

2   The police are more likely to arrest and charge Afro-Caribbeans, who therefore experience injustice.

A number of points should be raised in discussion:

■   There is considerable circumstantial evidence and research evidence to suggest that the police are racist, either institutionally or personally. Public debate on this issue surrounded police mishandling of enquiries into the murder of a young Afro-Caribbean student, Stephen Lawrence, by racists in the 1990s

■   Afro-Caribbeans are likely to be working-class (the link between class and criminal statistics has already been made).

■   Afro-Caribbeans are younger in terms of population distribution and there is a link between youth and crime statistics.

■   **Stuart Hall** has pointed out that the media stereotype street crime as being a 'black' crime. Smith (1997) develops this point to say that this reinforces discriminatory practices.

■   The Asian population is young, working-class and discriminated against, and yet does not seem to enter the statistics in the same numbers.

You should also note that members of ethnic minorities are particularly likely to appear in criminal statistics as victims of criminal behaviour, particularly racist attack. This tends to be an under-represented area in the research. Racism and racist acts tend to be under-recorded. There is a common belief that the police are unwilling to record attacks as being racially motivated and a degree of suspicion of the police prevails among

certain ethnic minority groups. However, Figure 12.6, which was drawn from the *British Crime Survey*, was based on victim self-reporting and may be more accurate than police data.

ACTIVITY — PROBLEM SOLVING

IDENTIFICATION AND INTERPRETATION | ANALYSIS AND EVALUATION

Percentage of incidents seen as racially motivated[1]: by ethnic group, 1995 (England and Wales)

Percentages

	White	Black	Indian	Pakistani/Bangladeshi
Threats	4	36	35	70
Violence[2]	2	16	12	29
Vandalism	1	9	21	23
Burglary	–	2	3	2
All incidents	1	9	13	26

[1] Respondents were asked 'Do you think the incident was racially motivated?'
[2] Comprises wounding, common assault, robbery and snatch thefts from the person

Source: *British Crime Survey*, Home Office

Figure 12.6   Percentage of incidents seen as racially motivated by ethnic group, 1995

1   Which racial group is most vulnerable to racist incidents?
2   Which racial group is least vulnerable to racist attack?
3   What evidence is there to suggest that white people can be the victims of racism?
4   To which crime are members of ethnic minorities most vulnerable?
5   How useful are the racial groupings used in the table as an understanding of the various racial and ethnic groups living in modern Britain?
6   Suggest reasons why people from ethnic minority groups are reported by *Social Trends* as tending to 'worry about crime much more than white people'.
7   Sociologically evaluate the suggestion that the fears of members of ethnic minority groups with relation to crime are realistic.

It is clear that, although the statistics offer a view of the typical criminal type as being working-class, male, possibly Afro-Caribbean and young, this may tell us more about how criminal statistics are gathered than about crime and criminal behaviour. All statistics should be treated with the utmost caution, as the next part of this area shows.

Locality

One of the earliest American sociological studies into locality was associated with the University of Chicago in the 1920s. Burgess claimed that a city could be divided into a series of concentric rings. Although the model has been adapted by a number of writers, it still remains valid as a model of city development (see Figure 12.7). The most recent adaptation was by Mike Davis (1994), who uses the rings as a basis for a study of fear of crime in cities. He sees the inner cities as an area that many people fear for the possibility of crime and urban riot. Cities have developed to protect the wealthy in out of town suburbs and the inner cities are now zones of social control though CCTV and overt policing or of crime associated with gangs, ethnic minorities, and youth violence.

There is a clear link between social geography and crime. Poor areas have higher crime rates and those who live in poor areas are most likely to be the victims

Figure 12.7 Adaptation of the Burgess model of city development

of crime. This can be illustrated by the fact that car and house insurance fees will vary with postcode or district. The very poorest areas of any town or city are also the most vulnerable to crime; this is a point emphasised by the *Islington Crime Survey* (Crawford et al. 1986). The inner city may be characterised by pubs, clubs and areas where prostitutes may make themselves available. This means that the poor areas are likely to be more heavily policed. Throughout the 1980s, there was a series of urban riots in British cities, some of them with a racial element because ethnic groups are among the most economically deprived. It has been noted elsewhere in this area that heavy-handed policing of the inner cities may have contributed to the riots. However, rural surveys such as that of Koffman (1996) suggest that crime is not an urban phenomenon alone; in the country, the nature of the crime itself changes.

The official statistics debate

This debate underlies a far deeper problem in sociology – the validity and reliability of all statistically gathered data. Ideas raised in this section could well be applied to other sections of the examination paper, in particular theory and methods. However, it is known that official statistics do not tell the whole story about the amount or nature of crime in that society. There are a number of reasons why crime data may be unreliable:

- An increase in crime figures could suggest that more crime is being committed or that more people are reporting crime. There are area differences in crime reporting, with people in areas of high crime risk reporting crime less often.

- Different countries regard different activities as criminal or may collect their figures differently.

- Changes in the law may mean that changes over time cannot be tracked. Abortion, homosexuality and suicide were once all considered to be criminal acts. Until very recently, there could be no rape within marriage because it was considered to be the right of a man to have sex with his wife.

- Criminal statistics may be affected by the purpose for which they are collected. For instance, the police are more likely to record crime if it is proof that they require more funding and will be less inclined to record crime if it reflects on their performance.

Dark figure of crime

The crime which does not feature in official statistics because it is not reported to the police is known as the **dark figure of crime**. Ironically, the crime about which we know the most is car crime because all cars must be insured by law and a crime number given in cases of insurance claims. Muncie in 1966 suggested that crimes might not be reported for the following reasons:

- The crime might not be noticed, for instance embezzlement and fraud.
- Many crimes are 'victimless', such as prostitution or drug selling.
- The event may be too trivial to report.
- The victim is frightened of the criminal and is unable to report.
- The victim distrusts the police, for instance in racial attacks.
- The victim is frightened and ashamed of the stigma that reporting the crime could bring. Rape is one of the best examples of a seriously under-reported crime.

ACTIVITY   KS **WORKING WITH OTHERS**

ANALYSIS AND EVALUATION

Ask people if they have been the victim of crime and if they have reported it to the police. Ask them for the reasons for their actions. Avoid asking for details about the personal crime because this could upset them. Concentrate on crimes against property.

- Do you find that Muncie has covered all the possibilities or can you add other suggestions for under-reporting of crime to this list?

- What have you learned about the relationship between crime that has taken place and crime that has been committed?

- Develop this study by asking people about the nature of their reactions to the fact that they were the victims of a crime.

Victim studies

Using the factor of the dark figure of crime as a starting point, a number of researchers attempted to discover more about the incidence of crime. The official statistics of the *British Crime Survey* involve data collected from a range of respondents who report on crime that they experienced in the preceding 12 months. The results tend to suggest that there is a vast amount of under-reporting. In 1998, only 44% of crimes were reported and of those crimes the police recorded just over half.

Some people are far more likely to be the victims of crime than others, with locality being one of the variables. Young men, for instance, are most likely to be the victims of street crime because they are out at night in places where crime takes place. However, they are also most likely to be the aggressors. Hough and Mayhew (1983) suggest that the average person is more frightened of being the victim of a crime than likely to experience it. However, radicals point out that fear of crime is not exaggerated because the events can be so catastrophic for the victim.

The most famous local victimisation study was the *Islington Crime Survey* (1986), and others have followed. These suggest that crime is a fact of life for certain sections of the community, with nearly a third of all households reporting robbery, burglary or assault within a year. Feminists such as Genn (1988) suggested that many women experience long-term victimisation and violence, often from ex-partners and men they knew, and much of which they did not report.

Self-report studies

The self-reporting of crime has a long history in sociology. In self-report studies people are asked to report on their own criminality and often the samples are large so the data is quantitative. These studies suggest that a vast amount of crime takes place, but that much of it is petty. They also suggest that a small number of people commit a huge amount of crime, a finding that is supported by the notoriety of some young people in their communities for being 'out of control'.

Moore, in *Investigating Crime and Deviance* (1996), suggests that the value of self-report studies is that they shed light on official statistics in the following ways:

■ crime figures are equal across classes

■ there is no relationship between family breakdown and crime

■ rates of offending do not vary between ethnic groups

In evaluating victim and self-report studies, you should consider the following:

■ Do people remember and report cases accurately?

■ Are all people likely to consider the same acts to be criminal?

■ Do people self-glorify by exaggerated reporting?

Explanations for criminal behaviours

Five types of theory account for crime in our society:

1 **Biological theories**, which suggest that the physical make-up of criminals is different from that of 'normal' people. This predisposes them to crime.

2 **Social psychological theories** suggest that criminals are different in their mental structure in some way and commit crime because they are somehow damaged.

3 **Functionalist and subcultural theories** suggest that criminal behaviours arise through adjustments that individuals and groups have to make to the workings of society. They create their own rules and subcultures to survive and attain the goals that others take for granted.

4 **Societal theories** such as Marxist theories suggest that the workings of society are at fault and people are criminal for reasons that are logical to them. Laws and social structures create criminals.

5 **Interactional and critical theories** reject the positivism or scientific approach of functionalism and Marxism because they suggest that the reaction of society to those labelled as criminals creates a hardening of criminal behaviour and does not allow people to escape from their own self-definition as criminal. Feminists are interested in the meanings of criminal behaviour.

Biological and social psychological suggestions as to the genesis of crime are generally rejected by sociologists for the reasons listed below. However, people in broader society, when faced with crime and criminal behaviours, will often resort to common-sense explanations such as 'they must be mad' or 'they are animals', both of which suggest that these sociobiological views are widely held.

> **HINTS AND TIPS** *Superficially, you will be attracted to biological and psychological theories of crime. They tend to offer simple answers, which satisfy our desire to consider criminals as sick and different from the rest of us. Ignore this temptation, however, because these theories are not required for examination answers and quoting them will waste time.*

Sociologists tend to reject biological 'they are born different' and psychological 'they are all mad' theories for the origin of crime.

■ These theories concentrate on individual explanations of crime. Clearly they are not an adequate explanation of criminal behaviour because social patterns of criminal activity can be seen from looking at statistics.

■ They tend to assume a division between 'criminal' and 'not criminal' but the case is not nearly as clear-cut as this. Many people are merely slightly criminal or marginally dishonest under certain circumstances. Few of us are totally honest and therefore a 'them' and 'us' approach offers no deep understandings.

Discussion exercise

Jack Nobbs in *Modern Society* suggested some of the following as causes of **delinquency** and delinquent behaviour. Add common-sense ideas of your own collected from class and group discussion.

- Instincts of aggression
- Lack of affection
- Illegitimacy
- Bad examples from older brothers
- Feelings of low self-esteem
- Spoiling of children
- Working mothers
- Poverty
- Single parenthood
- Living in bad areas
- Emotional disturbance
- Mental and physical inadequacies
- Neglectful upbringing
- Weak parental discipline

- Injustice of unequal society
- Loneliness
- Misunderstood at school
- Over-identification with media figures

1 Fit each suggested cause of delinquency to a type of theoretical perspective. Not all the views will fit neatly into one of the categories identified above. Discuss in your groups which type of view seems to fit which category and make a simple note of your discussions. If necessary, the idea can fit into more than one category.
2 From a common-sense point of view, what type of theory is most popularly held to be the cause of deviance and delinquency in our society?
3 From a sociological point of view, which type of theory do you feel most comfortable with? Suggest reasons for your point of view.
4 Are there any types of theory that you are willing to reject at this early stage in your studies? Explain why you feel that some theories do not offer a satisfactory explanation for criminal behaviour.

- These theories are deterministic. This means that they suggest that crime is caused by a specific factor and has a genesis in either biology or upbringing. The logic offered is that a factor such as a personality defect or a poor upbringing will cause crime. However, many people will experience similar circumstances and yet will not turn to criminal actions.

- Many of these studies began by looking at people in prison and attempting to discover a common factor. This ignores the fact that many criminals never go to prison, so the sample was biased in favour of the unlucky or low-ability criminal. A cross-section of people in prison cannot be held to be a cross-section of the criminal population.

HINTS AND TIPS *You may find that some of these criticisms of biological and psychological theories offer you a starting point for evaluating positivist research into criminology.*

From this point we need to study the two main sociological approaches in some detail. These two approaches can be described as positivist and interpretivist. Despite the very obvious differences between Marxism and functionalism, sociologists working within these traditions share the belief that deviance can be studied scientifically. However, critical analysts such as labelling theorists are concerned with the nature of the meaning of deviance for society.

HINTS AND TIPS *Collect a cuttings file of press releases and articles about famous criminal cases to support your theoretical discussions with factual evidence of recent issues and awareness of current affairs. These references will score well under examination conditions.*

Durkheim

Émile Durkheim is one of the most significant figures in sociology and his work will be revisited in later discussions of suicide. Durkheim's views can be summarised simply and they are of significance because they inform positivist methodological understandings of crime and crime data. They also underlie structural functionalist thought.

■ Crime is inevitable because no society is without crime.

■ A small amount of crime is, in some ways, good for society because it can force recognition that society needs to change, and it reinforces collective morality. We need criminals to jolt us into new ways of seeing the world or simply to make us feel better for hating them.

■ A crime is any act that offends common collective morality. Note that this view needs very careful examination because collective morality is not always correct (consider the witch hunts of the Middle Ages!).

■ Society will judge infringements of its codes with the utmost severity. People who break the rules may be deemed to be no longer protected by society.

■ People can judge themselves against the moral codes of society. We can tell by understanding the views of other people whether our acts are correct or incorrect.

■ The deviant can often be a creative and valuable individual who challenges the moral codes and creates the possibility for change.

However sympathetic some of these views may seem, there are also some critical questions which need to be asked if Durkheim's assumptions are to be evaluated properly.

Does everyone share moral codes?

The answer to this is that they obviously do not. One needs only to look at the differing moral codes of black and white Americans in the southern USA to realise that they can differ very much within societies. Many white people considered it perfectly moral to treat black people as though they were animals and to hang black men without benefit of trial. It is difficult to imagine many black people sharing those values.

Does this theorising account for the causes of crime?

It takes a very liberal view of criminal behaviour, but it is difficult to imagine that the victim of a rapist or an abuser is going to share Durkheim's positive views of crime as a force for moral good in society.

Does this theory explain why some are more likely to be criminal than others?

The answer would seem to be that it does not really account for social differences in criminality because it sees society as cohesive and consensual.

HINTS AND TIPS Ensure that your notes on Émile Durkheim are excellent. You will find discussions of his work on CD-ROM and on the Internet. You are unlikely to have a question that centres directly on the work of Durkheim, but you might need to refer to him in much of your examination writing.

Functionalists

For the purposes of examination you must be able to evaluate the usefulness of functionalist theories. However, functionalist theories have developed a critical debate, which can sometimes cause confusion. Be aware that although subcultural theories are given a separate subheading in this area, they developed from functionalist theory.

The underlying characteristics of functionalist theory on crime are derived without much development from the ideas of Durkheim. Functionalist writers tend to assume that:

■ everyone in society shares norms and values

■ norms and values form the basis of social order.

You will need to revisit the notes on Durkheim to examine these propositions.

One of the most influential writers from the functionalist perspective was Robert Merton, who was active before the Second World War. A simple summary of his views is given below.

■ If everyone shares the same goals but some cannot attain them then **anomie**, which is a sense of **alienation** and disorientation from society, will result.

■ Rules will lose their impact and can be ignored by certain individuals who will adapt their beliefs and behaviours.

■ There may be, within American society, a distinction between aspiration and the ability to gain desired social goals. Americans are taught to believe in the 'American Dream', or myth, which suggests that anyone can get on in life if they have the will and work very hard. This is tied in with veneration of Abraham Lincoln, who represents this possibility: the phrase used to describe his life is 'from log cabin to the White House'.

- Some people will inevitably turn to criminal behaviour such as theft.

Merton described a variety of typical responses to the failure to achieve success, some of which he felt generated criminal behaviours.

- **Conformity** – people struggle to achieve success even if this is an unrealistic goal for them.
- **Innovation** – people break rules to achieve success and will break laws in the process.
- **Ritualism** – people follow the rules but do not believe they will achieve success.
- **Retreatism** – people abandon the aims of broader society and create their own rules, rejecting the values of society and risking becoming deviant.
- **Rebellion** – people challenge the goals of society and aim for different measures of success. This too can result in criminal behaviours.

In evaluating Merton's contribution to the study of crime a number of points of evaluation should be made.

- Merton's theorising cannot be said to apply fully to British society because it has always been rigidly class-based. No one can ever be said to have honestly believed that if they work hard that they could become a member of the British aristocracy.
- It is clear that it is not just the poor who commit crime. Very wealthy people who have gained all that they need to gain from society have also been involved in criminal activity.
- Much crime, such as vandalism, is pointless and not goal-centred in any way.
- This theorising cannot account for 'political' crimes, such as terrorism, or social crimes, such as domestic violence and abuse.
- These ideas are not easily testable.
- Many people who suffer from limited opportunities remain law-abiding, honest, and non-criminal.

Subculture

One of the most influential subculturalists was Albert Cohen (1955), who drew on the theories of functionalism but applied geographical principles to his work. This work should be discussed in the light of considerations of the development of youth culture in Area 4. His ideas were influential in Britain, although many people who adopted them used interactional methodologies in their work. Cohen was critical of Merton because he realised that much criminal delinquent behaviour is actually malicious and pointless. He suggested that:

- Delinquent behaviour is caused by a desire for material goods.
- Some crime is expressive of frustration (vandalism) rather than acquisitive.
- Schools embody middle-class values and goals.
- Working-class boys cannot succeed in school so they develop 'status frustration'.
- Alternative avenues for satisfaction must be sought and these include the creation of subcultures with aggressive male attitudes to the forefront of behaviours.
- This is a collective and social response, as opposed to Merton's idea of individual response.

- Ironically, delinquent behaviour actually represents conformity to the goals of society.

Cohen's work was developed by Cloward and Ohlin (1961), who argued that opportunities must be necessary for delinquent behaviour to develop.

- The working class is liable to form **subcultures**, and a variety of subcultures exists.

- There is greater pressure on working-class people to join subcultures than on the middle class because the latter has more chance of societally defined and accepted success.

- Some criminal subcultures exist where adult crime is linked to youth crimes.

- Conflict subcultures are not linked to adult criminality.

- Some subcultures are retreatist or escapist from all society.

To evaluate subcultural theory, consider the following points:

- There is little proof that subcultures (as opposed to gangs) actually exist.

- It is difficult to offer scientific proof of 'values'.

- Many working-class males are quietly conformist – consider the discussion of the 'lads' by Paul Willis in Area 8. The deviant 'lads' were very much a minority within their school environment.

- Most boys appear to grow out of delinquent behaviours, often when they acquire a steady girlfriend.

- There is evidence to suggest that many working-class males do adopt heavily masculine behaviours whereas middle-class males are not so strongly gendered in their attitudes.

TASK

Hypothesis – Young men are predisposed to criminal behaviour.

Context – As you are thinking in terms of subculture with this question, the task is inviting you to consider whether males have 'different' attitudes to crime. You need to think about the question more fully, in the sense of 'different from whom?'

Another area of serious concern, which always arises when considering crime, is the ethics of the research. You should not directly ask if people actually commit certain crimes, because if you find out that they do you become an accomplice to the act. It is your legal duty to report your discoveries, however impractical that is.

You can also be fairly certain that if you ask about actual crimes committed, some people will exaggerate their activities and others minimise them for personal reasons. This tendency will be more marked if you interview respondents rather than asking for anonymous completion of questionnaires.

Method – Consider comparing the views of two contrasting groups of people to investigate whether there are cultural differences between young men and any other single social grouping. For contrast, you could consider men over 45 years of age, or perhaps you could look at young men in comparison with young women.

Design your questionnaire with some care. Ask your two different groups of respondents about attitudes to crime and the importance of relationships with the peer group rather than about actual criminal activities. Where do people obtain their values and whose opinions do they care about with relation to illegal activities?

Evaluation – You will probably find little proof of young men having a different subculture from other people. In groups many young people tend to show bravado, but in practical terms are they so different from the rest of society? The advantage of this particular task is that you will have a lot to discuss in terms of ethics, reliability, and validity.

Marxist accounts of criminality

A number of writers are associated with Marxist thought and two general lines of argument can be detected.

1 Many writers point to the fact that the crimes of the working class are over-researched, but that little attempt is made to understand the nature and purpose of crime among the wealthy. This develops into two further lines of thought, which suggest that the antisocial behaviour of wealthy companies is not criminalised, and that the wealthy are not caught and punished on the same terms as the poor.

2 A second line of thought offers the view that working-class crime is somehow evidence of a rejection of the current unfair and unequal division of wealth and power in our society. This can be criticised as a somewhat over-romanticised view of the criminal and has been comprehensively rebutted by critical theorists.

> **HINTS AND TIPS** *Revise any notes that you have on Marxism to ensure that you fully understand the theory.*

Marxism is a conflict theory. It is macro-sociological in that it is concerned with the broader structures of society. Marxists consider that power is held by those who own and control. The state, as part of the superstructure of society, is run for the benefit of the wealthy and serves ruling-class interests. The state passes laws which protect these interests and are a reflection of ruling-class ideology. Commitment to the laws of society is an aspect of false class consciousness.

The main areas of concern and interest to Marxists are summarised below:

Who makes the laws?

Marxists suggest that laws are made by legislators who work in the interests of the wealthiest and the most powerful. Gramsci made this point in his work on the role of the intellectual in society, when he discussed the nature of **bourgeois hegemony**. This term refers to the idea that the wealthy have control over the production of our ideas about society and over its structures. Gramsci is profiled in Area 5. The French philosopher Althusser suggested that the legislature is a **repressive state apparatus** designed to oppress and hold people down. All Marxists will point to the view that laws protect property and not people. Snider, quoted in Heidensohn (1989), suggested that laws are not passed to control capitalism and the state is reluctant to offend large global corporations.

Do laws benefit the wealthiest?

Pearce (1976) in *Crimes of the Powerful* suggests that the ruling classes allow some degree of social equality legislation because if it did not exist then there would be strong development of class consciousness. Oppression is not obvious so the government can appear to offer a balance for different interest groups. Haralambos and Holbourn point out that capitalism may actually be forced to adapt to changing situations by passing legislation which is inevitable because of social change, but it will do so reluctantly and at the last moment. Examples of such laws being forced upon society by the changing nature of morality and culture include laws governing equality issues, which were not as effective as had been hoped. There are also laws that if not passed would result in revolution, such as the end of apartheid in South Africa.

How are laws enforced?

The police and legislature enforce the law. The police respond to media and public pressure and accept cultural stereotypes. They play a part in oppression because they are tools of state interest. This was pointed out by Hall et al. (1978) in their famous *Policing the Crisis*. Chambliss (1975) suggested that the police are under pressure to arrest and will often arrest the poorest sectors of society such as vagrants. Rich areas of the city are unpoliced, whereas the *Scarman Report* pointed out that policing of poor areas with high numbers of ethnic minority populations can be heavy-handed and unpopular.

Prosecutions for workplace accidents and deaths caused by poor health and safety standards in factories are rare and yet far more people die in this way than by murder. Polluting companies such as Union Carbide (whose factory in India gassed and killed over 3000 people in Bhopal) are rarely penalised heavily for industrial accidents, and certainly not in such a way as to affect the value of the company. The ruling classes define social relationships so they can define crime. We are able to accept a morality which suggests that vast differences in wealth and power are appropriate and so we do not, or are powerless to, legislate against such obvious injustice.

Who breaks the law?

Everyone breaks the law. However, some people are more likely to get caught and end up in prison than others because laws are applied unequally. Westergaard and Resler (1975) in their classic analysis point out that if you steal £1000 in an armed robbery you are likely to end up in prison, but **white-collar crime** such as embezzlement of large sums by fiddling company accounts is almost impossible to prove and rarely results in a custodial sentence. Poor people go to prison. Statistics show that black people and working-class people are far more likely to go to prison than anyone else. Criminals are therefore blamed for the ills of society and we can feel secure that individuals and not the system are at fault. Marxists argue that criminals are the victims of an unjust society because they carry the responsibility for all the ills created by an unjust state.

To evaluate Marxist theory it is necessary to consider some of the following ideas:

- Is there an undue interest in white-collar crime at the expense of studying the poorest?
- Are the poorest made into working-class heroes?
- How does this account for crimes against individuals such as rape or drug abuse?
- Is crime about the acquisition of wealth?

HINTS AND TIPS   There is much of interest in this type of theorising, but always remember when analysing Marxism that the poor may be the victims of criminal justice systems, but they also are the real victims of crime. Poor people are more likely to steal from each other than from the rich. It would seem that poor males victimise people even less fortunate than themselves, such as the elderly and women. Is crime simply a sane response to an unjust society?

Interpretivist and critical theory

All the above theories can be described as positivist because they are concerned with crime as a clear social phenomenon that can be understood through the application of scientific methodologies. However, now it is necessary to look at critical and anti-positivist

ideas, which take a different stance and attempt to understand criminal behaviours as part of social interaction. In this area the various perspectives include labelling theories, phenomenology, new criminology and feminist theories.

Labelling

One of the most significant writers in the symbolic interactional tradition was Howard S. Becker, who is associated with labelling theory (there is discussion of these ideas in Area 8 when the same ideas were applied to processes within schools). You should also return to the study of stigma or non-culpable deviance, discussed in Area 11, to develop these issues.

HINTS AND TIPS   This is a good point at which to revise symbolic interactionalism. Make sure your notes are in order and that you understand the ideas.

The basic principles of symbolic interactionalism as applied to the study of crime and deviance suggest that

- there is no such thing as crime or deviance until someone has labelled it as such
- it is the situation in which the act occurs (social context) that creates the deviance
- it is the interpretation by the witnesses that creates the crime

People may commit an act that leads others to define them as lawbreakers or as deviants. If people are so defined, they are seen as having been labelled. The label evaluates the person as good and valuable or bad and wicked. It can be a detailed label such as 'homosexual' or 'mentally ill' or can be a hidden label, which the individual can choose to reveal or not as desired. This label becomes the **master status** and once people are aware of it they assume that the person has all the characteristics associated with that label. This can happen through **stereotyping**. The understanding is then that if a person's self-concept is drawn from the reactions of others he or she will take on those characteristics. This becomes the **self-fulfilling prophecy**. Quentin Crisp illustrates this in his autobiography *The Naked Civil Servant*. He describes how his knowledge of his own homosexuality, in the days when this was a criminal offence, led him to take on attributes that we would describe as 'camp' as a way of signalling his status as deviant to himself and to others.

Once the deviant label is attached to people, they experience some of the symptoms of the damaged identity described by Goffman. When in contact with those in authority, they are rejected or treated in a way that confirms the deviance and the low status. They find it difficult to get a job. 'Conventional' people may reject them. Even ordinary behaviours will be seen in the light of the deviant label. Rosenhan's famous experiments where sane people had themselves committed to mental asylums showed how entirely unexceptional actions such as note-taking, chatting or reading were interpreted as evidence of mental instability by clinical staff.

The deviant person becomes confirmed in the label when he or she joins a deviant subgroup. A subculture develops with beliefs and values that are at variance with those of mainstream society. The subculture may help people within it with advice and support. Many of these groups become formalised and politicised as self-help groups, such as Alcoholics Anonymous or Mind. The deviant is now identified to him- or herself in terms of membership of the deviant group and behaves in terms of the deviancy so that the deviancy becomes part of that person's identity. An example could be membership of a gay liberation movement, where people's sexuality becomes self-defining and more significant than other elements of their personality.

ACTIVITY — WORKING WITH OTHERS

IDENTIFICATION AND INTERPRETATION	ANALYSIS AND EVALUATION

Look at the evidence of deviancy in your own institution. Ask teachers or lecturers what signals they would use to identify people as 'potential trouble makers'. Ask yourself which come first – the identifiably deviant behaviours or the labels?

Major writers in this perspective, with whom you should be familiar, include Howard Becker and Edwin Lemert.

Howard Becker

Becker is one of the key writers in this tradition becaue it is with his work that we have the notion of deviant behaviour as being socially defined by groups within society. In his study of drug use (*Becoming a*

Marijuana Smoker) Becker noted that people actively learned a criminal behaviour that seemed meaningful to them from people described as 'significant others'. In this case, the significant others were musicians who encouraged people who shared their lifestyle to share the drug. People cut back on their drug use if they moved away from their circle of friends.

Edwin Lemert

Lemert is associated with the notions of primary and secondary deviance. For Lemert, the primary deviance was the first deviant act: the breaking of a law. For many people there is no response because they are not caught; however, secondary deviance is the social response which occurs when the police, law courts, family and friends become aware of the primary deviance. Lemert's interest in the secondary deviance means that his analysis of the primary deviance remains underdeveloped.

Phenomenology

This perspective originated in European philosophical thinking, unlike symbolic interactionalism, which was developed from the thoughts of George Herbert Mead. However, ethnomethodological phenomenology, to give it its full title, gained much popularity in the USA because it shares many of the same understandings as interactionalism. Ethnomethodologists seek to describe behaviours and understandings. They analyse crime and criminal labelling processes but do not suggest that labelling causes further criminal activity.

One of the best known writers in this theoretical perspective is Aaron Cicourel, who also published much work with Kitsuse. Cicourel and Kitsuse do *not* see labelling as a process in which someone applies a label and the labelled person then acts according to the description. Rather, they describe a series of complex interactions between the delinquent and the authorities. Cicourel suggested that the judicial authorities interact with young people on the basis of preconceptions and stereotypes. Negotiation takes place and those who understand less of how the system works are more likely to become the victims of it. Middle-class children can define themselves to the authorities as basically 'good' people who are remorseful and foolish and are often let off or treated with courtesy. Hostility, however, will produce an aggressive and authoritarian stance from the police and probation service, who then perceive the offender to be a 'typical delinquent'.

In evaluating labelling theories, whether interactional or ethnomethodological, it is important to understand that, while they bring considerable insight into the processes of becoming a criminal and the processes involved in the treatment of young offenders, there is no consideration of why the original act took place. Social structures are ignored, so there is little understanding of how power relationships are involved in the labelling process.

'New' criminology

A common aim of many of the new young sociologists of the 1970s was to combine the insights that Marxism offers into the nature of the structure of society with the methods and understandings that interactionalism brings to sociology. This resulted in a series of studies and an approach that is often called 'realism'. Realism formed part of a broader rejection of structural functional analyses of society. In practical terms, realism also gave rise to some extremely influential work and some revolutionary studies, but the impetus has been lost in more recent writing and many of the original realists have moved into other spheres of work. One of the most influential studies taking this approach in the field of criminology was Taylor, Walton and Young's (1973) book *The New Criminology*. They suggested that the study of crime required consideration of the following elements:

- **The context in which the crime occurs**. This should take account of political, social and economic factors.

- **The social psychology of crime**. Individuals can make personal choices about whether to offend.

- **The social dynamics of crime**. Individuals may not have the social opportunity to commit crime.

- **The reactions of others to the criminal action**. Crimes have witnesses and studies should take account of responses to crimes on an individual level and on a wider societal basis.

- **The reaction of the state to the criminal action**. Crimes have public reactions and the state may influence the reactions of justice professionals and the definition of crime.

- **The social reaction and how it affects the deviant's later reactions**. Sociologists need to research the impact of reactions and how these affect the individual's later career and life choices.

- **The deviant process as a whole**. The 'new' criminologists felt that an overview of the whole process was needed and that the interaction between these elements should become part of criminology.

HINTS AND TIPS *Although the points made by the new criminologists were eminently sensible, they were actually of little practical use when it came to research design because they set almost impossible standards for the practice of research.*

One of the achievements of the new criminologists was to point to the significance of politics, in the broadest possible sense, to crime study.

New Left realism

This is mostly associated with the work of Jock Young in the early 1980s, which suggested that official statistics on crime that show high rates of inner-city criminality are realistic and should be treated with respect.

- There are high rates of crime by inner-city youths who prey on other weaker working-class people within the most deprived areas.

- The fears that people express about criminality are realistic and reflect actual experiences.

Young is a youth subculturalist in that he suggests that those who commit street crime develop subcultures to cope with problems. These problems tend to be created by the broad social and economic inequalities of society. The subcultures do not necessarily have values that are at variance with broader society, and this can cause a sense of deprivation in the young criminal. This is a significant and logical point in the argument because the emphasis of the work is on the development of subcultures and there is recognition that they arise in marginalised youth who experience a high degree of relative deprivation. The view is realistic because it has its roots in the observation of actual culture. Young suggests that each generation of young people creates its own subcultures, which are ephemeral (short-lived) and reflect the changing nature of society. Note that there is a similarity to Merton's thought in this position, except that Young tends towards conflict models and Merton is a consensual theoretician. Interestingly, and in contrast to Merton, critics of this position state that crime is still seen as working-class and that middle-class delinquency is overlooked.

New Right realism

This was the dominant cultural view of the Conservative government's thinking on crime and it is tremendously important because it affected legislation in the 1980s (there is also little evidence that the Labour government of the late 1990s took issue with this position). It offers a consensual view and assumes that people make rational choices based on an understanding of the consequences of their actions. This ideology has led to a number of beliefs and social consequences:

- People commit crime because it benefits them. They must therefore be made to pay a heavy price for their criminality if they are caught so that the cost of crime outweighs the benefits. Britain now has a very high proportion of people in prison.

- People commit crime because they have lost their sense of responsibility to the community. Government has initiated a number of community policing schemes so that informal controls will limit crime.

- Morality begins within the family and so traditional family bonds must be strengthened. It is the break-up of traditional family life that has led to increase in crime. Families need to learn to look to themselves rather than to the state for support, and so radical reforms which forced care of the children back on to absent fathers were instituted through the Child Support Agency. Note the application of traditional Christian morality to a social problem.

New Right realism is significant because it formed part the dominant political theorising of the 1990s. It translated into a series of legislative changes and social policies that were marked by the notion of 'zero tolerance'. Many people felt that the justice systems and social services had moved so far in the direction of seeing the criminal as the victim of an unjust system that the victims had been forgotten. Zero tolerance was an American expression which became part of the vocabulary of popular newspapers and politicians who argued that the only response to crime was to make the criminals suffer for their anti-social behaviour. The answer to crime was seen as increased social control and an authoritarian stance.

	New Left realism	New Right realism
Significant of research?	High reliance on analysing data and statistics to understand trends and patterns	Based on political and ideological theorising
What causes crime?	Inequality in society	Individuals commit crime because they feel they will get pleasure or benefit
Who commits crime?	Marginalised and deprived people	'Bad' and immoral people who have been poorly socialised
Which social groups commit crime?	Young working-class people	The children of broken families and disorganised and immoral people are responsible for crime
What solutions are available?	A more equal and just society, a better environment, trust between the police and the communities they serve	A moral society with a highly developed and structured system of punishments, rejection of liberal treatment of criminals, increase in the powers of the police to deal with criminals

Figure 12.9   New Left and New Right realism

Feminist thought on crime

Feminist criminology is concerned with addressing the malestream nature of knowledge. Some of the most significant writers are Carol Smart, Ann Campbell and Frances Heidensohn. Their work has been referred to throughout this area, particularly with reference to the study of women as victims of crime and the criminal justice system. Feminists begin by rejecting the view that the differences between male and female behaviours and patterns of offending can be ascribed to biological differences, a view which was widely held by early criminologists such as Lombroso. Heidensohn also makes the point that much early sociological theorising about crime is actually a criminology of males and not of society. She theorises that female crime is not interesting or exciting, concerned as it is with shoplifting and moral infringements, so many of the classical theories ignore the incidence of crime among women or their tendency to deviant activity. This growing awareness of the politics of gender in the study of crime has marked most recent work in the field. A number of issues are raised by feminists!

■ Women tend not to appear in crime statistics. Does this mean they are not criminal? Obviously not, but the nature of their criminal activity often seems to be self-damaging or self-destructive (drug abuse and prostitution).

■ Crime among women is increasing. Does this reflect changes in femininity or changes in the reactions of the judicial system? Changes in the role of women in society could lead young women to challenge male status by imitating male behaviour. Girls also have more freedom to misbehave or commit crime.

■ Women are over-represented in victim statistics. They also show far more fear of crime than do men. Are their fears realistic?

■ Women are often the victims of hidden crime such as domestic violence or sexual abuse. This is very serious because there is a marked tendency in society to consider the victim as the problem, so traditional and judicial explanations of rape have included 'she was asking for it'.

■ While women who offend are in the minority, they tend to be treated harshly by the system if convicted and seen as atypical of their gender. They are more likely to be considered in terms of psychological and biological accounts of the genesis of crime: they are 'mad' or 'bad'.

■ Male sociologists tend to concentrate on males because they are trained in malestream, or masculine, knowledge. Girls are therefore invisible.

■ Recent feminists have raised the suggestion that femininity and crime should be seen in terms of 'why do women fail to commit crime?' Heidensohn (1996) explains that women are more controlled socially than are men.

■ Should masculinity be seen to be the problem? This is a common theme in feminist research, especially that by Bea Campbell, and is particularly relevant in this field of work because the characteristics of a criminal tend also to be the characteristics which are valued by society: toughness, aggression, domination and action. This is an idea that has relevance to discussions of youth culture and the soccer hooligan.

ACTIVITY KS **COMMUNICATION**

IDENTIFICATION AND INTERPRETATION

Discuss the representations of criminals in television and film. Identify the characteristics, which are seen as typical of villains and gangsters. You could look at a recent crime or detective film release for analysis of one media text. The amusing but gruesomely violent British independent film *Lock, Stock and Two Smoking Barrels* is a good example of the genre.

■ Identify the physical stereotype, to what extent is the typical criminal or gangster displaying archetypal male behaviour?

■ To what extent are these criminal characteristics portrayed as amusing, clever, desirable or admirable?

SOCIOLOGY IN PRACTICE

Look at the case study of Boomerang Boy taken from an article in *The Guardian*.

Shaun Andrew McKerry began petty shoplifting at the age of 12. He started because he needed the money for drink. These days he steals bigger things, and now the money is for drugs. He takes cars too, but that's just for the buzz. Shaun is just 15 years old, and in the course of the three years since he started stealing he has become what police describe as a "mini-crimewave" in his own right. The local papers have dubbed him Boomerang Boy and Homing Pigeon Boy because he keeps coming back to court. No sooner has he returned to the former pit village that is his home in Co Durham than he is offending again. Shaun Andrew McKerry simply doesn't care.

The papers say that McKerry could be responsible for anything up to 1,000 crimes in this rural area. His mother says it is more like 100. Her son is, she admits, "no angel", but he's not as bad as everyone is making out.

Since 1995, McKerry, who has not been to school for two years, has been arrested 80 times. He has had two sentences of detention and a string of convictions for burglary, aggravated vehicle taking, sending indecent letters, threatening behaviour, assaulting a police officer, attempted robbery, shoplifting and criminal damage.

In the cocky way that is his wont, McKerry once even had the nerve to put on a dress and pose as a woman. He did it so well he managed to steal 22 charity boxes In this same manner, he flouts every form of authority, breaks all his curfews and continually tells police and magistrates to "fuck off". McKerry's age and a loop-hole in the law mean that he cannot be detained in custody unless his alleged offences involve sex, serious violence or are so bad that he could receive a sentence of at least 14 years.

Ordinarily, and again because of his age, he could not be named by newspapers, but his identity was revealed last week after the Northern Echo pleaded with the magistrates court that it was in the public interest that "the people of the local community are made aware of the identity of someone who is a habitual offender".

The living room of the McKerry family's council house is covered with photos of the kids. Shaun's face beams down benignly, like any other boy pushed in front of the school snapper.

McKerry's mother, who must remain nameless for the sake of her other son and two daughters, says she dreads picking up the phone. It's not the hassle of going down to the cop shop or the courts again; it's the worry that Shaun has come to a messy end in a hot-wired car. When he's in a Young Offenders' Institute she doesn't have to worry.

"When Shaun's inside I'm okay with myself because I know he's safe. When he's out, I go low to the bottom and it's horrible," she explains. She has just received a letter from him signed "love Shaun". This is a new departure, as before it was just "from Shaun". Perhaps he is softening a little. Written on thin blue paper, the letter says, "It's your first and I bet you wish your last child on the line. I have been trying to phone all week. What have you been doing? Going out celebrating [his conviction]?"

Shaun's mum — we'll call her Susan — is 32 now. She had Shaun when was 16. She says she feels trapped in this place that her son has terrorised. She has lived in this hopeless village (it too cannot be named) almost all her life, but now her son has made her the focus of neighbourhood ire. Speak to the locals as they tend their unruly allotments — the bizarre grazing grounds of pit ponies and sheep — and they will tell you that Shaun McKerry is a little bastard, bad through and through.

His mother says: "Shaun went bad at the age of 12, but it was just petty shoplifting then. He met up with a car thief and that was that. He liked twocking [stealing] cars, he got a buzz out of it." Susan says her son was clever at school and wanted to be an archaeologist. Now, if he doesn't spend the rest of his life inside, she thinks he will most likely end up working for his uncle as a sheet metal worker.

Like many persistent young offenders, Shaun has no father figure. David Smith, professor of criminology at Edinburgh University, says research has shown that "there are much stronger chances that young people will get involved in criminal offending if their parents are in conflict. Boys who spend time with their father at the age of 12 are much less likely to become involved in crime."

McKerry's parents split violently seven years ago, and now he sees nothing of his dad. Susan thinks this is the core of the problem. "Shaun sees me as a mate," she says. "I have no control over him whatsoever. He likes the attention. All the stuff in the papers hasn't helped – he's just been playing up to all of that."

Down on the village's main road, a group of tracksuited teenage boys are hanging about. Shaun McKerry is just mental, they say, and his mother lets him get away with murder. Most kids around here behave themselves because they would get "brayed" [hit] by their parents if they didn't.

What make McKerry worse is the drugs. Susan says he'll take anything. Cannabis she doesn't mind, but he also takes "phets" (amphetamine) ecstasy and even heroin. When he is in the house, Shaun has mood swings and swears a lot. His mother has taken to ignoring him. He comes and goes as he wants, and she can't tell him what to do.

"I used to be able to keep him quiet but he has his ways of getting you back. There were times when I used to hit him but he used his temper and put his fist through things. I pray that he will change, that he will come to his senses," she says. "When I walk on the streets I feel ashamed. When I see people who own the cars he had taken I cannot look them in the eyes."

She says her son needs "some sort of counselling" and that the fact that he keeps reoffending means he is not getting what he needs when he is inside. A lifer who started with petty crime at the age of 10 and got his current sentence at 25 has written to Shaun, pleading with him to pack it in. He says he doesn't want Shaun going the same way.

Detective Chief Inspector Paul Green, crime manager at Bishop Auckland police station, says: "He is just one of lots of kids at that age who once they have been to court several times feel that there's no action to be taken. He exploits the system knowing nothing can be done with him. Last time he was only out for six hours before we caught him again."

The police can only hope that the Home Secretary's Crime and Disorder Act will allow them to do more with recidivists like McKerry. Jack Straw has announced plans to allow courts to lock up 12- to 15-year-olds who commit hundreds of crimes, and the new Youth Justice Board has suggested the possibility of electronic tagging. However, the UN has already criticised Britain for locking up children and statistics show that 80 per cent of youngsters who are incarcerated reoffend within two years.

Green says McKerry "needs his head put right or he's just on the road to nowhere except long-term prison – or he'll be killed in a stolen car." He is also worried for Shaun's siblings, who, he says, could go off the rails too. Susan is aware of this, but says her kids know what Shaun is doing is wrong. Her youngest boy does play up, though. Just the other day, at the age of eight, he told a policeman: "When I get older I'll be a twocker, but I'll be able to run faster than Shaun." Someone will have to stop him before he begins.

Source: Audrey Gillan, *The Guardian*, 25 March 1999

1 List the crimes which Boomerang Boy has been identified as committing. **(2)**

2 Give reasons why the boy cannot be detained in custody. **(2)**

3 Why has the newspaper been allowed to print the boy's name? **(2)**

4 What are the possible consequences for the boy himself, his family and the community from the decision to publicise his name? Develop your discussion of each of these points as fully as possible. There are a number of issues to be developed. **(12)**

5 There is a gap between the boy's aspirations to be an archaeologist and the probable reality of his being a sheet-metal worker. Which sociological theory might this observation support? **(8)**

6 Go through the article very carefully and identify all the possible solutions that are offered as to why Boomerang Boy began his criminal career. You may choose to consider ideologies of family and the way that they affect this debate. **(12)**

7 Look at each of the perspectives in turn and suggest an explanation for the child's criminal activities based on the sociological insights that each offers. **(4 each)**

8 Should the boy's mother be held responsible for the crimes that her son commits? Evaluate this suggestion in the light of sociological theory. **(12)**

The mass media and crime

This is linked to the work of **Stanley Cohen** and Stuart Hall, which is discussed in Area 5. The key theme of this type of work is that the media are actually able to create crime and disorder in our society while at the same time appearing to criticise it and to be on the side of law and social order.

HINTS AND TIPS *Refer to the Sociology in Practice section 'The virgin and the vamp' (page 83) where there is a case study to consider.*

■ It is claimed that the media create **moral panics** by covering incidents, in particular those related to youth culture, in a hysterical and value-laden way. Reporting sensationalises incidents.

■ The trigger or deviant incident is known as a **folk devil**. The folk devil is reported in a way that makes the danger seem dangerous and exciting. While many people over-react and consider the folk devil to be a danger to the moral fabric of society, others are drawn to the action or behaviour because of its dangerous romance. Certain crimes become fashionable; for example 'joy-riding', a term for the crime of taking away and driving a car, or car theft and destruction.

■ Other approaches have included the idea that certain events are so exciting that people may imitate them (**copy cat**). Although this common-sense view is widely discussed there is not a great deal of evidence beyond the point that when a crime is widely reported, it may be repeated. However, many notorious crimes have not been imitated.

HINTS AND TIPS *Could any of the following activities be seen as moral panics?*

- *Drug abuse/misuse*
- *Gang warfare*
- *Urban riots*
- *Raves*

Collect examples of reporting which could be considered to be overblown and sensationalised with respect to criminal activities and the young. Use these examples in your examination answers.

ACTIVITY KS APPLICATION OF NUMBER

IDENTIFICATION AND INTERPRETATION	ANALYSIS AND EVALUATION

It is argued that the media in our society are obsessed with questions of crime and deviance. Attempt a simple analysis to test this thesis. Obtain a TV listings magazine such as *Radio Times*. Use a marker pen and note how many television programmes are either factual or fictional accounts of crime and criminal behaviour.

- How many hours each week are devoted to media accounts of criminal behaviour?
- What proportion is this of our total possible television watching?
- What conclusions can you come to about the way that people feel about crime and criminal behaviour?
- Develop this work by looking at magazines and newspapers and attempting content analysis as outlined in Area 2.

Youth cultures and crime

Albert Cohen's (1955) *Delinquent Boys* has already been discussed in this area in relation to subcultural theorising. Cohen used Merton's theory to create a case study and said working-class boys have three options:

- to try for upward mobility through education
- to become traditional working class with conventional values and few means of attaining them

PROFILE

Stanley Cohen

Stanley Cohen is the author of one of the best known studies of the relationship between the media and social responses to deviance: *Folk Devils and Moral Panics*. He teaches at the London School of Economics where he is Martin White Professor of Sociology. He was brought up in South Africa and gained his first degree in Sociology and Social Work from the University of Witwatersrand, Johannesburg, in 1958.

Cohen obtained his doctorate from the London School of Economics in 1968, a study of social reactions to juvenile delinquency. He taught sociology at the University of Durham, and from 1972 the University of Essex. From 1982–1997 he was Director of the Institute of Criminology at the Hebrew University, Israel.

Hs most recent books are **Visions of Social Control**, **Against Criminology** and **Punishment and Social Control**. He has a longstanding interest in human rights and has recently completed a book entitled *States of Denial*, which deals with public responses to atrocities.

Folk Devils and Moral Panics remains a classic and has undergone frequent reprint and two separate editions. This is a relatively accessible piece of academic research and there is much of interest in it for students of sociology.

- to become delinquent and join a subculture with values opposed to the mainstream

However, Cohen's work was criticised on the grounds that, although it seems to fit the facts, there is little empirical research to support his findings. His writing has stimulated work in both the USA and in Britain and has led to a long sociological concern with young people. Much of this work is concerned with the criminal activities of young men and it is fair to remark that the activities of young women are ignored in much of the debate. In the USA, Matza (1964) suggested that:

- people have free will and can choose whether or not to act in a delinquent fashion
- most delinquency is not tough or thrilling but boring and episodic

He suggested that juveniles tend to drift into delinquency through a psycho-social process, which he called a technique of neutralisation and which involves denying that social rules have any relevance to them. These techniques include:

- **denial of responsibility** – 'it was an accident'
- **denial of injury** – 'it doesn't hurt anyone'
- **denial of victim** – 'he deserved it'
- **condemnation of condemners** – judges, the police and lawyers are all 'bad'
- **appeal to higher loyalty** – 'I did it for my mate'

Matza takes the idea a step further by suggesting that once people have learned to break rules, they take part in further delinquency because they stop feeling powerless and take control of their own lives, even if it is in a negative sense. Delinquents develop subterranean values belonging to the criminal underworld, in the sense that they share the values of broader society but they misapply these values and their subsequent behaviour becomes socially inappropriate.

There is a distinctively British subcultural debate which differs from American discussions. In the USA, sociologists work on a notion of working-class subcultures, but in Britain the discussion is more likely to centre on youth subcultures. This work on youth culture was linked initially to educational ideas (and can be used in educational analyses) but has developed into a broader coverage of crime and control issues.

The anti-school culture debate

Writers such as Downes (1966) suggest that schools create delinquency by institutionalising inequality of access to rewards and creating individual self-concepts of failure among the young. Paul Willis (1978) suggested that an anti-school subculture develops which prepares pupils for the dull grind of the meaningless work to which they will be consigned. Failure within school becomes anti-social behaviour out of school.

British cultural and ethnographic studies

These tend to be linked with media presentations of deviance and 'youth' cultures. Phil Cohen (1978) said that distinctive youth subcultures of styles and dress signal delinquency to the police and create labelling. Corrigan (1979) claimed that working-class boys

manufacture excitement through acts of petty vandalism. Hebdige (1974) pointed out that the symbols of Nazism typical of 'punk' are used to shock; the users see different meanings in such insignia than older people and do not understand the reactions they evoke. Note that many famous studies with a cultural dimension – such as Hall's *Policing the Crisis*, Cohen's *Folk Devils and Moral Panics* and Willis's *Learning to Labour*, all of which are discussed in various areas within the text – are concerned with youth culture to a large extent.

Drug use and youth culture

Many of the early interactionist studies of deviancy, such as those of Becker in the USA and Jock Young in Britain, were conducted among drug users. The reason for this choice is that it offers a fine example to prove that certain forms of deviance are socially defined. Alcohol is perfectly acceptable in society, but the use of cannabis (called marijuana in the USA) is not. In the late 1960s and early 1970s, youth culture was marked by a tolerance of drug use and was typical of hippie culture, which rejected what it saw as the values of a repressive Middle America.

It is difficult to be certain of the role that illegal drugs play in modern youth culture, but it is claimed that drug use has increased among all young people. Ecstasy is strongly associated with the 'club scene' and there are regular reports of deaths in the press. The most commonly used drug would appear to be cannabis. Parker and Measham suggested in 1994 that nearly half of all 15–16-year-old people had used an illegal drug. This implies that, rather than an act of rebellion and rejection of the values of society, illegal drug use has become almost a norm and part of the prevailing culture of young people. There is some suggestion that West Indian youths are more likely to use cannabis and other drugs than other ethnic groups, but this could be explained either by reference to Rastafarianism, which advocates the use of mind-expanding drugs, or by racial stereotyping.

Girl gangs

Little has been published on the youth culture of girls in terms of their capacity for deviance. There has been interest into their socialisation as domestic creatures through media imagery, and one of the the best known studies was Sue Sharpe's 1970s study *Just Like a Girl*. Campbell, however, studied women in New York gangs in the 1980s and offered a picture of a life where gang membership offered some sense of status, purpose and significance to women's otherwise bleak and deprived lives. Box and Hale also noted that female offenders tended to come from working-class and deprived backgrounds, where they would be unaffected by social improvements in the lives of women. Carlen noted the pattern of female offending as a response to poverty and deprivation. She discovered that her small group of women offenders claimed to be criminal for one of the following reasons:

- poverty
- a childhood in the care of a local authority
- drug and alcohol problems
- a desire for excitement

Soccer culture

A recent debate, which ties into analyses of youth culture, is the rise of soccer hooliganism, which became a serious moral panic of the 1980s. Marsh, Rosser and Harris in *The Rules of Disorder* reported on a study of the violent behaviour of football fans who followed Millwall and Oxford United. Their research method was observational and they noted that:

- most fans had dull daily lives
- the match was a central topic of conversation
- being a fan brought on a sense of identity and belonging
- fans divided themselves into semi-formalised groups based on age and status
- the descriptions of violence that had taken place were often in the form of post-match boasting rather than in any reality
- violence was symbolic and ritualised, with few people willing to overstep the boundaries

It was suggested that with the break-up and loss of working-class community life (described in Area 6) solidarity could be achieved through support of a team. However, some critics have noted that considerable violence did take place at matches and suggest that it represents the nature of working-class values. The perceived increase in violence was probably associated with

- youth unemployment
- confrontational tactics by authorities which challenged the young
- increased ability of young people to travel away from home
- mass media creations of myths of masculinity and male violence, which the fans emulated

To summarise, it should be noted that the rise of football hooliganism made it possible for the police to change the nature of their behaviour. A whole range of surveillance techniques and covert strategies came into play at that stage, and are now part of social control in our society. Commentators also noted that the police gained status in some sectors of the community because their view of events became the official view of editors and politicians. This was very notable during coverage of the 1989 Hillsborough disaster, where more than 90 people were crushed to death as a result of confused crowd control. *The Sun* in particular was condemned for its 'blame the fans' stance in reporting, which was widely criticised as the full facts of the case began to emerge. Their reporting was in contrast to the views of many members of the general public, including people who had been present, who perceived the police as incompetent and largely to blame.

> **HINTS AND TIPS** *This is a hotly argued debate. A number of books have been published on the issue of football violence, must notably by the Leicester University group. One of the criticisms that has been made of the Marsh thesis is that some of the violence at football has been extreme, and that it is not always the actions of youths but that older people are also involved. This might be a fruitful area of study for coursework for a student who actively supports a football team.*

Evaluating the youth culture debate

As a point of evaluation to the whole debate, the presence of a distinctive youth culture with aims and values that are different from those of adult society is by no means proven. Heidensohn (1989) points out that youth cultures are often studied ethnographically with little reference to the social worlds in which the youth gangs move or consideration of the details of their daily routines. Explorations of youth culture fail at this point. Young people may behave or dress in a way that is at variance with adult social norms, but do they necessarily hold views that are radically different from the values and mores of adults? Many adults in their own youth were members of groups such as hippies or punks but does this have to be anything more socially significant than a fashion statement?

> **HINTS AND TIPS**   *You should remember that many writers have linked the development of youth culture with cultural processes involving the media. You are advised to read more about this in Area 5, where the work of Stanley Cohen and Stuart Hall is considered, because it has much relevance to this debate.*

ACTIVITY   KS WORKING WITH OTHERS

ANALYSIS AND EVALUATION

Organise class discussion around the following points. Make good clear notes.

■ Delinquents are merely responding to social circumstances beyond their control.

■ Male sociologists have ignored the experience of the adolescent female in subcultural studies of crime.

■ Is delinquency a male working class phenomenon?

■ Do schools really create criminal deviance?

Culture of the police

Policing varies considerably from country to country and so any essay remarking on the nature of the police should show this awareness. Pressures to study the activities of the police have come from people concerned with political issues of freedom and civic rights. Groups such as the Council for Civil Liberties and Amnesty International have drawn attention to abuses of power, many of which have involved the police at various levels. When considering the police, remember that these points may just apply to members

of the police force but that the police themselves represent a significant part of the whole structure of social control and order.

In Britain we sustained a myth of 'our policemen are wonderful' until the 1970s. Radio and television shows portrayed the police in paternal and avuncular roles. In the USA, the police were never accorded the same status and so early studies of the police came from the USA. Early sociologists did not in fact study the police because they were generally more concerned with criminals. Many tended to romanticise the criminal or underdog, coming as they did from a structural functionalist or Marxist perspective. This changed in the 1970s with the advent of critical criminologies and so most work is very recent.

Why study the police?

The significance of the police as an area of study came about for a number of reasons, due to the social upheavals of the late 1960s and early 1970s. However, many of the issues that were raised at that time have not been fully addressed and embarrassing scandals tend to recur. Heidensohn's analysis provides the framework for the following discussion.

Scandals and corruption

There were a number of allegations in the 1970s of scandal and corruption involving the police in drugs, bribery and pornography. Many of these were associated with the West Midlands force. Whether these allegations were true or not remains irrelevant in some ways: the significance is that they are widely believed.

Rising crime and urban riots

Crime rates appear to be rising while clear-up rates tend to remain the same or even fall. These statistics are now in the public domain as police forces are expected to collect and produce statistical information about their performance. They can be obtained from the local council or the police themselves. Remember that all statistics should be treated with extreme caution, however – they rarely show what they purport to show!

Race relations

Reiner, Harrison, Hall and others have all noted poor relationships between the police and ethnic communities and low recruitment rates among ethnic groups. This has been exemplified by the appalling blunders of the London Metropolitan Police in dealing with the murder of the black teenager Stephen Lawrence, which became a *cause célèbre* of the 1990s.

Stop and search

This is a very unpopular (and dubious) activity of the police, who have the right to stop and search anyone they feel has been acting suspiciously. Notoriously few arrests come out of stop and search activities, many of these are for refusal to co-operate with the police or for obstruction, and result from the victim objecting to the police activity. Smith and Gray (1983) found that the main victims are those who are in some way seen as at variance with mainstream society: young people, overt homosexuals and young black men in particular.

The role of the police in industrial actions

The government used the police in political and social unrest where they were forceful or aggressive, depending upon one's perspective. The miners' strike of the early 1980s, which was prompted by closures of coal-mines by the Conservative government, and labour disputes at Wapping (which became test cases for limiting the powers of trades unions) became famous for the way the role of the police changed. The police were seen by certain sections of the community as agents of what was at that time a deeply unpopular government.

Technological change

The police became removed from their communities by the use of cars and mobile radios. There has been a strong movement in the other direction – community policing has produced some very positive results.

The Irish Question

Some very violent terrorist bombings occurred on mainland Britain in the 1970s. The media put tremendous pressure on the police and a number of quick arrests were made, which later led to serious charges of miscarriages of justice. Famous cases such as that of the Birmingham Six (filmed as *The Name of the Father*) and the Guildford Four led to full pardons for the convicted, but not before great damage had been done to individuals and to the reputation of the police.

Student unrest and the anti-Vietnam movement

Many middle-class young people became politicised or criminalised as a result of student unrest in the late 1960s. This movement was also associated with some drug abuse. There were demonstrations, some of which were violent. The police came to be seen as oppressive and reactionary rather than as guardians of the population by many people who later took up influential positions in society.

> **HINTS AND TIPS** Collect opinions from older people who may remember some of the events described in the list above. There may be evidence that current dissatisfaction with police performance is linked with what are now mostly historical events.

The police: consensus or conflict accounts of their role

What are the police for? Do they represent the wider community or do they represent legal authority? Opinion is deeply divided on this point. Many commentators have suggested that the power of the

---

ACTIVITY KS COMMUNICATION

IDENTIFICATION AND INTERPRETATION

Collect views from people as to the kind of person that they consider would make a good police officer. How many of your sample think in terms of an authoritarian personality rather than one who is a supportive member of the local community? If you have access to police officers, you could even consider their views. What do your findings tell you about the relationship of the police to society and social expectations of the police? Write up your results.

police originated in the respect of the community. Critchley (1978) supported this position. Lord Scarman (1981) said that there was a tradition of consensual policing in Britain. In contrast, the eminent criminologist Phil Cohen (1981) suggested that there has been a history of dislike and distaste for the police in many working-class areas of London since Victorian times. Modern myths about the origins of the power of the police overlook this antipathy. Cohen's view is a more critical analysis of the role of the police, which perhaps originated in Marxist analyses.

The culture of the police

Heidensohn (1989) points out that the police have a powerful occupational culture, which has elements of

- authoritarianism, according to Skolnik (1966) and Westley (1970)
- hostility to and intolerance of the public and blacks in the USA (Westley, 1970)
- cohesive social groupings (Punch, 1979)
- physical power and control (Holdaway, 1983)
- a notion of masculinity including drinking, violence, misogyny and racism (Smith and Gray, 1983)
- a desire for excitement and sensation (Smith and Gray, 1983)
- law enforcement (Southgate, 1986)
- racial prejudice (Southgate, 1986)
- all the above (Jones, 1986)

There have been moves to retrain the police into more acceptable attitudes. The police need to have a good relationship with the public. Hough and Mayhew (1983) suggest that most crime (85–90%) is actually brought to the police in reports from the public. There are doubts as to the success of such strategies developed to humanise the police and some are resisted from within the police force. The job of a policeman is in reality likely to be boring, and yet recruitment and much media imagery tends to emphasise excitement and thrills.

TASK

Hypothesis – The police themselves are responsible for the lack of respect they are accorded by many sections of the community.

Context – You will have to prove 'lack of respect', as this is an investigation which makes an assumption that may or may not be true. Many people in society have the utmost regard for the work of the police.

More discussion will be needed to decide the sections of the community that you will need to investigate. This might be easier to consider if the work is set in the context of a possible subculture such as football fans who attend matches, members of ethnic minority groups or any other section of the community with known poor relations with the police. Avoid known criminals such as drug users, who arguably can be said to have brought problems on themselves. Your target is community relations with the police force.

Method – Attempt a small-scale qualitative research project identifying the views of the public towards the police force. Ask people if their views are based on personal experience as victims or potential lawbreakers or if they base their opinions on something more general or diffuse.

Your conclusions might consider whether policing is consensual. Does it represent a top-down exercise of social control in the view of your respondents? It might be that the police have an undeservedly bad reputation based on public concern with one or two well known cases of miscarriages of justice, or it might be that the police are interacting badly with the general public and have a serious image problem.

Evaluation – Obviously, with coursework your main concern is always with the appropriateness of the methods that you choose. From this method you will have to consider questions of reliability and validity. Was your sample representative of a subsection of the community? Can you draw wider conclusions from this one group to an understanding of society and the police as a whole? Is there a difference between public reaction to 'the police' as a concept and 'the police' who investigated their burglaries?

Suicide

HINTS AND TIPS *Suicide is not an appropriate area for you to consider for coursework. Your relative inexperience will inevitably lead to ethical problems with your work. However sensitive you are, or mature in your approach, you will have serious problems as a result of the nature of the topic.*

This area is fascinating to sociologists despite the fact that there is very little reliable work that can be used.

The issues regarding the act of **suicide** itself are that

- one cannot investigate the reasons behind a successful suicide
- suicide is, of itself, an astonishing act because it seems to go against human nature, which suggests that life must be preserved at all cost

In sociological terms the issue is interesting because:

- Suicide was once a criminal act in our society although it is no longer so. It is clearly a socially created act of deviance.
- Suicide is a culturally defined act of deviance. Many cultures honour it, and even within our society we revere certain forms of suicide, such as the person who undertakes a hopeless act of heroism, as admirable and necessary. A captain is expected to stay on board a sinking ship and to be the last to leave for safety.
- The successful study of suicide was the starting point for sociological methodology.
- There is a huge debate surrounding the definition of suicide and the reliability of suicide figures which illustrates the problems that face sociologists

ACTIVITY KS**WORKING WITH OTHERS**

KNOWLEDGE AND UNDERSTANDING

You could contact the Samaritans to find out more about their work. Do not use an emergency contact line but find out the office number from a telephone directory or write to the organisation for details of their work and any statistical information that they are willing to share with you.

in all areas who must deal with official statistics and which casts light on considerations of numbers and meaning.

Durkheim and *Le Suicide*

Arguably, Émile Durkheim's (1897) study of suicide triggered the development of sociology as a discipline in this country. Durkheim was concerned to prove that society existed and that social rules would govern individual behaviour. This theorising underlies structural functionalist thought and is consensual. He took the most dramatically individualistic behaviour that he could find (suicide) and then set himself the task of proving that suicide, far from being a gesture of personal despair, was in fact an act prompted by a response to social circumstances.

He took official statistics from a number of countries and processed them to demonstrate patterns in suicide rates. His three basic points require little explanation, given the familiarity that we have with statistical analysis.

1 Suicide rates remain remarkably constant within cultures over time.
2 Different countries have different suicide rates.
3 Suicide rates vary within certain social groups within countries.

To further develop the point, he made a number of other observations.

- Protestants have higher suicide rates than Catholics. He argued that this was because Catholics are more closely integrated into their religious groupings.
- Those who are not married are more likely to commit suicide. This, he argued, was because people who are members of families feel a sense of cohesion to their family group and to society.
- In times of war, even in countries that are actually at peace, there are lower suicide rates. This he suggested is because people draw together in times of external danger and look after one another.

He offered four explanations for suicide, all of which support his contention that there is a relationship between the act and the rules of society.

Altruistic suicide

This is typical of those who are over-integrated into the rules of society. Altruism is an act of unselfishness. Such people will naturally endanger themselves because they feel they are doing so for others. A soldier on a mission that will bring certain death is in this position.

Egoistic suicide

This is typical of people who are insufficiently integrated into the rules of society. An egoist is totally self-centred. Egoism is typical of modern societies and people commit suicide for selfish reasons because they lack a sense of belonging.

Fatalistic suicide

This is the act of one who no longer cares about or who feels unable to change or have an impact on society or the lives of other people.

Anomic suicide

This is by far the most interesting area of study. Anomie is the absence of rules and regulations and people who experience anomie have a sense of meaninglessness in their lives. This absence of rule and role is typical of all society so an anomic suicide is the act of one who is highly attuned to the nuances of culture. People who feel that society is unpredictable lose their sense of belonging. There is evidence that suicide rates rise in times of recession and of economic boom.

> **HINTS AND TIPS** *You may also like to note that Durkheim believed that some of these factors could work in concert with one another to propel people to their deaths.*

Interpretivist approaches to suicide

It is often claimed, incorrectly, that Durkheim did not criticise the official statistics he gathered but took them at face value. Durkheim (1897) states that he had little alternative but to accept them at face value. He fully understood a number of issues that were later to be used in criticism of his work.

Evaluations to support the importance of Durkheim's work	Evaluations which criticise the work
Durkheim was successful in proving a link between society and suicide	Halbwachs (1930), a student of Durkheim, suggested that he applied a simple cause and effect approach and that suicide is a more complex topic than Durkheim allowed it to be
Durkheim shifted attention away from the romanticised idea that suicide is an act of individual passion and shed light on the social processes involved	Durkheim did not define all his terms accurately because there is no adequate working definition of suicide that actually relates to the data being collected
Durkheim proved that statistical analysis is a viable methodological approach	Social integration is not something that can be measured accurately so some of the conclusions may not be scientifically valid
Durkheim laid the foundations of positivist methodology	It has been suggested that Durkheim gave way to the temptation to ignore data that did not fit his thesis. This is a common criticism of positivist writers

Figure 12.9 Evaluating Durkheim's study of suicide

Douglas (1967) pointed out that there are a number of factors which point to the fact that official statistics are at best a clumsy tool. Suicides are likely to be concealed, particularly in a society such as our own, which considers suicide to be a particularly upsetting and unpleasant mode of death at best and a mortal sin which ensures that the suicide will burn in hell for eternity at worst. So antagonistic has our society been to suicide that suicides have not been buried in churchyards even in historical times. It is important therefore to consider the feelings of the people who remain to grieve. Factors affecting the accuracy of suicide statistics include:

- attempts by those discovering the body to hide evidence pointing to suicide
- official reluctance to define a death as a suicide
- suicides hiding the mode of death from their families – a fatal car accident may be just that (an accident) but could be a hidden suicide

A study by Atkinson (1978) looked at the work of Coroners' courts and the social and legal processing that goes on before a death is finally decreed a suicide. Factors involved in identifying a death as a suicide include

- the discovery of a suicide letter
- the actual manner of death
- the state of mind prior to death
- the motive that the suicide may have had

Cases are not clear-cut and it may be very difficult to decide the motive and nature of death. Coroners, lawyers who must investigate sudden or mysterious death, will attempt to allow let-out clauses such as 'the balance of the mind was disturbed' or 'case not proven'.

Taylor (1988), who is well known for his conference work with A level students and a variety of excellent study videos, attempts a 'realistic approach' which is a combination of perspectives. He looks at the personal meaning that suicide has for people and relates it to social relationships. He uses complex language and offers four possible types of suicide (Figure 12.10).

He combined Durkheim's types of suicide with a sense of the meaning that suicide may have for those people who attempt this form of deviance.

	Inner directed suicide (ectopic)	**Socially directed suicide (symphysic)**
Desire to be dead is strong	Submissive suicide	Sacrifice suicide to provoke guilt in others
Desire to be dead is uncertain	Thanation which is a form of gambling with life	Appeal suicide is designed to make others improve life for suicide

Figure 12.10 Taylor's four types of suicide

Area summary

This area is one of enormous complexity. That crime and deviance exist is not an issue, but there are certainly difficulties with their definition given that all cultures have different norms and values. Even within our own culture, there is considerable variation between the values of different social groups. The cultural values that are accepted as the basis of our legal and criminal codes are defined by a small section of the whole community: mostly those who are white, male, middle-class and middle-aged.

Crime has great impact on the public consciousness because we fear its consequences. Disorder strikes at the root of our personal security and safety; we need to feel that we can trust our fellow human beings. The consequences of criminal activity on the victim or the victim's family may be lifelong physical or psychological damage. The loss of a child, for instance, to violent crime is probably one of the very worst things that most parents could imagine. Despite this, humans seem to have a fascination with crime and deviance. This appears in our storytelling. You can see it in morality tales, where the good person wins in the end, or in a morbid fascination with the details of real-life murder and horror.

It can be argued that many people limit their daily activities because of the fear of crime. Women are advised by the police to avoid putting themselves into situations where they may be attacked and have lost their individual freedom at night as a consequence. People who are the victims of crimes such as abuse and rape may even be blamed for having brought the attack on themselves.

Factors associated with criminal behaviours are also related to issues of poverty, alienation, and powerlessness. Young working-class men are taught to be dominant and masculine, but these are precisely the qualities which make them unsuitable for the highest-paid jobs. Criminal behaviour does not always result in a conviction and there may be a stronger link between conviction and the prejudices of the criminal justice system or the police than between conviction and actual criminal behaviour. Despite attempts at impartiality and fairness, social processes can interfere in the criminal justice system through labelling and stereotyping, and certain individuals lose their full place in society before they can fully understand the long-term consequences of their actions.

The study of deviance and crime is difficult: that is why it is so fascinating to the sociologist. It brings many of the broader theoretical debates about the value of nature versus nurture, the usefulness of official statistics and the nature of social construction to the study of an issue which has direct bearing on all our lives.

Definitions

Alienation	A Marxist concept which suggests that people do not feel part of society because they lack power or control over their daily lives
Anomie	A functionalist concept which suggests that people lose their sense of place and belonging and so are at odds with themselves and their society
Bourgeois hegemony	The control of ideas and the domination of society by the middle classes
Chivalry thesis	The belief that the law is kinder or more generous to women than to men
Consensus theory	The idea that society is held together by a set of shared values and beliefs
Copy cat	People will behave in a way that is similar to something that they have already seen
Corporate crime	Crime committed by large corporations
Crime	The act of breaking a law
Criminal	One who breaks a law
Criminal code	A legal system
Culpable	To carry guilt for something or to be at fault
Cultural relativity	The idea that there is no absolute meaning for right and wrong, that these concepts are culturally determined
Dark figure of crime	The unreported crime which does not appear in statistics
Delinquency	A criminal act which is typical of a young person
Deviance	The breaking of a social code
Folk devil	This inspires the moral panic and the fear that people experience
Formal punishment	A legal punishment put in place by a court or any other official body
Informal sanctions	The punishments we give in daily life such as ignoring those who break certain rules
Law	A written rule for behaviour which applies to a society
Legal code	The written rules of any society
Master status	The most significant status or characteristic that a person has and by which s/he can be defined as an individual
Moral panics	A mass social reaction to a phenomenon which is characterised by moral judgements
Mores	A set of rules for conduct which people believe apply to all people in society
Norms	The normal behaviour for a given situation
Repressive state apparatus	Part of the state which is used to dominate and control through the exercise of power and fear

Sanctions	Punishments which can be applied to people
Self-fulfilling prophecy	The idea that people will grow to fill a set of beliefs that others have of their behaviour and personality
Social code	The unwritten rules of society
Social control	The control that society has over individuals
Spoiled identity	A person who is said to be stigmatised has a spoiled identity
Stereotyping	Over-simplified views of people based on superficial characteristics rather than on their personalities such as gender or ethnicity
Stigma	A mark of some kind, either social or physical, which makes the non-stigmatised feel uncomfortable
Subculture	A small group within society with views and opinions at variance with the rest.
Suicide	The deliberate ending of one's own life
Values	A set of beliefs and moral judgements about the nature of society
White-collar crime	An American term used to describe crime committed by middle-class people

Data response questions

Item A

As for me personally, after 15 years, Crimewatch has taught me two important lessons. One is that the world is not divided into honest folk and criminals. At some time or other in our lives almost all of us have broken criminal laws, whether it is cheating on taxes, not paying a fare, driving when over the limit, or a bit of vandalism when we were young and foolish (in my case it was vandalism) … Second, we as a society could do a great deal more to prevent crime.

Nick Ross (9 January 1999: 27) *Radio Times*.

Item B

The fact that around 49% of imprisoned adult offenders and some 71% of incarcerated juvenile offenders are reconvicted within 2 years of their release is often presented as conclusive proof that prisons and custodial establishments have little or no deterrent effect. But standard reconviction rates are arbitrary and vague measures of both prison performance and levels of reoffending.

Matthews, R. (1997: 10) 'Does prison work?' *Sociology Review*, February.

Item C

Pollution also involves incalculable costs. Illegal factory emissions and river pollution poison wildlife and affect people; sea pollution renders many beaches unvisitable (Croall 1992). As with 'accidents' in the workplace, pollution is rarely seen as a 'criminal' problem, although some prosecutions can involve large fines.

Croall, H. (1993: 23) White Collar Crime. *Sociology Review*, November.

Item D

Sociologists are predictably at odds over the cause of the increase in youth crime, with diagnoses and prescriptions more often reflecting political differences between the 'short sharp shock' brigade on the right and the 'solving the cause of crime' carers on the left.

Several leading academics … insist that prosperity rather than poverty nurtures crime, that envy is a principal motivator.

Millar, P. et al. (11 October 1998: 14) Teenage Timebomb. *Sunday Times*.

a What is the difference between 'reconviction' and 'reoffending'? (4)

KNOWLEDGE AND UNDERSTANDING

b   What is the difference between 'crime' and 'deviance'?   (4)

> KNOWLEDGE AND
> UNDERSTANDING

c   Evaluate the usefulness of the reconviction rates as a measure of
reoffending rates.   (6)

> IDENTIFICATION AND
> INTERPRETATION

d   Offer sociological reasons to explain why offenders may reoffend within
a short time of release from prison.   (6)

> IDENTIFICATION AND
> INTERPRETATION

e   Suggest sociological reasons why industrial pollution is rarely seen as
a criminal offence.   (7)

> | KNOWLEDGE AND | IDENTIFICATION AND |
> | UNDERSTANDING | INTERPRETATION |

f   Using the items and your own knowledge, assess the usefulness of
official crime data.   (9)

> ANALYSIS AND
> EVALUATION

g   Sociologically evaluate the assertion in Item 4 that envy is a primary
cause of crime.   (9)

> ANALYSIS AND
> EVALUATION

Structured questions

a   What types of crimes are likely to be under-reported in Britain?   (4)

> **GUIDANCE**   You will need to consider a variety of categories of crime which are
> under-reported and offer suggestions why they are missing from official data. You
> might consider crimes which are undiscovered such as fraud and white-collar crime as well as the more
> usual crimes such as rape or victimless crimes.
>
> KNOWLEDGE AND
> UNDERSTANDING

b Using sociological knowledge, assess the view that Sir Paul Condon, Chief Commissioner for the Metropolitan Police, recently expressed when he suggested that increasing reports of racial attacks are a sign of growing confidence in the police. **(4)**

> **GUIDANCE** *There are two possibilities here. Either racially motivated crime is increasing or Sir Paul Condon is correct. It is difficult to tell which is true in this case; however, you will need to comment on a little evidence to support either possibility. There is evidence to suggest that the police may be institutionally racist, however, people will not report crime unless they feel that it is effective to do so.*
>
> IDENTIFICATION AND INTERPRETATION

c Suggest reasons why females are largely absent from the criminal conviction statistics. **(7)**

> **GUIDANCE** *This question requires some consideration of why women are missing from the statistics. It may be that the police are not pressing charges against women, or you could consider explanations that offer elements of the social control debate. Females do not have as much social freedom as males. There is also the question of the fact that women are likely to be the victims of crimes such as domestic violence. Refer to feminists and feminist thought as well as New Right theories of the origins of crime.*
>
> IDENTIFICATION AND INTERPRETATION | ANALYSIS AND EVALUATION

d To what extent do laws and the criminal justice system represent the interests of the dominant ideology in society? **(10)**

> **GUIDANCE** *This requires an evaluation of Marxist theories of the origins of crime which also shows knowledge of how the justice system works. It is a simple question and one which could appear as an essay question where you would have to tackle it in a detailed and more explanatory format.*
>
> KNOWLEDGE AND UNDERSTANDING | IDENTIFICATION AND INTERPRETATION | ANALYSIS AND EVALUATION

Essay titles

1 Evaluate the usefulness of studies of suicide to a sociological understanding of deviance in society. **(25)**

2 Is there a relationship between deviance and power? **(25)**

3 How useful is the concept of subculture to an understanding of crime in our society? **(25)**

4   To what extent can it be argued that crime is a working-class male phenomenon?

KNOWLEDGE AND UNDERSTANDING	IDENTIFICATION AND INTERPRETATION	ANALYSIS AND EVALUATION

GUIDANCE   *Avoid the obvious answer to this essay, which suggests that working-class males do commit more crime. You are being asked to question commonplace assumptions and once you realise that, then the essay is much easier than it first appears.*

This is a really simple catch-all question which allows you to spend some time discussing the nature of social definitions of deviance, the way that criminal statistics are gathered, labelling theory and also the reality of crime in inner cities and deprived areas. If you limit yourself to a discussion of the social class debate, there will be plenty to write, but your answers will not stand out from the crowd.

The danger is that if you attempt to apply ideas from all sections of this area, you will find that there is much to consider, so your planning under examination conditions will need to be precise.

You are addressing the question of whether crime actually is a working-class phenomenon or whether our society defines crime in such a way as to create victims of certain people. The evidence of the study of the Boomerang Boy suggests that some members of our society are completely out of control; however, is he a victim of poverty and deprivation or his own impulses and the attention that it brings him?

Make sure that you have an excellent plan in order to organise the material that you have at your disposal. It makes sense to choose a conclusion before you begin the essay so that your personal position will inform the debate. You will find that the essay you write will have more shape and structure.

Further reading and references

Heidensohn, F. (1989) *Crime and Society*. Macmillan.
You are advised to be very familiar with this book, which offers a detailed overview of criminology in a readable and knowledgeable way. Heidensohn develops the standard critiques by offering a feminist perspective on the debate. She is one of the most influential of the modern writers on criminology.

Muncie, J. and McLaughlin, E. (1996) *The Problem of Crime*. Sage.
Another book you might like to refer to if you are in the later stages of your course. It contains a number of fascinating articles, presented for an academic audience but in a readable and accessible fashion. It deals with a wider range of issues associated with criminology than many normal texts and features fictional representations of crime and social histories of crime. Those who intend to study law at university would be well advised to invest in this text.

Wincup, E. and Griffiths, J. (1999) *Crime and Deviance*. Hodder & Stoughton.
Hodder and Stoughton publish a series of pocket-sized texts suitable for students at A level, known as the Access to Sociology series. These are being written to the demands of the various substantive syllabus areas. This small text offers an up-to-date overview of the debate, which is both comprehensive and accessible.

Taylor, S. (1988) *The Sociology of Suicide*. Longman.
Steve Taylor's book is a very readable and interesting overview of the suicide debate and attempts to place Durkheim's work in a modern social context.

You should obtain recent editions of the *British Crime Survey*, which has a great deal to offer in terms of statistical analysis of trends and patterns. This should be available in libraries or over interlibrary loan as it is an HMSO publication using government data.

Moore, S. (1996) *Investigating Crime and Deviance*. Collins Educational.
One of the most detailed of the A level texts, which forms part of the Sociology in Action series by Collins Educational.

Internet sites

There are a number of Websites which will support your study. The most useful can be obtained through www.open.gov.uk, but you will need to do a search. For other sites ask for 'crime' and 'statistics'. Some of the American sites make fascinating reading, though not all are sociologically useful. For interest, contact the American FBI by typing 'Federal Bureau of Investigation' into a search engine.

Bibliography

Alderson, J. (1979) *Policing Freedom*. MacDonald and Evans.

Althusser, L. (1984) *Essays on Ideology*. London, Verso.

Atkinson, J. (1978) *Societal Reactions to Suicide* in Cohen, S. *Discovering Suicide*. London, Macmillan.

Becker, H. (1965) *Outsiders*. London, Free Press.

Blomberg, T. and Cohen, S. (1995) *Punishment and Social Control*. New York, Aldine de Gruyter.

Box, S. (1983) *Power, Crime and Mystification*. London, Tavistock.

Burgess, E. W. (1966) in Shaw, C. (reprinted 1966) *The Jack Roller: A Delinquent Boy's Own Story*. Chicago, Chicago University Press.

Campbell, A. (1981) *Deliquent Girls*. Oxford, Blackwell.

Campbell, A. (1984) *Girls in the Gang*. Oxford, Blackwell.

Chambliss, W. (1975) *Towards a Political Economy of Crime*. Theory and Society, Vol. 2.

Cicourel, A. V. (1968) *The Social Organisation of Juvenile Justice*. University of California, Berkeley.

Cicourel, A. and Kitsuse, J. (1963) *The Educational Decision-Makers*. Indianapolis, Bobbs-Merrill.

Cloward, R. and Ohlin, L. (1961) *Deliquency and Opportunity: A Theory of Delinquent Gangs*. London, Routledge and Kegan Paul.

Cohen, A. (1955) *Deliquent boys*. New York, Free Press.

Cohen, P. (1978) *Knuckle Sandwich: Growing Up in the Working Class City*. Harmondsworth, Penguin.

Cohen, P. (1981) *Policing the Working Class City* in Fitzgerald, M., McLennan, G and Pawson, J. eds. *Crime and Society: Readings in History and Theory*. London, RKP.

Cohen, S. (1972) *Folk Devils and Moral Panics*. London, Paladin.

Cohen, S. (1985) *Visions of Social Control*. Cambridge, Polity Press.

Cohen, S. (1988) *Against Criminology*. Oxford, Transaction Books.

Corrigan, P. (1979) *Schooling the Smash Street Kids*. London, Macmillan.

Cowell, D., Jones, T. and Young, J. (1982) *Policing the Riots*. London, Junction Press.

Crawford, A. et al. (1990) *Second Islington Crime Survey*. Middlesex, Middlesex Polytechnic.

Crisp, Q. (1968) *The Naked Civil Servant*. London, Cape.

Critchley, T. A. (1978) *A History of Police in England and Wales*. London, Constable.

Croall, H. C. (1992) *White Collar Crime: Criminal Justice and Criminology*. Buckingham, Open University Press.

Davis, M. (1994) *Beyond Blade Runner: Urban Control, the Ecology of Fear*. Open Magazine Pamphlet Series.

Dobash, R. E. and Dobash R. P. (1979) *Violence Against Wives*. London, Open Books.

Douglas, J. D. (1967) *The Social Meaning of Suicide*. New York, Princeton Press.

Downes, D. M. (1966) *The Delinquent Solution*. London, Routledge and Kegan Paul.

Durkheim, E. trs. Spaulding, A. and Simpson, C. (1970) *Suicide: A study in Suicide*. London, Routledge and Kegan Paul.

Emsley, C. (1996) *Crime and Society in England 1750–1900*. London, Longman.

Foucault, M. (1977) *Discipline and Punish*. London, Allen Lane.

Gelsthorpe, L. (1996) *Critical Decisions in the Criminal Courts* in McLaughlin, E. and Muncie, J. (eds) *Controlling Crime*. London, Sage.

Genn, H. (1988) *Multiple Victimisation*, in Maguire, M. and Ponting, J. (eds) *Victims of Crime: A New Deal*. Buckingham, Open University Press.

Gilroy, P. (1987) *There ain't no black in the Union Jack*. London, Hutchinson.

Goffman, E. (1963) *Stigma: Notes on the Management of a Spoiled Identify*. New York, Prentice-Hall.

Gramsci, A. edited by Forgacs, D. (1988) *An Antonio Gramsci Reader: Selected Writings 1916–1935*. New York, Schocken books.

Hall and Jefferson (1976) *Resistance Through Rituals*. London, Hutchinson.

Hall, S., Cutcher, C., Jefferson, T., and Roberts, B. (1978) *Policing the Crisis*. London, Macmillan.

Halbwachs, M. (1930) *The Causes of Suicide* tr. Goldblatt H. (1978). London, R.K.P.

Hanmer, J. and Maynard, M. eds. (1987) *Women, Violence and Social Control*. London, Macmillan.

Haralambos, M. and Holborn, M. (1995) *Sociology: Themes and Perspectives, 4th Ed*. London, Collins Educational.

Hebbige, D. (1976) *Sub-cultural Conflict and Criminal Performance in Fulham*. Birmingham, CCCS.

Hebdige, D. (1974) *Aspects of Style in the Deviant Subcultures of the Sixties*. Birmingham, University of Birmingham Library (unpublished).

Hebdige, D. (1976) *Reggae, Rastas and Rudies* in Hall and Jefferson (1976) *Resistance Through Rituals*. London, Hutchinson.

Heidensohn, F. (1996) *Women and Crime, 2nd Ed*. London, Macmillan.

Heidensohn, Frances (1989) *Crime and Society* London, Macmillan.

Hirschi, T. (1969) *Causes of Delinquency*. Berkeley, University of California Press. HMSO, *Social Trends 29*, 1999. London, HMSO.

Holdaway, S. (1983) *Inside the British Police: a Force at Work*. Oxford, Blackwell.

Hood, R. (1989) *The Death Penalty: a World-Wide Perspective*. Oxford, Clarendon.

Hough, M. and Mayhew, P. (1983) *The British Crime Survey*. London, HMSO.

Jones, G. (1987) *Elderly People and Domestic Crime. British Journal of Sociology*, Vol. 27, No. 2.

Jones, S. (1986) *Policewomen and Equality*. London, Macmillan.

Kinsey, R., Lea, J. and Young, J. (1986) *Losing the Fight against Crime*. Oxford, Blackwell.

Koffman, L. (1996) *Crime Surveys and Victims of Crime*. Cardiff, University of Wales Press.

Lemert, E. (1948) *The Administration of Justice to Minority Groups in Los Angeles Country*. Berkeley, University of California Press.

Marsh, P., Rosser, E., Harre Rom (1978) *The Rules of Disorder*. London, RKP.

Matza, D. (1964) *Deliquency and Drift*. New York, Wiley.

Measham, F., Parker, H., Aldridge, J. (1998) *Starting, Switching, Slowing and Stopping: Report for the Drugs Prevention Initiative Integrated Programme*. London, Home Office.

Merton, R. K. (1961) *Contemporary Social Problems: An Introduction to the Sociology of Deviant Behaviour and Social Disorganisation*. New York, Harcourt, Brace.

Milgram, S. (1974) *Obedience to Authority*. New York, Harper and Row.

Moore, C. and Brown, J. (1981) *Community vs. Crime*. London, Bedford Square Press.

Moore, S. (1996) *Investigating Crime and Deviance*. London, Collins Educational.

Muncie, J. (1966) *The Construction and Deconstruction of Crime* in Muncie, J. and McLaughlin, E. (eds.) (1996) *The Problem of Crime*. London, Sage.

Muncie, J. and McLaughlin, E. (eds) (1996) *The Problem of Crime*. London, Sage.

Nobbs, J. (1981) *Modern Society: Social Studies for CSE, 2nd Edition*. London, Allen and Unwin.

Pearce, F. (1976) *Crimes of the Powerful*. London, Pluto.

Punch, M. (1979) *Policing the Inner City: A Study of Amsterdam's Warmoesstraat*. Hamdon Conn, Archon Books.

Reiner, R. (1994) *Policing and the Police* in Maguire, M. et al. (eds.) *The Oxford Handbook of Criminology*. Oxford, Oxford University Press.

Rosenhan, D. (1984) *On Being Sane in Insane Places* in Paul Watzlawick (ed.) *The Invented Reality*. New York, Norton.

Scarman, L. (1982) *The Scarman Report: The Brixton Disorders*. London, HMSO.

Scraton, P. and Gordon, P. (1984) *Causes for Concern: Questions of Law and Justice*. Harmondsworth, Penguin.

Sharpe, S. (1976) *Just Like a Girl*. Harmondsworth, Penguin.

Shearing, C. and Stenning, P. (1985) *From the Panopticon to Disney World: The Development of Discipline* in Doob, A. and Greenspan, E. (eds.) *Perspectives in Criminal Law*. Canada Law Book Inc.

Skolnik, I (1966) *Justice Without Trial*. New York, Wiley.

Smith, D. (1997) *Ethnic Origins, Crime and Criminal Justice* in Maguire, M. Morgan, R. and Reiner, R. *The Oxford Handbook of Criminology*. Oxford, Oxford University Press.

Smith, D. and Gray, J. (1983) *Police and People in London IV: The Police in Action*. London, Policy Studies Institute.

Southgate, P. (with Ekblom P) (1986) *Police-Public Encounters*. London, HMSO.

Stanko, E. (1987) *Typical Violence, Normal Precaution: Men, Women and Interpersonal Violence in England, Wales, Scotland and the USA* in Hanmer, J. and Maynard, M. eds. (1987) *Women, Violence and Social Control*. London, Macmillan.

Taylor, I., Walton, P. and Young, J. (1973) *The New Criminology*. London, Routledge.

Taylor, S. (1988) *The Sociology of Suicide*. London, Longman.

Westergaard and Resler (1975) *Class in a Capitalist Society* Harmondsworth, Penguin.

Westley, W. A. (1970) *Violence and the Police: a Sociological Study of Law, Custom and Morality*. Cambridge, MASS., M.I.T.

Willis, P. (1978) *Learning to Labour*. Farnborough, Saxon House.

Wincup, E. and Griffiths, J. (1999) *Crime, Deviance and Social Control*. London, Hodder and Stoughton.

Young, J. and Matthews, R. (1992) *Rethinking Criminology: The Realist Debate*. London, Sage.

Area 13

World Sociology

This area covers:

- The socio-political theories of development and underdevelopment
- The global interrelationships between societies: economic, cultural and political
- The nature of the aid relationship, trade relationships and international agencies
- A range of central problems in the Third World, in relation to health, urbanisation, education, employment and demographic change.

By the end of this area you should be able to:

- understand modernisation theory, neo-modernisation theory, dependency theory, globalisation, reflective modernisation, cultural and political globalisation
- understand the work of Anthony Giddens and a range of Marxist writers such as Wallerstein
- understand a range of global issues and problems.

Key terms

development
underdevelopment
modernisation
dependency
colonialism

imperialism
globalisation
aid
debt crisis
Third World

Area 13   Contents

Introduction

Global issues have a long history within sociology. For many centuries Europeans were responsible for terrible misdeeds against non-white populations. Even in this post-colonial world, where the First-World countries no longer directly administer Third-World countries, the racist ideologies that underpinned the often violent and ruthless colonial expansion often remain. Frequently such ideologies were spread globally by European traders and Christian missionaries who were motivated not by cruelty but by a desire to help civilise 'primitive' peoples in 'backward' parts of the world. Whatever the cause, colonialism often ended in slavery and the destruction of the highly developed cultures of non-European peoples. Marxist writers, in particular, have discussed the economic consequences of colonialism or imperialism. Since Lenin in 1916, Marxists have argued that the development of capitalism has been dependent upon the economic exploitation of the labour and natural resources of the **Third World**. In addition, the Third World is used as a marketplace.

In more recent years, sociologists have looked at the problems that governments face in attempting to regulate their own economies. The political and economic structures that governments have used to control what goes on within their borders appear to be becoming increasingly irrelevant as a consequence of processes of globalisation.

The 'modern world', which was so fully and clearly described by Marx, Weber, Parsons and others, appears to be giving way to other forms of societal formation. Giddens and Beck talk about the formation of 'risk societies' and forms of 'reflexive modernisation'. Other writers view the contemporary world as a postmodern condition.

In this area we will look at the transformation of a traditional society into a modern society, which, according to Talcott Parsons and W.W. Rostow, is a process of modernisation. We shall compare these modernisation theories with the contribution of Marxist writers, who look at the world in terms of economic dependency. The contribution of these theorists to a range of global problems will be assessed. In addition, we shall look at the political, economic and cultural process of globalisation and examine critically the contributions of David Held, Roland Robertson,

Anthony Giddens, Francis Fukuyama, Samuel Huntington, Immanuel Wallerstein, David Harvey and other Marxist writers to the debates about globalisation. Finally, we shall look at the contribution of postmodernist writers to the issues of international relations and the often complex relationship between globalisation and postmodernity.

Modernisation theory

Modernisation theory is about the formation of the modern industrial society. For many sociologists the development of modern societies from traditional societies means progress, and this progress is brought about by industrialisation, urbanisation, bureaucratisation, rationalisation, the spread of capitalism, the spread of individualism and science.

This approach is adopted by a range of theories: modernisation theory, convergence theory, theories of the transition of the former Communist societies and other forms of neo-modernisation theories.

Most modernisation theorists assume that:

■ social change is along a single path which all societies follow, with the USA and western Europe seen as 'model countries' or 'reference societies'

■ social change is irreversible

■ social change is gradual and peaceful

■ social change is incremental, through a number of clearly defined stages

■ social change is evolutionary

■ social change is both progressive and beneficial

■ modernisation brings about tendencies towards convergence between societies

However, there is no agreement as to what constitutes progress. In the 1960s W.W. Rostow and Talcott Parsons assumed that progress was economic in nature. For these theorists, modernisation referred to the attempts of less developed countries to catch up with the USA. This transformation of a traditional society into a modern society is referred to as the process of **modernisation**, but it could easily be referred to as a process of Americanisation.

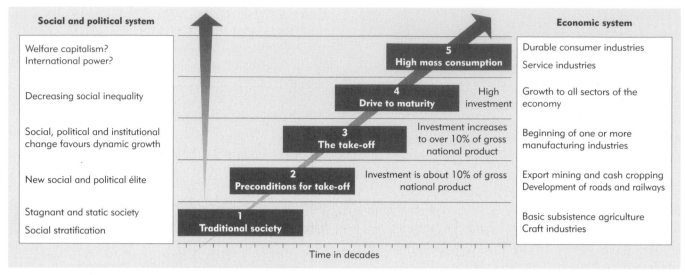

Figure 13.1   Rostow's stages of economic growth towards modernisation

Rostow: the five stages of economic growth towards modernisation

One of the most influential modernisation theorists is W.W. Rostow. He argues that all societies will be gradually transformed into modern industrial societies similar to western Europe and the USA. Figure 13.1 (from Cockerham 1995) summarises the argument. All countries go through five stages, from the traditional stage through to the **mature industrial stage** of high mass consumption.

Parsons: the functionalist approach to modernisation

As a functionalist, Parsons believed that the social system had to overcome four basic problems:

1 **Adaptation**, which was dealt with by the economy.
2 **Goal attainment**, which was dealt with by the political system.
3 **Pattern maintenance/tension management**, which was dealt with by the family.
4 **Integration**, which was dealt with by a range of cultural organisations such as schools and the media.

The social system was made up of individual people interacting with each other within institutions, and

these institutions performed functions both for individuals and for the social system itself. Underpinning the social system was a **common value system**. In a simple society Parsons describes the common value system as characterised by Pattern Variables A, whilst in a complex society the common value system is characterised by Pattern Variables B. The process of modernisation is the transition from Pattern Variables A to Pattern Variables B: in other words, from a simple/traditional society to a complex industrial society (see Cuff, E. et al. (1998) for a fuller picture). This was not an easy task for Parsons, because in the eyes of many people he had 'oversolved the problem of order' within the social system. This means that Parsons found it difficult to explain why a social system should change when everyone had a function, every function had a purpose, and all the people were socialised into a common value system. Why should such a society change?

In 1951, when Parsons published *The Social System* he clearly stated that he had no theory of social change:

> ... *a general theory of the processes of change of social systems is not possible in the present state of knowledge ... We do not have a complete theory of the processes of change in social systems .. when such a theory is available the millennium of social science will have arrived. This will not come in our time and most probably never.*

(Parsons, 1951:486)

Similar themes were taken up by Martin Lipset, with his notion of political man, and Daniel Bell with his end of ideology thesis. The assumption was that the USA had solved all the major problems of any social system, so no social change was needed. However, by the 1960s a whole range of groups was demanding change, not just in the USA but across the world: feminists, black civil rights activists, gay liberation activists, the peace movement and many more. This change had to be explained by sociologists.

Parsons makes his most clear and straightforward analysis of social change in his book *Societies: Evolutionary and Comparative Perspectives* (1970). For Parsons there were two overlapping types of social change:

1 **Structural differentiation**   Institutional change within the social system, usually involving institutions swapping functions. For example, the family losing its economic functions to the economy or its educational functions to the education system.
2 **Long-term evolution**   Movement of the social system along a long-term evolutionary path.

Structural differentiation was brought about by growing dissatisfaction with the outcomes of the social system and, at the same time, a growing realisation by some individuals that things could be done differently. As Parsons explains, this pressure to bring about change from within the social system had two principal sources:

- cultural sources of change
- motivational sources of change

These two factors generated 'strains' within the social system. Neil Smelser carried out a case study of the emergence of the cotton industry in Lancashire, making use of the Parsonian notion of structural differentiation. According to Smelser (1959), after the initial dissatisfaction with some aspects of the social system, the 'mechanisms of change and adjustment to change' proceeded thus:

- symptoms of disturbance such as negative emotional reaction
- covert attempts to handle the tensions
- tolerance of the new ideas in certain important groups

- positive attempts to translate the new ideas into concrete efforts at making profit
- implementation of the innovations
- adopting the innovation into society

According to Parsons, all social systems are on a long-term evolutionary path. Three basic assumptions underpin this movement of the social system along its evolutionary part: **differentiation**, **reintegration** and **adaptation**. Differentiation is the motor of social change for Parsons. It involves the establishment of more specialised and more independent units in social life. Smelser defines differentiation as a process in which one or more roles or organisations replace less well functioning roles or organisations. The new social units are structurally distinct, but taken together are functionally equivalent to the original unit.

More generally, Smelser describes the process of modernisation as multi-dimensional in nature. At the economic level modernisation

- is built upon scientific knowledge
- involves the change from subsistence farming to commercial farming
- replaces animal and human power with machines
- is the spread of urbanisation
- concentrates the industrial workforce in towns and cities

At the non-economic levels modernisation involves

- passing from tribal systems to democratic systems
- the development of education systems to provide training
- diminished religion and growing secularisation
- a shift from the extended family to the nuclear family
- greater social mobility, with class position based upon achievement

A number of theorists, for example Alex Inkeles (1976), have suggested that modernisation involves changes at a psychological level, with the emergence of a distinctly 'modern' personality that includes:

- refusal to accept dogmatic thinking
- consideration of public issues
- openness to new experiences

- conviction that science and reason are superior to emotion
- deferred gratification – recognising the value of saving up 'for a rainy day'
- high aspirations

This conception of the modern self, with its distinct personality traits, is very different from the self in pre-modern societies.

Critiques of modernisation theory

According to Piotr Sztompka (1993) there are many criticisms of modernisation theory:

- At an empirical level modernisation did not produce the results that the theory promised: poverty often persisted, as did dictatorial regimes. Modernisation also generated social disorganisation, deviance and delinquency.

- At a theoretical level the evolutionist assumptions were unacceptable: notably, the assumption of one single track of development. Instead of one development path there appeared to be several.

- The notion of regular stages of development is questionable.

- Finally, the goals of modernisation theory, that all societies have the goal of becoming like the USA, is seen as ethnocentric in nature.

Modernisation theories were often consistent with foreign policy initiatives of many industrial nations, notably in relation to aid. However, modernisation assumes that all technological advances are good for the nations concerned. The theory also does not take into account the unique history and culture of countries and how they may affect future development. Finally, many of the problems of the poorer countries cannot be solved by industrialisation alone.

ACTIVITY KS COMMUNICATION, PROBLEM SOLVING

IDENTIFICATION AND INTERPRETATION	ANALYSIS AND EVALUATION

List the criticisms of modernisation theory, together with a brief evaluative comment explaining if you agree with each point.

Convergence theory

Convergence theory is based upon the assumption that all societies are moving towards an industrial society, with very similar industrial organisation, economic organisation, political organisations and cultures. According to Raymond Aron (1967), an industrial society has five defining features:

1 The economy is separate from the family.
2 There is a technological division of labour within companies.
3 There is capital accumulation.
4 There is widespread acceptance of rationality.
5 Work is concentrated in designated workplaces.

The convergence is brought about by the demands the technology makes upon relations within industry, culture and the wider economy. Technological determinism is found within all convergence theories. The clearest statement of the convergence thesis is found in Kerr et al. (1960). All industrial systems are complex; they need high levels of investment in modern plant and machinery. In addition, they need highly skilled and motivated workforces trained to a high level. The workforce needs to be both geographically and socially mobile, living in urban centres which have to be administered by political agencies. There needs to be a work ethic which is accepted by all the people within the population. Because products need to be exported, communication systems need to be highly developed and as a consequence close links develop between countries. Cultural differences diminish between countries and a similar culture develops across the world.

Arnold S. Feldman and Wilbert E. Moore argue that industrial societies share a core set of social structures: factory system, stratification system (based upon specialisation in areas of different skills), commercialisation of goods and services, market systems, education systems that provide individuals with the skills to play a full and active role in the labour market.

However, there are three principal sources of variability, claim Feldman and Moore:

- The character of the pre-industrial social structure will help to shape the industrial society. Japan and

Russia have very different social structures because they have very different histories.

- The route or trajectory of industrialisation: different societies choose very different goals for their industrialisation process. Different societies want different things from industrialisation.

- The structure of industrial societies can be 'loose' or 'extensive'. This means that, despite the similarities, industrial societies have many differences.

Feldman and Moore argue that industrialisation is a single evolutionary process, but that there is 'selective retention'. This means that some aspects of the industrialisation process are accepted as valuable whereas other aspects are seen as having little desirability and are removed. The notion of complete convergence, for Feldman and Moore, is based upon three mistaken assumptions:

- In contrast to the view of convergence theorists, there is no stable and enduring terminus for the industrialisation process.

- The functional interdependence of social systems with convergence theory has been exaggerated.

- Industrialisation in itself causes **disequilibrium** within the social systems. In other words, the industrialisation process brings problems with it, but social systems deal with these problems in very different ways.

In the industrialisation of the USA, one of the problems was the lack of labour power. This was partly overcome by the use of slavery and a policy of encouraging immigration. In later years these policies caused racial conflict. In contrast, Russia had the problem of an agricultural population that was unwilling to participate in industrialisation. The solution to this was the forced collectivisation of farms and conscription of the labour force into factories.

Japanisation

Tim Leggatt (1985) argues that both Russia and Japan industrialised in the twentieth century. In addition, both were deliberate followers of the first industrialising

nations. However, each society found its own path to, and form of, industrial evolution distinct from that of the first industrial nations. The conclusion from this is that 'modernisation' may be an abstract and universal process but takes a variety of forms depending on the conditions.

Between November 1871 and September 1873, the Meiji government of Japan had a diplomatic team travelling around Europe and North America looking at all aspects of industrial societies to obtain advice on the path the Japanese should take in their modernisation. The report of the Iwakura Mission was published in 1878 under the title *Tokumei zsenken taishi Bei-O Kairan jikki* (*Journal of the Envoy Extraordinary Ambassador Plenipotentiary's Travels through America and Europe*), commonly known as the Jikki.

The Meiji government wanted a planned process of modernisation based upon what it found from the mission's observations of industrialisation in other parts of the world. The Jikki suggested that there should be selectivity in adopting western techniques and institutions. In essence what the Jikki suggested was that Japan should adopt western technology but not western values. The belief was not simply that Japanese culture and values were superior, but that major changes to traditional cultural patterns could result in social disorder. Chic Nakane (1985:15) says modernisation is a universal process, but cultural features of the society are independent from the modernising process:

> *Japanese working in all types of organisation are significantly different from their counterparts in the West and have not essentially changed since the Meiji period.*

Kozai points out the possible development paths faced by the Japanese at the end of the nineteenth century. Wakon is the 'spiritual power' or 'ideological core' of a people, yosai is the rational technology of the west. Japanisation is the combination of western technology with traditional Japanese culture and beliefs. Wakon is not anti-modern and yosai is not peculiar to the west. This is contrary to the modernisation theory of Parsons and Rostow, which suggests that traditional cultures are a brake on the modernisation process.

What is the traditional Japanese culture? Ruth Benedict (1946) claims that dominant cultural patterns are to be found in all regions and amongst all classes in Japanese society. Her book is called *The Chrysanthemum and the Sword*: the 'sword' symbolises Japanese militarism, the 'chrysanthemum' the culture of Japan. Japanese culture is thus a mixture of primitive militarism, which can produce violent forms of ultra-nationalism, and of aesthetic sensitivity – appreciation of things of great beauty.

> **ACTIVITY** **KS COMMUNICATION, PROBLEM SOLVING**
>
> | IDENTIFICATION AND INTERPRETATION | ANALYSIS AND EVALUATION |
> |---|---|
>
> In what sense does 'Japanisation' differ from the predictions of convergence theorists? Your answer should be both evaluative and interpretative in nature and will be in a form which can be used in an evaluation of convergence theory.

Neo-modernisation theory

After the collapse of the communist regimes across eastern Europe modernisation theories found a new focal point: the efforts of former communist countries to become capitalist countries. Sztompka (1993) argues that there are significant differences between the modernising processes in the Third World and those that are taking place in eastern Europe. Post-colonial societies were often starting from a traditional social formation, whereas post-communist societies had had a form of modernity imposed upon them by the former communist leaders. The communist societies experienced a form of flawed modernity, which has left the post-communist societies with many unwanted side-effects, such as environmental problems. In addition, the absence of private ownership and a functioning market system may hinder the modernisation process.

Neo-modernisation theory, as presented in the work of Eisenstadt (1992), Tiryakian (1985), Dahrendorf (1990), Etzioni (1991) and Sztompka (1991, 1992), is built upon a very different set of assumptions from that of Parsons, Smelser and Rostow. Neo-modernisation theory assumes that the driving force behind the process of

modernisation is the aspirations of ordinary people through spontaneous social movements. Modernisation needs a plentiful supply of convincing ideological resources. Modernisation is not a uniform process: there are several development paths, none of which is in itself better or worse than any other. The process is not solely economic in nature but is concerned with human values and aspirations. Neo-modernisation theory is not totally hostile to the place of tradition in social development: modernisation can make use of traditions within the society to bring about modernisation. The modern self or **modern personality** is not always regarded as a positive outcome. Neo-modernisation theory has no place for the evolutionary assumptions of the early modernisation theory of Parsons.

Marxist approaches

Dependency theory, which is Marxist in nature, suggests that the First World was undeveloped but never *under*developed. The First World keeps the Third World poor by exercising monopoly over world markets. There is an unequal exchange between the two worlds. Capitalist countries continue to exploit the labour and resources of the Third World.

Andre Gunder-Frank

Gunder-Frank (1969) argued that the modern world is dominated by capitalism and that within that global capitalist system there was a 'chain of dependency', between what he termed 'metropoles' and dependent 'satellites'. The USA and multi-national corporations based mainly in the USA were causing a permanent and irreversible process of underdevelopment. This underdevelopment was caused by the continual exploitation of Third-World resources. Therefore, the development of the First World and the underdevelopment of the Third World are outcomes of the same process. The Third World supplied raw materials to the developed world at very low prices and in return imported expensive manufactured goods.

This unequal exchange was possible because the First World was said to control world markets. Poverty and dependency were the inevitable outcome of this historical process. In Marxist terms, surplus value created in the Third World passed along the chain to the First World. Moreover, this 'chain of dependency' was supported by the political leaders in the Third World because they were co-opted into the service of the First World.

The incorporation of the Third World into the capitalist **chain of dependency** determined

- the shape and structure of social class and other economic structures
- the urban structures
- the structure of trade and investment

Gunder-Frank considered that the only group who could break the chain of dependency are the poor Third-World underclass.

This account is now considered to be both crude and inaccurate for several reasons.

- Gunder-Frank made little or no use of key Marxist concepts, the relationship between the First World and the Third World being one of unequal exchange in the world market rather than exploitation as explained by Marxists with the labour theory of value. If Frank had made use of the Marxist concept of exploitation, he would have had to explain how a surplus was created in the Third World for the First World to exploit.

- Gunder-Frank assumes that involvement in the world market made Latin America, for example, impoverished. In some cases this was true – Furtado gives the example of the Bolivian tin industry, which employed few miners and had no local processing plants. However, in many cases (Argentina, Uruguay and Colombia) British capital was used to build an infrastructure of railways which encouraged industrial development. Gunder-Frank cannot account for the range of development in the Third World, why some countries are getting poorer and others experience development. In some cases it is clear that global economic interconnections bring about significant economic development, as in the case of the Asian 'tiger'

economies Taiwan, South Korea, Singapore, Hong Kong.

Perhaps the clearest of these Marxist world system approaches, and certainly the most theoretically comprehensive approach, which rejects the idea of the unified nation state as a key factor in a global system of nation states, is that of Immanuel Wallerstein. Wallerstein (1979) argues that capitalism was never confined by national boundaries, it created a new world order with global interconnections which spread across the planet. He made a distinction between two types of world system:

- **World empires** – historical political units which colonised areas of the world by military means and imposed a rigid bureaucracy to extract taxes from local people. These empires were displaced by world economies that are much more flexible.
- **World economies** – this system is capitalistic in nature and based upon capital accumulation. The world economy is neo-colonial in nature, and is largely free from any influence of nation states.

In Wallerstein's view the modern world system is 'a single division of labour comprising multiple cultural systems, multiple political entities and even different modes of surplus appropriation' (Wallerstein, 1980:5) and is divided into three components:

1 **The core** – initially northern Europe and North America. This was the home of transnational corporations (TNCs), which dominated the global economy and exploited the world's population in their own interests.

2 **The semi-periphery** – initially the Mediterranean and eastern Europe. These were countries which did face exploitation from the core but had some capital that was not directly under the control of TNCs. This is a go-between between core and periphery.

3 **The periphery** – colonised and former colonised countries which are now clearly within neo-colonial economic relationships.

The transfer of surplus value from periphery to core can be achieved in two different ways, political or economic.

The political/economic arrangements within the world system are described by Ankie Hoogvelt (1982:192):

> *... the global distribution of wealth and poverty is seen as a result of market forces reinforcing an accident of history which gave a headstart to the European nations. But there is also political interference in the market. While the single world market rewards some activities and penalises others, the actors can and do interfere with the operation of the world market by appealing to their nation-states to interfere on their behalf. And once we get a difference in strength of the state machineries, we get the operation of unequal exchange imposed by strong states on weak ones in peripheral areas – by core areas on peripheral areas. In this way capitalism involves not only appropriation of the surplus value by an owner from a labourer but an appropriation of the whole world economy by core areas.*

In other words, the capitalist economy has built a global division of labour which is neo-colonial in nature. Moreover, all power and wealth is transferred to the core of the world system and the periphery and semi-periphery are left to be relatively poor and powerless.

Wallerstein's world system theory has been criticised by Anthony Giddens (1985), who explains that the appeal of Wallerstein's work is that he does not look upon nation states as isolated or solitary individual entities, but as part of a global structure which was brought about by the global spread of capitalism. However, Wallerstein's understanding of capitalism is questionable. His conception of capitalism is one of unequal exchange within a market rather than stressing exploitation via the labour theory of value. In other words, Wallerstein's view of capitalism is closer to Weber than to Marx.

In addition, for Wallerstein the existence of semi-peripheral regions is explained by the 'needs' of the world system. He assumes that the world system has 'agency' in the same fashion as individuals do – they do not. Wallerstein's account is both **functional** and **economically reductionist** in nature. In other words, the existence of the semi-periphery is explained by its functional necessity for the whole system, while the existence of the whole system explains the need for the semi-periphery.

Wallerstein also assumes that states have no sources of power to draw upon other than economic power.

He thus had difficulty in dealing with the former Soviet Union, which had to operate with a global economy dominated by capitalist institutions yet was militarily a superpower, which clearly meant that it was in a position to manipulate the world system. In general, it would be wrong to assume that nations outside the core are powerless, simply because of the lack of economic development; as was seen in the events leading up to the Gulf War, economically less developed nations can have a significance in the world.

Malcolm Waters (1995) also provides an informed evaluation of Wallerstein's analysis. Business, argues Waters, can unite geographically scattered producers and consumers. Capitalism is therefore economically globalising in nature. However, the declining contribution of world trade from Europe and the USA moved the dependency relationship in the direction of greater harmony or balance after 1945. Three recent globalising trends have challenged the validity of Walerstein's division of the world into core, semi-peripheral and peripheral societies.

- A number of less developed countries have become newly industrialising countries: Wallerstein would find it difficult to account for such development. Singapore, South Korea, Taiwan, Malaysia and Thailand are all examples.

- Some multi-national corporations have located production within less developed countries, which has brought about economic development.

- Taking their lead from OPEC, several less developed countries have managed to form cartels, which have given them the power to push up the price of their products on world markets.

Globalisation

Globalisation is the idea that the world is becoming a single place. As a process, globalisation directly affects the lives of all the people. Drugs, sex tourism, the nature of the work we do, eating disorders, plastic surgery, and more, all have a global dimension to them. As Roland Robertson (1994:8) has made clear:

> *The fact and the perception of ever increasing inter-dependence at the global level, the rising concern about the fate of the world as a whole and of the human species (particularly because of the threats of ecological degradation, nuclear disaster and AIDS), and the colonisation of the local by global life (not least via the mass media) facilitate massive processes of relativization of cultures, doctrines, ideologies and cognitive frames of reference.*

What Robertson means by this is that the world is becoming more connected, but at the same time we as individuals are becoming more concerned about the future of the human race. In addition, the global mass media are destroying local cultures to such a degree that people across the world are beginning to think in very similar ways.

In 1993 Leslie Sklair outlined and evaluated a number of different models of globalisation.

- Firstly, Sklair looks at Wallerstein's world system model which, as we have seen, is Marxian in orientation. In this model there is an international division of labour within the world economy. A nation's economy is linked in a number of ways to the international economy and can be at the core, semi-periphery or periphery. Nations at the periphery are much more likely to be in poverty. However, this model is said to be too determined by economic factors and ignores cultural factors.

- The second model Sklair evaluates is one of 'cultural imperialism', in which local or traditional cultures are destroyed by the cultural products of multi-national corporations in the advanced countries. Ulf Hannerz outlines a number of possible types of cultural unification, one of which is **global homogenisation** – this suggests complete domination in the world by 'lowbrow' western lifestyles, western products in the shops, western cars in the streets, western films at the cinema, western soaps on television, etc. This spread promotes *Dynasty* rather than Shakespeare.

- The third model is Sklair's own model, which is that the global system is built upon transnational practices. These practices are formed by transnational corporations and allow economic, political and cultural or ideological practices, such as consumerism, to travel across state borders.

According to David Held, governments find it difficult to regulate their own economies as global financial dealings can diminish the worth of a country's money. Environmental issues cross national boundaries. Although transnational governmental organisations like the United Nations, European Union, NATO and the WTO have expanded their influence in the world, bringing people together from diverse cultures can still increase the chances of conflict. Globalisation can diminish what were commonly accepted political and economic structures without inevitably leading to the foundation of new systems, which are clearly needed.

Globalisation can then generate nationalist conflict in the world, because political decisions are no longer taken by governments within nation states. In addition, as a process globalisation can destroy a person's cultural identity and force people to fight to protect their local ways of living. Although there is no one acceptable definition of nationalism from this perspective it is a counter-politics of the local.

Giddens: the world order

According to Giddens there are two general theories about the nature of the world order. The first is Marxist in nature, where states are viewed as mechanisms of class domination. The creation of a capitalist economy was brought about by the use of force. The second is termed 'International Relations'. In this perspective states are viewed as social actors. Internal struggles within states are not regarded as significant. However, unlike in the Marxist analysis, the territorial character of states and their geopolitical involvement is given a high priority.

Giddens rejects both of these perspectives; in his view, the world system has been influenced by several primary sets of processes '... associated with the nation state system, co-ordinated through global networks of information exchange, the world capitalist economy and the world military order' (Giddens, 1985:290).

Nation states appear to be more like 'actors' because in the modern world they have become **bounded administrative unities**. All states negotiate with each other. However, the actor-like qualities of the modern nation state have to be explained by looking at the internal characteristics of states. The actor-like qualities of nation states cannot be treated as 'given'.

In *The Nation State and Violence* (1985) Giddens explains that both the traditional imperialist state – such as the Ottoman Empire – and tribal societies have either become assimilated into more global units or have disappeared altogether, because of two processes:

- the global incorporation of industrial capitalism
- the global domination of the nation state

Nation states contain the four institutional clusterings of modernity:

- industrialised economy
- capitalistic production
- political integration
- military rule

and the world system was characterised by Giddens by an approximate transfer of these four institutional clusterings of modernity to the global setting, in the following way:

Symbolic orders/modes of discourse	→	Global information system
Political institutions	→	Nation-state system
Economic institutions	→	World capitalist economy
Law/modes of sanction	→	World military order

Modernity, for Giddens, is essentially 'globalising' in nature and his 'dimensions of globalisation' are, as suggested above, drawn from his four institutional clusterings of modernity (capitalism, the inter-state system, militarism and industrialism). In terms of the nature of 'globalisation', Giddens (1994:5) explains:

> *Globalization is not a single process but a complex mixture of processes, which often act in contradictory ways, producing conflicts, disjunctions and new forms of stratification. Thus, for instance, the revival of local nationalisms, and an accentuating of local identities, are directly bound up with globalizing influences, to which they stand in opposition.*

In Giddens' view, globalisation is a multiplicity of linkages and interconnections that surpass or exceed the nation states. As a concept, globalisation explains a process by which incidents, opinions and actions in one part of the world can have both meaningful and important repercussions for individuals and communities in quite distant parts of the world. In *Reflexive Modernization*, Giddens expands this point (1994:57–58):

> *The day to day activities of an individual today are globally consequential. My decision to purchase a particular item of clothing, for example, or a specific type of foodstuff, has manifold global implications. It not only affects the livelihood of someone living on the other side of the world but may contribute to a process of ecological decay which itself has potential consequences for the whole of humanity. This extraordinary, and still accelerating, connectedness between everyday decisions and global outcomes, together with its reverse, the influence of global orders over individual life, forms the key subject matter of the new agenda. The connections involved are often very close. Intermediate collectivities and groupings of all sorts including the state, do not disappear as a result; but they do tend to become reorganized or reshaped.*

Globalisation then, involves more than 'a diffusion of western institutions across the world, in which other cultures are crushed'. It involves '... a process of uneven **development** that fragments as it coordinates' (Giddens, 1990:175). The major feature of globalisation for Giddens is the compression of the world; this is the profound reordering of time and space in social life, what Giddens terms **time–space distanciation**.

Roland Robertson: the world as a single place

Robertson is one of the key thinkers in this area. He argues that the processes of globalisation have a long history and that the history of the world can be viewed as string of **miniglobalisations**: early imperialism, the formation of great empires and the unification of confiscated territories. He traces the trail of the globalisation process through five stages:

- the germinal phase
- the incipient phase

- the take-off phase
- the struggle for hegemony phase
- the uncertainty phase

The first stage is European in origin and lasted from about 1400 to the mid-eighteenth century. It is associated with such diverse global developments as the expansion of the Catholic church and development of the Gregorian calendar. The final stage is from the 1960s, with its expansion in demands for civil rights across the world, the moon landing, global environmental concerns and attempts to resolve them by events such as the Earth Summit, the end of the Cold War and the dissolution of the Soviet Union (and the subsequent uncertainty and doubt).

Globalisation is thus associated with both modernisation and postmodernity; as a concept it explains how the modern world came into being and at the same time explains the 'great global uncertainty' which people have observed since the beginning of the 1990s and which is becoming 'globally institutionalised'. As Robertson explains: '... there is an eerie relationship between postmodern theories and the idea of postmodernity, on the one hand, and the geopolitical 'earthquakes' that we (the virtually *global we*) have recently experienced, on the other' (1994:50). In his view, the concept of globalisation is about developments which have brought about 'the concrete structuration of the world as a whole' (1994:53) The notion of **structuration** was developed by Anthony Giddens and suggests that individual people (human agents) have the skills and ability to create structures which constrain their future behaviour. However, Robertson argues that Giddens' notion of structuration is shut into a 'quasi-philosophical context'. Structuration has to be moved out of the quasi-philosophical context:

> *It has to be made directly relevant to the world in which we live. It has to contribute to the understanding of how the global 'system' continues to be made. It has to be focused on the production and reproduction of 'the world' as the most salient plausibility structure of our time.*

(Robertson, 1994:53)

Robertson attempts to provide concrete examples of how Giddens' theory works in everyday life, to explain how the global system was made through a process of structuration. He attempts to identify the factors which have helped to bring about the structuration of the world global system:

> *More precisely, I argue that systematic comprehension of the structuration of world order is essential to the viability of any form of contemporary theory and that such comprehension must involve analytical separation of the factors that have facilitated the shift towards a single world – for example the spread of capitalism, Western imperialism and the development of a global media system – from the general and global agency-structure (and/or culture) theme. While the empirical relationship between the two sets of issues is of great importance (and, of course, complex), conflation of them leads us into all sorts of difficulties and inhibits our ability to come to terms with the basic but shifting terms of the contemporary world order, including the 'structure' of 'disorderliness'.*

(Robertson, 1994:55)

In other words, any valid social theory has to identify those factors which have made the world into a single place. These factors include the spread of capitalism or western imperialism, global media systems, individual human agents and the structures that we humans create, including the 'disorderliness' that we create yet find difficult to come to terms with. In Robertson's view, our conception of 'world politics' needs to take into account the 'meaning' of the 'global-human condition as a whole' – which he terms 'the new world order'. His belief is that issues of globality may form the basis of significant political, economic and military divisions in the twenty-first century. The once taken-for-granted boundary between the local and the global is not now so easy to distinguish, because in Robertson's view we have experienced the 'global institutionalisation of the life-world and the localisation of globality'. In other words, the world of everyday life (life-world) has a global feel to it: individuals have similar experiences in their local communities wherever they live in the world and at the same time issues and problems on the other side of the world feel no more distant than local events.

Waters explains that Robertson's conception of globalisation is built upon the 'establishment of cultural, social and phenomenological linkages between four elements' (1995:42):

- the individual human agent (self)
- the national society
- the international system of societies
- humanity in general

These four factors come together to create the global system. Waters explains the relationship between these four elements in the following way (1995:43):

> - *The individual self (1) is defined as a citizen of a national society (2), by comparison with developments in other societies (3), and as an instance of humanity (4).*
>
> - *A national society (2) stands in a problematical relationship to its citizens (1) in terms of freedom and control, views itself to be a member of a community of nations (3), and must provide citizenship rights that are referenced against general human rights (4).*
>
> - *The international system (3) depends on the surrender of sovereignty by national societies (2), sets standards for individual behaviour (1), and provides 'reality checks' on human aspirations (4).*
>
> - *Humanity (4) is defined in terms of individual rights (1) that are expressed in the citizenship provisions of the national societies (2) which are legitimated and enforced through the international system of societies (3).*

ACTIVITY KS **COMMUNICATION, PROBLEM SOLVING**

IDENTIFICATION AND
INTERPRETATION

- Take a look at the four points above and rewrite them in your own words.

ACTIVITY

IDENTIFICATION AND | ANALYSIS AND
INTERPRETATION | EVALUATION

Give a brief outline of what you consider to be the main points of the two concepts:

- Globalisation
- Postmodernism

David Held: globalisation and international governance

As political, social and economic action becomes global in breadth and there are much higher levels of interconnectedness between states, 'governance' may be now outside the reach of the modern nation state. International bodies diminish the scope of a nation state to govern its citizens. However, apparently, nation states still wish to join international bodies, rather than be isolated in the world. Early in 1995 Canada held a referendum on the future of Quebec, to decide if the area should become an independent French-speaking nation. French President Jacques Chirac said that France would recognise the new country if there was a 'yes' vote; however, as *The Independent* made clear:

> *For an independent Quebec, French recognition would have an important moral impact. But the separatists' first priority for formal recognition is the US. It will also be crucial for Quebec's industries to gain access to the North American Free Trade Agreement, an admission that the US and Canadian governments have said will not be automatic. Quebec has also said it will apply to the World Trade Organisation and that it would like to become a partner in both NATO and NORAD, the North American Air Defence pact.*

For Held, effective sovereignty is dependent upon the economic resources available to the nation state, yet economic globalisation has not been a uniform process across the globe. Some nation states have become economically powerful, and this gives them a greater say in the running of international bodies. The international bodies discussed above are not democratic in nature and they follow the interests of the economically powerful nations. Hence, globalisation can bring with it both fragmentation as well as integration. In Held's view it is essential to recognise three elements of globalisation:

KS **WORKING WITH OTHERS, COMMUNICATION, PROBLEM SOLVING**

These two concepts will allow you to make a range of evaluative points about most sociological theories of development, in the sense that both concepts undermine many of the key assumptions of both 'modernisation theory' as outlined by Parsons and Rostow and Marxist dependency theory.

- Economic, political, legal and military interconnectedness are changing the nation state from 'above'.

- New social movements and nationalist groups are questioning the credibility of the nation state from 'below'.

- Global bodies generate new relations between states and their citizens, as states have to take into account responses from international bodies when dealing with their citizens.

What Held suggests is a new 'cosmopolitan order'. This involves moving away from the idea that the nation state has sole jurisdiction over its territory and community. New bodies and new international relationships would have to be developed to provide a democratisation of the new international order. This involves:

- More democratic control over international bodies concerned with environmental, economic and security matters.

- Regional parliaments – for Africa, Latin America and a reformed European Parliament.

- A reformed UN, with an 'authoritative assembly' which will provide entrenched political, social and economic rights. This reformed UN will also provide accountability and regulation in national and international concerns.

Similar sentiments have been raised by journalist Michael Sheridan, who suggested:

> *The most important problem is the lack of a global public opinion before which international agencies may stand accountable. Part of the way forward may be for the national parliaments of the world's leading nations to set up scrutiny committees to review the work of all the international institutions of governance. Just as the EU has been kept, in some measure, on its toes by the European legislation committees of the national parliaments, so global bodies could be made subject to some measure of national political discipline.*
>
> *Until the international 'great and the good' feel that they are being closely watched by a lively political community, they will be tempted to take advantage of our lack of vigilance.*

(*The Independent* 11 May 1995)

Some key global issues

Health

Although cities in the Third World directly affect the health of the population by damaging the environment with pollution, within cities many traditional risks to health are reduced. Many modernisation theorists would suggest that economic development has brought with it a dramatic net increase in health when measured by indicators such as improved infant mortality and improved life expectancy.

However, many communicable diseases are still major killers in the Third World because of environmental factors such as poor water, air and food quality. Airborne diseases include tuberculosis, meningitis and whooping cough. Other diseases can be transmitted in human faeces (polio, hookworm and hepatitis). Some diseases are communicable by human contact – for example AIDS, leprosy and sexually transmitted diseases.

Water is often the key factor in many Third-World diseases. The World Health Organisation estimates that over 70% of hospital beds in the Third World are taken by people who are victims of waterborne diseases. Partly this is because sewage is given very little treatment before discharge into waterways. Solid wastes dumped into disposal sites can pollute groundwater that is used for drinking. In addition, as the WHO survey of 151 countries in 1988 suggests, only two-thirds of people in urban areas in the Third World had any form of sanitation service; the other third had to dispose of waste by their own means. Urbanisation often results in overpumping of ground water, which lowers water tables and increases the chance of encroachment and contamination.

Critics of modernisation theory would argue that increases in the number of hospital beds would do nothing to prevent these diseases, and little to cure people who have them, because western-style hospitals in the Third-World cities cater for the needs of affluent people. Such curative types of medicine provide little for the poor within the urban environment.

Education and employment

Third-World economies do not have large industrial sectors and many of the problems in Third-World cities are caused by the lack of well paid work. Many people in the Third World work in what is referred to as the informal sector: in domestic service, selling newspapers, drug dealing, cleaning shoes, prostitution and collecting rubbish for recycling. As Aidan Foster-Carter (1985) explains:

> The informal sector is characterised by ease of entry, indigenous resources, family ownership, small-scale, labour-intensive or adapted technology, skills acquired outside the formal school system, and unregulated and often highly competitive markets.

The formal sector is the opposite: difficult to enter, owned by large companies, capital-intensive, etc. However, we have to make clear that not all jobs in the informal sector are low-paid; in both sectors, people work long hours and working conditions are often dangerous. We also have to take into account that much work may be subcontracted from the formal to the informal sector.

The existence of the informal sector makes it difficult to measure the level of unemployment in the Third World. However, underemployment is described by Randinelli and Kasanda (1993) as 'an even more serious problem'; they estimate that up to 40% of the urban workforce in Third-World cities are underemployed. According to Gilbert and Guyler (1987), underemployment has three forms:

- Work is related to fluctuations in economic activity (i.e. seasonal work).

- There are so many workers in one type of occupation that a reduction in the number would not affect output (i.e. street vendors).

- 'Hidden unemployment', usually found in family firms where people are kept in employment, but with little to do.

Bienefield (1994) suggests that the economy of the Third-World city is like the feudal city of medieval Europe with its large number of pedlars, beggars, jugglers and thieves.

In First-World countries rates of unemployment are highest amongst people who lack education and skills, and entry into the formal sector is usually through the education system. There is a number of studies which suggest that this is also true in the Third World – for example, Smith and Cheung (1986) in their study of the Philippines and Wolpert's (1991) study of India. For these reasons demand in most Third-World countries for education is high.

For modernisation theory, modern education systems in the Third World are one of the most important factors in the process of development, as education improves the 'human capital' within the country. In contrast, dependency theory argues that western-style education systems in the Third World cause both economic and cultural damage. They are expensive to run and provide academic education for a minority of the population which, according to Frantz Fanon (1967), produces a **colonised personality** – individuals who are culturally dependent upon the west.

The environment

The physical environment is a key factor in the quality of life of all people in the world and it includes such things as the houses we live in, the air we breathe, the public services we use and the dangers we face in our everyday lives.

Air pollution is a major difficulty that people in a number of Third-World cities have to cope with. In Mexico City air pollution levels are said to be six times above WHO-defined agreeable levels while in Manila air pollution is three to four times above. Even in cities without large industrial sectors, like Caracas or Sao Paulo, air quality is poor because of vehicle emissions. In many Chinese cities air quality is poor because coal is used to heat homes: in Shanghai the smog is known by local people as the 'Yellow Dragon'.

Water is also heavily polluted in many Third-World cities, often because of inadequate sewerage systems. The Huangpu River in Shanghai, the Han River in Seoul and the Bogotá River in Colombia all have mostly untreated sewage deposited in them. In addition, drinking water is often expensive. Water from tankers in Port-au-Prince costs about 15% of a poor family's monthly income. If there is a street tap nearby, all water has to be collected and carried, mostly by women. Finally, if a family has no piped water it is much more likely to make use of polluted supplies.

Housing is expensive. Even for people who live in shanty towns, or spontaneous settlements, on the fringe of a city, building materials are expensive and their homes are often pulled down by landowners. Such settlements have limited access to public services, a greater chance of disease outbreaks and a greater risk of industrial injury – remember, for example, the explosion and gas escape from the Union Carbide pesticide plant at Bhopal, India.

Within rural areas desertification has been recognised as a major environmental issue. As Smith (1991) explains, as long ago as the 1930s the vegetation in many areas of West Africa was deteriorating: this became known as the 'advance of the Sahara'. As Smith stresses (1991:77), this is not due solely to changes in climate but also to changes in agricultural techniques and overgrazing:

> Problems of desertification are widespread, and principally result from farmers pushing into lands where rainfall is too low for crop cultivation without irrigation. Environmental refugees, the result of deterioration of agricultural land caused by unsustainable methods, now form the largest class of refugees in the world, estimated at over 10 million.

Smith estimates, for example, that:

- 61% of India's cultivated land is experiencing land degradation including the build-up of salts in the soil water – **salinisation**.

- 80% of the grass and crop areas of Madagascar have falling productivity because new soil is not formed as quickly as the old soil is lost – **soil erosion**.

- 50% of the agricultural land in Australia is being degraded, often as a result of the build-up of metals (magnesium, potassium and sodium) in the soil – **soil alkalinity**.

Even in the USA most farmers cannot afford to resolve these problems, and many conclude that traditional farming techniques gave better protection to the soil.

Urbanisation

Urbanisation refers to the tendency of people to move from rural areas into cities. The United Nations assessment of urbanisation trends (UNDIESA, 1991) shows that between 1970 and 1990 the estimated number of city dwellers in the Third World more than doubled, from 675 million to 1.5 billion. Today more than one in three people in the Third World lives in a city. According to modernisation theory, urbanisation is part of an evolutionary global process of modernisation which is the same across the world. However, contrary to what modernisation theory would suggest, rates of urbanisation in the Third World in the 1990s were faster than they ever were in the First World. In addition, this urbanisation often takes place without meaningful industrialisation.

Some factors 'push' people from rural to urban areas:

- rural population increase
- unemployment
- low wages

Other factors 'pull' people from rural to urban areas:

- high wages
- employment prospects
- amenities

A.S. Oberai has cast doubt upon rural population increase as a significant factor in the growth of third world cities (1993:63):

> Rapid population growth was once considered a major cause of rural–urban migration, with rural poverty caused by excess labour supply providing a 'push' to the cities (e.g. Lewis 1970). But rural out-migration now seems less strongly associated with rural population increase than with overall economic growth, changes in agricultural productivity, and land tenure systems that promote marked inequalities in landholdings and landlessness.

The nature of rural–urban migration differs between countries. In Central America most migrants make a permanent move to the city and never return to their rural homes (this was also the case in what were to become First-World countries). In Africa and South East Asia most rural–urban migration is of a temporary nature.

However, it has been suggested that poor rural conditions are the key factor in migration trends. Third-World cities offer their residents a better quality of life than is usually available in the rural areas. For example, in India in the 1980s infant mortality rates were 50%

higher in rural areas; in Indonesia almost 50% of rural families were in poverty whereas in urban areas the figure was 20%; in Brazil over 40% of rural families were in poverty whereas for urban families the figure was less than 25%. Moreover, urban populations are more likely to own a refrigerator, a television set and a car.

Demographic change

Population change is a product of three factors: births, deaths and migration. According to Frank Notestein's (1990) demographic transition theory, population growth has taken place across the world in three stages:

- **Pre-modern stage**   Population increase is limited because high birth rates are counterbalanced by high death rates.

- **Early industrial stage**   Industrialisation is associated with high rates of population in its early phase, when birth rates are still high but death rates decline because of improved living conditions and improved public health.

- **Mature industrial stage**   Growth in the population declines as birth rates fall to a similar level as death rates.

However, according to Scott Fosler (1990), many Third-World countries have a demographic profile which does not fit this model. Accelerated population increase exceeds the capacity of the economy to support such increases and the general economic well-being, suggested by the theory, is never reached because resources are never enough to maintain the population increase in comfort.

Edward Mburugu (1986) found that the fertility rate – the average number of children that women are anticipated to give birth to during their lifetimes – has continued to increase as economic development expands. However, many Third-World societies never develop to the point of mature industrialisation and the population increase never stabilises. In other words, demographic transition theory cannot explain the situation of rapid population growth without economic development, which we find in many Third-World countries.

The consequences of this situation were outlined in the 1991 Human Development Report of the United Nations Development Programme, which reported that in the Third World

- income per head in sub-Saharan Africa declined in the 1980s

---

ACTIVITY   KS WORKING WITH OTHERS, COMMUNICATION, PROBLEM SOLVING, APPLICATION OF NUMBER

| IDENTIFICATION AND INTERPRETATION | ANALYSIS AND EVALUATION |

> Fertility rates in member nations of the European Union for 1990 show an EU average of 1.58 children per woman of childbearing age. In contrast, fertility rates in Rwanda stand at 8.5 children per woman of childbearing age; Kenya 7.4; Zambia 7.2; Tanzania and Niger 7.1; Niger, Benin and Malawi 7.0.

Source: Cockerham (1995) *The Global Society*

- Why is the number of children per mother so much higher in Africa than in the EU?

William C. Cockerham gives us the following case study which is worth considering:

> Rwanda is a male-dominated society. The majority of women work in agriculture, and more than half are illiterate. Rwandan men believe that fathering children is a sign of manhood; they

object to birth control measures for their wives not only because they want to continue to father children but also because they think birth control pills will make their wives weak and unable to work in the fields. From the women's viewpoint, the more children they have, the more stable their marriages; children also help in the fields, thereby lightening the mother's work load and helping protect her from abuse from the father. Since women cannot inherit property under Rwandan law, children are about the only measure of status that accrues directly to a woman. Therefore, the women also feel they benefit from having large families.

Source: Cockerham (1995)

- What do you believe is the message of the above quote?

- more than one billion people are in poverty
- two billion people live without an adequate or safe sanitation system
- one and a half billion people do not have access to a clean and safe water supply
- 180 million children experience continuous and extreme malnutrition

World trade and aid

World trade is another area in which there are international bodies which diminish the sovereignty of national governments. In 1947, 35 countries signed up for the General Agreement on Tariffs and Trade (GATT), in which all members agreed not to increase tax, duties or impose restrictions on each other's goods. In 1986, the members held a meeting in Uruguay, with the intention of making significant changes to the GATT agreement. This 'Uruguay Round' dragged on into the 1990s. In the end a new organisation was formed – the World Trade Organisation (WTO). This has two aims: firstly, to continue the GATT agreements on opening up world trade to competition and, secondly, to make world trade more responsible for the environment. On 24 March 1995 Renato Ruggiero became head of the WTO, and was reported by *The Times* as saying: 'We cannot go back to the protectionism of the 1930s. Trade is the main tool of globalisation.' He was also reported as saying that the world had a vested interest in bringing both China and Russia fully into the world system: 'They must respect the rules of the game. But we have to adapt all international institutions to globalisation.' *(The Times* 24 March 1995)

One of the major global issues in the 1980s and 1990s was that of **aid**. This issue shows more clearly than any other the argument between sociologists over global issues. Aid is the giving of resources from one country to another and can take a number of forms.

- **Development aid** This is given to help a country develop its economy or services in an effort to improve the quality of life for all people in that country.

- **Emergency aid** Given after a disaster, such as famine or flood.
- **Military aid** This can include expertise as well as weapons.
- **Project aid** Aid given for specific projects such as a dam, a school or a road. It is often referred to as 'tied' aid because the donor country usually has some control over the project, such as insisting that purchases made with the aid come from the donor country.
- **Programme aid** Aid which is not linked to specific projects. It could be used to improve a country's trade imbalance.

Aid can be bilateral, when one country gives help to another, or aid can be multilateral, in which several countries give money to an international organisation such as the World Bank.

According to Teresa Hayter (1989), western governments use aid to support pro-capitalist governments in the world:

> *The World Bank and the IMF ... are dominated by the major Western powers; the United States and half a dozen other governments have an effective veto over their lending decisions through the weighted voting system, and other more subtle ways. In addition, the World Bank raises around 80 per cent of its money through Wall Street and other private financial markets; this means that they must defend the interests of those markets.*

(Hayter, 1989:28)

The World Bank and the IMF will give aid or loans only if the country is willing to run its economy in a way that they approve of. They will insist upon 'structural adjustments' or 'stabilisation programmes'. Again, as Hayter explains:

> *The stabilisation, or structural adjustment, programmes have been programmes to control government spending and the balance of payments by orthodox liberal means: by limiting credit, cutting public social expenditure and sometimes public investment, keeping down or cutting wages, eliminating subsidies, and devaluation. Cuts in military expenditure are not demanded; the issue is said to be 'too sensitive'. For example the government*

of Morocco, with the approval of the World Bank and the IMF, has been carrying out a programme of cuts in domestic public expenditure, especially on food subsidies which benefit the poor; at the same time it has been spending large sums on the war in the Sahara."

(Hayter, 1989:30–31)

Perhaps the most surprising fact about aid is that most goes to countries that are well off. For example, in 1992 the British government gave more aid to Oman, which is an oil-rich state, than to Ethiopia. In addition, many of the aid projects have 'strings attached'. A controversial case in recent years was the Pergau Dam project in Malaysia, built by Balfour Beatty and Cementation. The dam cost £397 million to build, of which Britain gave £234 million in aid. However, it was suggested that the aid package was linked to arms deals worth £1.3 billion to British companies.

Modernisation theorists tends to argue that aid can be used to help the process of economic development 'take off'. Dependency theorists argue that aid makes Third-World countries more dependent upon the First World, and hampers economic development.

SOCIOLOGY IN PRACTICE

Read the article below and attempt the questions:

Where now for the world's poor? The years since the collapse of Communism have seen the emergence of an apparent global consensus about the inescapable role of markets in economic life. But they have also brought a steadily developing sense of unease about how to respond to the losers in the increasingly ferocious competitive market place.

On the 25th September 1995 in Lambeth Palace a collection of the great and the good, led by Douglas Hurd and the Archbishop of Canterbury, gathered to debate how to respond to growing economic globalisation.

Economic globalisation has come about through the interactions of high technology in communications, and other parts of industry, with the large-scale financial deregulation that was lost in the Thatcher/Reagan era. National boundaries and habits are becoming increasingly irrelevant to business decisions as investment flows and production facilities move in search of the highest possible returns or market share. Marketing has become global – the whole world is sold the same McDonald's, Ford Mondeo, Coca-Cola or Michael Jackson album. Transnational companies grow ever larger, with their subsidiaries spanning the globe.

As a result the movement of money round the world is constantly speeding up – current foreign exchange dealings exceed 1 trillion dollars a day. And investors are moving their cash, known in financial jargon as foreign direct investment (FDI), around the unregulated world market in such quantities that FDI has overtaken trade as the engine of world growth. Jobs follow the cash, which is invested wherever labour is cheapest. Thus one of France's largest electronics groups employs three times as many people in Asia as it does at home. And Swissair has moved its accountancy department to Delhi. Good news for the poor? Up to a point. For when living standards begin to rise – and local wages with them – the jobs move elsewhere. Japanese investment is already shifting from South Korea and Taiwan to Malaysia and Thailand, which have one-tenth of the wage costs. The commercial logic is hard to defy. In September 1995 the UK firm Morgan Crucible, one of the world's largest suppliers of industrial carbons and ceramics, announced that it was moving production from Germany and Japan to eastern Europe and China. Wages were $31 an hour in Japan and $26 in Germany; in eastern Europe, rates were $1.50 an hour; at its new Shanghai plant $1 a day.

In such a process of heightened competition between countries, the strong do well and those left behind find it ever harder to catch up. The need to remain competitive in an open global economy will lead to a downward pressure on standards (of living, working and products) and national and local cultures will come under attack.

The resultant world system works perfectly well without bothering about Africa, where rates of malnutrition, child mortality and illiteracy – in decline until a few years ago – have begun to rise again. According to Kevin Watkins, senior policy adviser at Oxfam, less than 2 per cent of all FDI goes to Africa, so 15 per cent of the world's population is consigned to oblivion.

The idea that women in Shanghai – and their equivalents in the carpet sweatshops of Bangladesh – are working for about 65 pence a day provokes moral outrage in the aid agency world but no one seems very sure any more what to do about it. 'They do not have an intellectually coherent response,' says Vincent Cable, a senior economist with the Royal Institute of International Affairs.

He acknowledges the negative side: low wages, poor conditions, bronchial complaints from heavy wool dust in the air, saris caught up in cutting machines, piecework, no security. But if these women were not earning 65p a day what would they be doing? The alternatives would be subsistence farming, domestic service or prostitution. Cable sees labour-intensive, export-oriented growth as the only hope for the poor world. Their conditions will improve with overall economic growth. When the tide comes in, all boats rise.

To Kevin Watkins at Oxfam that sounds suspiciously like the old discredited 'trickle-down' theory in new clothes. There has been more than a decade of economic growth in the US and UK and yet at the same time significant increases in poverty. All boats rise, except those which are anchored to the river bed. Economic growth is a necessary condition for poverty reduction but it is not sufficient, unless accompanied by economic redistribution measures that empower poor people. Watkins sees globalisation as a euphemism for a race to maximise profit by lowering environmental standards and workers' pay and conditions.

But others in the aid agencies feel that the only realistic option is to work with the grain of the new economics. The poor nations can't opt out of globalisation, argues George Gelber, head of policy at the Catholic agency Cafod. 'They've got to be skilled up. Some will criticise us for saying that, but there are no alternative models in the wings.'

That is very much the approach of fair-trade organisations such as Oxfam Trading, Equal Exchange, Twin Trading and Traidcraft. Traidcraft also offers a business development service to struggling Third-World producers. The idea here is to use the market to create not only wealth but also community, by bringing pressure to bear on the commercial sector from all who have a stake in the business – consumers, staff and trading partners. But such initiatives will always be symbolic. The cost of unfair trade and unequal competition to developing countries' labour, according to the UN Development Programme, is the equivalent of $500bn a year. Compare that with the total aid the rich world gives: $54bn. And compare that with the global budget for all voluntary agencies: $5bn. With their tiny resources, aid organisations can hope to make only a very limited contribution.

Increasingly the agencies are seeing their role as one of campaigning and advocacy on behalf of their poor partners. The internal debate is therefore on how much they should shift their emphasis from grassroots projects to campaigning for the relief of Third World debt, for institutions such as the International Monetary Fund to become more transparent and more sensitive to the poor, and for the developing world to be given a fairer deal by the new World Trade Organisation.

Source: Adapted from Paul Vallely 'How to halt the global money-go-round? As big capital chases profit and low wages around the world, aid agencies are left with a dilemma: fund-raise, trade or campaign?' *The Independent* 25 September 1995

1 Extract the key arguments and debates from the passage. **(5)**

> IDENTIFICATION AND
> INTERPRETATION

2 Do you agree or disagree that: 'The years since the collapse of Communism have seen the emergence of an apparent global consensus about the inescapable role of markets in economic life'? Give at least three reasons for your answer. **(8)**

> ANALYSIS AND
> EVALUATION

3 Why do you think some nation states continue to be involved in world trade and to join international bodies when not all nation states seem to benefit from membership? **(8)**

> IDENTIFICATION AND
> INTERPRETATION

4 Draw up a list of international bodies or organisations with which you are familiar. **(8)**

> KNOWLEDGE AND | IDENTIFICATION AND
> UNDERSTANDING | INTERPRETATION

5 Apart from increasing the profits of multi-national companies, describe two advantages that 'pooling' or 'sharing' sovereignty may have for each of the following:

- a nation state
- a local community
- an individual **(6)**

> IDENTIFICATION AND
> INTERPRETATION

6 What do you think is one strength and one weakness of the statement that: 'National boundaries and habits are becoming increasingly irrelevant? **(6)**

> ANALYSIS AND
> EVALUATION

7 Why did Morgan Crucible, one of the world's largest suppliers of industrial carbons and ceramics, announce that it was moving production from Germany and Japan to eastern Europe and China? **(6)**

> IDENTIFICATION AND
> INTERPRETATION

8   Do you agree or disagree with the statement that in the new world order: '… the strong do well and those left behind find it even harder to catch up? Give at least two reasons for your answer.   **(6)**

ANALYSIS AND
EVALUATION

9   According to the study: 'The need to remain competitive in an open global economy will lead to a downward pressure on standards (of living, working, and products) and national and local cultures will come under attack from economic globalisation.' Which sociological perspective is expressed within this quotation? Give three reasons for your answer.   **(6)**

ANALYSIS AND
EVALUATION

10   According to the passage, Vincent Cable acknowledges the negative side of economic globalisation: low wages, poor conditions, bronchial complaints from heavy wool dust in the air, saris caught in cutting machines, piecework, no security. However, if the women in the study were not earning 65p a day what would they be doing? The alternatives would be subsistence farming, domestic service or prostitution. What do you think are the strengths and weaknesses of Vincent Cable's statement?   **(8)**

ANALYSIS AND
EVALUATION

11   The approach of organisations such as Oxfam Trading, Equal Exchange, Twin Trading and Traidcraft is described as 'fair trade'. What do you understand by the term fair trade?   **(8)**

| KNOWLEDGE AND UNDERSTANDING | IDENTIFICATION AND INTERPRETATION | ANALYSIS AND EVALUATION |

SOCIOLOGY IN PRACTICE

Read the following item and attempt the questions:

The annual summit of the heads of the seven leading rich countries, the G7, is the nearest thing there is to global government. As governing bodies go, it is singularly emaciated. Since it gave up trying to co-ordinate economic policy a decade ago, it has generated photo opportunities rather than decisions. Even if there were decisions, there is no G7 administration – no equivalent of the Brussels bureaucrats – to follow them through. The agenda is limited: mainly economic. And attendance reflects the convention of a self-electing, like-minded, rich man's club, rather than a realistic weighing of economic and political power, which is why Italy and Canada attend and not China and India, and why Russia is allowed in only on sufferance.

Emaciated or not, the G7 summit has assumed one heavy burden in 1995, a commitment to reform the international public sector: the UN; the Bretton Woods institutions (the IMF and World Bank); and the new World Trade Organisation (the successor of GATT). The question has become compelling since these institutions originated half a century ago, in the aftermath of war, in reaction to the Great Depression and in an intellectual climate that vested much faith in public institutions, national and global. The current mood is quite different. When such solid bastions of national public service and enterprise as the British Treasury, Deutsche Telecom, Air France and the US Federal Housing Department are being prepared for the auctioneer's hammer or the management consultant's knife, international civil servants are not going to be spared from rationalisation and 'downsizing'.

The international economic institutions are especially vulnerable to critical review, since the market-led global economic integration of the last few decades has, in key respects, marginalised them. Global integration has occurred through national deregulation – mainly of capital markets, partly of trade. Foreign exchange markets, for example, are effectively self-regulating. With a daily turnover of a trillion dollars, more than the total official reserves of all governments, there is no longer any serious pretence, least of all by the IMF whose responsibility this once was, that exchange rates can be 'managed' (short of complete monetary union). This is largely true also of the market in internationally traded securities, which grew in little over a decade to $20 trillion at the end of the 1980s and has since multiplied many times through derivatives. These markets operate and expand without any supranational supervision.

The other dynamic elements in the international economic system have also been market-driven, a product of liberalisation policies, mainly in G7 countries that owe little to global institutions; for example, the rapid growth of direct foreign investment flows – which multiplied by 400 per cent over six years during the 1980s and are now growing strongly again. And while the formal process of multinational trade negotiations can be credited with some of the trade expansion which has taken place, the most rapid growth of world trade has occurred in services – such as telecommunications and banking – without the help of a multilateral agreement. Furthermore, global standards are being created – for accounting; telecommunications interconnection, and quality control – on a largely voluntary, improvised, informal basis by the market players themselves.

The international public sector has been left with a diminished role and status. The IMF may seem overpowering to the small, mainly African and former Communist countries, for whom it has become a lender of last resort, but it is a shrunken shadow of the institution conceived by Keynes and his contemporaries. Its currency, the SDR, accounts for a tiny part of international liquidity. No industrial country of any importance has been subject to its policy conditions since Britain in the 1970s. Responsibility for systemic financial stability has been shifted elsewhere: to *ad hoc* committees of central bank officials meeting in Basel. The World Bank, despite its prestige, has also been marginalised. It is struggling to maintain its share of the shrinking pot of foreign aid, now down to 0.3 per cent of rich countries' GNP. Other UN agencies never had much of an economic role and are fighting to avoid outright closure.

Worse, the international institutions find they have few friends in the G7 countries. Free-market fundamentalists see no need for them. The left, and the environmental movement, has demonised them for some real, mostly imagined, sins against the world's poor and the planet. National politicians and officials, especially in the US, are jealous of their resources and their perks. The idealism and political energy that was once channelled into global multilateralism are now diverted into building regional institutions in Europe, North Africa, Latin America and the Asian Pacific. The global institutions have no popular constituency.

A world of highly integrated markets supported only by weak rules and institutions is a precarious one. It could crack. There are signs of this happening even within the G7. One line of weakness is trade policy, as the World Trade Organisation seeks to establish a stronger sense of international legality in the face of a direct challenge from the United States (which is endeavouring to force open the Japanese market unilaterally). Whatever the particular rights and wrongs in the Japan-US dispute, a fundamental issue of principle has arisen: unless the world's most powerful country can be made to conform to the rules of a multilateral institution, the way would be open to a fragmentation of the world economy into bilateral and regional arrangements. This is an issue that the G7 cannot duck.

Adapted from Vincent Cable 'Last orders for a rich man's club?' *The Independent* 15 June 1995

1   Vincent Cable suggests that, in the era of globalisation, international bodies like G7 are being marginalised. Outline the possible reasons given by Cable as to why this might be the case.   (6)

IDENTIFICATION AND INTERPRETATION

2   Why should the G7 be regarded as 'the nearest thing we have to a world government'?   (7)

IDENTIFICATION AND INTERPRETATION

3   According to the text: '... since these institutions originated half a century ago, in the aftermath of war, in reaction to the Great Depression and in an intellectual climate that vested much faith in public institutions, national and global. The current mood is quite different.' Making use of the information that Cable provides, why should there have been a change in the international mood?   (7)

IDENTIFICATION AND INTERPRETATION

4   What possible consequences does he suggest accompany this international change of mood?   (7)

IDENTIFICATION AND INTERPRETATION

5   According to the passage: 'The international economic institutions are especially vulnerable to critical review, since the market-led global economic integration of the last few decades has, in key respects, marginalised international economic institutions.' Which sociological perspective is expressed in this quotation? Give three reasons for your answer.   (7)

ANALYSIS AND EVALUATION

6   What do you understand by the term 'downsizing'?   **(2)**

> KNOWLEDGE AND UNDERSTANDING | IDENTIFICATION AND INTERPRETATION

7   According to the passage what are the problems with current world trade policy? **(8)**

> IDENTIFICATION AND INTERPRETATION

8   Why are Japan and the USA in dispute over world trade?   **(4)**

> IDENTIFICATION AND INTERPRETATION

9   What do you understand by the term 'global multilateralism'?   **(2)**

> KNOWLEDGE AND UNDERSTANDING | IDENTIFICATION AND INTERPRETATION

10   According to the item what is *the* issue that the G7 cannot duck?   **(2)**

> IDENTIFICATION AND INTERPRETATION

Area summary

We have looked at the assumptions and theories contained within modernisation theory, dependency theory, convergence theory and how Japan opted for a very different development path.

We have studied the concept of 'globalisation' in the work of Anthony Giddens, Roland Robertson, in terms of the economic, political and cultural dimensions including an outline of David Held's conception of a new 'cosmopolitan order'.

International bodies are active in all areas of social life and diminish the scope of a nation state to govern its citizens; examples include EU, IMF, WTO and World Bank, and the role that such bodies may play in the aid relationship.

We also looked at a range of problems that Third-World countries have to deal with: health, education, underemployment, environmental change, demographic change and urbanisation.

Definitions

Adaptation	Changes within a social system which bring about a closer harmony the environment
Aid	An economic arrangement between one country and another, or international agency, believed to bring about economic growth or some other specified improvement
Bounded administrative unit	A locality which has a form of authority which is responsible for the actions that take place with the locality
Chain of dependency	The links of reliance between people in the Third World and people in the rich, industrial countries
Colonialism	Direct political control of one society by another
Colonised personality	An individual, living in the Third World, who changes some key aspect of their 'self' to become more like people in the rich, industrial world
Common value system	A set of shared standards or principles which underpin a social system
Debt crisis	The inability of Third-World countries to prevent spiralling interest on debt
Dependency theory	A theory to explain the conditions that make Third-World societies helpless and constantly in need of help from western societies
Development	In western societies this is assumed to mean economic and political advancement
Differentiation	Changes within a social system which involves institutions either specialising in some of its functions or developing new functions
Disequilibrium	When the balance within social system is damaged in some way
Early industrial stage	The first phase in the process of a society developing the characteristics of a modern society

Economically reductionist	A way of theorising common to Marxists which involves excluding all factors other than economic factors in any explanation
Functional	A relationship within social systems which involves both individuals and institutions working for the benefit of the wider social system
Global homogenisation	A set of processes which are making political, cultural and economic differences in the world diminish
Globalisation	The whole world becoming a single place
Imperialism	The process of colonisation based on a belief in empire
Long-term evolution	Social change over a long period of time
Mature industrial stage	A later phase in the process of a society developing the characteristics of a modern society
Miniglobalisation	A term used by Robertson (1992) to describe the range of processes throughout history which have helped to brings about a process of globalisation
Modernisation	A process whereby societies develop the characteristics of a modern western society
Modernity	A society which is industrial, capitalist, has a central administrative power and is democratic
Modern personality	A set of characteristics of the 'self' common within people who live in advanced industrial societies
Pre-modern stage	A phase of social development that exists before modernity
Reintegration	A term used by Parsons (1970) to describe the process of a social systems regaining its stability after a period of change
Salinisation	A process in which salt becomes present in soil and water preventing crop growth and encouraging the spread of dessert
Soil alkalinity	The process of soils becoming more acid in nature preventing crop growth and encouraging the spread of dessert
Soil erosion	The breaking down of the structure of soil to the degree that it is no longer an effective growing medium
Structural differentiation	A term used by Parsons (1970) to changes within a social system at the institutional level, this may involve institutions either specialising in some of its functions or developing new functions
Structuration	A term used by Giddens to describe how individual people are capable of creating structures within a society
Third World	Countries mainly in the southern hemisphere which have undeveloped economies from a western perspective
Time-space distanciation	A term used by Giddens to describe the stretching of time and space across the globe; as people travel through space they also travel through time. As we can now travel a great speed over space we can travel through time
Underdevelopment	A process used to describe a country's growing poverty and industrial decline

Data response questions

In 1993 Leslie Sklair outlined a number of different models of globalisation. Firstly, there is a world system model which is Marxist in orientation, as put forward by Immanuel Wallerstein. In this model there is an international division of labour within the world economy. A nation's economy is linked in a number of ways to the international economy and can either be at its core, semi-periphery or periphery. Those nations which are at the periphery are much more likely to be in poverty. However, this model is said to be too determined by economic factors and ignores cultural factors.

The second model is one of 'cultural imperialism', in which local or traditional cultures are destroyed by the cultural products of multi-national corporations in the advanced countries. Ulf Hannerz (1996) outlines a number of possible types of cultural unification; one of which is 'global homogenisation' – this suggests complete domination in the world by 'lowbrow' western lifestyles, western products in the shops, western cars in the streets, western films at the cinema, western soaps on television, etc. This spread involves Dynasty rather than Shakespeare.

The third model is Sklair's own model, which is that the global system is built upon transnational practices. These practices are formed by transnational corporations and they allow economic, political and cultural or ideological practices, like consumerism, to travel across state borders.

The fact and the perception of ever-increasing inter-dependence at the global level, the rising concern about the fate of the world as a whole and of the human species (particularly because of the threats of ecological degradation, nuclear disaster and AIDS), and the colonisation of the local by global life (not least via the mass media) facilitate massive processes of relativisation of cultures, doctrines, ideologies and cognitive frames of reference.

Robertson (1994: 84)

a   What do you understand by the term 'globalisation'?   (5)

IDENTIFICATION AND
INTERPRETATION

b   Outline the arguments for and against the notion of 'cultural globalisation'?   (9)

ANALYSIS AND
EVALUATION

c   To what extent is the concept of globalisation similar to the notion of social, cultural and economic convergence?   (11)

| IDENTIFICATION AND INTERPRETATION | ANALYSIS AND EVALUATION |

Structured questions

1 What do you understand by the term Modernity? **(5)**

> **GUIDANCE** *Modernity simply means 'the modern world'. However, there is some disagreement amongst sociologists as to what are the central elements of the modern world. Durkheim, Weber and Marx had very different interpretations of modernity and how the modern world functions.*
>
> | KNOWLEDGE AND UNDERSTANDING | IDENTIFICATION AND INTERPRETATION |

2 What are the central components of 'globalisation'? **(10)**

> **GUIDANCE** *This concept is built upon the idea that the whole world is becoming a single place, and that you need to explore the processes that take place at an economic level: the activities of transnational corporations; at cultural level with the global media, and politically with the development of transnational bodies that have sovereignty over some aspects of the nation state's activities.*
>
> | KNOWLEDGE AND UNDERSTANDING | IDENTIFICATION AND INTERPRETATION |

3 According to Anthony Giddens (1991) we are living in an era of high or late modernity. What do you consider to be the key elements of Giddens' conception of high or late modernity? **(20)**

> **GUIDANCE** *Anthony Giddens is one of the most widely read, intellectually and politically influential sociologists in the world today. His conception of high or late modernity forms the back-drop to most sociological problems and issues. In your answer you need to explain that the central characteristics are: capitalism; industrialism; a central administrative power; and surveillance. Late Modernity differs from the modernity described by Durkheim, Weber and Marx in that Modernity is now global and reflexive.*
>
> | KNOWLEDGE AND UNDERSTANDING | IDENTIFICATION AND INTERPRETATION |

Essay titles

1 Evaluate the view that education is the most critical factor in the shift from under-development. **(40) AQA Specimen Unit 2000**

> **GUIDANCE** *In this essay you need to give an outline of the provision of education in the underdeveloped world. In addition, you need to compare the contrast the two key perspectives in the area. The modernisation view argues that education can be an important stimulus to economic growth and wider development. In contrast, dependency theorists are inclined to argue that the unequal economic relationship between the rich First World and the poor Third World will prevent economic growth and enforce dependency irrespective of the level of education with the Third World country. Some authors, such as Ivan Illich have discussed the development of a First World mentality in highly educated people living in the Third World, which can have a detrimental effect upon the culture of a Third World country. Finally, your essay must evaluate both of these positions and look at the activities of international bodies such as the World Bank and the IMF which are likely to finance education as a key element in project aid packages.*
>
> | KNOWLEDGE AND UNDERSTANDING | IDENTIFICATION AND INTERPRETATION | ANALYSIS AND EVALUATION |

2 "Contacts between rich and poor nations encourages development." To what extent do sociologists agree with this statement?   **(25) AEB Summer 1999**

GUIDANCE *In this answer you need to describe the strengths and weaknesses of the major*	KNOWLEDGE AND UNDERSTANDING	IDENTIFICATION AND INTERPRETATION	ANALYSIS AND EVALUATION

perspectives on social change: modernisation theory and dependency theory. You need to explain if either theory can provide a convincing explanation for why there is Third World poverty – how does each theory explain the 'Third-World/First World' divide.

3 Evaluate sociological approaches to the causes and effects of urbanisation in Third-World societies.   **(25)**

Further reading and references

Elger, T. and Smith, C. (Eds.) (1994) *Global Japanization: The Transnational Transformation of the Labour Process*. London, Routledge.

Scott, J. (1997) *Corporate Business and Capitalist Class*. Oxford, Oxford University Press.

Grint, K. (1991) *The Sociology of Work: An Introduction*. Cambridge, Polity.

Internet sites

www.sis.wau.nl/crds/cant-res.html
Centre for Rural Development Sociology
Has a great deal of information on all areas of the World Sociology specification, with a number of very good links to other sites of interest

www.unesco.org
United Nations Educational, Scientific and Cultural Organisation and

www.un.org/esa
United Nations Economic and Social Development
These two UN sites have a great deal of interdisciplinary information, especially up to date maps, statistics and news events

Bibliography

Aron, R. (1967) *Progress and Disillusion: The Dialectics of Modern Society*. New York, Mentor Books.

Bell, D. (1974) *The Coming of Post-industrial Society*. London, Heinemann.

Benedict, R. (1946) *The Chrysanthemum and the Sword*. Boston, Mass., Houghton Mifflin.

Bienefield, M. (1994) 'Capitalism and the Nation State in the Dog Days of the Twentieth Century' in R. Miliband and L. Panitch (Eds.) 'Between Globalism and Nationalism'. *Socialist Register*. London, Merlin Press.

Cockerham, W. (1995) *The Global Society*. New York, McGraw-Hill.

Cuff, E., Sharrock, W. and Francis, D. (1998) *Pertspectives in Sociology*. London, Routledge.

Dahrendorf, R. (1990) *Reflections on the Revolutions in Europe*. London, Chatto and Windus.

Eisenstadt, S. N. (1992) 'The Breakdown of Communist Regimes and the Vicissitudes of Modernity'. *Daedalus*, Spring.

Etzioni, A. (1991) *Socio-economic Perspectives on Friction*. Washington, IAREP/SASE Conference (Mimeo).

Fanon, F. (1967) *The Wreched of the Earth*. Harmondsworth, Penguin.

Feldman, A. S. and Moore, W. E. (1962) 'Industrialisation and Industrialism: Convergence and Differentiation'. *Transactions of the Fifth World Congress of Sociology*. Washington, ISA.

Fosler, S. (1990) in Carr, M. *New Patterns: Processes and Change in Human Geography*. Walton-on-Thames, Nelson.

Foster-Carter, A. (1985) *The Sociology of Development*. Ormskirk, Causeway Press.

Furtado, C. (1971) *Economic development of Latin America: a Survey from Colonial Times to the Cuban Revolution*. Cambridge, Cambridge University Press.

Giddens, A. (1985) *The Nation State and Violence*. Cambridge, Polity Press.

Giddens, A. (1990) *The Consequences of Modernity*. Cambridge, Polity Press.

Giddens, A. (1994) *Reflexive Modernization*. Cambridge, Polity Press.

Gilbert, A. and Guyler, J. (1987) *Cities, Poverty, and Development: Urbanisation in the Third World*. Oxford, Oxford University Press.

Gunder-Frank, A. (1969) 'Latin America: Underdevelopment or Revolution'. *Monthly New York Review Press*.

Hannerz, U. (1989) 'Notes on the Global Economy'. *Public Culture*, 1, 2.

Hayter, T. (1989) *Aid*. London, Earthscan Press.

Held, D. (1992) 'Democracy: From City States to a Cosmopolitan Order. *Political Studies*, XL.

Hoogvelt, A. (1982) *The Third World in Global Development*. London, Macmillan.

Inkeles, A. (1976) 'A Model of the Modern Man: Theoretical and Methodological Issues' in C. Black (Ed.) *Comparative Modernizations*. New York, Free Press.

Kerr, C., Dunlop, J. T., Harbison, H. and Myers, C. A. (1960) *Industrialism and Industrial Man*. Cambridge, Mass., Harvard University Press.

Kozai, T. (1984) *Wakon-ron-noto*. Tokyo, Iwanami shoten.

Leggatt, T (1985) *The Forking Paths*. London, Macmillan.

Mburugu, D. (1986) in Inmberlake, L. and Holmberg, J. (1991) *One World for One Earth: Overcoming Environmental Degradation*. London, Earthscan/Open University.

Lewis, O. (1970) 'The Culture of Poverty' in Lewis, O. *Anthropological Essays*. New York, Random House.

Lipset, S. M. (1967) *The First New Nation*. New York, Basic Books.

Nakane, C. (1985) *Japanese Society*. Berkeley, University of California Press.

Notestein, F. (1990) in Inmberlake, L. and Holmberg, J. (1991) *One World for One Earth: Overcoming Environmental Degradation*. London, Earthscan/Open University.

Oberai, A. S. (1993) 'Urbanisation, Development, and Economic Efficiency' in Kasarda, J. D. and Parnell, A. M. (Eds.) *Third World Cities: Problems, Policies and Prospects*. London, Sage.

Parsons, T. (1951) *The Social System*. London, Routledge.

Parsons, T. (1970) *Societies: Evolutionary and Comparative Perspectives*. Englewood Cliffs, Prentice Hall.

Randinelli, D. A. and Kasanda, J. D. (1993) 'Job Creation Needs in Third World Cities' in J. D. Kasards and A. Parnell (Eds.) *Third World Cities: Problems, Policies and Prospects*. London, Sage.

Robertson, R. (1994) *Globalisation*. London, Sage.

Rostow, W. W. (1960) *The Five Stages of Economic Growth: A Non-Communist Manifesto*. Cambridge, Cambridge University Press.

Sklair, L. (1993) 'Going global: Competing Models of Globalisation.' *Sociological Review*, November.

Smelser, N. (1959) *Social Change in the Industrial Revolution*. London, Routledge.

Smith, A. D. (1991) 'Towards a Global Culture?' in M. Featherstone (Ed.) *Global Culture: Nationalism, Globalisation and Modernity*. London, Sage.

Smith, H. L. and Cheung, P. L. (1986) 'Trends in the Effects of Family Background on Educational Attainment in the Philippines'. *American Journal of Sociology*, 91.

Sztompka, P. (1991) 'The Intangibles and Impoderables of the Transition to Democracy'. *Studies in Comparative Communism*, 24, 3.

Sztompka, P. (1992) 'Dilemmas of the Great Transition'. *Working Paper Series* No. 19. Cambridge, Mass., Harvard Centre for European Studies.

Sztompka, P. (1993) *The Sociology of Social Change*. Oxford, Blackwell.

Tiryakian, E. (1985) 'The Changing Centres of Modernity' in E. Cohen, M. Lissak and U. Almagor (Eds.) *Comparative Social Dynamics*. Boulder, Westview Press.

United Nations Department of International and Social Affairs (UNDIESA) (1991) 'World Urbanisation Prospects 1990: Estimates and Projections of Urban and Rural Populations of Urban Agglomerations.' *Population Studies* No. 121. New York.

UN Development Programme (1991) *Human Development Report*. New York, United Nations.

Wallerstein, I. (1979) *The Modern World System II*. New York, Academic Press.

Wallerstein, I. (1980) *The Modern World System*. New York, Academic Press.

Waters, M. (1995) *Globalisation*. London, Routledge.

Wolpert, S. (1991) *India*. Berkeley, University of California Press.

Power, Politics and Protest

This area covers:

- Explanations of the nature and distribution of power and ideology in the modern world
- The role of the state
- The changing nature of political participation
- The nature of new social movements and their role in the political process.

By the end of this area you should be able to:

- outline and evaluate traditional sociological theories of power within modernity
- understand the shift from class-based politics to a 'new' politics based upon new social movements and their politics of identity and trust – as distinct from old social movements
- be aware of the 'Third Way' and reflexive modernisation in the work of Giddens, the nature of polyarchy, the 'pure' relationship and democracy – the shift from emancipatory politics to life politics
- understand communitarianism, with reference to the work of Giddens, Etzioni and Macmurray, with critiques from Rorty and Campbell
- understand sociological theories of voting behaviour.

Key terms

power
authority
the state
polyarchy
new social movements

the third way
emancipatory politics
life politics
Communitarianism
class dealignment

Area 14 Contents

Introduction

What is power? What is *politics* about now? In the 1990s the world became a much more uncertain and dangerous place. In this area we will attempt to identify the forces and factors that brought about this uncertainty and danger. Many writers have implied that the political uncertainty is part of a postmodern condition in which people feel as if *the social* is dissolving, that the constraints we once had, which held together communities, do not have the force they once had and that individuals have to create their own bonds of community.

We will look at the changing nature of politics in the transition from modernity to postmodernity, the ways in which individuals cope with the consequences of factors such as the changing nature of their everyday lives. This is related to the global nature of modernity and some of the political issues raised by processes of globalisation; most notably attempts by politicians in Britain and the USA to enhance or recreate the bonds of community with the political ideology known as 'communitarianism' or the 'Third Way'. Most of these issues have been investigated by Anthony Giddens, whose influence on governments in Britain and the USA is considerable. We will use his work as a guide to understanding the range of complex factors which now make up the political world.

Power within modernity: traditional sociological theories of power

Max Weber was one of the founders of modern sociology and a key theorist of modernity. One of his many contributions to the sociology of politics was his theory of **power**. Simply stated, for Weber power is the ability to make somebody do something which you want them to do. He goes on to make the further distinction between **coercion** and **legitimate authority**.

For Max Weber, authority is the legitimate use of power. Individuals accept and act upon orders which are given to them because they believe that the order is right. Coercion, on the other hand, is where people are forced by others into an action, often by the threat of violence and this is always regarded as illegitimate.

Max Weber on legitimate authority

Weber outlined three ideal types of legitimate rule:

1 **Charismatic authority** For Weber a political system can be established by the fervour of a leader's character. In many cases, charismatic leaders are believed to have almost supernatural qualities.
2 **Traditional authority** This is a political system which is upheld by continual reference to traditional conventions and habits.
3 **Rational legal authority** Weber regards this political system as legitimate because it is believed to be 'legal' and built upon rational processes; the ideal type discussed by Weber is the bureaucracy.

Weber's analysis suggests that modernity always results in government by **bureaucracy**. The two most 'modern' societies in the twentieth century – Hitler's Germany and Stalin's Soviet Union – both relied heavily on the state bureaucracy to run efficiently. The basis of bureaucratic power, claimed Weber, is knowledge, which he said was the technical ability to make use of information that is protected by secrecy. Hence there is a need, he claimed, for a strong parliament as a guarantor of individual rights and independence. Weber was always in favour of political democratisation, and that included supporting votes for women. Weak parliaments generate fanatical divisions between parties, which Weber termed 'negative politics' because it was little more than an ideological masquerade, with the important decisions taken by the state bureaucracy.

Weber's ideal type of bureaucracy

An ideal type is a useful model by which to measure other forms of administration. Weber's model includes the following features:

- The bureaucratic administration is in the shape of a hierarchy – a structure in the shape of a pyramid, with a small group of people at the top with most of the power and a large group of people at the bottom with limited power.

- The procedures of any bureaucratic administration are based on a system of abstract rules, with all bureaucrats having a rigid number of recorded duties.

- The ideal officials within any bureaucratic administration do their job without friendship or favour to any clients: they treat all people the same.

- Employment in a bureaucratic administration is by appointment based on qualifications, not by election.

- Bureaucratic administration has the highest degree of efficiency.

Within the bureaucratic administration, officials have their own set of convictions or values, which Weber referred to as its *Amtsehre*. This includes:

- a recognition of the significance of the tasks they carry out

- a conviction that their qualifications and ability are better than those of people outside the bureaucracy

- belief that parliament is merely a 'talking shop'

- conviction that bureaucrats are above party politics

- conviction that bureaucrats are the only faithful interpreters of the national interest

- bureaucrats have their own concerns, which Weber calls their *Staatsraison*.

ACTIVITY

KS COMMUNICATION, WORKING WITH OTHERS, PROBLEM SOLVING

| IDENTIFICATION AND INTERPRETATION | ANALYSIS AND EVALUATION |

Weber argued that the bureaucratic administration is the most efficient form of administration. Do you accept or reject this view? What possible advantages do you think that a bureaucracy can have over other forms of administration?

Within the Weberian conception of bureaucracy, administration is clearly defined and soulless, machine-like. It makes use of rational means in accomplishing preconceived objectives. However, Weber's fear was that all bureaucracies have an inherent inclination to surpass their purpose, and to become an independent force within modern society.

ACTIVITY

KS COMMUNICATION, WORKING WITH OTHERS, PROBLEM SOLVING

| IDENTIFICATION AND INTERPRETATION | ANALYSIS AND EVALUATION |

In Weber's view all bureaucratic structures make use of secrecy. What value do you think a bureaucracy can gain from secrecy?

Many of Weber's critics neglect to take into account the nature of the ideal type as a research tool. The ideal type is a model, put together from a list of features which the researcher believes are the most important. Creation of the ideal type as a model built upon what Weber termed **value relevance**, which is the informed personal feelings of the researcher. This is the starting point from which the researcher goes on to consider real bureaucracies. Weber's critics assume that the ideal type is the end point of the research process. It is not: it is the start.

KNOWLEDGE AND UNDERSTANDING	INTERPRETATION	EVALUATION

This activity outlines Zygmunt Bauman's (1989) critique of Weber's conception of bureaucracy:

> *... In Weber's exposition of modern bureaucracy, rational spirit, principle of efficiency, scientific mentality, relegation of values to the realm of subjectivity etc. no mechanism was recorded that was capable of excluding the possibility of Nazi excesses; that, moreover there was nothing in Weber's ideal types that would necessitate the description of the activities of the Nazi state as excesses. For example, no horror perpetuated by the German medical technocrats was inconsistent with the view that values are inherently subjective and that science is intrinsically instrumental and value free.*

(Bauman, 1989:10)

> I propose to treat the Holocaust as a rare, yet significant and reliable, test of the hidden possibilities of modern society ... *Modern civilization was not the Holocaust's sufficient*

condition: it was, however, most certainly its necessary condition. Without it the Holocaust would be unthinkable. It was the rational world of modern civilization that made the Holocaust thinkable. The Nazi mass murder of the European Jewry was not only the technological achievement of an industrial society, but also the organisational achievement of a bureaucratic society ... bureaucratic rationality is at its most dazzling once we realize the extent to which the very idea of the Endlosung was an outcome of the bureaucratic culture ... At no point of its long and tortuous execution did the Holocaust come into conflict with the principles of rationality. The 'Final Solution' did not clash at any stage with the rational pursuit of efficient, optimal goal implementation. On the contrary, it arose out of a genuine rational concern, and it was generated by bureaucracy true to its form and purpose.

(Bauman, 1989:12, 13, 15 and 17)

In your own words, outline Bauman's critique of Weber's ideal type of bureaucracy.

Guenther Roth, an eminent Weberian scholar, has said of these views that his disagreement is 'total' and that he could not agree with one sentence on the grounds that: 'Weber was a liberal, loved the constitution and approved of the working class's voting rights (and thus, presumably, could not be in conjunction with a thing so abominable as the Holocaust)' (Bauman, 1989:10).

Steven Lukes argues that Weber's conceptions of power, authority and legitimacy are too restricted in their focus. Lukes (1974) argues that power has three dimensions, and that Weber is concerned only with the first.

- **Decision-making**, which is concerned with the actions of the decision makers.
- **Non-decision-making**, which is concerned with the way in which power is applied to restrict the decisions that the so-called decision-makers can select from.
- **Shaping desires**, which is concerned with the extent to which individuals may have their attitudes and beliefs directed by others, to make them agree to a decision which may not be in their own interests.

IDENTIFICATION AND INTERPRETATION	ANALYSIS AND EVALUATION

Bauman is a postmodernist. Before we move on, it might be interesting to look at what a postmodern organisation would/should look like. Reread the

section on postmodernism from Area 1, the section on bureaucracy above, and attempt to draw up a list of characteristics that you would expect to find in a postmodern organisation.

> ## Some points you might want to consider about postmodernist organisations
>
> The postmodern organisation should contain de-demarcated and multi-skilled jobs. Unlike the Prussian-style bureaucracy as outlined by Weber the postmodern organisation should be 'de-Prussianised'; it should be free of formal rationality, loosely coupled and complexly interactive; it should be a 'collegial formation' with no vertical authority, but with forms of 'networking'. These networks should reflect the new 'cultural and social specialists' needs and cultural capital and allow the specialists to resist control by traditional bureaucracy.
>
> In a post-Fordist world, which has an uncertain or postmodern feel to it, new forms of pluralistic or non-hierarchical organisation are possible. People can work within quality circles, in which workers are not constrained and powerless as they would be under some form of Tayloristic scientific management. They are not 'deskilled' as Braverman would suggest, but work within structures which empower individuals by allowing democratic participation in decision-making.

Élite theory

Classical élite theories reject democracy and assume that in any political system there will invariably be a small, purposeful élite with the skills and resources to dominate a large mass which has very little power. The key assumption of classical élite theory is that in all forms of society the 'rule of the few' is inevitable.

Classical élite theorists assume that the mass is psychologically weak and therefore incapable of holding power. The mass has an instinctive compulsion to be dominated: only the élite can fulfil that need. Robert Michels has termed this **The Iron Law of Oligarchy**. For this reason democracy is not a practical option for any political system.

Vilfredo Pareto (1847–1939)

Pareto started his analysis of society with his theory of non-logical actions. Pareto assumed that all individuals have six basic instincts, which he terms **residues**. These residues are guided by the élite with the use of four political operations which Pareto names the **derivations**.

The residues:

- **Residues of combination** – people have an instinct to live together in groups.
- **Persistence of aggregates** – once a group is established there is instinctual need to preserve it.
- **Sentiments of activity** – individuals strengthen the bonds that hold groups together by the use of ceremonies.
- **Residues of sociality** – groups have an instinctual animosity towards outsiders and a need for uniformity.
- **Self-preservation** – people desire to preserve their safety, possessions and social standing.
- **Sexuality** – sexuality has a part to play in supporting social control within society.

The derivations:

- **Simple assertion** – the élite announce that something is correct, and this is accepted without question.
- **Authority** – the mass do not disagree with what they are told by the élite because élite power is seen as legitimate.
- **Sentiments or principles** – élite decisions are said to be in harmony with widely held public feelings.
- **Verbal proof** – the mass are persuaded by the élite.

Pareto maintains that the élite are able to rule either by their cunning or by the use of force. He calls them 'foxes' or 'lions'.

Gaetano Mosca (1858–1911)

Mosca was also anti-democratic and argued that society divided into an organised élite and a large mass. Mosca outlined several kinds of élite group: military, priestly, wealthy and landowners. Moreover, although the élite might have a near-monopoly over the use of violence, they do not need to make constant use of violence to maintain their élite position. It is manipulation of the ideas of the mass which gives the élite their ability to keep power.

In Mosca's opinion, the élite are essential for the continuation of civilisation, as they are able to hold off forces which could overthrow it. Inside any community there will always be a number of conflicting and competing social forces and the stability of a community is maintained by the ability of the élite to restrict the damaging effects of these social forces. The élite try to perform this role by imposing a **political formula**, a set of principles and ideals which, if accepted, bring about political stability. In modern western societies the political formula is based on the principle 'government by due process of law'.

Criticisms of élite theory

■ Neither Mosca nor Pareto clearly defines his key terms. For example, a residue can be a sentiment, an instinct or a principle, social force. The theory of non-logical actions, upon which the theory is based, is not convincing because of this lack of clarity.

■ They do not discuss practical political situations, providing only a minimal description of the structure of political institutions.

■ In addition, many people find the way élite theory has been used as a justification for fascism very offensive.

Marxist theories of power

From the Marxist viewpoint, if a class owns the means of production it has not only economic power, but also political power. The state's role is to maintain capitalist society in the interests of the capitalists. In Veblen's words the capitalist state is a 'Soviet of capitalists'. The authority of the capitalist system is maintained by a dominant ideology, in which working-class people are said to have ideas and beliefs imposed upon them. Institutions that are involved in this ideological manipulation include the media, schools and organised religion.

Ralph Miliband (1973) argued that there is a well organised capitalist class, which controls top posts in both industry and government; most of these people were educated in top private schools before going on to Oxford or Cambridge. This narrow group of individuals uses the state as an instrument for its own lasting capitalist supremacy.

Nicos Poulantzas (1973), in contrast, asserts that the class background of people in the top government jobs

is not important. What is most significant is the organisation of capitalist society, and in particular the role of the state in maintaining capitalism, irrespective of the background of those doing the task at hand. The state must have a significant degree of **autonomy** from individual capitalists so as to be able to choose effectively between the rival requirements for state action.

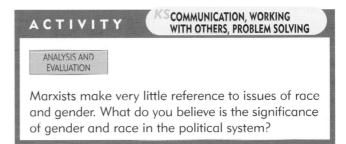

ACTIVITY   KS **COMMUNICATION, WORKING WITH OTHERS, PROBLEM SOLVING**

ANALYSIS AND EVALUATION

Marxists make very little reference to issues of race and gender. What do you believe is the significance of gender and race in the political system?

Gramsci (1977), rejected the 'economic determinism' in the traditional Marxian analysis. While imprisoned by the Italian fascist dictator Mussolini in the 1930s, Gramsci attempted to provide a theoretical basis to his activism in the Italian Communist Party. Gramsci's view was there should be a division between two parts of the state:

■ All the centrally controlled agencies of social control, which he termed **political society**. These include all the repressive state institutions such as the police and the military.

■ **civil society** is made up of institutions attempting to manipulate people's ideas and beliefs – the creation and distribution of ideology. It includes creative artists, philosophers and church thinkers.

The capitalist state rules by consensus, although it can use violence if and when required. However, Gramsci argued that the state would always seek a resolution to any conflict by peaceful means if at all possible. To this end, the capitalist state attempts to form a **historic bloc**, which involves striking a balance with distinct groups in an attempt to generate widespread feelings of communal solidarity. Such agreement is sustained by **hegemony** – Gramsci's conception of the Marxist notion of dominant ideology. Capitalism can be overthrown only by challenging hegemony and creating a new historic bloc. A key element in this process was to be provided by the Communist Party, which should provide the working class with leadership and become 'the modern prince'.

Abercrombie, Turner and Hill (1981) reject approaches which emphasise the ideological importance of the state: there are many studies, they argue, which show how working-class people can discard any dominant ideology. Paul Willis's study *Learning to Labour* is an example, which clearly demonstrates how a group of working-class 'lads' introduced masculine shop-floor culture into their school, in direct opposition to the philosophy that the teachers attempted to impose on them. For Abercrombie, financial considerations such as anxiety about unemployment are more significant in maintaining inequalites within capitalism.

Giddens' critique of Marxism

Since his 1985 book *The Nation State and Violence* Anthony Giddens has developed a number of critiques of Marxism. Later in this area we will assess the work of Giddens, but we outline some of his key criticisms here:

- Marxists do not have a satisfactory account of power, in particular they have no real analysis of military power or of the use of violence by individuals.
- Within the Marxist analysis there is no real account of administrative power or what is distinctive about administrative power within the nation state.
- Marxists do not take into account non-economic sources.
- Marxists do not take into account conflicts which are not related to class issues.
- Marxists do not take into account non-class-based politics – such as the Green movement or gender politics.

New Right theory of the state

Conservative philosophy or ideology in the UK has been dominated by Margaret Thatcher since the 1970s. It is commonly assumed that she broke the post-war consensus established by the Labour government of Attlee (1945–51) which was based on redistribution of income via the tax and benefits systems and the establishment of health care and education free at the point of issue as central elements of a comprehensive welfare state.

Thatcherism was seen as conviction politics; as enterprise culture pushing back the 'nanny state'; as

giving unions back to their members. Many on the left, notably Stuart Hall (1983), came to view Thatcherism as **authoritarian populism** where Thatcher recreated common sense in the minds of the working class by the use of 'hegemonic messages'.

Finer (1987) explained that all post-war governments accepted the triangle of public corporations, social services and full employment. However, the Thatcher governments had a very different vision of politics and the role of the state:

- Keynesian deficit financing was out.
- Physical controls and/or subsidies to ailing industries were out.
- Money supply economics and financial management of the economy were in.
- Unions were cold-shouldered.
- Public expenditure was restrained.
- Nationalised industries were told to make profits.
- Privatisation.
- Exchange controls were abolished.
- The maximum possible scope was given to market forces.

Finer explains: '…nothing – neither the rising unemployment that had stricken Macmillan and Heath with panic, nor waves of strikes such as had paralysed former governments – simply nothing was allowed to stand in the way of these policies.' (1987:129).

In many respects this was because, from a Thatcherite perspective, unemployment was blamed on the unemployed themselves: they had priced themselves out of jobs by demanding higher wages.

Other writers argued that Thatcher brought about a major change in values, attitudes and beliefs. Stephen Haseler (1989), for example, argued that Thatcherism was a reaction to the dominant paternalist stance of the major political parties in Britain from 1945 onwards. We could add that Thatcher attempted to turn the political into the personal. 'Don't spend more than you earn' became economic policy; 'Don't trust foreigners' became foreign policy. Is this the hallmark of postmodern politics?

However, what is most important for our purposes is that the New Right favours a minimal state. This is in sharp contrast to the Marxist view that capitalism as a system can only survive if there is a strong state.

A C T I V I T Y   **KS** COMMUNICATION, WORKING
WITH OTHERS, PROBLEM SOLVING

IDENTIFICATION AND
INTERPRETATION

ANALYSIS AND
EVALUATION

What is the role of violence in the political system:
for Marxists? Do you accept or reject this view?
Give a reason for your answer.

Summary of the similarities and differences between Marxism and élite theory

Similarities:

- Both Marxism and élite theory have a small ruling class which holds power, and a large group of powerless individuals.

- Both Marxism and élite theory are zero-sum conceptions of power. In other words, they presume that there is an unchanging quantity of power in society.

- Both Marxism and élite theory presume that the ruling class sustains its power by manipulating the thoughts and ideas of the powerless.

Differences:

- In the Marxist analysis the dominant class is invariably an economic class; in élite theory this is not the case.

- Marxism has a very promising view of the future – the powerless will one day arise from their exploitation and take power. In élite theory, oligarchy (the rule of the few) is inescapable: the mass will never rise up and take power.

- In the Marxist analysis, the connection between the bourgeoisie and the proletariat is always based upon economic exploitation. In contrast, in élite theory the mass has a psychological compulsion to be dominated.

- Marxism is used as a political defence for socialism. Élite theory is used as a political apology for fascism.

Source: Best (1997)

State-centred theories

The **state** is the most powerful organisation in society and it is believed to have interests of its own. The modern state is not the product of capitalism, or of class relations. There is no power in society forcing the state in any specific direction. Michael Mann (1993) suggests that there are several sources of social power: the economic, the political, the military and the ideological. He argues that one of the central factors in the process of state formation is the military danger from the outside world. Eric Nordlinger (1981) suggested that the state can develop greater independence from other groups in society by:

- concealing its methods of decision-making

- manipulating the honours system, or giving funding of government contracts to persuade people that government policies and programmes are right

- making use of the state's assets to pre-empt criticism, and set the agenda for public opinion – for example the increased use of government advertising in Britain since 1979

- changing policy to meet new circumstances

Theda Skopol (1979) is one of the most convincing state-centred theorists. She describes a number of states behaving independently to fulfil their own interests. Like Gramsci, who we discussed above, Skopol argues that state development is dependent upon how well organised other groups are in society. However, in contrast to the Marxian analysis, she thinks that states do not have to constantly secure advantages for the bourgeoisie because, she claims, a powerful state can mould the action of all classes, including the bourgeoisie.

However, the theoretical assumptions of state-centred theorists are often vague. They are critical of the assumptions of Marxists, pluralists and élite theorists but their own assumptions about the links between the state and society are not clear. At times they are neo-Weberian in nature, at times neo-Marxist.

Pluralism

Pluralism is a theory of power which stands in opposition to both Marxism and élite theory. It describes a situation in which power is diffuse or widely shared between any number of individuals, groups and organisations. In addition, for the pluralist the amount of power in society is not fixed.

All the participants within a pluralistic system have their own sectional interests and ideas on how to achieve their objectives. Unlike Marxist and élite theories, pluralism is a 'non-zero-sum' conception of power. For the pluralist the amount of power in society is not fixed, but can expand. Talcott Parsons (1951), for example, argued that every social action that a person carried out had to make use of power because every social action makes a difference in the world and whatever we do will affect other people. Social action is performed within roles – for example you may be reading this book whilst playing your role as a student. For Parsons, if the number of social roles within a social system were to increase, then the amount of power within that social system would also increase because more power would be needed to make all the additional differences in the world. The amount of power can also decrease: if the number of social roles were to decline, then the amount of power within that social system would also decline. Marxists and élite theorists, in contrast, believe that there is a fixed amount of power in society. If the ruling class gains power then the mass or proletariat must lose some power; if the proletariat gains power then the bourgeoisie must have lost some.

The pluralist maintains that the state is not there to support class interests – it is the rule-maker and umpire within society, the 'honest broker' that attempts to balance sectional interests and opinions within the political society. For the pluralist there is always political competition and a balance is needed between competing interests.

Dahl (1971) proposes four primary patterns of competition within pluralism:

- All active groups (political parties, pressure groups, for example) have the ability to exercise some influence over decision-makers
- Formal democracy, in which competition takes place between organised groups. Again the most often quoted examples include political parties
- The 'inclusive hegemony', usually a one-party state in which we find competition within the state

bureaucracy and between party members and party officials

- 'Competitive oligarchy' in which élite groups, such as party leaders or the very wealthy, compete for power

The most advanced form of pluralism is known as **polyarchy**. According to Robert Dahl (1971) polyarchy is the government of a state or city by the many rather than by a monarchy. People are citizens with citizenship rights, which the government cannot take away. The citizenship rights rest upon a set of authoritative rules, which are themselves based upon the citizens' wishes. This is necessary for the democratic process to work. The rules guarantee our civil and political rights, which, according to Lindblom (1977), include:

- freedom to form organisations
- freedom of speech and publication
- the right to vote
- the right to stand for public office, such as parliament or the local council
- the right of political leaders to ask for financial support
- the right of political leaders to compete for votes
- elections to decide who is to hold the top authority
- a range of sources of information available to people, who have the right to read whatever they wish
- government departments that make an effort to carry out whatever policies will help them get re-elected

These rules are based on choices which are created by the citizens themselves through a process of negotiation. According to Charles Lindblom (1977) – who had a significant influence upon the thinking of Anthony Giddens – these choices form a common core of four **volitions**:

- **Simple preference** – when a person holds a view that they like something and dislike another thing with no justification, for example 'I like Blair better than Hague'.
- **Complex judgement** – when someone comes to an opinion after some consideration and analysis. For example, when a person claims to want closer

ties with the European Union after an examination
of the relevant policies, issues and consequences.

- **Moral or ethical rules** – individuals choose an
  opinion on the basis of a moral code. For example
  being for or against IVF or abortion.

- **Simple preference between complex
  judgements** – individuals choose from a range of
  complex judgements as they would choose a
  simple preference. Lindblom gives the example of
  a person saying 'No, I don't believe in foreign aid,
  but don't ask me why.' (1977:135).

Giddens (1985) argues that nation states have a
tendency towards polyarchy; as all governments must
have the approval of the people in order to rule. Dahl
argues that polyarchy is both a product of the
democratising of nation states and a type of regime.
Within these societies, there are many opportunities for
participating in the political process and influencing the
actions of the government. This is because political
institutions within polyarchy have developed to aid the
democratic political process.

Critiques of pluralism and polyarchy

There are several criticisms of pluralism and polyarchy.
Pluralistic research is said to be concerned only with
decision-making and to have no conception of non-
decision-making. People in power may have the ability
to manipulate the decision-making process. It may
appear open and democratic but it is not. Notably,
pluralists are said to ignore the effects of ideology, that
individual ideas (volitions) may be manipulated by
capitalists via the mass media. Dahl does accept that
the unequal pattern of wealth distribution could help to
support an unequal division of political power.

Paul Hirst (1988) outlines the nature of pluralism and
polyarchy and evaluates the critiques. He argues that
Marxists view pluralism as 'misdescription of the
realities of power', which:

- disregards inequality of income and wealth – is the
  key characteristic of western societies

- focuses on the surface aspects of the political
  system – actual decision-making and efforts to
  influence decision-making processes by individuals
  and groups – rather than on the 'deep' causes such
  as class factors.

The 'new' politics

The 'new' politics involves a number of major shifts
in how we view the political relationships in the
world. The key characteristics are outlined by Best
(1997:587):

- A new foundation for authority and a need to re-
  evaluate the sociological established theories of
  authority such as Weber

- A shift away from class-based politics to identity
  politics

- A shift of support from old social movements such
  as political parties to **new social movements**

- The declining significance of the nation state in the
  face of processes of globalisation

- A loss of faith in grand narratives or big ideologies
  such as socialism

This situation can bring with it new forms of
community, which may be very rewarding and very
fulfilling for the individuals involved. Within
modernity individuals relate to each other in rational
ways. This is most clearly seen in the way people
relate to each other in Weber's ideal type of
bureaucracy. Moreover, because of the processes of
globalisation (see Area 13), rationality is said to be
common across the world. But in the postmodern
condition the foundations of rationality are said to be
undermined and people have to invent new ways of
relating to each other; and this means new forms of
politics. However, this condition can also generate
new forms of hostility towards individuals or groups
who are seen to be outsiders, and because human
behaviour is free from rationality, the scope for
misunderstanding human behaviour and intentions is
almost infinite.

What is the 'new' politics?

Within the 'new' politics of the postmodern condition
there is a great emphasis on issues of identity,
which appear to be more significant than class-based
issues. Nationalism in particular dominated the
politics of Europe in the last decade of the twentieth
century.

Nationalism

Nationalism is a return to the 'local', by which we mean a respect for local roots, in which people attempt to maintain or assert their local identity.

Nationalism has become synonymous with intolerance, inhumanity and violence. However, for many people nationalism brings feelings of hope, justice and liberation. If we take the example of Balkanisation (discussed below), it could be argued that the people of Slovenia and Croatia chose to secede from Yugoslavia because of the unwillingness of Serb and Montenegrans to put together an economic reform package which would have allowed Slovenia and Croatia to reap the full benefits of western tourism. What gave their nationalism its strength was the recognition of statehood by the European Union.

Giddens on nationalism

Giddens (1981) makes a distinction between the nation state and nationalism – although both are European in origin. The **nation state** is essentially an institution, what Giddens terms the dominant 'power container', whereas **nationalism** is a psychological phenomenon '… involving felt needs and dispositions' which '… feeds upon, or represents an attenuated form of … primordial sentiments.' (Giddens, 1981:193). Therefore '… nationalism is not merely a set of symbols and beliefs force fed to an unwilling or indifferent population' (Giddens, 1981:192).

For Giddens, in the modern world the foundations of everyday life are built upon routines. If the security these routines give is broken in some way, by any form of 'radical social disruption', then individuals can be attracted to the security that nationalistic symbols provide, most notably when this is associated with strong leadership. Giddens states that nationalism can provide reassurance for 'repressed anxieties' which are primitive in nature.

Balkanisation

Within the social sciences the term 'community' refers to:

■ locality

■ set of social relationships

■ shared identity

Conflicts can emerge over all three of these notions of community. This is most clearly seen in the analysis of the conflict in the former Yugoslavia by Stjepan G. Mestrovic's *The Balkanization of the West: The Confluence of Postmodernism and Postcommunism* (1994).

In contrast to modernist thinkers such as Anthony Giddens, Mestrovic argues that the world is becoming less cosmopolitan, less global and less rational. The world is moving towards smaller and smaller units with greater hostility towards each other. This is the process of **Balkanisation**, which is both a postmodern phenomenon and a rebellion against the grand narratives of the Enlightenment – it is a process of disintegration and against the optimistic faith of the Enlightenment. A key element of Balkanisation is 'narcissism': people feel that their religion (group, city, cultural group, etc.) is superior to all others. Together with the collective feeling that 'others' have ambitions to exterminate the whole of your group, such narcissis leads directly to hostility and the breakdown of society. The USA and western Europe are not Balkanising along geographical lines, but along ethnic, gender and other lines. Many native Americans, Kurds, Haitians, Bosnians, Croats and Palestinians (amongst others) feel that the western notion of universal human rights has passed them by.

In both the west and the Soviet Union there was a popular belief that their system was superior to the other. In the former Soviet Union the culture which helped to maintain the belief in the superiority of communism has not gone away, but is now manifest in aggressive forms of nationalism and ethnic conflict, which in the west we refer to as **tribalism**. Such views underline the need to **demonise** the 'other'. To explain this, Mestrovic draws upon the work of a number of writers such as Lasch – and notably Jovan Raskovic's 'Luda Zemlja' ('Crazy Land') (1990), which looks at the narcissistic nature of communism. When communism came to an end, people in the former Soviet Union experienced a collapse of hope and self-worth; their ontological security was shaken. Taking his starting point from Freud, Raskovic claims that:

- The Croats have a castration anxiety – they are driven by fears that something will happen to humiliate them and take away what they have worked for.
- The Moslems have an anal frustration – which makes them desire to be clean and good.
- The Serbs have Oedipal conflicts – which make them aggressive and authoritarian.

The interaction between these forces is what underpins the Balkan conflict, making violence inevitable. However, as we suggested above, Balkanisation is not confined to eastern Europe. In the USA, for example, after the 1993 Superbowl there was rioting on the streets of Dallas: black Americans pulled white Americans out of their cars and beat them up – as a revenge for slavery, they claimed. Dallas is not Sarajevo 'but disturbing similarities exist already' (Mestrovic, 1994:109). In addition, the postmodern television camera provokes the evils within traditional cultures to come to the surface. Television does not reduce racism, sexism or violence, but enhances the need for faith, which is asserted as fundamentalism.

In Area 4 we suggested that issues of culture and identity are central in defining:

- who we are as individuals
- who we are as community
- whom we do not accept as part of 'us'

We can say, then, that postmodern politics is a non-institutional participatory politics which is outside the established political institutions, which is not motivated by working-class people struggling to improve their economic situation but rather is motivated by people concerned with issues of identity and culture.

Within the postmodern condition there is no consistent moral discipline and this means that there is little to prevent individuals from becoming involved in acts such as ethnic cleansing; the extermination of people who are regarded as 'not one of us'. This is very much the dark side of postmodernity, the great danger that politics, as in the Balkans, can become a politics without rules or morality and in which people are capable of acts of great cruelty.

The breakdown of 'grand narratives' has a number of consequences.

1. The postmodern political condition becomes pluralistic in nature, with many 'cultures and discourses', each with its own 'small narrative'. These may be local, cultural, ethnic, religious or ideological in nature.
2. A foundation for what Habermas (1973) termed 'domination-free' discourse becomes possible; people can talk to each other free from ideology. This is what Habermas terms 'communicative competence'.
3. The replacement of the state as a 'class agency'. Class politics was always rational and calculable because it was based upon economic interests. However, without the economic interests of classes, politics becomes irrational and unpredictable.
4. Politics loses its sense of 'taboo'. Racism becomes politicised within a form of 'moral relativism' in which: '… even the assessment of a mass deportation and genocide becomes a matter of taste.'

In a more positive view, Heller and Feher (1988) argue that the postmodern political ethos is democratic in nature. With the decline in the grand narratives there is a greater emphasis upon the individual person actively making choices, rather than being pushed about by forces outside their control. It is this which upholds the postmodern democracy.

According to **Zygmunt Bauman** postmodern politics has four characteristics:

1. **Tribal politics**   Individuals come together with others who they feel share an identity. Often these communities are nationalistic in nature, and are referred to as tribes or imagined communities.
2. **Politics of desire**   Individuals need to obtain tribal tokens – something trivial like wearing the right kind of clothes, or something more unpleasant like involvement in ethnic cleansing – to show that they are part of the community.
3. **Politics of fear**   This is concerned with avoidance of potentially harmful effects. New political issues emerge which have nothing to do with social class, for example the possible link between BSE and CJD.
4. **Politics of certainty**   We have a need for expert advice, but in the postmodern condition we are unwilling to place our trust in experts. Loss of trust becomes a major political issue.

Zygmunt Bauman

According to Anthony Giddens, Zygmunt Bauman is *the* theorist of postmodernism. Born in Poland, he did his PhD at the London School of Economics in the 1950s under the supervision of Robert McKenzie. He taught sociology in a number of universities, including Manchester and Tel Aviv, before he became Professor of Sociology at Leeds University in 1970. He is at present Emeritus Professor of Sociology at Leeds University.

Now in his 70s, Bauman continues to write books, articles and reviews. His books include *Modernity and Ambivalence* (1991), *Intimations of Postmodernity* (1992), *Mortality, Immortality and Other Life Strategies* (1992), *Postmodern Ethics* (1993), *Life in Fragments* (1995), and *Postmodernity and Its Discontents* (1997), *Globalisation* (1998) and *Work, Consumerism and the New Poor* (1998). Bauman has also written about freedom, culture, thinking sociologically, and the Holocaust. For a critical review of his work look at 'Zygmunt Bauman: personal reflections from the mainstream of modernity' *British Journal of Sociology* (1998).

Postmodern politics is much more irrational and emotional than the politics that went before it.

IDENTIFICATION AND INTERPRETATION

Are there people in your area who are classed as 'outsiders'?

You could attempt to outline and evaluate the values of people in your neighbourhood who behave in relation to people who are classed as outsiders. Do they behave in a tribal fashion?

Politics in the postmodern world could be becoming **neo-medieval** in nature – suggesting a return to the politics of the Middle Ages. For Baudrillard (1993), the

curve of history may become so great that we have a reverse trajectory. The turn that history is now taking is one of reversal and elimination:

> *Restoration, regression, rehabilitation, the revival of old frontiers, differences, specificities and religious beliefs – and everywhere, even on the level of social mores, the change of heart: apparently all the marks of liberation won over the last century are now fading, and perhaps are all destined to disappear altogether one after the other. We are in the midst of an immense process of revisionism ...*

(Baudrillard, 1993:98)

What is neo-medieval?

In the postmodern condition, because of the process of reversal and elimination, politics appears to be developing a number of characteristics that are similar to the characteristics of the political system within medieval Europe:

- no nation state
- no democracy
- violent challenge to the power of the central authority (the king at that time) from various sources
- conflict between very different belief systems: church ideology versus secular ideology
- tension between the major institutions of the day: king versus church
- individuals unclear about their identity
- politics without established rules
- frequent resort to violence to resolve issues

In addition, because of the process of **implosion**, postmodern politics becomes not about class-based issues but about the single-issue campaigns of 'new' social movements, and political parties become increasingly irrelevant.

Baudrillard on implosion

According to Baudrillard (1993), the mass media are opposed to mediation. They are concerned with one-way communication, there is no exchange. This simple emission/reception of information can be viewed as the forced silence of the masses. The 'stupor' which the masses appear to be in is said by Baudrillard to make the masses radically uncertain as to their own desires. The media images are no longer differentiated from 'reality' or 'human nature', not because of some simple manipulation in a Marxian sense but because the masses have an almost infinite abundance of entertainment and other forms of useless information. The masses have a greater and greater desire for spectacle, and it is because of this demand that films become more and more expensive to produce, have better and better special effects, the promotion and hype is more intense, the merchandising covers all possible commodities. We have a televisually created politics of disillusion and disaffection. The end result is a series of implosions: conflict between labour and capital, politics and entertainment, high culture and low culture. All such divisions collapse in on themselves to form a political void. The result of this is often the 'sudden crystallisation of latent violence' (Baudrillard, 1993:76), which appears as irrational episodes. Spectators turn themselves into actors; they invent their own spectacle for the gaze of the media. Baudrillard discusses examples such as violence at the Heysel stadium, the Real Madrid–Naples European Cup final and Thatcher's conflict with the miners.

In summary, postmodernists would argue that political life is becoming more 'decentred' and that there has been a twofold postmodernisation of political life:

- The decline of class-based politics and the politics of other grand narratives, such as socialism and feminism, which tell large groups of people what to think.
- The breaking down of rigid barriers between political and private life allowing the emergence of 'identity politics'.

It is not only postmodernists who are concerned with these issues. Heir to the Frankfurt School, Jurgen Habermas, also makes a distinction between a 'new politics' and an 'old politics', in which old social movements are concerned with the economic issues such as the social security system. Habermas also

outlines a 'new politics' which is concerned with issues such as identity politics and human rights. This 'new politics' is the area of activity for the new social movements, and Habermas draws parallels between these and what he terms the 'social-romantic' movements from the nineteenth century, which rejected modern rational capitalism (these include groups of craftsmen and 'escapist' movements often supported by middle-class people).

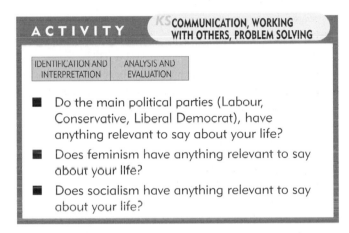

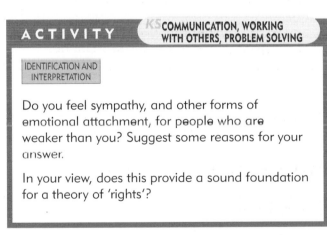

This suggests that the politics of the new social movements has more meaning for the individual than the politics of the class-based political parties. There are similarities here with the 'postmaterialist' thesis of Ronald Inglehart, who argues that the political changes in advanced societies can be tracked back to a transformation in 'the values of western publics … an overwhelming emphasis on material well-being and physical security towards greater emphasis on the quality of life' (Inglehart, 1971:3).

Inglehart also argues that this change has resulted in a decline of the Left/Right social class division and a rise in new social movements, together with a greater emphasis on lifestyle problems, individual freedom and liberty.

Jurgen Habermas: new social movements and communicative competence

New social movements attempt to defend the quality of life of people by becoming concerned with issues of personal and collective achievement which the process of rationalisation is taking away from them, issues such as equality, self-realisation, participation and human rights. These may take the form of **particularistic** concerns; these are concerns which are specific to followers of a new social movement rather than the wider society. However, social movements are also concerned with re-establishing a **communicative ethics**, which is about the sharing of community norms. Although new social movements may have differences of opinion and be in conflict over a range of issues, any dispute can be resolved only as long as each movement is able and willing to listen to the other; what Habermas termed the **ideal speech situation** – a form of shared communication between people who want to resolve their differences.

The Third Way

Anthony Giddens has a very different view of politics in an uncertain world. The election of the Blair government in Britain and the Clinton and Gore administration in the USA has made Giddens very influential politically. The **Third Way** is an alternative approach to politics, developed by Giddens, which is neither right-wing nor traditional social democracy. Influenced by **communitarianism**, the Third Way is about radically changing our notions of citizenship, away from something which is 'given' as of 'right' to something which must be 'achieved' through work and contributions to the community. In addition, the

Social democracy	Neoliberalism	Third Way
(the old left)	(the new right)	(the centre-left)
Class politics of the left	Class politics of the right	Modernising movement of the centre
Old mixed economy	Market fundamentalism	New mixed economy
Corporatism: state dominates civil society	Minimal state	New democratic state
Internationalism	Conservative nation	Cosmopolitan nation
Strong welfare state, protecting 'from cradle to grave'	Welfare safety net	Social investment state

Source: Giddens 'After the left's paralysis' New Statesman 1 May 1998:18

Figure 14.1 The Third Way

Third Way is about the creation of a 'social investment state' by eliminating social exclusion and segregation through training and reskilling the young unemployed via the New Deal.

Giddens (1998) notes that people at the bottom of the class ladder have become increasingly excluded from social and political life. The children of the poor make limited use of the education system and have fewer opportunities to become socially mobile. In a similar fashion, professional people increasingly exclude themselves from public institutions: they do not use the NHS; their children do not use state schools.

The New Deal

The New Deal was one of Labour's election pledges. Its intention was to reduce youth unemployment through a programme of welfare-to-work. The principal aim was to assist the transition from benefit to work for 18–24-year-olds who have been in receipt of benefit for over six months. After an initial interview, the young unemployed person will be invited into the 'Gateway': a four-month period of personal assessment, which is used to determine what the individual is already capable of and what option is suitable to his or her needs. It is also a stage where difficulties such as literacy can be dealt with, any personal problems such as drug or alcohol abuse can be identified and any rehabilitation, often with the use of mentors, can be provided.

After the Gateway there are four options:

- work in the private or public sector
- work in the voluntary sector
- work with the Environmental Task Force – cleaning rubbish from rivers, cleaning graffiti etc.
- full-time education or training.

If the young person goes into full-time work, the employer will receive a subsidy of £60 per week plus £750 training expenses, to allow the young person to receive one day a week training over a six-month period. If young people choose one of the other options, they will receive an extra £15 per week.

It is commonly assumed by people on the right that the benefits system created a dependency culture and that reform of the benefits system had not broken the cycle of dependency. The New Deal involves investing in individual people through training and increasing employment skills. As a consequence, employment opportunities are gained by the individual, which in turn creates economic prosperity and competitiveness in the global market. The communitarian edge to this policy is that for a person to take from the community they must give something back. Hence, citizenship rights are earned via work. As Raymond Plant (1998:30) explained:

> *The ideas of reciprocity and contribution are at the heart of this concept of citizenship: individuals do not and cannot have a right to the resources of society unless they contribute to the development of that society through work or other socially valued activities, if they are in a position to do so.*

As Tony Blair himself said in a party political broadcast: 'Everybody who has a contribution to make can.'

The Labour government claims that it is committed to eradicating social exclusion. As David Muligan, director of Demos, has explained, the unemployed 'are more properly defined as excluded because they live outside the worlds of work, of education, of sociability itself' (quoted in Lloyd, 1997:14).

Anthony Giddens' politics of 'reflexive modernisation': from emancipatory politics to life politics

> *Life politics is a politics, not of life chances, but of life-style. It concerns disputes and struggles about how (as individuals and as collective humanity) we should live in a world where what used to be fixed either by nature or tradition is now subject to human decisions.*

(Giddens, 1994:14–15)

Life politics emerges from **emancipatory politics** and is a politics of self-actualisation; in other words, life politics '... concerns debates and contestations deriving from the reflexive project of the self,' (Giddens, 1991:215). Emancipatory politics has two main elements:

1 An effort to break free from the shackles of the past.
2 Overcoming illegitimate domination, which adversely affects the life chances of individuals.

For Giddens, nation states are becoming more polyarchic in nature, citizenship rights have been won by participation in forms of 'emancipatory politics'. There is a high tolerance of opposition and widespread opportunities for influencing the conduct of government. Giddens argues that within nation states democracy is moving towards a 'dialogic democracy', which is similar in many respects to the 'pure relationship'. He explains:

> *... there is a close tie between the pure relationship and dialogic democracy. Dialogue, between individuals who approach one another as equals, is a transactional quality central to their mutuality. There are remarkable parallels between what a good relationship looks like, as developed in the literature of marital and sexual therapy, and formal mechanisms of political democracy. Both depend on the development of ... a principle of autonomy.*

(Giddens, 1994:118–119)

In Giddens' view, we need a theory of democratisation that takes into account both everyday life and globalising systems. Towards this end Giddens develops his notion of 'dialogic democracy', which stands in opposition to all forms of fundamentalism and attempts to '... create active trust through an appreciation of the integrity of the other. Trust is a means of ordering social relations across time and space' (Giddens, 1994:116). We attempt to live with others in a relation of 'mutual tolerance'. As Giddens suggested, our political relationships take on many of the characteristics of the 'pure' relationship. All individuals strive for a 'pure' relationship in Giddens' analysis; this is a relationship based solely upon trust and cannot be underpinned by any guarantee.

An important element in the changing nature of politics for Giddens is the rise of new social movements.

The distinction between old social movements and new social movements

Old social movements (OSMs), such as the trades union movement, were class-based movements and focused on the state to bring about change. In contrast, new social movements (NSMs) are not class-based movements, but are concerned, on the whole, with issues of identity and lifestyle. Examples include gay and lesbian groups such as Stonewall or OutRage, which direct their activities at a range of institutions, not just the state.

The distinction between OSMs and NSMs has been summarised by Paul Bagguley, who demonstrates that:

- OSMs are influenced by economic factors which directly affect economic advancement of their members. NSMs, in contrast, are 'post-materialist' in that they are influenced by problems that do not immediately affect the financial interests of their members, such as peace, the environment and human rights.

- Support for OSMs was mainly from working-class people, whilst support for NSMs is mainly drawn from the 'new' middle classes, in particular from public-sector professionals.

- OSMs were bureaucratic in nature, with a national committee structure. NSMs are built upon 'networks', which are predominantly informal, or 'polycephalus' in nature. They rely upon active participation rather than representation by delegates.

- OSMs are motivated by influencing significant people who have been elected or by influencing

some group which is powerful within a corporate structure. In contrast, NSMs are concerned with direct action, often involving symbolic protests such as climbing trees to prevent motorways from being built.

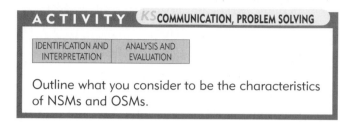

ACTIVITY KS **COMMUNICATION, PROBLEM SOLVING**

| IDENTIFICATION AND INTERPRETATION | ANALYSIS AND EVALUATION |

Outline what you consider to be the characteristics of NSMs and OSMs.

Classification of new social movements: Mario Diani

Mario Diani has attempted to pull together much of the relevant research and theories in the area and to produce a clear view of the nature of the NSM. Firstly, he explains that such diverse events and organisations as revolutions, religious and political groups, single issue campaigns have been defined as new social movements. Diani identifies four main trends within NSM analysis.

Collective behaviour approaches

An example is the work of Turner and Killian, who define an NSM as 'a collectivity acting with some continuity to promote or resist a change in the society or organisation of which it is part' (Diani, 1992:4). These groups do not have a clearly defined membership or leadership and their actions and views are determined by informal responses of the current supporters rather than by any formal management plan. In other words, this approach suggests that NSMs are networks of communication and action rather than formal organisations.

Resource mobilisation theory

An example is the work of Zald and McCarthy, who place much more attention on the role of the organisational factors within NSMs, which they define as 'a set of opinions and beliefs which represents preferences for changing some elements of the social structure and/or reward distribution of a society. A counter movement is a set of opinions and beliefs in a population opposed to a social movement' (quoted in Diani, 1992:4). In other words, this approach suggests that NSMs attempt to draw together resources in an effort to change some aspect of society.

Political process approaches

This may be seen in the work of Tilly, who associates the development of NSMs with the exclusion of individual interests from the established political processes and political channels. NSMs are a product of social unrest amongst people with a shared identity who are ignored by traditional political parties. Tilly defined NSMs as 'a sustained series of interactions between power holders and persons successfully claiming to speak on behalf of a constituency lacking formal representation, in the course of which those persons make publicly visible demands for changes in the distribution or exercise of power, and back those demands with public demonstrations of support' (quoted in Diani, 1992:5). In other words, this approach suggests that NSMs are groups made up of individuals who are ignored by the major political parties.

New social movement approaches

The work of both Touraine and Melucci attempts to link the rise of NSMs to wider structural and cultural changes within society. NSMs emerge as a consequence of the new contradictions which replace the class conflict – between the bourgeoisie and the proletariat – that we find with modern/organised capitalism, as this form of society gives way to a post-industrial society. Touraine views the NSM as 'a combination of a principle of identity, a principle of opposition and a principle of totality' (quoted in Diani, 1992:6). In other words, in the post-industrial society, individuals develop their own view of the world, their rivals and the winnings that can be gained from any conflict. NSMs are a product of the rise of a post-industrial society. In this post-industrial society, classes disappear and the space they leave is filled by NSMs.

Summary

For Mario Diani an NSM is not an organisation, it is:

- a network of informal interactions involving links between a number of individuals, groups and organisations
- a form of solidarity built upon shared beliefs
- a form of collective action outside the traditional political institutions, promoting or resisting social change
- a basis for a collective identity

ACTIVITY

IDENTIFICATION AND INTERPRETATION	ANALYSIS AND EVALUATION

Diani argues that NSMs are based upon a collective identity achieved through self-understanding and interpretation. If there is no collective identity we might conclude that there is no social movement. Tim Jordan has argued that 'It is not clear why a collective identity is constructed by actors in a movement' (Jordan, 1995:677).

Read the following passages and answer the questions that follow, giving reasons for your answers.

Item 1

❝ In the 1990s there has been a significant increase in the level of political activism amongst gay and lesbians who have 'come out' since the beginning of the AIDS epidemic. In Britain the activist group OutRage captured the news headlines because of its tactic of 'outing' closet homosexuals (using a number of methods to force unwilling individuals to admit publicly that they were homosexual). OutRage has also been active in other areas fighting anti-gay discrimination, prejudice and violence. In particular, building on the work of Michel Foucault (1977), OutRage has attempted to remake and remodel the identity of the homosexual man and lesbian woman, moving away from the notion of 'gay' and labelling themselves as 'queer'. Individuals who describe themselves as 'homosexual', in the eyes of OutRage, are accepting a heterosexual and false-scientific view of sexuality, in which homosexuals are marginalised and can be accepted as people only if they reject their 'queerness' or deny the legitimacy of their chosen sexuality. People who describe themselves as homosexuals are merely attempting to assimilate themselves into heterosexual life by accepting a role as a member of a distinct minority who ask for tolerance; but will always be regarded as sexually wrong. How do we characterise 'queer' culture?

- It is highly political, but above party politics.

- It rejects the rational sexual categories imposed upon us all, both homosexual and straight, male and female, in which we are asked to define ourselves as sexually 'normal'/heterosexual or otherwise.

- It aims to destabilise the power relations that maintain these categories, which force homosexuals into a private world.

- It refuses to accept homosexuality as a minority group in the population.

However, many lesbians and gays have questioned the notion of 'queer' and the identity that goes with it.

Item 2

‘ Assimilationism, as a term used to apply to minority groups in society, is the desire to merge – or the practice of merging – with the dominant majority.

Toby Manning (1995) *Gay Times*, April:19–20

Item 3

‘ Assimilationism is generally used in a slightly pejorative way to describe efforts amongst lesbian and gay men to become part of society. My own feeling is that (at Stonewall) we're not aiming towards a situation where everyone becomes the same – it's all about recognition and respect for difference. That's what makes life and society interesting. We're campaigning for social justice and equality. I don't see that as collaborating.

Angela Mason, Executive director of the Stonewall Group (1995). *Gay Times*, April:19–20

Item 4

‘ Assimilationism has been the dominant lesbian and gay rights strategy for the last 30 years, emphasising law reform, and the idea that the best way to advance our interests is by quietly blending in with mainstream heterosexual society. However, since the legal system has been devised by and is dominated by heterosexuals, that inevitably means that we win equality on terms

which are dictated by straights. The end result is the phenomenon of 'hetero homos' – queer versions of heterosexual lifestyle and morality.

The opposite of assimilation is not separatism. It is the proud assertion of a distinctive queer identity and culture. Assimilation implies that there is nothing worthwhile or valuable in the lesbian and gay experience. Queer emancipation does not depend on us adapting to the heterosexual status quo, but on us radically transforming it. In questioning and rejecting the predominant social view that homosexuality is wrong and inferior, many of us also end up challenging other social assumptions. While equal rights are an important first step, they do not amount to full queer emancipation. There's a need for a complete overhaul of all the laws and values around sex – a post-equality agenda. This would benefit both heterosexuals and homosexuals and it creates the possibility of a new radical consensus for social change which transcends sexual orientation.

Peter Tatchell, OutRage activist (1995)
Gay Times, April:19–20

Item 5

‘ Most of us would agree that we should do what ever we can to protect members of our community. If 'outing' can help destroy the power and credibility of gay homophobes who harm other lesbians and gay men, then it is arguably the morally right thing to do. By not 'outing' gay public figures who are homophobic, we are effectively allowing them to continue to hurt other gay people. Our silence and inaction make us accomplices by default.

Peter Tatchell (1995) The ethics of 'outing'.
Gay Times, February:37

1 What do you understand by the term 'queer'?
2 What do you understand by the term 'outing'?
3 What are the reasons, according to the items, why groups attempt to 'out' closet homosexuals?
4 Can we identify such a group as 'the gay community'?
5 Do homosexuals/gays/queers have any form of collective identity built upon shared beliefs?
6 Is the 'gay liberation' movement a new social movement? Give a reason for your answer.

ANALYSIS AND
EVALUATION

NSM: The anti-poll tax movement in Leeds

In 1989 the Conservative government introduced a
local tax, which they named the Community Charge,
although this was commonly known as the Poll Tax. It
was a regressive tax in that it hit the poorest the
hardest. Everybody in a local area would pay the
same amount of local taxation for local government
services, irrespective of their ability to pay. The
response to this tax was organised demonstrations,
often violent, and a campaign of non-payment. Paul
Bagguley (1995) conducted a case study of the Anti-
Poll Tax Movement (APTM) in Leeds. Read this outline
of his case study and attempt the questions below.

In Leeds local APTM groups were highly informal
organisations, co-ordinated by a city-wide
Federation which was run by three elected officers:
a secretary, a treasurer and a chairperson. Local
organisations sent two representatives to the city-
wide Federation although there was no control of the
local groups from the centre. The Federation
organised demonstrations – notably public poll tax
bill burnings – transport, leaflets and held advice
sessions for people who were facing legal problems
for non-payment.

Some of the local groups had formal membership
schemes, issuing membership cards and collecting

dues; other local groups were more informal
operating like a 'telephone tree'. Bagguley
describes the structure as a 'series of concentric
rights with a core of committed activists,
surrounded by a ring of people who turn up for
public meetings, demonstrations etc. and finally
those who didn't pay but did not go to meetings
etc.' (Bagguley, 1995:713). Some local groups had
the active support of left-wing groups, for example
Socialist Organizer or the Communist party. In other
areas of the city radical Christians, the peace
movement, CND and other single-issue groups
were involved. Council estates often had the
support of tenants' associations. Finally, the Leeds
Trades Club provided the Federation with office
premises. However, the Labour party and most
trades unions, apart from NALGO, were unwilling
to give support to the Federation as often its
activities – notably its most effective weapon of non-
payment – involved breaking the law.

1 To what extent was the APTM in Leeds
   bureaucratic in nature? Did it share any
   characteristics with Weber's ideal type of
   bureaucracy?
2 To what extent was the APTM in Leeds like the
   postmodern organisation outlined at the start of
   this area?
3 Is the APTM an 'old' social movement or a 'new'
   social movement? Give reasons for your answer.

What factors hold the NSM together if such groups
are not class-based movements? According to Julian
McAllister-Groves, NSMs are held together by
emotional factors, which are not found in the
recruitment to old class-based movements or
traditional political parties.

New social movements: emotional recruitment

There is an emotional aspect to NSM recruitment. Julian
McAllister-Groves outlines what he calls the 'emotions
approach to social movement recruitment'. He draws
upon Erving Goffman's work on 'framing' to explain
NSM recruitment.

What is 'framing'?

Goffman's book *Frame Analysis: An Essay on the
Organisation of Experience* (1974) is concerned with
how people make sense of their personal experiencing.
Goffman explains:

> *I assume that definitions of the situation are built up
> in accordance with principles of organisation which
> govern events – at least social ones – and our
> subjective involvement in them; frame is the word I
> use to refer to such of these basic elements as I am
> able to identify. That is the definition of frame. My
> phrase 'frame analysis' is a slogan to refer to the
> examination in these terms of the organisation of
> experience.*

(Goffman, 1974:10–11)

It is important to note that in this book there is a very definite shift away from symbolic interactionism and towards structuralism in Goffman's analysis. 'Frameworks' are viewed as **schemata of interpretation**: organising principles that people draw upon or use as a resource to give their life meaning. McAllister-Groves argues that the frame also helps NSMs to organise involvement by 'constructing sets of beliefs that encourage potential recruits to act because these beliefs appeal to them.' (McAllister-Groves, 1995:436). By the use of a 'frame' the NSM can make ways of thinking and feeling acceptable for an ordinary person which might otherwise be classed as 'emotional deviance'. An example he gives is that of men who joined NSMs because they were embarrassed to show emotion about animals outside such a group. McAllister-Groves explains:

> ' The animal rights activists that I studied experienced affection and empathy for the animals portrayed in animal rights literature as helpless victims of cruelty. Most of them, however, were attracted to the movement because of its ability to legitimate their affection and empathy for animals in a way that reduced difficult interactions with outsiders who viewed them as being too emotional and therefore irrational.

(McAllister-Groves 1995:438).

In contrast to this emotional position, Day and Robbins argue that the public-service professionals (teachers, social workers etc.) who joined CND and the Peace Movement in the 1980s did so, not out of any emotional attachment to 'peace' but because of economic self-interest. As they explain (1987:232):

> ' The mobilisation of welfare professionals must be seen in the context of the crises of social democracy and the sharpening of conflicts within the British state, between its repressive and productive arms. There has been a shift of resources from welfare services to the police and the military, and an accompanying tendency to legitimate the role of the state in terms of 'law and order' rather than social welfare. In the face of this material and ideological threat it is hardly surprising that the Peace Movement provides an avenue of mobilisation that is particularly attractive to members of the caring professions.

For Day and Robbins, the rise of NSMs is directly related to the economic interests of their members; the Peace Movement is then a form of institutionalised class action.

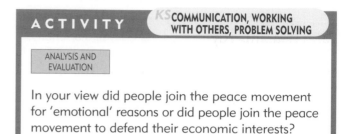

ACTIVITY KS COMMUNICATION, WORKING WITH OTHERS, PROBLEM SOLVING

ANALYSIS AND EVALUATION

In your view did people join the peace movement for 'emotional' reasons or did people join the peace movement to defend their economic interests?

David Held has made several critical points about Giddens' examination of NSMs, notably that many social movements are not included in Giddens' analysis, for example, the feminist movement and religious groups. However, in an earlier book (*The Nation State and Violence*, 1985) Giddens *did* discuss both the women's movement and religious movements. He argued that the struggles these groups were involved in had expanded our democratic rights.

In Giddens' political thought, 'life politics' has as its central principle enhancing personal independence, breaking down all forms of exploitation, inequality and oppression and promoting justice, equality and participation. Individuals thus have greater control over their own lives. Giddens recognises that nation states are restricted in their power. If a nation state, even a very powerful one such as the USA, were to ban IVF research or nuclear power, for example, this would have limited significance for global scientific developments.

Giddens adopts a rather optimistic view of the issues which emerge with globalisation (1994:253):

> ' Unpredictability, manufactured uncertainty, fragmentation: these are only one side of the coin of a globalizing order. On the reverse side are the shared values that come from a situation of global interdependence, organised via the cosmopolitan acceptance of difference.

'Manufactured uncertainty' means uncertainties created by people which have no real precedents, for example over the issue of global warming or nuclear power.

Tony Blair has argued that his politcs was influenced by the Scottish moral philosopher John Macmurray)who Blair first met during his time at Oxford University.

John Macmurray

Macmurray says that every person has a choice in every area of life: they can choose to do good or to do bad. Every person is a human agent living within a community. To behave morally is to behave in a fashion that benefits the community. Macmurray defines three modes of morality:

- The **communal mode** – if you carry out an action which is of benefit to others without benefiting yourself, then this is moral.

- The **contemplative mode** – if you behave in a way which is acceptable within the community, then this is moral.

- The **pragmatic mode** – if you choose to limit your own independence for the benefit the community, then this is moral.

Communitarianism

There are many people, both sociologists and others, who are concerned about the state of our communities. One of these people is Tony Blair. The concern here is that communities are breaking down and people are left with no moral code, no advice about how to live their lives in peace and with respect for others. This is what has become known as Balkanisation. The response to this breakdown of morality and stability within our communities is commonly known as communitarianism. The communitarians want to rebuild morality and social stability by combatting the liberal tendencies and extreme individualism of the Thatcher years. According to Etzioni this can be done by:

- strengthening local institutions such as schools, voluntary organisations and churches

- strengthening the family by returning to traditional gender roles and educating people to be good parents

- people becoming active citizens, taking responsibility for their own actions and being 'stakeholders' in the community, and especially in the community's children

According to communitarians, in the Thatcher years people spent a great deal of time at work and over-emphasised the material things their money could buy. As a consequence people became selfish and bad parents. Individual people loved their children and provided them with material things, but did not spend time with them. Neglected children grew up to be poor citizens. Hence we need a re-moralisation of the communities that we live in. For communitarian thinkers, to act morally is to act with the community in mind – any action that benefits others without benefiting oneself is moral.

Critiques of communitarianism

There are, however, a number of critiques of liberalism and the liberal society found within communitarianism, which we should look at.

Rorty (1991) argues that individuals who are labelled as 'communitarians' reject the 'individualistic rationalism of the Enlightenment', and reject the idea of 'rights'. In other words, from the point of view of communitarianism, liberal institutions and culture need the philosophical justification of the Enlightenment. Without this justification they cannot survive. In a post-Enlightenment world there is no guarantee that individuals will behave rationally and no automatic conception of rights. For these reasons the institutions and culture of democratic states are now without foundation.

Rorty defines three strands within communitarianism:

1 The argument that no society in which individuals do not share the same notion of 'moral truth' can endure. Such societies often turn to 'pragmatism,' which is not a 'strong enough philosophy to make [a] moral community possible,' (Rorty, 1991:177). Rorty quotes Bellah and others, who suggest that 'pragmatism' leads to ideological fanaticism and extreme political oppression.

2 The individuals produced by a liberal society are undesirable. Such a society is dominated by the rich, managers and therapists, who are the only people who wish to defend such a society. Rorty

argues that there is no reason to measure democratic institutions by the type of person they may produce (1991:190):

> *... even if the typical character types of liberal democracies are bland, calculating, petty and unheroic, the prevalence of such people may be a reasonable price to pay for political freedom.*

What is important for Rorty is that personhood involves having the capacity to choose, and this ability is 'prior to the ends it chooses.' (Rorty, 1991:185).

3 Liberal society presupposes a number of assumptions about the nature of human beings: in other words, it has an unstated theory of the self. Liberals generalise about the nature of self from the philosophical foundations of liberal institutions, which they admire. Rorty develops a notion of 'the self' in which the community is constitutive of the self. In other words, our notion of self is generated from factors within the wider society. This notion is widely accepted within both philosophy and sociology and is found in the work of G.H. Mead, Erving Goffman, Anthony Giddens and others. See Area 4 for a fuller discussion.

Rorty goes on to develop a notion of the self as a 'web':

> *think of human minds as webs of beliefs and desires, of sentential attitudes – webs which continually reweave themselves so as to accommodate new sentential attitudes ... All there is to the human self is just that web.*

(Rorty, 1991:93).

This means that, for Rorty, there is no thing called 'the self' that is different from 'the web of beliefs and desires that that self has' (Rorty, 1991:185). This idea was further developed in his book *Irony, Contingency and Solidarity* (1989).

Rorty describes his argument as an attempt to 'dissolve the metaphysical self in order to preserve the political one' (1991:185). Liberal social theory does not need a notion of self. The notion of self does not provide a basis for liberal social theory. However, if we desire a notion of self, then the 'self as web' model will fit with other assumptions that Rorty makes about the liberal society.

In defence of liberalism, Rorty reports Thomas Jefferson as saying: ... 'it does me no injury for my neighbour to say that there are twenty gods or no God.' This set the tone for American liberal politics, shared beliefs about issues such as religion were not necessary for the smooth and efficient running of liberal society. What was necessary was that individuals had a 'conscience'. As Rorty explains, the liberal society can get along without the need for political philosophies. In a similar fashion, questions about human nature, the self, motives for moral behaviour and the meaning of life are also irrelevant to the politics of a liberal society. This neutralises many of the criticisms made about liberalsim by communitarians and others.

Taking his lead from Rawls, Rorty suggests that 'justice' is the first virtue of the liberal society and that the need for such legitimation decreases as liberal society encourages the 'end of ideology'. 'Reflective equilibrium', or the balance of opinion, principles and argument, is the only method needed in discussing policy. In addition, Rorty argues that fanaticism threatens both freedom and justice and it is for this reason that liberals will use force against fanatics. Fanatics threaten liberal democratic institutions, because they challenge the individual conscience. The absence of fanaticism is one of the conditions of citizenship in a liberal society. This is built upon the notion that: '... anybody who is willing to listen to reason – to hear out all the arguments – can be brought around to the truth' (Rorty, 1991:188).

Voting behaviour

For many political scientists the era 1945–1970 was one of two-party supremacy and class voting. However, since 1970 there has been escalating electoral volatility and, above all, **class dealignment**. The connection between an individual's social class position and voting intention, which traditionally meant working-class people voting Labour and middle-class people voting Conservative, is broken. With class dealignment, this class-based voting was said to be steadfastly breaking down: so much so that by 1983 social class could 'correctly' be used to predict the votes of less than half of the British electorate. Voters were said to be politically leaving their 'natural' class party.

For Ivor Crewe, transformation of the social structure and the growth of a 'new' working class associated with the growth of working-class home ownership, produced a declining class consciousness. Working-class people were losing the taste for class-based politics.

More working-class people were finding themselves under cross-class tensions because they had diverse class characteristics, for example, home owners with manual occupations and children with ambitions to study at university. According to Crewe, this 'new' working class was likely to expand in future years. In Crewe's view, since 1970 the party choices of working-class people have become more closely associated with their positions on a range of issues. As we shall discuss below, voters are now said to be rational voters. Individuals use their vote in the same way that consumers use their money in the supermarket: to get maximum benefit for minimum cost.

However, some criticism can be made of the way in which Crewe defines social class: the **social grade schema**. The origins of the social grade schema are found in the *Annual Report of the Registrar General* (1911), and consisted of five hierarchical grades. Under the influence of Research Services Limited in the 1950s, this was modified into a sixfold categorisation (A, B, C1, C2, D, and E) of occupations (unskilled manual workers are in group E and professionals in group A). This way of defining 'class' takes the family as its unit of analysis, not the individual, and the occupation of the head of household is used as the indicator of the class position of all family members. This is a respectful way of saying that the social grade schema disregards women, and presumes that all people in the household have the same social class position as the oldest male. This is not only sexist but it ignores the fact that, according to Marshall's Essex Mobility Study (1988), up to 50% of people live in cross-class marriages. In other words, half of married people have a spouse with an occupation in a different social class.

No valid sociological research has been conducted to show if Crewe's conception of class reflects the structure of classes in society. Critics could call them 'arbitrary market research categories', rather than a class system. Outside the area of voting behaviour, the social grade schema is not used by any reputable social scientist.

Political scientists who make use of the social grade schema have left themselves open to the allegation that the class dealignment thesis is a product of attempts to measure the relationship between voting and class with defective measurement devices.

However, Ivor Crewe's view that people no longer vote on the basis of social class, but on the basis of 'issues' is now the accepted view within the social sciences.

Assumptions upon which the issue voting model is built

We might want to cast doubt upon some of the assumptions upon which 'issue voting' models are based. It is assumed that the issue voter is a rational voter, who attempts to get maximum personal benefit for minimum cost – the rational voter is a 'rational utility maximiser'. According to Anthony Downes (1957) rational individuals have a number of characteristics:

- a person can always make a decision when confronted with a range of alternatives
- a person can rank alternatives in order of preference
- the preferences are logically consistent
- the choice is always from the highest preference available
- the person will always make the same decision when confronted with the same alternatives

---

One important problem for this type of rational analysis is attempting to explain why people vote for parties when it is not in their economic interest to do so. For example, working-class people voting Conservative when they have a policy of raising money from VAT rather than income tax, or middle class Labour voters.

Another significant issue with this type of investigation is **rational abstention** in which the rational voter will understand that the significance of one vote is very small, and the cost of going to vote will always exceed the advantage gained from voting. In other words, it is always rational for the rational voter not to vote. One vote will not determine the outcome of an election and it is rational to let other people bear the cost of voting.

In the 1980s, Heath, Jowell and Curtice carried out the British Election Surveys and attempted to demonstrate that social class continued to be the most significant determinant in explaining how people vote. Taking their starting point from the research of John Goldthorpe, they redefined social class, and asserted that the working class made up about 34% of the electorate. In addition, they made an important separation between two forms of class voting: **absolute class voting** and **relative class voting**. Absolute class voting is the total number of working-class people voting Labour: this declined at each election from 1964 to 1983, with a slight increase in 1987, 1992, and 1997. Relative class voting is the strength of Labour support within the working class. Absolute class voting has decreased but relative class voting has shown 'trendless fluctuation', because the sum total of people within the working class is getting smaller at each election although the working class remains loyal to Labour. Heath et al. argue that this means there has been no significant class dealignment.

However, all the theories of voting behaviour assume that people are pushed about by forces outside their control, for example by class factors or rationality. If we accept that individuals live within a postmodern condition then we could argue that people's behaviour is not determined, and that voting is a question of personal, non-rational and total choice.

A C T I V I T Y KS **COMMUNICATION, WORKING WITH OTHERS, PROBLEM SOLVING**

IDENTIFICATION AND INTERPRETATION	ANALYSIS AND EVALUATION

As Johnston, Pattie and Allsopp make clear in *A Nation Dividing* (1988:269):

People are socialised into particular sets of political attitudes that reflect their occupational class origins and local contexts within which they learn the political meanings of their class positions. This produces the general pattern of voting by occupational class that is known as the class cleavage. That cleavage is far from complete, because of a variety of other influences, but it remains the single most important influence on the development of political attitudes and the identification of voters with particular political parties that follows.

■ Would you accept or reject this view?

Give a reason for your answer.

Understanding voting behaviour

For many psephologists (people who study voting behaviour) the period from 1945 to 1970 was one of:

■ two-party dominance

■ uniformity – people voted in a similar fashion all over Britain

■ class alignment – people voted on the basis of social class, with working-class people voting Labour and middle-class people Conservative

However, many researchers argue, the period since 1970 has been one of:

■ increasing electoral volatility — people vote differently at different elections

■ class dealignment and the rise of 'issue voting' – people no longer vote on the basis of social class, but on the basis of parties' policies on the key issues of the day

Most of the research into voting behaviour is concerned with examining the condition of the link between an individual's social class position and voting intention. Traditionally, working-class people were said to have a Labour identification, hence voting Labour in much greater numbers that other groups in the population. In contrast, middle-class people were said to have an identification with the Conservatives and this led to higher rates of Conservative voting. People who did not vote for their 'natural' class party were said to be 'deviant voters'. However, much of the research in the area now suggests that class alignment has been steadily breaking down since the 1970s, so much so that by 1983 social class could 'correctly' be used to predict the votes of less than half of the British electorate. Voters were said to be moving away from their 'natural' class party. Since the early 1980s the common view amongst psephologists is that people vote on the basis of issues rather than class alignment or identification.

However, before we look at the research into voting behaviour since the Second World War, we need to put into context what happened at the 1997 general election. During the 1980s many (if not all) researchers in the area seemed to assume that the Conservatives would always win general elections. Mark Kirby (1995) outlined the arguments for the Conservatives' continued electoral dominance:

- The Conservatives won four successive election victories (1979, 1983, 1987 and 1992), irrespective of the economic circumstances that the country was in.

- Traditional class identification was said to be breaking down, the link between class and voting no longer existed.

- Electorally, the working class was divided, with skilled manual workers voting Conservative in greater numbers.

- New divisions had replaced social class within the electorate, such as home ownership, which were to the benefit of the Conservatives electorally.

The 1997 general election

In 1997 Labour won a landslide victory, and Tony Blair became the first Labour Prime Minister since 1979. In addition, Paddy Ashdown's Liberal Democrats gained more than 25 seats. The Conservatives lost all their MPs in Scotland and Wales: in terms of representation in parliament, for the first time the Conservatives became an English party. Many Conservative cabinet ministers lost their seats, including Michael Portillo, who was seen by many as the obvious successor to John Major.

The campaign was dominated by 'sleaze'. Martin Bell (a BBC war reporter at the start of the campaign) stood as an independent candidate and, with the support of both Labour and the Liberal Democrats, who stood down their candidates against him, easily won Tatton, one of the safest Conservative seats in the country, defeating former minister Neil Hamilton.

According to Peter Kellner (1997):

> At the heart of the 1997 election result is a conundrum. The defending government was presiding over steady growth, low inflation, falling unemployment, a buoyant housing market, cheap mortgages and falling income tax rates – yet it lost power; and not only was it ejected from office, it secured a lower share of the vote than any governing party this century. How come?

Peter Kellner's analysis of the BBC's Exit Poll, conducted by NOP on 2356 individuals as they left the polling stations around Britain on election day 1997, is interesting. This study is important for sociologists

because NOP not only asked about people's voting intentions; they also asked the sample to anonymously supply personal information about themselves (their age, social class, gender, and their housing). This information let NOP compare the representatives of their sample and put together a detailed description of how different groups voted. In addition, as the same information was collected at the 1992 election exit poll, it was possible to make some valid statements about how the allegiance of different groups in the electorate changed between 1992 and 1997.

According to Kellner, the NOP survey suggests that:

- Memories of the recession in the early 1990s were more important in shaping attitudes about the Conservatives and affecting how people voted than feelings about the following recovery. As Kellner explains: 'The Conservative slogan, "Britain is booming", may have been counterproductive for it induced some voters to react: "Maybe it is, but I am not." Of those voters who said the economy was stronger, but their family's standard of living had deteriorated, more than eight out of 10 voted Labour or Liberal Democrat.'

- Labour succeeded in neutralising many of the negative perceptions that people had of them at the 1992 general election. The Blair leadership struck a chord with the electorate which the Kinnock leadership did not.

- The Conservative party was perceived as divided, while Labour was seen as united. As Kellner explains: 'A majority of more than two-to-one thought the Conservatives good for one class, rather than good for all classes; but a similar majority thought Labour good for all classes, not just one. Worse even than that for the Tories, as many as 84% saw the Tories as divided – whereas 66% saw Labour as united.'

- Tony Blair was seen as a much stronger and more competent leader than John Major: he outscored John Major by 14 points, although Major was perceived to be more trustworthy. A Tory advertisement depicting Tony Blair as a puppet of Chancellor Helmut Kohl did not strike the intended chord with the electorate.

- The majority thought Labour policies would make the situation better; in contrast, a considerable number of people in the sample thought that

Election Facts 1997

The final overall results were:

Labour:	419 seats (on a 44.4% share of the vote)
Conservative:	165 seats (on a 31.4% share of the vote)
Liberal Democrat:	46 seats (on a 17.2% share of the vote)
SNP:	6 seats
Plaid Cymru:	4 seats
Others:	19 seats

Turnout : 71.3%
Labour majority: 179
Swing: 10% Conservative to Labour

There are 117 women MPs in the House of Commons – approximately twice as many as in the previous parliament.

There were five women in the new Cabinet:
- Margaret Beckett (President of the Board of Trade)
- Harriet Harman (Social Security)
- Mo Mowlam (Northern Ireland)
- Clare Short (International Development)
- Ann Taylor (Leader of the Commons)

Non-cabinet appointments:
- Helen Liddell (Minister of State for the Treasury)

A total of 494 out of 659 constituencies were fought on new boundaries at the 1997 general election.

The following constituencies had majorities of under 1000:

Rank	Member	(Party, Constituency)	Majority
1	M.J. Oaten	(L Dem, Hampshire, Winchester)	2
2	A.M. Sanders	(L Dem, Torbay)	12
3	E. Davey	(L Dem, Kingston-upon-Thames, Kingston and Surbiton)	56
4	I.C. Bruce	(C, Dorset, South Dorset)	77
5	D. Heath	(L Dem, Somerset, Somerton and Frome)	130
6	Sir W.D. Madel	(C, Bedfordshire, South West Bedfordshire)	132
7	P.D. Stinchcombe	(Lab, Northamptonshire, Wellingborough)	187
8	P.A. Sawford	(Lab, Northamptonshire, Kettering)	189
9	P.L. Atkinson	(C, Northumberland, Hexham)	222
10	M.L.D. Fabricant	(C, Staffordshire, Lichfield)	238
11	B. White	(Lab, Buckinghamshire, North East Milton Keynes)	240
12	P.C.M. Nicholls	(C, Devon, Teignbridge)	281
13	D. Ruffley	(C, Suffolk, Bury St. Edmunds)	368
14	A. King	(Lab, Warwickshire, Rugby and Kenilworth)	495
15	Hon. D.P. Heathcoat-Amory	(C, Somerset, Wells)	528
16	Mrs. C.A. Spelman	(C, West Midlands, Meriden)	582
17	Sir R.B.F.S. Body	(C, Lincolnshire, Boston and Skegness)	647
18	Mrs E. Gordon	(Lab, Havering, Romford)	649
19	C.J. Fraser	(C, Dorset, Mid Dorset and Poole North)	681
20	Sir J.M. Shersby	(C, Hillingdon, Uxbridge)	724
21	T. Clark	(Lab, Northampton, South)	744
22	D.W.G. Chidgey	(L Dem, Eastleigh)	754
23	J.D. Cran	(C, Humberside, Beverley and Holderness)	811
24	Sir A.D. Steen	(C, Devon, Totnes)	877

Source: David Boothroyd's Website

Conservative policies would make the situation 'a lot worse'. As Kellner suggests: 'Labour was seen as the party of hope.'

- The swing in favour of the Labour Party amongst women was greater than amongst men.

Area summary

- Modernity generated a range of interesting theories of power, some of which assumed that the amount of power in society was fixed – such as Weber, Marx and élite theory. Pluralists, such as the functionalist Talcott Parsons, developed a non-zero-sum conception of power. All these theories made a distinction between 'authority' as the legitimate use of power and coercion. However, a number of postmodern writers argue that modernity gave way to a postmodern condition, in which there are no grand narratives, such as socialism or feminism, and no enforced identity. Hence a very different politics, a politics of identity.

- The postmodern condition undermines traditional theories of power because they undervalue the role of the individual human agent, and assume that individuals are pushed about by forces beyond their control.

- Within the postmodern condition there is a 'new' politics, which is uncertain and based upon issues of identity, which individual people often construct within new social movements.

- Politics within the postmodern condition can be very cruel and often tribal in nature; this form of politics can be seen as neo-medieval.

- Anthony Giddens argues that we do not yet live in a postmodern society, but within a 'reflexive modernity' in which there has been a shift from 'emancipatory politics' to 'life politics' and in which the self is highly reflexive and involved in a 'dialogic democracy' that is similar to the 'pure' relationship, a love relationship based on trust between equals.

- In Giddens' analysis all nation states have a tendency towards 'polyarchy'. As outlined by Giddens, social class has declined in significance and people join new social movements in which the bonds between people are emotional rather than economic.

- In order to resolve many of the problems of the 'new' politics, a number of politicians, most notably Tony Blair, have suggested that politics should become communitarian in nature.

- These issues affect theories of voting that assume voters are rational and vote on the basis of issues, which is said to undermine class-based voting. These theories also undervalue the role of the individual human agent and assume that people are pushed about by forces beyond their control, such as rationality and class.

Definitions

Absolute class voting
The total number of people voting for a political party within a given social class

Authoritarian populism
A term used by some Marxists to describe the style of the Thatcher governments, which was said to be very dictatorial but at the same time very well liked

Authority
The legitimate use of power

Autonomy
Freedom to take appropriate action or independence

Balkanisation
The process of states losing power to control the various forces within their locality, as is said to have happened within the former Yugoslavia

Bureaucracy
An authority system which takes the form of a rigid set of offices in the shape of a hierarchy

Civil society
A term used initially by Marxist Antiono Gransci in the 1930s to describe the legal and political institutions within a state

Class dealignment
The idea that social class is no longer a significant factor in determining how people vote

Coercion
The use of force and violence to secure one's ends

Communicative ethics
A set common principles on how to conduct oneself within a community

Communitarianism
A term used to describe an approach to politics which is concerned with rebuilding communities

Demographic transition theory
Explains population over time using birth and death rates

Demonise
The process of making a person or institution appear to be evil in the eyes of others

Derivations
A term used by Pareto to described the four strategies that the elite use to describe how the elite keep control

Emancipatory politics
A term used by Giddens to describe the politics of the Conservatives, old Labour and Liberals. This type of politics was concerned with liberating people from oppression

Hegemony
A term used initially by Marxist Antiono Gransci in the 1930s to describe a form of ideological distortion in which the ruling class create a form of consent within the working class

Historic bloc
A term used initially by Marxist Antiono Gransci in the 1930s to describe a compromise between groups in an effort to preserve capitalism

Ideal speech situation
A term initially used by Jurgen Habermas in the 1970s to describe a form of communication free of ideological distortion

Implosion
A term used initially by Jean Baudrillard in the 1980s to describe the world as a world of signs me cannot escape from

Legitimate authority
Authority which is legally sanctioned or seen as 'right'

Life politics
Politics of self-liberation and lifestyle

Nationalism	An often irrational state of feeling based upon the assumption that one's own nation state is superior to any other
Nation state	A geographical area with a centralised administrative power which exercises control of the locality
Neo-medieval	A situation used to draw similarities between the political system in the medieval world and the political system in the contemporary world, most notably in terms of the decline of the state and a shared state ideology
New social movements	Informally organised single-issue groups who favour direct action rather than legitimate means of getting their message across
Particularistic	A set of values which are said to support to views of New Social Movements over the views of others in a community
Political formula	A term used initially by elite theorist Mosca in the 1900s to describe the set of conventions, etc. imposed by the elite onto the mass, in order to maintain civilisation
Political society	A term used initially by Marxist Antiono Gransci in the 1930s to describe the coercive institutions within capitalism which are used to keep order
Polyarchy	A form of pluralism in which power is widely shared and politics is conducted on the basis of given rules
Power	The ability to make people do what you want them to do
Rational abstention	A logical flaw within the theory of rational voting which suggests that the rational voter will not vote because voting is not the rational thing to do
Relative class voting	A measure of the strength of class voting, in which the proportion of people in the working class voting Labour is contrasted with the proportion of middle-class people voting Conservative
Residues	A term used initially by elite theorist Pareto in the 1900s to describe the instincts and sentiments which people have
Schemata of interpretation	A set of thought categories that people make use of when making sense of the world
Social grade schema	A model of social class which classifies people on the basis of the occupation of their head of household
State	No agreed definition of the state exists, but it can mean the government and its agencies who have control over a given location
'Third Way'	An approach to politics which is neither right-wing (such as the New Right) nor left-wing (such as the traditional Labour Party), but based upon rebuilding communities and empowering individuals
Tribalism	A form of political association which shares a great deal in common with pre-modern clans
Value relevance	A term used initially by Max Weber in the 1920s to describe the initial stage in the process of constructing an ideal type, in which people select on the basis of their own personal opinion what the characteristics of the ideal type should be
Volitions	A term used by pluralists since the 1960s to describe the shared values and opinions upon which the rules that govern a democratic political system are built

TASK

Hypothesis – 'New social movements have been characterised as postmodern because they reject modernist political discourses and class identities' (Bagguley, 1995:606).

Context – There is much more to politics than politicians and the established political parties. Every community has politics. You could investigate who makes the decisions that directly affect your life.

Method – Select a decision which you feel has directly affected you and attempt a case study of that decision: who made it and why; what were the other options? Who benefited and who lost out because of that decision? It is possible to do this on a local or a global level. Did any group emerge to fight the decision and to point out alternatives?

You could investigate the role, purpose and organisation of this group. Is it a new social movement? Was the group involved in 'direct action',

such as climbing trees or hiding in tunnels? If not, why not? Is this form of direct action ever likely to be successful?

Such questions lend themselves to a variety of different research methods depending upon your interests and expertise: a content analysis of local and national newspapers; a series of interviews and/or observations of local groups; or a participant observation.

Evaluation – Was the group successful? Were the group members working inside or outside the normal political channels – such as writing letters to MPs and local councillors – or using forms of direct action? Did the group have a formal structure or was it more informal like a postmodern organisation?

You may well find that the answers to these questions are not so clear-cut as to be able to say 'yes' or 'no'. However, you may find that you are confronted with elements of the postmodern condition.

Data response questions

Item A   COMMUNITARIANISM

By and large, citizens like the idea of the welfare state to be there if they fall on hard times. But, increasingly, governments everywhere are realising that the public purse cannot afford it at present levels.

Right-wingers say that health, education and social security should be cut because it induces a dependency culture and saps individual initiative. But social ills are not merely the product of moral turpitude. Left-wingers say that if unemployment were reduced then governments would have extra taxation income to pay for existing levels of payments. But nobody is simply a helpless victim – everybody has some contribution to make.

A midway position is quite possible, however. Some services now provided by the welfare state should and could be undertaken by people on their own. At the same time, society must continue to share the burdens.

Communitarians propose a principle of subsidiary in which the primary responsibility belongs to the individuals nearest the problem; if a solution cannot be found, then the responsibility moves to the family; if there is still no solution, then to the community; then and only then, when no solution is possible at all, should the state be involved.

Habitats-mini articles
http://www.on-the-net.com/interskills/minis/habitat.htm#comm

Item B   *… by the strength of our common endeavour we achieve more than we achieve alone, so as to create for each of us the means to realise our true potential and for all of us a community in which power, wealth and opportunity are in the hands of the many, not the few, where the rights we enjoy reflect the duties we owe, and where we live together, freely, in a spirit of solidarity, tolerance and respect.*

Labour Party Constitution, Clause Four

Item C   *Amitai Etzioni's book* **The Spirit of Community** *says that about 20 years ago mothers did what men did: they ran away from their children by going out to get paid work. Their children were abandoned, as Etzioni puts it, to 'the drinks cabinet and the television'… But is it true?*

We need to test the hypothesis. The most substantive work on what parents actually do in their everyday life has been researched in Britain by Jonathan Gershung at the Centre for Micro-Social Research at Essex. Mapping, hour by hour, the activities of parenting and household responsibilities, he has come up with a very different picture from the one painted by Etzioni.

The work of parenting and housework has indeed changed. In 1961 women spent an average of 217 minutes a day and men 17 minutes a day on housework. In 1985 women spent 162 minutes a day and men something like double their previous figure – considerably more than they did, but considerably less than women.

The important thing here is the relationship between routine housework and routine parenting and dedicated parenting. How much time do parents spend eye-ball to eye-ball with their children? The average mother now with a full-time job spends more dedicated time with her children than the average homemaker of 30 years ago...

She may have been permanently present but she was also probably permanently 'absent'. Mothers were not people you played with or had conversations with. You played with and produced your culture with other children, your own generation... Parenting has indeed been refashioned... the kind of mother who is lodged in the nostalgic crusade of the communitarians didn't exist.

Adapted from Beatrix Campbell (1996)
The dangers of New Labour's communitarian ideas

a What do you understand by the term communitarian? **(3)**

> KNOWLEDGE AND
> UNDERSTANDING

b Can you identify any communitarian assumptions within the new Clause four? **(5)**

> IDENTIFICATION AND
> INTERPRETATION

c In your own words, could you write a paragraph which outlines Beatrix Campbell's critique of communitarianism. **(5)**

> IDENTIFICATION AND
> INTERPRETATION

d The research which Campbell reviews on parenting provides us with information from several years ago. Do you agree that the 'normal' mother today has more 'dedicated time' with her children than parents in the past? **(7)**

> KNOWLEDGE AND | IDENTIFICATION AND | ANALYSIS AND
> UNDERSTANDING | INTERPRETATION | EVALUATION

Structured questions

a   What are the identifying features of 'class dealignment'?   (4)

> **GUIDANCE**   A range of features would do here, you could highlight the loss of working class consciousness, the changing nature of the class structure in which we have both 'proletarianisation' of many in the middle classes and increasing affluence amongst many in the working classes.
>
> IDENTIFICATION AND INTERPRETATION

b   Assess the extent to which social class is still a key factor in the analysis of voting behaviour.   (9)

> **GUIDANCE**   This is a popular question, which gives you an opportunity to look at some of the traditional theories of social class that sociologists have used since the nineteenth century – Marx, Weber, the Registrar General's Classification of Occupations – and evaluate if they are still useful today. Do they hold up to the postmodernist's critique and redefinition of class? In addition, the question assumes that class is a central factor in determining how people vote. Theories of 'class alignment', which assume that people vote on the basis of their social class position, assume that individual people have very limited 'human agency'. You can discuss if people's ideas are determined by class factors, as for example Marxists would suggest, or are people free to think whatever they wish. However, at some point in your answer you will be expected to compare and contrast the position of Crewe with that of Heath, Jowell and Curtice. You will need to explain which you find the most convincing and why. Part of this evaluation should involve looking at how they define class.
>
> ANALYSIS AND EVALUATION

c   Assess the role of the mass media in the political process.   (9)

> **GUIDANCE**   This question is also very popular. It asks you to outline the role of the mass media. Does the mass media inform people so that they can make an informed choice in terms of how to vote and where the political parties stand on a range of issues? Or, alternatively, does the mass media manipulate people's ideas, putting pressure on people to think in particular ways?
>
> IDENTIFICATION AND INTERPRETATION | ANALYSIS AND EVALUATION
>
> There is a clear contrast here between a pluralist view, that there are a wide range of media products which people can choose from in order to make an informed choice, and Marxist views, derived from The Frankfurt School and others, which suggest that people are victims of ideology. You will need to explain which you find the most convincing and why.

Essay titles

1   Assess the strengths and weakesses of the pluralist theory of power.   (25)

2   Compare and contrast Marxist and New Right perspectives on the role of the state in society.   (25)

SOCIOLOGY IN PRACTICE

Giddens on New Social Movements

' *New forms of social movement mark an attempt at a collective reappropriation of institutionally repressed areas of life. Recent religious movements have to be numbered among these, although of course there is great variability in the sects and cults which have developed. But several other new social movements are particularly important and mark sustained reactions to basic institutional dimensions of modern social life. Although – and in some part because – it addresses questions which antedate the impact of modernity, the feminist movement is one major example. In its early phase, the movement was pre-eminently concerned with securing equal political and social rights between women and men. In its current stage, however, it addresses elemental features of existence and creates pressures towards social transformations of a radical nature. The ecological and peace movements are also part of this new sensibility to late modernity, as are some kinds of movements for human rights. Such movements, internally diverse as they are, effectively challenge some of the basic presuppositions and organising principles which fuel modernity's juggernaut.*

(Giddens 1991:208–209)

… new social movements cannot readily be claimed for socialism. While the aspirations of some such movements stand close to socialist ideals, their objectives are disparate and sometimes actively opposed to one another. With the possible exception of some sections of the green movement, the new social movements are not 'totalizing' in the way socialism is (or was), promising a new 'stage' of social development beyond the existing order. Some versions of feminist thought, for example, are as radical as anything that went under the name of socialism. Yet they don't envisage seizing control of the future in the way the more ambitious versions of socialism have done.

(Giddens, 1994:3)

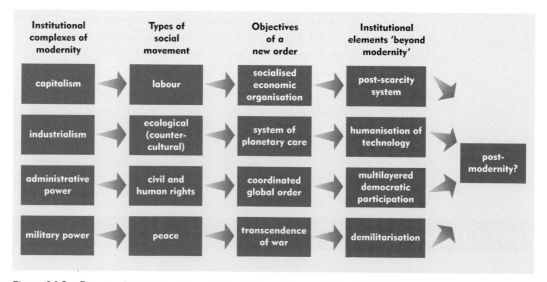

Figure 14.2   From modernity to post-modernity: Giddens' scheme (Held, 1992:34)

1 Why does Giddens believe that NSMs are not socialist in nature? Write a paragraph in which you make use of his notion of *life politics* and his notion of *dialogic democracy.* (9)

2 Would you suggest the NSMs in Giddens' view have *particular* or *universal* motives? Suggest a number of reasons for your answer. (9)

Spend a few minutes thinking about the following points. Discuss them with other sociology students.

1 What do you think Giddens understands by 'community'? (5)

2 According to Giddens, individuals seek a 'pure relationship' and this could provide the model for a new form of solidarity which he terms 'dialogic democracy'. (7)

3 Does Giddens' notion of solidarity based upon 'dialogic democracy' rest upon a solid ethical or sociological basis? (9)

Further reading and references

Kirby, M. (1995) *Investigating Political Sociology*. Although this book is a little dated in terms of its statistics, the evaluations, outline of central arguments and summaries of a range of writers is still very good.
A detailed book on the less traditional approaches to sociological research. A useful text for the more confident, inquisitive and 'aspiring researcher' student.

Internet sites

www.stile.lut.ac.uk/~gyobs/GLOBAL/t0000006.html This site is from Global Observatory Resource Information, and it gives a great deal of excellent information on the nature of new social movements with a good range of links.

www.abacon-com/sociology/soclinks/politics.html Allen and Bacon provide an excellent range of links to sites which are relevant to all topics looked at in this area.

Bibliography

Abercrombie, N., Hill, S. and Turner, B. (1981) *The Dominant Ideology Thesis*. London, Allen and Unwin.
Annual Report of the Registrar-General (1911). London, HMSO.
Bagguley, P. (1995) 'Protest, Poverty and Power: a Case Study of the Anti-poll Tax Movement in Leeds'. *Sociological Review*, 43. 4.
Baudrillard, J. (1993) *Simulations*. New York, Semiotexte.
Bauman, Z. (1989) *Modernity and the Holocaust*. Cambridge, Polity.
Bauman, Z. (1998) *Work, Consumerism and the New Poor*. Buckingham, Open University Press.
Bauman, Z. (1991) *Modernity and Ambivalence*. Cambridge, Polity.
Bauman, Z. (1992) *Intimations of Postmodernity*. London, Routledge.
Bauman, Z. (1992) *Mortality, Immortality and Other Life Strategies*. Cambridge, Polity.
Bauman, Z. (1993) *Postmodern Ethics*. Oxford, Blackwell.
Bauman, Z. (1995) *Life in Fragments*. Oxford, Blackwell.
Bauman, Z. (1997) *Postmodernity and Its Discontents*. Cambridge, Polity.
Bauman, Z. (1998) *Globalisation*. Cambridge, Polity.
Bellah, R. (1970) *Beyond Belief*. New York, Harper and Row.
Best, S. (1997) 'Agency and Structure in the Writings of Anthony Giddens'. *The Social Science Teacher* 26
Best, S. (1998) 'Zygmunt Bauman: Personal Reflections from the Mainstream of Modernity' *British Journal of Sociology*.
Campbell, B. (1996) 'The Dangers of New Labour's Communitarian Ideals'. *Sociological Research On-line*.
Crewe, I. (1992) 'Why Did Labour Lose Yet Again?' *Politics Review*, September.
Dahl, R. (1971) *Polyarchy*. Yale, Yale University Press.

Day, G. and Robbins, D. (1987) 'Activists for Peace: the Social Basis of a Local Peace Movement' in C. Creighton and M. Shaw (Eds.) *The Sociology of War and Peace*. London, Macmillan.

Diani, M. (1992) 'The Concept of Social Movements'. *Sociological Review*, 40, 1.

Downes, A. (1957) *An Economic Theory of Democracy*. New York, Harper and Row.

Etzioni, A. (1995) *The Spirit of Community*. London, Fontana.

Finer, S.E. (1979) *Five Constitutions*. Harmondsworth, Penguin.

Finer, S. (1987) 'State and Nation-building in Europe: the Role of the Military' in Tilly, C. (ed.) *The Formation of Nation States in Europe*. Princeton, NJ Princeton University Press.

Foucault, M. (1977) *Discipline and Punish: The Birth of the Prison*. New York, Pantheon.

Giddens, A. (1981) *Social Theory and Modern Sociology*. Cambridge, Polity.

Giddens, A. (1985) *The Nation State and Violence*. Cambridge, Polity.

Giddens, A. (1990) *The Consequences of Modernity*. Cambridge, Polity.

Giddens, A. (1994) *Beyond Right and Left*. Cambridge, Polity.

Goffman, E. (1974) *Frame Analysis: An Essay on the Organisation of Experience*. Harmondsworth, Penguin.

Gramsci, A. (1977) *The Modern Prince*. New York, International Publishers.

Habermas, J. (1973) *Legitimation Crisis*. London, Heinemann.

Hall, S. and J. (Eds.) (1983) *The Politics of Thatcherism*. London, Lawrence and Wishart.

Hall, S. et al. (1992) *Modernity and its Futures*. Milton Keynes, Open University Press.

Haseler, S. (1989) cited in Horsman, M. and Marshall, A. (1994) *After the Nation State*. London, Harper Collins.

Heath, A., Curtice, J., Evans, G., Jowell, R. and Witherspoon, S. (1991) *Understanding Political Change*. Oxford, Pergamon.

Heath, A., Jowell, R. and Curtice, J. *How Britain Votes*. Oxford, Pergamon.

Held, D. (1992) in Hall, S. (ed.) *Modernity and Its Futures*. Cambridge, Polity.

Heller, A. and Feher, F. (1988) *The Postmodern Political Condition*. Cambridge, Polity.

Hirst, P. (1988) *Politics After Thatcherism*. London, Macmillan.

Hirst, P. (1993) *Pluralist Theory of the State*. London, Routledge.

Inglehart, R. (1971) 'The Silent Revolution in Europe: Intergenerational Change in Post-industrial Societies'. *American Political Science Review*.

Inglehart, R. (1990) 'Values, Ideology and Cognitive Mobilisation in New Social Movements' in Dalton, R.J. *Challenging the Political Order*. Cambridge, Polity.

Johnston, R.J., Pattie, C.J. and Allsopp, J.G. (1988) *A Nation Dividing?* Harlow, Longman.

Jordan, B. (1987) *Rethinking Welfare*. Oxford, Blackwell.

Kellner, P. (1997) *The 1997 General Election*. http://bbc.co.uk/news.

Kirby, M. (1995) *Investigating Political Sociology*. London, Collins Educational.

Lasch, C. (1980) *The Culture of Narcissism: American Life in an Age of Diminishing Expectations*. London, Abacus.

Lindblom, C. (1977) *Politics and Markets*. New York, Basic Books.

Lloyd, J. (1997) 'New Deal'. *New Statesman and Society*, February.

Lukes, S. (1974) *Power: A Radical View*. London, Macmillan.

Macmurry, J. (1962) Self as Agent. London, Faber and Faber.

Mann, M. (1993) *The Sources of Social Power*. Cambridge, Cambridge University Press.

Manning, T. (1995) [untitled] *Gay Times*.

Marshall, G., Newby, H., Rose, D. and Vogler, C. (1988) *Social Class in Modern Britain*. London, Hutchinson.

Mason, A. (1995) [untitled] *Gay Times*.

McAllister-Groves, J. 'Learning to Feel: the Neglected Sociology of Social Movements'. *Sociological Review'*, 43, 3.

Mestrovic, S. (1994) *Balkaization of the West: The Confluence of Postmodernism with Postcommunism*. London, Routledge.

Melucci, A. *Anti-Nuclear Protest*. Cambridge, Cambridge University Press.

Michels, R. (1949) *Political Parties*. Glencoe, The Free Press.

Miliband, R. (1973) *State in Capitalist Society*. London, Quartet.

Nordlinger, E. (1981) *The Autonomy of the Democratic State*. Cambridge, Mass., Harvard University Press.

Parsons, T. (1951) *The Social System*. New York, Free Press.

Parsons, T. (1970) *Societies: Evolutionary and Comparative Perspectives*. Englewood Cliffs, Prentice-Hall.

Poulantzas, N. (1973) *Political Power and Social Classes*. London, Verso.

Raskovic, (1990) *Diministing Expectations*. London, Abacus.

Rorty, R. (1991) 'Objectivity, Relativism and Truth: Philosophical Papers.

Rorty, R. (1989) *Irony, Contingency and Solidarity*. Cambridge, Cambridge University Press.

Roth, A., *Parliamentary Profiles*. London Parlimentary Profiles.

Volume 1'. Cambridge, Cambridge University Press.

Skopol, T. (1979) *States and Social Revolutions*. Cambridge, Cambridge University Press.

Turner and Killian (1986) *Sovereign Individuals of Capitalism*. London, Allen and Union.

Tilly, C. (ed.) *The Formation of nation States in Europe*. princeton, NJ Princeton University Press.

Veblen, T. (1912) *The Theory of the Leisure Class*. New York, Macmillan.

World Health Organisation, (1988) *Application of the International Classification of Diseases*. Geneva, W.H.O.

Willis, P. (1977) *Learning to Labour*. Farnborough, Saxon House.

Index